Advanced Management Accounting

Text, Problems & Cases

About the Author

Prof. Jawahar Lal was formely Professor at the Department of Commerce, Delhi School of Economics, University of Delhi, Delhi. He also served as head, Department of Commerce and Dean, Faculty of Commerce and Business, University of Delhi. Prior to above associations, he taught at Shri Ram College of Commerce, University of Delhi. He has over forty-five years of teaching and research experience. He has been associated with teaching of postgraduate commerce and management courses, and imparting dissertation and thesis guidance to MPhil. and PhD Students.

Professor Lal is member of many academic and professional bodies; he is on the Editorial Board of many reputed journals, member of the Board of Studies and Research Committees of Indian Universities, member of Indian Commerce Association and member and fellow of the Indian Accounting Association. He has been conferred with IAA fellowship Award 2007 for lifetime dedication to Accounting Education and Research.

Prof. Lal has contributed seventy papers in reputed journals and has presented papers in sixty national and international conferences. He has also chaired technical sessions in many conferences. He has authored over a dozen reputed books. Some of his publications are *Accounting Theory and Practice; Cost Accounting; Managerial Accounting; Accounting for Management; Financial Accounting: Principles and Practices; Financial Accounting: Text and Problems; Corporate Annual Reports, Theory and Practice; Financial Reporting by Diversified Companies; Understanding Indian Investors and Corporate Financial Accounting*.

Advanced Management Accounting

Text, Problems & Cases

(M.Com., MBA, CA, ICWA, CS, CFA and other Professional Courses)

Prof. JAWAHAR LAL
Formerly Head, Department of Commerce
Formerly Dean, Faculty of Commerce & Business
Delhi School of Economics
University of Delhi
Delhi - 110 007

S. CHAND
PUBLISHING
empowering minds

S Chand And Company Limited
(ISO 9001 Certified Company)
RAM NAGAR, NEW DELHI - 110 055

S Chand And Company Limited
(ISO 9001 Certified Company)

S. CHAND PUBLISHING
empowering minds

Head Office: 7361, RAM NAGAR, QUTAB ROAD, NEW DELHI - 110 055
Phone: 23672080-81-82, 66672000 Fax: 91-11-23677446
www.**schandpublishing.com**; e-mail: **info@schandpublishing.com**

Branches:

Ahmedabad	:	Ph: 27541965, 27542369, ahmedabad@schandpublishing.com
Bengaluru	:	Ph: 22268048, 22354008, bangalore@schandpublishing.com
Bhopal	:	Ph: 4209587, bhopal@schandpublishing.com
Chandigarh	:	Ph: 2625356, 2625546, 4025418, chandigarh@schandpublishing.com
Chennai	:	Ph: 28410027, 28410058, chennai@schandpublishing.com
Coimbatore	:	Ph: 2323620, 4217136, coimbatore@schandpublishing.com (Marketing Office)
Cuttack	:	Ph: 2332580, 2332581, cuttack@schandpublishing.com
Dehradun	:	Ph: 2711101, 2710861, dehradun@schandpublishing.com
Guwahati	:	Ph: 2738811, 2735640, guwahati@schandpublishing.com
Hyderabad	:	Ph: 27550194, 27550195, hyderabad@schandpublishing.com
Jaipur	:	Ph: 2219175, 2219176, jaipur@schandpublishing.com
Jalandhar	:	Ph: 2401630, jalandhar@schandpublishing.com
Kochi	:	Ph: 2809208, 2808207, cochin@schandpublishing.com
Kolkata	:	Ph: 23353914, 23357458, kolkata@schandpublishing.com
Lucknow	:	Ph: 4065646, lucknow@schandpublishing.com
Mumbai	:	Ph: 22690881, 22610885, 22610886, mumbai@schandpublishing.com
Nagpur	:	Ph: 2720523, 2777666, nagpur@schandpublishing.com
Patna	:	Ph: 2300489, 2260011, patna@schandpublishing.com
Pune	:	Ph: 64017298, pune@schandpublishing.com
Raipur	:	Ph: 2443142, raipur@schandpublishing.com (Marketing Office)
Ranchi	:	Ph: 2361178, ranchi@schandpublishing.com
Sahibabad	:	Ph: 2771235, 2771238, delhibr-sahibabad@schandpublishing.com

First Edition 2003; Subsequent Editions and Reprints 2006, 2008, 2009, 2010, 2013, 2014, 2015

Fourth Edition 2016
Reprint 2018

ISBN : 978-93-525-3308-4

PRINTED IN INDIA

By Vikas Publishing House Pvt. Ltd., Plot 20/4, Site-IV, Industrial Area Sahibabad, Ghaziabad-201010 and Published by S Chand And Company Limited, 7361, Ram Nagar, New Delhi-110 055.

Dedicated to the
Sacred Memory of
My Parents

PREFACE TO THE FOURTH REVISED EDITION

Management accounting is concerned with gathering, classifying, developing and reporting information to managers and others inside an organisation to help them in all their managerial activities. It focuses on the use of financial and related information for making plans and taking strategic and operational decisions, and performance evaluation. It helps management in evaluating different decision alternatives and measuring success in relation to business missions, goals and strategies. Although management accounting follows an accounting process to accumulate and design information, it is more of a managerial tool for formulating and executing business strategy than a mere accounting process or activity.

Modern-day business is greatly influenced by global competition, continuous improvement, technological changes, customer focus and process reengineering. In this complex and dynamic environment, organisations have to take adequate steps to face major challenges and to formulate appropriate strategies to keep pace with the changing scenario. Management accounting provides information to organisations, managers, decision makers and others within an organisation to enable them to overcome organisational problems and successfully deal with a changing environment. Managers in all types of organisations – profit, not–for–profit, service – depend on management accounting. Management accounting is both an information provider and also part of an organisations's control mechanisms.

The text **Advanced Management Accounting – Text, Problems and Cases** provides a comprehensive and updated coverage of important topics, current trends, latest ideas and researches in management accounting. It presents the concepts, techniques and use of financial and other information in a clear, concise and logical sequence. The basic theme of the book is how management accounting helps managers in making improved decisions. It contains rich explanation of concepts and discusses principles and techniques involved in management accounting.

The fourth edition of the text continues its leading-edge and comprehensive coverage of management accounting topics within a decision-making framework. This revision is in response to extensive and encouraging feedback from teachers and students who have found it to be an indispensable text. Changes in this edition, have been motivated with a view to make the discussion more relevant and interesting to the students and to make this edition the most up-to-date and teachable text for the readers.

Structure of the Book

The text is structured into six parts.

1: *Introduction to Management Accounting* introduces the subject of management accounting and discusses its Nature and Scope, Cost Concepts and Classification.

2: *Cost Accumulation Systems and Product Costing* focuses on Cost Allocation and Overhead Absorption, Activity-based Costing and differences between Absorption and Variable Costing.

3: *Managerial Decision–making* discusses Cost-Volume-Profit Analysis, Relevant Information and Decision-Making and Pricing Decisions.

4: *Planning, Control and Performance Measurement* covers Budgeting, Standard Costing and Variance Analysis, Performance Measurement in Divisionalised Companies, Transfer Pricing,

Performance Measurement–Balanced Seorecard, Strategic Management Accounting and Management Control Systems.

5: ***Managerial Uses of Financial Statements*** deals with Cash Flow Statement and Financial Statement Analysis.

Chapter Organisation

All the chapters in the book have been carefully and logically organised to enable students to understand concepts and theories underlying management accounting. Each chapter has the following components:

- ***Comprehensive and Updated Coverage:*** The book presents the latest and adequate content on management accounting concepts, techniques and use of information for planning and decision making.
- ***Examples and Illustrative Numerical Problems:*** Real-world illustrative problems have been included in the chapters for better understanding of management accounting principles and techniques.
- ***Critical Analysis and Discussion Questions:*** Thought-provoking and real-life theory questions are given at the end of each chapter to test students' understanding of the content presented in the chapter. These questions require critical analysis and can be used as written assignments or as a basis for classroom/group discussion.
- ***Self-Assessment Questions:*** These questions aid students to judge their knowledge and understanding of subject – text discussed in the chapters.
- ***Multiple Choice Questions:*** Multiple choice questions given at the end of chapters help students in reviewing the important concepts and explanations presented therein.
- ***Numerical Problems:*** Problems with answers with varying degrees of difficulty have been given in the concerned chapters. Students are required to apply their understanding and knowledge of chapter materials to solve these problems since they would help them in better learning and understanding of the subject matter. These numerical problems generally involve more than one issue and contain difficult computations, straightforward requirements calling for decisions, interpretations or 'what if' answers.
- ***Cases:*** Almost all chapters in the book have managerial cases implying more complexity, analysis and synthesis. They would help students to extend their thought process to new situations and to shift from classroom to the business world to enhance their analytical power and to use multiple concepts to solve them.

With the above pedagogical features, the text presents a balanced blend of conceptual framework, management accounting techniques and use of accounting information. The organisation and discussion of materials are clear, concise, readable and finetuned.

Changes and New Features in the Fourth Edition

1. Improved and Updated Chapters

All the chapters have been ameliorated and updated. The following table summarizes the chapters significantly changed and improved.

Chapter 1: Management Accounting: Nature and Scope

Chapter 2: Cost Concepts and Classifications

Chapter 4: Activity-based Costing
Chapter 5: Absorption Versus Variable Costing
Chapter 6: Cost-Volume-Profit(CVP) Analysis
Chapter 7: Relevant Information and Decision Making
Chapter 8: Pricing Decisions
Chapter 9: Budgeting
Chapter 10: Standard Costing and Variance Analysis
Chapter 11: Performance Measurement in Divisionalized Companies
Chapter 12: Transfer Pricing
Chapter 13: Performance Measurement – Balanced Scorecard
Chapter 14: Strategic Management Accounting
Chapter 15: Management Control Systems
Chapter 16: Cash Flow Statement

2. **Inclusion of More Examples, Problems and Cases**
   Each chapter includes more thought-provoking real-world theory questions, numerical solved problems, Unsolved numerical problems, Cases.
   Most of the illustrative problems and end-of-chapter material have been revised in this edition.

3. **Adapted Problems**
   Numerous adapted CMA (USA), CA, ICWA, MBA, M.Com. problems are included to help students prepare for these examinations.
   With improved and updated materials, new examples and problems and assignment materials and redesigned pedagogy, the book will be very useful for post-graduate students of commerce and management who are pursuing the following courses:
   — M.Com.
   — MBA, MFC, MIB, MHROD and other management programmes.
   — CA, ICWA, CS and other similar professional programmes.

ACKNOWLEDGEMENTS

My long years of teaching and association with the subject of Mangement Accounting has prompted me to write this book. A large number of books on management accounting have been published. But I believe that there is a need for an ideal text with discussion of quality materials, contemporary concepts and approaches and student–friendly presentation.

In preparing the text, I have been benefited by opinions of colleagues in accounting and other disciplines in University of Delhi and also other institutions, interactions with practicing managers, and speakers at management development seminars and programmes. I have also been motivated greatly by writings of many reputed researchers and writers who have contributed to management accounting through their scholarly studies and publications. The text has included their writings and recommendations to provide students updated knowledge and theoretical understanding. I appreciate the views and feedback of my students as the subject matter contained in the book have been class-tested.

I express my deep appreciation of assistance provided by the Institute of Certified Management Accountants of the Institute of Management Accountants, USA and permission to use questions and answers from their past CMA examinations. I express my sincere thanks to Priscilla S. Payne, Managing Director of the Institute of Certified Management Accountants, USA for providing prompt assistance and enabling me to complete this text.

I am thankful for the continuous support and encouragement from all the members of my family – Pratibha, Sanjay, Seema, Rajnish, Ashish, Anupriya, Akshita, Siddharth, Anirudh — in all my academic activities and in completing this project as well. I sincerely acknowledge and appreciate their valuable cooperation.

I am thankful to Mrs. Nirmala Gupta, Chairperson S. Chand & Company Ltd., and other staff for giving warm cooperation and displaying professionalism in publishing this book.

I am thankful to the editorial team of S. Chand & Company Pvt. Ltd., New Delhi for bringing out this book in such an excellent form.

Prof. Jawahar Lal

WALKTHROUGH

3

COST ALLOCATION AND OVERHEAD ABSORPTION

LEARNING OBJECTIVES

After reading this chapter, you should be able to:

- Understand the Concept of Overhead Absorption
- Explain the Following Stages in Absorption of Overheads
  - ➢ Allocation and Apportionment of Overhead
  - ➢ Apportionment of Service Departments Overhead to Producing Departments
  - ➢ Absorption of Overhead Costs
- Distinguish between Actual and Predetermined Overhead Rate
- Explain the Treatment of Under/Over-absorption of Overheads
- Explain the Methods of Accounting for Administrative Overheads, Selling and Distribution Overheads

Every chapter begins with **Learning Objectives** which help you to understand the intended learning outcomes

Management accounting is that field of accounting which deals with providing information including financial accounting information to managers for their use in planning, decision-making, performance evaluation, control, management of costs, and cost determination. Management accounting contains reports prepared to fulfil the needs of management.

Management accounting is concerned with data collection from internal and external sources, analysing, processing, interpreting and communicating the information for use within the organization so that management can more effectively plan, make decisions and control operations.

The Institute of Management Accountants (IMA) in Statement No. 1 A (Statements on Management Accounting, 1982), has first defined management accounting as:

> *...the process of identification, measurement, accumulation, analysis, preparation and communication of financial information used by management to plan, evaluate, and control within the organization and to assure appropriate use and accountability for its resources.*

However, in recognition of the increasingly strategic role that management accounting plays in today's organizations, the IMA issued the following revised definition in December 2008.

Margin Notes help recapitulate important points effortlessly

Depending on the requirements, management accounting has evolved to fulfil the needs of management. Accordingly, some areas of its coverage may become outdated and be discarded and some newer areas may come within the management accounting activities.

Areas of Activity Considered to be Part of Management Accounting

Budgeting, planning and forecasting
Calculating the profitability of products, services and operations
Measuring organizational, divisional and departmental performance
Comparing results and performance within and between organizations
Assisting in the process of increasing effectiveness and efficiency
Assessing the performance of past and future capital investments
Advising on decisions about product mix, markets to be served and selling prices
Advising on decisions on whether to outsource products, components, activities and services
Advising on decisions involving the investment of scarce funds between a range of possible alternatives
Assisting in the making of a wide range of strategic decisions

Source: Hugh Combs, David Hobbs and Ellis Jenkins, Management Accounting, Principles and Applications, Sage Publications, 2005, p. 7.

As stated earlier, management accounting aims to provide information used by management. In this regard, the term 'management' may include the activities of individuals in a number of positions, such as:

- Senior managers
- Mid-level managers
- Lower-level managers
- Executive directors with management responsibilities
- Employees not usually considered to be 'manager' such as production line workers, call-centre operatives and sales people

Boxed Content – important information have been highlighted in boxes to help understand the contextual practices and processes.

Gray and Ricketts[1] illustrate the relationship between cost accounting and manag ing in these words:

> The data base (for cost accounting and management accounting) includes comr i.e., the same data are used, by managerial accounting and by cost accountir different ways. *For example*, historical data on labour costs are used by cost a to determine inventory values and cost of goods sold. The historical data on la might be used to estimate the labour cost for the coming year to determine tl workforce needed to meet anticipated production requirements and to estimate requirements to meet weekly payrolls. This represents the use of cost accountir develop managerial accounting data for planning decisions. The historical data costs might be compared with the estimated labour costs to determine if labou used effectively and efficiently. This represents the use of cost accounting data t managerial accounting data for control decisions. The data base also include..... sp for cost accounting and special data for managerial accounting, obviously calle because they are data used only by either cost accounting or by managerial accc

Quoted content throws light on important views and developments in the topic.

MANAGEMENT FUNCTIONS AND MANAGEMENT ACC

The management process implies four basic functions of (1) Planning (2) Organising and (4) Decision Making. Management accounting plays a vital role in these mana performed by managers.

1. *Planning:* Planning is formulating short-term and long-term plans and actions to achieve a particular end. A budget is the financial planning showing how resources are to be acquired and used over a specified time interval.

> **Planning** is formulating sh long-term plans and actior particular end.

Management accounting is closely interwoven in planning both because it provides information for decision-making and because the entire budgeting process is developed around accounting-related reports.

> **Basic functions of Manage** Planning, Organising, Contr sion making.

Management accounting helps managers in planning by providing reports which esti of alternative actions on an enterprise's ability to achieve desired goals. *For exampl* enterprise determines a target profit for a year, it should also determine how to reach *example*, what products are to be sold at what prices? The management accountant de

decision-making. On the other hand, financial accounting, also known as external accounting, produces information and reports for external users. The subject matter and scope of management accounting and financial accounting are displayed in Figure 1.1.

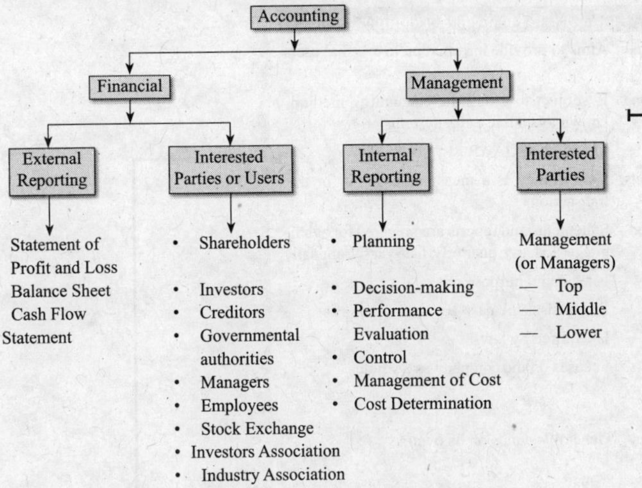

Figure 1.1: Scope of Management Accounting and Financial Accounting

Management accounting and financial accounting differ from each other in the following respects:

1. *Necessity:* Financial accounting must be done. Enough effort must be expended to collect data in acceptable form and with an acceptable degree of

> **Management accounting,** also known as internal accounting, identifies, col - lects, measures, classifies and reports

Numerous **illustrations and exhibits** to clearly understand the concepts discussed.

Merchandising Organizations

A merchandising organisation purchases products for resale. Generally, a merchandising firm provides a link in the physical distribution chain acting as a wholesaler or retailer. It keeps inventories of merchandise only. Exhibit 2.3 displays income statement of a merchandising firm. In merchandising firms, product cost includes the cost of merchandise plus inward freight and possibly certain internal merchandise handling costs. All other expenses are treated as period costs.

Exhibit 2.3: Income Statement in a Merchandising Firm

Income Statement of a Merchandising Firm

			(₹)
Sales			25,00,000
Less:	Cost of goods sold:		
	Beginning inventory	₹ 5,00,000	
Add:	Purchases	15,00,000	
	Goods available for sale	20,00,000	
Less:	Closing inventory	4,25,000	
			15,75,000
	Gross margin		9,25,000
Less:	Operating expenses:		
	Selling expenses	2,50,000	
	Administrative expenses	3,75,000	6,25,000
	Net Income		3,00,000

Cost flows pattern in a merchandising firm has been displayed in Figure 2.12. Operating Costs, as incurred, are immediately expensed. Merchandise, however, is acquired and first transferred to the inventory account. Subsequently, when the merchandise is sold, the cost flows, and it is transferred to an expense account.

The difference between management accounting and financial accounting has been summarised and presented in Table 1.1 below.

Table 1.1: Management Accounting Vs Financial Accounting

	Management Accounting	Financial Accounting
1.	Aims to provide information to internal users	Aims to provide information to external users
2.	Is not subject to any specific accounting method	Is subject to a definite accounting method, known as double-entry system
3.	Is not subject to GAAP	Is subject to GAAP
4.	Can use any measurement unit such as units, labour hours, machine hours	Uses money as a measurement unit for the transactions
5.	Statements and reports are prepared whenever needed	Statements and reports are prepared for a definite period, say, quarterly, half-yearly, annually
6.	Is a specific purpose report	Is a general purpose report
7.	Has more emphasis on the future	Emphasises the past
8.	Is not mandatory by law	Is required by law
9.	Focuses on parts, departments, products, divisions, etc. as well as on the company as a whole	Focuses on the company as a whole
10.	Depends on other disciplines such as economics, finance, operations research, statistics, etc.	Generally stands on its own
11.	Concentrates on relevance and flexibility of data	Concentrates on generating accurate and timely data

SIMILARITIES BETWEEN MANAGEMENT ACCOUNTING AND FINANCIAL ACCOUNTING

Despite the differences between financial accounting and management accounting as stated above, there are some similarities between the two which are as follows:

Several **tables** and **additional information** to help understand with clarity.

its sales mix and, thus, increase its operating profit, profit margin, and rate of return on investment.

If a division's investment turnover increases, and all other factors remain the same, the division's rate of return on investment will increase. *For example*, a division might attempt to increase sales through special sales promotions and thus increase operating efficiency, investment turnover, and rate of return on investment.

The rate of return on investment, profit margin, and investment turnover operate in relationship to one another. Specifically, more income can be earned by either increasing the investment turnover, increasing the profit margin, or both.

Figure 11.4 traces the origin of du pont formula of ROI.

In the early 1900s, the E.I. Du Pont de Nemours Powder Company was the leading firm manufacturing high explosives and was later to grow into one of the world's largest chemical companies. To control and evaluate its operations, Du Pont managers developed the concept of *return on investment*

The financial staff traced the cost and revenues for each product produced. This gave management accurate information on profits, which provided a more precise way of evaluating financial performance. However, managers found product-line profits to be an incomplete measure of performance because these did not indicate the rate of return on capital invested. One manager said, "The true test of whether the profit is too great or too small is the rate of return on the money invested in the business and not the per cent of profit on the cost."

Developing a rate of return on each segment of business required accurate data on investment. Du Pont undertook a careful valuation of each of its plants, properties, and inventories by product line. These data, along with profits, allowed management to track ROI by product line. In addition, Du Pont managers decomposed ROI (Profits ÷ Investment) into its component parts to understand the underlying changes in ROI. Figure 11.4 illustrates this decomposition.

ROI is the product of sales turnover (Sales ÷ Total investment) and return on sales (Earnings ÷ Sales). Given these data, managers could detemine the causes of a product's change in ROI. Du Pont managers used these data to evaluate new capital appropriations tby establishing the policy that there "be no expenditures for additions to the earnings equipment if the same amount of money could be applied to some better purpose in another branch of the company's business."

CRITICAL ANALYSIS AND DISCUSSION QUESTIONS, SELF-ASSESSMENT QUESTIONS, MULTIPLE CHOICE QUESTIONS, PROBLEMS, AND CASES

CRITICAL ANALYSIS AND DISCUSSION QUESTIONS

1. What is activity-based costing? Why is it needed?
2. What is a cost driver? What is the role of cost driver in tracing costs to products? *(M. Com., Delhi, 2008)*
3. Explain the steps in applying activity-based costing (ABC) in a manufacturing company.
4. How are activities grouped in a manufacturing company? *(M. Com., Delhi, 2005, 2008)*
5. Distinguish between activity-based costing and traditional costing system. *(M. Com., Delhi, 2007)*
6. What are the benefits of activity-based costing? *(M. Com., Delhi, 2007)*
7. Define unit-level activities, batch-level activities, product-level activities and facility-level activities.
8. "Overhead costs are source of product cost distortion." Do you agree? Explain.
9. What are the four basic steps required for activity-based costing?
10. Give the criterion for choosing cost drivers for allocating costs to products.
11. Why are conventional product-costing systems more likely to distort product costs in highly automated plants? How do activity-based costing systems deal with such a situation?
12. "Activity-based costing systems yield more accurate product costs than conventional systems because they use more cost drivers to assign support costs to products." Do you agree with this statement? Explain.
13. What are unit-level activities? Batch-level activities? Product-level activities? Facility-level activities?

A reflective section to facilitate critical thinking and self-evaluation.

REFERENCES

1. Joseph G. Louderback III and Jay S. Holmen, *Managerial Accounting*, Thomson and South Western, 2004, p. 90.
2. Joseph G. Louderback III and Jay S. Holmen, *Ibid*, p. 89.
3. Lane K. Anderson and Harold M. Sollenberger, *Managerial Accounting*, South Western Publishing Co., 1992, p. 37.
4. Charles T. Horngreen, Srikant M. Dattar and George Foster, *Cost Accounting, A Managerial Emphasis*, Pearson Education, 2008, p. 39.
5. Lane K. Anderson and Harold M. Sollenberger, *Ibid*, p. 44.
6. Wayne J. Morse, James R. Davis and Al L. Hartgraves, *Management Accounting*, Thomson, 2003, p. 128.
7. James Jiambalvo, *Managerial Accounting*, John Wiley and Sons, 2001, p. 213.

Referencs, Bibliography and **Index** to facilitate easy access and help learn beyond.

Required:

(a) Calculate the total cost of each product, if all overhead costs are absorbed on machine hour rate basis.

(b) Calculate the total cost of each product using activity base costing.

(c) Comment briefly on differences disclosed between overhead traced by present system and those traced by activity based costing. (CA Final, Nov., 2013)

Answer:

(a) A ₹ 89, 280, B ₹ 64,800, C ₹ 39,840 D ₹ 37,296

(b) A ₹ 69,750, B ₹ 60,825, C ₹ 47,100, D ₹ 53,541.

CASES

1. The controller of Apollo System Co. devised a new costing system based on tracing the cost of activities to products. The controller was able to measure post-manufacturing activities, such as selling, promotional, and distribution activities, and allocate these activities to products in order to have a more complete view of the company's product cost. This effort produced better strategic information about the relative profitability of product lines. In addition, the controller used the same product cost information for inventory valuation on the financial statements. Surprisingly, the controller discovered that the company's reported net income was larger under this scheme than under the traditional costing approach.

   Why was the net income larger, and how would you react to the controller's action? (M. Com, Delhi, 2013, 2015)

2. Oriental Insurance Co. is an insurance brokerage company that classified insurance products as either "Standard" or "Deluxe." Which are defined as follows:

   Standard: Electronic claims, few inquiries, mature product

   Deluxe: Paper claims, complex claims to process, many inquiries, a new product with complex options

   The company originally allocated processing and service expenses on the basis of revenue.

Cases to enhance real-world theoretical application and problem-solving.

BRIEF CONTENTS

PART ONE: INTRODUCTION

PART TWO: COST ACCUMULATION SYSTEMS AND PRODUCT COSTING

PART THREE: MANAGERIAL DECISION MAKING

PART FOUR: PLANNING, CONTROL AND PERFORMANCE MEASUREMENT

PART FIVE: MANAGERIAL USES OF FINANCIAL STATEMENTS

DETAILED CONTENTS

PART ONE: INTRODUCTION

PART TWO: COST ACCUMULATION SYSTEMS AND PRODUCT COSTING

PART THREE: MANAGERIAL DECISION MAKING

PART FOUR: PLANNING, CONTROL AND PERFORMANCE MEASUREMENT

PART FIVE: MANAGERIAL USES OF FINANCIAL STATEMENTS

PART

1

INTRODUCTION TO MANAGEMENT ACCOUNTING

1

MANAGEMENT ACCOUNTING: NATURE AND SCOPE

LEARNING OBJECTIVES:

After reading this chapter, you should be able to:

- Define Management Accounting, its Scope and its Role in Management Functions
- Distinguish between Cost Accounting and Management Accounting
- Identify the users of Management Accounting Information
- Explain Financial Accounting, its Limitations and its Differences and Similarities with Management Accounting
- Understand the Role of Management Accountant, Controller and Treasurer
- Explain Management Accounting in Service and Not-For-Profit Organizations, Banks and Merchandiser
- Identify International Aspects of Management Accounting
- Understand Current Focus of Management Accounting

DEFINITIONS OF MANAGEMENT ACCOUNTING

Management accounting is that field of accounting which deals with providing information including financial accounting information to managers for their use in planning, decision-making, performance evaluation, control, management of costs, and cost determination. Management accounting contains reports prepared to fulfil the needs of management.

> **Management accounting** is concerned with data collection from internal and external sources, analysing, processing, interpreting and communicating the information for use within the organization so that management can more effectively plan, make decisions and control operations.

The Institute of Management Accountants (IMA) in Statement No. 1 A (Statements on Management Accounting, 1982), has first defined management accounting as:

- *...the process of identification, measurement, accumulation, analysis, preparation and communication of financial information used by management to plan, evaluate, and control within the organization and to assure appropriate use and accountability for its resources.*

However, in recognition of the increasingly strategic role that management accounting plays in today's organizations, the IMA issued the following revised definition in December 2008.

- *Management accounting is a profession that involves partnering in management decision making, devising planning and performance management system, and providing expertise in financial reporting and control to assist management in the formulation and implementation of an organization's strategy.*

The CIMA (UK) defines the term 'management accounting' in the following manner:

- *Management accounting is an integral part of management concerned with identifying, presenting and interpreting information used for:*
    - *Formulating strategy*
    - *Planning and controlling activities*
    - *Decision taking*
    - *Optimising the use of resources*
    - *Disclosure to shareholders and others external to the entity*
    - *Disclosure to employees*
    - *Safeguarding assets*

Thus, management accounting is concerned with data collection from internal and external sources, analysing, processing, interpreting and communicating the information for use within the organization so that management can more effectively plan, make decisions and control operations.

SCOPE OF MANAGEMENT ACCOUNTING

In management accounting, the objective is to have a data pool which will include any and all information that management may need. *For example*, if management decides to depend on long-term debt for expansion of business, it may be investigated as to what effect this decision will have upon the earnings per share? Should debt in the equity structure be too large or small? Similarly, management may be interested in knowing the adequacy of cash flow receipts to pay current obligations or the effect of inflation on business decisions and performances. Thus, management accounting helps management in the total situation. In achieving this goal, management accounting makes use of information that is drawn from financial accounting and other disciplines, such as economics, finance, statistics, operational research and the like. Management accounting is not confined to the area of product costing, cost and price data.

Depending on the requirements, management accounting has evolved to fulfil the needs of management. Accordingly, some areas of its coverage may become outdated and be discarded and some newer areas may come within the management accounting activities.

Areas of Activity Considered to be Part of Management Accounting

- Budgeting, planning and forecasting
- Calculating the profitability of products, services and operations
- Measuring organizational, divisional and departmental performance
- Comparing results and performance within and between organizations
- Assisting in the process of increasing effectiveness and efficiency
- Assessing the performance of past and future capital investments
- Advising on decisions about product mix, markets to be served and selling prices
- Advising on decisions on whether to outsource products, components, activities and services
- Advising on decisions involving the investment of scarce funds between a range of possible alternatives
- Assisting in the making of a wide range of strategic decisions

Source: Hugh Combs, David Hobbs and Ellis Jenkins, Management Accounting, Principles and Applications, Sage Publications, 2005, p. 7.

As stated earlier, management accounting aims to provide information used by management. In this regard, the term 'management' may include the activities of individuals in a number of positions, such as:

- Senior managers
- Mid-level managers
- Lower-level managers
- Executive directors with management responsibilities
- Employees not usually considered to be 'manager' such as production line workers, call-centre operatives and sales people

COST ACCOUNTING AND MANAGEMENT ACCOUNTING

> **Cost accounting** is cost accumulation for inventory valuation and income determination. **Management accounting** uses cost data for planning, controlling and decision making purposes.

Cost accounting is mainly concerned with ascertainment of product costs and the techniques of product costing and deals with only cost and price data. It is limited to product costing procedures and related information processing. The major function of cost accounting is cost accumulation for inventory valuation and income determination. Management accounting, however, emphasises the use of cost data for planning, control and decision making purposes. It helps management in planning and controlling costs relating to both production and distribution activities.

Linkage between Cost and Management Accounting

In spite of the differing parameters of cost accounting and management accouning, cost accounting is generally indistinguishable from what is known as management or managerial accounting. Both these accounting systems are closely linked as they use common basic data and reports to a material degree. Much of the information used to prepare accounting statements and reports in cost accounting are also used in management accounting reports. Cost accounting largely uses data about production, sales, wages, overhead services. Management accounting utilises the same (and also additional) data to prepare budgets, performance reports, control reports, data analyses for decision-making purposes. Special decision methods, use of highly quantitative methods, behavioural techniques, information systems, budgeting are areas of management accounting.

Gray and Ricketts[1] illustrate the relationship between cost accounting and management accounting in these words:

> The data base (for cost accounting and management accounting) includes common data, i.e., the same data are used, by managerial accounting and by cost accounting, but in different ways. *For example*, historical data on labour costs are used by cost accounting to determine inventory values and cost of goods sold. The historical data on labour cost might be used to estimate the labour cost for the coming year to determine the size of workforce needed to meet anticipated production requirements and to estimate the cash requirements to meet weekly payrolls. This represents the use of cost accounting data to develop managerial accounting data for planning decisions. The historical data on labour costs might be compared with the estimated labour costs to determine if labour is being used effectively and efficiently. This represents the use of cost accounting data to develop managerial accounting data for control decisions. The data base also include..... special data for cost accounting and special data for managerial accounting, obviously called special because they are data used only by either cost accounting or by managerial accounting.

MANAGEMENT FUNCTIONS AND MANAGEMENT ACCOUNTING

The management process implies four basic functions of (1) Planning (2) Organising (3) Controlling and (4) Decision Making. Management accounting plays a vital role in these managerial functions performed by managers.

1. *Planning:* Planning is formulating short-term and long-term plans and actions to achieve a particular end. A budget is the financial planning showing how resources are to be acquired and used over a specified time interval.

> **Planning** is formulating short-term and long-term plans and actions to achieve a particular end.

Management accounting is closely interwoven in planning both because it provides information for decision-making and because the entire budgeting process is developed around accounting-related reports. Management accounting helps managers in planning by providing reports which estimate the effects of alternative actions on an enterprise's ability to achieve desired goals. *For example*, if a business enterprise determines a target profit for a year, it should also determine how to reach that target. *For example*, what products are to be sold at what prices? The management accountant develops data that help managers identify the more profitable products. Similarly, the effects of alternative prices and selling efforts (say, what will the profit be if we cut prices by 5% and increase volume by 15%, etc.) can easily be determined by the management accountant. As part of the budgeting process, management accountants prepare budgeted (forecasted) financial statements, often called proforma statements.

> **Basic functions of Management Process:** Planning, Organising, Controlling and Decision making.

2. *Organising:* Organising is a process of establishing an organizational framework and assigning responsibility to people working in an organization for achieving business goals and objectives.

> **Organising** is a process of establishing an organizational framework and assigning responsibility to people working in an organization for achieving business goals and objectives.

The type of organizational structure differs from one business enterprise to another. In the organising process, departmentalisation can be done by setting up divisions, departments, sections, branches. Organising requires clarity about each manager's responsibility and lines of authority. The various departments and units are inter-related in a hierarchy, with a formal communication structure in which information and instructions are passed downwards to lower level management and upwards to top management level.

Management accounting helps managers in organising by providing reports and necessary information to regulate and adjust operations and activities in the light of changing conditions. *For example*, the reports under management accounting can be prepared on product lines on which basis, managers can decide whether to add or eliminate a product line in the current product mix. Similarly, management accountant can provide sales report, production report to the respective manager for taking suitable action about the sales and production position.

> **Control** is the process of monitoring, measuring, evaluating and correcting actual results to ensure that a business enterprise's goals and plans are achieved.

3. *Controlling:* Control is the process of monitoring, measuring, evaluating and correcting actual results to ensure that a business enterprise's goals and plans are achieved. Control is accomplished with the use of feedback. Feedback is information that can be used to evaluate or correct the steps being taken to implement a plan. Feedback allows the managers to decide to let the operations and activity continue as they are, take remedial actions to put some actions back in harmony with the original plan and goals or do some rearranging and replanning at midstream.

> **Feedback** is information that can be used to evaluate or correct the steps being taken to implement a plan.

Management accounting helps in the control function by producing performance reports and control reports which highlight variances between expected and actual performances. Such reports serve as a basis for taking necessary corrective action to control operations. The use of performance and control reports follows the principle of management by exception. In case of significant differences between budgeted and actual results, a manager will usually investigate to determine what is going wrong and possibly, which subordinates or units might need help.

> **Decision making** is a process of choosing among competing alternatives.

4. *Decision Making:* Decision making is a process of choosing among competing alternatives. Decision-making is inherent in each of the three management functions described above, namely, planning, organising and controlling. A manager cannot plan without making decisions and has to choose among competing objectives and methods to carry out the chosen objectives. Similarly in organising, managers need to decide on an organization structure and on specific actions to be taken on day-to-day operations. In control function, managers have to decide whether variances are worth investigating. The decision-making process includes the following steps:

- Identifying a problem requiring managerial action
- Specifying the objective or goal to be achieved (e.g. maximising return on investment)
- Listing the possible alternative courses of action
- Gathering the information about the consequences of each alternative
- Making a decision, by selecting one of the alternatives

Management accounting plays a critical role in step 4 of the decision-making process. Management accounting system contains a storehouse of valuable information for predicting the results of various courses of action. Management accounting can assist management in formally structuring decision problems as well as placing the alternatives and their consequences in a form that will be easier for management to evaluate. While developing and gathering information for decision making purposes, the management accountant should include qualitative information also in his report to help managers better in their decision-making tasks. Dominiak and Louderback III observe:[2]

> Although managers use accounting data extensively as they make decisions, such data do not answer the questions that managers face. People make decisions and people bring to decision making their experience, values and knowledge which often cannot be incorporated into quantitative analyses. An action that seems best based on an analysis of the accounting data might not be taken because of some factor not captured in those data. *For example*, because the managers of a firm want the company to maintain technological leadership, they might launch a new product that is expected to be unprofitable. Quantifying the benefits of such leadership is not easy. It is unlikely that such a quantification would be included in the management accountant's analysis of the desirability of bringing out the new product. It is , however, quite likely that a report of that analysis would include a comment about the inability to quantify such benefits. That is, reports from managerial accountants are very likely to recognise factors whose financial implication are not incorporated in the reports.

Horngreen, Foster and Datar[3] state that management accountants perform three important roles– problem solving, scorekeeping and attention directing.

- ***Problem Solving:*** Comparative analysis for decision making. This role asks, of the several alternatives available, which is the best
- ***Scorekeeping:*** Accumulating data and reporting reliable results to all levels of management. This role asks how am I doing
- ***Attention Directing:*** Helping managers properly focus their attention. This role asks which opportunities and problems should I look into

Atkinson, Banker, Kaplan and Young[4] infer that management accounting information assists several different organizational functions, operational control, product and customer costing, management control and strategic control, as shown below.

Functions of Management Accounting Information

Operational Control	→	Provide feedback information about the efficiency and quality of tasks performed.
Product and Customer Costing	→	Measure the cost of resources used to produce a product or service and market and deliver the product or service to customers.
Management Control	→	Provide information about the performance of managers and operating units.
Strategic Control	→	Provide information about the enterprise's financial and long run competitive performance, market conditions, customer preferences and technological innovations.

Source: Anthony A. Atkinson, Rajiv D. Banker, Robert S. Kaplan, S. Mark Young, Management Accounting, Prentice Hall International, Inc., 2000, p. 12

USERS OF MANAGEMENT ACCOUNTING INFORMATION

Anyone who needs information to plan, control, coordinate, decide and manage an organization becomes the user of management accounting information. Hugh Combs *et al*[5] have recognised the following as users of information in management accounting for a manufacturing enterprise:

1. A *sales manager* would require information about sales trends, profitability, stock levels, stock turnover rates, salespeople's performance (measured in a variety of ways), customer 'hit rates', sales volumes and values by customer, area, sector, product line, etc.
2. A *production manager* would require information about production rates, production efficiencies, machine capacity usage, productive employee performance, quality measures and trends, stock levels, throughput rates, wastage rates, etc.
3. A *human resources manager* would require information about absenteeism rates, lateness, sickness levels and trends, staff turnover rates, recruitment costs and the effectiveness of the recruitment process, training rates and success rates, comparative salary and wage levels, etc.
4. An *office manager*, in addition to the types of information relevant to the human resources manager, would require information about matters such as the performance of the particular office, however measured, the extent to which service level agreements with other offices had been met, the overall effectiveness of the processes carried out by the office, budgets for the office and the extent to which these are being met, the cost implications of future services to be provided by the office, comparisons between the costs of services provided by the office and those of potential external providers, etc.
5. A *procurement manager* would require information about stock and procurement order levels, the effectiveness and costs of procurement processes, the cost implications of alternative procurement approaches, the comparative costs of alternative suppliers, procurement channels, etc.
6. A *director* or other high-level manager would require information on all of the above matters but, of course, at a more aggregated, summarised level. The high-level manager needs to be able to 'see the wood for the trees' and hence her/his information requirements will have a more strategic bias. Additionally, this type of manager would be more interested in the wider, longer-term and political aspects of the organization's business and thus the appropriate information requirements may be broader in scope, less accurate, and more frequently exhibit a non-financial bias.

Additionally, information of many types will be required, or at least be of interest, to employees of the organization, whether or not they are considered to be 'managers' in the formal sense. The following are examples of such uses of management information by employees:

1. Efficiency of the employee's department, production line, division, etc., as compared to that of others – particularly if the employee's monetary or other rewards are dependent upon performance.
2. Comparative wage levels – particularly if wage negotiations are impending.
3. The profitability and general performance of the organization, as compared with that of competitors – particularly when job security is being considered.
4. The employee's own performance, however measured, as compared with that of other employees – particularly when the employee is considering applying for promotion.

FINANCIAL ACCOUNTING

Financial Accounting is concerned with providing information to external users. It refers to the preparation of general purpose reports for use by persons outside a business enterprise, such as shareholders (existing and potential), creditors, financial analysts, labour unions, government authorities, and the like. Financial accounting is oriented towards the preparation of financial statements which summarise the results of operations for selected periods of time and shows the financial position of the business at particular dates. The following points are important to understand the scope and nature of financial accounting.

Contents

The end product of the financial accounting process are the financial statements that communicate useful information to decision-makers. The financial statements reflect a combination of recorded facts, accounting conventions and personal judgements of the preparers. There are three primary financial statements for a profit making entity in India, viz., the Statement of Profit and Loss (statement of revenues, expenses and profit), and the Balance Sheet (statement of assets, liabilities and owner's equity) and cash flow statement. The accounting information* generated by financial accounting is quantitative, formal, structured, numerical and past-oriented material.

Accounting System

> **Financial Accounting** is concerned with providing information to external users.

The accounting system includes various techniques and procedures used by the accountant (preparer) in measuring, describing and communicating financial data to users. Journals, ledgers and other accounting techniques used in processing financial accounting information depend upon the concept of the double-entry system. This technique includes Generally Accepted Accounting Principles (GAAP).** The standard of generally accepted accounting principles includes not only broad guidelines of general application but also detailed practices and procedures.

Measurement Unit

Financial accounting is primarily concerned with measurement of economic resources and obligations and changes in them. Financial accounting measures in terms of monetary units of a society in which it operates. *For example*, the common denominator or yardstick used for accounting measurement is the rupee in India and dollar in the USA. The assumption is that the rupee or the dollar is a useful measuring unit.

Users of Financial Accounting Information

As stated earlier, financial accounting information is intended primarily to serve external users. Some users have direct interest in reported information. Examples of such users are owners, creditors, potential owners, suppliers, management, tax authorities, employees, customers. Some users need financial accounting information to help those who have direct interest in a business enterprise. Examples of such users are financial analysts and advisers, stock exchanges, financial press and reporting agencies, trade associations, labour unions. These user groups having direct/indirect interest have different objectives and diverse informational needs. The emphasis in financial accounting

---

* The accounting information in a very broad sense means "economic information." See American Association's Committee Report on Basic Auditing Concepts, Supplement to the Accounting Review. 1972. p. 23.

** Generally Accepted Accounting Principles (GAAP) encompass the conventions, rules and procedures necessary to define accepted accounting practice at a particular time.

has been on general-purpose information which, obviously, is not intended to satisfy any specialised needs of individual users or specific user groups.

LIMITATIONS OF FINANCIAL ACCOUNTING

Financial accounting is significant for management as it helps them to direct and control the firm's activities. It also helps business managements in determining appropriate managerial policies in different areas such as production, sales, administration and finance. Financial accounting suffers from the following limitations which have been responsible for the emergence of cost and management accounting:

1. Financial accounting does not provide detailed cost information for different departments, processes, products, jobs in the production divisions. Management may need information about different products, sales territories and sales activities which are also not available in financial accounting.

2. Financial accounting does not set up a proper system of controlling materials and supplies. Undoubtedly, if material and supplies are not controlled in a manufacturing concern, they will lead to losses on account of misappropriation, misutilisation, scrap, defectives, etc.

3. The recording and accounting for wages and labour is not done for different jobs, processes, products, departments. This creates problems in analysing the costs associated with different activities.

4. It is difficult to know the behaviour of costs in financial accounting as expenses are not classified into direct and indirect and therefore cannot be classified as controllable and uncontrollable. Cost management which is the most important objective of all business enterprises, cannot be achieved with the aid of financial accounting alone.

5. Financial accounting does not possess an adequate system of standards to evaluate the performance of departments and employees working in departments. Standards need to be developed for materials, labour and overheads so that a firm can compare the work of workers, supervisors and executives with what should have been done in an allotted period of time.

6. Financial accounting contains historical cost information which is accumulated at the end of the accounting period. The historical cost is not a reliable basis for predicting future earnings, solvency, or overall managerial effectiveness. Historical cost information is relevant but not adequate for all purposes.

7. Financial accounting does not provide information to analyse the losses due to various factors, such as idle plant and equipment, seasonal fluctuations in volume of business, etc. It does not help management in taking important decisions about expansion of business, dropping of a product, alternative methods of production, improvement in product, etc.

8. Financial accounting does not provide necessary cost data to determine the price of the product being manufactured or the service being rendered to the consumers.

In spite of the above limitations, financial accounting has utility and is an important and conceptually rich area. Because of growing business complexities and advances in knowledge of human behaviour and decision processes, the scope and methods of financial accounting are changing. Financial accounting theory and practice will probably be broadened and improved considerably in the future.

DIFFERENCES BETWEEN MANAGEMENT ACCOUNTING AND FINANCIAL ACCOUNTING

As stated earlier, management accounting, also known as internal accounting, identifies, collects, measures, classifies and reports information that is useful to managers in planning, control and decision-making. On the other hand, financial accounting, also known as external accounting, produces information and reports for external users. The subject matter and scope of management accounting and financial accounting are displayed in Figure 1.1.

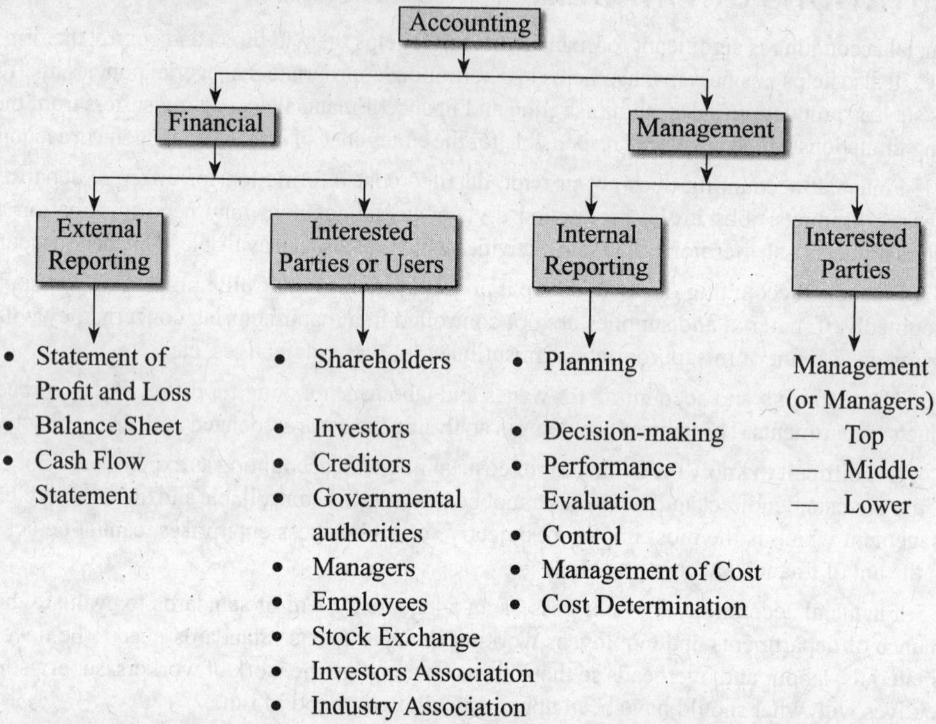

Figure 1.1: Scope of Management Accounting and Financial Accounting

Management accounting and financial accounting differ from each other in the following respects:

> **Management accounting,** also known as internal accounting, identifies, collects, measures, classifies and reports information that is useful to managers in planning, control and decision-making. **Financial accounting,** also known as external accounting, produces information and reports for external users.

1. *Necessity:* Financial accounting must be done. Enough effort must be expended to collect data in acceptable form and with an acceptable degree of accuracy to meet the requirements of the accounting standards bodies, and other outside parties, whether or not the management regards this information as useful. Management accounting, by contrast, is entirely optional: No outside agencies specify what must be done or that anything need be done. Because it is optional, there is no point in collecting a piece of management accounting information unless its value to management is believed to exceed the cost of collecting it.

2. *Purpose:* The purpose of financial accounting is to produce financial statements for outside users. When the statements have been produced, this purpose has been accomplished. Management accounting information, on the other hand, is only a means to an end, the end being the planning, implementing, and controlling functions of management.

3. ***Primary Users of Information:*** The users of financial accounting statements are mainly external to the business enterprise. External users include shareholders, creditors, financial analysts, government authorities, stock exchange, labour unions, etc. These financial statements are relevant to managements but are not adequate for the purpose of planning, control and decision-making. The information generated under the management accounting system is used by members of management at different levels. The nature of internal reports and data varies for different levels of management in conformity with their information requirements for analysing business operations and for planning and control purposes.

4. ***Accounting Structure and Method:*** Financial accounting is built around one fundamental equation : Assets = Liabilities and owners' equity. Financial accounting follows the double-entry system for recording, classifying and summarising business transactions. Management accounting is not based on the double-entry system. The only constraint regarding management accounting principles and methods is that they should be useful for management purposes.

5. ***Accounting Principle:*** Financial accounting information must be reported in accordance with Generally Accepted Accounting Principles (GAAP). GAAP are important in financial accounting and are used extensively while recording, classifying, summarising, and reporting business transactions. The use of GAAP adds credibility and reliability to financial statements and creates confidence among the financial statement users.

On the contrary, management accounting is not bound to use the "generally accepted accounting principles." It can use any accounting technique or practice which generates useful information. Besides, data developed in management accounting may be facts, estimates, projections, analyses, etc.

6. ***Unit of Measurement:*** All information under financial accounting is in terms of money. That is, transactions measured in terms of money have already occurred. In comparison, management accounting applies any measurement unit that is useful in a particular situation. Besides the monetary unit, the management accountant may find it necessary to use such measures, such as number of labour hours, machine hours and product units for the purpose of analysis and decision-making. Historical cost and past transactions are essential to financial accounting but may be secondary to management accounting as they are not of much use to management.

7. ***Time Orientation:*** Financial accounting data and statements are developed for a definite period, usually a year or a half-year or a quarter. It requires that financial statements be developed and presented at regular time intervals.

Management accounting reports and statements are prepared whenever needed. Reports may be prepared on a monthly, weekly or even daily basis. Frequency of reports is determined by particular planning, controlling and decision-making needs.

8. ***Information Content:*** Financial accounting systems capture only a few characteristics (i.e., datc, account, and amount in rupees) about only a subset of organizational events, those defined by financial accountants to be "accounting transactions." Financial accounting reports summarize the effects of these events in primarily monetary form.

Management accounting reports, on the other hand, summarize many different kinds of information that is useful for decision makers. They include non-monetary as well as monetary information. They show quantities of material as well as its monetary cost, number of employees and hours worked as well as labor costs, units of products sold as well as amounts of revenue, defect rates as well as scrap costs, and so on. Some of the information is strictly non-monetary; examples include new product development times, production yields, percentages of shipments made on time, product failure rates, numbers of customer complaints received, and competitors' estimated market shares.

9. *Information Precision:* Management needs information rapidly and is often willing to sacrifice some precision to gain speed in reporting. Thus, in management accounting, approximations are often as useful as, or even more useful than, numbers that are more precise. Although financial accounting cannot be absolutely precise either, the approximations used in management accounting are broader than those in financial accounting.

10. *Report Timeliness:* Because of the need for precision and a review by outside auditors, plus the time requirements of printing and distribution, financial accounting reports are distributed several weeks after the close of the accounting period. Larger companies annual reports for a fiscal year ending March 31 are often not received by shareholders until June or July. By contrast, because management accounting reports may contain information on which management needs to take prompt action, these reports are usually issued within a few day of the end of a month (or the next morning for a daily report).

11. *General Purpose Report vs. Specific Purpose Report:* Financial accounting produces information and reports which are general purpose reports in order to serve the informational needs of many external users such as shareholders, creditors, potential investors, customers, suppliers, regulatory authorities, employees and the general public. Financial accounting is concerned with overall firm performance rather than individual segments or departments.

On the contrary, the reports and data developed in management accounting are known as specific purpose reports designed for a particular user (manager) or particular decision. Management accounting uses internal reports to evaluate the performance of entities, product lines, departments and managers.

12. *Historical vs. Futuristic Data:* Financial accounting has a historical orientation and records and reports what has happened. Financial accounting concentrates on the results of past decisions.

Management accounting has a futuristic orientation and concentrates on what is likely to happen in the future. This is due to the fact that management accounting emphasises on developing information for planning, control and decision-making purposes. Therefore, management accounting focuses on the future more than the financial accounting.

13. *Report Entity:* Financial accounting focuses on the company as a whole. Sometimes, in financial accounting, some information is given about different products or lines of activity due to financial reporting requirements as provided in the Companies Act/Other rules and regulations.

Management accounting provides detailed and disaggregated information about products, individual activities, divisions, plants, operations, tasks or any other responsibility centres.

14. *Use of Disciplines:* Management accounting uses other disciplines to prepare the most useful reports and analyses for the managers. Some such disciplines are economics, finance, management, information system, industrial engineering, operations research, marketing, computer science, production management, statistics, psychology and sociology etc. In this way, management accounting is much broader than financial accounting.

15. *Liability Potential:* Although it happens infrequently, a company may be used by its shareholders or creditors for allegedly reporting misleading financial information in its annual report or in filings with Registrar of Companies. By contrast, as previously stated, management accounting reports need not be in accord with GAAP and are not public documents. Although a manager may be held liable for some illegal or unethical action and management accounting infomration conceivably may have played some role in his or her taking that action, it is the action itself, not the management accounting documents, that gives rise to the liability.

The difference between management accounting and financial accounting has been summarised and presented in Table 1.1 below.

Table 1.1: Management Accounting Vs Financial Accounting

	Management Accounting	Financial Accounting
1.	Aims to provide information to internal users	Aims to provide information to external users
2.	Is not subject to any specific accounting method	Is subject to a definite accounting method, known as double-entry system
3.	Is not subject to GAAP	Is subject to GAAP
4.	Can use any measurement unit such as units, labour hours, machine hours	Uses money as a measurement unit for the transactions
5.	Statements and reports are prepared whenever needed	Statements and reports are prepared for a definite period, say, quarterly, half-yearly, annually
6.	Is a specific purpose report	Is a general purpose report
7.	Has more emphasis on the future	Emphasises the past
8.	Is not mandatory by law	Is required by law
9.	Focuses on parts, departments, products, divisions, etc. as well as on the company as a whole	Focuses on the company as a whole
10.	Depends on other disciplines such as economics, finance, operations research, statistics, etc.	Generally stands on its own
11.	Concentrates on relevance and flexibility of data	Concentrates on generating accurate and timely data

SIMILARITIES BETWEEN MANAGEMENT ACCOUNTING AND FINANCIAL ACCOUNTING

Despite the differences between financial accounting and management accounting as stated above, there are some similarities between the two which are as follows:

1. Both deal with economic and business events.
2. Both try to quantify the results of business activity and transactions.
3. Both deal with financial statements, revenues, expenses, assets, liabilities, and cash flows.
4. Both are part of total accounting information system and the same accounting information system which is used in financial accounting can be used in management accounting to prepare some reports/analysis needed therein, if not all the reports.
5. Further, the reports prepared in management accounting and financial accounting are based on the same data base which are originally created to fulfil the accounting and reporting requirements of financial accounting. This is the reason that when the accounting system in an organization collects and classifies information, it does so in a manner and format which can be appropriate for both the accounting systems. To achieve this dual purpose in developing the data base, many business enterprises expand this data base so as to fulfil adequately the informational needs of their managers and decision-makers. *For example*, investors and

other users are primarily interested in the overall profitability of a company. However, the managers within the company are more interested in the profitability of individual products. In this situation, the accounting system can be developed and designed so as to provide both the total company profits as well as profits for the individual products. The vital point about the accounting system is the flexibility, that is, accounting system should be flexible to provide different data to different persons for different purposes.

6. Management and financial accounting are also similar with regard to determination and measurement of costs, their assignment to different accounting periods and allocation of costs to different departments and segments. The concepts and principles which are used in the area of financial accounting for the purposes of cost accumulation and cost allocation may also be suitable for management accounting as well. It means any method, principle or concept which are developed for financial accounting, can be used for preparing reports and analyses in management accounting if they are found useful for managerial purposes.

MANAGEMENT ACCOUNTANT — STATUS AND FUNCTIONS

The management accountant, often referred to as controller, is the manager of accounting information used in planning, control and decision-making areas. He is responsible for collecting, processing and reporting information that will help managers/decision makers in their planning, controlling and decision-making activities. He participates in all accounting activities within the organization.

Line vs. Staff Position

The role and responsibility of a management accountant is one of support. They provide help to those managers who have primary responsibility to fulfil basic managerial functions. Positions that have direct responsibility for the basic objectives of an organization are known as line positions. Positions that are supportive in nature and have only indirect responsibility for an organization's basic objectives are called staff positions. For instance, a manager of a production department holds a line position and has responsibility and authority to make decisions concerning his department. The production manager and similar other managers holding line positions formulate policies and goals and make decisions that have impact on production. The management accountant, however, has no authority over the production manager and other line positions managers. But since the management accountants have the responsibility of providing and interpreting accounting information, they can have significant influence on the policies and decisions made by production and similar line managers.

Functions of Management Accountant

Management accountants perform many vital responsibilities and functions within an organization such as:

1. Providing help in the design of an accounting information system
2. Collecting data
3. Helping in the maintenance of accounting records, preparation of financial statements
4. Helping in the budget preparation
5. Preparation of performance reports, control reports, special managerial reports/analyses for planning, control and decision-making
6. Coordinating budget-making and report preparation activities
7. Interpreting accounting data based on the particular requirements of a manager in a given situation
8. Ensuring that the accounting information system is adequate and useful in accordance with the budgets, plans, policies and decision requirements

Proactive Role

According to Hilton[6], managerial accountants add value to an organization by pursuing five major objectives:

1. Providing information for decision making and planning, and proactively participating as part of the management team in the decision-making and planning processes
2. Assisting managers in directing and controlling operational activities
3. Motivating managers and other employees towards the organization's goals
4. Measuring the performance of activities, subunits, managers, and other employees within the organization
5. Assessing the organization's competitive position, and working with other managers to ensure the organization's long-run competitiveness in its industry

Nowadays, managerial accounting analysis is considered so crucial in managing an enterprise that in most cases, management accountants are integral members of the management team. Far from playing a passive role as information providers, management accountants take a proactive role in both the strategic and day-to-day decisions that confront an enterprise.

Different Data/Analysis Needed

The management accountant should clearly understand that different decisions made in the organization require different types of data. Short-run decisions need different data than long-run decisions. Similarly, decisions affecting the total company such as product lines to be added in the existing product mix need more aggregate data than some other decisions, say, the optimum use of a particular machine. Therefore, the management accountant should ensure that the information system of the organization meets the need of all decision makers within the organization who require information for the performance of their jobs. *For example*, managers responsible for the sales of particular product might need weekly sales report for each territory. Their supervisor, who also supervises other managers, might need a weekly report for a group of products. The chief sales executive may require monthly reports of sales by product groups and sales territories. The management accountant must ensure that the information system meets these varying needs.

The management accountant is also required to make/prepare special analyses when managers consider non-routine decisions. In some decisions, such as the possibility of building a new plant, all relevant data might not be available in a format that enables managers to select the best course of action. The management accountant should develop relevant information to serve such special decisions and purposes. In fact, with regard to creating suitable information system, the management accountant is himself a decision-maker and decides what data should be gathered for the managers to help them in their decisions. If it is found that data given in a report to a manager is not useful for taking decisions, the accounting system can be changed/modified appropriately.

Financial and Non-financial Data

Although much of the information provided by the management accounting system is financial, there is a strong trend towards the presentation of substantial non-financial data as well. Management accountants supply all kinds of information to management and act as strategic business partners in support of management's role in decision making and managing the organization's activities.

Because of the vital functions performed and role played by a management accountant in an organization, the management accountant is often recognised as a member of the top-management team and encouraged to participate in planning, control and decision-making activities. Thus, it can be said that a management accountant is not only a service arm to management but also he is a part of the management.

Gary Siegel Organization in its report observes:

> Growing numbers of management accountants spend the bulk of their time as internal consultants or business analysts within their companies. Technlogical advances have liberated them from the mechanical aspects of accounting. They spend less time preparing standardized reports and more time analyzing and interpreting information. Many have moved from the isolation of accounting departments to be physically positioned in the operating departments with which they work. Management accountants work on cross-functional teams, have extensive face-to-face communications with people throughout their organizations, and are actively involved in decision making. . . . They are trusted advisors.[7]

MANAGEMENT ACCOUNTANT, CONTROLLER & TREASURER

Most often, a person discharging the functions of management accountant may not be titled as management accountant in an organization. There may be a top executive incharge of all finance and accounting activities, known as finance manager/chief finance officer. The treasurer is generally concerned with the organization's financial matters such as raising and management of cash. On the other hand, the Controller looks after operating matters with a view to assist management in decision making. The Controller provides managers with specialised services such as advice and help in budgeting, analysing variances, pricing decisions, special decisions, etc. The Controller is considered an organization's top accounting officer. Sometimes, the Controller prepares the annual accounts and financial statements for external users.

The Financial Executives Institute of USA, an association of corporate treasurers and controllers, distinguishes its functions as follows[8]:

Table 1.2: Controllership Vs Treasurership

Controllership	Treasurership
Planning for control	Provision of capital
Reporting and interpreting	Investor relations
Evaluating and consulting	Short-term financing
Tax administration	Banking and custody
Government reporting	Credits and collections
Protection of assets	Investments
Economic appraisal	Risk management (insurance)

Management accounting is the primary means of implementing the first three functions of controllership.

MANAGEMENT ACCOUNTING IN SERVICE AND NOT-FOR-PROFIT ORGANIZATIONS

Service organizations are those organizations that do not produce or sell tangible goods. Many not-for-profit organizations such as hospitals, educational institutions, government agencies and departments are also considered service organizations. There are some service organizations who are profit seeking organizations such as banks, transportation companies, insurance companies, hotels, real estate companies, accounting and auditing firms, management consultants, etc. Generally, service organizations are the organizations other than manufacturers, wholesalers and retailers.

In service organizations, managements perform the same functions as in profit seeking organizations. Accountants' roles are almost identical in both types of organization. Budgets are prepared, accounting system is designed, adequate planning and control systems and decision-making tools are used in both the organizations.

Horngreen *et al*[9] has identified the following characteristics of both profit seeking and not-for-profit service organizations:

1. ***Labor is Intensive:*** The highest proportion of expenses in schools and law firms are wages, salaries, and payroll-related costs, not the costs relating to the use of machinery, equipment and physical facilities.
2. ***Output is usually Difficult to Define:*** The output of a university might be defined as the number of degrees granted, but many critics would maintain that the real output is "what is contained in the students' brains." Therefore, measuring output is often considered impossible.
3. ***Major Inputs and Outputs Cannot be Stored:*** An empty airline seat cannot be saved for a later flight, and a hotel's available labour force and rooms are either used or unused as each day occurs.

MANAGEMENT ACCOUNTING IN OTHER ORGANIZATIONS: BANKS AND MERCHANDISING FIRMS

Generally, it is customary to consider manufacturing enterprises while discussing management accounting. However, management accounting can be used in any business, in any organization from a large-sized company to a family grocery shop. As stated earlier, service organizations, such as banks, hotels, accounting and auditing firms, insurance companies etc. require internal accounting data to determine the costs of providing their services and the price to charge. Similarly, not-for-profit and government units and agencies use internal accounting information to develop budgets and performance reports during normal operations. In fact, every person employed in a management-related job must help develop and rely on management accounting information. In the following paragraphs, the management accounting information needs of a bank and a merchandiser have been analysed. Subsequently, the information needs of managers in a manufacturing company, a bank and a merchandiser have been compared.

Banks

Banks typically provides its customers with various services for a fee. Banks provide the loans and charge interest as payment for the service. Bank managers require many types of data and reports relating to different activities of banks. Accounting information system is critical to managing bank's resources. Managers are responsible for safeguarding customers deposits and accounts opened by them, monitoring cash reserves, and doing cash balancing and monitoring. Bank managers use budgets and service-line analysis reports extensively. Cash management for internal use is also important. Bank managers make capital expenditure decisions in much the same way as managers in manufacturing. Although normal operating decisions differ in many ways, the bank manager must continually analayze the services provided and the optimal service mix of the bank, just as the manufacturing manager must analyse the products manufactured and the optimal product mix to be produced. Loan activities require an effective system for credit verification with related reporting. Monitoring of loan payments and defaulting loans is very important.

Since a bank's products are its services, it needs information to determine if its services operate efficiently and are cost effective. Therefore, information on cost per loan, cost per savings transaction, and cost per account maintenance has become increasingly important to bank managers.

Merchandising Firms

Merchandising concerns focus on management of three things — merchandise, personnel, customers. For merchandisers, the most important asset is merchandise. Managers need to perform the following functions with regard to merchandise

1. Ordering proper items in economical quantities
2. Storing merchandise safely after it is received
3. Displaying items to attract customers
4. Deciding about marketing efforts to promote sales
5. Delivering / Distributing items sold to customers

Managers require adequate and reliable information to perform / manage above responsibilities. Reports, requisitions, statements, analysis are needed to help the managers. Information is also needed about inventory records, economic order quantity to reduce costs, merchandise quality, deterioration, losses caused by theft, quantity on hand, customers demand, reorder point. Managers in merchandising firms are engaged in other activities as well, such as budgeting, cash management, product wise analysis, capital expenditure decisions, product selling cost analysis, preparing reports for different levels of management, preparing reports for government and taxation authorities, operating decisions concerning special orders, sales mix, personnel placement. Management accounting helps managers by providing accounting information concerning their areas of responsibility.

To conclude, information needs of managers in manufacturing firms, banks, merchandising firms differ from each other to a large extent due to varying objectives and needs, and business activities involved. However, in some respects, they have similar needs. Exhibit 1.1 displays and compares the information needs of managers in manufacturing company, banks and merchandising firms.

Exhibit 1.1: Comparative Analysis of Information Needs of Different Managers

Data, Reports and Analyses	*Manufacturing Company*	*Bank*	*Merchandising Concerns*
(*i*) Product/service costing:			
For cost control	×	×	×
For pricing decisions	×	×	
For inventory valuation	×		
(*ii*) Budget preparation	×	×	×
(*iii*) Cash management system:			
Normal operating funds	×	×	×
Funds held/managed for others		×	
(*iv*) Production planning	×		
(*v*) Product-line management	×		
(*vi*) Service-line management		×	
(*vii*) Merchandise-line management			×

(*viii*)	Capital expenditure analysis	×	×	×
(*ix*)	Distribution/selling :			
	Expense analysis	×		×
(*x*)	Special reporting activities	×	×	×
(*xi*)	Inventory control systems:			
	Raw materials	×		
	Work in process	×		
	Finished goods	×		
	Merchandise			×
	Funds on deposit		×	
(*xii*)	Operating decisions:			
	Special orders	×		×
	Sales mix	×		×
	Service mix		×	
	Make or buy	×		
	Sell or process further	×		
(*xiii*)	Preparation of tax reports	×	×	×

INTERNATIONAL ASPECTS OF MANAGEMENT ACCOUNTING

In today's globalised world and economy, business managers encounter new and more difficult decisions. Should Indian company raise capital in India or elsewhere. Where the products produced by Indian manufacturers be sold and to customers in which countries. Should a company manufacture its components in one country and do the assembly in another country. How far products should be changed and modified to accommodate tastes, cultures of other different customers. Multinational companies face other variety of decisions such as management of foreign currency. The above mentioned situations expand the information needs of managers. Therefore, in today's global economy management accountants have now greater responsibility to develop and provide adequate information to managers. This is further influencing the development of management accounting in today's competitive business world.

CURRENT FOCUS OF MANAGEMENT ACCOUNTING

Management accounting is required to change to satisfy the demands of the current economic environment. There is a need for more innovative and useful management accounting techniques to improve productivity, to reduce costs, to improve quality, to determine accurate product costs to satisfy managerial needs of planning, decision making and control. Hansen and Mowen[10] observe that management accounting has the following focus in today's business environment.

1. ***Activity-based Costing (ABC) and Activity-based Management (ABM):*** The demand for more accurate and relevant management accounting information has led to the development of activity-based costing and activity-based management. Activity-based costing improves the accuracy of assigning costs by first tracing costs to activities and then to products or customers that consume these activities. Process value analysis, on the other hand, emphasizes activity analysis—trying to determine why activities are performed and how well they are performed. The objective is to find ways to perform necessary activities more efficiently and to eliminate those that do not create customer value. Activity-based management is a system wide, integrated approach that focuses management's attention on activities with the objective

of improving customer value and the resulting profit. Activity-based management emphasizes activity-based costing (ABC) and process value analysis.

2. *Increasing Customer Value:* Globalisation has brought a wave of change in the way business operates and create value for the customer. Now the market is not firm-centric but customer-centric. Customer value is a key focus because firms can establish a competitive advantage by creating better customer value for the same or lower cost than that of competitors or creating equivalent value for lower cost than that of competitors. Customer value is the difference between what a customer receives (customer realization) and what the customer gives up (customer sacrifice). Increasing customer value means increasing customer realization or decreasing customer sacrifice, or both.

Increasing customer value to create a sustainable competitive advantage is achieved through selection of strategies. Cost information plays a critical role in this process and does through a process called strategic cost management. Strategic cost management is the use of cost data to develop and identify superior strategies that will produce a sustainable competitive advantage. A focus on customer value means that the management accounting system should produce information about both realization and sacrifice.

3. *Cross-functional Perspective:* Management accounting has a cross-functional perspective and management accountant must understand many functions of the business, from manufacturing to marketing to distribution to customer service. When customer value is attempted to be increased, all the functions of a business become interrelated; a decision affecting one affects the others. A cross-functional perspective helps us to see the forest, not just one or two of the trees. This broader vision allows managers to increase quality, reduce the time required to service customers and improve efficiency. In this perspective, management accounting helps other business functions through providing useful information and analysis.

4. *Total Quality Management:* Continuous improvement is fundamental for establishing a state of manufacturing excellence. Manufacturing excellence is the key to survival in today's world-class competitive environment. A philosophy of **total quality management,** in which manufacturers strive to create an environment that will enable workers to manufacture perfect (zero-defect) products, has replaced the "acceptable quality" attitudes of the past. Quality cost measurement and reporting are key features of a management accounting system for both manufacturing and service industries. In both cases, the management accounting system should be able to provide both operational and financial information about quality, including information such as the number of defects, quality cost reports, quality cost trend reports, and quality cost performance reports.

5. *Improving Efficiency and Reducing Time:* Improving efficiency in business activities is of vital concern in all business enterprises. Both financial and non-financial measures of efficiency are needed. Cost is a critical measure of efficiency. Trends in costs over time and measure of productivity changes can provide important measures of the efficiency of continuous improvement decisions. (output measured in relation to the inputs).

Reducing time in all phases of production cycles, selling and distribution should be an important target for all businesses. Firms should deliver products or services quickly by eliminating nonvalue-added time and time of no-value to the customer. Decrease in nonvalue added time has correspondence with increase in quality.

Now-a-days, the technological innovation has increased for many industries, and the life of a particular product can be quite short. Managers must be able to respond quickly and decisively to changing market conditions. Information to allow them to accomplish this must be available from a management accounting information system.

6. *Electronic Business (E-Business):* E-business is doing business transaction through information and communication technology. E-commerce is buying and selling products using information and communication technology. Business firms can expand sales and lower costs through e-business compared to paper-based transactions. Management accounting plays signification role in e-business through providing relevant cost information about its benefits, risks and opportunities. *For example*, business managers need to know the cost per electronic transaction versus cost per paper transaction.

7. *Focus on Value Creation Chain:* Strategic managment involves organizational planning for deployment of resources (such as fixed assets, employees, and working capital) to create value for customers and shareholders. The strategic management of resources is concerned with the following issues:[11]

- how to deploy resources to support strategies
- how resources are used in, or recovered from, change processes
- how customer value and shareholder value will serve as guides to the effective use of resources
- how resources are to be deployed and redeployed over time

These areas cannot be measured by financial accounting because they often relate to non-monetary information and measurements. Thus, management accounting provides the necessary estimates to help managers address these issues and focus on strategic objectives.

The foundation of the strategic management of resources is the value creation chain or the set of processes and activities that convert resources into products and services that have value to the organization's customers. An organizational value chain focuses on the key value-creating activities within an organization. It is less concerned with the traditional functions of organizational boundaries, instead encouraging a wider perspective to be taken by both operational managers and support areas such as accounting. From a management accounting perspective, that would mean considering the wider implications of a decision rather than just the impact at the local level. The value creation chain includes suppliers, internal processes, and customers. Managers can use the value creation chain to determine which activities create customer value as reflected in product/service prices and thus, revenues earned. By reducing or eliminating activities that do not add value within the value creation chain, organizations can become more efficient and effective. Management acconting provides information to managers on value creation.

REFERENCES

1. Jack Gray and Don Ricketts, *Costs and Management Accounting*, McGraw Hill Publishing Co., 1982, p. 12
2. Geraldine F-Dominiak and Joseph G. Louderback III, *Managerial Accounting*, PWS Kent Publishing Co., 1991, pp. 4-5
3. Charles T. Horngreen, George Foster and Srikant M. Datar, *Cost Accounting, A Managerial Emphasis*, Pearson Education, p. 9
4. Anthony A. Atkinson, Rajiv D. Banker, Robert S. Kaplan, S. Mark Young, *Management Accounting*, Prentice Hall International, 2000, p. 12
5. Hugh Combs *et al*, *Management Accounting*, Sage Publications, 2005, p. 9
6. Ronald W. Hilton, *Managerial Accounting*, Tata McGraw Hill, 2005, p. 6

7. Gary Siegel Organization, *Counting More, Counting Less: Transformatons in the Management Accounting Profession. The 1999 Practice Analysis of Management Accounting.* Institute of Managment Accountants, Montvale, NJ, August 1999, p. 3

8. Charles T. Horngreen, Gary L. Sundem and William O. Stratton, *Introduction to Management Accounting*, Prentice Hall, 2006, p. 18

9. Charles T. Horngreen, Gary L. Sundem and William O. Stratton, *Ibid*, p. 10

10. Don R. Hansen and Maryanne M. Mowen, *Management Accounting*, Thomson South Western, 2005, pp. 9-15

11. Brenda M. Mallouk, Gary Spraakaman, Cecily A Raiborn, Jesse T. Barfield, Michael R. Kinney *Managerial Accounting*, IInd Canadian Edition, 2007, p. 14.

CRITICAL ANALYSIS AND DISCUSSION QUESTIONS, SELF-ASSESSMENT QUESTIONS, MULTIPLE CHOICE QUESTIONS AND CASES

CRITICAL ANALYSIS AND DISCUSSION QUESTIONS

1. What is management accounting? Discuss the role of management accounting in the areas of planning, control and decision-making. *(M. Com., Delhi, 2005)*
2. How do management accounting and financial accounting differ? *(M. Com., Delhi, 2010, 2015)*
3. What are the steps involved in the managerial decision-making process? What role does management accounting play in that process?
4. "The best management accounting system is one that provides managers with all of the information they would like to have." Do you agree with this statement? Give reasons.
5. Why is financial accounting subject to more strict rules and regulations than management accounting?
6. "A management accountant is both an information provider and a part of management." Explain.
7. What are the four basic functions of the management process? How does management accounting help in this process?
8. "Management accounting is an extension of financial accounting techniques for special uses." Explain this statement with suitable illustrations. *(M. Com., Delhi)*
9. What brought about the change from simple cost accounting to management accounting? Briefly explain the principal techniques employed by the management accountant to help the management in their attention-directing and problem-solving functions. *(M. Com., Delhi)*
10. "The emphasis of financial accounting and management accounting differ." Explain. *(M. Com., Delhi University, 2009)*
11. "Management accounting is an extension of financial accounting." Critically examine this statement and bring out the difference between management accounting and financial accounting? *(M. Com., Delhi)*
12. Explain the role and responsibilities of a management accountant in a large-scale business enterprise. *(M. Com., Delhi, 2001)*
13. "Management accounting is nothing else but financial and cost accounting tailored to the requirements of management." Defend or criticise the statement. Give reasons. *(M. Com., Delhi, 2011)*
14. Examine the role of management accounting in a fast changing business environment. In what manner can management accounting be considered as an extension of financial accounting. Give salient points of distinction between the two. *(M. Com., Delhi)*
15. Explain the difference between financial accounting and management accounting. What is the role of a management accountant in a business firm? *(M. Com., Delhi, 2002, 2008)*

16. Explain the nature and scope of management accounting. In what ways do the roles and responsibilities of management accountants differ from those of financial accountants?
17. What types of organizations need management accounting information system?
18. Why do a company's operators/workers, managers and executives have different information needs than do shareholders and external suppliers of capital.? (*M. Com., Delhi* 2006)
19. Why financial accounting information alone may be insufficient for the informational needs of managers and executives? (*M. Com., Delhi* 2003, 2007)
20. How does the role for management accounting change as the environment becomes more competitive?
21. Why does management need measures besides financial measurements to assess how well their business performed?
22. What are the differences between the management accounting information needed in manufacturing organizations and that needed in service organizations.?
23. "Good accounting provides automatic control of operations." Do you agree? Explain.
24. "The Management Accountant does control in a special sense". Explain.
25. What is a service organization? What are their characteristics? In what way a service organization is different from other organizations?
26. "The management accountant is not important in non-profit organizations, such as departments of central government and state governments, and non-profit hospitals, because they do not have to earn profit." Do you agree with this statement? Why or why not.?
27. "It is important for management accountants to understand the uses of accounting data and for users of data to understand accounting. Only in this way can accounting provide the appropriate accounting data for the correct uses". Do you agree with this statement? Why or why not?
28. "The best management accounting system provides managers with all the information they would like to have." Do you agree with this statement? Why or why not?
29. A student planning a career in marketing wondered why it was important to learn about accounting. How would you respond?
30. Should a management accounting system provide both financial and nonfinancial information. Explain.
31. The management accountant should be a member of the top management staff? Do you agree or disagree?
32. What is ethical behaviour? Is it possible to teach ethical behaviour in a management accounting course?
33. List and describe the four basic management activities.
34. Distinguish between line and staff positions. Give two examples of each in a university setting.
35. What is the difference between manufacturing and service industry firms?
36. Can management accounting play an important role in a not-for-profit organization? Expain.
37. How can a management accountant help in formulating a strategy?
38. In an organization that has a Sales Department and a Personnel Deportment, among others, which of the two departments has (i) line responsibility and (ii) staff responsibility?

39. The following statement was made by Finance Director of Hindustan Engineering Ltd.

    "The managers of a company should use the same information as the shareholders of the firm. When managers use the same information in guiding their internal operations as shareholders use in evaluating their investments, the managers will be aligned with the shareholders' profit objectives." Comment on the above statement.

40. Explain the similarities and differences between financial accounting and management accounting. (*M. Com., D.U.*, 2013)

41. Discuss the current focus of management accounting. (*M. Com., D.U.*, 2014)

42. Explain the factors influencing the management accounting information system.

43. Write short notes on:

    (*i*) Activity-based management

    (*ii*) Total quality management

    (*iii*) Customer value

    How do they affect management accounting?

44. Explain the nature and scope of management accounting. In what way do the role and responsibilities of management accountants differ from those of financial accountants? (*M. Com., D.U.*, 2012)

45. What is the role of information in decision making?

46. Why would operating in a global (rather than a strictly domestic) marketplace create a need for additional information? Discuss some of the additional information you think managers would need and why such information would be valuable.

47. Discuss the validity of the following statement: "Only large companies (such as those that are publicly held and listed on a major stock exchange) have the opportunity to operate in a global marketplace."

48. Why is an effective management information system a key element of an effective managment control system?

49. Why do managers require both internal and external information to manage effectively?

50. Why would an organization have multiple control systems in place?

51. Management accountants are actively involved in the process of managing the entity. This process includes making strategic, tactical, and operating decisions while helping to coordinate the efforts of the entire organization. To fulfill these objectives, the management accountant accepts certain responsibilities that can be identified as (1) planning, (2) controlling, (3) evaluating performance, (4) ensuring accountability of resources, and (5) external reporting.

Required:

Describe each of these responsibilities of the management accountant, and identify examples of practices and techniques.

52. "I was trained as an engineer, I work as an engineer, and I intend to retire as an engineer. Why on earth would I want to learn accounting?" Amit Ghoshal, a senior production engineer at a large sized company, clearly is unhappy that his boss asked him to attend a one-week seminar or managerial accounting before taking on his new position. Amit's new duties deal with managing tools. He has over-all authority for when to replace tools, whether to buy them or make them, and what quantities to purchase or produce.

Required:

The following list presents five decisions that Amit might face in his job. How can managerial accounting information help with these decisions? For each decision, list at least one information item that Amit might use and whether the item is financial or nonfinancial in nature.

1. Whether actual costs are in line with expectations?
2. Whether to make a tool in-house or buy it from a supplier?
3. How many tools to purchase for making 100,000 units of a product?
4. What is the right inventory level for a given tool?
5. Whether to make a new tool or to refurbish an existing tool?

SELF-ASSESSMENT QUESTIONS

A. Fill in the blanks with appropriate words given in the brackets.

1. .... primarily serves the interest of internal management (Management/Financial accounting).
2. Management accounting concentrates on .... (preparation of financial statements/ control of business).
3. Planning and control are done by .... (top management/middle management/all levels of management).
4. Planning, control and other management functions are performed in .... (business organizations/service organizations/non-profit organizations/all organizations).
5. Budgets are .... (future/past) financial plan to achieve the business objectives.
6. Performance reports are required in .... (planning/control).
7. Performances corresponding to plans are (covered/not covered) in management by–exception approach.
8. Decision-making concerns the .... (future/past/future and past both).
9. Management accounting emphasises on providing .... (historical/futuristic) data to managers.
10. In all management decision the quantity of .... (future/past) revenue is a deciding factor.
11. Financial accounting provides .... purpose report. (Specific/general/specific and general both).
12. All business transactions are recorded in terms of money in .... accounting (financial/management/cost/all types of accounting).
13. .... accounting does not provide day- to day information about costs (management/ cost/financial).
14. The users of financial statement are mainly .... to the business enterprise. (internal/external).
15. Double entry system is used in .... accounting. (financial/management/cost).
16. .... accounting does not use any definite set of accounting principles. (Financial/ management).

17. Accounting data and statement are prepared at regular time intervals in .... accounting. (financial/cost/management).
18. Long range plans of action to achieve goals are referred to as .... plans. (strategic/operational).
19. The function of the management process that involves the development of a course of action to attain enterprise goals is referred to as .... (planning/controlling).
20. The head of production department occupies a .... position within a manufacturing company (line, staff).
21. The field of accounting that specialises in providing accounting information for use by managers in making decisions is .... (financial accounting/management accounting).
22. The function of management process that involves selecting one course of action from alternatives is referred to as .... (directing/decision-making).
23. The comparison of actual results with expected results is referred to as .... (controlling/feedback).
24. The management accountant occupies a .... position within an organization (line/staff).

B. Indicate whether each phrase is more descriptive of financial accounting or management accounting.

1. May be subjective
2. Decision making tool
3. Often used to describe company goal
4. Future oriented
5. Must comply with external standards and accounting principles
6. Income statement, balance sheet and statement of cash flows
7. Specific purpose report
8. High consolidated or aggregated reports
9. Prepared generally quarterly or half yearly or annually
10. May measure time or customer satisfaction
11. Subject to cost benefit analysis
12. Keeps records of assets and liabilities

C. For each item below, explain how you think management accounting and financial accounting may be the same and/or may differ.

1. The frequency with which reports are prepared
2. The timeliness of the information to the user when he or she receives a report
3. The degree of emphasis on precision and accuracy
4. The necessity of being audited
5. The existence of a conceptual framework
6. The knowledge of who the user is and exactly what the user is doing with the information
7. The delineation of activities

(M. Com., Delhi 1994)

D. The actions that follow are associated with a firm's accounting information system.

1. Preparing a report that details profit by customer
2. Preparing an income statement that complies with GAAP
3. Preparing a monthly cash budget
4. Voluntarily reporting safety costs to potential and existing investors
5. Research to determine how to report an uninsured facility destroyed by flood
6. Reporting on the trends in defect rates to the plant manager
7. Determining the cost of dropping a product
8. Determining the cost of producing a new product
9. Determining the cost of bad debts for the balanc sheet
10. Assessing post-purchase costs
11. A report that shows a trend in warranty costs
12. Reporitng the value of marketable securities
13. Determining how to consolide the financial reports of two subsidiaries
14. A report comparing the activity-based product costs with traditional product costs

Required:

Classify the above actions as belonging either to management accounting or financial accounting.

Answer:

1. Management
2. Financial
3. Management
4. Financial
5. Financial
6. Management
7. Management
8. Management
9. Financial
10. Management
11. Management
12. Financial
13. Financial
14. Management

E. The following words and phrases describe or are associated with either financial or managerial accounting. Indicate for each item whether it is more closely associated with financial (F) or management (M) accounting.

a. Verifiable
b. Largely historical
c. Relevant
d. Internally focused
e. Accounting standards
f. Forecasted
g. Formal
h. Focus is an organizational segments
i. Cost/benefit analysis
j. Focus is on serving external users
k. Emphasis is on timeliness
l. Emphasis is on consistency
m. Largely future oriented
n. Flexible

MULTIPLE CHOICE QUESTIONS

Select the correct answer for the following multiple choice questions.

1. Management accounting differs from financial accounting in that financial accounting is
   (a) More oriented toward the future.
   (b) Primarily concerned with external financial reporting.
   (c) Concerned with nonquantitative information.
   (d) Heavily involved with decision analysis and implementation of decisions.
2. Cost and management accounting systems are goods in the economic sense and, as such, their benefits must exceed their costs. When management accounting systems change, the cost that is frequently ignored is the cost of
   (a) Educating users.
   (b) Gathering and analysing data.
   (c) Training accounting staff.
   (d) Preparing reports.
3. The primary goal of management accounting is to:
   (a) Provide information to current and potential investors in the company.
   (b) Provide information to creditors as well as current and prospective investors.
   (c) Provide information to creditors, taxing authorities and current and prospective investors.
   (d) Provide information for planning, control and decision making.
4. Which of the following statements is false?
   (a) Management accounting statements do not necessarily comply with GAAP.
   (b) Financial accounting statements normally reflect more detail than would be found in management accounting reports.
   (c) Management accounting reports emphasise future activities and future costs.
   (d) Financial accounting data are directed primarily at external users rather than internal users.

Answer to Multiple Choice Questions

1. (b) 2. (a) 3. (d) 4. (b)

CASES

1. The management accountant of Allywin Automobile Company, situated in Chennai was not satisfied with the historical cost depreciation being used for charging cost of expensive machinery to individual components and products. Therefore, the management accountant calculated each year the replacement cost of each machine and calculated depreciation, based on the machine's replacement cost which was subsequently included in calculating machine hour rate. The machine hour rate calculated in this way was considered to assign machine expenses to the components produced on that machine. The management accountant also included an interest charge, based on 50% of machine replacement value, into the machine hour rate. The interest rate was an average of 7-9 interest rate on government securities.

As a consequence of these two decisions (charging replacement cost rather than historical cost and imputing a capital charge for the use of capital equipment), the product cost figures used internally by company managers were inconsistent with the numbers that were needed for inventory valuation for financial and tax reporting. The accounting staff had to perform a tedious reconciliation process at the end of each year to back out the interest and replacement value costs from the cost of goods sold and inventory values before they could prepare the financial statements.

Required:

(*a*) Why would the management accountant introduce additional complications into the company's costing system by assigning replacement value depreciation costs and imputed interest costs to the company's parts and products?

(*b*) Why should management accountants create extra work for the organization by deliberately adopting policies for internal costing that violate the generally accepted accounting principles that must be used for external reporting? (*M. Com. Delhi*)

2. Narula is a fast food company located in New Delhi with around 500 outlets in the states of Maharashtra, Karnataka, Andhrapradesh, Gujrat, West Bengal, Tamil Nadu and New Delhi. Identify the management accounting information needs for

   (*a*) The manager of a local fast food outlet that prepares food and serves it to customers who walk in or pick it up in a drive-through window.

   (*b*) The regional manager who supervises the operations of all the retail outlets in a particular state region.

   (*c*) Senior management located at the company's headquarters. Consider in particular the information needs of the Managing Director and Chief General Manager of Production and Marketing.

   Discuss the content, frequency and timeliness of information needed by the above management personnel.

3. Vikas has been promoted to product manager for detergents and soaps at Indian Lever Ltd. He has worked earlier as a sales representative and has competence in marketing research. However, his accounting background is limited to filing his income tax return, reviewing his salary slip, understanding his bank passbook and reviewing his company's profit and loss account and balance sheet. He has observed.

   "While the financial statements are no doubtful useful to investors, he does not see how accounting can help him be a good product manager."

Required:

Based on his remarks, it is obvious that Vikas's background of accounting is limited to financial accounting. Discuss some of the important differences between financial and management accouning and suggest some ways management accounting can help Vikas be a better product manager.

4. The Chief Finance Officer (CFO) of Vivekanand Central University, New Delhi is complaining about the heavy work that he is required to do at the beginning of each month. The Vice-Chancellor of the University requires the Chief Finance Officer (CFO) to submit a monthly report by the fifth day of the following month. The monthly report contains financial data. The CFO was heard saying, "why does the Vice - Chancellor need all this information? He

probably does not read half of the report. He is an old Botany professor and probably does not know the difference between cost and revenue."

Required:

(*i*) What is the importance of monthly report?

(*ii*) What is the responsibility of Chief Finance Officer with respect to a Vice-Chancellor who does not know much accounting? (*M. Com. Delhi* 2006)

5. Accounting has a long history of being an ethical profession. In recent years, however, some companies have asked their accountants to help "manage earnings."
   (*a*) What does it mean to "manage earnings".
   (*b*) Who is more likely to be involved in such a situation? the financial accountant or the management accountant? Why?
   (*c*) Do you believe that "managing earnings" is ethical? Discuss the rationale for your answer.
6. Consider the operation of Reliance Fresh. Identify the management accounting information needs for
   (*a*) Category manager of frozen goods, responsible for all the frozen food product lines, brands and individual product units (stock-keeping units).
   (*b*) Manager of a single Reliance Fresh Store.
   (*c*) Aman Damodaran, Managing Director of Reliance Fresh.
7. In a meeting of Departmental managers in a large sized diversified manufacturing company, the production manager made the following statement about the cost variance report.

   "Cost variances are useless. I don't want to ever have to look at a cost variance, monthly or weekly. Daily, I look at sales, bookings, and on-time delivery. Weekly, I look at a variety of quality reports including the outgoing quality control report on items passing the final test before despatch to the customer, in-process quality, and yields. Yield is a good surrogate for cost and quality. Monthly, I do look at the financial reports. I look closely at my fixed expenses and compare these to the budgets, especially on discretionary items like travel and maintenance. But the financial accounting don't tell me where I am wasting money. I expect that if I make operating improvements, costs should go down. The organizational dynamics make it difficult to link cause and effect precisely".

Required:

Comment on the production manager's assessment of his limited use for financial and cost summaries of performance. For what purposes, if any, are cost and financial information helpful to operating people? (*M.Com., Delhi University, 2010*)

8. You are the newly hired controller of QT Products, a large manufacturer of industrial products. Yesterday morning the president of the company called you and othr senior executives to her office where she stated that a competitor was about to file suit against QT for patent infringemnt. Regardless of the merits of the case, it will tie up company talent for a long while and will be quite costly to fight. The effects on the company's prospects cannot be measured, but it is possible that they will be severe.

   This evening your father called from Chennai, where he and your mother have lived in retirment for a few years. You chatted about the weather, the children, dad's golf game, and other such things. Then he told you that he had just bought shares in QT Products because he knew that any company you worked at would do well.

Required:

What do you say to your father?

9. Anjali Khare has decided to purchase a personal computer. She has narrowed the choice to two: HP and Dell. Both brands have the same processing speed, 6.4 gigabytes of hard-disk capacity, a 3.5-inch disk drive, a CD ROM drive, and each comes with the same basic software support package. Both come from mail-order companies with good reputations. The selling price for each is identical. After some review, Anjali discovers that the cost of operating and maintaining HP over a three-year period is estimated to be Rs 3000. For Dell, the operating and maintenance cost is Rs 6000. The sales agent for HP, emphasized the lower operating and maintenance costs. The agent for Dell, however, emphasized the service reputation of the product and the faster delivery time. (Dell can be purchased and delivered one week sooner than HP.) Based on all the available information, Anjali has decided to buy Dell.

Required:

(*i*) What is the total product purchased by Anjali?

(*ii*) How does the strategic positioning differ for the two companies?

(*iii*) When asked why she decided to buy Dell, Anjali responded, "I think that Dell offers more value than HP." What are the possible sources of this greater value? What implications does this have for the management accounting information system?

(*iv*) Suppose that Anjali's decision was prompted mostly by the desire to receive the computer quickly. Informed that it was losing sales because of the longer time to produce and deliver its products, the management of the company producing HP decided to improve delivery performance by improving its internal processes. These improvements decreased the number of defective units and the time required to produce its product. Consequently, delivery time and costs both decreased, and the company was able to lower it prices on HP. Explain how these actions translate into strengthening the competitive position of the HPPC relative to the Dell PC. Also discuss the implications for the management accounting information system.

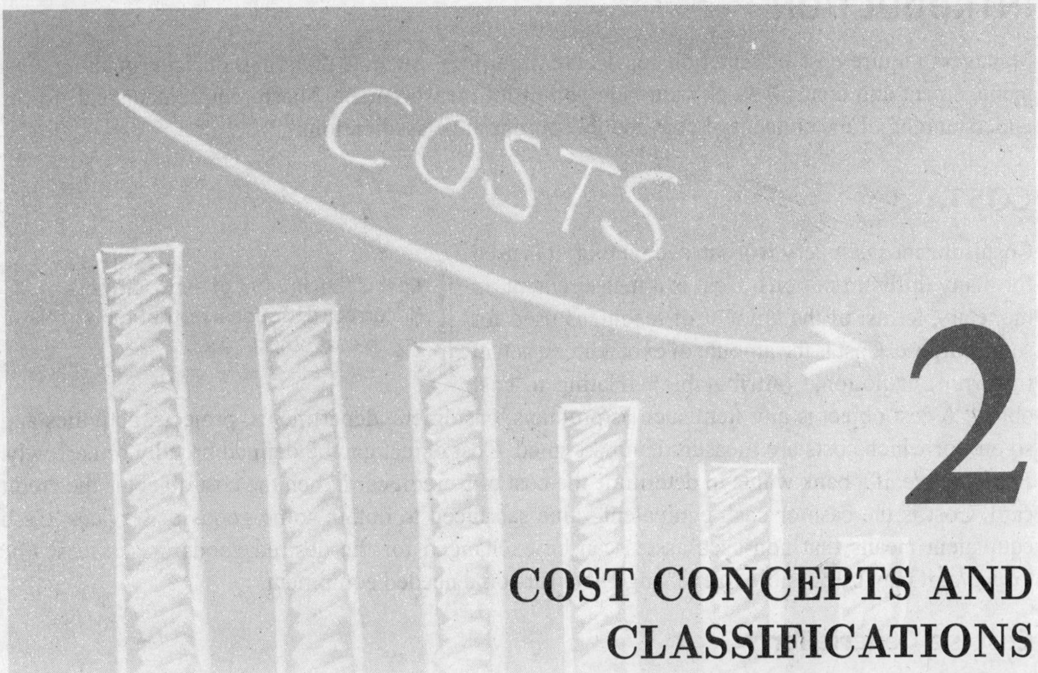

2

COST CONCEPTS AND CLASSIFICATIONS

LEARNING OBJECTIVES:

After reading this chapter, you should be able to:

- Define Cost, Deferred Cost, Expired Cost, Expense and Loss
- Distinguish between Cost Incurrence and Cost Recognition
- Explain different Types of Costs in terms of Traditional Classification, Cost Behaviour, Traceability to a Cost Object, Timing of Charges, Management Function, Decision Making and Control, Cost Control and Relationship with the Accounting Period
- Understand Cost Flows in Manufacturing, Merchandising and Service Organizations

INTRODUCTION

Managers require cost information for different purposes such as planning, decision-making, cost management and control, stock valuation and profit measurement. These requirements call for an understanding of the concept of cost and its appropriate classifications.

COST

Cost is the most slippery word in accounting; it is used for many different notions. Cost is a measurement, in monetary, terms, of the amount of resources used for some purpose. Cost is the amount of expenditure, actual (incurred) or notional (attributable), relating to cost object. A cost object is any item such as products, customers, departments, projects, activities and so on, for which costs are measured and assigned. Cost object can be defined broadly or narrowly. *For example*, if a bank wants to determine the cost of a credit card, then the cost object is the credit card. Cost is the cash or cash equivalent value sacrificed to obtain some goods or services. Cash equivalent means that non-cash assets can be exchanged for the desired goods or services. *For example*, it may be possible to exchange land for some needed equipment.

> **Cost** is the amount of expenditure, actual (incurred) or notional (attributable), relating to cost object.

Cost is a Generic Term

The term 'cost' is a generic term purposely defined and used in a variety of ways so as to include various types of costs. The term 'cost' itself is without any significant meaning and, therefore, it is always advisable to use it with an adjective, phrase or modifier that will convey the meaning intended. When the term is used specifically, it is always modified by such descriptions as prime, direct, indirect, fixed, variable, controllable, opportunity, imputed, sunk, differential, marginal, replacement and the like. Each modifier implies a certain attribute or characteristic which is important in computing, measuring and analysing the cost for its proper usage.

DEFERRED COST AND EXPIRED COST

Basically, when a cost is incurred, it could be in the form of deferred cost (asset) or expired cost (expense). Deferred costs are unexpired cost which provide benefit in the future periods. They are capitalised costs and known as assets and hence appear on the balance sheet. Examples of deferred or unexpired cost are plant, equipment, building, inventory, prepaid rent and insurance. When these deferred costs (assets) are used up or give up their usefulness, they are written off or expensed and to that extent, they become expenses and appear on the income statement and deducted from revenues.

> **Deferred costs** are unexpired cost which provide benefit in future periods.
>
> **Expired costs** are those which have been used in generating revenue and benefits have been received immediately.

Expired costs are those which have been used in generating revenue and benefits have been received immediately. They are not capitalised but deducted from revenues.

EXPENSES

Expenses are expired costs. When a cost or expenditure is incurred and totally used up in generation of revenue, the total expenditure will become expense and shown in the income statement.

> **Expenses** are expired costs.

Examples of expired costs are cost of goods sold expense, selling and administrative expense. Expenses need not necessarily have to be paid in cash immediately, even a promise to pay could be made for benefits obtained. The manufacturing costs are capitalised in the form of finished goods inventory and when a sale is made, they expire (becoming expenses). The cost of unsold inventory which was an asset earlier, now becomes expenses (cost of goods sold) as it has contributed to the generation of revenues.

Factory (manufacturing) overhead is treated as cost (an asset) because this is included in the cost of finished goods inventory which is an asset unless sale is made. Selling and administrative expenses are generally not included in the cost of finished goods inventory and therefore are only expenses and not cost (asset). Factory overheads are assets because they are supposed to add utility to the goods manufactured. *For example*, depreciation of a factory machine increases the utility of the goods manufactured which are therefore included in work-in-progress and finished goods inventory. But selling and distribution overheads do not add to the utility of goods manufactured and are treated merely as expenses and are deducted from revenues whenever incurred. Similarly, depreciation of a factory building is a cost, but depreciation of an office building is an expense.

The difference between expired costs (expenses) and unexpired costs (assets) is illustrated in Figure 2.1.

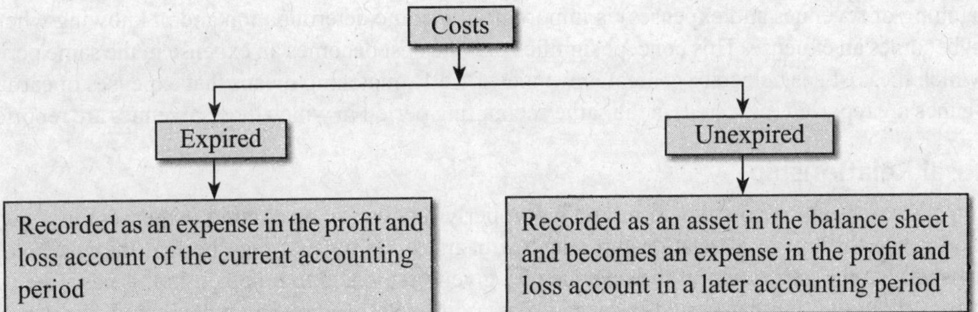

Figure 2.1: Expired and Unexpired Costs

LOSS

Loss is lost cost, i.e., cost which expires without giving any revenue benefit. That is, if no benefit is received from the cost incurred or it becomes definite then no benefit will accrue, the cost becomes a lost cost i.e., loss.

The term 'loss' is used to describe mainly two accounting events. In traditional financial accounting, it is used to denote a situation where expenses exceed revenues for an accounting period, that is, the opposite of net income (earnings) for the accounting period. Secondly, a loss arises due to the cost of an asset being more than the sale proceeds when the asset is sold. This unfavourable event does not arise from a normal business activity but due to non-operating transactions or events. This definition of loss is used to identify the opposite of gain.

Loss is unrelated to revenue generation and is only offset against revenue of the period in which the loss occurred. Examples of loss are loss on sale of fixed asset, loss of stock due to fire.

COST INCURRENCE AND COST RECOGNITION

Cost incurrence and cost recognition are different from each other. Cost incurrence refers to the receipt of goods or services at a bargained price in an exchange. Cost recognition is the identification of a cost as expired and showing it as an expense or loss (lost cost) in a given year's income statement. Cost incurrence logically precedes cost recognition, and when the benefits associated with cost (goods or services received in the exchange) extends into the next year, cost incurrence is reflected by a debit to an asset account, a deferred cost. Cost recognition is then effected subsequently next year by making an entry: debiting an expense (or loss) and crediting the deferred-cost asset (or contra-asset) account in total or partially. In cases in which the beneficial life of the incurred cost is short, that is, not beyond the current year, both cost incurrence and cost recognition are reflected concurrently in the current year and a debit to expense in place of asset is made. Next year no entry is needed.

> **Cost incurrence** refers to the receipt of goods or services at a bargained price in an exchange.
>
> **Cost recognition** is the identification of a cost as expired and showing it as an expense or loss (lost cost) in a given year's income statement.
>
> **Matching concept** signifies that the cost becomes an expense in the same period in which the cost has helped to generate revenues.

Matching Concept

The expensing of deferred costs (assets) i.e., when a deferred cost becomes an expense, is a function, not of cost incurrence but rather, of application of matching concept. The matching concept (matching of revenues and expenses) is important in income determination and in knowing when a cost becomes an expense. This concept signifies that the cost becomes an expense in the same period in which the cost has helped to generate revenues. Briefly, matching means that expenses of earning revenues are reported (matched) in the same accounting period in which those revenues are reported.

Causal Relationship

The reason why a cost would in fact be properly recognised as expired (expenses) in a given period relate to the causal relationship which it bears to revenue. It may be that the cost relates exclusively to the generation of the revenue of a given period and to no other. In this case, the cost expires wholly within that period because it has a direct association, on a cause and effect basis, with its revenues. Another possibility is that the cost is jointly related to the revenue of several periods so that it must be allocated against those periods revenues on some systematic and rational basis. Such a cost would have an indirect association with the revenues of a particular period. These two types of cost expirations, direct and indirect, are shown in the periodic income statements as expense, that is, used for generation of revenue. A third possibility is that a cost relate to no revenue whatsoever, that is, it was non-productive. Such a cost expires in the period in which its loss of utility is discovered. This last type of cost expiration is designated as a loss, or lost cost, in the income statement, as stated earlier.

DIFFERENT COST CONCEPTS AND CLASSIFICATIONS

In the following sections, we will understand different cost objectives and different cost classification.

Different Cost Objectives

The achievement of the managerial objectives require that cost should be ascertained, classified and grouped. Different cost objectives lead to different approaches to cost classifications and cost accumulation. A cost per unit devised for valuation of stock and profit measurement may be different from a cost per unit required for cost volume profit analysis. There are many objectives of cost classifications depending on the requirements of many managements. However, the following cost objectives are considered very useful and significant in classifying costs:

- Determining product costs for stock valuation and profit measurement
- Planning
- Decision making
- Control

Different cost concepts and classification are as follows:

1. Traditional Classification of costs:
   (*i*) Direct material
   (*ii*) Direct labour
   (*iii*) Direct expenses
   (*iv*) Factory overhead
   (*v*) Selling and distribution and administrative overheads.

The above cost classification is also used for the purpose of stock valuation and profit measurement.

2. Cost Behaviour (In Relation to Changes in Output, Activity):
   (*i*) Fixed Cost
   (*ii*) Variable Cost
   (*iii*) Mixed Cost (Semi-variable and Semi-fixed cost)
3. Degree of Traceability to a Cost Object i.e., Product, or job:
   (*i*) Direct Cost
   (*ii*) Indirect Cost
4. Timing of Charges against Sales Revenue:
   (*i*) Product Cost
   (*ii*) Period Cost

This cost classification is also used for the purpose of stock valuation and profit measurement.

5. Management function:
   (*i*) Manufacturing Cost
   (*ii*) Selling and Distribution Cost
   (*iii*) Administrative Cost
6. Relationship with the Accounting Period:
   (*i*) Capital Cost
   (*ii*) Revenue Cost
7. Cost for Decision-Making and Planning:
   (*i*) Opportunity Cost
   (*ii*) Sunk Cost
   (*iii*) Relevant Cost
   (*iv*) Differential Cost
   (*v*) Imputed Cost
   (*vi*) Out-of-pocket Cost
   (*vii*) Fixed, Variable and Mixed Cost
   (*viii*) Direct Cost and Indirect Cost
   (*ix*) Shutdown Cost

8. Cost for Control:
   (*i*) Controllable and Uncontrollable Cost
   (*ii*) Standard Cost
   (*iii*) Fixed, Variable and Mixed Cost
9. Other Costs:
   (i) Joint Cost
   (*ii*) Common Cost

TRADITIONAL CLASSIFICATION OF COSTS

The term "traditional classification" refers to the basic physical characteristics of the cost. In a manufacturing concern, the total cost of a product includes the following four elements:

1. *Direct Material:* Direct materials refers to the cost of the materials which becomes a major part of the finished product. They are raw materials that are conveniently and economically traceable to specific units of output, Some examples of direct materials are: raw cotton in textiles, crude oil to make diesel, steel to make automobile bodies. The following group of materials fall within this definition:

(*i*) All materials specially purchased for a particular job, order, process or product
(*ii*) All materials (including primary materials and raw materials) acquired and subsequently requisitioned from the stores for production
(*iii*) Components or part purchased or produced and requisitioned from the storeroom
(*iv*) Material passing from one process to another process
(*v*) Primary packing materials, e.g., wrapping, cardboard boxes, etc.

Items, such as import duties, dock charges, transport cost of materials, storing of materials, cost of purchasing and receiving materials are properly added to their invoiced price and thus, the materials are charged out at this increased cost.

2. *Direct Labour:* Direct Labour is defined as:

- *the labour of those workers who are engaged in the production process. It is the labour costs for specific work performed on products that is conveniently and economically traceable to end products.*

Direct labour is expended directly upon the materials comprising the finished product. Examples are the labour of machine operators and assemblers. However, a worker may be performing direct labour for a certain number of hours but be an indirect worker for the balance of the day.

3. *Direct Expenses:* These include any expenditure, other than direct material and direct labour, directly incurred on a specific cost unit (product or job). Such special necessary expenses can be identified with cost units and are charged directly to the product as part of the prime cost. These expenses are sometimes known as chargeable expenses. Examples of direct expenses are:

(*i*) Cost of hiring special machinery or plant
(*ii*) Cost of special moulds, designs and patterns
(*iii*) Experimental costs and expenditure on model and pilot schemes
(*iv*) Fees paid to architects, surveyors and other consultants
(*v*) Cost of transport and conveyance to the site of job or operations
(*vi*) Inward carriage and freight charges on special materials
(*vii*) Cost of patents and royalties

(*viii*) Cost of defective work, e.g., where several trials are necessary before an appropriate one is obtained. The cost of such trials is taken as direct expense

(*ix*) License fees

(*x*) Hire charges for plant and equipment for a specific product or job

(*xi*) Components and parts processed for a special job

(*xii*) Insurance charges on special materials chargeable to a job

The above (and similar other) direct expenses are incurred for a product or job and therefore are a part of the prime cost. Other things remaining the same, the term 'direct expenses' (chargeable expenses) whenever used in costing, refers to a specific product or job. That is, whether some expenses are direct or not, is decided in terms of specific job or product as product or job is considered the cost unit.

The total of the above three elements of costs (*i*) direct materials, (*ii*) direct labour and (*iii*) direct expenses, are prime cost.

According to Official Terminology of Chartered Institute of Management Accountants (London), prime cost is the total cost of direct material and direct labour. Thus, direct expenses are not included in prime cost as per CIMA Terminology. The CIMA defines direct cost as:

- *the expenditure which can be economically identified with a specific saleable cost unit.*

4. *Factory Overhead:* Factory overhead also called manufacturing expenses or factory burden may be defined as:

- *the cost of indirect materials, indirect labour and indirect expenses.*

The term 'indirect materials' refer to materials that are needed for the completion of the product but whose consumption with regard to the product is either so small or so complex that it would not be appropriate to treat it as a direct materials item. They are production supplies and other materials that cannot conveniently or economically be charged to a specific unit of output. Examples of such items are lubricants, cotton waste, hand tools, works, stationery, etc.

The term 'indirect labour' may be defined as:

- *that labour which does not affect the construction or the composition of the finished products. In other words, it is the labour cost of production-related activities that cannot be associated with or conveniently and economically traced to end products. Some examples of indirect labour are: foremen, shop clerks, general helpers, cleaners, material handlers, plant guards, employees engaged in maintenance work or other service work.*

The term 'indirect expenses' covers all indirect expenditure incurred by the manufacturing enterprise from the time production has started to its completion and transfer to the finished goods store. Any expenses not classified as direct expenses are known as indirect expenses. The Institute of Cost and Management Accountants (UK) defines indirect expenses as:

- *the expenses which cannot be allocated but which can be apportioned to or absorbed by cost centres or cost units.*

They are incurred for the benefit of more than one product, job or activity and must be apportioned by appropriate bases to the various functions. Expenses of this types include items such as heat, light, maintenance, factory manager's salary, etc.

The total of (*i*) prime cost and (*ii*) factory overhead is known as 'Factory Cost.' Direct labour and factory overhead together are known as conversion costs because they are the costs of converting raw materials into finished products.

5. *Selling and Distribution and Administrative Overheads:* Selling and distribution overheads usually begin when the factory costs end. Such expenses are generally incurred when the product is in saleable condition. It covers the cost of making sales and delivering/despatching products. These costs include advertising, salesman's salaries and commissions, packing, storage, transportation, and sales administrative costs.

Administrative overhead includes costs of planning and controlling the general policies and operations of a business enterprise. Usually, all costs which cannot be charged either to the production or sales division are considered as administrative costs. Typical of such items are fees of the board of directors, the Chairman's salary, the rent for general offices and costs of the general accounting department. Sometimes, some of such expenses as manager's salary are often allocated to manufacturing and included in factory overhead.

The sum of (*i*) Prime Cost, (*ii*) Factory Overhead and (*iii*) Selling and Distribution and Administrative Overhead is the Total Cost i.e., the cost "to make and sell". Exhibit 2.1 presents the traditional classification of costs as discussed above.

Exhibit. 2.1: Traditional Classification of Costs in a Manufacturing Concern

Direct Material	+ Direct Labour	+ Direct Expenses = (1) Prime Cost
		+
Indirect Materials	+ Indirect Labour	+ Indirect Expenses = Factory Overhead
↓	↓	↓
Threads, lubricants, glue, other factory supplies	Supervision, inspection superintendence, salary of factory clerks, experimental work, general helpers, cleaners employees engaged in maintenance work	Rent, insurance — fire and liability, taxes, depreciation, maintenance and repair, power, light, heat, misc. factory overhead, small tools, hire of machinery
		(2) Factory Cost
		+
Selling and Distribution Overhead +	Administrative Overhead =	Selling and Distribution and Administrative Overhead.
↓	↓	
Advertising, samples, salesmen's salaries, travel, depreciation of sales equipment, rent of branches, telephone, telegraph, supplies, stationery and printing, freight and carriage out, sales promotion, sales accounting, misc. expenses.	Office salaries, rent, executive's salaries, depreciation of equipment, telephone and telegraph, travel, property taxes, auditing expenses, stationery and printing postage, other administrative expenses.	
		(3) Total Cost

COST BEHAVIOUR (IN RELATION TO CHANGES IN OUTPUT OR ACTIVITY)

Cost can be classified into (*i*) fixed, (*ii*) variable and (*iii*) mixed costs, in terms of their variability or changes in cost behaviour in relation to changes in output, or activity or volume. Activity may be indicated in any form such as units of output, hours worked, sales, etc.

Fixed Cost

Fixed cost is a cost which does not change in total for a given time period despite wide fluctuations in output or volume of activity. The ICMA (UK) defines fixed cost as:

- *a cost which tends to be unaffected by variations in volume of output. Fixed costs depend mainly on the affluxion of time and do not vary directly with volume or rate of output.*

> **Fixed cost** is a cost which does not change in total for a given time period despite wide fluctuations in output or volume of activity.

These costs, also known as standby costs, capacity costs or period costs, arise primarily because of the provision of facilities, physical and human, to carry on business operations.

Fixed costs enable a business firm to do business, but they are not purely incurred for manufacturing. Examples of fixed costs are rent, property taxes, supervising salaries, depreciation on office facilities, advertising, insurance, etc. They accrue or are incurred with the passage of time and not with the production of the product or the job. This is the reason why fixed costs are expressed in terms of time, such as per day, per month or per year and not in terms of unit. It is totally illogical to say that a supervisor's salary is so much per unit.

By nature, the total fixed costs are constant which means that the fixed costs per unit will vary. Figure 2.2 shows the behaviour of fixed costs in total and on a per unit basis. When a greater number of units are produced, the fixed cost per unit decreases. On the contrary, when a lesser number of units are produced, the fixed cost per unit increases. This variability of fixed cost per unit creates problems in product costing. The cost per unit depends on the number of units produced or the level of activity achieved.

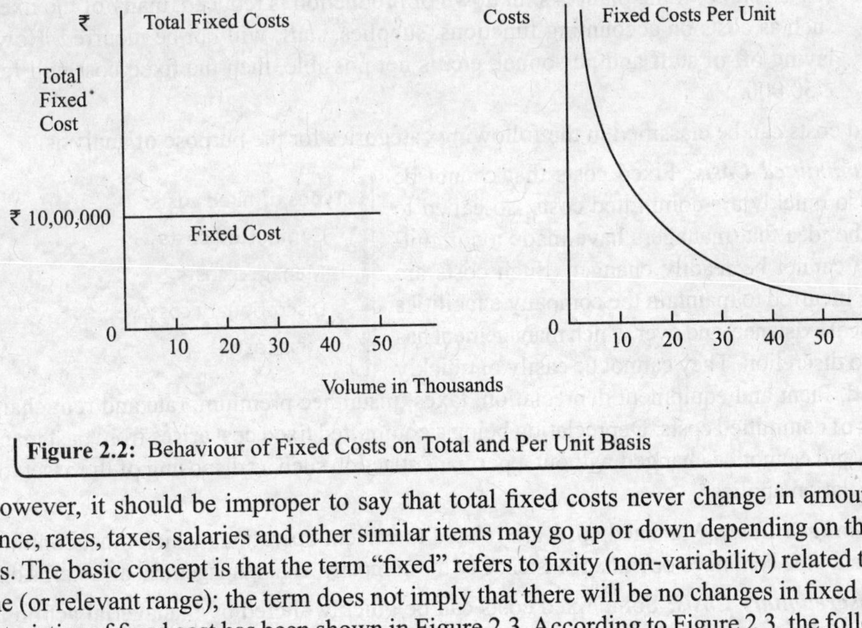

Figure 2.2: Behaviour of Fixed Costs on Total and Per Unit Basis

However, it should be improper to say that total fixed costs never change in amount. Rents, insurance, rates, taxes, salaries and other similar items may go up or down depending on the circumstances. The basic concept is that the term "fixed" refers to fixity (non-variability) related to specific volume (or relevant range); the term does not imply that there will be no changes in fixed cost. This characteristics of fixed cost has been shown in Figure 2.3. According to Figure 2.3, the following are the fixed costs at different levels of production:

1. ₹ 50,000 fixed cost between 20,000 and 80,000 units of production.

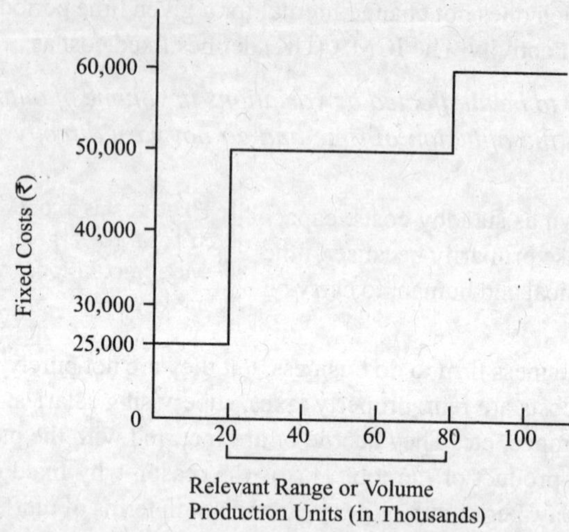

Figure 2.3: Total Fixed Costs at Different Levels of Production

2. ₹ 60,000 fixed cost in excess of 80,000 units. This assumes that increases in production after a certain level (80,000 units) requires increase in fixed expenses which have been fixed earlier, e.g., additional supervision, increase in quality control costs.
3. ₹ 25,000 fixed cost from zero units (shut down) to 20,000 units. This explains that if the level of activity comes to less than 20,000 units, some fixed costs may not be incurred. *For example*, if the plant is shut down or production is reduced, many of the fixed costs, such as costs on accounting functions, supplies, staff, will not be incurred, However, if laying off of staff and personnel, etc. is not possible, then the fixed cost will remain at ₹ 50,000.

Fixed costs can be classified in the following categories for the purpose of analysis:

> **Types of fixed costs:**
> - Committed costs
> - Managed costs
> - Discretionary costs
> - Step costs

1. *Committed Costs:* Fixed costs that cannot be changed so quickly are committed costs, so called to express the idea that managers have made a commitment that cannot be readily changed. Such costs are primarily incurred to maintain the company's facilities and physical existence, and over which management has little or no discretion. They cannot be easily or quickly eliminated. Plant and equipment depreciation, taxes, insurance premium, rate and rent charges are examples of committed costs. Depreciation being a committed fixed cost arises from past managerial decisions and cannot be changed without a permanent action such as disposing of the asset to which the depreciation applies.

2. *Managed Costs:* Managed costs are related to current operations which must continue to be paid to ensure the continued operating existence of the company, e.g., management and staff salaries.

3. *Discretionary Costs:* Some fixed costs can be quickly altered by managerial action and are called discretionary costs. They are also known as programmed costs. Discretionary costs are not related to current operations or activities and are subject to management discretion and control. These costs result from special policy decisions, management programmes, new researches, etc. Such costs can be avoided at management's discretion in a relatively short period of time as compared to committed costs. Some examples of such costs are research and development costs, marketing programmes, new system development costs, etc.

Deciding whether a cost is committed or discretionary, is not always possible just by knowing what the cost is for (rent, salaries, research and development, etc.). *For example*, rent might or might not be committed cost depending on the terms of the rental agreement.

Discretionary costs present unique problems in cost management because managers must determine whether the level of the discretionary activity—the cost driver—is appropriate. For example, should the company hire another research scientist? Should it reduce the number of pages in the annual report? Should it discontinue a particular training program? The larger question is often whether the company should even be performing the activity at all. Should the company pay tuition for employees taking courses? Should the company make charitable contributions?

Unfortunately, discretionary costs are often the first to be attacked in cost-reduction programs, perhaps partly because their effects are not immediately apparent. Managers must consider the long-run effects of cutting such discretionary costs as research and product development, management training programs, and programs to upgrade worker skills.[1]

4. *Step Costs:* Step costs are also known as step-fixed costs or step-variable costs. A step cost is constant for a given amount of output and then increased in a fixed amount at a higher output level. *For example*, in a manufacturing company, one supervisor is required at a salary of ₹ 10,000 p.m. for every 50 workers. So long as 50 workers or less than that are working, the supervision costs will be ₹ 10,000 p.m. But as soon as the 51st worker is employed, the cost of supervision increases by ₹ 10,000 p.m. to ₹ 20,000. The cost of supervision remains fixed at ₹ 20,000 if not more than 100 workers are working. But it will go up if more than 100 workers have been employed. Figure 2.4 exhibits the behaviour pattern of step costs.

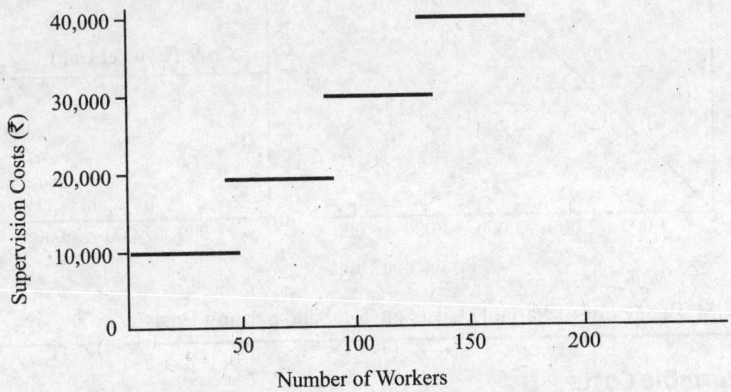

Figure 2.4: Step Costs

Step-fixed costs or step-variable costs exist because of indivisibility of resources; many resources cannot be acquired in infinitely divisible increments. An airline can't fly fractions of planes to provide exactly as many seats as passengers demand; it can fly only an entire airplane. Similarly, companies usually cannot rent space one square foot at a time. Nor can they hire part-time people for some jobs; it is difficult to hire a sales manager or controller for six or eight months of the year. However, the growing use of temporary employees ("temps") is a way of confronting the indivisibility problem.

Should we plan step-variable costs as if they were mixed, though the fixed component changes within the relevant range? Should we consider them variable, even though they do not vary between steps? Both approaches are used in practice, which means that actual costs will differ from cost predictions under either alternative. Managers are more likely to treat a cost as variable if the steps are relatively short and as fixed if the steps are relatively long (measured horizontally).[2]

Variable costs are those costs that vary in total amount directly and proportionately with the output.

Variable Cost

Variable costs are those costs that vary in total amount directly and proportionately with the output. There is a constant ratio between the change in the cost and change in the level of output. Direct material cost and direct labour cost are the costs which are generally variable costs. *For example*, if direct material cost is ₹ 50 per unit, then for producing each additional unit, a direct material cost of ₹ 50 per unit will be incurred. That is, the total direct material cost increases in direct proportion to increase in units manufactured. However, it should be noted that it is only the total variable costs that change as more units are produced; the per unit variable cost remains constant. Variable cost is always expressed in terms of units or percentage of volume, it cannot be stated in terms of time. Figure 2.5 shows behaviour of variable costs in total and on a per unit basis.

Figure 2.5 shows graphically the behaviour pattern of direct material cost. For every increase in the units produced, there is a proportionate increase in the cost when production increases in direct proportion at the constant rate of ₹ 50 per unit. The variable cost line is shown as linear rather than curvilinear. That is, on a graph paper, a variable cost line appears as unbroken straight line in place of a curve. Variable cost per unit is shown by constant.

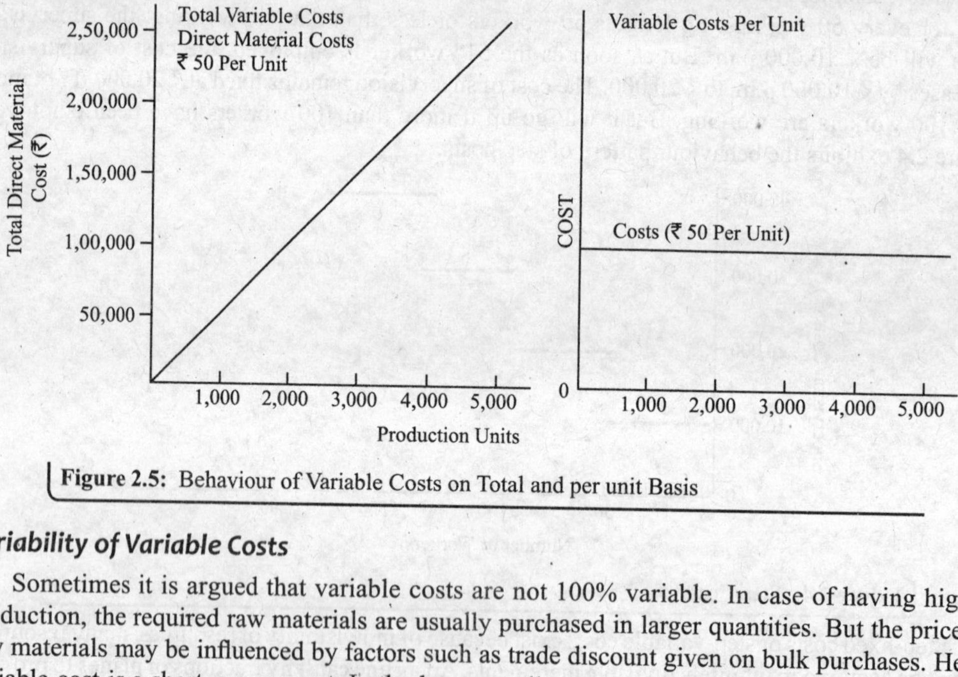

Figure 2.5: Behaviour of Variable Costs on Total and per unit Basis

Variability of Variable Costs

Sometimes it is argued that variable costs are not 100% variable. In case of having higher production, the required raw materials are usually purchased in larger quantities. But the price of raw materials may be influenced by factors such as trade discount given on bulk purchases. Here, variable cost is a short-run concept. In the longrun, all costs are variable, so accountants need to clarify the time horizon envisioned in identifying a cost as variable. If total variable cost always increases in proportion to changes in volume, then average variable cost must remain constant as volume changes. For a variable cost described by a curved line in place of a straight line, however, average variable cost will vary, as illustrated in column (3) of Table 2.1. The variable cost of the first 1,000 units produced is high, ₹ 50. As the total variable cost curve levels off, the increase in cost is less than proportional to the increase in volume, and average variable cost decreases. Total variable cost begins to climb more rapidly again at a volume of 7,000 units per week, and average variable cost starts to increase.

Table 2.1: Average Variable Cost

(1) Weekly Volume (units)	(2) Weekly Variable Cost (₹)	(3) Average Variable Cost 2/1 (₹)
1,000	50,000	50.0
2,000	90,000	45.0
3,000	1,20,000	40.0
4,000	1,50,000	37.5
5,000	1,80,000	36.0
6,000	2,10,000	35.0
7,000	2,45,000	35.0
8,000	2,92,000	36.5
9,000	3,60,000	40.0
10,000	4,60,000	46.0

Figure 2.6 shows two possible relations between total volume and average variable cost per unit of activity based on cost and units data as given in Table 2.1. Figure 2.6 shows average variable cost per unit (remaining constant) as straight line in one situation and in the alternate situation as a curved line for average variable cost as in Column 3 of Table 2.1.

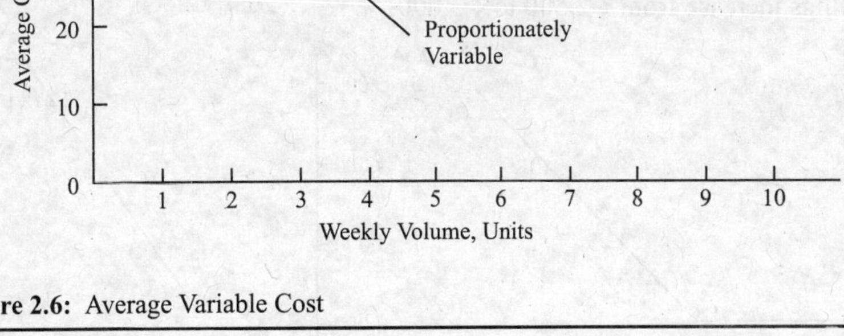

Figure 2.6: Average Variable Cost

Therefore, the concept of variability under variable costs or fixity in fixed costs is not absolute, it is only relative and an approximation. If circumstances differ from those upon which variability or fixity was determined, they will not be correct under changed conditions. Anderson and Sollenberger[3] observe:

Managers can, with time and interest, change the behaviour of certain activities costs in a firm. *For example*, variable direct labour costs can be converted to a fixed cost by guaranteeing employees, job security for some period of time such as a three year union contract or equipment could be leased on a short-term basis (day-to-day or even hourly) in place of purchasing/converting a fixed cost to a variable cost. Also, fixed cost automated equipment could be installed to replace high variable cost manual operations. Variable costs may be increased or decreased based on long-term competitive strategies and overt management decisions. Thus, analysts should recognise that managers have alternatives and can act to change cost behaviour patterns."

Relevant Range

The cost relationships, i.e., change in cost to change in output or activity explained above with regard to fixed and variable costs hold true only for a relevant range – a narrower range of activity. A relevant range indicates the normal range of expected activity. It is hoped that expected activity will not exceed a certain upper bound nor fall below a certain lower bound. Production activity is expected to be within this range and costs are budgeted for these levels. In many cases, fixed costs are fixed and variable costs are variable within the relevant range. Outside the upper range limit, additional fixed costs may be incurred. *For example*, another supervisor may be hired if a second shift is started in the factory, Similarly, the variable cost per unit may change (decrease) due to economies of larger volume purchases or higher overtime premiums if more work is added.

Mixed Costs

Mixed costs are costs made up of fixed and variable elements. They are a combination of semi-variable costs and semi-fixed costs. Because of the variable component, they fluctuate with volume; because of the fixed component, they do not change in direct proportion to output. Semi-fixed costs are those costs which remain constant up to a certain level of output after which they become variable as shown in Figure 2.7. Semi-variable cost is the cost which is basically variable but whose slope may change abruptly when a certain output level is reached as shown in Figure 2.8. An example of a mixed cost is the earnings of a worker who is paid a salary of ₹ 1,500 per week (fixed) plus ₹ 1 for each unit completed (variable). If he increases his weekly output from 1,000 units to 1,500 units, his earnings increase from ₹ 2,500 to ₹ 3,000.

Mixed costs are a combination of semi-variable costs and semi-fixed costs.

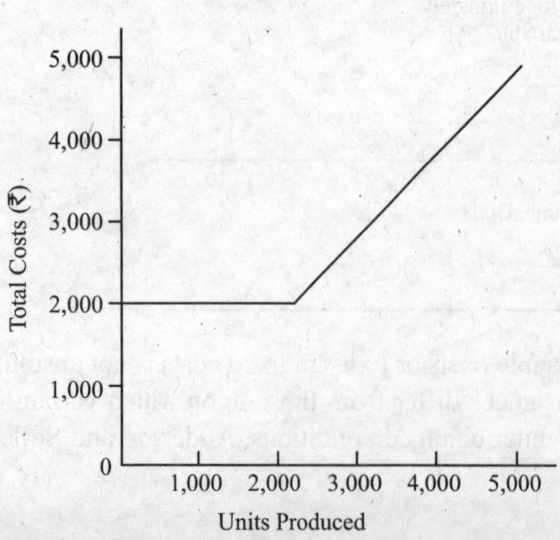

Figure 2.7: Semi-fixed Cost

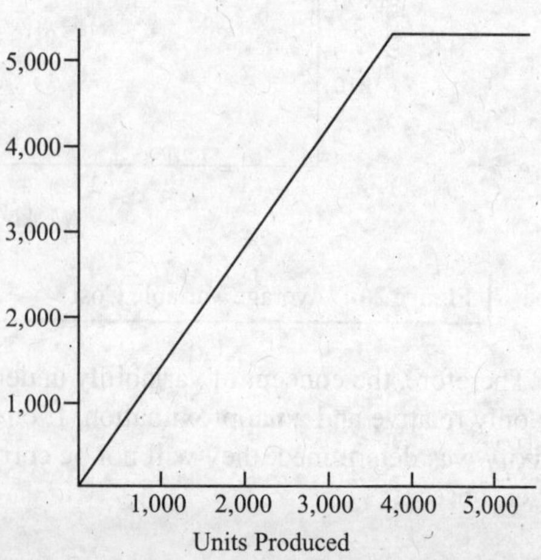

Figure 2.8: Semi-variable Cost

Earnings	*Units Produced*	
	1,000 units	1,500 units
Fixed component	₹ 1,500	₹ 1,500
variable component	1,000	1,500
Total:	2,500	3,000

An increase of 50% in output brings only a 20% increase in his earnings. Mathematically, mixed costs can be expressed as follows:

Total Mixed Cost = Total Fixed Cost + (Units × Variable Cost per Unit)

DEGREE OF TRACEABILITY TO A COST OBJECT – PRODUCT OR JOB

Cost is divided into direct and indirect cost in terms of degree of traceability to cost object i.e. product or job.

> **Direct costs** are easily traceable or identifiable with a product.

1. ***Direct Cost:*** An important problem in cost accounting is to determine the costs that are clearly identifiable and traceable to a costing object, such as units of product, company segments or some other specific activity. Costs which are easily traceable or identifiable with a product are called direct costs. If output units are the objects of costing, then direct costs represent costs and resources that can be traced to or identified with the finished product. Direct materials, direct labour and direct expenses are examples of direct costs.

> **Indirect costs** are those costs which cannot be identified with, or traced to a single product.

2. ***Indirect Cost:*** Indirect costs are those costs which cannot be identified with, or traced to a single product because they are common to several products. The example of indirect costs are: indirect materials (lubricants and scrap material), salary of factory supervisors (indirect labour), rent, rates and depreciation (indirect expenses). Indirect costs are often referred to as overheads. Overhead costs are indirect costs with respect to a specific product since they are incurred for all products manufactured in a company.

Costs also may be direct or indirect with respect to particular company segments or divisions. That is, some costs which are indirect for a product, may be traced to a segment or department and thus, will be direct costs for that department. A segment may mean any one of a number of things, viz., department, division, specific activity, sales territory and the like. *For example*, the salary of the plant manager of Plant A is a direct cost of plant A. But if multiple products are produced in plant A, the manager's salary is indirect to the specific products. Thus, what is a direct cost for one purpose, may be an indirect cost for another purpose.

Indirect costs (overhead costs) by nature create problems in cost determination and analysis. Direct cost related with a product can be measured with a high degree of accuracy. In the absence of appropriate direct measurement techniques, indirect costs have to be apportioned to different products. *For example*, suppose in a manufacturing concern, there are three separate production departments and a Head Office of the company. Each of these four segments will have costs which can be directly traced to their own departments. The direct or traceable costs of departments can be identified with the help of source documents and accounting records. What portion of the company Head Office expenses should be charged to different departments? Since the Managing Director's salary and other Head Office expenses benefits all three operating departments, these costs should be charged to all three departments. These indirect costs can be traced to different production departments only by apportionment involving some formula or base which may not be 100% accurate and reliable.

TIMING OF CHARGES AGAINST SALES REVENUE

Costs are classified into (*a*) product costs and (*b*) period costs, by their timing of charges against revenue or by whether they are inventoriable.

1. *Product Costs:* Product costs are inventoriable costs, identified as part of inventory on hand. Product costs are those costs which are identified with the product and included in stock valuation. All manufacturing costs are product costs. In a manufacturing concern, it is composed of four elements: (*i*) direct materials, (*ii*) direct labour, (*iii*) direct expenses and (*iv*) manufacturing overhead. That is, product cost is a full factory cost. Prior to sale, product costs are deferred as inventories and until the goods are sold, are shown on the balance sheet as assets. As finished inventory goods are sold, product costs are transferred from the inventory accounts to the cost of goods sold account, thus becoming part of the period costs at the time revenue is realised.

> **Product costs** are those costs which are identified with the product and included in stock valuation.

2. *Period Costs:* Period costs are those costs which are not included in stock valuation and are treated as expenses during the period in which they are incurred. They are not carried forward as a part of value of stock to the next accounting period. In a manufacturing organization, period costs include many selling and administrative costs needed to keep the business operating. These costs are necessary to generate revenues but they cannot be directly associated with units of product. Rather they can be assigned with periods of times in which they are consumed (expired). They are treated as expenses in the same period in which the costs are incurred.

> **Period costs** are those costs which are not included in stock-valuation and are treated as expenses during the period in which they are incurred.

It is significant to point out that product costs may be direct cost as well as indirect costs (direct costs with regard to direct material and direct labour, and indirect costs with regard to factory overhead). Similarly, period costs *i.e.* selling and distribution and administrative overheads may be direct and indirect costs.

The differences between product and period costs and their treatment are illustrated in Figure 2.9.

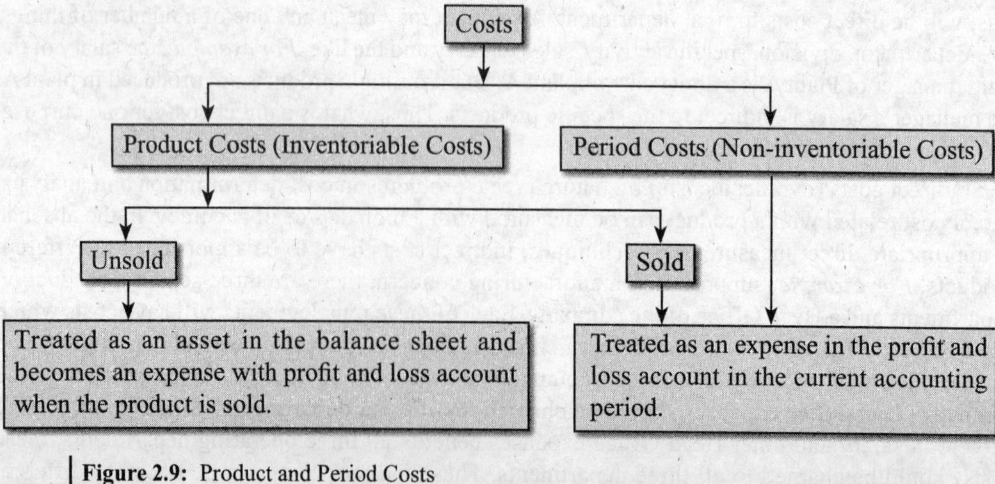

Figure 2.9: Product and Period Costs

Difference of opinion exists regarding whether certain costs should be considered as product or period costs. It is generally accepted that non-manufacturing costs such as selling and administrative costs should not be included in stock valuation and be treated as period costs. The reasons for such treatment are as follows:

(*i*) It is difficult to select equitable bases to apportion these costs to products. On the other hand, product costs can be assigned to specific products through objective and direct measurement and some by allocation.

(*ii*) The majority of these expenses are fixed regardless of the change in production or activity.

(*iii*) It is difficult, if not impossible, to determine the relationship between the incurrence of these costs and the production of individual units of output.

(*iv*) It is difficult to get evidence as to any future benefits that would be obtained from these expenses at the end of the accounting period. Such is the case with clerical salaries, used postage, office supplies, rent and the like. Even if it is argued that there will be future benefits, it is difficult to make accurate measurements of such benefits. Therefore objectivity and conservatism demand that such costs be treated as period costs and expensed. *For example*, costs like advertising, sales promotion, consulting fees may be expected to provide future benefits, but they are usually expensed when incurred.

Effect of Product Costs and Period Costs

The net income of a business enterprise is influenced by the amount of product cost and period costs. Therefore, the manner in which some costs are divided as product or period will surely have a bearing on reported net income of a business firm. Product costs, in the first instance, influence the value of inventory as such costs by nature should be included in the cost of product. Product costs affect net income in the period in which products representing the product costs have been sold. Apparently this may be a subsequent accounting period and not necessarily the period in which the product has been manufactured and product costs have been incurred. In other words, products costs do not reach the income statement and will not influence net income of a business enterprise until the product is sold. This event of influencing net income may take place in the current accouting period or subsequent accounting period. However, period costs appear directly on the income statement in the month or the period in which they expire.

Different Purposes Require Different Product Costs

The term 'product cost' has a broader concept and different purposes can result in different measures of product cost[4], as given below.

1. ***Pricing and Product Emphasis Decisions:*** For this purpose, the costs included are all areas of the value chain.

2. ***Contracting with Government Agencies:*** Government agencies frequently provide detailed guidelines on the allowable and non-allowable items in a product cost. *For example*, some government agencies explicitly exclude marketing costs from reimbursement to contractors and may reimburse only a part of R&D costs. Hence, the second bracket in Figure 2.10 shows how a specific contract may allow for all design and production costs and part of R&D costs.

(3) ***Preparing Financial Statements for External Reporting under Generally Accepted Accounting Principles:*** The focus here is on inventoriable costs. Under generally accepted accounting principles, only manufacturing costs are assigned to inventories in the financial statements.

Figure 2.10 illustrates how a product cost for external reporting can include only inventoriable costs in the financial statements, or a broader set of costs for reimbursement under a government contract, or a still broader set of costs for the pricing and product-emphasis decisions.

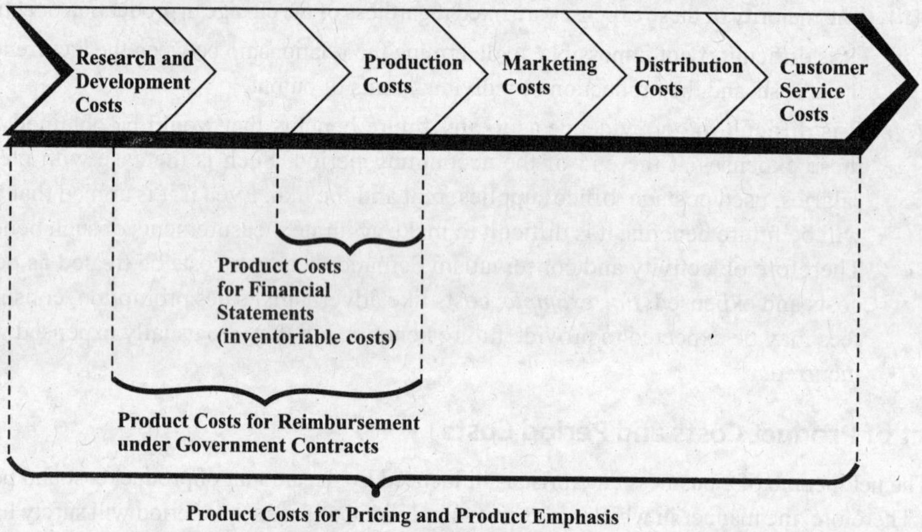

Figure 2.10: Different Product Costs for Different Purposes

Source: Charles T. Horngreen *et al*, Cost Accounting A Managerial Emphasis, Pearson Eduction, 2008, p. 38.

Product Costs in Different Firms

The nature of the business, to a great extent, determines which costs should be included in the product cost. Basically, there are three types of firms, viz. (1) merchandising firms, (2) service firms, and (3) manufacturing firms.

1. ***Merchandising Firms:*** Merchandising firms purchase readymade goods or products to resell them to their customers. Department stores, grocery stores, drug stores are some examples of merchandising firms. The cost incurred, i.e., purchase price paid by a merchandising firm in buying merchandise is the product cost. This product cost (purchase price) appears on the balance sheet as an asset (unexpired cost) till a sale is made. When products are sold, the product cost becomes an expense which is known as cost of goods sold. The cost of unsold products at the end of the accounting period appear as an asset on the balance sheet. The matching concept decides when the product cost becomes an expense. If the revenue from the sale of a product is reported in the income statement, then the corresponding cost of that product should be cost of goods sold in the same income statement.

2. ***Service Firms:*** Service firms, such as firms of chartered accountants, cost accountants, doctors, lawyers, etc. sell their services only (and no products) to generate revenues. In such service firms, there is not such thing as the product cost. All expenses are classified as operating expenses which expire during the current accounting period. These are deducted from the revenues to determine the net income.

3. ***Manufacturing Firms:*** A manufacturing firm does not purchase readymade products or goods for sale. Rather, production resources like materials and other resources are purchased and used in the manufacturing process to convert them into finished products. In a manufacturing firm, product costs include all costs necessary for the manufacture of the product. These product costs appear as assets on the balance sheet until the product is sold. When a sale is recorded, these product costs are transferred to cost of goods sold. The difference between sales and cost of goods sold is the gross margin from which selling and administrative expenses are deducted to determine the net income for the accounting period.

MANAGEMENT FUNCTION

Classification of costs according to management functions refers to how the cost was used (manufacturing, administration or selling). A functional classification implies that the business performs many functions for which costs are incurred. In measuring net income, expenses are usually classified by function and grouped under the headings of manufacturing, selling and administrative costs. Manufacturing costs are all production costs incurred to manufacture the products and to bring them to a saleable condition, including direct materials, direct labour and indirect manufacturing (factory overhead) costs. Selling and administrative charges may be treated as expenses when incurred or charged to prepaid expense accounts such as prepaid insurance. Functional classification is also important because it provides an opportunity to the management to evaluate the efficiency of departments performing different functions in the organization.

RELATIONSHIP WITH ACCOUNTING PERIOD: CAPITAL COST AND REVENUE COST

Costs can also be divided into two broad classes on the basis of the accounting period to which they relate: (*i*) capital expenditures and (*ii*) revenue expenditures. A capital expenditure provides benefit to future periods and is classified as an asset; a revenue expenditure is assumed to benefit the current period and is classified as an expense. A capital expenditure will flow into the cost stream as an expense when the asset is used up or written off.

The distinction between capital and revenue expenditures is vital to the proper matching of costs and revenue and to the accurate measurement of periodic net income.

COSTS FOR DECISION-MAKING AND PLANNING

Cost for decision making and planning include the following.

Opportunity Cost

Opportunity cost is the cost of opportunity lost. An opportunity cost is the benefit given up or sacrificed when one alternative is chosen over another. It is the income foregone by selecting another alternative. An opportunity cost is the net cash inflow that could be obtained if the resources committed to one action were used in the most desirable other alternative.

> **Opportunity cost** is the cost of opportunity lost; the benefit given up or sacrificed when one alternative is chosen over another.

Opportunity costs are not incorporated into formal financial accounting records. Why? Because historical record keeping is limited to transactions involving alternatives that were actually selected, rather than alternatives that were rejected. Rejected alternatives do not produce transactions and so they are not recorded.

Market Values, Profit Sacrificed

Opportunity costs are often market values. Alternatively, they are measured by the profit that would have been earned had the resources been used for the other purpose. *For example*, choosing to attend college instead of working has an opportunity cost equal to the salary foregone. Further, assume that a manufacturer can sell a semi-finished product to a customer for ₹ 50,000. He decides, however, to keep it and finish it. The opportunity cost of the semi-finished product is ₹ 50,000 because this is the amount of economic resources foregone by the manufacturer to complete the product. Similarly, capital which is invested in plant and inventories cannot now be invested in shares and debentures that will earn interest and dividends, the loss of interest and dividend that would be earned is the opportunity cost. Other examples of opportunity cost are when the owner of a business forgoes the opportunity to employ himself elsewhere; or a machine used to make product A is said to have an opportunity cost if the machine can be sold or if it can also make product B. Similarly, suppose a person has three job offers one for ₹ 40,000 p.m., another for ₹ 35,000 p.m and a third for ₹ 28,000 p.m., By selecting the best offer of ₹ 40,000, the opportunity cost will be ₹ 35,000, the next best alternative. ₹ 35,000 was given up to get 40,000. The general rule is that the opportunity cost should not exceed the value of option selected.

Opportunity costs are important in decision-making and evaluating alternatives. Decision-making is selecting the best alternative which is facilitated by the help of opportunity costs. Such costs do not require cash outlays and are only imputed costs.

Opportunity costs is not usually entered in the accounting records of an organisation, but it is a cost that must be explicitly considered in every decision a manager makes. Virtually every alternative has some opportunity cost attached to it.

Opportunity Costs and Scarce Resources

It is important to note that opportunity costs apply to the use of scarce resources. If resources are not limited or scarce, no sacrifice exists from using these resources. Further, if no alternative use of resources exists, then the opportunity cost is zero, But if resources have an alternative use, and are scarce, then an opportunity cost does exist. *For example* assume a factory is producing a product working at 75% capacity and has an opportunity to obtain a contract for the production of a special component. Accepting the contract will not affect in any way the revenue of existing product. Also, the available capacity cannot be put to any other use. Then the opportunity cost of accepting the contract will be zero. However, in case, the factory is working at 100% capacity and the output of the existing product needs to be reduced to accept the contract, giving a revenue loss of ₹ 10,00,000, then opportunity cost will be ₹ 10,00,000.

Example:

Sameer is a full-time student at a local university. He wants to decide whether he should attend at university a four-week summer session, where tuition is ₹ 2,500 or take a break and work full time at a local departmental store, where he could make as much as ₹ 1,500 a week: How much would going to the summer session cost him from a decision-making standpoint? What is the opportunity cost?

Solution:

The total cost of going to summer school would be ₹ 8,500 p.m. that is, ₹ 2,500 tuition plus ₹ 6,000 which he would give up by attending the university. The opportunity cost would be ₹ 6,000, since this is the amount he gives up by rejecting the alternative of working full time.

Relevant Costs

Relevant costs are those future cost which differ between alternatives. Relevant costs may also be defined as:

- *the costs which are affected and changed by a decision.*

> **Relevant costs** are those future cost which differ between alternatives.
>
> **Irrelevant costs** are those costs which remain the same and not affected by the decision whatever alternative is chosen.

If a cost increases, decreases, appears or disappears as different alternatives are compared, it is a relevant cost. On the countrary, irrelevant costs are those costs which remain the same and not affected by the decision whatever alternative is chosen. Irrelevant costs do not mean that such costs are forgotten or that such costs need not be evaluated. It simply means that irrelevant cost is not one of the factors that will quantitatively affect the decision. Relevant costs have the following two features:

1. ***Future Costs:*** Relevant costs are only future costs, i.e., those costs which are expected to be incurred in future. Relevant costs, therefore, are not historic (sunk) costs which have already been incurred and cannot be changed by a decision.
2. ***Incremental or Avoidable Costs:*** Relevant costs are only incremental (additional) or avoidable costs. Incremental costs refer to an increase in cost between two alternatives. Avoidable costs are those which are not incurred from one alternative to another.

To take an example, assume a business firm purchased a plant for ₹ 1,00,000 and has now a book value of ₹ 10,000. The plant has become obsolete and cannot be sold in its present condition. However, the plant can be sold for ₹ 15,000 if some modification is done on it which will cost ₹ 6,000.

In this example, ₹ 6.000 (modification costs) and ₹ 15,000 (sales values) both are relevant as they reflect future, incremental costs and future revenues respectively. The firms will have increamental benefit of ₹ 9,000 (₹ 15,000 – ₹ 6,000) on sale of the plant.

₹ 1,00,000 has already been incurred and being a sunk cost is not relevant to the decision, i.e., whether modification should be done. Similarly, the book value of ₹ 10,000 which has to be written off whatever alternative future action is chosen, is also not relevant because it cannot be changed by any future decision.

Differential Cost

Differential cost is the difference in total costs between any two alternatives. Differential costs are equal to the additional variable expenses incurred in respect of the additional output, plus the increase in fixed costs, if any. This means that differential cost is only the difference in the amount of the two costs. This cost may be calculated by taking the total cost of production without the additional contemplated output and comparing it with the total costs incurred if the extra output is undertaken.

Incremental and Decremental Costs

Differential costs are also known as incremental costs, although technically an incremental cost should refer only to an increase in cost from one alternative to another; decrease in cost should be referred to as decremental cost. Differential cost is a broader term, encompassing both cost increases (incremental çosts) and cost decreases (decremental costs) between alternatives.

The concept of differential costing is vital in planning and decision-making. It is an important tool in evaluating the profitability of alternative choice decisions and helping management in choosing the best alternative. The differential cost analysis can assist management in knowing the additional profit that would be earned if idle or unused capacity is used for extra production or if some additional investments are made by the firm.

Example:

A printer is considering replacing an old machine, which he purchased for ₹ 1,50,000 three years ago, with some labour-saving equipment. The old machine is being depreciated at ₹ 15,000 a year. The following alternative equipment options are available *for consideration.*

Machine A. The purchase price of machine A is ₹ 2,50,000 and yearly cash operating costs are ₹ 50,000.

Machine B. The purchase price of machine B is ₹ 2,80,000 and yearly cash operating costs are ₹ 45,000.

(*a*) What are the incremental costs, if any, in this alternative-choice situation?

(*b*) What are the sunk costs, if any, in this situation?

Solution:

(*a*) The following schedule will identify the incremental costs in this decision problem.

	Machine A	*Machine B*	*Incremental Costs (B–A)*
Purchase price (₹)	2,50,000	2,80,000	30,000
Cash operating costs (₹)	50,000	45,000	(5,000)
Depreciation of old equipment (₹)	15,000	15,000	—

(*b*) The depreciation on old equipment ₹ 15,000 (on the total purchase price of ₹ 1,50,000), is a sunk cost because it represents an investment outlay made in the past.

Sunk Cost

A sunk cost is the cost that has already been incurred. It is a past or committed cost, cost gone forever. Sunk costs (past costs) are costs that have been created by a decision in the past and cannot be changed once they have been incurred and cannot be avoided (changed) by any decision that is made in the future. Any asset obtained from the incurred cost can be used or sold, but its value is its present or future value — not the cost paid. Sunk costs are costs which are the result of previous decisions of the enterprise and which will be unaffected by any future decision as they have already been incurred.

Sunk costs (past costs) are costs that have been created by a decision in the past and cannot be changed once they have been incurred and cannot be avoided (changed) by any decision that is made in the future.

Thus, any historical cost is a sunk cost. Examples of sunk costs are book values of existing assets such as plant and equipment, inventory, investment in securities, etc. For example, if a plant was purchased five years ago for ₹ 5,00,000 with the expected life of 10 years and nil scrap value, then the written down value will be ₹ 2,50,000 if straight line method of depreciation has been used. This written down value (₹ 2,50,000) will have to be written off, no matter, what alternative future action is chosen. For instance, if the plant is to be used in the future, ₹ 2,50,000 will be written off and if the plant is decided to be scrapped, again ₹ 2,50,000 will be written off. Even though in hindsight the purchase of the machine may have been unwise, no amount of regret can undo that decision. This historical cost cannot be changed by any future decision and therefore becomes sunk cost. Therefore, they can and should be ignored when making a decision.

Anderson and Sollenberger[5] observe:

> Historical costs, which are fundamental to most balance sheet asset values and income measurement, have little or no significance in management analysis. A past cost has no meaning in decisions to hold, use or sell. Only current and future values have meaning. Even tax issues uses historical costs only to determine current and future tax costs. The temptation to continue to use historical costs in decision is great. But using any past cost will only distort the decision-making process.

Sunk Costs and Irrelevant Costs

The costs which are irrelevant for decision-making are not necessarily sunk costs. Some costs may be found irrelevant but not sunk costs. For example, a comparison of two alternative production methods may result in identical direct material costs for both the alternatives. In this case, the direct material cost will remain the same whichever alternative is chosen. In this situation, though direct material cost is the future cost to be incurred in accordance with the production, it is irrelevant, but, it is not a sunk cost.

Sunk Costs and Salvage Value

It is significant to mention that while book value of the old asset remains irrelevant, disposal and salvage values may be relevant as it involves relevant cash inflow. It is obtained only if the replacement alternative is selected. Any salvage value available at the end of useful life of a machine is relevant. A loss on disposal may have a favourable tax impact if the loss can be offset against taxable gains or taxable income. Thus, the book value of the old asset remains irrelevant but the expected tax reduction would be relevant.

Sunk Costs, Differential Costs, Opportunity Costs

A **sunk cost** is one that has already been incurred and therefore will be the same no matter which alternative a manager selects. Sunk costs are *never* relevant for decision -making because they are not differential cost.

Even though the historical cost of a resource is sunk, the resource can have a cost for dicision-making purposes. If a resource can be used in more than one way, it has an opportunity cost. An opportunity cost is the benefit lost by taking one action as opposed to another. The 'other' action is the best alternative availâble other than the one being contemplated.

A company that owns a warehouse (which is a sunk cost) can use it either to store its own products or rent it to another company. Using the space for storage requires that the company forego the opportunity to rent it. When the company considers any action that requires using the space for storage, the relevant cost of the space is its opportunity cost, the rent the company will not collect. Of course, the space might have other uses.

Sunk Costs and Ethical Dilemmas

Although the book value of the old machine has no economic significance, the accounting treatment of past costs may make it psychologically difficult for managers to regard them as irrelevant. Morse, Davis and Hartgraves[6] observe:

From an economic viewpoint, the analysis should focus on future costs and revenues that differ. The decision should not be influenced by sunk costs. Although there is no easy solution to this behavioral and ethical problem, managers and management accountants should be aware of its potential impact.

> The possibility of recording an accounting loss may place managers in an ethical dilemma. Although an action may be desirable from the long-run viewpoint of the organization, in the short run, choosing the action may result in an accounting loss. Fearing the loss will lead superiors to question his or her judgement, a manager might prefer to use the old machine (with lower total profits over the four-year period) as opposed to replacing it and being forced to record a loss on disposal. Although this action may now avoid raising trouble-some questions, the cumulative effect of many decisions of this nature will be harmful to organization's long-run economic health.

Similarly, Jiambalvo[7] advises:

> When managers make decisions, they need to be careful that they are not influenced by sunk costs. That's difficult because, psychologically, people are pre-disposed to take sunk costs into account. Psychologists refer to this "irrational" economic behavior as the *sunk cost effect*. Consider an immensely expensive waterway project. Proponents of the project may suggest that its elimination would be inappropriate because so much money had already been spent on its completion. That is, proponents rationalize continuation of the project in terms of sunk costs!

Imputed Cost

Imputed costs are costs not actually incurred in some transaction but which are relevant to the decision as they pertain to a particular situation. These costs do not enter into traditional accounting systems. But they being related with economic reality help in making better decisions. Interest on internally generated funds, rental value of company-owned property and salaries of owners of a single proprietorship or partnership are some examples of imputed costs. Costs paid or incurred are not imputed costs. *For example*, if ₹ 50,000 is paid for purchase of raw materials it is an outlay cost but not an imputed cost, because it would enter into accounting systems. By itself, ₹ 50,000 measures the monetary impact of this particular event. When a company uses internally generated funds, no actual interest payment is required. But if the internally generated funds are invested in some projects, interest would have been earned. The revenue foregone (loss of interest) represents an opportunity cost, and thus, imputed costs are opportunity costs. Similarly, the owner or manager should deduct from the profits of the business, an amount equivalent to the salary the owner would have earned by working in some other profession and the interest which the owner's capital would have earned in an alternative business.

> **Imputed costs** are costs not actually incurred in some transaction but which are relevant to the decision as they pertain to a particular situation.

Out-of-pocket Cost

While imputed costs do not involve cash outlays, out-of-pocket costs signify the cash cost associated with an activity. Non-cash costs such as depreciation are not included in out-of-pocket costs. This cost concept is significant for management in deciding whether or not a particular project will at least return the cash expenditures associated with the project selected by management. Similarly, acceptance of a special order for production may necessitate the consideration of out-of-pocket costs that need not be incurred if the special order proposal is not accepted. Depreciation on plant and equipment is not relevant in decision-making because no cash goes outside the business.

> **Out-of-pocket costs** signify the cash cost associated with an activity.

Fixed, Variable and Mixed Costs

Fixed, variable and mixed costs have been explained in the preceding sections.

Direct Cost and Indirect Cost

Direct cost and indirect cost have been explained in the preceding sections.

Example:

Proposal A is being evaluated against Proposal B. Fill up column IV of the following table:

I	II	III	IV
Sl. No.	*Type of Cost*	*Classification*	*Condition under which the classification happens*
(i)	Variable cost per unit	Irrelevant	
(ii)	Unavoidable fixed costs	Relevant	
(iii)	Out of pocket costs in future	Relevant	
(iv)	Sunk cost	Irrelevant	

(Only Columns I and IV are required to be presented in the answers)

(CA. Final, Nov. 2015)

Solution:

Analysis of Costs for Evaluation of Proposal A against the Proposal B

Sl. No.	*Condition under which classification happens*
(i)	Variable Cost per unit that will not differ between the options or Variable Cost has already been incurred in the past.
(ii)	Fixed Cost that is not committed and differ between the options.
(iii)	Additional future cost that Differs between alternatives.
(iv)	Costs already have been incurred and it will not affect any current or future action.

Shut Down Cost

> **Shut down costs** are those costs which have to be incurred under all situations in the case of stopping manufacture of a product or closing down a department or division.

Shut down costs are those costs which have to be incurred under all situations in the case of stopping manufacture of a product or closing down a department or division. Shut down costs are always fixed costs. If the manufacturing of a product is stopped, variable cost like direct materials, direct labour, direct expenses, variable factory overhead will not be incurred. However, a part of fixed costs (if not total fixed costs) associated with the product will be incurred such as rent, watchman's salary, property taxes, etc. Such fixed costs are unavoidable. Some fixed costs associated with the product become avoidable and need not be incurred in case production is stopped such as supervisor's salary, factory manager's salary, lighting, etc. Shut down costs, thus, refer to minimum fixed costs which are incurred in the event of closure of a department or division.

COST FOR CONTROL

Costs used for control are generally grouped as follows:

Controllable and Uncontrollable Cost

The concept of controllable cost is very important in cost accounting and contributes effectively to the achievement of the objectives of cost control and responsibility accounting. The ICMA (UK) defines controllable cost as:

- *a cost which can be influenced by the action of a specified member of an under taking* and uncontrollable cost as:

- *a cost which cannot be influenced by the action of a specified member of an undertaking*

Basically, a controllable cost is the cost over which a manager has direct and complete decision authority. That is, controllable costs can be controlled (reduced) by a manager at a given organizational level. Controllable costs do not imply that they are 100% controllable.

> **Controllable cost** is the cost over which a manager has direct and complete decision authority. They are generally fixed costs

As an example of controllable and uncontrollable costs, consider a plant supervisor. This individual influences labour and material costs by scheduling workers and assuring an efficient production process. Thus, labour and material costs are a supervisor's controllable costs. However, the supervisor cannot determine insurance for a plant. A plant manager or an insurance specialist makes decisions regarding insurance. Therefore, insurance cost is a supervisor's non-controllable cost but a plant manager's or an insurance specialist's controllable cost.

1. ***Partly Controllable Cost:*** Some costs are partly controllable by a responsibility centre manager. Maintenance cost is such an example which can be influenced (controlled) on one hand, by the production manager through minimising misuse of plant and machinery, and, on the other hand, by the maintenance manager by providing skilled repairmen. Such jointly controllable costs are found in business firms, manufacturing and non-manufacturing. *For example*, the cost of raw materials is controlled by the production managers as well as purchase managers. The production manager controls at quantity level, and the purchase manager at the price level. Such costs are reported to both of them, but one responsible manager should be held accountable for those costs which he can control.

Service organizations also have jointly controllable costs. Branch manager of a bank might have little to say about the hiring of their employees; nonetheless, they control scheduling and assignment of work. Accordingly, a responsibility cost system might reasonably include the expense for branch salaries as controllable on branch statements.

2. ***Controllable Cost and Variable Cost:*** The term 'controllable cost' should not be confused with the terms 'variable cost'. These terms are not synonymous. Variable costs vary with the output but are not necessarily controllable. A cost is controllable by one who monitors it. A cost is variable when it is a function of output. The two are not the same. *For example*, the cost of containers may not be controllable by the manager of the container department. The cost of cans varies mostly with the price of aluminium rather than with production. Similarly, factory supplies used for servicing plant and equipment may vary with the output in the production department, but the production manager cannot control them.

3. ***Controllable Cost and Direct Cost:*** Similarly, Controllable costs and direct costs are not necessarily the same. A cost may be a direct cost of a given department but may not be controlled by the department supervisor. *For example*, the salary of a department supervisor, which is a direct cost of the department, is controlled at a higher level of management rather than by the supervisor. The direct costs of a machining department include the salary of the manager and depreciation of machinery, as opposed to joint departmental costs, such as building occupancy and corporate overheads. Depreciation of machinery is a direct cost but not controllable. Likewise, the manager's salary is direct but not controllable because a higher authority approves it. Direct costs need not be controllable at the departmental level.

4. *Uncontrollable Cost and Fixed Cost:* Further, it should not be assumed that all fixed costs are uncontrollable. While a fixed cost, such as property insurance may be uncontrollable at certain managerial levels, it is nevertheless subject to control by manager who has the authority to obtain insurance coverage. Costs resulting from decisions of prior periods are not controllable in the short run by anyone. The control over a fixed asset acquisition, *for example*, occurs when management approves its purchase. The subsequent depreciation expense is not controllable.

Controllable and uncontrollable cost, in fact, should not be viewed as variable costs or fixed costs and as direct costs or indirect costs as well.

5. *Factors Making Cost Controllable/Uncontrollable:* Sometimes it is contended that two factors: (*i*) the time period factor, and (*ii*) the decision- making authority, can make a cost controllable or uncontrollable. If the time period is long enough, all costs can be controllable and curtailed. *For example*, the manager of an insurance department can control the insurance cost on a yearly basis but he cannot control the cost on a monthly or weekly basis. Similarly, the decision-making authority influences the cost. If a responsibility centre manager has been delegated authority to spend the cost, he can control it. Proper delegation helps in establishing clear responsibility and controllability. All costs can be said to be controllable by somebody in the organization. The managing director of a company is responsible for all costs. But practically, the responsibility and authority of controlling costs is delegated to different levels in the organization.

Example:

Which of the following costs are likely to be *fully* controllable, *partially* controllable, or *not* controllable by the manager of the production department?

(*a*) Wages paid to direct labour
(*b*) Rent on factory building
(*c*) Manager's salary
(*d*) Utilities
(*e*) Direct materials used
(*f*) Supplies
(*g*) Insurance on factory equipment
(*h*) Advertising
(*i*) Price paid for materials and supplies
(*j*) Idle time due to machine breakdown

Solutions:

(*a*) fully
(*b*) not
(*c*) not
(*d*) partially
(*e*) fully
(*f*) partially
(*g*) not
(*h*) not
(*i*) not
(*j*) partially

Standard Costs

Standard costs are those costs which are planned or predetermined cost estimates for a unit of output in order to provide a basis for a comparison with actual costs. Standard costs are used to prepare budgets. Standard cost is a unit concept and indicates standard

> **Standard costs** are those costs which are planned or predetermined cost estimates for a unit of output in order to provide a basis for a comparison with actual costs.

cost per unit of output, per labour hour, etc. On the contrary, the term 'budgeted cost' is total concept and indicates total budgeted cost of an item, at activity level or output level such as budgeted cost of material is ₹ 80,000 if 8,000 units are manufactured.

Fixed, Variable and Mixed Cost

Fixed, Variable and Mixed Costs have been discussed earlier in this chapter.

OTHER COSTS

Other costs can be broadly bifurcated into Joint and Common Costs.

Joint Costs

Joint costs relate to two or more products produced from a common production process or element—material, labour, or overhead or any combination thereof, or so locked together that one cannot be produced without producing the other(s).

Joint costs arise where the processing of a single raw material or production resources results in two or more different products simultaneously. Sometimes, joint costs and common costs are used having identical meaning. However, both the terms have different meanings. Joint costs relate to a situation in which the factors of production by their basic nature result in two or more products. The jointness results from there being more than one product, and these multiproducts are the result of the method of production or the nature of raw material and not of a decision by management to produce both. In other words, joint costs relate to two or more products produced from a common production process or element—material, labour, or overhead or any combination thereof, or so locked together that one cannot be produced without producing the other(s).

Thus, joint cost is the cost of two or more products that are produced simultaneously by a single process and are not identifiable as individual types of products until a certain stage of production known as the split off point (point of separation) is reached. *For example*, kerosene, fuel oil, gasolene and other oil products are derived from crude oil. Joint costs are total costs incurred up to the point of separation. Sometimes it is found that one product is of major importance and the others are of minor importance. In such situations, products of lesser importance are known as by-products.

Joint costs can be apportioned to different products only by means of some suitable bases of apportionment. Total costs of production of multiple products combine both joint costs and separable individual product costs. The latter are easily identified and traced to the individual products, and no problem of apportionment is involved in such costs.

Common Costs

Common costs are those costs which are incurred for more than one product, job, territory or any other specific costing object.

Common costs are those costs which are incurred for more than one product, job, territory or any other specific costing object. Common costs are not easily identifiable with individual products and, therefore, are generally apportioned. The National Association of Accountants (USA) defines the term 'common cost' as:

- *the cost of services employed in the creation of two or more output which is not allocatable to those outputs on a clearly justified basis.*

The important distinguishing characteristic of a common cost is that there is no clearly definable association between the incurrence of the cost and the cost object that benefit from use of the facilities.

Common costs are not only common to products, but they may be common to processes, functions, responsibilities, customers, sales territories, periods of time and similar costing units. *For example*, the salary of a manager of a production department which is manufacturing three products is an example of common cost with respect to the products. But salary is direct cost to the production department. Similarly, the rent of the factory is common to all departments located in the factory. The basic point is that a particular (common) cost may be direct to one object and common as far as other objects are concerned.

Although both the terms, 'common cost' and 'joint cost' are sometimes used interchangeably, they differ from each other. Joint costs emerge when multiple products are manufactured in a common process and when common inputs are used. The multiple products have a definite quantitative relationship to each other and the production of one product influences the output of the other product, though in a lesser proportion. Common costs are not the result of any manufacturing compulsion or the use of any single raw material. Besides common costs can be apportioned to costing objects like products, jobs, department, etc. without much difficulty. But the apportionment of joint costs involves many complexities and difficulties in cost accounting. The incurrence of common costs are influenced by management decisions. But joint costs are influenced by common production process and use of common raw materials.

COST FLOWS IN MANUFACTURING, MERCHANDISING AND SERVICE ORGANIZATIONS

Costs are accounted for from the point they are incurred to their recognition as expenses on the income statement. The process is referred to as cost flows. The cost flows in a manufacturing firm are more complex than those of a merchandising firm or a service firm.

Manufacturing Organizations

Manufacturing firms have the most complex cost of goods sold activities. The manufacturing firm will buy materials or components and convert these inputs into a saleable product. Manufacturing requires three types of inventories – materials, work-in-progress and finished products. For a manufacturing firm, the selling and administrative costs are expensed immediately, Exhibit 2.2 and Figure 2.11 display the income statement and cost flow pattern in a manufacturing firm.

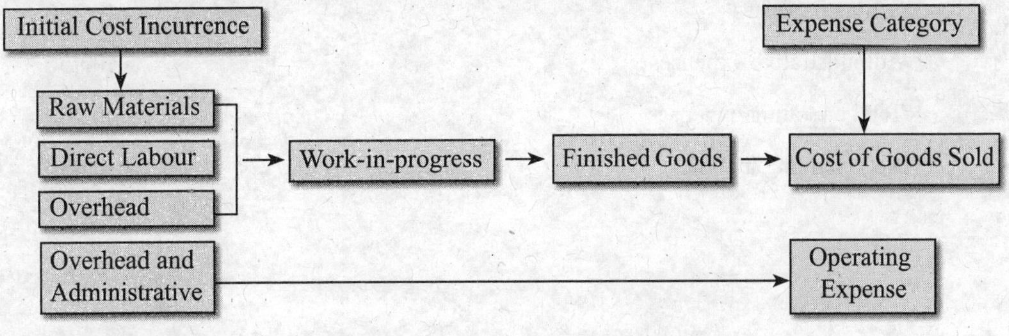

Figure 2.11: Cost Flows in a Manufacturing Organization

Exhibit 2.2: Income Statement in a Manufacturing Organization

Income Statement for the year ending December 2016

		₹
Sales		4,00,000
Cost of Sales:		
Cost of goods manufactured:		
Opening materials inventory		23,250
Add:	Purchase of materials	1,16,150
	Materials available for use	1,39,400
Less:	Closing materials inventory	25,500
	Materials used	1,13,900
Add:	Direct labour	44,750
Add:	Manufacturing (factory) overhead	1,05,850
	Manufacturing cost	2,64,500
Add:	Opening working progress	21,350
	Total manufacturing (factory) costs	2,85,850
Less:	Closing work-in progress	20,400
	Cost of goods manufactured	2,65,450
Add:	Opening finished goods inventory	37,600
	Goods available for sale	3,03,050
Less:	Closing finished goods inventory	39,700
	Cost of goods sold	2,63,350
	Gross profit (margin)	1,36,650
	Operating expenses:	
	Selling expenses	49,250
	Administrative expenses	50,950
	Total operating expenses	1,00,200
	Net operating income	36,450

Merchandising Organizations

A merchandising organisation purchases products for resale. Generally, a merchandising firm provides a link in the physical distribution chain acting as a wholesaler or retailer. It keeps inventories of merchandise only. Exhibit 2.3 displays income statement of a merchandising firm. In merchandising firms, product cost includes the cost of merchandise plus inward freight and possibly certain internal merchandise handling costs. All other expenses are treated as period costs.

Exhibit 2.3: Income Statement in a Merchandising Firm

Income Statement of a Merchandising Firm

			(₹)
Sales			25,00,000
Less:	Cost of goods sold:		
	Beginning inventory	₹ 5,00,000	
Add:	Purchases	15,00,000	
	Goods available for sale	20,00,000	
Less:	Closing inventory	4,25,000	
			15,75,000
	Gross margin		9,25,000
Less:	Operating expenses:		
	Selling expenses	2,50,000	
	Administrative expenses	3,75,000	6,25,000
	Net Income		3,00,000

Cost flows pattern in a merchandising firm has been displayed in Figure 2.12. Operating Costs, as incurred, are immediately expensed. Merchandise, however, is acquired and first transferred to the inventory account. Subsequently, when the merchandise is sold, the cost flows, and it is transferred to an expense account.

Figure 2.12: Cost Flows in a Merchandising Firm

Service Organizations

A service organisation performs an activity or provides service for a fee. The costs of performing the service may include salaries of professionals and support personnel, supplies, purchased specialised services and routine costs such as rent and utilities. An income statement for a service firm is shown in Exhibit 2.4.

Exhibit 2.4: Income Statement in a Service Firm

Income Statement of a Service Firm

		(₹)
Revenues		1,50,000
Less: Expenses:		
Cost of services sold:		
Direct materials (Supplies)	₹ 25,000	
Direct labour	50,000	
Overhead	50,000	1,25,000
Gross margin		25,000
Less: Operating expenses:		
Selling expenses	2,000	
Administrative expenses	8,750	10,750
Net Income		14,250

Some service firms can identify direct costs of performing the service, while most service organizations treat all expenses as operating expenses. *For example*, if a service firm has undertaken to provide service to a client, the direct costs in this regard will include chargeable time of the firm's professional staff and any other costs that are traceable directly to specific client. Unlike a manufacturing firm, the service firm has no finished goods inventory because it is not possible to inventory services. Service firms maintain only supplies inventories.

Cost Flows

The cost flows pattern in a service firm is displayed in Figure 2.13. Raw materials, materials directly needed for providing service generally known as supplies, are purchased and their cost flows into the Inventory Account. As materials and supplies are used along with direct labour and overhead, these costs immediately become expenses, known as cost of services. The operating costs of selling and administration become expenses as they are incurred.

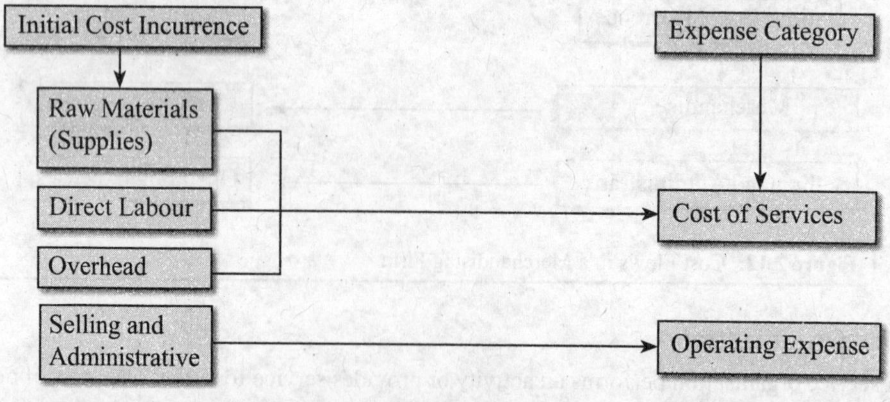

Figure 2.13: Cost Flows in Service Organizations

Illustrative Problem 1

A manufacturing company manufactures and sells a number of products. The following cost data relating to a company's activities and one of the company's production department (Department No. 5) have been taken from the company records.

1. Salary of factory manager
2. Supervisor's salary (Department 5)
3. Materials used on products in Department 5
4. Depreciation on building
5. Depreciation on equipment in Department 5
6. Wages of production Employees in Department 5
7. Salary of sales manager
8. Factory taxes and insurance
9. Wages of maintenance employees for factory plant and equipment
10. Sales commission paid on product sales
11. Lubricating oils for equipment in Department 5
12. Computer operating costs
13. Advertising agency costs
14. Expenses on travel and entertainment
15. Factory heat and power
16. Salary of Vice-President–Finance

You are required to classify each cost into:

(*a*) Variable or fixed cost

(*b*) Product or period cost

(*c*) Direct or indirect cost to the cost objective (product or department in relation to the answer to part (*b*) above)

(*d*) Controllable or non-controllable by the manager of Department 5.

Solution:

Items of cost	*Varia-ble cost*	*Fixed cost*	*Pro-duct cost*	*Period cost*	*Direct cost*	*Indirect cost*	*Controllable by Manager of Deptt. 5*		*Remarks*
							Yes	*No*	
(1)	(2)	(3)	(4)	(5)	(6)	(7)			
1. Salary of factory manager		√	√			√		√	
2. Supervisor's salary (Department 5)		√	√			√		√	It will be direct cost of department 5 but manager (of Department 5) does not control his own salary.
3. Materials used on product in Department 5	√	√	√	√					

Items of cost (1)	*Variable cost* (2)	*Fixed cost* (3)	*Product cost* (4)	*Period cost* (5)	*Direct cost* (6)	*Indirect cost* (7)	*Controllable by Manager of Deptt. 5*		*Remarks*
							Yes	*No*	
4. Depreciation on building		√				√		√	It will be product cost if building is factory; if building is office, then cost is period cost and if it is factory and office building both this cost should be allocated between factory and office cost.
5. Depreciation on equipment in Department 5.		√	√		√			√	It is non-controllable cost because manager of Deptt. 5 cannot buy/sell equipment.
6. Wages of production employees in Department 5	√		√		√		√		It is assumed that wages are paid hourly and hours vary with output.
7. Salary of sales manager		√		√		√		√	It has been assumed as fixed.
8. Factory taxes and insurance		√	√			√		√	
9. Wages of maintenance employees		√	√			√		√	
10. Sales commission paid on product sales	√			√	√			√	It is considered direct with relation to specific products. It is generally semi-variable.
11. Lubricating oils for equipment of Department 5	√		√			√	√		
12. Computer operating costs		√		√		√		√	Computer centre provides service to all departments of a company. The manager of Department 5 may influence only a small portion of such costs.
13. Advertising		√		√		√		√	It is considered fixed due to contract with the advertising agency.

Items of cost (1)	*Variable cost* (2)	*Fixed cost* (3)	*Product cost* (4)	*Period cost* (5)	*Direct cost* (6)	*Indirect cost* (7)	*Controllable by Manager of Deptt. 5* *Yes*	*No*	*Remarks*
14. Expenses on travel and entertainment		√		√		√		√	It may be semi-Variable cost if it is related to sales. It may be semi-fixed within relevant range.
15. Factory heat and power		√		√		√		√	
16. Salary of the Vice-President-Finance		√		√		√		√	

Illustrative Problem 2

Louise Marsh is a student at State University. Recently, she purchased a used car for ₹ 50,000 cash. Being concerned over the costs of owning and operating a car, she prepared the following estimates:

Licence fees and taxes — ₹ 500 per year

Maintenance and repairs — ₹ 2,500

Insurance — ₹ 2,500 per year

Tyres — ₹ 2,400 per set of four, useful life of tyres — 15000 kms, Cost of petrol — ₹ 0.90 per km. Annual mileage to be driven — 10,000 kms.

Also, Marsh expect to keep the car for three years and sell it for ₹ 5,000. She bought a set of new tyres for the car during the first week of ownership and does not intend to replace tyres at time of final sale.

Required:

(*a*) Classify the costs of Marsh's car as either direct or indirect assuming that she selects the 'car-km' as her cost objective and that she uses straight line depreciation.

(*b*) What is the full cost of a car-km for Marsh's automobile ?

(*c*) Marsh and a classmate, Janet Bond, plan a weekend at a beach resort and agree to share transportation costs equitably for the 500 km trip. Actual expenditures were:

Petrol ₹ 450.

Overspeeding ticket while Bond was driving ₹ 500

Replacement of broken fan belts ₹ 150. If you were Marsh, how much would you expect Bond to pay? Do you think Bond would agree? Why? (*M. Com. Delhi*)

Solution:

(*a*)

Cost Items	***Direct***	***Indirect***
Licence fees and taxes	No	Yes
Maintenance and repairs	No	Yes
Insurance	No	Yes
Tyres	No	Yes
Cost of petrol	Yes	No

Note: Cost of tyres is indirect cost but if this cost is related to useful life of tyres (15000 kms), it may be treated as direct cost.

(*b*) Full Cost of Marsh's Used Car

Items of Cost	*Annual* (₹)	*Per Car Km* (₹)
Depreciation (including tyres)	15,000	
Licence fees and taxes	500	
Maintenance and repairs	2,500	
Insurance	2,500	
Tyres (₹ 2,400 per set of 4 for 15000 kms)	1,600	
Cost of petrol	9,000	
	31,100	
Annual mileage (₹ 31,100 ÷ 10000 kms)		3.11
(*c*) Full cost of 500 km trip		
₹ 3.11 × 500 kms = ₹ 1,555		
(*i*) Marsh would expect Bond to pay ½ of transportation costs on the basis of full costing:		
½ of full cost (500 kms trip) =	₹ 777.50	
Add: Overspeeding ticket of Bond =	500.00	
Total:	1,277.50	
(*ii*) Whereas Bond would not like to pay ₹ 1,277.50, the maximum amount that Bond would like to pay will be:		
Petrol (1/2) =	₹ 225	
Fan belt (1/2)	₹ 75	
	300	
Add: Overspeeding ticket	500	
Maximum amount	₹ 800	

Illustrative Problem 3

For a new product, Mega Manufacturing is deciding whether to buy 500 units of a component from an outside supplier or to make them in-house. If Mega buys the component from an outside supplier, it will pay the supplier ₹ 12 per unit. Mega will also pay ₹ 1 per unit to inspect the componnt and spend an additional ₹ 9 per unit in materials and labor to convert each component into a finished product. Mega will sell the finished product to consumers for ₹ 30 per unit.

Making the component in-house requires ₹ 6 worth of steel and ₹ 3 worth of a special alloy. Mega routinely purchases and uses steel in its operations, and it does not currently have any steel in inventory. The special alloy is unique to the component in question, and Mega currently has ₹ 2,000 worth in stock. If it chooses the buy option, Mega will dispose of the special alloy. Disposal costs equal salvage value, meaning that Mega's net proceeds from disposal are ₹ 0. Making the component in-house also requires that Mega hire new workers at a cost of ₹ 16 per hour—workers can make four units of the component per hour.

As under the buy option, Mega will pay ₹ 1 per unit to inpsect the component and spend an additional ₹ 9 per unit in materials and labor to convert each component into a finished product. Mega will then sell the finished product to consumers for ₹ 30 per unit.

(*a*) *What are the controllable costs and benefits associated with the buy option? What are the controllable costs and benefits associated with the make option?*

A cost or benefit is controllable if it changes relative to current expenses and revenues. Compared to current profit, the following costs and benefits change under the buy and make options:

Costs and Benefits–Buy Option

Item	*Amount per unit*	*Total (500 units)*
Revenues—Finished Units	₹ 30	₹ 15,000
Total Controllable Benefits		₹ 15,000
Purchase Price	₹ 12	₹ 6,000
Inspection	₹ 1	₹ 500
Additional Materials and Labor	₹ 9	₹ 4,500
Total Controllable Costs		₹ 11,000
Value (benefits–costs)		₹ 4,000

Costs and Benefits–Make Option

Item	*Amount per unit*	*Total (500 units)*
Revenues—Finished Units	₹ 30	₹ 15,000
Total Controllable Benefits		₹ 15,000
Steel	₹ 6	₹ 3,000
Special Alloy*	₹ 0	₹ 0
Labor**	₹ 4	₹ 2,000
Inspection	₹ 1	₹ 500
Additional Materials and Labor	₹ 9	₹ 4,500
Total Controllable Costs		₹ 10,000
Value (benefits-costs)		₹ 5,000

* The ₹ 2,000 of special alloy in inventory is a sunk cost, and Mega does not plan to purchase additional special alloy if it makes the component in house. Thus, the cost is non-controllable.

** ₹ 4 per unit = ₹ 16 per hour / 4 units per hour.

(*b*) *What is the value of the make option? What is the value of the buy option?*

Value = Controllable benefits - Controllable costs. Based on calculations in part (*a*):

Value (buy) = ₹ 15,000 – ₹ 11,000 = ₹ 4,000

Value (make) = ₹ 15,000 – ₹ 10,000 = ₹ 5,000

Mega should choose the make option because it has the higher value.

(*c*) *Compared to the buy option, what are the relevant costs and revenues associated with the make option?*

The revenues received from the finished product do not differ between the two options. Given this, *the relevant revenues are* ₹ 0.

In addition, three of the costs do not differ between the make and buy options: (1) the inspection cost, (2) the additional labor and materials required to convert the component to a finished product, and (3) the sunk cost of the special alloy. Accordingly, these costs are irrelevant. The three costs that differ are: (1) the steel, (2) the labor, and (3) the purchase price. Thus, we have:

Relevant Costs–Make Option

Item	*Amount per unit*	*Total (500 units)*
Steel	₹ 6	₹ 3,000
Labor	₹ 4	₹ 2,000
Purchase Price	(₹ 12)	(₹ 6,000)
Total Relevant Cost		(₹ 1,000)

Using the principle of relevance, we find that Mega still prefers the make option because its cost is ₹ 1,000 less than the cost of the buy option. Notice that we subtracted the purchase price in our computations. We did so because, compared to buying, Mega *saves* ₹ 12 per unit by making the component.

Thus, the principles of relevance and controllability give us the same ranking of options. Relevance also preserves the difference in value between the two options, or ₹ 1,000. Finally, notice that compared to controllability, relevance allows us to focus our attention on fewer items.

(*d*) *Suppose Mega did not have the alloy in stock and had to purchase it. How does this information change your analysis?*

This information means that the cost of alloys is now controllable. It also is relevant. Thus, the controllable costs of the make option would increase to ₹ 11,500, making the buy option more attractive. Likewise, the relevant cost of making versus buying is ₹ 500, again meaning that buy is the preferred option. Both analyses show that Mega gains ₹ 500 by buying the component over making it, if the firm has to purchase the alloy.

Illustrative Problem 4

A company can make any one of the 3 products X, Y or Z in a year. It can exercise its option only at the beginning of each year.

Relevant information about the products for the next year is given below:

	X	*Y*	*Z*
Selling Price (₹ / unit)	10	12	12
Variable Costs (₹ / unit)	6	9	7
Market Demand (unit)	3,000	2,000	1,000
Production Capacity (unit)	2,000	3,000	900
Fixed Costs (₹)		30,000	

You are required to compute the opportunity costs for each of the products.

(*M. Com. Delhi 2011*)

Solution:

		X	Y	Z
(i)	Contribution per unit (₹)	4	3	5
(ii)	Units (Lower of Production/Market Demand	2,000	2,000	900
(iii)	Possible Contribution (₹) [I × II]	8,000	6,000	4,500
(iv)	Opportunity Cost* (₹)	6,000	8,000	8,000

* Opportunity cost is the maximum possible contribution forgone by not producing alternative product i.e. if Product X is produced then opportunity cost will be maximum of (₹ 6,000 from Y, ₹ 4,500 from Z).

Illustrative Problem 5

A company can produce any of its 4 products, A, B, C and D. Only one product can be produced in a production period and this has to be determined at the beginning of the production run. The production capacity is 1,000 hours. Whatever is produced has to be sold and there is no inventory build-up to be considered beyond the production period. The following information is given:

	A	B	C	D
Selling Price (₹/unit)	40	50	60	70
Variance Cost (₹/unit)	30	20	20	30
No. of units that can be sold	1,000	600	900	600
No. of production hours required per Unit of product	1 hour	1 hour and 15 minutes	1 hour and 15 minutes	2 hours

(CA Final, Nov. 2013)

What are the opportunity costs of A, B, C and D?

Solution:

Calculation of Opportunity Cost

	A	B	C	D
Selling Price (₹ per unit)	40	50	60	70
Variance Cost (₹ per unit)	30	20	20	30
Contribution (₹ per unit) ...[A]	10	30	40	40
Demand (units)	1,000	600	900	600
No. of Units can be Produced (within 1,000 hours of production capacity)	1000 $\left(\frac{1,000 \text{ hrs.}}{1 \text{ hr.}}\right)$	800 $\left(\frac{1,000 \text{ hrs.}}{1.25 \text{ hr.}}\right)$	800 $\left(\frac{1,000 \text{ hrs.}}{1.25 \text{ hr.}}\right)$	500 $\left(\frac{1,000 \text{ hrs.}}{2 \text{ hr.}}\right)$
No. of Units can be Sold (lower of demand and product [B]	1,000	600	800	500
Possible Contribution of Product (₹) ...[A] × [B]	10,000	18,000	32,000	20,000
Opportunity Cost (₹)	32,000	32,000	20,000	32,000

Illustrative Problem 6

A company has decided to launch a new product X which is, expected to have demand of 10,000 units during the year at ₹ 160 per unit. The following information is furnished by the company:

(*i*) Material: The manufacture of one unit of X requires one unit of each of materials A, B and C.

Raw Material	*Current Stock (units)*	*Cost per unit (₹)*		
		Original Cost	*Current Purchase Price*	*Resale Value*
A. Regularly being used	10,000	16	20	14
B. Old stock (Not in use)	6,000	28	24	8
C. New stock	–	–	48	–

(*ii*) *Direct labour:* Skilled labour is paid at ₹ 80 per hour. It takes 0.25 hours/unit. Skilled labour has to be drawn from another product line which has a contribution of ₹ 240 per unit, with each unit requiring 2 hours of skilled labour

Unskilled labour: 2 hours/unit ₹ 56 per hour. There is abundant Unskilled labour in the factory, but according to an agreement with the labour union, no unskilled worker can be retrenched.

(*iii*) Variable overhead – ₹ 10 per unit

(*iv*) Fixed Costs – no increase

Using relevant cost approach, you are required to find out the average variable cost per unit of X.

(*CA Final, May 2012*)

Solution:

(a) Average Variable Cost Per Unit of X

Cost Element	*Relevancy*		*Total Cost (10,000 units)* ₹	*Average Cost per unit* ₹
Raw material A	Replacement Cost	Current purchase price	2,00,000	20.00
Raw material B	Opportunity Cost	Opportunity Cost (6000 units × ₹ 8 per unit)	48,000	
Raw material B	Incremental Cost	Current Purchase	96,000	
		Price (4,000 units × ₹ 24 per unit)		
		Subtotal Raw material B	1,44,000	14.40
Raw material C	Incremental Cost	Current Purchase	4,80,000	48.00
		Price (10,000 units × ₹ 48 per unit)		
		Subtotal Raw material B	1,44,000	14.40
Skilled Labour	Opportunity Cost	Contribution Lost	3,00,000	30.00
		10,000 × 0.25 × 240/4		
Unskilled Labour	Sunk Cost		NIL	NIL
Variable Overhead	Incremental Cost	10,000 × ₹ 10 per unit	1,00,000	10,00
		Total	12,24,000	122,40

REFERENCES

1. Joseph G. Louderback III and Jay S. Holmen, *Managerial Accounting*, Thomson and South Western, 2004, p. 90.
2. Joseph G. Louderback III and Jay S. Holmen, *Ibid*, p. 89.
3. Lane K. Anderson and Harold M. Sollenberger, *Managerial Accounting*, South Western Publishing Co., 1992, p. 37.
4. Charles T. Horngreen, Srikant M. Dattar and George Foster, *Cost Accounting, A Managerial Emphasis*, Pearson Education, 2008, p. 39.
5. Lane K. Anderson and Harold M. Sollenberger, *Ibid*, p. 44.
6. Wayne J. Morse, James R. Davis and Al L. Hartgraves, *Management Accounting*, Thomson, 2003, p. 128.
7. James Jiambalvo, *Managerial Accounting*, John Wiley and Sons, 2001, p. 213.

CRITICAL ANALYSIS AND DISCUSSION QUESTIONS, SELF-ASSESSMENT QUESTIONS, MULTIPLE CHOICE QUESTIONS, EXERCISES AND CASES

CRITICAL ANALYSIS AND DISCUSSION QUESTIONS

1. Define the term 'cost'. How is it different from expense?
2. Define the terms 'fixed costs', 'variable costs', 'semi variable costs' and give example of each one.
3. Define and illustrate the following concepts of cost:
   (*a*) Direct and indirect cost
   (*b*) Product and period cost
   (*c*) Controllable and non-controllable cost
   (*d*) Joint cost and common cost (*M. Com., Delhi,* 2005, 2010, 2013)
4. "Cost may be classified in a variety of ways according to their nature and the information needs of management." Explain and discuss this statement. Illustrate with examples the classifications required for different purposes.
5. What is the meaning of the term "incremental cost"? Does incremental cost mean the same thing as variable cost?
6. Bring out clearly the significance of the following costs for management:
   (*a*) Opportunity cost
   (*b*) Sunk cost
   (*c*) Imputed cost
   (*d*) Out-of-pocket costs
7. Why is classification of costs into controllable and uncontrollable heads vital in the institution of responsibility accounting? (*M. Com., Delhi*)
8. Which manufacturing costs are classified as product costs under absorption costing? Under direct costing? (*M. Com., Delhi*)
9. Why are sunk costs not relevant in decision-making? (*M. Com., Delhi*)
10. "All controllable costs are direct costs. Not all direct costs are controllable, however", Do you agree? Explain with the help of suitable examples. (*M. Com., Delhi*)
11. Distinguish between the variable costs and differential costs and highlight the importance of differential costs in non-routine decisions. (*M. Com., Delhi*)
12. What are the differences between a controllable cost and a non-controllable cost? (*M. Com., Delhi,* 2008, 2012)
13. Discuss the various costs used in decision-making and explain their characteristics.
14. Distinguish between period costs and product costs. Why is this distinction considered important ? (*M. Com., Delhi,* 2001, 2008)
15. (*a*) Distinguish between out of pocket cost and opportunity cost.
    (*b*) Explain and illustrate the distinction between 'direct cost' and 'indirect cost' specially from the point of view of decision-making.

16. Why should the term "cost" have an adjective attached to it to have meaning for a manager? (*M. Com., Delhi,* 2002)
17. Define an opportunity cost and explain its relevance to decision-making. When would a decision maker look at the opportunity cost of a decision?
18. Explain whether the following statements are true?
    (*a*) All future costs are relevant costs.
    (*b*) All sunk costs are irrelevant.
    (*c*) A cost can be relevant for one decision and irrelevant for another decision.
    (*d*) All relevant costs are present or future amounts.
    (*e*) All irrelevant costs are past costs .
19. Explain how time has an effect upon the controllability of cost.
20. Expenses and costs are often used interchangeably, yet they do not always mean the same thing. Distinguish between the two terms.
21. Identify and describe the three elements that make up manufacturing costs.
22. "All differential costs are variable costs". Comment.
23. Why is the idea of controllability important when accounting data are used for performance evaluation and decision-making?
24. What effect does an increase in output have on:
    (*i*) Unit fixed costs
    (*ii*) Unit variable costs
    (*iii*) Total fixed costs
    (*iv*) Total variable costs
25. Explain why knowledge of cost behaviour is useful information for a manager to have?
26. On a per unit basis fixed costs are variable and variable costs are fixed. Do you agree? Explain your reasoning.
27. What is the difference between a loss and an expense?
28. Explain what is meant by cost flow? How do the cost flows of the three different organizations differ?
29. How do the income statements of a manufacturing firm, merchandising firm and service firm differ from each other?
30. A cost that is not controllable at one level may be controllable at a higher level. Explain.
31. Explain why the salary of a plant manager would be classified as an overhead cost, not an administrative cost.
32. Use the letters given below for each of the following cost groups to create a formula for each of the terms listed.
    (*a*) Fixed manufacturing overhead
    (*b*) Direct materials used
    (*c*) Total manufacturing overhead
    (*d*) Variable manufacturing overhead
    (*e*) Direct materials purchases

(*f*) Beginning finished goods inventory

(*g*) Direct Labour

(*h*) Ending work-in-progress

(*i*) Ending finished goods inventory

Terms—Prime costs, conversion costs, direct costs, indirect costs, total factory costs to be accounted for, cost transferred to finished goods inventory, goods available for sale.

33. Explain whether you agree with each of the following statements:

    (*i*) 'All direct costs are variable.'

    (*ii*) 'Variable costs are controllable and fixed costs are not.'

    (*iii*) 'Sunk costs are irrelevant when providing decision-making information.'

34. Lists two costs which are used in decision-making but not entered in the accounting system under designation.

35. Name a cost which is reflected in the accounting system but not used in decision-making.

36. 'The cost of my trip to Mumbai was ₹ 50,000'. Using the concept of cost developed in this chapter, explain why this statement is ambiguous. (*M. Com., Delhi*, 2003)

37. It is commonly suggested that a management accounting system should be capable of supplying different measures of cost for different purposes. You are required to set out the main types of purpose for which cost information may be required in a bussiness organisation, and to discuss the alternative measures of cost which might be appropriate for each purpose.

38. "Issues of product costing are irrelevant for service organizations since they can not build up inventories of services and all costs for providing services are expensed in the period they are used." Evaluate this statement.

39. Why is a cost referred to as variable if it remains constant per unit for all volume levels within the relevant range?

40. Define and describe the relevance of following costs:

    (*i*) Sunk-cost and Relevant cost

    (*ii*) Controllable and uncontrallable cost (*M. Com., Delhi University, 2009*)

41. What is meant by 'product costing accuracy'?

42. Why are product costs also called inventoriable costs?

43. For what particular management function is relevant cost information needed?

44. Why might the term average cost be misleading?

45. Should managers be responsible for the costs they can not control directly? Why or why not?

46. Why do managers consider direct cost to be more accurate than indirect costs?

47. "The concept of shortrun costs and longrun costs are relative—short run could mean a day, a month, a year or even 10 years, depending on what you are looking at." Comment.

48. "My variable costs are ₹ 5 per unit. If I want to increase production from 1,00,000 units to 1,50,000 units, my total costs should go up by only ₹ 2,50,000." Comment.

49. At two levels of activity within the relevant range, average costs are ₹ 192 and ₹ 188 respectively. Assuming the cost function is linear, what can be said about the existence of fixed and variable costs?

50. You are about to complete Master Degree from college, and you have been fortunate to receive three job offers. How will you make your decision? Briefly discuss your goals and how you would rank your options.
51. Enlarging the number of options available can never reduce opportunity cost. Is this statement true?
52. You have a final exam in managerial accounting tomorrow. What is the opportunity cost of watching television tonight?

SELF-ASSESSMENT QUESTIONS

A. Identify the following items of cost as a product or period costs for a manufacturing enterprise.

1. Depreciation on computerised telephone call system
2. Factory heat, light and power
3. Advertising expenditure
4. Boxes used to package the finished product
5. Lubricating materials for factory machines
6. Depreciation of sales person's automobiles
7. Wages of machine operators
8. Payroll of finished goods warehouse employees
9. Depreciation of the company president's cars
10. Costs incurred for reserving conference rooms at a resort hotel for the annual executive's conference
11. Insurance on factory machines
12. Depreciation of factory building
13. Wages of sales persons
14. Factory machines repairs
15. Production Superintendent's wages
16. Salary of factory storeroom clerk
17. Company-level research and development costs
18. Pencils and paper clips for production manager
19. Direct materials used during production
20. Factory supervisor's salaries

B. Which of the following costs are likely to be controllable by the head of the Production department?

1. Price paid for materials
2. Charge for floor space
3. Raw materials used
4. Electricity used for machinery
5. Machinery depreciation
6. Direct labour
7. Insurance on Machinery
8. Share of cost of industrial relations department.

C. The following data are taken from the records of a manufacturing company:

Inventories:	Jan. 1, 2016	Jan. 31, 2016
Direct materials	₹ 18,000	₹ 15,000
Work-in-progress	₹ 9,000	₹ 6,000
Finished goods	₹ 27,000	₹ 36,000

Additional information for the month of January 2016

Direct materials purchased	₹ 42,000
Direct labour cost	₹ 30,000
Direct labour rate per hour	₹ 7.50
Factory overhead rate per direct Labour hour	₹ 10.00

Based on the above data for the month of January 2016

1. Prime cost incurred was
   (*a*) ₹ 75,000 (*b*) ₹ 69,000
   (*c*) ₹ 45,000 (*d*) ₹ 39,000
2. Conversion cost incurred was
   (*a*) ₹ 30,000 (*b*) ₹ 40,000
   (*c*) ₹ 70,000 (*d*) ₹ 72,000
3. Cost of goods manufactured was
   (*a*) ₹ 1,18,000 (*b*) ₹ 1,15,000
   (*c*) ₹ 1,12,000 (*d*) ₹ 1,09,000

D. For the relevant cost data in items 1 to 7 listed below, indicate which of the following is the best classification:

(*a*) Sunk cost (*b*) Incremental cost
(*c*) Variable cost (*d*) Fixed cost
(*e*) Semi-variable cost (*f*) Semi-fixed cost
(*g*) Controllable cost (*h*) Non-controllable cost
(*i*) Opportunity cost

1. A company is considering selling an old machine. The machine has a book value of ₹ 20,00,000. In evaluating the decision to sell the machine, the ₹ 20,00,000 is a ....
   ....
2. As an alternative to the old machine the company can rent a new one. It will cost ₹ 3,00,000 a year. In analysing the cost-volume behaviour the rental is a ....
   ....
3. To run the firm's machine, there are two alternative courses of action. One is to pay the operator a base salary plus a small amount per unit produced. This makes the total cost of the operators a ....
4. As an alternative, the firm can pay the operators a flat salary. It would then use one machine when volume is low, two when it expands and three during peak periods. This means that the total operator cost would now be a ....
5. The machine mentioned in (1) could be sold for ₹ 8,00,000. If the firm considers retaining and using it the ₹ 8,00,000 is a ....

6. If the firm wishes to use the machine any longer, it must be repaired. For the decision to retain the machine, the repair cost is a ....

7. The machine is charged to the foreman of each department at a rate of ₹ 3,00,000 a year, In evaluating the foreman the charge is a ....

E. Indicate what cost term is being defined in each of the following cases:

1. Cost per unit that decreases as more units are produced in a given time period.
2. Activity levels within which the firm is expected to operate and can predict costs.
3. Costs that are expensed within a given time period and not inventorised.
4. Cost that management has obligated itself to incur in the future.
5. A cost that will go away if activity is eliminated.
6. Profit that is given up by accepting a different option.
7. A cost that is managed by a specific manager.
8. A cost incurred to produce more than one product that cannot be easily traced to each product.
9. Total product cost divided by total units produced.
10. The cost of adding one more unit of output.
11. A cost that is traceable to a particular cost objective but cannot be controlled by manager responsible for that cost objective .
12. Product cost is not materials or direct labour.

F. From the words given in the brackets, choose the appropriate term for completing each of the following sentences:

1. Disbursement of cash or its equivalent or the commitment to pay cash in the future for the purpose of generating revenues are (costs, expenses).
2. A product, sales territory, department or activity to which costs are traced is referred to as a (cost driver, cost object).
3. The increase or decrease in cost that is expected from a particular course of action as compared with an alternative is referred to as a (differential cost, sunk cost).
4. Insurance premiums on factory equipment would be a (controllable, non-controllable) cost for an assembly line supervisor.
5. Research and development costs are usually viewed as (discretionary, opportunity) costs.
6. Factory overhead costs combined with direct labour costs are called (prime, conversion) costs.
7. The implementation of automated factory equipment normally (increases, decreases) the direct labour component of product costs.
8. A cost that has been incurred and cannot be reversed by subsequent decision is an example of a (fixed, sunk) cost.
9. If the activity base is the number of units produced, the wages of assembly workers are considered a (fixed, variable) cost.
10. The (opportunity, prime) cost of not investing in government securities that yields 11.5% is the interest foregone on the possible investment.
11. Direct materials costs combined with direct labour costs are called (prime, conversion) costs.
12. The wages of assembly workers are normally considered (period, product) cost.

13. The cost of management consulting is normally considered an example of a (discretionary, sunk) cost.
14. Straight line depreciation on factory equipment is considered a (fixed, variable) cost for the activity base, number of units produced.
15. The cost of materials that are integral part of the manufactured final product is classified as part of the (direct materials, factory overhead) cost.
16. The cost of wages of employees who are directly involved in converting raw materials into the manufactured end product is classified as (direct labour, factory overhead) cost.
17. Product costs would normally not include (depreciation on factory equipment, salary of the controller).
18. For a television manufacturer, the cost of picture tubes is a (direct materials, factory overhead) cost.
19. An assembly line worker's hourly wages for an automobile manufacture is an example of (direct labour, factory overhead).
20. The cost that is common to both prime costs and conversion costs is (direct materials, direct labour) cost.

G. Match the items in column 1 with the best choice in column 2.

Column 1	***Column 2***
1. Total fixed Costs 2. Incurred Costs 3. Cost of goods manufactured 4. Total manufacturing Costs 5. Unit variable Cost	*(A)* Costs incurred during a period *(B)* Total amount remains constant *(C)* Expired Costs *(D)* Direct materials and direct labour *(E)* Costs of completed production after adjustment for work in progress inventory
6. Prime Costs 7. Expenses that are matched 8. Materials, Labour and factory overhead 9. Conversion Costs	*(F)* Direct labour and factory overhead *(G)* Added cost of a new product *(H)* Remains constant per unit *(I)* Direct materials, direct labour and factory overhead
10. Cost of goods sold	*(J)* Cost of goods manufactured adjusted for changes in finished goods stock.

MULTIPLE CHOICE QUESTIONS

Select the correct answer for the following multiple choice questions:

1. For a manufacturing company, which of the following is an example of a period rather than a product cost?
   (*a*) depreciation on factory equipment
   (*b*) wages of sales people
   (*c*) wages of machine operators
   (*d*) insurance on factory equipment

2. Prime costs and conversion costs share what common element of total cost?
   (a) Variable overhead (b) Fixed overhead
   (c) Direct materials (d) Direct labour
3. Indirect materials are
   (a) A prime cost (b) A fixed cost
   (c) An irrelevant costs (d) A factory overhead cost
4. Factory overhead
   (a) Is a prime cost (b) Can be a variable cost or a fixed cost
   (c) Can only be a fixed cost (d) Includes all factory labour
5. Direct material costs are

	Conversion	***Manufacturing***	***Prime***
(a)	Yes	Yes	No
(b)	Yes	Yes	Yes
(c)	No	Yes	Yes
(d)	No	No	No

6. Fixed cost per unit increases when
   (a) Production increases (b) Production decreases
   (c) Variable cost per unit decreases (d) Prime cost per unit decreases
7. The cost of rent for a manufacturing plant is a

	Prime Cost	***Product Cost***
(a)	No	Yes
(b)	No	No
(c)	Yes	No
(d)	Yes	Yes

8. The fixed portion of the semivariable cost of electricity for a manufacturing plant is a

	Period Cost	***Product Cost***
(a)	Yes	No
(b)	Yes	Yes
(c)	No	Yes
(d)	No	No

9. HCL Co. develops computer programmes to meet customer's special requirements. How should HCL categorize payments to employees who develop these programme?

	Direct Costs	***Value-added Costs***
(a)	Yes	Yes
(b)	Yes	No
(c)	No	No
(d)	No	Yes

10. Wages paid to a time keeper in a factory are:

	Prime Cost	***Conversion Cost***
(a)	Yes	No
(b)	Yes	Yes
(c)	No	No
(d)	No	Yes

11. Factory supplies for a manufacturing plant are generally

    (*a*) Prime costs (*b*) Period costs

    (*c*) Variable costs (*d*) Excluded from product cost

12. Costs that increase as the volume of activity decrease within the relevant range are:

    (*a*) Average cost per unit (*b*) Average variable cost per unit

    (*c*) Total fixed costs (*d*) Total variable costs

13. Those costs referred to as controllable costs are:

    (*a*) Costs that management decides to incur in the current period to enable a company to achieve objectives

    (*b*) Costs that are likely to respond to the amount of attention devoted to them by a specified manager

    (*c*) Costs that fluctuate in total in response to small changes in the rate of utilisation of capacity

    (*d*) Costs that will be unaffected by current managerial decisions

14. Costs that are inventoriable are:

    (*a*) Manufacturing costs incurred to produce units of output.

    (*b*) All manufacturing costs other than direct labour costs and raw materials costs.

    (*c*) The sum of direct labour costs and all factory overhead costs.

    (*d*) The sum of raw materials costs and direct labour costs.

15. The term conversion costs refers to:

    (*a*) Manufacturing costs incurred to produce units of output

    (*b*) All costs associated with manufacturing other than direct labour costs and raw materials costs

    (*c*) Costs associated with marketing, despatching, warehousing and billing activities

    (*d*) The sum of raw material costs and direct labour costs

    (*e*) Total of direct labour costs and all factory overhead costs

16. The term prime costs refers to:

    (*a*) Manufacturing costs incurred to produce units of output

    (*b*) All costs associated with manufacturing other than direct labour costs and raw material costs

    (*c*) Costs that are predetermined and should be attained

    (*d*) The sum of direct labour costs and all factory overhead costs

    (*e*) The sum of raw material costs, direct labour costs and direct expenses

17. The term 'variable costs' refers to:

    (*a*) All costs that are likely to respond to the amount of attention devoted to them by a specified manager

    (*b*) All costs associated with marketing, despatching, warehousing and billing activities

    (*c*) All costs that do not change in total for a given period of time and relevant range but become progressively smaller on a per unit basis as volume increases

    (*d*) All manufacturing costs incurred to produce units of output

    (*e*) All costs that fluctuate in total in response to small change in the rate of utilisation of capacity

18. The term 'committed costs' refers to:
    (*a*) Costs that management decides to incur in the current period to enable the company to achieve objectives other than the filling of orders placed by customers.
    (*b*) Costs that are likely to respond to the amount of attention devoted to them by a specified manager.
    (*c*) Costs that are governed mainly by past decisions, which established the present levels of operating and organizational capacity, and that only changes slowly in response to small changes in capacity.
    (*d*) Costs that fluctuate in total in response to small changes in the rate of utilisation of capacity.
    (*e*) Amortisation of costs that were capitalised in previous periods.
19. The term discretionary costs refers to :
    (*a*) Cost that management decides to incur in the current period to enable the company to achieve objectives other than the filling of order placed by customers.
    (*b*) Costs that are likely to respond to the amount of attention devoted to them by a specified manager.
    (*c*) Costs that are governed mainly by past decisions, which established the present levels of operating and organizational capacity, and that only change slowly in response to small changes in capacity.
    (*d*) Amortisation of costs that were capitalised in previous periods.
    (*e*) Costs that will be unaffected by current managerial decisions.
20. Conversion cost is equal to the total of:
    (*a*) Direct labour and raw materials (*b*) Direct labour and factory overhead
    (*c*) Indirect labour and factory overhead (*d*) Factory overhead and raw materials
21. Which type of cost is a vital part of decision-making but omitted from conventional accounting records?
    (*a*) Out of pocket cost (*b*) Sunk cost
    (*c*) Opportunity cost (*d*) Direct cost
22. Which one of the following is least likely to be an objective of a cost accounting system?
    (*a*) Product costing. (*b*) Department efficiency.
    (*c*) Inventory valuation. (*d*) Sales commission determination.
    (*e*) Income determination.
23. In cost terminology, prime costs consist of:
    (*a*) Direct materials and variable factory overhead.
    (*b*) Direct labour and indirect labour.
    (*c*) Indirect labour and fixed factory overhead.
    (*d*) Direct labour and direct materials.
    (*e*) Direct labour and variable factory overhead.
24. In cost terminology, conversion costs consists of:
    (*a*) Direct and indirect labour
    (*b*) Direct labour and direct materials
    (*c*) Direct labour and factory overhead

(d) Indirect labour and variable factory overhead
(e) Prime costs and fixed factory overhead

25. Which one of the following categories of cost is most likely not considered a component of fixed factory overhead?
(a) Rent (b) Property taxes
(c) Depreciation (d) Supervisory salaries
(e) Power

26. 'Committed costs' are costs that
(a) Were capitalized and amortized in prior periods.
(b) Are responsive to management's attention.
(c) Management decides to incur in the current period that do not have a clear cause and effect relationship between inputs and outputs.
(d) Result from a clear measurable relationship between inputs and outputs.
(e) Establish the present level of operating capacity and cannot be altered in the short run.

27. The difference between variable costs and fixed costs is:
(a) Variable costs per unit fluctuate and fixed costs per unit remain constant.
(b) Variable costs per unit are fixed over the relevant range and fixed costs per unit are variable.
(c) Total variable costs are variable over the relevant range and fixed in the long term, while fixed costs never change.
(d) Variable costs per unit change in varying increments, while fixed costs per unit change in equal increments.
(e) Total variable costs can be varied by management, while fixed costs are uncontrollable.

28. A cost that bears an observable and known relationship to a quantifiable activity base is a(n)
(a) Engineered cost (b) Indirect cost
(c) Sunk cost (d) Target cost
(e) Fixed cost

29. The term that refers to costs incurred in the past which are not relevant to a future decision is:
(a) Discretionary cost (b) Full absorption cost
(c) Underallocated indirect cost (d) Sunk cost
(e) Incurred marginal cost

30. Conversion costs do not include
(a) Depreciation (b) Direct materials
(c) Indirect labour (d) Indirect materials
(e) Direct labour

31. The cost of scrap, rework, and tooling charges in a product quality cost system are catergorized as a(n)
(a) Training cost (b) External failure cost
(c) Internal failure cost (d) Prevention cost
(e) Appraisal cost

32. The term that best refers to past costs that have been incurred and are not relevant to any future decisions is
    (*a*) Discretionary costs
    (*b*) Full absorption costs
    (*c*) Incurred marginal costs
    (*d*) Underallocated indirect costs
    (*e*) Sunk costs
33. Relevant costs are
    (*a*) All fixed and variable costs.
    (*b*) Costs that would be incurred within the relevant range of production.
    (*c*) Past costs that are expected to be different in the future.
    (*d*) Anticipated future costs that will differ among various alternatives.
34. Incremental costs is
    (*a*) The difference in total costs that results from selecting one choice instead of another.
    (*b*) The profit forgone by selecting one choice instead of another.
    (*c*) A cost that continues to be incurred in the absence of activity.
    (*d*) A cost common to all choices in question and not clearly or feasibly allocable to any of them.
35. A company will produce 20,000 units of product A at a unit variable cost of ₹ 7 and a unit selling price of ₹ 13. Fixed costs are ₹ 40,000. However, the company will still have 40% idle capacity. The company can use this idle capacity to produce 6,000 units of a different product B, which it can sell for ₹ 7 per unit. The incremental variable cost of producing a unit of B is ₹ 6. Present fixed costs that will be allocated to B amount to ₹ 10,000. To decide whether to produce B, the company should use
    (*a*) Differential cost analysis
    (*b*) Information economics
    (*c*) Regression analysis
    (*d*) Markov chain analysis
36. Which one of the following costs would be relevant in short-term decision-making?
    (*a*) Incremental fixed costs
    (*b*) All costs of inventory
    (*c*) Total variable costs that are the same in the considered alternatives
    (*d*) Costs of fixed assets to be used in the alternatives
37. When a decision is made in an organization, it is selected from a group of alternative courses of action. The loss associated with choosing the alternative that does not maximize the benefit is the
    (*a*) Net realizable value
    (*b*) Expected value
    (*c*) Opportunity cost
    (*d*) Incremental cost
38. Controllable costs
    (*a*) Arise from periodic appropriation decisions and have no well-specified function relating inputs to outputs.
    (*b*) Are primarily subject to the influence of a given manager of a given responsibility center for a given time span.
    (*c*) Arise from having property, plant, and equipment, and a functioning organization.
    (*d*) Result specifically from a clear-cut measured relationship between inputs and outputs.

39. A cost that bears an observable and known relationship to a quantifiable activity base is a(n)

(*a*) Engineered cost (*b*) Indirect cost
(*c*) Target cost (*d*) Fixed cost

40. The following data apply to Items (*i*) to (*iii*)

Management accountants are frequently asked to analyze various decision situations including the following:

I. The cost of a special device that is necessary if a special order is accepted.

II. The cost proposed annually for the plant service for the grounds at corporate headquarters.

III. Joint production costs incurred, to be considered in a sell-at-split versus a process-further decision.

IV. The costs associated with alternative uses of plant space, to be considered in a make/buy decision.

V. The cost of obsolete inventory acquired several years ago, to be considered in a keep-versus-disposal decision.

(*i*) The costs described in situations I and IV above are

(*a*) Prime costs (*b*) Sunk costs (*c*) Discretionary costs.
(*d*) Relevant costs (*e*) Imputed costs

(*ii*) The costs described in situations III and V above are

(*a*) Prime costs (*b*) Sunk costs (*c*) Discretionary costs.
(*d*) Relevant costs (*e*) Imputed costs

(*iii*) The cost described in situations II above is a

(*a*) Prime cost (*b*) Sunk cost (*c*) Discretionary cost.
(*d*) Relevant cost (*e*) Imputed cost

(CMA, USA, Adapted with permission)

Answer to Multiple Choice Questions:

1. (b)	2. (d)	3. (d)	4. (b)	5. (c)
6. (b)	7. (a)	8. (c)	9. (a)	10. (d)
11. (c)	12. (a)	13. (b)	14. (a)	15. (e)
16. (e)	17. (e)	18. (c)	19. (b)	20. (b)
21. (c)	22. (d)	23. (d)	24. (c)	25. (e)
26. (e)	27. (b)	28. (a)	29. (d)	30. (b)
31. (c)	32. (e)	33. (d)	34. (a)	35. (a)
36. (a)	37. (c)	38. (b)	39. (a)	

40. (i) (d) (ii) (b) (iii) (c)

EXERCISES

1. In a company, an advertising budget is fixed at ₹ 9,00,000 and is apportioned among departments on the basis of sales revenue. A Department to which ₹ 2,00,000 of this budget was charged, has been eliminated. Does this mean that the advertising cost of ₹ 9,00,000 will be reduced. Explain.

   Are there circumstances under which the ₹ 9,00,000 of advertising could be reduced by elimination of a department ? *(M. Com., Delhi,* 2002)

2. A construction company has equipment that can be rented to another contractor for ₹ 50,000 a month whereby the company pays the operating costs estimated at ₹ 15,000 a month. This equipment can be used by the company to earn ₹ 80,000 a month with operating costs estimated at ₹ 15,000 a month. Identify the sunk cost in this decision situation. What is the opportunity cost? Compute the profit advantage from the better alternative.

3. Miss Sangita is considering the possibility of obtaining a two-year Master Degree from an Institute. In order to do this, however, she must give up her job that pays a salary of ₹ 2,40,000 per year. Living costs, whether she goes on for the degree or not, are estimated at ₹ 1,50,000 per annum. However, the cost of tuition and books at the institute will amount to ₹ 50,000.

   (i) What is the opportunity cost if Sangita decides to go for the degree.

   (ii) What is the sunk cost in this decision.

   (iii) Identify the differential costs in this decision.

4. Rajan is manager of Department 7 and has the authority to buy supplies, hire labour and incur telephone and postage charges for the department. Various costs for the month of March 2016 are as follows:

Plant superintendent's salary	₹ 80,000
Factory health and light	₹ 32,000
Maintenance and repair — Dept. 7	₹ 26,000
Telephone and postage — Dept. 7	₹ 11,000
Plant maintenance and repairs	₹ 17,000
Supplies used — Dept. 7	₹ 14,000
Salary (Rajan)	₹ 25,000
Labour cost — Dept. 7	₹ 1,46,000
Plant depreciation	₹ 30,000
Equipment depreciation — Dept. 7	₹ 23,000
Total	₹ 4,04,000

Required:

(i) List the costs that can be controlled by Rajan.

(ii) Lists the costs that can be directly identified with Department 7.

(iii) List the cost that can directly be identified with the plant.

(iv) To determine the full cost to operate department 7, which costs were to be apportioned.

5. A manufacturing company has budgeted fixed costs for the year at ₹ 12,00,000. It is estimated that no less than 40,000 units of product are to be manufactured next year. In a relatively poor year 50,000 units would be made. If the company were to operate at an average or normal level it could make 60,000 units. With very good conditions, it would be possible to make 80,000 units. Which unit cost would you be inclined to use in the determining product cost in the long run? Explain.
6. You were told that materials costing ₹ 20 for each unit of product are needed to produce a certain product line. Three units of product can be manufactured in each hour with a labour cost of ₹ 15 per hour. Total fixed costs of manufacturing amounts to ₹ 3,00,000 per year. No other costs are incurred in manufacturing. Why are you unable to determine the total unit cost to manufacture the product.
7. A manufacturing company can manufacture any one of three different products A, B, C, with the equipment currently installed in one of the divisions. The annual depreciation of the equipment is ₹ 32,400 and the annual cost to operate the equipment, regardless of which product is manufactured is ₹ 7,200.

   Product A is expected to give sales revenue of ₹ 1,76,000 per year with additional costs of production amounting to ₹ 39,000. Product B will yield sales revenue of ₹ 1,30,000 per year with additional costs of ₹ 38,000. Product C will yield sales revenue of ₹ 3,14,000 with additional costs of ₹ 2,30,000.

Required:

(*i*) Which of the three products offers the best profit potential based on the information given?

(*ii*) Identify the irrelevant costs.

(*iii*) What is the opportunity cost of selecting the most profitable product line?

8. Rahul is the manager of photocopying at State Bank of India Regional Office, New Delhi. He purchased a photocopy machine last year for ₹ 5,00,000. This year, a new photocopier, which is faster and more reliable than the current photocopier is available in the market. In deciding whether or not to purchase the new machine, should Rahul consider how much he paid for the old machine? Should Rahul consider the value of the old machine in the used photocopier market? (*M. Com., Delhi*, 2003, 2007, 2014)
9. Asian Paints Co. produces a chemical which is used to retard fading in interior house paint. In the past year the company produced 2,00,000 litres at a total cost of ₹ 20,00,000 (₹ 10 per litre). The company is currently considering an order for 10,000 litres from a paint company in Sri Lanka. Explain why the incremental cost associated with this order is likely to be less than ₹ 1,00,000. (*M. Com., Delhi University*, 2013)
10. A leading newspaper, The Time of India, ran an advertisement for itself. The advertisement stated that the paper, which cost the customer ₹ 2, was a good bargain because it cost the publisher nearly ₹ 2.50 (₹ 1.03 for paper, ₹ 0.27 for printers' labour, ₹ 0.20 for ink, ₹ 0.45 for salaries of editorial employees and ₹ 0.52 for other operating expenses such as executives' salaries, rent, depreciation and taxes).

    Is the buyer actually paying less than cost? What assumptions do you make to arrive at your answer? How can the publisher be so generous to readers? (*M. Com., Delhi*, 2005)

11. Unitech Developer purchased a plot of land for ₹ 50 crores near Delhi to build residential flats for prospective buyers because it came to know that a shopping mall was going to be built on the other side of the road. As it turned out, the rumour was false. A sanitary landfill was located on the other side of the road, and the purchased plot of land was worthless.

    Required : What type of cost is the ₹ 50 crores that Unitech Developer paid for the vacant land?

12. Assume you purchased a ticket for ₹ 200 to see your Delhi University's cricket team participating in a national competition. Someone has offered to buy your ticket for ₹ 300. But you decided to go to the game.

Required:

(*i*) What did it really cost you to see the game?

(*ii*) What type of cost is this?

13. Punjab Plumbing Services provides plumbing services to residential customers in south areas of New Delhi from Monday to Friday. Ramesh, the owner believes that it is important for his employees to have Saturday and Sunday off to spend with their families. However, he also recognises that this policy has implications for profitability and he is considering staying open on Saturday. Ramesh estimates that if his company stays open on Saturday, it can generate ₹ 20,000 of daily revenue each day for 52 days per year. The incremental daily costs will be ₹ 6,000 for labour, ₹ 4,000 for parts, ₹ 400 for transportation and ₹ 1,000 for office staff. These costs do not include a share of monthly rent, or a share of depreciation related to office equipment. Ramesh is not in favour of employees working on Sunday, but he would like to know the opportunity cost of not working on Saturday.

    Provide Ramesh with an estimate of the opportunity cost and explain why you do not have to consider rent or depreciation of office equipment in your estimate.

    (*M. Com., Delhi University*, 2009)

14. Two years ago, the manager of a Super Market purchased a new scanner costing ₹ 50,000. A sales person recently tried to sell the manager a new computer-integrated checkout system for the store. The new system would save the store a substantial amount of money each year. The recently purchased scanner could be sold for ₹ 25,000 in the second hand market. The manager refused to listen to the sales person, saying "I just bought these scanners. I can not get rid of them until I get my money's worth out of them".

    What type of cost is the cost of purchasing the old scanners? What common behavioural tendency is the manager displaying?

15. Suppose you are going to drive home this weakend a round trip of 200 Kms. Your car gets 15 Kms per litre of Petrol and you expect petrol to cost ₹ 60 per litre. Insurance and depreciation are ₹ 50,000 per year. You usually drive 12000 Kms per year. A friend asks you to take him along. He lives 5 Kms from your home.

Required:

(*i*) What are the costs of taking your friend along, as opposed to going by your self?

(*ii*) Suppose now that you are not planning on going home. Your friend asks for a ride and you are willing to go. What are the costs of going, as opposed to not going?

16. Rakesh operates a covered parking structure that can accommodate up to 600 cars. He charges ₹ 6 per hour for parking. Parking attendants cost ₹ 12 per hour each to staff the cashier's booth at the Parking. The facility has two parking attendants who each work eight hours per day. Utilities and other fixed costs average ₹ 4000 per month.

    Recently, the manager of a nearby Taj Hotel approached Rakesh concerning the reservation of 100 spots over an upcoming weekend for a lump sum of ₹ 3,600. This particular weekend will be a cricket weekend, and the structure would be full for only the six hours surrounding the game. Other than those six hours, the structure would have more than 100 empty spots available. The facility would have the same number of parking attendants whether or not Rakesh takes the offer from the Taj Hotel. What is the opportunity cost of accepting the offer?

17. A computer manufacturer is deciding whether to produce a large monitor with a thin flat screen. One of the managers suggested that the incremental costs for this line of manufacturing will be primarily variable because the company currently has a lot of idle capacity.

Required:

(*a*) What is the cost object in this decision?

(*b*) Is the accounting system likely to have the information needed to develop a cost function? Explain.

(*c*) What might be an appropriate estimation technique for this cost? Explain.

(*d*) What is the opportunity cost for using this idle capacity? Explain.

18. Anil is a handyman who does odd jobs such as painting, installing ceiling fans, and minor electrical work. Suresh recently contracted with Anil to paint the outside of his home, and chose a unique color that few persons would consider.

    The day before he planned to paint, Anil purchased an initial batch of 20 litres of the paint. The local hardware store, which mixed the paint to order, charged Anil ₹ 3,250, the store also noted its policy of "no refunds or exchanges on custom colors." Unfortunately, Anil threw his back out that evening. By the time he recovered a month later, Suresh had sold his home.

Required:

(*a*) What is Anil's opportunity cost of using the paint for a new job?

(*b*) Suppose Anil decides to throw the paint out because no one else wants the color that Suresh had picked out. As a hazardous substance, paint has to be properly disposed. The landfill will charge Anil ₹ 400 to dispose of the paint. In light of this new information, what is Anil's opportunity cost of using the paint for a new job?

(*c*) Suppose Suresh had paid a nonrefundable advance of ₹ 3500 to Anil. How, if at all, does this information affect Anil's opportunity cost of using the paint for another job?

19. Rajnish is leaving tomorrow for a three-day business trip and is trying to decide the most economical way to get to and from the airport and his home. Rajnish could either drive (using his own car) or take the Metro. If Rajnish drives, then he estimates that it will cost ₹ 3 per kilometer driven in operating costs (e.g., for oil) and ₹ 75 per day for parking. The one-way cost of the Metro is ₹ 250. Rajnish's home is exactly 30 kilometer from the airport.

Required:

(*a*) What are the controllable costs for Rajnish's decision?

(*b*) What are the relevant costs and benefits for Rajnish's decision?

(*c*) Are the controllable costs the same as the relevant costs for Rajnish's decision? If so, why? Can controllable and relvance give the same costs and benefits even when the status quo is not a feasible option?

20. Seeking to find gainful part-time employment, Johnson is choosing between two job offers. The first, a sales position at a department store, pays a flat salary of ₹ 8 per hour. As Johnson plans to work 80 hours per month, he expects to earn ₹ 640 per month. The second job, at a stereo store, pays a monthly salary of ₹ 400 for a 1/2 time position (20 hours per week or 80 hours per month) plus commissions. The store manager informs Johnson that, on average, 1/2 time salespeople earn commission of ₹ 300 per month.

    Both job sites are about 25 kilometers from Johnson's home, and Johnson estimates that, regardless of the position taken, he will incur about ₹ 125 in travel costs per month. Johnson currently shares an apartment with three friends. His share of the rent and utilities is ₹ 250 per month.

Required:

(*a*) Classify the following costs and benefits as to their controllability and relevance for Johnson's decision: (1) Job salaries; (2) commissions; (3) transportation costs; (4) rent and utilities.

(*b*) Using controllable costs and benefits, estimate the value and opportunity cost of Johnson's two decision options.

(*c*) Evaluate Johnson's decision using relevant costs and benefits.

CASES

1. Pawan Kumar has just joined as a manager at the XYZ manufacturing company at Hyderabad. The company makes the jewel cases. Earlier, before joining this company, Pawan Kumar had worked for fifteen years in production engineering. Now, Pawan Kumar would be reporting directly to his managing director, Rakesh.

    On a day, Rakesh advised Pawan Kumar to prepare and present an analysis of impact of new automated machines in place of the old machines. The new machines would reduce direct labour costs considerably and also there would be efficiency gains in direct materials. Overheads like depreciation and insurance will increase. The Managing Director desired savings in other costs such as supervision, maintenance, materials handling, quality inspection.

    Pawan Kumar visited the accounting department to check accounting records and behaviour of different type of costs when the new machine was purchased.

Required:

(*i*) Identify the areas as referred to in the above paragraphs, about which Pawan Kumar should be knowledgeable.

(*ii*) Explain the importance of areas identified in point (*i*) above for a manager like Pawan Kumar in a large sized manufacturing firm.

2. Raghvendra, Manager of Electronics Division in an Electronics Company discussed with the Division Controller, Somender some issues recently brought to his attention. The discussion between the two was as follows:

   Raghvendra: Somender, you have been my controller for 10 years. You should be able to answer to some of the problems that are coming to our notice. Our division has Engineers, Production Managers and Marketing Manager who are no longer comfortable with our Cost Accounting System. Customer demand is forcing to create new technology with increased capability. However, prices of our products are decreasing regularly. Yet, some Managers are saying that these costs are useless and they do not reflect the difference in product features such as colour, capabilities, packaging and services. Does our Cost Accouting System really allow us to determine product line profitability accurately?

   Somender: I notice that in aggregate our product costing are accurate. What we report on our balance sheet and income statement is much on target. However, I am not confident that our cost assignment procedures allow us to make strong statements about individual product profitability. Many of the costs are assigned using assumed relationship and may not reflect a cause and effect relationship.

   Raghvendra: If what you are saying is right, how can we rely on individual costing for decision making? *For example*, can we use them to help us price our products and determine the right product mix. Can these costs be used to help us improve product designs?

   Somender: The points you are making are good. But there is difference between decision and accuracy. If the costs are not assigned correctly, using them for pricing and design decisions could be harmful. We do not know the real cost of product differences and real cost differences between distribution channels and customers.

   Raghvendra: Somender, something must be done. Can we improve the accuracy of our product costing. We must know how much each product is costing. It is also vital to have accurate cost information about our distribution channels and customers. It seems important that we need to learn more about costs and then make decisions relating to those cost. Understanding the nature of cost is fundamental to make good management and I need your help.

Required:

(*i*) What is meant by product costing accuracy?

(*ii*) How will increasing accuracy of product costing improve decision making?

(*iii*) Why does Somender feel that the division's product costs are not very accurate?

(*iv*) Is assigning cost accurately as important for services as it is for tangible products?

3. You have been hired by Dabur India Ltd. to fill a new position that has been created in response to rapid growth in sales. It is your responsibility to coordinate despatch of finished goods from the factory to distribution warehouses located in various parts of India so that goods will be available as orders are received from customers.

   The company is unsure how to classify your annual salary in its cost accounting records. The company's cost accountant says that salary should be classified as a manufacturing (product) cost; the controller says that it should be classified as a selling expense; and the managing director says that it does not matter which way your salary is classified?

Required:

(*i*) Which viewpoint is correct?

(*ii*) From the point of view of the reported net income for the year, is the managing director correct in his statement that it does not matter which way your salary cost is classified? Explain. (*M. Com., Delhi*, 2012, 2014)

4. PQR Ltd., a manufacturer of tool kits has just completed XY's domestic order of 100 kits at a price of ₹ 1,650 per kit. The details of cost for XY's order are:

	Cost (₹)
Direct Material	90,000
Direct Labour	32,000
Tools and Consumables	16,400
Variable overheads	9,600
Fixed overheads (allocated)	15,000
Total	1,63,000

The company wishes to evaluate a special export order from Expo Ltd. of similar 300 kits at ₹ 1,600 per kit. For the export order, special packing has to be done at ₹ 20 per kit. An additional fixed inspection cost specific to this export order has to be incurred. The allocation of fixed overheads will be revised to increase by ₹ 25,000. Tools, and Consumables above include special purpose tools costing ₹ 10,000 incurred for XY's order and these can be reused for the export order and the remaining portion is variable. PQR Ltd. wishes to accept the export order at 10% profit on the selling price.

What should be the maximum amount that can be incurred as inspection cost for making such an acceptance possible? If Expo Ltd. offers to take the products without inspection, what is the maximum discount (as a percentage of the existing export price) that PQR Ltd. can offer to retain its 10% profit, on the revised selling price? (Round of calculations to two decimal places). (*CA Final, May, 2014*)

Answer: Maximum inspection cost ₹ 40

Maximum discount 2.77%

5. A Company manufacturing several products for regular sales, has conducted a market survey of cost of ₹ 1,00,000 to introduce a new product NP. The market Survey suggests that there is a demand for the sale of 1,00,000 units of NP at ₹ 18 each for one year.

The following information has been furnished by the Company:

(*i*) Raw Materials: Each article of NP requires one unit of each of the three types of the raw materials namely A, B, and C. Material 'A' is in regular use of the Company and the stocks are replaced as and when exhausted. Material 'B' is not in regular use of the Company at present and holds a stock of 60,000 units. Material 'C' is used only in NP and hence the Company has to purchase the same as per the requirement of production of the new product.

The data relating to the three items of raw materials are as under:

Raw Material	Current Stock (Units)	Cost per unit of raw material		
		Original Cost	Current Replacement Cost	Current Resale
		₹	₹	₹
A	1,00,000	2.00	2.50	1.75
B	60,000	3.50	3.00	1.00
C	—	—	6.00	5.00

(*ii*) Direct Labour: NP requires for each article:

Skilled labour 0.25 hour of ₹ 3 per hour and unskilled labour 2 hours at ₹ 2 per hour. Due to shortage of skilled labour, the Company has, in the event of deciding to take up the production of NP, to divert the skilled labour from some other product which earns a contribution of ₹ 2 per hour of skilled labour. The Company has a surplus of 3,00,000 hours of unskilled labour for which payment is being made on time basis as per contract and it is not possible to terminate the surplus worker.

(*iii*) Additional staff required for the manufacture of NP:

One Foreman at ₹ 36,000 p.a.

One Supervisor at ₹ 24,000 p.a.

(*iv*) Machines: Two machines namely Machine Type 'P' and Machine Type 'Q' are required to produce NP. Machine Type 'P' is in regular use on other products also and Machine Type 'Q' is now idle. If NP is not produced Machine Type 'Q' can be sold immediately. The relevant data relating to each type of machine are as under:

	At the start of the year	At the close of the year
	₹	₹
Type 'P' Replacement Cost	1,60,000	1,30,000
Resale value	1,20,000	94,000
Type 'Q' Replacement Cost	26,000	18,000
Resale value	22,000	17,000

The Company charges depreciation on straight line basis.

(*v*) **Overheads:**

Fixed Overheads of the Company ₹ 18,000 per anum.

Variable Overheads s 1,50 per unit of the new product NP.

Required:

Using the concept of relevancy of costs, prepare a cost sheet to show the cost per unit of the new product NP. Substantiate the figures with necessary explanation.

Answer: Total cost ₹ 14,00,000

Cost per unit:

Direct material ₹ 10.30

Direct labour ₹ 1.25

Variable overheads ₹ 1.50

Fixed overheads ₹ 0.60

Depreciation ₹ 0.35

Total cost per unit ₹ 14

PART 2

COST ACCUMULATION SYSTEMS AND PRODUCT COSTING

PART

2

COST ACCUMULATION SYSTEMS AND PRODUCT COSTING

3

COST ALLOCATION AND OVERHEAD ABSORPTION

LEARNING OBJECTIVES

After reading this chapter, you should be able to:

- Understand the Concept of Overhead Absorption
- Explain the Following Stages in Absorption of Overheads
  - ➢ Allocation and Apportionment of Overhead
  - ➢ Apportionment of Service Departments Overhead to Producing Departments
  - ➢ Absorption of Overhead Costs
- Distinguish between Actual and Predetermined Overhead Rate
- Explain the Treatment of Under/Over–absorption of Overheads
- Explain the Methods of Accounting for Administrative Overheads, Selling and Distribution Overheads

ABSORPTION OF OVERHEADS

The full cost of a product consists of direct costs and indirect costs. The direct costs are easily traced or identified with the product or job without any difficulty. In a manufacturing organization, direct materials, direct labour and direct expenses are examples of direct costs. The assignment of a complete specific cost to a cost centre or cost unit is known as 'cost allocation'. All direct costs are allocated to a cost centre or cost unit.

> **Absorption of overheads** is the procedure of distributing or sharing out overhead costs to different products.

Indirect costs or overhead costs are not directly traceable to product or job because they are incurred for two or more products; their clear identification with one product is not possible. There is no direct and observable way of determining how much of overhead costs belong to each product. Due to these features, overhead costs are termed 'indirect costs'.

The procedure of distributing or sharing out overhead costs to different products is known as absorption of overheads. There is a need to develop methods to decide the share of overhead costs for different products.

STAGES IN ABSORPTION OF OVERHEADS

There are three stages in the absorption of overheads.

Stage I: Allocation and Apportionment of Overhead

The first stage in the absorption of overhead costs is to identify and collect overhead costs for different production and cost centres. The first stage is known as 'primary distribution.'

Primary Distribution

> Stages in Absorption of Overheads:
>
> - **Primary Distribution:** Identification and collection of overhead costs for different production and cost centres
> - **Secondary Distribution:** Overhead cost of service department are apportioned to production departments

Some overhead costs can be directly identified with a particular department or cost centre as having been incurred for that cost centre. These items of overhead cannot be traced to products or jobs but can be allocated specifically to departments. Examples of such overhead costs are repairs and maintenance expenses incurred in specific departments, supervision, indirect labour, overtime, indirect materials and factory supplies, equipment depreciation, etc.

Expenses, such as power, light, rent, depreciation of factory building, expenses shared by all departments, cannot be charged directly to a department, be it production or service. They are incurred for all and must, therefore, be apportioned or prorated to any or all departments using such items. Cost apportionment is the process of charging expenses in an equitable proportion to the various cost centres or departments. The Institute of Cost and Management Accountant (UK) defines cost apportionment as:

■■ *the allotment of proportions of items of cost to cost centres or cost units.*

The apportionment should be done on some rational and equitable bases. In cost accounting, this is known as primary distribution of overhead.

It would be difficult to give a comprehensive list of the bases of apportionment, but the following bases are in common use:

1. ***Floor Area Occupied:*** Overheads such as lighting and heating, rent and rates, depreciation on building, building repairs, caretaking, watching and patrolling.
2. ***Capital Values:*** Depreciation on plant and machinery, insurance on building, and plant and machinery, maintenance of plant and machinery.

3. ***Direct Labour Hours and /or Machine Hours:*** Insurance on Jigs, tools and fixtures, power, works management remuneration, repairs and maintenance cost.
4. ***Number of Workers Employed:*** Canteen, accident insurance, medical, dental and first aid, pensions, personnel department expenses, profit sharing payments, recreation, supervision, time office, wages department.
5. ***Technical Estimate:*** Fire prevention, oil and grease, steam, water without meter.

Example:

Modern Company has four departments. A, B and C are the production departments and D is a servicing department. The actual costs for a period are as follows:

		(₹ '000)
***Indirect Materials*:**		
Production department	A	950
	B	1,200
	C	200
Servicing department		1,500
Indirect Wages:		
Production department	A	900
	B	1,100
	C	300
Servicing department		1,000
Rent		2,000
Repair		1,200
Depreciation		900
Light		200
Supervision		3,000
Insurance		1,000
Employees Insurance (employer's Liability)		300
Power		1,800

The following data are also available in respect of four departments:

	Departments			
	A	***B***	***C***	***D***
Area (sq. feet)	150	110	90	50
No. of workers	24	16	12	8
Total wages (₹ '000)	₹ 8,000	₹ 6,000	₹ 4,000	₹ 2,000
Value of plant (₹ '000)	24,000	₹ 18,000	₹ 12,000	₹ 6,000
Value of stock (₹ '000)	₹ 15,000	₹ 9,000	₹ 8,000	—

Apportion the above costs to the various departments on the most equitable method.

Solution:

Departmental Distribution Summary

(₹ '000)

Items	Basis	Total	Production department service dept.			
			A	B	C	D
Indirect materials	Allocation	3,850	950	1,200	200	1,500
Indirect wages	Allocation	3,300	900	1,100	300	1,000
Rent	Area	2,000	750	550	450	250
Repairs	Plant Value	1,200	480	360	240	120
Depreciation	Plant value	900	360	270	180	90
Light	Area	200	75	55	45	25
Supervision	No. of workers	3,000	1,200	800	600	400
Insurance	Value of stock	1,000	500	300	200	–
Employees Insurance	Wages	300	120	90	60	30
Power	Plant value	1,800	720	540	360	180
	Total	17,550	6,055	5,265	2,635	3,595

Note: (*i*) It has been asumed that insurance has been taken for stock.

(*ii*) Power expenses have been apportioned on the basis of value of plant because no other infomation has been given.

Stage II: Apportionment of Service Departments Overhead to Producing Departments

In stage II, overhead costs of service departments are apportioned to production departments. Such apportionment is termed as 'Secondary Distribution'.

Secondary Distribution

The primary distribution of factory overhead apportions all overhead costs to the different departments or cost centres — production and service departments. It is necessary that overhead costs of service departments (accumulated through direct allocation or primary distribution) should be further assigned to producing departments. This is due to the reason that service departments do not themselves manufacture anything and it is the production departments or cost centres which are involved in manufacturing activities. The reassignment or reapportionment of service departments overhead to producing departments or centres is termed as secondary distribution.

Secondary distribution is useful in the following matter:

1. It helps in determining the cost of products or jobs sold and inventory figures.
2. It helps in determining the effect of various managerial decisions and actions on the total cost of the business firm. *For example*, decisions as to add or to drop a product line require information about its cost effect which can be estimated after secondary distribution has been made.
3. It helps subsequently in determining the price of the product or job. In case of contracts based on cost in place of market price, secondary distribution helps in fixing a selling price which is advantageous to the parties concerned.
4. It promotes motivation among employees of the producing departments to take up service department activities.

Bases for Secondary Distribution

It is difficult to suggest a sample list of service departments and equitable bases of distribution of overhead costs. The objective is to find the allocation base that best measures the causal or beneficial relationship between the departments whose costs are being apportioned and the departments receiving the service. The general basis for apportioning service department overheads to producing department are the following:

1. ***Service Rendered (Benefits Obtained):*** This is perhaps the most popular method of apportioning service department costs. The service rendered to different departments, *i.e.*, benefits obtained by them can be a suitable basis.

2. ***Ability to Pay:*** This method suggests that a large share of servicing departments overhead costs should be assigned to those producing departments whose product contributes the most to the income of a business enterprise. However, it is difficult to measure the ability to pay of different departments and also this method is not based on equity.

3. ***Survey or Analysis:*** This method is applied where a suitable base is difficult to find or it would be too costly to select a method which is considered suitable. *For example*, the postage cost could be apportioned on a survey of postage used during a year.

4. ***Efficiency or Incentives:*** This method uses standards and budgets and apportions the overhead costs on the basis of a present budget or standard. Sometimes this method is used along with the bases of services rendered or ability to pay method.

In selecting a suitable base for apportioning service department overheads, consideration should be given to practicability, simplicity, economy, theoretical soundness and assistance in accurate costing and cost control. If a service department overhead is allocated on the basis over which the production manager has no control, the prorated cost may result in an inappropriate charge to the producing department.

The following list gives a few service departments and bases commonly used to apportion the respective overhead costs:

Table 3.1: Service Department and Apportionment Base

Service Department	*Apportionment Base*
Personnel	Number of employees, labour hours, labour cost
Purchasing	Number of orders, cost of materials
Receiving	Cost of materials, number of units, number of orders
Stores	Cost of materials, number of requisitions filled, number of units handled
Factory Office	Number of employees, labour hours, labour cost
Machine Maintenance and Repair	Machine hours, labour hours, labour cost, services rendered
Engineering	Machine hours, labours hours, service rendered
Payroll or Time-keeping Department	Total labour or machine hours or number of employees in each department
Welfare, Canteen, Recreation, Medical	Number of employees in each department
Building Service Department	Relative area of each department
Internal Transport Service	Weight, value, graded products, weight and distance

Inter-departmental Services

While apportioning service departments overheads, one may notice two situations: (*i*) Firstly, the entire amount of a servicing department is to be distributed to only producing departments. This does not involve any practical difficulty and provides the simplest and quickest method for apportioning overheads of servicing department (*ii*) Secondly, service provided by some servicing departments are used partly by other servicing departments. That is, many service departments serve each other. *For example*, the payroll department in a firm prepares payroll for the entire organization, but it depends on the building maintenance department for repair and maintenance services. Similarly, the building maintenance department provides service for all departments using the building, but it gets service from departments like stores, factory office, and personnel. This second situation is known as inter-department services.

Arguments have also been advanced to suggest that service department overheads must be apportioned to the other service departments as well as to producing department who have received benefit from the servicing department. The main argument in support of this opinion are the following:

1. Failure to charge a given service department with the cost of services rendered by other service departments causes an understatement of the cost of operating the department receiving the service.
2. If the costs of a service department are controlled through the use of a budget, the cost of services rendered to it by other service departments should be incorporated in the budget. Only by so doing, can the efficiency of operation of a particular service department be measured.

Methods to Deal with Interdepartmental Service

There are mainly two methods to deal with inter-departmental service – continuous apportionment and Algebraic Method.

Continuous Apportionment

In this method, the process of apportioning service departments overhead is continued until the figures become immaterial or totally exhausted. The following steps are involved in this method:

1. Use the given percentages to apportion the original total of the first service department. This closes the account of the first service department and transfers prorated amounts to other departments.
2. Use the given percentage to all other service departments whose total is made up of original amount plus prorated amounts of service department first. This closes the accounts of second service department and assigns prorated amounts to the other departments including servicing department first also.
3. Follow the same procedure to all other service departments.
4. Repeat a second cycle of apportionment starting with the service department first, whose total consists, at present, only of amounts prorated from other service departments. In this way, the service department total become less and less with each cycle of apportionment because each time a substantial amount is apportioned to the producing departments.
5. Stop the above cycle at any point where it is found that the remaining figures (to be apportioned) are too small to be of any consequence or when the figures are totally exhausted.

Example:

The overhead of a manufacturing company has been analysed to the point of primary distribution shown below.

		(₹)
Production departments:	Machine	10,000
	Assembly	4,000
Service department:	Canteen	2,000
	Powerhouse	3,000

The canteen is to be apportioned on the basis of employees:

	Employees	%
Machine	240	60
Assembly	140	35
Powerhouse	20	5
	400	100

The powerhouse is to be apportioned on the basis of electricity used

	Thousand Kilowatts	%
Machine	270	75
Assembly	36	10
Canteen	54	15
	360	100

Apportion service departments overhead to production departments.

Solution:

	Machine ₹	*Assembly* ₹	*Canteen* ₹	*Powerhouses* ₹
Primary apportionment	10,000	4,000	2,000	3,000
Apportion: Canteen	1,200	700	–2,000	100
Powerhouse	2,325	310	465	–3,100
Canteen	279	163	– 465	23
Powerhouse	18	2	3	–23
Canteen	2	1	–3	
Total Service Depts.	3,824	1,176		
Total Production Overhead	13,824	5,176		

Algebraic Method or Simultaneous Equation

This method helps in finding out the amount of overhead of each servicing department by solving simultaneous equations. The total expenses of service departments can be directly transferred to production departments.

Example:

PH Ltd. is a manufacturing company having three production departments, A, B and C and two service departments X and Y. The following is the budget for December 2016.

	Total	*A*	*B*	*C*	*X*	*Y*
	₹	₹	₹	₹	₹	₹
Direct Material		1,000	2,000	4,000	2,000	1,000
Direct Wages		5,000	2,000	8,000	1,000	2,000
Factory Rent	4,000					
Power	2,500					
Depreciation	1,000					
Other overheads	9,000					
Additional Information:						
Area (sq. ft.)		500	250	500	250	500
Capital value (₹ 1 lakh) of Assets		20	40	20	10	10
Machine hours		1,000	2,000	4,000	1,000	1,000.
Horsepower of machines		50	40	20	15	25

A technical assessment of the apportionment of expenses of service departments is as under:

	A	*B*	*C*	*X*	*Y*
	%	%	%	%	%
Service dept. X	45	15	30	—	10
Service dept. Y	60	35	—	5	—

Required:

(*i*) A statement showing distribution of overheads to various departments.

(*ii*) A statement showing re-distribution of service department expenses to production departments.

(*iii*) Machine hour rates of the production departments A, B and C.

Solution:

(i) Overhead Distribution Summary

	Basis	*Total*	*A*	*B*	*C*	*X*	*Y*
		₹	₹	₹	₹	₹	₹
Direct Materials	Direct	—	—	—	—	2,000	1,000
Direct Wages	—	—	—	—	—	1,000	2,000
Factory Rent	Area	4,000	1,000	500	1,000	500	1,000
Power	H.P.X M/c hr.	2,500	500	800	800	150	250
Depreciation	Cap. Value	1,000	200	400	200	100	100
Overheads	M/c hr.	9,000	1,000	2,000	4,000	1,000	1,000
			2,700	3,700	6,000	4,750	5,350

(ii) Re-distribution of Service Department's Expenses

	A ₹	B ₹	C ₹	X ₹	Y ₹
Total Overheads	2,700	3,700	6,000	4,750	5350
Dept. X overhead apportioned in the ratio (45:15:30:10)	2,138	712	1,425	–4,750	475
Dept Y overhead apportioned in the ratio (60:35:-:5)	3,495	2,039	—	291	–5,825
Dept. X Overhead apportioned in the ratio (45:15:30:10)	131	44	87	–291	29
Dept. Y Overhead apportioned in the ratio (60:35:-:5)	17	10	—	2	–29
Dept. X Overhead apportioned in the ratio (45:15:30:10)	1	—	1	–2	—
Total	8,482	6,505	7,513	—	—

(iii) Machine Hour Rate

	A	B	C
Machine hours	1,000	2,000	4,000
Machine hour rate (₹)	8.48	3.25	1.88

Stage III: Absorption of Overhead Costs

After all service departments overhead costs have been apportioned to producing departments, the next step is to spread factory overhead to different products or jobs produced. This is termed as: Overhead absorption' in cost accounting. The Institute of Cost and Management Accounts (UK) has defined overhead absorption as:

- *the allotment of overhead to cost units.*

Known by different names such as recovery, overhead application, overhead costing, levy, burden rate, etc. the term 'absorption' implies that expenses pertaining to a producing department or cost centre are finally charged to or absorbed in the cost of products, jobs, etc. passing through it. As a result of absorption, the cost of each unit of product of the producing department includes an equitable share of the total overhead of that department.

METHODS OF ABSORPTION

The rate which is used to charge overhead costs to the products or jobs is known as absorption rate. The following are the generally recognised methods of absorption or absorption rate.

Methods of Absorption:

- Percentage on Direct Materials
- Percentage on Direct Wages
- Prime cost percentage
- Unit of Production basis
- Labour Hour / Production Hour Rate
- Machine Hour Rate

Percentage on Direct Materials

In some manufacturing concerns, a study of past costs will reveal a correlation between direct materials cost and factory overhead. Therefore, an absorption rate based on materials cost might be applicable. In such a case, the rate is obtained by dividing total estimated factory overhead by total direct materials cost expected to be used in the manufacturing process. If factory overheads is ₹ 3,00,000 and materials cost is 2,50,000, the absorption rate will be:

$$\frac{₹\ 3,00,000}{₹\ 2,50,000} \times 100 = 120\%$$

Each job or product would be charged on the basis of 120% absorption rate. For example, if the materials cost of a product is ₹ 5,000, the factory overhead to be charged for that product would be ₹ 6,000 (5,000 × 120%).

Advantages

The "percentage on direct material cost" method is simple and easy to understand and apply. This method will give correct overhead cost figures where the prices of materials do not differ significantly, where quantity, and cost of materials in each product are uniform, and where processing for the different products is also uniform. It is useful in very simple types of small business firms.

Disadvantages

This method has the following disadvantages:

1. There is no logical relationship between materials cost of a product and factory overhead used in production.
2. Materials prices are subject to fluctuations quite often and this phenomenon leads to high or low overhead costs, even though overhead figures remain unchanged. This does not help in making a proper comparison of cost of production from period to period.
3. Most of the overhead expenses vary with time. For example, a product or job using cheap materials but longer period of processing should bear more for overhead as compared to a job or product which uses expensive materials but a shorter period of processing. Thus, most overhead costs accrue on a time basis and not on materials consumed. But the use of direct materials costs totally ignores the time factor which is an important factor in allocation/apportionment of overhead costs.
4. This method is not proper where part of the materials passes through all processes, and part through only some processes.
5. The mere fact that a job consumes materials of a very expensive nature does not imply that the overhead incurred on that job will also be heavier.

Percentage on Direct Wages

The direct labour cost basis is the widely used method of applying overhead to jobs or products. This is computed in the following manner:

$$\frac{\text{Factory overhead}}{\text{Direct labour cost}} \times 100$$

If factory overhead is ₹ 20,000 and the direct labour cost is also ₹ 20,000, then absorption rate based on direct wages will be 100%.

$$\frac{₹\ 20,000}{₹\ 20,000} \times 100$$

A job or a product with a direct labour cost of ₹ 3,000 would be charged with ₹ 3,000 for factory overhead.

Advantages

This method is beneficial where production is uniform, all the workers in the organisation work more or less on the same hourly rate, and labour is predominantly used.

This method has the following advantages:

1. It is simple to operate and understand.
2. It considers the time factor, as labour cost is computed by multiplying number of hours spent on work by an hourly labour rate, the more hours worked, the higher the labour cost and the greater use and therefore the charge for factory overheads.
3. Labour rates fluctuate but less frequently than that of price of materials.

Disadvantages

The disadvantages are as follows:

1. It depends on cost of direct labour which may not reflect accurately the contribution of factory overhead in the cost of product. Many expenses such as taxes, property insurance, depreciation are functions of time.

2. It does not consider the share of other factors of production in production other than direct labour factor, for example, machinery. In many business firms, it is machinery and not the labour which is the major factor of production.

3. It does not take into account variations, if any, in the rates of remuneration for different types of labour and therefore, the wages incurred on different jobs are not necessarily in the same ratio as the hours spent. This fact would be clear where workers are paid on a piece-rate basis as in this system, wages depend on output and not upon time. This limitation is clear from the following example:

	Job A *(16 hr)* ₹	*Job B* *(20 hr)* ₹
Direct Materials	600	600
Direct Labour	400	400
Prime Cost	1000	1000
Factory Overhead (75% on direct wages)	300	300
Factory Cost	1300	1300

As job B has taken 25% extra time to complete work than A, the job carried out by B must have occupied the factory for a longer period than A's, but as is clear from the above statement, the charge for factory overhead is the same in each case.

4. Total direct labour cost represents the sum of high-and low-wage production workers. By applying overhead on the basis of direct labour cost, a job or product is charged with more overhead when a high rate operator performs work instead of a low-rate worker. Such a method can lead to incorrect distribution of factory overhead particularly when numerous operators, with different hourly rates in the same department, perform similar operations on different jobs or products.

Prime Cost Percentage

The prime cost basis combines the total of direct materials cost and direct labour cost and uses this total as a basis for charging overhead. The formula used in determining the rate is:

$$\frac{\text{Factory overhead}}{\text{Prime Cost}} \times 100$$

If in a case the factory overhead is ₹ 4,56,000 and prime cost is 6,00,000, then prime cost percentage rate will be

$$\frac{4,56,000}{6,00,000} \times 100 = 76\% \text{ of Prime Cost}$$

Advantages

The advantages are:

1. This method is simple to operate
2. It considers both materials and labour in charging overhead to each job or product
3. The prime cost data are easily available without any additional problem of accumulation

Disadvantages

The disadvantages are:

1. Two items, i.e., materials and labour both of which possess many disadvantages influence the charging of factory overhead to jobs and products.
2. Where the cost of materials is a larger part of the prime cost, the time factor (direct labour costs) will be ignored which is more related to the factory overhead.
3. It ignores time factor in absorbing factory overhead.
4. It can be useful to only a few departments where the type of labour and value of materials used are constant. But this method is not suitable for the entire plant. Unless a standard article is produced requiring a constant quantity of materials and number of hours engaged in its manufacture, the method will give inaccurate result.

Unit of Production Basis

The unit of production method is the simplest and most direct method of charging factory overhead. The unit might be a kilo, a foot, a machine, a hundred pieces or whatever unit of measure is used for the product. As a formula, the computation is as follows:

$$\frac{\text{Factory overhead}}{\text{Units of production}}$$

If factory overhead is ₹ 3,00,000 and the company intends to produce 250 units during the next period, each unit completed would be charged with ₹ 1200 (3,00,000 ÷ 250 units) as its share of factory overhead. Thus, an order with 1,000 completed units would be charged ₹ 12,00,000 (1,000 units × ₹ 1200) for factory overhead.

This method is the simplest one. But its usefulness is limited normally to those situations where only one product is produced. It is used most satisfactorily in small manufacturing concerns having relatively simple manufacturing process or in large concerns manufacturing few articles in large quantities. If several products manufactured are alike or closely related, absorption of factory overhead can be made on a weight or point basis, such as in the following example:

Factory Overhead	₹ 5,50,000
Points value of product A	5 points
Points value of product B	7 points
Production units A 4000, B 5,000	

$$\text{Rate per unit} = \frac{₹\ 5,50,000}{(4,000 \times 5)+(5,000 \times 7)} = ₹\ 10$$

Rate per unit of A = 5 × ₹ 10 = ₹ 50

Rate per unit of B = 7 × ₹ 10 = ₹ 70

Labour Hour/Production Hour Rate

One of the most widely used methods for overhead application is the labour hour basis. The equation for determining the overhead rate under this method is:

$$\frac{\text{Factory overhead}}{\text{Direct labour hours}}$$

If factory overhead is ₹ 4,00,000 and direct labour hours are 2,000, then overhead rate based on direct labour hours would be ₹ 200 per hour of direct labour (₹ 4,00,000 ÷ 2,000 hours). A product that requires 5,000 direct labour hours would be charged with ₹ 10,00,000 (5,000 hours × ₹ 200) for factory overhead.

Advantages

The following are the advantages:

1. As long as direct labour is the chief factor in manufacturing process, the direct labour hour method is useful as the most equitable basis for charging overhead.
2. This method uses the time factor and production taking the same time charged with the same amount of overhead, though the direct labourer may be getting different wage rates.

Disadvantages

The disadvantages are:

1. The method requires accumulation of direct labour hours by job, product or department. Timekeeping should be adequate to provide this information.
2. This method cannot be used where machines are used extensively for production. In other words, this method assume that direct labour is only the major factor of production.

Machine Hour Rate

The machine hour rate is similar to the labour hour rate method and is used where the work is performed primarily on machines. The formula used in computing the rate is:

$$\frac{\text{Factory overhead}}{\text{Machine hours}}$$

If factory overhead is ₹ 3,00,000 and total machine hours are 1,500, the machine hour rate is ₹ 200 per machine hour (₹ 3,00,000 ÷ 1500 hours).

Advantages

The advantages are:

1. This method can be used advantageously where the machine is the major factor in production.
2. In capital intensive industries, plants and machines are used in large quantities and one operator may attend to several machines or several operators may attend to a single machine.
3. By making the machine the basis, therefore, overhead costs can be equitably absorbed among different products.

Disadvantages

The disadvantages are:

1. Machine hour data have to be collected; therefore it requires additional clerical work. The cost of collection and accounting activities goes up and therefore, is not workable for small business firms.
2. The method cannot be used universally by all business concerns. It can be used where production is mainly through a machine. Comparatively, direct labour hours can be used widely by the organizations.

Computing Machine Hour Rate

For the purpose of computing the machine hour rate, each machine (or a group of similar machines) becomes a cost centre and all overheads are charged to a machine cost centre or to different machine cost centres if many such centres have been created within the department. A machine hour rate for a specific machine cost centre is computed by dividing the total overhead estimated or incurred for that machine divided by actual or estimated machine hours.

The machine hour rate may have different concepts such as:

1. ***Ordinary Machine Hour Rate:*** This rate takes into account only those overhead expenses which are variable and directly attributed to the running of a machine. Such expenses are power, fuel, repair, maintenance and depreciation. The total of all these expenses is divided by the total machine hours.

2. ***Composite Machine Hour Rate:*** This method takes into account not only expenses directly connected with the machine as mentioned above, but also other expenses which are known as standing or fixed charges. Such expenses are rent and rates, supervisory, labour, lighting and heating, etc. These expenses being fixed in nature are determined for a particular period and then apportioned among different departments on some equitable bases. The overhead expenses thus apportioned to each department are further apportioned among the machines (machine cost centres) in that department on an equitable basis.

The following are bases used for the apportionment of expenses for computing machine hour rate.

Table 3.2: Basis for Apportionment of Expenses

	Overhead Expenses	Basis
1.	**Standing Charges:**	
(i)	Supervision	Estimated time devoted to each machine
(ii)	Rent and Rates	Floor area occupied by each machine
(iii)	Heating and Lighting	Number of points or floor occupied by each machine
(iv)	Lubricating oil and consumable stores	Capital value, machine hours or past experience
(v)	Insurance	Insured value of each machine
(vi)	Miscellaneous Expenses	Equitable basis depending on facts
2.	**Machine or Variable Expenses:**	
(i)	Depreciation	Machine hours
(ii)	Repairs	Machine hours or captial values or cost of repairs spread over the working life of a machine
(iii)	Power	Horse power of machines or machine hours or meter readings

Selecting an Absorption Rate

The above absorption rates have their own merits and demerits. The method to be used depends on the factors and circumstances prevailing in a manufacturing firm. Whatever method is selected by a firm, it must achieve the following objectives:

1. The basic objective is to select an absorption base which helps in determining the accurate amount of factory overhead to be charged to individual products, jobs, processes, etc. The base should have cause and effect relationship with the incurrence of the overhead costs and should be physically related to the production of the products. If overhead items mainly relate to the use of machinery, a machine hour rate will be suitable. If overhead items originate due to purchasing and handling materials, then the materials cost may be selected as the base.

2. A secondary objective in selecting a method of absorption is to minimise clerical effort and cost. When two or more absorption rates tend to charge the same amount of overhead, the simplest base could be used. Generally speaking, the direct labour cost or materials cost base do involve least clerical effort and cost, whereas direct labour hour and machine hour involve more clerical work and are expensive. In a standard costing system, the usual bases are standard direct labour cost, standard labour hours, and standard machine hours.

3. The selection of an absorption base is also influenced by other factors, such as type of industry, legal requirements, if any, policy of management, etc. in addition to the suitability of a method under specific circumstances.

Illustrative Problem 1

The Genetry Company produces two products, X and Y. Estimated costs are presented below for a year in which 12,500 units of each product are expected to be sold:

	Total	*Product X*	*Product Y*
Direct production cost	₹ 4,50,000	₹ 3,00,000	₹ 1,50,000
Overhead cost	1,80,000	1,20,000	60,000
Selling and administrative cost	1,20,000	80,000	40,000

An annual profit of ₹ 1,50,000 for the whole company is considered satisfactory. The company uses the same gross margin percentage (*i.e.* mark-on) to arrive at the price for both products.

Required:

(*a*) Calculate selling prices for both products X and Y.

(*b*) Using the prices calculated above, how much profit would result if sales were 15,000 units of X and 10,000 units of Y instead of 12,500 units of each?

(*c*) Comment on the effect of changes in the product mix on total profit when the same margin percentage is used (*M. Com., Delhi,* 1993)

Solution:

Determination of selling price

	Products		*Total*
(*a*)	*X* (₹)	*Y* (₹)	(₹)
Direct production cost	3,00,000	1,50,000	4,50,000
Overhead cost	1,20,000	60,000	1,80,000
cost of production	4,20,000	2,10,000	6,30,000
add : gross margin			
$\left(\frac{2,70,000}{6,30,000} \times 100 = 42.86\%\right)$	1,80,000	90,000	2,70,000
	6,00,000	3,00,000	9,00,000
Selling Price per unit	$\frac{6,00,000}{12,500} = 48$	$\frac{3,00,000}{12,500} = 24$	
(*b*)	*A*	*B*	*Total*
Selling Price per unit	₹ 48	₹ 24	
Less: Variable Cost per unit	24	12	
Contribution per unit	24	12	
Total Contribution15,000 × 24, 10,000 × 12	3,60,000	1,20,000	4,80,000
Less: Fixed Cost (Overhead and Selling and Administrative Cost)	2,00,000	1,00,000	3,00,000
Total Company profit	1,60,000	20,000	1,80,000

(c) The total company profit is ₹ 180,000 in situation (B) as compared to ₹ 1,50,000 in (A)

Note: Gross profit will be ₹ 2,70,000 as total profit is ₹ 1,50,000 after paying selling and administrative cost of ₹ 1,20,000. Thus,

Gross profit = Selling and Admn. + Company profit

= 1,20,000 + 1,50,000 = ₹ 2,70,000.

$$\text{Variable cost per unit} = X, \frac{3,00,000}{12,500} = ₹\ 24,\ Y, \frac{1,50,000}{12,500} = ₹\ 12$$

Illustrative Problem 2

Topside Limited has two production departments A and B and two service departments—Factory Office and Materials Handling. All factory overhead costs are traceable to departments with the exception of building occupancy.

According to the managerial policy, Department A has to absorb factory overhead on a machine-hour basis and Department B has to absorb them on direct labour hour basis.

At normal capacity of 10,000 machine hours in Department A and of 20,000 direct labour hours in department B, the budgeted allowances for the direct department costs for a year are as follows:

	Non-Variable ₹	*Variable* ₹
Factory Office	28,400	Nil
Materials Handling	11,000	Nil
Department A	27,000	10,000
Department B	15,600	6,000

Building occupancy costs have been budgeted at ₹ 20,000 per year and are nonvariable with volume.

The following data concerning production operation have been made available:

	Area Occupied	*No. of Employees*	*Units of Materials Issued*
Factory Office	8 per cent	3	Nil
Materials Handling	20 per cent	4	Nil
Department A	40 per cent	12	3,000
Department B	32 per cent	8	2,000

You are required to —

(i) Prepare on Overhead Distribution Summary departmentalizing factory overhead costs.

(ii) Determine departmental non -variable and variable absorption rates at normal capacity

(*M. Com, Delhi,* 1995)

Solution:

(i) Overhead Distribution Summary

Particulars	*Departments (₹)* A	B	Factory Office	Materials Handling
Variable cost	10,000	6,000	—	—
Non-variable cost	27,000	15,600	28,400	11,000
Building occupancy cost (₹ 20,000 apportioned in the ratio of area occupied i.e. 40:32:8:20)	8,000	6,400	1,600	4,000
Total factory overhead	45,000	28,000	30,000	15,000
Apportioning factory office overheads (on the basis of no. of employees) (i.e. 12: 8: 4)	15,000	10,000	–30,000	5,000
	60,000	38,000	NIL	20,000
Apportioning materials handling overheads (on the basis of unit of materials issued i.e. 3:2)	12,000	8,000		–20,000
	72,000	46,000	NIL	NIL

(ii) Departmental Absorption Rate

	Deptt. A	*Deptt. B*
Variable overhead	₹ 10,000	₹ 6,000
Non-variable overheads	₹ 62,000	₹ 40,000
Normal capacity	10,000 machine hrs.	20,000 direct labour hrs.
(*a*) Variable absorption rate	$\frac{₹ 10,000}{10,000 \text{ hrs.}}$	$\frac{6,000}{20,000 \text{ hrs.}}$
	₹ 1 per machine hr.	₹ 0.30 per direct labour hr.
(*b*) Non-variable absorption rate	$\frac{₹ 62,000}{10,000 \text{ hrs.}}$	$\frac{40,000}{20,000}$
	₹ 6.20 per machine hr.	₹ 2 per direct labour hr.

Illustrative Problem 3

In a machine shop, the machine hour rate is worked out at the beginning of a year on the basis of a 13-week period which is equal to three calendar months. The Following estimates for operating a machine are relevant:

Total working hours available per week	48 hours
Maintenance time included in the above	2 hours
Setting up time included in the above	2 hours
Costs details:	
Operators wages (per month)	₹ 650
Supervisory salary (per month) (common supervisor for 3 machines)	₹ 1,800
W.D.V. of machine (Depreciation at 10% plus 2% on an average for extra shift allowance)	₹ 1,80,000
Repairs and maintenance (per annum)	₹ 16,000
Consumable stores (per annum)	₹ 30,000
Rent, rates and taxes (for the quarter apportioned)	₹ 5,000

Power consumed is @ 15 units per hour @ 40 paise per unit. Power is required for productive hours only, setting -up time is part of productive time but no power is required for setting up jobs.

The operator and supervisor are permanent. Repairs and maintenance and consumable stores are variable.

You are required to:

(*a*) Work out the machine hour rate.

(*b*) Work out the rate for quoting to the outside party for utilising the ideal capacity in the machine shop assuming a profit of 20% above variable cost.

Solution:

(a) Computation of Machine Hour Rate

Standing charges:		
Rent, Rates and Taxes	₹ 5,000.00	
Supervision	₹ 5,400.00	
Operator's wages	₹ 1,950.00	
Total standing charges	₹ 12,350.00	
Effective hours (46 × 13) = 598		
Fixed costs per hour (12,350/598)		₹ 20.65
Variable costs per hour:		
Power: $\frac{15 \times 44 \times 0.40}{46}$	₹ 5.74	
Repairs and maintenance: 4,000/598	6.69	
Consumable stores 7,500/598	12.54	
Depreciation: $21/4 \times 600/598 = \frac{21,600}{598 \times 4}$	9.03	34.00
		54.65

(b) Quotation for outside parties:

variable cost per hour	34.00
Add: 20% profit	6.80
Minimum to be quoted	₹ 40.80

Note: (1) Depreciation has been treated as a variable expense:
(2) Depreciation per annum is ₹ 21,600 @ 12% on ₹ 1,80,000

Illustrative Problem 4

An engineering company, engaged in the manufacturing of various heavy engineering products, has installed one Pegard Numerical Control Horizontal Borer for specialised manufacturing operations. Calculate the machine hour rate on the basis of the following particulars:

(*i*) F.O.B. cost of the machine ₹ 24 lakhs. (*ii*) Customs duty, insurance, freight, etc. ₹ 11 lakhs. (*iii*) Installation expenses ₹ 3 lakhs. (*iv*) Cost of tools adequate for 2 years only ₹ 4 lakhs. (*v*) Cost of machine room ₹ 3 lakhs. (*vi*) Cost of air conditioning for machine room ₹ 2 lakhs. (*vii*) Rate of interest on term loan to finance the above captial expenditure 12% per annum. (*viii*) Salaries, etc. for operators and supervisory staff ₹ 2 lakhs per year. (*ix*) Cost of electricity ₹ 11 per hour. (*x*) Consumption of stores ₹ 5000 per month. (*xi*) Other expenses ₹ 5 lakh per annum (*xii*) Assume rate of depreciation as 10% per annum on fixed assets. (*xiii*) Total working hours in the machine room is 200 hours in a month (*xiv*) Loading and unloading time is 10% of machine time. (*xv*) You can make suitable assumptions if necessary, for the purpose of your computation.

Solution:

Computation of Machine Hour Rate

		Per hour
Machine Expenses:		
Cost of Machine	₹ 24,00,000	
Custom duty, insurance, freight, etc.	11,00,000	
Installation expenses	3,00,000	
Cost of machine room	3,00,000	
Cost of airconditioning of the machine room	2,00,000	
Total Capital Cost	43,00,000	
(*i*) Depreciation @ 10% p.a.	4,30,000	₹ 199.07
(*ii*) Cost of electricity		11.00
(*iii*) Cost of tools	2,00,000	92.13
Standing Charges:		
(*i*) Salaries	2,00,000	
(*ii*) Interest @ 12%, p.a. on total capital Investment including cost of tools, i.e., on ₹ 47,00,000	₹ 5,64,000	
Consumption of stores	60,000	
Other Expenses	5,00,000	
Total Standing Charges	13,24,000	
Cost per hour of standing charges (13,24,000 ÷ 2,160 hrs.)		613.00
Machine hour rate		₹ 915.20

Note: 1. Total working hours per annum are 200 × 12 = 2,400.
2. Loading and unloading time is 10% of machine time.
3. Effective working hours are 2,160 hours (2,400 – 10% of 2,400).
4. It is assumed that there is no consumption of electricity during loading and unloading time.
5. Interest has been treated as an element of cost. It could be ignored also.

Illustrative Problems 5

Consider the following budgeted data for a client case of an accounting firm. The client wants a fixed price quotation.

Direct professional labour	₹ 20 000
Direct support labour	10 000
Fringe benefits for direct labour	13 000
Telephone calls	2 000
Computer lines	6 000

Overhead is allocated at the rate of 100 per cent of direct labour cost.

Required:

(*a*) Prepare a schedule of the budgeted total costs for the client. Show subtotals for total direct labour costs and total costs as a basis for mark-up.

(*b*) Assume that the partner's policy is to quote a fixed fee at 10 per cent above the total costs. What fee would be quoted?

(*c*) Explain why the listed estimates for costs might not be similar to the actual costs for the job. What factors could affect the accuracy of these estimates? List as many factors as you can.

Solution:

(*a*)

Direct labour costs:		
Professional labour	₹ 20 000	
Support labour	10 000	
Total	30 000	
Other direct costs	23 000	(fringe benefits + copying + phone + computer*)
Allocated overhead	30 000	(100% of ₹ 30 000)
Budgeted costs	₹ 83 000	

* This assumes that computer lines and costs can be traced. If these cannot be traced, then this cost would be assigned to overhead.

(*b*) Fee = 110% × ₹ 83 000 = ₹ 91 300

(*c*) Many factors could affect these costs. Because they are estimations, any relevant factors that were left out of the estimate could influence cost. It is difficult to predict how efficient the resources will be used. It is possible that the professional labour hours required are more or less than estimated, depending on the skills of the professionals and the accuracy with which the amount of work was estimated. If something was overlooked that requires more hours, the estimate will be off. Phone costs and computer costs may be different because rates change, or the job requires more or less telephone or computer work.

Factors that could affect the actual costs: price changes for any of the resources, and unforeseen complications such as computer crashes, problems with communication systems, illness of key professional and support employees, and unforeseen problem in the actual work.

OVERHEAD RATES: ACTUAL VS. PREDETERMINED

The basic purpose of overhead absorption rates is to absorb total overhead in products or jobs manufactured. This objective can be achieved through actual overhead rate or predetermined overhead rate.

Actual Overhead Rate

When the absorption is based on actual overhead, it is known as actual overhead rate. This can be calculated only after the end of the accounting period when all cost and production figures have been collected. This method has the following disadvantages:

> When the absorption is based on actual overhead, it is known as **actual overhead rate.**

1. Product costs cannot be determined until some considerable time after the end of the accounting period. This may not help in controlling cost and in fixing selling prices.

2. There are likely to be variations in the overhead incurred because of the seasonal nature of some overhead costs, change in the volume of production and efficiency of factory for different periods. If actual overhead costs from individual month is used, the overhead cost per unit will vary because of seasonal costs. Where actual costs are used to calculate selling prices, difficulties arise because the product cost fluctuates from period to period and there is a considerable delay in product cost determination.

3. Some overhead costs are of fixed nature, such as depreciation, supervision, property taxes, etc. These overhead costs being constant give a different per unit cost when divided by differing production volumes. Also some overheads like fire insurance premium are paid in advance but this should be charged to all work done/products manufactured during the year. How should the absorption be done? It creates an inequitable situation. Similar absorption problems would result if actual cost incurred for repairs and maintenance were charged directly to a job or product processed during the month when the repairs were done. This is not equitable. Ordinarily, repairs are necessary because of wear and tear over a much larger period than one month and are done to permit continuous production.

Predetermined Overhead Rate

A different overhead cost per unit (higher or lower) is misleading as it prompts one to conclude that management is less efficient in one period as compared to the other. But the variation in total cost and unit cost just reflect the time of year the units were manufactured, a factor outside the control of management. Cost accountants aim to average out these variations through the use of a predetermined overhead rate calculated on an annual basis. All the seasonal overhead costs are merged together and spread over (charged to) the production for the entire year.

Predetermined overhead rate is a rate calculated in advance of the period in which it is to be used, by dividing the estimated period overhead is to be absorbed by the estimated period production. Production may be measured on any of the absorption bases, such as prime cost, labour hours, etc. A predetermined overhead rate provides the only feasible method of computing product overhead cost promptly enough to serve management needs and eliminates uncontrollable and illogical month to month fluctuations in unit costs.

> **Predetermined overhead rate** is a rate calculated in advance of the period in which it is to be used.

Predetermined overhead rates can be used with advantage for both job order and process cost accounting. The primary objective of predetermined overhead rates is to provide a reasonably constant unit cost and to avoid unit cost fluctuations caused by seasonal overhead cost fluctuations, changes in volume, or accounting methods.

Secondly, predetermined overhead rates also make possible the immediate costing of job or products completed during the month. When a job is finished, the absorption rate is multiplied by the absorption base to find out the total amount to be charged to the product or job. Under a process costing system, predetermined overhead rate is used to charge overhead to the output of the process in question.

Thirdly, predetermined rates contribute effectively to standard costing and budgetary control programmes as these programmes use estimated costs and standard cost to measure production activities.

Under- or Over-absorption of Overhead

Where the actual overhead of a period is absorbed at an absorption rate based on actual production during that period, the overhead absorbed must, if all calculations have been correctly made, exactly equal the overhead incurred. This is not so, however, when a predetermined rate is used. The amount absorbed in cost accounts may not be equal to actual overhead relating to an accounting period. The use of a predetermined rate may, therefore, result in under-absorption or over-absorption. When the amount absorbed is less than the actual overhead, there is under-absorption. Over absorption arises when the amount absorbed is more than the actual overhead. Since actual overheads are not recorded in cost accounts, under-absorption and over-absorption can be treated in any one of the following ways:

1. In a seasonal business firm, the balance (due to under - or over-absorption) may be carried forward to the subsequent period with the expectation that it will be counterbalanced at the end of accounting period. This is clear from the following example.

Months	*Production units*	*Overhead absorbed @ ₹ 2 per unit*	*Actual overhead*	*Under- or over-absorption*
July	1000	2000	3,000	−1,000
August	1500	3000	4,200	−1,200
September	3000	6000	3,800	+2,200

2. A supplementary rate can be used to adjust the amount of under- or over-absorption. The supplementary rate is determined by dividing the amount of under - or over-absorption by the actual absorption base. Under-absorption is adjusted by using a plus supplementary rate while a minus supplementary rate in used to correct over-absorption. For instance, in the above example, a plus supplementary rate of ₹ 1 per unit $\frac{₹\ 1{,}000}{1{,}000 \text{ units}}$ can be used to increase the recorded overhead by ₹ 1,000 for the month of July. Similarly, a minus supplementary rate of ₹ 0.733 $\frac{2{,}200}{3{,}000}$ can be used to decrease the recorded overhead by ₹ 2,200 for the month of September.

3. The amount of under- or over-absorption can be transferred to the costing profit and loss account to arrive at the accurate net profit for an accounting period. When over-or under absorption has been due to abnormal factors, the amount of under- or over-absorption is necessarily transferred to the costing profit and loss account.

Example:

In a manufacturing company, overhead was recovered at predetermined rate of ₹ 25 per man-day. The total factory expenses incurred and the mandays actually worked were ₹ 41.50 lakhs and 1.50 lakh days respectively.

Out of the 40,000 units produced during a period, 30,000 were sold.

On analysing the reasons, it was found that 60% of the unabsorbed over-heads were due to defective planning and the rest were attributable to increases in overhead costs.

How would unabsorbed overheads be treated in cost accounts?

Solution:

Recovered Overheads = Actual mandays × Rate

= 1.50 lakhs × ₹ 25 = ₹ 37.50 lakhs

Actual Overheads = ₹ 41.50 lakhs

Under-recovery of overhead = 41.50 – 37.50 = 4 lakhs

Reasons for under-absorption:

(*i*) Defective Planning $= \frac{4 \text{ lakhs} \times 60}{100}$

= ₹ 2.40 lakhs

(*ii*) Increase in Overhead cost $= \frac{4 \text{ lakhs} \times 40}{100}$

= 1.60 lakhs

Treatment of under-absorption in cost account:

(*i*) ₹ 2.40 lakhs should be transferred to the costing profit and loss account as under absorption has arisen because of abnormal factors.

(*ii*) The under-absorption due to increases in overhead costs should be charged to units produced in the company. The amount of ₹ 1.60 lakhs will be distributed in the following manner:

Cost of sales A/c = 1.60 lakhs × $\frac{3}{4}$ = ₹ 1.20 lakhs

Finished goods stock A/c = $\frac{1.60 \text{ lakhs} \times 1}{4}$ = ₹ 0.40 lakhs

Example:

Your company uses a historical cost system and applied overheads on the basis of 'predetermined' rates. The following are the figures from the Trial Balance as on 31st March 2016.

Manufacturing Overheads	₹ 4,26,544 Dr.
Manufacturing Overheads applied	₹ 3,65,904 Cr.
Work-in-Progress	₹ 1,41,480 Dr.
Finished goods stock	₹ 2,30,732 Dr.
Cost of goods sold	₹ 8,40,588 Dr.

Give two methods for the disposal of the under-absorbed overheads and show the profit implications of each method.

Solution:

Actual Overheads	₹ 4,26,544
Overheads recovered	₹ 3,65,904
Under-absorbed Overheads	₹ 60,640

The under- absorbed overheads may be treated by following any one of the following methods:

1. Transferring to the costing profit and loss account.
2. Using a supplementary rate to recover the under-absorbed overhead.

According to first method, the total unabsorbed overhead amount of ₹ 60,640 will be written off to the costing profit and loss account. The use of this method will reduce the profits of the concern by ₹ 60,640 for the period.

According to second method, a supplementary rate may be used to adjust the overhead cost of each unit. The under-absorbed amount in total may, at the end of the accounting period, be apportioned on a ratio basis to the three control accounts, viz., work-in-progress, finished goods stock and cost of goods sold account. Prorated figures of under-absorbed overhead for work-in-progress, finished goods stock and cost of goods sold in this question on the basis of values of the balances in each of these accounts are as follows:

Additional Overhead (under absorbed)

	₹	₹	*Total* ₹
Work-in-progress	1,41,480	7,074 *	1,48,554
Finished goods stock	2,30,732	11,537 **	2,42,269
Cost of goods sold	8,40,588	42,029 ***	8,82,617
	12,12,800	60,640	12,73,440

By using this method, the profit for the period will be reduced by ₹ 42,029 and the value of stock will increase by ₹ 18,611 (₹ 7074 + ₹ 11,537). The later will affect the profit of the subsequent period.

Working Notes

The apportionment of under-absorbed overhead over work-in-progress, finished goods stock and cost of goods sold on the basis of their value in the respective amount is as follows:

* Overhead to be absorbed (work-in-progress)

$$= \frac{60,640}{12,12,800} \times 1,41,480 = ₹\ 7,074$$

** Overhead to be absorbed (finished goods stock)

$$= \frac{60,640}{12,12,800} \times 2,30,732 = ₹\ 11,537$$

*** Overhead to be absorbed (cost of goods sold)

$$= \frac{60,640}{12,12,800} \times 8,40,588 = ₹\ 42,029$$

ADMINISTRATIVE OVERHEAD

Office and administrative overhead will normally be smaller than the overhead of the factory and therefore the adoption of scientific and complicated system for charging such overhead is not so essential. Generally, there are three methods of accounting for administrative overhead.

1. ***As a Separate Item of Cost:*** Under this method, administrative overhead is treated as additional item of cost. A rate is generally determined for absorption of overhead following one of the following bases:

$$\frac{\text{Total administrative overheads}}{\text{Total factory cost or}} \times 100$$

   Total factory overheads or
   Total sales or
   Total gross profit or
   Total conversion costs
   Conversion costs include the cost of direct labour, direct expenses and factory overheads.

2. ***Apportionment between Manufacturing and Selling Divisions:*** Under this method, administrative overhead is divided between manufacturing and selling divisions on some suitable basis. However, it is difficult to find a suitable basis for apportionment. The method of apportioning manufacturing overhead can be applied for apportioning administrative overhead.

3. ***Transfer to Costing Profit and Loss Account:*** Under this method, administrative costs are not treated as product cost but as periods cost. However, this method understates the cost of product even though logically this cost should be charged to products because it is incurred for the product or job.

SELLING AND DISTRIBUTION OVERHEADS

Often it is suggested that selling and distribution overheads should be treated as direct charges to the profit and loss account of the period during which they occur. However, it is appropriate that products or jobs should be charged for their portion of selling and distribution costs. Selling overheads are incurred to generate and increase sales among the customers for the products. Distribution overheads are incurred after the sales to make the packed product available for despatch. However, for the purpose of apportionment, both the overheads can be taken together.

The most common types of classification used in the analysis of selling and distribution costs are:

1. Products or product groups
2. Sales territories
3. Channels of distribution (e.g., wholesale, retail, chain store, etc.) in order to ensure an equitable price structure
4. Order sizes (to assess whether savings on large orders warrant the allowance of quantity discounts, etc.)
5. Salesmen
6. Delivery methods (e.g., road, rail, air, etc.)
7. Customer or customer type (chemists, grocers, etc.)
8. Credit terms (e.g., cash, credit and hire-purchase sales)
9. Warehouse or store

Some items of selling and distribution overheads can be directly charged to products if they are specifically incurred for them such as, advertising for a definite product, dealer service, packing, transport. Overhead items which cannot be charged directly to products, are apportioned first by different sales territories or channels of distribution. And for this one of the following methods can be applied:

1. ***Rate per Article:*** If this method is adopted, the overhead costs are divided, as equitably as possible over the types of product sold. For this purpose, each cost must be considered separately and the benefits derived therefrom by each article determined. The total expenditure allocated to each type of article is then divided by the quantity of the article sold to give a rate per article.

2. ***A Percentage on the Selling Price of Each Article:*** This is suitable for apportionment of direct selling costs, general administration, finance costs, etc. If selling overhead of a sales zone is ₹ 5,000 and the sales of that Zone are ₹ 20,000, an addition should be made to the cost of products by 25% of the selling price of that product. This method can be adopted successfully only where the products of a business are sold at standard prices and the proportion of each type of products is constant.

3. ***A Percentage of Work Costs:*** This method is very simple to operate. Where selling overheads are small, this method can be adopted, even though various articles are produced, as little advantage would be gained by using a more complicated system.

4. ***According to the Number of Order:*** Under this method, overheads can be apportioned on the basis of services rendered.

BACKFLUSH COSTING

Companies may have some inventory despite using just-in-time (JIT) production method. Companies that record costs directly in cost of goods sold can use a method called backflush costing to transfer any costs back to the inventory accounts, if necessary. Backflush costing is a method that works backward from the output to assign manufacturing costs to work-in-process inventories. The term 'backflush' is used because costs are flushed back through the production process to allocate costs between cost of goods sold and inventory.

> **Backflush costing** is a method that works backward from the output to assign manufacturing costs to work-in-process inventories.

Backflush costing avoids detailed accounting transactions. In conventional product costing system costs are assigned with the movement of the products from direct materials to work-in-progress to finished goods. However, in backflush costing, we focus first, on the output of the organisation and work backwards to allocate costs between costs of goods sold and inventories. No separate accounts are maintained for work-in-progress in backflush accounting.

CRITICAL ANALYSIS AND DISCUSSION QUESTIONS, SELF-ASSESSMENT QUESTIONS, MULTIPLE CHOICE QUESTIONS, PROBLEMS AND CASES

CRITICAL ANALYSIS AND DISCUSSIONS QUESTIONS

1. What do you mean by full costing? What are its uses?
2. Distinguish between direct cost and indirect cost.
3. What is the need of absorption?
4. Discuss different stages in absorption of overheads.
5. How is apportionment of overhead costs done?
6. Explain the bases for apportionment of service department overheads to producing departments.
7. What is inter-department services? How are they treated for the purpose of absorption?
8. Discuss the different methods of absorption of overhead costs.
9. What do you mean by predetermined overhead rate? Why is such a rate used?
10. Explain the meaning of under-absorption and over-absorption. How are they treated in cost accounting?
11. Explain backflush costing.
12. What is the difference between production department and service department?
13. What are different stages of cost absorption in conventional product-costing system?
14. Why do conventional product-costing system apportion service department overheads first to the production departments before assigning them to products?

SELF-ASSESSMENT QUESTIONS

I. The following Data apply to Items 1 to 2

Zeta Company is preparing its annual profit plan. As part of its analysis of the profitability of individual products the controller estimates the amount of overhead that should be allocated to the individual product lines from the information given below:

	Wall Mirrors	*Specially Windows*
Units produced	25	25
Materials moves per product line	5	15
Direct labour hours per unit	200	200

Budgeted material handling costs ₹ 50,000

1. Under a costing system that allocates overhead on the basis of direct labour hours, the materials handling costs allocated to one unit of wall mirrors would be

(*a*) ₹ 1,000 (*b*) ₹ 500 (*c*) ₹ 2,000
(*d*) ₹ 5,000 (*e*) ₹ 0

2. Under activity-based costing (ABC), the materials handling costs allocated to one unit of wall mirrors would be

   (*a*) ₹ 1,000 (*b*) ₹ 500 (*c*) ₹ 1,500 (*d*) ₹ 2,500 (*e*) ₹ 0

II. The following Data apply to Items 3 to 7

Madtack Company's beginning and ending inventories for the month of November 2016 are

	November 1	***November 30***
Direct Materials	₹ 67,000	₹ 62,000
Work-in-Process	1,45,000	1,71,000
Finished Goods	85,000	78,000
Production data for the month of November follows:		
Direct Labour		₹ 2,00,000
Actual factory Overhead		1,32,000
Direct Materials purchased		1,63,000
Transportation in		4,000
Purchase returns and allowances		2,000

Madtack uses one factory overhead control account and charges factory overhead to production at 70 per cent of direct labour cost. The company does not formally recognize over/underapplied overhead until year end.

3. Madtack Company's prime cost for November is

   (*a*) ₹ 3,70,000 (*b*) ₹ 1,68,000 (*c*) ₹ 3,63,000
   (*d*) ₹ 1,70,000 (*e*) ₹ 3,68,000

4. Madtack Company's total manufacturing cost for November is

   (*a*) ₹ 5,02,000 (*b*) ₹ 5,03,000 (*c*) ₹ 3,63,000
   (*d*) ₹ 4,95,000 (*e*) ₹ 5,10,000

5. Madtack Company's cost of goods transferred to finished goods inventory for November is

   (*a*) ₹ 4,69,000 (*b*) ₹ 4,77,000 (*c*) ₹ 4,95,000
   (*d*) ₹ 4,84,000 (*e*) ₹ 4,76,000

6. Madtack Company's cost of goods sold for November is

   (*a*) ₹ 4,84,000 (*b*) ₹ 4,91,000 (*c*) ₹ 5,02,000
   (*d*) ₹ 4,76,000 (*e*) ₹ 4,69,000

7. Madtack Company's net charge to factory overhead control for month of November is

   (*a*) ₹ 8,000 debit, overapplied
   (*b*) ₹ 8,000 debit, underapplied
   (*c*) ₹ 8,000 credit, overapplied
   (*d*) ₹ 8,000 credit, underapplied
   (*e*) ₹ 1,32,000

(CMA, USA, Adapted with permission)

Answers to Self-Assessment Questions

I. 1. (*a*) 2. (b)

II. 3. (a) 4. (e) (5) (d) 6. (b) 7. (c)

MULTIPLE CHOICE QUESTIONS

Select the correct answer for the following multiple choice questions.

1. Which of the following statements best describes cost allocation?
   (*a*) A company can maximize or minimize total company income by selecting different bases on which to allocate indirect costs.
   (*b*) A company should select an allocation base to raise or lower reported income on given products.
   (*c*) A company's total income will remain unchanged no matter how indirect costs are allocated.
   (*d*) A company should ordinarily allocate indirect costs randomly or based on an ability-to-bear criterion.
2. The allocation of cost to particular cost objects allows a firm to analyze all of the following except
   (*a*) Whether a particular department should be expanded
   (*b*) Why the sales of a particular product have increased
   (*c*) Whether a product line should be discontinued
   (*d*) Why a particular product should be purchased rather than manufactured in-house
3. Costs are allocated to cost objects in many ways and for many reasons. Which one of the following is a purpose of cost allocation?
   (*a*) Evaluating revenue center performance
   (*b*) Measuring income and assets for external reporting
   (*c*) Budgeting cash and controlling expenditures
   (*d*) Implementing activity-based costing
4. The allocation of general overhead costs to operating departments can be least justified in determining
   (*a*) Income of a product or functional unit
   (*b*) Costs for short-term decisions
   (*c*) Costs of products sold and remaining in inventory
   (*d*) Costs for Government's cost plus contracts
5. To identify costs that relate to a specific product, an allocation base should be chosen that.
   (*a*) Does not have a cause-and-effect relationship
   (*b*) Has a cause-and-effect relationship
   (*c*) Considers variable costs but not fixed costs
   (*d*) Considers direct materials and direct labour but not factory overhead
6. Allocation of support department costs to the production departments is necessary to
   (*a*) Control costs
   (*b*) Determine overhead rates
   (*c*) Maximize efficiency
   (*d*) Measure use of plant capacity
7. The most accurate method of allocating service department costs is the
   (*a*) Reciprocal method
   (*b*) Step method

(*c*) Direct method
(*d*) Accretion method
(*e*) Composite method

8. Multiple or departmental overhead rates are considered preferable to a single or plant-wide overhead rate when
   (*a*) Manufacturing is limited to a single product flowing through identical departments in a fixed sequence
   (*b*) Various products are manufactured that do not pass through the same departments or use the same manufacturing techniques
   (*c*) Cost drivers, such as direct labour, are the same over all processes
   (*d*) Individual cost drivers cannot accurately be determined with respect to cause-and-effect relationships
   (*e*) The single or plant-wide rate is related to several identified cost drivers
9. Generally, individual department rates rather than a plant-wide rate for applying overhead would be used if
   (*a*) A company wants to adopt a standard cost system
   (*b*) A company's manufacturing operations are all highly automated
   (*c*) A company's manufacturing operations are basically labour based
   (*d*) Manufacturing overhead is the largest cost component of its product cost
   (e) The manufactured products differ in the resources consumed from the individual departments in the plant
10. Because the allocation method recognizes that service departments often provide each other with inter departmental service, it is theoretically considered to be the most accurate method for allocating service department costs to production departments. This method is the
   (*a*) Direct method
   (*b*) Variable method
   (*c*) Reciprocal method
   (*d*) Linear method
   (*e*) Step-down method
11. When allocating service department costs to production departments, the method that does **not** consider different cost behavior patterns is the
   (*a*) Step method
   (*b*) Reciprocal method
   (*c*) Direct method
   (*d*) Single-method
   (*e*) Dual-rate method

(*CMA, USA, Adapted with permision*)

Asnwers to Multiple Choice Questions

1. (c)	2. (b)	3. (b)	4. (b)	5. (b)
6. (b)	7. (a)	8. (b)	9. (e)	10. (c)
11. (d)				

PROBLEMS

1. Mid-City College is organised into three instruction centres and two service centres. The instruction centres are arts and sciences, education and business administration. The service centres are buildings and grounds and central administration. The president wants to know the cost per student in each of the three instruction centres. As a part of the task, you have been asked to assist with the reassignment of overhead costs from the service centres to instruction centres. The following data represent estimates for the current school year:

(₹ '000)

	Total	***Arts and Science***	***Education***	***Business Adminis-tration***	***Buildings and Grounds***	***Central Adminis-tration***
	₹	₹	₹	₹	₹	₹
Overhead cost (₹ 000)	10,000	3,000	2,250	2,500	1,500	750
Per cent of space occupied	100	30	25	20	10	15
Number of employees	300	90	65	45	60	40
Number of students	8,000	4,000	2,500	1,500	—	—

Required:

(*a*) Reassign the overhead costs from the service centres to the instruction centres, with building and ground allocated first.

(*b*) Calculate the overhead cost for each instruction centre on a number-of-student basis.

(M. Com., Delhi, 1993)

2. Collins company has two service and three production centres in its production operations. The following data present estimates for the coming year:

		Service Centre		***Production Centre***		
	Total	***1***	***2***	***A***	***B***	***C***
	₹	₹	₹	₹	₹	₹
Overhead cost (₹ 000)	3,000	360	310	650	800	880
Number of employees	310	10	15	90	95	100
Square feet of space occupied	20,000	1,600	2,000	3,400	6,000	7,000
Direct labour hours				1,80,000	1,90,000	2,00,000

The company allocates Service Centre I first. It allocates Service Centre I costs on the basis of number of employees and Service Centre 2 on the basis of space occupied.

Required:

(*i*) Reassign the overhead cost from the service to the production centres.

(*ii*) Calculate the overhead rate per direct labour-hour for each of the three production centres.

(M. Com., Delhi)

CASES

Computer Information Services is a computer software consulting company. Its three major functional areas are computer programming, information systems consulting and software training. Carol Birch, a pricing analyst in the Accounting Department, has been asked to develop total costs for the functional areas. These costs will be used as a guide in pricing a new contract. In computing these costs, Birch is considering three different methods of allocating overheads costs—the direct method, the step method, and the reciprocal method. Birch assembled the following data on overhead from its two service departments, the Information Systems Department and the Facilities Department.

	Service Department		***Production Department***			
	Information Systems	Facilities	Computer Programming	Consulting	Training	Total
Budgeted overhead (₹)	50,000	25,000	75,000	110,000	85,000	345,000
Information Systems* (hours)		300	1,200	600	900	3,000
Facilities** (thousand square feet)	200		400	600	800	2,000

*Allocated on the basis of hours of computer usage.

**Allocated on the basis of floor space.

Required:

A. Using computer usage time as the application base for the Information Systems Department and square feet of floor space for the Facilities Department, apply overhead from these service departments to the production departments, using the following two methods.

1. Direct method 2. Step method

B. 1. Define the reciprocal method of allocating the costs of service departments.

2. Would the reciprocal method be appropriate for Computer Information Services?

C. Rather than allocating costs, how might Computer Information Services better assign the Information Systems Department's costs? *(CMA, USA, Adapted with permission)*

Answer:

A.	Programming	Consulting	Training
1. Direct Method	₹ 1,02,778	1,29,444	1,12,778
2. Step Method	₹ 1,01,667	1,30,000	1,13,333

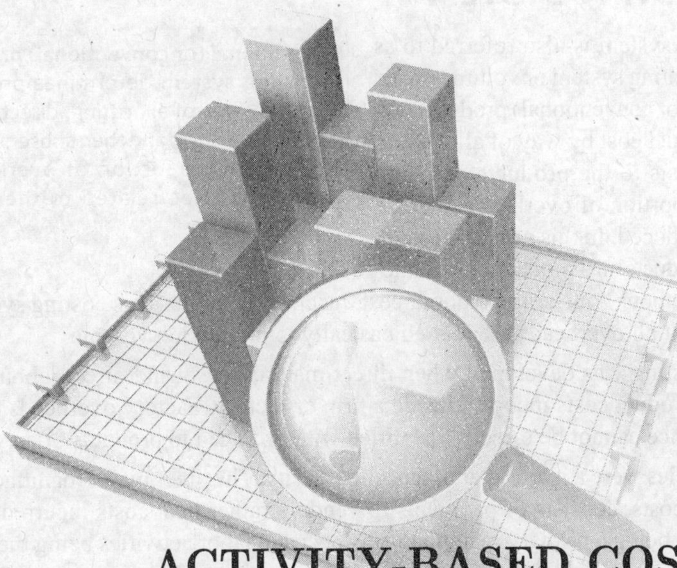

4

ACTIVITY-BASED COSTING (ABC)

LEARNING OBJECTIVES :

After reading this chapter, you should be able to:

- Understand Traditional Product Costing, its Concept, Limitations, and Situation Under which it can be used
- Explain the Concept of Activity-based Costing
- Describe Stages and Flow of Costs in ABC
- Explain Classification of Activities in a Manufacturing Organization
- Compare ABC With Traditional Costing System
- Discuss Merits and Demerits of ABC
- Understand the Role of ABC in Service Industry
- Explain the Criteria for Successful Implementation of ABC
- Elaborate upon the use of ABC for External Reports

TRADITIONAL COSTING SYSTEM

Traditional (or conventional) product costing system determines product cost by way of allocating, direct costs to the products and then subsequently adding a proportion of overheads deemed to be related to the units produced.

Traditional product costing system is also referred to as functional-based cost accounting system or volume-based costing system. Traditional (or conventional) product costing system determines product cost by way of allocating, in the first stage, direct costs to the products and then subsequently adding a proportion of overheads deemed to be related to the units produced. In this costing system, overheads are charged to products on a production volume-related basis such as direct labour hours, direct labour cost, machine hour etc. This costing system is based on the assumption that all overheads are related basically to production volume.

Traditional product costing was developed when direct material costs and direct labour costs accounted for the bulk of product costs incurred inside a firm or factory. Factory overheads tend to serve all production and hence cannot be directly identified with or traced to products or services.

In the past, labor activities were a major manufacturing activity. The other major manufacturing cost item, direct materials costs, consists of payments to vendors rather than costs incurred inside the factory. With labor costs being a primary manufacturing cost and labor activities being the major activity in the manufacture of a product, volume-based costing systems focus on measuring and controlling direct labor costs. Factory overheads have been a small fraction of the labor cost and are deemed as resources expended to support labor activities. Using direct labor costs, a traditional overhead costing system becomes a volume-based costing system. As volumes (units) change, direct labor costs, as do overhead costs, vary in proportion to changes in units of production.

Functional-based (volume-based) costing system has the following features:

1. It assumes simple labour-based production norm and low level of mechanisation
2. Direct costs i.e. direct material and direct labour have larger proportion in the total costs of production
3. Overhead costs are in small proportion because support or servicing functions such as planning, purchasing, accounting, finance, administration, etc. are less
4. Standardised products are generally assumed to be produced
5. This costing system is assumed not to be affected much by technology changes and production methods and products are subject to slow rate of changes

Volume-based Overhead Rate

The factory overhead rate in a volume-based costing system is either a single overhead rate for the entire operation (plantwide rate) or a set of overhead rates with various rates for different departments or divisions (departmental rates). These overhead rates use an output-volume-based activity or activities to assign (or to spread) factory overhead costs to products or services. An output-volume-based costing system spreads costs evenly so that each cost object (product or service) receives the same amount. (Absorption of overheads has been discussed in previous Chapter 3).

Limitations of Volume-based Costing System

Volume-based costing system has served well since the inception of cost accounting. However, remarkable changes have taken place in production methods, organisational structure, cost behaviour and magnitudes. Production is now automated and computerised. Overheads now-a-days constitute a very high proportion of total costs as compared to direct labour. Support functions and their costs have shown increasing trends continually. Thus, at present, overheads are less affected by production volume (as in conventional costing), but more by range and complexity of products manufactured.

The following are the limitations of volume-based costing sysem:

1. Different products utilize different amount of resources, which is not recognized in traditional costing system.
2. Overheads now constitute the largest share of cost, often greater than 50% and is typically applied to products as percentage of the smallest cost (direct labour) leading to serious distortion of product cost.
3. By relying on volume-related measures to determine product costs, traditional costing system do a poor job in reflecting supporting costs for manufucturing and distribution of products or services.More and more factory overheads such as setup cost, materials handling cost, and product design and research and development costs are unrelated to the number of units produced.
4. Traditional costing system tends to overcost standard, high volume products and undercost low volume products, leading to incorrect pricing and product mix decisions.
5. It creates a bias toward direct labor reduction as a cost reduction technique rather than overall productivity improvement.
6. It provides no information useful in either identifying productivity improvement opportunities or determining if productivity improvement efforts have yielded significant results. Indeed, often traditional costing system indicates higher cost in the presence of known productivity improvement or vice versa.

Thus, companies that apply plantwide and departmental overhead rates to assign overhead costs to products often do not produce reliable cost data. Conventional product costing system follows a cost smoothening or peanut-butter costing which describes a costing approach that uses broad averages for distributing the cost of resources uniformly to cost objects (such as product or services) when the individual products or services, in fact, use those resources in a non-uniform way. For some companies, product cost distortions can be damaging, particularly for those characterized by intense or increasing competitive pressures, continuous improvement, total quality management, total customer satisfaction and sophisticated technology. As firms operating in this competitive environment adopt new strategies to achieve competitive excellence, their cost accounting systems often must change to keep pace. Cost accounting systems that worked reasonably well in the past may no longer be acceptable[1].

Blocher, Chen, Cokins and Lin[2] observe:

> *A volume-based overhead costing system, whether plantwide or departmental, often leads to inaccurate product costs, especially for firms with complex manufacturing operations—firms with varieties of products or heterogeneous production processes. As firms increase in variety of product, volume, size, or complexity, resources used and costs spent on supporting activities, increase. Distortions of volume-based overhead cost systems increase as product diversity increases because the cost system (i) is designed to cost products in the aggregate, not to ralate to unique manufacturing characteristics in different operations; (ii) uses a common plantwide or departmental cost driver and ingnores differences in activities for differrent products or production runs within the plant or department; (iii) employs a common activity volume for all operations such as direct labor-hours or dollars as the base to distribute overhead costs to all products while the selected activity is a small portion of the overall production activities; and (iv) deemphasizes long-term product analysis.*

Users of traditional volume-based cost data who are aware of likely distortions in cost data from a volume-based costing system, often attempt to make intuitive, and likely, imprecise adjustments to the volume-based cost information without understanding their complete effect and, thereby, distort the cost information further. Inaccurate cost information can lead to undesirable strategic results, such as wrong product-line decisions, unrealistic pricing, and ineffective resource allocations.

Situations Under Which Traditional Costing System can be used

A volume-based costing system may provide reasonably accurate costs when a business firm possesses the following characteristics:

1. Few and very similar product and service lines
2. Low overhead expenses
3. Similar distribution channels, customer demands and customers
4. Similar conversion process for all products or services
5. High margins of products and services

Example to Illustrate Erroneous Costing with Traditional Costing System

- Four friends A, B, C, D go to a restaurant. Each one of them orders different items to eat and drink. Obviously, each item's price is different. So, at the end of the meal, the waiter brings a common bill totalling all the items consumed by all the four. Say the bill is ₹ 1080. What do they do? They divide ₹ 1080 by 4 and each one gives his share of the bill i.e. ₹ 270.
- The question to ask is: has each one really eaten worth ₹ 270?
- The answer is: 'No'.
- Had you kept an account of who ate what, you could have got the exact bill for the individual accurately. Suppose, one of them kept an account of who ate what, he could calculate his share of total bill by looking at the prices of the ordered items from the menu cards. So knowing this, one of them kept an account like this and he found that the four friend ate like this: first one ate worth ₹ 150, the second one worth ₹ 420, the third one ₹ 270 and fourth one ₹ 240. The total is the same but each one costs differently than the earlier (average) ₹ 270 each.
- Now, replace the four friends by four products being manufactured in a company. With conventional costing system, the cost of each will be ₹ 270. Selling price of each would be decided by the market trend. Therefore, we will calculate the profit or loss made by the sales of each item with reference to ₹ 270 as the cost of each one of them. However, suppose we are in a position to keep a track of exact costing of each product by using a costing system like ABC and suppose that the exact cost found by ABC happens to be ₹ 150 for first product, ₹ 420 for second product, ₹ 270 for third item and ₹ 240 for fourth items, your profit calculations now will give you an entirely different picture for each product.
- You will now be able to find as to which product is really making the profit or loss and exactly how much?
- Now, based on this information of exact profitability and cost of each product by using ABC, management decisions on product mix, cost reduction, product design modification, marketing/sales strategies can be taken more correctly. In absence of this information, by using the information given earlier by the conventional costing system, all these decisions were being taken as 'shot in the dark'- literally blindly. They were misleading.

ACTIVITY-BASED COSTING (ABC): MEANING OF

> **Activity-based Costing (ABC)** is a costing system which focuses on activities performed to produce products.

The activity-based costing (ABC) is a costing system which focuses on activities performed to produce products. ABC is that costing in which costs are first traced to activities and then to products. This costing system assumes that activities are responsible for the incurrence of costs and products create the demands for activities. Costs are charged to products based on individual product's use of each activity. In traditional product costing system, costs are, first, traced not to activities but to an organisational unit, such as department or plant and then to products. ABC, as compared to traditional cost system is based on one fundamental difference. Under ABC, activity and product/service costs are determined based on the primary principle that activities consume resources (costs). Products and servises (cost objects), in turn, consume the activities. This principle is fundamentally different from traditional costing systems whose premise is that product/services consume resources directly, and activity costs are not calculated at all.

STAGES AND FLOW OF COSTS IN ABC (STEPS IN ABC)

There are two primary stages in ABC – first tracing costs to activities; and second, tracing activities to products. The different steps in the two stages of ABC are as follows:

Step 1: Identify Activities

An activity is a unit of work. If you go to a restaurant for lunch/dinner, a waiter or waitress might perform the following units of work:

- Seat customer and offer menu
- Take your order
- Send orders to kitchen
- Bring food
- Replenish beverages
- Determine and bring bill
- Collect money and give change
- Clear table

Each of these in an activity and the performance of each activity consumes resources that cost money.

The first step in developing activity-based product costs is to identify the activities performed in the organization. Think of activities as "verbs" that answer the question "What do you do?" If you had to answer the question, what might be some of your responses? "I study, I sleep, I eat." Asking this question to employees is one way to determine the activities they perform; another is to observe what they do. Either way, this step is the most time consuming part of implementing an activity based costing system and the one that can generate the greatest error.

In addition to identifying the activities, you need to determine how much time employees spend performing each activity. Let's go back to your answer to the question "What do I do?" While you might find it easy to list what you do, saying how much time you spend on each activity might be harder. For instance, the amount of time you spend studying probably varies each week, depending on what class tests you have. The same is true for many employees; the time they spend on certain tasks varies from one month to the next. Nevertheless, employees must make such an estimate so that the resources consumed by the activities (that is, their salaries and other costs) can be calculated.

As activities are identified, the time spent on that activity and the resources consumed by that activity must be tracked.

Step 2: Develop Activity Cost Pools

After all the activities have been identified and the appropriate level of detail has been selected, the activities are combined into activity cost pools based on their cost drivers. For example, Apollo Sports Co.'s managers determined that "moving materials from the storeroom to the cutting room" and "packing finished products" were both batch activities. Because pants, jerseys, and jackets are produced in batches, the number of batches produced determines the frequency of these warehousing and packaging activities and the resources consumed. Therefore, managers combined those two activities into one pool. After gathering all the relevant information about activities and their drivers, Apollo Sports Co.'s managers determined that the company had the following five activity pools:

Activity Pool	**Activity Driver**
Product design	Number of product lines
Warehousing/packaging	Number of batches
Cutting	Number of cuts
Sewing	Direct labour hours
General	Not assigned to products

Once the activity pools have been determined, manufacturing overhead costs can be assigned to them. This is referred to as a first-stage allocation because costs are assigned first to the activity pools before being assigned to cost objects. Table 4.1 shows the first-stage allocation of manufacturing overhead resources for Apollo Sports. These allocations were based on employee estimates of time spent and the resources used to complete the activities. Notice that the ₹ 13,26,000 that relates to the machine is not included in the costs allocated to the activity pools, since those costs are traceable directly to the jackets. All the remaining manufacturing overhead costs are allocated to the activity pools.

Table 4.1: Step 2: Allocation of Manufacturing Overhead Costs to Activity Pools

	Machine Costs Traceable to Jackets	Product Design	Warehouse/ Packaging	Cutting	Sewing	General	Total
Indirect labor	₹ 25,140	₹4,00,000	₹4,00,000	₹75,000	₹1,50,000	₹10,59,860	₹21,10,000
Depreciation	₹40,920		₹73,960		₹3,46,960		₹4,61,840
Indirect material	₹12,59,940	₹3,75,120	₹11,08,690	₹13,58,610	₹10,10,640		₹51,13,000
Rent						₹11,00,000	₹11,00,000
Utilities					₹4,13,300	₹1,70,000	₹5,83,300
Insurance						₹5,50,000	₹5,50,000
Other		₹63,770	₹1,22,970	₹37,470	₹1,47,300	₹42,850	₹4,14,360
Total	₹13,26,000	₹8,38,890	₹17,05,620	₹14,71,080	₹20,68,200	₹29,22,710	₹1,03,132,500

Step 3: Calculate Activity Cost Pool Rates

After the manufacturing overhead costs have been assigned to activity cost pools, the next step in developing activity-based product costs is to calculate an activity rate for each cost pool. Activity rate is calculated as follows:

$$\text{Activity Rate} = \frac{\text{Total activity cost pool resources}}{\text{Total activity driver volume}}$$

Table 4.2 shows the calculation of the four activity rates for Apollo Sports. Let's review the calculations. For product design, the activity cost total ₹ 8,38,890 (see Table 4.1). Since the number of product lines is the cost driver and Apollo has three product lines (pants, jerseys and jackets), the denominator is 3 product lines. The calculation of the activity rate is:

$$\frac{₹\,8,38,890}{3 \text{ product line}} = ₹\,2,79,630 \text{ per product line}$$

Table 4.2: Step 3: Calculation of Activity Rates

	Total Cost (A)	Total Activity (B)	Activity Rate (A)/(B)
Product design	₹ 8,38,890	3 product lines	₹ 2,79,630 per product line
Warehousing/Packaging	₹ 17,05,620	9,170 batches	₹ 186 per batch
Cutting	₹ 14,71,080	56,580 cuts	₹ 26 per cut
Sewing	₹ 20,68,200	86,175 direct labor hours	₹ 24 per direct labor hour

For warehousing/packaging, the activity cost total ₹ 17,05,620. The number of batches produced is the cost driver for this activity pool. It is calculated as follows:

	Budgeted Production		Units per Batch		Number of Batches
Pants	1,83,500	÷	50	=	3,670
Jerseys	66,500	÷	35	=	1,900
Jackets	18,000	÷	5	=	3,600
Total					9,170

Given this number of batches, the activity rate for this pool is calculated as:

$$\frac{₹\,17,05,620}{9,170 \text{ batches}} = ₹\,186 \text{ per batches}$$

For cutting, the activity cost total is ₹ 14,71,080. The number of cuts is the cost driver for this activity pool; it is calculated as follows:

	Batches		Cuts per Batch		Total Cuts
Pants	3,670	×	4	=	14,680
Jerseys	1,900	×	5	=	9,500
Jackets	3,600	×	9	=	32,400
Total					56,680

Given this number of cuts, the activity rate is calculated as:

$$\frac{₹\,14,71,080}{56,580 \text{ cuts}} = ₹\,26 \text{ per cut}$$

Finally, for sewing, the activity cost total is ₹ 20,68,200. Direct labor hours is the cost driver for this activity pool, and it is calculated as follows:

	Budgeted Production	Direct Labor Hours per Unit		Total Direct Labor Hours
Pants	1,83,500	0.25 hours	=	45,875
Jerseys	66,500	0.20 hours	=	13,300
Jackets	18,000	1.50 hours	=	27,000
Total				86,175

Given this number of direct labor hours, the activity rate is calculated as:

$$\frac{₹\ 20,68,200}{86,175 \text{ direct labour hours}} = ₹\ 24 \text{ per direct labour hour}$$

Step 4: Allocate Costs to Products or Services

With the activity rates calculated, one can allocate the costs to products or services. The following formula can be used to allocate costs to products or services.

Allocated Cost = Activity rate × Activity driver consumption

Table 4.3 shows the cost allocations to the three products. Notice that each product has four allocations, one for each of the activity pools. Notice, too, that the activity rate column for each product is the same, since the activity rates are constant, regardless of the product that is consuming the resource. However, each product uses the activities to different degree, and those differences in usage drive the differences in allocated costs. For example, the cutting cost allocated to pants is ₹ 26 × 14680 cuts = ₹ 3,81,680; to jackets, it is ₹ 8,42,400 – why? The answer is that jackets require many more cuts than pants, even though the company makes fewer jackets than pants. Let's reconcile how the overhead costs from the first-stage allocation (see Table 4.1) were allocated to the three products:

		Overhead Costs
Pants		₹ 24,44,930
Jerseys		11,99,230
Jackets		
ABC allocation	₹ 24,39,630	
Machine costs	₹ 13,26,000	37,65,630
Total costs allocated		₹ 74,09,790
General costs not allocated		29,22,710
Total overhead costs		₹ 1,03,32,500

All the overhead costs have been accounted for. When the overhead cost allocated to the jackets is added to the machine costs traced to the jackets, the total overhead cost of the jackets becomes ₹ 37,65,630. Notice that this amount is more than the overhead cost allocated to pants. Even though budgeted production called for only 18,000 jackets as compared to 1,83,500 pants, jacket production requires many more activities than pants production.

Table 4.3: Step 4: Allocating Activity Costs to Products

Pants	Activity Rate	Activity		ABC Cost
Product design	₹ 2,79,630 per product line	× 1 line	=	₹ 2,79,630
Warehousing/packaging	₹ 186 per batch	× 3,670 batches	=	6,82,620
Cutting	₹ 26 per cut	× 14,680 cuts	=	3,81,680
Sewing	₹ 24 per direct labor hour	× 45,875 direct labor hours	=	11,01,000
				₹ 24,44,930

Jerseys	Activity Rate	Activity		ABC Cost
Product design	₹ 2,79,630 per product line	× 1 line	=	₹ 2,79,630
Warehousing/packaging	₹ 186 per batch	× 1,900 batches	=	3,53,400
Cutting	₹ 26 per cut	× 9,500 cuts	=	2,47,000
Sewing	₹ 24 per direct labor hour	× 13,300 direct labor hours	=	3,19,200
				₹ 11,99,230

Jackets	Activity Rate	Activity		ABC Cost
Product design	₹ 2,79,630 per product line	× 1 line	=	₹ 2,79,630
Warehousing/packaging	₹ 186 per batch	× 3,600 batches	=	6,69,600
Cutting	₹ 26 per cut	× 32,400 cuts	=	8,42,400
Sewing	₹ 24 per direct labor hour	× 27,000 direct labor hours	=	6,48,000
				₹ 24,39,630

Step 5: Calculate Unit Product Costs

The last step in the preparation of activity-based costing data is to calculate the unit product cost. In Step 4, we calculated the total overhead allocated to each product. For decision-making purposes, we need to convert that amount to a unit cost by dividing the total overhead cost by the total number of units produced. For example, the overhead cost for a pair of pants would be ₹ 13.3 (rounded), calculated as:

$$\frac{₹\ 24{,}44{,}930}{1{,}83{,}500 \text{ pants}} = ₹\ 13.3 \text{ per pair of pants.}$$

To calculate the total product cost per unit, we need to add the direct materials and direct labor costs to this overhead cost. The total activity-based cost for a pair of pants would be:

Direct materials	₹ 44.7
Direct labor	24.0
Overhead	13.3
Total product cost per unit	₹ 82.0

Table 4.4 shows the calculation of the total product costs and unit costs for all the three products based on the budgeted production for 2017.

Table 4.4: Step 5: Calculating Unit Product Costs

	Pants	Jerseys	Jackets	Total Costs
Traceable overhead			₹ 13,26,000	₹ 13,26,000
Allocated overhead	₹ 24,44,930	₹ 11,99,230	₹ 2439630	₹ 60,83,790
Total overhead costs	₹ 24,44,930	₹ 11,99,230	₹ 37,65,630	₹ 74,09,790
Unit produed	÷ 1,83,500	÷ 66,500	÷ 18,000	
Overhead per unit	₹ 13.3	₹ 18.0	₹ 209.2	
Direct materials	44.7	68.5	447.2	
Direct labor	24.0	19.2	144.0	
	₹ 82	₹ 105.7	₹ 800.4	

Let us compare the activity-based overhead allocation to Apollo's original allocation, based on direct labor cost. Table 4.5 shows the manufacturing overhead costs allocated to each of the products under the two methods. Notice that the total amount of manufacturing overhead allocated to the products differ between the two methods– ₹ 1,03,32,500 under the traditional approach and ₹ 74,09,790 under the activity-based approach. The difference between the amount of manufacturing overhead allocated under the two methods is ₹ 29,22,710 general overhead cost pool that was not allocated to products under activity-based costing.

Figure 4.5: Comparison of Traditional and Activity-based Costing

Traditional	Pants	Jerseys	Jackets	Total
Direct labor cost	₹ 44,00,000	₹ 12,74,000	₹ 25,92,000	₹ 82,66,000
Overhead rate	125%	125%	125%	125%
= Allocated overhead	₹ 55,00,000	₹ 15,92,500	₹ 32,40,000	₹ 1,03,32,500
% of total overhead	53.23%	15.41%	31.36%	
ABC				
Traceable			₹ 13,26,000	₹ 13,26,000
+ Product design	₹ 2,79,630	₹ 2,79,630	₹ 2,79,630	₹ 8,38,890
+ Warehousing/packaging	6,82,620	3,53,400	6,69,600	17,05,620
+ Cutting	3,81,680	2,47,000	8,42,400	14,71,080
+ Sewing	11,01,000	3,19,200	6,48,000	20,68,200
= Allocated overhead	₹ 24,44,930	₹ 11,99,230	₹ 37,65,630	₹ 74,09,790
% of allocated overhead	33.00%	16.18%	50.82%	
+ Organizational-level Overhead (not allocated)				29,22,710
= Total overhead				₹ 1,03,32,500

Although the total amount of allocated overhead differs between the two methods, we can still compare the percentage of overhead allocated to each product. Notice where the big differences occur in Table 4.5. Under the traditional costing method, pants were allocated 53.23% of manufacturing overhead, yet under activity-based costing, pants received just 33% of manufacturing overhead. The other major difference between the two methods was for jackets, which were allocated 31.36% of total overhead under the traditional method and 50.82% under activity-based costing. What caused the differences in the relative amount of manufacturing overhead allocated under the two methods to pants, a high-volume product, and jackets, a low-volume product? One obvious cause is the cost associated with the machine. Under traditional costing, these costs were shared by all three products. However, under activity-based costing, these costs are traced directly to jackets, reducing the amount of overhead allocated to pants and increasing the amount of overhead allocated to jackets.

A second cause of difference in costs results from the cutting operation. Jacket production required more cutting than pant production, even though Apollo produced only one-tenth the number of jackets as pants. The shift in cost from a high-volume to a low-volume product is quite common in newly implemented activity-based costing systems. That is because low-volume products, such as jackets, tend to use as many product-level activities as other products, while generating as many or more batch-level activities.

ACTIVITY COST DRIVERS

> Cost drives is an activity which generates cost. It is a factor such as the level of activity or volume that causally affect costs.

Like a resource driver that is used to trace resource to activities, an activity cost driver is used to trace activity costs to cost objects. Activity driver is defined as a

- *measure of the frequency and intensity of the demands placed on activities by cost objects. An activity driver is used to assign costs to cost objects.*

A cost driver is an activity which generates costs. A cost driver is a factor, such as the level of activity or volume, that causally affects costs (over a given time span). That is, a cause-and-effect relationship exists between a change in the level of activity or volume and a change in the level of the total costs of that cost object. Thus, cost drivers signify factors, forces or events that determine the costs of activities. Based on activity usage (consumption), activity costs are traced to cost objects. In a manufaturing organization, the following are examples of some activity cost drivers (see Exhibit 4.1).

Exhibit 4.1: Activity Cost Drivers

Examples of Activity Cost Drivers

1. Number of receiving orders for the receiving department.
2. Number of purchase order for the cost of operating the purchase department.
3. Number of dispatch orders for the dispatch department.
4. Number of units.
5. Number of setups.
6. Amount of labour cost incurred.
7. Value of materials in a product.
8. Number of materials handling hours.
9. Number of inspections.
10. Number of schedule changes.
11. Number of parts received per month.
12. Number of machine hours used on a product.
13. Number of set up hours.
14. Number of direct labour hours.
15. Number of sub-assemblies.
16. Number of vendors.
17. Number of purchasing and ordering-hours.
18. Number of units scrapped.
19. Number of labour transactions.
20. Number of customer orders processed.
21. Number of parts.
22. Number of employees.

It should be understood that direct costs do not need cost drivers as they can be traced directly to a product. Direct costs are themselves cost drivers. However, all other factory or manufacturing costs need cost drivers. The cost driver of variable costs is the level of activity or volume whose change cause the variable costs to change proportionately.

Costs that are fixed in the short run have no cost driver in the short run but may have cost drivers in the long run. For instance, costs of testing personal computers (which comprise costs of testing department equipment and staff costs) may not change with changes in the volume of production. Therefore, these costs would be fixed in the short run. In the long run, however, an organization may need to increase/decrease testing department's equipment and staff to the levels needed to support future production volumes. So, in the long run, volume of production or activity becomes cost drivers of these testing and staff costs.

SELECTION OF ACTIVITY COST DRIVERS

In traditional product costing, the number of cost drivers used are few such as direct labour hours, machine hours, direct labour cost, units produced. But ABC may use a multitude of cost drivers that relate costs more closely to the resources consumed and activities occurring. There are difficulties in choosing realistic cost drivers. There are no simple rules that pertain to the selection of cost drivers. The best approach is to identify the resources that constitute a significant proportion of the product costs and to determine their cost behavior. When identifying and selecting activity drivers, match the activity to the activity level, which is defined as a description of how an activity is used by a cost object (product/service) or activity. Some activity levels describe the cost object that uses the activity and nature of its use.

According to Hilton,[3] the following three factors are important in selecting appropriate cost drivers:

1. *Degree of Correlation:* The central concept of an activity-based costing system is to assign the costs of each activity to product lines on the basis of how each product line consumes the cost driver identified for that activity. The idea is to infer how each product line consumes the activity by observing how each product line consumes the cost driver. Therefore, the accuracy of the resulting cost assignment depends on the degree of correlation between consumption of the activity and consumption of the cost driver.

2. ***Cost of Measurement:*** Designing any information system entails cost-benefit trade-offs. The more activity cost pools there are in an activity-based costing system, the greater will be the accuracy of the cost assignments. However, more activity cost pools also entail more cost drivers, which results in greater costs of implementing and maintaining the system. Similarly, the higher the correlation between a cost driver and the actual consumption of the associated activity, the greater the accuracy of the cost assignments. However, it may also be more costly to measure the more highly correlated cost driver.

3. ***Behavioural Effects:*** Information systems have the potential not only to facilitate decisions but also to influence the behaviour of decision maker. This can be good or bad, depending on the beavioural effects. In Identifying cost drivers, an ABC analyst should consider the possible behavioural consequences. For example, in a JIT production environment, a key goal is to reduce inventories and material handling activities to the absolute minimum level possible. The number of material moves may be the most accurate measure of the consumption of the material handling activity for cost assignment purpose. It may also have a desirable behavioural effect of motivating managers to reduce the number of times materials are moved, thereby reducing material.

Dysfunctional behavioural effects are also possible. For example, the number of vendor contacts may be a cost driver for the purchasing activity of vendor selection. This could induce purchasing managers to contact fewer vendors, which could result in the failure to identify the lowest-cost or highest-quality vendor.

ABC focuses on the drivers which cause overheads and traces overheads to products in terms of usage of cost drivers. Therefore, under ABC, a large proportion of overheads are product related. In traditional costing systems, however, most support overheads are assigned to products in a general arbitrary manner and therefore cannot be related to products. ABC by identifying appropriate cost drivers and cost pools makes the product costs more accurate and reliable. Further, ABC, in this way, helps in better cost management and cost control by managing the activities which cause costs.

Miller[4] observes that tips for identifying activity drivers include the following:

- Pick activity drivers that correlate with the actual consumption of the activity
- Minimize the number of unique drivers. Cost and complexity are directly correlated with the number of drivers
- Pick activity drivers that encourage improved performance
- Pick activity drivers that are already available and/or have a low cost of collection

TYPES OF COST DRIVERS

Customer demand is considered to be the basic cost driver. Without customer demand for products or services, an organization cannot exist. To serve customers, managers and employees make a variety of decisions and perform many actions/activities. These decisions and activities, undertaken to satisfy demand, drive costs. Morse, Davis and Hartgraves[5] suggest that cost drivers should be divided into three categories:

1. Structural Cost Drivers: They are fundamental choices about the size and scope of operations and technologies employed in delivering products or services to customers. Decision affecting structural cost drivers are made infrequently and once made, an organization is committed to a course of action that will be difficult to change. For a chain of super market stores, the following may be structural cost drivers:

(*i*) Determining the size of stores. This will affect types of merchandise that can be provided to customers and operating costs.

(*ii*) Determining the type of construction. A small size store will involve less cost. But it may not be suitable to store many other needed items.

(*iii*) Determining the location of the store. Location in a high class shopping complex will cost more but will attract more customers.

(*iv*) Determining the kind of technology used in the stores. A system involving clerks to keep all records of sales, purchases and inventory may be cheaper. A computerised system in the beginning requires higher investment and fixed operating costs. But, later, it may be less expensive due to high sales volume. Also, it will provide latest information about all operations.

2. Organisational Cost Drivers: They are choices concerning the organization of activities and involvement of persons inside and outside the organisation in decision making. Like structural cost drivers, organisational cost drivers influence costs by affecting the type of activities and cost of activities performed to satisfy customer needs. Decisions that affect organisational cost drivers are made within the context of previous decisions affecting structural cost drivers. In a manufacturing organization, previous decisions about plant, equipment and location are taken as given when decisions impacting organizational cost drivers are made. In a manufacturing company, examples of organizational cost drivers are:

- Preferring a limited number of suppliers. This may be useful in ensuring proper supplies in proper quantities at proper time.
- Authorizing employees to make decisions and giving them cost and other data. This will make employees customer-oriented, reduce costs and improve decision speed. Production workers, for example, may take steps to reduce manufacturing cost and defects and spoilage.

- Deciding components of a product to fit them in the most correct manner. This will save assembly time and cost and reduce defects.
- Deciding to manufacture a low-volume product on low speed, general purpose equipment; rather than high-speed, special purpose equipment.
- Deciding to reorganise the existing equipment in the factory so that sequential operation are nearer. This will reduce cost of moving inventory between different machines.

3. Activity Cost Drivers: Activity cost drivers are specific units of work (activities) performed to serve customer needs that consume costly resources. The customer may be outside the organisation, such as a client of an advertising firm or inside the organization, such as an accounting office that receives maintenance services. Because the performance of activities consumes resources and resources cost money, the performance of activities drives cost.

CLASSIFICATION OF ACTIVITIES IN MANUFACTURING ORGANIZATIONS

As stated earlier, activities are identified and classified into different categories or segments of the production process. The grouping of activities is preferably done using the different levels at which activities are performed. Broadly, activities are classified into one of four activity categories:

1. *Unit-level activities:* Activities which are performed each time a unit is produced. They are repetitive activities. For example, direct labour hours, machine hours, power are used each time a unit is produced. Direct materials and direct labour activities are also unit-level activities, although they are not overhead costs. Costs of unit level activities vary with the number of units produced.

2. *Batch-level activities:* Activities which are performed each time a batch of goods or products is produced. The costs of batch-level activities vary with the number of batches but are fixed with respect to the number of units in each batch. Machine setups, inspections, production scheduling, materials handling are examples of batch-level activities which are related to batches but not to individual products.

3. *Product-level activities:* Activities which are performed to support the production of each different type of product. Maintenance of equipment, engineering charges, testing routines, maintaining bills of materials, handling materials are some examples of batch-level activities.

4. *Facility-level activities:* Activities which are needed to sustain a factory's general manufacturing process. These activities are common to a variety of products and are most difficult to link to product-specific activities. Examples of facility-level activities are factory management, maintenance, security, plant depreciation, etc.

Several additional examples of the costs driven by activities at each above level are presented in Table 4.6.

Table 4.6: Activity Levels and Associated Activity Costs

Activity Level	Reason for Activity	Examples of Activity Cost
1. Unit-level	Performed for each unit of product produced or sold	Cost of raw materials Cost of inserting a component Utilities cost of operating equipment Some costs of packaging Sales commissions

2.	Batch-level	Performed for each batch of product produced or sold	Cost of processing sales order Cost of issuing and tracking work order Cost of equipment setup Cost of moving batch between work stations Cost of inspection (assuming same number of units inspected in each batch)
3.	Product-level	Performed to support each different product that can be produced	Cost of product development Cost of product marketing such as advertising Cost of specialized equipment Cost of maintaining specialized equipment
4.	Facility-level	Performed to maintain general manufacturing capabilities	Cost of maintaining general facilities such as buildings and grounds Cost of non-specialized equipment Cost of maintaining non-specialized equipment Cost of real property taxes Cost of general advertising Cost of general administration such as the plant manager's salary

Source: Wayne J. Morse, James R. Davis, Al. L. Hartgraves, Management Accounting, A Strategic Approach, South Western College Publishing, 2000, P. 54.

In ABC system, facility-level activities and costs are treated as period cost as they are found difficult to assign to different products. The costs associated with the first three categories — unit-level, batch-level, product-level — are assigned to products, using cost drivers that reflect the cause and effect relationship between activity consumption and cost.

COMPARISION BETWEEN TRADITIONAL COSTING AND ACTIVITY-BASED COSTING SYSTEM

In the following sections, the differences between the two costing systems are described.

Cost Assignment

Both the costing sytems do the costing of a cost object which may be a finished or semifinished product, a component, an activity, a process consisting of series of activity, a customer, a supplier, etc. However, the methodology of costing in the two costing systems is different. Let us take the example of a component as a cost object for doing its costing.

The component consumes certain amount of certain material and labor and that can be exactly measured. So, the costing of direct material and direct labor can be done in ABC exactly in the same manner as is done in conventional costing system i.e. by multiplying total material consumed by the component by material's unit price and by multiplying total labor hours used by the component by the per hour labor rate.

To this will be added, the portion of overheads of the organization that actually got consumed by this component. In conventional costing system, it is done by loading a percentage of the total overhead cost of the organization to the component. Generally, this percentage is either the percentage of the labor cost or as the percentage of the material cost of the component or labor or machine hours as compared to the overall labor cost or overall material cost or total labour or machine hours of the entire orgonization. In fact, there is no rationale to it since the component may not have actually attracted the overheads to it in this manner of percentages.

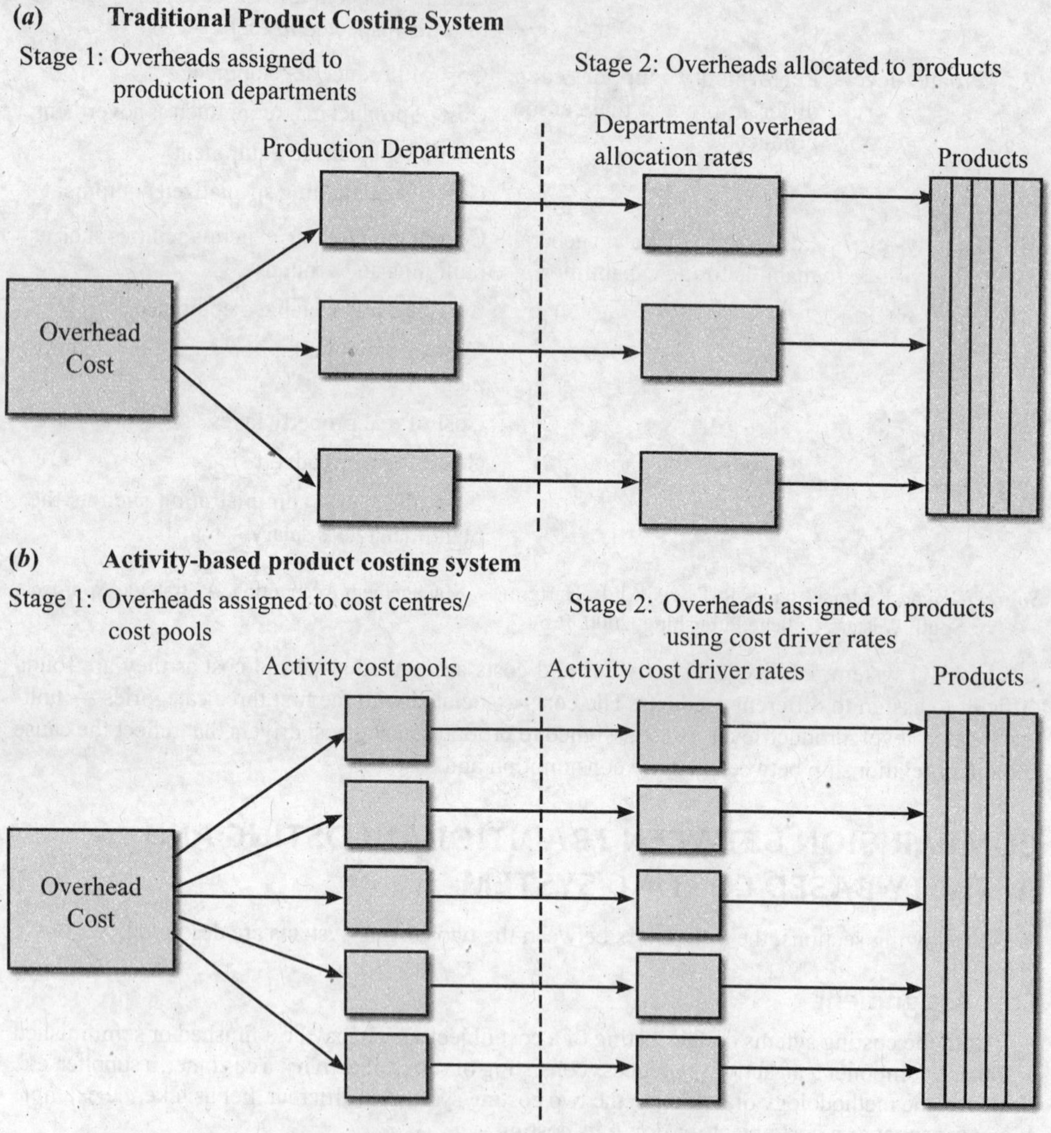

Figure 4.1: Comparison of Traditional and Activity-based Costing Systems

Source: J. Innes and F. Mitchell, *Activity-Based Costing: A Review with Case Studies*, 1990, CIMA,UK.

In ABC, there is a need to find out the actual overhead activities performed on the component. Each overhead activity is measured in terms of its cost driver i.e. how many units of that cost driver were actually used by the component. On each overhead activity, the total cost of that overhead activity is collected at the organizational level. This is called the overhead cost pool of that activity. Also, unit cost of each activity driver is worked out by dividing the total overhead cost pool of that activity by the total units of the cost driver used at the organizational level. This gives the actual cost per unit of the cost driver of that activity. Now, by multiplying the units of cost driver actually used by the component by this cost driver rate, one can get the actual cost of that overhead activity performed on the component. The overhead cost is allocated, in this manner, to the component for all the overhead activities the component used.

In summary, in ABC, each overhead activity has a overhead cost pool at the organizational level, each overhead activity has a cost driver with its unit of measurement and each cost driver has its unit cost i.e. the cost driver cost. In this way, ABC improves product costing procedure (as compared to traditional costing) because it recognises that many so-called fixed overhead costs vary in proportion to changes other than production units. By establishing the link between these cost drivers and fixed overhead costs, they are finally traced to individual products.

Figure 4.1 presents an overview of product cost determination under traditional costing and ABC system.

Two-Stage Allocation

It can be observed that both the costing systems follow a two stage allocation procedure. In traditional costing, in the first stage, overhead costs are allocated to production departments. But in ABC, in the first stage, overhead costs are assigned to each major activity and not to departments. In traditional costing, overheads are pooled/collected department-wise. But, in ABC, many activity-based cost pools or cost centres are created. In traditional costing, overhead costs of service departments are allocated/reapportioned to production departments and therefore in this costing system finally only fewer cost pools exist. But ABC creates separate cost pools for service activities as well and overhead costs of these service activities (service departments) are assigned directly to specific products through applying cost driver rates. Thus, in ABC, there is no need to allocate/reapportion overheads of service departments.

Use of Historical Costs

Another difference between traditional and activity-based costing is the historical orientation. It is not unusual for an organization to use actual historical cost as the basis for developing manufacturing cost standards. These historical costs often include rework, duplication, waste, redundancy, and inefficiency. Accepting historical costs as a given and reflecting these costs in standards does not support continuous improvement. In a competitive situation, where competitors have been proactive in eliminating waste and improving activities, an organization can go out of business while meeting its standards. While activity-based costs are also calculated using historical resource costs, the orientation is different. Proponents of ABC are concerned about future competitive positions and use historical cost only as a baseline for improvement.[7] Table 4.7 summarizes the major differences between the two costing system.

Table 4.7: Traditional and ABC Systems

	Traditional	ABC
1. Cost pools	1. One or a limited number	1. Many, to reflect different activities
2. Applied rate	2. Volume-based cost drivers	2. Activity-based, non-financial
3. Suited for	3. Labour-intensive, low-overhead companies	3. Capital-intensive, product-diverse, widely diverse set of operating activities, variation in numbers of production runs, high-overhead companies
4. Benefits	4. Simple, inexpensive	4. Accurate product costing, possible elimination of non-value-added activities
5. Cost assignment	5. Allocates overhead costs first to departments and second to products or services	5. Assigns overhead costs first to activity cost pools and second to products or services
6. Focus	6. Focuses on managing costs of functional departments or responsibility centres	6. Focuses on managing processes and activities and solutions of cross-functional problems

Advantages of ABC

The following are the advantages of ABC:

1. Accurate Product Cost — ABC brings accuracy and reliability in product cost determination by focussing on cause and effect relationship in the cost incurrence. It recognises that it is activities which cause costs, not products and it is product which consume activities.

   In advanced manufacturing environment and technology where support functions overheads constitute a large share of total costs, ABC provides more realistic product costs. ABC produces reliable and correct product cost data in case of greater diversity among the products manufactured such as low-volume products, high-volume products. Traditional costing system is likely to bring errors and approximation in product cost determination due to using arbitrary apportionment and absorption methods.
2. Information about Cost Behaviour — ABC identifies the real nature of cost behaviour and helps in reducing costs and identifying activities which do not add value to the product. With ABC, managers are able to control many fixed overhead costs by exercising more control over the activities which have caused these fixed overhead costs. This is possible since behaviour of many fixed overhead costs in relation to activities now become more visible and clear.
3. Tracing of Activities for the Cost Object — ABC uses multiple cost drivers, many of which are transaction based rather than product volume. Further, ABC is concerned with all activities within and beyond the factory to trace more overheads to the products.
4. Tracing of Overhead Costs — ABC traces costs to areas of managerial responsibility, processes, customers, departments besides the product costs.

5. Better Decision Making — ABC improves greatly the manager's decision making as they can use more reliable product cost data. ABC helps usefully in fixing selling prices of products as more correct data of product cost is now readily available.
6. Cost Management — ABC provides cost driver rates and information on transaction volumes which are very useful to management for cost management and performance appraisal of responsibility centres. Cost driver rates can be used advantageously for the design of new products or existing products as they indicate overhead costs that are likely to be applied in costing the product.
7. Use of Excess Capacity and Cost Reduction — ABC, through the processes of pooling of activity costs and the identification of cost drivers, can lead to a range of applications. These include the identification of spare capacity and the fostering of cost reduction by comparing the resources required under ABC with the resources that are currently provided. This provides a platform for the development of activity-based budgeting in which the resource relationships identified by ABC are used to project future resource requirements.
8. Benefit to Service Industry — Service organizations, such as banks, hospitals and government departments, have very different characteristics than manufacturing firms. Service organizations have almost no direct costs, most of the costs are overheads and they do not hold stocks of service as the service is consumed when it is produced. Traditional costing has generally been considered inappropriate for these organizations, whereas ABC offers the potential of benefits from improved decision making and cost management[7].

An ABC system can provide better costing information and help management manage efficiently and gain a better understanding of the firm's competitive advantages, strengths and weaknesses. Often, managers recogize needs for a better costing system such as ABC when they are experiencing increased lost sales due to erroneous pricing that resulted from inaccurate costing data. An ABC system has the most impact on firms that have areas with large, increasing expenses or have numerous products, services, customers, processes, or a combination of these. Example are plants that produce standard and custom products, high-volume and low-volume products, or mature and new products. Firms that accept small and large orders, offer standard and customized deliveries, or satisfy all customers including those who demand frequent changes and services either before or after the delivery, and customers who hardly ever request special services can benefit substantially from activity-based costing systems.[8]

Colin Drury[9] observes:

> *ABC provides not only a base for calculating more accurate product costs but also a mechanism for managing costs. An ABC system focuses management attention on the underlying causes of costs. It assumes that resource-consuming activities cause costs and that products incur costs through the activities they require for designing, engineering, manufacturing, marketing, delivery, invoicing and servicing. By collecting and reporting on the significant activities in which a business engages, it is possible to understand and manage costs more effectively.*
>
> *With an ABC system, costs are managed in the long run by controlling the activities that drive them. In other words, the aim is to manage the activities rather than costs. By managing the forces that cause the activities (i.e., cost drivers), costs will be managed in the long-term. The application of activity-based systems may have the greatest potential for contributing to cost management, budgeting, control and performance evaluation.*

According to Weil and Maher:[10]

> *Activity-based costing plays an important role in companies' strategies and long-range plans to develop a competitive cost advantage. While activity-based costing focuses attention on activities in allocating overhead costs to products, activity-based management focuses on managing activities to reduce costs. Cost reduction generally requires a change in activities. Top management can send notices to company employees to reduce costs, but the implementation requires a change in activities. If you have lived in a city that has had to reduce costs, you know that achieving the reduction required a change in activities such as fewer police patrols, a cut in library hours, and reduced social services. An entity cannot know the effect of a change in activities on costs without the type of cost information provided by activity-based costing.*

Demerits of ABC

The following are the demerits of ABC:

1. ***Expensive and Complex:*** ABC has numerous cost pools and multiple cost drivers and therefore can be more complex than traditional product costing systems. It can prove costly to manage ABC system.
2. ***Selection of Drivers:*** Some difficulties emerge in the implementation of ABC system such as selection of cost drivers, assignment of common costs, varying cost driver rates. etc.
3. ***Disadvantageous to Smaller Firms:*** ABC has different levels of utility for different organisation such as large manufacturing firm can use it more usefully than the smaller firms. Also, it is likely that firms depending on cost-plus pricing can take advantages from ABC as it gives accurate product cost. But those firms who use market based prices may not favour ABC. The level of technology and manufacturing environment prevailing in different firms also affect the application of ABC.
4. ***Measurement Difficulties:*** The main costs and limitations of an ABC system are the measurements necessary to implement it. ABC systems require management to estimate costs of activity pools and to identify and measure cost drivers to serve as cost allocation bases. Even basic ABC systems require many calculations to determine costs of products and services. These measurements are costly. Activity cost rates also need to be updated regularly.

ABC in the Service Industry

Although initially developed and implemented by manufacturers, activity-based costing has been widely adopted in service industries as well. ABC is used by airlines, railroads, hotels, hospitals, banks, insurance companies, telephone companies, and financial services firm. The overall objective of ABC in service firms is no different than it is in a manufacturing company. That objective is to identify the key activities that generate costs and to keep track of how many of those activities are performed for each service provided (by job, service, contract, or customer).

ABC can prove very useful to many service organizations because in these service organizations managers need accurate information about the cost of service being provided by them. Further, such service firms require to use this information to improve their operations and to fulfil the needs of tneir customers in a more costeffective manner.

The general approach to identifying activities, activity cost pools, and cost drivers is the same for service companies and for manufacturers. Also, the labeling of activities as value-added and non-value-added, and the attempt to reduce or eliminate non-value-added activities as much as possible, is just as valid in service industries as in manufacturing operations. What sometimes makes implementation of activity-based costing difficult in service industries is that, compared to manufacturers, a larger proportion of overhead costs are company-wide costs that cannot be directly traced to specific services provided by the company.

Kaplan and Cooper[11] suggest that service companies are ideal candidates for ABC, even more than manufacturing companies. Earlier, service organizations were government-owned or operated in highly regulated, protected and non-competitive environment. Thus, service organizations were not under any pressure to improve profitability by eliminating non-value added or non-profit activities. The prices of services were simply increased to cover cost increases. No efforts was made to design a cost system that accurately measures the costs and profitability of individual services.

However, due to privatisation, deregulation and increasing competition, the service organizations need to have cost and management accounting systems which can help them to accurately measure cost and resulting profitability for their services, customers and markets. Therefore, ABC would prove advantageous to service organizations to understand their cost base and to make decisions on value-added/non-value added activities. Kaplan and Cooper illustrate the use of ABC in banks for product and customer profitability analysis. The following are some of the activities and cost drivers in bank as identified by Kaplan and Cooper[12]:

Activity	*Cost Driver*
Provide ATM services	No. of ATM transactions
Clear Debit items	No. of debits processed
Clear Credit items	No. of credit processed
Issue cheque books	No. of cheque books issued
Computer processing	No. of computer transactions
Prepare statements of account transactions	No. of statements issued
Administer mortgages	No. of mortgages maintained

Drury and Taylers[13] after making survey of UK Companies have concluded that service organizations are more likely to implement ABC systems. They found that 51% of the financial and service organizations surveyed, compared with 15% of manufacturing organizations, had implemented ABC.

Criteria for Successful Implementation of ABC System

For an ABC system to be successful, a business organization must embrace this system and use it for all management decision making. According to Guin[14], the success of ABC system depends on the following key factors:

1. The system has top management support
2. The ABC methods are understandable and explainable
3. The system is accessible
4. Internal people take ownership of the system
5. ABC data is linked to how people are evaluated and rewarded
6. A cross-functional team should be created to design and implement the ABC system

1. Top management support is critical. Top managers must strongly support the ABC implementation because their leadership is instrumental in properly motivating all employees to embrace the need to change. An ABC system changes a company's perspective of its business. As such, the organization has winners and losers. The losers are likely to fight the system unless senior management voices confidence in it. Senior executives should provide briefings and training classes about ABC to their employees. In addition, most people are resistant to change, and unless change is forced, a new idea can whither away.

2. For the ABC system to be successful, the company's employees must understand it and its results. The ABC system must represent how the company's activities consume resources and how its products or customers trigger those activities. Simiplifying assumptions are not only allowable but neccesary; the system cannot become too complex. If a system is not understandable, it is not credible.

At the same time, the system must accurately report product costs. The results must appear intuitively correct. Assignment schemes should not be arbitrary. If one part is more expensive than another, and the difference cannot be explained, the system will not have credibility. Without credibility, the system will fail.

3. The ABC system must be accessible by all potential users. All potential users of an ABC system must have timely, convenient access to the cost system. This is one important reason an integrated cost system is superior to a standalone syatem. Integrated cost systems are accessible from any information system terminal in the company. No non-integrated system can match this availability.

Restricting access to the system also breeds distrust. Users are naturally skeptical of new systems. Many users only feel comfortable with the system after prolong experimentation.

4. The implementation site's personnel must gain ownership to the system. This holds true for all new systems. Unless someone is committed to the new idea and champions it, overcoming all obstacles to its implementation, the idea bogs down and withers away. A cost system is no exception. In addition, only with in-house expertise will the system become an evolving entity, growing and responding to new company needs.

5. Top management should ensure that ABC data is linked to how people are evaluated and rewarded. If employees continue to be evaluated and rewarded using traditional (not ABC) cost data, they will quickly get the message that ABC is not important.

6. Cross-functional team should be created to design and implement the ABC system. The team should include representatives from each area that will use ABC data, such as a marketing, production, engineering, and accounting department. These cross-functional employees possess intimate knowledge of many parts of an organization's operations that is necessary for designing an effective ABC system. Furthermore, tapping the knowledge of cross-functional managers lessens their resistance to ABC because they feel included in the implementation process. Time after time, when accountants have attempted to implement an ABC system on their own without top-management support and cross-functional involvement, the results have been ignored.[15]

ACTIVITY-BASED COSTING AND EXTERNAL REPORTS

ABC produces more reliable cost data than traditional costing method. However, data produced under ABC is rarely used for preparing external reports meant for external users. Garrison, Noreen and Brewer[16] have found the following reasons of not using ABC data for external reports by business firms.

Firstly, external reports are less detailed than internal reports prepared for decision making. On the external reports, individual product costs are not reported. Cost of goods sold and inventory valuations are disclosed, but they are not broken down by product.

If some products are undercosted and some are overcosted, the errors tend to offset each other when the product costs are added together.

Secondly, it is often very difficult to make changes in a company's accounting system. The official cost accounting systems in most large companies are usually embedded in complex computer programmes that have been modified in-house over the course of many years. It is extremely difficult to make changes in such computer programs without causing numerous bugs.

Thirdly, an ABC system does not conform to Generally Accepted Accounting Principles (GAAP), Product costs computed for external reports must include all of the manufacturing costs and only manufacturing costs; but in an ABC system, product costs exclude some manufacturing costs and include some non-manufacturing costs. It is possible to adjust the ABC data at the end of the period to conform to GAAP, but that requires more work.

Fourthly, auditors are likely to be uncomfortable with allocations that are based on interviews with the company's personnel. Such subjective data can be easily manipulated by management to make earnings and other key variables look more favourable.

For all of these reasons, most companies confine their ABC efforts to special studies for management, and they do not attempt to integrate activity-based costing into their formal cost accounting systems.

Illustrative Problem 1

ABC Company manufactures a variety of handcrafted bed frames. the company's manufacturing activities and related data for the current year are as follows:

Manufacturing Activity	Estimated Cost	Cost Driver used as Allocation Base	Estimated Volume for Cost Driver
Materials handling	₹ 4,00,000	Number of parts	8,00,000 parts
Cutting	12,00,000	Machine hours	8,00,000 hours
Assembly	30,00,000	Direct labour hours	1,50,000 hours
Wood staining	13,20,000	Number of frames stained	60,000 frames

Two styles of bed frames were produced in July: a wood frame with fewer parts, and a metal frame that required no staining activities. Direct labour is paid ₹ 25 per hour. Their quantities, direct material costs and other data follow:

	Unit Produced	Direct Material	Machine Hours	Number of Part	Direct labour Hours
Wood frames	5,000	₹ 600,000	5,000	100,000	6,000
Metal frames	1,000	200,000	500	10,000	3,000

Required:

(*a*) Compute the ABC cost allocation rates and then calculate total manufacturing costs and unit costs of the wood and metal frames.

(*b*) Suppose non-manufacturing activities, such as product design, were analysed and allocated to the wood frame at ₹ 10 each and the metal frame at ₹ 15 each. Moreover, similar analyses were conducted of other non-manufacturing activities, such as distribution, marketing and customer service. The support costs allocated were ₹ 50 per wood frame and ₹ 80 per metal frame. Calculate the product cost per unit including the non-manufacturing costs.

Solution:

(a) Resource of Activity	Wood Frames (₹)		Metal Frames (₹)	
Direct materials		600,000		2,00,000
Direct labour	6000 × ₹ 25	1,50,000	3,000 × ₹ 25	75,000
Materials handling	1,00,000× ₹ 0.50	50,000	10,000 × ₹ 0.50	5,000
Cutting	5,000 × ₹ 30	1,50,000	500 × ₹ 30	15,000

Assembly	6,000 × ₹ 20	1,20,000	3,000 × ₹ 20	60,000
Wood staining	5,000 × ₹ 22	1,10,000	0 × ₹ 22	0
Total		₹ 1,1,80,000		₹ 3,55,000
Per unit	₹ 11,80,000 ÷ 5,000	₹ 236 per unit	₹ 3,55,000 ÷ 1,000	₹ 355 per unit

(b) Product cost per unit including manufacturing and non-manufacturing costs:

Wood frame = ₹ 236 + ₹ 10 + ₹ 50 = ₹ 296

Metal frame = ₹ 355 + ₹ 15 + ₹ 80 = ₹ 480

Illustrative Problem 2

S. Chand & Co., a leading publisher, publishes two versions of a text book. One is paperback and the other is hard bound. Management is considering publishing only the higher quality book. The firm assigns its ₹ 500,000 of overhead to the two types of books. The overhead is composed of ₹ 2,00,000 of utilities and ₹ 3,00,000 of quality control inspectors' salaries. Some additional data follow:

	Paperback	*Hard Bound*
Revenues	₹ 16,00,000	₹ 14,00,000
Direct costs	₹ 12,50,000	₹ 6,00,000
Production (units)	5,00,000	3,50,000
Machine hours	42,500	7,500
Inspections	2,500	12,500

Required:

a. Compute the overhead cost that should be allocated to each type of text book using cost drivers appropriate for each type of overhead cost.

b. The firm has used machine hours to allocate overhead in the past. Should the publisher stop producing the paperback books? Explain why management was considering this action and what its decision should be.

Solution:

a.	*Paperback*	*Hard Bound*	*Total*
Machine hours	42,500	7,500	50,000
Rate per MH (₹ 2,00,000 ÷ 50,000)	× ₹ 4	× ₹ 4	× ₹ 4
Utility cost	₹ 170,000	₹ 30,000	₹ 200,000
Number of inspections	2,500	12,500	15,000
Rate per inspection (₹ 3,00,000 ÷ 15,000)	× ₹ 20	× ₹ 20	× ₹ 20
Quality inspection cost	₹ 50,000	₹ 250,000	₹ 300,000
Total traceable overhead costs	₹ 220,000	₹ 280,000	₹ 500,000

b. Income calculation using machine hours to allocate utilities and inspection hours to allocate inspectors' salaries to products:

Using the traditional cost driver (machine hours), the following results had been achieved, given a ₹ 10 charge (₹ 5,00,000 ÷ 50,000) per MH:

	Paperback	Hard Bound
Revenue	₹ 16,00,000	₹ 14,00,000
Direct costs	₹ 12,50,000	₹ 6,00,000
Overhead	₹ 4,25,000	75,000
Total Costs	₹ 16,75,000	₹ 6,75,000
Margin	₹ (75,000)	₹ 7,25,000

The reason paperbacks were erroneously thought to be unprofitable was caused by the method of allocating overhead. The firm should continue producing paperbacks as shown in the following calculations.

	Paperback	Hard Bound
Revenue	₹ 16,00,000	₹ 14,00,000
Direct costs	₹ 12,50,000	₹ 6,00,000
Overhead	₹ 2,20,000	₹ 2,80,000
Total costs	₹ 14,70,000	₹ 8,80,000
Margin	₹ 1,30,000	₹ 5,20,000

Illustrative Problem 3

Canon Manufacturing produces two different models of cameras. One model has an automatic focus; the other requires the user to focus manually. The two products are produced in batches (an equal number of batches is used for each product).

Each time a batch is produced, the equipment must be configured (set up) for the specifications of the camera model being produced. The machine configuration required for the automatic focus model is more complex and consumes more of the setup activity resources than the manual focus camera. Total setup costs are ₹ 100,000 per year. Total setup hours are 10,000 with 7,000 hours needed for the automatic focus camera and 3,000 hours needed for the manual focus camera.

The manual focus model is more labor-intensive and requires much more assembly time and less machine time. Total direct labor hours used for both products are 100,000 with 70,000 hours used for the manual model and 30,000 used for the automatic model. There are 40,000 units of the manual model and 60,000 units of the automatic model produced each year. Canon currently assigns only manufacturing costs to the two products. Overhead costs are assigned to the two products in preparation to the direct labor hours used by each product. All other costs are viewed as period costs.

Canon budgets costs for all departments within the plant—both support departments like maintenance and purchasing—as well as production departments like machining and assembly. Department managers are evaluated and rewarded based on their ability to control costs. Individual managerial performance is assessed by comparing actual costs with budgeted costs.

Required:

(*i*) Is Canon using a functional-based or an activity-based management accounting system? Explain.

(*ii*) Canon's Setup costs are overhead costs. What is the setup cost assigned per unit for each model using current method of assigning overhead costs to products? Would you classify this cost assignment as direct tracing, driver tracing, or allocation? Explain.

(*iii*) Can you suggest a better way of assigning setup costs? Provide calculations, and explain why you think this method is better. Is this method compatible with production-based costing or with activity-based costing? Explain.

Solution:

(i) As per the information given in the question, it can be said that Canon uses a functional-based accounting system. It is found that product costs are only determined by production costs. Apparently, the financial accounting system is driving the type of product cost information being produced. Second, only direct labor hours, a unit-level driver, are used to assign overhead costs. Since many overhead costs are likely to be caused by nonunit-level drivers, this also suggests a strong reliance on allocation for cost assignment. Third, the company attempts to control costs by encouraging departmental managers to meet budgeted levels of expenditures. The focus is on departmental performance rather than systemwide performance. Further, departmental performance is measured only by financial parameters. An ABC system emphasizes controlling costs by managing activities and their causes; it also uses nonfinancial measures of performance.

(ii) Setup cost per direct labor hour = ₹ 100,000/100,000

= ₹ 1.00 per DLH

Setup cost assigned:

	Automatic Model	Manual Model
₹ 1.00 × 30,000 DLH	₹ 30,000	—
₹ 1.00 × 70,000 DLH	—	70,000
Total	₹ 30,000	₹ 70,000
Units produced	÷ 60,000	÷ 40,000
Setup cost per unit	₹ 0.50	₹ 1.75

It is not direct tracing because there is no exclusive physical association. If direct labor hours is a causal factor that measures the consumption of setup resources, then it could be classified as driver tracing. However, there appearse to be little association between direct labor hours and setup cost consumption. The automatic model uses more setup resources and less direct labor hours than the manual model uses, respectively. Thus, this assignment should be classified as allocation.

(iii) Setup hours is a more likely cause-and-effect measure of resource consumption. The use of setup hours obtains an assignment rate of ₹ 10 per setup hour (₹ 100,000/10,000 setup hours) and the following assignment:

	Automatic Model	Manual Model
₹ 10.00 × 7,000 setup hrs.	₹ 70,000	₹ —
₹ 10.00 × 3,000 setup hrs.	—	30,000
Total	₹ 70,000	₹ 30,000
Units produced	÷ 60,000	÷ 40,000
Setup cost per unit	₹ 1.17	₹ 0.75

The assignment of cost is compatible with an ABC approach and not functional based approach (setup hours is a nonunit-level driver).

Illustrative Problem 4

The Hindustan Corporation manufactures oxygen tanks for deep sea divers. Information regarding resources for the month of March are as follows.

	Resources Used	Resources Supplied
Marketing	₹ 28,000	₹ 30,000
Depreciation	24,000	40,000
Outside Contracts	12,000	12,000
Materials	60,000	60,000
Setups	14,000	20,000
Energy	20,000	21,000
Parts Management	15,000	16,000
Engineering Charges	10,000	12,000
Short-term Labor	7,000	7,000
Long-term Labor	10,000	14,000
Administative	20,000	26,000

In addition, ₹ 22,000 was spent on 800 quality inspections with a cost driver rate of ₹ 25, and ₹ 8,000 was spent on 200 customer-service cost driver units with a cost driver rate of ₹ 30. Sales for March were ₹ 350,000.

Required:

a. Prepare a traditional income statement.

b. Prepare an activity-based income statement.

c. Explain briefly why the activity-based income statement provides better information to managers.

Solution:

a.

HINDUSTAN CORPORATION

Traditional Income Statement for the Month Ending March 31

Sales		₹ 350,000
Costs:		
Marketing	₹ 30,000	
Depreciation	40,000	
Outside Contracts	12,000	
Materials	60,000	
Setups	20,000	
Energy	21,000	
Parts Management	16,000	
Engineering Changes	12,000	
Short-Term Labor	7,000	
Long-Term Labor	14,000	
Administrative	26,000	

Quality Inspections	22,000	
Customer Service	8,000	
Total Costs		288,000
Operating Profits		₹ 62,000

b. Activity-Based Income Statement for the Month Ending March 31

	Resources Used	Unused Capacity	Resources Supplied	
Sales				₹ 350,000
Costs:				
Marketing	₹ 28,000	₹ 2,000	₹ 30,000	
Depreciation	24,000	16,000	40,000	
Outside Contracts	12,000	0	12,000	
Materials	60,000	0	60,000	
Setups	14,000	6,000	20,000	
Energy	20,000	1,000	21,000	
Parts Management	15,000	1,000	16,000	
Engineering Changes	10,000	2,000	12,000	
Short-Term Labor	7,000	0	7,000	
Long-Term Labor	10,000	4,000	14,000	
Administrative	20,000	6,000	26,000	
Quality Inspections	20,000	2,000	22,000	
Customer Service	6,000	2,000	8,000	
Total Costs	₹ 246,000	₹ 42,000	₹ 288,000	
Operating Profits				₹ 62,000

c. Activity-based reports differentiate between resources used and those supplied. Providing information on unused resources helps managers make better decisions to lower costs or use resource more efficiently.

Illustrative Problem 5

DEF Bank operated for years under the assumption that profitability can be increased by increasing Rupee volumes. But that has not been the case. Cost analysis has revealed the following:

Activity	Activity Cost (₹)	Activity Driver	Activity Capacity
Providing ATM service	1,00,000	No. of transaction	2,00,000
Computer processing	10,00,000	No. of transactions	25,00,000
Issuing Statements	8,00,000	No. of statements	5,00,000
Customer inquiries	3,60,000	Telephone minutes	6,00,000

The following annual information on three products was also made available;

	Checking Accounts	Personal Loans	Gold Visa
Units of product	30,000	5,000	10,000
ATM transactions	1,80,000	0	20,000
Computer transactions	20,00,000	2,00,000	3,00,000
Number of statements	3,00,000	50,000	1,50,000
Telephone minutes	3,50,000	90,000	1,60,000

Required:

(*i*) Calculate rates for each activity.

(*ii*) Using the rates computed in requirement (*i*), calculate the cost of each product.

(CA Final, May 2013)

Solution:

CALCULATION OF ACTIVITY RATES

Activity	Activity Cost [*a*] (₹)	Activity Driver	No. of Units of Activity Driver [b]	Activity Rate [a]/[b] (₹)
Providing ATM Service	1,00,000	No. of ATM Transactions	2,00,000	0.50
Computer Processing	10,00,000	No. of Computer Transactions	25,00,000	0.40
Issuing Statements	8,00,000	No. of Statements	5,00,000	1.60
Customer Inquiries	3,60,000	Telephone Minutes	6,00,000	0.60

CALCULATION OF COST OF EACH PRODUCT

Activity	Checking Accounts (₹)	Personal Loans (₹)	Gold Visa (₹)
Providing ATM Service	90,000	—	10,000
	(1,80,000 tr. × ₹ 0.50)		(20,000 tr. × ₹ 0.50)
Computer Processing	8,00,000	80,000	1,20,000
	(20,00,000 tr. × ₹ 0.40)	(2,00,000 tr. × ₹ 0.40)	(3,00,000 tr. × ₹ 0.40)
Issuing Statements	4,80,000	80,000	2,40,000
	(3,00,000 tr. × ₹ 1.60)	(50,000 tr. × 1.60)	(1,50,000 tr. × 1.60)
Customer Inquiries	2,10,000	54,000	96,000
	(3,50,000 tr. × ₹ 0.60)	(90,000 tr. × ₹ 0.60)	(1,60,000 tr. × ₹ 0.60)
A. Total Cost	₹ 15,80,000	₹ 2,14,000	₹ 4,66,000
B. Units of Product	30,000	5,000	10,000
C. Cost of each Product [A/B]	52.67	42.80	46.60

Illustrative Problem 6

NDPL Electric manufactures power distribution equipment for commercial customers, such as hospitals and manufacturers. Activity-based costing was used to determine customer profitability. Customer service activities were assigned to individual customers, using the following customer service activities, activity base, and activity rate.

Customer Service Activity	Activity Base	Activity Rate
Bid preparation	Number of bid requests	₹ 220/request
Despatch	Number of despatches	₹ 18/despatch
Support standard items	Number of standard items ordered	₹ 24/std.item
Support nonstandard items	Number of nonstandard items ordered	₹ 82/nonstd.item

Assume that the company had the following gross profit information for three representative customers:

	Customer 1	Customer 2	Customer 3
Revenue	₹ 24,250	₹ 18,000	₹ 40,000
Cost of good sold	11,640	9,360	24,800
Gross profit	₹ 12,610	₹ 8,640	₹ 15,200
Gross profit as a percent of sales	52%	48%	38%

The administrative records indicated that the activity-base usage quantities for each customer were as follows:

Activity Base	Customer 1	Customer 2	Customer 3
Number of bid requests	20	6	8
Number of Despatch	34	22	16
Number of standard items ordered	48	35	52
Number of non-standard items ordered	50	25	15

Required:

a. Prepare a customer profitability report dated for the year ended December 31, 2016 showing (1) the income from operations after customer service activities, (2) the gross profit as a percent of sales, and (3) the income from operations after customer service activities as a percent of sales. Round percentages to the nearest whole percent.

b. Interpret the report in part (a).

Solution:

a. **NDPL ELECTRIC**

Customer Profitability Report For the Year Ended December 31, 2016

	Customer 1	Customer 2	Customer 3
Revenue	₹ 24,250	₹ 18,000	₹ 40,000
Cost of goods sold	11,640	9,360	24,800
Gross profit	₹ 12,610	₹ 8,640	₹ 15,200

Customer service activities:			
Bid preparation..................................	₹ 4,400[a]	₹ 1,320	₹ 1,760
Despatch..	612[b]	396	288
Support standard items........................	1,152[c]	840	1,248
Support non-standard items..................	4,100[d]	2,050	1,230
Total customer service activities...............	₹ 10,264	₹ 4,606	₹ 4,526
Income from operations after customer service activities..................................	₹ 2,346	₹ 4,034	₹ 10,674
Gross profit as a percent of sales...............	52%	48%	38%
Income from operations after customer service activities as a percent of sales	10%	22%	27%

[a]₹ 2,200 × 20 bid requests

[b]₹ 18 × 34 Despatches

[c]₹ 24 × 48 standard items

[d]₹ 820 × 50 nonstandard items

b. The gross profit as a percent of sales indicated that Customer 3 was the least profitable, while Customer 1 was the most profitable. After deducting the activity costs associated with customer service activities, these positions reversed. Customer 3 became the most profitable, while Customer 1 became the least profitable. The reason is because Customer 3 consumed much fewer customer service activities than did Customer 1. Apparently, Customer 3 ordered standard products that required few specialized bid requests. In addition, Customer 3 required fewer despatches, indicating larger loads to a single location, rather than many smallar despatches to different locations.

Illustrative Problem 7

MST Limited has collected the following data for its two activities. It calculates activity cost rates based on cost driver capacity.

Activity	*Cost Driver*	*Capacity*	*Cost*
Power	Kilowatt hours	50,000 kilowatt hours	₹ 2,00,000
Quality Inspections	Number of Inspections	10,000 Inspections	₹ 3,00,000

The company makes three products M, S and T. For the year ended March 31, 2016, the following consumption of cost drivers was reported:

Product	*Kilowatt hours*	*Quality Inspections*
M	10,000	3,500
S	20,000	2,500
T	15,000	3,000

Required:

(*i*) Compute the costs allocated to each product from each activity.

(*ii*) Calculate the cost of unused capacity for each activity.

(iii) Discuss the factors the management considers in choosing a capacity level to compute the budgeted fixed overhead cost rate.

Solution:

(*i*) ***Statement of cost allocation to each product from each activity***

	Product			
	M ₹	**S** ₹	**T** ₹	**Total** ₹
Power (Refer to working note)	40,000 (10,000 kwh × ₹ 4)	80,000 (20,000 kwh × ₹ 4)	60,000 (15,000 kwh × ₹ 4)	1,80,000
Quality Inspections (Refer to working note)	1,05,000 (3,500 inspections × ₹ 30)	75,000 (2,500 inspections × ₹ 30)	90,000 (3,000 inspections × ₹ 30)	2,70,000

Working note:

Rate per unit of cost driver:

Power : (₹ 2,00,000 / 50,000 kwh) = ₹ 4/kwh

Quality Inspection : (₹ 3,00,000 / 10,000 inspections) = ₹ 30 per inspection

(*ii*) ***Computation of cost of unused capacity for each activity:***

	₹
Power (₹ 2,00,000 – ₹ 1,80,000)	20,000
Quality Inspections (₹ 3.00,000 – ₹ 2,70,000)	30,000
Total cost of unused capacity	50,000

(*iii*) ***Factors management consider in choosing a capacity level to compute the budgeted fixed overhead cost rate:***

— Effect on product costing & capacity management

— Effect on pricing decisions.

— Effect on performance evaluation

— Effect on financial statements

— Regulatory requirements.

— Difficulties in forecasting chosen capacity level

Illustrative Problem 8

A company makes three main products using broadly the same production methods and equipment for each product. A conventional product costing system is used at present, although an activity-based costing (ABC) system is being considered. Details of the three products for a typical period are:

	Hours per unit		*Materials per Unit*	*Volume units*
	Labour Hrs	*Machine Hrs*	*(₹)*	
Product P	.50	1.50	20	750
Product Q	1.50	1.00	12	1250
Product R	1.00	3.00	25	7000

Direct labour costs ₹ 6 per hour and production overheads are absorbed on a machine hour basis. The rate for the period is ₹ 28 per machine hour.

Further analysis shows that the total of production overheads can be divided as follows:

	%
Cost relating to set ups	35
Cost relating to machinery	20
Cost relating to materials	15
Cost relating to inspection	30
Total production overhead	100

The following activity volumes are associated with the product line for the period as a whole. Total activities for the period are:

	No. of set-ups	*No. of movement of materials*	*No. of inspections*
Product P	75	12	150
Product Q	115	21	180
Product R	480	87	670
	670	120	1000

Required:

(*I*) Calculate the cost per unit for each product using conventional methods.

(*II*) Calculate the cost per unit for each product using activity-based costing.

(*III*) Comment on the reasons for any differences in the costs in the two costing methods.

Solution:

I. Conventional Costing Method

Product Costs per Unit	*Products*		
	P	***Q***	***R***
Material (₹)	20	12	25
Direct labour @ ₹ 6	3	9	6
Production overhead	42	28	84
(Machine hrs. @ ₹ 28, 1.5, 1, 3 hrs.)			
	65	49	115

II. Activity-based Costing

First, find out total production overhead

Total production overhead based on machine hours weightage

Total machine hrs × Machine hour rate

(750 × 1.50 + 1250 × 1 + 7000 × 3) × ₹ 28 = ₹ 6,54,500

Production Overhead Classification:

		₹
Set up costs	35%	2,29,075
Machining	20%	1,30,900
Material handling	15%	98,175
Inspection	30%	1,96,350
		6,54,500

Product-wise Production Overhead Analysis (₹)

	Products			
	P	***Q***	***R***	***Total***
				₹
Set ups (75 : 115 : 480)	25,643	39,319	1,64,113	2,29,075
Machining (Total machine hours) (1125 : 1250 : 21000)	6,300	7,000	1,17,600	1,30,900
Materials handling (12 : 21 : 87)	9,817	17,181	71,177	98,175
Inspection (150 : 180 : 670)	29,452	35,343	1,31,555	1,96,350
Total	71,212	98,843	4,84,445	6,54,500
Number of Units	750	1250	7000	
Production overhead Per unit (rounded) ₹	95	79	69	

	Product Cost Per Unit (ABC)		
	P	***Q***	***R***
Direct Materials	20	12	25
Direct Labour	3	9	6
Production overhead	95	79	69
	118	100	100

Reasons for Difference:

- Set up costs has been distributed based on no. of set ups, which is more logical than conventional approach.
- Materials handling cost is logically distributed based on no. of movement of materials.
- Inspection cost is also based on inspection activity.

Hence, Products P and Q have received proportionally more production overheads under ABC than conventional product costing methods.

Working Notes: (Machine hrs of different products)

Product P	750 × 1.50	=	1,125
Product Q	1250 × 1.00	=	1,250
Product R	7000 × 3.00	=	21,000
			23,375

2. In conventional costing, production overhead charged per unit are different from production overhead per unit in ABC. However, total production overhead charged i.e. ₹ 6,54,500 is same in both costing methods. This is proved by using data from conventional costing.

Total Machine Hrs.

Product P	= 750 × 1.50	=	1,125
Product Q	= 1250 × 1	=	1,250
Product R	= 7000 × 3	=	21,000
			23,375 Hrs.

Machine Hr. Rate $= \frac{6,54,500}{23,375} =$ ₹ 28 per hour

Production Overhead Charged Under Conventional Costing

	Product P	Product Q	Product R
Overhead rate per unit (₹)	42	28	84
Product Units	750	1,250	7,000
Total production overhead charged to Products (Rate × Total Units)	31,500	35,000	5,88,000

Total Production overhead charged under conventional costing = ₹ 31,500 + ₹ 35,000 + ₹ 5,88,000 = ₹ 6,54,500

Illustrative Problem 9

Fasteners Ltd. produces and sells four products A, B, C and D. Details of the four products and relevant information are given below for the year ended 2016.

Products	***A***	***B***	***C***	***D***
Output (units)	120	100	80	120
Cost per unit: (₹)				
Direct Material	40	50	30	60
Direct Labour	28	21	14	21
Machine-hours (per unit)	4	3	2	3

The four products are similar and are usually produced in production runs of 20 units and sold in batches of 10 units.

The production overheads during the period are as follows:

	₹
Factory Works Expenses	20,860
Set up costs	10,500
Stores receiving	7,200
Inspection/Quality Control	4,200
Material handling and dispatch	9,240

The production overhead is currently absorbed by using a Machine-hour rate and the company wishes to introduce Activity Based Costing (ABC) system and has identified major cost pools for production overheads and their associated cost drivers.

Information in these activity cost pools and their drivers is given below:

Activity Cost Pools	*Cost Drivers*
Factory Works Expenses	Machine-hours
Set up Costs	Number of production runs
Stores receiving	Requisition raised
Inspection/Quality Control	Number of production runs
Material handling & dispatch	Number of orders executed

The number of requisitions raised on the stores was 20 for each product and number of orders executed was 42, each order being for a batch of 10 of a product.

Required:

(*i*) Total cost of each product assuming the absorption of overhead on Machine-hour basis.

(*ii*) Total cost of each product assuming the absorption of overhead by using activity-based costing.

(*iii*) Show the differences between (*i*) and (*ii*) and Comment

(CA Final)

Solution:

Fasteners Limited

(*i*) Statement showing Total Cost of different products assuming absorption of overhead on a Machine Hour Rate basis:

(Figure in ₹)

Particulars	*Product*				*Total*
	A	*B*	*C*	*D*	
Output (units)	120	100	80	120	420
Direct Material	40	50	30	60	180
Direct Labour	28	21	14	21	84
Overheads @ ₹ 40 per Machine hr.	160	120	80	120	480
Total Cost per Unit	228	191	124	201	
Total Cost	27360	19100	9920	24120	80500

$$\text{Overhead Rate} = \frac{₹\,52000}{1300} = ₹\ 40 \text{ per Machine hour}$$

[Total Machine hours = $(120 \times 4 + 100 \times 3 + 80 \times 2 + 120 \times 3) = 1300$]

(*ii*)

Total Overheads	*(₹)*	*Drivers*	*No.*	*Cost/Unit of Drivers*
Factory Works Expenses	20860	Machine hrs	1300	20860 ÷ 1300 = ₹ 16.05
Set up Costs	10500	Production runs	21	10500 ÷ 21 = 500.00
Stores receiving	7200	Requisitions	80	7200 ÷ 80 = 90.00
Inspection / Quality Control	4200	Production runs	21	4200 ÷ 21 = 200
Material Handling and dispatch	9240	Orders	42	9240 ÷ 42 = 220.00
Total	52000			

Statement Showing Total Cost of each product assuming activity-based costing:

Particulars	***Product***			
	A	***B***	***C***	***D***
Output (units)	120	100	80	120
No. of Production runs	6	5	4	6
No. of Stores requisitions	20	20	20	20
No. of Sales Orders	12	10	8	12
Machine hours	4	3	2	3
Direct materials (₹)	40.00	50.00	30.00	60.00
Direct labour (₹)	28.00	21.00	14.00	21.00
Particulars	***Product***			
	A	***B***	***C***	***D***
Factory Works Expenses (₹)	64.18	48.14	32.09	48.14
Set ups (₹)	25.00	25.00	25.00	25.00
Store receiving (₹)	15.00	18.00	22.50	15.00
Inspection / Quality Control (₹)	10.00	10.00	10.00	10.00
Handling / dispatch (₹)	22.00	22.00	22.00	22.00
Unit Cost (₹)	204.18	194.14	155.59	201.14
Total cost (₹)	24501.60	19414.00	12447.20	24136.80

(*iii*) Statement Showing differences (in ₹)

Particulars	***Product***			
	A	***B***	***C***	***D***
Cost per Unit Under MHR (i)	228.00	191.00	124.00	201.00
Costper Unit Under ABC (ii)	204.18	194.14	155.59	201.14
Difference	23.82	(3.14)	(31.59)	(0.14)
Total Cost-MHR (*i*)	27360.00	19100.00	9920.00	24120.00
Total Cost-ABC (*ii*)	24501.60	19414.00	12447.20	24136.80
Difference	2858.40	(314.00)	(2527.20)	(16.80)

The difference is that A consumes comparatively more of machine hours.

The use of activity-based costing gives different product costs than what were arrived at by utilizing traditional costing. It can be argued that product costs using ABC are more precise as overheads have been identified with specific activities.

Illustrative Problem 10

Fairdeal produces a product specially for its three customers, P, Q, R requiring 20,000 units, 15,000 units and 10,000 units respectively per annum.

The data in 2015-16 about the product are:

Production cost	₹ 48 per unit	
Sale price (net)	₹ 90 per unit	
Overhead not connected with production:		₹ (for the year)
Quality inspection		2,62,500

Delivery	2,55,600
Salesmen	74,000
After-sales service	93,720

Fairdeal apportions these non-production overhead costs on the basis of the production cost. The CEO is unhappy about this and asks you for an analysis upon ABC method.

You find the following activity volumes in the period:	*P*	*Q*	*R*
Number of inspections	8,330	420	0
Number of deliveries	2,080	40	10
Number of salesmen visits	160	20	5
After-sales visits	160	84	40

Required:

(*a*) Re-work the apportionment of non-production overheads to find the comparative costs of sales.

(*b*) Comment on the results so obtained in (*a*).

Solution:

(*a*) Working for apportionment of non-production overhead:

Cost driver rates:	***(Total ohd./total no.)***	***Rate per service***
	₹	₹
Inspection	2,62,500 / 8,750	30
Delivery	2,55,600 / 2,130	120
Salesmen visits	74,000 / 185	400
After-sales visits	93,720 / 284	330
	₹ 6,85,820	

Apportionment of Non-production Overhead on the Basis of ABC Method (above rate x relative number of service)

Customer	***P***	***Q***	***R***
	₹	₹	₹
Inspection	2,49,900	12,600	—
Delivery	2,49,600	4,800	1,200
Salesmen visit	64,000	8,000	2,000
After-sales visits	52,800	27,720	13,200
Total overhead	6,16,300	53,120	16,400
Units supplied	20,000	15,000	10,000
Non-production Overhead per unit	30.82	3.54	1.64

Apportionment of non-production overhead as per practice of Fairdeal:

Total non-production overhead	=	₹ 6,85,820
Total units sold	=	45,000
Rate per unit = ₹ 6,85,820 / 45,000)	=	₹ 15.24

Total Cost of Sales on the basis of

	Uniform production cost	ABC method applied to non-production overhead
P	₹ (48 + 15.24) = ₹ 63.24	₹ (48 + 30.82) = ₹ 78.82
Q	₹ (48 + 15.24) = ₹ 63.24	₹ (48 + 3.54) = ₹ 51.54
R	₹ (48 + 15.24) = ₹ 63.24	₹ (48 + 1.64) = ₹ 49.64

(*b*) As per practice of the firm, for each unit of the product as supplied to the three customers, the cost of sales is uniform at ₹ 63.24 p.a., irrespective of their varying requirements of non-production services. Non-production service costs vary widely among the customers according to their relative demand for such services.

As against the generalized view of the cost of sales under the usual method of distribution of non-production overheads followed by Fairdeal, the ABC method of apportionment of the service costs reveals the cost of sales to different customers in realistic perspective and offers a better basis of pricing products for Fairdeal. The CEO's fear of un-fair deal to customers warrants a closer view.

Illustrative Problem 11

Statusline & Company is a manufacturer of a range of white goods. Cost structure of its different products is as follows:

Standard Cost of the Products

Particular	*Product P*	*Product Q*	*Product R*
Direct Materials	25.00	20.00	20.00
Direct Labour @ ₹ 5 per hour	15.00	20.00	25.00
Production Overheads	15.00	20.00	25.00
	55.00	60.00	70.00
Quantity produced (units)	10,000	20,000	30,000

Production overhead is absorbed on the basis of Direct Labour Hours. Statusline & Company wishes to introduce activity-based costing (ABC) system and has identified four major cost pools for production overhead and their associated cost drivers. Information on these activity cost pools and their drivers is given below:

Activity Cost Pool	*Cost Driver*	*Cost Associated with Activity Cost Pool (₹)*
Stores Receiving	Purchase requisition	1,48,000
Inspection / Quality Control	Number of production runs	4,47,000
Material Handling & despatch	Orders executed	1,05,000
Production scheduling/Machine set-ups	Number of set-ups	6,00,000

Further relevant information on the three products is also given below:

Particular	*Product P*	*Product Q*	*Product R*
No. of Purchase requisitions	300	450	500
No. of Production runs	750	1050	1200
No. of Orders Executed	180	270	300
No. of set-ups	360	390	450

Required:

(*i*) Calculate the activity-based production cost of all the three products.

(*ii*) Comment on the differences between the original traditionally calculated costs and Activity Based Costs (ABC) you calculated.

Solution:

(i) Statusline & Company

Overhead Cost Per Cost Driver Unit:

Activity Cost Pool	*Cost Driver units*	*Overheads (₹)*	*Overhead cost per driver unit (₹)*
Stores Receiving	1250	1,48,000	118.40 per purchase requisition
Inspection/Quality Control	3000	4,47,000	149.00 per production run
Material handling & despatch	750	1,05,000	140.00 per order executed
Production scheduling/machine set up	1200	6,00,000	500 per set up

Details of production Overheads (Activitywise) under ABC

Particulars	*Products*		
	P	*Q*	*R*
Quantity produced (units)	10,000	20,000	30,000
Stores receiving	$\frac{118.4 \times 300}{10,000}$ = ₹ 3.552	$\frac{118.4 \times 450}{20,000}$ = ₹ 2.664	$\frac{118.4 \times 500}{30,000}$ = ₹ 1.9733
Inspection/quality Control	$\frac{149 \times 750}{10,000}$ = ₹ 11.175	$\frac{149 \times 1050}{20,000}$ = ₹ 7.8225	$\frac{149 \times 1200}{30,000}$ = ₹ 5.96
Material handling & despatch	$\frac{140 \times 180}{10,000}$ = ₹ 2.52	$\frac{140 \times 270}{20,000}$ = ₹ 1.89	$\frac{140 \times 300}{30,000}$ = ₹ 1.40
Production Scheduling/Machine Set-ups	$\frac{500 \times 360}{10,000}$ = ₹ 18.00	$\frac{500 \times 390}{20,000}$ = ₹ 9.75	$\frac{500 \times 450}{30,000}$ = ₹ 7.50

ABC Production Costs Statement (₹ per unit)

Particulars	*Products*		
	P	*Q*	*R*
Direct Materials	25	20	20
Direct labour @ ₹ 5 / hr	15	20	25

Production overheads:			
Stores Receiving	3.55	2.66	1.97
Inspection / quality control	11.18	7.82	5.96
Material handing & despatch	2.52	1.89	1.4
Production Scheduling/machine set-up	18	9.75	7.5
Total Cost of Production	75.25	62.12	61.83

(*ii*) Comparison of the ABC cost with the original traditionally calculated cost reveals that product-R was significantly overcosted by the traditional system relative to the ABC system while product-P was seriously undercosted. Product-R is high-volume product with a high direct labour content, whilst Product-P is a low-volume product with a low direct labour content; this result is therefore expected.

ABC reflects reality in its allocation of production overhead costs to the product. The traditional approach allocated all production overhead costs to products as if the overheads were driven by unit level activities i.e. the number of direct labour hours worked.

In the light of above criteria, it may be commented that ABC gives a better insight into the cost of producing the products than traditional costs.

Illustrative Problem 12

ABC Ltd. manufactures two types of machinery equipments Y and Z and applies/absorbs overheads on the basis of direct-labour hours. The budgeted overheads and direct-labour hours for the month of December, 2016 are ₹ 12,42,500 and 20,000 hours respectively. The information about Company's products is as follows:

	Equipment Y	***Equipment Z***
Budgeted Production volume	2,500 units	3,125 units
Direct material cost	₹ 300 per unit	₹ 450 per unit
Direct labour cost		
Y : 3 hours @ ₹ 150 per hour	₹ 450	
X : 4 hours @ ₹ 150 per hour		₹ 600

ABC Ltd.'s overheads of ₹ 12,42,500 can be identified with three major activities:

Order Processing (₹ 2,10,000), machine processing (₹ 8,75,000), and product inspection (₹ 1,57,500). These activities are driven by number of orders processed, machine hours worked, and inspection hours, respectively. The data relevant to these activities is as follows:

	Orders processed	***Machine hours worked***	***Inspection hours***
Y	350	23,000	4,000
Z	250	27,000	11,000
Total	600	50,000	15,000

Required:

(*i*) Assuming use of direct-labour hours to absorb/apply overheads to production, compute the unit manufacturing cost of the equipments Y and Z, if the budgeted manufacturing volume is attained.

(*ii*) Assuming use of activity-based costing, compute the unit manufacturing costs of the equipments Y and Z, if the budgeted manufacturing volume is achieved.

(*iii*) ABC Ltd. 's selling prices are based heavily on cost. By using direct-labour hours as an application base, calculate the amount of cost distortion (under-costed or over- costed) for each equipment.

(*iv*) Discuss, how an activity-based costing might benefit ABC Ltd.

Solution:

(*i*) Overheads application base: Direct labour hours

	Equipment Y ₹	*Equipment* Z ₹
Direct material cost	300	450
Direct labour cost	450	600
Overheads*	186.38	248.50
	936.38	1,298.50

$$\text{Pre-determined rate} = \frac{\text{Budgeted overheads}}{\text{Budgeted direct labour hours}}$$

$$= \frac{₹12,42,500}{20,000\text{ hours}} = ₹\ 62.125$$

(*ii*) Estimation of Cost-Driver Rate

Activity	*Overhead cost* ₹	*Cost-driver level*	*Cost driver rate* ₹
Order processing	2,10,000	600 Orders processed	350
Machine processing	8,75,000	50,000 Machine hours	17.50
Inspection	1,57,500	15,000 Inspection hours	10.50

	Equipment Y ₹	*Equipment* Z ₹
Direct material cost	300	450
Direct labour cost	450	600
Prime cost	750	1,050
Overhead cost		
Order processing 350 : 250	1,22,500	87,500
Machine processing 23,000 : 27,000	4,02,500	4,72,500
Inspection 4,000 : 11,000	42.000	1,15,500
Total overhead cost	5,67,000	6,75,000

Per unit cost		
= 5,67,000/2,500	226.80	
= 6,75,500/3,125		216.16
Unit manufacturing cost	976.80	1,266.16

(iii)

	Equipment *Y* ₹	*Equipment* *Z* ₹
Unit manufacturing cost-using direct labour hours as an application base	936.38	1,298.50
Unit manufacturing cost-using activity based costing	976.80	1,266.16
Cost distortion	(–) 40.42	(+) 32.34

Low volume product *Y* is under-costed and high volume product *Z* is over-costed using direct labour hours as a basis for overheads absorption. It is due to the limitation of traditional costing system.

(*iv*) Activity-based costing system is suitable in case of ABC Ltd. because it is a multi-product company and overheads costs are substantial portion of total cost. The use of activity based costing will avoid cost distortion as ABC Ltd. has a large proportion of non-unit- level activities such as orders processed and inspection hours.

Illustrative Problem 13

The following are Product Nova Shaft's data for next year budget:

Activity	*Cost Driver*	*Cost Driver volume/year*	*Cost Pool*
Purchasing	Purchase orders	1,500	₹ 75,000
Setting	Batches produced	2,800	₹ 1,12,000
Materials handling	Materials movements	8,000	₹ 96,000
Inspection	Batches produced	2,800	₹ 70,000
Machining costs	Machine hours	50,000	₹ 1,50,000

Purchase orders	25
Output	15,000 units
Production batch size	100 units
Materials movements per batch	6
Machine hours per unit	0.1

Required:

(i) Calculate the budgeted overhead costs using activity based costing principles.

(ii) Calculate the budgeted overhead costs using absorption costing (absorb overhead using machine hours).

(iii) How can the company reduce the ABC for Product Nova Shaft?

Solution:

(i) Computation of Activity-based Overheads

Step 1: Compute cost per unit of cost driver = Cost pool / cost driver volume

Activity	*Cost Driver*	*Cost Pool (a) ₹*	*Cost driver volume/yr (b)*	*Cost/Unit of cost driver (a)/(b) ₹*
Purchasing	Purchase orders	75,000	1,500	₹ 50/purchase order
Setting	Batches produced	1,12,000	2,800	₹ 40/batch
Materials handling	Material movements	96,000	8,000	₹ 12/movement
Inspection	Batches produced	70,000	2,800	₹ 25/batch,
Machining	Machine hours	1,50,000	50,000	₹ 3/machine hour

Step 2: Compute the volume of cost drivers consumed by Product Nova Shaft

Purchase orders (given) = 25

Batches = 15,000/100 = 150

Materials movement = 150 batches × 6 = 900

Machine hours = 15,000 units × 0.1 = 1,500

Step 3: Compute the Activity Based Overheads Cost for Product Nova Shaft

Activity	*Cost Driver*	*Cost/ Cost Driver Unit ₹*	*Activities Cost Driver rate*	*Total Cost*
Purchasing	Purchage orders	50	25 order × ₹ 50	₹ 1,250
Setting	Batches produced	40	150 batches × ₹ 40	₹ 6,000
Material handling	Material movements	12	900 movement × ₹ 12	₹ 10,800
Inspection	Batches produced	25	150 batches × ₹ 25	₹ 3,750
Machining	Machine hours	3	1,500 hours × ₹ 3	₹ 4,500
				₹ 26,300

(ii) Compution of Budgeted Overheads Costs for Product Nova Shaft using Absorption Costing

Budgeted overheads = (₹ 75,000 + ₹ 96,000 + ₹ 112,000 + ₹ 70,000 + ₹ 150,000) = ₹ 503,000

Budgeted absorption cost/machine hour = ₹ 503,000 / 50,000 = ₹ 10.06

Budgeted machining hours for Product Nova Shaft = 1,500

Budgeted absorbed overhead = 1,500 × ₹ 10.06 = ₹ 15,090

(iii) Ways in which the Company can Reduce the activity-based Cost for Product Nova Shaft:

- Reduce the number of batches by increasing the batch size which will then reduce the setting up overhead, materials handling and inspection costs.

- Reduce the number of purchase orders
- Innovate ways of speeding up production so that the machining hours are reduced.

Illustrative Problem 14

A company manufactures three types of products namely P, Q and R. The data relating to a period are as under:

	P	*Q*	*R*
Machine hours per unit	10	18	14
Direct labour hours per unit @ ₹ 20	4	12	8
Direct Material per unit (₹)	90	80	120
Production (units)	3,000	5,000	20,000

Currently, the company uses traditional costing method and absorbs all production overheads on the basis of machine hours. The machine hour rate of overheads is ₹ 6 per hour.

The company proposes to use activity-based costing system and the activity analysis is as under:

	P	*Q*	*R*
Batch size (units)	150	500	1,000
Number of purchase orders per batch	3	10	8
Number of inspections per batch	5	4	3

The total production overheads are analysed as under:

Machine set up costs	20%
Machine operation costs	30%
Inspection costs	40%
Material procurement related costs	10%

Required:

(i) Calculate the cost per unit of each product using traditional method of absorbing all production overheads on the basis of machine hours.

(ii) Calculate the cost per unit of each product using activity-based costing principles:

Solution:

(i) Cost per unit using traditional method of absorbing all production overheads on the basis of machine hours:

Products	*P*	*Q*	*R*
	₹	₹	₹
Direct materials	90	80	120
Direct labour (4:12:8 hours) × ₹ 20	80	240	160
Production Overheads (10:18:14 hours) × ₹ 6	60	108	84
Cost per unit	230	428	364

(ii) 1. Cost per unit of each product using activity based costing:

	Products	*P*	*Q*	*R*	*Total*
A.	Production (units)	3,000	5,000	20,000	
B.	Batch size (units)	150	500	1000	
C.	Number of batches [A ÷ B]	20	10	20	50
D.	Number of purtchase order per batch	3	10	8	
E.	Total purchase orders [C × D]	60	100	160	320
F.	Number of inspections per batch	5	4	3	
G.	Total inspections [C × F]	100	40	60	200

2. Total Production overhead

		P	Q	R
A.	Machine hours per unit	10	18	14
B.	Production units	3,000	5,000	20,000
C.	Total machine hours [A × B]	30,000	90,000	2,80,000

Total machine hours = 4,00,000

Total production overheads = 4,00,000 × ₹ 6 = ₹ 24,00,000.

3. Cost driver rates:

Cost Pool	*%*	*Overheads* ₹	*Cost Driver Units*	*Cost Driver Rate* ₹
Set up	20%	4,80,000	50	9,600 per set up
Inspection	40%	9,60,000	200	4,800 per inspection
Purchases	10%	2,40,000	320	750 per purchase
Machine hours	30%	7,20,000	4,00,000	1.80 per Machine Hour

4. Cost per unit of P, Q and R:

Products	*P*	*Q*	*R*
Production (units)	3,000	5,000	20,000
	₹	₹	₹
Direct Materials (90:80:120)	2,70,000	4,00,000	24,00,000
Direct Labour (80:240:160)	2,40,000	12,00,000	32,00,000
Overheads:			
Machine related costs @ ₹ 1.80/hour (30,000:90, 000:2, 80,000)	54,000	1,62,000	5,04,000
Set-up cost @ ₹ 9600/ set up (20:10:20)	1,92,000	96,000	1,92,000
Inspection costs @ ₹ 4800/ inspection (100:40:60)	4,80,000	1,92,000	2,88,000
Purchase ralated costs @ ₹ 750/ purchase (60:100:160)	45,000	75,000	1,20,000
Total costs	12,81,000	21,25,000	67,04,000
Costs per unit (Total cost ÷ units)	427.00	425.00	335.20

Illustrative Problem 15

ABC Bank is examining the profitability of its Premier Account, a combined Savings and Cheque account. Depositors receive a 7% annual interest on their average deposit. ABC Bank earns an interest rate spread of 3% (the difference between the rate at which it lends money and rate it pays to depositors) by lending money for home loan purpose at 10%.

The Premier' Account allows depositors unlimited use of services such as deposits, withdrawals, cheque facility, and foreign currency drafts. Depositors with Premier Account balances of ₹ 50,000 or more receive unlimited free use of services. Depositors with minimum balance of less than ₹ 50,000 pay ₹ 1,000-a-month service fee for their Premier Account. -

ABC Bank recently conducted an activity-based costing study of its services. The use of these services in 2016-17 by three customers is as follows:

	Activity-Based Cost Per Transaction	***Account***	***Usage***	
		Customer X	***Customer Y***	***Customer Z***
	₹	₹	₹	₹
Deposits/withdrawal with teller	125	40	50	5
Deposits/withdrawal with automatic teller machine (ATM)	40	10	20	16
Deposits/withdrawal on pre-arranged monthly basis	25	0	12	60
Bank Cheques written	400	9	3	2
Foreign Currency drafts	600	4	1	6
Inquiries about Account balance	75	10	18	9
Average Premier Account balance for 2016-17		55,000	40,000	12,50,000

Assume Customer X and Z always maintains a balance above ₹ 50,000, whereas Customer Y always has a balance below ₹ 50,000.

Required:

(*i*) Compute the 2016-17 profitability of the customers X, Y and Z Premier Account at ABC Bank.

(*ii*) What evidence is there of cross-subsidisation among the three Premier Accounts? Why might ABC Bank worry about this cross-subsidisation, if the Premier Account product offering is profitable as a whole?

(*iii*) What changes would you recommend for ABC Bank's Premier Account?

Solution:

(*i*) Customer Profitability Analysis

ABC Bank — Premier Account

Activity	***Activity based cost***	***Customers***		
		X	***Y***	***Z***
		₹	₹	₹
Deposits/withdrawal with teller	125	5,000 (40 × 125)	6,250 (50 × 125)	625 (5 × 125)

Deposits/withdrawal with ATM	40	400 (10 × 40)	800 (20 × 40)	640 (16 × 40)
Deposits/withdrawal on prearranged monthly basis	25	0 (0 × 25)	300 (12 × 25)	1,500 (60 × 25)
Bank cheques written	400	3,600 (9 × 400)	1,200 (3 × 400)	800 (2 × 400)
Foreign currency drafts	600	2,400 (4 × 600)	600 (1 × 600)	3,600 (6 × 600)
Inquiries about Account balance	75	750 (10 × 75)	1,350 (18 × 75)	675 (9 × 75)
Customer cost (A)		**12,150**	**10,500**	**7,840**
Spread on Average balance maintained	3%	1,650 (3% × 55,000)	1,200 (3% × 40,000)	37,500 (3% × 12,50,000)
Service fees	₹ 1,000 p.m.		12,000	
Customer benefit		**1,650**	**13,200**	**37,500**
Customer Profitability (Benefits – Costs)		(10,500)	2,700	29,660

(*ii*) Customer *Z* is most profitable and is cross-subsidising the most demanding customer X. Customer *Y* is paying for the services used, because of not being able to maintain minimum balance. No doubt, 'Premier Account' product offering is profitable as a whole, but the worry is of not finding customers like customer *Z* who will maintain a balance higher than the stipulated minimum. It appears, the minimum balance stipulated is inadequate considering the services availed by depositors in 'Premium Account'.

(*iii*) The changes suggested to ABC Bank's 'Premier Account' are as follows:

- Increase the requirement of minimum balance from ₹ 50,000 to ₹ 1,00,000.
- Charge for value added services like Foreign Currency Drafts.
- Do not allow deposits/withdrawal below ₹ 10,000 at the teller. Only ATM machine withdrawal be allowed.
- Inquiries about account balance to be entertained only through Phone Banking/ATM.

Illustrative Problem 16

A company produces three products A, B and C for which the standard costs and quantities per unit are as follows:

Products	**A**	**B**	**C**
Quantity produced	10,000	20,000	30,000
Direct material/p.u. (₹)	50	40	30
Direct labour/p.u. (₹)	30	40	50

Labour hours/p.u.	3	4	5
Machine hours/p.u.	4	4	7
No. of purchase requisitions	1,200	1,800	2,000
No. of set ups	240	260	300

Production overhead split by department — Department 1 = ₹ 11,00,000

— Department 2 = ₹ 15,00,000

Department 1 is labour intensive and Department 2 is machine intensive

Total labour hours in Department 1 = 1,83,333

Total machine hours in Department 2 = 5,00,000

Production overhead split by activity	— Receiving/inspecting	₹ 14,00,000
	— Production scheduling/machine set up	₹ 12,00,000
		₹ 26,00,000

Number of batches received/inspected = 5,000

Number of batches for scheduling and set-up = 800

You are required to:

(i) Prepare Product Cost Statement under traditional absorption costing and Activity Based Costing method.

(ii) Compare the results under two methods. (CA Final)

Soluton:

Traditional absorption costing

Absorption rates:

$$\text{Department 1} = \frac{₹\,11{,}00{,}000}{1{,}83{,}333 \text{ labour hours}} = ₹\,6 \text{ per labour hour}$$

$$\text{Department 2} = \frac{₹\,15{,}00{,}000}{5{,}00{,}000 \text{ machine hours}} = ₹\,3 \text{ per machine hour}$$

Product cost statement

Products	A (₹)	B (₹)	C (₹)
Direct materials	50	40	30
Direct labour	30	40	50
Overhead:			
Department 1	18 (3 hrs × ₹ 6)	24 (4 hrs × ₹ 6)	30 (5 hrs × ₹ 6)
Department 2	12 (4 hrs × ₹ 3)	12 (4 hrs × ₹ 3)	21 (7 hrs × ₹ 3)
Total cost p.u.	110	116	131

Activity-based costing

Cost driver rates:

Receiving/inspecting $= \dfrac{₹\,14{,}00{,}000}{5{,}000 \text{ (No. of batches received/inspected)}}$

$= ₹\,280$ per requsition

Production scheduling/Machine set ups $= \dfrac{₹\,12{,}00{,}000}{800 \text{ (No. of setups)}} = ₹\,1{,}500$ per set up

Product cost statement (per unit)

Products	A (₹)	B (₹)	C (₹)
Direct materials (₹)	50	40	30
Direct labour (₹)	30	40	50
Overhead:			
Receiving	34*	25	19
Production scheduling	36**	20	15
Total cost per unit	150	125	114

{₹ 280 × 1,200) ÷ 10,000 units = ₹ 34*; similarly ₹ 25 and ₹ 19

{₹ 1,500 × 240) ÷ 10,000 units = ₹ 36**; similarly ₹ 20 and ₹ 15

	A	B	C
Traditional System	110.00	116.00	131.00
ABC	150.00	125.00	114.00
Difference	(40.00)	(9.00)	17.00

The two absorption methods produce different results. Product C appears to be much more expensive using the traditional method than it does with ABC, while product A is the opposite. If it is assumed that ABC is more accurate, which it may or may not be, then product C would be overpriced on the traditional method and sales would presumably be poor as a consequence-assuming competitors supply more cheaply. Product A would be the opposite: sales would be high and it is possible that the company would unknowingly make a loss per unit on product A.

Illustrative Problem 17

Apollo Test Laboratories does Heat Testing (HT) and Stress Testing (ST) on materials. Under its current costing system, Apollo aggregates all operating costs of ₹ 1,20,00,000 into a single overhead cost pool. Apollo calculates a rate per test-hour of ₹ 150 (₹ 1,20,00,000/80,000 total test-hours). HT uses 50,000 test-hours, and ST uses 30,000 test-hours. Apollo controller believes that there is enough variation in test procedures and cost structures to establish separate costing and billing rates for HT and ST. The market for test services is becoming competitive. Without this information, any miscosting and mispricing of its services could causes Apollo to lose business. Vikas divides Apollo's costs into four activity-cost categories.

a. Direct-labour costs, ₹ 24,00,000. These costs can be directly traced to HT, ₹ 18,00,000 and ST ₹ 6,00,000.

b. Equipment-related costs (rent, maintenance, energy, and so on), ₹ 40,00,000. These costs are allocated to HT and ST on the basis of test-hours.

c. Setup costs, ₹ 35,00,000. These costs are allocated to HT and ST on the basis of the number of setup-hours required. HT requires 13,500 setup-hours, and ST required 4,000 setup-hours.

d. Costs of designing tests, ₹ 21,00,000. These costs are allocated to HT and ST on the basis of the time required to design the tests. HT requires 2,800 hours, and ST requires 1,400 hours.

Required:

(i) Classify each activity cost as output unit-level, batch-level, product or service-sustaining, or facility sustaining.

(ii) Calculate the cost per test-hour for HT and ST. Explain briefly the reasons why these numbers differ from ₹ 150 per test-hour that Apollo calculated using its existing costing system.

(iii) Explain the accuracy of the product costs calculated using the existing costing system and the ABC system. How might Apollo's management use the cost hierarchy and ABC information to manage its business better?

Solution:

(i) Output unit-level costs

Direct-labour costs, ₹ 24,00,000

Equipment-related costs (rent, maintenance, energy, and so on), ₹ 40,00,000

These costs are output unit-level costs because they are incurred on each unit of materials tested, that is, for every hour of testing.

Batch-level costs

Setup costs, ₹ 35,00,000

These costs are batch-level costs because they are incurred each time a batch of materials is set up for either HT or ST, regardless of the number of hours for which the tests are subsequently run.

Service-sustaining costs

Costs of designing tests, ₹ 21,00,000.

These costs are service-sustaining costs because they are incurred to design the HT and ST tests, regardless of the number of batches tested or the number of hours of test time.

(ii)

Particulars	*Heat Testing (HT)* Total(1)	Per Hour(2) (1) ÷ 50,000	*Stress Testing (ST)* Total (3)	Per Hour (4) (3) ÷ 30,000
Direct labour costs (given)	₹ 18,00,000	₹ 36	₹ 6,00,000	₹ 20
Equipment-related costs				
₹ 50 per hour × 50,000 hours				
₹ 50 per hour* × 30,000 hours	25,00,000	50	15,00,000	50
*₹ 40,00,000 ÷				

(50,000 + 30,000 hour) = ₹ 50 per test hour				
Setup Costs				
₹ 200 per setup-hour × 13,500 setup-hour ₹ 200 per setup-hour × 40,000 setup-hours	27,00,000	54	8,00,000	26.67
(₹ 35,00,00) ÷ (13,500 + 4,000) set up hours = ₹ 200 per set up hour				
Costs of designing tests				
₹ 500 per hour × 2,800 hours ₹ 500 per hour × 1,400 hours	14,00,000	28	7,00,000	23.33
*₹ 21,00,000 ÷ (2,800 + 1,400) hours = ₹ 500 per hour				
Total costs	84,00,000	168	36,00,000	120

At a cost per test-hour of ₹ 150, the existing costing system undercosts heat testing (₹ 18) and overcosts stress testing (₹ 30). The reason is that heat testing uses direct labor, setup, and design resources per hour more intensively than stress testing. Heat tests are more complex, take longer to set up, and are more difficult to design. The existing costing system assumes that testing costs per hour are the same for heat testing and stress testing.

(iii) The ABC system better captures the resources needed for heat testing and stress testing because it identifies all the various activities undertaken when performing the test and recognizes the levels of the cost hierarchy at which costs vary.

Apollo's management can use the information from the ABC system to make better pricing and product mix decisions. For example, it might decide to increase the prices charged for the more costly heat testing and consider reducing prices on the less costly stress testing. Apollo should watch if competitors are underbidding Apollo in stress testing, and causing it to lose business. Apollo can also use ABC information to reduce costs by eliminating processes and activities that do not add value, identifying and evaluating new methods to do testing that reduce the activities needed to do the tests, reducing the costs of doing various activities, and planning and managing activities.

Illustrative Problem 18

Sujata Co. sells two versions, Deluxe and Premium, of his firm's only product, the GoGoJuicer. The GoGoJuicer uses patented technology to extract the last drop of juice from most fruits. The Premium version can handle larger fruit and has more options relative to the Deluxe version. The following table provides the financial results for the most recent year of operations. Labour costs ₹ 16 per hour, and each product requires one hour of labour. Sujata currently allocates all fixed manufacturing costs to products, using labour hours as the allocation basis. It also allocates all fixed selling and administrative expenses, using revenue as the allocation basis.

Units	Deluxe 90,000	Premium 10,000	Total 100,000
Revenue	₹ 63,00,000	₹ 9,00,000	₹ 72,00,000
Materials	10,80,000	2,50,000	13,30,000
Labour	14,40,000	1,60,000	16,00,000
Contribution margin	₹ 37,80,000	₹ 4,90,000	42,70,000
Allocated fixed manufacturing costs	34,20,000	3,80,000	38,00,000
Allocated fixed selling and administrative expenses	2,51,563	35,937	2,87,500
Profit margin	₹ 1,80,437	₹ 74,063	₹ 1,82,500
Unit profit margin	₹ 1.2048	₹ 7.4063	

Required:

(a) Although the unit profit margin of the Deluxe Juicer is rather low, Sujata, the managing director, believes that it is important to keep this model in the product mix. However, Sujata believes that she can tailor her promotion and sales strategies to improve the sales mix to a 6:4 ratio from the current 9:1 ratio of Deluxe to Premium juicers, with total volume staying the same at 100,000 units. Using the current fixed manufacturing costs activity rate and the current fixed selling and administrative costs activity rate, compute Sujata's expected profit if sales change to 60,000 Deluxe Juicers and 40,000 Premium Juicers.

(b) Sujata is pleased to discover that, as per the existing costs estimates, the new sales mix is expected to more than double her profit. When Sujata shares her insight with his staff, they express some reservations. Her production manager, Debra, indicates that ₹ 11 lakhs of the ₹ 38 lakhs in fixed manufacturing costs (approximately 30%) pertains to batch-related activities such as scheduling production runs. Because the Premium Juicer is run in smaller batches (250 per batch rather than 500 per batch for the Deluxe model), she conjectures that fixed manufacturing costs are unlikely to stay at ₹ 38 lakhs if the sales mix changes as proposed. Likewise, Bijoy, the marketing manager, indicates that while it takes 10 sales visits to sell 1,000 units of the Deluxe Juicer, it takes 25 visits to sell 1,000 Premium Juicers. Reverting to the original problem data, determine the cost per batch if ₹ 11 lakhs of fixed manufacturing costs relate to batch-level activities. It addition, determine the cost per sales visit if all selling and administrative costs are allocated using sales visits, rather than revenue, as the cost driver. Finally, determine the activity rate per labour hour for the remaining fixed manufacturing costs of ₹ 27 lakhs.

(c) Using the original product mix (i.e., 90,000 Deluxe Juicers and 10,000 Premium Juicers), determine Sujata's expected profit using the three cost pools and cost drivers you derived in part (b). Compare your profit estimate sith Sujata current profit of ₹ 182,500.

(d) Using the proposed product mix (i.e. ₹ 60,000 Deluxe and 40,000 Premium Juicers), determine Sujata's expected profit using the three cost pools and cost drivers you derived in part (a) How does this profit estimate compare to the profit you computed in part (a)?

Solution:

(a) The current fixed manufacturing costs activity rate = ₹ 38,00,000/1,00,000 labour hours = ₹ 38 per labour hour. (Because each product requires 1 hour of labour, the total labour hours equals the total number of units produced). The current fixed selling and administrative expenses activity rate = ₹ 2,87,500/₹ 72,00,000 = ₹ 0.03993 per ₹ 1 of revenue. Finally, we calculate the unit prices, materials, and labour costs by dividing revenue, materials costs, and labour costs by the number of units. For example, the materials cost per unit of a premium juicer = ₹ 2,50,000/10,000 units = ₹ 25 per unit.

The following tables provides the income statement for the new product mix:

	Deluxe	Premium	Total
Units	**60,000**	**40,000**	**100,000**
Revenue	₹ 42,00,000	₹ 36,00,000	₹ 78,00,000[2]
Materials	7,20,000	10,00,000	17,20,000[3]
Labour	9,60,000	6,40,000	16,00,000[4]
Contribution margin	₹ 25,20,000	₹ 19,60,000	₹ 44,80,000
Allocated fixed manufacturing costs	22,80,000	15,20,000	38,00,000[5]
Allocated fixed selling and administrative expenses	1,67,706	1,43,748	3,11,454[6]
Profit margin	₹ 72,294	₹ 2,96,252	₹ 3,68,546

[1] 100,000 units sold in a 6 : 4 ratio

[2] (60,000 Deluxe × ₹ 70 per unit) + (40,000 Premium × ₹ 90 per unit)

[3] (60,000 Deluxe × ₹ 12 per unit) + (40,000 Premium × ₹ 25 per unit)

[4] (60,000 Deluxe × ₹ 16 per unit) + (40,000 Premium × ₹ 16 per unit)

[5] (60,000 Deluxe × 1 hour × ₹ 38 per hour) + (40,000 Premium × 1 hour/unit × ₹ 38 per hour)

[6] (42,00,000 × ₹ 0.03993) + (₹ 36,00,000 × ₹ 0.03993)

Notice that we also could have used the unit profit margins to calculate expected profit under the proposed product mix. Specifically, ₹ 368,546 ≈ (60,000 × ₹ 1.2048) + (40,000 × ₹ 7.4063).

Note: The total profit numbers do not agree by ₹ 6 due to rounding of the selling and administrative costs in the summary table.

(b) We now have three cost pools instead of two. We have split the fixed manufacturing costs into two pools: batch costs (allocated by the number of batches) and other manufacturing costs (allocated by labour hours). We also have changed the cost driver for selling costs from revenue to the number of sales visits. We have:

Total number of batches: (90,000 deluxe unit/500 unit per batch) + (10,000 premium unit/250 unit per batch) = 220 batches

Total number of sales visits: [(90,000 deluxe units/1,000) × 10] + [(10,000 premium units/1,000) × 25] = 1,150 visits

Using these estimates of activity volumes, we have:

Rate per batch = ₹ 11,00,000/220 = ₹ 5,000 per batch

Rate per labor hour = ₹ 27,00,000/1,00,000 labor hours = ₹ 27 per labor hour

Rate per sales visit = ₹ 2,87,500/1,150 visits = ₹ 250 per visit

(c) The following table provides the income statement for the old product mix with the new cost pools and cost drivers:

Units	Deluxe 90,000	Premium 10,000	Total 100,000[1]
Revenue	₹ 63,00,000	₹ 9,00,000	₹ 72,00,000[2]
Materials	10,80,000	2,50,000	13,30,000[3]
Labor	14,40,000	1,60,000	16,00,000[4]
Unit-related fixed manufacturing costs	24,30,000	2,70,000	27,00,000[5]
Batch-related fixed manufacturing costs	9,00,000	2,00,000	11,00,000[6]
Fixed selling and administrative expenses	2,25,000	62,500	2,87,500[7]
Profit margin	₹ 2,25,000	(₹ 42,500)	₹ 1,82,500

[1] 100,000 units sold in the original 9:1 ratio

[2] (90,000 Deluxe × ₹ 70 per unit) + (10,000 Premium × ₹ 90 per unit)

[3] (90,000 Deluxe × ₹ 12 per unit) + (10,000 Premium × ₹ 25 per unit)

[4] (90,000 Deluxe × ₹ 16 per unit) + (10,000 Premium × ₹ 16 per unit)

[5] (90,000 Deluxe × 1 hour × ₹ 27 per hour) + (10,000 Premium × 1 hour/unit × ₹ 27 per hour)

[6] [(90,000 Deluxe/500 units per batch) + (10,000 Premium/250 units per batch)] × ₹ 5,000 per batch

[7] [900 visits for Deluxe + 250 visits for Premium] × ₹ 250 per sales visit

Although we changed the number of cost pools and the drivers used, our profit estimate equal Sujata's original profit. The reason is that the changes in the allocation system merely redistributes the costs between the two products.

Notice, however, that the change in our allocation system dramatically alters the profit attributable to each of the two product lines. The revised data indicate that the Deluxe model is highly profitable while the Premium model loses money.

(d) The following table provides the income statement for the new product mix with the new cost pools and cost drivers.

Units	Deluxe 60,000	Premium 40,000	Total 100,000[1]
Revenue	₹ 42,00,000	₹ 36,00,000	₹ 78,00,000[2]
Materials	7,20,000	10,00,000	17,20,000[3]
Labor	9,60,000	6,40,000	16,00,000[4]
Unit-related fixed manufacturing costs	16,20,000	10,80,000	27,00,000[5]
Batch-related fixed manufacturing costs	6,00,000	8,00,000	14,00,000[6]
Fixed selling and administrative expenses	1,50,000	2,50,000	4,00,000[7]
Profit margin	₹ 1,50,000	₹ (1,70,000)	₹ (20,000)

[1] 100,000 units sold in the proposed 6:4 ratio

[2] (60,000 Deluxe × ₹ 70 per unit) + (40,000 Premium × ₹ 90 per unit)

[3] (60,000 Deluxe × ₹ 12 per unit) + (40,000 Premium × ₹ 25 per unit)

[4] (60,000 Deluxe × ₹ 16 per unit) + (40,000 Premium × ₹ 16 per unit)

[5] (60,000 Deluxe × 1 hour × ₹ 27 per hour) + (40,000 Premium × 1 hour/unit × ₹ 27 per hour)

[6] [(60,000 Deluxe/500 units per batch) + (40,000 Premium/250 units per batch)] × ₹ 5,000 per batch

[7] [600 visits for Deluxe + 1,000 visits for Premium] × ₹ 250 per sales visit

Our revised profit estimate clearly shows that it is unwise to change the product mix to favor the premium model.

The old method for estimating capacity costs used unit-level drivers only. Thus, most of the capacity costs are allocated to the Deluxe line because it accounts for most of the labor costs and units. Consequently, when Sujata projects future capacity costs, her estimates do not change much. After all, the total volume in terms of labor hours and in terms of units has not changed. However, the detailed activity analysis information provided by Debra and Bijoy indicate a significant increase in the activities needed to support the new product mix. The increase in activity volume will naturally trigger an increase in capacity costs. By partitioning the capacity costs into smaller pools and using cost drivers that capture the underlying activities, the revised cost system provides a better estimate of the capacity costs needed to support the new product mix.

Illustrative Problem 19

The following information provides details of the costs, volume and cost drivers for a particular period in respect of ABC Co. a hypothetical company:

	Product X	Product Y	Product Z	Total
1. Production and sales (units)	30,000	20,000	8,000	
2. Raw material usage (units)	5	5	11	
3. Direct material cost	₹ 25	₹ 20	₹ 11	₹ 1,238,000
4. Direct labour hours	1⅓	2	1	88,000
5. Machine hours	1⅓	1	2	76,000
6. Direct labour cost	₹ 8	₹ 12	₹ 6	
7. Number of production runs	3	7	20	30
8. Number of deliveries	9	3	20	32
9. Number of recepits (2 × 7)[a]	15	35	220	270
10. Number of production orders	15	10	25	50
11. Overhead costs:				
Set-up	30,000			
Machines	7,60,000			
Receiving	4,35,000			
Packing	2,50,000			
Engineering	3,73,000			
	₹ 18,48,000			

[a]The company operates a just-in-time inventory policy, and receives each component once per production run.

In the past the company has allocated overheads to products on the basis of direct labour hours.

However, the majority of overheads are more closely related to machine hours than direct labour hours.

The company has recently redesigned its cost system by recovering overheads using two volume-related bases: machine hours and a materials handling overhead rate for recovering overheads of the receiving department. Both the current and the previous cost system reported low profit margins for product X, which is the company's highest-selling product. The management accountant has recently attended a conference on activity-based costing, and the overhead costs for the last period have been analysed by the major activities in order to compute activity-based costs.

Required:

(a) Compute the product costs using a traditional volume-related costing system based on the assumptions that:

(i) All overheads are recovered on the basis of direct labour hours (i.e. the company's past product costing system);

(ii) The overheads of the receiving department are recovered by a materials handling overhead rate and the remaining overheads are recovered using a machine hour rate (i.e. the company's current costing system).

(b) Compute product costs using an activity-based costing system.

(c) Briefly explain the differences between the product cost computations in (a) and (b).

Solution:

(a) (i)

$$\text{Direct labour overhead rate} = \frac{\text{total overheads (₹ 18,48,000)}}{\text{total direct labour hours (88,000)}}$$

$$= \text{₹ 21 per direct labour hour}$$

Product costs

Product	**X** (₹)	**Y** (₹)	**Z** (₹)
Dirct labour	8	12	6
Direct materials	25	20	11
Overhead[a]	28	42	21
Total cost	61	74	38

Note:

[a]X = 1⅓ hours × ₹ 21

Y = 2 hours × ₹ 21

Z = 1 hour × ₹ 21

(ii) Materials handling

$$\text{Overhead rate} = \frac{\text{receiving department overheads (₹ 4,35,000)}}{\text{direct material cost (₹ 12,38,000)}}$$

$$= 35.14\% \text{ of direct material cost}$$

$$\text{Machine hour overhead rate} = \frac{\text{other overheads (₹ 14,13,000)}}{\text{76,000 machine hours}}$$

$$= \text{₹ 18.59 per machine hour}$$

Product costs

Product	**X** (₹)	**Y** (₹)	**Z** (₹)
Direct labour	8.00	12.00	6.00
Direct materials	25.00	20.00	11.00
Materials handling overhead	8.78 (₹ 25 × 35.14%)	7.03 (₹ 20 × 35.14%)	3.87 (₹ 11 × 35.14%)
Other overheads[a] (machine hour basis)	24.79	18.59	37.18
Total cost	66.57	57.62	58.05

Note:

[a]X = 1⅓ × ₹ 18.59

Y = 1 × ₹ 18.59

Z = 2 × ₹ 18.59

(b) The cost per transaction or activity for each of the cost centres is as follows:

Set-up cost

$$\text{Cost per setup} = \frac{\text{setup cost (₹ 30,000)}}{\text{number of production runs (30)}} = \text{₹ 1,000}$$

Receiving

$$\text{Cost per receiving order} = \frac{\text{receiving cost (₹ 4,35,000)}}{\text{number of order (270)}} = \text{₹ 1,611}$$

Packing

$$\text{Cost per packing order} = \frac{\text{packing cost (₹ 2,50,000)}}{\text{number of order (32)}} = \text{₹ 7,812}$$

Engineering

$$\text{Cost per production order} = \frac{\text{engineering cost (₹ 3,73,000)}}{\text{number of production orders (50)}} = \text{₹ 7,460}$$

The total set-up cost for the period was ₹ 30,000 and the cost per transaction or activity for the period is ₹ 1,000 per set-up. Product X required three production runs, and thus ₹ 3,000 of the set-up cost is traced to the production of product X for the period. Thus the cost per set-up per unit produced for product X is ₹ 0.10 (₹ 3000/30,000 units).

Similarly, product Z required 20 set-ups, and so ₹ 20,000 is traced to product Z. Hence the cost per set-up for product Z is ₹ 2.50 (₹ 20,000/8,000) units).

The share of a support department's cost that is traced to each unit of output for each product is therefore calculated as follows:

$$\text{cost per transaction} \times \frac{\text{number of transactions per product}}{\text{number of units produced}}$$

The unit standard costs for products X, Y and Z using an activity-based costing system are:

	X	Y	Z
Direct labour	₹ 8.00	₹ 12.00	₹ 6.00
Direct materials	25.00	20.00	11.00
Machine overhead[a]	13.33	10.00	20.00
Set-up costs	0.10	0.35	2.50
Receiving[b]	0.81	2.82	44.30
Packing[c]	2.34	1.17	19.53
Engineering[d]	3.73	3.73	23.31
Total manufacturing cost	53.31	50.07	126.64

Notes:

[a]Machine hours × machine overhead rate (₹ 760,000/76,000 hrs)

[b]X = (₹ 1611 × 15)/30,000

Y = (₹ 1611 × 35)/20,000

Z = (₹ 1611 × 220)/8,000

[c]X = (₹ 7812 × 9)/30,000

Y = (₹ 7812 × 3)/20,000

Z = (₹ 7812 × 20)/8,000

[d]X = (₹ 7460 × 15)/30,000

Y = (₹ 7460 × 10)/20,000

Z = (₹ 7460 × 25)/8,000

(c) The traditional product costing system assumes that products consume resources in relation to volume measures such as direct labour, direct materials or machine hours. The activity-based system recognizes that some overheads are unrelated to production volume, and uses cost drivers that are independent of production volume. For example, the activity-based system assigns the following percentage of costs to product Z, the low volume product:

Set-up-related cost	66.67%	(20 out of 30 set-ups)
Delivery-related costs	62.5%	(20 out of 32 deliveries)
Receiving costs	81.5%	(220 out of 270 receiving orders)
Engineering-related costs	50%	(25 out of 50 production orders)

In contrast, the current costing system assigns the cost of the above activities according to production volume, measured in machine hours. The total machine hours are:

Product X 40,000 (30,000 × 1⅓)

Product Y 20,000 (20,000 × 1)

Product Z 16,000 (8,000 × 2)

76,000

Therefore 21% (16,000/76,000) of the non-volume-related costs are assigned to product Z if machine hours are used as the allocation base. Hence the traditional system undercosts the low-volume product, and, on applying the above approach, it can be shown that the high-volume product (product X) is overcosted. *For example*, 53% of the costs (40,000/76,000) are traced to product X with the current system, whereas the activity-based system assigns a much lower proportion of non-volume-related costs to this product.

REFERENCES

1. Don R. Hansen and Maryanne M. Mowen, *Management Accounting*, Thomson South Western, 2005, p. 118.
2. Edward J. Blocher, Kung H. Chen, Gary Cokins and Thoms W. Lin, *Cost Management*, Tata Mc Graw Hill, 2005, pp. 134-135.
3. Ronald W. Hilton, *Managerial Accounting*, Tata Mc Graw Hill, 2005, pp. 182-183.
4. John A. Milter, *Implementing Activity-Based Management in Daily Operations*, John Wiley & Sons, 1996, p. 54.
5. Wayne J. Morse, James R. Davis, AL.L. Hartgraves, *Management Accounting, A Strategic* Approach, South Western College Publishing, 2000, p. 16.
6. John A. Miller, Ibid, p. 66.
7. Hugh Combs, David Hobbs and Ellis Jen Kins, *Management Accounting, Principles and Applications*, 2005, p. 67.
8. Edward J.Blocher, Kung H. Chem, Gary Cokind and Thomas W. Lin, Ibid, p. 138.
9. Colin Drury, *Management and Cost Accounting*, Thomson Learning, 2000, p. 285.
10. Roman L. Weil and Michael W. Maher, *Handbook of Cost Management*, John Willy and Sons, 2005, p. 23.
11. R. S. Kaplan and R. C. Cooper, "Cost and Effect, Using Integrated Systems to Drive Profitability and Performance", Harvard Business School Press, 1998.
12. R. S. Kaplan and R. Cooper, Ibid.
13. Colin Drury and M. Tayler, "Cost Systems Design and Profitability Analysis in UK Companies, Chartered Institute of Management Accountants", 2000.
14. Michael C.O'Guin, *The Complete Guide to activity-based costing*, Prentice Hall, New Jersey, 1991, pp. 128-130.
15. Ray H. Garrison, Eric W. Noreen and Peter C. Brewer, *Managerial Accounting*, 13th Edition, McGrawHill Education (India) Private Ltd., 2011, p. 312.
16. Ray H. Garrison, Eric W. Noreen and Peter C. Brewer, Ibid, pp. 332-333.

CRITICAL ANALYSIS AND DISCUSSION QUESTIONS, SELF-ASSESSMENT QUESTIONS, MULTIPLE CHOICE QUESTIONS, PROBLEMS, AND CASES

CRITICAL ANALYSIS AND DISCUSSION QUESTIONS

1. What is activity-based costing? Why is it needed?
2. What is a cost driver? What is the role of cost driver in tracing costs to products? (*M. Com., Delhi*, 2008)
3. Explain the steps in applying activity-based costing (ABC) in a manufacturing company.
4. How are activities grouped in a manufacturing company? (*M. Com., Delhi*, 2005, 2008)
5. Distinguish between activity-based costing and traditional costing system. (*M. Com., Delhi*, 2007)
6. What are the benefits of activity-based costing? (*M. Com., Delhi*, 2007)
7. Define unit-level activities, batch-level activities, product-level activities and facility-level activities.
8. "Overhead costs are source of product cost distortion." Do you agree? Explain.
9. What are the four basic steps required for activity-based costing?
10. Give the criterion for choosing cost drivers for allocating costs to products.
11. Why are conventional product-costing systems more likely to distort product costs in highly automated plants? How do activity-based costing systems deal with such a situation?
12. "Activity-based costing systems yield more accurate product costs than conventional systems because they use more cost drivers to assign support costs to products." Do you agree with this statement? Explain.
13. What are unit-level activities? Batch-level activities? Product-level activities? Facility-level activities?
14. "Attributing direct costs and absorbing overhead costs to the product/service through an activity-based costing approach will result in a better understanding of the true cost of final output." You are required to explain and comment on the above statement.
15. What is an activity-based approach to designing a costing system?
16. Describe four levels of cost hierarchy.
17. What are the key reasons for product cost differences between traditional costing systems and ABC systems.
18. "ABC systems only apply to manufacturing companies." Do you agree? Explain.
19. "Activity-based costing is the wave of the present and the future. All companies should adopt it." Do you agree? Explain.
20. The following are six cost pools established for a company using activity-based costing. The pools are related to the company's product using cost drivers:

Cost Pools:

(*a*) Inspection of raw materials

(*b*) Production equipment repairs and maintenance

(*c*) Raw materials storage
(*d*) Plant heat, light, water and power
(*e*) Finished product quality control
(*f*) Production line setups

Required:

For each of the preceding cost pools, identify a possible cost driver.

21. Explain why overcosting and undercosting products occur with traditional costing systems.
22. What is activity-based costing ? Distinguish between ABC and traditional costing system. Explain advantages of activity-based costing. (M.Com., Delhi, 2010, 2014)
23. Why might ABC be useful in a company with only one product?
24. Explain why a costing system that uses either a plant wide or a departmental overhead rate is likely to produce distorted product costs.
25. Explain why overcosting and undercosting products occur with traditional costing systems.
26. Explain how a traditional, Volume-based product costing system operates.
27. What are cost drivers? What is their role in an activity-based costing systems?
28. What is the role of an activity dictionary in an ABC project?
29. Explain why a manufacturer with diverse product lines may benefit from an ABC system?
30. Are ABC systems appropriate for the service industry?
31. Why would management be concernerd about the accuracy of product costs?
32. Under what conditions would the multiple production department factory overhead rate method provide more accurate product costs than the single plantwide factory overhead rate method?
33. Under what circumstances might the activity-based costing method provide more accurate product costs than the multiple production department factory overhead rate method?
34. How can activity-based costing be used in service companies?
35. "Activity-based costing is great for manufacturing companies but it does not really address the needs of the service sector." Do you agree? Explain.
36. "One of the lessons learned from activity-based costing is that all costs are really a function of volume." True, False, Uncertain? Explain.
37. Would you expect companies that adopt ABC to add value to shareholders? How would you measure such added value?
38. "Activity-based costing is for accountants and production managers. I plan to be a marketing manager, so ABC would not help me." Do you agree with this statement? Explain.
39. In a televised cricket game, what activities are value added? What activities are non-value added? Would everyone agree with your choices? Why or why not?
40. Are all companies likely to benefit to an equal extent from adopting ABC. Discuss.
41. What is the basis that ABC systems use to form cost pools?
42. What is the primary criterion that we should use when choosing a driver to allocate costs from an activity pool to produces?
43. Why does allocating costs using an ABC system not change the total reported income for the organization as a whole?
44. What is cross-subsidization?
45. List three ways in which a company can improve profitability using ABC data.

46. What are the two key customer-planning decisions that companies face?
47. What are the differences between product-level profit analysis and customer-level profit analysis?
48. Suppose we are choosing between two drivers to allocate the costs in the 'perform setup' cost pool: the number of setups or the number of setup hours. When will the choice not matter (i.e., will result in the same amount costs being allocated to the various products from this pool?) What factors do we need to consider when making this choice?
49. How are costs determined under activity-based costing. Explain the advantages and disadvantages of activity-based costing. (M. Com., D.U., 2012, 2015)
50. "Activity-based costing systems yield more accurate product costs than conventional systems because they use more cost drivers to assign support costs to products." Explain this statement and discuss the stages and flow of costs in activity-based costing. (M. Com., D.U., 2013)

SELF-ASSESSMENT QUESTIONS

I. Match the following lettered terms on the left with the appropriate numbered description on the right.

(*a*) Activity driver	1. Non-value-added use of time
(*b*) Cost driver analysis	2. Cost explained well by traditional cost drivers
(*c*) Cycle time	3. Driver of some costs
(*d*) Idle time	4. Time from receipt of order to delivery of product
(*e*) Long-term variable cost	5. Cost not usually assigned to products under ABC
(*f*) Mass customization	6. Personalized production
(*g*) Product complexity	7. Establishing cost causality
(*h*) Organizational-level cost	8. Measure of activity demand
(*i*) Unit-level cost	9. Indicator of activities and their time
(*j*) Value chart	10. Costs traditionally known as fixed

II. Match the following lettered terms on the left with the appropriate numbered description on the right.

(*a*) Activity analysis	1. Setup cost
(*b*) Activity-based costing	2. A costing system that uses multiple cost drivers
(*c*) Attribute-based costing	3. A process of involving all affected personnel from the beginning of a project
(*d*) Batch-level cost	4. An approach to associate costs with activities
(*e*) Manufacturing cycle efficiency	5. A tool to find the cost of product features
(*f*) Non-value-added activity	6. A flowchart indicating all steps in producing a product or performing a service
(*g*) Process map	7. Idle time, transfer time, or storage time
(*h*) Research and development	8. Actual production time divided by total cycle time
(*i*) Simultaneous engineering	9. Product/process level cost
(*j*) Value-added activity	10. Something that increases worth of a product or service

III. Match each of the following activities to the most likely activity level for a bank. Suggest a feasible cost-driver base and activity level for each.

Activity	**Activity Level**
1. Sales calls—existing commercial customers	a. Unit
2. Sales calls—new commercial customers	b. Batch
3. Commercial loan negotiation	c. Product
4. Commercial loan review	d. Customer
5. Customer file maintenance	e. Facility
6. Community involvement	
7. Employee relations	
8. Commercial loan customer service	
9. Consumer loan customer service	
10. Consumer loan review	
11. Consumer deposit/withdrawal processing	
12. Commercial deposit/withdrawal processing	
13. Advertising particular products	

Answer:

Matching activity levels and possible cost-driver bases to activities (The possible cost-driver bases are suggestions, there is often more than one correct answer).

Activity	Possible cost-driver base	Activity Level
Sales calls--existing commercial customers	No. of calls	Customer
Sales calls--new commercial customers	No. of calls	Customer
Commercial loan negotiation	No. of applications	Unit
Commercial loan review	No. of applications	Unit or Batch
Customer file maintenance	No. of customers	Customer
Community involvement	Hours of time	Facility
Employee relations	No. of employees	Facility
Commercial loan customer service	No. of commercial customers	Customer
Consumer loan customer service	No. of commercial customers	Customer
Consumer loan review	No. of applications	Unit or Batch
Consumer deposit/withdrawal processing	No. of deposits/withdrawals	Unit
Commercial deposit/withdrawal processing	No. of deposits/withdrawals	Unit
Advertising particular products	No. of products being advertised	Prosuct or Customer

MULTIPLE CHOICE QUESTIONS

Select the correct answer for the following multiple choice questions.

1. Cost drivers in activity-based costing:
   (*a*) Are always related to production volume
   (*b*) Are workers who influence cost control
   (*c*) Often assign more costs to low-volume products than traditional allocation methods.
   (*d*) None of the above
2. Most companies that use an activity-based costing systems use
   (*a*) No cost pools
   (*b*) One or two cost pools
   (*c*) Two to five cost pools
   (*d*) More than five cost pools
3. Activity-based cost systems
   (*a*) Always lead to improvements in cost control
   (*b*) Are less expensive to develop and maintain than traditional costing systems
   (*c*) Allow managers to see the costs of key activities
   (*d*) Are used to develop the full cost of products which provides clear cut information for decision making
4. In an activity-based costing system, what should be used to assign a department's manufacturing overhead costs to products produced in varying lot sizes?
   (*a*) A single cause and effect relationship
   (*b*) Multiple cause and effect relationships
   (*c*) Relative net sales values of the products
   (*d*) A product's ability to bear cost allocations
5. In an activity-based costing system, cost reduction is accomplished by identifying and eliminating

	All cost drivers	***Non-value-adding activities***
(*a*)	No	No
(*b*)	Yes	Yes
(*c*)	No	Yes
(*d*)	Yes	No

6. ABC Co.'s cost allocation and products costing procedures follow activity-based costing principles. Activities have been identified and classified as being either value-adding or non-value-adding as to each product. Which of the following activities, used in ABC Co. production process, is non-value-adding?
   (*a*) Design engineering activity (*b*) Heat treatment activity
   (*c*) Drill press activity (*d*) Raw materials storage activity
7. An accounting system that collects financial and operating data on the basis of the underlying nature and extent of the cost drivers is
   (*a*) Activity-based costing (*b*) Target costing
   (*c*) Cycle-time costing (*d*) Variable costing

8. Multiple or departmental manufacturing overhead rates are considered preferable to a single or plantwide overhead rate when
   (*a*) Manufacturing is limited to a single product flowing through identical departments in a fixed sequence.
   (*b*) Various products are manufactured that do not pass through the same departments or use the same manufacturing techniques.
   (*c*) Individual cost drivers cannot accurately be determined with respect to cause-and-effect relationships.
   (*d*) The single or plantwide rate is related to several identified cost drivers.
9. Activity-based costing (ABC) has become increasingly more feasible because of technological advances that allow managers to obtain better and more timely information at a relatively low cost. For this reason, a manufacturer is considering using barcode identification for recording information on parts used by the manufacturer. A reason to use bar codes rather than other means of identification is to ensure that
   (*a*) The movement of all parts is recorded
   (*b*) The movement of parts is easily and quickly recorded
   (*c*) Vendors use the same part numbers
   (*d*) Vendors use the same identification methods
10. Cost drivers are
    (*a*) Activities that cause costs to increase as the activity increases.
    (*b*) Accounting techniques used to control costs.
    (*c*) Accounting measurements used to evaluate whether performance is proceeding according to plan.
    (*d*) A mechanical basis, such as machine hours, computer time, size of equipment, or square footage of factory, used to assign costs to activities.
11. Process value analysis is a key component of activity-based management that links product costing and
    (*a*) Reduction of the number of cost pools
    (*b*) Continuous improvement
    (*c*) Accumulation of heterogeneous cost pools
    (*d*) Overhead rates based on broad averages
12. Which of the following statements about activity-based costing is not true?
    (*a*) Activity-based costing is useful for assigning marketing and distribution costs.
    (*b*) Activity-based costing is more likely to result in major differences from traditional costing systems if the firm manufactures only one product rather than multiple products.
    (*c*) In activity-based costing, cost drivers are what cause costs to be incurred.
    (*d*) Activity-based costing differs from traditional costing systems in that products are not cross-subsidized.
13. The use of activity-based costing normally results in
    (*a*) substantially greater unit costs for low-volume products than is reported by traditional product costing.
    (*b*) substantially lower unit costs for low-volume products than is reported by traditional product costing.
    (*c*) decreased set-up costs being charged to low-volume products.

(*d*) equalizing set-up costs for all product lines.

(*e*) making pricing decisions more difficult. (*CMA, USA, Adapted with permission*)

Answer to Multiple Choice Questions

1. (*c*)	2. (*d*)	3. (*c*)	4. (*b*)	5. (*c*)
6. (*d*)	7. (*a*)	8. (*b*)	9. (*b*)	10. (*a*)
11. (*b*)	12. (*b*)	13. (*a*)		

EXERCISES

1. The Commissioner of Municipal Corporation, Delhi is dissatisfied with rising costs and deteriorating quality of the services provided by the municipal workers, particularly in the Public Works Department; paving roads, repairing potholes, and cleaning the streets. He is contemplating privatizing these services by outsourcing the business to independent, private contractors. The Commissioner has demanded that his staff develop an activity-based cost system for municipal services. However, before proceeding with his privatization initiative, he declared, "Introducing competition and privatization to government services requires real cost information. You can't compete out if you are using fake cost." Currently, the accounting and financial systems of Delhi City report only how much is being spent in each department, by type of expenditure, payroll, benefits, materials, vehicles, equipment (including computers and telephones) and supplies. (M. Com, Delhi, 2011, 2014)

Required:

(a) Before outsourcing to the private sector, why does the Commissioner want to develop activity-based cost estimates of the current cost of performing these municipal services?

(b) After building activity-based cost models, should this information be shared with the municipal workers? Why or why not? How might the workers use ABC information?

2. Determine whether each of the following activities is likely to be value-added or non-value-added, and explain your choice.

(a) Inspection activities

(b) Moving materials to workstations

(c) Manufacturing extra inventory to keep employees busy

(d) Packing to fill a customer order

(e) Product design initiatives

3. You have been asked to analyse your brother's preschool operation to determine in what ways he can improve quality and reduce costs. You decide to analyse the activities provided by the preschool and use an ABC system to assign costs to the activities. The following list contains potential activities from which to choose.

- *Learning activities.* At times during the day, children are listening to stories, learning to sing simple songs, following simple directions as part of games or art activities, and playing interactively with special toys developed to enhance eye-hand coordination or understanding of spatial relations.
- *Resting:* The children rest on mats during this activity while one teacher monitors and the other teachers prepare lesson plans.
- *Snack and meal activities:* Snacks and meals are prepared by teachers and one food-service employee. Sometimes the students prepare their own snacks and practice following directions.

- *Free play activities:* While children play inside or outside, a few teachers monitor their progress while others prepare learning activities to be used later.
- *Art and craft activities:* These daily activities promote some of the same skills as the learning activities, but children are encouraged to be more creative.
- *Miscellaneous:* These activities include greeting the children, helping them with their dress, helping them use the restroom, interacting with parents and conferencing with parents.
- *Music activity:* This weekly activity encourages the children's interest in music and dance.
- *Conferencing with parents:* This quarterly activity consists of the head teacher (your brother) meeting with each child's parents for half an hour.

Required:

(a) Choose several activities to use for cost pools. Explain your choices.

(b) Choose cost drivers for these pools. Explain your choices.

(c) Identify possible reasons why measurement error might exist in the ABC costs.

(d) How would you estimate the increase in future costs if your brother plans to expand his operations?

4. Delhi Jal Board (DJB), Delhi offers waste management services, specializing in construction waste. DJB has two product lines: regular waste disposal and hazardous waste disposal. Because hazardous waste requires extra handling and care, DJB has specialized equipment for handling materials such as asbestos and lead-based paint.

In a typical engagement, DJB places one or more dumpsters at the client's construction site. These dumpsters are emptied every week. The dumpsters may be emptied sooner if the construction crew informs DJB that the dumpster is full. DJB then hauls the waste to the landfill, disposing of it properly. The landfill charges DJB a fee based on the number of Kilograms dumped as well as the type of waste dumped (the landfill fee for hazardous waste is higher than the fee for regular waste).

The following table lists eight costs incurred by DJB:

Cost	*Description of Cost*
1	Diesel costs for hauling waste to the landfill
2	Landfill fee for dumping regular waste
3	Landfill fee for dumping hazardous waste
4	Cost of weekly scheduled pickups
5	Annual city permit fee to handle hazardous materials
6	Cost of the truck to haul waste (DJB's truck can haul dumpsters with either regular or hazardous waste)
7	Cost of new dumpster to handle hazardous waste
8	Salary to receptionist at the DJB's office

Required:

Classify each cost as per the cost hierarchy—that is, classify each cost as being a unit, batch, product, or facility-level cost. In addition, classify each cost as being direct (D) or indirect (I) with respect to DJB's two product lines. Provide a brief rationale for each classification.

PROBLEMS

1. Sony Corporation produces two types of flat-screen televisions. The standard televisions are designed for durability. The company recently began producing the higher-quality, high-grade model to appeal to dedicated watchers. Since the introduction of the high-grade product, profits have steadily declined. Management believes that the accounting system might not be accurately allocating costs to products, particularly since sales of the high-grade product have been increasing.

   Management has asked you to investigate the cost allocating problem. You find that manufacturing overhead is currently assigned to products based on the direct-labour costs in the products. For your investigation, you have data from last month. Last month's manufacturing overhead was ₹ 22,00,000 based on the production of 3,200 standard units and 1,000 high-grade units. Direct-labour and direct-material costs were as follows:

	Standard	***High-Grade***	***Total***
Direct labour (₹)	17,40,000	6,60,000	24,00,000
Direct material (₹)	12,50,000	11,40,000	23,90,000

   Management believes that overhead costs are caused by three cost drivers. The cost drivers and their costs for last month were as follows:

		Activity Level		
Cost Driver	***Costs Assigned***	***Standard***	***High Grade***	***Total***
Number of production runs	₹ 1,000,000	40	10	50
Quality tests performed	900,000	12	18	30
Despatch orders processed	300,000	100	50	150
Total overhead	₹ 2,200,000			

Required:

a. How much of the overhead will be assigned to each product if these three cost drivers are used to allocate overhead? What is the total cost per unit produced for each product?

b. How much of the overhead was assigned to each product if direct-labour cost had been used to allocate overhead? What is the total cost per unit produced for each product?

c. How might the results from using activity-based costing in requirement (a) help management understand Sony's declining profits?

Answer :

(*a*) Total cost per unit, Standard ₹ 1359; High Grade ₹ 2640.

(*b*) Total cost per unit, Standard ₹ 1433; High Grade ₹ 2,405.

(*c*) On the basis of direct labour, the company has been understating the cost to produce High-Grade Units and therefore overstating High-Grade's profits.

2. The law firm of Sagar & Co. provides legel services for clients. During the year, corporate clients required 5,000 hours of legal services, while individuals required 3,000 hours. The firm has traditionally used direct labor hours to assign overhead.

   However, the manager believes services to businesses cost more than services to individuals and wishes to adopt activity-based costing. The firm's revenues and costs for the year are shown below:

	Corporate	Individual	Total
Revenue	₹ 150,000	₹ 150,000	₹ 300,000
Expenses:			
Lawyer's salaries	₹ 100,000	50,000	₹ 150,000
Overhead:			
Filing			10,000
Quality control			5,000
Data entry			25,000
Total overhead			₹ 40,000

The accountant has kept records of the following data for use in the new activity-based costing system:

		Activity Level	
Overhead Cost	Cost Driver	Corporate	Individual
Filing	Number of Clients	5	5
Quality control	Number of hours spent	75	75
Data entry	Number of pages entered	1,000	1,500

Required:

(a) Prepare an income statement showing profits by segments using the traditional direct-hour allocation base.

(b) Prepare an income statement showing profits by segments using the three cost drivers in the ABC mode.

(c) Discuss the best way to allocate costs in this example and include the approximate difference in profits between corporate and Individual clients. Why would Activity-based costing be preferred as a cost allocation method?

Answer:

Ans. (a) Operating profit, corporate ₹ 25,000; Individual ₹ 85,000.

(b) Profit, corporate ₹ 31,250; Individual ₹ 78,750.

(c) ABC method shows a more accurate allocation of costs based on the activity needed to earn the revenue.

3. Larsen & Toubro makes a single product—a fire-resistant commercial filing cabinet—that it sells to office furniture distributors. The company has a simple ABC system that it uses for internal decision making. The company has two overhead department whose costs are as follows.

Manufacturing overhead	₹ 5,000,000
Selling and administrative overhead	3,000,000
Total overhead costs	₹ 8,000,000

The company's ABC system has the following activity cost pools and activity measures:

Activity Cost Pool	Activity measure
Assembly units	Number of units
Processing orders	Number of orders
Supporting customers	Number of customers
Other	Not applicable

Costs assigned to the 'Other' activity cost pool have no activity measure; they consist of the costs of unused capacity and organization-sustaining cost—neither of which are assigned to order, customers, or the product.

The company distributes the costs of manufacturing overhead and of selling and admin istrative overhead to the activity cost pools based on employee interviews, the results of which are reported below:

Distribution of Resource consumption Across Activity Cost Pools

	Assembling Unit	Processing Order	Supporting Customers	Other	Total
Maunfacturing overhead	50%	35%	5%	10%	100%
Selling and administrative overhead	10%	45%	25%	20%	100%
Total activity	1,000 units	250 orders	100 customers		

Required:

(a) Perform the first-stage allocation of overhead costs to the activity cost pools.

(b) Compute activity rates for the activity cost pools.

(c) OfficeMart is one of Larsen & Toubro's customers. Last year, Office Mart ordered filing cabinets four different times. OfficeMart ordered a total of 80 filing cabinets during the year. Show the overhead costs attributable to OfficeMart.

(d) The selling price of a filing cabinet is ₹ 5950. The cost of direct materials is ₹ 1800 per filing cabinet, and direct labor is ₹ 500 per filing cabinet. What is the customer margin of OfficeMart?

Answer:

Customer margin ₹ 8400.

4. Balaji Hospital has two types of patients: normal care and intensive care. On a daily basis, both types of patients consume resources necessary for their care. For example, they occupy beds, receive nursing help, use care supplies (lotion, guaze, tissues, etc.), have bedding, towels, and clothes laundered, eat meals, etc.

Mohan Kumar, the hospital administrator, wants to calculate the cost per patient day for each type of patient.

To illustrate how daily care costs can be assigned to each type of patient, information has been gathered for nursing care. There are always four nurses on duty. There are three shifts, each lasting eight hours. Nurses work 40 hours per week and are paid an average of ₹ 45,000 per year, including benefits. Full-time nurses work 50 weeks per year. The hospital employs only one part-time nurse, who is paid ₹ 22,500 for the hours worked during the year (only the amount needed to ensure that the four-nurse coverage policy is satisfied). Assume that a year is exactly 52 weeks. During the year, normal care patients accounted for 8,000 patient days, and intensive care patients accounted for 2,000 patient days. Intensive care patients use half of the nursing care hours.

Required:

(i) Calculate the nursing cost per patient day for each patient type using patient days to assign the cost.

(ii) Calculate the nursing cost per patient day for each patient type using nursing hours used to assign the cost. Is this cost assignment more accurate than the one using patient days? Explain your reasoning.

(iii) Suppose that one nurse on each shift is dedicated to the intensive care unit and that the other three nurses provide additional help as needed. What additional information would you like to have to assign nursing costs so that a cost per patient day can be calculated for each patient type? Which of the three assignment methods are you using?

(iv) Suppose that the hospital administrator asks you to calculate the cost of laundry per patient day for each patient type. Describe how you assign laundry cost, and specify the information that would be needed to do so. Did you use direct tracing or driver tracing? Explain.

Answer:

(i) ₹ 78.75 per day (for either type of patient)

(ii) Cost per patient day, Intensive care ₹ 196.88 per day, Normal care ₹ 49.22 per day

(iii) Hours of additional usage will be needed

(iv) Total laundary costs divided by total pounds of laundary provides a rate that can be used to assign the laundary cost.

5. Zenith Co., manufactures desk lamps and floor lamps. Information regarding resources for the month of March follows:

	Resources Used	Resources Supplied
Parts Management........................	₹ 3,000	₹ 3,500
Energy........................	5,000	5,000
Quality Inspections........................	4,500	5,000
Long-term Labor........................	2,500	3,500
Short-term Labor........................	₹ 2,000	₹ 2,400
Setups........................	7,000	10,000
Materials........................	15,000	15,000
Depreciation........................	6,000	10,000
Marketing........................	7,000	7,500
Customer Service........................	1,000	2,000
Administrative........................	5,000	7,000

In addition, ₹ 2,500 was spent on 10 engineering changes with a cost driver rate of ₹ 250, and ₹,3,000 was spent on four outside contracts with a cost driver rate of ₹ 750. There was no unused capacity for these two activities. Sales for March were ₹ 100,000. Management has requested that you:

a. Prepare a traditional income statement.

b. Prepare an activity-based income statement.

c. Write a short report explaining why the activity-based income statement provides better information to manegers.

Answer:

(a) Operating profit ₹ 23,600

(b) Operating profit ₹ 23,600

(c) ABC reports provides information about resources used and those supplied which can help managers make better decisions to use resources efficiently and to lower costs.

6. ABB, Inc., produces headlamps for campers, and other people who want the convenience of a light at night without carrying a flashlight. It currently allocates overhead costs using direct-labor hours, but the controller has recommended an activity-based costing system using the following data:

Activity	*Cost Driver*	*Cost*	*Activity Level*	
			Product A	*Product B*
Production setup	Number of setups	₹ 50,000	10	15
Materials handling and requisition	Number of parts	15,000	18	36
Packaging and dispatching	Number of units dispatched	30,000	45,000	75,000
Total overhead		₹ 95,000		

Required:

a. Compute the amount of overhead to be allocated to each product under activity-based costing.

b. Compute the amount of overhead to be allocated to each product using direct-labour hours as the allocation base. Assume that the number of direct-labor hours required to assemble each unit is 0.5 per unit of Product A and 1.0 per unit of Product B. The company producted 45,000 units of Product A and 75,000 units of Product B.

c. Should the company follow the controller's recommendations?

Answer:

	Product A	*Product B*
(a) Total overhead	₹ 36,250	₹ 58,750
(b) Direct labour hours basis	₹ 21,923	₹ 73,077

(c) The ABC system should be adopted if the benefits from improved information exceed the additional costs required to obtain the information.

7. ABC Limited manufactures two radio models, the Nova which has been produced for five years and sells for ₹ 900, and the Royal, a new model introduced in early 2016, which sells for ₹ 1,140. Based on the following Income statement for the year 2016-17, a decision has been made to concentrate ABC Limited's marketing resources on the Royal model and to begin to phase out the Nova model.

ABC Limited

Income Statement for the year ending March 31, 2017

	Royal Model ₹	*Nova Model* ₹	*Total* ₹
Sales	45,60,000	1,98,00,000	2,43,60,000
Cost of Goods sold	31,92,000	1,25,40,000	1,57,32,000
Gross margin	13,68,000	72,60,000	86,28,000
Selling & Administrative Expenses	9,78,000	58,30,000	68,08,000
Net Income	3,90,000	14,30,000	18,20,000
Unit Produced and sold	4,000	22,000	
Net Income per unit sold	97.50	65	

The standard unit costs for the Royal and Nova models are as follows:

	Royal Model ₹	*Nova Model* ₹
Direct Materials	584	208
Direct Labour Royal (3.5 hrs × ₹ 12)	42	
Nova (1.5 hrs × ₹ 12)		18
Machine usage		
Royal (4 hrs × ₹ 18)	72	
Nova (8 hrs × ₹ 18)		144
Manufacturing overheads (applied on the basis of machine hours at a pre-determined rate of ₹ 25 per hour)	100	200
Standard Cost	798	570

ABC Ltd.'s Controller is advocating the use of activity-based costing and activity-based cost management and has gathered the following information about the company's manufacturing overheads cost for the year ending March 31, 2017.

Activity centre (Cost driver)	*Traceable Costs ₹*	*Number of Events*		
		Royal	*Nova*	*Total*
Soldering (Number of solder joints)	9,42,000	3,85,000	11,85,000	15,70,000
Shipments (Number of shipments)	8,60,000	3,800	16,200	20,000
Quality Control (Number of inspections)	12,40,000	21,300	56,200	77,500
Purchase orders (Number of orders)	9,50,400	1,09,980	80,100	1,90,080
Machine Power (Machine hours)	57,600	16,000	1,76,000	1,92,000
Machine setups (Number of setups)	7,50,000	14,000	16,000	30,000
Total Traceable costs	48,00,000			

Required:

(i) Prepare a Statement showing allocation of manufacturing overheads using the principles of activity-based costing.

(ii) Prepare a Statement showing product cost profitability using activity-based costing.

(iii) Should ABC Ltd. continue to emphasize the Royal model and phase out the Nova model? Discuss.

Answer:

(i) Manufacturing overhead cost per unit, Royal ₹ 409.98, Nova ₹ 143.64.

(ii) Net income, Royal, ₹ 8,49,920; Nova ₹ 26,69,920.

(iii) Nova Model should continue to be emphasised and Royal Model should not be over emphasised.

8. MNP suits is a ready-to-wear suit manufacturer. It has four customers: two wholesale-channel customers and two retail-channel customers.

MNP suits has developed the following activity-based costing system:

Activity	*Cost driver*	*Rate in 2016*
Order processing	Number of purchase orders	₹ 1,225 per order
Sales visits	Number of customer visits	₹ 7,150 per visit
Delivery-regular	Number of regular deliveries	₹ 1,500 per delivery
Delivery-rushed	Number of rushed deliveries	₹ 4,250 per delivery

List selling price per suit is ₹ 1000 and average cost per suit is ₹ 550. The CEO of MNP suits wants to evaluate the profitability of each of the four customers in 2015 to explore opportunities for increasing profitability of his company in 2016. The following data are available for 2015:

Item	*Wholesale customers*		*Retail customers*	
	W	*H*	*R*	*T*
Total number of orders	44	62	212	250
Total number of sales visits	8	12	22	20
Regular deliveries	41	48	166	190
Rush deliveries	3	14	46	60
Average number of suits per order	400	200	30	25
Average selling price per suit	₹ 700	₹ 800	₹ 850	₹ 900

Required:

(i) Calculate the customer-level operating income in 2015.

(ii) What do you recommend to CEO of MNP suits to do to increase the company's operating income in 2016?

(iii) Assume MNP suits' distribution channel costs are ₹ 17,50,000 for its wholesale customers and ₹ 10,50,000 for the retail customers. Also, assume that its corporate sustaining costs are ₹ 12,50,000. Prepare Income statement of MNP suits for 2015.

Answer:

(i)	W	H	R	T
Customer level operating income (₹)	24,54,650	28,06,750	10,46,500	11,98,250

(ii) Total operating income ₹ 34,56,150.

9. Green Garden Co., is a lawn and garden care service. It originally specialized in serving small residential clients but recently started contracting for work on office building grounds. Since Ramesh (owner) believes that commercial lawn care is more profitable, he is considering dropping residential services altogether.

   Employees worked a total of 20,000 hours last year, 13,000 on residential jobs and 7,000 on commercial jobs. Wages amounted to ₹ 9 per hour for all work done. Materials are included in overhead. All overhead is allocated on the basis of labor-hours worked, which also is the basis for customer charges. Ramesh can charge ₹ 22 per hour for residential work but only ₹ 19 per hour for commercial work.

Required:

a. If overhead for the year was ₹ 62,000, what were the profits of commercial and residential service using labour-hours as the allocation base?

b. Overhead consists of costs of transportation, equipment use, and supplies, which can be traced to the following activities:

Activity	*Cost Driver*	*Cost* ₹	*Activity Level* *Commercial*	*Activity Level* *Residential*
Transportation	Number of clients serviced	8,000	15	45
Equipment use	Equipment hours	18,000	3,500	2,100
Supplies	Area serviced in square yards	36,000	130,000	70,000
Total overhead		62,000		

Recalculate profits for commercial and residential services based on these activity bases.

c. What recommendations do you have for management regarding the profitability of these two types of services?

Answer:

	Commercial	**Residential**
(a) Profits (₹)	48,300	1,28,700
(b) Profits (₹)	33,350	1,43,650

(c) Continue the residential business which has a profit margin of 50% as compared to commercial work which has a profit margin of 25%.

10. Ranbaxy Point Manufacturing has just completed a major change in its quality control (QC) process. Previously, products had been reviewed by QC inspectors at the end of each major process, and the company's ten QC inspectors were changed as direct labor to the operation or job. In an effort to improve efficiency and quality, a computer video QC system was purchased for ₹ 250,000. The system consists of a minicomputer, 15 video cameras, other peripheral hardware, and software.

    The new system uses cameras stationed by QC engineers at key points in the production process. Each time an operation changes or there is a new operation, the cameras are moved, and a new master picture is loaded into the computer by a QC engineer. The camera takes pictures of the unit in process, and the computer compares them to the picture of a "good" unit. Any differences are sent to a QC engineer who removes the bad units and discusses the flaws with the production supervisors. The new system has replaced the 10 QC inspectors with two QC engineers.

The operating costs of the new QC system, including the salaries of the QC engineers, have been included as factory overhead in calculating the company's plant-wide factoty overhead rate, which is based on direct labor cost.

The company's president is confused. His vice president of production has told him how efficient the new system is, yet there is a large increase in the factory overhead rate. The computation of the rate before and after is shown below.

	Before	***After***
Budgeted overhead	₹ 19,00,000	₹ 21,00,000
Budgeted direct labor	10,00,000	7,00,000
Budgeted overhead rate	190%	300%

'Three hundred percent,' lamented the president. 'How can we compete with such a high factory overhead rate?'

Required:

a. Discuss the development of factory overhead rates. Why do we need Factory overhead rates and how are they computed? Discuss the accuracy of the computation of a factory overhead rate.

b. Explain why the increase in the overhead rate should not have a negative impact on Ranbaxy Manufacturing.

c. Explain, in detail, how Ranbaxy Manufacturing could change its overhead accounting system to eliminate confusion over product costs.

d. Discuss how an activity-based costing system might benefit Ranbaxy Manufacturing.

11. XYZ Ltd. manufactures four products, namely A, B, C and D using the same plant and process. The following information relates to a production period:

Product	***A***	***B***	***C***	***D***
Output in units	720	600	480	504
Cost per unit:	₹	₹	₹	₹
Direct Material	42	45	40	48
Direct labour	10	9	7	8
Machine hours per unit	4 hrs.	3hrs.	2hrs.	1hr.

The four products are similar and are usually produced in production runs of 24 units and sold in batches of 12 units. Using machine hour rate currently absorbs the production overheads. The total overheads incurred by the company for the period is as follows:

	₹
Machine operation and Maintenance cost	63,000
Setup costs	20,000
Store receiving	15,000
Inspection	10,000
Material handling and dispatch	2,592

During the period the following cost drivers are to be used for the overhead cost:

Cost	Cost driver
Setup cost	No. of production runs
Store receiving	Requisition raised
Inspection	No. of production runs
Material handling and dispatch	Orders executed

It is also determined that:

- Machine operation and maintenance cost should be apportioned between setup cost, store receiving and inspection activity in 4:3:2.
- Number of requistion raised on store is 50 for each product and the no. of order executed is 192, each order being for a batch of 12 of a product.

Required:

(a) Calculate the total cost of each product, if all overhead costs are absorbed on machine hour rate basis.

(b) Calculate the total cost of each product using activity base costing.

(c) Comment briefly on differences disclosed between overhead traced by present system and those traced by activity based costing. (CA Final, Nov., 2013)

Answer:

(a) A ₹ 89, 280, B ₹ 64,800, C ₹ 39,840 D ₹ 37,296

(b) A ₹ 69,750, B ₹ 60,825, C ₹ 47,100, D ₹ 53,541.

CASES

1. The controller of Apollo System Co. devised a new costing system based on tracing the cost of activities to products. The controller was able to measure post-manufacturing activities, such as selling, promotional, and distribution activities, and allocate these activities to products in order to have a more complete view of the company's product cost. This effort produced better strategic information about the relative profitability of product lines. In addition, the controller used the same product cost information for inventory valuation on the financial statements. Surprisingly, the controller discovered that the company's reported net income was larger under this scheme than under the traditional costing approach.

   Why was the net income larger, and how would you react to the controller's action?

   (M. Com, Delhi, 2013, 2015)

2. Oriental Insurance Co. is an insurance brokerage company that classified insurance products as either "Standard" or "Deluxe." Which are defined as follows:

   Standard: Electronic claims, few inquiries, mature product

   Deluxe: Paper claims, complex claims to process, many inquiries, a new product with complex options

   The company originally allocated processing and service expenses on the basis of revenue.

Under this traditional allocation approach, the product profitability report revealed the following:

	Standard Product	Deluxe Product	Total
Revenue	₹ 600	₹ 400	₹ 1,000
Processing and Service expenses	420	280	700
Income from operations	₹ 180	₹ 120	₹ 300
Operating income margin	30%	30%	30%

The company decided to use activity-based costing to allocate the processing and service expenses. The following activity-based costing analysis of the same data illustrates a much different profit picture for the two types of products.

	Standard Product	Deluxe Product	Total
Revenue	₹ 600	₹ 400	₹ 1,000
Processing and service expenses	183	517	700
Income from operations	₹ 417	₹ (117)	₹ 300
Operating income margin	70%	(29%)	30%

Explain why the activity-based profitability report reveals different information from the traditional sales allocation report.

3. The Controller of Konark Elecronics ltd. prepared the following product profitability report for management, using activity-based costing methods for allocating both the factory overhead and the marketing expenses. As such, the controller has confidence in the accuracy of this report. In addition, the controller interviewed the vice president of marketing, who indicated that the floor loudspeakers were an older product that was highly recognized in the marketplace. The ribbon loudspeakers were a new product that was recently launched. The ribbon loudspeakers are a new technology that have no competition in the marketplace, and it is hoped that they will become an important future addition to the company's product portfolio. Initial indications are that the product is well received by customers. The controller believes that the manufacturing costs for all three products are in line with expectations.

	Floor Loudspeakers	Bookshelf Loudspeakers	Ribbon Loudspeakers	Totals
Sales	₹ 10,00,000	₹ 7,50,000	₹ 5,00,000	₹ 22,50,000
Less cost of goods sold	7,00,000	4,12,500	4,50,000	15,62,500
Gross profit	₹ 3,00,000	₹ 3,37,500	₹ 50,000	₹ 6,87,500
Less marketing expenses	3,80,000	75,000	40,000	4,95,000
Income from operations	₹ (80,000)	₹ 2,62,500	₹ 10,000	₹ 1,92,500

Required:

(*i*) Calculate the gross profit and income from operations to sales ratios for each product.

(*ii*) Write a memo using the product profitability report and the calculations in (*i*) to make recommendations to management with respect to strategies for the three products.

4. The following news item appeared in Indian newspaper MINT on May 2, 2008.

DABUR MANAGES COST PRESSURES

Dabur India Ltd. like many of its peers in the FMCG space, has managed to maintain profit margins despite soaring input costs. Adjusted for its investments in its retail venture, a chain of health and beauty stores, operating margin improved by about 20 basis points during the March 2008 quarter. Operating profit as a result grew 15.6% more or less tracking the 14.3% growth in revenues. Both sales growth and margin expansion had been better in the first three quarters of financial year 2007-2008 at 16% and 66 basis points, respectively, leading to 20% growth in operating profit.

According to analysts, the company has been able to contain raw material cost pressures through better supply chain management. For the whole year, raw material costs fell by as much as 90 basis points, helped partly by an average 3% increase in selling prices. The company's consumer health division recorded strong double-digit growth in the March quarter, after having recorded 5% growth in the December quarter and negative growth in the first half of the year. Growth slowed compared with that in the first three quarters owing to a drop in growth rates in international and in its food business.

The company has said that it expects revenues to grow by 15-20% this financial year, which, based on its ability to maintain profit margin, should lead to a similar increase in profit. A recent report by Merrill Lynch notes that the company is well placed to grow profit by about 20% even after accounting for costs related to the retail venture, thanks largely to the company's rich pipeline of new products and variants. But, note that at current levels, the stock trades at nearly 28 times trailing earnings, which more than adequately captures the estimated growth in profit.

Required:

(*i*) Explain how Dabur Co. was able to manage costs.

(*ii*) Distinguish between cost management techniques adopted by Dabur as stated in the News above and the ones that are suggested by activity-based costing (ABC).

5. Sony, manufactures portable radios. Last year the firm sold 25,000 radios at ₹ 250 each. Total costs amounted to ₹ 52,50,000 of wihch ₹ 15,00,000 were considered fixed. An activity-based costing study recently revealed that Radio's fixed costs include the following components:

Setup (40 setups at ₹ 4,000 per setup)	₹ 1,60,000
Engineering (500 hours at ₹ 250 per hour)	1,25,000
Inspection (1,000 inspections at ₹ 300 per inspection)	3,00,000
General factory overhead	6,15,000
Total	₹ 12,00,000
Fixed selling and administrative costs	3,00,000
Total	₹ 15,00,000

Management is considering both the installation of new, highly automated manufacturing equipment and a move toward just-in-time inventory and production management. If the new equipment is installed, setups will be quicker and less expensive. Under the proposed JIT approach, there would be 300 setups per year at ₹ 500 per setup. Because a total quality program would accompany the move toward JIT, only 100 inspections are anticipated at a cost of ₹ 450 each.

After the installation of the new system, 800 hours of engineering would be required at ₹ 280 per hour. General factory overhead would increase to ₹ 16,61,000; however, the automated equipment would allow Sony, to cut its unit variable cost by 20 percent. Finally, the overall improvement in product quality would support a selling price of ₹ 260 per unit.

Required:

(a) Upon seeing the analysis given in the problem, the vice-president for manufacturing exclaimed to the controller, "I thought you told me this ₹ 15,00,000 cost was fixed. These don't look like fixed costs at all. What you're telling me now is that setup costs us ₹ 4,000 every time we start a production run. What gives?" As the controller, write a short memo to the vice-president that clarifies the situation.

(b) Compute Sony's new break-even point in units if the proposed automated equipment is installed.

(c) Calculate how many units Sony will have to sell to show a profit of ₹ 14,00,000 assuming the new technology is adopted.

(d) If Sony, adopts the new manufacturing technology, will its break-even point be higher or lower? Will the number of sales units required to earn a profit of ₹ 14,00,000 be higher or lower? Are the results in this case consistent with what you would typically expect to find in a modern high-tech manufacturing facility? Explain.

Answer:

(b) 17,000 units.

(c) 27,000 units.

(d) The breakeven point will be higher (17,000 units in place of 15,000 units).

6. During the last 20 years, KL's manufacturing operation has become increasingly automated with computer-controlled robots replacing operatives. KL currently manufactures over 100 products of varying levels of design complexity. A single, plant-wide overhead absorption rate (OAR), based on direct labour hours, is used to absorb overhead costs.

In the quarter ended March 2016, KL's manufacturing overhead costs were:

	(₹ 000)
Equipment operation expenses	125
Equipment maintenance expenses	25
Wages paid to technicians	85
Wages paid to storemen	35
Wages paid to dispatch staff	40
	310

During the quarter, Hari Bhakti Management Consultants were engaged to conduct a review of KL's cost accounting systems. Hari Bhakti's report includes the following statement:

'In KL's circumstances, absorbing overhead costs in individual products on a labour hour absorption basis is meaningless. Overhead costs should be attributed to products using an activity based costing (ABC) system. We have identified the following as being the most significant activities:

(1) Receiving component consignments from suppliers

(2) Setting up equipment for production runs

(3) Quality inspections

(4) Dispatching goods orders to customers.

Our research has indicated that, in the short term, KL's overheads are 40% fixed and 60% variable. Approximately half the variable overheads vary in relation to direct labour hours worked and half vary in relation to the number of quality inspections. This model applies only to relatively small changes in the level of output during a period of two years or less.'

Equipment operation and maintenance expenses are apportionable as follows:

- Component stores (15%), manufacturing (70%) and goods dispatch (15%).

Technician wages are apportionable as follows:

- Equipment maintenance (30%), setting up equipment for production runs (40%) and quality inspections (30%).

During the quarter

- A total of 2000 direct labour hours were worked (paid at ₹ 12 per hour),
- 980 component consignments were received from suppliers,
- 1020 production runs were set up,
- 640 quality inspections wer carried out, and
- 420 goods orders were dispatched to customers.

Part One

KL"s production during the quarer included components R, S and T. The following information is available:

	Component R	Component S	Component T
Direct labour hours worked	25	480	50
Direct material costs	₹ 1 200	₹ 2 900	₹ 1 800
Component consignments received	42	24	28
Production runs	16	18	12
Quality inspections	10	8	18
Goods orders dispatched	22	85	46
Quantity produced	560	12 800	2 400

In April 2016 a potential customer asked KL to quaote for the supply of a new component Z to a given specificaion. 1000 units of Z are to be supplied each quarter for a two-year period. They will be paid for in equal instalments on the last day of each quarter. The job will involve an initial design cost of ₹ 40 000 and production will involve 80 direct labour hours, ₹ 2000 materials, 20 component consignments, 15 production runs, 30 quality inspections and 4 goods dispatches per quarter.

KL's Sales Director comments:

'Now we have a modern ABC system, we can quote selling prices with confidence. The quarterly charge we quote should be the forecast ABC production cost of the units plus the design cost of the Z depreciated on a straightline basis over the two years of the job-to which we should add a 25% mark-up for profit. We can base our forecast on costs experinced in the quarter ended March.'

Required:

(a) Calculate the unit cost of components R, S, T using KL's existing cost accounting system (single factory labour hour OAR).

(b) Explain how an ABC system would be developed using the information given. Calculate the unit cost of components R, S, T under ABC system.

(c) Calculate the charge per quarter that should be quoted for supply of component Z in a manner consistent with the Sales Director's comments. Advise KL's management on the merits of this selling price, having regard to factors you consider relevant.

Note: KL's cost of capital is 3% per quarter.

Answer:

(a) Cost per unit
R, ₹ 9.60
S, ₹ 6.49
T, ₹ 4.23

(b) Cost per unit
R, ₹ 18.68
S, ₹ 2.08
T, ₹ 5.82

(c) Incremental cost attributable to the order ₹ 16,737.

7. Scott Manufacturing produces two items in its Virginia Beach plant: Tuff Stuff and Ruff Stuff. Since inception, Scott has used only one manufacturing overhead cost pool to accumulate costs. Overhead has been allocated to products based on direct labor hours. Until recently, Scott was the sole producer of Ruff Stuff and was able to dictate the selling price. However, last year, Marvella Products began marketing a comparable product at a price below the cost assigned by Scott. Market share has declined rapidly, and management must now decide whether to meet the competitive price or to discontinue the product line. Recognizing that discontinuing the product line would place an additional burden on its remaining product, Tuff Stuff, management is using activity-based costing to determine if it would show a different cost structure for the two products.

The two major indirect costs for manufacturing the products are power usage and setup costs. Most of the power is used in fabricating, while most of the setup costs are required in assembly. The setup costs are predominantly related to the Tuff Stuff product line.

The plant manager, Kati Scott, has decided to separate the Manufacturing Department costs into two activity cost pools as follows:

Fabricating: machine hours will be the cost driver.

Assembly: number of setups will be the cost driver.

Jack Riley, the controller, has gathered the following information.

MANUFACTURING DEPARTMENT
Annual Budget before Separation of Overhead

		Product Line	
	Total	**Tuff Stuff**	**Ruff Stuff**
Number of units		20,000	20,000
Direct-labor hours*		2 hours per unit	3 hours per unit

Total direct-labor cost	₹ 24,00,000		
Direct material		₹ 15.00 per unit	₹ 9.00 per unit
Budgeted overhead:			
Indirect labor	72,000		
Fringe benefits	15,000		
Indirect material	93,000		
Power	5,40,000		
Setup	2,25,000		
Quality assurance	30,000		
Other utilities	30,000		
Depreciation	45,000		

*Direct-labor hourly rate is the same in both departments.

MANUFACTURING DEPARTMENT

Cost Structure after Separation of Costs into Activity Cost Pools

	Fabricating	**Assembly**
Direct-labor cost	74%	26%
Direct material (no change)	100%	0%
Indirect labor	76%	24%
Fringe benefits	80%	20%
Indirect material	₹ 60,000	₹ 33,000
Power	₹ 480,000	₹ 60,000
Setup	₹ 15,000	₹ 210,000
Quality assurance	80%	20%
Other utilities	50%	50%
Depreciation	78%	22%

Cost driver:

	Product Line	
	Tuff Stuff	**Ruff Stuff**
Machine-hours per units	4.4	6.0
Setups	1,000	272

Required:

1. Assigning overhead based on direct-labor hours, calculate the following:
   a. Total budgeted cost of the Manufacturing Department.
   b. Unit cost of Tuff Stuff and Ruff Stuff.
2. After separation of overhead into activity cost pools, compute the total budgeted cost of each department: fabricating and assembly.
3. Using activity-based costing, calculate the unit costs for each product.
4. Discuss how a decision regarding the production and pricing of Ruff Stuff will be affected by the results of your calculations in the preceding requirements.

(CMA USA adapted)

Answers:

1. (a) ₹ 39,30,000

   (b) Unit cost, Tuff stuff ₹ 84

   Ruff stuff ₹ 112.50

2. Total budgeted cost

   Fabricating ₹ 29,76,000

   Assembly ₹ 9,54,000

3. Unit cost, Tuff stuff ₹ 91.71

   Ruff stuff ₹ 104.94

4. ABC may lead the company to decide to lower its price for Ruff Stuff in order to be more competitive in the market and continue production of the product.

8. Ultratech Co. manufactures several different types of printed circuit boards; however, two of the boards account for the majority of the company's sales. The first of these boards, a television circuit board, has been a standard in the industry for several years. The market for this type of board is competitive and price-sensitive. Ultratech plans to sell 65,000 of the TV boards in 2015 at a price of ₹ 300 per unit. The second high-volume product, a personal computer circuit board, is recent addition to Ultratech's product line. Because the PC board incorporates the latest technology it can be sold at a premium price. The 2015 plans include the sale of 40,000 PC boards at ₹ 600 per unit.

   Ultratech's management group is meeting to discuss how to expand the sales and do promotion for 2015. The sales manager believes that the market share for the TV board could b expanded by concentrating Ultratech's promotional efforts in this area. In response to this suggestion, the production manager said, "Why don't you go after a bigger market for the PC board? The cost sheets that I get show that the contribution from the PC board is more than double the contribution from the TV board. I know we get a premium price for the PC board. Selling it should help overall profitability."

   The cost-accounting system shows that the following costs apply to the PC and TV boards.

	PC Board	**TV Board**
Direct material	₹ 280	₹ 160
Direct labor	4 hr.	1.5 hr.
Machine time	1.5 hr.	.5 hr.

   Variable manufacturing overhead is applied on the basis of direct-labor hours. For 2015, variable overhead is budgeted at ₹ 22,40,000, and direct-labor hours are estimated at 280,000. The hourly rates for machine time and direct labor are ₹ 20 and ₹ 28, respectively. The company applies a material-handling charge at 10 percent of material cost. This material-handling charge is not included in variable manufacturing overhead. Total 2015 expenditures for direct material are budgeted at ₹ 2,12,00,000.

   Andrew Fulton, Ultratech's controller, believes that before the management group proceeds with the discussion about allocating sales and promotional expenses to individual products, it might be worth-while to look at these products on the basis of the activities involved in their production. Fulton has prepared the following schedule to help the management group understand this concepts.

"Using this information," Fulton explained, "we can calcuate an activity-based cost for each TV board and each PC board and then compare it to the standard cost we have been using. The only cost that remains the same for both cost methods is the cost of direct material. The cost drivers will replace the direct labor, machine time, and overhead costs in the old standard cost figures."

Budgeted Cost		**Cost Driver**	**Budgeted Annual Activity for Cost Driver**
Procurement	₹ 8,00,000	Number of parts	40,00,000 parts
Production scheduling	4,40,000	Number of boards	1,10,000 boards
Packaging and shipping	8,80,000	Number of boards	1,10,000 boards
Total	₹ 21,20,000		
Machine setup	₹ 8,92,000	Number of setups	2,78,750 setups
Hazardous waste disposal	96,000	Pounds of waste	16,000 pounds
Quality control	11,20,000	Number of inspections	1,60,000 inspections
General supplies	1,32,000	Number of boards	1,10,000 boards
Total	₹ 22,40,000		
Machine insertion	₹ 24,00,000	Number of parts	30,00,000 parts
Manual insertion	80,00,000	Number of parts	10,00,000 parts
Wave-soldering	2,64,000	Number of boards	1,10,000 boards
Total	₹ 1,06,64,000		

Required per Unit	**PC Board**	**TV Board**
Parts:	55	26
Machine insertions	36	25
Manual insertions	19	1
Machine setups	3	2
Hazardous waste disposal	.40 lb.	.03 lb.
Inspections	2	1

Required:

1. Identify at least four general advantages associated with activity-based costing.
2. On the basis of Ultratech's unit cost data given in the problem, calculate the total amount that each of the two product lines will contribute toward covering fixed costs and profit in 2015. (In other words, for each product line calculate the total sales revenue minus the total *variable* costs. This amount is often referred to as a product's total *contribution margin*.)
3. Repeat requirement (2) but now use the cost data from the activity-based costing system.
4. Explain how a comparison of the results of the two costing methods may impact the decisions made by Ultratech's management group. (*CMA, USA adapted*)

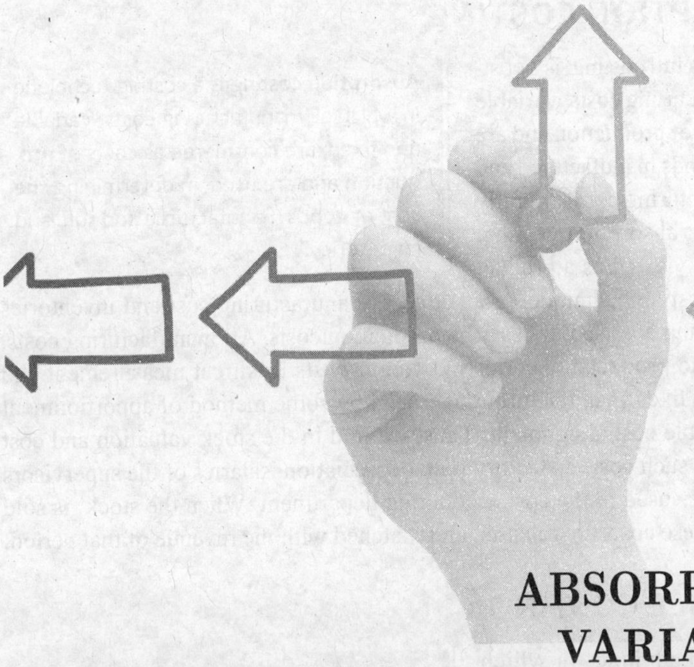

5

ABSORPTION VERSUS VARIABLE COSTING

LEARNING OBJECTIVES:

After reading this chapter, you should be able to:

- Explain the Concepts of Absorption and Variable Costing
- Distinguish Between Absorption Costing and Variable Costing
- Explain Preparation of Income Statement in Absorption and Variable Costing
- Describe the Advantages and Disadvantages of Absorption and Variable Costing, Precautions in Using Absorption Costing
- Explain the Impact of JIT Method
- Explain the Methods of Determining Cost Behaviour

CONCEPT OF ABSORPTION COSTING

Absorption costing, also known as full costing, is a costing technique in which all manufacturing costs, variable and fixed, are considered as costs of production and are used in determining the cost of goods manufactured and sold and inventories. All manufacturing costs are fully absorbed into finished goods. In absorption costing, fixed manufacturing overhead is viewed as a product cost, not a period cost. In this costing technique, product cost, manufacturing cost and inventories cost all have the same meaning and are used to describe production costs. All manufacturing costs, variable and fixed, are charged to products; material and labour costs by direct measurement and identification with products; and fixed manufacturing overhead by some method of apportionment which aims to provide an equitable cost assignment. Thus, we find in the stock valuation and cost of goods manufactured and sold, such costs as factory rent, depreciation, salaries of the supervisors and night watchman and supplies used in the cost accounting department. When the stock is sold in the next accounting period, these costs are released and matched with the revenue of that period.

> **Absorption costing** is a costing technique in which all manufacturing costs, variable and fixed, are considered as costs of production and are used in determining the cost of goods manufactured and sold and inventories.

CONCEPT OF VARIABLE COSTING

Variable costing is a costing technique in which only variable manufacturing costs are considered and used while valuing inventories and determining cost of goods sold. That is, only variable manufacturing costs are considered as product costs and are allocated to products manufactured. These costs include direct materials, direct labour and variable factory overhead. Fixed factory (manufacturing) overheads are not considered product costs and are not used to value inventories and determine the cost of goods sold and are excluded from the cost of product. Fixed manufacturing costs are treated as period costs in variable costing i.e costs which are a function of a time rather than of production, These fixed manufacturing costs are necessary to provide only facilities and are the costs of maintaining a readiness to produce or service to which they relate. These costs are not affected by changes in the quantity of product manufactured and therefore are considered an expense of the period and written off to profit and loss account in the period they are incurred. Some examples of fixed manufacturing overhead are plant depreciation, supervisors' salaries, property taxes, insurance, etc.

> **Variable costing** is a costing technique in which only variable manufacturing costs are considered and used while valuing inventories and determining cost of goods sold.

Variable Costing, Direct Costing, Marginal Costing

Variable costing is referred to, frequently in practice, by different names such as direct costing, marginal costing. However, the use of the term 'variable costing' is most appropriate.

1. *Direct Costing:* The term 'direct costing' refers to those costs which can be identified and traced directly to the units of output. The word 'direct' implies a high degree of traceability and, in this regard, both variable and fixed costs can be direct cost which are traceable to a costing centre. For example, in a department that makes only one product, direct product costs are all costs which can be traced to the department including supervision, depreciation and other fixed costs as well as variable costs. Variable costing is a more appropriate term because it emphasises 'cost variability' and requires that distinction should be made between fixed and variable cost.

2. *Prime Costing:* Variable costing also differs from prime costing in which only direct materials, direct labour and direct expenses are considered for inventory valuation and variable factory overhead is excluded.

3. *Marginal Costing:* The use of the term 'marginal costing' interchangeably with the term 'variable costing' is also not appropriate. In fact, the terms 'marginal cost' and marginal costing originated first in the area of economics. These terms in economics mean the aggregated costs expected to be incurred when the production quantity is increased or decreased by one more unit. In economics, therefore, marginal costs include both fixed and variable costs resulting from producing an extra unit if producing an additional unit results in an increase in fixed costs as well. Increase in fixed costs may be due to situations such as appointment of additional supervisor or increase in capacity due to purchase of an additional machine. Clearly, therefore, the term 'marginal costing' has a different concept than that of variable costing which considers only variable production costs in all situations and never considers fixed costs as in marginal costing.

Some argue that if an extra unit is produced, the costs which could be incurred for producing this extra unit will be only variable costs as fixed costs remain constant. In this way, marginal costing may be interpreted in the same manner as variable costing. However, the use of the term' marginal costing' in accounting will create confusion because the economists have been using this term having an accepted definition in economics. Therefore, any attempt by the accountants and accounting practitioners in using the term 'marginal costing' (assuming their own or restricted concept) will not bring clarity to the interpretation but only add more confusion.

4. *Incremental Costing and Differential Costing:* It should be further understood that the terms 'incremental costing', 'differential costing' imply similar meaning as that of marginal costing. It is better, therefore, not to use these terms also when referring to variable costing.

Variable costing is not a distinct method of cost determination as job or process costing are. It is simply a technique where the cost of goods manufactured is composed only of variable manufacturing costs–those manufacturing costs that increase or decrease as the volume of production rises or falls. This technique of variable costing can be used simultaneously in all methods of costing including job or process costing. Besides job or process costing, variable costing can be used in historical (actual) cost system and standard cost system. With a standard costing system, scientific estimates of an efficient level of performance are established. By applying variable costing to standards, business enterprises have an excellent tool for managerial decision making.

DIFFERENCES BETWEEN ABSORPTION COSTING AND VARIABLE COSTING

Variable costing and absorption costing differ from each other with regard to (*i*) cost elements included in product costs, (*ii*) difference in inventory values and (*iii*) difference in net income.

Cost Elements in Product Cost

Conceptually, variable costing and absorption costing differ only in the treatment of fixed factory (manufacturing) overhead in the accounting records and financial statement. In both the costing, it is agreed that selling and administrative overhead, whether variable or fixed, are period costs and these costs are not treated as product costs with the result that selling and administrative overheads are not included in the costs of inventories, and costs of goods sold. Similarly, it is also agreed that variable manufacturing costs are product costs, *i.e.*, costs to be charged to the product. The disagreement between the two, is only in regard to the treatment of fixed manufacturing costs. Under absorption costing, fixed manufacturing costs are charged to inventory and cost of goods sold. Under variable costing, these costs are not charged to inventory and cost of goods sold but are treated as period expenses when incurred. Exhibit 5.1 illustrates the treatment of different cost elements in the two costing techniques and clearly indicates that both differ only about treatment of fixed factory overhead.

Exhibit 5.1: Treatment of Cost Elements in Absorption Costing and Variable Costing

	Cost Elements as Product or Period Costs	*Absorption Costing*	*Variable Costing*
(*i*)	Direct Materials	Product	Product
(*ii*)	Direct Labour	Product	Product
(*iii*)	Direct Expenses	Product	Product
(*iv*)	Variable factory overhead	Product	Product
(*v*)	Fixed factory overhead ⟶	Product	Period
(*vi*)	Variable Selling Expenses	Period	Period
(*vii*)	Fixed Selling Expenses	Period	Period
(*viii*)	Variable Administrative Expenses	Period	Period
(*ix*)	Fixed Administrative Expenses	Period	Period

Differences in Inventory Values

Variable costing and absorption costing do influence inventory value differently. As stated earlier, inventories under absorption costing absorb fixed factory overhead, whereas, inventories under variable costing include only variable production costs, An example is given here in order to make the difference in inventory valuations of absorption and variable costing more visible and concrete. The following data are taken from the records of a manufacturing company.

Direct Material	₹	50	
Direct Labour	₹	100	
Variable factory overhead	₹	50	
Variable selling and administrative overhead	₹	50	
Fixed Overheads:			
Fixed manufacturing overhead (at normal output level)	₹	2,50,000	
Fixed selling and administrative overhead	₹	1,00,000	
Units produced		10,000	units
Units sold (₹ 300 per unit)		8,000	units
Units in the beginning inventory		NIL	
Normal output (Capacity) Level		10,000	units

Based on the above information, the unit costs for inventory valuation under the two costing techniques will be as follows:

	Absorption Costing (₹)	*Variable Costing* (₹)
Direct Materials	50	50
Direct Labour	100	100
Variable factory overhead	50	50
Fixed factory overhead (₹ 2,50,000/10,000 units)	25	—
Total per unit cost	225	200

Under absorption costing, inventories will be valued and reported on the balance sheet at ₹ 225 per unit; under variable costing, the unit cost for inventory valuation is ₹ 200. The difference of ₹ 25 in the unit cost is due to the treatment of fixed manufacturing overhead ₹ 2,50,000, Under absorption costing, fixed manufacturing overhead is spread over all the units manufactured, whereas variable costing does not charge fixed manufacturing overhead to production.

It is significant to note that, under both the techniques, selling and administrative expenses, variable and fixed both, are not charged to product but are treated merely as expenses (period costs) in the period when they are incurred.

Difference in Net Income

Difference in the computation of product cost (due to difference in the treatment of fixed factory overhead) bring differences in net income figures in the two costing techniques.

Fixed Manufacturing Cost per unit and Change in Inventory Levels

The magnitude of any difference in net income is a function of the fixed manufacturing costs per unit and the change in inventory levels.

The arrangement of data in the conventional absorption costing income statement differs considerably from the format of the variable costing income statement. Under absorption costing, all costs are divided into three categories: manufacturing, selling, and administrative costs. In the income statement, all manufacturing costs (variable and fixed) are subtracted from the sales revenue to get a gross margin/gross profit on sales; and selling and administrative expenses (variable and fixed) are deducted from gross margin to arrive at the net operating income.

Further, fixed manufacturing overhead in absorption costing are charged to units produced on the basis of per unit fixed manufacturing overhead rate obtained by dividing the standard fixed manufacturing overhead by normal output level as follows:

$$\frac{\text{Standard Fixed Manufacturing Overhead}}{\text{Normal Output (Capacity)}}$$

Capacity (Volume) Variance

If actual production is equal to normal output level, the total fixed manufacturing overhead (budgeted at normal output level) will be charged to units produced. If actual production is more or less than the normal output level, greater (if actual production is greater) or lesser (if actual production is lesser) fixed manufacturing will be first charged to units produced. Subsequently, if actual production is above or below the normal or standard capacity, adjustments are made for capacity (volume) variance since the amount of fixed manufacturing overhead incurred will always be equal to actual fixed manufacturing overhead. However, by showing the absorbed/chargeable amount of fixed manufacturing overhead in terms of actual units produced, the value of closing inventories stands already affected to that extent.

If the volume (capacity) variance is favourable, i.e., over-absorption (actual production being higher than normal capacity production), the amount of over-absorption is deducted from the total cost of goods manufactured and sold. If the volume (capacity) variance is unfavourable, i.e., under absorption (actual production being lesser than normal capacity production) the amount of under -absorption is added to the cost of goods manufactured and sold. A proforma of income statement prepared under absorption costing is given in Exhibit. 5.2.

No Capacity Variance in Variable Costing

Under variable costing, only variable costs of production (direct material, direct labour and variable manufacturing overhead) are subtracted from sales revenue to determine a balance which is known by different names, such as marginal contribution, marginal income (profit), marginal revenue, marginal balance, profit pick-up, etc. All fixed costs, and variable selling, distribution and administrative costs are deducted from this balance to arrive at the net income. Since fixed manufacturing costs are not charged to products under variable costing, there can be no volume (capacity) variance. Marginal contribution/marginal income under variable costing is greater than the gross profit/gross margin under absorption costing. Exhibit 5.3 depicts a proforma of income statement prepared under variable costing.

Exhibit 5.2: Income Statement (Absorption Costing)

		Amount ₹
	Sales	—
Less:	Cost of goods sold:	
1.	Variable production costs:	
	Direct material cost	—
	Direct labour cost	—
	Variable manufacturing overhead	—
2.	Fixed factory (manufacturing) overhead	—
	Cost of goods manufactured	—
Add:	Beginning inventory	—
	Cost of goods available for sale	—
Less:	Closing inventory	—
	Cost of goods sold	—
	± Over-or under-applied factory (manufacturing) overhead (over absorption to be deducted and under-absorption to be added)	—
	Cost of goods sold at actual	—
	Gross profit on sales	—
Less:	Fixed selling and administrative expenses	—
	Variable selling and administrative expenses	—
	Net Income	—

Exhibit 5.3: Income Statement (Variable Costing)

		Amount ₹
	Sales	—
Less:	Cost of goods sold:	
	Variable production costs:	
	Direct material cost	—
	Direct labour cost	—

	Variable manufacturing (factory) overhead	—
	Cost of goods manufactured	—
Add:	Beginning inventory	—
	Cost of goods available for sale	—
Less:	Closing inventory	—
	Variable Cost of goods sold	—
	Marginal contribution	—
Less:	Fixed manufacturing overhead	—
	Variable selling and administrative expenses*	—
	Fixed selling and administrative expenses	—
	Net Income	—

* In income statement (variable costing), variable selling and administrative expenses, alternatively, can be added to variable cost goods bold before finding the contribution margin. However, this treatment will not make any differences in the value of closing stocks, cost of goods sold and net income under variable costing. Further, variable selling and administrative expenses remains a period cost, and does not become a product cost because of this treatment.

The relationship between production and sales determines the difference in net income under the two costing techniques. In order to understand production, sales and income relationship, the following possibilities, found in practice, have been explained.

1. *Production Equals Sales:* If production and sales are equal, net income will be the same under absorption costing and variable costing. Since the units manufactured are all sold, absorption costing, like variable costing, will treat the total fixed manufacturing overhead as an expense of the period. No fixed manufacturing overhead flows into or out of inventory.

Further, in this situation, stocks will neither increase nor decrease. If there is opening stock, an amount of fixed manufactured overhead will be carried forward as an expense to be included in the current period. But at the same time, an equivalent amount included in closing stock valuation will be deducted from the cost of production as production is equal to sales and opening stock, if any, will be equal to closing stock. Thus, under absorption costing, the net effect is that the only fixed manufacturing overhead which is included as an expense for the period will be the amount of fixed manufacturing overhead which has been incurred in the period. Thus, production being equal to sales, net income in the two costing techniques will not differ.

2. *Production More than Sales:* When production is greater than sales, net income reported under absorption costing will be greater than net income reported under variable costing. Under absorption costing, as production exceeds sales, closing stocks increase. The effect of this is that a greater amount of fixed manufacturing overheads in the closing stock will be deducted from the expenses (cost of goods sold) of the current period than the amount of fixed manufacturing overheads included in opening stock of the current period. Variable costing, however, always recognises the total fixed manufacturing overhead of the period as an expense and values closing stock in terms of only variable production costs, i.e., at a smaller valuation. As a result of this, if production is more than the sales, absorption costing will show a higher net income than the variable costing.

3. *Sales More than Production:* If sales are more than the production, variable costing will show higher net income than the absorption costing. Selling more than was produced means that units in the opening stock are being sold. Under absorption costing, opening inventory carries with them a part of fixed manufacturing overhead of the previous period. In addition to it, units produced in the current period and sold are also charged with the total fixed manufacturing overhead of the current period. Therefore, under absorption costing, the amount of fixed manufacturing overhead shown as expense is more (by the amount of fixed overhead included in opening stock) than the current period's fixed manufacturing overhead. In variable costing, inventory is valued in terms of only variable production costs, not including fixed manufacturing overhead. Thus, fixed manufacturing overhead of the current period will only be charged under variable costing. Accordingly, variable costing net income is greater than the absorption costing net income by the amount of fixed manufacturing overhead included in the opening stock units which are being sold.

The relationship between production, sales and the net incomes under the two costing techniques can be summarised as follows:

		Net Income Absorption Costing (AC)		Net Income Variable Costing (VC)
(i)	Production = sales	AC	=	VC
(ii)	Production > sales (Production more than sales)	AC	>	VC
(iii)	Production < sales (Production less than sales)	AC	<	VC

The difference in net income in the two costing techniques can also be found in case of constant production (but sales fluctuating) or constant sales (but production fluctuating) situation over a period. In case of a constant production schedule over time while sales are allowed to fluctuate each period, the absorption costing net income will fluctuate up and down with sales but the constant production will have a levelling effect on the swings. In other words, the peaks will neither be as high nor as low as the corresponding sales. Variable costing net income, on the other hand, will have swings that match those of sales, in both direction and relative height and depth. For the situation, where production fluctuates while sales remain rather constant, a different story is told. In this case, absorption costing net income will fluctuate with production in both directions and relative height and depth. Variable costing net income will remain constant to correspond with sales[1].

The differences between absorption costing and variable costing have been further clarified in Table 5.1.

Table 5.1: Absorption Costing vs Variable Costing

Criteria	*Absorption Costing*	*Variable Costing*
1. Separation of costs	Costs separated into those which can be traced to the cost centre (i.e., allocated costs) and those which cannot be traced, which have to be apportioned using some arbitrary basis	Costs need to be separated into variable cost and fixed costs. This is not always an easy task.
2. Product costs :		
(i) Variable production costs	Included	Included
(ii) Fixed manufacturing	Included	Excluded
(iii) Other costs	Written off direct to the profit and loss account, e.g. administration cost, selling cost and research and development expenditure, fixed and variable both	All costs (except variable production costs) are treated as period costs, i.e., written off in the period to which they relate

Criteria	Absorption Costing	Variable Costing
3. Stock valuation: (*i*) Variable production costs (*ii*) Fixed manufacturing costs	 Included Included (carried forward to next accounting period)	 Included Excluded (not carried forward to next accounting period)
4. Recovery of costs	Attempts to make sure that all manufacturing costs are recovered. However, there is likely to be an under-or over-recovery of overheads, because absorption rates have to be predetermined	Uses only costs which can be traced to the product. Avoids having any under-or over-recovery of manufacturing overheads.
5. Profit	Computed as gross profit and net profit	Computed as a contribution and net profit
6. Decision-making	Unsuitable The costs can never really be described as accurate	Suitable The costs used are realistic and more accurate
7. Reporting	Recommended for external-reporting	Recommended as being more meaningful for internal reporting
8. Makes use of budgeted figures	Yes	Yes
9. Inventorization of fixed manufacturing costs	Yes	No
10. Effect of changes in unit inventory levels on operating income Production = Sales Production > Sales Production < Sales	 Equal Higher Lower	 Equal Lower Higher
11. Effects on cost-volume-profit relationship (for a given level of fixed costs and a given contribution margin per unit)	Driven by (*a*) sales units (*b*) production units (*c*) chosen denominator level	Driven by sales units

THROUGHPUT COSTING

Throughput costing is also known as super–variable costing. Throughput costing considers only direct materials as true variable cost and other remaing costs as period costs to be charged in the period in which they are incurred. Thus, in throughput costing, only direct materials costs are inventoriable costs. In this costing, contribution is equal to revenue minus all variable direct materials cost of goods sold. Throughput costing is not used for external reporting because it gives significant different net income figures than those revealed by absorption costing. It provides less incentive to produce for inventory than variable or absorption costing since inventory value figures are very low. Throughput costing has relevance only for internal uses of management.

Example:

Based on the following data relating to a company, prepare income statement for the first month, second month, third month, fourth month using absorption costing and variable costing.

Normal capacity 20,000 units per month.

Variable costs (direct materials, direct labour, variable factory overhead) per unit ₹ 60.

Fixed factory overhead ₹ 2,50,000 per month or 12.5 per unit at normal capacity. Fixed selling and administrative expenses are ₹ 50,000 p.m.

Variable selling and administrative expenses are ₹ 2 per unit sold.

Sales prices per unit is ₹ 100.

Actual production, sales and inventories in units are:

	First month	*Second month*	*Third month*	*Fourth month*
Unit in beginning Inventory	—	—	3,000	1,000
Units produced	17,500	21,000	19,000	20,000
Units sold	17,500	18,000	21,000	16,500
Units in closing Inventory	—	3,000	1,000	4,500

Solution:

Income Statement (Absorption Costing)

	First month	*Second month*	*Third month*	*Fourth month*
Sales (₹ 100 per unit)	₹ 17,50,000	18,00,000	21,00,000	16,50,000
Variable cost per unit ₹ 60	10,50,000	12,60,000	11,40,000	12,00,000
Fixed factory overhead @ ₹ 12.5	2,18,750	2,62,500	2,37,500	2,50,000
Cost of goods Manufactured	12,68,750	15,22,500	13,77,500	14,50,000
Add: Beginning Inventory	—	—	2,17,500	72,500
Cost of goods available for sales	12,68,750	15,22,500	15,95,000	15,22,500
Less: Ending Inventory	—	2,17,500	72,500	3,26,250
Cost of goods sold	12,68,750	13,05,000	15,22,500	11,96,250
Over-or-under applied factory overhead	31,250	(12,500)	12,500	—
Cost of goods sold at actual	13,00,000	12,92,500	15,35,000	11,96,250
Gross profit on sales	4,50,000	5,07,500	5,65,000	4,53,750
Less: Selling and administrative expenses (fixed and variable)	85,000	86,000	92,000	83,000
Net income for the month	3,65,000	4,21,500	4,73,000	3,70,750

Note: In absorption costing income statement, fixed factory expenses are included in the unit cost and also in the inventory values.

(*i*) Ending Inventory: Second month $\frac{3,000}{21,000} \times 15,22,500 = ₹\ 2,17,500$

Third month $\frac{1,000}{22,000} \times 15,95,000 = ₹\ 72,500$

Fourth month $\frac{4,500}{21,000} \times 15,22,500 = ₹\ 3,26,250$

(*ii*) In the first month ₹ 31,250 is under-absorbed factory overhead due to production being less than normal capacity and is added to the cost of goods sold.

(*iii*) In the second month, ₹ 12,500 is over-absorbed due to higher production and has therefore been substracted.

(*iv*) In the third month, ₹ 12,500 is under-absorbed and has been added back to cost of goods sold.

(*v*) In the fourth month, production is at normal capacity and there is no under or over -absorption.

Income Statement (Variable Costing)

	First month	*Second month*	*Third month*	*Fourth month*
Sales (₹ 100 per unit)	17,50,000	18,00,000	21,00,000	16,50,000
Variable manufacturing costs ₹ 60 per unit	10,50,000	12,60,000	11,40,000	12,00,000
Cost of goods manufactured	10,50,000	12,60,000	11,40,000	12,00,000
Add: Beginning Inventory	—	—	1,80,000	60,000
Cost of goods available for sales	10,50,000	12,60,000	13,20,000	12,60,000
Less: Closing Inventory	—	1,80,000	60,000	2,70,000
Cost of goods sold	10,50,000	10,80,000	12,60,000	9,90,000
Contribution	7,00,000	7,20,000	8,40,000	6,60,000
Less: Fixed factory Overhead	2,50,000	2,50,000	2,50,000	2,50,000
Fixed Selling and Administrative Expenses	50,000	50,000	50,000	50,000
Variables Selling and Administrative Expenses	35,000	36,000	42,000	33,000
Total fixed costs and Non-manufacturing variable costs	3,35,000	3,36,000	3,42,000	3,33,000
Net income for the month	3,65,000	3,84,000	4,98,000	3,27,000

Note: Under variable costing, fixed factory (manufactured) overhead costs are not included in the product unit costs and costs of inventories.

(*i*) Valuation of closing inventory

Second month = 3,000 × ₹ 60 = ₹ 1,80,000

Third month = 1,000 × ₹ 60 = ₹ 60,000

Fourth month = 4,500 × ₹ 60 = ₹ 2,70,000

(*ii*) The question of under or over–absorption of factory overhead does not arise under variable costing.

A comparison of the income statements leads to the following conclusions:

1. Under variable costing, the closing inventory is costed at a smaller figure because only variable costs are charged to the product.
2. Both costing methods report the same amount of profit in periods in which production and sales are equal and there is no inventory change (first month). This is because the amount of fixed factory overhead costs charged to the period was the same in each case. Under variable costing ₹ 2,50,000 was deducted from sales as period costs. Under absorption costing ₹ 2,50,000 was charged to the sales in two parts: (*a*) ₹ 2,18,750 as part of the cost of sales (17,500 units × ₹ 12.5) and (*b*) ₹ 31,250 as unfavourable volume (capacity) variance.
3. When inventory of manufactured goods fluctuates from period to period, net income will differ somewhat under the two methods because absorption costing requires that part of the period costs (Fixed manufacturing overhead) be included in inventory, whereas variable costing excludes this costs. Therefore:
   (*i*) When production exceeds sales (the inventory is increased), the net income reported under absorption costing is higher than reported under variable costing. This follows because under absorption costing, a portion of the fixed costs budgeted for the period is shifted to the following period in the closing inventories whereas under variable costing thc total fixed costs are charged against income. This is clear from comparing the net income of the second and fourth month.
   (*ii*) When sales exceeds production (the inventories are decreased), variable costing shows a higher profit because only current period costs are being charged against current revenues whereas under absorption costing the period costs previously included in inventory are now being charged against current revenues. This situation is illustrated by the income of the third month.
4. Under variable costing profits always move in the same direction as sales volume. They cannot, of course, increase or decrease in direct proportion because unit fixed costs do not remain constant. Profit reported under absorption costing behave irregularly and sometimes in the opposite direction from sales. For example, sales of the fourth month are lower than the sales of the first month, yet the net income reported for the fourth month is higher than the net income for the first month.
5. The above income statements are prepared on the assumption that selling prices remained constant and that there were no changes in either the manufacturing costs or the selling and administrative expenses. Further, it has been assumed that overheaded costs are absorbed at predetermined rates based on normal capacity.
6. The aggregate net income (of different month or periods taken together) will be the same under both costing techniques provided production and sales, in total, are equal. In the above example, total production are 77,500 units and total sales are 73,000 units. Since production and sales are unequal, the combined net income is not the same.

RECONCILIATION OF NET INCOME

The differences in the net income between absorption costing and variable costing are due to: (*i*) amount of fixed factory overhead charged to inventory, (*ii*) over-or under-absorbed fixed factory overhead having been deferred in absorption costing. That is, the entire difference in net income can be explained by the amount of fixed factory overhead that is included in the beginning and closing inventories.

Reconciliation of Differences between Absorption and Variable Costing Income

	Second month (₹)	*Third month* (₹)	*Fourth month* (₹)
Variable Costing Income	3,84,000	4,98,000	3,27,000
Absorption costing income	4,21,500	4,73,000	3,70,750
Difference to be explained	(37,500)	25,000	(43,750)
1. Differences in the value of opening and closing inventories in variable and absorption costing:			
(*a*) Second month :			
Opening	0	—	—
Closing ₹ 1,80,000 – 2,17,500	(37,500)		
(*b*) Third month			
Opening ₹ 1,80,000 – 2,17,500	—	37,500	—
Closing ₹ 60,000 – 72,500	—	(12,500)	—
(*c*) Fourth month:			
Opening ₹ 60,000 – 72,500	—	—	12,500
Closing ₹ 2,70,000 – 3,26,250	—	—	(56,250)
	(37,500)	25,000	(43,750)

Note: There are no opening and closing inventory for the first month.

Income may be influenced under absorption costing if a large inventory is kept even if such inventory build-up is not needed for business purposes. In other words, by building up finished goods and work-in process inventories, it is possible to shift a part of fixed factory overhead to a subsequent period, and thus manipulate income for the current period.

Inventory Values

As stated earlier, inventories under absorption costing absorb a part of the fixed manufacturing costs of a period, whereas inventories under variable include only the variable manufacturing costs. Closing inventories calculated from the data given above would be as follows:

Closing Inventories

	First month	*Second month*	*Third month*	*Fourth month*
Absorption costing @ ₹ 72.5 per unit	—	2,17,500	72,500	3,26,750
Variable costing @ ₹ 60 per unit	—	1,80,000	60,000	2,70,000

Difference are caused by the elimination of fixed factory expenses from inventories in variable costing.

VARIABLE COSTING AND CONTRIBUTION MARGIN

Contribution can be considered and determined from two angles.

1. *Manufacturing Margin:* First, contribution is determined with the objective of income measurement and from the standpoint of what costs are to be considered product costs and thus included in inventory, and what costs are to be considered period costs and treated simply as expenses of the period. The variable costing follows this format of determining contribution. Accordingly, under variable costing, contribution is obtained after deducting variable production costs, which are treated product cost, from sales. Subsequently, from this contribution all other costs (fixed manufacturing overhead, fixed and variable selling and administrative overheads) which are treated as period costs are deducted to finally find out the net income. This format of determining contribution is useful to management when it is concerned with cost volume relationship from production activities only. Since management is considering only the production area under variable costing, non-manufacturing variable costs (variable selling and administrative costs) are excluded while determining contribution. Such contribution can be better referred to as manufacturing margin or contribution margin from production.

2. *Contribution Margin from Total Operations:* Second, contribution can be determined from the viewpoint of a firm's total-cost-volume- profit relationship or total operations. A broader view of contribution determination is taken and here the contribution margin is the amount remaining after deducting all variable costs, both production and selling, from sales, This contribution margin should cover fixed costs and provide a satisfactory profit. When management is concerned with cost-volume profit relationship for the entire firm, the variable non-production costs become relevant, as well as the variable production costs. Such a contribution margin can be referred to as contribution margin from total operations. Generally, the use of the term contribution margin refers to contribution margin from total operations.

The contribution margin from total operations is used in calculating the break even point. The variable costing approach (contribution margin from production approach) is useful in making incremental production decisions. The contribution margin approach (total contribution margin from total operations approach) is useful in making both incremental production and incremental selling decisions, in addition to its value in the study of cost-volume profit relationships for the firm as whole.[2]

Variable Costing for Service Firms

Unlike a manufacturing company, a service company does not make or sell a product. Thus, service companies do not have inventory. Since, service companies have no inventory, they do not use absorption costing to allocate fixed costs. In addition, variable costing reports of service companies do not report a manufacturing margin.

To illustrate variable costing for a service company, Indigo Airlines, which operates as a domestic airlines, is used. The variable and fixed costs of Indigo Airlines are shown below.

Cost	Cost Behavior	Activity Base
Depreciation expense	Fixed	
Food and beverage service expense	Variable	Number of passengers
Fuel expense	Variable	Number of kilometres flown
Rental expense	Fixed	
Selling expense	Variable	Number of passengers
Wages expense	Variable	Number of kilometres flown

As discussed in Chapter 2, a cost is classified as a fixed or variable cost according to how it changes relative to an activity base. A common activity for a manufacturing firm is the number of units produced. In contrast, most service companies use several activity bases.

To illustrate, Indigo Airlines uses the activity base of number of passangers for food and beverage service and uses number of kilometres flown for fuel and wage expenses.

The variable costing income statement for Indigo Airlines, assuming revenue of ₹ 1,92,38,000 is shown below in Table 5.2.

Table 5.2: Variables Costing Income Statement for a Service Company

Indigo Airlines Variable Costing Income Statement for the Month ended March 31, 2016		
Revenue		₹ 192,38,000
Variable costs:		
Fuel expense	₹ 40,80,000	
Wages expense	61,20,000	
Food and beverage service expense	4,44,000	
Selling expense	32,56,000	
Total variable costs		1,39,00,000
Contribution margin		53,38,000
Fixed costs:		
Depreciation expense	₹ 36,00,000	
Rental expense	8,00,000	
Total fixed costs		44,00,000
Income from operations		₹ 9,38,000

Unlike a manufacturing company, Table 5.2 does not report cost of goods sold, inventory, or manufacturing margin. However, as shown in this table, contribution margin is reported separately from income from operations.

ADVANTAGES OF VARIABLE COSTING

The following are the advantages of variable costing:

1. ***Planning and Control:*** Financial planning requires managers to estimate future sales, future production levels, future costs, etc. Sales forecasts determine production plans, which in turn determine the level of expenditures required for raw materials, direct labour and variable manufacturing overhead. In order to determine the level of expenditure at different production levels, knowledge of cost behaviour and distinguishing between fixed and variable costs is essential for making accurate cost estimates at different levels of production and sales. Thus, a financial plan will highlight expected production level and related expected costs. This financial plan can be used to monitor the actual performance as it is done. In case actual performance is different from the budgeted activity level, corrective action can be taken by management. Thus, control is exercised by management through taking corrective actions. But, for the control function to work and succeed, cost should be divided into fixed and variable components which is achieved only under variable costing and not under absorption costing.

Absorption costing ignores cost behaviour and is not able to isolate and relate accurate costs to different sales and product volumes. It is not reliable because of the arbitrary allocation of manufacturing overhead. These allocations may not reflect accurate charging of manufacturing overhead to different production levels.

Variable costing income statements are more useful internally for short-term planning, controlling and decision making than absorption costing statements. To carry out their functions, managers need to understand and be able to project how different costs will change in reaction to changes in activity levels. Variable costing, through its emphasis on cost behaviours, provides that necessary information.

2. *Managerial Decision-making:* Management requires knowledge of cost behaviour under various operating conditions and business decisions. The identification and classification of costs as either fixed or variable, with semi-variable expenses properly subdivided into this fixed and variable components, provide useful framework for the accumulation and analysis of costs and further for making decisions. Relevant costs are required for a variety of short-term decision such as changes in production levels, make or buy, entry into new markets, product mix, plant expansion or contraction or special promotional activities. These decisions require that costs be split into their fixed and variable components and this is possible only under variable costing. Therefore, projection of future costs and revenues for different activity levels and the use of relevant cost decision-making techniques are facilitated and highlighted in variable costing and not in absorption costing. The utility of variable costing rests upon the fact that, within a limited volume range, fixed costs tend to remain constant in total when activity level changes, Under such conditions, only variable costs are relevant in ascertaining costs of additional output and sales or in other short-term decisions.

Another benefit of variable costing is that the favourable margin between selling prices and variable cost should provide a constant reminder of income forgone because of lack of sales volume. A favourable margin justifies a higher production level.

3. *Product Pricing Decisions:* Variable costing provides more useful information to management for pricing decisions than absorption costing. It is rightly contended that the best or optimum price is that which produces the maximum excess of total sales revenue over total cost. The optimum production volume is that at which increase in total cost due to the addition of one more unit of volume is just equal to the increase in total revenue or a zero increase in total profit. The price at which this volume can be achieved is the optimum product price. A higher price will decrease the sales revenue, a lower price tends to increase the sales volume and leads to abnormal production costs due to overtime, production inefficiencies, etc. Variable costing serves as the basis of product pricing in many cases. Under variable costing, management has the data to determine when it is advisable to accept orders if other than normal conditions exist. In some cases, a sales order can be accepted even if it contributes partly to fixed costs. New short-term businesses or orders should be accepted as long as the variable cost of making and selling are recovered—variable costs represent the minimum sales price under these conditions. Knowledge of the contribution margin provides guidelines for the most profitable pricing policies. However, the full cost and not only the variable cost should be the basis of product pricing in the long-run. The full cost is the cost which includes variable manufacturing cost and fixed manufacturing cost incurred in the production process.

4. *Cost Control:* For the purpose of cost control, costs should be pooled into separate variable and fixed totals. Separation of variable and fixed costs supports the use of standards, budgets and responsibility reporting to help management in controlling costs. All costs are controllable in the long run by someone within a business enterprise. But they are not all controllable at the same level of management. For example, supervisors in production department are responsible for controlling the use of direct materials in their departments. They have no control, however, over insurance costs related to the production department building. For a specific level of management, controllable costs are costs that it controls directly and non-controllable costs are costs that another level of management controls. This distinction, as applied to specific levels of management, is useful in fixing the responsibility for incurrence of costs and then for reporting cost data to those responsible for cost control.[3]

The variable costing includes only variable manufacturing costs, which varies with change in the volume of production, in the cost of product and thus makes variable manufacturing costs controllable at cost centre level by operating management. Fixed production costs may not be controllable at departmental level and therefore should not be included in the production costs at cost centre level, as it is important to match control with responsibility. The fixed manufacturing costs are reported as separate item in the variable costing income statement, they are easier to identify and control (by a higher level of management) than when they are spread among units of product as in absorption costing. Similarly, under variable costing, each other variable and fixed operating expenses (e.g., variable and fixed selling and administrative expenses) are reported separately and thus become easier to identify and control than in absorption costing where they are not reported separately but combined together.

5. *Inventory Changes Do Not Affect Profit:* In variable costing, profit is a function of sales volume only. But under absorption costing sales and production (production creates inventory) both influence profit of a period. Profit in variable costing is not affected by changes in inventory as in absorption costing. Other things remaining the same (i.e., selling prices, costs, sales mix, etc), profit move in the same direction as sales when variable costing is used. In absorption costing, profit may decline although sales have increased. When inventory levels fluctuate greatly, profits calculated under absorption costing may be distorted since inventory changes will influence the amount of fixed manufacturing overheads charged to an accounting period.

6. *Avoiding the Impact of Fixed Manufacturing Costs:* Variable costing avoids the arbitrary apportionment of fixed factory overheads and also avoids problem of determining a suitable absorption basis which is needed for a predetermined overhead absorption rate. Fixed production costs are charged to the period in which they are incurred and are not carried forward in stock which may be unsaleable, resulting in earlier profits being overstated. It is argued that managerial decisions can be easily made if fixed production costs are separated and are not mixed in inventory or cost of sales. Since most fixed manufacturing costs are committed and can not be avoided, these costs should not be part of inventory. These fixed manufacturing costs are incurred to have the *capacity* to make products during a particular period and will be incurred even if nothing is made during the period. Moreover, whether a unit is made or not, the fixed manufacturing costs will be exactly the same. Therefore, variable costing advocates argue that fixed manufacturing costs are not part of the costs of producing a particular unit of product and thus the matching principle dictates that fixed manufacturing costs should be charged to the current period. In addition, the presentation of the total amount of fixed manufacturing costs on variable costing income statement emphasizes their full impact on net income, an effect partially hidden in inventory values under absorption costing. Another benefit of variable costing is that production managers cannot manipulate income by producing more or fewer product units than needed during a period. Under absorption costing, however, a production manager could increase income simply by producing more units than are currently needed for sales.

Morse, Davis and Hartgraves[4] observe:

> *when considering the financial accounting principle of matching, variable costing has advantage over absorption costing because it matches revenue with the direct cost of producing those revenues. This results in net income varying only with sales and not with both sales and production, as is often found in absorption costing. In absorption costing, overproduction especially distorts net income during a period because the excess inventory is assigned fixed costs that would otherwise be assigned to the units produced and sold.*

7. *Performance Evaluation of Managers:* The evaluation of managers is often linked with the profitability of units they manage and control. The changes in income from one period to another and difference between the actual income and budgeted income are used to judge managerial performance and efficiency. For example, if a manager has worked hard and has increased sales while controlling costs simultaneously, income will increase indicating the success and better performance of manager. The variable costing income statement highlights the relationship between sales and income whereas the absorption costing income statement does not generally show any association between sales and income. For example, under absorption costing income may decrease although sales have increased or sales may decrease but income reported may be higher due to large inventory being created due to higher production. Variable costing always produces an increase in income corresponding to the improved sales performance.

Furthermore, the variable costing can be used to evaluate the profit contributions of plants, product lines and sales territories. The separation of fixed and variable costs which are basic to variable costing is critical for making accurate evaluations. Thus, variable costing can make a significant contribution to management decision-making in such and similar areas.

8. *Segmental Reporting:* Segmented reporting provides information about the contribution of organizational subunits. Segmented income statements differ from other income statements because they display amounts for direct (traceable) fixed costs (costs avoidable if the segment is eliminated) and for common or allocated fixed costs (costs that will continue to be incurred even if the segment is eliminated). Presenting segmented income statements on a variable-costing rather than on absorption-costing basis is preferable because it results in more accurate studies of relative profitability of divisions, plants, products, territories, activities, and other segments of an organization. It concentrates on the contribution (the segment margin) that each segment makes to the recovery of common fixed costs. Marginal income data facilitate appraisal of segments without the bias (cross-subsidies) introduced by allocated common fixed costs.

9. *Customer Profitability Analysis:* Customer profitability analysis is an application of segmented reporting in which a customer group is treated as a segment. This analysis may be done using variable costing to determine a customer contribution margin or absorption costing to determine a customer gross margin based on full-cost cost of sales. It is especially helpful when combined with an activity-based costing approach that determines which activities are performed for each group and assigns costs based on appropriate drivers. Activities include those required to gain new customers and to maintain relationships with current customers as well as ordering, packaging, handling, customer service, etc. Furthermore, assignment of costs for a customer profitability analysis is based on cost-hierarchy concepts similar to those used in product profitability analysis. For example, activities, their drivers, and their costs may be classified as order level, customer level, channel level, market level, or enterprise level. Assignment of revenues is also a critical concern in customer profitability analysis. Thus, sales returns and allowances, the effects of coupon offers, price discounts, etc., should be traced to specific customer groups.

LIMITATIONS OF VARIABLE COSTING

The following are the limitations of variable costing:

1. ***Separation of Costs into Fixed and Variable:*** The variable costing method requires that all costs should be divided into fixed and variable elements. Also variable costing assumes that the relation between the sales and the variable costs is direct, proportionate, linear. It cannot be true under all circumstances. Examples of factors that might affect this assumption include quantity discounts on materials, and labour efficiency variance.
2. ***Product Costs Not without Fixed Costs:*** Complete product cost does not depend only on variable production costs. Fixed costs should be considered in determining the product cost and for long-range pricing and other long-run policy decisions. The product is not complete until it is in a form and place and at a time desired by the customer, and this product completion involves distribution just as essentially as it does manufacturing.
3. ***Temptation to Cut prices:*** It is also argued that if managers are given only variable cost (as is done in variable costing) they will be tempted to cut prices to the degree that company profits will suffer. Despite the many other advantages of the method for internal purposes, variable costing generates product figures providing little basis for long range pricing policies[5].

4. ***Use of Net Income Figure:*** Income figures obtained under variable costing have to be used carefully if management decides to expand business or drop a product line. Management has to consider other factors also before deciding to drop a product line such as customer goodwill. The loss in customer goodwill which might result from dropping a product with a low contribution margin could easily offset any gain from products with higher contribution ratios. Thus, the variable costing although useful is not a perfect managerial tool.
5. ***Unwise Decisions:*** Sometimes variable costing may be unnecessarily given a broader significance than it deserves. For instance, when sales are higher than production, variable costing net income will be more than absorption costing net income. In this case, sometimes, management may take unwise actions due to 'increased profits' reported by variable costing. It may prompt the marketing managers to go for lower selling prices, may inspire the managers and employees to demand higher salary or bonus. But, in fact, there can be no justification for such actions. At the other extreme, variable costing results may mislead management during a business recession during which variable costing profit will be minimised due to sales being extremely lower than production.

ADVANTAGES OF ABSORPTION COSTING

The following are the advantages of absorption costing:

1. ***Consideration of Fixed Costs:*** Absorption costing rightly recognises the importance of including fixed production costs in product cost determination and in determining a suitable pricing policy. Supporters of absorption costing argue that fixed production costs are just as much used in the production of goods and services as the variable production costs.

   The pricing based on absorption costing similarly ensures that all costs are covered. The pricing determined in terms of only variable costs (as is advocated in variable costing) may, in the long-run, result in a contribution margin failing to cover the fixed costs. It is important, however, that sales are equal to or exceed the budgeted production level otherwise all fixed manufacturing costs will not be covered and will be under-absorbed.
2. ***Seasonal Sales:*** In a situation where production is done to have sales in future (e.g., seasonal sales), absorption costing will show correct profit calculation than the variable costing. In such a case, under variable costing, sales will be zero but all fixed costs will be shown as an expense in the same accounting period. The result is that losses will be reported during out of season periods and large profits will be reported in the periods when the goods are sold.

   On the contrary in absorption costing, fixed manufacturing overheads are included in closing stock valuation and are deferred and recorded as an expense only in the period in which goods are sold. Losses, therefore, will not be reported in absorption costing when sales are nil or quite low and stocks are being builtup. Thus, absorption costing will report correct profit situation than variable costing.
3. ***Conformity with Accrual and Matching Concepts:*** Absorption costing conforms with accrual and matching accounting concepts which requires matching costs with revenue for a particular accounting period.
4. ***External Reporting and Income Taxes:*** Absorption costing has been recognised for the purpose of preparing external reports and for stock valuation purpose. For instance, FASB (USA), ASC (UK), ASB (India) have recommended the use of absorption costing for these purposes.

It is also required that business firms should use absorption costing when filing out income tax returns. Even if a company uses absorption costing for its external reports, a manager can use variable costing income statements for internal reports. No Particular accounting problems are created by using *both* costing methods—the variable costing method for internal reports and the absorption costing method for external reports.

Top executives are typically evaluated based on the earnings reported to shareholders on the company's external financial reports. This creates a problem for top executives who might otherwise favour using variable costing for internal reports. They may feel that because they are evaluated based on absorption costing reports, decisions should also be based on absorption costing data.

5. ***No Need to Separate Costs as Fixed and Variable:*** Absorption costing avoids the separation of costs into fixed and variable elements which cannot be easily and accurately done.
6. ***Relevance of Under-absorption and Over-absorption:*** The presentation of under-absorption and over-absorption of factory overheads in absorption costing discloses inefficient or efficient utilisation of production resources which is not possible in variable costing.
7. ***Accountability of Departmental Managers:*** The allocation and apportionment of fixed factory overheads to cost centres or departments makes managers more aware and responsible for the costs and services provided to their centres/departments.

LIMITATIONS OF ABSORPTION COSTING

Absorption costing is criticised on some valid grounds:

1. ***Fixed Costs are Period Costs:*** Many accountants argue that fixed costs, whether related to manufacturing or to selling and administration, are period costs which produce no future benefits and therefore, should not be included in the cost of the product and inventory.

2. ***Apportionment of Overhead Costs:*** The validity of product costs determined under absorption costing depends upon the appropriateness of apportionment of overhead costs in a reasonably correct manner. But in practice, many overhead costs are apportioned by using arbitrary methods. The resulting costs figures, therefore, are doubtful and if included in the costs of products can make the product costs inaccurate and unreliable.

3. ***Not Useful in Decision Making:*** Absorption costing is not helpful to management in decision making. Various types of managerial problems, such as selection of production volume and optimum capacity utilization, selection of product-mix, whether to buy or manufacture, evaluation of performance, choice of alternatives can be solved only with the help of variable costing analysis.

McWatters, Morse and Zimmerman[6] comment that managers who rely on product costs from absorption costing system are likely to misprice products and choose inappropriate product mixes. They further argue:

> *A common result of the misuse of product costs from full absorption cost system is the death spiral, which occurs when an organisation drops a product because its full costs exceeds its price. Once the product is eliminated, the fixed overhead that has been allocated to it is redistributed to the remaining products. This redistribution might make other products appear to be unprofitable because of the increased overhead that these products now must bear. When these products are dropped, more overhead is again allocated to the remaining products. So, the cycle continues, until the organisation has no profitable production left.*

4. ***Not Useful in Cost Control:*** Absorption costing is not helpful in control of costs and planning and control function. It is not useful in fixing the responsibility for incurrence of costs. It is not practical to hold a manager accountable for costs over which he has no control. Once he learns that he cannot control part of the costs with which he is charged, his sense of responsibility for controlling his direct cost somehow seems to weaken. Allocating indirect costs also distorts results of operations besides complicating control and decision-making. Distortion occurs because different bases of apportionment produce different allocation to products and affect different results.

5. ***Inflated, Not Real, Profit:*** Absorption costing helps a manager to increase operating income in a specific period by increasing the production, even if there is no customer demand for the additional production. When absorption costing method is used, fixed production overheads are charged to products and are included in product costs. Consequently, the closing stocks are valued on total cost (including fixed overheads) basis. The net effect is that the charge of fixed overheads to P/L account gets reduced, if the closing stock is greater than the opening stock. This situation has the effect of inflating the profit for the period. One motivation could be a manager's bonus plan that is based on reported operating income.

Critics of absorption costing refer to this phenomenon as one that creates illusionary or phantom profits. Phantom profits are temporary absorption-costing profits caused by producing more inventory than is sold. When sales increase to eliminate the previously produced inventory, the phantom profits disappear.

The undesirable effect of producing for inventory may be sizeable and they can arise in several ways. For examples[7],

(*i*) A plant manager may switch production to those orders that absorbs the highest amount of fixed manufacturing costs, regardless of the customer demand for these products (called "cherry picking" the production line). Production of items that absorb minimal fixed manufacturing costs may be delayed, resulting in failure to meet promised customer delivery dates (which, in itself, can reduce long term customer loyalty).

(*ii*) A plant manager may accept a particular order to increase production even though another plant in the same company is better suited to handle that order.

(*iii*) To meet increased production, a manager may defer maintenance beyond the current accounting period. Although operating income may increase now, future operating income will probably decrease because of increased repairs and less efficient equipment.

Garrison, Noreen and Brewer[8] observe:

> *Absorption costing income statements can be confusing and are easily misinterpreted. A manager might wonder why net operating income went up from one period to another period even though sales were exactly the same. Was it a result of lower selling costs, more efficient operations, or was it some other factor? In fact, it was simply because the number of units produced exceeded the number of units sold in later period and so some of the fixed manufacturing overhead costs were deferred in inventories in that period. These costs have not gone away—they will eventually flow through to the income statement in a later period when inventories go down. There is no way to tell this from the absorption costing income statements.*
>
> *In contrast, the variable costing income statements are clear and easy to understand. All other things the same, when sales go up, net operating income goes up. When sales go down, net operating income goes down. When sales are constant, net operating income is constant.*
>
> *To avoid mistakes when absorption costing is used, readers of financial statements should be alert to changes in inventory levels. Under absorption costing, if inventories increase, fixed manufacturing overhead costs are deferred in inventories, which in turn increases net operating income. If inventories decrease, fixed manufacturing overhead costs are released from inventories, which in turn decreases net operating income. Thus, when absorption costing is used, fluctuations in net operating income can be due to changes in inventories rather than to changes in sales.*

6. *Impact on Long-term Profit:* Mcwatters, Morse and Zimmerman[9] demonstrate that managers can increase short term reported income and harm the organisation at the same time. In the long term, reported income will be lower as the higher inventory costs are passed on to subsequent years. However, not all managers remain with the organisation long enough to bear the costs of earlier over production. As long as managers are evaluated based on short term income and have the potential to leave the organisation, absorption costing creates an incentive to overproduce. Managers who are evaluated based on long term performance and are committed to the organisation for the long term have less incentive to overproduce.

On the debate between variable costing and absorption costing, Anderson and Sollenberger[10] aptly comment:

> *Neither variable costing nor absorption costing is correct or incorrect. Their usefulness correlates with management's attitudes and with philosophies of organisational behaviour. This means that some companies will find variable costing extremely useful while other companies will find it less meaningful. Since the major difference between the two methods is the treatment of fixed costs as product or period costs, the difference in net profits disappears where little or no inventory of work in process or finished goods exists. For companies implementing JIT production procedure, inventories will be eliminated or substantially reduced. Hence, the difference in costing method loses significance in this environment. Also, this controversy is irrelevant to service organisation*

According to Garrison and Noreen[11],

> *At any rate, absorption costing is the generally accepted method for preparing mandatory external financial reports and income tax returns. Probably because of the cost and possible confusion of maintaining two separate costing systems—one for external reporting and one for internal reporting—most companies use absorption costing for both external and internal reports.*

PRECAUTIONS IN USING ABSORPTION COSTING

Horngreen, Foster and Datar[12] suggest the following guidelines for revising performance evaluation and controlling dysfunctional aspects associated with absorption costing:

1. *Careful Budgeting and Inventory Planning to Reduce Management's Latitude for Gaming:* For example, the budgeted monthly balance sheets have estimates of the inventories. These could be used in a management –by-exception way to highlight unplanned inventory buildups.

2. *Change the Accounting System:* Discontinue the use of absorption costing for internal reporting and instead use variable costing. This change will reduce the incentives of managers to produce for inventory.

3. *Incorporate a Carrying Charge for Inventory into the Internal Accounting System:* For example, an inventory carrying charge of 1% per month could be assessed for resources tied up in inventory assets.

4. *Change the Time Period used to Evaluate Performance:* Critics of absorption costing give examples in which managers take actions that maximize quarterly or annual income at the potential expense of long run income. By evaluating performance over a 3-5 year period, managers will be less tempted to produce for inventory.

5. *Include Non-financial as well as Financial Variables in the Measures used to Evaluate Performance:* Companies are currently using non-financial variables, such as the following, to monitor manager's performance in key areas:

a. $\dfrac{\text{Ending inventory in units this period}}{\text{Ending inventory in units last period}}$

b. $\dfrac{\text{Sales in units this period}}{\text{Ending inventory in units this period}}$

Any buildup of inventory at the end of the year would be signalled by tracking the month-to-month behaviour of these two non-financial inventory measures. Companies that manufacture or sell several products could report the two measures on a product by-product basis.

McWatters, Morse and Zimmermen[13] suggest the following methods to check the manager's incentive to overproduce.

1. ***Charge Managers for Holding Inventory:*** The net income reported in financial statement does not consider explicitly the opportunity cost of using cash to hold inventory. The residual income performance measure is one example of a charge for holding inventory because the manager is responsible for the opportunity cost of capital.

2. ***Follow a Strict Senior Management Policy against Adding to or Building Inventories:*** Compensation plans can contain a clause that bonuses tied to net income will not be paid if inventories exceed a certain amount. However, such strict conditions are cumbersome and costly to monitor. In some circumstances such as new product innovation and unexpected orders, the organization prefers high inventory levels.

3. ***Choose Performance Measures other than Short-term Reported Income to Evaluate Managers:*** Long term profit, change in share price, total sales or percentage of defects also could be used as measures of managerial performance.

4. ***Use Just-in-Time (JIT) Production System to Reduce Inventory Levels:*** In JIT system, manufacturing generally does not begin until a customer orders the part or the final product. If the production schedule is determined by demand, the plant manager or product line manager does not have the discretion to set production levels in excess of demand. In essence, a JIT system removes the responsibility from managers to set production levels. These responsibilities are replaced by demand -driven market orders.

IMPACT OF JIT INVENTORY METHOD AND LEAN PRODUCTION

As discussed earlier, absorption costing and variable costing will give different net profit figures whenever there is a difference between production units and sales units. This brings change in the number of units in inventory. It is also true that absorption costing profit may be erratic and may be in opposite direction than that of sales.

When JIT methods (also known as lean production method) are used by the companies, difference of profit between absorption costing and variable costing will be reduced. Under JIT, goods are produced to customers' orders and the goal is to eliminate finished goods inventory entirely and reduce work in process inventory to almost nothing. If there is very little inventory, then changes in inventory will be very small and both variable costing and absorption costing will generally show the same net income figure. In that case, absorption costing net income will move in the same direction as movements in sales. It is significant to observe that the erratic movement of net income under absorption costing and the difference in net income between absorption and variable costing happen because of changes in the number of units in inventory.

However, per unit cost of product will still be different between absorption and variable costing. But, in case JIT and lean production are used, the difference in net income will largely disappear.

COST BEHAVIOUR

Cost behaviour can be defined as:

- *the manner in which cost changes due to changes in volume or activity.*

In relation to cost behaviour analysis, fixed and variable cost classifications are basically two extremes. Between these two classes of cost behaviour are various costs that imply both fixed and variable cost characteristics. Such costs are known as semi variable or mixed costs such as salaries of supervisors, accountants, typists, clerks, employees, insurance, pension plans, maintenance of building and grounds, purchased power, water, gas, telephone and telegraph, fuel, oil and other supplies. Semi-variable costs present the biggest problem in cost analysis as they do not show any definite relationship between cost and volume.

Importance of Cost Behaviour Analysis

A proper analysis of cost behaviour patterns is the basis of all profit planning and cost control. The determination of fixed and variable elements of a semi-variable cost and the creation of total fixed and total variable costs is of value in cost accounting. The separation of costs into fixed, variable and semi-variable is necessary in order to determine, analyse, control, measure or evaluate the following:

1. Departmental expenses allowed at various levels of production
2. Operating efficiency of a department
3. Use of variable costing method
4. Utilisation of facilities
5. Break-even point
6. Relative profitability of territories, departments and customers
7. Company profit position
8. Cost-volume-profit analysis
9. Marginal or differential cost for various decision- making purposes
10. Effect of proposed capital expenditures
11. Effect of alternative courses of action

Methods of Determining Cost Behaviour

Several methods are used for segregating semi-variable costs into fixed and variable. There are four major techniques that are found in practice and they are listed as follows:

1. High and low points method, 2. Scattergraph method, 3. Least squares regression method, 4. Accounting or analytical approach.

High and Low Points Methods

This approach considers the difference in total cost between two different volumes, and divides the incremental cost by the volume. As the words 'high' and 'low' imply, the two levels of volume chosen are the highest and the lowest for the periods under review. The result of this division is the estimated variable cost per unit. Then, the average activity level is computed together with the average cost for the periods in the data base. The fixed cost is estimated by taking the total average cost and subtracting the variable cost for the average activity level. The variable cost is computed by multiplying the average activity level by the variable cost per unit as determined above.

As an illustration, assume that a company incurred the following costs in two periods (high and low) in which 5,000 units and 10,000 units were produced:

Cost	Cost Incurred 5,000 units	10,000 units
	₹	₹
Insurance on factory building	3,00,000	3,00,000
Depreciation of machinery (units of output method @ ₹ 80 per unit)	4,00,000	8,00,000
Indirect Material	4,50,000	7,00,000

Since insurance remained constant at the two volumes, there is no variable component. Since a 100% increase in volume resulted in a 100% increases in depreciation, there is no fixed component. Indirect materials contain both a fixed and variable component.

Separation is made as follows:

Variable component:	₹
Indirect material cost of 10,000 units	7,00,000
Indirect material cost of 5,000 units	4,50,000
Cost of production of additional 5,000 units	2,50,000
Variable cost per unit ₹ 2,50,000 ÷ 5,000 units	50.0

Fixed components:	5,000 units	10,000 units
Total indirect materials cost	4,50,000	7,00,000
Variable components @ ₹ 50 per unit	2,50,000	5,00,000
Fixed components	2,00,000	2,00,000

Scattergraph Method

Another approach to the estimation of the fixed and variable components of a mixed cost is the scattergraph method. With this procedure, various costs are plotted on a vertical line, the y-axis, and measurement figures (activity levels such as direct labour hours, units of output, percentage of capacity or direct labour cost) are plotted along a horizontal line, the x-axis. A straight line is fitted to this scatter of points by visual approximation. The slope of the line is used to estimate the variable costs and the intercept of the line with the vertical axis is considered as the estimated fixed cost. The following examples illustrates the scattergraph method.

Month	*Direct labour hours*	*Costs* (₹)
January	17,000	3,20,000
February	15,000	3,10,000
March	17,000	3,10,000
April	19,500	2,95,000
May	21,000	2,50,000
June	16,000	2,65,000
July	13,000	2,50,000
August	13,000	2,50,000
September	15,500	2,65,000
October	17,500	2,75,000
November	21,500	2,90,000
December	24,000	3,40,000
	2,10,000	34,20,000

The first step in constructing a scattergraph requires plotting each of the observation on graph paper (see Figure 5.1). The second step is fitting a regression line or trend line to the data. In the chart, line B is plotted by visual inspection. Ideally, there should be as many dots above as below the line. Another line is drawn parallel to the base line from the point of intersection on the y-axis, which is at ₹ 2,20,000. This line A represents the fixed portion of the expenses for all levels of activity within a reasonable range. The triangle formed by line A and B shows the increase in the expenses as direct labour hours increase.

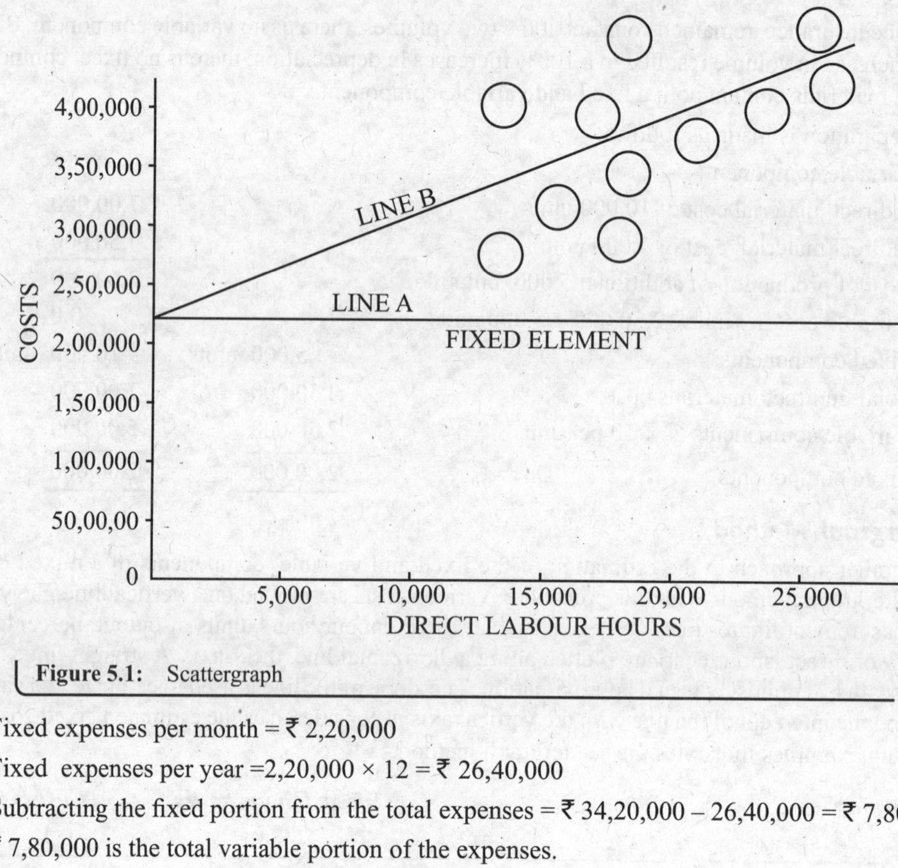

Figure 5.1: Scattergraph

Fixed expenses per month = ₹ 2,20,000

Fixed expenses per year =2,20,000 × 12 = ₹ 26,40,000

Subtracting the fixed portion from the total expenses = ₹ 34,20,000 – 26,40,000 = ₹ 7,80,000

₹ 7,80,000 is the total variable portion of the expenses.

$$\text{Variable cost per direct labour} = \frac{₹\,7{,}80{,}000}{2{,}10{,}000\,\text{hr}} \quad ₹\,3.7 \text{ per hour.}$$

Thus, expenses consist of ₹ 2,20,000 fixed expenses and variable factor ₹ 3.7 per direct labour hour.

On the scattergraph, although the points are scattered, a definite upward line or cost trend in relation to volume is clearly apparent. Placing transparent ruler over the points, the accountant tries to fit a line to the points in such a way that the areas above and below the line are about equal. Interaction of the trend line with the cost axis determines the fixed component. The variable components can be found by subtracting the fixed component from the total cost at any volume. In the scattergraph method, data being irregular, the trend line would not be so obvious and drawing the line would be difficult.

A definite trend upward is apparent but exactly where the trend line should fall is not so easy to locate.

The scattergraph is a simple device requiring no complicated formula or calculation. It shows a cost behaviour pattern graphically and is easily understood. As a graph it does not possess a high degree of accuracy. It has within itself a measure of reliability. Correlation, if any, that exists between cost and volume is apparent. If costs are behaving irregularly, this fact will be known as soon as the observations are plotted. The Scattergraph has, however, one drawback. Fitting the trend line by observation introduces a personal bias which can be removed only by fitting the line mathematically.

Least Squares Regression Method

The method of least squares uses the equation for a straight line: $Y = a + bx$, with a as the fixed element, and b the degree of variability. For many accounting application, regression provides an accurate estimate of fixed and variable costs.

The answer under regression differs from the scattergraph method because observation does not offer so accurate an answer as this mathematical procedure. Individuals cannot differ in their separation of fixed and variable components. However, this method has drawbacks, it fits a straight line to any set of cost data no matter how erratic the cost behaviour pattern may be. Further, unless a computer is available for this work, the calculations required by the method of least squares are laborious and time-consuming.

Accounting or Analytical Approach

This approach to cost behaviour analysis is close scrutiny of the chart of accounts and a classification of costs into their fixed and variable components according to their basic characteristics determined by the accountant using good judgement, knowledge, and experience. This approach is simple and inexpensive but in its simplicity lies its inherent weakness. The results obtained are not accurate and may happen to be mere guesses. To improve this method, costs over a period of time can be watched. The time selected must be long enough to provide valuable data over a wide range of activity. Having collected cost data at different production levels, the accountant then proceeds to identify fixed and variable costs. Costs which appear to be semi-variable must be set aside for further analysis into fixed and variable components.

Example:

The following are the Maintenance Costs incurred in a Machine shop for the six month with corresponding machine hours:

Month	*Machine Hours*	*Maintenance Costs* ₹
January	2,000	3,00,000
February	2,200	3,20,000
March	1,700	2,70,000
April	2,400	3,40,000
May	1,800	2,80,000
June	1,900	2,90,000
Total	12,000	18,00,000

Analyse the Maintenance Cost, which is semi-variable, into fixed and variable element.

Solution:

Computation of Variable Cost and Fixed Cost has been done according to Range Method.

	Machine Hours	*Maintenance Costs*
		₹
Highest point, April	2,400	3,40,000
Lowest point, March	1,700	2,70,000
	700	70,000

$$\text{Variable Cost per Machine hour} = \frac{\text{Change in Maintenance Costs}}{\text{Change in Hours}}$$

$$₹\,70{,}000/700 = ₹\,100$$

Total Variable Cost for 2,400 machine hours will be

$$2{,}400 \times ₹\,100 = ₹\,2{,}40{,}000$$

Hence, Fixed Cost is (₹ 3,40,000 – ₹ 2,40,000) = ₹ 1,00,000

Analysis of Maintenance Cost into Fixed and Variable Element

	Machine Hours	*Maintenance Cost*	*Fixed Cost*	*Variable Cost*
January	2,000	3,00,000	1,00,000	2,00,000
February	2,200	3,20,000	1,00,000	2,20,000
March	1,700	2,70,000	1,00,000	1,70,000
April	2,400	3,40,000	1,00,000	2,40,000
May	1,800	2,80,000	1,00,000	1,80,000
June	1,900	2,90,000	1,00,000	1,90,000

Illustrative Problem 1

Your company has a production capacity of 2,00,000 units per year. Normal capacity utilisation is reckoned as 90%. Standard variable production costs are ₹ 11 per unit. The fixed costs are ₹ 3,60,000 per year. Variable selling costs are ₹ 3 per unit and fixed selling costs are ₹ 2,70,000 per year. The unit selling price is ₹ 20. In the year just ended on 30th June 2016 the production was 1,60,000 units and sales were 1,50,000 units. The closing inventory on June 30, 2016 was 20,000 units. The actual variable production costs for the year were ₹ 35,000 higher than the standard:

1. Calculate the profit for the year by absorption costing method and variable costing method.
2. Explain the difference in the profits.

Solution: (1)

Income Statement (Absorption Costing)
for the Year Ending 30th June 2016

	Amount (₹)	*Amount* (₹)
Sales		30,00,000
Less: Cost of goods sold :		
(1,60,000 × ₹ 11)	17,60,000	
Increases in Variable Cost	35,000	
Fixed Cost	3,20,000	
Opening stock (10,000 × ₹ 13)	1,30,000	
Cost of goods available for sale	22,45,000	
Less: Closing stock (20,000 units)	2,64,118	
Cost of goods sold	19,80,882	
Add: Under-absorption	+ 40,000	20,20,882
Gross Profit		9,79,118
Less: Fixed selling expenses	2,70,000	
Variable selling expenses	4,50,000	
		7,20,000
Net profit		2,59,118

Working Notes

1. Fixed costs (₹ 3,60,000) has been treated as fixed manufacturing costs and therefore has been included in the valuation of closing stock under absorption costing. In absorption costing income statement ₹ 3,20,000 (1,60,000 units × ₹ 2) is charged as fixed cost.
2. In the absence of information concerning opening stock, it is valued at variable costs at ₹ 11 per unit plus an apportionment of fixed costs at normal capacity, i.e., $\frac{₹\ 3,60,000}{1,80,000 \text{ units}}$
3. Cost of closing stock (20,000) units

$$\frac{20,000 \text{ units}}{1,70,000 \text{ units}} \times ₹\ 22,45,000 = ₹\ 2,64,118$$

Income Statement (Variable Costing)
for the Year Ending 30th June 2016

	Amount (₹)	*Amount* (₹)
Sales		30,00,000
Less: Cost of goods sold;		
Variable production costs	17,60,000	
Additional variable production costs	35,000	

Variable production costs of opening stock	1,10,000	
Cost of goods available for sale	19,05,000	
Less: Closing stock	2,24,118	
Cost of goods sold		16,80,882
Marginal Contribution		13,19,118
Less: Fixed Costs	3,60,000	
Fixed Selling Expenses	2,70,000	
Variable Selling Expenses	4,50,000	10,80,000
Net Profit		2,39,118

Note: Value of closing stock (20,000 units) $= \frac{20,000}{1,70,000} \times ₹\,19,05,000 = ₹\,2,24,118$

(2) *Comment:* The difference in profit under absorption costing and variable costing is ₹ 20,000 (₹ 2,59,118 – 2,39,118). This difference in profit is due to the difference in values of opening stock and closing stock in these two costing techniques as shown below:

	Opening Stock (₹)	***Closing Stock*** (₹)
Absorption Costing	1,30,000	2,64,118
Variable Costing	1,10,000	2,24,118
Difference	20,000	40,000

Net Difference = ₹ 40,000 – 20,000 = ₹ 20,000.

Illustrative Problem 2

A company has produced 1,500 units against a budgeted quantity of 2,000 units. Actual sales were 1,300 units. The company's policy is to value stocks at standard absorption cost.

Other data are:

Direct material	₹ 100 per unit
Direct labour	₹ 100 per unit at normal efficiency
Variable OH	₹ 50 per unit
Fixed OH at budgeted capacity	₹ 1,00,000
Variable selling OH	₹ 26,000
Budgeted fixed selling OH	₹ 30,000
Actual fixed selling OH	₹ 25,000
Selling price	₹ 400 per unit

There was no opening stock.

(*i*) Present the profitability statement under absorption costing system.

(*ii*) Assuming actual labour was 25% below normal efficiency and that 100 units of production had to be scrapped after complete manufacture, compute the actual profit or loss.

(*iii*) Reconcile the profits under (*i*) and (*ii*) above.

Profit under Absorption Costing System

Particulars	₹ '000
Sales (1,300 × 400)	520
Absorption costs:	
Opening Stock	Nil
Cost of production	
1,500 units × 300	450
Less: Closing Stock (200 × 300)	60
Net Absorption costs	390
Add: Under-absorption (500 × 50)	25
Total absorption costs	415
Gross profit	105
Less: Selling overhead variable	26
Selling overhead fixed	25
Profit/(loss)	54

Actual Profit and Loss Account

Particulars	₹ '000
Sales (1,300 × 400)	520
Closing Stock (100 × 300)	30
Total	550
Cost:	
Direct materials (1,500 × 100)	150
Direct labour (1,500 × 100/75%)	200
Variable overhead (1,500 × 50)	75
Fixed manufacturing overhead	100
Fixed Selling overhead	25
Variable Selling overhead	26
Total costs	576
Profit / (Loss)	(26)

Working Notes

	₹
Absorption cost per unit	
Direct materials	100
Direct labour	100
Variable overhead	50
Fixed Overhead (1,00,000 / 2,000)	50
Total	300

	Units
Budgeted capacity	2,000
Production	1,500
Under-absorption	500
Sales	1,300
Closing stock	200

Reconciliation

	₹'000
Profit under absorption costing	54
Less: Labour inefficiency**	(50)
Less: Value of units scrapped	(30)
Actual profit / (loss)	(26)

** Cost of labour inefficiency is calculated for 1500 units as follows:

25% below normal efficiency means $133\frac{1}{3}\%\left(\frac{100}{75\%}\right)$ i.e.

$$\frac{100 \times 100}{75} = 133\frac{1}{3}$$

Therefore, for 1500 units, $1500 \times \left(133\frac{1}{3}\% - 100\right) = 1500 \times 33\frac{1}{3} =$ ₹ 50,000

In actual profit and loss statement, closing stock units will be 100 (200 units – 100 scrapped units).

Actual labour is 25% below normal efficiency

Therefore actual direct labour cost for 1500 units will be $\frac{1500 \times 100}{75\%} = \frac{1500 \times 100 \times 100}{75}$ = ₹ 2,00,000

Note: In case budgeted fixed selling overheads are considered while arriving at absorption profit a saving of ₹ 5,000 shall need to be identified as part of reconciliation.

Illustrative Problem 3

A company manufactures a single product which it sells for ₹ 50 per unit. The production process is automated and there are no variable costs. The company's production cost are ₹ 2,00,000 per month. Normal activity is 10,000 units per month and the standard fixed cost per unit is ₹ 20. The company has no selling and administrative expenses. The company began May with no inventory. Its activity for May, June and July is summarised as follows, in units.

	May	*June*	*July*
Production	11,000	10,000	9,000
Sales	9,000	10,000	11,000

Required:

(*i*) Prepare income statements for each of the three months using standard absorption costing.
(*ii*) Prepare income statements for each of the three months using standard variable costing.

Solution:

	May	*June*	*July*
Production units	11,000	10,000	9,000
Sales units	9,000	10,000	11,000

Income Statement (Absorption Costing)

Sales (₹) @ ₹ 50/-	4,50,000	5,00,000	5,50,000
Less: Cost of goods sold:			
Opening Stock	—	40,000	40,000
Variable production cost	—	—	—
Fixed production cost @ ₹ 20	2,20,000	2,00,000	1,80,000
Cost of goods available for sales	2,20,000	2,40,000	2,20,000
Less: Closing Stock	40,000	40,000	NIL
Cost of goods sold	1,80,000	2,00,000	2,20,000
± Capacity variance	(20,000)	NIL	+ 20,000
Actual/Adjusted cost of goods sold	1,60,000	2,00,000	2,40,000
Gross Profit/Net Profit	2,90,000	3,00,000	3,10,000

Valuation of closing stock:

$$\text{May} = \frac{2{,}000 \text{ units}}{11{,}000 \text{ units}} \times ₹\,2{,}20{,}000 = ₹\,40{,}000$$

$$\text{June} = \frac{2{,}000 \text{ units}}{12{,}000 \text{ units}} \times ₹\,2{,}40{,}000 = ₹\,40{,}000$$

July = Nil Closing inventory

Income Statement (Variable Costing)

	May	June	July
Sales @ ₹ 50	4,50,000	5,00,000	5,50,000
Less: Variable cost of goods sold:			
Opening inventory	—	—	—
Variable production cost	—	—	—
Cost of goods available for sales	—	—	—
Less: Closing inventory			—
Variable cost of goods sold	NIL	NIL	NIL
Margin	4,50,000	5,00,000	5,50,000
Less: Fixed production cost	2,00,000	2,00,000	2,00,000
Net income	2,50,000	3,00,000	3,50,000

Reconciliation Statement

	May	June	July
Absorption costing net income	↑ 2,90,000	3,00,000	3,10,000
Variable costing net income	2,50,000	3,00,000	↓ 3,50,000
	40,000	NIL	40,000
Inventory Values:			
Absorption:			
Opening		40,000	40,000
Closing	40,000	40,000	—
	40,000	NIL	40,000
Variable costing:			
Opening	—	—	—
Closing	—	—	—
	—	—	—
Difference in net income (Net effect)	40,000	NIL	40,000

Illustrative Problem 4

Daniel Crowley, the vice president of Master key products Inc, has just received the financial statements for the second quarter of 2016 and is disturbed by the result.

With an increase in sales volume in the second quarter and with no change in prices on the cost structure, we make less money? No way' he exclaims.

He asks you to see where the mistake has been made and to give him corrected statements. The income statements, as presented for the first and second quarters of 2016 are as follow.

Master Key Products Inc

Comparative Income Statement for the First Two Quarters of 2016

	Second Quarter	*First Quarter*
Number of units sold	50,000	40,000
Sales	₹ 6,00,000	₹ 4,80,000
Cost of goods sold:		
Inventory, beginning of quarter (10,000 units)	₹ 1,60,000	₹ 80,000
Current production cost	3,20,000	4,00,000
Cost of merchandise available for sale	4,80,000	4,80,000
Less: Inventory, end of quarter	80,000	1,60,000
Cost of goods sold	4,00,000	3,20,000
Capacity variance	50,000	—
Total	4,50,000	3,20,000
Gross margin	1,50,000	1,60,000
Selling and administrative expenses	50,000	40,000
Income before income tax	1,00,000	1,20,000
Income tax (40%)	40,000	48,000
Net Income	60,000	72,000

The company operated at normal capacity and made 50,000 units of product during the first quarter and 40,000 units of product during the second quarter. All selling and administrative expenses are variable and vary at ₹ 1 per unit of product sold.

(*i*) Explain to Crowley that no mistake was made and show him how the income before income taxes decrease in spite of increased sales volume.

(*ii*) Revise the statement for the each of the two quarters, to show the result on a variable costing basis.

Solution:

$$\text{Fixed manufacturing overhead rate} = \frac{\text{Am. of capacity variance}}{\text{Capacity variance units}}$$

$$= \frac{₹\ 50,000}{10,000\ \text{units}} = ₹\ 5$$

Fixed manufacturing overhead in opening inventory = ₹ 5 × 10,000 units = ₹ 50,000

Variable manufacturing overhead = 80,000 – 50,000 = ₹ 30,000

$$\text{Variable manufacturing rate will be ₹ 3 per unit} = \frac{₹\ 30,000}{10,000\ \text{units}} = ₹\ 3$$

(*i*) The income statement prepared by the absorption costing tends to conceal the fact that fixed manufacturing cost from 2016 (first quarter) in the amount of ₹ 50,000 (10,000 × ₹ 5) has been shifted to 2016 (second quarter) as a part of the inventory carry over to 2016 (second quarter). The reduction in income before taxes of ₹ 20,000 can be explained as follows:

		₹
Increased revenue (10,000 more units × ₹ 12) =		1,20,000
Less: increased variable costs		
Manufacturing (10,000 units × ₹ 3) = ₹ 30,000		
Selling and administrative (10,000 × ₹ 1) = ₹ 10,000		40,000
Increased contribution margin		80,000
	₹	₹
Less: (*i*) Shift of fixed cost out of 2016 (first quarter by inventory carryover =	1,00,000	
Less: Shift of fixed cost out of 2015 **(IV quarter)**	50,000 =	50,000
(*ii*) Shift of fixed cost into 2016 **(II quarter)** by inventory carryover	1,00,000	
Less: Shift of fixed cost into 2016 (IIIrd quarter) by ₹ 50,000 =	50,000	50,000
		1,00,000
Decreases in income before tax		20,000

(II) Income Statement for the First Two Quarters of 2016 (Variable Costing)

	Ist Quarter	*2nd Quarter*
Production units	50,000	40,000
Number of units sold	40,000	50,000
Sales @ ₹ 12 per unit (₹)	4,80,000	6,00,000
Cost of goods sold:		
Opening inventory	30,000	60,000
Add: Current production cost variable @ ₹ 3	1,50,000	1,20,000
Cost of merchandise available for sale	1,80,000	1,80,0000
Closing inventory	60,000	30,000
Cost of goods sold	1,20,000	1,50,0000
Manufacturing margin	3,60,000	4,50,000
Selling and Adm. Expenses	40,000	50,000
Contribution margin	3,20,000	4,00,000
Less: Fixed costs	2,50,000	2,50,000
Income before taxes	70,000	1,50,000
Income tax (40%)	28,000	60,000
Net Income	42,000	90,000

Illustrative Problem 5

Modi Zerox Co. manufactures toner used in photocopy machines. The company's product is sold at ₹ 50 per unit. The company uses an actual costing system, which means that the actual costs of direct material, direct labor, and manufacturing overhead are entered into work-in-process inventory. The actual application rate for manufacturing overhead is computed each year; actual manufacturing overhead is divided by actual production (in units) to compute the application rate. Information for first two years of operations is as follows:

	Year 1	Year 2
Sales (in units)	2,500	2,500
Production (in units)	3,000	2,000
Production costs:		
Variable manufacturing costs	₹ 21,000	₹ 14,000
Fixed manufacturing overhead	42,000	42,000
Selling and administrative costs:		
Variable	25,000	25,000
Fixed	20,000	20,000

Required:

Modi Zerox Company had no beginning or ending work-in-process inventories for either year.

(*a*) Prepare operating income statements for both years based on absorption costing.

(*b*) Prepare operating income statements for both years based on variable costing.

(*c*) Prepare a numerical reconciliation of the difference in income reported under the two costing methods used in requirements (*a*) and (*b*).

(*d*) Reconcile income reported under absorption and variable costing, during each year, by comparing the following two amounts on each income statement.

* Cost of goods sold
* Fixed cost (expensed as a period expense)

(*e*) What was Company's total income across both years under absorption costing and under variable costing? Comment on this result.

Solution:

a. **Absorption-costing income statements:**

	Year 1 (₹)	Year 2 (₹)
Sales revenue	125,000[a]	125,000[d]
Less: Cost of goods sold:		
Beginning finished-goods inventory	0	10,500[e]
Cost of goods manufactured	63,000[b]	56,000[f]
Cost of goods available for sale	63,000	66,500
Ending finished-goods inventory	10,500[c]	0
Cost of goods sold	52,500	66,500
Gross margin	72,500	58,500
Selling and administrative expenses	45,000	45,000
Operating income	27,500	13,500

[a] 2,500 units × ₹ 50 per unit

[b] ₹ 21,000 + ₹ 42,000 (i.e. both variable and fixed costs)

[c] 500 units × (₹ 63,000 / 3,000 units)

[d] 2,500 units × ₹ 50 per unit

[e] Same as year 1 ending inventory

[f] ₹ 14,000 + ₹ 42,000 (i.e, both variable and fixed costs)

b. **Variable-costing income statements:**

	Year 1 (₹)	Year 2 (₹)
Sales revenue	125,000[a]	125,000[d]
Less: Cost of goods sold:		
Beginning finished-goods inventory	0	3,500[e]
Cost of goods manufactured	21,000[b]	14,000[f]
Cost of goods available for sale	21,000	17,500
Ending finished-goods inventory	3,500[c]	0
Cost of goods sold	17,500	17,500
Add: Variable selling and administrative costs	25,000	25,000
Total variable costs:	42,500	42,500
Contribution margin	82,500	82,500
Less: Fixed costs:		
Manufacturing	42,000	42,000
Selling and administrative	20,000	20,000
Total fixed costs	62,000	62,000
Operating income	20,500	20,500

[a]2,5000 units × ₹ 50 per unit
[b]The variable manufacturing cost only, ₹ 21,000
[c]500 units × (₹ 21,000 / 3,000 units)
[d]2,500 units × ₹ 50 per unit
[e]Same as year 1 ending inventory
[f]The variable manufacturing cost only, ₹ 14,000.

c. **Reconciliation of reported income under absorption and variable costing:**

Year	Change in Inventory (in units)		Actual Fixed-Overhead Rate (₹)	Difference in Fixed Overhead Expense (₹)	Absorption-Costing Income Minus Variable-Costing Income (₹)
1	500 increase	×	14	7,000	7,000
2	500 decrease	×	14*	(7,000)	(7,000)

*The 500 units which were sold in year 2, but which were manufactured in year 1, include an absorption-costing product cost of ₹ 14 per unit for fixed overhead,. Since these 500 units were manufactured in year 1, it is the year 1 fixed-overhead rate that is relevant to this calculation, not the year 2 rate.

Explanation: At the end of year 1, under absorption costing ₹ 7,000 of fixed overhead remained stored in finished-goods inventory as a product cost (year 1 fixed-overhead rate of ₹ 14 per unit × 500 units = ₹ 7,000). However, in year 1, under variable costing, that fixed overhead was expensed as a period cost.

In year 2, under absorption costing, that same ₹ 7,000 of fixed overhead was expensed when the units were sold. However, under variable costing that ₹ 7,000 of fixed overhead cost had already been expensed in year 1 as a period cost.

d. Reconciliation of income by comparison of cost of goods sold and fixed manufacturing overhead under absorption and variable costing.

Year 1

(₹)

	Absorption	Variable	Difference	
Cost of goods sold	52,500	17,500		
Fixed manufacturing overhead (period cost)	0	42,000		
Total	52,500	59,500	7,000	Expenses greater under variable costing
Operating income	27,500	20,500	7,000	Operating income greater under absorption costing

Year 2

(₹)

	Absorption	Variable	Difference	
Cost of goods sold	66,500	17,500		
Fixed manufacturing overhead (period cost)	0	42,000		
Total	66,500	59,500	7,000	Expenses greater under absorption costing
Operating income	13,500	20,500	7,000	Operating income greater under variable costing

e. Total operating income across years 1 and 2 is ₹ 41,000 under both absorption and variable costing. This highlights the fact that the key difference between these two costing methods is the timing with which fixed manufacturing overhead costs are expensed. Since the company sold the same number of units that it produced, across the two years taken together, the same amount of fixed manufacturing overhead is expensed, under both absorption and variable costing.

Illustrative Problem 6

For several months, top management of a company has been puzzled by fluctuation in the income as reported by the accountant . The results for February, March and April as reported are as follows:

		February	*March*	*April*
		₹	₹	₹
Sales		18,00,000	18,00,000	9,00,000
Less:	Manufacturing cost of sales	16,60,000	13,60,000	4,30,000
	Selling and Admn. Expenses	4,40,000	4,40,000	4,40,000
	Total Expenses	21,00,00	18,00,000	8,70,000
	Net Income (loss)	(3,00,000)	0	30,000

There has been no change in sales price during the 3 month period. During the months of February and March, the plant sold 3,00,00,000 units. In April it sold 1,50,00,000 units.

The production for the 3 months was as follows:

	February	*March*	*April*
Opening Inventory (units)	3,01,00,000	1,00,000	1,00,000
Production during the month	0	3,00,00,000	6,00,00,000
	3,01,00,000	3,01,00,000	6,01,00,000
Units sold	3,00,00,000	3,00,00,000	1,50,00,000
Ending Inventory	1,00,000	1,00,000	4,51,00,000

The standard cost for the units sold discloses the following information:

	Cost per 1,000 units
	₹
Direct material and labour	30
overhead:	
variable	2
Fixed	10
	42

The fixed manufacturing costs budgeted for each of the months were ₹ 4,00,000. There were no spending or efficiency variances during three months. All selling and administrative expenses were of a fixed nature.

You are required to prepare comparative income statements for the 3 months, using (*i*) absorption costing, and (*ii*) variable costing. (*M. Com., Delhi*)

Solution: (i) Absorption Costing

Profit Statement for 3 Months

	February ₹	*March* ₹	*April* ₹
Sales	18,00,000	18,00,000	9,00,000
Less: Cost of goods sold:			
Opening Inventory:			
VC @ ₹ 32	9,63,200	3,200	3,200
FC @ ₹ 10	3,01,000	1,000	1,000
Cost of goods manufactured : VC	Nil	9,60,000	19,20,000
: FC	Nil	3,00,000	6,00,000
	12,64,200	12,64,200	25,24,200
Less: Closing inventory	4,200	4,200	18,94,200
	12,60,000	12,60,000	6,30,000
Add: ± capacity variance	+ 4,00,000	+ 1,00,000	– 2,00,000
Adjusted cost of goods sold	16,60,000	13,60,000	4,30,000
Gross Margin	1,40,000	4,40,000	4,70,000
Less: Selling and Adm. Exp.	4,40,000	4,40,000	4,40,000
Net profit before tax (loss)	(3,00,000)	Nil	30,000

Note: 1. In absorption costing opening inventory is valued at variable cost plus fixed cost unit, i.e., ₹ 42 per 1,000 units.

2. In March unabsorbed fixed cost of ₹ 1,00,000 has been added to cost of goods sold whereas in April over-absorbed fixed cost of ₹ 2,00,000 has been deducted.

(ii) Variable Costing

Profit Statement for 3 Months

	February		*March*		*April*	
Sales		18,00,000		18,00,000		9,00,000
Less: Cost of goods sold:						
Opening inventory	9,63,200		3,200		3,200	
Add: Cost of goods mfd.	Nil		9,60,000		19,20,000	
Cost of goods available for sale	9,63,200		9,63,200		19,23,200	
Less: Closing inventory	3,200		3,200		14,43,200	
Cost of goods manufactured and sold		9,60,000		9,60,000		4,80,000
Contribution Margin		8,40,000		8,40,000		4,20,000
Less: Selling and Adm. Exp		4,40,000		4,40,000		4,40,000
Less: Fixed Cost		4,00,000		4,00,000		4,00,000
Net Profit/Loss		Nil		Nil		(4,20,000)

Note: 1. In variable costing opening and closing inventory are valued at variable costs only, i.e ₹ 32 per 1,000 units

2. The fixed costs are charged as a periods cost.

Comments: It would be clear from the above statements of profit that under absorption costing, profit is inflated by including fixed costs in the inventory valuation, under variable costing, fixed costs are treated as period costs and hence are written off in the period they occur.

Illustrative Problem 7

The Shahenshash Superstars Ltd. uses direct costing for internal control and absorption costing for external reporting purposes.

At the Month of March 2015, it was anticipated that sales would rise 20% the next year. Therefore, production was increased from 20,000 units to 24,000 units to meet this expected demand. However, economic conditions were not especially fruitful; only 20,000 units were sold.

The following data pertain to the year ended March 2016

	₹
Selling price per unit	30
Beginning finished goods units	0
Sales (units)	20,000
Production (units)	24,000
Ending finished goods inventory (units)	4,000
Variable manufacturing costs per unit for the year ending March 2016:	
Direct labour	7.50
Direct materials	4.50
Variable manufacturing costs	3.0

Total variable manufacturing costs	15.00
Annual fixed costs for 2015-2016	
Manufacturing	96,000
Selling and Administrative	1,00,000
Total	1,96,000

There were no variable selling and administrative costs. All taxes are to be ignored.

You are required to:

(*i*) Prepare an income statement based on direct costing for the year ended March 2016.

(*ii*) Prepare an income statement based on absorption costing for the year ended March 2016

(*iii*) Explain the difference, if any, in the net income figures by an analysis of the inventories.

Solution:

(i) The Shahenshah Superstars Ltd.
Income Statement for Year Ended 31st March 2016
(Direct Costing)

	₹	₹
Sales revenue (20,000 units @ ₹ 30)		6,00,000
Variable cost of goods sold:		
Cost of goods produced (24,000 units @ ₹ 15)	3,60,000	
Ending finished goods (4,000 units @ ₹ 15)	(60,000)	(3,00,000)
Contribution margin		3,00,000
Less: Fixed Costs :		
Manufacturing	96,000	
Selling and Administration	1,00,000	1,96,000
Net Income		1,04,000

(ii) The Shahenshah Superstars Ltd.
Income Statement for Year Ended 31st March 2016
(Absorption Costing)

	₹	₹
Sales revenue (20,000 units @ ₹ 30)		6,00,000
Cost of goods sold:		
Cost of goods produced (24,000 units @ ₹ 19)	4,56,000	
Ending finished goods (4,000 units @ ₹ 19)	76,000	
		3,80,000
Gross margin		2,20,000
Selling and Administrative Expenses		1,00,000
Net Income		1,20,000

(iii) Reconciliation between Direct Costing and Absorption Incomes

	₹
Net income — Direct costing	1,04,000
Net income — Absorption costing	1,20,000
Difference	16,000
Fixed Manufacturing cost — beginning inventory	0
Fixed Manufacturing cost — ending inventory (4,000 units @ ₹ 4)	16,000
Difference	–16,000
Variable Manufacturing cost	= ₹ 15 per unit
Fixed Manufacturing cost (₹ 96,000 ÷ 24,000 units)	4 per unit
Total Manufacturing cost	19 per unit

Since the inventory level increases, part of 2016 fixed manufacturing costs are retained on the balance sheet by absorption costing.

Illustrative Problem 8

From the information given below relating to the India Integration Ltd., you are required to prepare profit statements for the year ending March 2016 based on:

(*i*) Marginal costing

(*ii*) Absorption costing

Comment on the difference in the profit figures you report for (*i*) and (*ii*) above.

India Integration Ltd., produces a single product which is bottled and sold in cases. The normal annual level of operations, on which the production fixed overhead absorption is based, is 36,000 cases. Data for the last financial year were as follows:

Production	40,000 cases
Sales	32,000 cases

	₹ Per case
Selling Price	60
Costs:	
Production:	
Direct Labour	12
Direct Material	14
Variable Overhead	8
Fixed Overhead (Budgeted and incurred)	2,16,000
Selling and Administrative Costs:	
Fixed	₹ 50,000
Variable	15% of sales revenue

There was no opening stock of finished goods and the work-in-progress stock may be assumed to be the same at the end of the year as it was at the beginning of the year.

Solution:

(i) Profit Statement based on Marginal Costing

		₹ (000)
Sales (32,000 @ ₹ 60 each)		1,920
Less: Cost of production:		
Direct Material	560	
Direct Labour	480	

	Variable overhead	320	
		1,360	
Less:	Closing stock 8,000 cases @ 34	272	
	Variable cost of goods sold		1,088
	Contribution		832
Less:	Fixed production overhead	216	
	Variable Selling and Administration Costs	288	
	Fixed Selling and Admn. Costs	50	554
	Net Profit		278

(ii) Profit Statement based on Absorption Costing

		₹ ('000)	₹ ('000)
Sales			1,920
Less:	Cost of production:		
	Direct Labour	480	
	Direct Material	560	
	Variable Overhead	320	
Fixed Overhead $\left(40{,}000 \times \frac{2{,}16{,}000}{36{,}000}\right)$		240	
		1600	
Less:	Closing Stock $\left(\frac{8000}{40{,}000} \times ₹1{,}600\right)$	320	
	Production cost of goods sold	1,280	
Less:	Over-absorption	24	
			1,256
	Gross profit		664
Less:	Selling and Administrative costs:		
	Fixed	50	
	Variable	288	338
	Net Profit		326

(*iii*) The difference in two profit figures is caused by the differing treatment of fixed production overheads. Under Marginal Costing, these overheads are treated as period expenses and written off totally in the year's profit statement. Under Absorption costing, they are treated as a part of the cost of production and charged in the year's accounts only to the extent that production is sold consequently, a proportion is carried forward to the next year in the form of closing stock. A profit reconciliation statement explains the situation:

		₹ ('000)
Net Profit per Marginal Cost Approach		278
Add:	Proportion of fixed production Overhead included in closing stocks: (₹ 6 × 8,000)	48
	Net profit under absorption costing	326

Illustrative Problem 9

The Seers Can Company has two plants, one in Bombay, and the other in Calcutta. The physical characteristics of plants are similar, and the results of operation of the two plants are compared each month in order to judge the performance of the two managements. The April income statements of the two plants were as follows:

	Bombay Plant ₹	Calcutta Plant ₹
Sales	18,00,000	18,00,000
Less: Manufacturing Cost of Sales	12,60,000	13,60,000
Selling and Adm. Expenses	4,40,000	4,40,000
Total Expenses	17,00,000	18,00,000
Net Income	1,00,000	- 0 -

Each plant sells its product for the same price. During the month of April, each plant sold and shipped 3,00,00,000 cans. The production for the month at the two plants was as follows:

	Bombay Plant	Calcutta Plant
Opening Stock (no of cans)	1,00,000	1,00,000
Production during the month	4,00,00,000	3,00,00,000
	4,01,00,000	3,01,00,000
Cans Shipped during the month	3,00,00,000	3,00,00,000
Closing Stock (no, of cans)	1,01,00,000	1,00,000

The Bombay plant built up its stock in April in anticipation of the canning season, which begins in May on the West Cost. The East Cost canning season begin in the middle of June.

The Standard cost for the type of can sold in April discloses the following information:

Standard Cost Card (For Both Plants)

	Cost per 1,000 Cans ₹
Direct Material	25
Direct Labour	5
Variable Overhead	2
Fixed Overhead	10
	42

For each plant, the manufacturing fixed costs budgeted for the month were ₹ 4,00,000. There were no spending or efficiency variances.

All Selling and Adm. expenses were of a fixed nature.

Required:

Prepare revised income statements for the two plants, using variable costing. Explain the difference in income between the two plants. Which statements do you feel would be more useful to management in evaluating the operations of plants?

Solution:

Income Statement for the Month of April (Variable Costing Basis)

	Bombay Plant	*Calcutta Plant*
Production (Cans)	4,00,00,000	3,00,00,000
Sales (Cans)	3,00,00,000	3,00,00,000
	(₹)	(₹)
Sales (₹)	18,00,000	18,00,000
Less: Variable production costs:		
Direct Material	10,00,000	7,50,000
Direct Labour	2,00,000	1,50,000
Variable Overheads*	80,000	60,000
	12,80,000	9,60,000
Add: Opening Inventory (at standard variable cost of ₹ 32 per 1000 cans)	3,200	3,200
	12,83,200	9,63,200
Less: Closing Inventory (at standard variable cost ₹ 32 per 1,000 cans)	3,23,200	3,200
Cost of cans sold	9,60,000	9,60,000
Contribution	8,40,000	8,40,000
Less: Fixed Costs:		
Fixed Overheads	4,00,000	4,00,000
Selling and Administrative Expenses	4,40,000	4,40,000
Total Fixed Cost	8,40,000	8,40,000
Net Income	Nil	Nil

* Variable overheads has been assumed as variable production overhead.

Difference in net incomes of Bombay and Calcutta Plant is NIL. There is difference in net income of Bombay Plant on the basis of variable costing and absorption costing. For this, reconciliation statement is as follows:

Reconciliation Statement (Bombay Plant)

	₹	
Net Income (absorption costing)	1,00,000	
Net Income (variable costing)	Nil	
Difference	1,00,000	

This difference is due to including fixed overhead in inventory change quantity, i.e.,

Opening Inventory	1,00,000	cans
Closing Inventory	1,01,00,000	
Increase in Inventory	1,00,00,000	

Value of Increased Inventory

= 1,00,00,000 × ₹ 10 fixed overhead rate (per 1000 cans)

= ₹ 1,00,000

The Bombay Plant has produced 4,00,00,000 cans and therefore has absorbed the total budgeted fixed overheads of ₹ 4,00,000. The Calcutta Plant operated at below its normal capcity and produced only 3,00,00,000 cans. In case of Calcutta Plant therefore, there is unfavourable capacity variance (under absorption) of ₹ 1,00,000 which is causing difference in net income of the two plants on absorption costing basis.

However, in case of Calcutta Plant, since opening and closing inventory are equal, there is no difference in net income between absorption costing and variable costing.

The variable costing statement would be more useful for evaluating the operation of the plants.

Illustrative Problem 10

A company produces an item which it sells for ₹ 52 per unit. The production cost are as follows: Fixed costs per year ₹ 22,50,000, variable cost per unit ₹ 12.5, normal activity is 1,50,000 units per year. At the beginning of the year, the position statement was as follows:

Position Statement as at January 1

	₹		₹
Capital	8,00,000	Other assets	7,50,000
Retained earnings	2,25,000	Finished goods	2,75,000
	10,25,000		10,25,000

Note: Finished goods represent 10000 units (₹ 1,25,000 of variable costs and ₹ 1,50,000 of fixed costs).

The information for the years 1,2,3 are as follows:

Years	*Sales (units)*	*Sales (₹)*	*Production (units)*
1.	1,00,000	52,00,000	1,25,000
2.	1,00,000	52,00,000	80,000
3.	1,00,000	52,00,000	1,70,000

The manufacturing cost of each were as stated above. You are required to

1. Prepare an income statement for each of the three years, using normal activity as the basis of overhead absorption.
2. Prepare an income statement for each of three years, using variable costing. (*M. Com., Delhi*)

Solution:

Income Statement (Variable Costing)

	Year 1 (₹)	*Year 2 (₹)*	*Year 3 (₹)*
Sales (₹)	52,00,000	52,00,000	52,00,000
Less: Cost of goods sold : Opening Inventory	1,25,000	4,37,500	1,87,500
Add: Variable Costs	15,62,500	10,00,000	21,25,000
	16,87,500	14,37,500	23,12,500
Less: Closing Inventory	4,37,500	1,87,500	10,62,500
Cost of goods sold	12,50,000	12,50,000	12,50,000
Contribution	39,50,000	39,50,000	39,50,000
Less: Fixed Cost	22,50,000	22,50,000	22,50,000
Net Income	17,00,000	17,00,000	17,00,000

Income Statement (Absorption Costing)

	Year 1	*Year 2*	*Year 3*
Sales (₹)	52,00,000	52,00,000	52,00,000
Less: Cost of goods sold:			
Opening Inventory	2,75,000	9,62,500	4,12,500
Add: Variable costs	15,62,500	10,00,000	21,25,000
Fixed Overhead	18,75,000	12,00,000	25,50,000
Cost of goods available	37,12,500	31,62,500	50,87,500
Less: Closing Inventory	9,62,500	4,12,500	23,37,500
Cost of goods sold	27,50,000	27,50,000	27,50,000
Capacity variance	3,75,000	10,50,000	(3,00,000)
Adjusted cost of goods sold	31,25,000	38,00,000	24,50,000
Gross margin/Net Income	20,75,000	14,00,000	27,50,000

Note: (*i*) All fixed costs have been assumed as fixed manufacturing overheads
(*ii*) Variable manufacturing overhead rate is ₹ 12.5
(*iii*) Fixed manufacturing overhead rate is ₹ 15 (₹ 1,50,000/ 10,000 units)

Illustrative Problem 11

You are given below the income statement of Modern Fashions Ltd. for the years 2015 and 2016:

	2015	**2016**
Number of units sold	15,000	20,000
Sales	₹ 7,50,000	₹ 10,00,000
Cost of goods sold:		
Beginning inventory	₹ 57,600	₹ 2,37,600
Current cost of production	7,20,000	5,40,000
Cost of merchandise available for sale	7,77,600	7,77,600
Less: Ending Inventory	2,37,600	57,600
Cost of goods sold	5,40,000	7,20,000
Capacity Variance	—	1,25,000
Total	5,40,000	8,45,000
Gross margin	2,10,000	1,55,000
Selling and Administrative Expenses	46,000	56,000
Income before taxes	1,64,000	99,000

In 2015 the President of the company planned to increase inventory in anticipation of increased sales volume in the year 2016. The sales volume increased as expected but the president was surprised to find that instead of having increased profits the profit was lower than what it was for 2015. In as much as selling price and costs did not change, he believes the income statements are incorrect. During 2015, the company operated at normal capacity and manufactured 20,000 units, the total manufacturing cost per unit amounted to ₹ 36 at normal capacity with fixed cost per unit at ₹ 25. 15,000 units were manufactured in 2016. The fixed selling and administrative expenses were ₹ 8,000 in both the years.

You are required to:

(*i*) Explain the profit difference to the president, particularly the reason for the decrease.

(*ii*) Revise the statement for the two years to show the operating results on a variable costing basis

(*iii*) Explain the difference, if any, between the incomes for the two years under variable and absorption costing. (*M. Com., Delhi,* 2008)

Solution:

	2015	**2016**
Opening Inventory units	1,600	6,600
Current production	20,000	15,000
Total units available for sales	21,600	21,600
Less: Sales units	15,000	20,000
Closing Inventory units	6,600	1,600

Statement of Difference in Absorption Profit

Difference in net income ₹ 1,64,000 – ₹ 99,000 = ₹ 65,000

	(₹)
Additional sales revenue in 2016	
(5000 units × ₹ 50) =	2,50,000
Less: Variable manufactured costs @ ₹ 11	55,000
Contribution margin	1,95,000
Less:	
(*i*) Current year fixed manufacturing overhead applicable to 5000 units @ ₹ 25 (actual production is less than normal production, however under all situations, the total fixed manufacturing overhead (₹ 5,00,000) will be incurred. Therefore, a proportionate part of ₹ 5,00,000 (current year fixed manufacturing overhead) applicable to 5000 units will be charged to these 5000 units)	(1,25,000)
(*ii*) Fixed manufacturing overhead shifted to 2016 from 2015 via opening inventory for 5000 units *(opening units 6600 – closing units 1 600 = 5000 units)	(1,25,000)
(*iii*) Increases in selling and adm - exp.	(10,000)
Difference (decreases) in profit.	(–) 65000

*Alternatively fixed manufacturing overhead for 6600 units can be directly deducted and then fixed manufacturing overhead for 1600 closing inventory units should be added.

The above answer can be derived alternatively in the following manner.

Statement of Difference in Profit (Absorption Costing)

			(₹)
	Increased sales revenue in 2016 over 2015 (5000 units × ₹ 50) =		2,50,000
Less:	Variable cost (manufacturing) @ ₹ 11 =		55,000
	Increased contribution margin		1,95,000
Less:	(*i*) Fixed manufactured costs shifted to 2016 via opening inventory (6600 units × ₹ 25) =	165,000	
	Minus: Fixed manufacturing costs included in closing inventory in 2016 (1600 units × ₹ 25) =	40,000	(1,25,000)
(*ii*)	Fixed manufacturing costs shifted from 2015 to 2016 by inventory carry over (6600 units × ₹ 25) = 1,65,000		
	Minus : Fixed manufacturing costs included in closing inventory of 2014 and shifted to 2015 via opening inventory (1600 units × ₹ 25) =	40,000	(1,25,000)
(*iii*)	Increase in selling & Adm. exp.		(10,000)
	Difference (decrease) in profit		(–) 65,000

Income Statement (Variable Costing)

		2015 (₹)	2016 (₹)
Sales (₹)		7,50,000	10,00,000
Less:	Cost of goods sold:		
	Opening Inventory (1600 units @ ₹ 11)	17,600	72,600
	Variable production cost @ ₹ 11	2,20,000	1,65,000
	Cost of goods available for sale	2,37,600	2,37,600
Less:	Closing Inventory (6600 units @ ₹ 11, 1600 units ₹ 11)	72,600	17,600
	Costs of goods sold	1,65,000	2,20,000
	Contribution margin	5,85,000	7,80,000
Less:	Fixed manufacturing Overhead	(5,00,000)	(5,00,000)
	Selling and Adm-Exp	(46,000)	(56,000)
Inccme before tax		39,000	2,24,000

Reconciliation statement

	2015 (₹)	2016 (₹)
Net Income (Absorption Costing)	↑ 1,64,000	99000
Net Income (Variable Costing)	39,000	↓ 2,24,000
Difference	1,25,000	1,25,000

In 2015 absorption costing income is higher by ₹ 1,25,000. However, in 2016 absorption costing income is less by ₹ 1,25,000

	2015 (₹)	2016 (₹)
Absorption Costing:		
Opening Inventory	57,600	2,37,600
Closing Inventory	2,37,600	57,600
	(+) 1,80,000	(–) 1,80,000
Variable Costing:		
Opening Inventory	17,600	72600
Closing Inventory	72,600	17600
	(+) 55,000	(–) 55,000
Net effect (difference)	(+) 1,25,000	1,25,000

Note: (*i*) In 2015, in absorption costing closing inventory increases by ₹ 1,80,000, but the profit does not go up by that amount because actual sales are less than the normal capacity sales.

(*ii*) In 2016, in absorption costing, closing inventory decreases by ₹ 180,000. But the profit does not decreases by this amount as more sales (equivalent to normal output units) are made.

Illustrative Problem 12

A company has prepared the following income statement on absorption costing basis:

		(₹)
Sales		4,70,000
Cost of goods sold:		
Opening Inventory (variable costs ₹ 42,000)	₹ 70,000	
Current production cost	2,56,000	
	3,26,000	
Less: Closing Inventory (Variable cost ₹ 31,200)	52,000	2,74,000
Gross margin (manufacturing / unadjusted)		1,96,000
Less: Capacity variance (unfavourable)		32,000
Gross margin (adjusted)		1,64,000
Less: Selling and distribution cost		20,000
Administrative cost		22,000
Net income before taxes		1,22,000

Additional Information:

(*i*) The fixed manufacturing overheads are absorbed at a standard rate per unit of product.

(*ii*) Total fixed cost of the current year (budgeted as well as actual) is ₹ 1,34,400

(*iii*) All units in inventory at the end of the year were manufactured during the year

Prepare an income statement on variable costing basis.

Solution:

Income Statement
(Variable Costing)

	(₹)	(₹)
Sales		4,70,000
Less: Cost of goods sold:		
Opening Inventory	42,000	
Current variable production cost	1,53,600	
	1,95,600	
Less: Closing Inventory	31,200	
		1,64,400
Contribution margin		3,05,600
Less: Other costs:		
(*i*) Fixed production overhead		
(*a*) ₹ 2,56,000 – 1,53,600 =	1,02,400	
(*b*) Unabsorbed fixed production overhead	32,000	(1,34,400)
(*ii*) Selling & distribution costs		(20,000)
(*iii*) Administrative costs		(22,000)
Net income before taxes		1,29,200

Note: There is less than normal capacity production. Therefore, total fixed production cost charged to current production will be ₹ 1,02,400 [1,34,400 — 32,000 unfavourable capacity variance]. Current variable production cost will be ₹ 1,53,600 (2,56,000 — 1,02,400). Further, it should be noted that unfavourable capacity variance is added to cost of goods sold or alternatively it is deducted from gross margin (as given in this question).

Illustrative Problem 13

Rumbles Ltd. manufactures a single product, with a variable manufacturing cost of ₹ 12 per unit and a selling price of ₹ 20 per unit. Fixed production overheads are ₹ 90,000 per period. The company operates a fully absorption costing system and the fixed overheads are absorbed into the cost of production, on the basis of a normal activity of 15,000 units per period, at a rate of ₹ 6 per unit. Any under or over absorbed overheads are written off to the profit and loss account at the end of a each period. It may be assumed that no other expenses are incurred.

Summarised below are the company's manufacturing and trading results showing quantities only, for periods 2 and 3.

	Period 2 (units)	*Period 3 (units)*
Opening Stock	5,000	11,000
Production	17,000	13,000
	22,000	24,000
Less: Closing Stock	11,000	6,000
Sales	11,000	18,000

The managing director of Rumbles Ltd. has calculated that as sales have increased by 7000 units in periods 3, the company's profit should increase by ₹ 56,000. However the results produced by the accountant show that profits in period 2 were ₹ 34,000 and in period 3 were ₹ 24000. The managing director is somewhat surprised.

Required:

(*i*) Produce columner revenue accounts, for both period, showing how profits of ₹ 24000 and ₹ 34000 were obtained .

(*ii*) Explain, with supporting calculations:

(*a*) Reasons for reduction in reported profits between the two periods.

(*b*) How the managing director has calculated that profits should increase by ₹ 56000 in periods 3.

(*c*) Why profits have not increased by ₹ 56000 in period 3. (*M. Com. Delhi,* 2003)

Solution:

Income Statement (Absorption Costing)

		Period 2 ₹	*Period 3* ₹
Sales		2,20,000	3,60,000
Less:	Cost of goods sold:		
	Opening stock	90,000	1,98,000
	Variable manufacturing cost	2,04,000	1,56,000
	Fixed overhead @ ₹ 6	1,02,000	78,000
		3,96,000	4,32,000
Less:	Closing stock	1,98000	1,08,000
	Cost of goods sold	1,98,000	3,24,000
	Capacity variance	(12,000)	+12,000
	Adjusted cost of goods sold	1,86,000	3,36,000
	Net Income	34,000	24,000

Statement Showing Reduction in Profit

Difference in profit = ₹ 34,000 – 24,000 = ₹ 10,000

Income Statement (additional 7,000 units)

			₹
Sales			1,40,000
Less:	Variable costs		84,000
	Contribution margin		56,000
Less:	(*i*) Related Fixed Costs		(42,000)
	(*ii*) Shifting of fixed costs from period 2 to period 3 via		
	Opening Inventory	11,000 units	
Less:	= Closing Inventory Period 3	(6,000) units	
			(24,000)
Less:	Closing Inventory Period 1	(1,000 units)	
		4,000 units	
	Decrease in profit		₹ 10,000

Or

Income Statement (Additional 7000 Units)

			₹
Sales			1,40,000
Less: Variable costs			84,000
			56,000
Less: (*i*) Shifting of fixed overhead costs from period 2 into period 3 by inventory carryover			₹
	Opening Inventory:	11,000 units	
Less:	Closing Inventory:	6,000 units	
	(i.e. shift of fixed costs into period 4)	5,000 units	(30,000)
	(*ii*) Shifting of fixed costs out of period 2 to period 3		
	Opening inventory:	11,000 units	
Less:	Closing inventory	5,000 units	
	(shifted from period 1 to period 2)	6,000 units	(36,000)
	Decrease in net profit		10,000

Note: Explaination is required to show how Period 2 profit is greater than Period 3 profit when sales are more in period 3 than in Period 2. In the first instance, Period 3 profit is negatively influenced because it has more opening units than closing units, i.e. 5000 units (11,000 – 6000). Secondly, period 2 is having more units in closing stock than in opening stock, i.e. 6,000 units (11000 – 5000). Taking Period 2 and Period 3 into account, it means Period 2 is additionally better off with possessing extra 1000 units (6,000 units – 5,000 units) which is increasing further the profit of Period 2 and decreasing the profit of Period 3. Period 3 profit declines because it carries negative effect to the extent of 5,000 units. Assuming Period 2 carrying positive effect to the extent of 5000 units, the difference in profit between the two periods will be smaller. The fact that Period 2 has additional positive effect (1,000 units), it will be considered to account for the reduction in profit in Period 3 over Period 2.

(*b*) The managing director has calculated profit of ₹ 56,000 equivalent to contribution margin of ₹ 56000, He has assumed that profit should go up by ₹ 56,000 because in period 2, profit has been ₹ 34000 at 11,000 sales units whereas in period 3 sales has been 18,000 units.

Illustrative Problem 14

Johnson company has just completed its first year of operations. The unit costs on a normal costing basis are as follows:

Manufacturing Costs (per unit):	₹
Direct Material (2 lbs @ ₹ 2)	4.00
Direct Labour (1.5 hrs @ ₹ 9)	13.50
Variable Overhead (1.5 hrs @ ₹ 2)	3.00
Fixed Overhead (1.5 hrs @ ₹ 3)	4.50
Total	25.00
Selling and Administrative costs:	
Variable	₹ 5 per unit
Fixed	₹ 1,90,000
During the year, the company has the following activity:	
Units produced	24,000
Units sold	21,500
Unit selling price	42
Direct labour hours worked	36,000

Actual fixed overhead was ₹ 12,000 less than budgeted fixed overhead. Budgeted variable overhead was ₹ 5,000 less than actual variable overhead. The company used expected actual activity level of 36000 direct labour hours to compute the predetermined overhead rates. Any overhead variance are closed to cost of goods sold.

Required:

(*i*) Compute the unit cost using (*a*) absorption costing (*b*) variable costing
(*ii*) Prepare an absorption costing income statement.
(*iii*) Prepare a variable costing income statement.
(*iv*) Reconcile the difference between the two income statements.

Solution:

(*i*) Absorption Unit Cost

	₹
Direct Materials	4.00
Direct Labour	13.50
Variable Overhead	3.00
Fixed Overhead	4.50
Total	25.00

Variable Unit Cost

	₹
Direct Materials	4.00
Direct Labour	13.50
Variable Overhead	3.00
Total	20.50

(*ii*) Absorption Costing Income Statement

		₹	₹
	Sales (21,500 units @ ₹ 42)		9,03,000
Less:	Cost of goods sold		
	(21,500 units @ ₹ 25.00)	5,37,500	
	minus over-absorption	7,000	5,30,500
	Gross margin		3,72,500
Less:	Selling and Administrative Expenses		2,97,500
	Net income		75,000

Note: Amount of the over-absorption has been calculated in the following manner.

Budgeted fixed Overhead = (36000 hours × ₹ 3 per hour) = ₹ 1,08,000

Actual fixed overhead was ₹ 12000 less than the budgeted fixed overheads

Therefore, actual fixed Overheads =1,08,000 – 12000 = ₹ 96,000

Similarly, budgeted variable Overhead = (36000 hrs × ₹ 2) = ₹ 72,000

Since actual variable overhead was ₹ 5,000 higher than the budgeted variable overhead, the actual variable overhead should be ₹ 72,000 + ₹ 5,000 = ₹ 77,000

Both variable and fixed overhead are applied on the basis of direct labour hours. Since 36,000 hours have been worked, the total applied overheads amount to ₹ 1,80,000 (36,000 hours × ₹ 5). Actual overhead are ₹ 96,000 + ₹ 77,000 = ₹ 1,73,000.

	₹
Applied Overhead	1,80,000
Actual Overhead	1,73,000
Over-absorbed Overhead	7,000

(*iii*) Variable Costing Income Statement

		₹
Sales (21,500 units @ ₹ 42)		9,03,000
Less: variable cost of goods sold (21,500 units @ ₹ 20.50)	4,40,750	
Add: Under -absorbed variable overhead	5,000	
Total cost of goods sold		4,45,750
Contribution margin		4,57,250
Less: Fixed factory overhead	96,000	
Selling and Administrative Exp.	1,90,000	
Variable selling expense (21,500 units × ₹ 5)	1,07,500	3,93,500
Net Income		63,750

Note: The under-applied variable overhead is simply the actual variable overhead of ₹ 77,000 minus the absorbed overheads of ₹ 72,000 (36000 hrs × ₹ 2). Also, in variable costing, the actual fixed overhead is charged in the income statement directly.

(*iv*) Difference in Net Income = ₹ 75000-₹ 63,750 = ₹ 11,250

This difference in net income (higher net income in absorption costing) is due to fixed factory overhead being included in closing stock in absorption costing and not in variable costing.

Therefore

Difference in net income = Fixed overhead rate × (Production – Sales)

₹ 11,250 = ₹ 4.50 (24,000 – 21,500)

₹ 11,250 = ₹ 4.50 × 2,500

₹ 11,250 = ₹ 11,250

Illustrative Problem 15

Topeless Products Ltd. has several product lines with a sales manager in charge of each product line and he is paid a bonus based on the net income generated by his product line.

In analysing performance of one product line, the General Sales Manager noted that although the sales declined larger bonus was paid than last year because net income increased from ₹ 90,000 last year to ₹ 1,20,000 for the current year.

The General Sales Manager wonders how the product line manager is entitled to a bonus with a decline in sales. He also wants to know how net income increased when sales declined.

As a Cost Accountant you are required to prepare the income statements, based on which the bonus was paid.

Explain with supporting figures why net income increased when sales declined. What do you think of the present method of paying bonus? Can you suggest some other method?

The data given in support for bonus payment are:

	Year 2	Year I
Units sold @ ₹ 20	30,000	40,000
Standard variable cost of production per unit (₹)	8	8
Fixed Factory Overhead Cost (₹)	2,00,000	2,00,000
Selling & distribution Expenses (assumed to be fixed) (₹)	1,40,000	1,40,000
Standard Fixed Factory Overheads per unit (₹)	5	5
Units produced	50,000	30,000
Opening finished goods Inventory-Units		10,000

All factory overhead variances are written off to cost of goods sold. (*M. Com., Delhi,* 2008)

Solution:

Statement showing income statement based on which the bonus was paid

		Year 1	*Year 2*
Units sold		40,000	30,000
Sales value @ ₹ 20		₹ 8,00,000	₹ 6,00,000
Cost of sales:			
Variable Cost			
	Year 1 : 30,000 × ₹ 8; Year 2 : 50,000 × ₹ 8	2,40,000	4,00,000
Fixed Factory Overhead		2,00,000	2,00,000
Cost of production		4,40,000	6,00,000
Add:	Opening stock:		
	Year 1,10,000 × ₹ 13; Year 2 Nil	1,30,000	
		5,70,000	6,00,000
Less:	Closing Stock		
	Year I Nil: Year 2 (20,000 × ₹ 13)		2,60,000
	Cost of goods sold	5,70,000	3,40,000
Add:	Selling and Distribution Expenses	1,40,000	1,40,000
	Cost of sales	7,10,000	4,80,000
	Income (Sales minus Cost of Sales)	90,000	1,20,000

The above statement shows that income in year 2 has increased in spite of decrease in sales because fixed *overheads* have been carried over to next year as part of the value of closing stock in year 2.

The above method of paying bonus to production manager cannot be considered appropriate. The relevant method for paying bonus to sales manager is the variable costing method as shown below:

		Year 1	**Year 2**
	Sales	₹ 8,00,000	₹ 6,00,000
Less:	Variable cost	3,20,000	2,40,000
	Contribution	4,80,000	3,60,000
Less:	Fixed costs	3,40,000	3,40,000
	Income	1,40,000	20,000

If bonus to sales manager is paid on the variable costing method, sales manager cannot get more bonus when sales decline.

Illustrative Problem 16

You are provided with the following information for Singh Enterprises during the first quarter of 2016.

	January	February	March
Unit sales	12,000	14,000	18,000
Sales price per unit	₹ 12	₹ 12	₹ 12
Variable manufacturing cost per unit	5	5	5
Unit production	15,000	18,000	13,000

Additional information:

(a) On January 1, there were 2,000 units on hand.

(b) Fixed overhead cost is ₹ 3.00 per unit and is applied to units of product on the basis of a production volume of 14,000 units per month. The cost of goods sold is adjusted for any over-or underapplied fixed manufacturing overhead.

(c) Singh Enterprises uses a FIFO inventory flow. Work in process inventories are immaterial and are to be ignored.

(d) Fixed selling and administrative expenses total ₹ 20,000 per month.

(e) Variable selling and administrative expenses is ₹ 2 per unit sold.

Required:

(i) For each of the above three months, prepare income statements using:

(a) Absorption costing;

(b) Contribution approach with direct costing.

(ii) Explain in detail why, under absorption costing, over the three-month period profits have moved erratically and have not moved in correlation with the changes in sales volume. In your answer you should include a reconciliation of net income under absorption costing with net income under direct costing.

Solutions:

(i) (a)

Income Statements For the months ended (Absorption Costing)

	January	February	March
Sales	₹ 144,000	₹ 168,000	₹ 216,000
Costs of goods sold:			
Beginning inventory	16,000	40,000	72,000
Variable Manufacturing Cost	75,000	90,000	65,000
Fixed manufacturing Cost	45,000	54,000	39,000
Cost of good manufactured	120,000	144,000	104,000
Goods available for sale	136,000	184,000	176,000
Less: ending inventory	40,000	72,000	32,000
	96,000	112,000	144,000
Under or (over) applied FOH	(3,000)	(12,000)	3,000
Adjusted Cost of goods sold	93,000	100,000	147,000
Gross margin	51,000	68,000	69,000
Selling and admin expenses:			
Variable	24,000	28,000	36,000
Fixed	20,000	20,000	20,000
	44,000	48,000	56,000
Net income (loss)	7,000	20,000	13,000

(b)

Income Statements For the months ended (Variable Costing)

	January	February	March
Sales	₹ 144,000	₹ 168,000	₹ 216,000
Costs of goods sold:			
Beginning inventory	10,000	25,000	45,000
Variable Manufacturing Cost	75,000	90,000	65,000
Goods available for sale	85,000	115,000	110,000
Less: ending inventory	25,000	45,000	20,000
Variable cost of goods sold	60,000	70,000	90,000
Contribution margin	84,000	98,000	1,26,000
Less: Fixed			
Manufacturing overhead	42,000	42,000	42,000
Selling and administration	20,000	20,000	20,000
Variable selling and administration	24,000	28,000	36,000
	62,000	62,000	62,000
Net income (loss)	(2,000)	8,000	28,000

(ii) As shown in the answer to part (a) under the absorption costing income statements, February's net income was ₹ 20,000 when 14,000 units were sold but in March when 18,000 units were sold, net income was ₹ 13,000; ₹ 7,000 less when in fact, 4,000 more units were sold. Under absorption costing, profits are affected by both sales and production. When production exceeds sales in a given month, a portion of the fixed overhead cost of these months is deferred to the future as opposed to being expensed as is done under variable costing. In absorption costing the fixed overhead is a product cost and is therefore not expensed until the product is sold. In variable costing, fixed overhead is treated as a period cost and is expensed in the period incurred.

January's net income under absorption costing was ₹ 7,000, but under variable costing there was a loss of ₹ 2,000. This ₹ 9,000 difference between these two net incomes is accounted for by the fact that in January 3,000 more units were produced than were sold. The fixed overhead cost per unit is ₹ 3.00. Under variable costing ₹ 9,000 more would have been expensed than under absorption costing since under absorption costing since under absorption costing the fixed overhead 'attaches' to the product and is not expensed until sold.

In February, the same happened as in January in that Singh produced 4,000 more units than sold, resulting in a difference of ₹ 12,000 (4,000 × ₹ 3) between the incomes reported.

In March, however, singh sold 5,000 units more than were produced, resulting in the variable costing approach showing ₹ 15,000 more income than was reported under absorption costing. This is because the fixed overhead component of these 5,000 units have already been expensed in a previous month under variable costing.

Illustrative Problem 17

The Gurgaon plant of Maruti Udyog Ltd., assembles Zen motor vehicle. The standard unit manufacturing cost per vehicle in 2016 is as follows:

Direct materials	₹ 60,000
Direct manufacturing labour	₹ 18,000
Variable manufacturing overhead	₹ 20,000

The Gurgaon plant is highly automated. Maximum production capacity per month is 4,000 vehicles. Fixed manufacturing overhead in 2016 is allocated on the basis of normal capacity utilisation of the plant. In 2016, the budgeted normal capacity is 3,000 vehicles per month. The budgeted monthly fixed manufacturing overhead is ₹ 7,50,000.

On January 1, 2016 there is zero beginning inventory of Zen vehicles. The actual unit production and sales figures for the first three months are:

	January	*February*	*March*
Production	3,200	2,400	3,800
Sales	2,000	2,900	3,200

Selling price per vehicle is ₹ 2,00,000.

Required:

(*i*) Prepare income statements for the three months under absorption costing and variable costing.

(*ii*) Prepare reconciliation statement to reconcile the differences in net income in the two costing techniques. (*M. Com. Delhi University, 2009*)

Solution:

Income Statement (Absorption)

		January	*February*	*March*
	Sales (₹)	40,00,00,00	58,00,00,000	64,00,00,000
Less:	Cost of goods sold:			
	Opening inventory		11,79,00,000	6,87,75,000
	Variable production cost (₹ 98,000 per car)	31,36,00,000	23,52,00,000	37,24,00,000
	Fixed manufacturing Overhead @ ₹ 250	8,00,000	6,00,000	9,50,000
	Cost of goods available for sales	31,44,00,000	35,37,00,000	44,21,25,000
Less:	Closing inventory	11,79,00,000	6,87,75,000	12,77,25,000
	Cost of goods sold	19,65,00,000	28,49,25,000	31,44,00,000
	± Capacity variance	(50,000)	1,50,000	(2,00,000)
	Cost of goods sold at actual	19,64,50,000	28,50,75,000	31,42,00,000
	Gross profit	20,35,50,000	29,49,25,000	32,58,00,000
Less:	Variable selling and distribution	—	—	—
	Fixed selling and distribution	—	—	—
	Next profit	20,35,50,000	29,49,25,000	32,58,00,000

Income Statement (Variable Costing)

	January	*February*	*March*
Sales (₹)	40,00,00,000	58,00,00,000	64,00,00,000
Less: Cost of goods sold:			
Opening inventory		11,76,00,000	6,86,00,000
Variable production cost	31,36,00,000	23,52,00,000	37,24,00,000
Cost of goods available for sales	31,36,00,000	35,28,00,000	44,10,00,000
Less: Closing inventory	11,76,00,000	6,86,00,000	12,74,00,000
Cost of goods sold	19,60,00,000	28,42,00,000	31,36,00,000
Margin	20,40,00,000	29,58,00,000	32,64,00,000
Less: Fixed production overhead	7,50,000	7,50,000	7,50,000
Fixed selling and distribution	—	—	—
Variable selling and distribution	—	—	—
Next Income	20,32,50,000	29,50,50,000	32,56,50,000

Reconciliation Statement

	January	*February*	*March*
Absorption Costing income	20,35,50,000	29,49,25,000	32,58,00,000
Variable costing income	20,32,50,000	29,50,50,000	32,56,50,000
Difference in net income	+ 3,00,000	(–) 1,25,000	1,50,000
Inventory Values:			
Absorption Costing:			
Opening	–	11,79,00,000	6,87,75,000
Closing	11,79,00,000	6,87,75,000	12,77,25,000
	11,79,00,000	4,91,25,000	5,89,50,000
Variable costing:			
Opening		11,76,00,000	6,86,00,000
Closing	11,76,00,000	6,86,00,000	12,74,00,000
	11,76,00,000	4,90,00,000	5,88,00,000
Net difference	3,00,000	(– 1,25,000)	1,50,000

Illustrative Problem 18

Apollo Laboratory Company is a family-owned business in which you own 20% of the common stock and your brothers and sisters own the remaining shares. The employment contract of company's new controller, Rahul stipulates a base salary of ₹160,000 per year plus 10% of income from operations in excess of ₹ 8,00,000. Rahul uses the absorption costing method of reporting income from operations, which has averaged approximately ₹ 11,00,000 for the past several years.

Sales for 2010, Rahul's first year as controller of Company, are estimated at 50,000 units at a selling price of 120 per unit. To maximize the use of Company's productive capacity, Rahul has decided to manufacture 60,000 units, rather than the 50,000 units of estimated sales. The beginning inventory at January 1,2010, is insignificant in amount, and the manufacturing costs and selling and administrative expenses for the production of 50,000 and 60,000 units are as follows:

50,000 Units to be Manufactured

	Number of Units	*Unit Cost*	*Total Cost*
Manufacturing costs:			
Variable	50,000	₹ 56	₹ 28,00,000
Fixed	50,000	12	6,00,000
Total		₹ 68	₹ 34,00,000
Selling and administrative expenses:			
Variable	₹ 12,00,000		
Fixed	4,00,000		
Total	₹ 16,00,000		

60,000 Units to be Manufactured

	Number of Units	*Unit Cost*	*Total Cost*
Manufacturing costs:			
Variable	60,000	₹ 56	₹ 33,60,000
Fixed	60,000	10	6,00,000
Total		₹ 66	₹ 39,60,000
Selling and administrative expenses			
Variable	₹ 12,00,000		
Fixed	4,00,000		
Total	₹ 16,00,000		

Required:

(*i*) Prepare an absorption costing income statement for the year ending December 31, 2010, based on sales of 50,000 units and the manufacture of 50,000 units. Also, do the same analysis, assuming production of 60,000 units.

(*ii*) Explain the difference in the income from operations reported in (*i*).

(*iii*) Compute Rahul's total salary for the year 2010, based on sales of 50,000 units and the manufacture of 50,000 units and 60,000 units. Compare your answers.

(*iv*) In addition to maximizing the use of Company's productive capacity, why might Rahul wish to manufacture 60,000 units rather than 50,000 units?

(*v*) Can you suggest an alternative way in which Rahul's salary could be determined, using a base salary of ₹ 160,000 and 10% of income from operations in excess of ₹ 8,00,000, so that the salary could not be increased by simply manufacturing more units?

(*M. Com., Delhi University,* 2012)

Solution: (i)

Absorption Costing Income Statement—50,000 Units Manufactured for the Year Ended December 31, 2010

Sales (50,000 × ₹ 120)	₹ 60,00,000
Cost of goods sold (50,000 × ₹ 68)	34,00,000
Gross profit	₹ 26,00,000
Selling and administrative expenses (₹ 12,00,000 + ₹ 4,00,000)	16,00,000
Income from operations	₹ 10,00,000

Absorption Costing Income Statement—60,000 Units Manufactured for the Year Ended December 31, 2010

Sales (50,000 × ₹ 120)		₹ 60,00,000
Cost of goods sold:		
Cost of goods manufactured (60,000 × ₹ 66)	₹ 39,60,000	
Less inventory, December 31 (10,000 × ₹ 66)	6,60,000	
Cost of goods sold		33,00,000
Gross profit		₹ 27,00,000
Selling and administrative expenses (₹ 12,00,000 + ₹ 4,00,000)		16,00,000
Income from operations		₹ 11,00,000

(*ii*) The ₹ 1,00,000 difference in the amount of income from operations (₹ 11,00,000 – ₹ 10,00,000) is due to the allocation of fixed manufacturing costs to ending inventory. The entire amount of the ₹ 600,000 of fixed manufacturing costs is included in the cost of goods sold when 50,000 units are manufactured. When 60,000 units are manufactured, ₹ 100,000 (10,000 units × ₹ 10) of the fixed manufacturing costs are included in ending inventory and are thus excluded from the cost of goods sold.

(*iii*) ***a.*** Base salary: ₹ 1,60,000

b.

Base salary	₹ 1,60,000
Bonus (₹ 11,00,000 – ₹ 8,00,000) × 10%	30,000
Total salary	₹ 1,90,000

(*iv*) By manufacturing 60,000 units, Rahul increased his salary by ₹ 30,000.
It can be observed that by increasing the ending inventory by 10,000 units, the Company will risk higher obsolescence and incur additional costs of carrying and storing inventory, and these costs will reduce future income of the Company.

(*v*) If Rahul's salary were ₹ 1,60,000 plus a bonus based on income from operations, and the variable costing method had been used, income from operations would have been ₹ 10,00,000, as displayed below, regardless of how many units were manufactured. Thus, Rahul would not have been able to increase his salary simply by manufacturing more units.
The variable costing income statements are as follows:

Variable Costing Income Statement—50,000 Units Manufactured for the Year Ended December 31, 2010

Sales (50,000 × ₹ 120)		₹ 60,00,000
Variable cost of goods sold (50,000 × ₹ 56)		28,00,000
Manufacturing margin		₹ 32,00,000
Variable selling and administrative expenses		12,00,000
Contribution margin		₹ 20,00,000
Fixed costs:		
Fixed manufacturing costs	₹ 6,00,000	
Fixed selling and administrative expenses	4,00,000	10,00,000
Income from operations		₹ 10,00,000

Variable Costing Income Statement—60,000 Units Manufactured for the Year Ended December 31, 2010

Sales (50,000 × ₹ 120)		₹ 60,00,000
Variable cost of goods sold:		
Variable cost of goods manufactured (60,000 × ₹ 56)	₹ 33,60,000	
Less inventory, December 31 (10,000 × ₹ 56)	5,60,000	
Variable cost of goods sold		28,00,000
Manufacturing margin		₹ 32,00,000
Variable selling and administrative expenses		12,00,000
Contribution margin		₹ 20,00,000
Fixed costs:		
Fixed manufacturing costs	₹ 6,00,000	
Fixed selling and administrative expenses	4,00,000	10,00,000
Income from operations		₹ 10,00,000

Illustrative Problem 19

Star Co. manufactures a small part that is widely used in various electronic products such as home computers. Operating results for the first three years of activity were as follows (absorption costing basis):

	Year 1	Year 2	Year 3
Sales	₹ 800,000	₹ 640,000	₹ 800,000
Cost of goods sold:			
Beginning inventory	—0—	—0—	200,000
Add cost of goods manufactured	580,000	600,000	560,000
Goods available for sale	580,000	600,000	760,000
Less ending inventory	—0—	200,000	140,000
Cost of goods sold	580,000	400,000	620,000
Gross margin	220,000	240,000	180,000
Selling and administrative expenses	190,000	180,000	190,000
Net income (loss)	₹ 30,000	₹ 60,000	₹ (10,000)

In the latter part of Year 2, a competitor went out of business and in the process dumped a large number of units on the market, As a result, Star's sales dropped by 20% during Year 2 even though production increased during that year, Management had expected sales to remain constant at 50,000 units; the increased production was designed to provide the company with a buffer of protection against unexpected spurts in demand, By the start of Year 3, management could see that inventory was excessive and that spurts in demand were unlikely. To work off the excessive inventories, Star cut back production during Year 3, as shown below:

	Year 1	Year 2	Year 3
Production in units	50,000	60,000	40,000
Sales in units	50,000	40,000	50,000

Additional information about the company follows:

(a) The company's plant is highly automated. Variable manufacturing costs (direct materials, direct labour, and variable manufacturing overhead) total only ₹ 2 per unit, and fixed manufacturing costs total ₹ 480,000 per year.

(b) Fixed manufacturing costs are applied to units of product on the basis of each year's production. (That is, a new fixed manufacturing overhead rate is computed each year).

(c) Variable selling and administrative expenses were ₹ 1 per unit sold in each year. Fixed selling and administrative expenses totalled ₹ 1,40,000 each year.

(d) The company uses a FIFO inventory flow assumption.

Star's management cannot understand why profits doubled during Year 2 when sales dropped by 20% and why a loss was incurred during Year 3 when sales recovered to previous levels.

Required:

(i) Prepare a new income statement for each year using the contribution approach, with variable costing.

(ii) Refer to the absorption costing income statements above.

(a) Compute the unit product cost in each year under absorption costing. (Show how much of this cost is variable and how much is fixed.)

(b) Reconcile the variable costing and absorption costing net income figures for each year.

(iii) Refer again to the absorption costing income statements. Explain why net income was higher in Year 2 than it was in Year 1 under the absorption approach, in light of the fact that fewer units were sold in Year 2 than in Year 1.

(iv) Refer again to the absorption costing income statements. Explain why the company suffered a loss in Year 3 but reported a profit in Year 1 although the same number of units was sold in each year.

(a) Explain how operations would have differed in Year 2 and Year 3 if the company had been using JIT inventory methods.

(b) If JIT had been in use during Year 2 and Year 3, what would the company's net income (or loss) have been in each year under absorption costing? Explain the reason for any differences between these income figures and the figures reported by the company in the statements above.

Solutions:

(i) **Income Statement (Variable Costing)**

	Year 1	**Year 2**	**Year 3**
Sales	₹ 800,000	₹ 640,000	₹ 800,000
Less variable expenses:			
Variable cost of goods sold @ ₹ 2	100,000	80,000	100,000
Selling and			
administrative expenses @ ₹ 1	50,000	40,000	50,000
Total Variable expenses	150,000	120,000	150,000
Contribution margin	650,000	520,000	650,000

Less fixed expenses:			
Manufacturing overhead	480,000	480,000	480,000
Selling and administrative expenses	140,000	140,000	140,000
Total fixed expenses	620,000	620,000	620,000
Net income (loss)	₹ 30,000	₹ (100,000)	₹ 30,000

Note: In the above income statement (prepared on variable costing), variable cost of goods sold has been computed directly for sales units, and not for production units (year 2). So, closing stocks need not to be shown in the income statement.

(ii) (a)

	Year 1	Year 2	Year 3
Variable manufacturing cost	₹ 2.00	₹ 2.00	₹ 2.00
Fixed manufacturing cost:			
₹ 480,000 ÷ 50,000 units	9.60		
₹ 480,000 ÷ 60,000 units		8.00	
₹ 480,000 ÷ 40,000 units			12.00
Unit product cost	₹ 11.60	₹ 10.00	₹ 14.00

(b)

	Year 1	Year 2	Year 3
Variable costing net income (loss)	₹ 30,000	₹ (100,000)	₹ 30,000
Add (Deduct): Fixed manufacturing overhead cost deferred in inventory from Year 2 to Year 3 under absorption costing (20,000 units × ₹ 8.00)		160,000	(160,000)
Add: Fixed manufacturing overhead cost deferred in inventory from Year 3 to the future under absorption costing (10,000 units × ₹ 12.00)			120,000
Absorption costing net income (loss)	₹ 30,000	₹ 60,000	₹ (10,000)

(iii) Production went up sharply in Year 2 thereby reducing the unit product cost, as shown in (iia) above. This reduction in cost per unit, combined with the large amount of fixed manufacturing overhead cost deferred in inventory for the year, more than offset the loss of revenue. The net result is that the company's net income increased.

The fixed manufacturing overhead cost deferred in inventory from Year 2 was charged against Year 3 operations, as shown in the reconciliation in (iib). This added charge against Year 3 operations was offset somewhat by the fact that part of Year 3's fixed manufacturing overhead costs were deferred in inventory to future years [again see (iib)]. Overall, the added costs charged against Year 3 were greater than the costs deferred to future years, so the company reported less income for the year even though the same number of units was sold as in Year 1.

(iv) (a) Several things would have been different if the company had been using JIT inventory methods. First, in each year production would have been geared to sales so that little or no inventory of finished goods would have been built up in either Year 2 or Year 3. Second, unit product costs probably would have been the same in all three years, since these costs would have been established on the basis of *expected* sales (50,000 units) for each year. Third, since only 40,00 units were sold in Year 2, the company would have produced only that number of units and therefore would have had some underapplied overhead cost for the year.

(b) If JIT had been in use, the net income under absorption costing would have been the same as under variable costing in all three years. The reason is that with production geared to sales, there would have been no ending inventory on hand, and therefore there would have been no fixed manufacturing overhead costs deferred in inventory to other years. Assuming that the company *expected* to sell 50,000 units in each year and that unit product costs were set on the basis of that level of expected activity, the income statements under absorption costing would have appeared as follows:

	Year 1	Year 2	Year 3
Sales	₹ 800,000	₹ 640,000	₹ 800,000
Less cost of goods sold:			
Cost of goods manufactured (@ ₹ 11.60)	580,000	464,000*	580,000
Add underapplied overhead		96,000**	
Cost of goods sold	580,000	560,000	580,000
Gross margin	220,000	80,000	220,000
Selling and administrative expenses	190,000	180,000	190,000
Net income (loss)	₹ 30,000	₹ (100,00)	₹ 30,000

* 40,000 units × ₹ 11.60 = ₹ 464,000.

** 10,000 units *not* produced × ₹ 9.60 fixed manufacturing overhead cost per unit = ₹ 96,000 fixed manufacturing overhead cost applied to products.

Illustrative Problem 20

Liberty Leather Company manufactures three sizes of extreme weather coats—small (S), medium (M) and large (L). The income statement has consistently indicated a net loss for the M size, and management is considering three proposals: (1) continue Size M, (2) discontinue Size M and reduce total output accordingly, or (3) discontinue Size M and conduct an advertising campaign to expand the sales of Size S so that the entire plant capacity can continue to be used.

If Proposal 2 is selected and Size M is discontinued and production curtailed, the annual fixed production costs and fixed operating expenses could be reduced by ₹ 64,000 and ₹ 44,800, respectively. If Proposal 3 is selected, it is anticipated that an additional annual expenditure of ₹ 48,000 for the rental of additional warehouse space would yield an increase of 130% in Size S sales volume. It is also assumed that the increased production of Size S would utilize the plant facilities released by the discontinuance of Size M.

The sales and costs have been relatively stable over the past few years, and they are expected to remain so for the foreseeable future. The income statement for the past year ended June 30, 2016, is as follows:

	Sizes			
	S	*M*	*L*	*Total*
Sales	₹ 9,28,000	₹ 10,24,000	₹ 13,28,000	₹ 32,80,000
Cost of goods sold:				
Variable costs	₹ 4,16,000	₹ 4,96,000	₹ 6,08,000	₹ 15,20,000
Fixed costs	1,04,000	1,92,000	2,40,000	5,36,000
Total cost of goods sold	₹ 5,20,000	₹ 6,88,000	₹ 8,48,000	₹ 20,56,000
Gross profit	₹ 4,08,000	₹ 3,36,000	₹ 4,80,000	₹ 12,24,000
Less operating expenses:				
Variable expenses	₹ 1,84,000	₹ 2,16,000	₹ 2,72,000	₹ 6,72,000
Fixed expenses	1,28,000	1,44,000	1,60,000	4,32,000
Total operating expenses	₹ 3,12,000	₹ 3,60,000	₹ 4,32,000	₹ 11,04,000
Income from operations	₹ 96,000	₹ (24,000)	₹ 48,000	₹ 1,20,000

Required:

(*i*) Prepare an income statement for the past year in the variable costing format.

(*ii*) Based on the income statement prepared in (*i*) and the other data presented, determine the amount by which total annual income from operations would be reduced below its present level if Proposal 2 is accepted.

(*iii*) Prepare an income statement in the variable costing format, indicating the projected annual income from operations if Proposal 3 is accepted.

(*iv*) By how much would total annual income increase above its present level if Proposal 3 is accepted? Explain.

Solution: (i)

Liberty Leather Company Variable Costing Income Statement for the Year Ended June 30, 2016

	Sizes			
	S	*M*	*L*	*Total*
Sales	₹ 9,28,000	₹ 10,24,000	₹ 13,28,000	₹ 32,80,000
Variable cost of goods sold	4,16,000	4,96,000	6,08,000	15,20,000
Manufacturing margin	₹ 5,12,000	₹ 5,28,000	₹ 7,20,000	₹ 17,60,000
Variable operating expenses	1,84,000	2,16,000	2,72,000	6,72,000
Contribution margin	₹ 3,28,000	₹ 3,12,000	₹ 4,48,000	₹ 10,88,000
Fixed costs:				
Manufacturing costs				₹ 5,36,000
Operating expenses				4,32,000
Total fixed costs				₹ 9,68,000
Income from operations				₹ 1,20,000

(*ii*) Annual income from operations would be reduced below its present level by ₹ 2,03,200 if Size M were to be discontinued (Proposal (*ii*), as indicated below:

Contribution margin for Size M .... ₹ 3,12,000

Less reduction in fixed production costs and fixed operating expenses (₹ 64,000 + ₹ 44,800)	1,08,800
Reduction in annual income from operations	₹ 2,03,200

If Size M is discontinued, ₹ 312,000 of contribution margin would be forgone and only ₹ 108,800 in fixed costs would be saved, resulting in a decrease of ₹ 203,200 in income from operations.

(*iii*)

Liberty Leather Company
Variable Costing Income Statement — Proposal (*iii*)

	Sizes		
	S	***L***	***Total***
Sales	₹ 21,34,400	₹ 13,28,000	₹ 34,62,400
Variable cost of goods sold	9,56,800	6,08,000	15,64,800
Manufacturing margin	₹ 11,77,600	₹ 7,20,000	₹ 18,97,600
Variable operating expenses	4,23,200	2,72,000	6,95,200
Contribution margin	₹ 7,54,400	₹ 4,48,000	₹ 12,02,400
Fixed costs:			
Manufacturing costs			₹ 5,36,000
Operating expenses (including ₹ 48,000 additional rent)			4,80,000
Total fixed costs			₹ 10,16,000
Income from operations			₹ 1,86,400

(*iv*) ₹ 66,400. A comparison of the amount of income from operations under present conditions, as indicated in (*i*), and under Proposal (*iii*), as indicated in (*iii*), suggest an increase of ₹ 66,400 if Proposal (*iii*) is accepted, as illustrated below:

Income from operations, Proposal (*iii*)	₹ 1,86,400
Income from operations, present conditions	1,20,000
Increase in income from operations	₹ 66,400

Alternatively, the ₹ 66,400 increase can be determined as follows:

Contribution margin, Size S, Proposal (*iii*)		₹ 7,54,400
Contribution margin, Size S, present operations		3,28,000
Increase in contribution margin		₹ 4,26,400
Less contribution margin, Size M, present operations	₹ 31,200	
Additional rent	48,000	3,60,000
Increase in income from operations		₹ 66,400

Illustrative Problem 21

Byrd Company is a manufacturer of small appliances for both residential and commercial use. The company's accounting and financial reporting system is primarily designed to meet external reporting requirements in accordance with generally accepted accounting principles. For inventory costing purposes. Byrd uses the absorption costing method in conjuction with a standard costing system. Relevant information on one of Byrd's product lines is provided below for the last two years. The standard costs for the product have not changed since 2015.

Unit information	2016	2017
Beginning Inventory	900	1,400
Production	2,000	400
Sales	1,500	1,700
Normal activity	2,000	2,000
Other data		
	(₹)	(₹)
Sales price per unit	100.00	100.00
Standard prime costs per unit	40.00	40.00
Standard variable overhead cost per unit	15.00	15.00
Variable marketing and administrative costs per unit sold	1.00	1.00
Total budgeted (and actual) fixed manufacturing costs	10,000	10,000
Total fixed marketing and administrative costs	3,000	3,000
Net unfavourable variance* pertaining to variable manufacturing costs	1,000	1,000

*All variances are expensed in the period incurred.

Currently, Byrd evaluates the performance of its product line managers and calculates bonuses on the basis of operating income computed on an absorption costing basis. It has been suggested that the use of variable costing for internal reporting purposes would more accurately reflect the performance of the product line managers.

Required:

A. Using the data provided above, calculate Byrd Company's operating income for 2011 and 2012 using.

1. Absorption costing. 2. Variable costing.

B. Discuss the features of variable costing that allow it to more accurately reflect the performance of Byrd Company product line managers. Be Sure to include in your discussion how absorption costing may influence a product line manager's behaviour differently from variable costing. *(CMA, USA, Adapted with permission)*

Solution:

Income Statement under Absorption Costing

	2016 (₹)	2017 (₹)
Sales[(1)]	1,50,000	1,70,000
Cost of goods sold:		
Beginning Inventory[(2)]	54,000	84,000
Cost of goods manufactured[(3)]	1,20,000	24,000
Cost of goods available	1,74,000	1,08,000
Less: Ending Inventory[(4)]	(84,000)	(6,000)
Cost of goods sold at standard cost	90,000	1,02,000
Net unfavourable variance	1,000	1,000
Production volume variance[(5)]	—	8,000
Adjusted cost of goods sold	91,000	111,000

Gross Margin	59,000	59,000
Variable marketing & administrative costs(6)	1,500	1,700
Fixed marketing & administrative costs	3,000	3,000
Operating income	54,500	54,300

Note:

	2016	2017
(1)	1,500 units × ₹ 100	1,700 units × ₹ 100
(2)	900 units × ₹ 60*	1,400 units × ₹ 60

*Unit cost is comprised of prime cost + variable overhead + fixed overhead ₹ 40 + ₹ 15 + ₹ 5**
= ₹ 60 per unit

**Fixed overhead per unit
₹ 10,000 ÷ 2,000 units = ₹ 5 per unit

	2016	2017
(3)	2,000 units × ₹ 60	400 units × ₹ 60
(4)	1,400* units × ₹ 60	100 units × ₹ 60

*Ending inventory, in units is comprised of beginning inventory + production-sales

2016	2017
900 + 2,000 – 1,500	1,400 + 400 – 1,700
= 1,400 units	= 100 units

	2016	2017
(5)	—	1,600* units × ₹ 5

*Unit production variance, in units, is comprised of normal activity – actual production.

2016	2017
—	2,000 – 400 = 1,600 units

	2016	2017
(6)	1,500 units × ₹ 1	1,700 units × ₹ 1

Income Statement under Variable Costing

		2016 (₹)	2017 (₹)
Sales(1)		150,000	170,000
	Cost of goods sold		
	Beginning inventory(2)	49,500	77,000
	Cost of goods manufactured (3)	110,000	22,000
	Cost of goods available	159,500	99,000
Less:	Ending inventory(4)	77,000	5,500
	Cost of goods sold at standard cost	82,500	93,500
	Net unfavorable variance	1,000	1,000
	Adjusted costs of goods sold	83,500	94,500
	Contribution margin	66,500	75,500
	Variable marketing & administrative costs (5)	1,500	1,700
	Fixed marketing & administrative costs	3,000	3,000
	Fixed manufacturing overhead	10,000	10,000
	Operating income	52,000	60,800

Note:

2016	2017
(1) 1,500 units × ₹ 100	1,700 unit × ₹ 100
(2) 900 units × ₹ 55*	1,400 units × ₹ 55
* Unit cost is comprised of prime cost + variable overhead.	
2016	**2017**
₹ 40 + ₹ 15 = ₹ 55 per unit	
(3) 2,000 units × ₹ 55	400 units × ₹ 55
(4) 1,400 units × ₹ 55	100 units × ₹ 55
(5) 1,500 units × ₹ 1	1,700 units × ₹ 1

B. Among the features that allow variable costing to more accurately reflect the performance of Byrd company's product line manager are

- That it more clearly distinguishes between fixed and variable costs: fixed manufacturing costs are not included in inventory.
- Inventory changes do not affect performance. Operating income is driven by fluctuations in sales volume alone; it is unaffected by fixed manufacturing cost that are released or held back in inventory.
- That it is not as susceptible to manipulation. Under absorption costing, a manager can increase income by increasing production or choosing a more favourable capacity denominator level, and thus capitalize fixed costs into inventory, deferring the expense.

REFERENCES

1. Lane K. Anderson and Harold M. Sollenberger, *Managerial Accounting*, South Western Publishing Co., 1992, p. 507.
2. Don T. Decoster, -et al, *Management Accounting, A Decision Emphasis*, John Wiley and Sons, 1988, p. 118.
3. Carl S. Warren and Philipe E. Fess, *Financial and Managerial Accounting*, South Western Publishing Co., 1992, p. 901.
4. Wayne J. Morse, James R. Davis, Al. Hartgraves, *Management Accounting, A Strategic Emphasis*, South Western College Publishing, 2000, p. 340.
5. Letricia Gayle Raburn, "Principles of Cost Accounting, using a Cost Management Approach[4]", Irwin, 1989, p. 730.
6. Cheryl S. McWatters, Dale C. Morse and Jerold L. Zimmerman, *Management Accounting*, McGraw Hill, 2001, p. 385.
7. Charles T. Horngreen, George Foster and SriKant M. Datar, *Cost Accounting. A Management Emphasis.* Prentice Hall 2000, p. 298-299.
8. Ray H. Garrison, Eric W. Noreen and Peter C. Brewer, Managerial Accounting, 13th Edition, McGraw Hill Education (India) Pvt. Ltd., 2011, p. 287.
9. Cheryl S. McWatters, Dale Morse and Jerold L. Zimmerman, *Management Accounting.* McGraw Hill, 2001, p. 383.
10. Lame K. Anderson and Harold M. Sollenberger, *Managerial Accounting.*, South Western Publishing, 1992, p. 511.
11. Ray H. Garrison and EricW. Noreen, *Managerial Accounting*, Irwin McGraw Hill, 2000, p. 300.
12. Charles T. Hornegreen, George Foster and Sri Kant Datar, lbid, p.299.
13. Cheryl S. McWatters, Dale C. Morse and Jerold L. Zimmerman, *Management Accounting* McGraw Hill, 2001. p. 383-384.

CRITICAL ANALYSIS AND DISCUSSION QUESTIONS, SELF-ASSESSMENT QUESTIONS, MULTIPLE CHOICE QUESTIONS, PROBLEMS AND CASES

CRITICAL ANALYSIS AND DISCUSSION QUESTIONS

1. What do you mean by variable costing? Discuss its usefulness and limitation.
2. Distinguish between absorption and variable costing. What are the most important areas of management decisions helped by the application of variable (marginal) costing technique? *(M. Com., Delhi, 2014)*
3. "Variable Costing reveals the lowest price at which a product can be sold during a trade depression, but they also reveal to management the most profitable lines during the period of intense trade activity." Explain with examples.
4. How do income statement prepared under absorption costing and variable costing differ?
5. Compared with absorption costing, when will variable costing report lower profits, higher profits, the same profits?
6. In what ways is variable costing better adapted to managerial uses in planning and control, decision making, pricing policy?
7. "Absorption costing obscures the total amount of fixed costs whereas variable costing highlights it" Explain this statement.
8. "In classifying a particular cost as fixed or variable, the volume of activity levels is extremely important." Discuss and illustrate this statement.
9. Explain the concept of marginal (variable) costing. Describe the characteristics and limitations of marginal costing.
10. Explain the advantage of variable costing over absorption costing. Give suitable illustrations. *(M. Com., Delhi)*
11. Why do some persons prefer the phrase 'variable costing to the phrase' direct or marginal costing? *(M. Com., Delhi)*
12. Why is it impossible for a company to incur an overhead capacity variance when variable costing is used?
13. Explain whether variable costing or absorption costing will have the higher net profit under each of the following conditions:
    (*i*) Production equals sales (*ii*) Production exceeds sales
    (*iii*) Production is less than sales
14. How is it possible to increase net profit using absorption costing when sales are not increasing?
15. Discuss the arguments for and against the inclusion of fixed overheads in stock valuation for the purpose of internal profit measurement.
16. How are marketing and administrative costs treated under variable costing? Under absorption costing?
17. How can a company using absorption costing manipulate profit without changing sales?
18. Does variable costing imply that every variable cost associated with a product is reflected in its inventory cost?
19. Indicate several questions or decisions for which the use of variable costing would be more appropriate than use of absorption costing. *(M. Com., Delhi, 2011)*

20. What factors related to manufacturing costs causes the difference in net income computed using absorption costing and using variable costing?
21. What are the features associated with variable costing income measurement that a marketing manager should find attractive?
22. What is the only difference between the way costs are assigned under variable and absorption costing?
23. Why is variable costing better than absorption costing for the evaluation of managerial performance?
24. Why is variable costing better than absorption costing for the evaluation of segment performance?
25. Explain how income under absorption costing can increase from one period to the next even though selling prices and costs have remained the same.
26. Discuss the important areas of management decisions helped by the application of variable costing technique. Also, explain its limitations. (*M. Com., Delhi,* 2001)
27. Why is variable costing better than absorption costing for planning, controlling and evaluation of managerial performance. (*M. Com., Delhi,* 2002)
28. Discuss the advantages and disadvantages of absorption costing over variable costing. What precautions are essential in using absorption costing? (*M. Com., Delhi,* 2004, 2008, 2010)
29. What is the impact of JIT on absorption costing profit?
30. "Absorption costing regards more categories of costs as product costs." Explain.
31. Why is variable costing used only for internal reporting and not for external financial reporting or tax purposes?
32. "Variable costing is consistent with cost-volume profit analysis." Explain.
33. Why is variable costing a more descriptive term for the product costing method popularly known as direct costing?
34. The fixed manufacturing Overhead expense recognized on an income statement was ₹ 5,00,000. The fixed manufacturing overhead for the period was ₹ 4,00,000. Was the income statement prepared using absorption costing or variable costing. Explain.
35. The term direct costing is a misnomer. Variable costing is a better term for the product costing method. Do you agree or disagree? Why?
36. Explain how throughput costing differs from absorption and variable costing.
37. Will variable and absorption costing result in significantly different income measures in a JIT setting? Why?
38. Why do proponents of variable costing prefer variable costing when making pricing decisions?
39. Which is more consistent with cost-volume-profit analysis, variable costing or absorption costing? Why?
40. Tough times always seem to bring out the worst in people. When companies are desperate to stay in business or to report more favourable earnings to their shareholders, some managers just can't seem to resist the temptation to manipulate reported profits. Unfortunately, inventory is sometimes a tempting source of such manipulations. It is important to know how such earnings distortions can occur, whether they result from intentional actions or innocent miscalculation.

Required:

(*i*) What product cost concept is the basis for inventory valuation and cost of goods sold determination for external financial reporting purposes?

(*ii*) Explain the concept of 'phantom' or 'illusory' profits. Excluding inflation and changes in the selling prices of products, how could a firm with the same sales as last year report significantly higher profits without cutting any costs? Could a firm with sales below the break-even point report profits? Explain.

(*iii*) Are all such 'fictitious' profits an attempt to distort profits and mislead investors and creditors? If not, under what economic conditions would this most likely occur?

(*iv*) Could the reverse situation occur? That is, could lower accounting profits be reported even though the firm is not economically worse off? Under what economic conditions would this most likely occur?

SELF–ASSESSMENT QUESTIONS

I. A company developed the following direct costing income statement for year 2012.

	₹	Per unit ₹
Sales (1,50,000 units at ₹ 30)	45,00,000	30.00
Variable costs :		
Direct Materials	10,50,000	7.00
Direct Labour	15,00,000	10.00
Manufacturing Overhead	3,00,000	2.00
Selling and Marketing	3,00,000	2.00
	31,50,000	21.00
Contribution Margin	13,50,000	9.00
Fixed Costs:		
Manufacturing Overhead	600,000	4.00
Selling and Marketing	300,000	2.00
	900,000	6.00
Net Income	4,50,000	3.00

The company based its 2013 budget on the assumption that fixed costs, unit sales, and the sales price would remain as they were in year 2012, but with net income being reduced to ₹ 3,00,000. By July of 2013 the manager predicted that units sales would increase over 2012 levels by 10%. Based on the 2013 budget and the new information, the predicted 2013 net income would be:

(*a*) ₹ 3,00,000 (*b*) ₹ 3,30,000

(*c*) ₹ 4,20,000 (*d*) ₹ 5,85, 000

II. ABC Company began operations on January 3, 2012. Standard costs were established in early January assuming a normal production volume of 1,60,000 units.

However, the company produced only 1,40,000 units of product and sold 100,000 units at a selling price of ₹ 180 per unit during 2012. Variable costs totalled ₹ 70,00,000 of which 60 per cent were manufacturing and 40 per cent were selling. Fixed cost totalled ₹ 1,12,00,000 of which 50 per cent were manufacturing and 50 per cent were selling. The company had no Raw Materials or Work in Process Inventories at December 31, 2012. Actual input price per unit of product and actual input quantities per unit of product were equal to standard.

Based on the above data, Find out the following items:

1. Cost of goods sold at standard cost for 2012 using full absorption costing is:
   (*a*) ₹ 82,00,000 (*b*) ₹ 72,00,000
   (*c*) ₹ 65,00,000 (*d*) ₹ 70,00,000
   (*e*) Some amount other than those given above
2. The value assigned to December 31, 2012 inventory using variable (direct) costing is
   (*a*) ₹ 28,00,000 (*b*) ₹ 12,00,000
   (*c*) ₹ 20,00,000 (*d*) ₹ 30,00,000
   (*e*) Some amount other than those given above
3. Manufacturing overhead volume variance in 2012 using full absorption costing is:
   (*a*) ₹ 8,00,000 unfavourable (*b*) ₹ 8,00,000 favourable
   (*c*) ₹ 7,00,000 unfavourable (*d*) ₹ 7,00,000 favourable
   (*e*) Some amount other than those given above
4. 2012 income from operations using variable (direct) costing is:
   (*a*) ₹ 34,00,000 (*b*) ₹ 18,00,000
   (*c*) ₹ 26,00,000 (*d*) ₹ 10,00,000
   (*e*) Some amount other than those given above

III. A Company planned and actually manufactured 2,00,000 units of its single product in 2012, its first year of operations. Variable manufacturing cost were ₹ 30 per unit of product. Planned and actual fixed manufacturing costs were ₹ 6,00,000 and selling and administrative costs totalled ₹ 4,00,000 in 2012. The company sold 1,20,000 units of product in 2012 at a selling price of ₹ 40 per unit.

Based on the above data, find out the following items:

I. 2012 operating income using absorption (full) costing is
   (*a*) ₹ 2,00,000 (*b*) ₹ 4,40,000
   (*c*) ₹ 6,00,000 (*d*) ₹ 8,40,000
   (*e*) Some amount other than those given above

II. 2012 operating income using variable (direct) costing is:
   (*a*) ₹ 2,00,00 (*b*) ₹ 4,40,000
   (*c*) ₹ 8,00,000 (*d*) ₹ 6,00,000
   (*e*) Some amount other than those given above

IV. Nash Glassworks Company has budgeted fixed manufacturing overhead of ₹ 100,000 per month. The company uses absorption costing for both external and internal financial reporting purposes. Budgeted manufacturing overhead rates for cost allocations for the month of April 2012 using alternative unit output denominator levels are shown below.

Budgeted Capacity Levels	***Budgeted Denominator Level (Units of output)***	***Budgeted Overhead Cost Rate*** ₹
Theoretical	15,00,000	.0667
Practical	12,50,000	.0800
Normal	7,75,000	.1290
Master-budget	8,00,000	.1250

Actual output for the month of April was 8,00,000 units of glassware.

1. When Nash Glassworks Company allocates fixed costs, management will select a capacity level to use as the denominator or volume. All of the following would be appropriate as the capacity level that approximates actual volume level except

   (*a*) normal capacity (*b*) expected annual activity

   (*c*) theoretical capacity (*d*) expected annual capacity

   (*e*) master-budget capacity

2. The choice of production volume level as a denominator in the computation of fixed overhead rates can significantly affect reported net income. Which one of the following statements is correct for Nash Glassworks Company ? The choice of

   (*a*) Practical capacity as the denominator level will result in a lower net income amount than if master-budget capacity is chosen.

   (*b*) Normal capacity as the denominator level will result in a lower net income amount than if any other capacity volume is chosen.

   (*c*) Master -budget capacity as the denominator level will result in a lower net income amount than if theoretical capacity is chosen.

   (*d*) Practical capacity as the denominator level will result in a higher net income amount than if normal capacity is chosen.

   (*e*) Normal capacity as the denominator level will result in a higher net income amount than if any other capacity is chosen. (*CMA, USA, Adapted with permission*)

Answer:

1. (c), 2. (a).

MULTIPLE CHOICE QUESTIONS

Select the correct answer for the following multiple choice questions:

1. Profits under absorption costing and variable costing will be the same if

   (*a*) There are no opening and closing stocks

   (*b*) There is opening stock and no closing stock

   (*c*) There is closing stock and no opening stock

   (*d*) There are opening and closing stocks

2. What cost are treated as product costs under variable (marginal) costing?

   (*a*) Direct Costs

   (*b*) Variable Production Costs

   (*c*) All Variable

   (*d*) All Variable and Fixed Manufacturing Costs

3. Which of the following must be known about a production process in order to institute variable costing technique?

   (*a*) Variable and fixed components of all costs related to production

   (*b*) Controllable and uncontrollable components of all costs related to production

   (*c*) Standard production rates and times for all elements of production

   (*d*) Contribution margin and break even point for all goods in production

4. In an income statement prepared as an internal report using absorption costing, which of the following terms should appear?

	Contribution Margin	***Gross profit Margin***
(*a*)	No	Yes
(*b*)	No	No
(*c*)	Yes	No
(*d*)	Yes	Yes

5. Which of the following is an argument against the use of variable costing?
   (*a*) Absorption costing overstates the balance sheet value of inventories?
   (*b*) Variable factory overhead is a period cost
   (*c*) Fixed factory overhead is difficult to allocate properly
   (*d*) Fixed factory overhead is necessary for the production of a product
6. Stocks and work -in -progress should be valued using an absorption approach for
   (*a*) External reporting purposes (*b*) internal reporting purposes
   (*c*) Internal and external purposes (*d*) Decision-making purposes
7. Fixed costs of ₹ 18 per unit were included in the opening and closing stocks for absorption costing purposes. For the period under review there were 1,800 units opening stock and 1,200 units closing stock. The Absorption costing profit would be:
   (*a*) ₹ 10,800 greater than the marginal costing profit
   (*b*) ₹ 21,600 greater than the marginal costing profit
   (*c*) ₹ 10,800 less than the marginal costing profit
   (*d*) ₹ 21,600 less than the marginal costing profit
8. The concept that considers the cost of product manufactured to be composed only of those manufacturing costs that vary with the rate of production is known as:
   (*a*) Absorption costing (*b*) Variable costing
   (*c*) Replacement cost (*d*) None of the above
9. In an income statement prepared under the variable costing concept, the deduction of the variable cost of goods sold from sales yields an intermediate amount referred to as:
   (*a*) Gross profit (*b*) Contribution margin
   (*c*) Manufacturing margin (*d*) None of the above
10. During a year in which the number of units manufactured exceed the number of units sold, the operating income reported under the absorption costing concept would be:
   (*a*) Larger than the operating income reported under variable costing
   (*b*) Smaller than the operating income reported under the variable costing concept
   (*c*) The same as the operating income reported under variable costing concept
   (*d*) None of the above
11. Sales were ₹ 7,50,000, variable cost of goods sold was ₹ 4,00,000, Variable selling and administrative expenses were ₹ 90,000 and fixed costs were ₹ 2,00,000. The contribution margin was:
   (*a*) ₹ 60,000 (*b*) ₹ 2,60,000
   (*c*) ₹ 3,50,000 (*d*) None of the above

12. In an income statement prepared as an internal report using the variable costing method, variable selling and administrative expenses would:
    (*a*) Not be used
    (*b*) Be used in computation of the manufacturing margin
    (*c*) Be used in the computation of operating income but not in the computation of the contribution margin
    (*d*) Be treated the same as fixed selling and administrative expenses
13. A company manufactures 50,000 units of a product and sells 40,000 units. Total manufacturing cost per unit is ₹ 50 (variable manufacturing cost ₹ 10 fixed manufacturing cost ₹ 40). Assuming no beginning inventory, what is the effect on net income if absorption costing is used instead of variable costing?
    (*a*) Net income is ₹ 4,00,000 lower (*b*) Net income ₹ 4,00,000 higher
    (c) Net income is the same (d) Net income is ₹ 2,00,000 higher
14. Using the variable costing method, which of the following costs are assigned to inventory?

	Variable selling and administrative cost	***Variable factory overhead costs***
(*a*)	Yes	Yes
(*b*)	Yes	No
(*c*)	No	No
(*d*)	No	Yes

15. At the end of ABC Co's., first year of operations, 1,000 units of inventory remained on hand. Variable and fixed manufacturing costs per unit were ₹ 90 and ₹ 20, respectively. If company uses absorption costing rather than variable (direct) costing, the result would be a higher pretax income of
    (*a*) ₹ 0 (*b*) ₹ 20,000
    (*c*) ₹ 70,000 (*d*) ₹ 90,000
16. A manufacturing company prepares income statements using both absorption and variable costing methods. At the end of a period actual sales revenues, total gross profit and total contribution margin approximated budgeted figures, whereas net income was substantially greater than the budgeted amount. There were no beginning or ending inventories. The most likely explanation of the net income increase is that, compared to budget, actual.
    (*a*) Manufacturing fixed costs had increased
    (*b*) Selling and administrative fixed expenses had decreased
    (*c*) Sales prices and variable costs had increased proportionately
    (*d*) Sales prices had declined proportionately less than variable costs
17. A single– product company prepares income statement using both absorption and variable costing methods. Manufacturing overhead cost applied per unit produced in 2011 was the same as in 2010. The 2011 variable costing statement reported a profit whereas the 2011 absorption costing statement reported a loss. The difference in reported income could be explained by units produced in 2011 being
    (*a*) Less than units sold in 2011
    (*b*) Less than activity level used for allocating overhead to the product
    (*c*) In excess of the activity level used for allocating overhead to the product
    (*d*) In excess of units sold in 2011

18. Which of the following statement is true for a firm that uses variable costing?
    (*a*) The cost of unit of product changes because of changes in number of units manufactured
    (*b*) Profits fluctuate with sales
    (*c*) An idle facility variance is calculated
    (*d*) Product costs include direct (variable) administrative costs
19. Which method of inventory costing treat direct manufacturing cost and manufacturing overhead costs, both variable and fixed, as inventoriable cost?
    (*a*) Direct costing (*b*) Variable costing
    (*c*) Absorption costing (*d*) Conversion costing
20. Using absorption costing, fixed manufacturing overhead costs are best described as:
    (*a*) Direct period costs (*b*) Indirect period costs
    (*c*) Direct product costs (*d*) Indirect product costs
21. When a firm prepares financial reports by using absorption costing
    (*a*) Profits will always increase with increases in sales
    (*b*) Profits will always decreases with decreases in sales
    (*c*) Profits may decrease with increased sales even if there is no change in selling price and costs
    (*d*) Decreased output and constant sales result in increased profits
22. Which one of the following statements is correct regarding absorption costing and variable costing?
    (*a*) Administrative overhead costs are treated in the same manner under both costing methods.
    (*b*) If finished goods inventory increases, absorption costing results in higher income
    (*c*) Variable manufacturing costs are lower under variable costing.
    (*d*) Gross margins are the same under both costing methods.
23. Absorption costing and variable costing are different methods of assigning costs to units produced. Which cost item listed below is not correctly accounted for as a product cost?

	Part of Product Cost under	
	Absorption Cost	***Variable Cost***
(*a*) Manufacturing supplies	Yes	Yes
(*b*) Insurance on factory	Yes	No
(*c*) Direct Labour cost	Yes	Yes
(*d*) Packaging and Shipping costs	Yes	Yes

24. The upper limit of a company's productive output capacity given its existing resources is called
    (*a*) Excess capacity (*b*) Cycle time capacity
    (*c*) Relevant range capacity (*d*) Practical capacity
    (*e*) Theoretical capacity
25. Which costing method is properly classified as to its acceptability for both external and internal reporting?

	External Reporting	Internal Reporting
(a) Activity-based costing	Yes	Yes
(b) Job costing	No	Yes
(c) Variable costing	Yes	No
(d) Process costing	No	Yes

(CMA, USA, Adapted with permission)

Answer to Multiple Choice Questions

1. (a)	2. (b)	3. (a)	4. (a)	5. (d)
6. (a)	7. (c)	8. (b)	9. (c)	10. (a)
11. (b)	12. (d)	13. (b)	14. (d)	15. (b)
16. (b)	17. (a)	18. (b)	19. (c)	20. (d)
21. (c)	22. (b)	23. (d)	24. (d)	25. (a)

PROBLEMS

1. Consider the following facts:

	Year 2015	Year 2016
Sales volume	70,000 units	1,30,000 units
Production volume	1,00,000 units	1,00,000 units
	₹	₹
Selling price	20 per unit	20 per unit
Variable Manufacturing	13 per unit	13 per unit
Fixed Manufacturing	3,40,000	3,40,000
Non Manufacturing costs (all fixed)	1.50,000	1,50,000

Prepare comparative income statement under variable costing and full absorption costing.

Answers:

Net Income: Variable costing 2015, ₹ 0, 2016, ₹ 420

Absorption costing 2015, ₹ 102, 2016, ₹ 318

2. Using the information given below, calculate the net income for the month of October, November and December and the value of finished goods on hand at the end of period using absorption costing and marginal costing. Also, comment on the difference in profits under these two methods.

	October	November	December
Production units	45,000	36,000	45,000
Sales units	36,000	42,000	48,000
Opening stock units	—	9,000	3,000
Closing stock units	9,000	3000	
Additional information:			
Selling price per unit	₹ 50		
Variable cost per unit	₹ 30		
Fixed cost per unit	₹ 10		
Total fixed costs per month	₹ 3,90,000		
Normal output per month	39,000 units		

Answers:

Profit under absorption costing, October ₹ 4,20,000, November ₹ 3,90,000, December ₹ 5,40,000 profit under marginal costing. October ₹ 3,30,000, November ₹ 4,50,000, December ₹ 5,70,000. Difference in profits of different month is due to differences in values of closing stocks which are determined differently under both the methods.

3. The director of a company have been studying the following condensed profit reports for the years 2015 and 2016

	2015	2016
Sales (₹)	3,00,000	4,50,000
Profit or Loss (₹)	55,000	35,000

The directors are perturbed over the trend, for a 50% increases in sales resulted in a decrease in profit in 2016. The chief cost accountant explains that unabsorbed overhead was charged to operations. His statement was based on the following data:

	2015	2016
Sales (units)	20,000	30,000
Production (units)	30,000	20,000
Sales price per unit (₹)	15	15
Variable cost per unit (₹)	5	5
Fixed factory overhead (₹)	1,80,000	1,80,000
Fixed factory overhead per unit (standard)	6	6
Fixed selling and administrative expenses	25,000	25,000

Prepare: (*a*) Income statement by the conventional methods to which the chief cost accountant referred.

(*b*) Income statements by variable costing method.

Answers:

Net Profit, Absorption Costing, 2015 ₹ 55,000, 2016 ₹ 35,000 Variable Costing 2015 ₹ 5,000 loss, 2016 ₹ 95,000

4. The data below relates to a company which makes and sells a component:

	March units	*April* units
Sales	5,000	10,000
Production	10,000	5,000
	₹	₹
Selling price per unit	100	100
Variable Production cost per unit	50	50
Fixed Production overheads incurred	1,00,000	1,00,000
Fixed Production overheads costs, per unit, being the pre-determined overhead absorption rate	10	10
Selling distribution and administration cost (all fixed)	50,000	50,000

You are required to present comparative profit statements for each month using:

(*i*) Absorption costing

(*ii*) Marginal costing

(*b*) Comment on the following statement using the figures contained in your answer to (*a*) "marginal costing rewards sales whereas absorption costing rewards production".

Answer:

	March	***April***
Absorption costing profit (₹)	1,50,000	3,00,000
Marginal costing profit (₹)	1,00,000	3,50,000

5. The following data relate to the operations of Hindustan Manufacturers Ltd. for the year ending 31st March 2016.

	₹ (000)
Units produced	600
Units sold	500
Direct Materials incurred	₹ 900
Direct Labour incurred	300
Variable factory overhead	750
Fixed factory overhead incurred	1200
Selling and Administrative Expenses (fixed)	275
Selling price per unit	6
Raw materials inventory (beginning)	100
Raw materials inventory (ending)	100
Work in process inventories (beginning and ending)	Nil
Finished goods inventory (beginning)	Nil

You are required to prepare income statements, using absorption costing and variable costing.

Answer:

Absorption costing profit (₹) 1,00,000

Variable costing loss (₹) 1,00,000

6. The Bestobell Manufacturing Company showed the following results for the four quarters of 2016:

	Ist Quarter	***IInd Quarter***	***IIIrd Quarter***	***IVth Quarter***
Sales, units	40,000	60,000	60,000	30,000
Production units	70,000	50,000	60,000	10,000
		₹		
Selling price per unit		10		
Variable manufacturing cost per unit		4		
Fixed manufacturing cost per quarter		1,50,000		
Fixed selling and Administrative cost per quarter		90,000		
Normal capacity per quarter (units)		50,000		

There are no work-in-progress inventories and the level of raw materials inventories has remained constant throughout.

With this information you are required to prepare quarterly and year's total income statement:

(*a*) on absorption costing basis

(*b*) on a variable costing basis

Answer:

Absorption costing I ₹ 90,000; II ₹ 90,000; III ₹ 1,20,000; IV Loss ₹.1,20,000

Variable costing I Zero, II ₹ 1,20,000; III ₹ 1,20,000; IV Loss ₹ 60,000

7. The operations of Indo-Nelson Ltd. for April 2016 revealed the following:

	₹
Sales	15,00,000
Fixed costs:	
Manufacturing overhead	1,00,000
Selling expenses	30,000
General expenses	20,000
Variable costs:	
Raw materials used in production	4,00,000
Direct labour used in production	5,00,000
Factory overhead	1,50,000
Selling expenses	40,000
General expenses	10,000

The inventory on April 1, 2016 was ₹ 3,00,000 which included fixed manufacturing expenses of ₹ 35,000, the April 30, inventory was ₹ 6,00,000 which included fixed manufacturing expenses of ₹ 45,000.

You are required to works out income statement under (*i*) Absorption Costing, and (*ii*) Direct Costing. (*M. Com., Delhi*)

8. Summer and Sounds Ltd. furnished the following production, costs and sales data:

Direct labour	₹ 20 per unit
Materials	40 per unit
Overheads:	
Variable	30 per unit
Fixed	₹ 24,00,000 per month
Selling expenses	₹ 21,00,000 per month
Administrative expenses	₹ 22,00,000 per month
Sales price	150 per unit

During March 2012, the company experienced the following :

Beginning Inventory	20,000 units
Production	190,000 units
Sales	2,05,000 units

Assuming the denominator used in arriving at the fixed overhead rate was 2,00,000 units per month,

(*a*) Prepare a direct costing income statement for March 2016.

(*b*) Determine the absorption costing net income for March 2016.

Answer:

Net Income, Direct costing ₹ 56,00,000. Absorption costing ₹ 54,20,000.

9. From the following information, prepare a statement of income under (*i*) Direct Costing and (*ii*) Absorption Costing.

Sales 50,000 units @ ₹ 12,000 each

Actual production 90,000 units

Manufacturing costs:	₹
(*i*) Depreciation on straight line basis	15,00,000
(*ii*) Office expenses	5,00,000
(*iii*) Other indirect expenses :	2,00,000
(*iv*) Direct costs (per unit):	
Material Consumed	5,000
Labour cost	3,000
Other direct expenses	1,000

Assume, there is no beginning inventory. Explain the causes of difference between the two profit figures. (*M. Com., Delhi*)

Answer:

Net Income: Direct Costing ₹ 14,78,00,000, Absorption Costing ₹ 14,87,78,000. Value of Closing Stock. Direct Costing ₹ 36,00,00,000, Absorption Costing, ₹ 36,09,78,000. Difference in income is due to the difference in the value of closing stock in the two costing concepts.

10. Examine the following income statements based on direct costing. Assume that the denominator volume for absorption costing in 2015 and 2016 was 1300 units and that total fixed costs were identical in 2015 and 2016. There is no beginning or ending work -in-process.

Income Statement for the Year Ending December 31, 2016

	₹
Sales 1180 units @ ₹ 10	11,800
Deduct variable costs:	
Beginning inventory 120 units @ ₹ 6	720
Variable manufacturing cost of goods manufactured, 1,100 units @ ₹ 6	6,600
Variable manufacturing cost of goods available for sale	7,320
Ending inventory 40 units @ ₹ 6	240
Variable manufacturing cost of goods sold	7,080
Variable selling and Administrative Expenses	500
Total variable cost	7,580
Contribution margin	4,220
Deduct fixed costs:	
Fixed factory overhead at budget	2,600
Fixed selling and administrative expenses	400
Total fixed costs	3,000
Operating Income	1,220

With this information prepare an income statement on absorption costing. Assume that actual costs were equal to budgeted fixed costs. Also explain the difference in operating income between absorption costing and direct costing.

11. Vikas manufacturing company has a standard variable manufacturing cost of ₹ 8 per unit produced. Fixed production costs are ₹ 1,10,000 per month (for standard volume of 11,000 units per month) and fixed selling and administrative expenses are ₹ 70,000 per month. The firm begins January with no inventories and had the following activity in January, February and March:

	January	*February*	*March*
Production (units)	12,000	10,000	11,000
Sales (units)	10,000	11,000	11,000

The selling price was ₹ 30 per unit in each month. You are required to prepare monthly income statements using both variable and absorption costing methods. You are required to account for the difference, if any, in the results reported under the two methods.

(*M. Com., Delhi*)

Answer:

Net Income, Absorption Costing, January ₹ 60,000, February ₹ 52,000, March ₹ 62,000. Variable Costing, January ₹ 40,000 , February ₹ 62,000, March ₹ 62,000.

12. During the current period, Johnson Company sold 60,000 units of product at a selling price of ₹ 30 per unit. At the beginning of the period there were 10,000 units in inventory and Johnson Company manufactured 50,000 units during the period. The manufacturing costs and selling and administrative expenses were as follows:

	Total Cost ₹	***No. of Units***	***Unit Cost*** ₹
Beginning inventory:			
Direct Materials	67,000	10,000	6.70
Direct Labour	155,000	10,000	15.50
Variable factory overhead	18,000	10,000	1.80
Fixed factory overhead	20,000	10,000	2.00
Total	2,60,000		26.00
Current period costs;			
Direct Materials	3,50,000	50,000	7.00
Direct Labour	8,10,000	50,000	16.20
Variable factory overhead	90,000	50,000	1.80
Fixed factory overhead	1,00,000	50,000	2.00
Total	13,50,000		27.00
Selling and administrative expenses:			
Variable	65,000		
Fixed	45,000		
	1,10,000		

Required:

(*i*) Prepare an income statement based on absorption costing concept.

(*ii*) Prepare an income statement based on variable costing concept.

(*iii*) Explain the reason for the difference in the amount of operating income between the two costing concepts.

Answer:

(*i*) ₹ 80,000 (*ii*) 1,00,000 (*iii*) The difference of ₹ 20,000 in the amount of income is due to the different treatment of fixed manufacturing costs. The beginning inventory in the absorption costing income statement includes ₹ 20,000 (10000 units × ₹ 2) of fixed manufacturing costs incurred in the preceding period. This ₹ 20,000 was included as an expense in the variable costing statement in the prior period and therefore has not been included as an expense in the current period variable costing income statement, resulting in higher net income by ₹ 20,000 under the variable costing.

13. The selling price and cost data, which are identical for each of the three years, are given below in respect of a manufacturing company.

	₹
Selling price per unit	150
Manufacturing costs:	
Direct Materials cost per unit	28
Direct Labour cost per unit	47
Variable factory overhead per unit	5
Fixed factory overhead in total ₹ 12,00,000	
Marketing and Administrative Expenses:	
Variable	25% of sales
Fixed	₹ 3,50,000

	Units	
Year	***Production***	***Sales***
2015	60,000	50,000
2016	60,000	55,000
2017	50,000	60,000

The Company uses a predetermined overhead rate for fixed costs based on normal capacity of 60,000 units per year.

Required:

(*i*) Prepare a three-year comparative income statement using absorption costing.

(*ii*) Prepare a three year comparative income statement using variable costing.

(*iii*) Reconcile the net income figures of absorption costing and variable costing for each of the three years.

14. X Limited commenced business on Ist March making one product only, the standard cost of which is as follows:

	₹
Direct Labour	5
Direct Material	8
Variable Production overhead	2
Fixed Production overhead	5
Standard Production cost per unit	20

The Fixed production overhead figure has been calculated on the basis of budgeted normal output of 36,000 units per annum.

You are to assume that all budgeted fixed expenses are incurred evenly over the year. March and April are to be taken as equal period months.

Selling, distribution and administration expenses are:

Fixed	₹ 1,20,000 per annum
Variable	15% of sales value

The selling price per unit is ₹ 35 and the number of units produced and sold were:

	March (units)	***April (units)***
Production	2,000	3,200
Sales	1,500	3,000

You are required to:

(*a*) Prepare profit statements for each of the months of March and April, using (*i*) Marginal costing and (*ii*) Absorption costing

(*b*) Present a reconciliation of profits or loss figures given in your answer to (*a*)

15. Production and cost data are given below for Oak Valley Parts Co.

	2016	**2015**
Number of units produced	60,000	75,000
Number of units sold	75,000	60,000
Unit selling price	₹ 25	₹ 25
Unit variable manufacturing cost	8	8
Total fixed manufacturing cost	7,50,000	7,50,000

In 2015 the company operated at a normal level of capacity. There was not inventory on hand at the beginning of 2015.

Required:

(*i*) Prepare a comparative income statement for the manufacturing operation for the 2 years on a standard absorption costing basis.

(*ii*) Explain the difference in income from the manufacturing operations, pointing out why the income for 2016 was higher or lower than what it was in 2015.

Answer:

Absorption costing Net income 2015, ₹ 4,20,000, 2016 ₹ 3,75,000 difference in net income is due to the fact that fixed overheads included in closing stock of 2015 has been charged as an expenses of 2016 in the form of opening stock of that year.

16. ABC Ltd. can produce 4,00,000 units of a product per annum at 100% capacity. The variable production costs are ₹ 40 per unit and the variable selling expenses are ₹ 12 per sold unit. The budgeted fixed production expenses were ₹ 24,00,000 per annum and the fixed selling expenses were ₹ 16,00,000. During the year ended 31st March, 2016, the company worked at 80% of its capacity. The operating data for the year are as follows:

Production	3,20,000 units
Sales @ ₹ 80 per unit	3,10,000 units
Opening stock of finished goods	40,000 units

Fixed production expenses are absorbed on the basis of capacity and fixed selling expenses are recovered on the basis of period.

You are required to prepare Statements of Cost and Profit for the year ending 31st March, 2016:

(*i*) On the basis of marginal costing (*ii*) On the basis of absorption costing

Answer:

Profit under marginal costing ₹ 46,80,000 profit under absorption costing ₹ 47,40,000

17. During the first month of operations ended March 31, 2016, The Kenley Bottle Company produced 33,600 designer water bottles, of which 31,200 were sold. Operating data for the month are summarized as follows:

Sales		₹ 2,87,040
Manufacturing Costs:		
Direct materials	₹ 1,74,720	
Direct labor	47,040	
Variable manufacturing cost	21,840	
Fixed manufacturing cost	20,160	2,63,760
Selling and administrative expenses:		
Variable	₹ 13,728	
Fixed	9,984	23,712

During April, The Kenley Company produced 28,800 designer water bottles and sold 31,200 bottles. Operating data for April are summarized as follows:

Sales		₹ 2,87,040
Manufacturing costs:		
Direct materials	₹ 1,49,760	
Direct labor	40,320	
Variable manufacturing cost	18,720	
Fixed manufacturing cost	20,160	2,28,960
Selling and administrative expenses:		
Variable	₹ 13,728	
Fixed	9,984	23,712

Required:

(*i*) Using the absorption costing concept, prepare income statements for (*a*) March and (*b*) April.

(*ii*) Using the variable costing concept, prepare income statements for (*a*) March and (*b*) April.

(*iii*) (*a*) Explain the reason for the differences in the amount of income from operations in (*i*) and (*ii*) for March.

(*b*) Explain the reason for the differences in the amount of income from operations in (*i*) and (*ii*) for April.

(*iv*) Based on your answers to (*i*) and (*ii*), did Kenley Bottle Company operate more profitably in March or in April? Explain.

Answer:

(*i*) Absorption costing profit March ₹ 18,408; April ₹ 15,528

(*ii*) Variable costing profit March ₹ 16,968; April ₹16,968

(*iii*) Difference in income is due to treatment of fixed manufacturing costs in the valuation of inventory.

(*iv*) The company was equally profitable in March and April under variable costing.

18. During the first month of operations ended July 31, 2017, Britania Co. baked 7,000 cakes, of which 6,400 were sold. Operating data for the month are summarized as follows:

Sales		₹ 128,000
Baking costs:		
Direct materials	₹ 53,900	
Direct labor	25,900	
Variable manufacturing cost	14,000	
Fixed manufacturing cost	18,200	112,000
Selling and administrative expenses:		
Variable	₹ 14,080	
Fixed	6,400	20,480

During August, Britania Co. baked 5,800 cakes and sold 6,400 cakes. Operating data for August are summarized as follows:

Sales		₹ 128,000
Baking costs:		
Direct materials	₹ 44,660	
Direct labor	21,460	
Variable manufacturing cost	11,600	
Fixed manufacturing cost	18,200	95,920
Selling and administrative expenses:		
Variable	14,080	
Fixed	6,400	20,480

Required:

(*i*) Using the absorption costing concept, prepare income statements for (*a*) July and (*b*) August.

(*ii*) Using the variable costing concept, prepare income statements for (*a*) July and (*b*) August.

(*iii*) (*a*) Explain the reason for the differences in the amount of income from operations in (*i*) and (*ii*) for July.

(*b*) Explain the reason for the differences in the amount of income from operations in (*i*) and (*ii*) for August.

(*iv*) Based on your answer to (*i*) and (*ii*) did Britania Co. operate profitably in July or in August? Explain.

Answer:

Absorption costing profit July ₹ 5120 August ₹ 2000

Variable costing profit July ₹ 3560; August ₹ 3560.

19. Action Shoe Company is concerned with changing to the variable costing method of inventory valuation for making internal decisions. The absorption costing income statements for January and February are shown below.

	January (₹)	*February* (₹)
Sales (8,000 units)	16,00,000	16,00,000
Cost of goods sold	(9,92,000)	(10,88,000)
Gross profit	6,08,000	5,12,000
Selling & Administrative Expenses	3,00,000	3,00,000
Net Income	3,08,000	2,12,000

Production data are as shown below:

Production units	10,000	6,000
Variable Production cost per unit	₹ 100	₹ 100
Fixed Production overhead costs	₹ 2,40,000	₹ 2,40,000

The selling and administrative expenses shown above include variable costs of ₹ 10 per unit sold.

Required:

(a) Prepare income statements for both months using variable costing.

(b) Explain why the net income under absorption costing for January was higher than the net income for February when sales units are same in each month.

(c) Reconcile the absorption costing and variable costing net income figures for each month.

Answer:

(a) Variable costing income January ₹ 2,60,000; February ₹ 2,60,000.

(b) Income for January is higher in absorption costing due to closing inventory and lower for February due to opening inventory.

20. Videocon Manufacturing Co. had wide fluctuations in production and sales of televisions. Variable manufacturing costs per unit were as follows for the first three quarters of 2016.

	Quarter		
	First	***Second***	***Third***
Direct Materials (₹)	1500	2000	2500
Direct Labour (₹)	2000	2000	3000
Variable Manufacturing Overhead (₹)	500	1000	2000

The television sells for ₹ 10,000 each. The fixed manufacturing costs were ₹ 25,00,00,000 each quarter, The variable selling and administrative expenses were ₹ 600 for each unit sold and the fixed selling and administrative expenses were ₹ 8,00,00,000 per quarter. Beginning inventory at the start of the first quarter of 20,000 units was recorded at ₹ 11,00,00,000 including ₹ 3,00,00,000 of fixed costs. The company uses the FIFO inventory method. Production and sales data are as follows:

Quarter	***Produced***	***Sold***
First	1,50,000	1,40,000
Second	1,60,000	1,50,000
Third	1,60,000	1,70,000

Required:

(a) Prepare income statements for each quarter using variable costing and absorption costing.

(b) Reconcile the incomes for each quarter between the two methods. *(M.Com. Delhi 2006)*

Answer:

	Quarter		
Net Income	***First***	***Second***	***Third***
(a) Absorption costing (₹)	4,46,000	3,72,500	77,375
Variable costing (₹)	4,26,000	3,60,000	93,000

(b) Difference in net income in the two costing techniques is due to respective inventory values.

21. Ms. Raghavan is the manager of the Chemical division of National Fertilizer Industries. She is one of several managers being considered for the Chief Operating Officer of the company, as the current president is retiring in a year.
All divisions use standard absorption costing; normal capacity is the basis for application of fixed overhead. Normal capacity in the Division is 40,000 units per quarter, and quarterly fixed overhead is ₹ 500,000. Variable production cost is ₹ 50 per unit. Raghavan has been looking at the report for the first three months of the year and is not happy with the results.

Chemical Division Income Statement for First Quarter

	₹	₹
Sales (25,000 units)		25,00,000
Cost of goods sold :		
Beginning Inventory (10,000 units)	6,25,000	
Production costs applied	15,62,500	
Total	21,87,500	
Less ending Inventory	6,25,000	15,62,500
Gross profit		9,37,500
Volume variance		(1,87,500)
Selling and General Expenses		(5,00,000)
Income		2,50,000

The sales forecast for the second quarter is 25,000 units. Raghavan had budgeted second quarter production at 25,000 units but changes it to 50,000 units, which is practical capacity for a quarter. The sales forecasts for each of the last two quarters of the year are also 25,000 units. Costs incurred in the second quarter are the same as budgeted, based on 50,000 units of production.

Required:

(*a*) Prepare an income statement for the second quarter.

(*b*) Does the statement for the second quarter reflect Raghavan's performance better than that for the first quarter? Can you make any suggestions for reporting in the future? Do you think Raghavan should be seriously considered for the Chief Operating Officer? Why or why not? (*M. Com Delhi,* 2013)

Answer:

(*a*) Net profit for second quarter ₹ 5,62,500; Variable costing profit ₹ 2,50,000 for both the quarters.

22. 'This makes no sense at all,' said Rajnish, president of ITC Company. 'We sold the same number of units this year as we did last year, yet our profits have more than doubled. Who made the goof- the computer or the people who operate it?' The statements to which Mr. Rajnish was referring are shown below (absorption costing basis):

(₹)

	Year 1	*Year 2*
Sales (20,000 units each year)	700,000	700,000
Less Cost of goods sold	460,000	400,000
Gross margin	240,000	300,000
Less Selling and Administrative Expenses	200,000	200,000
Net income	40,000	100,000

The statements above show the results of the first two years of operation. In the first year, the company produced and sold 20,000 units; in the second year, the company again sold 20,000 units, but it increased production in order to have a stock of units on hand, as shown below:

	Year 1	*Year 2*
Production in units	20,000	25,000
Sales in units	20,000	20,000
Variable production cost per unit	₹ 8	₹ 8
Fixed Manufacturing Overhead Costs (total)	₹ 300,000	₹ 300,000

ITC Company produces a single product, fixed manufacturing overhead costs are applied to the product on the basis of each year's production. (Thus, a new fixed manufacturing overhead rate is computed each year. Variable selling and administrative expenses are ₹ 1 per unit sold.

Required:

(*i*) Compute the unit product cost for each year under:

a. Absorption costing *b.* Variable costing

(*ii*) Prepare an income statement for each year, using the contribution approach with variable costing.

(*iii*) Reconcile the variable costing and absorption costing net income figures for each year.

(*iv*) Explain to the president why, under absorption costing, the net income for Year 2 was higher than the net income for Year 1 although the same number of units was sold in each year.

23. Ms. Sarika Ghosh opened ABB Telecommunication, a small manufacturing company at the beginning of the year. To get the company through its first quarter of operations, it has been necessary for Sarika Ghosh to place a considerable strain on her own personal finances. The following income statement for the first quarter was prepared by a friend who has just completed a course in management accounting at Delhi University.

ABB Telecommunications Income Statement

For the Quarter Ended March 31

	₹	₹
Sales (28,000 units)		11,20,00,000
Less Variable Expenses:		
Variable cost of goods sold*	4,62,00,000	
Variable Selling and Administrative	1,68,00,000	6,30,00,000
Contribution margin		4,90,00,000
Less: Fixed Expenses:		
Fixed Manufacturing Overhead	3,00,00,000	
Fixed Selling and Administrative	2,00,00,000	5,00,00,000
Net loss		(10,00,000)

*Consists of direct materials, direct labour, and variable manufacturing overhead.

Ms. Sarika is discouraged over the loss shown for the quarter, particularly since she had planned to use the statement as support for a bank loan. Another friend, a chartered accountant, insists that the company should use absorption costing rather than variable costing, and argues that if absorption costing had been used, the company would probably have reported at least some profit for the quarter.

At this point, Ms. Sarika is manufacturing only one product, a swimsuit. Production and cost data relating to the swimsuit for the first quarter follow:

Units produced	30,000
Units Sold	28,000
Variable costs per unit:	
Direct Materials	₹ 350
Direct Labour	1200
Variable Manufacturing Overhead	100
Variable Selling and Administrative	600

Required:

(*i*) Complete the following:

a. Compute the unit product cost under absorption costing.

b. Prepare the company's income statement for the quarter using absorption costing.

c. Reconcile the variable and absorption costing net income (loss) figures.

(*ii*) Was the chartered accountant correct in suggesting that the company really earned a 'profit' for the quarter? Explain.

(*iii*) During the second quarter of operations, the company again produced 30,000 units but sold 32,000 units. (Assume no change in total fixed costs.)

a. Prepare an income statement for the quarter using variable costing

b. Prepare an income statement for the quarter using absorption costing

c. Reconcile the variable costing and absorption costing net income figures

24. The demand for shampoo, one of numerous products manufactured by Himalaya Care Product Co. has dropped sharply because of recent competition from a similar product. The company's chemists are currently completing tests of various new formulas, and it is anticipated that the manufacture of a superior product can be started on March 1, one month hence. No change will be needed in the present production facilities to manufacture the new product because only the mixture of the various materials will be changed.

The controller has been asked by the president of the company for advice on whether to continue production during February or to suspend the manufacture of shampoo until March 1. The controller has assembled the following pertinent data:

Income Statment – Shampoo
For the Month Ended January 31, 2016

Sales (245,000 units)	₹ 1,07,80,000
Cost of goods sold	1,00,62,000
Gross profit	₹ 7,18,000
Selling and administrative expenses	15,22,000
Loss from operations	₹ (8,04,000)

The production costs, selling and administrative expenses, based on production of 245,000 units in January, are as follows:

Direct materials	₹ 8.00 per unit
Direct labor	10.00 per unit
Variable manufacturing cost	19.60 per unit
Variable selling and administrative expenses	5.60 per unit

Fixed manufacturing cost	850,000	for January
Fixed selling and administrative expenses	150,000	for January

Sales for February are expected to drop about 30% below those of the preceding month. No significant changes are anticipated in the fixed costs or variable costs per unit. No extra costs will be incurred in discontinuing operations in the portion of the plant associated with shampoo. The inventory of shampoo at the beginning and end of February is expected to be inconsequential.

Required:

(*i*) Prepare an estimated income statement in absorption costing form for February for shampoo, assuming that production continues during the month.

(*ii*) Prepare an extimated income statement in variable costing form for February for shampoo, assuming that production continues during the month.

(*iii*) What would be the estimated loss in income from operations if the shampoo production were temporarily suspended for February?

(*iv*) What advice should the controller give to management?

Answer:

(*i*) Operating loss ₹ 8,62,800

(*ii*) Operating loss ₹ 8,62,800

(*iii*) ₹ 10,00,000

(*iv*) Production of shampoo should be continued.

25. Anil Malhotra, manager of Zen Products' Bangalore Division, is trying to decide what production schedule to set for the last quarter of the year. The Banglore Division had planned to sell 3,600 units during the year, but by September 30 only the following activity had been reported:

	Units
Inventory, January 1	—0—
Production	2,400
Sales	2,000
Inventory, September 30	400

The division can rent warehouse space to store up to 1,000 units. The minimum inventory level that the division should carry is 50 units. Mr Anil is aware that production must be at least 200 units per quarter in order to retain a nucleus of key employees. Maximum production is 1,500 units per quarter.

Demand has been soft, and the sales forecast for the last quarter is only 600 units. Due to the nature of the division's operations, fixed manufacturing overhead is a major element of product cost.

Required:

1. Assume that the division is using variable costing. How many units should be scheduled for production during the last quarter of the year? Show computations and explain your answer. Will the number of units scheduled for production affect the division's reported income or loss for the year? Explain.
2. Assume that the division is using absorption costing and that the divisional manager is given an annual bonus based on divisional operating income. If Mr. Anil wants to maximize his division's operation income for the year, how many units should be

scheduled for production during the last quarter? Show computations and explain your answer.

3. Identify the ethical issues involved in the decision Mr. Anil must make.

Answer:

1. Required production 250 units.
2. 1200 units.

CASES

1. The Outdoor Division of Home Appliances Ltd. uses absorption costing for profit reporting. The general manager of the Outdoor Division is concerned about meeting the income objectives of the division. At the beginning of the reporting period, the division had an adequate supply of inventory. The general manager has decided to increase production of goods in the plant in order to allocate fixed manufacturing cost over a greater number of units. Unfortunately, the increased production cannot be sold and will increase the inventory. However, the impact on earnings will be positive because the lower cost per unit will be matched against sales. The general manager has come to Narainswamy, the controller, to determine exactly how much additional production is required in order to increase net income enough to meet the division's profit objectives. Narainswamy analyzes the data and determines that the inventory will need to be increased by 30% in order to absorb enough fixed costs and meet the income objective. Narianswamy reports this information to the division manager.

   Discuss whether the behaviour of Narainswamy is an ethical one?

2. Amitabh was a divisional controller at Tata Chemicals Company. He was upset by recent memo he received from the divisional manager, Mukesh. Amitabh was scheduled to present the divisional's financial performance at headquarters in one week. In the memo, Mukesh had given Amitabh some instructions for this upcoming report. In particular, he had been told to emphasize the significant improvement in the division's profits over last year. Amitabh, however, did not believe that there was any real underlying improvement in the division's performance and was reluctant to say otherwise. He knew that increase in profits was because of Mukesh's conscious decision to produce for inventory.

   In an earlier meeting, Mukesh had convinced his plant managers to produce more than they knew they could sell. He argued that by deferring some of this period's fixed costs, reported profits would jump. He pointed out two significant benefits. First, by increasing profits, the division could exceed the minimum level needed so that all the managers would qualify for the annual bonus. Second, by meeting the budgeted profit level, the division would be better able to compete for much-needed capital. Amitabh had objected but had been overruled. The most persuasive counter argument was that the increase in inventory could be liquidated in the coming year as the economy improved. Amitabh, however, considered this event unlikely. From past experience, he knew that it would take at least two years of improved market demand before the productive capacity of the division was exceeded.

Required:

(*i*) Discuss the behaviour of Mukesh, the divisional manager. Was the decision to produce for inventory correct and ethical one?

(ii) What should Amitabh do? Should he comply with the directive to emphasise the increase in profits? If not, what options does he have?

3. Ranbaxy Company uses an actual absorption cost system to apply all production costs to units produced. The plant has a maximum production capacity of 4,00,00,000 units but produced and sold only 1,00,00,000 units during year 2016. There were no beginning or ending inventories. The Company's income statement for year 2016 follows:

Ranbaxy Company Income Statement
For the Year Ending December 31, Year 2016

	₹	₹
Sales (1,00,00,000 units at ₹ 6)		6,00,00,000
Cost of goods sold:		
Direct costs, material, and labor (1,00,00,000 at ₹ 2)	2,00,00,000	
Manufacturing overhead	4,80,00,000	
Cost of goods sold		6,80,00,000
Gross Margin		(80,00,000)
Selling and Administrative costs		1,00,00,000
Operating profit (loss)		(1,80,00,000)

The board of directors is concerned about the ₹ 1,80,00,000 loss. A consultant approached the board with the following offer: "I agree to become president for no fixed salary. But I insist on a year-end bonus of 10 per cent of operating profit." The board of directors agreed to these terms and hired the consultant as Ranbaxy's new president.

The new president promptly stepped up production to an annual rate of 3,00,00,000 units. Sales for year 2017 remained at 1,00,00,000 units. The resulting Ranbaxy Company absorption-costing income statement for year 2017 follows:

Income Statement
For the Year Ending December 31, Year 2017

	₹	₹
Sales (1,00,00,000 units at ₹ 6)		6,00,00,000
Cost of goods sold :		
Cost of goods manufactured :		
Direct costs, material and labour (3,00,00,000 at ₹ 2)	6,00,00,000	
Manufacturing overhead	4,80,00,000	
Total cost of goods manufactured	10,80,00,000	
Less: Ending inventory		
Variable (2,00,00,000 at ₹ 2)	4,00,00,000	
Indirect (20/30 × ₹ 4,80,00,000)	3,20,00,000	
Total ending Inventory	7,20,00,000	
Cost of goods sold		3,60,00,000
Gross Margin		2,40,00,000

Selling and Administrative costs	1,00,00,000
Operating profit before bonus	1,40,00,000
Bonus	14,00,000
Operating profit after bonus	1,26,00,000

The day after the statement was verified, the president took his cheque for ₹ 14,00,000 and resigned to take a job with another company. He remarked, "I enjoy challenges. Now that Ranbaxy Company is in the black, I'd prefer tackling another challenging situation."

Required:

(*a*) Step back, and look at this overall situation. In general, what do you think is going on here? More specifically, how would you evaluate the company's year 2017 performance.

(*b*) Using variable costing, what would operating profit be for year 2016, for year 2017. (Assume that all selling and administrative costs are committed and unchanged.) Compare those results with the absorption-costing statements.

Answer:

For both the years, under variable costing operating loss will be ₹ 1,80,00,000

4. Tata Petroleum Company Ltd's. board of directors was meeting to select a new vice-president of operations. The leading candidate was Rahul Sharma, manager of the Tata Petroleum's largest division. Rahul had been divisional manager for three years. The managing director, Vivek Kumar was impressed with the significant improvements in the division's profit since Rahul became its manager. In the first year of operations, divisional profits had increased by 20%. They had shown significant improvements for the following two years as well. To gather support for Rahul, the managing director circulated the following divisional income statement.

(₹ '000)

	2014	**2015**	**2016**
Sales	30,000	32,000	34,000
Less: Costs of goods sold*	26,250	26,400	27,200
Gross Margin	3,750	5,600	6,800
Less: Selling and Administrative Overheads (fixed)	3,000	3,600	3,800
Net income	750	2000	3000

* Assumes a LIFO inventory flow:

Vivek commented at the board of directors meeting, "as you can see, Rahul has increased profits by a factor of four since 2014. And it is so far the most impressive performance of any divisional manager. We could certainly use someone with that kind of drive. I definitely believe that Rahul should be the new Vice-President."

Hemant, the Vice-President of finance responded, "I am not quite as convinced that Rahul's performance is as impressive as it appears. I could hardly believe that Rahul's division could show the magnitude of improvement revealed by the income statements. So I asked the divisional controller to supply some additional information. As the data suggest, the profits realised by Rahul's division may be attributable to a concerted effort to produce for inventory. In fact, I believe it can be shown that the division is actually showing a loss each year and that real profits have declined by as much as 15% since 2014". Hemant showed the following information to the board members.

	2014	2015	2016
Sales (units)	1,50,000	1,60,000	1,70,000
Production*	2,00,000	2,50,000	3,00,000
Actual (and budgeted) fixed overhead (₹)	1,50,00,000	1,50,00,000	1,50,00,000
Fixed overhead Rate	75	60	50
Unit variable Production costs	100	105	110

*This represents both expected and actual production. Fixed overhead rates are computed using expected actual production.

Required:

(*a*) Explain what Hemant meant by "producing for inventory".

(*b*) Recast the income statements in a variable-costing format. Now how does the performance of the division appear?

(*c*) Reconcile the differences in income figures using the two methods for each of the three years.

Answer:

(*a*) Producing for inventory means producing more units than are sold, increasing inventory.

(*b*) Variable costing net income

year	₹
2014	Loss (3000)
2015	Loss (3,400)
2016	Loss (3,500)

5. Hitkari Ceramic Ltd. produces ceramic coffee mugs. The company has the capacity to produce 50 lakhs mugs per year but the results of a downturn has cut production and sales in the current year to 15 lakhs mugs. The operating statement for the year 2016 is as follows:

Income Statement for the Year Ending 2016

	₹ ***(lakhs)***
Sales (15 lakhs @ ₹ 20)	300
Less: Cost of goods sold :	
Variable cost 15 lakhs @ ₹ 5	(75)
Fixed Cost	(200)
Gross Margin	25
Less: Selling and Administration	(40)
Operating profit	(15)

At the end of 2016, there was no ending inventory of finished goods.

The board of directors is very concerned about the ₹ 15 lakhs operating loss and hires an outside consultant who reports that the company suffers from two problems. First, Hitkari Ceramics chairman receives a fixed salary and since he does not hold any share in the company, he does not worry about profits. Second, the company has not aggressively marketed its product. The board of director makes an offer to the chairman to retire so that the company can hire a new chief general manager to turn the company around. The current chairman accepts the offer to retire and the board immediately hires chief general manager cum chairman.

The new chairman is to get a fixed salary of ₹ 5,00,000 a year plus 15% of the firm's operating profits, if any, operating profits are calculated using absorption costing. In 2017, the new chairman doubles selling and administrative budget to ₹ 80 lakhs (which includes his salary of ₹ 5,00,000). He expands inventory and the number of distributors handling the mugs. Production is increased to 45 lakhs mugs and sales of mugs climb to 18 lakhs at ₹ 20 each. Variable costs per mug in 2017 remain at ₹ 5 and fixed cost at ₹ 200 lakhs. At the end of 2017, the new chairman meets with the board of directors , and announces that he has accepted another Job. He believes that he has successfully put Hitkari back on track and thanks the board for giving him the opportunity. His new job is helping to turn around another struggling company.

Required:

(*i*) Calculate the new chairman's bonus for 2017, using appropriate income statement.

(*ii*) Evaluate the new chairman's performance for 2017. Did he do as good a job as the numbers in part (*i*) suggest.

(*iii*) Which technique(s)–absorption costing or variable costing or both -is (are) correct measure (s) of profit and performance. Give reasons. (*M. Com., Delhi*, 2007)

Answer:

Bonus, ₹ 16.5 lakhs.

6. Prakash, the new manager of the Oliver Division of General Products Company, was .greatly displeased at the income statements that his controller, Shiv Shankar had been giving him. Prakash recently had been placed in charge of the division because it had not been showing satisfactory results. Prakash was upset because, although sales had risen in each of the last two months, profits had not kept pace. Income statements for the last three months are as follows:

(₹)

	March	*April*	*May*
Sales	36,00,000	44,00,000	56,00,000
Cost of Sales	19,80,000	26,40,000	38,10,000
Gross Profit	16,20,000	17,60,000	17,90,000
Other Expenses	14,20,000	15,00,000	16,20,000
Profit before taxes	2,00,000	2,60,000	1,70,000

Prakash asked Shiv Shanker why profits had declined when sales had increased and why a substantial increase in sales from March to April had produced only a small increase in profits. Shiv Shankar's reply was simply that operations had gone according to plans that Prakash had set, and that the problems that Prakash wanted to know about were due to the method of accounting for product costs and the relationships of sales to production.

Prakash was unimpressed with this explanation and rather testily pointed out that he had been put in charge of the division to "turn it around". He was not about to let accounting conventions give corporate management second thoughts about placing him in charge, Shiv Shankar who was fully aware of the claims Prakash had made when being considered for the manager's job, had not liked Prakash from the start. To the suggestion that accounting conventions were standing in the way of Prakash's performance, Shiv Shankar replied only that the reports for all divisions were prepared from the same uniform accounting system and in the form required for corporate reporting. He told Prakash that the reports were prepared using GAAP, which was necessary because the company was publicly held and had to issue reports to shareholders. He did not tell Prakash that he believed the methods used by the company for external reporting were inappropriate for internal purposes.

Later, at lunch with Raghav, the division's sales manager, Shiv Shanker narrated the conversation that he had had with Prakash. Raghav, who had also wondered about the company's accounting methods, asked Shiv Shanker why he didn't just explain the statements to Prakash. "Not on your life," said Shiv Shanker. "I see no reason to help that braggart. Let him explain to the top boss why things aren't going the way he said they would if he were put in charge instead of me."

"Actually," Shiv Shanker continued, "what he's worried about just isn't a difficult problem. Cost of sales included both standard cost and the adjustment needed when production for the month did not equal the 25,000-unit volume that was used to set the standard fixed cost of ₹ 90 per unit. In fact, things have gone very well. We had no variances at all except for volume. Selling prices held very well at ₹ 200 per unit, and the division is doing much better now. But would I like to be there when the boss asks Prakash why things are not going well! Why, even production in April was right on target at 25,000 units budgeted."

Required:

(*a*) Explain the results in the three-month period. You may wish to compute standard fixed costs per unit and production in each month.

(*b*) Prepare income statements for the three months using variable costing.

7. "These statements can't be right," said Prem Narayan, president of Jayco Watch Co. "Our sales in the second quarter were up by 25% over the first quarter, yet these income statements show a precipitous drop in net income for the second quarter. Those accounting people have fouled something up." Mr. Narayan was referring to the given statements.

After studying the statements briefly, Mr. Narayan called in the controller to see if the mistake in the second quarter could be located before the figures were released to the press. The controller stated, "I' am sorry to say that those figures are correct. I agree that sales went up during the second quarter, but the problem is in production. You see, we budgeted to produce 15,000 units each quarter, but a strike in Maharastra among some of our suppliers forced us to cut production in the second quarter back to only 9,000 units. That's what caused the drop in net income."

Jayco Watch Co.
Income Statements
For the First Two Quarters

(₹)

	First Quarter		***Second Quarter***	
Sales		4,80,00,000		6,00,00,000
Less cost of goods sold:				
Beginning Inventory	80,00,000		1,40,00,000	

Add cost of goods manufactured	3,00,00,000		1,80,00,000	
Goods available for sale	3,80,00,000		3,20,00,000	
Less ending Inventory	1,40,00,000		20,00,000	
Cost of goods sold		2,40,00,000	3,00,00,000	
Add under applied overhead			72,00,000	3,72,00,000
Gross Margin		2,40,00,000		2,28,00,000
Less Selling and Administrative Expenses		2,00,00,000		2,15,00,000
Net income		40,00,000		13,00,000

Mr. Narayan was confused by the controller's explanation. He replied, "This doesn't make sense. I ask you to explain why net income dropped when sales went up and you talk about production! So what if we had to cut back production? We still were able to increase sales by 25%. If sales go up, then net income should go up. If your statements can't show a simple thing like that, then it's time for some changes in your area!"

Budgeted production and sales for the year, along with actual production and sales for the first two quarters, are given below:

	Quarter			
	First	***Second***	***Third***	***Fourth***
Budgeted sales (units)	12,000	15,000	15,000	18,000
Actual sales (units)	12,000	15,000	—	—
Budgeted production (units)	15,000	15,000	15,000	15,000
Actual production (units)	15,000	9,000	—	—

The company's plant is heavily automated, and fixed manufacturing overhead amounts to ₹ 1,80,00,000 each quarter. Variable manufacturing costs are ₹ 800 per unit. The fixed manufacturing overhead is applied to units of product at a rate of ₹ 1200 per unit (based on the budgeted production shown above). Any under or overapplied overhead is taken directly to cost of goods sold for the quarter. The company had 4,000 units in inventory to start the first quarter and uses the FIFO inventory flow assumption. Variable selling and administrative expenses are ₹ 500 per unit.

Required:

(*a*) What characteristic of absorption costing caused the drop in net income for the second quarter and what could the controller have said to explain the problem more fully?

(*b*) Prepare income statements for each quarter using the variable costing.

(*c*) Reconcile the absorption costing and the variable costing net income figures for each quarter.

(*d*) Identify and discuss the advantages and disadvantages of using the variable costing method for internal reporting purposes.

8. "Now this doesn't make any sense at all," said Mona Dhar, financial vice president for Bajaj Company. "Our sales have been steadily rising over the last several months, but profits have been going in the opposite direction. In September, we finally hit ₹ 2,00,00,000 in sales, but the bottom line for that month drops off to a ₹ 10,00,000 loss. Why aren't profits more closely correlated with sales?"

The statements to which Ms. Mona Dhar was referring are shown below:

Bajaj Company
Monthly Income Statements

	July (₹)	August (₹)	September (₹)
Sales (@ ₹ 250)	1,75,00,000	1,87,50,000	2,00,00,000
Less cost of goods sold:			
Beginning Inventory	8,00,000	32,00,000	40,00,000
Cost applied to production:			
Variable manufacturing costs (@ ₹ 90)	76,50,000	72,00,000	54,00,000
Fixed manufacturing overhead	59,50,000	56,00,000	42,00,000
Cost of goods manufactured	1,36,00,000	1,28,00,000	96,00,000
Goods available for sale	1,44,00,000	1,60,00,000	1,36,00,000
Less ending Inventory	32,00,000	40,00,000	8,00,000
Cost of goods sold	1,12,00,000	1,20,00,000	1,28,00,000
Underapplied or (overapplied) fixed			
Overhead cost	(3,50,000)		14,00,000
Adjusted cost of goods sold	1,08,50,000	1,20,00;000	1,42,00,000
Gross margin	66,50,000	67,50,000	58,00,000
Less Selling and Administrative Expenses	62,00,000	65,00,000	68,00,000
Net Income (loss)	4,50,000	2,50,000	(10,00,000)

Rajiv Dhawan a recent Honours graduate from Delhi University who has just been hired by Bajaj Company, has stated to Ms. Dhar that the contribution approach, with variable costing, is a much better way to report profit data to management. Sales and production data for the last quarter follow:

	July	August	September
Production in units	85,000	80,000	60,000
Sales in units	70,000	75,000	80,000

Additional information about the company's operations is given below:

a. Five thousand units were in inventory on July I.

b. Fixed manufacturing overhead costs total ₹ 1,68,00,000 per quarter and are incurred evenly throughout the quarter. This fixed manufacturing overhead cost is applied to units of product on the basis of a budgeted production volume of 80,000 units per month.

c. Variable selling and administrative expenses are ₹ 60 per unit sold. The remainder of the selling and administrative expenses on the statements above are fixed.

d. The company uses a FIFO inventory flow assumption. Work in process inventories are insignificant and can be ignored.

"I know production is somewhat out of step with sales," said Gagandeep, the company's controller. "But we had to build inventory early in the quarter in anticipation of a strike in September. Since the union settled without a strike, we then had to cut back production in September in order to work off the excess inventories. The income statements you have are completely accurate,"

Required:

(*i*) Prepare an income statement for each month using the contribution approach with variable costing.

(*ii*) Explain to Ms. Mona Dhar why profits have moved erratically over the three-month period shown in the absorption costing statements above and why profits have not been more closely related to changes in sales volume.

(*iii*) Reconcile the variable costing and absorption costing net income (loss) figures for each month. Show all computations, and show how you derive each figure used in your reconciliation. (M. Com., Delhi, 2015)

9. The demand for solvent, one of numerous products manufactured by Mathews Industries Co., has dropped sharply because of recent competition from a similar product. The company's chemists are currently completing tests of various new formulas, and it is anticipated that the manufacture of a superior product can be started on May 1, one month hence. No changes will be needed in the present production facilities to manufacture the new product because only the mixture of the various materials will be changed.

   The controller has been asked by the Managing Director of the company for advice on whether to continue production during April or to suspend the manufacture of solvent until May 1. The controller has assembled the following pertinent data:

Mathews Industries Co.
Income Statement
For the Month Ended March 31, 2012

Sales (2,500 units)	₹ 1,75,00,000
Cost of goods sold	1,56,50,000
Gross profit	₹ 18,50,000
Selling and administrative expenses	36,60,000
Loss from operations	₹ (18,10,000)

The production costs and selling and administrative expenses, based on production of 2,500 units in March, are as follows:

Direct materials	₹ 2730 per unit
Direct labour	950 per unit
Variable manufacturing cost	900 per unit
Variable selling and administrative expenses	500 per unit
Fixed manufacturing cost	₹ 42,00,000 for March
Fixed selling and administrative expenses	₹ 24,10,000 for March

Sales for April are expected to drop about 25% below those of the preceding month. No significant changes are anticipated in the fixed costs or variable costs per unit. No extra costs will be incurred in discontinuing operations in the portion of the plant associated with solvent. The inventory of solvent at the beginning and end of April is expected to be inconsequential.

Required:

(*i*) Prepare an estimated income statement in absorption costing form for April for solvent, assuming that production continues during the month.

(*ii*) Prepare an estimated income statement in variable costing form for April for solvent, assuming that production continues during the month.

(*iii*) What would be the estimated loss in income from operations if the solvent production were temporarily suspended for April?

(*iv*) What advice should the controller give to management?

Answer:

(*i*) Loss ₹ 30,100

(*ii*) Loss ₹ 30,100

(*iii*) Loss ₹ 66,100

(*iv*) Production of solvent should be continued.

10. Maruti manufactures control panels for the electronics industry and has just completed its first year of operations. The following discussion took place between the controller, Smith, and the company president, Rahul.

Rahul: I've been looking over our first year's performance by quarters. Our earnings have been increasing each quarter, even though our sales have been flat and our prices and costs have not changed. Why is this?

Smith: Our actual sales have stayed even throughout the year, but we've been increasing the utilization of our factory every quarter: By keeping our factory utilization high, we will keep our costs down by allocating the fixed plant costs over a greater number of units. Naturally, this causes our cost per unit to be lower than it would be otherwise.

Rahul: Yes, but what good is this if we have been unable to sell eveything that we make? Our inventory is also increasing.

Smith: This is true, However, our unit costs are lower because of the additional production, When these lower costs are matched against sales, it has a positive impact on our earnings.

Rahul: Are you saying that we are able to create additional earnings merely by building inventory? Can this be true?

Smith: Well, i've never thought about it quite that way, but I guess so.

Rahul: And another thing. What will happen if we begin to reduce our production in order to liquidates the inventory? Don't tell me our earnings will go down even though our production effort drops!

Smith: Well

Rahul: There must be a better way. I'd like our quarterly income statements to reflect what's really going on, I don't want our income reports to reward building inventory and penalize reducing inventory.

Smith: I'm not sure what I can do—we have to follow generally accepted accounting principles.

Required:

(*i*) Why does reporting income under generally accepted accounting principles "reward" building inventory and "penalize" reducing inventory?

(*ii*) What advice would you give to Smith in responding to Rahul's concern about the present methods of profit reporting?

11. Jaishanker left his job as the production manager of medium-sized firm two year ago to join a new firm that was manufacturing a revolutionary type of fitness equipment. Jaishanker was made the general manager at the start of operation, and the firm seemed to be doing extremely well. The president was extremely pleased with the company's first-year performance, and at the beginning of the second year (2016) promised Jaishanker a ₹ 20,000 bonus if the company's net income were to increase by 25% in 2016.

During 2016, Jaishanker sold 25% more units than he had in 2015 and was so confident that he would receive his bonus that he bought non-refundable airline tickets to Europe for his wife and son.

At the end of 2016, Jaishanker received fiscal 2016 income statement, which showed that the company's income had decreased from 2015 even though it had sold considerably more units, Jaishanker did not get along very well with the accountant and felt that he had deliberately distorted the financial statements for 2016. The following are the reports that Jaishanker received:

	2015	2016
Production (in units)	6,000	3,000
Sales (in units)	4,000	5,000
Unit selling price	₹ 500	₹ 500
Unit costs:		
Variable manufacturing	₹ 300	₹ 300
Variable selling	20	20
Fixed manufacturing	180,000	210,000
Fixed selling	100,000	140,000

Income Statement (FIFO)

	2015	2016
Sales	₹ 20,00,000	₹ 25,00,000
Cost of goods sold	13,20,000	17,70,000
Gross margin	6,80,000	7,30,000
Selling	1,80,000	2,40,000
Net income	₹ 5,00,000	₹ 4,90,000

Required:

(*i*) Prepare variable costing income statements for fiscal 2015 and 2016.

(*ii*) Preapare a reconciliation for 2015 and 2016 for the differences between the net income as determined by the income statements you have prepared in part (a) and the income statements prepared by the accountant.

(*iii*) Explain to Jaishanker why he lost his ₹ 20,000 bonus. Which set of income statements more accurately measures performance? Why?

12. Jayco Industrial Co. manufactures three sizes of industrial work benches—small (S), medium (M), and large (L). The income statement has consistently indicated a net loss for the M size, and management is considering three proposals: (1) continue Size M, (2) discontinue size M and reduce total output accordingly, or (3) discontinue Size M and conduct an advertising campaign to expand the sales of Size S so that the entire plant capacity can continue to be used.

If proposal 2 is selected and Size M is discontinued and production curtailed, the annual fixed production costs and fixed operating expenses could be reduced by ₹ 210,000 and ₹ 42,000, respectively. If Proposal 3 is selected, it is anticipated that an additional annual expenditure of ₹ 126,000 for the salary of a assistant brand manager (classified as a fixed operating expense) would yield an increase of 130% in Size S sales volume. It is also assumed that the increased production of Size S would utilize the plant facilities released by the discontinuance of Size M.

The Sales and costs have been relatively stable over the past few years, and they are expected to remain so for the foreseeable future. The income statement for the past year ended March 2016, is as follows:

	Size			
	S	**M**	**L**	**Total**
Sales	₹ 14,70,000	₹ 16,10,000	₹ 14,00,000	₹ 44,80,000
Cost of goods sold:				
Variable costs	₹ 7,98,000	₹ 10,64,000	₹ 8,40,000	₹ 27,02,000
Fixed costs	3,57,000	4,27,000	3,71,000	11,55,000
Total cost of goods sold	₹ 11,55,000	14,91,000	12,11,000	38,57,000
Gross profit	₹ 3,15,000	₹ 1,19,000	₹ 1,89,000	₹ 6,23,000
Less operating expenses:				
Variable expenses	₹ 1,75,000	₹ 1,61,000	₹ 1,26,000	₹ 4,62,000
Fixed expenses	₹ 47,600	₹ 63,000	₹ 21,000	₹ 1,31,600
Total operating expenses	₹ 2,22,600	₹ 2,24,000	₹ 1,47,000	₹ 5,93,600
Income from operations	₹ 92,400	₹ (1,05,000)	₹ 42,000	₹ 29,400

Required:

(*i*) Prepare an income statement for the past year in the variable costing format.

(*ii*) Based on the income statement prepared in (i) and the other data persented above, determine the amount by which total annual income from operations would be reduced below its present level if Proposal 2 is accepted.

(*iii*) Prepare an income statement in the variable costing format, indicating the projected annual income from operations if Proposal 3 is accepted.

(*iv*) By how much would total annual income increase above its present level if Proposal 3 is accepted? Explain.

13. Amit Dhawan was proud of the way he had guided Screen Technology Company over the past year since he had accepted the job as the company's president. Under Amit's direction, the privately held company's sales had grown each quarter, and several new sales contacts in Europe looked promising for future business. Amit had taken a personal interest in developing new business, and the company's future looked bright. Amit had also seen to it that the company's costs had remained in check. One of the new president's first moves had been to benchmark several of Screen Technology's performance measures against other high-tech electronics firms. Amit was convinced that the company's production technology and business practices were as efficient as any firm in the business.

Screen Technology had been formed some five years earlier to manufacture aperture masks, which are an important component in computer monitors and TV picture tubes. Aperture masks direct a beam of electrons to the red, blue, and green phosphor stripes on the inside face of a picture tube. Thus, the aperture mask is a critical component in the creation of a color picture on the computer monitor or TV tube. Ranging in size from 18 to 90 centimeters, Screen Technology's masks are manufactured from nickel alloy. Several patented manufacturing steps are used to produce the aperture masks, including highly accurate photographic and etching processes, chemical coating processes, and cleaning processes. Screen Technology's masks already were being marketed in Africa and Asia, and negotiations were proceeding with several potential European customers.

At the beginning of his second year on the job, Amit had been lookng forward to the fourth-quarter financial statements. Upon reading the financial reports, though, Amit was dismayed when he saw the Screen Technology's fourth-quarter profit was actually lower than that reported in the third quarter. "What's going on here?" he thought. Amit picked up the phone to call Siddharth, Screen Technology's controller, for an explanation.

Shown here are the third and fourth-quarter income statements that were perplexing Amit.

SCREEN TECHNOLOGY COMPANY
Income Statements
For the 3rd and 4th Quarters of 2016

	3rd Quarter	**4th Quarter**
Sales revenue	₹ 5,040,000	₹ 7,920,000
Less: Cost of goods sold (at standard absorption cost)	3,780,000	5,9,40,000
Gross margin (at standard)	₹ 1,260,000	₹ 1,980,000
Adjust for: Fixed overhead volume variance*	3,60,000	3,60,000
Gross margin (at actual)	₹ 1,620,000	₹ 1,620,000
Less: Selling and administrative expenses	7,20,000	9,60,000
Net income	₹ 9,00,000	₹ 6,60,000

*There were no other variances during the 3rd or 4th quarters of 2016. The 3rd-quarter volume variance is negative (or favorable) and the 4th-quarter volume variance is positive (or unfavourable)

When Siddharth arrived at Amit's office, he could see the president was upset and puzzled. "You're the controller, Siddhart," began Amit, "I hope you have a good explanation for this.

When sales go up from one quarter to the next, and production efficiency and standard costs remain about the same, I would expect profits to increase also. And I can assure you that our owners will expect inreased profits, too, when I go to the quarterly meeting next week."

Siddharth tried to explain to Amit why Screen Technology's profit had fallen, even though sales had risen substantially. "Our financial statements are prepared using absorption costing," explained Siddharth. "This mean that all manufacturing costs are treated as product costs. Direct material, direct labor, and all manufacturing overhead costs are stored in inventory until the units are sold. It's true that sales rose during the fourth quarter, but production did not keep pace with sales. In fact, actual fourth-quarter production was somewhat lower even than our planned production for the quarter. When that happens, we end up expensing fixed manufacturing overhead during the current period, even though it was incurred during a previous period."

"Well, I'm no accountant," retorted Amit. "I'm an engineer and I've spent most of my career in marketing. But this just doesn't seem reasonable to me. If sales go up, and production efficiency remains more or less the same, then I still think income ought to go up. I was counting on a bonus this quarter, and I would think you would've been expecting one, too. Can't you produce an income statement where profits increase when sales increase?"

"Yes, I can, Amit," replied the controller. "I can use a method called variable costing instead of absorption costing. Under the method, fixed manufacturing overhead is expensed during the period it's incurred. That effectively eliminates the kind of distortion that's bothering you. Since Screen Tech is a privately held company, we can use either method we want. The owners should be informed if we change methods, though. And they should also be made aware of the effect of the change on executive bonuses."

"I think we should change to the other method, then," respond Amit. "What's d you call it? Variable costing, was it?"

"That's right, Amit. It's called variable costing because only variable manufacturing costs are inventoried."

"Okay, here's what I would like you to do, Siddharth. Please prepare third-quarter and fourth-quarter income statements for me using variable costing. Then come along with me to next week's meeting and explain to our bosses why the results differ."

"You got it," replied Siddharth. "And I'll show you the effect of the accounting method change on the balance sheet also."

"That sounds good," replied Amit. "By the way, is there a down side to variable costing? What do you see as the advantages and disadvantages?"

Before Siddhart could respond, Amit got a phone call from an important customer. Before meeting with Amit again to answer his last question, Siddharth prepared the following third-quarter and fourth-quarter income statements. He also summarized the effect of the proposed accounting method change on Screen Technology's comparative balance sheets.

SCREEN TECHNOLOGY COMPANY
Income Statements
For the 3rd and 4th Quarters of 2016
(prepared using Variable Costing)

	3rd Quarter	4th Quarter
Sales revenue	₹ 50,40,000	₹ 79,20,000
Less: Variable expenses:		
Variable manufacturing costs (at standard variable cost)*	25,20,000	39,60,000
Variable selling and administrative costs	4,20,000	6,60,000
Contribution margin	₹ 21,00,000	₹ 33,00,000
Less: Fixed expenses:		
Fixed manufacturing overhead	18,00,000	₹ 18,00,000
Fixed selling and administrative costs	3,00,000	3,00,000
Net income	₹ 0	₹ 12,00,000

*There were no variances during the 3rd or 4th quarters of 2016.

SCREEN TECHNOLOGY COMPANY
Selected Balance Sheet Information
For the Quarters Ending September 30 and December 31, 2016

Balance sheets prepared using absorption costing	**30 September**	**31 December**
Inventory	₹ 2,700,000	₹ 1,080,000
Retained earnings	3,400,000	4,060,000
Balance sheets prepared using variable costing		
Inventory	₹ 1,800,000	₹ 7,20,000
Retained earnings	2,500,000	3,700,000

Required:

1. How would you respond to the president's last question to the controller regarding the pros and cons of variable and absorption costing?
2. Prepare a reconciliation of the reported fourth-quarter income under variable and absorption costing.
3. Explain how and why the balance sheets differ under variable and absorption costing.
4. Would there be differences in reported income under variable and absorption costing if the statements had been annual statements instead of quarterly statements? Explain.
5. Discuss the following comment made by Amit to Siddharth the next afternoon. Citing specific ethical standards for management accountants, explain how Siddharth should respond.

   "Siddharth, I've been thinking about this whole issue some more. Why don't we just choose between variable and absorption costing each quarter, depending on which will report the highest profit for the quarter and give us the biggest bonuses?" *(CMA, USA, Adapted)*

PART

3

MANAGERIAL DECISION MAKING

CHAPTER 6:

Cost-Volume-Profit (CVP) Analysis

CHAPTER 7:

Relevant Information and Decision Making

CHAPTER 8:

Pricing Decisions

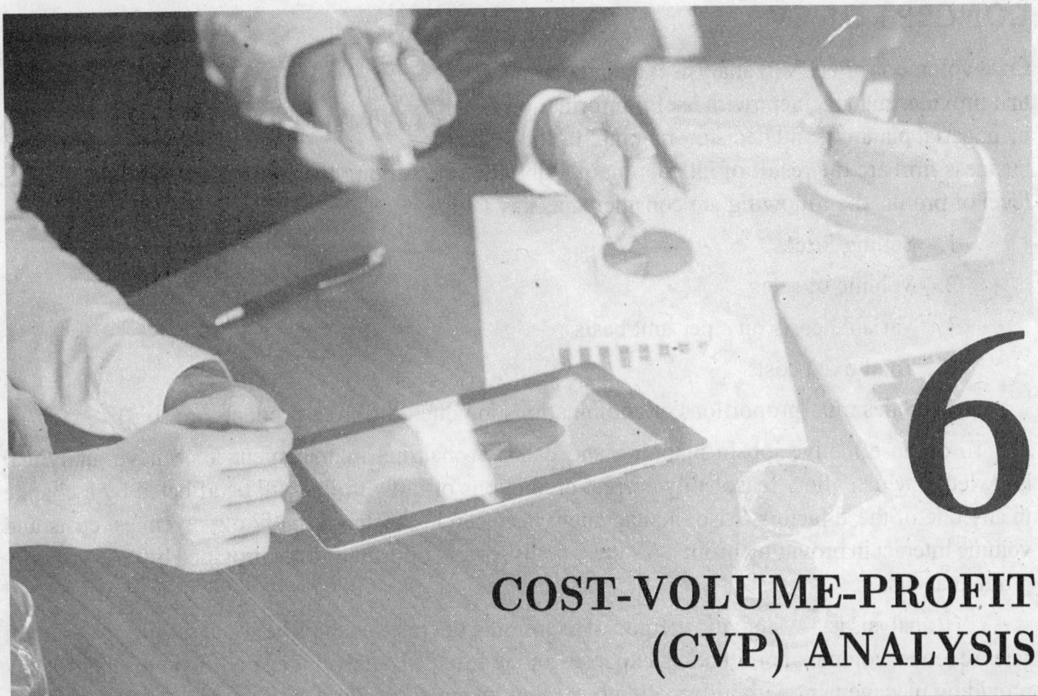

6

COST-VOLUME-PROFIT (CVP) ANALYSIS

LEARNING OBJECTIVES

After reading this chapter, you should be able to:

- Explain the Concept of Cost-Volume-Profit Analysis
- Describe the Techniques of CVP Analysis—Contribution Margin, Break-even Analysis, Profit-Volume (P/V) Analysis
- Identify the Role of CVP Analysis, its use in Scarce Resources
- Understand the Economist's View on CVP Analysis
- Explain the Importance of CVP Analysis in Service and Non-profit Organizations
- List Limitations of CVP Analysis

CONCEPT OF CVP

> **CVP analysis** is a systematic method of examining the relationships between selling prices, total sales revenue, volume of production, expenses and profit.

Cost-Volume-Profit (CVP) analysis is an important tool that provides management with useful information for managerial planning and decision-making. Profits of a business firm are the result of interaction of many factors. Among the many factors influencing the level of profits, the following are considered as key factors:

1. Selling Prices
2. Volume of sales
3. Variable costs on a per unit basis
4. Total fixed costs
5. Sales mix (proportions or combinations in which different products are sold).

To do an effective job in planning and decision-making, management must have analytical knowledge which allow reasonably correct predictions of how profits will be affected by a change in any one of these factors. Also, management needs an understanding of how revenues, costs and volume interact in providing profits. All these analyses and information are provided by cost-volume-profit analysis.

CVP analysis is a systematic method of examining the relationships between selling prices, total sales revenue, volume of production, expenses and profit. CVP analysis can play an important role by providing management with information regarding financial results if a specified level of activity or volume fluctuates, information on relative profitability of its various products, information on probable effects of changes in selling price and other variables. Such information can help management improve the relationship between these variables. Similarly, CVP analysis may be used in setting selling prices, selecting the products mix to sell, choosing among alternative marketing strategies, and analysing the effects of cost increases or decreases on the profitability of the business enterprise.

TECHNIQUES OF CVP ANALYSIS

CVP analysis uses the following techniques or analyses while answering many questions in the area of managerial planning and decision-making:

1. Contribution Margin Concept
2. Break-Even Analysis
3. Profit-Volume (P/V) Analysis

Each of these techniques are discussed independently in great depth below.

CONTRIBUTION MARGIN CONCEPT

> **Contribution margin** is the excess of sales revenue over variable expenses.

Contribution margin concept indicates the profit potential of a business enterprise and also highlights the relationship between cost, sales and profit. Contribution margin is the excess of sales revenue over variable expenses. From the contribution margin, fixed expenses are deducted giving finally operating income or loss. Contribution margin is thus used to recover fixed costs. Once the fixed costs are recovered, any remaining contribution margin adds directly to the operating income of the firm. Contribution margin is a highly useful technique for planning and decision-making by the management.

Contribution Margin Ratio (Also Known as C/S Ratio or P/V Ratio)

The contribution margin can also be expressed in the form of a percentage. The contribution margin ratio is also known as 'Contribution to Sales' (C/S) ratio or Profit-Volume (P/V) ratio. This ratio denotes the percentage of each sales Rupee available to cover the fixed costs and to provide operating income to a firm. Taking an example, assume the following information in the case of a company.

	₹
Sales	10,00,000
Variable Costs	6,00,000
Fixed Costs	3,00,000

In this case, contribution margin is ₹ 4,00,000, profit ₹ 1,00,000 and contribution margin is 40% as shown by the following computation:

		₹
(*i*)	Sales	10,00,000
Less:	Variable Costs	6,00,000
	Contribution margin	4,00,000
Less:	Fixed Costs	3,00,000
	Profit	₹ 1,00,000

(*ii*) Contribution margin Ratio (or C/S or P/V ratio)

$$= \frac{\text{Sales} - \text{Variable Costs}}{\text{Sales}}$$

$$= \frac{₹\ 10,00,000 - 6,00,000}{10,00,000}$$

$$= \frac{₹\ 4,00,000}{10,00,000}$$

$$= 40\%$$

The P/V ratio helps in knowing the effect on income of a firm due to increase or decrease in sales volume. For instance, in the above example, a business enterprise may be interested in studying the effect of having additional sales of ₹ 4,00,000 on the income of the firm. Multiplying the P/V ratio (40%) by the change in sales volume (₹ 4,00,000) indicates an increase in operating income by ₹ 1,60,000 if additional sales is possible. The total income will be ₹ 2,60,000 as is clear from the following computation:

		₹
	Sales	14,00,000
Less:	Variable Costs (₹ 14,00,000 × 60%)	8,40,000
	Contribution margin (₹ 14,00,000 × 40%)	5,60,000
Less:	Fixed costs	3,00,000
	Net Income	2,60,000

In the above example, variable costs as percentage are 60% of sales (100% – P/V ratio which is 40%). Thus, variable cost as a percentage of sales are always equal to 100% minus the P/V ratio.

The P/V ratio is useful to management in deciding whether to increase sales voulme. *For example*, if the P/V ratio of a business enterprise is large and the enterprise is operating at less than 100% capacity, it will be advantageous for the firm to go for increase in sales volume as net income will go up because of higher sales volume. On the other hand, a firm with a small P/V ratio will not find increase in sales volume much profitable. In fact enterprises having a lower P/V ratio should aim at reducing costs and expenses before thinking of increasing the sales volume.

The use of P/V ratio in a specific analysis is based on the assumption that except sales volume, other factors such as the unit selling price, percentage of variable cost to sales, amount of fixed costs remain constant. If there are changes in any of these factors, the effect of such change should be considered in making the analysis involving P/V ratio.

Unit Contribution Margin

Unit contribution margin or contribution margin on per unit basis is equally useful as it also indicates the profit potential of a product or activity. The unit contribution margin is the money available from sale of each unit to cover fixed costs and provide profits to a firm. *For example*, if a selling price of a company's product is ₹ 100 and variable costs per unit ₹ 60, the unit contribution margin will be ₹ 40 (₹ 100 – 60).

> **Unit contribution margin** or contribution margin indicates the profit potential of a product or activity.

While the P/V ratio is most useful when the increase or decrease in sales volume is measured in terms of Rupees, the unit contribution margin is most useful when increase or decrease in sales volume is measured in sales units (quantities). If a business firm has been able to cover fixed costs, the net income of the firm will increase by unit contribution margin multiplied by additional sales units.

BREAK EVEN ANALYSIS

Break-even analysis stresses the relationship and the factors affecting profit. A break-even analysis indicates at what level cost and revenue are in equilibrium. It is a simple and easily understandable method of presenting to management the effect of changes in volume on profits.

> **Break even analysis** stresses the relationship and the factors affecting profit.

Break-even Point

The break-even point can be defined as:

- *the point or sales level at which losses cease and profits begin or vice versa.*

Or it can be described as that level of sales at which profits are zero and there is no loss. The break-even point serves as a base indicating how many units of product must be sold if a company is to operate without loss.

At the break-even point profit being zero, contribution (sales—variable cost) is equal to the fixed cost. If the actual volume of sales is higher than the break-even volume, there will be a profit. The break-even point is reached when the fixed costs have been fully met, beyond the break-even point, all the marginal contribution represents income.

> **Break-even point** is the level of sales at which profits are zero and there is no loss.

Assume that a company manufactures and sells a single product as follows:

Selling price per unit = ₹ 20

Variable cost per unit = ₹ 10

Total fixed cost = ₹ 1,00,000

The break-even sales to cover fixed costs will be 10,000 units.

Selling price per unit = ₹ 20

Variable cost per unit = ₹ 10

Contribution = ₹ 10

$$\text{Break-even volume} = \frac{₹\ 1,00,000 \text{ fixed cost}}{₹\ 10 \text{ contribution margin}}$$

$$= 10,000 \text{ units.}$$

If the company can sell more than 10,000 units, it will earn profits because fixed costs remain constant. If less than 10,000 units are sold, a loss will be incurred. The profits will be equal to the number of units sold in excess of 10,000 units multiplied by the unit contribution margin. *For example*, if 25,000 units are sold, the company will be operating at 15,000 units above its break-even point and will earn a profit of ₹ 1,50,000 (15,000 units × ₹ 10 contribution margin).

Break-even Formula

The break-even point can be obtained directly by a mathematical formula. The basic formula to find out the break-even point is:

$$\text{Break-even sales (units)} = \frac{\text{Fixed costs}}{\text{Contribution margin per unit}}$$

$$\text{Break-even sales (volume)} = \frac{\text{Fixed costs}}{\text{C/S ratio (also known as P/V ratio)*}}$$

or

$$\text{Break-even sales volume} = \frac{\text{Total fixed expenses}}{1 - (\text{total variable expenses/Total sale volume})}$$

Break-even Chart

Total revenues and total costs at different sales volume can be estimated and plotted on a break-even chart. This chart is constructed as follows:

1. A horizontal base line, the *x*-axis, is drawn and spaced into equal distances representing either plant capacity, sales volume or number of units. A physical index of output (units of product) is preferable because it is not influenced by changes in selling price, but when many products are involved, a sales value index may be selected.
2. A vertical line, the *y*-axis is drawn on the left side of the chart and also spaced into equal parts. This line indicates sales revenue and also costs.
3. A line parallel to the horizontal line (*x*-axis) is drawn for fixed costs.

* C/S ratio is popularly known as P/V ratio because after fixed costs are fully recovered i.e. after break-even point, all contributions (sales—variable costs) become profit. However, before break-even point, all contributions will not become profit since fixed costs are yet to be recovered.

4. A total cost line is drawn starting at the y-axis fixed cost point and moving to the right. This total cost line represents at each point the total of all items of cost, fixed and variable.
5. The sales line is drawn starting at the zero point on the vertical axis and ending at the top on the right side.
6. The total cost line intersects the sales line at a point which is known as the break-even point.
7. The area to the left of the break-even point between the total cost line and the sales line is the loss area: the profit area lies to the right of the break-even point, above the total cost line.

The data from the previous example are presented on the break-even chart (see Figure 6.1).

From Figure 6.1, it can be observed that the break-even point occurs when sales are 10,000 units at ₹ 2,00,000.

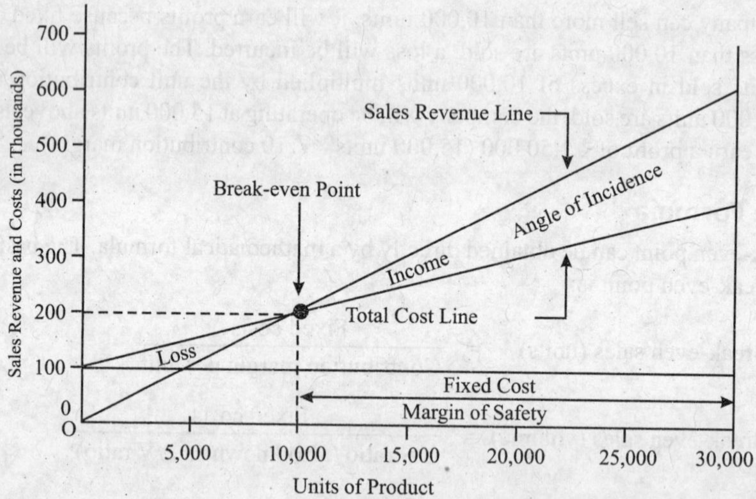

Figure 6.1: Break-even Chart

Margin of Safety

This is the difference between sales and the break-even point. If the distance is relatively short, it indicates that a small drop in production or sales will reduce profit considerably. If the distance is long, it means that the business can still make profits even after a serious drop in production. It is important that there should be a reasonable margin of safety, otherwise a reduced level of production may prove dangerous. The margin of safety can be found by using the following formula:

$$\text{Margin of Safety} = \text{Profit} \div \text{P/V ratio}$$

or

$$\text{Margin of Safety} = \frac{\text{Profit} \times \text{Sales}}{\text{Sales} - \text{Variable cost}}$$

Angle of Incidence

This is the angle at which the sales line cuts the total cost line. Management's aim will be to have as large an angle of incidence as possible because a large

> **Margin of Safety** is the difference between sales and break-even point
>
> **Angle of Incidence** is the angle at which the sales line cuts the total cost line.

angle of incidence shows a high rate of profit. A narrow angle would show that even fixed overheads are absorbed and profit accrues at a relatively low rate of return, indicating that variable costs form a large part of cost of sales.

Sales Formula

Often, it is necessary to know what level of sales is required to satisfy certain conditions of costs, contributions, etc. The desired sales can be expressed in various ways:

Sales = Fixed cost + Variable cost + Profit

or

Sales = (Profit + Fixed cost)/P/V ratio

Break-even Analysis through Equations

Cost-Volume-Profit relationships can be expressed in equation form also. A general form of expressing costs-volume-profit relationships is as follows:

Sales – Fixed Costs – Variable Costs = Income

Sales = Fixed Costs + Variable Costs + Income

In fact, total sales and variable costs are a function of the units produced or the activity undertaken. Therefore, the equation can be restated as:

SP (X) = FC + VC (X) + I

Where SP = Selling price per unit

X = Number of units sold

FC = Total fixed costs

VC = Variable cost per unit

I = Total income

To illustrate the above relationship, assume the following information about a company:

Selling price per unit ₹ 125

Variable costs per unit ₹ 75

Total fixed costs ₹ 30,00,000

Break-even point in units can be found using the above equation, the calculation is shown below:

SP (X) = FC + VC (X) + I

₹ 125 (X) = ₹ 30,00,000 + ₹ 75 (X) + 0

₹ 125 (X) – ₹ 75 (X) = ₹ 30,00,000

₹ 50 X = ₹ 30,00,000

X = ₹ 30,00,000 ÷ 50

X = 60,000 units

It can be noticed from the above equation that ₹ 30,00,000 fixed cost is being divided by contribution margin per unit ₹ 50 (₹ 125 – ₹ 75). This break-even equation, in fact, is in the form of following formula, which is generally used to find out break-even point in units:

$$\text{Break-even point in units} = \frac{\text{Total fixed costs}}{\text{Contribution margin per unit}}$$

Cash Break-even Point

Cash break-even point indicates the solvency or liquidity position of a business enterprise. Cash break-even point indicates break-even sales to cover only the fixed costs involving cash payments and to break-even. Cash break-even point is computed by using the following formula:

$$\text{Cash break-even point (units)} = \frac{\text{Total cash fixed costs}}{\text{Cash contribution margin per unit}}$$

$$\text{Cash break-even point (₹)} = \frac{\text{Total cash fixed costs}}{\text{P/V ratio}}$$

Total cash fixed costs do not include expenses which do not involve cash outflows or which are non-cash in nature such as depreciation, amortisation, etc. In fact, break-even sales should primarily aim at recovering only cash outlays and therefore, non-cash fixed costs like depreciation should be deducted from total fixed costs. It can be said that as long as a firm has adequate cash inflows to pay necessary cash outflows, the firm may continue its operation although the firm's profit and loss account shows loss. Cash break-even point is always lower than the normal break-even point which is based on accrual accounting concept and takes into account non-cash fixed expenses also such as depreciation.

Impact of Income Taxes

If target income is given on an after-tax basis, the target income volume formula would be as follows:

$$\text{Target income volume} = \frac{\text{Fixed costs} + [\text{Target income after tax} / (1 - \text{Tax rate})]}{\text{Unit contribution margin}}$$

Detailed Break-even Charts

Break-even charts are sometimes drawn to show more details. The profit area can be divided into section to show income before and after taxes, costs can be separated by elements such as material, labour, indirect manufacturing costs, and selling and administrative expenses. Costs can be further divided into out-of-pocket costs which will require cash outlays and other costs such as depreciation which are non-cash expenditure. A desired profit before taxes can also be added as a fixed cost. Using the same data as before, assume the costs are broken down into the following categories:

Unit variable cost :	₹
Direct material	4
Direct labour	2
Variable manufacturing overhead	2
Variable selling and administrative expenses	2
Total unit variable costs	10
Fixed manufacturing overhead	80,000
Fixed selling and administrative expenses	20,000
Total fixed expenses	1,00,000

The desired profit before income tax is ₹ 1,00,000. The company must sell 10,000 units to break-even and must sell another 10,000 units to earn ₹ 1,00,000 profit before taxes. In other words, the company must sell 20,000 units if it expects to earn a profit of ₹ 1,00,000 before income tax. The break-even chart showing cost and profit details is shown in Figure 6.2.

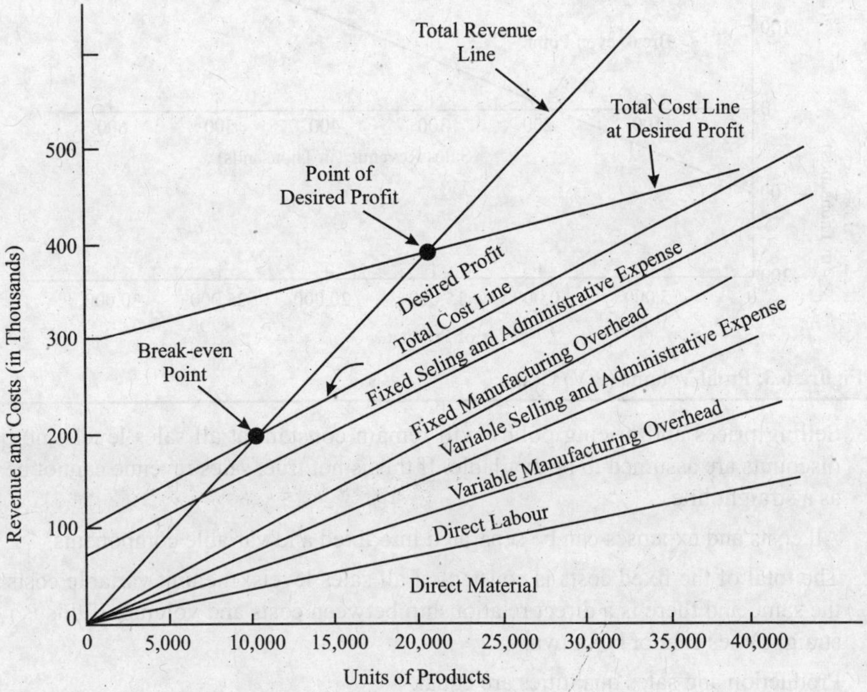

Figure 6.2: Break-even chart showing cost and profit details

PROFIT VOLUME (P/V) ANALYSIS

A P/V graph is sometimes used in place of or along with a break-even chart. Profits and losses are given on a vertical scale, and units of products, sales revenue or percentage of activity are given on a horizontal line. The horizontal line is drawn on the graph to separate profits from losses. The profits and losses at various sales levels are plotted and connected by the profit line. The break-even point is measured at the point where the profit line intersects the horizontal line. The P/V graph may be preferred to the break-even chart because profit and losses at any point can be read directly from the vertical scale, but the P/V graph does not clearly show how costs vary with activity.

Data used earlier to prepare the break-even chart are also used in preparing the P/V graph (see Figure 6.3).

Basic Assumption in CVP Analysis

CVP analysis is based on several assumptions. Whether income is computed under the absorption or marginal (variable) costing concept, these assumptions include the following:

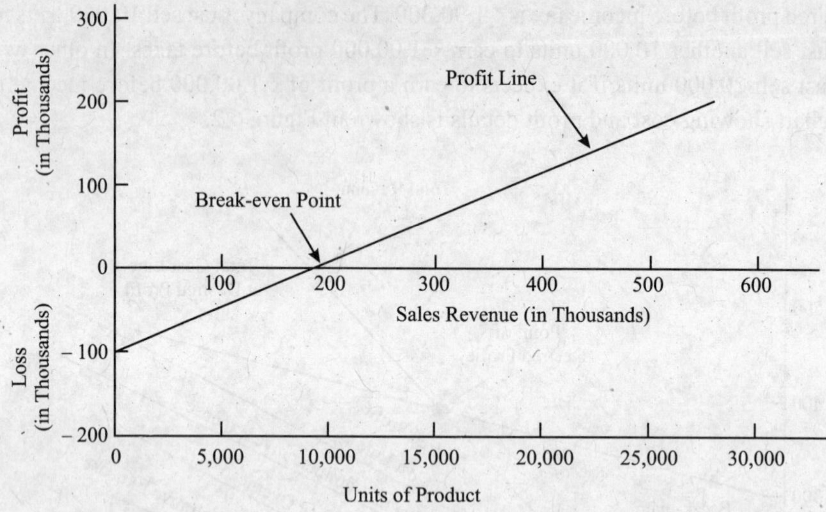

Figure 6.3: Profit Volume (P/V) Graph

1. Selling prices and pricing policy will remain constant at all sales levels; no quantity discounts are assumed to be available. If this is not true, sales revenue cannot be plotted as a straight line.
2. All costs and expenses can be separated into fixed and variable components.
3. The total of the fixed costs is constant at all sales levels; the unit variable costs remain the same and there is a direct relationship between costs and volume. If this is not true, straight lines cannot be drawn.
4. Production and sales quantities are equal.
5. Managerial policies, technological methods, and efficiency of men and machines will not change and cost control will be neither strengthened nor weakened.
6. Volume is assumed to be the only important factor affecting cost behaviour, other influencing factors such as unit prices, sales-mix, labour-strikes, and production methodology are ignored. Any change in cost behaviour will need the break-even point to be modified.
7. In case of multiple products being manufactured by the enterprises, the sales-mix should remain unchanged. That is, the calculation of the break-even point in the case of multiple products predetermines the number of units to be sold in respect of each product. This multiproduct sales-mix should remain unchanged.

The role of CVP analysis is discussed in great depth in the following section.

ROLE OF CVP ANALYSIS

As stated earlier, a cost-volume-profit analysis can be used to measure the effect of factor changes and management decision alternatives on profits. These factors include possible changes in selling prices, changes in variable or fixed cost, expansion or contraction of sales volume, or other changes in operating methods or policies. Cost-volume profit analysis is also useful for problems of product pricing, sales-mix, adding or deleting product lines, and accepting special orders. Some situations where CVP analysis can be used, are explained below:

Changes in Selling Prices

The CVP graph is frequently used to illustrate the potential profit effect of contemplated price changes. A change in the selling price of a product changes its P/V ratio, which in turn has two effects on the profit pattern, first, a new break-even point is established, second, profits above and below the break-even sales volume are different. Effects on the profit pattern are as follows:

1. ***Increase in Selling Price:*** If the selling price is increased, it increases the P/V ratio, and the rate of fixed costs recovery is increased. The break-even point (break-even volume) declines, profits beyond the break-even point increases; losses below the break-even point decreases.
2. ***Decreases in Selling Price:*** If the selling price decreases, it decreases the P/V ratio and the rate of fixed cost recovery declines. The break-even point moves at a higher point; profits beyond the break-even point decreases, losses below the break-even point increases.

Assume, *for example*, that a company produces a product with a selling price of ₹ 10 per unit and a variable cost of ₹ 4 per unit. Fixed costs are ₹ 36,000 per year. The effect of a 20% increase and a 20% decrease in the present selling price is given below:

Table 6.1: Effect of Changes in Selling Prices

	Selling price		
	Present	***20% Increase***	***20% Decrease***
Selling price per unit	₹ 10.00	₹ 12.00	₹8.00
Variable cost per unit	4.00	4.00	4.00
Marginal contribution per unit	6.00	8.00	4.00
P/V Ratio	60%	$66^2/_3$%	50%
Fixed costs	36,000	36,000	36,000
Break-even point in units	6,000	4,500	9,000
In volume	60,000	54,000	72,000
Changes in break-even Point:			
In units	0%	–25%	+50%
In sales volume	0%	–10%	+20%

The effects of the above changes in selling prices can also be shown on a CVP graph (Figure 6.4).

Changes in Variable Costs

The CVP graph is used to evaluate the impact of increases and decreases in variable costs per unit. Changes in variable cost change the P/V ratio, change the break-even point and affect profit and loss at different volumes. The effects of changes in variable costs can be summarised as follows:

1. ***Increase in Variable Costs:*** An increase in variable costs has the same effect as a decrease in the selling price. It decreases the P/V ratio and the rate of fixed cost recovery is slower. The break-even point moves to a higher level, profits after the break-even point decreases; losses before the break-even point increases.
2. ***Decrease in Variable Costs:*** A decrease in variable costs has the same effect as an increase in the selling price. A higher P/V ratio is achieved and the rate of fixed costs recovery is increased. The break-even point declines; profits beyond the break-even point are higher; losses before the break-even point are lower.

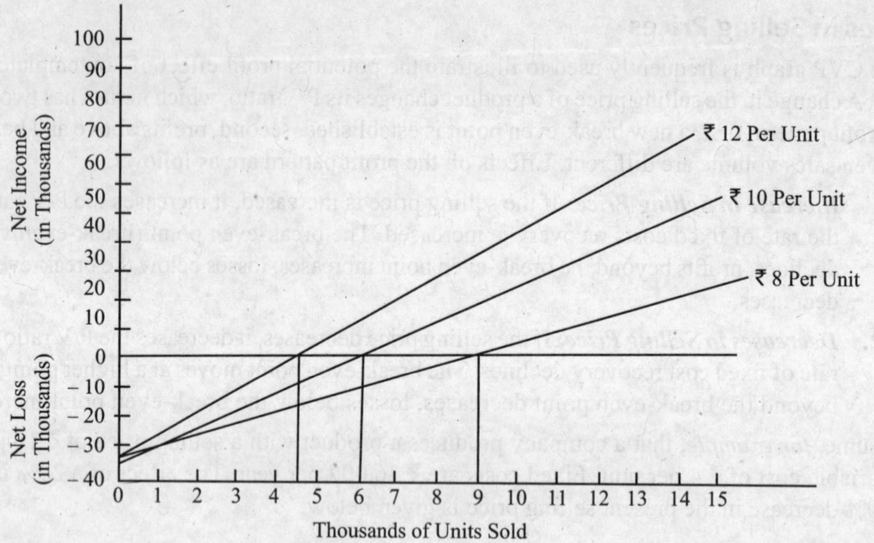

Figure 6.4: Effect of Changes in Selling Prices on Profits

To illustrate the effect of change in variable costs, assume a company is selling a product for ₹ 40 a unit and has a variable cost of ₹ 20 per unit. Fixed costs total ₹ 48,000 per year. The effects of a 20% increase and a 20% decrease in variable cost are given in the following table:

	Present variable cost (₹)	***20% Increase*** (₹)	***20% Decrease*** (₹)
Unit selling price	40.00	40.00	40.00
Variable cost per unit	20.00	24.00	16.00
Marginal contribution	20.00	16.00	24.00
P/V ratio	50%	40%	60%
Fixed costs	48,000	48,000	48,000
Break-even point:			
Sales volume	96,000	1,20,000	80,000
Units	2,400	3,000	2,000

Changes in Fixed Cost

Increase and decrease in the fixed cost do not have any impact on the P/V ratio, but they change the break-even point. With the same P/V ratio, the rate of the fixed costs recovery remains the same.

1. ***Increase in Fixed Costs:*** If fixed costs are increased, the break-even point (break-even volume) is higher. Profits above the break-even point are lower by the amount of the increase in fixed costs; below the break-even point losses increase by the amount of increase.
2. ***Decrease in Fixed Costs:*** If fixed costs are decreased, it lowers the break-even point. The profits are greater by the amount of the decrease, and losses are smaller by the amount of the decrease in fixed costs.

Assume that a company has a P/V ratio of 40% and present fixed costs of ₹ 50,000. The effects of change in the fixed costs by ₹ 10,000 are as follows:

	Present fixed Costs	*Increase by ₹ 10,000*	*Decrease by ₹10,000*
Fixed costs	₹ 50,000	₹ 60,000	₹ 40,000
P/V ratio	40%	40%	40%
Break-even point	1,25,000	1,50,000	1,00,000
Decrease	0	+25,000	–25,000

From the above example it is clear that the P/V ratio is the same in each situation and break-even point can be determined by dividing the amount of the change by the P/V ratio:

$$\frac{\text{Change in fixed costs}}{\text{P/V ratio}}$$

$$= \frac{₹\,10{,}000}{40\%} = ₹\,25{,}000$$

Desired or Target Profit

Sometimes, management faces two decisions: (*i*) to increase sales volume through reduction in selling prices, and (*ii*) to increase selling prices in case the P/V ratio is low, with the expectation that a higher profit will be earned. These decisions should be taken carefully after studying the profit pattern and other factors, otherwise the results can be harmful particularly for those companies whose P/V ratios are already low. Also, if reduction in selling prices does not increase the sales volume, the price reduction will result only in lower profits. Price cuts, like increase in variable unit costs, decrease the contribution margin. On a unit basis, price decreases may appear to be insignificant, but when the unit differential is multiplied by thousands of units, the total effect may be significant. Perhaps, many more units will have to be sold to make up the loss in profit or to earn a target profit.

Assume Company *A* hopes to increase its profits by selling more units, and to sell more, it plans to reduce its prices by 10%. The present price and cost structure and the desired one is given below:

	Present price and cost	*Desired price and cost*
Selling price	₹ 50	₹ 45
Variable cost	25	25
Contribution margin	25	20
Contribution margin (%)	50%	44.4%

At present, the contribution margin being 50 %, Company *A* will break-even when sales are twice the fixed costs. This means that if fixed costs are ₹1,00,000, 4000 units must be sold to earn a revenue of ₹ 2,00,000. But when the price is reduced to recover ₹1,00,000 in fixed costs, sales revenue must amount to ₹ 2,25,000. Not only must the revenue be higher but with a lower price per unit, more units must be sold to obtain that revenue; 5000 units must be sold just to break-even. To overcome the effect of the cut in price, sales volume in physical units must be increased by 25%.

5000 units to be sold at a lower price to break-even.

4000 units to be sold at present price to break-even.

1000 Increase in number of units.

$$\frac{1000}{4000} = 25\%$$

Sales revenue must be increased by 12-1/2%.

₹ 2,25,000 sales revenue at new break-even point.

₹ 2,00,000 sales revenue at present break-even point.

₹ 25,000 increase in sales revenue.

$$\frac{₹\ 25,000}{₹\ 2,00,000} = 1/8 = 12\text{-}1/2\%$$

The increase in sales volume required to overcome the effect of a price reduction is relatively greater when the rate of the contribution margin per unit is relatively low. If a product makes only a small contribution, then a reduction in selling price makes it all the more difficult to recover the fixed costs and to earn profits.

Similarly, a business firm may think of increasing the selling price if the P/V ratio is low. However, increase in selling price may reduce the sales volume.

Suppose a company has the following present and proposed costs and selling price structure:

	Present	***Proposed***
Selling price per unit	₹ 100	₹ 120
Variable cost per unit	70	70
Contribution per unit	30	50
P/V Ratio	30%	41.67%
Increase in contribution	—	20

Decrease in the present sales volume without effecting the present $= \frac{20}{50} = 40\%$

If there is a 20% increase in the selling price, the sales volume should not decline by more than 40 %. If decline in sales volume is less than 40% the profit position would be improved. Thus, any company with a P/V ratio of 30% can raise its selling prices by 20% and absorb a 40% reduction in sales volume without reduction in net income regardless of the amount of fixed costs involved.

Multi-Product Situations

When there are multiple products with different contribution margins, the mix of the product has a direct effect on the fixed costs recovery and total profits of the firm. Different products have different P/V ratios because of different selling prices and variable costs. Some products make larger contributions to fixed cost recovery and profit than others. The total profits depends to some extent upon the proportions in which the products are sold.

For example, assume that a company with fixed costs of ₹ 25,000 per year manufactures two products A and B with P/V ratios as follows:

	Product A	***Product B***
Unit selling price	₹ 10	₹ 20
Variable costs	4	16
Marginal contribution	6	4
P/V Ratio	60%	20%

With comparatively low variable costs, product A has a relatively high P/V ratio, each unit of product A sold contributes ₹ 6 to fixed costs recovery and profit. Product B, with comparatively high variable costs, has a low P/V ratio, each unit sold contributes only ₹ 4 to fixed costs recovery and profit. Other things being equal, the sale of product A is more profitable than that of product B, despite the fact that the selling price of product B is twice that of product A. It is correct to say that profits will decline as the sales mix shifts from product A to product B. This also implies, however, that new analyses of profit volume relationship must be made as the product-mix changes.

Different combinations of sales-mix (based on the above figure) will result in different net income. *For example*, if the total sales volume is ₹ 1,00,000 equally divided between the two products, the net income would be ₹ 15,000.

	Product A	*Product B*	*Total*
Per cent of sales revenue	50%	50%	100%
Sales revenue	₹ 50,000	50,000	1,00,000
P/V ratio	60%	20%	40%
Marginal contribution	30,000	10,000	40,000
Fixed costs			25,000
Net income			₹ 15,000

$$\text{Break-even point} = \frac{\text{Fixed cost}}{\text{P / V ratio}}$$

$$= \frac{25{,}000}{40\%} = ₹\ 62{,}500$$

If the sales mix is changed so that product A has 60% of the sales revenue, the profit on sales of ₹ 1,00,000 would increase to ₹ 19,000.

	Product A	*Product B*	*Total*
Per cent of sales revenue	60%	40%	100%
Sales revenue	₹ 60,000	40,000	1,00,000
P/V ratio	60%	20%	44%
Marginal contribution	36,000	8,000	44,000
Fixed cost			25,000
Net income			₹ 19,000

$$\text{BEP} = \frac{25{,}000}{44\%} = ₹\ 56{,}818$$

Sales Mix and Break-even Point

Sales mix is the relative proportion of each product line to the total sales of various products sold by an enterprise.

Break-even point is computed for a specified sales mix.

Sales mix is the relative proportion of each product line to the total sales of various products sold by an enterprise. As stated earlier, if there are no constraints or limitations, management should try to maximise the sales of the product (s) with higher P/V ratio. However, a sales mix results because there are limits to the quantities of any given product that can be produced and there may also be certain market limitations on how much can be sold.

When different products have their own different production facilities, selling prices, variable costs and fixed costs separately, cost-volume-profit analysis can be done for each product separately. But, in many situations, this is not found and different products share common facilities and have common fixed costs. In such a situation, CVP analysis is performed by averaging the data using the sales mix as weights. The break-even point is computed for a specified sales mix and break-even chart and P/V graph are constructed for any specified sales mix. But any one break-even chart or P/V graph will show a constant sales mix for the total sales of different products, covering the cost and revenue lines as well. The sales necessary to achieve desired or target levels of operating profit can also be computed on the basis of specified sales mix. If the sales mix changes, CVP analysis, break-even point, desired sales for target profit, costs and revenue lines will also change accordingly.

To illustrate the computation of break-even point in a sales mix situation, an example is given here. Assume, for a company, the fixed costs are ₹ 6,75,000. Further, assume that the units sales volume, units selling prices, unit variable costs, unit contribution margins for products A, B and C are as follows:

Products	*Sales Volume (units)*	*Unit Selling (price) (₹)*	*Unit Variable Cost (₹)*	*Contribution per unit (₹)*	*Margin % (P/V ratio) (₹)*
A	20,000	50	20	30	60
B	10,000	50	30	20	40
C	10,000	50	40	10	20
	40,000				

Break-even points (in units) will be computed using a weighted average contribution margin as follows:

Products	*Sales Mix (%)*		*Contribution Margin*	*Weighted Contribution Margin per unit (₹)*
A	50%	×	30	15
B	25%	×	20	5
C	25%	×	10	2.50
Total weighted contribution margin				₹ 22.50

$$\text{BEP (Units)} = \frac{\text{Fixed Cost}}{\text{Weighted contribution margin}}$$

$$= \frac{₹\,6,75,000}{₹\,22.50} = 30,000 \text{ units}$$

The detailed composition of sales and contribution margins at this level (30,000 units) are as follows:

Products	*Sales Mix*		*Total Units*	*Units of Products*		*Contribution Margin per unit (₹)*	*Total Contribution ₹*
A	50%	×	30,000 =	15,000	×	30	4,50,000
B	25%	×	30,000 =	7,500	×	20	1,50,000
C	25%	×	30,000 =	7,500	×	10	75,000
Break-even contribution margin.							₹ 6,75,000

Break-even point (in sales Rupees) can also be calculated. For this, first, total P/V ratio is required and then divide the fixed costs by total P/V ratio. Using the above information, calculation is shown below:

	Products			
	A	*B*	*C*	*Total*
Sales (units)	20,000	10,000	10,000	40,000
Selling Price (₹) Per unit	50	50	50	
Sales (₹)	10,00,000	5,00,000	5,00,000	20,00,000
Less: Variable Costs (₹)	4,00,000	3,00,000	4,00,000	11,00,000
Contribution margin	6,00,000	2,00,000	1,00,000	9,00,000
Less: Fixed Costs				6,75,000
Profit before tax				2,25,000

$$\text{Total P/V ratio} = \frac{\text{Total Contribution}}{\text{Total Sales}}$$

$$= \frac{₹\ 9,00,000}{₹\ 20,00,000}$$

$$= 45\%$$

$$\text{Break-even sales (₹)} = \frac{\text{Fixed Cost}}{\text{Total P/V ratio}}$$

$$= \frac{₹\ 6,75,000}{45\%} = ₹\ 15,00,000$$

₹ 15,00,000 as break-even sales can be verified by computing break-even sales of individual products as follows:

Product	*Break-even Units*	*Selling Price (₹)*	*Break-even Sales (₹)*
A	15,000	50	7,50,000
B	7,500	50	3,75,000
C	7,500	50	3,75,000
Total break-even sales:			15,00,000

If there is any change in the above sales mix, the break-even point, P/V ratio, amount of profit before tax may change. For instance, assume that the quantities sold of products A, B and C are 5,000 units, 20,000 units and 15,000 units, respectively. Further, assume, that there are no changes with regard to fixed costs, variable cost per unit and selling price per unit. The change in the sales mix will influence the factors of CVP analysis as shown below:

Products	*Sales Volume (units)*	*Sales Mix % unit*	*Contribution margin per unit*	*Total contribution (₹)*	*Sales Revenue (₹)*
A	5,000	12.50%	30	1,50,000	2,50,000
B	20,000	50%	20	4,00,000	10,00,000
C	15,000	37.5%	10	1,50,000	7,50,000
Total contribution margin				7,00,000	20,00,000
Less: Fixed Costs				6,75,000	
Profit before tax				25,000	

$$\text{Total P/V ratio} = \frac{\text{Total Contribution}}{\text{Total Sales}}$$

$$= \frac{₹\ 7,00,000}{₹\ 20,00,000} = 35\%$$

$$\text{Break-even sales} = \frac{\text{Fixed Costs}}{\text{Total P/V ratio}}$$

$$\text{Break-even sales} = \frac{₹\ 6,75,000}{35\%}$$

$$= ₹\ 19,28,571$$

Break-even point in units will be computed using a weighted average contribution margin, as stated earlier.

The calculation is shown below:

Products	*Sales Mix (%)*		*Contribution Margin Per unit (₹)*	*Weighted Contribution margin (₹)*
A	12.50%	×	30	3.75
B	50%	×	20	10.00
C	37.50%	×	10	3.75
Total weighted contribution margin				17.50%

$$\text{BEP (units)} = \frac{\text{Fixed Cost}}{\text{Weighted contribution margin}}$$

$$= \frac{₹\ 6,75,000}{₹\ 17.50}$$

$$= 38,571 \text{ units}$$

It can be observed that due to change in sales mix, profit before tax is considerably lower (₹ 25,000) although the amount of sales revenue is the same. The total contribution is less than the earlier ones. P/V ratio has decreased (35%) and break-even-point in units has increased to 38,571 units. These differences are due to changes in sales mix. On the need of promoting products having different P/V ratios, Anderson and Sollenberger advise:

> One way to encourage the sales force to sell more of the high contribution margin lines is to compute sales commissions on the contribution margin and not on sales revenue. If sales commissions are based on sales revenue, a sales force may have a high volume of sales of less profitable product lines and still earn a satisfactory commission. But if sales commission are related to contribution margin, the sales force is encouraged to strive for greater sales of more profitable products, and, in doing so, will help to improve total company profits.[1]

Desired Profit and Tax

The amount of desired profit before income taxes is treated as if it were additional fixed costs in finding out the sales units or sales revenue required to give the amount of desired profit. The usual formula is:

$$\text{Desired sales units} = \frac{\text{Fixed cost + Profit before Tax}}{\text{Contribution Margin per unit}}$$

$$\text{Desired sales revenue} = \frac{\text{Fixed Cost + Profit before tax}}{\text{P/V ratio}}$$

The amount of desired profit can be mentioned as a profit after income taxes. In such a case, the profit before tax is calculated by the following formula:

$$\text{Profit before tax} = \frac{\text{Profit after tax}}{(1 - \text{tax rate})}$$

For instance, if profit after tax is ₹ 1,20,000 and tax rate 40%, profit before tax will be ₹2,00,000 as calculated below:

$$\text{Profit before tax} = \frac{1{,}20{,}000}{(1 - .40)}$$

$$= ₹\ 2{,}00{,}000$$

Sometimes management is interested in knowing the sales units required to give a specified amount of profit on per unit basis. The formula for computing such number of sales units to give desired profit per unit is as follows:

$$\text{Sales units for desired profit per unit} = \frac{\text{Fixed cost}}{(\text{Contribution margin per unit} - \text{desired profit per unit})}$$

Say, if fixed costs are ₹ 1,00,000 and contribution margin per unit ₹ 10 and the desired profit per unit ₹ 2, then the sales units required to give this profit will be 12,500 units, as calculated below:

$$\text{Sales units for desired profit per unit} = \frac{₹\ 1{,}00{,}000}{(₹\ 10 - ₹\ 2)}$$

$$= \frac{₹\ 1{,}00{,}000}{₹\ 8}$$

$$= 12{,}500 \text{ units}$$

Similarly, if the desired profit is stated not on a per unit basis, but as a percentage of sales, the relevant formula for calculating the required sales volume is:

$$\text{Sales Volume for desired profit (as percentage of sales)} = \frac{\text{Fixed cost}}{(\text{P/V ratio} - \text{profit margin})}$$

Say, if fixed costs are ₹ 1,00,000, P/V ratio 40% and profit margin (percentage of sales) 20%, the required sales revenue will be ₹5,00,000 as calculated below:

$$\text{Sales volume (for desired profit margin)} = \frac{₹\ 1{,}00{,}000}{(40\% - 20\%)} = ₹\ 5{,}00{,}000$$

CVP analysis plays a vital role in different managerial decision areas, as discussed above. It can help the managers to understand impact of different decision factors on costs and profits. Many firms, especially cost leadership firms, through CVP analysis, can decide to increase volume by lower selling prices to achieve lower overall operating costs, particulary lower unit fixed costs.

Also, CVP analysis is important in using both life-cycle costing and target costing. In life-cycle costing, CVP analysis is used in the early stages of the product's cost life cycle to determine whether the product is likely to achieve the desired profitability. Similarly, CVP analysis can assist in target costing at these early stages by showing the effect on profit of alternative product designs at expected sales levels.

In addition, CVP analysis can be used at later phases of the life cycle, during manufacturing planning, to determine the most cost-effective manufacturing process. Such manufacturing decisions include when to replace a machine, what type of machine to buy, when to automate a process, and when to outosource a manufacturing operation. CVP analysis is also used in the final stages of the cost life cycle to help determine the best marketing and distribution systems. *For example*, CVP analysis can be used to determine whether paying salespeople on a salary basis or a commission basis is more cost effective. Similarly, it can help to assess the desirability of a discount programme or a promotional plan.

CVP analysis also has a role in strategic positioning. A firm that has chosen to compete on cost leadership needs CVP analysis primarily at the manufacturing stage of the cost life cycle. The role of CVP analysis here is to identify the most cost-effective manufacturing methods, including automation, outsourcing, and total quality management. In contrast, a firm following the differentiation strategy needs CVP analysis in the early phases of the cost life cycle to assess the profitability of new products and the desirability of new features for existing products.[2]

CVP ANALYSIS IN SERVICE AND NON-PROFIT ORGANIZATIONS

CVP analysis can be usefully applied by service and non-profit organisations besides the manufacturing and merchandising firms. In service and non-profit organisations, their output needs to be measured which is different from tangible units sold in a manufacturing and merchandising firm. *For example*, output in some service and non-profit industries are as follows:

Industry	**Measure of Output**
Hotels	Room nights occupied
Hospitals	Patient Days
Airlines	Passanger Kms.

The working of CVP analysis and its assumptions are identical to service and non-profit organisations as they apply to manufacturing and merchandising organisations.

CONTRIBUTION MARGIN ANALYSIS

Managers often use contribution margin in planning and controlling operations. In doing so, managers use contribution margin analysis. Contribution margin analysis focuses on explaining the differences between planned and actual contribution margins.

> **Contribution margin analysis** focuses on explaining the differences between planned and actual contribution margins.

As stated earlier, contribution margin is defined as sales less variable costs. Thus, a difference between the planned and actual contribution margin may be caused by an increase or a decrease in:

1. Sales
2. Variable costs

An increase or a decrease in sales or variable costs may in turn be due to an increase or a decrease in the:

1. Number of units sold
2. Unit sales price or unit cost

The effects of the preceding factors on sales or variable costs may be stated as follows:

1. ***Quantity Factor:*** The effect of a difference in the number of units sold, assuming no change in unit sales price or unit cost. The *sales quantity factor* and the *variable cost quantity factor* are computed as follows:

   Sales Quantity Factor = (Actual Units Sold – Planned Units of Sales) × Planned Sales Price

   Variable Cost Quantity Factor = (Planned Units of Sales – Actual Units Sold) × Planned Unit Cost

   The preceding factors are computed so that a positive amount increases contribution margin and a negative amount decreases contribution margin.

2. ***Unit Price Factor or Unit Cost Factor:*** The effect of a difference in unit sales price or unit cost on the number of units sold. The *unit price factor* and *unit cost factor* are computed as follows:

   Unit Price Factor = (Actual Selling Price per Unit – Planned Selling Price per Unit) × Actual Units Sold

   Unit Cost Factor = (Planned Cost per Unit – Actual Cost per Unit) × Actual Units Sold

   The preceding factors are computed so that a positive amount increases contribution margin and a negative amount decreases contribution margin.

Market Segment Analysis for Service Company

A contribution margin report for service companies can be used to analyze and evaluate market segments. Typical segments for various service companies are shown below.

Service Industry	*Market Segments*
Electric power	Regions, customer types (industrial, consumer)
Banking	Customer types (commercial, retail), products (loans, savings accounts)
Airlines	Products (passengers, cargo), routes
Railways	Products (commodity type), routes
Hotels	Hotel properties
Telecommunications	Customer type (commercial, retail), service type (voice, data)
Health care	Procedure, payment type (Medicare, insured)

To illustrate a contribution margin report for Indigo Airlines (segmented by route), the following data is being considered for June 2016.

Routes

	New Delhi/ Mumbai	*Mumbai/ Chennai*	*Chennai/ New Delhi*
Average ticket price per passenger	₹ 40,000	₹ 30,000	₹ 50,000
Total passengers served	9,000	5,000	11,000
Total kilometres flown	90,000	40,000	1,20,000

The variable costs per unit are as follows:

Fuel	₹ 1,000 per kilometre
Wages etc.	₹ 1,500 per kilometre
Food & Beverage service	₹ 150 per passenger
Selling	₹ 500 per passenger

Based on the above data, a contribution margin analysis statement for Indigo Airlines is shown below. The statement is segmented by the routes (city pairs) flown.

Indigo Airlines
Contribution Margin by Route for the Month June 2016

(₹ 000)

	New Delhi/ Mumbai	*Mumbai/ Chennai*	*Chennai/ New Delhi*
Revenue (Ticket price × No. of passengers)	3,60,000	1,50,000	5,50,000
Fuel (No. of kilometres flown × ₹ 1)	90,000	40,000	1,20,000
Wages etc. (No. of kilometres flown × ₹ 1.5)	1,35,000	60,000	1,80,000
Food & Beverage service (No. of passengers × ₹ .15)	1,350	750	1,650
Selling expenses (No. of passengers × ₹ .5)	4,500	2,500	5,500
Total Variable costs	2,30,850	1,03,250	3,07,150
Contribution margin	29,150	46,750	2,42,850
Contribution margin ratio (rounded)	8 %	31 %	44 %

It is found from the analysis that the New Delhi/Mumbai route has the lowest contribution margin ratio of 8% where as the Chennai/New Delhi route has the highest contribution margin ratio of 44%. Using this contribution margin analysis, managers of Indigo Airlines can take actions to improve the contribution margin of its New Delhi/Mumbai route in the future such as decreasing ticket prices. The other factors such as likelihood of increase in fuel prices, wages etc. should be considered while doing contribution margin analysis. Under the changed situations, new contribution margin report needs to be prepared by the managers of Indigo Airlines.

OPERATING LEVERAGE

Operating leverage is a measure of the effect of a percentage change in sales on profit before taxes. Operating leverage can help the management with relatively large P/V ratio and larger fixed cost to increase the net income with a small increase in sales volume. Operating leverage is computed as a ratio of contribution margin divided by profit.

Operating leverage is a measure of the effect of a percentage change in sales on profit before taxes.

$$\text{Operating leverage} = \frac{\text{Contribution margin}}{\text{Profit before tax}}$$

Since the difference between contribution margin and profit is fixed costs, companies with large amounts of fixed costs will generally have a high operating leverage. A high operating leverage indicates that a small increase in sales will give a large percentage increase in net income.

On the other hand, a low operating leverage indicates that a large increase in sales is necessary to have significant percentage increase in net income. An example is given here to illustrate the concept of operating leverage.

	A Co.	*B Co.*
Sales	₹ 4,00,000	₹ 4,00,000
Less: Variable costs	3,00,000	3,00,000
Contribution	1,00,000	1,00,000
Less: Fixed costs	80,000	50,000
Profit	20,000	50,000

Both the companies have identical amounts of sales, variable costs, contribution margin and P/V ratios. However, A company has more fixed costs than B Co. and therefore, lower net income than B Co. The operating leverage for both the companies are as follows:

	A Co.	*B Co.*
Operating Leverage	$\frac{₹\ 1{,}00{,}000}{₹\ 20{,}000}$	$\frac{₹\ 1{,}00{,}000}{₹\ 50{,}000}$
	= 5	= 2

A Co. has higher operating leverage (5 times) and B Co. has lower operating leverage (2 times). This simply means that in case of A Co., the net income will increase by 5 times and in case of B Co., it will increase by 2 times to the percentage increase in sales. For instance, if sales increase by 10%, the net income of A Co. will go up by 50% and the net income of B Co. will increase by 20%. The company with a higher level of fixed costs receives the benefits of leveraging because fixed costs influence the profit and then the operating leverage as is clear from the expanded formula:

$$\frac{\text{Contribution margin}}{\text{Profit}} = \frac{\text{Contribution margin}}{\text{Contribution margin} - \text{fixed costs}}$$

As fixed costs increase, the denominator of the formula gets smaller which means higher operating leverage. The higher the fixed costs, the closer the company is to break-even. Therefore, increase in sales will bring greater percentage increase in profits. A Co. will have higher percentage change in profit than B Co. because its fixed costs are higher. The following computations based on increased sales illustrates this fact.

	A Co. (₹)	*B Co.* (₹)
Sales	4,40,000	4,40,000
Less: Variable costs	3,30,000	3,30,000
Contribution margin	1,10,000	1,10,000
Less: Fixed costs	80,000	50,000
Net Income	30,000	60,000
Percentage increase in net income	50%	20%

From the above analysis, it is clear that for A Co., even a small increase in sales will generate a large percentage increase in net income. Thus, A Co. will be motivated to work hard to increase sales. On the contrary B Co. will not have large increase in its net income due to increased sales.

B Co. may concentrate on reducing variable costs and fixed costs and thus improving contribution margin which in turn will improve its operating leverage.

In a declining market situation, the situation will be reverse. That is, if sales decreases by 10%, the profit of A Co. (with relatively high fixed costs) will decrease by 50%, and the profit of B Co. (with smaller fixed costs) will decrease by 20%. It means profit of A Co. will be ₹ 10,000 and profit of B Co. will become ₹ 40,000.

CVP ANALYSIS AND SCARCE RESOURCE

In a multiple-product situation, product mix decision cannot be made in terms of contribution margin only when some resources or factors of production are found to be limited. Such situations are frequently seen in business enterprises. In this case, management should try to achieve the best contribution margin per unit of the scarce or limited factor. The scarce factors are likely to be: labour hours, machine hours, space used for production, etc. If there are no constraints or marketing limitations, product (s) having the highest contribution margin per unit should be manufactured. An example is given here to illustrate product mix decision in case of limiting factors.

Products	*Contribution margin per unit (₹)*	*Production hours per unit of product*	*Contribution margin per hour*
A	10	5	2
B	6	2	3
C	4	1	4

Assume that production hours available is 10,000. Considering the contribuition margin per production hour, it can be said that the firms should manufacture all possible units of product C, then all units of product B and finally all units of product A. Assume that the market for product C is only for 1000 units and 750 units of product B has to be produced to fulfil some prior agreements or commitments, the appropriate product mix will be as follows in terms of available production time.

Production time available	= 10,000 hrs
Product C (1000 units × 1 hour)	= 1,000 hrs
Product B (750 units × 2 hrs)	= 1,500 hrs
Product A (1500 units × 5 hrs)	= 7,500 hrs
	= 10,000 hours

From the above analysis, the most appropriate product mix which can be advised for utilising 10,000 production hours is: Product A 1,500 units. Product B 750 units and Product C 1000 units. In a changed situation (than the one assumed here), generally, business enterprise should increase the production of product C and decrease the production of Product A.

INDIFFERENCE POINT

> **Indifference point** is the level of volume at which total costs, and hence profits, are the same under both cost structures.

Another important tool that managers use to help them choose between alternative cost structures is the indifference point. The indifference point is the level of volume at which total costs, and hence profits, are the same under both cost structures. If the company operated at that level of volume, the alternative used would not matter because income would be the same either way. At the cost indifference point, total costs (fixed cost and variable cost) associated with the two alternatives are equal. There may be two methods or two alternatives of doing a thing, say two methods of production. It is also possible at a particular level of activity, one production method is superior to another, and vice versa. There is a need to know at which level of production, it will be desirable to shift from one production method to another production method. This level or point is known as cost indifference point and at this point total cost of two production methods is same. Cost indifference point can be calculated as follows:

$$\text{Cost Indifference Point} = \frac{\text{Differential fixed cost}}{\text{Differential variable cost per unit}}$$

Alternatively, we may calculate the indifference point by setting up an equation where each side represents total cost under one of the alternatives. (Because selling price is the same under both of these alternatives, profits will be the same when total costs are the same.) At unit volumes below the indifference point, the alternative with the lower fixed cost gives higher profits; at volumes above the indifference point, the alternative with the higher fixed cost is more profitable. *For example*, assume indifference point for a company's new product is 18,333 units, calculated as follows, with Q equal to unit volume.

Assume the following details about two methods of production, A and B, for the new product.

Production Method A = Fixed ₹ 40,000; Variable cost per unit ₹ 7

Production Method B = Fixed cost ₹ 95,000; Variable cost per unit ₹ 4

Selling price for both production methods ₹ 10 per unit

The indifference point will be 18,333 units, calculated as follows. Q indicates unit Volume.

$$\begin{aligned} \text{Total Cost for Production A} &= \text{Total Cost for Production B} \\ \text{Fixed cost + variable cost} &= \text{Fixed cost + variable cost} \\ ₹\ 40{,}000 + ₹\ 7\ Q &= ₹\ 95{,}000 + ₹\ 4Q \\ ₹\ 3\ Q &= ₹\ 55{,}000 \\ Q &= 18{,}333 \text{ units (rounded)} \end{aligned}$$

At volumes below 18,333 units, production A gives lower total costs (and higher profits); above 18,333 units, production B gives higher profits.

The line ₹ 3Q = ₹55,000 gives a clue to the trade-off between the alternatives: The company gains ₹ 3 per unit in reduced variable costs by increasing fixed costs ₹ 55,000. The indifference point shows that the company needs 18,333 units to make the trade-off desirable.

It may be noticed that break even point for the two methods are

Production method A

₹ 40,000/₹ 3 = 13,333 units

Production method B

₹ 95,000/₹ 6 = 15,833 units

Managers may have no correct answer in their choice of cost structure. Analytical tools such as the indifference point, margin of safety, and CVP graph help them evaluate alternatives, but the decision depends on their attitudes about risk and return. If they want to avoid risk, they will choose production A, forgoing the potential for higher profits from production B. If they are venturesome, they probably will be willing to take some risk for the potentially higher returns and choose production B.

Cost indifference point is useful in many decision situations, such as quality improvement programmes, different marketing plans, production plans or methods etc.

Cost indifference point should be distinguished from break-even point. Break-even point compares total sales and total cost of a product. Also, at break-even point total cost line intersects total sales line. As stated above, cost indifference signifies equality of total costs of two alternatives. At cost indifference point, total cost lines of two alternatives intersect each other.

CVP ANALYSIS AND ECONOMIST'S VIEW

In economics, economists give more attention to the problem of determining the optimum level of a firm. Accepting the objective of profit maximisation, the optimum level of activity is when marginal cost (MC) equals marginal revenue (MR). Economist's approach as compared to accountant's approach in CVP analysis has the following assumptions:

1. Economic approach, similar to accounting approach assumes that volume is the sole determinant of cost and revenue changes.
2. Economic approach assumes that total cost function is curvilinear and not linear as is assumed in accounting approach. The main reasons for the difference in the two assumptions of cost functions is the range of activity levels assumed in both economic model and accounting model. The economic model considers a range of outputs sufficient to cause significant changes in efficiency whereas the CVP relationship is assumed over a smaller range of activity.

   Break-even point under the economic approach has been shown in Figure 6.5.

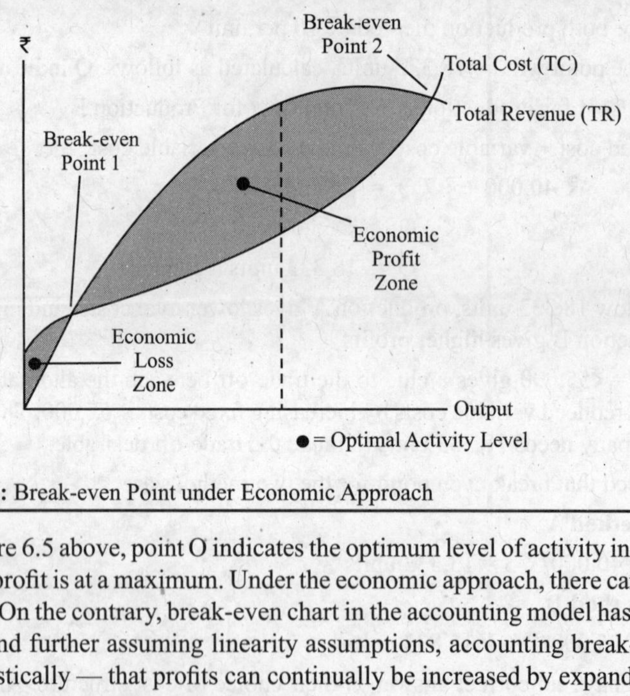

Figure 6.5: Break-even Point under Economic Approach

3. In Figure 6.5 above, point O indicates the optimum level of activity in economic approach where profit is at a maximum. Under the economic approach, there can be two break-even points. On the contrary, break-even chart in the accounting model has a single break-even point and further assuming linearity assumptions, accounting break-even chart predicts unrealistically — that profits can continually be increased by expanding output. Without further analysis, the accounting break-even approach can not be used to establish the optimum output level.
4. The economic approach is based on opportunity costs which include a normal rate of profit. A normal rate of profit is considered by economists to be a cost that has to be met if the firm is to stay in business.

   The accounting break-even point does not include any profit element but it merely balances accounting costs and revenues. This break-even chart, to serve as a base for decision-making, should be based on expected future costs and revenues and not on historical costs.

5. The economic approach, assuming a curvi-linear relationship, shows increasing profits at low activity and decreasing profits at higher levels. The economic approach displayed in Figure 6.5 assumes imperfect competitions where pricing and output decisions are inter-dependent.

   Accounting break-even point assumes a linear revenue function with a constant price per unit at all production levels and therefore profit increases proportionately with output. The assumption is that the firm operates under perfect competition and is a price taker.

The validity of either model depends upon the type of market in which the firm operates although in practice the position is more complicated than the simplistic assumptions contained in both of the models. Product differentiation, promotion policies, tactical pricing, changes in the marketing mix, foreign competition at subsidised prices and other such operating disturbances all tend to cloud the clear cut relationships embodied in both models[3].

Lucy[4] observes:

> The economist's approach produces a general analytical model which is designed to produce predictions about the behaviour of market variables (price, output, etc.) whereas the accountant's model has the more limited objective of attempting to provide practical assistance for decision making within a given firm. Both models suffer from the disadvantage that they are based on single cost and revenue values for every output level and thus ignore the uncertainties which exist in every planning and decision-making situation. Provided that the relevant activity range is being considered and the cost and revenue functions are valid then both models are likely to give similar solutions to a given problem although care will be needed in the interpretation because of the inclusion of normal profits in the cost function of the economic model.

LIMITATIONS OF CVP ANALYSIS

CVP analysis is a useful planning and decision-making device, usually in the form of a chart, showing how revenue, costs, and profit fluctuate with volume. The CVP technique is useful to management in areas of budgeting, cost control and decisiong-making. Further, CVP is used to evaluate the profit impact of alternative decisions. In spite of CVP being a useful technique, it suffers from some limitations.

1. Because of the many assumptions, CVP is only an approximation at best. CVP analysis needs estimates and approximation in assembling necessary data and thus lacks accuracy and precision.

2. In CVP analysis, it is assumed that total sales and total costs are linear and can be represented by straight lines. In some cases, this assumption may not be found true. For instance, if a business firm sells more units, the variable costs per unit may decrease due to more operating efficiencies in the factory.

3. CVP analysis is performed within a relevant range of operating activity and it is assumed that productivity and efficiency of operations will remain constant. This assumption may not be valid.

4. CVP analysis assumes that costs can be accurately divided into fixed and variable categories. Such categorisation is sometimes difficult in practice.

5. CVP analysis assumes no change in the inventory quantities, during the period. That is, opening inventory units equal the closing inventory units. This also means that units produced during the

period are equal to units sold. When changes take place in inventory level, CVP analysis becomes more complex.

6. If prices, unit costs, sales-mix, operating efficiency, or other relevant factors change, then the overall CVP analysis and relationships also must be modified. Because of these assumptions, cost data are of limited significance.

7. Furthermore, a number of problems arise while making a multi-product analysis under CVP analysis. The first problem is identifying the facilities which are shared by unrelated products. If fixed expenses and facility usages can be identified directly with individual products, the analysis will be satisfactory. A second problem occurs if there is a non-linear relationship in the units of measurement. Different products typically yield different contribution margins and are produced in various volumes with differing costs. As a result neither the revenue curve nor the cost curve is necessarily straight and the break-even point is difficult to find. A third problem lies in the assumption of certainty in demand projections. Most analyses performed by accountants and managers are deterministic, certainty is assumed although uncertainty is the environment of operation. A fourth problem is the complexity of analysis where several products are concerned. The make of revenue and cost curves for each product plotted on the conventional break-even group results generally in a meaningless hodgepodge.

Therefore, while preparing or interpreting cost-volume profit analysis all assumptions and limitations should be carefully considered. A series of CVP analysis based on different sets of assumptions and circumstances may be prepared to reflect situations prevailing in different business enterprises. When circumstances change, CVP analysis should also be revised to reflect the changing situations. It is also necessary to have up-to-date analysis so that it can act as a useful device in profit forecast, budgeting, cost control and managerial decision-making.

Illustrative Problem 1

A financial analyst is studying two packaging systems, basic and deluxe. The basic system has variable operating costs of ₹ 6 per unit and annual committed costs of ₹ 6,00,000; in contrast, the deluxe system has variable costs of ₹ 3 and committed costs of ₹ 8,00,000. The company sells its products for ₹ 40 per unit, subject to a 10 per cent sales commission. Ignore taxes.

Required:

(*a*) Which of the two systems will be more profitable for the firm if sales are expected to average 1,20,000 units per year?

(*b*) How many units must the company sell to break even if it selects the deluxe system?

(*c*) At what volume level will management be indifferent to the basic system and the deluxe system?

Solution:

(*a*) The Deluxe system would be more profitable, as shown below.

	Basic	*Deluxe*
Annual sales (1,20,000 units × 40)	₹ 48,00,000	₹ 48,00,000
Less variable costs:		
Operating		
1,20,000 units × 6.00	7,20,000	
1,20,000 units × 3.00		3,60,000
Commissions (4,800,000 × 0.10)	4,80,000	4,80,000
Total variable cost	12,00,000	8,40,000
Contribution margin	36,00,000	39,60,000
Less annual committed costs	6,00,000	8,00,000
Annual net income	30,00,000	31,60,000

(*b*) Break-even point (in units): Committed Cost ÷ Unit Contribution Margin

Basic : ₹ 6,00,000 ÷ [₹ 40 – (₹ 6.00 + (₹ 40 × 0.10))] = 20,000 units per year.

Deluxe : ₹ 8,00,000 ÷ [₹ 40 – (₹ 3.00 + (₹ 40 × 0.10))] = 24,242 units per year

(*c*) The point of indifference will produce equal levels of profitability. On the basis of the information presented in part (a), the Basic system has a unit contribution margin of ₹ 30 (₹ 40 – 6.00 – 4.00), and the Deluxe system has a unit contribution of ₹ 33 (₹ 40 – 3.00 – 4.00). Thus, if X = the volume level that equates profits, at the point of indifference, profits are equal as follows:

₹ 30 X – ₹ 6,00,000 = ₹ 33X – ₹ 8,00,000

₹ 3X = ₹ 2,00,000

X = 66,667 units per year.

Illustrative Problem 2

A Ltd. has been offered a choice to buy a machine between M1 and M2. The following data are provided:

	M1	M2
Annual output in units	10,000	10,000
Fixed Cost	₹ 60,000	₹ 32,000
Profit at above level	₹ 60,000	₹ 48,000

The market price of the product is expected to be ₹ 20 per unit.

You are required to compute:

(*i*) Break Even Point of each machine.

(*ii*) The level of sales at which both the machines earn equal profit.

(*iii*) The range of sales at which one is more profitable from the other.

Solution:

(*i*) Machines

	M1	M2
	₹	₹
Sales value 10,000 × ₹ 20	2,00,000	2,00,000
Contribution (Fixed Cost + Profit)	1,20,000	80,000
Variable Cost	80,000	1,20,000
P/V Ratio (Contribution/Sales)	60%	40%
Break Even Point (Fixed Cost/PV ratio)	1,00,000	80,000
Break Even Points (Units)	5,000	4,000
Contribution per unit (₹)	12	8
Variable Cost per unit	8	12

(*ii*) Since the selling price of the product produced by machine M1 and M2 are same, the machine will earn equal profit when the total costs of operation of both the machines are same.

If x be the output at which total cost of the machines are same we have total cost of

Machine M1 $= 8x + 60,000$

And Machine M2 $= 12x + 32,000$

Therefore, $8x + 60,000 = 12x + 32,000$

Or, $4x = 28,000$

Or, $x = 7000$

At a production level of 7000 units the profits made by M1 and M 2 would be the same.

(*iii*) The Break Even Point of M1 is 5000 units and compared to that of 4000 units in case of M 2 and at a production level of 7000 units they earn equal profits. Therefore, M2's profit earning capacity is more in the region 4000 to 6999 units because it starts earning profit at a lower point as BEP is lower here. Beyond 7000 units M 1 will earn more profits because it has a higher P/V ratio which enables it to earn more contribution of the increasing sales.

Illustrative Problem 3

Happy Holidays company contracts to take children on excursion trips Relevant information for a proposed excursion trip is given below:

Revenue per trip per child	4,000
Expenses that have to be incurred:	
Train fare per child per trip	1,700
Meals per child per trip	300
Craft Materials per child per trip	600
Room rent per trip (4 children can be accommodated in a room)	760
Local Transport at Picnic spots (per vehicle)	1,200
(each vehicle can seat 6 children excluding the driver)	
Fixed costs that are required to be covered in a trip ₹ 5,18,130.	

Find the minimum number of children to cross the break-even point and start earning a profit.

(CA Final Nov. 2011)

Solution:

Item Description	₹
Revanue per trip	4,000
Less Variable costs:	
Train fare	1700
Meals per Child	300
Craft Materials	600
Total Variable Cost	2,600
Contribution per child	1,400

Relevant range = ₹ 5,18,130/1010 = 513

Total Step Fixed Cost = Room Rent (760/4) + Transport Cost (1200/6) = ₹ 190 + ₹ 200 = ₹ 390

Net Contribution = (₹ 1,400 – ₹ 390) = ₹ 1010.

Contribution = Sales – Variable Cost = ₹ 4,000 – ₹ 2,600 = ₹ 1,400.

Profitability at 513 Students		₹
General Fixed Cost		5,18,130
Room Rent	(129×760)	98,040
Transportation	(86×1200)	103,200
Total Fixed Cost		7,19,370
Gross Contribution	(513×1400)	7,18,200
Loss		(1,170)

BEP = 513 + 170/1400 = 513.83. Hence the Minimum Students will be 514

Relevant Range for Earning Profit will be 514 to 516

Particulars	*514*	*516*
General Fixed Cost	5,18,130	5,18,130
Room Rent	98,040	98,040
Transportation	1,03,200	1,03,200
Total Fixed Cost	7,19,370	7,19,370
Gross Contribution	7,19,600	7,22,400
Profit	230	3,030

Illustrative Problem 4

The following are cost data for three alternative ways of processing work cases in an office system:

	A *Manual* (₹)	B *Semi-Automatic* (₹)	C *Fully Automatic* (₹)
Total fixed cost per month	3,000	9,000	25,000
Variable cost per case	48	28	8

Calculate cost indifference points, Interpret your result. State for what volumes of cases will you prefer each of A, B, and C. *(CA Final, Nov., 2015)*

Solution:

(*i*) ***Statement Showing "Cost Indifference Point"***

	A and B	*A and C*	*B and C*
Differential Fixed Cost (₹) ...(I)	6,000 (9,000 – 3,000)	22,000 (25,000 – 3,000)	₹16,000 (25,000 – 9,000)
Diff. Variable Costs (₹) ...(II)	20 (48 – 28)	40 (48 – 8)	20 (28 – 8)
Cost Indifference Point ...(I/II) (Differential Fixed Cost / Differential Variable Costs per case)	300 Cases	550 Cases	800 Cases

(*ii*) Interpretation of Results

At activity level below the indifference points, the alternative with lower fixed costs and higher variable costs should be used. At activity level above the indifference point alternative with higher fixed costs and lower variable costs should be used.

No. of Cases	*Alternative to be Chosen*
Cases ≤ 300	Alternative 'A'
300 ≥ Cases ≤ 800	Alternative 'B'
Cases ≥ 800	Alternative 'C'

Illustrative Problem 5

X Ltd. makes a single product with the following details:

Description	*Current Situation*	*Proposed Change*
Selling Price (₹/unit)	10	
Direct Costs (₹/unit)	5	
Present number of setups per production period, (before each production run, setup is done)	42	
Cost per set up (₹)	450	Decrease by ₹ 90
Production units per run	960	1,008
Engineering hours for production period	500	422
Cost per engineering hour(₹)	10	

The company has begun activity-based costing of fixed costs and has presently identified two cost drivers, viz. production runs and engineering hours. Of the total fixed costs presently at ₹ 96,000, after the above, ₹ 72,100 remains to be analyzed. There are changes as proposed above for the next production period for the same volume of output.

(i) How many units and in how many production runs should X Ltd. produce in the changed scenario in order to break-even?

(ii) Should X Ltd. continue to break up the remaining fixed costs into activity based costs? Why?

(CA Final, Nov. 2015)

Solution:

Working: Statement Sharing 'Non-unit level Overhead Costs'

Particulars	*Current Situation*	*Proposed Situation*
No. of Production Runs/Setups	42	40 $\left(\frac{960 \text{ run} \times 42 \text{ setup}}{1,008 \text{ units}}\right)$
Cost per Setup	₹ 450	₹ 360
Production Units *per run*	960 units	1,008 units
Production Units	40,320 (960 units × 42)	40,320
Engineering Hrs.	500	422
Engineering Cost *per hour*	₹ 10	₹ 10

(*i*) Break Even Point (Changed Scenario)

Break Even Point

$$= \frac{\text{Fixed Cost} + (\text{Setup Cost} \times \text{No. of Setups}) + (\text{Engineering Costs} \times \text{No. of Engineering Hrs.})}{(\text{Price - Unit Variable Cost})}$$

$$= \frac{₹\ 72,100 + (₹\ 360 \times 40 \text{ Setups}) + (₹\ 10 \times 422 \text{ hrs.})}{(₹\ 10 - ₹\ 5)} = 18,144 \text{ units}$$

Break Even Point (No of Production Runs)

$$= \frac{\text{Break Even (units)}}{\text{Production (units per run)}} = \frac{18,144 \text{ units}}{1,008 \text{ units}}$$

$= 18$ Runs

(*ii*) A company should adopt Activity-based Costing (ABC) system for accurate product costing, as traditional volume based costing system does not take into account the Non-unit Level Overhead Costs such as Setup Cost, Inspection Cost, and Material Handling Cost, etc. Cost Analysis under ABC system showed that while these costs are largely fixed with respect to sales volume, but they are not fixed in respect of other appropriate cost drivers. If break up of the remaining ₹ 72,100 fixed costs consist of only a small portion of these costs, ABC need not be applied.

However, it may also be noted that the primary study has resulted in cost savings. If the savings in cost are expected to exceed the cost of study and implementing ABC, it may be justified. Further it is pertinent to mention that ABC offers no increase in product-costing accuracy for single-product setting.

Illustrative Problem 6

ZED Ltd. produces two products, *P* and *Q*. The budgeted selling price per unit for *P* and *Q* are ₹ 3600 and ₹ 4320 respectively. Variable costs of production and sales for *P* and *Q* are ₹ 1800 and ₹ 3600 respectively. Annual fixed cost of the company amounts to ₹ 1,76,000. The company has two different production sales options as under:

Option 1 – A mix of 2 units of *P* for every 3 units of *Q*

Option 2 – A mix of 1 unit of *P* for every 3 units of *Q*

Find out the combined Break Even Point under each option and the optimal mix that the company should adopt.

Solution:

Contribution per unit of product

	Product P	***Product Q***
Budgeted Selling Price	3600	4320
Less variable cost	1800	3600
Contribution	1800	720

Option–1 (2 units of P and 3 units of Q)

Total contribution = ₹ 1800 × 2 + ₹ 720 × 3 = ₹ 3600 + ₹ 2160 = ₹ 5760

Break-even Point = (Fixed Cost × Total sales) / Contribution

Total sales value of 2 units of P and 3 units of Q = ₹ (2 × 3600 + 3 × 4320) = ₹ 20160

Combined Break Even Point = ₹ 1,76,000/5760 × 20,160 = ₹ 6,16,000

(Represented approximately by 61 units of P and 92 units of Q)

Option – 2 (1 unit of P and 2 units of Q).

Total contribution = ₹ 1800 × 1+ ₹ 720 × 2 = ₹ 1800 + ₹ 1440 = ₹ 3240

Total sales value = ₹ 3600 × 1 + ₹ 4,320 × 2 = ₹ 3,600 + ₹ 8,640 = ₹ 12,240

Combined Break Even Point = ₹ 1,76,000/3,240 × 12,240 = ₹ 6,64,889

(Represented approximately by 54 Units of *P* and 108 units of *Q*)

Conclusion:

As Option–1 results in lower BEP and in this option average contribution per total number of units is higher, the company should adopt this option.

Illustrative Problem 7

Liberty company has three product lines of belts: X, Y and Z with contribution margins of ₹ 15, ₹ 10 and ₹ 5 respectively. The Marketing Director foresees sales of 1,00,000 units in the coming period, consisting of 10,000 units of X, 50,000 units of Y and 40,000 units of Z. The company's fixed costs for the period are ₹ 5,10,000.

Required:

(*i*) What is the company's break-even point in units, assuming that the given sales mix is maintained ?

(*ii*) If the sales mix is maintained, what is the total contribution when 1,00,000 units are sold? What is the operating income ?

(*iii*) What would operating income be if 10,000 units of X, 40,000 units of Y and 50,000 units of Z were sold ? What is the new break-even point in units if these relationships persist in the next period ?

Solution:

(*i*) Sales of X, Y and Z are in the ratio 10,000 : 50,000 : 40,000. So every 1 unit of X, 5 units of Y and 4 units of Z are sold.

Let Q = Number of units of X to break-even

5Q = Number of units of Y to break-even

4Q = Number of units of Z to break-even

Total Contribution – Fixed costs = Zero operating income

₹ 15 × Q + ₹ 10(5Q) + ₹ 5(4Q) – ₹ 5,10,000 = 0

85Q – ₹ 5,10,000 = 0

Q = 5,10,000/85 = 6,000 units

Q = 6,000 units of X

5Q = 30,000 units of Y

4Q = 24,000 units of Z

Total 60,000 units

(*ii*) Total Contribution and Operating Income

X: 10,000 × ₹ 15	₹ 1,50,000
Y: 50,000 × ₹ 10	5,00,000
Z: 40,000 × ₹ 5	2,00,000
Total contribution	8,50,000
Fixed costs	5,10,000
Operating income	3,40,000

(*iii*) Operating income

X: 10,000 × 15	₹ 1,50,000
Y: 40,000 × 10	4,00,000
Z: 50,000 × 5	2,50,000
Total contribution	₹ 8,00,000
Fixed costs	5,10,000
Operating income	2,90,000

Let Q = Number of units of X to break-even

4Q = Number of units of Y to break-even

5Q = Number of units of Z to break-even

Contribution margin – Fixed costs = Break-even point

₹ 15(Q) + ₹ 10(4Q) + ₹ 5(5Q) – ₹ 5,10,000 = 0

80Q = ₹ 5,10,000

Q = 6,375 units of X

4Q = 25,500 units of Y

5Q = 31,875 units of Z

Total = 63,750 units

Break-even point indicates that the new mix contains less of the higher contribution margin per unit, product Y, and more of the lower contribution margin per unit, product Z.

Illustrative Problem 8

Deepika is a distributor of brass picture frames. For current year, she plans to purchase frames for ₹ 60 each and sell them for ₹ 90 each. The fixed costs for current year are expected to be ₹ 4,80,000. The only other costs will be variable costs of ₹ 120 per order for preparing the invoice and delivery documents, organizing the delivery, and following up for collection of accounts receivable. The ₹ 120 cost will be incurred each time Deepika despatches an order of picture frames, regardless of the number of frames in the order.

Required:

(*i*) (*a*) Suppose Deepika sells 40,000 picutre frames in 1,000 orders in current year. Calculate Deepika's current year operating income.

(*b*) Suppose Deepika sells 40,000 picture frames in 800 orders in current year. Calculate current year operating income.

(*ii*) Suppose Deepika anticipates making 500 orders in current year. How many picture frames must she sell to breakeven in current year ?

(*iii*) Calculate another break-even point for current year different from the one described in requirement (*ii*). Explain briefly why Deepika has multiple breakeven points.

Solution:

(*i*) (*a*) Operating income = Revenues – (Cost of picture frames × Quantity of picture frames) – (Cost of despatches × Number of despatches) – Fixed costs

= (₹ 90 × 40,000) – (₹ 60 × 40,000) – (₹ 120 × 1,000) – ₹ 4,80,000

= ₹ 36,00,000 – 24,00,000 – 1,20,000 – 4,80,000

= ₹ 6,00,000

(*b*) Operating income = (₹ 90 × 40,000) – (₹ 60 × 40,000) – (₹ 120 × 800) – ₹ 4,80,000

= ₹ 36,00,000 – 24,00,000 – 96,000 – ₹ 4,80,000

= ₹ 6,24,000

(*ii*) Number of picture frames sold by Q, then

₹ 90Q – ₹ 60Q – 500 × ₹ 120 – ₹ 4,80,000 = 0

₹ 30Q – ₹ 60,000 – ₹ 4,80,000 = 0

₹ 30Q = ₹ 5,40,000

Q = ₹ 5,40,000/30 = 18,000 picture frames

(*iii*) Suppose Deepika had 1,000 despatches

₹ 90Q – ₹ 60Q – (1,000 × ₹ 120) – ₹ 4,80,000 = 0

30Q = 1,20,000 + 4,80,000

Q = ₹ 6,00,000/30 = 20,000 picture frames.

There are multiple BEP, as there are two cost drivers – quantity of picture frames and number of orders. Various combinations of the two cost drivers can yield zero operating income.

Illustrative Problem 9

XY Hotel has 40 bedrooms with a maximum occupancy of 490 sleeper nights per week. Average occupancy is 60% throughout the year. Meals provided to guests have been costed and the average food cost per person per day is as follows:

	₹
Breakfast	72.00
Lunch	222.00
Dinner	268.00
	560.00

Direct wages and staff meals per week are as under:

	₹
Housekeeping	39,040.00
Restaurant and kitchen	68,600.00
General	35,200.00

Direct expenses per annum are ₹ 9,15,200 for housekeeping and ₹ 10,40,000 for restaurant. Indirect expenses amount to ₹ 68,22,400, which should be apportioned on the basis of floor area. The floor areas are as follows:

	Sq. Mt.
Bed rooms	3,600
Restaurant	1,200
Service Area	600

A net profit of 10% must be made on the restaurant taking and also on accommodation takings. Required: Calculate what per person should be charged per day and also show the split between meals and accommodation charges. *(CA Final, Nov. 2012)*

Solution:

Particulars	*Total (₹)*	*House keeping (₹)*	*Restaurant (₹)*	*General & Services (₹)*
Direct Wages and Staff Meal per week	1,42,840	39,040	68,600	35,200
Other Direct Expenses per week [₹ 9,15,200/52; ₹ 10,40,000/52]	37,600	17,600	20,000	–
Sub Total – Direct Expenses	1,80,440	56,640	88,600	35,200
Direct Expenses per week (General)* [39,040:68,600]	–	12,767	22,433	(35,200)
Indirect Expenses per week (Based on floor area) [3,600 : 1,200]	1,31,200	98,400	32,800	–
Total	3,11,640	1,67,807	1,43,833	–

Average Occupancy (490 × 60% = 294 Sleeper nights per week)

Particulars	*Total (₹)*	*House keeping (₹)*	*Restaurant (₹)*
Cost per person per day [₹ 1,67,807/294; ₹ 1,43,833/294]	1,060.00	570.77	489.23
Food Cost per person per day	560.00	–	560.00
Total Cost per person per day	1,620,00	570.77	1,049.23
Add : 1/9th of Cost	180.00	63.42	116.58
Charges per person per day	1,800.00	634.19	1,165.81

Illustrative Problem 10

A company manufactures two types of herbal products, A and B. Its budget shows profit figures after apportioning the fixed joint cost of ₹ 15 lacs in the proportion of the numbers of units sold. The budget for 2016, indicates:

	A	B
Profit (₹)	1,50,000	30,000
Selling price / unit (₹)	200	120
P/V ratio (%)	40	50

You are required to advise on the best option among the following, if the company expects that the number of units to be sold would be equal.

(*i*) Due to exchange in a manufacturing process, the joint fixed cost would be reduced by 15% and the variables cost would be increased by 7½ %.

(*ii*) Price of A could be increased by 20 % as it is expected that the price elasticity of demand would be unity over the range of price.

(*iii*) Simultaneous introduction of both the option, viz, (*i*) and (*ii*) above.

(CA Final, Nov, 2001)

Solution:

(*i*) Contribution per unit of each product:

	Product A	Product B
	₹	₹
Contribution per unit	80	60
(Sales × P/V ratio)	(₹ 20 × 40 %)	(₹ 12 × 50 %)

(*ii*) Number of units to be sold:

We know that:

Total contribution – Fixed cost = Profit

Let x be the number of units of each product sold, therefore:

$(80x + 60x)$ – ₹ 15,00,000 = ₹ 1,50,000 + ₹ 30,000

or x = 12,000 units

(*a*) ***Option:*** **Increase in profit, when due to change in a manufacturing process, there is reduction in joint fixed cost and increase in variable costs.**

	₹
Revised contribution from 12,000 units of A due to 7.5% increase in variable cost (12,000 units (₹ 200 – ₹ 129)	8,52,000
Revised contribution from 12,000 units of B due to 7.5% increase in variable cost 12,000 units (₹ 120 – ₹ 64.50)	6,66,000
Total revised contribution	15,18,000
Less: Fixed cost (₹ 15,00,000 – 15% × ₹ 15,00,000)	12,75,000
Revised Profit	2,43,000
Less: Existing profit	1,80,000
Increase in profit	63,000

(*b*) ***Option:*** **Increase in profit when the price of product A increased by 20% and the price elasticity of its demand would be unity over the range of price.**

	₹
Budgeted revenue from Product A (12,000 units × ₹ 200)	24,00,000
Revised demand (in units) (₹ 24,00,000 / ₹ 240)	10,000
Revised contribution (in ₹) [10,000 units × (₹ 240 – ₹ 120)]	12,00,000
Less: Existing contribution (12,000 units × ₹ 80)	9,60,000
Increase in profit (contribution)	2,40,000

******Note:*** **Since price elasticity of demand is 1, therefore the revenue in respect of products will remain same.**

(*iii*) ***Option:*** Increase in profit on the simultaneous introduction of above two options

	₹
Revised contribution from Product A [10,000 units (₹ 240 – ₹ 129)]	11,10,000
Revised contribution from Product B [12,000 units (₹ 120 – ₹ 64.50)]	6,66,000
Total revised contribution	17,76,000
Less: Revised fixed cost	12,75,000
Revised profit	5,01,000
Less: Existing profit	1,80,000
Increase in profit	3,21,000

Advice: A comparison of increase in profit figures under above three options clearly indicates that the option (*iii*) is the best as it increases the profit of the concern by ₹ 3,21,000.

Note: The budgeted profit (loss) for 2016 in respects of Products A and B should be ₹ 2,10,000 and (₹ 30,000) respectively instead of ₹ 1,50,000 and ₹ 30,000.

Illustrative Problem 11

XYZ Ltd., is selling three brands of its product in the brand name X, Y and Z. The details regarding unit costs and selling prices are as under:

	X (₹)	***Y*** (₹)	***Z*** (₹)
Direct materials	6	12	16
Direct labour	8	8	20
Variable overhead	6	20	14
Selling price	36	50	96

The monthly fixed expenditure is ₹ 5,40,000. Sales volume for the months of July and August of 2016 are as follows:

	X	***Y***	***Z***
July	20,000	20,000	20,000
August	40,000	26,000	10,000

Find out the monthly profits and if your computation brings out that higher profit was earned in the month having lower sales volume. Kindly justify the finding with reasons.

Solution:

XYZ Limited

Statement of Contribution per unit

	X (₹)	*Y* (₹)	*Z* (₹)
Direct Materials	6	12	16
Direct Labour	8	8	20
Variable Overheads	6	20	14
Marginal Cost	20	40	50
Selling Price	36	50	96
Contribution	16	10	46

Statement of Profit

July	*Products*			
	X	*Y*	*Z*	*Total*
Sales (Units)	20,000	20,000	20,000	60,000
Contribution (₹)	3,20,000	2,00,000	9,20,000	14,40,000
Fixed Cost (₹)				5,40,000
Profit (₹)				9,00,000
August				
Sales (Units)	40,000	26,000	10,000	76,000
Contribution (₹)	6,40,000	2,60,000	4,60,000	13,60,000
Fixed Cost (₹)				5,40,000
Profit				8,20,000

The Profit Statement shows that although the sale quantity has been more in August at 76,000 units than 60,000 units in July, both contribution and profit were lower in August. The reason for this apparent anomaly is drop in sale of Product Z having the highest contribution of ₹ 46 per unit. The contribution per unit from Products X and Y amounts to only ₹ 16 and ₹ 10 respectively. This means one unit of Z earns ₹ 20 more compared to one unit of X and Y taken together. Thus, the increase in sales of X and Y though significant in quantity could not compensate the loss in contribution due to reduction of sales of Z in the month of August.

Illustrative Problem 12

The following miscellaneous information regarding the operations of 2016 has been made available form the records of the Acme corporation:

Sales	₹ 1,00,000
Direct materials used	40,000
Direct labour	15,000
Fixed manufacturing overhead	20,000

Fixed selling and administration expenses	10,000
Gross profit	20,000
Net loss	5,000

There are no beginning or ending inventories.

It is required to calculate:

(i) Variable factory overhead

(*ii*) Variable selling and administration expenses

(*iii*) Contribution margin in rupees

(*iv*) Break-even point in rupee sales

(*v*) Factory cost of goods sold

Solution:

Cost of production of goods sold = Sales – Gross profit

= 1,00,000 – 20,000

Cost of production of goods sold = 80,000

(*i*) Variable Factory Overheads:

Let they be X.

Then the cost of goods sold will be: = 40,000 + 15,000 + 20,000 + X = 80,000

or 75,000 + X = 80,000

or X = 5,000

(*ii*) Variable Selling and Administration Expenses:

Let they be X

Gross profit – selling and Admn. expenses (Fixed and Variable) = Net loss

or 20,000 – 10,000 – X = 5,000

or 10,000 + 5,000 = X

or X = ₹15,000

(*iii*) Contribution Margin: Sales – Variable costs

= 1,00,000 – (40,000 + 15,000 + 5,000 + 15,000)

= 1,00,000 – 75,000

= ₹ 25,000

(*iv*) Break-even Point

$$= \frac{\text{Fixed costs}}{1 - \dfrac{\text{Variable costs}}{\text{Corresponding sales}}}$$

$$= \frac{30,000}{1 - \dfrac{75,000}{1,00,000}}$$

= 30,000 × ₹ 4 = ₹ 1,20,000

(v)	Factory Cost of Goods Sold:		
	Direct material	40,000	
	Direct labour	15,000	
			55,000
Add:	Factory overheads:		
	Fixed	20,000	
	Variable	5,000	25,000
	Factory cost		80,000

Illustrative Problem 13

The Chief Cost Accountant of Vikas Limited found to his surprise that the actual profit for the period ending 30th June 2016 was the same as budgeted inspite of realising 10% more than the budgeted selling prices. The following were the results:

Particular	*Budget* ₹	*Actuals* ₹
Sales	5,00,000	8,25,000
Variable costs of sales	3,00,000	5,75,000
Fixed costs	1,00,000	1,50,000
Profit	1,00,000	1,00,000

You are required to assist the Chief Cost Accountant in preparing the necessary explanations as to why the profit remained the same despite an increase in sales.

Solution:

In order to assist the Chief Cost Accountant of Vikas Ltd., in preparing the necessary explanations, for the profit remaining the same, in spite of an increase in sales revenue, the following factors may be considered:

Factors contributing to the increase in profit:

		₹
(i)	Increase in Sales revenue due to increased selling price (Working Note 1)	75,000
(ii)	Increase in Contribution on account of increased sales volume (Working Note 4)	1,00,000
		1,75,000

Factors contributing to the increase in cost:

(i)	Increase in Variable Cost: (Working Note 5)	1,25,000
(ii)	Increase in Fixed Cost	50,000
		1,75,000

Working Notes

1. Increase in Sales Revenue due to price increase (10% more than the Budgeted)

$$= \frac{₹\ 8,25,000}{110} \times 10 = ₹\ 75,000$$

2. Increase in Sales Volume:

$=$ (Actual Sales – Sales Revenue due to increased Selling Price – Budgeted Sales)

$= ₹\ 8,25,000 - ₹\ 75,000 - ₹\ 5,00,000 = ₹\ 2,50,000$

3. $$\text{Budgeted P/V Ratio} = \frac{\text{Budgeted Contribution}}{\text{Budgeted Sales}} \times 100$$

$$= \frac{₹\ 5,00,000 - ₹\ 3,00,000}{₹\ 5,00,000} \times 100 = 40\%$$

4. Increase in contribution due to higher sales volume

$= ₹\ 2,50,000 \times 40\% = ₹\ 1,00,000$

5. Budgeted proportion of Variable Cost (on the sale of ₹ 7,50,000)

$$= \frac{\text{Budgeted Cost} \times \text{Actual Sales Volume}}{\text{Budgeted Sales}}$$

$$= \frac{₹\ 3,00,000 \times ₹\ 7,50,000}{₹\ 5,00,000} = ₹\ 4,50,000$$

Increase in Variable Cost

$=$ (Actual Variable Cost of Sale – Budgeted proportion of Variable Cost)

$= ₹\ 5,75,000 - ₹\ 4,50,000 = ₹\ 1,25,000$

A perusal of the above-mentioned factors clearly shows that the profit of M/s. Vikas Ltd., has increased by ₹ 1,75,000 due to increase in selling price (₹ 75,000) and contribution on increased volume (₹ 1,00,000). At the same time the cost of the firm has also increased to the tune of ₹ 1,75,000 (increase in variable cost ₹ 1,25,000 and increase in fixed cost ₹ 50,000). Since the increase in profit equals to the increase in cost, therefore, the profit of the firm has remained the same as shown in the budget.

Illustrative Problem 14

Morton Company's income statement for last month is given below:

Sales (15,000 units × ₹ 30)	₹ 450,000
Less variable expenses	315,000
Contribution margin	135,000
Less fixed expenses	90,000
Net income	₹ 45,000

The industry in which Morton Company operates is quite sensitive to cyclical movements in the economy. Thus, profits vary considerably from year to year according to general economic conditions. The company has a large amount of unused capacity and is studying ways of improving profits.

Required:

1. New equipment has come onto the market that would allow Morton Company to automate a portion of its operations. Variable costs would be reduced by ₹ 9 per unit. However, fixed costs would increase to a total of ₹ 2,25,000 each month. Prepare two contribution-type income statements, one showing present operations and one showing how operations would appear if the new equipment is purchased.
2. Refer to the income statements in (1) above. For both present operations and the proposed new oprations, compute (a) the degree of operating leverage, (b) the break-even point in Rupees, and (c) the margin of safety in both amount and percentage terms.
3. Refer again to the data in (1) above. As a manager, what factor would be paramount in your mind in deciding whether to purchase the new equipment? (You may assume that ample funds are available to make the purchase.)
4. Refer to the original data. Rather than purchase new equipment, the president is thinking about changing the company's marketing method. Under the new method, sales would increase by 20% each month and net income would increae by one-third. Fixed costs could be slashed to only ₹ 48,000 per month. Compute the break-even point for the company after the change in markting method.

Solution:

1. The income statements would be:

	Present			Proposed		
	Amount	Per Unit	%	Amount	Per Unit	%
Sales	₹ 450,000	₹ 30	100%	₹ 450,000	₹ 30	100%
Less variable expenses	315,000	21	70	180,000	12*	40
Contribution margin	135,000	₹ 9	30%	270,000	₹ 18	60%
Less fixed expenses	90,000			225,000		
Net income	₹ 45,000			₹ 45,000		

₹ 21 – ₹ 9 = ₹ 12.

2. (*a*)

	Present	Proposed
Degree of operating leverage	$\frac{₹\,135{,}000}{₹\,45{,}000} = 3$	$\frac{₹\,270{,}000}{₹\,45{,}000} = 6$

(*b*)

	Present	Proposed
Break-even point in Rupees	$\frac{₹\,90{,}000}{0.30} = ₹\,3{,}00{,}000$	$\frac{₹\,225.000}{0.60} = ₹\,3{,}75{,}000$

(*c*)

	Present	Proposed
Margin of safety = Total sales less Break-even sales:		
₹ 450,000 – ₹ 300,000	₹ 150,000	
₹ 450,000 – ₹ 375,000		₹ 75,000

Margin of safety percentage = Margin of safety divided by Total sales:		
₹ 150,000 ÷ ₹ 450,000	33 1/3%	
₹ 75,000 ÷ ₹ 450,00		16 2/3%

3. The major factor would be the sensitivity of the company's operations to cyclical movements in the economy. In years of strong economic activity, the company will be better off with the new equipment. The reason is that the new equipment will increase the CM ratio, thereby permitting profits to rise more rapidly in years that sales are strong. However, in periods of economic recession, the company will be worse off with the new equipment. The greater fixed costs created by the new equipment will cause losses to be deepr and sustained more quickly than at present. Thus, management must decide whether the potential for greater profits in good years is worth the risk of deepers losses in bad years.
4. Notice that no information is given on either the new variable expenses or the new contribution margin ratio. Both of these items must be determined before the new break-even point can be computed. The computations are:

New variable expenses:

Sales = Variable expenses + Fixed expenses + Profits

₹ 5,40,000* = Variable expenses + ₹ 48,000 + ₹ 60,000**

₹ 4,32,000 = Variable expenses

*New level of sales: ₹ 4,50,000 × 1.20 = ₹ 5,40.000

**New level of net income: ₹ 45,000 × 11/3 = ₹ 60,000

New CM ratio:

Sales	₹ 5,40,000	100%
Less variable expenses	4,32,000	80%
Contribution margin	₹ 1,08,000	20%

With the above data, the new break-even point can be computed:

$$\frac{\text{New level of fixed costs, ₹ 48,000}}{\text{New CM ratio, 0.20}} = ₹\ 240,000$$

Illustrative Problem 15

Satish Enterprises is a leading exporter of Kid's Toys. J Ltd. of USA, has approached Satish Enterprises for exporting a special toy named "Jumping Monkey". The order will be valid for the next three years at 3,000 toys per month. The export price of the toy will be $ 4.

Cost data per toy is as follows:

Materials	₹ 60
Labour	₹ 25
Variable overheads	₹ 20
Primary packing of the toy	₹ 15

The toys will be packed in lots of 50 each. For this purpose, a special box, which will contain 50 toys will have to be purchased, cost being ₹ 400 per box.

Satish Enterprises will also have to import a special machine for making the toys. The cost of the machine is ₹ 24,00,000 and duty thereon will be at 12%. The machine will have effective life of 3 years and depreciation is to be charged on straight-line method. Apart from depreciation, annual fixed overheads is estimated at ₹ 4,00,000 for the first year with increase in the second year. Fixed overheads are incurred uniformly over the year.

Assuming the average conversion rate to be ₹ 50 per $. You are required to:

(*i*) Prepare a monthly and yearly profitability statement for the first year and second year assuming the production at 3,000 toys per month.

(*ii*) Compute a monthly and yearly break-even units in respect of the first year.

(*iii*) In what contingency can there be a second break-even point for the month and for the year as a whole?

(*iv*) Have you any comments to offer on the above?

(CA Final, Nov. 1999)

Solution:

(*i*) Profit Statement for First and Second Year on Monthly and Yearly Basis

(Amount in '000)

	First Year		Second Year	
	***Monthly* (₹)**	***Yearly* (₹)**	***Monthly* (₹)**	***Yearly* (₹)**
Sales Revenue	600 {3,000 units × ($4 × ₹ 50)}	7,200	600	7,200
Material	180 (3,000 units × ₹ 60)	2,160	180	2,160
Labour	75 (3,000 units × ₹ 25)	900	75	900
Variable Overheads	60 (3,000 units × ₹ 20)	720	60	720
Primary Packing	45 (3,000 units × ₹ 15)	540	45	540
Boxes Cost	24 $\left(\frac{3{,}000 \text{ units}}{50 \text{ units}} \times ₹\,400\right)$	288	24	288
Total Fixed Overheads (W.N.-1)	108 $\left(\frac{₹\,1{,}296}{12 \text{ months}}\right)$	1,296	110 $\left(\frac{₹\,1{,}320}{12 \text{ months}}\right)$	1,320
Profit	108	1,296	106	1,272

(*ii*) Statement of Monthly Break-Even Units for the First Year

(Amount in '000)

		Levels No. of Units (See W.N.-2)			
		1,351-1,400 (₹)	1,401-1,450 (₹)	1,451-1,500 (₹)	1,501-1550 (₹)
1	Fixed Costs: Total Fixed Overheads per month	1,08,000	1,08,000	1,08,000	1,08,000
2	Semi-Variable Costs: (Special Boxes Cost) (W.N.-2)	11,200 (28 Boxes × ₹ 400)	11,600 (29 Boxes × ₹ 400)	12,000 (30 Boxes × ₹ 400)	12,400 (31 Boxes × ₹ 400)
3	Total Fixed and Semi Variable Costs ...(1) + (2)	1,19,200	1,19,600	1,20,000	1,20,400
4	Break-even Level (in units) $\left(\frac{\text{Total Fixed and Semi-Variable Cost}}{\text{Contribution per unit}}\right)$	1,490 (₹ 1,19,200 / ₹ 80)	1,495 (₹ 1,19,600 / ₹ 80)	1,500 (₹ 1,20,000 / ₹ 80)	1,505 (₹ 1,20,400 / ₹ 80)

The above statement shows that the first and second break-even level of units, viz., 1,490 and 1,495 units falls outside the range of 1,351-1,400 and 1,401-1,450 units respectively. In the present case, a monthly break-even level of units is 1,500 units which lies in the range of 1,451-1,500 units.

Statement of Yearly Break-Even Units for the First Year

		Levels No. of Units (See W.N.-3)			
		17,851-17,900 (₹)	17,901-17,950 (₹)	17,951-18,000 (₹)	18,001-18,050 (₹)
1	Fixed Costs	12,96,000	12,96,000	12,96,000	12,96,000
2	Semi-Variable Costs: (Special Boxes Cost)	1,43,200 (358 Boxes × ₹ 400)	1,43,600 (359 Boxes × ₹ 400)	1,44,000 (360 Boxes × ₹ 400)	1,44,400 (361 Boxes × ₹ 400)
3	Total Fixed and Semi Variable Costs ...(1) + (2)	14,39,200	14,39,600	14,40,000	14,40,400
4	Break-even Level (in units)	17,990 (₹ 14,39,200 / ₹ 80)	17,995 (₹ 14,39,600 / ₹ 80)	18,000 (₹ 14,40,000 / ₹ 80)	18,005 (₹ 14,40,400 / ₹ 80)

The above table shows that yearly break-even units is 18,000 units which lies in the range of 17,951-18,000 units. The other first two figures do not lie in the respective ranges. Hence, they are not acceptable.

(*iii*) In case the number of toys goes beyond the level of 1,500, one more box will be required to accommodate each 50 additional units of toys. In such a case, the additional cost of a box will be ₹ 400. This amount can be recovered by the additional contribution of 5 toys. Thus, the second break-even point in such a contingency is 1,505 toys.

In case the number of toys goes beyond the level of 18,000 number, one more box will be required. The additional cost of this box will be ₹ 400; which can be recovered by the additional contribution of 5 toys. Thus, the second break-even point is 18,005 toys.

(*iv*) Yearly break-even point of 18,000 units of toys in the first year is equal to 12 times the monthly break-even point of 1,500 units. Thus, both the monthly and yearly figures of break-even point fall on the upper limit of their respective range.

In the second case, it is not so because the monthly and yearly break-even point fall within the range of 50 toys.

Working Notes

(1)

Fixed Overheads	1st Year	2nd Year
Depreciation $\left\{\frac{₹\,24,00,000 + ₹\,2,88,000\ (\text{Duty})}{3\ \text{Years}}\right\}$	₹ 8,96,000	₹ 8,96,000
Other Fixed Overheads	₹ 4,00,000	₹ 4,24,000
Total Fixed Overheads	₹ 12,96,000	₹ 13,20,000

(2)

Fixed Overhead in the first year	₹ 12,96,000
Fixed Overhead per month	₹ 1,08,000
Contribution per unit (₹ 200 – ₹ 120)	₹ 80

Hence the Break-even Number of Units will be above 1,350 units $\left(\frac{₹\,1,08,000}{₹\,80}\right)$

(3)

Fixed Overhead in the first year	₹ 12,96,000
Contribution per unit (₹ 200 – ₹ 120)	₹ 80

Hence the Break-even Number of Units to recover fixed cost will be above 16,200 units $\left(\frac{₹\,12,96,000}{₹\,80}\right)$

But, at this break-even point, another fixed cost will be incurred on Boxes.

Number of Boxes Required $\left(\frac{16,200\ \text{units}}{50\ \text{units}}\right)$	324 units
Cost of Boxes (324 units × ₹ 400)	₹ 1,29,600
Now the Total Fixed Cost (₹ 12,96,000 + ₹ 1,29,600)	₹ 14,25,600
Therefore, the new Break-even Point $\left(\frac{₹\,14,25,600}{₹\,80}\right)$	17,820 units

Illustrative Problem 16

Zet Airline provides passenger airline service, using small jets. The airline connects four major cities: Pune, Bangalore, Chennai and Kolkata. The company expects to fly 125,000 kilometre during a month. The following costs are budgeted for a month:

Fuel	₹ 95,00,000
Ground personnel	71,43,000
Crew salaries	62,80,000
Depreciation	17,20,000
Total costs	₹ 2,46,43,000

The management wishes to assign these costs to individual flights in order to gauge the profitability of its service offerings. The following activity bases were identified with the budgeted costs:

Airline Cost	Activity Base
Fuel, crew, and depreciation costs	Number of kilometre flown
Ground personnel	Number of arrivals and departures at an airport

The size of the company's ground operation in each city is determined by the size of the workforce. The following monthly data are available from corporate records for each terminal operation:

Terminal City	Ground Personnel Cost	Number of Arrivals/Departures
Pune	₹ 24,80,000	320
Bangalore	9,10,000	130
Chennai	12,30,000	150
Kolkata	25,23,000	290
Total	₹ 71,43,000	890

Three recent representative flights have been selected for the profitability study. Their characteristics are as follows:

Description	Kilometre Flown	Number of Passengers	Ticket Price per Passenger
Flight 101Pune to Kolkata	1,850	23	₹ 13,750
Flight 102 Chennai to Pune	600	29	5,900
Flight 103 Pune to Bangalore	350	14	4,250

Required:

1. Determine the fuel, crew, and depreciation cost per kilometre flown.
2. Determine the cost per arrival or departure by terminal city.
3. Use the information in (1) and (2) to construct a profitability report for the three flights.
4. Evaluate flight profitability by determining the break-even number of passengers required for each flight assuming all the costs of a flight are fixed.

Solution:

1. The depreciation and maintenance cost per kilometre is calculated as follows:

$$\frac{\text{Monthly fuel, crew, and depreciation}}{\text{Monthly number of kilometres flown}}$$

$$\frac{₹\,95,00,000 + ₹\,62,80,000 + ₹\,17,20,000}{125,000 \text{ Kilometres}} = 140 \text{ Kilometres}$$

2.

Terminal City	Monthly Ground Personnel Cost per City	÷	Number of Arrivals/Departures	=	Arrival/Departure Rate per City
Pune	₹ 24,80,000	÷	320	=	₹ 7750
Bangalore	9,10,000	÷	130	=	7000
Chennai	12,30,000	÷	150	=	8200
Kolkata	25,23,000	÷	290	=	8700
Total	₹ 71,43,000		890		

3.

Flight Profitability Report
For Three Representative Flights

	Flight 101	Flight 102	Flight 103
Passenger revenue (passengers × fare)	₹ 3,16,250	₹ 1,71,100	₹ 59,500
Fuel, crew, and depreciation costs (kilometres × ₹ 140 per kilometre)	₹ 2,59,000	₹ 84,000	₹ 49,000
Ground personnel (sum of departure plus arrival charges)	16,450[1]	15,950[2]	14,750[3]
	₹ 2,75,450	₹ 99,950	₹ 63,750
Flight income from operations	₹ 40,800	₹ 71,150	₹ (4,250)

[1] ₹ 7,750 + ₹ 8,700 (Pune to Kolkata)

[2] ₹ 8,200 + ₹ 7,750 (Chennai to Pune)

[3] ₹ 7,750 + ₹ 7,000 (Pune to Bangalore)

4. The break-even formula is:

$$\frac{\text{Break-Even Number of}}{\text{Passengers per Flight}} = \frac{\text{Fixed Costs of a Flight}}{\text{Seat Fare} - \text{Variable Cost per Seat}}$$

None of the costs in a flight are variable to the number of seats. Essentially, the costs will be incurred regardless of the number of passengers on the flight. Thus, the costs of the flight are all fixed. Given this assumption, the break-even number of passengers is a straightforward division of the costs by the fare. The results are (rounded to the nearest whole number):

Flight	Approximate Break-Even
101	₹ 2,75,450 / ₹ 13,750 = 20 passengers
102	₹ 99,950 / ₹ 5,900 = 17 passengers
103	₹ 63,750 / ₹ 4,250 = 15 passengers

Note that Flight 103 is losing money because only 14 seats were sold, which is below the break-even point. Thus, this flight must have a higher proportion of seats sold in order to earn a profit. This is a key feature of service companies. They must manage the revenue earned from a fixed capacity. The technique for doing this is termed "yield management." *For example,* when a hotel offers a weekend discount to attract volume during the slower weekend, it is practicing yield management.

Illustrative Problem 17

Taurus Ltd. produces three products — A, B, and C, from the same manufacturing facilities. The cost and other details of the three products are as follows:

	A	*B*	*C*
Selling Price/unit (₹)	200	160	100
Variable Cost/unit (₹)	120	120	40
Fixed Expenses/month (₹)			2,76,000
Maximum production per month (units)	5,000	8,000	6,000
Total hours available for the month			200 hours
Maximum demand per month (units)	2,000	4,000	2,400

The processing hours cannot be increased beyond 200 hours per month.

You are required to:

(*a*) Compute the most profitable product-mix:

(*b*) Compute the overall break-even sales of the company for the month based on the mix calculated in (*a*) above.

Solution:

M/s Taurus Limited
(a) Computation of Most Profitable Product Mix

Product	*Number of Units to be produced (Note 1)*	*Contribution per unit (₹)*	*Total Contribution (₹)*
A	2,000	80	1,60,000
B	1,600	40	64,000
C	2,400	60	1,44,000
		Total Contribution:	3,68,000
		Less: Fixed Expenses:	2,76,000
		Profit	92,000

(b) Computation of Overall Break-even Sales

$$\text{Break-even Sales} = \frac{\text{Fixed Costs} \times \text{Total Sales}}{\text{Total Contribution}}$$

$$= \frac{₹\ 2,76,000}{₹\ 3,68,000} \times ₹\ 8,96,000$$

$$= ₹\ 6,72,000$$

Working Notes:

(1) Statement Showing Units to be produced

Products	*A*	*B*	*C*
(*i*) Selling price per unit (₹)	200	160	100
(*ii*) Variable cost per unit (₹)	120	120	40
(*iii*) Contribution per unit (*i*) – (*ii*)	80	40	60
(*iv*) Maximum Production per hour (units)	$\frac{5,000}{200}$ = 25	$\frac{8,000}{200}$ = 40	$\frac{6,000}{200}$ = 30
(*v*) Contribution per hour (₹) (Maximum production per hour × Contribution per unit)	₹ 80 × 25 = 2,000	₹ 40 × 40 = 1,600	₹ 60 × 30 = 1,800
(*vi*) Ranking	I	III	II
(*vii*) Units to be produced	2,000	1,600	2,400
(*viii*) Time required for the units to be produced (hrs)	80	40	80

(2) Statement of Contribution

Products	*Units*	*Selling price per unit*	*Variable cost per unit*	*Sales revenue*	*Variable cost*	*Contribution*
A	2,000	200	120	4,00,000	2,40,000	1,60,000
B	1,600	160	120	2,56,000	1,92,000	64,000
C	2,400	100	40	2,40,000	96,000	1,44,000
Total				8,96,000	5,28,000	3,68,000

Illustrative Problem 18

Vinak Ltd. which produces three products furnishes you the following data for 2016-2017.

	Products		
	A	*B*	*C*
Selling price per unit (₹)	100	75	50
Profit/Volume ratio (%)	10	20	40
Maximum sales potential (Units)	40,000	25,000	10,000
Raw material content as percentage of variable costs (%)	50	50	50

The fixed expenses are estimated at ₹ 6,80,000. The Company uses a single raw material in all the three products. Raw material is of short supply and the company has a quota for the supply of raw material for the value of ₹ 18,00,000 for the year 2016-2017 for the manufacture of its products to meet its sales demand.

You are required to:

(*i*) Set a product mix which will give the maximum overall profit keeping the short supply of raw material in view. (*ii*) Compute that maximum profit. (*M. Com., Delhi,* 2002)

Solution:

Marginal Cost Statement

	Products		
	A	***B***	***C***
(*i*) Selling price per unit	₹ 100	75	50
(*ii*) Profit/volume ratio	10 %	20 %	40 %
(*iii*) Contribution	10	15	20
(*iv*) Variable cost	90	60	30
(*v*) Raw material cost (50% of variable cost)	45	30	15
(*vi*) Contribution as a percentage of raw material cost	22.22 %	50 %	133.33 %

The above statement shows that on the basis of percentage of contribution to material, the priorities of products will be C, B and A respectively. The output of the different products should, therefore, be as shown in the following statement of product mix.

(*i*) Statement of Product Mix

Product	*Units*	*Cost of raw material*
C	10,000	₹ 1,50,000
B	25,000	7,50,000
A	20,000	9,00,000
	55,000	18,00,000

(*ii*) Statement of Profit

Products	*A*	*B*	*C*	*Total*
Sales	₹ 20,00,000	18,75,000	5,00,000	43,75,000
Less: Variable costs	18,00,000	15,00,000	3,00,000	36,00,000
Contribution	2,00,000	3,75,000	2,00,000	7,75,000
Less: Fixed costs				6,80,000
Profit				₹ 95,000

Contribution as percentage of material content, A 10/45 × 100 = 22.2%, B 15/30 × 100 = 50% C 20/15 × 100 = 133.33%.

Illustrative Problem 19

The budgeted income statement by product lines of Multiproducts Ltd. for 2016 is as follows:

	Product A (₹)	*Product B* (₹)	*Product C* (₹)
Sales	2,00,000	5,00,000	3,00,000
Variable Expenses:			
Cost of goods sold	90,000	2,70,000	1,50,000
Selling	30,000	90,000	45,000

Fixed Expenses:			
Overhead	36,000	90,000	54,000
Administrative	16,000	40,000	24,000
Income before Tax	28,000	10,000	27,000
Income Tax @ 40%	11,200	4,000	10,800
Net Income	16,800	6,000	16,200

All products are manufactured in the same facilities under common administrative control. Fixed expenses are allocated among the products in proportion of their budgeted sales volume:

(*a*) Compute the budgeted break-even point of the company as a whole, from the data provided.

(*b*) What would be the effect on Budgeted Income if half of the budgeted sales volume of product B were shifted to product A and C in equal rupee amounts, so that the total budgeted sales in rupees remain the same.

(*c*) What would be the effect of the shift in the product mix suggested in (*b*) above on the budgeted break-even point of the whole company?

Solution:

(*a*) Budgeted BEP for the company as a whole

$$\text{Composite PV ratio} = \frac{\text{Total contribution}}{\text{Total sales}} \times 100$$

$$= \frac{80{,}000 + 1{,}40{,}000 + 1{,}05{,}000}{10{,}00{,}000} \times 100$$

$$= \frac{3{,}25{,}000}{10{,}000} \times 100 = 32.5\%$$

$$\text{BEP for the company} = \frac{\text{Total fixed costs}}{\text{Composite PV ratio}}$$

$$= \frac{52{,}000 + 1{,}30{,}000 + 78{,}000}{32.5\%}$$

$$= \frac{2{,}60{,}000 \times 100}{32.5} = ₹\ 8{,}00{,}000$$

(*b*) Effect on Budgeted Income if half the sales of Product B is shifted equally to Products A and C.

	Product A	***Product B***	***Product C***
Sales (*i*)	3,25,000	2,50,000	4,25,000
Variable expenses:			
Cost of goods sold	1,46,250	1,35,000	2,12,500
Selling	48,750	45,000	63,750

Fixed expenses: (apportioned according to sales)			
Overhead	58,500	45,000	76,500
Administrative	26,000	20,000	34,000
Total cost (*ii*)	2,79,500	2,45,000	3,86,750
Income before tax (*i*) – (*ii*)	45,500	5,000	38,250
Income tax @ 40%	18,200	2,000	15,300
Net Income	27,300	3,000	22,950
Total Net Income			₹ 53,250

The original budgeted income is ₹ 39,000. Hence the income would increase by ₹ 14,250 as a result of the proposed change.

(*c*) Break-even after shift in the product mix

$$\text{Composite PV Ratio} = \frac{\text{Total Contribution}}{\text{Total Sales}} \times 100$$

$$= \frac{1,30,000 + 70,000 + 1,48,750}{10,00,000} \times 100$$

$$= \frac{3,48,750}{10,00,000} \times 100 = 34.87\%$$

Break-even point of the company as a whole

$$= \frac{\text{Total Fixed Expenses}}{\text{Comnposite PV Ratio}}$$

$$= \frac{2,60,000}{34.87\%}$$

$$= ₹\ 7,45,627$$

Thus, the break-even point will stand reduced to sales of ₹ 7,45,627 from ₹ 8,00,000 as a result of shift in the total production-mix.

Illustrative Problem 20

The executive of B. Co., a small manufacturer of one product are developing the annual profit plan. They have just reviewed the 'first cut' at the annual income statement and are concerned with the ₹ 1,10,000 indicated profit on a sales volume of 20,000 units. The fixed cost structure of ₹ 9,90,000 appears to be high and they have some doubts about departing from the unit sales price of ₹ 100. There is a general agreement that the "profit target should be ₹ 2,20,000." This case deals with several tentative alternatives suggested during the meeting of the executive's committee that just reviewed the tentative profit plan.

You are required to compute:

(*a*) The budgeted break-even point in rupees and in units and the number of units that would have to be sold to earn the target profit.

(*b*) You are also required to respond directly to each of the following two alternatives under consideration by the management.

Consider each above part independent of the other and state any assumptions that you would like to make.

Alternative (1). A sales price increase of 20% is contemplated; the sales executive estimates that this will cause a drop in units that can be sold by 15%. What would be the new break-even point in rupees and in units. What would be the new profit figures? How many units would have to be sold to earn the target profit?

Alternative (2). A decrease in fixed costs of ₹ 55,000 and a decrease of variable costs of 6% are contemplated. What would be the new BEP in rupees? How many units must be sold to earn the target profit?

Solution:

Units Sold 20,000

Particulars	*Per Unit* ₹	*Total* ₹
Fixed Cost	49.50	9,90,000
Profit	5.50	1,10,000
Contribution	55.00	11,00,000
Sales	100.00	20,00,000
Variable Cost	45.00	9,00,000

Profit Volume Ratio = 55/100 × 100 = 55%

$$\text{Break-even point (in rupees)}:= \frac{\text{Fixed Cost}}{\text{P/V Ratio}} = \frac{9,90,000}{55} \times 100 = ₹\ 18,00,000$$

Break-even point (in units):

$$= \frac{\text{Break - even Sales}}{\text{Selling price per unit}} = \frac{₹\ 18,00,000}{₹\ 100} = 18,000 \text{ units}$$

(*ii*) Number of units to be sold for target profit

$$= \frac{\text{Fixed Cost + Target Profit}}{\text{Contribution per unit}}$$

$$= \frac{2,20,000 + 9,90,000}{55} = \frac{12,10,000}{55} = 22,000 \text{ units}$$

(b) Alternative I

	Original Sales Price per unit	₹ 100
Add:	20% increase	20
	New Selling Price	₹ 120
	Variable cost per unit	45
	Contribution per unit	75

$$\text{BEP (in units)} = \frac{\text{Fixed Cost}}{\text{Contribution per unit}} = \frac{9,90,000}{75} = 13,200 \text{ units}$$

BEP (in ₹) = Break-even Units × Selling price per unit

= 13,200 × 120 = ₹ 15,84,000

New Sales in units = 20,000 less 15% = 17,000

New profit = 17,000 × 75 – 9,90,000 = 12,75,000 – 9,90,000

= ₹ 2,85,000

$$\text{Units to be sold for Target profit} = \frac{\text{Fixed Cost + Target Profit}}{\text{Contribution per Unit}}$$

$$\frac{2,20,000 + 9,90,000}{75} = 16,133 \text{ units}$$

Alternative II

Sales price per unit	₹ 100.00
Variable cost per unit	42.30
Contribution per unit	57.70

Break-even point (in ₹):

$$= \frac{\text{New Fixed Cost} \times \text{Sales Price per Unit}}{\text{New Contribution per Unit}}$$

$$= \left(\frac{9,90,000 - 55,000}{57.70}\right) \times ₹\,100 = ₹\,16,20,451$$

$$\text{Units to be sold for Target profit} = \frac{2,20,000 + 9,35,000}{57.70}$$

$$= \frac{11,55,000}{57.70} = 20,017 \text{ units}$$

Illustrative Problem 21

A Company manufactures three different products and the following information has been collected from the books of accounts:

	Product		
	S	***T***	***Y***
Sales mix	35 %	35 %	30 %
Selling price	₹ 30	40	20
Variable cost	₹ 15	20	12
Total fixed costs		₹ 1,80,000	
Total sales		₹ 6,00,000	

The company has currently under discussion, a proposal to discontinue the manufacture of product Y and replace it with product M. when the following result are anticipated:

	Product		
	S	*T*	*M*
Sales mix	50 %	25 %	25 %
Selling price	₹ 30	40	30
Variable cost	₹ 15	20	15
Total fixed costs	₹ 1,80,000		
Total sales	₹ 6,40,000		

Will you advise the company to changeover to production of M? Give reasons for your answer.

Solution:

Existing Production

	Product			
	S	*T*	*Y*	*Total*
Selling price (₹)	30	40	20	
Variable cost (₹)	15	20	12	
Contribution per unit (₹)	15	20	8	
P/V Ratio $\frac{\text{Contribution} \times 100}{\text{Sales}}$	50%	50%	40%	
Sales mix	35%	35%	30%	
Contribution per rupee of sales (P/V ratio × sales mix)	17½	17½	12%	47%
Total Sales	₹ 6,00,000			
Total Contribution (6,00,000 × 47%)	₹ 2,82,000			
Fixed Costs	₹ 1,80,000			
Profit at present production	₹ 1,02,000			

$$\text{Break-even point} = \frac{\text{Fixed cost}}{\text{P/V ratio}} = \frac{1,80,000}{0.47} = ₹\ 3,83,000$$

Proposed Production

	Product			
	S	*T*	*M*	*Total*
Selling price (₹)	30	40	30	
Variable cost (₹)	15	20	15	
Contribution per unit (₹)	15	20	15	
P/V Ratio	50%	50%	50%	
Sales mix	50%	25%	25%	
Contribution per rupee of sales (P/V ratio × Sales mix)	25%	12½%	12½%	50%

Total sales	₹ 6,40,000
Total contribution (6,40,000 ×.50)	₹ 3,20,000
Fixed Cost	₹ 1,80,000
Profit	₹ 1,40,000

$$\text{Break-even point} = \frac{\text{Fixed cost}}{\text{P/V ratio}} = \frac{1,80,000}{0.50} = ₹\ 3,60,000$$

The proposal can be accepted becasue after replacement of Y with products M: (*i*) the break even point of the company is reached at a lower level of the total sales as compared to the present situation, and (*ii*) also there is an increase of profit by ₹ 38,000.

Illustrative Problem 22

The Budgeted result of 'X' Ltd. is set out below in respect of the various products processed at the Plant.

Product	*Sales in ₹ Lakh*	*Variable Cost as % of Sales Value*
A	5	60%
B	4	50%
C	8	65%
D	3	80%
E	6	75%
Total	26	65.77%

Fixed Costs for the period are estimated at ₹ 9 lakhs. Furnish:

(*a*) a statement showing the loss that would result.

(*b*) recommend a change in sales volume of each product which will eliminate the expected losses on the basic assumption that the sales of only one product can be increased at a time.

Solution:

X Limited
Statement Showing Expected Losses

Product ₹	*Sales (in lakhs)*	*Variable Cost as % of sales*	*Variable Cost* ₹ *(in lakhs)*	*Contribution* ₹ *(in lakhs)*	*P/V*
A	5	60%	3.0	2.0	40%
B	4	50%	2.0	2.0	50%
C	8	65%	5.2	2.8	35%
D	3	80%	2.4	0.6	20%
E	6	75%	4.5	1.5	25%
	26	65.77%	17.1	8.9	35.24%

	₹
Total Fixed Cost targeted	9,00,000
Total contribution	8,90,000
Loss/Under recovery of fixed cost	10,000

$$\text{Additional value of sales required} = \frac{\text{Under recovery of fixed cost}}{\text{P/V Ratio}}$$

Product

A $\quad \frac{10,000}{40\%} = \frac{100}{40} \times 10,000 = ₹\ 25,000$

B $\quad \frac{10,000}{50\%} = \frac{100}{50} \times 10,000 = ₹\ 20,000$

C $\quad \frac{10,000}{35\%} = \frac{100}{35} \times 10,000 = ₹\ 28,570$

D $\quad \frac{10,000}{20\%} = \frac{100}{20} \times 10,000 = ₹\ 50,000$

E $\quad \frac{10,000}{25\%} = \frac{100}{25} \times 10,000 = ₹\ 40,000$

The above calculations clearly show that if 'X' Ltd. can increase the sale of Product A by ₹ 25,000 or Product B by ₹ 20,000 its business operations can be pulled up to the B/E point.

The P/V ratio for each of the various products has been arrived at as under using the formula

$$\frac{\text{Sale} - \text{Variable cost}}{\text{Sales}} = \text{P/V Ratio}$$

Product

A $\quad \frac{5-3}{5} \times 100 = 40\%$

B $\quad \frac{4-2}{4} \times 100 = 50\%$

C $\quad \frac{8-5.20}{8} \times 100 = 35\%$

D $\quad \frac{3-2.4}{3} \times 100 = 20\%$

E $\quad \frac{6-4.5}{6} \times 100 = 25\%$

The B/E point on the basis of a change in product mix is valuable in decisions to determine the relative priorities for various products in a diversified product mix and where there are production constraints.

Illustrative Problem 23

X Co., Ltd. manufactures and sells two types of products, A and B. An increase in the sale of one depresses sales of the other on a unit basis and vice versa.

The following data in respect of a period are presented to you:

	Per unit A ₹	Per unit B ₹
Sales price	45.00	55.00
Fixed overhead (₹ 4,80,000 allocated on 1 : 2 basis)	4.00	8.00
Variable cost of sales	24.00	30.00
Sales commission (20% of sales)	9.00	11.00
Net profit	8.00	6.00

Required:

(*a*) Work out the number of units of A and B used in the above cost data.

(*b*) Show clearly the actual operating results.

(*c*) State, with arguments, whether the management should increase the sales of A or B.

(*d*) If the units of A actually sold are increased by 20% or alternatively decreased by 10% how would this increase or decrease affect the quantum of profit or loss?

(*M. Com., Delhi,* 2014)

Solution:

(*a*) The total fixed overhead of ₹ 4,80,000 has been allocated on 1:2 basis, i.e., ₹ 1,60,000 (₹4,80,000 × 1/3) to product A and ₹ 3,20,00 (₹ 4,80,000 × 2/3) to product B.

Number of units manufactured = Fixed overhead allocated to product/fixed overhead per unit.

For product A, number of units = ₹ 1,60,000/4 = 40,000 units.

For product B, number of units = ₹ 3,20,000/8 = 40,000 units.

(*b*) Statement of operating results:

	Product	***A***	***B***	***Total***
	Sales (units)	40,000	40,000	
		₹ (*in lakh*)	₹ (*in lakh*)	₹ (*in lakh*)
Sales		18.00	22.00	40.00
Less:	Sales Commission	3.60	4.40	8.00
		14.40	17.60	32.00
Less:	Variable cost of sales	9.60	12.00	21.60
	Contribution	4.80	5.60	10.40
Less:	Fixed cost	1.60	3.20	4.80
	Profit	3.20	2.40	5.60

(c) Statement of contribution per unit:

	Product	***A***	***B***
	Sales price	45.00	55.00
Less:	Commission	9.00	11.00
	Net sales revenue	36.00	44.00
Less:	Variable cost of sales	24.00	30.00
	Contribution per unit	12.00	14.00

Since the contribution from product B is higher, management would be advised to increase the sales of that podouct.

(d) (*i*) When the sales of A increase by 20%, i.e., 8,000 units, the sales of product B decrease corrrespondingly by 8,000 units. The revised sales figures will, therefore, be:

Product A — 48,000 units Product B — 32,000 units

The position will be as follows:

	Product	***A***	***B***	***Total***
	Sales (units)	48,000	32,000	
	Contribution per unit	12.00	14.00	
	Total contribution	5,76,000	4,48,000	10,24,000
Less:	Fixed overhead			4,80,000
	Profit			5,44,000

(*ii*) When the sales of product A decrease by 10%, i.e., 4,000 units, the sales of product B increase by 4,000 units. The revised sales figures will thus be:

	Product	***A***	***B***	***Total***
	Sales (units)	36,000	44,000	
	Contribution per unit	12.00	14.00	
	Total contribution	4,32,000	6,16,000	10,48,000
Less:	Fixed overhead			4,80,000
	Profit			5,68,000

It is thus seen that in case (*i*), the profit is reduced to ₹ 5,44,000 as against the existing profit of ₹ 5,60,000. In case (*ii*) however, there is an increase of profit from the existing level of ₹ 5,60,000 to ₹ 5,68,000. Alternate (*ii*) *i.e.* decreasing the sales of product A by 10% and increasing the sales of product B correspondingly by 4,000 units is recommended.

Illustrative Problem 24

The present annual net income of Zinc Diecasting Company is as follows:

	₹
Sales	₹ 1,20,00,000
Variable Costs	72,00,000
	48,00,000
Non-variable costs	36,00,000
Net Income	12,00,000

The present facilities allow expansion of sales upto ₹ 1,50,00,000 per year. Sales prospects indicate that sales could be increased to ₹ 2,00,00,000 per year.

Under consideration is a plan to expand plant facilities by building a new factory.

The following estimates have been prepared for a plant capable of meeting a sales demand of ₹ 50,00,000 per year:

Investment required		₹ 20,00,000
Desired return on investment		10% per year
Annual non-variable costs:		
Depreciation – 5%	₹ 1,00,000	
Others	₹ 7,00,000	₹ 8,00,000

Variable costs in the new plant are expected to remain on the same basis as at present.

You are required to determine the:

(*i*) break-even sales volume with the present facilities and with the additional plant

(*ii*) additional sales volume required to break-even on new facilities

(*iii*) additional sales volume needed to cover the desired return on investment in the new plant

(*iv*) annual sales volume after proposed expansion to earn the present net income of ₹ 12,00,000.

Solution:

(*i*) (*a*) Break-even sales volume $= \dfrac{\text{Non variable Costs}}{\text{Contribution}} \times \text{Sales}$

$$= \frac{₹\ 36,00,000}{₹\ 48,00,000} \times ₹\ 1,20,00,000$$

$$= ₹\ 90,00,000$$

(*b*) Break-even on new facilities

$$= \frac{\text{Existing Nonvariable Cost + Additional Nonvariable cost}}{\text{Contribution}} \times \text{Sales}$$

$$= \frac{₹\ 36,00,000 + ₹\ 8,00,000}{₹\ 48,00,000} \times ₹\ 1,20,00,000$$

$$= \frac{44,00,000}{48,00,000} \times 1,20,00,000$$

$$= ₹\ 1,10,00,000$$

(*ii*) Additional Sales volume

= Sales volume with additional plant–Sales volume wihout additional plant

= ₹ 1,10,00,000 – ₹ 90,00,000

= ₹ 20,00,000

(*iii*) Break-even sales =

$$\frac{\text{Existing non variable costs + Additional non variable costs + Desired return on investment}}{\text{Contribution}} \times \text{Sales}$$

$$= \frac{₹\ 36,00,000 + ₹\ 8,00,000 + ₹\ 2,00,000}{₹\ 48,00,000} \times ₹\ 1,20,00,000$$

$$= \frac{46,00,000}{48,00,000} \times 1,20,00,000$$

$$= ₹\ 1,15,00,000$$

Additional sales volume

$$= ₹\ 1,15,00,000 - ₹\ 1,10,00,000 = ₹\ 5,00,000$$

(*iv*) Break-even Sales Volume

$$= \frac{\text{Existing Nonvariable Cost + Additional Nonvariable Cost + Desired Return}}{\text{Contribution}} \times \text{Sales}$$

$$= \frac{₹\ 36,00,000 + ₹\ 8,00,000 + ₹12,00,000}{₹\ 48,00,000} \times 1,20,00,000$$

$$= \frac{56,00,000}{48,00,000} \times 1,20,00,000 = ₹\ 1,40,00,000$$

Illustrative Problem 25

Faxtronics is a New Delhi-based company that produces and sells two models — FM 101 and FM 102, of high quality for fax machines. The following information about these two models are given below:

	Cost per Unit	
	***FM* 101**	***FM* 102**
	₹	**₹**
Direct materials	120	160
Direct labour		
(₹ 20 per hour)	50	80
Variable overhead		
(₹ 5 per machine hour)	20	40
Fixed overhead	20	20
Total costs per unit	210	300
Price per unit	₹ 260	₹ 400

Demand for the two models has grown rapidly in recent years and Faxtronics can no longer meet the demand with its current production capacity. At present, the monthly demand is 8,000 units for FM 101 and 5,000 units for FM 102. Monthly capacity is limited to 60,000 machine hours.

Required:

(*i*) Determine the product mix that maximises profits.

(*ii*) Suppose Faxtronics has received a special order from a new customer willing to buy 2,000 units of FM 101 at ₹ 300 each. What is the opportunity cost associated with this order?

(*iii*) Should Faxtronics accept this order ? Give reasons. (*M. Com., Delhi,* 2001)

Solution:

(*i*) **Contribution Margin Per Unit**

	***FM* 101 (₹)**	***FM* 102 (₹)**
Selling price per unit	260	400

Less: Variable cost per unit:		
Direct materials	120	160
Direct labour	50	80
Variable overhead	20	40
Total variable cost	190	280
Contribution margin per unit	70	120

Contribution Margin Per Unit of Scarce Resource

	FM 101	*FM 102*
Contribution per unit of product	₹ 70	₹ 120
No of Machine hours per unit	₹ 20/₹ 5	₹ 40/₹ 5
	= 4 hrs.	8 hrs.
Contribution margin per machine hour	70/4 hrs	120/8
	= ₹ 17.50	₹ 15

When capacity fully utilised, Model FM 101 is a more profitable product because it has a higher contribution margin per unit of scarce resource (machine hours) than FM 102. Therefore, Faxtronics should first satisfy all the demands for FM 101 and then use the remaining machine hours of capacity to manufacture FM 102. The optimum production plan is as follows:

Product	*Hours*
8000 units of FM 101	32,000 hrs.
3500 units of FM 102	28,000 hrs. (Remaining)
	60,000 hrs.

(*ii*) Faxtronics has no surplus capacity available for the production of an additional 2000 units of FM101 which requires 8000 machine hrs (2000 units × 4 hrs.). Because FM 102 has the lowest contribution margin per machine hour, Faxtronics can make available the capacity (8000 machine hrs) necessary for the special order by reducing the production of FM 102 by 1000 units (8000 hrs. ÷ 8). The contribution margin for these 1000 units of FM 102 is ₹ 120 per unit. Therefore, the opportunity cost to make 2000 additional units of FM 101 is ₹ 120 × 1000 units = ₹ 1,20,000.

(*iii*) **Special Order Costs (2000 units)**

	Amount (₹)
Variable cost	2000 units × ₹ 190 = 3,80,000
Opportunity cost	1,20,000
Relevant Cost	5,00,000

Relevant cost per unit ₹ 5,00,000/2000 units = ₹ 250

Therefore, Faxtronics should accept this order because the price of ₹ 300 is higher than the relevant cost of ₹ 250 per unit. Faxtronics will enjoy increased profits by ₹ 1,00,000 [(₹ 300 – ₹ 250) × 2000 units] by accepting the special order.

Illustrative Problem 26

The operating results of B M Ltd., for the year 2016 were as under:

	Sales mix (%)	*P/V ratio (%)*
A	40	20
B	10	6
C	30	12
D	20	10

Total sales value of all the products was ₹ 80 lakhs. Total fixed overheads amounted to ₹ 10 lakhs. The raw material content of each of the products represented 50% of the respective variable costs. The forecast for the year 2017 is as under:

(*i*) The raw material costs will go up by 10%.

(*ii*) The company has been able to obtain an import quota of raw materials of the value of ₹ 35 lakhs.

(*iii*) The maximum sale potentiality of any of the above four products is 40% of the 2016 sales value.

(*iv*) The company expects to secure an increase of 5% in the selling prices of all the products uniformly.

Required:

(*i*) Prepare a statement showing the profitability of 2016.

(*ii*) Set a product-mix to maximise profits in 2017.

(*iii*) Prepare a statement showing the profitability of 2017. (*M.Com. Delhi*, 2003)

Solution:

(*i*) **Profitability of 2016**

Product	*Sales-mix %*	*Sales value ₹*	*P/V ratio %*	*Contribution ₹*
A	40	32,00,000	20	6,40,000
B	10	8,00,000	6	48,000
C	30	24,00,000	12	2,88,000
D	20	16,00,000	10	1,60,000
	100	80,00,000		11,36,000
Less: Fixed expenses				10,00,000
Profit				1,36,000

The raw material being controlled by an import quota is the factor. So the optimum product-mix is:

Product	*Sales (₹)*	*Variable Cost (100-P/V ratio)*	*Raw material Content (50% of V.C) %*	*Contribution %*	*Contribution as % of raw material*
A	32,00,000	80	40	20	50.0
B	8,00,000	94	47	6	12.8
C	24,00,000	88	44	12	27.3
D	16,00,000	90	45	10	22.2

(*ii*) **Product-mix at 2017 costs and prices to maximise profits**

Product	*Sales* %	*Sales Value* (₹)	*Variable Cost* (₹)	*Raw material* (₹)	*Raw Material with10 % increase* (₹)
A	40	32,00,000	25,60,000	12,80,000	14,08,000
B	—	—	—	—	—
C	40	32,00,000	28,16,000	14,08,000	15,48,800
D	20	16,00,000	14,40,000	7,20,000	7,92,000
		80,00,000			37,48,800

Optimum product-mix subject to raw materials as key factor

Product	*Sales* (₹)	*Raw Materials* (₹)	*Sales at 5% increase* (₹)
A	32,00,000	14,08,000	33,60,000
B	—	—	—
C	32,00,000	15,48,800	33,60,000
D	10,97,374	5,43,200	11,52,243
		35,00,000	78,72,243

$$\text{Product D Sales} = \frac{\text{New Raw Materials Cost with increase} \times \text{Previous Sales}}{\text{Old Raw Materials Cost with increase}}$$

$$= \frac{5,43,200 \times ₹\,16,00,000}{₹\,7,92,000} = ₹\,10,97,374$$

(*iii*) **Profitability of 2017**

Product	*Sales* (₹)	*Raw Materials* (₹)	*V. costs* (₹)	*Total V.C.* (₹)	*Contribution* (₹)
A	33,60,000	14,08,000	12,80,000	26,88,000	6,72,000
B	—	—	—	—	—
C	33,60,000	15,48,800	14,08,000	29,56,800	4,03,200
D	11,52,243	5,43,200	4,93,818	10,37,018	1,15,225
	78,72,243	35,00,000	31,81,818	66,81,818	11,90,425
Fixed expenses					10,00,000
Profit					1,90,425

Illustrative Problem 27

(*a*) Mark Ltd. has a chain of fast food restaurants with the following income pattern:

Average sales revenue for each customer ₹ 15

Cost of food material per customer servicing ₹ 5

Cost of cooking and direct labour per servicing	₹ 3
Other variable expenses per servicing	₹ 4
Fixed costs per week comprise of the following:	
Manager's salaries at all the outlets	₹ 75,000 per week
Depreciation cost	₹ 15,000 per week
Establishment expenses	₹ 10,000 per week
Interest and bank charges	₹ 5,000 per week

With this information calculate the following:

(*i*) Break-even level in terms of number of customers.

(*ii*) The desired level of operation in terms of number of customers if the management wants to earn a net profit of ₹ 3,000 per week after tax (assuming tax rates to be 50% of the income from this business).

(*b*) Jagdish has a soft drink stall located at the Department of Commerce premises. He sells Campa Cola only @ ₹ 3 per bottle, which he purchases from the factory van on wholesale basis @ ₹ 2.25 each. His other costs (non-variable) are ₹ 1,500 per week. Calculate his break-even level per week.

(*c*) Jagdish is considering also selling hamburgers. His reasons are two-fold: First hamburgers would attract lunchtime customers. A hamburger and a Campa Cola are quick lunch. Second, he has to meet competition from other stalls located nearby, some of which provide more extensive menus.

Jagdish analysed the cost as follows:

Monthly fixed expenses:	
Wages of a cook	₹ 1,500
Other	₹ 300
Total	₹ 1,800
Variable expenses (per hamburger):	
Rolls	1.50
Vegetables @ ₹ 9.00 per kilo	
(15 hamburgers per kilo)	₹ 0.60
Other	₹ 0.40
Total	₹ 2.50

Jagdish plans to sell hamburgers at a price of ₹ 4.00 each. Assuming thirty days stall opening period in a month you are required to state with calculations:

(*i*) The daily and monthly break-even points in number of hamburgers and in rupee sales.

(*ii*) If adding this new product (*i.e.*, hamburger) has resulted in additional sale of 500 Campa Cola bottles a day what would be its impact on profits of Jagdish on daily and monthly basis.

(*iii*) If adding hamburger requires fixed investment of ₹ 25,000 in equipment (which is subject to 50% depreciation on straight line basis, and the cost of raising this amount from bank is 24% per annum interest, would you advise Jagdish to add hamburger to its sales line? Give reasons. (*M. Com., Delhi*)

Solution:

(*a*) Contribution = Sales – Variable costs = ₹ 15 – 12 = ₹ 3

(*i*) C/S ratio $= \dfrac{\text{Contribution}}{\text{Sales}} = 3/15 = 1/5$

BEP (Customers) $= \dfrac{\text{Fixed cost}}{\text{Contribution margin per customer}}$

$= \dfrac{₹\ 1,05,000}{₹\ 3} = 35,000$ customers

(*ii*) Desired Level of operations (for ₹ 3,000 after tax profit)

Profit after tax = ₹ 3,000

Tax rate = 50%

Profit before tax = ₹ 6,000

Desired level of Operations (No. of Customers) $= \dfrac{\text{Fixed Cost + desired profit}}{\text{Contribution margin per customer}}$

$\dfrac{₹\ 1,05,000 + 6,000}{3} = \dfrac{₹\ 1,11,000}{3}$

= 37,000 customers.

(*b*) Selling price = ₹ 3

Variable cost = ₹ 2.25

Contribution margin = ₹ 3 – 2.25 = ₹ 0.75

C/s ratio $= \dfrac{0.75}{3} = 1/4$

BEP (per week) $= \dfrac{\text{Fixed cost}}{\text{C / S ratio}} = \dfrac{₹\ 1,500}{1/4}$

= ₹ 6,000

BEP (No. of bottles) $= \dfrac{\text{Fixed cost}}{\text{Contribution margin per bottle}}$

$= \dfrac{₹\ 1,500}{0.75} = 2,000$ bottles

(*c*) **(*i*) BEP on daily basis**

BEP (No. of hamburgers) $= \dfrac{\text{Fixed cost for one day}}{\text{Contribution margin per hamburger}}$

$= \dfrac{₹\ 1,800 \div 30\text{ days}}{(₹ 4.00 - ₹ 2.50)}$

$= \dfrac{₹\ 60}{₹\ 1.50}$

= 40 hamburgers

BEP (₹) $= \dfrac{\text{Fixed cost}}{\text{C/s ratio}} = \dfrac{₹ 60}{3/8} = \dfrac{60 \times 8}{3}$

$= ₹ 160$

BEP on Monthly Basis

BEP (No. of hamburgers) $= \dfrac{\text{Fixed cost}}{\text{Contribution margin per hamburger}}$

$= \dfrac{₹ 1,800}{₹ 1.50} = 1200$ humburgers

BEP (₹) $= \dfrac{\text{Fixed cost}}{\text{c/s ratio}}$

$= \dfrac{1,800}{3} = \dfrac{1,800 \times 8}{3} = ₹ 4,800$

***(ii)* Effect of Additional sales of 500 Campa bottles**

Increase in profit = No. of bottles × contribution margin per bottle

On Daily basis = 500 × ₹ 0.75

= ₹ 375

Increase in Monthly Profit = ₹ 375 × 30 days

= ₹ 11,250

***(iii)* Total fixed cost after the Investment**

Monthly Basis: Previous fixed cost	= ₹ 1,800
Depreciation $\dfrac{12,500}{12}$	= ₹ 1,042
Interest $\dfrac{₹ 6,000}{12}$	= ₹ 500
	₹ 3,342
Annual Basis = 1800 × 12	= ₹ 21,600
Depreciation	= ₹ 12,500
Interest	= ₹ 6,000
	= ₹ 40,100

BEP (units) $= \dfrac{\text{Fixed cost}}{\text{Contribution margin per unit}}$

BEP (units) Monthly $= \dfrac{₹ 3,342}{₹ 1.50} = 2228$ hamburgers

BEP (units) Annual basis $= \dfrac{₹ 40,100}{₹ 1.50} = 26,733$ hamburgers

Comment: 2228 hamburgers are required to be sold per month to break-even. Additional investments are advised if Jagdish is sure of selling more than 2228 hamburgers per month to have some/desired profit through this sale.

Illustrative Problem 28

A hospital operates a separate department for private patients. The department has 60 beds and the hospital charges a fee of ₹ 170 per day per patient. The patients will however make their own arrangement for payments of physician's fees. During 2014, the hospital collected a total revenue by way of fees of ₹ 28,12,650. The actual expenses incurred were as under:

	Allocation basis	
	Patient days	Bed capacity
	Variable (₹)	Fixed (₹)
Food	4,40,000	
Staff other than nurses		24,000
Laundry	2,40,000	
Laboratory & Pharmacy	5,20,000	
Maintenance	74,000	
General Administration		4,74,000
Others	49,600	
Total	13,23,600	4,98,000

Besides, rent of premises in which the department is housed is ₹ 8,00,000 p.a. During the next year, it is expected that the aforesaid fixed and variable expenses will go up by 10%. The rent will increase to ₹ 10,00,000.

The requirement of nursing staff is as under:

Annual patient days.	No. of nurses
Less than 8,000	3
8,000 – 10,000	4
11,000 – 12,000	5
Over 12,000	8

The average salary of nursing staff which was ₹ 13,000 per nurse p.a. in 2014 will increase to ₹ 14,000 per nurse p.a. in 2015.

Because of the insufficient demand, the hospital is contemplating to close the department.

Required:

(*i*) Present a statement of

(a) actual profitability for 2014,

(b) projected profitability for 2015.

(*ii*) Calculate the break-even patient days of occupancy for 2015.

(*iii*) What increase in fees is required to break-even at 2014 patient days of occupancy in 2015?

Solution:

(*i*) Maximum Bed days = 365 × 60 = 21,900

Collections = 28,12,650

Bed days occupancy = 28,12,650/170 = 16,545

Variable costs = 13,23,600/16,545 = 80

Contribution/bed day = 170 – 80 = 90

Increase next year = 80 × 110/100 = 88

(a) Profitability 2014 –

Contribution (16,545 × 90)	14,89,050
FC: Staff & Gen. Adm.	4,98,000
Nurses (8 × 13,000)	1,04,000
Rent	8,00,000
	14,02,000
Profit	87,050

(b) Profitability 2015 –

Contribution [16,545 × (170 – 88) i.e. 16,545 × 82]	13,56,690
FC: Staff & Gen. Adm. (4,98,000 × 110/100)	5,47,800
Nurses (8 × 14,000)	1,12,000
Rent	10,00,000
	16,59,800
Loss	30,03,110

(*ii*) BEP assuming a minimum of 3 Nurses –

FC Admn.	5,47,800
Rent	10,00,000
Nurses (8 × 14,000)	42,000
	15,89,800

BEP 15,89,800 ÷ 82 = 19,388 patient days

Since it exceeds 12,000 patient days, 8 nurses have to be employed

Hence, BEP = 16,59,800 ÷ 82 = 20,241 patient days

20,241/365 = 55 bed

55 bed occupancy / per day is required.

(*iii*) If demand is same as in 2014 i.e., 16,545 patient days, the fees have to be increased:

Contribution required = ₹16,59,800 ÷ 16,545 = ₹ 100.32.

Fee should be VC + C = 88 + 100.32 = ₹ 188.32.

Illustrative Problem 29

Flyway Ltd. has hired an aircraft to specially operate between cities A and B. All the seats are economy class.

The following information is available:

Seating capacity of the aircraft	:	260 passengers
Average number of passengers per flight	:	240 passengers
Average one-way fare from A to B	:	₹ 5,000 per passenger
Fuel costs per flight from A to B	:	₹ 90,000
Food cost (A to B sector) (no charge to passenger)	:	₹ 300 per passenger
Commission to travel agents (All tickets are through agents)	:	10% of the fare
Annual lease costs allocated to each flight	:	₹ 2,00,000
ground services, baggage handling/checking in service costs per flight A to B	:	₹ 40,000
Flight crew salaries per flight A to B	:	₹ 48,000

There is an offer from another airlines operator, Haltgo Ltd. for a stop-over at destination D, which is on the way from A to B. Due to this, the flight will operate from A to D, then from D to B.

The following terms are considered for the stop-over:

50 seats from D to B will be booked by Haltgo at ₹ 2,700 per ticket, whether or not Haltgo is able to sell them to its customers. No agents' commission is payable on these tickets. However, Snacks must be provided to these passengers also by Flyway Ltd. at no further charge to Haltgo or the passengers.

A maximum of 60 tickets can be sold by Flyway's travel agents for the A to D sector at a fare of ₹ 3,000 per passenger.

Since the stop-over wastes more time, 25 of Flyway's original passengers in the A to B sector will voluntarily drop out in favour of other airlines offering direct flights between A and B.

Due to the stop-over, fuel costs will increase from ₹ 90,000 to ₹ 1,35,000. Additional airport landing/ baggage handling charges of ₹ 19,000 per stop over will have to be incurred by Flyway Ltd.

Flyway Ltd. will have to serve snacks to all the passengers in the D to B sector at no charge to passengers. Each snack will cost Flyway ₹ 200. This will be in addition to the original food at ₹ 300 served in the A to D sector.

You may assume that fuel costs are not affected by the actual number of passengers in the flight, ignore non-financial considerations, additional wear and tear to aircraft due to extra landing/take-off.

Without considering Haltgo's offer,

(*i*) What is the profit earned by Flyway Ltd. per flight form A to B?

(*ii*) What is the break-even number of passengers for each flight from A to B, considering the effects of Haltgo's offer.

(*iii*) Evalute whether Flyway should accept the offer.

Solution:

Allocation of Seats in the Aircraft

Existing Situation	
For Destination A to B	
Seating Capacity of the Aircraft	260 passengers
Average Number of Passengers per flight	240 passengers
Proposed Situation	
For Destination D to B	
Seats Booked by Haltgo Ltd.	50 Seats
For Destination A to B	
Seats Available {260 (capacity) – (booked by Haltgo Ltd. for destination D to B)}	210 Seats
Requirement of Regular Passengers {240 (original no. of passengers) – 25 (no. of passengers drop out due to wastage of time)}	215 Seats
Possible Allocation of Seats to Regular Passengers	210 Seats
For Destination A to D	
Seat Available {260 (capacity) – 210 (seats allocated to regular passengers of destination A to B)}	
Requirement of Agents (tickets can be sold by Flyway's travel agents)	60 Seats
Possible Allocation to Agents of Flyway Ltd.	50 Seats

Contribution per Flight

Particulars	*Existing* ₹	*Proposed* ₹
Revenue *per passenger* (Gross Fare)	5,000	3,000
Less : Total Variable Cost *per passenger*:		
10% Commission on Fare	500	300
Food	300	300
	800	600
Contribution per passenger	4,200	2,400

Profit per Flight Under Existing Situation

Contribution per flight (24 × ₹ 4200)		10,08,000
Less: Fixed Costs *per flight*		
Fuel Cost	90,000	
Annual Lease Cost	2,00,000	
Ground Service, Baggage Handling/Checking in	40,000	
Flight crew Salaries	48,000	3,78,000
Profit *per flight*		6,30,000

$$\text{Break-even No. of Passengers} = \frac{\text{Total Fixed Cost per Flight}}{\text{Contribution per Passenger}} = \frac{₹\,3,78,000}{₹\,4,200} = 90 \text{ passengers}$$

Additional Revenue/Expenditure from Haltgo Ltd.'s offer under Proposed Situation

Particulars	*Additional*	
	Cost (₹)	*Revenue (₹)*
Revenue from Destination D to B (50 Seats × ₹ 2,700)		1,35,000
Contribution from Destination A to D (50 Seals × ₹ 2,400)		1,20,000
Contribution Lost for Destination A to B (30 Seals* × ₹ 4,200)	1,26,000	
Snacks (260 Passengers × ₹ 200)	52,000	
Fuel Cost	45,000	
Airport Landing/Baggage Handing Charges	19,000	
Total	2,42,000	2,55,000

Recommendation: Accept Haltgo's offer since Flyway Ltd. will gain ₹ 13,000 (₹ 2,55,000 – ₹ 2,42,000) per flight.

Illustrative Problem 30

A company manufactures two products. Each product passes through two departments A and B before it becomes a finished product. The data for a year are as under:

Products	**Aristocrat**	**Deluxe**
(*i*) Maximum sales potential in units	7,400	10,000
(*ii*) Product unit data:		
Selling price per unit	₹ 90	₹ 80
Machine hours per unit:		
Department A Hours	0.50	0.30
Department B Hours	0.40	0.45

(*iii*) Maximum capacity of Department A is 3,400 hours and of Department B is 3,840 hours.

(*iv*) Maximum quantity of direct materials available is 17,000 kg. Each product requires 2 kg of direct materials. The purchase price of the direct materials is ₹ 5 per kg.

(*v*) Variable costs are budgeted at ₹ 50 per hour for Department A and ₹ 60 per hour for Department B.

In view of the aforesaid production capacity constraints, the company has decided to produce only one of the two products during the year under review.

Required:

(*i*) Which of the two products should be produced and sold in the year under review to maximize the profit. State the number of units of that product and the resultant contribution.

(*ii*) The suplus capacity available in Department A or Department B after manufacture of either Aristocrat or Deluxe is proposed to be hired out to earn a contribution of ₹ 40 per hour in the case of Department A and ₹ 60 per hour in the case of Department B. Prepare a statement to show whether Aristocrat or Deluxe should now be produced to maximize the total contribution. Calculate such total contribution.

(*iii*) The company has been advised to produce 4,250 units of each product and also to hire out the surplus capacity of Department A and/or Department B. You are required to examine the feasibility of this proposal and to prepare a budget analysis showing the total contribution for the year.

Solution:

(*i*) **Statement of maximum number of units of two products to be produced and sold to maximize the resultant contribution**

	Aristocrat	**Deluxe**
Maximum possible production (in units) (Refer to working note 3)	6,800	8,500
Maximum resultant contribution (in ₹) (Refer to working notes 2)	2,10,800 (6,800 units × ₹ 31)	2,38,000 (8,500 units × ₹ 28)

Decision: The sale of 8,500 units of Deluxe model of product produces a resultant contribution of ₹ 2,38,000, which is maximum within the capacity and material constraints. Hence 8,500 units of Deluxe model of the product should be manufactured.

(*ii*) **Statement showing maximum contribution on the sale of Aristocrat or Deluxe models and hiring out the surplus capacity in department A and B**

	Aristocrat ₹	**Deluxe** ₹
Contribution on the sales of maximum possible production (Refer to working notes 2 and 3)	2,10,800	2,38,000
Contribution available on hiring the spare capacity		
(When 6,800 units of Aristocrat and 8,500 units of Deluxe model were manufactured and sold)		
Department A (Refer to working note 4)	Nil	34,000 (850 hours × ₹ 40)
Department B (Refer to working note 4)	67,200 (1, 120 hours × ₹ 60)	900 (15 hours × ₹ 60)
Total contribution	2,78,000	2,72,900

Decision: The above statement shows that the contribution of the company would be maximum ₹ 2,78,000 on sale of 6,800 units of Aristocrat model and hiring out the spare capacity of departments.

(iii) Statement showing contribution on the sale of 4,250 units of each model and hiring out the surplus capacity in departments A and B

	Aristocrat ₹	Deluxe ₹	Total
Contribution on the sale of 4,250 units of each model (Refer to working note 2)	1,31,750 (4,250 units × ₹ 31)	1,19,000 (4,250 units × ₹ 28)	2,50,750
Contribution available on hiring the surplus capacity (227.5 hours × ₹ 60)			13,650
Total contribution			2,64,400

Working Notes

1. **Variable cost (per unit):**

	Aristocrat ₹	Deluxe ₹
Direct material cost per unit	10,00 (2 kgs × 5)	10,00 (2 kgs × 5)
Variable costs:		
Department A	25.00 (0.50 hours × ₹ 50)	15.00 (0.30 hours × ₹ 50)
Department B	24.00 (0.40 hours × ₹ 60)	27.00 (0.45 hours × ₹ 60)
Total variable cost (per unit)	59.00	52.00

2. **Contribution (per unit):**

Selling price (per unit)	90.00	80.00
Less: Variable cost (per unit)	59.00	52.00
Contribution (per unit):	31.00	28.00

3. **Maximum possible production of each product (in units):**
(Under maximum capacity and material constraints)

	Department A	Department B
Maximum available hours	3,400	3,840

	Aristocrat	Deluxe
Maximum possible production (in units) (under maximum capacity constraint of each department)		
Department A	6,800 $\left(\frac{3{,}400 \text{ hours}}{0.5 \text{ hours}}\right)$	11,333 $\left(\frac{3{,}400 \text{ hours}}{0.3 \text{ hours}}\right)$
Department B	9,600 $\left(\frac{3{,}840 \text{ hours}}{0.4 \text{ hours}}\right)$	8,533 $\left(\frac{3{,}840 \text{ hours}}{0.45 \text{ hours}}\right)$

Maximum possible production (in units)	8,500	8,500
(By utilizing the available material)	$\left(\frac{17,000 \text{ kgs.}}{2 \text{ kgs.}}\right)$	$\left(\frac{17,000 \text{ kgs.}}{2 \text{ kgs.}}\right)$
Maximum possible production (in units) (Under capacity and material constraints)	6,800	8,500

4. Surplus capacity statement (in hours):

	Department A	Department B
Surplus capacity hours available	Nil	1,120
(When 6,800 units of Aristocrat model are produced)	(3,400 hours – (0.5 hours × 6,800 units)	(3,840 hours – (0.4 hours × 6,800 units)
Surplus capacity hours available	850	15
(When 8,500 units of Deluxe model are produced	(3,400 hours – (0.3 hours × 8,500 units)	(3,840 hours – (0.45 hours × 8,500 units)

5. Surplus capacity statement (in hours):

(On the production and sale of 4,250 units of each product)

	Aristocrat	Deluxe	Total
Hours utilized on the production of 4,250 units			
Department A	2,125 (4,250 units × 0.5 hours	1,275 (4,250 units × 0.3 hours)	3,400
Department B	1,700 (4,250 units × 0.4 hours)	1,912.5 (4,250 units × 0.45 hours)	3,612.5
Total hours	3,825	3,187.5	
Surplus capacity hours:			
Department A: (3,400 hours – 3,400 hours)		NIL	
Department B: (3,840 hours – 3,612.5 hours)		227.5	

Illustrative Problem 31

Bharat Seat Ltd. manufactures and sells one product–an infant car seat called Babycomfort–at a price of ₹ 500. Variable costs equal ₹ 200 per car seat. Fixed costs are ₹ 49,50,000. Bharat Seats Ltd. manufactures Babycomfort upon the receipt of orders from its customers. In year 1, it sold 30,000 units of Babycomfort. One of Bharat Seats Ltd. customers, Hyundai Motor Co., has asked if in year 2 Bharat Seats will manufacture a different style of car seat called Babyluxury. Hyundai will pay ₹ 250 for each unit of Babyluxury. The variable costs for Babyluxury are estimated at ₹ 150 per seat. Bharat Seats has enough capacity to manufacture all the units of Babycomfort it can sell as well as the units of Babyluxury that Huyndai wants and will thus incur no additional fixed costs. Bharat Seats estimates that in year 2 it will sell 30,000 units of Babycomfort (assuming the same price and variable costs in year 1) and 20,000 units of Babyluxury.

Siddharth, the president of Bharat Seats, checked the effect of accepting Hyundai's offer on the break-even revenues for year 2. Using the planned sales mix for year 2, he was surprisd to find that the revenues required to break even appeared to increase. He was not sure that his numbers were correct, but if they were, Siddharth felt inclined to reject Hyundai's offer. He asks for your advice.

Required:

(*i*) Calculate the break-even point in units and in revenues for year 1.

(*ii*) Calculate the break-even point in units and in revenues for year 2 at the planned sales mix.

(*iii*) Explain why the break-even point in revenues calculated in requirements (i) and (ii) are different.

(*iv*) Should Siddharth accept Hyundai's offer? Provide supporting computations.

(*M. Com., Delhi University*)

Solution:

(*i*) Break-even point in year 1 (units) = Fixed costs/Contribution margin per unit = ₹ 49,50,000/₹ 300 = 16,500 units

Break-even point in year 1 (in revenues) = 16,500 × ₹ 500 = ₹ 82,50,000

(*ii*) Break-even point in year 2 (in units)

Bharat Seats expects to sell 3 units of Babycomfort for every 2 units of Babyluxury in year 2, so consider a bundle consisting of 3 units of Babycomfort and 2 units of Babyluxury.

Unit contribution Margin from Babycomfort = ₹ 500 – 200 = ₹ 300

Unit contribution Margin from Babyluxury = ₹ 250 – 150 = ₹ 100

The contribution margin for the bundle is

₹ 300 × 3 units of Babycomfort + ₹ 100 × 2 units of Babyluxury = ₹ 1,100

So bundles to be sold to break-even = ₹ 49,50,000/1,100 = 4,500 bundles

Breakeven point in year 2 (in units)

Babycomfort, 4,500 × 3 = 13,500 units

Babyluxury, 4,500 × 2 = 9,000 units

Break-even point in revenues:

Babycomfort 13,500 units × ₹ 500 per unit	67,50,000
Babyluxury 9,000 unts × ₹ 250 per unit	22,50,000
Total	₹ 90,00,000

(*iii*) Contribution margin percentage in year 1 = Contribution margin per unit in year 1/Selling price in year 1

= ₹ 300/₹ 500 = 60 per cent

Contribution margin percentage in year 2 = Contribution margin of bundle in year 2/ Selling price of bundle in year 2

= ₹ 1,100/(3 × ₹ 500) + (2 × ₹ 250) = 1,100/2,000 = 55 per cent

The break-even point in year 2 increases because fixed costs are the same in both years but the contribution margin generated by each rupee of sales revenue at the given product mix decreases in year 2 relative to year 1.

(*iv*) Despite the breakeven sales revenue being higher, Bharat Seats should accept Hyundai's offer. The breakeven points are irrelevant because Bharat Seats is already above the break-even sales volume in year 1. By accepting Hyundai's offer, Bharat Seats has the ability to sell all the 30,000 units of Babycomfort in year 2 and make more sales of Babyluxury to Hyundai without incurring any more fixed costs.

Operating Income in year 2 with and without Babyluxury are expected to be as follows:

	Without Babyluxury	With Babyluxury
Sales	₹ 1,50,00,000	₹ 2,00,00,000 (₹ 500 × 30,000 + ₹ 250 × 20,000)
Variable costs	60,00,000	90,00,000 (₹ 200 × 30,000 + ₹ 150 × 20,000)
Contribution margin	90,00,000	1,10,00,000
Fixed costs	49,50,000	49,50,000
Operating income	40,50,000	60,50,000

Illustrative Problem 32

Tata Power produces the same power take off units in two plants, a new plant in Punjab and an older plant in Delhi. The Tata Power is expected to produce and sell 1,92,000 power takeoff units during the coming year. The following data are available for the two plants.

	Punjab		Delhi	
Selling price		₹ 15,000		₹ 15,000
Variable manufacturing cost per unit	₹ 7,200		₹ 8,800	
Fixed manufacturing cost per unit	3,000		1,500	
Variable marketing and distribution cost per unit	1,400		1,400	
Fixed marketing and distribution cost per unit	1,900		1,450	
Total cost per unit		13,500		13,150
Operating income per unit		1,500		1,850
Production rate per day	400 units		320 units	

All fixed costs per unit are calculated based on normal year consisting of 240 working days. When the number of working days exceeds 240, variable manufacturing costs increase by ₹ 300 per unit in Punjab and ₹ 800 per unit in Delhi. Capacity for each plant is 300 working days per year.

Wishing to take advantage of the higher operating income per unit at Delhi, Tata Power's manager has decided to manufactures 96,000 units at each plant. This production plan results in Delhi operating at capacity (320 units per day × 300 days) and Punjab operating at its normal volume (400 units per day × 240 days).

(*i*) Calculate the break-even point in units for the Punjab and Delhi plants.

(*ii*) Calculate the operating income that would result from the production manager's plan to produce 96,000 units at each plant.

(*iii*) Determine how the production of the 1,92,000 units should be allocated between Punjab and Delhi plants to maximize operating income for Tata Power. Show your calculations.

(*M. Com., Delhi University, 2012*)

Solution:

(*i*) **Calculation of Break-even Point in units**

Contribution Margin per unit calculation

Particulars	Punjab	Delhi
Selling price	15,000	15,000
Less: variable costs :		
Manufacturing	7,200	8,800
Marketing and distribution	1,400	1,400
Contribution margin per unit	₹ 6,400	₹ 4,800

Fixed Costs Calculation

Total fixed costs = (Fixed manufacturing costs per unit + Fixed marketing and distribution cost per unit) × Production rate per day × Normal working days

Punjab = (₹ 3,000 + 1,900) × 400 × 240 = ₹ 47,04,00,000

Delhi = (₹ 1,500 + 1,450) × 320 × 240 = ₹ 22,65,60,000

Break-even Calculation:

Break-even units = Fixed costs/Contribution margin per unit

Punjab = ₹ 47,04,00,000/6,400 = 73,500 units

Delhi = ₹ 22,65,60,000/4,800 = 47,200 units

(*ii*) The operating income that would result from the division production manager's plan to produce 96,000 units at each plant is ₹ 36,28,80,000. The normal capacity at the Punjab plant is 96,000 units (400 × 240); however, the normal capacity at the Delhi plant is 76,800 units (320 × 240). Therefore, 19,200 units (96,000 – 76,800) will be manufactured at Delhi at a reduced contribution margin of ₹ 4,000 per unit (4,800 – 800).

Contribution Margin per plant:

Punjab, 96,000 × ₹ 6,400	₹ 61,44,00,000
Delhi, 76,800 × ₹ 4,800	36,86,40,000
Delhi, 19,200 × ₹ 4,000	7,68,00,000
Total contribution margin	1,05,98,40,000
Deduct fixed costs ₹ 47,04,00,000 + 22,65,60,000	69,69,60,000
Operating income	36,28,80,000

(*iii*) The optimal production plan is to produce 1,20,000 units at the Punjab plant and 72,000 units at the Delhi plant. The full capacity of the Punjab plant, 1,20,000 units (400 units × 300 days), should be utilized as the contribution from these units is higher at all levels of production than the contribution from units produced at the Delhi plant:

Contribution Margin per plant:

Punjab, 96,000 × ₹ 6,400	₹ 61,44,00,000
Punjab, 24,000 × (₹ 6,400 – 300)	14,64,00,000
Delhi, 72,000 × ₹ 4,800	34,56,00,000
Total contribution margin	1,10,64,00,000
Deduct total fixed costs	69,69,60,000
Operating income	₹ 40,94,40,000

The contribution margin is higher when 1,20,000 units are produced at the Punjab plant and 72,000 units at the Delhi. As a result, operating income will also be higher in this case since total fixed costs for the division remain unchanged regardless of the quantity produced at each plant.

Illustrative Problem 33

Lavasa Manufacturing Company produces two products: squares and cirlces. The projected income for the coming year, segmented by product line, follows:

	Squares	Circles	Total
Sales	₹ 3,00,000	₹ 25,00,000	₹ 28,00,000
Less: Variable expenses	1,00,000	5,00,000	6,00,000
Contribution margin	₹ 2,00,000	₹ 20,00,000	₹ 22,00,000
Less: Direct fixed expenses	28,000	15,00,000	15,28,000
Product margin	1,72,000	5,00,000	6,72,000
Less: Common fixed expenses			1,00,000
Operating income			₹ 5,72,000

The selling prices are ₹ 30 for sqares and ₹ 50 for circles.

Required:

(*i*) Compute the number of units of each product that must be sold for the Company to break even.

(*ii*) Compute the revenue that must be earned to produce an operating income of 10 per cent of sales revenues.

(*iii*) Assume that the marketing manager changes the sales mix of the two products so that the ratio is three squares to five circles. Repeat Requirements (*i*) and (*ii*).

(*iv*) Refer to the original data. Suppose that Lavasa can increase the sales of squares with increased advertising. The extra advertising would cost an additional ₹ 45,000, and some of the potential purchasers of circles would switch to squares. In total, sales of squares would increase by 15,000 units, and sales of circles would decrease by 5,000 units. Would the company be better off with this strategy?

Solution:

(*i*) Sales mix:

Squares: ₹ 3,00,000/₹ 30 = 10,000 units
Circles: ₹ 25,00,000/₹ 50 = 50,000 units

Product	P	–	V*	=	P – V	×	Sales Mix	=	Total CM
Squares	₹ 30		₹ 10		₹ 20		1		₹ 20
Circles	50		10		40		5		200
Package									₹ 220

₹ 1,00,000/10,000 = ₹ 10

₹ 5,00,000/50,000 = ₹ 10

Break-even packages = ₹ 16,28,000/₹ 220 = 7,400 packages

Break-even squares = 7,400 × 1 = 7,400

Break-even circles = 7,400 × 5 = 37,000

(*ii*) Contribution margin ratio = ₹ 22,00,000/₹ 28,00,000 = 0.7857

0.10 Revenue = 0.7,857 Revenue – ₹ 16,28,000

0.6857 Revenue = ₹ 16,28,000

Revenue = ₹ 23,74,216

(*iii*) New mix:

Product	P –	V =	P – V ×	Sales Mix =	Total CM
Squares	₹ 30	₹ 10	₹ 20	3	₹ 60
Circles	50	10	40	5	200
Package					₹ 260

Break-even packages = ₹ 16,28,000/₹ 260 = 6,262 packages

Break-even squares = 6,262 × 3 = 18,786

Break-even circles = 6,262 × 5 = 31,310

CM ratio = ₹ 260/₹ 340* = 0.7647

*(3) (₹ 30) + (5) (₹ 50) = ₹ 340 revenue per package

0.10 Revenue = 0.7647 Revenue – ₹ 16,28,000

0.6647 Revenue = ₹ 16,28,000

Revenue = ₹ 24,49,225

(*iv*)		
	Increase in CM for squares (15,000 × ₹ 20)	₹ 3,00,000
	Decrease in CM for circles (5,000 × ₹ 40)	(2,00,000)
	Net increase in total contribution margin	₹ 1,00,000
	Less: Additional fixed expenses	45,000
	Increase in operating income	₹ 55,000

The company would gain ₹ 55,000 by increasing advertising for the squares. This is a good strategy.

Illustrative Problem 34

In 2010, the turnover of a company, which operated at a margin of safety of 25% amounted to ₹ 9,00,000 and profit volume ratio was 33%. During 2011, the company estimated that although the same volume of sales as 2010 would be maintained, the sales value would go down due to decrease in selling price. There will be no change in variable costs. The company proposes to reduce its fixed costs through an intensive cost reduction programme. These changes will alter the profit volume ratio and margin of safety to 30% and 40% respectively in 2011.

Even if the company closed down its operation in 2011, it would incur a minimum fixed cost of ₹ 50,000.

Required:

(*i*) Present a comparative statement indicating the sales, variable costs, fixed costs, and profit for 2010 and 2011.

(*ii*) At what minimum sales will the company be better off by locking up in business in 2011?

(*M. Com., Delhi,* 2008)

Solution:

Working Notes:

Year 2010 (₹)

Sales	9,00,000
Less: Variable cost	6,00,000
Contribution	3,00,000

Break-even sales

₹ 9,00,000 × 75/100 = ₹ 6,75,000

$$\text{P. V. ratio ₹ } \frac{3,00,000}{9,00,000} = 33.33\%$$

Fixed cost

$$\frac{\text{Fixed cost}}{\text{P V ratio}} = \text{Break-even sales}$$

B.E. Sales × PV ratio = Fixed cost

₹ 6,75,000 × 33.33% = ₹ 2,25,000

Profit = Contribution – Fixed cost

= ₹ 3,00,000 – ₹ 2,25,000 = ₹ 75,000

Year 2011

Let sales be x

Variable cost = ₹ 6,00,000

Contribution = x – ₹ 6,00,000

$$\text{PV ratio} = \frac{\text{Contribution}}{\text{Sales}}$$

$$\frac{30x}{100} = x - ₹\ 6,00,000$$

$$30x = 100\,x - 6,00,00,000$$

$$100x - 30x = 6,00,00,000$$

$$x = 6,00,00,000/70$$

∴ Sales = ₹ 8,57,143

(₹)

Sales	8,57,143
Less: Variable cost	6,00,000
Contribution	2,57,143

Break-even sales

₹ 8,57,143 × 60/100 = 5,14,286

Fixed cost

= Break-even sales × PV ratio

= ₹ 5,14,286 × 30/100 = 1,54,286

Profit

= Contribution – Fixed cost

= ₹ 2,57,143 — ₹ 1,54,286 = ₹ 1,02,857

(*i*) Comparative Statement indicating sales, variable costs, fixed costs, and profit

(₹)

Particulars	2010	2011
Sales	9,00,000	8,57,143
Less: Variable cost	6,00,000	6,00,000
Contribution	3,00,000	2,57,143
Less: Fixed cost	2,25,000	1,54,286
Profit	75,000	1,02,857

(*ii*) Calculation of minimum sales which will lock up minimum fixed cost of ₹ 50,000 in year 2011 when Company closed down its operation.

Relevant fixed cost = ₹ 1,54,286 – ₹ 50,000 = ₹ 1,04,286

PV ratio = 30%

Minimum sales required to recover relevant fixed cost

$$= \frac{\text{Contribution}}{\text{P V ratio}} = \frac{₹\,1,04,286}{0.30} = ₹\,3,47,620$$

Illustrative Problem 35

Calculate the effect of change in 'Sales Mix' from the following data:

	Products				
	M	***N***	***O***	***P***	***Total***
	₹	₹	₹	₹	₹
Sales	40,000	50,000	20,000	10,000	1,20,000
Variable Cost	24,000	34,000	16,000	4,000	78,000
Fixed Cost					29,400

The sales mix changed to:

	₹
M	30,000
N	44,000
O	40,000
P	6,000
	1,20,000

Solution:

(*a*) **Statement of Profit/Loss on Sales Mix — current**

Total	(₹)			*Products*	
	₹	*M*	*N*	*O*	*P*
(*i*) Sales	1,20,000	40,000	50,000	20,000	10,000
(*ii*) Variable Cost	78,000	24,000	34,000	16,000	4,000
(*iii*) Contribution (*i–ii*)	42,000	16,000	16,000	4,000	6,000
(*iv*) Fixed Cost	29,400				
(*v*) Profit (*iii–iv*)	12,600				
(*vi*) Percentage of contribution on Sales (P/V ratio)	35%	40%	32%	20%	60%

(*b*) **Statement of profit/loss due to change in Sales Mix**

	Total			*Products*	
		M	*N*	*O*	*P*
	₹	₹	₹	₹	₹
(*i*) Sales	1,20,000	30,000	44,000	40,000	6,000
(*ii*) Variable Cost	82,320	18,000	29,920	32,000	2,400
(*iii*) Contribution (*i–ii*)	37,680	12,000	14,080	8,000	3,600
(*iv*) Fixed Cost	29,400				
(*v*) Profit (*iii–iv*)	8,280				

Difference in Profit = ₹ 12,600 – 8,280 = ₹ 4,320

Note: Variable costs per rupee of sales are as follows:

M = ₹ 24,000 ÷ 40,000 = ₹ 0.60

N = ₹ 34,000 ÷ 50,000 = ₹ 0.68

O = ₹ 16,000 ÷ 20,000 = ₹ 0.80

P = ₹ 4,000 ÷ 10,000 = ₹ 0.40

It would be clear from the above two statements that due to change in Sales Mix the total profit has decreased by ₹ 4,320. The reasons are as follows:

(*i*) Sale of product P which makes maximum percentage of contribution on sales (i.e. ₹ 0.60 per rupee on sales) has dropped.

(*ii*) Similarly, sales of products M and N which make significant contribution to profit have also fallen resulting in a fall of profit.

(*iii*) Product whose sale has been increased makes a contribution of 20% on sales but it does not compensate the fall of profit.

The effect of variation in Sales Mix can be ascertained in a different manner as shown below:

(*c*) **Changed Sales Mix**

	Total	***Products***		***(₹)***	
	₹	*M*	*N*	*O*	*P*
(*i*) Sales	1,20,000	30,000	44,000	40,000	6,000
(*ii*) Percentage of contribution to sales (current)		40 %	32 %	20 %	60 %
(*iii*) Contribution (*i*× *ii*)	37,680	12,000	14,080	8,000	3,600
(*iv*) Current contribution	42,000	16,000	16,000	4,000	6,000
(*v*) Variation in contribution	(–)4,320	(–)4,000	(–)1,920	4,000	(–)2,400

Illustrative Problem 36

Partial income statements of Delhi University Dining Hall Food Service for the first two quarters of Year 2016 are as follows:

Partial Income Statements for First and Second Quarters of Year 2016

	First Quarter	**Second Quarter**
Sales at ₹ 36 per Meal (unit)	₹ 3,60,000	₹ 6,30,000
Total Costs	4,90,000	6,70,000
(Loss)	₹ (1,30,000)	₹ (40,000)

Each rupee of variable cost per meal comprises 50 per cent direct labor, 25 per cent direct materials, and 25 per cent variable overhead costs. University Dining Hall expects sales units, price per unit, variable cost per unit, and total fixed costs to remain at the same level during the third quarter as during the second quarter. University Dining Hall sold 17,500 meals in the second quarter.

(*a*) What is the quarterly break-even point in meals (units)?

(*b*) The dining hall has just received a special order from the university officials that requests 7,500 meals for visitors to campus at a price of ₹ 32 per meal (unit). If the dining hall accepts the order, it will not affect the regular market for 17,500 meals in the third quarter. The dining hall can produce the additional meals with existing capacity, but direct labor costs per meal will increase by 10 per cent for all meals produced because of the need to hire and use new labor. Fixed costs will increase by ₹ 30,000 per quarter if the dining hall accepts the new order. Should it accept the university officials' order?

(*c*) Assume that the dining hall accepts the order in part (*b*) What level of sales volume to student customers provides third-quarter profit of ₹ 68,000? (The third quarter would be just like the second quarter if the dining hall does not accept the university officials' order.)

Solution:

(*a*) First Quarter Sales = ₹ 3,60,000 / ₹ 36 = 10,000 Units.

Total Costs = Fixed Costs (F) + Variable Cost per Unit (V) × Unit Sales (X).

V = (₹ 6,70,000 – ₹ 4,90,000) / (17,500 – 10,000) = ₹ 24 per Unit.

F = ₹ 6,70,000 – (₹ 24 × 17,500) = ₹ 2,50,000.

Breakeven Point = ₹ 2,50,000 / (₹ 36 – ₹ 24) = 20,833 Units.

(*b*)

	University Officials Order Accepted	University Officials Order Not Accepted
Units	25,000	17,500
Revenue	₹ 8,70,000[a]	₹ 6,30,000
Variable Costs:		
Materials	(1,50,000)[b]	(1,05,000)[b]
Labor	(3,30,000)[c]	(2,10,000)[d]
Overhead	(1,50,000)	(1,05,000)
Fixed Costs	(2,80,000)[e]	(2,50,000)
Operating Profit (Loss)	₹ (40,000)	₹ (40,000)

[a]₹ 8,70,000 = ₹ 6,30,000 + (₹ 32 × 7,500).

[b]Amounts = ₹ .6 per meal × number of meals.

₹ 6 per meal = 25% of ₹ 24 variable cost per meal according to Part (a) of the solution.

[c]₹ 3,30,000 = ₹ 12 per meal × 1.1 for cost increase × 25,000 meals.

₹ 12 per meal = 50% of ₹ 24 variable cost per meal according to Part (a) of the solution.

[d]₹ 2,10,000 = ₹ 12 per meal × 17,500 meals.

[e]₹ 2,80,000 = ₹ 2,50,000 + ₹ 30,000 cost increase.

No change in Operating Profit (Loss) if the order is accepted.

(*c*) V = (₹ 1,50,000 + ₹ 3,30,000 + ₹ 1,50,000)/25,000 = ₹ 25.2 per unit.

Find X:

₹ 68,000 = ₹ 36X + ₹ 2,40,000 – ₹ 25.2X – ₹ 1,89,000 – ₹ 2,80,000

₹ 68,000 = ₹ 10.8X – ₹ 2,29,000

₹ 2,97,000 = ₹ 10.8X

X = ₹ 2,97,000/₹ 10.8

X = 27,500 student meals.

Illustrative Problem 37

Lighthouse Company, maker of quality flashlights, has experienced a steady growth in sales for the past five years. However, increased competition has led Mr. Das, the CEO, to believe that to maintain the company's present growth requires an aggressive advertising campaign next year. To prepare the next year's advertising campaign, the company's accountant has prepared and presented to Mr. Das the following data for the current year, Year 1:

Cost Schedule

Variable Costs:	
Direct Labor	₹ 10.00 per Flashlight
Direct Materials	4.50
Variable Overhead	2.00
Total Variable Costs	₹ 16.50 per Flashlight

Fixed Costs:	
Manufacturing	₹ 40,000
Selling	30,000
Administrative	80,000
Total Fixed Costs	₹ 1,50,000
Selling Price, per Flashlight	40.00
Expected Sales, Year 1 (25,000 Flashlights)	₹ 10,00,000
Tax Rate: 35 Per cent	

Mr. Das has set the sales target for year 2 at a level of ₹ 11,20,000 (or 28,000 flashlights).

Required:

(*a*) What is the projected after-tax operating profit for Year 1?

(*b*) What is the after-tax break-even point in units for Year 1?

(c) Mr. Das believes that to attain the sales target (28,000 flashlights) requires an additional selling expense of ₹ 40,000 for advertising in year 2, with all other costs remaining constant. What will be the after-tax operating profit for Year 2 if the firm spends the additional ₹ 40,000?

(*d*) What will be the after-tax break-even point in sales Rupees for Year 2 if the firm spends the additional ₹ 40,000 for advertising ?

(*e*) If the firm spends the additional ₹ 40,000 for advertising in Year 2, what is the sales level in Rupees required to equal Year 1 after-tax operating profit ?

(*f*) At a sales level of 28,000 units, what is the maximum amount the firm can spend on advertising to earn an after-tax operating profit of ₹ 75,000 ?

Solution:

(*a*)

Sales	₹ 10,00,000	(= ₹ 40 × 25,000)
Variable Costs	4,12,500	(= ₹ 16.50 × 25,000)
Contribution Margin	₹ 5,87,500	
Fixed Costs	1,50,000	
Before-Tax Profit	₹ 4,37,500	
Taxes (35% Rate)	1,53,125	
After-Tax Profit	₹ 2,84,375	

(*b*) Break-even in Units

$$= \frac{(\text{Fixed Costs})(1-t)}{(\text{Unit Contribution Margin})\ (1-t)}$$

$$= \frac{(₹150{,}000)(1-.35)}{(₹40-₹16.50)(1-.35)}$$

$$= ₹\,97{,}500/₹\,15.275$$

= 6,383 Units (Rounded)

(*c*)

Sales	₹ 11,20,000	(= ₹ 40 × 28,000)
Variable Costs	4,62,000	(= ₹ 16.50 × 28,000)
Contribution Margin	₹ 6,58,000	
Fixed Costs	1,90,000	(= ₹ 1,50,000 + ₹ 40,000)
Before-Tax Profit	₹ 4,68,000	
Taxes (35% Rate)	1,63,800	
After-Tax Profit	₹ 3,04,200	

(*d*) Break-even in Units $= \dfrac{(\text{Fixed Costs})(1-t)}{(\text{Unit Contribution Margin})(1-t)}$

= [₹ 1,90,000 (1 – 0.35)]/[(₹ 40 – ₹ 16.50)(1 – 0.35)]

= ₹ 1,23,500/₹ 15.275

= 8,085 Units (Rounded)

Break-even in Sales ₹ = Sales Units × Sales Price

= 8,085 × ₹ 40

= ₹ 3,23,400

(*e*) Target Profit in Units $= \dfrac{(\text{Fixed Costs + Target Profit})(1-t)}{(\text{Unit Contribution Margin})(1-t)}$

= [(₹ 1,90,000 + ₹ 4,37,500)(1 – 0.35)]/₹ 15.275

= ₹ 4,07,875/₹ 15.275

= 26,702 Units (Rounded)

Target Profit in Sales ₹ = Sales Units × Sales Price

= 26,702 × ₹ 40

= ₹ 10,68,080

(*f*)

Sales	₹ 11,20,000	(= ₹ 40 × 28,000)
Variable Costs	4,62,000	(= ₹ 16.50 × 28,000)
Contribution Margin	₹ 6,58,000	
Advertising Costs	?	
Other Fixed Costs	1,50,000	
Before-Tax Profit	₹ 1,15,385	[= ₹ 75,000/(1 – .35)]
Taxes (35% Rate)	40,385	
After-Tax Profit	₹ 75,000	

To find the maximum advertising cost to maintain after-tax profit of ₹ 75,000, solve as follows:

Contribution Margin (₹ 6,58,000) – Advertising Costs – Other Fixed Costs (₹ 1,50,000) = Before-Tax Profits (₹ 1,15,385)

₹ 6,58,000 – ₹ 1,50,000 – ₹ 1,15,385 = Advertising Costs

Maximum Advertising Costs = ₹ 3,92,615.

Illustrative Problem 38

Philips Radio Co. manufactures portable radios. Last year the firm sold 25,000 radios at ₹ 2500 each. Total costs amounted to ₹ 5,25,00,000 of which ₹ 1,50,00,000 were considered fixed. An activity-based costing study recently revealed that Radio's fixed costs include the following components:

	(₹)
Setup (40 setups at ₹ 40,000 per setup)	₹ 16,00,000
Engineering (500 hours at ₹ 2,500 per hour)	12,50,000
Inspection (1,000 inspections at ₹ 3000 per inspections)	30,00,000
General Factory overhead	61,50,000
Total	₹ 1,20,00,000
Fixed selling and administrative costs	30,00,000
Total	₹ 1,50,00,000

Management is considering both the installation of new, highly automated manufacturing equipment and a move toward just-in-time inventory and production management. If the new equipment is installed, setup will be quicker and less expensive. Under the proposed JIT approach, there would be 300 setups per year at ₹ 5000 per setup. Because a total quality programme would accompany the move toward JIT, only 100 inspections are anticipated at a cost of ₹ 4500 each.

After the installation of the new system, 800 hours of engineering would be required at ₹ 2800 per hour. General factory overhead would increase to ₹ 1,66,10,000, however, the automated equipment would allow the company, to cut its unit variable cost by 20 per cent. Finally, the overall improvement in product quality would support a selling price of ₹ 2600 per unit.

Required:

(*a*) Upon seeing the analysis given in the problem, Philip Radio's vice-president for manufacturing told to the controller, "I thought you told me this ₹ 1,50,00,000 cost was fixed. These don't look like fixed costs at all. What you're telling me now is that setup costs us ₹ 40,000 every time we start a production run. As company controller, you are required to prepare a brief explanation to the vice-president-manufacturing that clarifies the situation.

(*b*) Compute Philip Radio's new break-even point in units if the proposed automated equipment is installed.

(*c*) Calculate how many units Philip Radio, will have to sell to show a profit of ₹ 1,40,00,000 assuming the new technology is adopted.

(*d*) If Philip Radio adopts the new manufacturing technology, will its break-even point be higher or lower? Will the number of sales units required to earn a profit of ₹ 1,40,00,000 be higher or lower? Are the results in this case consistent with what you would typically expect to find in a modern high-tech manufacturing facility? Explain.

Solution:

(*a*) The ₹ 1,50,00,000 cost that has been characterized as "fixed" will not increase with increases in sales volume. However, as the activity-based costing analysis demonstrates, these costs are not fixed with respect to other important cost drivers. This is the difference between a traditional costing system and an ABC system. The latter recognizes that costs vary with respect to a variety of cost drivers, not just sales volume.

(*b*) New breakeven point if automated equipment is installed:

Sales price	₹ 2,600
Costs that are variable (with respect to sales volume):	
Unit variable cost [₹ 5,25,00,000 – ₹ 1,50,00,000 = ₹ 3,75,00,000; (₹ 3,75,00,000 × 0.8) ÷ 25,000 units]	1,200
Unit contribution margin	₹ 1,400
Costs that are fixed (with respect to sales volume):	
Setup (300 setups at ₹ 5000 per setup)	₹ 15,00,000
Engineering (800 hours at ₹ 2800 per hour)	22,40,000
Inspection (100 inspections at ₹ 4,500 per inspection)	4,50,000
General factory overhead	1,66,10,000
Total	₹ 2,08,00,000
Fixed selling and administration costs	30,00,000
Total	₹ 2,38,00,000

Break-even Point (in Units): Fixed Cost ÷ Unit Contribution Margin

₹ 2,38,00,000 ÷ ₹ 1400 = 17,000 units.

(*c*) Number of units = (Fixed Cost + Target Profit) ÷ Unit Contribution Margin

(₹ 2,38,00,000 + ₹ 1,40,00,000) ÷ ₹ 1400 = 27,000 units.

(*d*) If Philip Radio, adopts the new manufacturing technology:

1. The breakeven point will be higher (17,000 units instead of 15,000 units). The 15,000-unit figure is derived as follows:

   Unit variable cost = ₹ 1500 [= (₹ 5,25,00,000 – ₹ 1,50,00,000) ÷ 25,000 units]

   Unit contribution margin = ₹ 1000 (= ₹ 2500 – ₹ 1500).

   Breakeven units = 15,000 (= ₹ 1,50,00,000 ÷ ₹ 1000)

2. The number of units sold to show a profit of ₹ 1,40,00,000 will be lower than before (27,000 units instead of 29,000 units). The 29,000-unit figure is computed as follows: [(₹ 1,50,00,000 + ₹ 1,40,00,000) ÷ ₹ 1000].

3. These results are typical of situations where firms adopt advanced manufacturing equipment and practices. The breakeven point increases because of the increased fixed costs associated with the large investment in equipment. However, at higher levels of sales after fixed costs have been covered, the larger unit contribution margin (₹ 1400 instead of ₹ 1000) earns a profit at a faster rate. (The higher contribution is usually the result of increased operating efficiencies.) The overall outcome is that the firm needs to sell fewer units to reach a given target profit level.

Illustrative Problem 39

GoGo Juice is a combination gas station and convenience store that is located at a busy intersection. Recently, a national chain opened a similar store only a block away; consequently, sales have decreased for GoGo. In an effort to reclaim the lost sales, GoGo has implemented a promotional effort where for every ₹ 10 in sales, the customer receives a coupon worth ₹ 1 towards the next purchase of gasoline. The average gasoline customer purchases 15 gallons of gasoline at ₹ 1.129 per gallon, for a total sale of ₹ 16.94. This promotional effort should encourage the gasoline customer to purchase additional items, for a total sale of ₹ 20. At ₹ 20, the customer is entitled to two coupons rather than one. The results of an average month, prior to this coupon promotion, are shown in the chart below.

	Sales	Cost of sales
Gasoline	₹ 100,000	₹ 0.84675 per gallon
Food and beverages	60,000	60%
Other products	40,000	50%
		Other costs
Labor - station attendants		₹ 9,000
Labor - supervision		2,500
Rent, power, supplies, interest, and miscellaneous		46,500
Depreciation (pumps, computers, counters, fixtures, and building)		2,500

Not included in the costs shown in the chart is the monthly cost of printing the coupons which is estimated to be ₹ 500. Coupons are issued on the basis of total purchases regardless of whether the purchases are paid in cash or paid by redeeming coupons. Assume that coupons are distributed to customers for 80 per cent of the total sales. Also assume that all coupons distributed are used to purchase gasoline.

Required:

A. If GoGo Juice implements the promotional coupon effort, calculate the profit (loss) before tax if the sales volume remains constant and the coupons are used to purchase gasoline. Assume the product mix, percentage of gasoline, food and beverages, and other products, remains the same.

B. Calculate the break-even sales for GoGo Juice if the promotional effort is implemented. Assume that the product mix will remain constant.

C. Disregarding your responses to Requirements A. and B., assume the weighted contribution margin, after implementation of the coupon program, is 30 percent. Calculate the profit (loss) before tax for GoGo Juice, assuming sales increase 20 per cent due to the new program. Assume that the sales mix remains constant.

D. GoGo Juice is considering using sensitivity analysis in combination with cost-volume-profit analysis. Discuss the use of sensitivity analysis with cost-volume-profit analysis. Include in your discussion at least three factors that make sensitivity analysis prevalent in decision making. *(CMA., USA, Adapted with permission)*

Solution:

A. GoGo Juice's profit (loss) before tax, from implementing the promotional coupon offer with no change in sales volume is (₹ 8,000), as calculated below.

	Gasoline	Food and Beverage	Other	Total
Sales Revenue	₹ 100,000	₹ 60,000	₹ 40,000	₹ 200,000
Coupons Redeemed	(16,000)(1)			(16,000)
Cost of Sales	75,000(2)	36,000	20,000	131,000
Contribution Margin	₹ 9,000	₹ 24,000	₹ 20,000	53,000

Fixed Costs	61,000(3)
Loss Before Tax	₹ (8,000)

(1) Coupons redeemed:

Total sales ₹ 200,000 × 80% distribution × 10% (₹ 1 off for every ₹ 10 purchased) = ₹ 16,000.

(2) Gasoline Cost of Sales:

₹ 100,000 sales ÷ ₹ 1.129 price per gallon = 88,574 gallons.

88,574 gallons × ₹ 0.84675 per gallon = ₹ 75,000.

(3) Fixed Costs:

Labor-station attendants	₹ 9,000
Labor-supervision	2,500
Rent, power, supplies, etc.	46,500
Depreciation (pumps, etc.)	2,500
Coupon printing cost	500
Total Fixed Costs	₹ 61,000

B. The break-even sales for GoGo Juice, if the promotional effort is implemented, is ₹ 2,30,189, calculated as follows.

Current contribution margin ratio = ₹ 53,000 ÷ ₹ 200,000 = 26.5%

Break-even sales = Fixed costs ÷ Contribution margin ratio

= ₹ 61,000 ÷ .265

= ₹ 2,30,189

C. Profit before tax, assuming a 20 per cent sales increase and a 30 per cent wighted contribution margin, would be ₹ 11,000, calculated as follows.

Sales revenue	(₹ 200,000 × 1.20)	₹ 240,000
Contribution margin	(₹ 240,000 × 30%)	₹ 72,000
Less: Fixed costs		61,000
Profit before tax		₹ 11,000

D. Sensitivity analysis is used to deal more effectively with uncertainty or risk. Sensitivity analysis is a "What-if" type of analysis used to determine the outcome if any parameters change from the initial assumptions. *For example*, revenues or costs could be changed from the initial assumptions and a new break-even sales volume calculated.

At least three factors that make sensitivity analysis prevalent in decision making includes the following.

- The availability of computers and spreadsheet software has made it very quick and easy to compute the impact of changing one or more assumptions in a financial model.
- As the business environment is becoming more dynamic and competitive, sensitivity analysis provides managment with an understanding of the impact of changes in the environment. The increased emphasis on productivity, competitive market place, changing consumer demand, shorter product life cycle times, and faster obsolescence of technology makes senstivity analysis more prevalent.

- Sensitivity analysis aids management in identifying the key variables and assumptions, so the variables can be monitored or a decision made to obtain additional information on them.

Illustrative Problem 40

After several stagnant years, Kimbeth Heating and Cooling (KHC) is actively pursuing new business. KHC operates a single manufacturing facility which produces the firm's two product lines, heating and cooling systems for residential and commercial use. KHC is competing with another firm to become the second largest supplier of heating and cooling systems in North America. Bill Roberts, general manager and former controller of Commercial systems, is particularly interested in the company's goal to expand the commercial product line as his bonus would be directly affected by this growth.

Ann Tremont was recently named Chief Operating Officer (COO) following the retirement of her predecessor. Aware of the upcoming opportunities in the construction industry, Tremont has asked Roberts to work with Barbara Chase, a new assistant controller reporting to Roberts, to develop current product line costs and sales projections for the next fiscal year. Roberts had already prepared the information shown below. KHC uses the straight line method of depreciation for all of its assets and has an effective income tax rate of 40 percent.

	Residential Systems	***Commercial Systems***
Estimated unit sales	37,500	12,500
Per unit		
Average price	₹ 5,000	₹ 25,000
Variable manufacturing cost	3,000	16,000*
Variable selling cost	1,000	4,000
* Represents a ₹ 2,000 per unit savings resulting from the expected purchase of new equipment.		
Number of units required for break–even operations	15,000	5,000
Fixed costs		
Product costs	₹ 2,40,00,000 **	
Selling cost	1,10,00,000	
General & administrative costs	50,00,000	
Expected after-tax income	₹ 3,60,00,000	

** Includes ₹ 12,50,000 annual depreciation for new equipment expenditures of ₹ 50,00,000 for the commercial product line.

Unfamiliar with KHC's product lines and costs, Chase spoke with several engineering and sales personnel to gather information. Subsequent to these meetings, Chase approached Roberts with the following suggested modifications to his report.

- The projected sales should be 40,000 residential units and 10,000 commercial units.

- Engineering reports provided by the manufacturer of the proposed new equipment for the commercial product line indicate that the variable manufacturing cost should be approximately ₹ 17,000 per commercial unit, not the ₹ 16,000 included in Roberts projections.
- Engineering personnel believe that a 20 per cent savings per unit of variable manufacturing costs could be achieved for the residential units if new four-year life robotics equipment were purchased for this line. The new equipment could be obtained at 28 per cent of the ₹ 50,00,000 that Roberts proposes to spend on the commercial line. (KHC's Board of Directors will not approve two major capital equipment improvements in the same fiscal year. Thus, only one of the two product lines will have robotics equipment installed in this budget period).

After reviewing this data, Roberts told Chase that her suggested modifications were incorrect because many of the people she interviewed were new to KHC and did not adequately understand the process. In addition, the senior people she consulted on the residential product line were resistant to the success of the commercial product line. Accordingly, Roberts told Chase to assist him in preparing the presentation using the information he had originally developed and not to mention her reservations about his projections again.

Required:

Although directed differently, Barbara Chase wants to revise Bill Roberts' analysis using her revisions from the data she gathered on Kimbeth Heating and Cooling (KHC).

1. Assume that Roberts purchases the equipment for the commercial line. Compute KHC's expected after-tax income.
2. Assume instead that Roberts purchases the equipment for the residential line. Compute KHC's expected after-tax income.
3. Without prejudice to your response to Requirement 2, assume that Roberts purchases the equipment for the residential line only and makes some minor changes to fixed costs, resulting in total fixed costs of ₹ 3,81,00,000. If the sales mix remains constant, determine the number of units needed from each product line for KHC to achieve an after-tax income of ₹ 4,20,00,000. *(CMA, USA, Adapted with permission)*

Solution:

1. Assuming that Kimbeth Heating and Cooling (KHC) purchases the equipment for the commercial line, the expected after-tax income of ₹ 2,40,00,000 is computed as follows.

Calculation of Contribution Margins

	Residential	***Commercial***
Estimated sales units (1)	40,000	10,000
Variable unit costs:		
Manufacturing	₹ 3,000	₹ 17,000 (2)
Selling	1,000	4,000
Total variable cost	4,000	21,000
Sales price	5,000	25,000
Contribution margin	1,000	4,000

(1) Revised volume estimate
(2) Revised manufacturing cost from selling new equipment

Calculation of Fixed Costs

Fixed costs = ₹ 2,40,00,000 + ₹ 1,10,00,000 + ₹ 50,00,000 = ₹ 4,00,00,000

Calculation of After-tax Income

After-tax income = (Contribution margin – Fixed cost) × (1 – tax rate)
= [₹ 1,000 (40,000) + ₹ 4,000 (10,000) – ₹ 4,00,00,000] × (1– .40)
= [₹ 4,00,00,000 + ₹ 4,00,00,000 – ₹ 4,00,00,000] × .60
= ₹ 4,00,00,000 × .60
= ₹ 2,40,00,000

2. Assuming that KHC purchases the equipment for the residential line, the expected after-tax income of ₹ 3,29,40,000 is computed as follows.

Calculation of Contribution Margins

Residential:

Revised variable manufacturing cost = ₹ 3,000 – (₹3,000 × .20) = ₹ 2,400
Revised contribution margin = ₹ 1,000 + ₹ 600 = ₹ 1,600

Commercial:

Revised variable manufacturing cost = ₹ 16,000 + ₹ 2,000 = ₹ 18,000 without benefit of new equipment
Revised contribution margin = ₹ 4,000 – 1,000 = ₹ 3,000

Calculation of Differential Fixed Cost

Residential equipment = (₹ 50,00,000 × .28) ÷ ₹ 4 years = ₹ 3,50,000 depreciation/year
Differential fixed cost = ₹ 4,00,00,000 – ₹ 12,50,000 + ₹ 3,50,000 = ₹ 3,91,00,000

Calculation of After-Tax Income

After-tax income = [₹ 1,600 (40,000) + ₹ 3,000 (10,000) – ₹ 3,91,00,000] × (1– .40)
= (₹ 6,40,00,000 + ₹ 3,00,00,000 – ₹ 3,91,00,000) × .60
= ₹ 5,49,00,000 × .60
= ₹ 3,29,40,000

3. Assuming a sales mix of four residential units to one commercial unit, then 11,500 commercial units and 46,000 residential units will be needed to achieve an after-tax income of ₹ 4,20,00,000, computed as follows.

Calculation of Contribution Margin

Contribution margin = After-tax net income + tax + fixed costs
Tax = [₹ 4,20,00,000/ (1– .40)] – ₹ 4,20,00,000 = ₹ 2,80,00,000
Contribution margin = ₹ 4,20,00,000 + ₹ 2,80,00,000 + ₹ 3,81,00,000 = ₹ 10,81,00,000

Calculation of Number of units of Each Product Line needed

4X (Residential contribution margin) + 1X (Commercial contribution margin) = ₹ 10,81,00,000

4X (₹1,600) + X (₹ 3,000) = ₹ 10,81,00,000

₹ 9,400X = ₹ 10,81,00,000

X = 11,500 commercial units

4X = 46,000 residential units.

REFERENCES

1. Lane K. Anderson and Harold M. Sollenberger, *Managerial Accounting,* South Western Publishing Co. 1992, pp. 156-157.
2. Edward J. Blocher, Kung H. Chen, Gàry Cokins and Thomas W. Lin, *Cost Management,* Tata McGraw Hill Publishing Co. Ltd., 2006, pp. 240-241.
3. T. Lucy, *Management Accounting,* 2000, p. 297.
4. T. Lucy, *Ibid,* p. 297.

CRITICAL ANALYSIS AND DISCUSSION QUESTIONS, SELF-ASSESSMENT QUESTIONS, MULTIPLE CHOICE QUESTIONS, PROBLEMS AND CASES

CRITICAL ANALYSIS AND DISCUSSION QUESTIONS

1. Explain cost-volume-profit analysis. What are its assumptions?
2. Discuss the types of analyses undertaken under CVP analysis.
3. Describe the components of a break-even chart.
4. How does a P/V graph differ from break-even chart? Which form of presentation is superior.
5. Discuss the following terms:
   (*a*) Key factor,
   (*b*) P/V ratio, and
   (*c*) margin of safety.
6. (*a*) What do you understand by the term margin of safety with reference to volume of production?
   (*b*) How do the following reflect on a break-even volume and on a P/V ratio: (*i*) increase in total fixed cost: (*ii*) increase in total physical sales, (*iii*) decrease in variable costs per unit?
7. What do you understand by the term "break-even analysis"? Enumerate its uses.
8. Discuss the uses of CVP analysis and its significance to management.
9. "The contribution approach is the foundation of CVP logic and related techniques." Discuss.
10. Discuss the role of contribution in marginal costing in decisions relating to fixation of selling price.
11. State with reasons whether the following propositions are correct:
    (*a*) In an undertaking with a high fixed cost, break-even point can be attained at a lower level of activity.
    (*b*) Profit is represented by the product of the margin of safety and the P/V ratio.
    (*c*) In relation to normal sales, a low margin of safety along with a high P/V ratio is generally an indication of high fixed costs.
12. "The effect of a price reduction is always to reduce the P/V ratio, to raise the break-even point, and to shorten the margin of safety." Explain with a suitable illustration.
13. Define break-even point. How can the break-even point be computed?
14. How is a break-even chart prepared? What information does the break-even chart give?
15. For product-mix decisions, what criteria can be used to select product that will maximise net income?
16. "Break-even analysis assumes that variable costs and revenues are linear and that fixed costs are fixed. "Briefly explain why these assumptions may not be realistic.
    (*M.Com., Delhi*, 2003)
17. A well-known writer commenting on the break-even chart said: "It (the break-even chart) must be applied with an intelligent discrimination. with an adequate grasp of the

assumptions underlying the technique and of the limitations surrounding its practical applications." Expand on this statement giving illustrations of the points which the writer has in mind.

18. Briefly explain the uses of break-even analysis in business. Give real life illustration.
19. Examine the concept of Margin of Safety and give its uses for decision-making. *(M.Com., Delhi)*
20. Briefly explain the limitations of break-even analysis. *(M. Com., Delhi)*
21. Using imaginary figures, explain and illustrate the calculation of break-even point in a multi product situation. *(M. Com., Delhi)*
22. The accountant's approach to cost volume profit analysis has been criticised in that, among other matters, it does not deal with the following:
    (*a*) situations where sales volume differs radically from production volume.
    (*b*) situations where the sales revenue and the total cost functions are marked by non-linear.
    (*c*) changes in product mix.
    (*d*) risk and uncertainty.
    Explain these objections to the accountant's conventional cost-volume-profit model and suggest how they can be overcome or ameliorated.
23. What is the meaning of a break-even point where multiple products are present? Explain the meaning in terms of individual products.
24. What is operating leverage? How can it work against a company?
25. Explain why contribution margin per unit becomes profit per unit above the break-even point.
26. Explain how CVP analysis developed for single product can be used in a multiple product setting.
27. Explain how a change in sales mix can change a company's break-even point.
28. If a firm's degree of operating leverage is 3 and it experiences a 20 per cent increase in sales, by what percentage will the firm's profits increase?
29. (*a*) How is operating leverage computed? What does operating leverage measure?
    (*b*) Does a high operating leverage indicate that a small increase in sales will yield a large increase or a small increase in profit?
30. Compare cost-voulme-profit analysis with profit-volume analysis. How do they differ?
31. Fixed costs are often defined as "fixed over the short run." Does this mean that they are not fixed over the long run? Why or why not?
32. What effect could the following changes, occurring independently, have on (*i*) break-even point (*ii*) contribution margin and expected profit?
    (*a*) An increase in fixed costs.
    (*b*) A decrease in wage rates applicable to direct, strictly variable labour.
    (*c*) An increase in the selling price of the product.
    (*d*) An increase in production volume.
33. "The assumption of linearity of costs negates much of the usefulness of the accountant's work in the area of cost-volume-profit analysis." Discuss.

34. Compare and contrast the break-even chart and the profit-volume chart as providers of useful information to management.
35. Discuss the economist's contribution to cost-volume-profit analysis.
36. Discuss the practical problems involved in using break-even charts and profit-volume charts for multiproduct firms.
37. "In CVP analysis, gross margin is a less useful concept than contribution margin." Do you agree? Explain.
38. "Cost volume-profit analysis is an over simplification of the real world. For this reason, it has little to offer to a decision marker." Comment.
39. Why is CVP analysis a short-run tool? Why is it inappropriate as a long-run model?
40. "In CVP analysis, gross margin is a less useful concept than contribution margin." Do you agree? Explain.
41. When sales volume increases, which company will experience a larger percentage increase in profit: Company X which has mostly fixed expenses or Company Y. which has mostly variable expenses?
42. Explain how activity-based costing (ABC) affects cost-volume profit analysis.
43. Your classmate is having trouble with CVP analysis and asks for your help. He has the following comments:

    "How can CVP analysis work when you really do not know what is going to happen? You might change your selling price. Your suppliers might change their prices. Inflation can cause other costs to go up. You might not sell the number of units you need to sell in order to earn a target profit. All sorts of things can happen that can invalidate your calculations." Answer your classmate's questions.
44. "The relevant range pertains to fixed costs, not variable costs." Do you agree. Explain.
45. If a new product does not require any new fixed costs because the company utilizes the existing capacity of facilities and personnel, what is the breakeven point?
46. Is CVP analysis used in profit planning, cost planning or revenue planning?
47. How is CVP analysis is used to calculate the breakeven point for multiple products?
48. Explain why contribution margin per unit becomes profit per unit above the breakeven point.
49. Define the term margin of safety. Explain how it can be used as a crude measure of operating risk?
50. Why does the activity-based costing approach to CVP analysis offer more insight than the conventional approach?
51. Both, A Company and B Company had the same sales, total costs and income from operations for the current financial year, yet A Company had a lower break even point than B Company. Explain the reason for this difference in breakeven points.
52. If companies that are operating below the breakeven points can not raise prices, what must they do to breakeven?
53. Which action has a greater effect on the unit contribution margin: (1) increasing the unit selling price by 10% or (2) reducing the unit variable cost by 10%?
54. We could readily extend CVP analysis to consider cash breakeven by considering cash fixed costs only. That is, we exclude noncash items such as depreciation from the analysis. Which kinds of firms would value this approach?

55. If fixed costs increase, but the unit contribution margin stays the same, can we calculate the additional volume needed to break even by dividing the change in fixed costs by the unit contribution margin? Why or why not?
56. Could we modify the CVP relation to include step costs? What complications might arise in the context of CVP analysis with step costs?
57. Is the contribution margin ratio of a software firm such as Infosys Ltd. likely to be higher or lower than the contribution margin ratio of an auto maker such Hundai? What does this imply about the sensitivity of profit to sales?
58. How might managers use the margin of safety concept in decision making?
59. Why does operating leverage decrease as sales volume increases?
60. Why is operating leverage viewed as a measure of risk?
61. Consider a large multidivisional firm such as ITC or HUL Ltd. Does it make sense to perform CVP analysis for such firms as a whole? More generally, how could such firms use CVP insights effectively?

SELF-ASSESSMENT QUESTIONS

A. The following statements relate to cost-volume-profit analysis. Indicate whether each statement is true or false and write a brief explanation supporting your answer.

(*a*) Break-even calculations have little practical value because most managers have to do better than break-even.

(*b*) If you decided to rent a truck for ₹ 36,000 a year for all mileage up to 10,000 and 10 p. for each additional mile, user rental would be a semivariable cost of the user.

(*c*) If fixed costs are ₹ 5,00,000 a year, variable costs are ₹ 15 per unit, and the selling price is ₹ 20 per unit, it will be necessary to sell 1,00,000 units to break-even.

(*d*) The main purpose of cost-volume-profit analysis is to pinpoint the position at which the firm neither makes a profit nor suffers a loss.

(*e*) Data for break-even analysis can be taken directly from the conventionally prepared (absorption cost) income statement.

(*f*) A successful business manager should set a goal of achieving the break-even point in each period's operations.

B. The following statements relate to several concepts of cost-volume-profit relationships. Indicate whether you agree or disagree with each statement and give a brief explanation supporting your answer.

(*a*) The variable cost ratio is determined by dividing sales revenue by variable costs, and the ratio is the component of the contribution margin ratio.

(*b*) Break-even sales in units can be computed by dividing total fixed costs by the contribution margin per unit.

(*c*) The break-even chart can be regarded as a dynamic analysis in the sense that total fixed costs and the relationship between variable costs and sales revenue will hold true for any and all levels of sales.

(*d*) In applying cost-volume-profit analysis, managers should understand that an increase in fixed costs will cause both the break-even point and the contribution margin ratio to increase.

(*e*) A fundamental concept in cases of multiple products is that changes in the break-even point are casued by changes in sales prices and are not affected by any changes in the sales mix of the various products.

C. For each of the following numbered items, identify the item in the right-hand column that best matches the numbered item. No item in the right-hand column should be used more than once.

1. Indicate the point at which the company neither makes a profit nor incurs a loss.	(*a*) Relevant range
2. A graphic analysis of the relationship of costs and sales revenue to profit.	(*b*) Unit profit volume graph
3. Determined by dividing the contribution margin by sales revenue.	(*c*) Departmentalization
4. Determined by dividing total fixed costs by the contribution margin ratio.	(*d*) Cost-volume profit analysis
5. The amount of total fixed costs and unit variable costs, as well as the slope of the revenue line, are meaningful only within this area.	(*e*) Variable costs
6. When a shift in this aspect occurs, a change in profit can also be expected using the same contribution margin ratio.	(*f*) Break-even chart
7. Determined by dividing fixed costs by the contribution margin per unit.	(*g*) Price Reduction
8. Indicates how much sales may decrease from a particular sales figure before a loss is incurred.	(*h*) Break-even analysis.
9. The margin of safety expressed as a percentage of sales.	(*i*) Margin of safety ratio
10. This change will not necessarily lead to an increase in volume sufficient to increase profits.	(*j*) Contribution
11. A measure of the effect of price changes on volume sold.	(*k*) Sales mix
12. Products make a favourable contribution as long as the sales revenue exceeds this.	(*l*) Break-even point in rupees.
	(*m*) Elasticity of demand
	(*n*) Break-even point in units
	(*o*) Break-even point

D. A Company sold 1,00,000 units of its product at ₹ 20 per unit. Variable costs are ₹ 14 per unit (manufacturing costs of ₹ 11 and selling costs of ₹ 3). Fixed costs are incurred uniformly throughout the year and amount to ₹ 7,92,000 (manufacturing costs of ₹ 5,00,000 and selling costs of ₹ 292,000). There are no beginning or ending inventories.

(*i*) The break–even point for this product is

(*a*) ₹ 36,40,000 or 1,82,00 units (*b*) ₹ 26,00,000 or 1,30,000 units

(*c*) ₹ 18,00,000 or 90,000 units (*d*) ₹ 17,60,000 or 88,000 units

(*e*) None of the above.

(ii) The number of units that must be sold to earn a net income of ₹ 60,000 for the year before income taxes would be

(a) 1,42,000 (b) 1,32,000
(c) 1,00,000 (d) 38,000

(iii) If the income tax rate is 40%, the number of units that must be sold to earn an after-tax income of ₹ 90,000 would be

(a) 1,69,000 (b) 1,57,000
(c) 1,44,000 (d) 1,04,777
(e) None of the above

(iv) If labour costs are 50% of variable costs and 20% of fixed costs, a 10 % increase in wages and salaries would increase the number of units required to break-even (in fraction form) to

(a) 8,07,840/5.3 (b) 8,31,600/5.78
(c) 8,07,600/14.7 (d) 8,31,600/14.28
(e) None of the above.

E. The following data pertain to two types of products manufactured by a company:

	Per Unit	
	Sales Price	**Variable Costs**
Product Y	₹ 120	₹ 70
Product Z	₹ 500	₹ 200

Fixed costs total ₹ 3,00,000 annually. The expected mix in units is 60 per cent for product Y and 40 per cent for product Z.

(i) How much is break-even sales in units?

(a) 857 (b) 1,111
(c) 2,000 (d) 2,459

(ii) How much is break-even sales in rupees?

(a) ₹ 3,00,000 (b) ₹ 4,20,000
(c) ₹ 4,75,000 (d) ₹ 5,44,000

F. Bimal Electronic Co., is developing a new product, surge protectors for high-voltage electrical flows. The following cost information relates to the product.

	Unit Costs
Direct meaterials	₹ 325
Direct labour	₹ 400
Distribution	75

The company will also be absorbing ₹ 1,20,00,000 of additional fixed costs associated with this new product. A corporate fixed charge of ₹ 20,00,000 currently absorbed by other products will be allocated to this new product:

(i) If the selling price is ₹ 1,400 per unit, the break-even point in units (rounded to the nearest hundred) for surge protectors is

(a) 8,500 units (b) 10,000 units
(c) 15,000 units (d) 20,000 units
(e) 23,300 units

(ii) How many surge protectors (rounded to the nearest hundred) must Bimal Electronics sell at a selling price of ₹ 1,400 per unit to gain ₹ 30,00,000 additional income before taxes?

(a) 10,700 units (b) 12,100 units
(c) 20,000 units (d) 25,000 units
(e) 28,300 units

(iii) How many surge protectors (rounded to the nearest hundred) must Bimal Electronics sell at a selling price of ₹ 1,400 per unit to increase after-tax income by ₹ 30,00,000? Bimal Electronics effective income tax rate is 40 percent.

(a) 10,700 units (b) 12,100 units
(c) 20,000 units (d) 25,000 units
(e) 28,300 units

(CMA, USA, Adapted with permission)

Answer: F.

(i) (d) (ii) (d) (iii) (e)

MULTIPLE CHOICE QUESTIONS

Select the correct answer for the following multiple choice questions:

1. Contribution margin is known as
   (a) Marginal income (b) Gross profit
   (c) Net income (d) Net profit
2. The break-even analysis may be described as
   (a) Comparison between production and sales
   (b) Comparison to make out capacity utilisation
   (c) Comparison between target set and actual achievement
   (d) Comparison between sales and costs
3. An increase in sales price
   (a) Does not affect the break-even point
   (b) Lowers the net profit
   (c) Increase the break-even point
   (d) Lowers the break even point
4. A decrease in sales price
   (a) Does not affect the break-even point
   (b) Lowers the net profit
   (c) Increases the break-even point
   (d) Lowers the break-even point
5. Fixed cost per unit decreases when
   (a) Production volume increases
   (b) Production volume decreases
   (c) Variable cost per unit decreases
   (d) Prime cost per unit decreases
6. Margin of safety is referred to as
   (a) Excess of budgeted or actual sales over the variable expenses and fixed expenses, at break-even.

(*b*) Excess of budgeted or actual sales revenue over the fixed expenses
(*c*) Excess of actual sales over budgeted sales
(*d*) Excess of sales revenue over the variable expenses

7. The most useful information desired from a break-even chart is the
(*a*) Amount of sales revenue needed to cover variable costs
(*b*) Amount of sales revenue needed to cover fixed costs
(*c*) Relationship among revenues, variable costs and fixed costs of various levels of activity
(*d*) Volume or output level at which the enterprise breaks even

8. Each of the following would affect the break-even point except a change in the
(*a*) Number of units sold (*b*) Variable cost per unit
(*c*) Total fixed costs (*d*) Sales price per unit

9. The method of cost accounting that lends itself to break-even analysis is
(*a*) Variable (marginal) (*b*) Standard
(*c*) Absolute (*d*) Absorption

10. Cost-volume profit analysis allows management to determine relative profitability of a product by
(*a*) Highlighting potential bottlenecks in the production process
(*b*) Keeping fixed costs to an absolute minimum
(*c*) Determining contribution margin per unit and projected profits at various levels of production
(*d*) Assigning costs to a product in a manner that maximises the contribution margin

11. To obtain the break-even point in rupees, total fixed costs are divided by which of the following:
(*a*) Variable cost per unit
(*b*) Fixed cost per unit
(*c*) Variable cost per unit ÷ sales price per unit
(*d*) (Sales price per unit – Variable cost per unit) ÷ sales price per unit

12. Given the following notations, what is the break-even sales in rupees?
(*a*) $\frac{SP}{FC - VC}$ (*b*) $\frac{VC}{SP - FC}$
(*c*) $\frac{FC}{VC - SP}$ (*d*) $\frac{FC}{\frac{SP - VC}{SP}}$

13. Which of these alternative would generally decrease contribution margin
(*a*) A 15% increase in selling price (*b*) A 15% increase in variable expense
(*c*) A 15% decrease in variable expense (*d*) A 15% decrease in fixed expense

14. If fixed expenses decrease while variable expense per unit remains constant, the new contribution margin in relation to the old will be
(*a*) Unchanged (*b*) Higher
(*c*) Lower (*d*) Indeterminate
(*e*) None of the above

15. Cost volume-earnings analysis includes some inherent, simplifying assumptions. Which of the following is not one of these assumptions?
    (*a*) Cost and revenues are predictable and are linear over the relevant range
    (*b*) Variable costs fluctuate proportionally with volume
    (*c*) Changes in beginning and ending inventory levels are insignificant in amount.
    (*d*) Sales mix changes as fixed costs increase beyond the relevant range
16. The cost-volume-profit analysis underlying the conventional break-even chart does not assume that
    (*a*) Price will remain fixed
    (*b*) Production will equal sales
    (*c*) Some costs vary inversely with volume
    (*d*) Cost are linear and continuous over the relevant range
17. Which of the following would cause the break-even to change ?
    (*a*) Sales units increased
    (*b*) Total production units decreased
    (*c*) Total variable costs increased as a function of higher production
    (*d*) Fixed costs increased due to addition to physical plant
18. If the fixed costs for a product decrease and the variable costs (as a percentage of sales) decrease, what will be the effect on the contribution margin ratio and the break-even point, respectivley?

	Contribution Margin Ratio	***Break-even Point***
(*a*)	Decreased	Increased
(*b*)	Increased	Decreased
(*c*)	Decreased	Decreased
(*d*)	Increased	Increased

19. If the fixed costs attendant to a product increase while variable costs and sales price remain constant what will happen to (1) contribution margin and (2) break-even point?

	Contribution Margin Ratio	***Break-even Point***
(*a*)	Unchanged	Increase
(*b*)	Unchanged	Unchanged
(*c*)	Increase	Decreased
(*d*)	Decrease	Increase

20. The contribution margin per unit is the difference between the selling price and the variable cost per unit, and the contribution margin ratio is the ratio of the contribution margin to the selling price per unit. If the selling price and the variable costs per unit both increase 20% and fixed costs do not change, what is the effect on the contribution margin per unit and the contribution margin ratio?
    (*a*) Contribution margin per unit and the contribution margin ratio both remain unchanged.
    (*b*) Contribution margin per unit and the contribution margin ratio both increase.

(c) Contribution margin per unit increases and the contribution margin ratio remains unchaged.

(d) Contribution margin per unit increases and the contribution margin ratio decreases.

21. The following information is available for a Company.

Sales	₹ 350,000
Cost of goods sold	₹ 120,000
Total fixed expenses	₹ 60,000
Total variable expenses	₹ 100,000

Which amount would you find on company's CVP income statement?

(a) Contribution margin of ₹ 250,000

(b) Contribution margin of ₹ 190,000

(c) Gross profit of ₹ 230,000

(d) Gross profit of ₹ 190,000

22. If sales are ₹ 5,00,000, variable costs are ₹2,00,000 and fixed costs are ₹2,40,000 what is the contribution margin ratio (P/V) ratio)?

(a) 40% (b) 40%

(c) 60% (d) None of the above

23. If the unit selling price is ₹16, the unit variable cost is ₹12 and fixed costs are ₹ 60,000, what are break-even sales (units)?

(a) 10,000 units (b) 15,000 units

(c) 20,000 units (d) 45,000 units

24. Based on the following data, what is operating leverage

	Sales	₹ 6,00,000
Less:	Variable costs	₹ 2,40,000
	Contribution margin	3,60,000
	Fixed costs	1,60,000
	Operating income	2,00,000

(a) .8 (b) 1.2 (c) 1.8 (d) 4.0

25. At the break-even point, the contribution margin equals total

(a) Variable costs (b) Sales revenues

(c) Selling and administrative costs (d) Fixed costs

26. The most likely strategy to reduce the breakeven point would be to

(a) Increase both the fixed costs and the contribution margin

(b) Decrease both the fixed costs and the contribution margin

(c) Decrease the fixed costs and increase the contribution margin

(d) Increase the fixed costs and decrease the contribution margin

27. Del Co. has fixed costs of ₹ 1,00,000 and break-even sales of ₹ 8,00,000. What is its projected profit at ₹ 12,00,000 sales?

(a) ₹ 50,000 (b) ₹ 1,50,000

(c) ₹ 2,00,000 (d) ₹ 4,00,000

28. In calculating the breakeven point for a multi-product company, which of the following assumptions are commonly made when variable costing is used?
    I. Sales volume equals production volume.
    II. Variable costs are constant per unit.
    III. A given sales mix is maintained for all volume changes.
    (*a*) I and II (*b*) I and III
    (*c*) II and III (*d*) I, II, and III
29. Break-even analysis assumes that over the relevant range
    (*a*) Unit revenues are nonlinear (*b*) Unit variable costs are unchanged
    (*c*) Total costs are unchanged (*d*) Total fixed costs are nonlinear
30. A Company has sales of ₹ 200,000, a contribution margin of 20%, and a margin of safety of ₹ 80,000. What is Company's fixed cost?
    (*a*) ₹ 16,000 (*b*) ₹ 24,000
    (*c*) ₹ 80,000 (*d*) ₹ 96,000
31. On January 1, 2017, Lake Co. increased its direct manufacturing labour wage rates. All other budgeted costs and revenues were unchanged. How did this increase affect Lake's budgeted break-even point and budgeted margin of safety?

	Budgeted breakeven point	***Budgeted margin of safety***
(*a*)	Increase	Increase
(*b*)	Increase	Decrease
(*c*)	Decrease	Decrease
(*d*)	Decrease	Increase

32. The ratio of fixed costs to the contribution margin is the
    (*a*) break-even point (*b*) profit margin
    (*c*) operating profit (*d*) contribution margin ratio
    (*e*) margin of safety
33. When an organization is operating above the break-even point, the degree or amount that sales may decline before losses are incurred is called the
    (*a*) residual income rate (*b*) marginal rate of return
    (*c*) margin of safety (*d*) target (hurdle) rate of return
    (*e*) variable sales ratio
34. The term "gross margin" for a manufacturing firm refers to excess of sales over
    (*a*) cost of goods sold, excluding fixed indirect manufacturing costs
    (*b*) all variable costs, including variable selling and administrative expenses
    (*c*) cost of goods sold, including fixed indirect manufacturing costs
    (*d*) variable costs, excluding variable selling and administrative expenses
    (*e*) manufacturing costs, excluding fixed manufacturing costs
35. A depreciation tax shield is
    (*a*) an after-tax cash outflow
    (*b*) a reduction in income taxes
    (*c*) the cash provided by recording depreciation
    (*d*) the expense caused by depreciation
    (*e*) caused by the fact that depreciation does not affect cash flow

36. United Industries manufactures three products at its highly automated factory. The products are all popular with demand far exceeding the company's ability to supply the market place. To maximize profit, management should focus on each product's
    (*a*) gross margin
    (*b*) segment margin
    (*c*) contribution margin
    (*d*) contribution margin ratio
    (*e*) contribution margin per machine hour
37. Marston Enterprises sells three chemicals: petrol, septine; and tridol. Petrol is the company's most profitable product: tridol is the least profitable. Which one of the following events will definitely decrease the firm's overall break-even point for the upcoming accounting period?
    (*a*) The installation of new computer-controlled machinery and subsequent layoff of assembly line workers
    (*b*) A decrease in tridol's selling price
    (*c*) An increase in the overall market for septine
    (*d*) An increase in anticipated sales of petrol relative to sales of septine and tridol
    (*e*) An increase in petrol's raw material cost
38. The following information relates to Clyde Corporation which produced and sold 50,000 units during a recent accounting period.

Sales	₹ 8,50,000
Manufacturing costs	
Fixed	2,10,000
Variable	1,40,000
Selling and administrative costs	
Fixed	3,00,000
Variable	45,000
Income tax rate	40%

    For the next accounting period, if production and sales are expected to be 40,000 units, the company should anticipate a contribution margin per unit of
    (*a*) ₹ 0.55
    (*b*) ₹ 3.10
    (*c*) ₹ 7.98
    (*d*) ₹ 9.10
    (*e*) ₹ 13.30.
39. Cost-volume-profit analysis is a key factor in many decisions, including choice of product lines, pricing of products, marketing strategy, and use of productive facilities. A calculation used in a CVP analysis is the break-even point. Once the break-even point has been reached, operating income will increase by the
    (*a*) Gross margin per unit for each additional unit sold
    (*b*) Contribution margin per unit for each additional unit sold
    (*c*) Variable costs per unit for each additional unit sold
    (*d*) Sales price per unit for each additional unit sold
40. In preparing a cost-volume-profit analysis for his candle manufacturing business, Ramesh is considering raising his prices ₹ 2 per candle. He is worried about the impact the increase will have on his revenues from trade fairs. He is concerned about the
    (*a*) Elasticity of demand
    (*b*) Substitution effect
    (*c*) Nature of supply
    (*d*) Maximization of utility

(CMA, USA, Adapted with permission)

Answer to Multiple Choice Questions

1. (a)	2. (d)	3. (d)	4. (c)	5. (a)
6. (a)	7. (d)	8. (a)	9. (a)	10. (c)
11. (d)	12. (d)	13. (b)	14. (a)	15. (d)
16. (c)	17. (c)	18. (d)	19. (a)	20. (b)
21. (a)	22. (c)	23. (b)	24. (c)	25. (d)
26. (c)	27. (a)	28. (c)	29. (b)	30. (b)
31. (b)	32. (a)	33. (e)	34. (c)	35. (b)
36. (e)	37. (d)	38. (e)	39. (b)	40. (a)

PROBLEMS

1. Quality Cabinet Construction is considering introducing a new cabinet-production seminar with the following price and cost characteristics:

Tuition	₹ 200 per Student
Variable Costs (wood, supplies, etc.)	₹ 120 per Student
Fixed Costs (advertising, instructor's salary, insurance, etc.)	₹ 4,00,000 per Year

Required:

(*a*) What enrollment enables Quality Cabinet Construction to break even?

(*b*) How many students will enable Quality Cabinet Construction to make an operating profit of ₹ 2,00,000 for the year?

(*c*) Assume that the projected enrollment for the year is 8,000 students for each of the following situations:

(1) What will be the operating profit for 8,000 students?

(2) What would be the operating profit if the tuition per student (that is, sales price) decreased by 10 percent? Increased by 20 percent?

(3) What would be the operating profit if variable costs per student decreased by 10 percent? Increased by 20 percent?

(4) Suppose that fixed costs for the year are 10 per cent lower than projected, whereas variable costs per student are 10 per cent higher than projected. What would be the operating profit for the year?

Answer:

(*a*) 5000 students

(*b*) 7500 students

(*c*) (1) ₹ 2,40,000

(2) Decrease by 10%, profit decreases by ₹ 1,60,000

Increase by 20%, profit increases by ₹ 3,20,000

(3) Decrease by 10%, profit increases by ₹ 96,000

Increase by 20%, profit decreases by ₹ 1,92,000

(4) Profit decreases by ₹ 56,000

2. Hastinapur Engineering Limited manufactures and sells four products — A, B, C and D. The sales mix in value comprises $33\frac{1}{3}$%, $41\frac{2}{3}$%, $16\frac{2}{3}$% and $8\frac{1}{3}$% of A, B, C and D respectively. The total budgeted sales (100%) are ₹ 60,000 per month.

Operating costs are as thus:
Product A – 60% of selling price
Product B – 68% of selling price
Product C – 80% of selling price
Product D – 40% of selling price
Fixed costs are ₹ 14,700 per month.

The firm proposes to change the sales mix for the next month as follows and it is estimated that total sales would be maintained at the same level as the current month:

Product A	25%	Product C	30%
Product B	40%	Product D	5%

You are required to calculate:

(*i*) Break-even point for the products on an overall basis for the current month.
(*ii*) Break-even point for the products on an overall basis for the next month assuming that the proposal is implemented and
(*iii*) Explain the shift in the break-even point to a new position.

Answer:

(*i*) Composite break-even point ₹ 42,000
(*ii*) BEP ₹ 46,226
(*iii*) The upward shift in BEP is due to the fact that there has been larger decline in sales mix proportion of two products A and D, and in case of product D there has been increase in its sales mix ratio.

3. Akbar Ali Multiproducts Ltd., produces three products with the following characteristics:

	Product I	**Product II**	**Product III**
Price per unit	₹ 50	₹ 60	₹ 70
Variable cost per unit	₹ 30	₹ 20	₹ 40
Expected sales (units)	1,00,000	1,50,000	2,50,000

Total fixed costs for the company are ₹ 1,24,00,000. Assuming that the product mix would be the same at break-even point, compute the B.E. Point in (i) units: (ii) Sales revenue.

(*M. Com., Delhi*)

Answer:

(*i*) 4,00,000 units
(*ii*) ₹ 2,52,00,000

4. The Saurashtra Chemicals, Rajkot produces two products, X and Y, whose selling price and expenses are given below:

	X	**Y**
Sales Price	100	140
Variable expenses per unit	60	80
Contribution margin	40	60

Fixed expenses ₹ 7,00,000 per year

Unit sales of the two products historically have been almost identical. Management is considering the possibility of increasing its advertising budget for Product Y by ₹ 1,00,000 in hope of changing the product mix to 1.5 units of Y sold for each unit of X sold.

Required:

(*i*) Assuming unit sales are divided evenly between the two products, calculate the break-even point in sales rupees.

(*ii*) Assuming the additional ₹ 1,00,000 is spent on advertising product Y and the product mix is 1.5 units of Y for each unit of X sold, calculate the break-even point.

(*M. Com., Delhi*)

Answer:

(*i*) ₹ 16,80,000 (*ii*) ₹ 19,07,692.3

5. The cost per unit of the three products A, B and C of a company is as follows:

	A	*B*	*C*
			(₹)
Direct materials	10	8	9
Direct labour	6	7	6
Variable expenses	4	5	3
Fixed expenses	3	3	2
Total cost	23	23	20
Profit	9	7	6
Selling price	32	30	26
No. of units manufactured	10,000	5,000	8,000

Production arrangements are such that if one product is given up, the production of the others can be raised by 50%. The directors propose that C should be given up because the contribution in that case is lowest. Do you agree?

Answer:

The proposal that product C should be given up, is not correct.

6. Alfa Ltd. had prepared the following budget for the year 2016 based on full capacity utilisaton.

		(₹ lakhs)
Sales of whole production		40.00
Direct materials	8.00	
Direct wages	12.00	
Direct consumables	4.00	24.00
Gross profit		16.00
Commission	2.00	
Delivery	1.20	
Maintenance	0.80	
Depreciation	1.60	
Salaries and indirect wages	5.20	
Others costs	2.40	13.20
Net profit		2.80

Commission and delivery costs are fixed at 50%. The remaining 50% varies directly with sales. Maintenance costs are also fixed and variable in the same proportion with reference to production as in the case for commission. All other indirect costs are fixed.

Owing to current uncertainties in the economic situation, it is now envisaged that during 2016 only 60% of production will be achieved and all of it will be sold.

You are required to:

(*a*) Prepare a revised budget for 2016

(*b*) Determine the break-even level of production.

Answer:

Loss on revised budget ₹ 2.80 lakh, BEP (Sales) ₹ 32,00,000

7. A company is producing an identical product in two factories. The following are the details in respect of both the factories.

	Factory X ₹	***Factory*** Y ₹
Selling price per unit	50	50
Variable cost per unit	40	35
Fixed cost	2,00,000	3,00,000
Depreciation included in above	40,000	30,000
Sales (units)	30,000	20,000
Production capacity (units)	40,000	30,000

You are required to determine:

(*a*) Break-even point (BEP) for each factory, individually.

(*b*) Which factory is more profitable?

(*c*) Cash BEP for each factory individually.

(*d*) BEP for the company as a whole, assuming the present product-mix.

(*e*) BEP for the company as a whole, assuming the product-mix can be altered as desired.

(*f*) Consequences on profits and BEP if the product-mix is changed to 2:3 and total demand remains constant.

Note: BEP may be indicated in number of units.

8. The following information of a company is available for the year 2016:

	₹
Sales	40,000
Raw materials	20,000
Direct wages	6,000
Variable and fixed OH	10,000
Profit	4,000
Units sold	200

In the year 2017, wages rate will increase by 50% and fixed cost will decrease by ₹ 600. If 300 units are sold in 2017, the total fixed and variable OH will be ₹11,400. How many units should be sold in 2017, so that the same amount of profit per unit as in year 2016 may be earned?

Answer:

360 units

9. A company is deciding which of two new thermostat systems to produce and sell. The Basic system has variable costs of ₹ 8.00 per unit, excluding sales commissions, and annual fixed costs of ₹ 520,000; the Deluxe system has variable costs of ₹ 6.40, excluding sales commissions, and fixed costs of ₹ 672,000. The company's selling price is ₹ 32 per unit for the Basic model and ₹ 38 for the Deluxe model. The company pays a 10 per cent sales commission.
   (*a*) Which of the two systems will be more profitable for the firm if sales for either system are expected to average 150,000 units per year?
   (*b*) How many units must the company sell to break even if it selects the Deluxe system?
   (*c*) Suppose the Basic system requires the purchase of additional equipment that is not reflected in the preceding figures. The equipment will cost ₹ 224,000 and will be depreciated over a 10-year life by the straight-line method. How many units must the company sell to earn ₹ 40,000 of income, after considering depreciation, if the Basic system is selected?
   (*d*) Now, ignore the information presented in part (c). Write a report that explains to management the level of volume at which it should be indifferent between the Basic system and Deluxe system.

Answer:

(*a*) Deluxe model will be profitable
Net inome Basic, ₹ 26,00,000
Deluxe ₹ 34,98,000
(*b*) 24,173 units
(*c*) 28,000 units
(*d*) Indifference point 21,714 units

10. Jindal Company has one product: printing logos on sweatshirts for businesses. The sales price of ₹ 2,000 remains constant per unit regardless of volume, as does the variable cost of ₹ 1,200 per unit. The company is considering operating at one of the following three monthly levels of operations:

	Volume Range (production and sales)	Total Fixed Costs	Increase in Fixed Costs from Previous Level
Level 1	0 – 10,000	₹ 40,00,000	—
Level 2	10,001 – 25,000	80,00,000	₹ 40,00,000
Level 3	25,001 – 40,000	1,00,00,000	20,00,000

(*a*) Calculate the break-even point(s) in units.

(*b*) If the company can sell everything it makes, should it operate at level 1, level 2, or level 3? Support your answer.

Answer:

(*a*) BEP, Level 1; 5000 units

Level 2; 10,000 units

Level 3; 12,500 units

(*b*) Profits is optimum at Level 3 ₹ 2,20,00,000

11. Cost-volume-profit analysis showed how much Auto, Ltd. had to improve just to break even in Year 1. In that year, the break-even point was 22 lakhs units, but the company was selling considerably fewer than 20 lakhs units. Faced with a severe recession in the industry, Auto Co. had virtually no chance to increase sales enough to break even. Meanwhile, the company had received loan guarantees from the government, which evoked considerable criticism that the government was supporting a 'failing' company.

By Year 4, Auto Co. reduced its break-even point to 11 lakhs units, and the company reported a profit for the first time in several years. The turnaround came despite continued low sales in the industry; it resulted primarily from severe cost cutting, which reduced fixed costs from ₹ 4,50,00,00,000 in Year 1 to ₹ 3,10,00,00,000 in Year 4. In addition, the company made improvements in its production methods, which enabled it to maintain its volume of output despite the reduction in fixed costs.

(*a*) If Auto Co. Break-even volume was 11 lakh units and its fixed costs were ₹ 3,10,00,00,000, what was its average contribution margin per unit?

(*b*) Why do you think management concentratd on readucing fixed costs to put Auto Co. above its break-even point?

(*c*) As a shareholder of Auto Co. what concerns might you have about the company's massive cost cutting?

Answer:

(*a*) ₹ 2818.18

(*b*) Management has correctly realized the increasing level of competition in the auto industry. The only alternative available is to reduce fixed costs.

(*c*) In the long run, cutting costs, sometimes, can lead to reduced profits.

12. Delhi Equipments Ltd., manufactures four components, the cost particulars of which are given below:

	Components			
	A	***B***	***C***	***D***
Elements of cost:				
Direct material	₹ 80	100	100	120
Direct labour	20	25	25	30
Variable overhead	10	12	15	10
Fixed overhead	15	23	20	20
	125	160	160	180
Output per machine hour (units)	4	2	3	3

The key factor is shortage of machine capacity.

You are required to advise management as to whether they should continue to produce all or some of these components (which are used in its main product) or they should buy them from a supplier who has quoted the following prices:

A, ₹ 115; B, ₹ 175; C, ₹ 135; D, ₹ 185.

Answer:

Component *C* should be purchased. Continue the production of components *A*, *B* and *D*.

13. Paradise Broadcasting operated at the break-even point of ₹ 22,50,000 during Year 1 while incurring fixed costs of ₹ 10,00,000. Management is considering two alternatives to reduce the break-even level. Alternative A trims fixed costs by ₹ 2,00,000 annually with no change in variable cost per unit; doing so, however, will reduce the quality of the product and result in a 10 per cent decreae in selling price, but no change in the number of units sold. Alternative B substitutes automated equipment for certain operations now performed manually. Alternative B will result in an annual increase of ₹ 300,000 in fixed costs but a 5 per cent decrease in variable costs per unit produced, with no change in product quality, selling price, or sales volume.

   (*a*) What was the total contribution margin (contribution margin per unit times number of units sold) during Year 1?

   (*b*) What is the break-even point in sales under alternative A?

   (*c*) What is the break-even point in sales under alternative B?

   (*d*) What should the company do?

Answer:

(*a*) ₹ 10,00,000

(*b*) ₹ 21,05,263

(*c*) ₹ 27,65,957

(*d*) The company should choose the alternative that yields the greatest profit in the projected range, probably alternative A.

14. Star Paper Company produces plastic mailboxes. The projected income statement for the coming year follows:

Sales	₹ 8,40,600
Less: Variable costs	3,53,052
Contribution margin	₹ 4,87,548
Less: Fixed costs	2,50,000
Operating income	₹ 2,37,548

Required:

(*i*) Compute the contribution margin ratio for the mailboxes.

(*ii*) How much revenue must the company earn in order to break even?

(*iii*) What volume of sales must be earned if the company wants to earn an after-tax income equal to 8 per cent of sales? Assume that the tax rate is 34 percent.

(*iv*) What is the effect on the contribution margin ratio if the unit selling price and unit variable cost each increase by 10 percent?

(*v*) Suppose that management has decided to give a 3 per cent commission on all sales. The projected income statement does not reflect this commission. Recompute the contribution margin ratio assuming that the commission will be paid. What effect does this have on the break-even point?

(*vi*) If the commission is paid as described in Requirement (v), management expects sales revenues to increase by ₹ 80,000. Is it a sound decision to implement the commission? Support your answer with appropriate computations.

Answer:

(*i*) C/M ratio 58%

(*ii*) ₹ 4,31,034

(*iii*) ₹ 5,44,900

(*iv*) Same C/M ratio 58%

(*v*) The effect is to increase the break-even point.

15. Johnson Company operates an assembly line to manufacture vacuum cleaners. It could set up a second line in currently idle space, if volume were big enough to justify it. The second line would require the following monthly costs at a production volume of 2,000 vacuum cleaners a month:

Supervisor	₹ 23,000
Inspector	₹ 18,000
Assemblers (6 workers)	₹ 1,00,000
Power	₹ 25,000
Total	₹ 1,66,000

In addition, materials and parts cost ₹ 300 for each vacuum cleaner made. The vacuum cleaners are sold to wholesalers for ₹ 400 each.

(*a*) What is the minimum monthly volume to justify starting the second line if all of the costs of assembly line are fixed.

(*b*) What is the minimum monthly volume to justify starting the second line if supervision and inspection costs are fixed and the costs of assemblers and power are proportionally variable with volume?

(*c*) What generalization can you draw from this exercise as to the imapct of the variations in the relative proportions of fixed and variable costs? (Suggestion: Consider how your answer to part (*a*) or (*b*) would change if you found that all production costs were proportionally variable with volume.)

Answer:

(*a*) Minimum monthly volume will be break-even volume which is 1660 units (*b*) break-even volume 1093.3 units. (*c*) If all costs are proportionally variable, then production is justified if only one unit can be sold, as long as the contribution margin per unit is positive. In this case, if all costs are proportionally variable, average variable cost will be ₹ 300 + (₹1,66,000/2,000) = ₹ 383, and the contribution margin will be ₹ 17.

Generalising from this, we can say that the higher the proportion of fixed costs in the cost mix at a specified volume, the higher will be the break-even volume.

16. A Ltd. manufactures three products and the cost particulars for a year are as follows:

	Product		(₹)
	X	Y	Z
Sales	2,00,000	4,00,000	2,50,000
Materials	1,00,000	1,50,000	1,25,000
Labour cost	30,000	50,000	40,000
Variable overhead	10,000	20,000	25,000
Fixed overhead	35,000	50,000	25,000

The company imports raw materials which is used in manufacture of all products. The consumption of materials is as follows:

X — 2000 kg; Y — 5000 kg; Z — 3000 kg.

There is restriction on import of materials. The management is planning to close down one of the lines of product and utilise the material for other two lines to improve the profitability. As the management accountant of the company, prepare a report for the closure of one line for improving the profitability.

Answer:

Contribution X—₹ 60,000, Y—₹ 1,80,000, Z—₹ 60,000. Contribution per kg. of material is minimum in case of Z. Hence manufacture of Z may be discontinued and this raw material should be utilised to manufacture Y which gives maximum contribution per kg. of material.

17. A company reported its operating results for 2016 and 2017 as follows:

	2016 (₹)	2017 (₹)
Sales	8,00,000	9,03,000
Less: Cost of sales	6,40,000	6,70,000
	1,60,000	2,33,000
Overhead	1,80,000	1,90,000
	(20000)	43000

During 2017 selling prices were raised by 5%. Prepare a statement bringing out the factors leading to change in profit earned in 2017 over 2016. *(M. Com., Delhi)*

Answer:

Profit increased due to price	₹ 43,000
Profit increased due to sales volume	₹ 12,000
Profit increased due to reduction in cost of sales	₹ 18,000
Profit reduced due to increase in overhead	₹ 10,000

18. Milton Ltd. produces a molded plastic casting, LX 201, for desktop computer. Summary data from its current year income statement are as follows:

Revenues	₹ 50,00,000
Variable costs	30,00,000
Fixed costs	21,60,000
Operating income	₹ (1,60,000)

Kamna, Milton's president, is very concerned about Milton's poor profitability. She asks Amit, production manager, and Sudhir, controller, to see if there are ways to reduce costs.

After two weeks Amit returns with a proposal to reduce variable costs to 52 per cent of revenues by reducing the costs Milton currently incurs for safe disposal of wasted plastic. Sudhir is concerned that this would expose the company to potential environmental liabilities. He tells Amit, "We would need to estimate some of these potential environmental costs and include them in our analysis." You can't do that," Amit replies. "We are not violating any laws. There is some possibility that we may have to incur environmental costs in the future, but if we ring it up now, this proposal will not go through because our senior management always assumes these costs to be larger than they turn out to be. The market is very tough, and we are in danger of shutting down the company. We don't want all our colleagues to lose their jobs. The only reason our competitors are making money is because they are doing exactly what I am proposing."

(*i*) Calculate Milton's break even revenues for the current year.

(*ii*) Calculate Milton's break even revenues if variable costs are 52 per cent of revenues.

(*iii*) Calculate Milton's operating income in current year if variable costs had been 52 per cent of revenues.

(*iv*) Given Amit's comments, what should Sudhir do?

Answer:

(*i*) ₹ 54,00,000

(*ii*) ₹ 45,00,000

(*iii*) ₹ 2,40,000

(*iv*) Incorrect reporting of environmental costs to continue business operation is unethical. Sudhir should bring it to the notice of management.

19. R. A. Rao and Company, makers of quality hand-made pipes, has experienced a steady growth in sales for the past five years. However, increased competition has led Mr. Rao, the president, to believe that an aggressive advertising campaign will be necessary next year to maintain the company's present growth.

To prepare for next year's advertising campaign, the company's accountant has prepared and presented Mr. Rao with the following data for the current year 2016.

Variable expenses:	
Direct labour	₹ 80.0 per pipe
Direct materials	₹ 32.5 per pipe
Variable overhead	₹ 25.0 per pipe
Total variable expenses	₹ 137.5 per pipe
Fixed expenses:	
Manufacturing	₹ 2,50,000
Selling	₹ 4,00,000
Administrative	₹ 7,00,000
Total fixed expenses	₹ 13,50,000
Selling price per pipe	₹ 250.0
Expected sales, 2016 (20,000 units)	₹ 50,00,000

Mr. Rao has set the sales target for 2017 at a level of ₹ 55,00,000 (or 22,000 pipes)

Required:

(*i*) What is the projected profit for 2016?

(*ii*) What is the break-even point for 2016 in units?

(*iii*) Mr. Rao believes an additional advertising expense of ₹ 1,12,500 in 2017, with all other expenses remaining constant, will be necessary to attain the 2017 sales target. What will the profit be for 2017 if additional ₹ 1,12,500 is spent and 22000 pipes are sold.

(*iv*) What will the break-even point in sales for 2017 be if the additional ₹ 1,12,500 is spent for advertising?

(*v*) If the additional ₹ 1,12,500 is spent for advertising in 2017, what is the required sales level in rupees sales to equal 2016 profit?

(*vi*) At a sales level of 22,000 units, what is the maximum amount which can be spent on advertising if a before tax profit of ₹ 10,00,000 is desired?

Answer:

(*i*) Profit ₹ 9,00,000 (*ii*) 12,000 units (*iii*) Profit ₹ 10,12,500

(*iv*) ₹ 32,50,000 (*v*) ₹ 52,50,000 (*vi*) ₹ 1,25,000

20. On the basis of the following information in respect of an engineering company, what is the product mix which will give the highest possible profit? Do you recommend overtime working upto a maximum of 15,000 hours at twice the normal wages (ignore overheads)?

Product manufactured	*A*	*B*	*C*
Raw materials per unit	10 kg	6 kg	15 kg
Labour hours per unit @ ₹ 1/= per hour	15	25	20
Sales price per unit (₹)	125	100	200
Maximum production possible (units)	6,000	4,000	3,000

1,00,000 kgs raw materials are available @ ₹ 10 per kg. Maximum production hours are 1,84,000 with facility for a further 15,000 hours on overtime basis at twice the normal wages rate. (*M.Com., Delhi*)

Answer:

Product mix ranking C, A, B

Maximum units, Product C 3000 units, Product A 6000 units, Product B 1360 units

Overtime hours for production of 600 additional units of product B should not be used as it will result in reduction of ₹ 6000 in total contribution.

21. Income statements for two different companies in the same industry are as follows:

		Company A	***Company B***
	Sales	₹ 50,00,000	₹ 50,00,000
Less:	Variable costs	40,00,000	20,00,000
	Contribution margin	10,00,000	30,00,000
Less:	Fixed costs	5,00,000	25,00,000
	Operating income	5,00,000	5,00,000

Required:

(*a*) Compute the degree of operating leverage for each company.

(*b*) Compute the break-even point for each company. Explain why the break-even point for company B is higher.

(*c*) Suppose that both companies experience a 50% increase in revenues. Compute the percentage change in profits for each company. Explain why the percentage increase in company B's profits is so much larger than that of company A.

Answer:

	Company A	Company B
(*a*) Operating leverage	2 times	6 times
(*b*) Break-even point (₹)	25,00,000	41,66,667
(*c*) Percentage increase in profit	100%	300%

22. Ranbaxy Ltd. Manufactures phamaceutical products that are sold through a network of sales agents. The agents are paid a commission of 18 per cent of revenues. The income statement for the current year ending March 31, is as follows:

Ranbaxy Limited Income Statement
for the Current Year Ended March 31

	₹	₹
Revenues		2,60,00,000
Cost of goods sold:		
Variable	1,17,00,000	
Fixed	28,70,000	1,45,70,000
Gross margin		1,14,30,000
Marketing costs:		
Commissions	46,80,000	
Fixed costs	34,20,000	81,00,000
Operating income		33,30,000

Ranbaxy is considering hiring its own sales staff to replace the network of sales agents. Ranbaxy would pay its salespeople a commission of 10 per cent of revenues and incur additional fixed costs of ₹ 20,80,000.

(*i*) Calculate Ranbaxy Ltd's break-even point in revenues for the current year.

(*ii*) Calculate Ranbaxy Ltd's break-even point in revenues for the current year if the company had hired its own sales force in the current year to replace the network of sales agents.

(*iii*) Calculate the degree of operating leverage at revenues of ₹ 2,60,00,000 if (*a*) Ranbaxy uses sales agents and (*b*) Ranbaxy employs its own sales staff. Describe the advantages and disadvantages of each alternative.

(*iv*) If Ranbaxy had hired its own sales staff and increased the commission paid to them to 15 per cent, keeping all other cost behaviour pattems the same, how much revenue would Ranbaxy have to generate to earn the same operating income as in the current year?

(*M. Com., Delhi University,* 2010)

Answer:

(*i*) BEP ₹ 1,70,00,000

(*ii*) BEP ₹ 1,86,00,000

(*iii*) Degree of operating leverage

(*a*) Sales agents 2.89 (*b*) Own sales staff 3.51

(*iv*) ₹ 2,92,50,000

23. Ezee Ltd makes two products, E and Z. All units produced are sold. There is no inventory build up. Production facilities may be used interchangeably for both the products. Sales units are the limiting factor. The following information is given:

	Price Level			*Proposed increase*
	E	*Z*	*Total*	*Total*
Contribution ₹/unit	25	20		
Fixed Cost ₹			46,000	47,500
Sales units	3,000	2,000	5,000	4,000

For increase in quantities above 4,000 units for each product, there will be an increase in variable selling costs, (for the increased portion only), thereby reducing the contribution per unit to the following figures:

Units	*Contribution per unit (₹)*	
	E	*Z*
4001-5000	20	15
5001-6000	15	10
Above 6000	No Sales possible	

(*i*) For the present level, find the break-even point with the present product.

(*ii*) What is the minimum number of incremental units to be sold to recover the additional fixed cost of ₹ 47,500 to be incurred? (Present product mix need not be maintained):

(*iii*) If you are allowed to choose the best product mix for the incremental level, (while taking the present mix given in the first table above for the present level), what would be the individual product quantities and the corresponding total contributions, the weighted average contribution per unit and the total profits for the complete production?

(CA Final, May 2012)

Answer:

(*i*) 2000 units

(*ii*) 2125 units, Product E. 1000 units, Product Z. 1125 units

(*iii*) Product mix, Product E 5,000 units, Product Z 4,000 units

Total contribution ₹ 1,20,000; Average contribution per unit ₹ 22.22; Total profits, ₹ 1,06,500

24. Northwood Company manufactures basketballs. The company has a standard ball that sells for ₹ 250. At present, the standard ball is manufactured in a small plant that relies heavily on direct labour workers. Thus, variable costs are high, totalling ₹ 150 per ball.

Last year, the company sold 30,000 standard balls, with the following results:

Sales (30,000 standard balls)	₹ 75,00,000
Less variable expenses	45,00,000
Contribution margin	30,00,000
Less fixed expenses	21,00,000
Net income	₹ 90,00,00

Required:

1. Compute (a) the CM ratio and the break-even point in balls, and (b) the degree of operating leverage at last year's level of sales.
2. Due to an increase in labour rates, the company estimates that variable costs will increase by ₹ 30 per ball next year. If this change takes place and the selling price per ball remains constant at ₹ 250, what will be the new CM ratio and break-even point in balls.
3. Refer to the data in (2) above. If the expected change in variable costs takes place, how many balls will have to be sold next year to earn the same net income (₹ 9,00,000) as last year?
4. Refer again to the data in (2) above. The president feels that the company must raise the selling price on the standard balls. If Northwood Company wants to maintain *the same CM ratio as last year*, what selling price per ball must it charge next year to cover the increased labour costs?
5. Refer to the original data. The company is discussing the construction of a new, automated plant to manufacture the standard balls. The new plant would slash variable costs per ball by 40%, but it would cause fixed costs to double in amount per year. If the new plant is built, what would be the company's new CM ratio and new break-even point in balls?
6. Refer to the data in (5) above.
   a. If the new plant is built, how many balls will have to be sold next year to earn the same net income (₹ 9,00,000) as last year?
   b. Assume the new plant is built and that next year the company manufactures and sells 30,000 balls (the same number as sold last year). Prepare a contribution income statement and compute the degree of operating leverage.
   c. If you were a member of top management, would you have voted in favour of constructing the new plant? Explain.

Answer:

1. (a) CM ratio 40%, 21,000 balls

   (b) 3.33
2. CM ratio 28%, 30,000 balls
3. 42,857 balls
4. Increase in selling price ₹ 50
5. CM ratio 64%, 26,250 balls
6. (a) 31,875 balls,

   (b) Degree of operating leverage : 8

25. Sava Health Centre runs an Intensive medical care unit. For this purpose, it has hired a building at a rent of ₹ 50,000 per month with the understanding that it would bear the repairs and maintenance charges also. The unit consists of 25 beds and 5 more beds can be comfortably accommodated when the occasion demands. The parmanent staff attached to the unit is as follows:

2 Supervisors, each at a salary of ₹ 5,000 per month; 4 nurses, each at a salary of ₹ 3,000 per month and 2 ward boys, each at a salary of ₹ 1,500 per month.

Though the unit was open for the patients all the 365 days in a year, scrutiny of account in 2014 revealed that only for 120 days in a year, the unit had the full capacity of 25 patients per day and for another 80 days, it had an average 20 beds only occupied per day. But there were occasions when the beds were full, extra beds were hired at a charge of ₹ 50 per bed per day and this did not come to more than 5 beds extra above the normal capacity on any one day. The total hire charges for extra beds incurred for the whole year amount to ₹ 20,000.

The unit engaged expert doctors from outside to attend on the patients and the fees were paid on the basis of the number of patients attended and time spent by them and on an average worked out to ₹ 20,000 per month in 2014.

The other expenses for the year were as under:

	₹
Repairs and maintenance	93,600
Food supplied to patients	4,44,000
Janitor and other services for them	1,12,500
Laundry charges for their bed linen	1,28,000
Medicines supplied	5,30,000
Cost of oxygen, x-ray etc., other than directly borne for treatment of patients	4,50,000
General administration charges allocated to the unit	1,50,000

Required:

(*i*) If the unit recovered overall amount of ₹ 1,000 per day on an average from each patient, what is the profit per patient day made by the unit in 2014.

(*ii*) The unit wants to work on budget for 2015. but the number of patients requiring intensive medical care is a very uncertain factor. Assuming that same revenue and expenses prevail in 2014, in the first instance, workout the number of patient days required by the unit to break-even.

Answer:

(*i*) Profit per parient day ₹ 386.38

(*ii*) 2260 patient days.

CASES

1. The Dean, Faculty of Management Studies at the University of Bombay at Mumbai was considering whether to offer 'one-month Executive Development Programmes' for corporate executives. The tuition was ₹ 65,000 per person. Variable costs, which included meals, materials and lodging were ₹ 8,000 per person. Certain costs of offering the programmes, including advertising the programmes, faculty members' fees, audiovisual equipment rent would not be affected by the number of people attending (within a relevant range). Such costs, which could be thought of as step costs, amounted to ₹ 8,00,000 for the programmes.

   In addition to these costs, a number of staff including Dean of Management Studies, worked on the programmes. Although the salaries paid to these staff were not affected by organising the programme, working on the programme took these people away from other duties, thus creating an opportunity cost, estimated to be ₹ 7,00,000 for this programme.

   Using this information, the Dean calculated the break-even point to be (₹ 8,00,000 + ₹7,00,000)/ (₹ 65,000 – ₹ 8,000) = 26.3 Students. If the Dean of the faculty wanted to at least break-even on this programme, it should offer the programme only if it expected at least 27 students to attend.

   Present a report to the Dean that evaluates the quality of this analysis. Your report should focus on concerns about the accuracy of data and limitations of cost-volume-profit analysis.

   (*M. Com., Delhi,* 2014)

2. Godrej Health Care Ltd. has launched a new cosmetic product. The management of the company is deciding its marketing strategies. The following information is available about the product.

Anticipated selling price per unit	₹ 120
Variable cost per unit	₹ 60
Anticipated volume (units)	12,00,000
Production cost	₹ 1,80,00,000
Anticipated advertising	₹ 60,00,000

   Two managers, Dhawan and Deshmukh had the following discussion to increase the profitability of the new product.

   Dhawan: I think we need to think of some way to increase profitability. Do you have any idea?

   Deshmukh: I think the best strategy would be to become aggressive on price.

   Dhawan: How aggressive?

   Deshmukh: If we drop the price to ₹ 84 per unit and maintain our advertising budget at ₹ 60,00,000, I think we will generate sales of 45,00,000 units.

   Dhawan: I think that is the wrong way to go. You are giving too much up on price. Instead, I think we need to follow an aggressive advertising strategy.

   Deshmukh: How aggressive?

   Dhawan: If we increase our advertising to a total of ₹ 1,80,00,000 we should be able to increase sales volume to 39,00,000 units without any change in price.

   Deshmukh: I don't think this is reasonable. We will never cover the increased advertising costs.

Required:

Which opinion is best? Do nothing, follow the advice of Deshmukh? or follow Dhawan's opinion?

3. ABC company manufactures pharmaceutical products that are sold through a network of sales agents located in India and Sri Lanka. The agents are currently paid an 18 per cent commission on sales; this percentage was used when the company prepared the following proforma income statement for the fiscal year ended June 30, 2016.

ABC Company
Proforma Income Statement
for the Year Ending June 30, 2016
(₹ 000 omitted)

	₹	₹
Sales		26,000
Cost of goods sold:		
Variable	11,700	
Fixed	2,870	14,570
Gross profit		11,430
Selling and admin. costs:		
Commissions	₹ 4,680	
Fixed advertising cost	750	
Fixed administrative cost	1,850	7,280
Operating income		4,150
Fixed interest cost		650
Income before income taxes		3,500
Income taxes (40%)		1,400
Net income		2,100

Since the completion of this statement, the company has learned that its agents are requiring an increase in the commission rate to 23 per cent for the upcoming year. As a result, the company's president has decided to investigate the possibility of hiring its own sales staff in place of the network of sales agents. He has asked Ramaswamy, the company's management accountant to gather information on the costs associated with this change.

Ramaswamy estimates that the company will have to hire eight salespeople to cover the current market area, and the annual payroll cost of each of these employees will average ₹ 80,000, including fringe benefit expenses. Travel and entertainment expenses are expected to total ₹ 6,00,000 for the year and the annual cost of hiring a sales manager and sales secretary will be ₹ 1,50,000. In addition to their salaries, the eight salespeople will each earn commissions at the rate of 10 per cent on the first ₹ 20,00,000 in sales and 15 per cent on all sales over ₹ 20,00,000. For planning purpose, Ramaswamy expects that all eight salespeople will exceed the ₹ 20,00,000 mark and that sales will be at the level previously projected. Ramaswamy believes that the company should also increase its advertising budget by ₹ 5,00,000.

Required:

(*a*) Calculate ABC Company's break-even point in sales Rupees for the fiscal year ended June 30, 2016, if the company hires its own sales force and increases its advertising costs.

(*b*) If ABC Company continues to sell through its netwrok of sales agents and pays the higher commission rate, determine the estimated volume in sales Rupees for the fiscal year ended June 30,2016, that would be required to generate the same net income as that projected in the proforma income statement presented.

(*c*) Describe the general assumptions underlying break-even analysis that might limit its usefulness in this case. (*CMA, USA, Adapted with permission*)

Answer:

(*a*) ₹ 1,80,25,000 (*b*) ₹ 3,00,63,000

4. Ms. Monika Iyer, director and owner of the Kids Education Center, has a master's degree in education. In the seven years, she has been running the Kids Education Center, her salary has ranged from nothing to ₹ 20,00,000 per year. "The second year," she says, "I made ₹ 62 an hour." (Her salary is what's left over after meeting all other expenses.)

Could she run a more profitable center? She thinks perhaps she could if she increased the student-teacher ratio, which is currently five students to one teacher. (Government rules for a center such as this set a maximum of 10 students per teacher.) She refuses to increase the ratio to more than six-to-one. "If you increase the ratio to more than six-to-one, the children don't get enough attention. In addition, the demands on the teacher are far too great," She does not hire part-time teachers.

Monika rents the space for her center in the basement of a Health Care Centre for ₹ 90,000 per month, including utilities. She estimates that supplies, snacks, and other nonpersonnel costs are ₹ 8,000 per student per month. She charges ₹ 38,000 per month per student. Teachers receive ₹ 1,20,000 per month, including fringe benefits. She has no other operating costs. At present, she cares for 30 students and employs six teachers.

(*a*) What is the present operating profit per month of the Kids Education Center before Ms. Monika's salary?

(*b*) What is (are) the break-even point(s), before Ms. Monika's salary, assuming a student-teacher ratio of 6:1?

(*c*) What would be the break-even point(s), before Ms. Monika's salary, if the student-teacher ratio increased to 10 : 1?

(*d*) Ms. Monika has an opportunity to increase the student body by six students. She must take all six or none. Should she accept the six students if she wants to maintain a maximum student-teacher ratio of 6 : 1?

(*e*) (Continuation of part d.) Suppose that Ms. Monika accepts the six children. Now she has the opportunity to accept one more, which requires hiring one more teacher. What would happen to profit, before her salary, if she accepts one more student?

Answer:

(*a*) ₹ 90,000

(*b*) 19 students

(*c*) 11 students

(*d*) Increase in total contribution ₹ 1,80,000

(*e*) Profit would decrease by ₹ 90,000

5. Prithvi Theatre Co. is located in Mumbai City. The company is housed in the Arts Center Building at Nariman Point in Mumbai. The company features five different folk dances cum music per year. For the upcoming season, the five different folk dances of different states in India are to be performed as given below.

   The president and general manager has tentatively sheduled the following number of performances for each variety of dance of different states for the coming season:

Assam	5
Manipur	5
Odissa	20
Punjab	10
Rajasthan	5

   To produce each performance, costs must be incurred for costumes, props, rehearsals, royalties, guest artist fees, choreography, salaries of production staff, music, and wardrobe. These costs are fixed for a particular dance regardless of the number of performances. The direct fixed costs are as follows for each of dance.

Assam	**Manipur**	**Odissa**	**Punjab**	**Rajasthan**
₹ 2,75,50,000	₹ 1,45,50,000	₹ 70,50,000	₹ 3,45,00,000	₹ 1,55,50,000

   Other fixed costs are incurred as follows:

Advertising	₹ 80,00,000
Insurance	15,00,000
Administrative salaries	2,22,00,000
Office rental, phone, and so on	84,00,000
Total	₹ 4,01,00,000

   For each performance of each dance, the following costs are also incurred:

Symphony	₹ 3,80,000
Auditorium rental	70,000
Dancers' payroll	4,00,000
Total	₹ 8,50,000

   The auditorium in which the performance is presented has 1,854 seats, which are classified as A, B, and C. The best viewing ranges from A seats to C seats. Information concerning the different types of seat follows:

	A seats	**B, Seats**	**C Seats**
Quantity	114	756	984
Price	₹ 3,500	₹ 2,500	₹ 1,500
Percentage sold for each performance:*			
Folk-dance	100	100	100
All others	100	80	75

* Based on past experience, the same percentages are expected for the coming season.

Required:

(*i*) Compute the expected revenues from the performances that have been tentatively scheduled. Prepare a variable-costing income statement for each variety of dance.

(*ii*) Calculate the number of performances of each dance required to produce the revenues needed to cover each dance's direct fixed costs.

(*iii*) Calculate the number of performances of each dance required for the company as a whole to break even. If you were the president and general manager, how would you alter the tentative schedule of performance?

(*iv*) Suppose that it is possible to offer a matinee of the popular Odissi dance. Seats would sell for ₹ 500 less than in the evening, and the rental of the auditorium would be ₹ 20,000 less. The president and general manager believes that five matinee performances are feasible and that 80 per cent of each type of seat can be sold. What effect will the matinee have on the company's profitability? On the overall break-even point?

(*v*) Suppose that no additional evening performances can be offered beyond those tentatively scheduled. Assume that the company will offer five matinee performances of Odissi. Also, the company expects to receive ₹ 60,00,000 in government grants and contributions from supporters of the fine arts. Will the company break even? If not, what actions would you take to bring revenues in line with costs? Assume that no additional performances of Odissi dance are feasible.

Answers:

(*i*)

Assam	Loss	₹ 1,67,10,000
Manipur	Loss	₹ 37,10,000
Odissa	Profit	₹ 5,12,50,000
Punjab	Loss	₹ 1,28,20,000
Rajasthan	Loss	₹ 47,10,000

(*ii*)

Assam	=	13
Manipur	=	7
Odissa	=	3
Punjab	=	16
Rajasthan	=	8

(*iii*) 7 (Assam, Manipur, Rajasthan)
14 (Punjab, Odissa)

(*iv*) Adding the matinee will increase profit by ₹ 72,020

New breakeven point 5.82 packages
or 6 (rounded up)

6 (Assam, Manipur, Rajasthan, Odissa matinees)
12 (Punjab)
24 (Odissa)

(*v*) No, the company will not break even and will have operating loss of ₹ 1,35,98,000. It may be suggested to hold as many performances of Odissa dance as possible. This action has already been taken. Other corrective steps could be to increase the prices of seats, to cut administrative costs, to offer a less expensive dance, to offer additional performances of some other variety of dances.

6. A company operates a hotel. It is spread over six floors of a building excluding the ground floor with a restaurant in the sixth floor. On the ground floor, the hotel operates a sports centre including a swimming pool and a shopping arcade.

   The hotel has a capacity of 100 single rooms and 20 double rooms. The average occupancy of bothe the single and double rooms is expected to be 80% throughtout the year of 365 days. The rent for double room has been fixed at 125% of the rent of a single room. Cost are as under:

Variable costs :	Single rooms ₹220 each per day
	Double rooms ₹ 350 each per day
Fixed costs :	Single rooms ₹ 120 each per day
	Double rooms ₹ 250 each per day

   The income and costs relating to the service centres are as under:

   (a) Restaurant:

   Estimated average sales per day ₹25,000

   Contribution 30% of sales

   Fixes costs ₹8,00,000 per annum.

   (b) Sports center:

   Average number of persons expected to use the centre per day is 50.

   Average contribution per day per person is ₹ 15.

   Fixed costs ₹ 4,00,000 per annum.

   (c) Shopping arcade:

   Average contribution per month is ₹ 35,000

   Fixed costs ₹ 4,00,000 per annum.

Required:

(*i*) Calculated the rent chargeable for single and double rooms per day in such a way that the hotel earns a margin of safety of 20% on hiring of rooms.

(*ii*) Evaluate the profitability of the three services centres and work ou the total profit of the hotel per annum based on the rent recommended by you in (i) above.

(*iii*) The hotel wants to reserve the normal occupancy of ten single rooms for its regular customer by allowing a discount of 10% on room rent. What increase in occupancy ratio is required in respect of the remaining rooms to earn the same envisaged in (ii) above.

(*iv*) An associate company wishes to take the entire complex hotel on lease for a total rent of ₹ 175 lacs for five years. The associate company is prepared to pay the entire lease rent in advance. Taking the capital recovery factor for 10% of return for 5 years at 3.79, advise the management of the hotel company whether or not leasing arrangement should be entered into.

Answer:

(*i*) Single room, ₹ 460; Double rooms, ₹ 575

(*ii*) Restaurant Profit ₹ 19,37,500; sports centre Loss ₹ 1,26,250; shopping arcade Profit ₹ 20,000. Total profit ₹ 51,89,250 per annum.

(*iii*) Increase in occupancy ratio 81.41%

(*iv*) Discounted income for 5 years ₹ 1,96,67,257 is less than rent of ₹ 1,75,00,000, Lease should not be accepted.

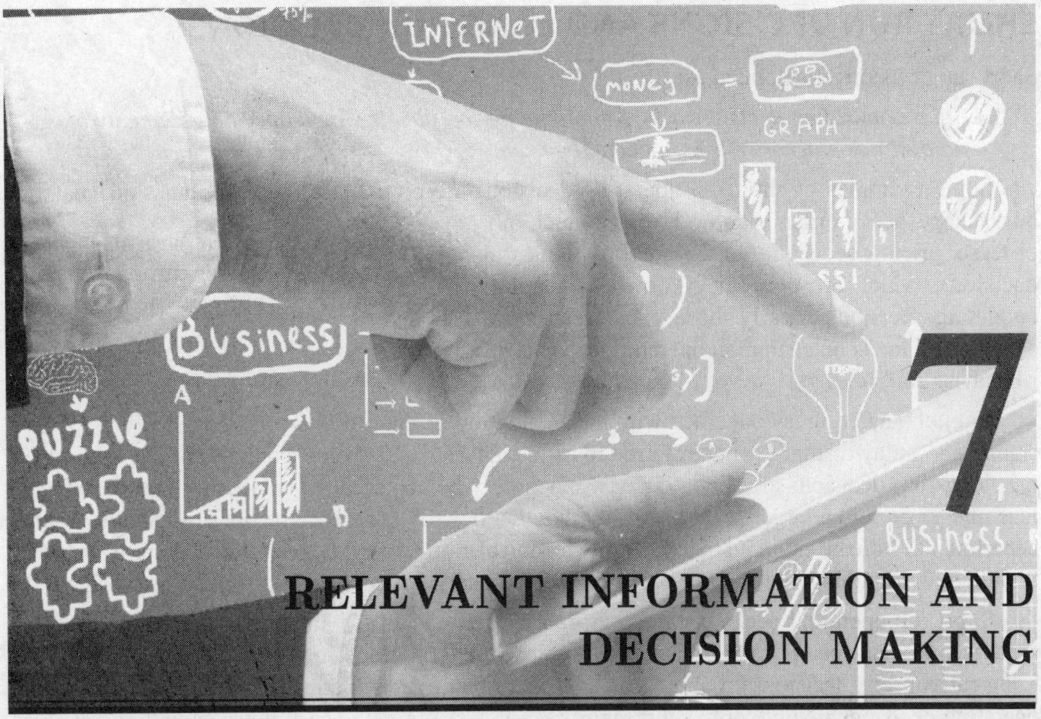

7

RELEVANT INFORMATION AND DECISION MAKING

LEARNING OBJECTIVES:

After reading this chapter, you should be able to:

- Distinguish between Short-run and Long-run Decisions
- Define Decision Making Process and Steps in this Process
- Explain the Concept of Relevant Information, Relevant Revenues, Relevant Costs and Differential Analysis
- Understand the Concept of Relevant Costs in Activity-based Costing
- Identify Precautions in Decision Making
- Discuss Behavioural Issues in Decision Making
- Explain the Relevance of Qualitative Factors in Managerial Decision Making

SHORT-RUN DECISIONS AND LONG-RUN DECISIONS

Short-run decisions *are* defined as:

- *those operating decisions which span the period during which operating capacity of a business enterprise is assumed to be fixed.*

Some examples of short-run operating decisions are optimal product mix decision, make or buy, accept special orders, add or drop a product, buy or lease, pricing decision. On the contrary, long-run decisions, which are popularly known as 'capital budgeting decisions', imply those managerial decisions which focus on change in operating capacity of a business enterprise.

> **Long-run decisions** are those managerial decisions which focus on change in operating capacity of a business enterprise.

Capital budgeting is concerned with the acquisition of long-term assets and usually involves a significant outlay of funds, often referred to as 'capital outlays'. Some examples of capital budgeting (long-run) decisions are: Should a new machinery be acquired to replace an old, less efficient machinery? Should a larger plant be built? Should a new branch office be opened? Should a retail departmental store be enlarged? Should more technical or other staff be recruited on long-term basis? Should new technology be acquired that will perform services currently performed by workers?

Short-run operating decisions and long-run capacity decisions are similar in that both rely on a differential analysis of cash inflows and outflows. There is one important difference, however. Long-run capacity decisions involve cash flows over several future periods, whereas typical short-run operating decisions involve only short range cash flows. When the cash flows extend over several future periods, some technique must be employed for making the cash flows comparable,[1] because one Rupee received now is more valuable than one Rupee received several years from now. This technique is known as net present value method in the long-run or capital budgeting decisions. Sometime it is also called Discounted Cash Flow (DCF) analysis.

DECISION-MAKING PROCESS

Decision making, is the process of evaluating two or more alternatives leading to a final choice, sometimes known as 'Alternative Choice Decisions'. It is a formal method for making a choice, frequently involving both quantitative and qualitative analyses. Decision-making is closely associated with planning for the future and is directed towards a specific objective or goal. The care put into each decision often determines the level of outcome. Still the best process and even the best decision does not guarantee a successful outcome. The future determines its own fate, but the best prepared decision is more likely to produce the desired result than any other selection.[2] The overall decision process (also referred to as decision model) contains the following decision-making steps.

> **Decision making** is the process of evaluating two or more alternatives leading to a final choice.

Step 1: Determine/Clarify the Decision Problem/Strategic Issues

The first step in the decision-making process, which is very important, is to identity and define the problem, or strategic issues which require making decisions. This helps the decision maker to focus on the right questions involved in decision. Greater managerial skill and expertise is required in defining a decision problem to subsequently address it correctly. For example, a production manager might wrongly consider the choice as make or buy a part for a product when the correct decision might be to determine whether the product should be redesigned so the part is not needed.

Sometimes, the decision problem is quite complex. For example, the demand for a company's popular product is declining. What are the reasons for it? Declining quality control? Decrease in customer satisfaction? Increasing competition? Availibility of alternative product in the market? Higher selling prices? etc. Before a decision can be made, the problem needs to be clarified and defined in more specific terms. In some situations, the decision problem may itself be clear. For example, a business firm may receive a special order for its product at a price below the regular market price. The decision under this situation is clear i.e. whether to accept or reject the order.

Step 2: Specify the Criteria

After identifying the decision problem, the decision maker should specify the criteria upon which a decision is to be made. Most often, the criteria or the objective can be easily quantified such as minimizing cost, improving profit through increased return on investment, increasing share of company product in the market. Sometimes the criteria or the objectives are in conflict with each other, such as where reducing cost, quality of the product needs to be maintained. Also, in some situations, other interested parties or stakeholders like shareholders, creditors may have their own separate criteria or objectives. Therefore, a manager most often is forced to think of multiple objectives, both the quantifiable short-term goals and the more strategic difficult-to-quantify goals.[3]

Step 3: Identify Alternatives as Possible Solutions to the Problem

Decision making is choosing between the alternatives. If the objective is to increase sales, there can be many alternatives to achieve this goal. If a machine breaks down, it could be repaired or replaced. Within the replacement, it may be bought or leased. Determining the possible alternatives is an important step in the decision making process.

Those alternatives that are clearly not feasible should be eliminated from the decision making process.

Step 4: Perform Relevant Information Analysis

In this fourth step, a manager collects relevant data (relevant costs and relevant benefits) associated with each feasible alternative. Selecting data relating to decision is one of the management accountant's most important roles in an organization. In this decision making step, manager performs an analysis of relevant costs and relevant benefits (revenues) and other pertinent strategic issues. Manager also makes predictions about relevant information corresponding to alternatives in terms of future values of relevant costs and relevant revenues.

Managers should also identify and analyze, to the extent possible, non-financial advantages and disadvantages (known as qualitative factors) about each feasible alternative while performing relevant information analysis.

Step 5: Select and Implement the Best Alternative

Based on the relevant cost and relevant revenue analysis, the manager, in the fifth step, selects the best alternative and executes it.

Step 6: Evaluate Performance

In the sixth and final step, the manager evaluates the performance of the implemented decision as a basis for feedback to a possible reconsideration of this decision as it relates to future decisions. The decision process is thus a feedback-based system in which the manager continually evaluates the results of prior analyses and decisions to discover any opportunities for improvement in decision making.

RELEVANT INFORMATION

Managerial decision making is a process of making choices. If a choice is to be made among alternatives, there must be differences among the alternatives. Relevant information should be used by the decision maker in evaluating the alternatives and in making decisions. Relevant information has two characteristics.

1. ***Impact on the Future:*** Relevant information has a bearing on the future. Relevant information focuses on the future because every decision deals with selecting courses of action for the future. Nothing can be done to alter the past. The consequences of decisions are borne in the future, not the past. Information to be relevant (i.e. relevant costs and benefits) to a decision should imply a future event.

> **Relevant information** has impact on the future and is different under different alternatives.

Since relevant information involves future events, the management accountant must predict the amounts of the relevant costs and benefits. In making these predictions, the accountant often will use estimates of cost behavior based on historical data. There is an important and subtle issue here. *Relevant* information must involve costs and benefits to be realized in the *future*. However, the accountant's *predictions* of those costs and benefits often are based on data from the *past*.[4]

2. ***Different under Different Alternatives:*** Relevant information includes costs and benefits that differ among the alternatives. Expected future revenues and costs that do not differ or remain the same across alternatives have no impact on the decision and therefore irrelevant and should be eliminated from the relevant information analysis.

Further, in relevant information, due weightage must be given to qualitative factors and quantitative non-financial factors.

According to Hilton[5], information to be useful for decision making should possess three characteristics.

1. Relevance
2. Accuracy
3. Timeliness

RELEVANT INFORMATION AND DIFFERENTIAL ANALYSIS

Relevant information implies relevant costs and relevant revenues (benefits) which are useful to evaluate alternatives, to ascertain the effect of various alternatives on profit and to finally select the alternative with the greatest benefit.

Relevant revenues and relevant costs are defined as:

- *the current and future values that differ among the alternatives under consideration.*

They are the differences between the alternatives under consideration. The amount of such differences are called differentials and the (accounting) analysis concerned with the effect of alternatives on revenues and costs is called differential analysis. Thus, differential analysis, known as relevant information analysis also, is defined as:

- *the use of relevant revenues and relevant costs in decision making.*

Relevant revenues and costs are also known as differential revenues and differential costs. This analysis provides a decision rule to managers in decision-making which is 'the alternative that gives the greatest incremental profit should be selected'. Incremental profit is the difference between the relevant revenues and relevant costs of each alternative.

A differential analysis of relevant costs is always preferable to complete analysis of all costs and revenues for a number of reasons[6].

- A differential analysis focuses on only those items that differ, providing a clearer picture of the impact of the decision at hand. Management is less apt to be confused by this analysis than by one that combines relevant and irrelevant items.
- A differential analysis contains fewer items, making it easier and quicker to prepare.
- A differential analysis can help to simplify complex situations (such as those encountered by multiple-product or multiple-plant firms), when it is difficult to develop complete firmwide statements to analyze all decision alternatives.

Relevant Revenues

Relevant (differential) revenue, as stated earlier, is the amount of increase or decrease in revenue expected from a particular course of action as compared with an alternative. *For instance*, assume that a plant is being used to manufacture product A, which gives revenue of ₹ 3,00,000. If the plant could be used to make product B, which will provide revenue of ₹ 3,50,000, the differential revenue from making and selling product B will be ₹ 50,000.

Accrual Profit and Cash Flow

Relevant revenues are like cash inflows. If the amount of accrual profit and cash flow differs, the manager should give importance to cash flow. For short-run managerial decisions, timing of cash flow, i.e., when the cash flows are received, are not so important. However, for long-run decisions where the time span is usually for more than one year, the timing of cash flows is important in the evaluation of alternatives and in making decisions.

Relevant Costs

Relevant Costs are also known as differential costs or decision making costs. Relevant or differential cost is the difference in the total costs between alternative choices. It is difference in total costs between two volumes. It is the cost that should be considered when a decision is made involving an increase or decrease of n units of output above a specified output. When a decision results in an increased cost, the differential cost may be referred to as an incremental cost. If the cost decreases, the differential cost may be referred to as a decremental cost. The incremental cost includes the change in fixed component as well as the variable component. Assume that a company has physical facilities to manufacture 20,000 units of a product; production beyond that point would require the installation of additional equipment, that is, fixed costs as well as variable costs will have to be incurred if management desires to produce more than 20,000 units.

> **Relevant or differential cost** is the difference in the total costs between alternative choices.
>
> When a decision results in an increased cost, the differential cost may be referred to as an **incremental cost.**

Differential and Incremental

The term *differential* is more inclusive than *incremental*. The latter term suggests increases, and some decisions produce decreases in both revenues and costs. But the terms are not as important as what they denote. Differential costs are *avoidable* costs. If a company can change a cost by taking one action as opposed to another, the cost is avoidable and therefore differential. Suppose a company could save ₹ 5,00,000 in salaries and other fixed costs if it stopped selling a product in a particular geographical region. The ₹ 5,00,000 is avoidable (differential) because it will be incurred if the company continues to sell in the region and will not be incurred if the firm stops selling in that region. Of course, the company will lose revenue if it discontinues sales in the region. Hence, the lost revenue is also differential in a decision to stop selling in the region.

Relevant costs vary with the type of decision. However, the following are the common characteristics of relevant costs:

1. Relevant costs are expected future costs
2. They differ between different decision alternatives

Expected future costs imply that the costs are expected to occur during the time period covered by the decision. *For example*, new product will need the incurrence of direct material, direct labour and other costs. Relevant costs also differ between decision alternatives. For example, a graduate may choose between higher education and immediate employment. The costs that are relevant in this decision and which differ between the two decisions are the costs of books, fees, etc., because these costs will not be incurred if the graduate takes up employment. However, irrelevant costs are costs of accommodation, clothings, etc. which will have to be incurred under both the decisions.

The differential cost concept is one of the most useful in planning and decision making. It provides a tool for testing the profitability of increased output for an acceptable alternative. In many short-run decisions, only costs, not revenues, will change. In this case, the most beneficial (profitable) decision will be one with the lowest cost because the lowest cost alternative will give the highest profit for the business enterprise, provided all other factors remain constant.

ACTIVITY-BASED COSTING AND RELEVANT COSTS

Activity-based costing can be used to help identify potentially relevant costs for decision-making purposes. Activity-based costing improves the traceability of costs by focusing on the activities caused by a product or other segment. Managers should exercise caution against reading more into this "traceability" than really exists. People have a tendency to assume that if a cost is traceable to a segment, then the cost is automatically an avoidable cost. That is not true. The costs provided by a well-designed activity-based costing system are only potentially relevant. Before making a decision, managers must still decide which of the potentially relevant costs are actually avoidable. Only those costs that are avoidable are relevant and the others should be ignored[7].

For example, depreciation of ₹ 80,000 on fixtures is a traceable cost of home appliances lines because it relates to activities in that department. However, ₹ 80,000 is not avoidable if the home appliances lines is dropped. The key lesson here is that the method used to assign a cost to a product or other segment does not change the basic nature of the cost. A sunk cost such as depreciation of old equipment is still a sunk cost regardless of whether it is traced directly to a particular segment on an activity basis, allocated to all segments on the basis of labor-hours, or treated in some other way in the costing process. Regardless of the method used to assign costs to products or other segments, the manager still must apply the correct principles to determine the costs that are avoidable in each situation.

PRECAUTIONS IN DECISION MAKING

As stated earlier, relevant revenues and relevant costs are important variables in decision making. However, sometimes managers may ignore relevant information or include irrelevant information in their decision making model. Hilton[8] advises to avoid the following four common mistakes in decision making.

1. ***Sunk Costs:*** The book value of an asset, defined as its acquisition cost less the accumulated depreciation, is a sunk cost. Sunk costs cannot be changed by any current or future course

of action, so they are irrelevant in decision making. Nevertheless, a common behavioral tendency is to give undue importance to book values in decisions that involve replacing an asset or disposing of obsolete inventory. People often seek to justify their past decisions by refusing to dispose of an asset, even if a better alternative has been identified. *The moral : Ignore sunk costs.*

2. ***Unitized Fixed Costs:*** For product-costing purposes, fixed costs often are divided by some activity measure and assigned to individual units of product. The result is to make a fixed cost appear variable. While there are legitimate reasons for this practice, from a *product-costing* perspective, it can create havoc in *decision making.* Therefore, in a decision analysis, it is usually wise to include a fixed cost in its total amount, rather than as a per-unit cost. *The moral* : *Beware of unitized fixed costs in decision making.*
3. ***Allocated Fixed Costs:*** It is also common to allocate fixed costs across divisions, departments, or product lines. A possible result is that a product or department may appear unprofitable when in reality it does make a contribution toward covering fixed costs and profit. Before deciding to eliminate a department, be sure to ask which costs will be avoided if a particular alternative is selected. A fixed cost that has been allocated to a department may continue, in total or in part, even after the department has been eliminated. *The moral : Beware of allocated fixed costs; identify the avoidable costs.*
4. ***Opportunity Costs:*** People tend to overlook opportunity costs, or to treat such costs as less important than out-of-pocket costs. Yet opportunity costs are just as real and important to making a correct decision as are out-of-pocket costs. *The moral : Pay special attention to identifying and including opportunity costs in a decision analysis.*

DECISION MAKING: BEHAVIOURAL ISSUES

Decision making in organizations has bearing on performance evaluation of managers and their behaviour. Managers might make decisions that have favourable impact on their perceived performances and compensation. There is a tendency among the managers to focus on short-term goals and ignore the long-term goals because their salary and compensation is based on short-term accounting results such as net profit. Without long-term or strategic considerations, management can incorrectly use relevant costs and revenues analysis to target a short-term benefit and in this way greatly suffer a significant long-term loss. *For example*, a firm might choose to accept a special order because of a positive relevant cost analysis without properly considering that the nature of the special order could have a significant negative impact on the firm's image in the market place and perhaps a negative effect on sales of the firm's other products. The important message for managers is to keep the long-term objectives in the forefront in any decision situation.

The treatment of sunk costs in decision making by some managers may create behavioural issues. As stated earlier, sunk costs are not relevant in decision making. For example, the book value of an outdated machine is irrelevant in making an equipment-replacement decision. Suppose, however, that a manager correctly ignores an old machine's book value and decides on early replacement of the machine he purchased a few years ago. Now suppose the helpless manager is criticized by his superior for "taking a loss" on the old machine, or for buying a 'not good' machine in the first place. What a manager will do the next time he faces a similar decision? If he is like many people, he will tend to keep the old machine in order to justify his prior decision to purchase it. In so doing, he will be compounding his error. However, he may also be avoiding criticism from a superior who does not understand the importance of optimal decision making and relevant information. It is advisable that in order to help the managers in making appropriate decisions through evaluation of relevant costs and revenues, their performance evaluation system and compensation policy should match with and be consistent with decision making perspective. If an organization desires managers to make optimal decisions; it must provide them incentives to do so. This requires that managers' performance should be evaluated in terms of factors that should be considered in making opitmal decisions.

TYPES OF DIFFERENTIAL ANALYSIS DECISIONS

> **Differential analysis decisions** cover situations where best alternative is selected from two or more alternative courses of action.

Differential analysis decisions, referred to as alternative choices decisions, cover situations with two or more alternative courses of action from which the manager (decision maker) must select the best alternative. A decision involving more than two alternatives is called a multiple-alternative choice decision. Some examples of alternative choice decisions are: make or buy, own or lease, retain or replace, repair or renovate, now or later, change versus status quo, slower or faster, export versus local sales, shutdown or continue, expand or contract, change the produce-mix, take or refuse orders, place special orders, select sale territories, replace present equipment with new machinery, sell at split-up point or process further, etc.

Some of the above alternative decisions and the information relevant to the decisions are discussed below.

Make or Buy/Insourcing Vs Outsourcing

Make or buy decisions, also referred to as insourcing vs outsourcing decisions, arise when a company with unused production capacity considers the following alternatives:

- To buy certain raw materials or subassemblies from outside suppliers
- To use available capacity to produce the items within the company

> **Outsourcing** is purchasing goods and services from outside vendors
>
> **Insourcing** is producing the same goods or providing the same services within the organisation.

The objective of a make or buy decision should be to best utilise the firm's productive and financial resources. The problem often arises in connection with the possible use of idle equipment, idle space and even idle labour. In such situations, a manager is inclined to consider making certain units instead of buying them in order to utilise existing facilities and to maintain work-force stability. Commitment of new resources may also be involved.

Reasons for Outsourcing

Outsourcing is purchasing goods and services from outside vendors rather than insourcing, which is producing the same goods or providing the same services within the organisation.

Organizations often have external opportunities to acquire services or components of products they manufacture rather than providing the service or manufacturing the component internally. The external acquisition of services or components is called outsourcing. There are three major reasons for outsourcing : (1) to focus on the key aspects of the business by outsourcing non-core activities, (2) to improve the quality of support activities, and (3) to better control costs.

Relevant information for insourcing vs outsourcing decisions include both quantitative and qualitative factors. Following box lists the motivating factors for organisations to go for outsourcing.

Top Ten Reasons to Outsource

Reduce and control operating costs
Improve company focus
Gain access to world-class capabilities
Free internal resources for other purposes
Obtain resources not available internally
Accelerate reengineering benefits
Eliminate a function difficult to manage/out of control
Make capital funds available
Share risks
Obtain cash infusion

Source: The Outsourcing Institute, *Survey of Current and Potential Outsourcing End-Users* 1998, http://www.outsourcing.com/howandwhy/research/survey results/main.htm (August 14, 1999).

According to Barfield, Raiborn and Kinney, the following factors listed in the box should be considered in the outsourcing decision.

Outsource Decision Considerations

Relevant Quantitative Factors:
Incremental production costs for each unit
Unit cost of purchasing from outside supplier (price less any discounts available plus shipping, etc.)
Number of available suppliers
Production capacity available to manufacture components
Opportunity costs of using facilities for production rather than for other purposes
Amount of space available for storage
Costs associated with carrying inventory
Increase in throughput generated by buying components

Relevant Qualitative Factors:
Reliability of supply sources
Ability to control quality of inputs purchased from outside
Nature of the work to be subcontracted (such as the importance of the part to the whole)
Impact on customers and markets
Future bargaining position with supplier(s)
Perceptions regarding possible future price changes
Perceptions about current product prices (are the prices appropriate or, in some cases with international suppliers, is product dumping involved?)

Source: Jesset T. Barfield, Cecily A. Raiborn and Michael R. Kinney, Cost Accounting, Traditions and Innovations, Thomson, 2003, p. 505

Example

For example, assume that a company can make a part that it has been purchasing at a unit cost of ₹ 300. The company has been operating at 75% of normal capacities and in the foreseeable future no use for the excess capacity is contemplated except for the possible production of the part. Fixed manufacturing cost amounts to ₹ 17,00,000 a year whether the plant operates at 75% or 100% of capacity. The cost to manufacture 50,000 units of the part that will be needed has been estimated as follows:

	Cost to Make	
	Unit cost ₹	Total Cost ₹
Direct materials	125	62,50,000
Direct labour	80	40,00,000
Variable manufacturing overhead	50	25,00,000
Total incremental cost	255	1,27,50,000
Cost to purchase part	300	1,50,00,000
Net advantage in parts production	45	22,50,000

Costs that will be incurred under both alternatives are not relevant to the analysis. In the above analysis the fixed manufacturing overhead has not been considered because it has to be incurred under both alternatives. The fixed manufacturing overhead is a sunk cost which is not relevant to the decision. Logically, the costs that will be increased or decreased as a result of making the part should be considered.

Some Other Factors in Make/Buy Decisions

Make or buy decisions are often complex, involving not only present costs but also projections of future costs resulting from such factors as capacity, trade secrets, technological improvements, product quality, seasonal sales, and production fluctuations. It is responsibility of top management to determine the basic factors that should be taken into account in make or buy decisions. Another factor to consider in make or buy decisions is the technical ability of the labour that will be utilised in making the product; it should be evaluated against any special training and skills needed. It may also be necessary to acquire specialised plant facilities and equipment to manufacture the new product. The firm should make an analysis of the cost, quality and quantity considerations of the individual make or buy decisions. Differential cost analysis is especially useful if the company has idle capacity and idle workers that can be used to make the tools or parts. Other potential use of available capacity should also be considered; and qualitative factors must be evaluated in the decision process. These considerations include price stability from suppliers, reliability of delivery and quality of the material or component involved.

In addition, new sources of materials suppliers may be required. To reduce the effect of limitations associated with make or buy decisions, it is necessary that make or buy decisions should always be reviewed by one control entity within the firm. Without this review process, all elements of planning, control and coordination with respect to the firm's goals are lost, which again is detrimental to the firms's long-range survival. The qualitative factors should be evaluated by more than one individual, so personal biases do not cloud valid business judgement.

Horngreen, Datar and Foster[9] observe:

Outsourcing is not without risks. As a company's dependence on its suppliers increases, suppliers could increase prices and let quality and delivery performance slip. To minimise these risks, companies generally enter into long-run contracts specifying costs, quality and delivery schedules with their suppliers. Intelligent managers build close partnerships or alliances with a few key suppliers. Toyota goes so far as to send its own engineers to improve suppliers' processes. Suppliers of companies such as Ford, Hyundai, Panasonic and Sony have researched and developed innovative products, met demands for increased quantities, maintained quality, and on time delivery, and lowered costs — actions that the companies themselves would not have had the competencies to achieve.

Outsourcing decisions invariably have a long-run horizon in which the financial costs and benefits of outsourcing become more uncertain. Almost always, strategic and qualitative factors become important determinants of the outsourcing decision. Weighing all these factors requires the exercise of considerable management judgement and care.

Similarly, Barefied, Raiborn and Kinney[10] comment:

Although companies may gain the best knowledge, experience, and methodology available in a process through outsourcing, they also lose some degree of control. Thus, company management should carefully evaluate the activities to be outsourced. Factors to consider include whether (1) a function is considered critical to the organization's long-term viability (such as product research and development); (2) the organization is pursuing a core competency relative to this function; or (3) issues such as product/service quality, time of delivery, flexibility of use, or reliability of supply cannot be resolved to the company's satisfaction.

Drop or Add Product

The decision to eliminate an unprofitable product is a special case of segment or product profitability evaluation. To evaluate the financial consequences of eliminating a product, it is necessary to concentrate on the differential or incremental profit effect of the decision. An important factor in the decision to add or drop a product is whether it will increase or decrease the future income of the business. Appropriate cost and profit measures must be developed for each alternative.

Care must be taken not only to consider the profitability of the product being analyzed but also to evaluate the extent to which sales of other products will be adversely affected when one product is removed. An unprofitable product may be part of a line of products that must be complete in order to attract customers to more profitable products. The unprofitable product may also be a complement to more profitable products, in which case some customers may buy the more profitable products because the unprofitable product is also available from the same company. If the expected sales decrease of related products is severe enough, it probably would be desirable to retain the product being scrutinized.

Management needs data that will permit development of warning signals for products that may be in trouble. Such warning signals include:[11]

1. Increasing number of customer complaints
2. Increasing number of dispatches returned
3. Declining sales volume
4. Product sales volume decreasing as a percentage of the firm's total sales
5. Decreasing market share

6. Malfunctioning of the product or introduction of a superior competitive product
7. Past sales volume not up to projected amounts
8. Expected future sales and market potential not favourable
9. Return on investment below a minimum acceptable level
10. Variable costs approaching or exceeding revenue
11. Various costs consistently increasing as a percentage of sales
12. Increasing percentage of executive time required
13. Price which must be constantly lowered to maintain sales
14. Promotional budgets which must be consistently increased to maintain sales

Example

To illustrate the product abandonment decision, assume a company is considering dropping product B from its line because accounting statements show that product B is being sold at a loss.

Income Statement

	Product A ₹	*Product B* ₹	*Product C* ₹	*Total* ₹
Sales revenue	50,000	7,500	12,500	70,000
Cost of sales:				
Direct material	7,500	1,000	1,500	10,000
Direct labour	15,000	2,000	2,500	19,500
Indirect manufacturing cost (50% of direct labour)				
	7,500	1,000	1,250	9,750
	30,000	4,000	5,250	39,250
Gross margin on sales	20,000	3,500	7,250	30,750
Administrative expenses				
(allocation on arbitrary basis)	12,500	4,500	4,000	21,000
Net income (loss)	7,500	(1,000)	3,250	9,750

Additional Information:

(*i*) Factory overhead costs are made up of fixed costs of ₹ 5,850 and variable costs of ₹ 3,900. Variable costs by products are: product A ₹ 3,000. Product B ₹ 400, and product C ₹ 500.

(*ii*) Fixed costs and expenses will not be changed if product B is eliminated.

(*iii*) Variable selling and administrative expenses to the extent of ₹ 11,000 can be traced to the product as follows: A, ₹ 7,500, B, ₹ 1,500: C ₹ 2,000.

(*iv*) Fixed selling and administrative expenses are ₹ 10,000.

The decision to drop product B cannot be reasonably made from the above data prepared under a conventional income statement. This information together with the following statement may be helpful to management.

	Product A ₹	Product B ₹	Product C ₹	Total ₹
Sales revenue	50,000	7,500	12,500	70,000
Less: Variable Product Cost:				
Direct material	7,500	1,000	1,500	10,000
Direct labour	15,000	2,000	2,500	19,500
Factory overhead	3,000	400	500	3,900
Selling and administrative expenses	7,500	1,500	2,000	11,000
	33,000	4,900	6,500	44,400
Contribution margin	17,000	2,600	6,000	25,600
Less: Fixed costs:				
Factory overhead				5,850
Selling and administrative expenses				10,000
Total fixed costs				15,850
Net income				9,750

This statement shows that product B exceeds its variable costs by ₹ 2,600. If the sale of product B were discontinued, this marginal contribution would be lost and the net income of the firm would be reduced by ₹ 2,600. That is, net income will be ₹ 7,150 (₹ 9,750 – ₹ 2,600). In this illustration, it has been assumed that sales of products A and C will not increase after product B is dropped. Further, it has been assumed that dropping product B will not change the fixed costs and expense. If these assumptions are not true, new analysis must be made. Assume, for example, that after droping product B, the sales of product A increase by 10%. The total profit of the firm will not increase by this sales increase. Product A makes only a marginal contribution of 34%.

	₹	
Sales revenue	50,000	100%
Variable costs	33,000	66%
Marginal contribution	17,000	34%

On additional sales of ₹ 5,000, the marginal contribution would be ₹ 1,700:

	₹
Sales revenue	5,000
Variable costs (66%)	3,300
Marginal contributions (34%)	1,700

This contribution is less than ₹ 2,600 now being realised on the sales of product B. It would take additional sales of product A of approximately ₹ 7,647 to equal the marginal contribution of ₹ 2,600 now being made by product B:

$$\frac{\text{Marginal contribution of production B}}{\text{Marginal contribution of product A}} = \frac{2,600}{34\%} = ₹\,7,647$$

It is possible that dropping product B may result in reduction in some of the fixed costs. Product B now contributes ₹ 2,600 towards recovery of fixed costs and expenses. Only if the fixed costs and expenses can be reduced by more than this amount, it will be advisable to drop product B.

Sell or Process Further

The decision whether a product should be sold at the split-off point or processed further is faced by many manufacturers. The choice between selling a product at split-off or processing it further is short-run operating decision. Additional processing adds value to a product and increases its selling price above the amount for which it could be sold at split-off. The decision to process further depends upon whether the increase in total revenues exceeds the additional costs incurred for processing beyond split-off. Generally speaking, there are two general conditions under which a sell or process further decision could occur:

1. The company is evaluating the possibility of processing beyond split-off and must incur certain equipment costs and other fixed costs if additional processing is to occur.
2. The company already processes a product beyond split-off and has invested in the equipment and required personnel.

The first situation is really a capital budgeting problem and here it is not sufficient to determine whether incremental revenues exceed incremental costs. Since new investment in machinery and building are involved, the rate of return on this investment must also be considered.

Relevant Costs

In the second situation, the relevant costs are only those costs which relate to the additional processing of each product beyond the split-off point. The joint costs are relevant to the further processing decisions. Certain fixed costs such as supervisory salaries are related to additional processing. If these costs are eliminated by selling products at split-off, they are incremental and should be included in the decision analysis. If salaried personnel are assigned other duties in the company when additional processing is discontinued, the salary costs are not incremental since they are incurred under either decision alternative. If the equipment used for additional processing sits idle or can be used in other processes, it should be ignored in the decision analysis. Depreciation expense is never relevant in short-run operating decisions, since depreciation is an allocation of costs incurred in a past time period.

In deciding upon which course of action to follow, the company compares the contribution margin from the sale of the partially processed product with the contribution margin from the sale of the completely processed product. The revenue to be derived from the sale of the partially processed product is the opportunity cost attached to the decision of further processing.

Example

A partially processed product can be sold for ₹ 90 per unit which is manufactured at a cost of ₹ 60. Further processing can be done at an additional cost of ₹ 30 per unit and the final product can be sold at ₹ 150 per unit. The firm can produce 10,000 units. The analysis is shown below:

	Sell ₹	*Process & Sell* ₹
Sales revenue	9,00,000	15,00,000
(₹ 10,000 units)		
Less: Manufacturing costs	6,00,000	9,00,000
	3,00,000	6,00,000

Net advantage in further processing ₹ 6,00,000 – ₹ 3,00,000 = ₹ 3,00,000

Thus, there is a net advantage of ₹ 3,00,000 in processing the product further. The market value of the partially processed product (₹ 9,00,000) is considered to be the opportunity cost of further processing.

The figure of net advantage of ₹ 3,00,000 can be arrived at in the following manner also:

		₹	₹
	Revenue from sale of final product (10,000 × ₹ 150)		15,00,000
Less:	Additional processing cost (10,000 × 30)	3,00,000	
	Revenue from sale of intermediate product (10,000 × 90)	9,00,000	12,00,000
	Net advantage in further processing		₹ 3,00,000

To take another example, suppose, a firm purchased some material for ₹ 1,00,000 sometime back which would realise ₹ 50,000 if sold now. If the material is not sold it could be used in making a product which would sell for ₹ 1,50,000 after incurring additional costs of ₹ 65,000. The analysis is as follows:

To Make Product

	₹	₹
Revenue from product		1,50,000
Costs:		
External opportunity cost (incremental cost)	65,000	
Internal opportunity cost	50,000	(1,15,000)
Net benefit		35,000

To Sell Material

	₹
Revenue from material	50,000
Costs:	
Internal opportunity cost (benefit foregone by not making product) (1,50,000 – 65,000)	(85,000)
Net loss	(35,000)

It is not always easy to identify all possible opportunities, and it can be even more difficult to impute values to these opportunities. An alternative approach to the above example is to use incremental costing, where the difference between incremental revenues and incremental costs is computed.

	Make Product (₹)	*Sell Material* (₹)	*Differential Costs* (₹)
Incremental revenue	1,50,000	50,000	1,00,000
Incremental cost	65,000	—	(65,000)
	85,000	50,000	35,000

The same decision is made, resulting in the manufacture of the product to provide a ₹ 35,000 net benefit.

Operate or Shutdown

Differential cost analysis is also used when a business is confronted with the possibility of a temporary shutdown. This type of analysis has to determine whether in the short-run a firm is better off operating than not operating. As long as the products sold recover their variable costs and make a contribution towards the recovery of fixed costs, it may be preferable to operate and not to shutdown. Also management should consider the investment in the training of its employees which would be lost in the event of temporary shutdown. Recruiting and training new workers would add to present costs. Another factor is the loss of established markets. Also, a temporary shutdown does not eliminate all costs. Depreciation, taxes, interest, and insurance costs are incurred during shutdown also. The other points (benefits) which should be considered are the following: avoiding operating losses, savings in maintenance and repair costs, savings in indirect labour costs, savings in fixed costs.

Even if sales do not recover the variable cost and the portion of fixed cost that is avoidable, the firm may still be better off operating than shutting down the facility. Closing a facility and subsequently reopening it is a costly process. The shutdown may necessitate the incurrence of maintenance procedures in order to preserve machinery and buildings during periods of inactivity (e.g. rust inhibitors, dust covers, security equipment, etc.). The shutdown also may require the incurrence of legal expenditures and employee maintenance pay. During the shutdown period, some employees will probably be lost (i.e., they may not wait until the facility is reopened to go back to work), in which case the investment in the training of those employees will be lost. The morale of other employees, as well as company goodwill, may be adversely affected, and the recruiting and training of replacement workers that must be incurred when the facility is later reopened, add to costs. Although difficult to quantify, the loss of established market share is also a factor to be considered. When a company leaves a market for a while, its customers tend to forget about the company's product. As a consequence, reentering the market at a latter time will probably require reeducating consumers about the company's product. These shutdown costs must be weighed against losses from continued operations.[12]

Example

To illustrate an analysis of possible temporary shutdown, assume that a company operating below 50% of its capacity expects that the volume of sales will drop below the present level of 10,000 units per month. Management is concerned that a further drop in sales volume will create a loss and has under consideration a recommendation that operations be suspended, until better market conditions prevail and also a better selling price. The present operating income statement is as follows:

		₹	₹
	Sales revenue (10,000 units @ ₹ 30)		3,00,000
Less:	Variable cost @ ₹ 20 per unit	2,00,000	
	Fixed costs	1,00,000	3,00,000
	Net income		0

The following income statements have been prepared for sales at different capacities:

Units Produced

	Shutdown	2,000	4,000	6,000	8,000	10,000
Sales revenue @ ₹ 30	0	60,000	1,20,000	1,80,000	2,40,000	3,00,000
Variable costs @ ₹ 20	0	40,000	80,000	1,20,000	1,60,000	2,00,000
Contribution	0	20,000	40,000	60,000	80,000	1,00,000
Fixed costs	40,000	1,00,000	1,00,000	1,00,000	1,00,000	1,00,000
Loss	(40,000)	(80,000)	(60,000)	(40,000)	(20,000)	0

It would appear that shutdown is desirable when the sale volume drops below 6,000 units per month, the point at which operating losses exceed the shutdown cost. This volume of 6,000 units could be arrived at without an income statement as follows:

	₹
Fixed costs if plant operates	1,00,000
Fixed costs if plant shuts down	40,000
Additional costs to be recovered when operating	60,000
Each unit of products sold contributes ₹ 10 to fixed costs recovery:	
Selling price per unit	30
Variable cost per unit	20
Contribution	10

Sales of 6,000 units is necessary to recover ₹ 60,000 of fixed costs.

$$\frac{60,000}{10} = 6,000 \text{ units}$$

If the selling price is cut to ₹ 28, the contribution margin will be ₹ 8 per unit.

Required sale to recover an additional ₹ 60,000 of fixed costs

$$\frac{60,000}{8} = 7,500 \text{ units}$$

That is, sale of 7,500 units would be necessary to recover an additional ₹ 60,000 of fixed costs.

Special Orders

All business decisions should not be evaluated in the same way. Sometimes special orders or one time orders have different characteristics from recurring orders. Therefore, each order should be evaluated based on costs relevant to the situation and the goals of the business firm. The question of special orders arises when a company has excess or idle production capacity and management considers the possibility of selling additional products at less than normal selling prices, provided that such a special order will not affect the regular sales of the same product.

The basic problem is to determine an acceptable price for the special order units. Cost analysis using the contribution approach is a useful technique to determine the short-run profit effects of special order transactions. In deciding the pricing of special orders where normal operations are not disturbed and where unused production capacity exists, it is not advisable to attach fixed costs to products. Price determination should take into account the recovery of incremental (variable) costs caused by accepting the special order. If the normal fixed costs are included in the price of the special order, the price may be too high and the business firm could lose the entire order and the contribution margin to be earned on the special order. Only the relevant (variable) costs should be used in the decision analysis to arrive at an appropriate price. Fixed cost are relevant only if incurred to facilitate the special order.

Importance of Time Span in Special Order

The special order is a one-time order for specific units, say 1,000 units that will use current excess capacity. Because no special setups or equipment are required to produce the order, it is appropriate to consider only variable costs in computing the order's profitability.

But what if the order giver wants the company to sign a multiyear contract to provide 1,000 units per month at ₹ 925 each? Under these circumstances, management would be well advised to reject the contract because there is a high probability that cost increases would make the order unprofitable in later years. At the very least, management should insist that a cost escalation clause be added to the purchase agreement, specifying that the selling price would increase to cover any cost increases and detailing the cost computation.

Of more concern is the variable nature of all long-run costs. Given adequate time, management must replace fixed assets and may adjust both the number of machines as well as the size of machines used in the manufacturing process. Accordingly, in the long run, all costs (including costs classified as fixed in a given period) are relevant. To remain in business in the long run, the company must replace equipment, pay property taxes, pay administrative salaries, and so forth. Consequently, management should consider *all costs* (fixed and variable, manufacturing and nonmanufacturing) in evaluating a long-term contract.[13]

Example

The following example illustrates the special order decisions.

A manufacturing company produces 20,000 units by operating at 60% of the capacity and sells at a price of ₹ 3000 per unit. The budgeted figures for the year 2017 are as follows:

	***Production* (20,000 *units*)** ₹
Raw materials @ 425	85,00,000
Direct labour@ 575	1,15,00,000
Variable factory overhead @ 775	1,55,00,000
Fixed factory overhead	1,25,00,000
Variable selling costs 2.75% of selling price	
Fixed selling and administrative costs	72,50,000

The company receives a special order for 10,000 units from a firm. The company desires to earn a profit of ₹ 100 per unit and no selling expenses are to be incurred for the special order. The minimum price on the special order and income statements are as follows:

Pricing of Special Order

	(10,000 *units*) ₹
Variable costs to be incurred:	
Raw materials	425
Direct labour	575
Variable overhead	775
Variable cost per unit (no selling expenses)	1775
Desired profit	100
Minimum price	1875
Increase in sales = 10,000 units × ₹ 1875 = ₹ 1,87,50,000	

Income Statement

	Without special order (₹)	*Special order* (₹)	*With special order* (₹)
Sales	6,00,00,000	1,87,50,000	7,87,50,000
Less: Variable costs:			
Raw materials	85,00,000	42,50,000	1,27,50,000
Direct labour	1,15,00,000	57,50,000	1,72,50,000
Variable factory overhead	1,55,00,000	77,50,000	2,32,50,000
Variable selling costs (2.75% of selling price)	16,50,000	—	16,50,000
Total variable costs	3,71,50,000	1,77,50,000	5,49,00,000
Less: Fixed costs:			
Fixed factory overhead	1,25,00,000	—	1,25,00,000
Fixed selling & administrative costs	72,50,000	—	72,50,000
Total fixed costs	1,97,50,000	—	1,97,50,000
Total costs	5,69,00,000	1,77,50,000	7,46,50,000
Net income before taxes	31,00,000	10,00,000	41,00,000

From the above analysis, it is clear that the acceptance of the special order will increase the profit by ₹ 10,00,000. Also the bid price (₹ 1875) is significantly less than the normal price of ₹ 3000.

Qualitative Considerations

Although an analysis of cost and revenue information may indicate that a special order would be profitable in the short run, management might still reject the order because of qualitative considerations. Any concerns regarding the order's impact on regular customers might lead management to reject the order even if there is excess capacity. If the order involves a special low price, regular customers might demand a similar price reduction and threaten to take their business elsewhere. Alternatively, management might accept the special order while operating at capacity if they believed there were long-term benefits associated with penetrating a new market. Legal factors must also be considered if the special order is from a buyer who competes with regular customers.

Replace or Retain

The decision to replace or retain plant and equipment is a capital investment or long-term decision and should be taken very carefully. The differential costs which are important in retain or replace decisions are the following: change in fixed overheads costs, loss on sale of old equipment, capital investment and related costs such as rate of return and interest. Management should also consider differential benefits likely to be derived such as higher production and increased sales, realisable value of old machine, saving in operating costs, tax advantages, if any.

Example

Suppose a company has purchased a plant for ₹ 1,00,000 five years ago which has a life of 10 years with no salvage value. The present book value is ₹ 50,000. Management is considering the replacement of this plant with a new plant costing ₹ 80,000 having a life of five years with no scrap value at the end of its life. The costs of operating present plant and the proposed plant are as follows:

	Present Plant ₹	Proposed Plant ₹
Variable costs:		
Labour, supplies, power, etc.	80,000	48,000
Fixed costs:		
Insurance, taxes, etc.	10,000	12,000
Depreciation	10,000	16,000
	1,00,000	76,000

It appears that the proposed plant would result into cost savings of ₹ 24,000 (1,00,000 – 76,000). However, the book value of the present equipment is a sunk cost and not relevant in the decision. The following analysis helps in making a better use of the data:

	₹	₹
Variable costs:		
Labour, supplies, power, etc.	80,000	48,000
Fixed costs:		
Insurance, taxes, etc.	10,000	12,000
Depreciation	0	16,000
	90,000	76,000

The purchase of the new plant results in a saving of ₹ 14,000 (₹ 90,000 – 76,000). Management has to consider whether this benefit is enough to justify the investment of ₹ 80,000 in new machinery.

To take another example, suppose, the management of a company wants to replace an old machine with a new one. Data are as follows.

	Old Machine ₹	New Machine ₹
Cost	2,40,000	1,20,000
Book value	80,000	—
Disposal value now	8,000	—
Disposal value at end of life	—	—
Variable costs	1,60,000	1,12,000
Annual revenue	2,00,000	2,00,000
Estimate life (remaining)	4 years (future)	4 years

The analysis is as follows:

<u>*Relevant costs:*</u>

(*a*) Disposal value now — represents a future cash inflow.

(*b*) Cost of new machine — represents a future cash outflow.

(*c*) Variable costs — incremental costs.

<u>*Irrelevant costs:*</u>

(*a*) Cost of old machine — past (historical) cost.

(*b*) Book value and gain or loss on disposal — both involve depreciation and original cost (that is, sunk cost).

Annual revenue — this would be relevant (as it represents a future cash inflow) if it differs between alternatives. But in this example it is common to both options, and not relevant.

On a Four-year Basis

Keep		*Replace*
₹		₹
6,40,000	Variable costs	4,48,000
—	Cost of new machine	1,20,000
		5,68,000
	Disposal value	(8,000)
6,40,000		5,60,000

Net benefit in replacement = ₹ 6,40,000 – 5,60,000 = ₹ 80,000

Decision – It should be replaced.

The amount of net benefit of ₹ 80,000 can be found using an alternative approach, as explained below:

		Replace
	₹	₹
Saving in variable costs:		
(₹ 1,60,000 – 1,12,000) × 4 years =		1,92,000
Less: Cost of new machine	1,20,000	
Less: Disposal value of old machinery	8,000	(1,12,000)
		80,000

Decision again is to replace the old machinery and buy the new machinery.

Buy or Lease

Another problem that management usually faces is whether to buy an asset or whether to lease it. The lease of an asset results into future cash payments (outflow) which should be discounted back to the present. Assume a company is considering whether to lease or buy an asset. The asset can be purchased for ₹ 6,75,00,000 or it may be leased for five years by paying rental payments of ₹ 2,50,00,000 per year for the first two years, ₹ 1,50,00,000 for the next two years and ₹ 1,00,00,000 for the last year. The company can borrow ₹ 6,75,00,000 from its bank. If the present value of the five years rental payments exceeds ₹ 6,75,00,000, the asset should be purchased and not leased; however, if the present value in aggregate is less than ₹ 6,75,00,000 it will be better to lease the asset.

If the lease of the asset is considered an operating lease, the lease payments would be deducted from the revenue annually to arrive at pretax income. This method lowers the tax liability in the earlier years of the asset life than would be allowed if the company were required to depreciate the asset. To determine the benefits in tax liability, it is necessary to consider the interest deductions that would be obtained if a company were to borrow the funds to acquire the asset. The interest payments would be tax deductible. In addition, the asset would be depreciated and the amount of depreciation would be deducted for income tax purposes. If the asset is to be leased, the total payments would be deducted for income tax purposes. The differences between these two floors must be analysed and the net present value of the difference in tax payments should be determined. This figure will guide management to decide whether to buy or to lease.

QUALITATIVE FACTORS IN DECISION MAKING

> **Qualitative factors** are those elements relating to a decision which cannot be expressed in monetary terms or can be expressed in monetary terms with great difficulty or inaccuracy.

Differential analysis or relevant information analysis should be considered as only one input for the final decision to be made by the managers. In fact, a number of qualitaitve factors may have vital impact on managerial decisions. Qualitative factors are those elements relating to a decision which cannot be expressed in monetary terms or can be expressed in monetary terms with great difficulty or inaccuracy. Managers should consider qualitative factors also while making decisions, otherwise it is likely that a wrong decision will be made.

For example, in a make or buy decision, decision-makers should consider many qualitative factors also such as quality of items being purchased from outside, reliability of supply sources, expected stability of prices over the next several years, service quality, labour relations in the supplier's company, etc. It may also be found that decision to purchase from outside could result in closing down of the company's facilities for manufacturing the component. Such a decision will influence adversely the morale of company's employees which may, in turn, affect future production and plans of the company. Dependence on an outside supplier is also risky as the suppliers sometimes may not supply the components on time. In such a case, the buyer-company will not be in a position to fulfill customers orders and thus the company may lose its goodwill in the market resulting, further, in poor future sales.

Qualitative factors are difficult to quantify in monetary terms. However, the decision-maker should try to have as much quantifiable information as possible in these situations. For instance, the effect on customer goodwill due to delay on the part of supplier in meeting orders can be estimated. If there are many suppliers available in the market for the components, this qualitative factor can be ignored as components can be purchased from any supplier in case of delay. However, if the components can be purchased from a single supplier, these qualitative factors will be of great importance. In this situation, the decision-maker should compare the cost savings due to purchasing the component from outside (rather than manufacturing within the company) with the risk associated with supplier delaying the fulfilment of orders. If cost savings are more than the (quantifiable) risk, the company may continue to purchase from outside; if cost savings are insufficient to cover the risk related with this qualitative aspect, probably it may not be advisable to purchase the component from outside.

Managers must study carefully the data to be used in decision-making. Other qualitative factors besides cost should also be given proper attention. The pressure of competition, the maintenance of source of supply and of certain marketing outlets, and the maintenance of the existing personnel organization and morale, opportunity to balance risk, benefit of providing complete product line to attract new customers may often be the real determinants of business decisions. The quantitative information alone does not provide a solution to all business problems. Sometimes, other factors are more important than cost factors. If the qualitative factors are essentially equal across alternatives, relevant costs become the deciding factor instead of being just one input among several factors to be considered for managerial decisions. The cost of developing information for decision-making should not exceed the potential benefits to be obtained. It should be ensured that accurate and timely information is available to managers for decision-making and planning at the least possible expense.

Illustrative Problem 1 (Outsourcing Decision)

Sterling Corporation is considering outsourcing its accounts receivable function, a support service in the finance department. The Co's cost management analyst expects annual benefits that include personnel cost savings of ₹ 1,21,000, facilities saving of ₹ 90,000, other support service cost savings of ₹ 60,000, and no loss of service quality. The analyst also estimated annual costs of the decision to include the contract cost to Mohan Co. of ₹ 1,60,000, severance costs of dismissed personnel of ₹ 20,000, and contract administration costs of ₹ 12,000.

Required:

(*a*) Based on the quantifiable benefits and costs of the decision, would you recommend that Sterling should outsource its accounts receivable function? What qualitative factors should the company also consider?

(*b*) Sterling did outsource the accounts receivable function and measured actual benefits to include personnel cost savings of ₹ 82,000, facilities cost savings of ₹ 1,00,000, support service cost savings of ₹ 70,000. Actual costs included ₹ 1,60,000 for the outsourced service, ₹ 30,000 for training costs, and ₹ 13,000 for contract administration. Furthermore, customer billing complaints were lower than in previous years; sales growth was lower; and employee turnover in other support service areas was higher. Prepare suitable analysis.

(*c*) On balance, do you agree with the outsourcing decision? Why or why not?

Solution:

(*a*) Expected benefits of the decision total ₹ 2,71,000 (₹ 1,21,000 + 90,000 + 60,000) while expected costs total ₹ 1,92,000 (₹ 1,60,000 + 20,000 + 12,000), with a net benefit of ₹ 79,000. Qualitative factors to consider include service quality (timeliness, accuracy), impacts on existing customers, contacts with existing customers, and impacts on current and future employees.

(*b*)

Benefits of outsourcing accounts receivable	**Expected amount**	**Actual amount**	**Variance**	**Qualitative Information**
	₹	₹	₹	
1. Personnel cost savings	1,21,000	82,000	(39,000)	
2. Facilities cost savings	90,000	1,00,000	10,000	
3. Support cost savings	60,000	70,000	10,000	
4. Quality of service	—	—	—	Fewer billing complaints
Total quantifiable benefits	2,71,000	2,52,000	(19,000)	

Costs of outsourcing	**Expected amount**	**Actual amount**	**Variance**	**Qualitative Information**
	₹	₹	₹	
1. Contracted service	1,60,000	160,000	0	
2. Training costs	20,000	30,000	10,000	
3. Contract administration	12,000	13,000	1,000	
4. Loss of direct contact with customers	—	—	—	Lower sales growth

5. Adverse effects of personnel reductions	—	—	—	Increased personnel turnover
Total quantifiable costs	1,92,000	2,03,000	11,000	
Net quantifiable annual benefits	79,000	49,000	(30,000)	

(c) Although quantitative benefits were lower than expected, they are still positive. Unknown is whether the outsourcing contract is responsible for lower sales growth and increased personnel turnover. This looks like a close call, and deserving of more investigation.

Illustrative Problem 2 (Closing a Division)

The Indian Defense Department has the difficult decision of deciding which military divisions to shut down. Military and political factors obviously matter, but cost savings are also an important factor. Consider two naval divisions, one located on the West Coast and the other on South Coast. The Navy has decided that it needs only one of those two divisions permanently, so one must be shut down. The decision regarding which divisions to shut down will be made on cost considerations alone. The following information is available.

(*a*) The West Coast division was built at a cost of ₹ 100 crore. The operating costs of the division are ₹ 400 crore per year. The divsion is built on land owned by the Navy, so the Navy pays nothing for the use of the property. If the division is closed, the land will be sold to developers for ₹ 500 crore.

(*b*) The South Coast division was built at a cost of ₹ 150 crore on land leased by the Navy from private citizens. The Navy can choose to lease the land permanently for a lease payment of ₹ 3 crore per year. If it decides to keep the South Coast division open, the Navy plans to invest ₹ 60 crore in a fixed income securities, which at 5% interest will earn ₹ 3 crore the government needs for the lease payments. The land and building will immediately revert back to the owner if the division is closed. The operating costs of the division excluding lease payments, are ₹ 300 crore per year.

(*c*) If the West Coast division is shut down, the Navy will have to transfer some personnel to the South Coast facility. As a result, the yearly operating costs at South Coast will increase by ₹ 100 crore per year. If the South Coast facility is closed down, no extra costs will be incurred to operate the West Coast facility.

The Defense Department argues that it is cheaper to shut down the South Coast division for two reasons:

(*i*) It would save ₹ 100 crore per year in additional costs required to operate the South Coast division, and

(*ii*) It would save the lease payment of ₹ 3 crore per year. The West Coast division requires no cash payments for use of the land because the land is owned by the Navy.

Do you agree with the Defense Department's arguments and conclusions? In your answer, identify and explain all costs that you consider relevant and all costs that you consider irrelevant for the closing decision of the division. *(M.Com., Delhi University)*

Solution:

Relevant Cost Analysis

The future outlay operating costs will be ₹ 400 crore regardless of which division is closed, given the additional ₹ 100 crore in costs at South Coast if West Coast is closed. Further, one of the divisions will permanently remain open while the other will be shut down. The only relevant revenue and cost comparisons are:

(*a*) ₹ 500 crore from sale of the West Coast division. Note that the historical cost of building the West Coast division (₹ 100 crore) is irrelevant. Note, also, that future increase in the value of the land at the West Coast division is also irrelevant. One of the divisions must be kept open, so if it is decided to keep the West Coast division open, the Defense Department will not be able to sell this land at a future date.

(*b*) ₹ 60 crore in savings in fixed income securities if the South Coast division is closed. Again, the historical cost of building the South Coast division (₹ 150 crore) is irrelevant.

The relevant costs and benefits analysis favours closing the West Coast division despite the objections raised by the Defense Department. The net benefit equals ₹ 440 (₹ 500 – ₹ 60) crore.

Illustrative Problem 3 (Decision About Sales Outlet Closure)

Apex Ltd has introduced a special pack of festival gift Hamper and priced each Hamper at ₹ 400. The standard cost of producing each hamper is ₹ 200. The Hampers are sold through three big outlets in 3 city Malls and also through a cluster of small neighborhood stores scattered over the city.

Data relating to each outlet is as under:

	City Mall-1	City Mall-II	City Mall-III	Neighbourhood Stores
Sales (in units)	1000	500	300	600
KM Travelled for delivery	1000	500	1200	7500
No. of emergency delivery	–	–	2	–
No. of orders taken	5	3	7	10
Discounts (% of sales value)	20	15	20	6
Sales commission (% of sales value)	10	10	10	10
Publicity Cost (₹)	30,000	40,000	45,000	60,000

The following additional information are provided:

(*i*) Delivery costs by the company's own transport vary according to distance and cost ₹ 5 per km over the standard product cost of ₹ 200 per hamper.

(*ii*) Out of standard product cost of ₹ 200, 40% represents fixed overhead.

(*iii*) When the sales outlets face emergency stock out situation, special deliveries are made and charged @ ₹ 500 per delivery.

(*iv*) Each outlet negotiates independently the discounts on sale price. Publicity Costs are specific to each outlet.

(*v*) Order taking costs are ₹ 200 per order.

Required:

Workout the profitability for each of the outlets and also give your opinion with reasoning whether sales through any outlet is to be stopped.

Solution:

Comparative profitability statement

	City Mall-1	*City Mall-II*	*City Mall-III*	*Neighbourhood Stores*
No. of units Sold	1000.00	500.00	300.00	600.00
		(₹ in THOUSANDS)		
Sales	400.00	200.00	120.00	240.00
Less : Variable Production Cost	120.00	60.00	36.00	72.00
Contribution	280.00	140.00	84.00	168.00
Delivery Costs	(5.00)	(2.50)	(6.00)	(37.50)
Emergency Delivery Cost	–	–	(1.00)	–
Order Taking Costs	(1.00)	(0.60)	(1.40)	(2.00)
Discounts	(80.00)	(30.00)	(24.00)	(14.40)
Sales Commission	(40.00)	(20.00)	(12.00)	(24.00)
Publicity Cost	(30.00)	(40.00)	(45.00)	(60.00)
Profit Before Fixed Overhead	124.00	46.90	(5.40)	30.10
Contribution/Sales (%)	70	70	70	70
Profit / Sales (%)	31.00	23.45	(4.50)	12.54

Comments:

1. For all outlets, contribution to sales Ratio is same (70%)
2. Profit to sales ratio varies from 31% to 4.50% for different outlets.
3. City Mall-III has incurred loss due to higher rate of discount given to it and also excess publicity cost. For this outlet the company had to make emergency delivery.
4. City Mall-III had placed small orders, but City Mall-I was most prudent in that respect. The publicity cost is lowest for City Mall-I.
5. Delivery costs for neighborhood stores are high due to several deliveries made to different stores.

In consideration of analysis above, about City Mall-III, the company should consider to renegotiate the existing contract in respect of it. Also, the company may consider whether City Mall-III should be discontinued as a sales outlet.

Illustrative Problems 4 (Make or Buy Decision)

The Theater Division of New Delhi School of Drama, employs five people in its Publication Department. These people lay out pages for pamphlets, brochures, and other publications for the productions of the school. The pages are delivered to an outside company for printing. The school is considering an outside publication service for the layout work. The outside service is quoting a price of ₹ 15 per layout page. The budget for the Publication Department for 2017 is as follows:

Salaries	₹ 2,20,000
Benefits	35,000
Supplies	30,000
Office expenses	25,000
Office depreciation	30,000
Computer depreciation	22,000
Total	₹ 3,62,000

The department expects to lay out 20,000 pages for 2017. The computers used by the department have an estimated residual value of ₹ 7,000. The Publication Department office space would be used for future administrative needs, if the department's function were purchased from the outside.

Required:

(*a*) Prepare a differential analysis report, for the make-or-buy decision, considering the 2017 differential revenues and costs.

(*b*) On the basis of your analysis in part (*a*), should the page layout work be purchased from an outside company?

(*c*) What additional considerations might factor into the decision making?

Solution:

(*a*)

Proposal to Purchase Outside Page Layout Services
For the year 2017

Differential revenue:		
Salvage of computer equipment		₹ 7,000
Differential expenses:		
Purchase price of layout work:		
Number of pages	20,000	
Price per page	× ₹ 15	
Total		₹ 3,00,000
Differential cost to perform internally:		
Salaries	₹ 2,20,000	
Benefits	35,000	
Supplies	30,000	
Office expenses	25,000	310,000
Cost savings from purchasing layout services		₹ 10,000
Total benefit from using an outside service		₹ 17,000

(*b*) The benefit from using an outside service is shown to be ₹ 17,000 greater than performing the layout work internally. The fixed costs (depreciation expenses) in the budget are irrelevant to the decision. Thus, the work should be purchased from the outside on a strictly financial basis. In addition, the decision to purchase from the outside would be further favoured if the need for administrative expansion space were great. If more administrative space were needed immediately, then any avoided lease costs would become a differential benefit to the decision to out-source.

(*c*) Before electing to terminate the five employees, the theatre division should consider the long-run impact of the decision. Specifically, future page layout rates may grow faster than the cost of internal salaries, thus favouring the use of employees over the long term. This would especially be the case if the outside company provided a low bid in order to win the initial business. In addition, the theatre division may wish to consider noneconomic factors such as the ability to more directly control the quality and timing of the layout work by internal employees.

Illustrative Problem 5 (Drop a Product)

A firm makes only three products and has no space to expand further. Its management wish to know which products are the most profitable so that they can concentrate their sales promotion accordingly. The following informations is available:

	A ₹ '000	*B* ₹ '000	*C* ₹ '000	*Total* ₹ '000
Sales	300	150	400	850
Less:				
Direct labour	20	20	30	70
Direct materials	100	60	100	260
Variable overheads	30	10	30	70
Allocated fixed overheads	75	25	155	255
Total costs	225	115	315	655
Profit	75	35	85	195
Space occupied (sq.m.)	3,000	1,000	6,000	10,000

Advise the management

Solution:

In this situation, the scarce resource is space and, therefore, the firm should aim to make the most profitable use of that space. This will be achieved, not by calculating the profit per square metre, but by calculating the contribution per square metre. The reasoning here is that fixed overheads are always somewhat arbitrarily apportioned to product lines. It is also the case that as soon as the volumes in the product mix change, then the profit does not change pro rata because of the very nature of fixed costs.

The information should therefore be presented in a marginal costing format to arrive at the contribution per square metre on each product:

(₹ '000)

		A ₹	*B* ₹	*C* ₹	*Total* ₹
	Sales	300	150	400	850
Less:	Variable costs	150	90	160	400
	Contribution	150	60	240	450
	Contribution ratio	50%	40%	60%	53%
	Space occupied (sq.m.)	3,000	1,000	6,000	10,000
	Contribution per sq.m.	.05	.06	.04	.045

Without any scarce resource we should rank the three products in order of their contribution ratio, which is the order CAB. When we take the scarce resource of space into account, and aim to maximize the contribution earned in that space, the contribution per square metre ranks the products in the different order of BAC.

A firm facing this situation should endeavour to switch productive resources away from Product C to Product B primarily, or, failing that, from C to A. Sales promotion and marketing effort should be biased to this end, but obviously there is no point in producing products, however profitable they may seem on paper, if there is no demand for them.

Another point to bear in mind is whether the individual products comprise a product range where demand is not discrete, but is either competitive or complementary. In the former case, the promotion of the most profitable product will reduce demand for the other less profitable products in the range, to the benefit of the firm overall. In the latter case demand for all three products may move in step with each other, so that one product should not be promoted in isolation.

Illustrative Problem 6 (Discontinuing a Product)

A company manufactures three products. The respective details are:

	A	*B*	*C*
Capacity engaged	(20%)	(40%)	(40%)
Units produced	2,000	5,000	6,000
Cost per unit:	(₹)	(₹)	(₹)
Material cost	20	32	36
Wages	10	12	16
Variable overheads	7	9	11
Fixed overheads	6	9	10
Total	43	62	73
Selling price per unit	40	75	85
Profit per unit (loss)	(3)	13	12

The management proposes to discontinue product A as for the last few years it is showing a loss. Future prospects of the other two products being good, it is intended to utilise the disengaged capacity in product A, in product B and product C equally.

	B	*C*
Expected rise in prices and cost (%) :		
Material	10%	10%
Wages	5%	5%
Selling Price	2%	5%

Fixed overheads shall remain the same. You are required to prepare a statement of projected profitability and advise the management as to whether the scheme may be adopted. (*M.Com., Delhi*)

Solution:

Statement of Projected Profitability with Products B and C Only

Particulars		*Products* B	C	*Combined*
Capacity engaged (%)		50	50	100
Units produced		6,250	7,500	
Selling price (₹)		76.50	89.25	
Sales revenue (₹)		4,78,125	6,69,375	11,47,500
Less:	*Variable costs:*			
	Material costs			
	B ₹ 35.20 per unit	2,20,000		2,20,000
	C ₹ 39.60 per unit		2,97,000	2,97,000
Wages:	B: ₹ 12.60	78,750		78,750
	C: ₹ 16.80		1,26,000	1,26,000
Variable overheads:				
	B: ₹ 9	56,250		56,250
	C: ₹ 11		82,500	82,500
Total		3,55,000	5,05,500	8,60,500
Contribution		1,23,125	1,63,875	2,87,000
Less:	*Fixed overheads:*			
	A: 2,000 × ₹ 6 = ₹ 12,000			
	B: 5,000 × 9 = ₹ 45,000			
	C: 6,000 × 10 = ₹ 60,000			1,17,000
	Net profit			1,70,000

Statement of Profitability with Products A, B and C

Particulars		*Products* A	B	C	*Combined*
	Capacity engaged	20%	40%	40%	100%
	Units produced	2,000	5,000	6,000	—
		₹	₹	₹	₹
	Sales revenue	80,000	3,82,500	5,35,500	9,98,000
Less:	Variable costs (new)	74,000	2,84,000	4,04,400	7,62,400
	Contribution	6,000	98,500	1,31,100	2,35,600
Less:	fixed costs				1,17,000
	Net profit				1,18,600

Notes:

(*i*) Selling price per unit as well as variable cost per unit pertaining to product A does not increase.

(*ii*) Profitability statement with products A, B and C taken together is prepared on the basis of revised cost data. The reason is that variable costs as well as selling prices in respect of products B and C will increase, irrespective of the fact whether product A is dropped or not. The only point of difference is the number of units produced.

Decision: After dropping product A, the total net profit increases to ₹ 1,70,000. Therefore, management should accept the scheme of dropping product A.

Illustrative Problem 7 (Further Processing Decision)

A company's plant processes 1,50,000 kgs. of raw material in a month to produce two products, viz, '*P*' and '*Q*'. The cost of raw material is ₹ 12 per kg. The process costs for a month are:

	₹
Direct Materials	90,000
Direct Wages	1,20,000
Variable Overheads	1,00,000
Fixed Overheads	1,00,000

The loss in process is 5% of input and the output ratio of *P* and *Q* which emerge simultaneously is 1 : 2. The selling prices of the two products at the point of split off are: *P* ₹ 12 per kg. And *Q* ₹ 20 per kg. A proposal is available to process *P* further by mixing it with other purchased materials. The entire current output of the plant can be so processed further to obtain a new product '*S*'. The price per kg. of *S* is ₹ 15 and each kg of output of *S* will require one kilogram of input *P*. The cost of processing of *P* into *S* (including other materials) is ₹ 1,85,000 per month.

You are required to prepare a statement showing the monthly profitability based both on the existing manufacturing operations and on further processing.

Will you recommend further processing?

Solution:

Working Notes:

	Kgs.
1. *Material input*	1,50,000
Less: Loss of Material in process (5% of 1,50,000)	7,500
Total output	1,42,500

2. Output of *P* and *Q* are in the ratio of 1 : 2 of the total output:

$$P = \frac{1,42,500 \times 1}{3} = 47,500 \text{ kg}$$

$$Q = \frac{1,42,500 \times 2}{3} = 95,500 \text{ kg}$$

3. *Joint Costs*:

	₹
Material (input) (1,50,000 kg. × ₹ 12)	18,00,000
Direct materials	90,000
Direct Wages	1,20,000
Variable overheads	1,00,000
Fixed overheads	1,00,000
	22,10,000

4. Sales Revenue of P, Q and S
   $P = 47{,}500 \times ₹\,12 = ₹\,5{,}70{,}000$
   $Q = 95{,}000 \times ₹\,20 = ₹\,19{,}00{,}000$
   $S = 47{,}500 \times ₹\,15 = ₹\,7{,}12{,}500.$
5. Apportionment of joint costs viz. ₹ 22,10,000 over P and Q in proportion of the sales value i.e. ₹ 5,70,000 and ₹ 19,00,000, i.e., 3 : 10 is :

	Total	*P*	*Q*
	₹	₹	₹
Joint cost apportionment	22,10,000	5,10,000	17,00,000
In the ratio of 3 : 10		$\left(\frac{₹\,22{,}10{,}000 \times 3}{13}\right)$	$\left(\frac{₹\,22{,}10{,}000 \times 10}{13}\right)$

6. Total Cost of 47,500 kg. of S = Joint Cost of P + Cost of Processing P into S.
   = ₹ 5,10,000 + ₹ 1,85,000
   = ₹ 6,95,000.

Statement Showing the Monthly Profitability

	Based on existing manufacturing operations			*Based on further processing of P into S*		
	Products			*Products*		
	P	*Q*	*Total*	*S*	*Q*	*Total*
Sales quantity (kgs.)	47,500	95,000	1,42,500	47,500	95,000	1,42,500
	₹	₹	₹	₹	₹	₹
Sales Revenue (Refer to working note 4)	5,70,000	19,00,000	24,70,000	7,12,500	19,00,000	26,12,500
Less: Joint Costs (Refer to working note 5 and 6)	5,10,000	17,00,000	22,10,000	6,95,000	17,00,000	23,95,000
Profit	60,000	2,00,000	2,60,000	17,500	2,00,000	2,17,500

Recommendation: Further processing of P is not recommended as it results in a lower profit of P.

Illustrative Problem 8 (Sell or Process Further Decision)

A company produces three joint products in one common process. Each product can be separately processed further after split-off point. The estimated data for a particular month are as under:

	Product		
	A	*B*	*C*
Selling price at split-off point (₹ litre)	100	120	150
Selling price after further processing (₹ litre)	200	200	250
Post separation point cost (₹)	3,50,000	4,50,000	2,00,000
Output in litres	3,500	2,500	2,000

Pre-separation point joint costs are estimated to be ₹ 2,40,000. As per current practice such costs are apportioned to the three products according to production quantity.

You are required to :

(*i*) Prepare a statement of estimated profit or loss for each product and in total for the month if all three products are processed further; and

(*ii*) From the profit statement comment how profit could be maximized if one or more products are sold at split-off points.

Solution:

(*i*) Profitability after further processing all three products:

	Product			(₹ in '000)
	A	*B*	*C*	*Total*
	₹	₹	₹	₹
Sales revenue	700	500	500	1700
Costs: Pre-separation*	– 105	– 75	– 60	– 240
post-separation	– 350	–450	–200	–1000
Profit / Loss (–)	245	–25	240	460

*apportioned on the basis of output ,i.e. @ (₹ 2,40,000/8,000 litres or ₹ 30 per litre).

(*b*) (*ii*) **Whether to process further or not**

Profitability by further processing

Product	*Incremental revenue*	*Incremental cost*	*Incremental profit*
	₹ '000	₹ '000	₹ '000
A	₹ 100 × 3,500 = 350350	nil	
B	₹ 80 × 2,500 = 200450	–250	
C	₹ 100 × 2,000 = 200200	nil	

It is seen that further processing will not be gainful for products *A* or *C*, while there will be loss of ₹ 2,50,000 in product *B*.

Note that instead of this product-wise analysis, one can find the same overall result if a study is made of the joint products together, as under:

	Product A	*Product B*	*Product C*	*Total*
	₹ '000	₹ '000	₹ '000	
Sales revenue (pre-separation)	350	300	300	950
Cost up to pre-separation	–105	–75	–60	– 240
Profit	245	225	240	710
Profit at post-separation, as worked in answer (*b*) (*i*)				460

Further processing will result in reduction of profit by ₹ 2,50,000 [7,10,000 – 4,60,000].

Illustrative Problem 9 (Replace or Retain)

Bajaj Co. purchased a new machine one year ago at a cost 60,00,000. Although the machine operates well, the president of the company is wondering if the company should replace it with a new electronically operated machine that has just come on the market. The new machine would slash annual operating costs by two-thirds, as shown in the comparative data below:

	Present Machine	*Proposed New Machine*
Purchase cost new	60,00,000	90,00,000
Extimated useful life new	6 years	5 years
Annual operating costs	42,00,000	14,00,000
Annual straight-line depreciation	10,00,000	18,00,000
Remaining book value	50,00,000	—
Salvage value now	10,00,000	—
Salvage value in 5 years	—0—	—0—

In trying to decide whether to purchase the new machine, the president has prepared the following analysis:

Book value of the old machine	₹ 50,00,000
Less salvage value	10,00,000
Net loss from disposal	₹ 40,00,000

"Even though the new machine looks good," said the president, "we can't get rid of that old machine if it means taking a huge loss on it. We'll have to use the old machine for at least a few more years."

Sales are expected to be ₹ 2,00,00,000 per year, and selling and administrative expenses are expected to be ₹ 1,26,00,000 per year, regardless of which machine is used.

Required:

1. Prepare a summary income statment covering the next five years, assuming:
   a. That the new machine is not purchased.
   b. That the new machine is purchased.
2. Determine the desirability of purchasing the new machine using only relevant costs in your analysis.

Solution:

1. a. and b.

	5 Years Summary		
	***Keep Old* Machine**	***Buy New Machine***	***Difference***
Sales (₹ 2,00,00,000 × 5 years)	₹ 10,00,00,000	₹ 10,00,00,000	—0—
Selling and administrative expenses (1,26,00,000 × 5 years)	6,30,00,000	6,30,00,000	—0—
Operating costs	21,0,00,000	70,00,000	1,40,00,000
Depreciation of the old machine, or loss write-off	50,00,000	50,00,000	—0—
Salvage value—old machine	—	(10,00,000)	10,00,000
Depreciation—New machine		90,00,000	(90,00,000)
Total expenses	8,90,00,000	8,30,00,000	60,00,000
Net operating income	₹ 1,10,00,000	₹ 1,70,00,000	₹ 60,00,000

* In a formal income statement, these two items should be shown as a single 40,00,000 "loss from disposal" figure.

The new machine should be purchased. The savings in operating costs over the next five years will exceed the net investment by ₹ 60,00,000.

2. Reduction in annual operating

(₹ 28,00,000 × 5 years)		₹ 1,40,00,000
Investment in the new machine:		
Original cost	₹ 90,00,000	
Less salvage value of the old machine	10,00,000	80,00,000
Net advantage of purchasing the new machine		₹ 60,00,000

All other costs are either sunk or do not differ between the alternatives.

Illustrative Problem 10 (Accept New Order)

A toy manufacturer earns an average net profit of ₹ 30 per piece in a selling price of ₹ 150 by producing and selling 60,000 pieces at 60% of the potential capacity. Composition of his cost of sales is:

	₹
Direct material	40
Direct wages	10
Works overhead	60 (50% fixed)
Sales	10 (25% variable)

During the current year, he intends to produce the same number but anticipates that:

(*a*) his fixed charge will go up by 10%

(*b*) rates of direct labour will increase by 20%

(*c*) rates of direct material will increase by 5%

(*d*) selling price cannot be increased.

Under these circumstances, he obtains an order for a further 20% of his capacity. What minimum price will you recommend for accepting the order to ensure the manufacture, an overall profit of ₹ 18,05,000?

Solution:

Marginal Cost for the Current year

	₹
Direct material	42
Direct wages	12
Variable overheads:	
Works overhead	30
Sales overhead	2.5
Total marginal cost	86.5
Contribution per unit	63.5
Selling price	150

Statement of Profit on Sale of 60,000 Units

	₹	₹
Sales		90,00,000
Less: Variable cost (60,000 × ₹ 86.5)		51,90,000
Contribution		38,10,000
Less: Fixed costs:		
Works overheads (18,00,000 + 1,80,000)	19,80,000	
Sales overheads (4,50,000 + 45,000)	4,95,000	24,75,000
Profit		13,35,000
Profit required	18,05,000	
Profit on 60,000 units	13,35,000	
Profit to be earned on 20,000 units	4,70,000	

Statement of Minimum Selling Price Per Unit for an Order of 20,000 Units

	₹
Variable costs (20,000 × 86.5)	17,30,000
Desired profit	4,70,000
Total sales	22,00,000
Selling price per unit = $\frac{₹\,22,00,000}{20,000}$	110

The above can be verified as under:

Sales 60,000 units × 150 = 90,00,000		
20,000 units × 110 = 22,00,000		1,12,00,000
Less: Variable costs:		
80,000 × 86.5 = 69,20,000		
Fixed costs = 24,75,000		93,95,000
Profit		18,05,000

Illustrative Problem 11 (Shutdown Decision)

TQM Limited makes engines for motor cars for its parent company and for two other motor car manufacturers.

On 31st December, the company has sufficient work order for January and one further order for 21,000 engines. Due to recession in the economy, no further order are expected until May when it is hoped economic prospect for the motor car industry will have improved. Recently factory has been working at only 75% of full capacity and the order for 21,000 engines represents about one month production at this level of activity.

The board of directors are currently considering following two options:

(*i*) Complete the order in February and close the factory in March and April.

OR

(*ii*) Operate at 25 per cent of full capacity for each of three months of February, March and April.

The costs per month at different levels of activities are as follows:

	At 75% (₹)	At 25% (₹)	Idle (₹)
Direct Material	5,25,000	1,75,000	—
Direct Labour	5,23,600	1,73,250	—
Factory overhead:			
Indirect material	8,400	4,900	4,900
Indirect labour	1,01,500	59,500	—
Indirect expenses:			
Repairs and maintenance	28,000	28,000	—
Others expenses	52,500	34,300	26,600
Office overheads:			
Staff salaries	1,48,400	98,000	67,550
Other overheads	28,000	19,950	11,200

Other information is as follows:

- Material cost and labour cost will not be incurred where there is no production.
- On the reopening of the factory, one time cost of training and engagement of new personnel would be ₹ 65,800 and overhauling cost of plant would be ₹ 14,000.
- Parent company can purchase engines from open market at reasonable price.

Required:

(*i*) To express your opinion, along with calculations, as to whether the plant should be shut down during the month of March and April or operate 25% of full capacity for three months.

(*ii*) To list and comment on cost and non-costs factors which might be relevant to the decision.

Solution:

(*i*)

	Option I ***At 75% in Feb and close in March and April (₹)***	***Option II*** ***At 25% each from Feb – April (₹)***
Direct Material	5,25,000	5,25,000
Direct Labour	5,23,600	5,19,750
	10,48,600	10,44,750
Factory Overhead :		
Indirect Material	8,400	14,700
Two months idle (₹ 4900 × 2)	9,800	
Indirect Labour	1,01,500	1,78,500
Training cost	65,800	
Indirect Exp. :		
Repairs & Maintenance	28,000	84,000

Overhauling cost	14,000	
Others Expenses	52,500	1,02,900
Idle × 2 months	53,200	
Office overhead:		
Staff Salaries	1,48,400	2,94,000
Idle 67,550 × 2 months	1,35,100	
Other overheads	28,000	59,850
Idle	22,400	
Total overhead cost	6,67,100	7,33,950
Total cost	17,15,700	17,78,700

The more economical course of action is to operate at 75% capacity for a month only, and close the plant for March and April. This option will save (₹ 17,78,700 – ₹ 17,15,700) = ₹ 63,000.

(*ii*) Cost Factors and Non-cost Factors

In regard to the decision on shut down of operations or contnuing with operations, the factors to be considered are:

1. The proposal which involves the lower total costs will be selected.
2. If the company has contracted the purchases from high quality and high price suppliers, a change in the procurement policy to 'shop around' may be considered to obtain economies in purchases.
3. The services of unskilled labour, if any, who do not require re-training may be dispensed with. They may be recruited and put on work without incurring training cost on re-opening of the factory. This will save training and idle time cost.
4. The possibility of wage freeze may reluctantly be considered as an extreme measure.

Illustrative Problem 12 (Make/Buy Decision)

X is a multiple product manufacturer. One product line consists of motors and the company produces three different models. *X* is currently considering a proposal from a supplier who wants to sell the company blades for the motors line.

The company currently produces all the blades it requires. In order to meet customer's needs, *X* currently produces three different blades for each motor model (nine different blades).

The supplier would charge ₹ 25 per blade, regardless of blade type. For the next year *X* has projected the costs of its own blade production as follows (based on projected volume of 10,000 units):

Direct materials	₹ 75,000
Direct labour	₹ 65,000
Variable overhead	₹ 55,000
Fixed overhead:	
Factory supervision	₹ 35,000
Other fixed cost	₹ 65,000
Total production costs	₹ 2,95,000

Assume (1) the equipment utilized to produce the blades has no alternative use and no market value, (2) the space occupied by blade production will remain idle if the company purchases rather than makes the blades, and (3) factory supervision costs reflect the salary of a production supervisor who would be dismissed from the firm if blade production ceased.

Required:

(*i*) Determine the net profit or loss of purchasing (rather than manufacturing), the blades required for motor production in the next year.

(*ii*) Determine the level of motor production where *X* would be indifferent between buying and producing the blades. If the future volume level were predicted to decrease, would that influence the decision?

(*iii*) For this part only, assume that the space presently occupied by blade production could be leased to another firm for ₹ 45,000 per year. How would this affect the make or buy decision?

Solution:

(*a*) This is make or buy decision, so compare the incremental cost to make with the incremental cost to buy.

Make the Blades

Incremental Costs Per Unit	
Direct materials (₹ 75,000 ÷ 10,000 units)	₹ 7.50
Direct labour (₹ 65,000 ÷ 10,000 units)	₹ 6.50
Variable overhead (₹ 55,000 ÷ 10,000)	₹ 5.50
Supervision (₹ 35,000 ÷ 10,000)	₹ 3.50
Total cost	₹ 23.00

Compare the cost to make the blades for 10,000 motors i.e. ₹ 23.00, with the cost to buy, ₹ 25.00. There is a net loss of ₹ 2.00 if '*X*' chooses to buy the blades.

(*b*) '*X*' will be indifferent between buying and making the blades when the total costs for making and buying will be equal at the volume level where the variable costs per unit times the volume plus the fixed avoidable costs are equal to the supplier's offered cost of ₹ 25.00 per unit times the volume.

(Direct materials + Direct labour + Variable overhead) × Volume + Supervision = Cost to buy × Volume.

Let volume in units $= x$

$$(7.50 + 6.50 + 5.50) \times x + 35{,}000 = 25.00\,x$$

$$19.50\,x + 35{,}000 = 25.00\,x$$

$$35{,}000 = 25.00 \times x - 19.50 \times x$$

$$35{,}000 = 5.50 \times x$$

$$x = 6{,}364 \text{ units of blades}$$

As volume of production decreases, the average per unit cost of in-house production increases. If the volume falls below 6,364 motors, then '*X*' would prefer to buy the blades from the supplier.

(*c*) If the space presently occupied by blade production could be leased to another firm for ₹ 45,000 per year. '*X*' would face an opportunity cost associated with in-house blade production for the 10,000 units of ₹ 4.50 per unit.

New cost to make = 23.00 + 4.50 = 27.50

Now '*X*' should buy because the cost to make, ₹ 27.50, is higher than the cost to buy, ₹ 25.00.

Illustrative Problem 13 (Selecting a Proposal)

Better and Best Ltd. manufacture only one product. Production is regular throughout the year and the capacity of the factory is 1,50,000 units per annum. The summarized Profit and Loss Account for the year ended 31st March is being reviewed by the Board of Directors.

	₹
Sales @ ₹ 10 per unit	10,00,000
Cost of sales:	
Direct materials	2,50,000
Direct labour	1,50,000
Production overheads:	
Variable	30,000
Fixed	2,30,000
Administrative overheads:	
Fixed	1,00,000
Selling and distribution overhead:	
Variable	50,000
Fixed	1,50,000

(*i*) The Production Director proposed to reduce selling price to ₹ 9 in order to utilize full capacity.

(*ii*) The Sales Director proposed to increase selling price by 20 percent. By spending ₹ 2,25,000 on advertisement, sales will be increased to 1,20,000 units per annum.

(*iii*) The Personnel Director pleaded for a change in the method of wage payment. For the present piece rate of ₹ 1.50 per unit, a bonus scheme (for each 2% increase in production over the target, there would be an increase of 1% in the basic wage of each employee) will be implemented. A target of 2,000 units per week for the company will be set for 50 week year. Selling price increase by 10%. With an Additional Advertisement cost of ₹ 1,60,000, 20% increase in present sales will be achieved.

(*iv*) The Chairman felt that the packaging of the product required improvement. He wanted to know the sales required to earn a target profit of 10% on turnover with the introduction of an improved packing at an additional cost of 20 paise per unit (no change in selling price).

You are required to evaluate individually the proposals of each of the board member and give your recommendation. (*CA Final, May 2013*)

Solution:

Evaluation of Proposals

	Particulars	*Proposal I*	*Proposal II*	*Proposal III*
A.	Sale units	1,50,000	1,20,000	1,20,000
B.	Selling Price per unit	₹ 9	₹ 12	₹ 11
C.	Sales	13,50,000	14,40,000	13,20,000
D.	*Less:* Variable cost	7,20,000	5,76,000	5,94,000
E.	Contribution	6,30,000	8,64,000	7,26,000
F.	*Less:* Fixed Cost	4,80,000	4,80,000	4,80,000
G.	*Less:* Advertising Cost	—	2,25,000	1,60,000
H.	Profit [E – F – G]	1,50,000	1,59,000	86,000

Working for Proposal II

Present Labour Rate = ₹ 1.50 *per unit*

Target Production Volume = 2,000 units × 50 weeks = 1,00,000 units

Production above the target volume = 1,20,000 units – 1,00,000 units = 20,000 units or 20% of Target Production Volume

Bonus (for each 2% increase in production over the target, there would be an increase of 1% in the basic wages of each employee) = $\frac{1\%}{2\%} \times 2\%$ = 10% increase in basic wages.

It means wages would be ₹ 1.65 (₹ 1.50 × 1.10) per unit.

Proposal (iv): Let Sales volumes is X units.

Particulars	*Amount* (₹)
Sales (X units × ₹ 10)	10X
Less: Variable cost [X units × ₹ (4.80 + 0.20)]	5X
Contribution	5X
Less: Fixed Cost	4,80,000
Profit	5X – 4,80,000

Profit equals to 10% of Turnover, it means

$$5X - 4,80,000 = 10\% \text{ of } 10X$$
$$4X = 4,80,000$$
$$X = 1,20,000 \text{ units}$$
$$\text{Turnover} = 1,20,000 \text{ units} \times ₹\ 10 = ₹\ 12,00,000$$
$$\text{Profit} = 10\% \text{ of } ₹\ 12,00,000 = ₹\ 1,20,000$$

Particulars	*Capacity Utilization*	*Profit* (₹)
Existing Situation	66.67%	40,000
Proposal (I)	100.00%	1,50,000
Proposal (II)	80.00%	1,59,000
Proposal (III)	80.00%	86,000
Proposal (IV)	80.00%	1,20,000

Company should accept Proposal (II).

Working Note:

Profitable Present Situation

Particulars	*Total* (₹)	*Per unit* (₹)
Sales (1,00,000 units × ₹ 10)	10,00,000	10,00
Less: Variable Cost:		
Direct Material	2,50,000	2.50
Direct Labour	1,50,000	1.50
Production Overheads	30,000	0.30
Selling and Distribution Overhead	50,000	0.50
Total Variable Cost	1,80,000	4.80

Particulars	Total (₹)	Per unit (₹)
Contribution	5,20,000	5.20
Less: Fixed Cost:		
Production Overheads	2,30,000	2.30
Administrative Overheads	1,00,000	1.00
Selling and Distribution Overhead	1,50,000	1.50
Total Fixed Cost	4,80,000	4.80
Profit	40,000	0.40

Illustrative Problem 14 (Machine Replacement Decision)

Compro Digital Components Company assembles circuit boards by using a manually operated machine to insert electronic components. The original cost of the machine is ₹ 60,000, the accumulated depreciation is ₹ 24,000, its remaining useful life is five years, and its residual value is negligible. In March 2016, a proposal was made to replace the present manufacturing procedure with a fully automatic machine that will cost ₹ 1,11,000. The automatic machine has an estimated useful life of five years and no significant residual value. For use in evaluating the proposal, the accountant accumulated the following annual data on present and proposed operations:

	Present Operations	*Proposed Operations*
Sales	₹ 2,90,000	₹ 2,90,000
Direct materials	₹ 86,000	₹ 86,000
Direct labor	40,000	—
Power and maintenance	8,000	30,000
Taxes, insurance, etc.	4.000	7,000
Selling and administrative expenses	65,000	65,000
Total expenses	₹ 2,03,000	₹ 1,88,000

Required:

(*a*) Prepare a differential analysis report for the proposal to replace the machine. Include in the analysis both the net differential change in costs anticipated over the five years and the net annual differential change in costs anticipated.

(*b*) Based only on the data presented, should the proposal be accepted?

(*c*) What are some of the other factors that should be considered before a final decision is made?

Solution:

Proposal to Replace Machine
March 2016

Annual costs and expenses—present machine	₹ 203,000
Annual costs and expenses—new machine	188,000
Annual differential decrease in costs and expenses	₹ 15,000*
Number of years applicable	× 5
Total differential decrease in costs and expenses	₹ 75,000

Cost of new equipment		111,000
Net differential increase in costs and expenses, five-year total		₹ 36,000
Annual differential increase in costs and expenses— new machine (₹ 36,000/5 years)		₹ 7,200

*The annual differential decrease in costs and expenses could be computed alternatively as follows:

Decrease in direct labor costs		₹ 40,000
Less: Increase in power and maintenance	₹ 22,000	
Increase in taxes, insurance, etc.	3,000	25,000
Annual differential decrease in costs and expenses		₹ 15,000

(*b*) The proposal should not be accepted.

(*c*) In addition to the factors given, consideration should be given to such factors as: Do both present and proposed operations provide the same capacity? What are the opportunity costs associated with alternative uses of the ₹ 1,11,000 outlay required to purchase the automatic machine? Is the product improved by using automatic machinery? Does the income tax have an effect on the decision?

Illustrative Problem 15 (Discontinuing a Product Line)

Larsen & Toubro Co. makes a machinery equipment, pump, and has been experiencing losses on this product for several years. The most recent quarterly income statement for the pump product line is given below:

Income Statement
For the Quarter Ended March 31

Sales		₹ 8,50,000
Less variable expenses:		
Variable manufacturing expenses	₹ 3,30,000	
Sales commissions	42,000	
Shipping	18,000	
Total variable expenses		390,000
Contribution margin		4,60,000
Less fixed expenses:		
Advertising	2,70,000	
Depreciation of equipment (no resale value)	80,000	
General factory overhead	1,05,000*	
Salary of product-line manager	32,000	
Insurance on inventories	8,000	
Purchasing department expenses	45,000†	
Total fixed expenses		5,40,000
Net loss		₹ (80,000)

*Common costs allocated on the basis of machine-hours.

†Common costs allocated on the basis of sales Rupees.

The discontinuance of the pump product line would not affect sales of other lines and would have no noticeable effect on the company's total general factory overhead or total Purchasing Department expenses.

Required:

Would you recommend that the pump product line be discontinued? Support your answer with appropriate computations.

Solution:

No, the pump product line should not be discontinued. The computations are:

Contribution margin lost if the line is dropped:		₹ (460,000)
Fixed costs that can be avoided if the line is dropped:		
Advertising	₹ 2,70,000	
Salary of the product line manager	32,000	
Insurance on inventories	8,000	3,10,000
Net disadvantage of dropping the line		(₹ 150,000)

The same solution can be obtained by preparing comparative income statements:

	Keep Product Line	Drop Product Line	Difference Net Income Increase or (Decrease)
Sales	₹ 8,50,000	—0—	₹ 8,50,000
Less variable expenses:			
Variable manufacturing expenses	3,30,000	—0—	42,000
Sales commissions	42,000	—0—	42,000
Shipping	18,000	—0—	18,000
Total variable expenses	3,90,000	—0—	3,90,000
Contribution margin	4,60,000	—0—	(4,60,000)
Less fixed expenses:			
Advertising	2,70,000	—0—	2,70,000
Depreciation of equipment	80,000	80,000	—0—
General factory overhead	1,05,000	105,000	—0—
Salary of product line manager	32,000	—0—	32,000
Insurance on inventories	8,000	—0—	8000
Purchasing department expenses	45,000	45,000	—0—
Total fixed expenses	5,40,000	2,30,000	3,10,000
Net loss	(80,000)	(230,000)	(1,50,000)

Illustrative Problem 16 (Discontinuing a Product Line)

The Northern Division of Jindal Furnishing Co. makes and sells tables and beds. The following estimated revenue and cost information from the division's activity-based costing system is available for 2016.

	4,000 Tables	*5,000 Beds*	*Total*
Revenues (₹ 1,250 × 4,000; ₹ 2,000 × 5,000)	₹50,00,000	₹1,00,00,000	₹1,50,00,000

Variable direct materials and direct manufacturing labor costs (₹ 750 × 4,000; ₹ 1,050 × 5,000)	30,00,000	52,50,000	82,50,000
Depreciation on equipment used exclusively by each product line	4,20,000	5,80,000	10,00,000
Marketing and distribution costs ₹ 4,00,000 (fixed) + ₹ 7,500 per consignment × 40 consignments; ₹ 6,00,000 (fixed) + ₹ 7,500 per consignment × 100 consignments	7,00,000	13,50,000	20,50,000
Fixed general administrative costs of the division allocated to product lines on the basis of revenues	11,00,000	22,00,000	33,00,000
Allocated corporate-office costs allocated to product lines on the basis of revenues	5,00,000	10,00,000	15,00,000
Total costs	57,20,000	1,03,80,000	1,61,00,000
Operating income (loss)	₹ (7,20,000)	₹ (3,80,000)	₹ (11,00,000)

Additional information includes:

(*a*) On January 1, 2016, the equipment has a book value of ₹ 10,00,000 and zero disposal value. Any equipment not used will remain idle.

(*b*) Fixed marketing and distribution costs of a product line can be avoided if the line is discontinued.

(*c*) Fixed general administrative costs of the division and corporate-office costs will not change if sales of individual product lines are increased or decreased or if product lines are added or dropped.

Required:

(*i*) On the basis of financial considerations alone, should the Northern Division discontinue the tables product line, assuming the released facilities remain idle? Show your calculations.

(*ii*) What would be the effect on Northern Division's operating income if it were to sell 4,000 more tables? Assume that to do so the division would have to acquire additional equipment costing ₹ 4,20,000 with a one-year useful life and zero disposal value. Assume further that the fixed marketing and distribution costs would not change but that the number of consignments would double. Show your calculations.

Solution:

(*i*) The incremental revenue losses and incremental savings in cost by discontinuing the Tables product line are as follows:

	Difference: Incremental (Loss in Revenues) and Savings in Costs from Dropping Tables Line
Revenues (loss)	₹ (50,00,000)
Savings in costs:	
Direct materials and direct manufacturing labor	30,00,000
Depreciation on equipment	0
Marketing and distribution	7,00,000
General administration	0
Corporate office costs	0
Total costs (Savings)	37,00,000
Operating income (loss)	₹ (13,00,000)

Dropping the Tables product line results in revenue losses of ₹ 50,00,000 and cost savings of ₹ 37,00,000. Hence, the operating income will be ₹ 13,00,000 higher if it does not drop the Tables line.

By dropping the Tables production line, the company will save none of the depreciation on equipment, general administration costs, and corporate office costs, but it will save variable manufacturing costs and all marketing and distribution costs on the Tables product line.

(*ii*) The Company will generate incremental operating income of ₹ 12,80,000 from selling 4,000 additional tables and, hence, should try to increase table sales.

	Incremental Revenues and (Costs)
Revenues	₹ 50,00,000
Direct materials and direct manufacturing labor	(30,00,000)
Cost of equipment written off as depreciation	(4,20,000)*
Marketing and distribution costs	(3,00,000)†
General administration costs	0**
Corporate office costs	0**
Operating income	₹ 12,80,000

*Note that the additional costs of equipment are relevant future costs for the "selling more tables decision" because they represent incremental future costs that differ between the alternatives of selling and not selling additional tables.

†Current marketing and distribution costs which varies with number of consignments = ₹ 7,00,000 – ₹ 4,00,000 = ₹ 3,00,000. As the sales of tables double, the number of consignments will double, resulting in incremental marketing and distribution costs of (2 × ₹ 3,00,000) – ₹ 3,00,000 = ₹ 3,00,000.

"General administration and corporate office costs will be unaffected if the company decides to sell more tables. Hence, these costs are irrelevant for the decision.

Illustrative Problem 17 (Allocation of a Scarce Resource)

Suppose you are taking an examination that contains three types of questions: (1) multiple choice, (2) short answer, and (3) essay. The examination will contain 14 multiple-choice questions worth 2 points each (28 points total), 8 short-answer questions worth 4 points (32 points total), and 4 essay questions worth 10 points each (40 points total). Thus, the maximum score is 100 points.

You believe that you can correctly answer 90% of the multiple-choice questions you attempt, receive 80% of the possible points on each short-answer question you attempt, and receive 70% of the possible points on each essay question you attempt. In addition, you need 4 minutes to answer each multiple-choice question, 5 minutes to answer each short answer question, and 10 minutes to answer each essay question. The examination is scheduled to last only two hours.

(*M. Com., Delhi University, 2012*)

Required:

To maximize your expected score, which type of questions should you answer first? Which type of questions should you answer last? What is your expected score?

Solution:

In this problem, time is in short supply. Thus, maximizing total points requires to maximize the points earned per available minute. The following analysis presents data.

Expected Points per Minute of Examination Time			
	Multiple Choice	***Short Answer***	***Essay***
Maximum points per question	2	4	10
Probability correct	0.90	0.80	0.70
Expected points if Question attempted	1.8	3.2	7
Time per question in minute	4	5	10
Expected points per minute	0.45	0.64	0.70

To maximize the expected score on the examination, one should attempt the essay questions first, followed by the short-answer questions and finish with the multiple-choice questions. Such a strategy leads to the following expected score:

Expected Examination Score			
	Allocated Time (min.)	***Expected Points***	***Time left (min.)***
Start of examination			120
Allocated to essay questions	40	28.00*	80
Allocated to short-answer questions	40	25.60**	40
Allocated to multiple-choice questions	40	18.00***	0
Expected Total Score		**71.60**	

*There are four essay questions worth 10 points each. Each question takes 10 minutes to answer, and, on average, one receives 70% of the possible points. Thus, it will take 4 × 10 = 40 minutes to answer these questions and one will receive 4 × 10 × .7 = 28.00 points (i.e., 40 minutes × 0.70 points per minutes = 28 points)

**There are 8 short – answer questions worth 4 points each. Each question takes 5 minutes to answer and, on average, one receives 80% of the possible points. Thus, it will take 5 × 8 = 40 minutes to answer these questions and receive 4 × 8 × .8 = 25.60 (i.e., 40 minutes × 0.64 points per minute = 25.6 points)

***There are 14 multiple-choice questions worth 2 points each. Each question takes 4 minutes to answer, and, on average, one will receive 90% of the possible points. With only 40 minutes remaining, however, one can answer only 10 multiple-choice questions. Thus, one will spend the remaining 40 minutes on multiple-choice questions and receive 2 × 10 × .9 = 18.00 points (i.e., minutes × 0.45 points per minute = 18 points)

This problem shows that even though there is a greater probability of being correct on the multiple-choice questions, they should be attempted last because they take too much time. Essentially, one will only get an average of 0.45 points per minute spent on the multiple-choice questions, whereas one can get an average of 0.70 points per minute spent on the essay questions.

Illustrative Problem 18 (Key Factor)

Vexed Ltd. is facing a short-term problem of insufficient raw materials to meet next months budgeted production of its three products A, B and C.

The original budgets for next month were:

	Product A ₹ 000	Product B ₹ 000	Product C ₹ 000	Total ₹ 000
Variable costs:				
Raw materials	340	180	260	780
Direct labour	400	310	580	1290
Variable overheads	160	110	120	390
Fixed cost apportionment	600	440	560	1600
Total costs	1500	1040	1520	4060
Profit	440	280	360	1080
Sales	1940	1320	1880	5140

The amount of raw materials available for next month's total production of all three products is unlikely to exceed ₹ 5,00,000.

You are required:

(*a*) to calculate the most profitable sales mix possible in this case, assuming that Vexed Ltd. want to produce a minimum of 50% of budget for all three products.

(*b*) to state your conclusions and the reasoning behind your approach.

Solution:

50% of budgeted levels will use up ₹ 3,90,000 of raw materials being 50% of the ₹ 7,80,000 total. The remaining Re. 1,10,000 of raw materials should be allocated to the products (s) with the highest contribution per ₹ 1 of raw material used on that product. We therefore need to calculate the contribution on individual product lines and then the contribution per Re. 1 of raw material used in the process, as follows:

	Product A	Product B	Product C	Total D
	₹ 000	₹ 000	₹ 000	₹ 000
Sales	1940	1320	1880	5140
Less: Variable costs	900	600	960	2460
Contribution	1040	720	920	2680
Raw material used	340	180	260	780
Contribution per Re. 1 of raw material	₹ 3.06	₹ 4.00	₹ 3.54	

Therefore more raw material should be allocated to product B up to its maximum budget potential. This will use up ₹ 90,000 of the ₹ 1,10,000 available. The remaining ₹ 20,000 of raw material should then be allocated to product C. The revised budget will now be:

	Product A ₹ 000	Product B ₹ 000	Product C ₹ 000	Total D ₹ 000
Sales	970	1320	1085	3375
Variable costs:				
Raw materials	170	180	150	500

Direct labour	200	310	335	845
Variable overheads	80	110	69	259
Total variable costs	450	600	554	1604
Contribution	520	720	531	1771
Fixed costs				1600
Profit				171

Illustrative Problem 19 (Decision about Mechanisation)

Management of a manufacturing unit is considering extensive modernisation of the factory through progressive mechanisation which would result in improved productivity and reduced strength. Through negotiations with the union, it was agreed that for every 1% increase in productivity, workers would be paid 0.5% incentive wages. It was also agreed that through voluntary retirement the staff strength would be reduced to 300 from the present level of 400. The following further comparative data are available before and after the proposed mechanisation:

	Before Mechanisation	*After Mechanisation*
	₹	₹
No. of articles produced per month	50,000	48,000
Fringe benefits	50% of wages	
Wages paid per month	4,00,000	
Sales per month (value)	24,00,000	
P/V ratio	25%	

Based on the above data, you are required to work out the annual financial implication of the proposal.

Solution:

Improvement in productivity after mechanisation:

Proportionate output of 300 workers on the basis of existing productivity level:

$$\frac{50,000 \times 300}{400} = 37,500 \text{ units}$$

Actual output of 300 workers envisaged after mechanisation = 48,000 units

$$\text{Improvement in productivity} = \frac{48,000 - 37,500}{37,500} \times 100\% = 28\%$$

Incentive Wages Payable:

Incentive Wages for 28% improvement in productivity

(1/2% for every 1% improvement) = 28% × 0.5% = 14%

Annual Wages payable to 300 workers before incentive

$$= \frac{₹\ 4,00,000}{400} \times 300 \times 12 = ₹\ 36,00,000$$

Selling price per unit = 24,00,000 ÷ 50,000 = ₹ 48 per unit

Computation of Saving (Loss) after Mechanisation

	Before Mechanisation ₹	After Mechanisation ₹
Wages payable per annum	48,00,000	36,00,000
Fringe benefits 50% of wages	24,00,000	18,00,000
Incentive wages @ 14% of wages	—	5,04,000
	72,00,000	59,04,000
Saving per annum		12,96,000
Less: Loss of Contribution due to lower sales:		
(50,000 units – 48,000 units) × 12 × 25/100 of ₹ 48		2,88,000
Increase in Annual Contribution due to mechanisation		₹ 10,08,000

Illustrative Problem 20 (Make or Buy Decision)

Auto Parts Ltd. has an annual production of 90,000 units for a motor component. The component's cost structure is as below:

	₹
Materials	270 per unit
Labour (25% fixed)	180 per unit
Expenses:	
Variable	90 per unit
Fixed	135 per unit
Total:	675 per unit

(*a*) The Purchase Manager has an offer from a supplier who is willing to supply the component at ₹ 540. Should the component be purchased and production stopped?

(*b*) Assume the resources now used for this component's manufacture are to be used to produce another new product for which the selling price is ₹ 485.

In the latter case the material price will be ₹ 200 per unit. 90,000 units of this product can be produced on the same cost basis as above for labour and expenses. Discuss whether it would be advisable to divert the resources to manufacture the new products, on the footing that the component presently being produced would, instead of being produced, be purchased from the market.

Solution:

(*a*) Statement Showing the Variable Cost and Purchase Cost of Component......Used by Auto Parts Ltd.

Variable cost	*Per unit* (₹)	*Total for 90,000 units* (₹)
Materials	270	2,43,00,000
Labour	135	1,21,50,000

Expenses	90	81,00,000
Total variable cost (when component is produced)	495	4,45,50,000
Cost of purchase (when component is purchased)	540	4,86,00,000
Difference, excess of purchase price over variable cost	45	40,50,000

Fixed expenses not being affected, it is evident from the above statement that if the component is purchased from the outside supplier, the company will have to spend ₹ 45 per unit more and on 90,000 units the company will have to spend ₹ 40,50,000 more. Therefore, the company should not stop the production of the component.

(*b*) The following statement shows the cost implications of the proposal to divert the available facilities for a new product.

Statement Showing the Contribution per Unit if the Existing Resources are Used for the Production of Another New Product

	(₹)	(₹)
Selling price of the new product per unit		485
Less: Materials cost	200	
Labour (variable)	135	
Expenses (variable)	90	425
Contribution per unit		60
Loss per unit if the present component is purchased:		
Purchase price of the existing product		540
Less: Total variable cost of producing the existing component		495
Excess cost		45

Thus, if the company diverts its resources for the production of another new product, it will benefit by ₹ 15, *i.e.*, ₹ 60 – 45 per unit. On 90,000 units the company will save ₹ 13,50,000. Therefore, it is advisable to divert the resources to manufacture the new product and the component presently being produced should be purchased from the market. This is also brought out by the following figures:

	₹
Total cost of producing the component (90,000 × 675) (A)	6,07,50,000
Cost of purchasing the component (90,000 × 540)	4,86,00,000
Fixed expenses, not having been saved (90,000 × 180, *i.e.*, 675 – 495)	1,62,00,000
	6,48,00,000
Less: Contribution from the new product (90,000 × 60)	54,00,000
Total cost if component is purchased and new product is made (B)	5,94,00,000
Saving (A – B)	13,50,000

Illustrative Problem 21 (Export Proposals)

Vinak Ltd. operating at 75% level of activity produces and sells two products A and B. The cost sheets of the two products are as under:

	Product A	Product B
	₹	₹
Units produced and sold	600	400
Direct materials	₹ 200	₹ 400
Direct labour	400	400
Factory overheads (40% fixed)	500	300
Selling and administration overheads (60% fixed)	800	500
Total cost per unit	1900	1600
Selling price per unit	2300	1900

Factory overheads are absorbed on the basis of machine hour which is the limiting (Key) factor. The machine hour rate is ₹ 200 per hour.

The company receives an offer from Canada for the purchase of product A at a price of ₹ 1750 per unit.

Alternatively, the company has another offer from the Middle East for the purchase of product B at a price of ₹ 1550 per unit.

In both the cases, a special packing charge of ₹ 50 per unit has to be borne by the company.

The company can accept either of the two export orders and in either case the company can supply such quantities as may be possible to be produced by utilising the balance of 25% of its capacity.

You are required to prepare:

(*i*) A statement showing the economics of the two export proposals giving your recommendations as to which proposal should be accepted.

(*ii*) A statement showing the overall profitability of the company after incorporating the export proposal recommended by you. (*M. Com. Delhi*, 2002)

Solution:

(i) Economics of the Two Export Proposals

	Order from Canada for Product A	*Order from the Middle East for product B*
Marginal cost per unit:		
Materials	₹ 200	₹ 400
Labour	400	400
Variable factory overheads	300	180
Variable selling and admn. overheads	320	200
Special packing charges	50	50
Total variable cost	1270	1230
Export price per unit	1750	1550
Contribution per unit	480	320

Since machine hour is the limiting (key) factor, the contribution should be linked with the machine hours. This has been worked out as follows:

Machine hour per unit	2.5 hours	1.5 hours
Contribution per machine hour	₹ 192	₹ 213

Product B yields a better contribution per machine hour.

The order from the Middle East should therefore be accepted as compared to the Canadian offer.

Working Notes

	A	*B*	*Total*
	₹	₹	
Factory overheads per unit	500	300	
Machine hour rate per hour	200	200	
Machine hour per unit	2.5	1.5	
Units produced	600	400	
Machine hours utilised	1,500	600	2,100
Leval of activity			75%

Maximum hours at 100% activity: $\frac{2,100}{75} \times 100 = 2,800$ hr

Capacity hours available for export 2,800 – 2,100 = 700 hr.

(ii) Statement of Overall Profitability

	Product A	*Product B*	*Total*
Units	**600**	**867**	
	(₹)	**(₹)**	**(₹)**
Materials	1,20,000	3,46,800	4,66,800
Labour	2,40,000	3,46,800	5,86,800
Factory overhead: Variable	1,80,000	1,56,100	3,36,100
Fixed	1,20,000	48,000	1,68,000
Selling & Admn. Overheads:			
Variable	1,92,000	1,73,400	3,65,400
Fixed	2,88,000	1,20,000	4,08,000
Special packing (@ ₹ 50 for 467 units)	—	23,400	23,400
Total costs	11,40,000	12,14,500	23,54,500
Sales	13,80,000	14,83,900	28,63,900
Profit	2,40,000	2,69,400	5,09,400

Working Notes

1. Number of units of B:

	₹
Sales in the home market	400
Export market 700 hrs/1.5	467
Total	867

2. Sales value of B:

	₹
400 units in the home market @ ₹ 1900	7,60,000
467 units for export @ ₹ 1550	7,23,900
Total:	14,83,900

Illustrative Problem 22 (Continue or Drop)

AudioMart is a retailer of radios, stereos, and televisions. The store carries two portable sound systems that have radios, tape players, and speakers, System A, of slightly higher quality than System B, costs ₹ 20 more. With rare exceptions, the store also sells a headset when a system is sold. The headset can be used with either system. Variable-costing income statements for the three products are as follows:

	System A	*System B*	*Headset*
Sales	₹ 45,000	₹ 32,500	₹ 8,000
Less: Variable expenses	20,000	25,500	3,200
Contribution margin	₹ 25,000	₹ 7,000	₹ 4,800
Less: Fixed costs*	10,000	18,000	2,700
Operating income	₹ 15,000	₹ (11,000)	₹ 2,100

*This includes common fixed costs totalling ₹ 18,000, allocated to each product in proportion to its revenues.

The owner of the store is concerned about the profit performance of System B and is considering dropping it. If the product is dropped, sales of System A will increase by 30 percent, and sales of headsets will drop by 25 percent.

Required:

(*i*) Prepare segmented income statements for the three products using a better format.

(*ii*) Prepare segmented income statements for System A and the headsets assuming that System B is dropped. Should B be dropped?

(*iii*) Suppose that a third system, System C, with a similar quality to System B, could be acquired. Assume that with C, the sales of A would remain unchanged; however, C would produce only 80 pcr cent of the revenues of B, and sales of the headsets would drop by 10 percent. The contribution margin ratio of C is 50 percent, and its direct fixed costs would be identical to those of B. Should System B be dropped and replaced with System C?

Solution:

(*i*)

	System A	*System B*	*Headset*	*Total*
Sales	₹ 45,000	₹ 32,500	₹ 8,000	₹ 85,500
Less: Variable expenses	20,000	25,500	3,200	48,700
Contribution margin	₹ 25,000	₹ 7,000	₹ 4,800	₹ 36,800
Less: Direct fixed costs*	526	11,158	1,016	12,700
Segment margin (loss)	₹ 24,474	₹ (4,158)	₹ 3,784	₹ 24,100
Less: Common fixed costs				18,000
Operating income				₹ 6,100

*₹ 45,000/₹ 85,500 × ₹ 18,000 = ₹ 9,474; ₹ 10,000 – ₹ 9,474 = ₹ 526

₹ 32,500/₹ 85,500 × ₹ 18,000 = ₹ 6,842; ₹ 18,000 – ₹ 6,842 = ₹ 11,158

₹ 8,000/₹ 85,500 × ₹ 18,000 = ₹ 1,684; ₹ 2,700 – ₹ 1,684 = ₹ 1,016

(*ii*)

	System A	*Headset*	*Total*
Sales	₹ 58,500	₹ 6,000	₹ 64,500
Less: Variable expenses	26,000	2,400	28,400
Contribution margin	₹ 32,500	₹ 3,600	₹ 36,100
Less: Direct fixed costs	526	1,016	1,542
Segment margin	₹ 31,974	₹ 2,584	₹ 34,558
Less: Common fixed costs			18,000
Operating income			₹ 16,558

System B should be dropped.

(*iii*)

	System A	*System C*	*Headset*	*Total*
Sales	₹ 45,000	₹ 26,000	₹ 7,200	₹ 78,200
Less: Variable expenses	20,000	13,000	2,880	35,880
Contribution margin	₹ 25,000	₹ 13,000	₹ 4,320	₹ 42,320
Less: Direct fixed costs	526	11,158	1,016	12,700
Segment margin	₹ 24,474	₹ 1,842	₹ 3,304	₹ 29,620
Less: Common fixed costs				18,000
Operating income				₹ 11,620

Replacing B with C is better than keeping B, but not as good as dropping B without replacement with C.

Illustrative Problem 23 (Multiple Decision Situations)

Shown below is a statement of profitability for the first quarter of 2016, for two products manufactured by a company.

	A	*B*	*Total*
Volume of production and sales	1,000	800	
Unit selling price (₹)	175	140	
Revenue (₹)	1,75,000	1,12,000	2,87,000
Manufacturing cost:			
Fixed/set-up costs for individual products	35,000	29,000	64,000
Variable A @ ₹ 60	60,000		
B @ ₹ 65		52,000	1,12,000
	95,000	81,000	1,76,000
Joint costs allocated in proportion to other manufacturing costs	19,000	16,200	35,200
Selling and administrative costs: allocated in proportion to revenue	26,250	16,800	43,050
Total costs	1,40,250	1,14,000	2,54,250
Product profit/(loss)	34,750	(2,000)	32,750

Provide recommendations for management, supported by appropriate calculations, in response to the following questions:

(*a*) What minimum price would make acceptance of an order for an additional 200 units of A worthwhile?

(*b*) As product B is recorded as making a loss, should production be terminated?

(*c*) Other manufacturers are willing to supply both A and B at the levels required, at a unit cost of ₹ 150 and ₹ 110. If production ceases, the Co. could offer the factory space for rent at ₹ 35,000 per quarter. Would this alternative be beneficial for the company?

Solution:

(A) Calculation of Minimum Price

Variable costs of product A= ₹ 60 per unit.

Therefore, minimum price for special order = that which is sufficient to cover variable costs. That is, ₹ 60 × 200 = ₹ 12,000.

(B) If B is terminated, only direct costs (₹ 81,000) will be saved. But the company will lose ₹ 1,12,000 of revenue. Therefore, loss will increase without B.

Contribution = 1,12,000 – 81,000 = ₹ 31,000

Other costs charged to Product B = 16,200 + 16,800

(Joint costs + selling & Adm. costs) = ₹ 33,000

So, amount of loss = ₹ 33,000

Current loss = ₹ 2,000

Decision: As B is making a positive contribution, it should be retained.

(C)

	Manufacture ₹	*Purchase and Sell* ₹
Net revenues from manufacturing (as given)	32,750	—
Purchase Alternative:		
Revenue from sales (as given)		2,87,000
Less: Purchase costs:		
Product A @ ₹ 150 (for units 1000)		(1,50,000)
Product B @ ₹ 110 (for 800 units)		(88,000)
		49,000
Less: Selling & Adm. costs (Total of Product A and B)		**(43,050)**
		5,950
Add: Rent received		35,000
Net Income	32,750	40,950

Decision: Purchase A and B rather than manufacture them.

Assumption: It has been assumed that selling and administrative costs would also be incurred in case of purchasing products A and B as these are the costs essentially being incurred for selling purposes. Further, manufacturing costs and joint costs will not be incurred in case products A and B are purchased from outside. Therefore, they have not been considered while ascertaining net income in alternative 'purchase and sell'.

Thus, purchase for resale would give a higher return than current manufacture. But other factors such as ability to rent, closure costs, continuity of supply and purchase price are important to the decision.

Illustrative Problem 24 (Special Order)

Nubo Manufacturing, Co. is presently operating at 50% of practical capacity producing about 50,000 units annually of a patented electronic component. Nubo recently received an offer from a company in Yokohama, Japan, to purchase 30,000 components at ₹ 600 per unit, FOB Nubo's plant. Nubo has not previously sold components in Japan. Budgeted production costs for 50,000 and 80,000 units of output follow:

Units	50,000	80,000
	₹	₹
Costs:		
Direct material	75,00,000	1,20,00,000
Direct labour	75,00,000	1,20,00,000
Factory overhead	2,00,00,000	2,60,00,000
Total costs	3,50,00,000	5,00,00,000
Cost per unit	₹ 700	₹ 625

The sales manager thinks the order should be accepted, even if it results in a loss of ₹ 100 per unit, because he feels that sales may build up future markets. The production manager does not wish to have the order accepted primarily because the order would show a loss of ₹ 25 per unit when computed on the new average unit cost. The treasurer has made a quick computation indicating that accepting the order will actually increase gross margin.

Required:

(*a*) Explain what apparently caused the drop in cost from ₹ 700 per unit to ₹ 625 per unit when budgeted production increased from 50,000 to 80,000 units. Show supporting computations.

(*b*) (1) Explain whether (either or both) the production manager or the treasurer is correct in his reasoning.

(2) Explain why the conclusions of the production manager and the treasurer differ.

(c) Explain why each of the following may affect the decision to accept or reject the special order

(1) The likelihood of repeat special sales and/or all sales to be made at ₹ 600 per unit

(2) Whether the sales are made to customers operating in two separate, isolated markets or whether the sales are made to customers competing in the same market.

(*M.Com. Delhi,* 2000)

Solution:

(*a*) The difference in unit cost was caused by the difference in the average unit cost of factory overhead. The computations for costs per unit follow:

	Cost per unit	
	50,000 units of output ₹	80,000 units of output ₹
Direct material:		
₹ 75,00,000/50,000 units	150	150
₹ 1,20,00,000/80,000 units		
Direct labour:		
₹ 75,00,000/50,000 units	150	
₹ 1,20,00,000/80,000 units		150
Factory overhead:		
₹ 2,00,00,000/50,000 units		
₹ 2,60,00,000/80,000 units	400	325
Cost per unit	700	625

The reason for the difference in average unit cost of factory overhead probably was caused by some of the overhead being fixed within the given levels of output. In this instance the fixed component of factory overhead may be estimated in the following manner:

Change in cost (₹ 2,60,00,000 – ₹ 2,00,00,000) = ₹ 60,00,000

Change in output (80,000 – 50,000) = 30,000 units

Variable costs per unit (₹ 60,00,000 ÷ 30,00,000) = ₹ 200

If variable factory overhead is incurred at ₹ 200 unit, the amount of fixed costs would be computed as follows:

₹ 2,00,00,000 factory overhead – (₹ 200 × 50,000 units) variable overhead = ₹ 1,00,00,000 fixed factory overhead.

₹ 2,60,00,000 factory overhead – (₹ 200 × 80,000 units) variable overhead = ₹ 1,00,00,000 fixed factory overhead.

At 50,000 units of output the fixed portion of factory overhead is ₹ 200 per unit (₹ 1,00,00,000 ÷ 50,000 units). And at 80,000 units of output the fixed portion of factory overhead is 125 per unit (₹ 1,00,00,000 ÷ 80,000 units). Thus, the ₹ 75 per unit decrease in average units cost apparently resulted from spreading the fixed costs over an increased number of units of production.

(*b*) (1) Both production manager's and treasurer's statements are correct as given. The new average unit cost of ₹ 625 is certainly more than the offered purchase price of ₹ 600; thus, a ₹ 25 per unit loss would result on this order. The resulting "book loss" on this order would be ₹ 7,50,000 (₹ 25 × 30,000 units) as indicated by the production manager. Notwithstanding, the remaining 50,000 units of regular sales would show an increased margin (gain) of ₹ 75 per unit because their average unit cost decreased from ₹ 700 to ₹ 625 per unit. Thus, regular sales would show an increased profit of ₹ 37,50,000 (₹ 75 × 50,000 units). The net result would be an increase of ₹ 30,00,000 in gross margin this period if the Yokohama company offer was accepted. Accordingly, the treasurer's statement is also correct because gross margin for this period will increase if the offer is accepted.

The treasurer's reasoning can also be illustrated by application of the marginal-income or contribution-margin technique. The extra units will generate a unit sales price of ₹ 600 and a unit variable cost of ₹ 500 (₹ 150 + 150 + 200): the result is a ₹ 100 per unit contribution margin to increase gross margin. Thus, by selling the extra 30,000 units gross margin will increase by ₹ 30,00,000 (₹ 30,000 units × ₹ 100 contribution margin per unit).

(2) The primary reason for the difference in conclusions by the production manager and the treasurer is in their respective method of analysis. The production manager is evaluating average unit cost in comparison with selling price to determine the profitability of the special order. The treasurer is comparing the difference in total costs at the two levels of output with the difference in total revenues at the two levels of output, in effect comparing marginal cost with marginal revenue, to determine the incremental effect on gross margin. The treasurer's reasoning is appropriate for the short-run while the production manager's reasoning is inappropriate for a short-range decision but is appropriate for a long-range decision. In this instance the decision appears to be a one-time thing indicating that the treasurer's reasoning is most appropriate.

(*c*) (1) Perhaps the most important consideration is the extent to which this short-range decision will have a long-range effect on Nubo. If the offer is rejected the chances of receiving another offer from the Yokohama company is considerably reduced. But if the offer is accepted, a repeat order is more likely in the future.

By accepting the offer, Nubo may be inadvertently establishing a market price of ₹ 600 per unit for its product which cannot be maintained in the long-run (average unit cost at 80,000 units is ₹ 625). If the customers who purchase the other 50,000 units become aware of the ₹ 600 unit sales price charged from the Yokohama firm they too may want a ₹ 600 unit price. If Nubo sold all 80,000 units at ₹ 600 each a negative gross margin of ₹ 20,00,000 would result, and it would have zero gross margin at 1,00,000 units, the practical capacity of the plant.

(2) Even if the ₹ 600 unit selling price does not have an effect on the unit selling price to present customers, it may depress the quantity of sales of other units at the normal price. If the Yokohama firm plans to compete for the same customers as Nubo's regular customers, the ultimate effect of making the 30,000 unit sales to the Yokohama firm at ₹ 600 a unit may give it an unfair competitive advantage. Ultimately, a shift of customers from Nubo's regular customers to the Yokohama firm would cause a decrease in unit sales at the regular price.

If the Yokohama firm is operating in a completely isolated market from Nubo's regular customers, no undesirable effects should result from this one-time sale. An exception to this reasoning would result if Nubo's regular customers desired to expand into this isolated market but found that they were at a competitive disadvantage because of the 30,000 unit sales made by Nubo to the Yokohama firm.

Illustrative Problem 25 (Contribution Margin Analysis)

Deccan Industries manufactures only one product. For the year ended December 31,2016, the contribution margin increased by ₹ 36,000 from the planned level of ₹ 7,20;000. The president of Deccan Industries has expressed some concern about such a small increase and has requested a follow-up report.

The following data have been gathered from the accounting records for the year ended December 31, 2016:

	Actual	*Planned*	*Difference-Increase (Decrease)*
Sales	₹ 14,70,000	₹ 14,40,000	₹ 30,000
Less:			
Variable cost of goods sold	₹ 5,60,000	₹ 5,92,000	₹ (32,000)
Variable selling and administrative expenses	1,54,000	1,28,000	26,000
Total	₹ 7,14,000	₹ 7,20,000	₹ (6,000)
Contribution margin	₹ 7,56,000	₹ 7,20,000	₹ 36,000

Number of units sold	14,000	16,000
Per unit:		
Sales price	₹ 105.00	₹ 90.00
Variable cost of goods sold	40.00	37.00
Variable selling and administrative expenses	11.00	8.00

Required:

(*i*) Prepare a contribution margin analysis report for the year ended December 31,2016.

(*ii*) At a meeting of the board of directors on January 30,2017, the president, after reviewing the contribution margin analysis report, made the following comment:

"It looks as if the price increase of ₹ 15.00 had the effect of decreasing sales volume. However, this was a favourable tradeoff. The variable cost of goods sold was less than planned. Apparently, we are efficiently managing our variable cost of goods sold. However, the variable selling and administrative expenses appear out of control. Let's look into these expenses and get them under control! Also, let's consider increasing the sales price to ₹ 120 and continue this favorable tradeoff between higher price and lower volume."

Do you agree with the president's comment? Explain.

Solution: (*i*)

Deccan Industries
Contribution Margin Analysis
For the Year Ended December 31, 2016

Planned contribution margin		₹ 7,20,000
Effect of change in sales:		
Sales quantity factor (14,000 – 16,000) × ₹ 90	– ₹ 1,80,000	
Unit price factor (₹ 105 – ₹ 90) × 14,000	2,10,000	
Total effect of change in sales		30,000
Effect of changes in variable cost of goods sold:		
Variable cost quantity factor (16,000 – 14,000) × ₹ 37.	₹ 74,000	
Unit cost factor (₹ 37 – ₹ 40) × 14,000	– 42,000	
Total effect of changes in variable cost of goods sold		32,000
Effect of changes in variable selling and administrative expenses:		
Variable cost quantity factor (16,000 – 14,000) × ₹ 8	₹ 16,000	
Unit cost factor (₹ 8 – ₹ 11) × 14,000	– 42,000	
Total effect of changes in variable selling and administrative expenses		– 26,000
Actual contribution margin		₹ 7,56,000

(*ii*) The president's first statement appears correct taken at face value. The president is incorrect regarding variable cost of goods sold. The majority of the decrease in the variable cost of goods sold was due to the variable cost quantity factor. However this decrease was offset by a ₹ 3.00 increase in the variable cost of goods sold per unit. The contribution margin improved, but some inefficiency reduced the expected amount of improvement from the variable cost quantity factor.

The president is correct in saying that an investigation of the increase in variable selling and administrative expenses is needed. The unit cost factor increased by ₹ 3.00, which more than offset the favorable variable cost quantity factor, resulting in an overall decrease in the contribution margin. The increase in the variable selling and administrative expenses is probably due to the additional selling effort required in the face of price increases. It will probably be very difficult to improve the efficiency of this effort as prices go up. Therefore, the president's suggestion is probably unwarranted. Increasing the price again will require even more selling effort to overcome this negative influence. In addition, there is a limit as to how much price increase the market will likely be able to support.

Illustrative Problem 26 (Close a Department)

The directors of Big Bazar Department Store Ltd are concerned at the poor results achieved in its toy department. They have noted that it has earned an income of ₹ 6.7% of sales, considerably less than the target set by the company. They are considering the closing of the department.

The income account of the department for the year just ended runs as follows:

	₹	₹
Sales		2,97,20,000
Less: Cost of sales		1,91,20,000
Gross profit		1,06,00,000
Less:		
Wages of sales assistants (2 @ ₹ 16,00,000)	32,00,000	
Salary of supervisor	21,00,000	
Establishment costs of the department (heating, repairs, insurance, etc.)	12,00,000	
Rent of store – allocated to department on basis of floor area occupied	10,00,000	
General oeverhead costs of store – allocation in proportion to sales in each department	12,00,000	87,00,000
Net income for the year		19,00,000

If the department were closed, the space it occupied could be used either for an extension of the clothing department, or for storage of inventory (in which case rent of ₹ 16,00,000 per annum for warehouse facilities could be saved). You are also given the following information:

1. The gross profit earned in the toy department would be expected to remain at the same level in future years. If the clothing department were extended, it would be expected to increase its sales by ₹ 1,80,00,000 and earn a gross profit of 50% on sales.
2. If the department were converted to storage, the sales assistance would be transferred to other departments at their present wages. This would avoid the need to employ new

assistants at a wage of ₹ 14,00,000 per annum each to make good normal losses of staff. If the department were turned over to clothing, the assistants would be employed in the extended department at their present wages and no additional assistants would be required.

3. In either event, the supervisor of the department would be redundant; the new department would come under other supervisors, already employed. In accordance with company policy, however, the supervisor would not be dismissed but would be found employment in general administrative duties, at the present salary.
4. Establishment costs of the department would be:
   if converted to storage ₹ 6,00,000 p.a.
   if converted to clothing ₹ 8,00,000 p.a.
5. If the department were converted to storage, general administrative costs for the store would fall by ₹ 2,00,000. Otherwise, they would continue at the present level.
6. It is to be assumed that there would be no material capital expenditure associated with any of the possibilities.

Required:

(*a*) Prepare calculations to indicate to the board of directors the best course of action. You may make and specify any reasonable assumptions that you consider necessary for your answer and you may add a *short* note on any considerations not reflected in your calculations.

(*b*) Prepare a short note on the suitability of judging department by their net income as percentage of sales.

Solution:

Alternative Annual Budgets

	Keep toy department (₹)	***Extend clothing department*** (₹)	***Use for storage*** (₹)
Benefits: Gross profit	26,50,000	22,50,000	–
Rent saved	–	–	4,00,000
General administrative costs saved	–	–	50,000
	26,50,000	22,50,000	4,50,000
Costs:			
Sales assistant's wage (Cost of replacements – existing assistants will be employed in any case)	7,00,000	7,00,000	0
Supervisor (Salary payable in any case so irrelevant. But value of general administrative duties are cost of keeping toy department – assume zero)	0	0	0
Establishment costs	3,00,000	2,00,000	1,50,000

Rent (Unaffected by decision)	0	0	0
	10,00,000	9,00,000	1,50,000
Surplus	₹ 16,50,000	₹ 13,50,000	₹ 3,00,000

Keeping the toy department open produces ₹ 3,00,000 more surplus than the next best alternative (extending the clothing department). However, if the value of the supervisor as a general administrator is more than ₹ 3,00,000 per annum, it may be better to close the toy department and to use the space to extend the clothing department. The directors should also consider possible interdependences between the demands for different products: for example, are customers who enter the store to buy toys more likely also to buy clothes or other products?

Net income as % of sales is only a partial measure of performance. Most organisations wish to maximise the income earned on each Re. of capital invested, not on each Re. of sales. So a department which earns an income of 10% of sales and produces only Re 1 of sales each year per Re of capital employed is doing less well than a department which earns an income of 5% of sales, but which makes ₹ 5 of sales each year per Re of capital employed.

Illustrative Problem 27 (Make or Buy)

Lotus Company produces two products, A and B. The segmented income statement for a quarter follows:

	Product A	*Product B*	*Total*
Sales	₹ 1,50,000	₹ 80,000	₹ 2,30,000
Less: Variable expenses	80,000	46,000	1,26,000
Contribution margin	₹ 70,000	₹ 34,000	₹ 1,04,000
Less: Direct fixed expenses*	20,000	38,000	58,000
Segment margin	₹ 50,000	₹ (4,000)	₹ 46,000
Less: Common fixed expenses			30,000
Operating income			₹ 16,000

* Includes depreciation.

Product A uses subassembly that is purchased from an external supplier for ₹ 25 per unit. Each quarter, 2,000 subassemblies are purchased. All units produced are sold, and there are no ending inventories of subassemblies. Lotus is considering making the subassembly rather than buying it. Unit variable manufacturing costs are as follows:

Direct materials	₹ 2
Direct labor	3
Variable overhead	2

Two alternatives exist to supply the productive capacity:

1. Lease the needed space and equipment at a cost of ₹ 27,000 per quarter for the space and ₹ 10,000 per quarter for a supervisor. No other fixed expenses are incurred.
2. Drop Product B. The equipment could be adapted with virtually no cost and the existing space utilized to produce the subassembly. The direct fixed expenses, including supervision, would be ₹ 38,000, ₹ 8,000 of which is depreciation on equipment. If Product B is dropped, the sales of Product A will not be affected.

Required:

(*i*) Should Lotus Company make or buy the subassembly? If it makes the subassembly, which alternative should be chosen? Explain and provide supporting computations.

(*ii*) Suppose that dropping B will decrease sales of A by 6 percent. What effect does this have on the decision?

(*iii*) Assume that dropping B decreases sales of A by 6 pcr cent and that 2,800 subassemblies are required per quarter. As before, assume that there are no ending inventories of subassemblies and that all units produced are sold. Assume also that the per-unit sales price and variable costs are the same as in Requirement (*i*). Include the leasing alternative in your consideration. Now, what is the correct decision?

Solution:

(*i*) ***Cost Item***	***Lease and Make***	***Buy***
Purchase cost		₹ 50,000
Variable manufacturing costs	₹ 14,000*	—
Lease	27,000	—
Supervisor salary	10,000	—
Total relevant costs	₹ 51,000	₹ 50,000

*₹ 7 × 2,000

	Drop B and Make
Purchase cost	—
Variable manufacturing costs	₹ 14,000
Lost contribution margin	34,000
Total relevant costs	₹ 48,000

Note: The ₹ 38,000 of direct fixed expenses is the same across all alternatives.

The most favorable alternative is to drop B and make the subassembly.

(*ii*) Analysis with complementary effect:

	Make	***Buy***
Lost sales for A[a]	₹ 9,000	—
Cost of making component[b]	₹ 13,160	—
Reduction of other variable costs[c]	(1,800)	—
Lost contribution margin for B	34,000	—
Cost to purchase[d]	—	₹ 50,000
Total relevant costs	₹ 54,360	₹ 50,000

[a]0.06 × ₹ 150,000

[b]0.94 × 2,000 × ₹ 7.00

[c]0.06 (₹ 80,000 – ₹ 50,000); since sales decrease by 6 pcr cent if the component is manufactured, the other variable costs (those other than the cost of the component) will decrease proportionately

[d]If the buy alternative is chosen, there is no reduction in sales and the same number of components will be needed.

The correct decision now is to Keep B and buy the component.

(*iii*) Variable manufacturing costs

	Lease and Make	*Buy*
Variable manufacturing cost	₹ 19,600[a]	—
Lease	27,000	—
Supervisor salary	10,000	—
Purchase cost	—	₹ 70,000[b]
Total relevant costs	₹ 56,600	₹ 70,000

[a]₹ 7 × 2,800
[b]₹ 25 × 2,800

	Drop B and Make
Lost sales from A	₹ 9,000
Variable cost of manufacturing[a]	18,424
Reduction of other variable costs[b]	(600)
Loss in contribution margin for B	34,000
Purchase cost	—
Total relevant costs	₹ 60,824

[a]0.94 × 2,800 × ₹ 7.00
[b]0.06 × (₹ 80,000 – ₹ 70,000)

The correct decision now is to lease and make the component.

Illustrative Problem 28 (Purchase of New Equipment)

A factory engaged in the manufacture of electronic goods has a ten-year old equipment depreciated on straight-line method. The useful life of the equipment was estimated to be 20 years with a residual value of ₹ 3 lakhs (original cost of the equipment being ₹ 23 lakhs). The output of the equipment is 1,200 units per hour.

The management now proposes to instal a new equipment worth ₹ 50 lakhs which has an estimated life of 15 years and a residual value of ₹ 5 lakhs. The payment terms for the new equipment include a part exchange provision of ₹ 6 lakhs in respect of the existing equipment. The output of the new equipment is 3,000 units per hour.

Other comparative annual cost data relating to the two-equipments are as under:

	Existing Equipment (₹)	*New Equipment* (₹)
Wages	1,00,000	1,20,000
Repair and Maintenance	20,000	52,000
Consumables	3,20,000	4,80,000
Power	1,20,000	1,50,000
Allocation of Fixed Costs	60,000	80,000
Total hours run per year	2,400	2,400

You are required to prepare a comparative schedule showing total conversion cost as well as cost per 1,000 units after considering interest @ 10% on net cash outflow for procuring the new equipment and also for providing for the yearly recovery of the loss suffered in the transaction.

Solution:

Comparative Statement of Conversion Cost

	Old Equipment (₹)	*New Equipment* (₹)
Annual Depreciation—New Equipment (WN1 [i])		3,00,000
Old Equipment (WN1 [ii])	1,00,000	70,000
Interest on Capital (WN-2)	—	4,40,000
Wages	1,00,000	1,20,000
Repairs and Maintenance	20,000	52,000
Consumables	3,20,000	4.80.000
Power	1,20,000	1,50,000
Allocation of Fixed Expenses	60,000	80,000
	7,20,000	16,92,000
Total Hours run per annum	2,400	2,400
Operating cost per hour	300	705
Output per hour (units)	1,200	3,000
Operating cost per 1000 units	250	235

Hence, there is a net saving in cost of ₹ 15 per 1,000 units on account of replacement of old equipment by a new equipment.

Working Notes:

1. *Depreciation:*

		₹
	(*i*) Existing Equipment:	
	Capital Cost	23,00,000
Less:	Residual Value	3,00,000
		20,00,000
	Life	20 years
	Annual Depreciation	1,00,000
	(*ii*) *New Equipment:*	
	Capital Cost	50,00,000
Less:	Residual Value	5,00,000
		45,00,000
	Life	15 years
	Annual Depreciation	₹ 3,00,000

Besides this the old equipment will be exchanged for ₹ 6,00,000 towards payment of cost of new equipment. Such sale will have to be written off over a period of 10 years (*i.e.*, the remaining life of the old equipment). The amount of such loss will be as under:

		₹
	Cost of old equipment	23,00,000
Less:	Depreciation written off over 10 years @ ₹ 1,00,000 every year	10,00,000
		13,00,000

Less: Exchange	6,00,000
	7,00,000
Loss per annum over remaining 10 years	70,000

2. Interest on net cash outflow as a result of purchase of new equipment:

Cost of new equipment:	50,00,000
Less: Exchange value of old equipment	6,00,000
New Cash Outflow	44,00,000
Interest @ 10%	= 4,40,000

Illustrative Problem 29 (Deciding Product Mix)

From the following particulars, find the most profitable product mix and prepare a statement of profitability of that product mix:

	Product A	*Product B*	*Product C*
Units budgeted to be produced and sold	1,800	3,000	1,200
Selling price per unit (₹)	60	55	50
Requirement per unit:			
Direct Materials	5 kg	3 kg	4 kg
Direct Labour	4 hr.	3 hrs.	2 hrs.
Variable Overheads	₹ 7	₹ 13	₹ 8
Fixed Overheads	₹ 10	₹ 10	₹ 10
Cost of Direct Material per kg	₹ 4	₹ 4	₹ 4
Direct Labour Hour Rate	₹ 2	₹ 2	₹ 2
Maximum Possible Units of Sales	4,000	5,000	1,500

All the three products are produced from the same direct material using the same type of machines and labour. Direct labour, which is the key factor is limited to 18,600 hours.

Solution:

Statement of Most Profitable Mix

Particulars	*Products*		
	A ₹	*B* ₹	*C* ₹
Selling price per unit (*i*)	60	55	50
Variable Cost:			
Direct Material	20	12	16
Direct Labour	8	6	4
Variable Overhead	7	13	8
Total Variable Cost (*ii*)	35	31	28
Contribution per unit (*i*)-(*ii*)	25	24	22
Contribution per hour (WN: 1)	6.25	8	11
Ranking of products according to profitability	III	II	I

Statement of Profitability of the Most Profitable Product Mix

Particulars	*Products*			
	A	*B*	*C*	*Total*
Ranking of Products	III	II	I	
Units produced (WN : 2)	150	5,000	1,500	
Contribution per unit (₹)	25	24	22	
Total contribution on units sold (₹)	3,750	1,20,000	33,000	1,56,750
	(150 × 25)	(5000 × 24)	(1500 × 22)	
Less: Fixed Cost (₹) (WN:3)				60,000
Profit (₹)				96,750

Working Notes:

(1) Computation of Contribution per hour

Particulars	*Products*		
	A	*B*	*C*
Contribution per unit (₹)	25	24	22
Direct labour per unit	4	3	2
Contribution per hour (₹)	25/4 = 6.25	24/3 = 8	22/2 = 11

(2) Computation of Output of Different Products

In the problem given direct labour hour is the key factor and only 18,600 hours are available to produce the three products. The available 18,600 hours will therefore be utilised in the order of the ranking assigned *i.e.,* (1) Product C (II) Product B and (III) Product A.

The number of units of the product to be produced, depends upon the maximum possible sale of each product. The details of the product to be produced keeping in mind available hours and ranking of the products are as given below:

		Total hours utilised
Product C	1,500 units × 2 hrs	3,000
Product B	5,000 units × 3 hrs	15,000
Product A	150 units × 4 hrs	600
Total Hours		18,600

(3) Computation of Total Fixed Costs

Particulars	*Products*			*Total*
	A	*B*	*C*	
Budget units to be produced and sold	1,800	3,000	1,200	
Fixed overhead (₹) per unit	10	10	10	
Total Fixed Overhead (₹)	18,000	30,000	12,000	60,000

Illustrative Problem 30 (Shut Down Decision)

When Alps Ltd. operates at normal capacity, it manufactures 2,00,000 units of product per year. The unit cost of manufacturing at normal capacity is as follows:

	(₹)
Direct materials	78
Direct labour	21
Variable overheads	25
Fixed overheads	40
Product cost (unit)	164
Selling price	210

During the next 3 months, only 10,000 units can be produced and sold. Management plans to shut down the plant, estimating that the fixed manufacturing overhead can be reduced to ₹ 7,40,000 for the quarter when the plant is not operating; the fixed overhead costs are incurred at a uniform rate throughout the year. Additional costs of plant shut down for the 3 months are estimated at ₹ 1,40,000.

You are required to answer:

(*a*) Should the plant be shut down for 3 months? Show computations.

(*b*) What is the shut down point for the three months in units of product?

(*M.Com., Delhi*)

Solution:

(a) Decision Analysis (Shut down plant)

Particulars		*Operating Plant* (₹) (₹)	*Shut down Plant* (₹) (₹)
(*i*) Estimated revenue (10,000 × ₹ 210)		21,00,000	—
(*ii*) Estimated cost:			
Direct materials	78		
Direct labour	21		
Variable overheads	25		
	124		
Total variable costs		(12,40,000)	—
(*iii*) Estimated contribution		8,60,000	—
Less: Fixed costs		(20,00,000)	(7,40,000)
Shut-down costs		—	(1,40,000)
Net profit (loss)		(11,40,000)	(8,80,000)

The plant should be shut down for 3 months as the loss is ₹ 8,80,000 only, while operating the plant would entail a greater loss (₹ 11,40,000)

(*b*) The shut down point is the point at which losses from continued operation are equal to the shut down costs. That is,

$$\frac{\begin{pmatrix}\text{Fixed cost when}\\ \text{plant is operating}\end{pmatrix}-\begin{pmatrix}\text{Shut down cost when}\\ \text{plant is not operating}\end{pmatrix}}{\text{Contribution margin per unit}}$$

$$=\frac{₹\,20,00,000-₹\,8,80,000}{₹\,86.0}=13,023 \text{ units}$$

Illustrative Problem 31 (Buy New Machine)

Perfect Product Ltd. is currently buying a component from a local supplier at ₹ 15 each. The supply is tending to be irregular. Two proposals are under consideration:

(*i*) Buy and instal a semi-automatic machine for manufacturing this component, which would involve an annual fixed cost of ₹ 9 lakh and a variable cost of ₹ 6 per manufactured component:

(*ii*) Buy and instal an automatic machine for manufacturing this component, incur an annual fixed cost of ₹ 15 lakh and a variable cost of ₹ 5 per manufactured component. Determine with necessary computations:

1. The annual volume required in each case to justify the switchover from "outside purchase" to "own manufacture."
2. The annual required volume to justify selection of the automatic machine instead of semiautomatic machine.
3. If the annual requirement for the coming year is expected to be 5,00,000 (units) and the volume is expected to increase rapidly thereafter, would you recommend the automatic or semiautomatic machine? Justify your recommendation.

Solution:

1. Volume required to justify own manufacture of a component is given by the following formula:

$$\frac{\text{Fixed costs (incremental)}}{\text{(Buying cost per unit- Variable cost per unit)}}$$

(*a*) Semi-automatic machine

$$\frac{₹\,9,00,000}{(₹\,15-₹\,6)}=1,00,000 \text{ units}$$

(*b*) Automatic machine

$$\frac{₹\,15,00,000}{(₹\,15-₹\,5)}=1,50,000 \text{ units}$$

2. 1,50,000 units as shown in (1) *b*.

3. Production Cost Statement

	Automatic machine	***Semi-automatic machine***
No. of units	5,00,000	5,00,000
Variable cost per unit (₹)	5	6
Total variable cost	25,00,000	30,00,000
Plus fixed cost	15,00,000	9,00,000
Total cost	40,00,000	39,00,000
Per unit cost	8.00	7.80

At the expected volume of 5,00,000 units, calculations suggest that the semi-automatic machine should be bought. However, as the demand is expected to increase rapidly after one year, from the long-term point of view, purchase of the automatic machine is recommended as cost per unit would be equal to 6,00,000 units as shown below:

Production Cost Statement (6,00,000 units)

Particulars	*Automatic machine* ₹	*Semi-automatic machine* ₹
Total variable cost	30,00,000	36,00,000
Plus fixed cost	15,00,000	9,00,000
Total cost	45,00,000	45,00,000
Cost per unit	7.50	7.50

Clearly, at the production volume of greater than 6,00,000 units total cost per unit would be lower in the automatic machine compared to the semi-automatic.

Illustrative Problem 32 (Use of Excess Capacity)

Barren Equipment Manufacturing built a new facility in 2016 but has only been able to use 60% of its capacity in manufacturing its major machine products. Management would like to use the excess capacity and has three possibilities. Only one of the three may be selected.

(*i*) The company could produce an additional 6,000 units per year of its most popular machine and develop a foreign market. Management estimates that additional freight costs would amount to ₹ 200 per machine and fixed factory overhead would increase by ₹ 60,000. To cover the additional cost, the selling price per machine would be increased by ₹ 300 per machine.

(*ii*) The company could produce and market a new laser lathe. The capacity could be used to produce 2,000 units per year that would sell for ₹ 1,800 each. Management has estimated the following unit variable costs:

	₹
Direct materials	600
Direct labour	300
Variable overhead	450
Variable selling	50
	1,400

The new lathe would require additional fixed costs ₹ 2,00,000 in fixed overhead and ₹ 80,000 in fixed selling.

(*iii*) The Paco-Pole Company has offered to lease the facilities at ₹ 30,000 per month plus 10% of the net revenues generated by the facilities. Net revenues are estimated at ₹ 15,00,000 per year.

Required:

(*i*) Which of the three alternatives should management select?

(*ii*) What is the opportunity cost of the decision?

Solution:

(*i*) The company could produce an additional 6,000 units (machines) per year of its most popular machine and develop foreign markets.

Additional freight cost ₹ 200/- per machine		
Total freight costs 6000 × ₹ 200	=	12,00,000
Fixed factory overhead would increase	=	60,000
Total costs		₹ 12,60,000

To cover the additional costs, the selling prices per machine would be increased by ₹ 300/- per machine.

Increased Sales Revenue = 6,000 × ₹ 300 = ₹ 18,00,000

Net advantage in producing 6,000 additional units of its most popular machine = ₹ 5,40,000 (₹ 18,00,000 – ₹ 12,60,000)

(*ii*) New Laser Lathe — The company could produce and market a new laser lathe. The capacity could be used to produce 2,000 units per year that would sell for ₹ 1,800 each.

Thus, estimated sales revenue = 2,000 units × ₹ 1,800 = ₹ 36,00,000

Management has estimated the following variable costs ₹ 1,400 per lathe.

Total variable costs of 2,000 units = 2,000 × ₹ 1,400
= ₹ 28,00,000

Estimated contribution margin of 2,000 laser Lathes
= 36,00,000 – 28,00,000 = ₹ 8,00,000

Additional fixed costs:

	₹
Fixed overhead	2,00,000
Fixed selling	80,000
	2,80,000

Estimated increase in net income = ₹ 8,00,000 – 2,80,000 = ₹ 5,20,000

(*iii*) Estimated Lease Rental of the Facility

			₹
	₹ 30,000 p.m. × 12 months	=	3,60,000
Add:	10% of ₹ 15,00,000	=	1,50,000
	Total estimated revenue to be realised from Paco-Pole Company		5,10,000

Decision: Thus, out of three alternatives, the management should select the first alternative of producing an additional 6,000 units (machines) per year of its most popular machine. Since this alternative is likely to result in the maximum increase in the net income of the company, *i.e.*, by ₹ 5,40,000. Besides, it will also be able to develop a foreign market.

Opportunity Cost of the Decision

The opportunity cost of the decision will be as follows:

(*i*) It would forgo the alternative of producing and marketing a new laser lathe which would have brought in a net increase in income to the extent of ₹ 5,20,000

(*ii*) It would also forgo the alternative of leasing the facilities which could have brought in the additional net revenue of ₹ 5,10,000 per year.

Thus the net advantage of selecting the first alternative, in comparison to the second alternative is of ₹ 20,000 and ₹ 30,000 compared with the third alternative.

Illustrative Problem 33 (Different Cost Calculations and Special Order)

Mr. Karan Mehta operates a small machine shop. He manufactures one 'standard product which is available from many other similar businesses and also manufactures another product referred to as 'universal'. His accountant prepared the annual income statement given as below:

	Universal Product ₹	*Standard Product* ₹	*Total* ₹
Sales	5,00,000	2,50,000	7,50,000
Material	1,00,000	80,000	1,80,000
Labour	2,00,000	90,000	2,90,000
Depreciation	63,000	36,000	99,000
Power	7,000	4,000	11,000
Rent	60,000	10,000	70,000
Heat and light	6,000	1,000	7,000
Other expenses	4,000	9,000	13,000
	4,40,000	2,30,000	6,70,000
Net profit	60,000	20,000	80,000

The depreciation charges are for machines used in the respective product lines. The power charge is apportioned on the estimate of power consumed. The rent is for the building space which has been leased for the ten years at ₹ 70,000 per year. The rent and heat and light are apportioned to the product lines based on amount of floor space occupied. All other costs are current expenses and are identified with the product line causing them.

A customer of 'Universal Product' has asked Karan Mehta if he would manufacture 5000 special units for him. Mr. Karan Mehta is working at capacity and would have to give up some other business in order to take this special order. Though he cannot reduce Universal Product orders already agreed to, he could reduce the output of his Standard Product by about one half for one year while producing the specially requested Universal Product'. The customer is willing to pay ₹ 70 for each part. The material cost will be ₹ 20 per unit and the labour will be ₹ 36 per unit. Mr. Karan Mehta will have to spend ₹ 20,000 for a special device which will be discarded when the job is done.

Required:

I. Calculate and present the following costs related to the 5,000 unit universal product order

(*a*) Incremental cost of the order

(*b*) Full cost of the order

(*c*) Opportunity cost of accepting the order

(*d*) Sunk costs related to the order

II. Should Karan Mehta accept the special order? Explain your answer. (*M.Com., Delhi* 2003)

Solution:

I: **(*a*) Incremental cost of the Order**

Cost Incurred to Fill Order (5,000 units)

Cost	*Per unit* ₹	*Total cost* (₹) ₹
Material	20	1,00,000
Labour	36	1,80,000
Special overhead	—	20,000
Total		3,00,000

Costs Reduced for 'Standard Product'

	₹
Material	40,000
Labour	45,000
Other	4,500
	89,500

Total Net incremental cost = Cost incurred to fill order — Costs reduced (saved)

₹ 3,00,000 — ₹ 89,500 = ₹ 2,10,500

Depreciation, heat and light, rent are not affected by the order, since they are committed fixed costs and thus continue regardless of the order. Power might be affected depending on the particular requirements of the special units. It is assumed that the same amount of power will be used in each case.

In case, power is taken as a cost to be incurred to fill order, then power (assuming 50% of power cost) will be taken as incremental cost and will be added. But, at the same time, power cost for Standard Product (say 50%) will be reduced or saved. So, it will have to be deducted from total incremental cost. So, it will not affect the answer. Therefore, alternatively, it may not be taken at all.

Alternate Solution

I (*a*) Incremental costs of the Order

Costs Incurred to Fill Order (5,000 units)

Cost	*Per unit*	*Total Cost* (₹)
Material	20	1,00,000
Labour	36	1,80,000
Special overhead	—	20,000
Power		2,000
Total		3,02,000

Costs Reduced for Standard Product

	₹
Material	40,000
Labour	45,000
Power	2,000
Other	4,500
	91,500

Total Incremental cost = ₹ 3,02,000 – 91,500 = ₹ 2,10,500

Note: **Incremental costs mean those additional costs which are required to be incurred in addition to existing costs being incurred. Incremental costs are different from direct costs which mean costs directly associated with some activity.**

In the above, solution 1(*a*), power costs may not be shown in both the part. Still, the answer would be the same.

(*b*) Full Cost of the Order

		(₹)
1.	Incremental Cost incurred to fill the order (taken from (*a*) above)	3,00,000
2.	Depreciaiton	18,000
3.	Rent	5,000
4.	Power	2,000
5.	Heat and light	500
		3,25,500

(*c*) Opportunity Cost of Accepting the Order

Opportunity cost is the net income sacrificed to select an alternative. Or opportunity costs also means net cash flow given up. In this case, opportunity costs arises in relation to Standard Product.

Opportunity cost in terms of net income given up

Total net profit of Standard Product is ₹ 20,000.

Therefore, profit given up = 50% of ₹ 20,000
= ₹ 10,000

Opportunity costs in terms of net cash flow given up will be as follows:

	₹	
50% sales of Standard Product =		₹ 1,25,000
Less: Costs involving Cashflow:		
Material	40,000	
Labour	45,000	
Power	2,000	
Heat & light	500	
Other	4,500	
Rent	5,000	97,000
Opportunity cost of Special order		28,000

Note: **Rent, Heat and light may not be included if one is taking the (right) assumption that discontinuance of 50% Standard product will not eliminate these costs as they relate to space occupied.**

(*d*) Sunk Costs Related to the Order

Sunk costs are the costs that do not change as a result of choosing one order or the other.

	(₹)
Depreciation	18,000
Power	2,000
Rent	5,000
Heat and light	500
Total	25,500

II Special Order Decision

		(₹)
	Sales Revenue	3,50,000
Less:	Full cost of the order	3,25,500
	Advantage in accepting the order	24,500
Less:	Opportunity cost (net profit sacrificed)	10,000
	Net advantage in special order	14,500

Note: **Full cost has been considered since 50% of 'Standard Product' has been cut. Therefore costs like depreciation, rent, heat and light (to the extent of 50%) are to be borne by special order units. These costs logically should not be borne by the remaining 50% Standard Product. Otherwise, the sale of remaining 50% standard product would wrongly be affected.**

Alternate Solution:

		₹
	New sales (5,000 × ₹ 70) =	3,50,000
Less:	Standard Product Sales	1,25,000
	Incremental Sales	2,25,000
Less:	Incremental costs from 1(*a*) above	2,10,500
Net advantage in special order		14,500

Other factors must also be considered, such as the longrun consequences of failing to satisfy standard product consumers, the reliability of the cost estimates and the importance of this valued customer.

Illustrative Problem 34 (Keep or Close)

Rakesh, an entrepreneur, runs two departmental stores, one in Delhi and the other in Noida. Operating income for each store in 2017 is as follows :

	Delhi Store	***Noida Store***
Revenues	₹ 1,07,00,000	₹ 86,00,000
Operating costs:		
Cost of goods sold	75,00,000	66,00,000
Lease rent (renewable each year)	9,00,000	7,50,000
Labour costs (paid on hourly basis)	4,20,000	4,20,000
Equipment depreciation	2,50,000	2,20,000
Utilities (Electricity heating)	4,30,000	4,60,000
Allocated corporate overhead	5,00,000	4,00,000
Total operating costs	1,00,00,000	88,50,000
Operating income (loss)	7,00,000	(2,50,000)

The equipment has zero disposal value. Mohan, the accountant makes the following comment. "Rakesh can increase his profitability by closing down the Noida store or by adding another store like it."

Required:

(*i*) By closing down the Noida store, Rakesh can reduce overall corporate overhead costs by ₹ 4,40,000. Calculate Rakesh's operating income if he closes the Noida store. Is Mohan's statement about the effect of closing the Noida store correct? Explain.

(*ii*) Calculate Rakesh's operating income if he keeps the Noida store open and opens another store with revenues and costs identical to the Noida store (including a cost of ₹ 2,20,000 to acquire equipment with a one-year useful life and zero disposal value). Opening this store will increase corporate overhead costs by ₹ 40,000. Is Mohan's statement about the effect of adding another store like the Noida store correct? Explain.

(*M.Com., Delhi University, 2009, 2011*)

Solution:

Relevant Revenues and Relevant Cost Analysis of Closing Noida Store and Opening Another Store

	(₹) *Closing NOIDA Store*	(₹) *Opening New Store like NOIDA Store*
	Loss in Revenue & savings in costs	*Incremental Revenue & Incremental Costs*
Revenues	(86,00,000)	86,00,000
Cost of goods sold	66,00,000	(66,00,000)
Lease rent	7,50,000	(7,50,000)
Labour costs	4,20,000	(4,20,000)
Equipment depreciation	NIL	(2,20,000)
Utilities (Electricity heating)	4,60,000	(4,60,000)
Corporate overhead costs	4,40,000	(40,000)
Total savings in costs/costs	86,70,000	84,90,000
Effect on operating income	70,000	1,10,000

1. The data presented above relating to NOIDA store presents the loss in relevant revenues and the relevant savings in costs from closing the NOIDA store. Mohan is correct that Rakesh's operating income would increase by ₹ 70,000 if he closes down the NOIDA store. Closing down the NOIDA store results in a loss of revenues of ₹ 86,00,000 but cost savings of ₹ 86,70,000 (from cost of goods sold, rent, labour, utilities and corporate costs.) Note that by closing down the NOIDA store, Rakesh will save none of the equipment related costs because this is a past cost.

Also, note that relevant corporate overheadcosts are the actual corporate overhead costs ₹ 4,40,000 that Rakesh expects to save by closing the NOIDA store.

The corporate overhead of ₹ 4,00,000 allocated to NOIDA store is irrelevant to the analysis.

2. The data relating to another store presented above presents the relevant revenues and relevant costs of opening another store like the NOIDA store. Mohan is correct that opening such a store would increase Rakesh's operating income by ₹ 1,10,000. Incremental revenues of ₹ 86,00,000 exceeds the incremental costs of ₹ 84,90,000 (from cost of goods sold, rent, labour, utilities and some additional corporate costs). Note that the cost of equipment (written off as depreciation) is relevant because it is an expected future cost that Rakesh will incur only if he opens the new store.

Also note that the relevant corporate overhead costs are ₹ 40,000 of actual corporate overhead costs that Rakesh expects to incur as a result of opening the new store. Rakesh may, infact, allocate more than ₹ 40,000 of corporate overhead to the new store but this allocation is irrelevant to the analysis.

The key reason that Rakesh's operating income increases either if he closes down the NOIDA store or if he opens another store like it, is the behaviour of corporate overhead costs. By closing down the NOIDA store Rakesh can significantly reduce corporate overhead costs presumably by reducing the corporate staff that overseas the NOIDA operation. On the other hand, adding another store like NOIDA does not increase actual corporate costs by much, presumably because the existing corporate staff will be able to oversee the new store as well.

Illustrative Problem 35 (Export Order)

An engineering company produces product P in its production shop 'A'. The overhead recovery rate is 100% of direct wages based on the following budgeted figures:

	₹
Direct wages	1,60,000
Variable overhead	64,000
Fixed overheads	96,000

The production plan for the same budget period envisages an output of 18,000 units of Product P whose sales and cost data are as under:

	₹ *per unit*
Selling Price	42
Direct Materials	12
Direct Wages	8
Total Overheads	8

The company proposes to use the balance capacity of shop A after completing the above said production plan, for the manufacture of component Q whose cost data are as under:

	₹ *per unit*
Direct Materials	8
Direct Wages	16
Total Overheads	16

The component Q is used by the company in the manufacture of some other product in another production Department.

The company receives an export order from abroad for the purchase of 2,000 units of Product P at ₹ 30 each. This offer can be accepted by diverting the capacity from component Q. In that event the company has to buy the component which is available from an outside supplier at a price of ₹ 40 each.

You are required to evaluate the alternative of action and state with reasons whether the spare capacity should be utilised for the manufacture of:

(*a*) The component Q or

(*b*) 2,000 units of product P for export and buying of the component Q from the outside supplier.

Solution:

Basic Calculations:

		₹
(*i*)	Total Direct Wages (given)	1,60,000
(*ii*)	Variable Overhead (given)	64,000
(*iii*)	Variable Overhead Recovery Rate: $\frac{64,000 \times 100}{1,60,000}$	
	= 40% of Direct Wages	
(*iv*)	Production of P as per budget units	18,000
(*v*)	Direct Wages per unit	8
(*vi*)	Total Wages cost of P	1,44,000
(*vii*)	Capacity available for Production of Q in terms of wages cost:	
	1,60,000 – 1,44,000 =	16,000
(*viii*)	Direct wage cost per unit of Q	= 16
(*ix*)	No. of units of Q that can be produced; 16,000/16	1,000 units
(*x*)	Marginal cost of component Q:	
	Direct Material	8
	Direct Wages	16
	Variable Overheads (40% of Direct wages)	6.40
		30.40
(*xi*)	Cost of purchasing component Q from the market	40.00
(*xii*)	Extra cost per unit to be paid for component Q, if purchased from market	₹ 9.60
(*xiii*)	Total Incremental Cost to be paid for 1,000 units of Component Q	9,600

Each unit of Product P costs ₹ 8 in direct wages. Each unit of Component Q cost ₹ 16 in direct wages. In other words, in terms of labour costs, in case 1,000 units of component Q is not produced, the capacity released can be utilised for manufacture of 2,000 units of product P, as desired.

Evaluation of Production of 2,000 units of Product 'P' for Export

	₹
Marginal Cost per unit of Product P:	
Direct Material	12
Direct Labour	8

	Variable overheads (40% of direct labour)	3.20
		23.20
	Selling price per unit	30.00
	Contribution per unit (₹ 30.00 - ₹ 23.20)	6.80
	Total Contribution for 2,000 units (2,000 × 6.80)	13,600
Less:	Extra Cost to be paid for purchase of component Q from the market as per calculation (xii) above	9,600
	Incremental Gain	4,000

The above analysis shows that manufacture and export of 2,000 units of Product P will be more profitable to the company as compared to manufacturing of component Q.

Illustrative Problem 36 (Sell or Process Further Decision)

Curn-Clean Company produces a variety of cleaning compounds and solutions for both industrial and household use. While most of its products are processed independently,a few are related, such as the company's A 337 and its Sparkle silver polish.

A 337 is a coarse cleaning powder with many industrial uses. It costs ₹ 16 a kilogram to make, and it has a selling price of ₹ 20 a kilogram. A small portion of the annual production of A 337 is retained in the factory for further processing. It is combined with several other ingredients to form a paste that is marketed as Sparkle silver polish. The silver polish sells for ₹ 40 per jar.

This further processing requires 250 grams of A 337 per jar of silver polish. The additional direct costs involved in the processing of a jar of silver polish are:

Other ingredients	₹ 6.5
Direct labour	14.8
Total direct cost	₹ 21.3

Overhead costs associated with the processing of the silver polish are:

Variable manufacturing overhead cost	25% of direct labour cost

Fixed manufacturing overhead cost (per month):

Production supervisor	₹ 16,000
Depreciation of mixing equipment	14,000

The production supervisor has no duties other than to oversee production of the silver polish. The mixing equipment is special-purpose equipment acquired specifically to produce the silver polish. It has only negligible resale value.

Direct labour is a variable cost at the Company

Advertising costs for the silver polish total ₹ 40,000 per month. Variable selling costs associated with the silver polish are 7.5 of sales.

Due to a recent decline in the demand for silver polish, the company is wondering whether its continued production is advisable. The sales manager feels that it would be more profitable to just sell of the A 337 as a cleaning powder.

Required:

1. What is the incremental contribution margin per jar from further processing of A 337 into silver polish?
2. What is the minimum number of jars of silver polish that must be sold each month to justify the continued processing of A 337 into silver polish? Show all computation in good form.

(CMA, USA Adapted)

Solution:

1. A product should be processed further so long as the incremental revenue from the further processing exceeds the incremental costs. The incremental revenue from further processing for A 337 is:

	₹
Selling price of the silver polish, per jar	40
Selling price of 250 grams of A 337 ₹ (20 ÷ 4)	5
Incremental revenue per jar	35

The incremental variable costs are:

Other ingredients	₹ 6.5
Direct labour	14.8
Variable manufacturing overhead (25% × ₹ 14.8)	3.7
Variable selling costs (7.5% × 40)	3.0
Incremental variable cost per jar	₹ 28.0

Therefore, the incremental contribution margin is ₹ 7.0 per jar (₹ 35 – ₹ 28). The ₹ 16.0 cost per kilogram (₹ 4 per 250 grams) required to produce the A 337 would not be relevant in this computation, since it is incurred regardless of whether A 337 is further processed into silver polish or sold outright.

2. Only the cost of advertising and the cost of the production supervisor are avoidable if production of the silver polish is discontinued. Therefore, the number of jars of silver polish that must be sold each month to justify continued processing of A 337 into silver polish is:

Producing supervisor	₹ 16,000
Advertising—direct	40,000
Avoidable fixed costs	₹ 56,000

$$\frac{\text{Avoidable Fixed Costs, ₹ 56,000}}{\text{Incremental CM perjar, ₹ 7.0}} = \textbf{8,000} \text{ jars per month}$$

Therefore, if 8,000 jars of silver polish can be sold each month, the company would be indifferent between selling it or selling all of the A 337 as a cleaning powder. If the sales of the silver polish are greater than 8,000 jars per month, then continued processing of the A 337 into silver polish would be advisable since the company's total profits will be increased. If the company can't sell at least 8,000 jars of silver polish each month, then production of the silver polish should be discontinued. To verify this, we show below the total contribution to profits of sales of 7,000, 8,000 and 9,000 jars of silver polish, contrasted to sales of equivalent amounts of A 337 sold outright (i.e., 7,000 jars of silver polish would require the use of 1,750 kilograms of A 337 that otherwise could be sold outright as cleaning powder, etc.):

	7,000 Jars of Polish; or 1,750 Kgs. of A 337	8,000 Jars of Polish; or 2,000 Kgs. of A 337	9,000 Jars of Polish; or 2,250 Kgs. of A 337
Sales of Silver Polish:			
Sales @ ₹ 40 per jar	₹ 2,80,000	₹ 3,20,000	₹ 3,60,000
Less variable expenses:			
Production costof A 337 @ ₹ 16 per kg	28,000*	32,000*	36,000*
Further procesing and selling costs of the polish @ ₹ 28 per jar	1,96,000	2,24,000	2,52,000
Total variable expenses	2,24,000	2,56,000	2,88,000
Contribution margin	56,000	64,000	72,000
Less avoidable fixed costs:			
Production supervisor	16,000	16,000	16,000
Advertising	40,000	40,000	40,000
Total avoidable fixed costs	56,000	56,000	56,000
Total contribution to common fixed costs and to profits	₹ -0-	₹ 8,000	₹ 16,000
Sales of A 337:			
Sales @ ₹ 2.00 per kg	₹ 35,000	₹ 40,000	₹ 45,000
Less variable expenses:			
Production cost of A 337 @ ₹ 16 per kg	28,000*	32,000*	36,000*
Contribution to common fixed costs and to profits	₹ 7,000	8,000	₹ 9,000

* This cost will be incurred regardless of whether the A 337 is further processed into silver polish or sold outright as cleaning powder; therefore, it is not relevant to the decision, as stated earlier. It is included in the computation above for the specific puposes of showing that it will be incurred under either alternative. The same thing could have been done with the depreciation on the mixing equipment.

Illustrative Problem 37 (Export Order)

A company currently operating at 80% capacity has the following profitability particulars:

		₹	₹
	Sales		12,80,000
Costs:			
	Direct Materials	4,00,000	
	Direct Labour	1,60,000	
	Variable Overheads	80,000	
	Fixed Overheads	5,20,000	11,60,000
	Profit		1,20,000

An export order has been received that would utilise half the capacity of the factory. The order has either to be taken in full and executed at 10% below the normal domestic prices, or rejected totally. The alternatives available to management are given below:

(*i*) Reject the order, and continue with the domestic sales only as at present.

(*ii*) Accept order, split capacity equally between overseas and domestic sales and turn away excess domestic demand.

(*iii*) Increase capacity so as to accept the export order, and maintain the present domestic sales by:

(*a*) buying an equipment that will increase capacity by 10% and fixed cost by ₹ 40,000 and

(*b*) work overtime at time and a half to meet balance of required capacity.

Prepare comparative statements of profitability and suggest the best alternative.

Solution:

			₹
	(*i*) Sales		12,80,000
Less:	Variable Costs:	₹	
	Direct Materials	4,00,000	
	Direct labour	1,60,000	
	Variable Overhead	80,000	6,40,000
	Contribution		6,40,000
Less:	Fixed Overhead		5,20,000
	Profit		1,20,000
	P/V ratio (contribution)	50%	
	(*ii*) Sales at 80% capacity		12,80,000
	Sales at 100% capacity		16,00,000
	Export Sales:		
	50% of capacity of factory		8,00,000
Less:	10% due to price reduction		80,000
			7,20,000
Add:	Domestic sales by utilzing 50% of balance capacity		8,00,000
	Total sale for utilizing 100% capacity under alternative (*ii*)		15,20,000

			₹
Less:	Variable Cost $\frac{6,40,000 \times 100}{80}$		8,00,000
	Contribution		7,20,000
Less:	Fixed Cost		5,20,000
	Profit		2,00,000
	(*iii*) Sales:		
	Domestic Sales		12,80,000
	Export Sales		7,20,000
			20,00,000
Less:	Marginal Cost	₹	
	(*a*) For Domestic Sales (as given in alternative (*i*)	6,40,000	
	(*b*) For overtime paid for meeting balance of required capacity, *i.e.*, 20% capacity (Refer to working note)	20,000	
	(*c*) For Exports Sales $\frac{6,40,000 \times 50\%}{80\%}$	4,00,000	
			10,60,000
	Contribution under alternative (*iii*)		9,40,000
Less:	Fixed Cost:		
	(*i*) Existing	5,20,000	
	(*ii*) Increase in Fixed Cost to meet 10% increase in capacity	40,000	5,60,000
	Profit		3,80,000

Alternative (*iii*) yields the highest profit. Hence, it is the best alternative.

Notes:

Calculation of Overtime:

Capacity required for Export Order is 50%

Capacity presently being used is 80%

Increase required in capacity is 30%. This is met as follows:

(*a*) Working full capacity	100%
(*b*) Buying new equipment	10%
(*c*) Working overtime	20%
	130%

	₹
Direct labour for 80% capacity	= 1,60,000
Direct labour for 20% capacity	= 40,000
Overtime Premium is half of the above	= 20,000

Illustrative Problem 38 (increase in Selling Price)

The profit for the year of Push on Ltd. works out to 12.5% of the capital employed and the relevant figures are as under:

	₹
Sales	5,00,000
Direct Materials	2,50,000
Direct Labour	1,00,000
Variable Overheads	40,000
Capital Employed	4,00,000

The new Sales Manager who has joined the company recently estimates for next year a profit of about 23% on capital employed, provided the volume of sales is increased by 10% and simultaneously their is an increase in Selling Price of 4% and on overall cost reduction in all the elements of cost by 2%.

Find out by computing in detail the cost and profit for next year, whether the proposal of Sales Manager can be adopted.

Solution:

Push On Limited

Statement Showing Cost and Profit for the Next Year

Particulars	*Existing Volume, etc.*	*Volume, costs, etc. after 10% increase*	*Estimated Sales, Cost, Profit, etc., for the next year after increase in selling price @ 4% and overall cost reduction by 2%*
	₹	₹	₹
Sales	5,00,000	5,50,000	5,72,000
Direct Materials	2,50,000	2,75,000	2,69,500
Direct Labour	1,00,000	1,10,000	1,07,800
Variable Overheads	40,000	44,000	43,120
Marginal Cost	3,90,000	4,29,000	4,20,420
Contribution	1,10,000	1,21,000	1,51,580
Fixed Cost	60,000	60,000	58,800
Profit	50,000	61,000	92,780
Percentage Profit on Capital Employed	12.5%	—	$\frac{92,780}{4,00,000} \times 100 = 23.19\%$

Since the profit of ₹ 92,780 is more than 23% of capital employed, the proposal of sales manager can be accepted.

Illustrative Problem 39 (Make or Buy)

The Lakme Company, which produces and sells to wholesalers a highly successful line of summer lotions and insect repellents, has decided to diversify in order to stabilize sales throughout the year. A natural area for the company to consider is the production of winter lotions and creams to prevent dry and chapped skin.

After considerable research, a winter products line has been developed. However, because of the conservative nature of the company management, the company's president has decided to introduce only one of the new products for this coming winter. If the product is a success, further expansion in future years will be initiated.

The product selected (called "Chap-off") is a lip balm that will be sold in a lipstick-type tube. The product will be sold to wholesalers in boxes of 24 tubes for ₹ 800 per box. Because of available capacity, no additional fixed charges will be incurred to produce the product. However, a ₹ 1,00,00,000 fixed charge will be absorbed by the product to allocate a fair share of the company's present fixed costs to the new product.

Using the estimated sales and production of 1,00,000 boxes of Chap-off as the standard volume, the accounting department has developed the following costs:

	(₹)
Direct labour	200 per box
Direct materials	300 per box
Total overhead	150 per box
Total	650 per box

Lakme has approached a cosmetics manufacturer to discuss the possibility of purchasing the tubes for Chap-off. The purchase price of the empty tubes from the cosmetics manufacturer would be ₹ 90 per 24 tubes. If the Lakme accepts the purchase proposal, it is estimated that direct labour and variable overhead costs would be reduced by 10 pcr cent and direct material costs would be reduced by 20 percent.

Required:

1. Should the Lakme Company make or buy the tubes? Show calculations to support your answer.
2. What would be the minimum purchase price acceptable to the Lakme Company for the tubes? Support your answer with an appropriate explanation.
3. Instead of sales of 1,00,000 boxes, revised estimates show sales volume at 1,25,000 boxes. At this new volume, additional equipment, at an annual rental of ₹ 10,00,000 must be acquired to manufacture the tubes. However, this incremental cost would be the only additional fixed cost required even if sales increased to 3,00,000 boxes. (The 3,00,000 level is the goal for the third year of production.) Under these circumstances, should the Lakme company make or buy the tubes? Show calculations to support your answer.
4. The company has the option of making and buying at the same time. What would be your answer to question 3 if this alternative was considered? Show calculations to support your answer.
5. What nonquantifiable factors should the Lakme Company consider in determining whether they should make or buy the lipstick tubes? (*CMA, USA adapated with permission*)

(*M.Com., Delhi, 2015*)

Solution:

Make or Buy Decision

1.

	(₹)
Cost saved by purchasing tubes:	
Material (20% × ₹ 300)	60
Labour (10% × ₹ 200)	20
Overhead (10% × ₹ 50)	5
Total	85
Cost to buy	90

*Total overhead ₹ 150 per unit
Allocated overhead ₹ 100 per unit (₹ 1,00,00,000 ÷ 1,00,000)
Variable overhead ₹ 50 per unit.
Decision: Lakme Co. should make the tube.

2. The problem asks for the minimum purchase price. The context of the problem implies that the maximum purchase price is what was really required. Lakme Company would not pay more than ₹ 85 each because that is the cost to make the product internally. Obviously, the company would be willing to pay any amount which was less than ₹ 85.
3. At a volume of 1,25,000 units, Lakme should buy the tubes. The cost of buying 1,25,000 tubes is ₹ 1,12,50,000 (1,25,000 × ₹ 90). The cost of making 1,25,000 tubes is

	₹
1,25,000 × ₹ 85	1,06,25,000
Added fixed cost	10,00,000
	1,16,25,000

Buying the tubes will save ₹ 3,75,000.

4. Lakme Co. needs 1,25,000 tubes. The cost to buy 1,25,000 tubes is ₹ 1,12,50,000. The cost to make 1,25,000 tubes is ₹ 1,16,25,000. The cost to make 1,00,000 (standard volume) and buy 25,000 tubes is

₹
85,00,000
22,50,000
1,07,50,000

Therefore, to supply its needs, Lakme Co. should choose this latter course of action.

5. There are many nonquantifiable factors which Lakme should consider in addition to the economic factors calculated above. Among such factors are:
   (*a*) The quality of the purchased tubes as compared to Lakme-produced tubes.
   (*b*) The reliability of delivery to meet production schedules
   (*c*) The financial stability of the supplier.
   (*d*) Development of an alternate source of supply
   (*e*) Alternate uses of tube-manufacturing capacity.
   (*f*) The long-run character and size of the market.

Illustrative Problem 40 (Discontinuance of a Product)

A limited company manufacturers three different products and the following information has been collected from the books of accounts:

	Products		
	S	***T***	***Y***
Sales mix	35%	35%	30%
	₹	₹	₹
Selling price	30	40	20
Variable cost	15	20	12
		₹	
Total fixed costs		1,80,000	
Total sales		6,00,000	

The company has currently under discussion, a proposal to discontinue the manufacture of product Y and replace it with product M, when the following results are anticipated:

	S	*T*	*M*
		Product	
Sales mix	50%	25%	25%
	₹	₹	₹
Selling price	30	40	30
Variable cost	15	20	15
Total fixed costs		1,80,000	
Total sales		6,40,000	

Will you advise the company to change over to production of M? Give reasons for your answer.

Solution:

Existing production		***Products***		
	S	*T*	*Y*	***Total***
Selling price (₹)	30	40	20	
Variable cost (₹)	15	20	12	
Contribution per unit (₹)	15	20	8	
P/V Ratio	50%	50%	40%	
Sales mix	35%	35%	30%	
Contribution per rupee of sales (P/V ratio × Sales mix)	17½%	17½%	12%	47%
Present total sales				₹ 6,00,000

	₹
Present total contribution (6,00,000 × .47)	2,82,000
Fixed cost	1,80,000
Present profit	1,02,000
Present Break-even Sales: Fixed cost/P/V Ratio: 1,80,000/0.47	3,83,000

Proposed production:

	S	*T*	*M*	
		Products		
Selling price (₹)	30	40	30	
Variable cost (₹)	15	20	15	
Contribution per unit (₹)	15	20	15	
P/V ratio	50%	50%	50%	
Sales mix	50%	25%	25%	
Contribution per rupee of sales (P/V ratio × Sales mix)	25%	12½%	12½%	50%

		₹
	Proposed total sales	6,40,000
	Proposed total contribution (6,40,000 × .50)	3,20,000
Less:	Fixed costs	1,80,000
	Profit	1,40,000

Proposed Break-even point: $\frac{\text{Fixed cost}}{\text{P/V ratio}} = \frac{1,60,000}{0.50} = 3,60,000$

The new proposal to replace product Y and M can be accepted because of the following reasons: (*i*) The break-even point of the company under the new proposal reaches at a lower level of the total sales as compared to the present situation, (*ii*) The profit under the new proposal also increases by ₹ 38,000.

Illustrative Problem 41 (Methods of Increasing Production)

TTD Ltd. manufacturing a single product has normal working capacity of 8,000 units per annum. The sales manager has projected a sales of 10,000 units for the year 2012-13 at a price of ₹ 250 per unit.

The operating budget for 2012-2013 is as under:

		₹ *lakhs*
Sales 8,000 units @ ₹ 250 each		20.00
Cost of production:	₹ *(lakhs)*	
Raw materials	12.00	
Direct wages	3.00	
Works overhead (50% fixed)	1.40	
Administration overhead (all fixed)	0.60	
Selling and distribution overhead (80% fixed)	1.00	18.00
Profit	18.00	2.00

In order to increase production to meet the sales demand, two proposals have been put forward as under:

(*i*) Sub-contracting the production of 2,000 units at ₹ 225 per unit.

(*ii*) Installing an additional machine which will entail the following expenses:

(*a*) cost of machine ₹ 2,00,000; life 20 years

(*b*) Recruitment of 10 workers including direct workers to operate the machine at a wage rate of ₹ 500 each per month. Add 25% towards fringe benefits. (None of the existing workers will be utilised for this purpose).

(*c*) Interest on capital required for the purchase of machine, 15% per annum.

The following additional fixed expenses will be incurred in respect of both the alternatives:

	₹
Administration expenses	10,000 per year
Selling and distribution expenses	20,000 per year

Required:

(*i*) A statement showing the respective profitability of the two method of increasing the production,

(*ii*) Comments upon the choice of one of the two proposals.

Solution:

(₹ *in lakhs*)

	Present	*Sub-contracting*	*Installing additional machine*
Sales units	8,000	10,000	10,000
Sales realisation	20.00	25.00	25.00
Variable costs:			
Raw materials	12.00	12.00	15.00
Direct wages	3.00	3.00	3.00
Works overhead	0.70	0.70	0.875
Selling and distribution overhead	0.20	0.20	0.25
	15.90	15.90	19.125
Add: For contract work for 2,000 units at ₹ 225 per unit		4.50	
	15.90	20.40	19.125
Contribution	4.10	4.60	5.875
Fixed Expenses:			
Works overhead	0.70	0.70	0.70
Administration overhead	0.60	0.60	0.60
Selling and admn. expenses	0.80	0.80	0.80
Additional admn. expenses	—	0.10	0.10
Selling and distribution	—	0.20	0.20
Wages			0.75
Interest			0.30
Depreciation			0.10
Total	2.10	2.40	3.55
Profit	2.00	2.20	2.325

Incremental profit will be ₹ 20,000 (2.20 – 2.00) in the case of sub-contracting and ₹ 32,500 (2.325 – 2.00) in the case of installing the additional machine.

The second alternative is favoured if the additional load of 2,000 units is continuous.

Illustrative Problem 42 (Make or Buy)

"In my opinion, we ought to stop making our own drums and accept the outside supplier's offer," said Arun, managing director of Laxmi' Machinary Ltd. "At a price of ₹ 1800 per drum, we would be paying ₹ 5 less than it costs us to manufacture the drums in our own plant. Since we use 60,000 drums a year, that would be an annual cost savings of ₹ 3,00,00,000." The present cost to manufacture one drum is given below (based on 60,000 drums per year):

	(₹)
Direct material	1035
Direct labour	600
Variable overhead	150
Fixed overhead (₹ 280 general company overhead,	

₹ 160 depreciation and,	
₹ 75 supervision)	515
Total cost per drum	2300

A decision about whether to make or buy the drums is especially important at this time since the equipment being used to make the drums is completely worn out and must be replaced. The choices facing the company are:

Alternative 1: Purchase new equipment and continue to make the drums. The equipment would cost ₹ 8,10,00,000; it would have a six-year useful life and no salvage value. The company uses straight-line depreciation.

Alternative 2: Purchase the drums from an outside supplier at ₹ 1800 per drum under a six-year contract.

The new equipment would be more efficient than the equipment that the company has been using and, according to the manufacturer, would reduce direct labour and variable overhead costs by 30%. The old equipment has no resale value. Supervision cost (₹ 45,00,000) per year and direct materials cost per drum would not be affected by the new equipment. The new equipment's capacity would be 90,000 drums per year. The company has no other use for the space being used to produce the drums.

The company's total general company overhead would be unaffected bythis decision.

Required:

1. To assist the managing director in making a decision, prepare an analysis showing what the total cost and the cost per drum would be under each of the two alternatives given above. Assume that 60,000 drums are needed each year. Which course of action would you recommend to the managing director?
2. Would your recommendation in (1) above be the same if the company's needs were: (a) 75,000 drums per year or (b) 90,000 drums per year? Show computations to support your answer, with costs presented on both a total and a per unit basis.
3. What other factors would you recommend that the company consider before making a decision?

Solution:

1. The ₹ 280 per drum general overhead cost is not relevant to the decision, since this cost will be the same regardless of whether the company decides to make or buy the drums. Also, the present depreciation figure of ₹ 160 per drum is not a relevant cost, since it represents a sunk cost (in addition to the fact that the old equipment is worn out and must be replaced). The cost (depreciation) of the new equipment is a relevant cost, since the new equipment will not be purchased if the company decides to accept the outside supplier's offer. The cost of supervision is relevant to the decision, since this cost can be avoided by buying the drums.

	Differential Costs Per Drum		***Total Differential Costs—60,000 Drums***	
	Make	***Buy***	***Make***	***Buy***
	(₹)	(₹)	(₹)	(₹)
Outside supplier's price		1800		10,80,00,000
Direct materials	1035		6,21,00,000	
Direct labour (₹ 600 × 70%)	420		2,52,00,000	

Variable overhead (₹ 150 × 70%)	105		63,00,000	
Supervision	75		45,00,000	
Depreciation	225*		1,35,00,000	
Total cost	1860	1800	11,16,00,000	10,80,00,000
Difference in favour of buying	60		36,00,000	

* ₹ 8,10,00,000 ÷ years = ₹ 1,35,00,000 per year; 135,00,000 per year ÷ 60,000 drums = ₹ 225 per drum.

2. (a) Notice that unit costs for both supervision and depreciation will change if the company needs 75,000 drums each year. The reason is that these fixed costs will be spread over a greater number of units, thereby reducing the cost per unit.

	Differential Costs Per Drum		***Total Differential Costs—75,000 Drums***	
	Make (₹)	***Buy*** (₹)	***Make*** (₹)	***Buy*** (₹)
Outside supplier's price		1800		13,50,00,000
Direct materials	1035		7,76,25,000	
Direct labour	420		3,15,00,000	
Variable overhead	105		78,75,000	
Supervision (₹ 45,00,000 ÷ 75,000 drums)	60		45,00,000	
Depreciation (₹ 1,35,00,000 ÷ 75,000 drums)	180		1,35,00,000	
Total cost	1800	1800	13,50,00,000	13,50,00,000
Difference	-0-		-0-	

The company would be indifferent between the two alternatives if 75,000 drums were needed each year.

(b) Again, notice that the unit costs for both supervision and depreciation decrease with the greater volume of units.

	Differential Costs Per Drum		***Total Differential Costs—90,000 Drums***	
	Make (₹)	***Buy*** (₹)	***Make*** (₹)	***Buy*** (₹)
Outside supplier's price		1800		16,20,00,000
Direct materials	1035		9,31,50,000	
Direct labour	420		3,78,00,000	
Variable overhead	105		94,50,000	
Supervision (₹ 45,00,000 ÷ 90,000 drums	50		45,00,000	
Depreciation (₹ 1,35,00,000 ÷ 90,000 drums)	150		1,35,00,000	
Total cost	1760	1800	15,84,00,000	16,20,00,000
Difference in favour of making	40		36,00,000	

The company should purchase the new equipment and make the drums if 90,000 units per year are needed.

3. Other factors which the company should consider include.
   (a) Will volume in future years be increasing, or will it remain constant at 60,000 units per year? (If volume increases, then buying the new equipment becomes more desirable, as shown in the computations above.)
   (b) Can quality control be maintained if the drums are purchased from the outside supplier?
   (c) Will costs for materials and labour increase in future years, thereby increasing the cost of making the drums? (The supplier will be locked into an ₹ 1800 price.)
   (d) Will the outside supplier bedependable in meeting shipping schedules?
   (e) Can the company begin making the drums again, if the supplier proves to be undependable; or are there alternate suppliers?
   (f) What is the labour outlook in the supplier's industry (e.g. are frequent labour strikes likely)?
   (g) If the outside supplier's offer is accepted and the need for drums increases in future years, will the supplier have the added capacity to provide more than 60,000 drums per year?

Illustrative Problem 43 (Special Order Decision)

A Co. Ltd. manufactures several different styles of jewllery cases. Management estimates that during the third quarter, the company will be operating at 80 pcr cent of the normal capacity. Because the company desires a higher utilisation of plant capacity, the company will consider a special order.

The company has received special order inquiries from two companies. The first order is from JCP Co. Ltd., which would like to market a jewellery case similar to one of A Co. Ltd's. jewellery cases. JCP jewellery case would be marketed under JCP's own label. JCP Co. Ltd. has offered A Co. Ltd. ₹ 57.50 per jewellery case for 20,000 cases to be shipped by the last date of the quarter. The cost data for A Co. Ltd, jewellery case that would be similar to the specifications of JCP special order are as follows:

	₹
Regular selling price per unit	90
Costs per unit:	
Raw Materials	25
Direct Labour 0.5 hour @ ₹ 60	30
Overhead 0.25 machine hour @ ₹ 40	10
Total Costs	65

According to the specifications provided by JCP Co. Ltd., the special order case requires less expensive raw materials. Consequently, the raw materials will only cost ₹ 22.50 per case. Management has estimated that the remaining costs, labour time and machine time will be the same as for A Co. Ltd. jewellery case.

The second special order was submitted by K Co. Ltd. for 7.500 jewellery cases at ₹ 75 per case. These jewellery cases, like the JCP cases, would be marketed under K label and have to be shipped by the last date of the quarter. However, the K Jewellery case is different from any jewellery case in A Co. Ltd. line. The estimated per unit cost of this case are as follows:

	₹
Raw Materials	32.50
Direct Labour 0.5 hour @ ₹ 60	30.00
Overhead 0.5 machine hour @ ₹ 40	20.00
Total Costs	82.50

In addition, A Co. Ltd will incur ₹ 15,000 in additional setup costs and will have to purchase a ₹ 25,000 special device to manufacture these cases, this device will be discarded once the special order is completed.

The A Co. Ltd.'s manufacturing capabilities are limited to the total machine hours available. The plant capacity under normal operations is 90,000 machine hours per year or 7,500 machine hours per month. The budgeted fixed overhead for the Current year amounts to ₹ 21,60,000. All manufacturing overhead costs are applied to production on the basis of machine hours at ₹ 40 per hour.

A Co. Ltd. will have the entire quarter to work on the special orders. Management does not expect any repeat sales to be generated from either special order. Company practice precludes from subcontracting any portion of an order, when special orders are not expected to generated repeat sales.

Required:

Should A Co. Ltd. accept either special order? Justify your answer and show the calculations.

(CA Final, Nov. 2000)

Solution:

Statement showing profits on the acceptance of special orders in 4,500 unutilised hours (Refer to working note 1)

Alternatives	I	II
	JCP Co. Ltd.	K. Co. Ltd.
Units made	18,000	7,500
	₹	₹
Selling price per unit	57.50	75.00
Less: Cost per unit (Refer to working note 2)	56.50	70.50
Profit per unit	1.00	4.50
Total profit	18,000	33,750
	(18,000 units × ₹ 1)	(7,500 units × ₹ 4.50)
Less: Costs of set up and special device	NIL	40,000
Net Profit / (Loss)	18,000	(6,250)

Note: For special orders allocation of fixed overhead costs are not relevant.

Decision:

(*i*) If special order of JCP Co. Ltd. can be bifurcated the company can supply 18,000 units of jewellery cases and can earn additional profit of ₹ 18,000. The remaining 2,000 units of order cannot be met due to capacity constant.

(*ii*) The special order from K Co. Ltd. is not acceptable as it results into loss to the extent of ₹ 6,250.

Working notes:

1. Total unutilized hours during the third quarter

Total hours of third quarter (7,500 hours × 3 months)	22,500
Hours utilized for 80% operating level (22,500 hours × 80%)	18,000
Total unutilized hours during the third quarter	4,500

2. Computation of fixed and variable overhead rate

Fixed overheads per annum (₹)	21,60,000
Normal capacity hours	90,000
Fixed overheads rate per hour (₹) (₹ 21,60,000 / 90,000 hours)	24
Manufacturing overhead application rate per hour (₹)	40
Therefore, variable overhead rate per hour ₹ (₹ 40 – ₹ 24)	16

3. Cost per unit of the order from JCP Co. Ltd. and K. Co. Ltd.

	JCP Co. Ltd.	K, Co. Ltd.
	₹	₹
Raw materials cost per unit	22.50	32.50
Direct labour	30.00	30.00
Variable overheads	4.00	8.00
	(0.25 hours × ₹ 16)	(0.5 hours × ₹ 16)
Total cost per unit	56.50	70.50

Illustrative Problem 44 (Product Mix Decision)

Hindustan Machine Tools (HMT) makes cutting tools for metal working operations. It makes two types of tools: R3, a regular cutting tool, and HP6, a high-precision cutting tool, R3 is manufactured on a regular machine, but HP6 must be manufactured on both the regular machine and a high precision machine. The following information is available.

	R3	HP6
Selling price	₹ 1,000	₹ 1,500
Variable manufacturing cost per unit	600	1,000
Variable marketing cost per unit	150	350
Budgeted total overhead costs	35,00,000	55,00,000
Hours required to produce 1 unit on the regular machine	1.0	0.5

Additional information includes:

(*a*) HMT faces a capacity constraint on the regular machine of 50,000 hours per year.

(*b*) The capacity of the high-precision machine is not a constraint.

(*c*) Of the ₹ 55,00,000 budgeted fixed overhead costs of HP6, ₹ 30,00,000 are lease payments for the high-precision machine. This cost is charged entirely to HP6 because HMT uses the machine exclusively to produce HP6. The lease agreement for the high-precision machine can be canceled at any time without penalties.

(*d*) All other overhead costs are fixed and cannot be changed.

Required:

1. What product mix,that is, how many units of R3 and HP6 will maximize HMT's operating income?
2. Suppose HMT can increase the annual capacity of regular machines by 15,000 machine-hours at a cost of ₹ 15,00,000. Should HMT increase the capacity of regular machines by 15,000 machine hours? By how much will HMT's operating income increase? Show your calculations.
3. Suppose that the capacity of the regular machines has been increased to 65,000 hours. HMT has been approached by Titan to supply 20,000 units of another cutting tool. S3, for ₹ 1,200 per unit. HMT must either accept the order for all 20,000 units or reject it totally, S3 is exactly like R3 except that its variable manufacturing costs are ₹ 700 per unit (It takes one hour to produce one unit of S3 on the regular machine, and variable marketing costs equal ₹ 150 per unit). What product mix should HMT choose to maximize operating income? Show your calculations.

Solution:

Product mix, relevant costs

1.

	R3	HP6
Selling price	₹ 1,000	₹ 1,500
Variable manufacturing cost per unit	600	1,000
Variable marketing cost per unit	150	350
Total variable costs per unit	750	1,350
Contribution margin per unit	₹ 250	₹ 150
Contribution margin per hour of the constrained resource (the regular machine)	$\frac{₹ 250}{1}$ = ₹ 250	$\frac{₹ 15}{0.5}$ = ₹ 300
Total contribution margin from selling only R3 or only HP6		
R3: ₹ 250 × 50,000, HP6. ₹ 300 × 50.000	₹ 1,25,00,000	₹ 1,50,00,000
Less: Lease costs of high-precision machine to produce and sell HP6	—	30,00,000
Net relevant benefit	₹ 1,25,00,000	₹ 1,20,00,000

Even though HP6 has the higher contribution margin per unit of the constrained resource, the fact that HMT must incur additional costs of ₹ 30,00,000 to achieve this higher contribution margin means that HMT is better off using its entire 50,000-hour capacity on the regular machine to produce and sell 50,000 units. (50,000 hours ÷1 hour per unit) of R3. The additional contribution from selling HP6 rather than R3 is ₹ 25,00,000 (₹ 1,50,00,000 – ₹ 1,25,00,000), which is not enough to cover the additional costs of leasing the high-precision machine. Note that, because all other overhead costs are fixed and cannot be changed, they are irrelevant for the decision.

2. If capacity of the regular machines is increased by 15,000 machine-hours to 65,000 machine-hours (50,000) originally + 15,000 new), the net relevant benefit from producing R3 and HP6 is as follows:

	R3	HP6
Total contribution margin from selling only R3 or only HP6		
R3:₹ 250 × 65,000: HP6: ₹ 300 × 65,000	₹ 1,62,50,000	₹ 1,95,00,000
Less: Lease costs of high-precision machine that would be incurred if HP6 produced and sold	—	30,00,000
Less: Cost of increasing capacity by 15,000 hours on regular machine	15,00,000	15,00,000
Net relevant benefit	₹ 1,47,50,000	₹ 1,50,00,000

Investing in the additional capacity increases HMT's operating income by ₹ 25,00,000 (₹ 1,50,00,000 calculated in requirement 2 minus ₹ 1,25,000 calculated in requirement 1), so HMT should add 15,000 hours to the regular machine. With the extra capacity available to it, HMT should use its entire capacity to produce HP6. Using all 65,000 hours of capacity to produce HP6 rather than to produce R3 generates additional contribution margin of ₹ 32,50,000 (₹ 1,95,00,000 – ₹ 1,62,50,000) which is more than the additional cost of ₹ 30,00,000 to lease the high-precision machine. HMT should therefore produce and sell 1,30,000 units of HP6 (65,000 hours ÷ 0.5 hours per unit of HP6) and zero units of HP6) and zero units of R3.

3.

	R3	HP	S3
Selling price	₹ 1,000	₹ 1,500	₹ 1,200
Variable manufacturing costs per unit	600	1,000	700
Variable marketing costs per unit	150	350	150
Total variable costs per unit	750	1,350	850
Contribution margin per unit	₹ 250	₹ 150	₹ 350
Contribution margin per hour of the constrained resource (the regular machine)	$\frac{₹ 250}{1} = ₹ 250$	$\frac{₹ 15}{0.5} = ₹ 300$	$\frac{₹ 350}{1} = ₹ 350$

The first step is to compare the operating profits that HMT could earn if it accepted the Titan Corporation offer for 20,000 units with the operating profits HMT is currently earning. S3 has the highest contribution margin per hour on the regular machine and requires no additional investment such as leasing a high-precision machine. To poduce the 20,000 units of S3 requested by Titan Corporation, HMT would require 20,000 hours on the regular machine resulting in contribution margin of ₹ 350 × 20,000 = ₹ 70,00,000.

HMT now has 45,000 hours available on the regular machine to produce R3 or HP6.

	R3	HP6
Total contribution margin from only selling R3 or only HP6		
R3: ₹ 250 × 45,000; HP6: ₹ 300 × 45,000	₹ 1,12,50,000	₹ 1,35,00,000
Less: Lease costs of high-precision machine to produce and sell HP6	—	30,00,000
Net relevant benefit	₹ 1,12,50,000	₹ 1,05,00,000

HMT should use all the 45,000 hours of available capacity to produce 45,000 units of R3. Thus, the product mix that maximizes operating income is 20,000 units of S3, 45,000 units of R3,and zero units of HP6. This optimal mix results in a contribution margin of ₹ 1,82,50,000 (₹ 70,00,000 from S3 and ₹ 1,12,50,000 from R3). Relative to requirement 2, operating income by ₹ 32,50,000 (₹ 1,82,50,000 minus ₹ 1,50,00,000 calculated in requirement 2). Hence, HMT should accept the Titan business and supply 20,000 units of S3.

Illustrative Problem 45 (Keep or Close Decision)

A company having its Head Office in Centown has three factories situated at Uptown, Middletown and Downtown. The operations of Middletown have been unprofitable for a number of years. The leasehold of Middletown will also expire by the end of the current year.

In view of the continued losses, the management has decided to close down the said factory rather than renew the lease. The factory's plant and machinery can be sold of at a price higher than the written down value and the surplus funds will be sufficient to cover all termination costs.

The projected profitability of the factories for the next year is as under.

(₹ Lakhs)

	Uptown	Middletown	Downtown	Total
Sales	400	100	300	800
Variable costs	220	75	195	490
Fixed costs:				
Factory	80	30	40	150
Selling and Admin.	30	5	15	50
Head Office expenses apportioned	25	15	25	65
Porfit	45	–25	25	45

The company however would like to continue to serve the customers now being served by the Middletown) if it could do so economically. Accordingly, the following proposals were put forward for consideration based on a selling price of ₹ 250 per unit.

(*i*) Close down Middletown factory and expand the operations of the Downtown factory for which capacity exists there. This proposal will involve the following changes:

(*a*) Sales revenue of Downtown factory will increase by 25%

(*b*) The factory fixed costs of Downtown factory will increase by 10%

(*c*) Fixed selling and administration of the said factory will increase by 5%

(*d*) Variable distribution costs of the additional output will increase by ₹ 4 per unit

(*ii*) Close down Middletown factory and expand the operations of the Uptown factory, subject to the following changes in case of the latter.

(*a*) Sales revenue will increase by ₹ 80 lakhs

(*b*) Factory fixed costs will increase by 20%

(*c*) Fixed selling & administration costs will increase by 10%

(*d*) Variable distribution costs in respect of the additional units will increase by ₹ 5 per unit.

(*iii*) Close down Middletown factory and enter into a long-term contract with an independent manufacturer to serve the customers of Middletown factory. The manufacturer will pay royalty of ₹ 5 per unit to the company. In that event, the sales of the area served by the Middletown factory will reduce by 25%.

(*iv*) Close down Middletown factory and discontinue serving the present customers of that area. You are required to evaluate each of these proposals and advise the management of the action to be taken in the interest of improving the profitability of the comapany.

(*CMA, India, Final*)

Solution:

(*i*) Close down Middletown factory and expand Downtown factory:

(₹ lakhs)

	Uptown	Downtown	Total
Sales	400	375.00	775.00
Variable costs			
Factory	220	243.75	463.75
Selling (Additional)	—	1.20@	1.20
Total	220	244.95	464.95
Contribution	180	130.05	310.05
Fixed costs:			
Factory	80	44.00	124.00
Selling & Admn.	30	15.75	45.75
Total	110	59.75	169.75
Factory contribution	70	70.30	140.30
H.O. Expenses			65.00
Profit			75.30

@ Sales $3,00,00,000 \times \frac{25}{100}$ = ₹ 75,00,000

No. of unit $\frac{75,00,000}{250}$ = 30,000, Selling variable costs 30000 × 4 = ₹ 7,20,000.

(*ii*) Close down Middletown factory and expand Uptown Factory:

(₹ lakhs)

	Uptown	Downtown	Total
Sales	480.00	300.00	780.00
Variable costs:			
Factory	264.00	195.00	459.00
Selling	1.60 @	—	1.60
Total	265.60	195.00	460.60
Contribution	214.40	105.00	319.40
Fixed costs:			
Factory	96.00	40.00	136.00
Selling & Admn.	33.00	15.00	48.00
Total	129.00	55.00	184.00
Factory contribution	85.40	50.00	135.40
H.O. Expenses			65.00
Profit			70.40

@ Sales = ₹ 80,00,000

Selling variable cost = $\frac{80,00,000}{250}$ = 32,000 units × 5 = ₹ 1,60,000

(*iii*) Closedown Middletown factory and subcontract production:

Sales of Middletown factory = ₹ 100 lakhs

Effective sales 100 × $\frac{75}{100}$ = ₹ 75 lakhs

/ Units $\frac{75,00,000}{250}$ = 30,000 × 5 = ₹ 1,50,000

(₹ lakhs)

	Uptown	**Downtown**	**Royalty**	**Total**
Sales	400.00	300.00	300	700.00
Variable costs	220.00	195.00		415.00
Contribution	180.00	105.00		285.00
Fixed costs:				
Factory	80.00	40.00		120.00
Selling and Admn.	30.00	15.00		45.00
Total	110.00	55.00		165.00
Factory Contribution	70.00	50.00	1.50	121.50
H.O. expenses apportioned				65.00
Porfit				56.50

(*iv*) Closedown Middletown Factory:

	Downtown	**Rayalty**	**Total**
Factory contribution as in (*iii*) above	70.00	50.00	120.00
H.O. Office expenses			65.00
Profit			55.00

It will be seen that the alternative to close down Middletown factory and ignore servicing of its customers itself results in profit of ₹ 55 lakhs as against ₹ 45 lakhs if it was continued to operate. However, the 'first' alternative to expand the operations of the Downtown factory along with closure of Middletown factory gives the best profit and the same has to be preferred.

In all the aforesaid computations, it is assumed that H.O. expenses will not reduce even marginally if the Middletown factory is closed.

Illustrative Problem 46 (Special Order Decision)

Award Plus Company manufactures medals for winners of athletic events and other contests. Its manufacturing plant has the capacity to produce 10,000 medals each month. Current production and sales are 7,500 medals per month. The company normally charges ₹ 150 per medal. Cost information for the current activity level is as follows:

Variable costs that vary with number of units produced:

Direct materials	₹ 2,62,500
Direct manufacturing labor	3,00,000

Variable costs (for setup materials, handling, quality control and so on) that vary with number of batches 150 batches × ₹ 500 per batch	75,000
Fixed manufacturing costs	2,75,000
Fixed marketing costs	1,75,000
Total costs	10,87,500

Award Plus has just received a special one-time-only order for 2,500 medals at ₹ 100 per medal. Accepting the special order would not affect the company's regular business. The company makes medals for its existing customers in batch sizes of 50 medals (150 batches × 50 medals per batch = 7,500 medals). The special order requires Award Plus to make medals in 25 batches of 100 each.

1. Should Award Plus accept this special order? Show your calculations.
2. Suppose plant capacity were only 9,000 medals instead of 10,000 medals each month. The special order must either be taken in full or rejected completely. Should Award Plus accept the special order? Show your calculations.
3. As in requirement (1), assume that monthly capacity is 10,000 medals. Award Plus is concerned that if it accepts the special order, its existing customers will immediately demand a price discount of ₹ 10 in the month in which the special order is being filled. They would argue that the company's capacity costs are now being spread over more units and that existing customers should get the benefit of these lower costs should Award Plus accept the special order under these conditions? Show your calculations.

(CMA, USA, Adapted with permission)

Solution:

1. Operating income statement under the alternatives of accepting/rejecting the special order are:

	Without One-time Only Special Order 7,500 Units	*With One-Time Only Special Order 10,000 Units*	*Difference 2,500 Units*
Revenues	₹ 11,25,000	₹ 13,75,000	₹ 2,50,000
Variable costs:			
Direct materials	2,62,500	3,50,000[1]	87,500
Direct manufacturing labor	3,00,000	4,00,000[2]	1,00,000
Batch manufacturing costs	75,000	87,500[3]	12,500
Fixed costs:			
Fixed manufacturing costs	2,75,000	2,75,000	—
Fixed marketing costs	1,75,000	1,75,000	—
Total costs	10,87,500	12,87,500	2,00,000
Operating income	₹ 37,500	₹ 87,500	₹ 50,000

[1] $\frac{₹\,2{,}62{,}500}{7{,}500} \times 10{,}000$ [2] $\frac{₹.\,3{,}00{,}000}{7{,}500} \times 10{,}000$ [3] ₹ 75,000 + (25 × ₹ 500)

Alternatively, we can calculate the incremental revenue and the incremental costs of the additional 2,500 units as follows:

Incremental revenue ₹ 100 × 2,500	₹ 2,50,000
Incremental direct manufacturing costs (₹ 2,62,500/7,500) × 2,500	87,500
Incremental direct manufacturing costs (₹ 3,00,000/7,500) × 2,500	1,00,000
Incremental batch manufacturing costs ₹ 500 × 25	12,500
Total incremental costs	2,00,000
Total incremental operating income from accepting the special order	₹ 50,000

Award plus should accept the one-time-only special order if it has no long-term implications because accepting the order increases operating income by ₹ 50,000.

If, however, accepting the special order would cause the regular customers to be dissatisfied or to demand lower prices, then Award Plus will have to trade off the ₹ 50,000 gain from accepting the special order against the operating income it might lose from regular customers.

2. Award Plus has a capacity of 9,000 medals. Therefore, if it accepts the special one-time order of 2,500 medals, it can sell only 6,500 medals instead of the 7,500 medals that it currently sells to existing customers. That is, by accepting the special order, Award must forgo sales of 1,000 medals to its regular customers. Alternatively, Award plus can reject the special order and continue to sell 7,500 medals to its regular customers.

The operating income from selling 6,500 medals to regular customers and 2,500 medals under one-time special order are as follows:

Revenues (6,500 × ₹ 150) + (2,500 × ₹ 100)	₹ 12,25,000
Direct materials (6,500 × ₹ 35[1]) + (2,500 × ₹ 35[1])	3,15,000
Direct manufacturing labor (6,500 × ₹ 40[2]) + (2,500 × ₹ 40[2])	3,60,000
Batch manufacturing costs (130[3] × ₹ 500) + (25 × ₹ 500)	77,500
Fixed manufacturing costs	2,75,000
Fixed marketing costs	1,75,000
Total costs	12,02,500
Operating income	₹ 22,500

[1]$₹\,35 = \dfrac{₹\,2,62,500}{7,500}$ [2]$₹\,40 = \dfrac{₹\,3,00,000}{7,500}$

[3]Award Plus makes regular medals in batch sizes of 50. To produce 6,500 medals requires 130 (6,500 ÷ 50) batches.

Accepting the special order will result in a decrease in operating income of ₹ 15,000 (₹ 37,500 – ₹ 22,500). The special order should, therefore, be rejected.

A more direct approach would be to focus on the incremental effects—the benefits of accepting the special order of 2,500 units versus the costs of selling 1,000 fewer units to regular customers. Increase in operating income from the 2,500-unit special order equals ₹ 50,000 (requirement 1). The loss in operating income from selling 1,000 fewer units to regular customers equals:

Lost revenue ₹ 150 × 1,000	₹ (1,50,000)
Savings in direct materials costs ₹ 35 × 1,000	35,000
Savings in direct manufacturing labor costs ₹ 40 × 1,000	40,000
Savings in batch manufacturing costs ₹ 500 × 20	10,000
Operating income lost	₹ (65,000)

Accepting the special order will result in a decrease in operating income of ₹ 15,000 (₹ 50,000 – ₹ 65,000). The special order should, therefore, be rejected.

3. Award Plus should not accept the special order.

Increase in operating income by selling 2,500 units under the special order (requirement 1)	₹ 50,000
Operating income lost from existing customers (₹ 10 × 7,500)	(75,000)
Net effect on operating income of accepting special order	₹ (25,000)

The special order should, therefore, be rejected.

Illustrative Problem 47 (Cost of Strike)

Bajaj Equipment Co. has recently suffered a strike which lasted for two weeks. During that time no equipments were produced. The company issued a press statement to the effect that the cost of the strike was ₹ 150 lakhs. This figure was arrived at by the managing director, who estimated that production lost was 1,000 equipments, each of which could have been sold for ₹ 15,000 giving a total loss of turnover of ₹ 1,50,00,000. The company's cost accountant feels that the managing director was overstating the cost of the strike and provides the following statement to support his view.

	₹ 000
Expenses avoided:	
Materials (₹ 3,000 per equipment)	3,000
Production labour (₹ 1,500 per equipment)	1,500
Depreciation of machinery	5,250
Overheads : 200% on labour	3,000
	12,750
Loss of sales revenue	15,000
Cost of strike	2,250

The following additional information is available:

(*i*) Depreciation of machinery is based on the conventional straight-line method of calculation. The plant manager estimates that the machinery will fall in value by ₹ 6,00,000 each week regardless of the level of production. In addition, it is felt that its value will fall by ₹ 4,50,000 for every 100 equipments that are produced.

(*ii*) Overhead expenses are recovered at the rate of 200% on production labour. Most of the overhead expenses are unaffected by the level of production (e.g. rent, rates, maintenance, staff wages), but some, such as power and lighting, vary directly with production. The general manager estimates that the latter type of overhead expense, varying directly with the level of production, amounts to ₹ 30,000 for every 100 equipments producted.

(*iii*) During the period of the strike the maintenance staff, whose wages are included in the fixed overhead expense, carried out a major overhaul on one of the company's machines using materials costing ₹ 30,000. This overhaul would normally have been performed by an outside contractor at a price, including materials, of ₹ 3,00,000.

(*iv*) The sales manager feels that about one-half of the production lost could be made up and sold in the next month by the production labour working overtime. Labour is paid at the rate of time-and-a-half for overtime working.

Prepare a statement clearly showing the cost to the company of the strike. State any assumptions which you make and explain any differences between your figures and those of the cost accountant.

Solution:

Cost of Strike

		₹	₹
Contribution lost:			
Sales revenue (1,000 equipments)			1,50,00,000
Less:	Materials (see note 1)	30,00,000	
	Production labour (see note 2)	15,00,000	
	Fall in machine value (see note 3)	45,00,000	
	Variable overheads (see note 4)	3,00,000	93,00,000
Loss of contribution			57,00,000
Less:	Saving on overhaul (see note 5)	2,70,000	
	Increased contribution next month (see note 6)	24,75,000	27,45,000
Cost of strike			29,55,000

Notes:

1. It is assumed that materials are freely available at a market price of ₹ 3,000 per equipment.
2. It is assumed that no payment is made to production labour during the strike.
3. Depreciation based on book value is not relevant as it merely represents an arbitrary writing off of historical cost. Assuming that the machinery is not sold at the beginning of the strike, the fall in value of ₹ 6,00,000 per week will occur whether or not production continues. It is therefore not relevant in assessing the cost of the strike. However, the fall in value due to use (sometimes called the user cost) is avoided and must be included as a saving, *i.e.* 10 × ₹ 4,50,000 = ₹ 45,00,000.
4. Those overheads which are fixed regardless of the level of production may be ignored as they are payable with or without the strike. The overheads which are avoided as a result of the strike must be included in the statement as a saving, *i.e.* 10 × ₹ 30,000 = ₹ 3,00,000.
5. By utilising the maintenance staff to carry out the major overhaul, the company pays only for materials (₹ 30,000). An outside contractor would have charged ₹ 3,00,000. A saving of ₹ 2,70,000 is effected which would not have been possible without the strike.
6. The sales manager feels that about one-half of the lost production could be made up and sold next month. The contribution from these sales will reduce the cost of the strike to the company, *i.e.*

	₹	₹
Sales revenue (500 Equipments)		75,00,000
Less		
Materials	15,00,000	
Production labour (at time and a half)	11,25,000	
Fall in machine value	22,50,000	
Variable overheads	1,50,000	50,25,000
Contribution		24,75,000

7. A number of other points should be considered. For example:
   (a) Was the overhaul really necessary?
   (b) Is machine capacity adequate to make up one-half of the lost production next month?
   (c) Will the market buy the extra production and the normal monthly production next month at the price assumed?
   (d) What interest costs are involved in delaying some production for one month?

Illustrative Problem 48 (Discontinue a Product Line)

Crimson Industries began operations 15 years ago as a manufacturer of athletic shoes. It later added a successfull line of athletic socks, and then introduced a line of athletic sportswear which has become its most profitable product line. Over the years, competition from Asia Corporation has forced Crimson to reduce the prices of its athletic shoes to the point where this product line now consistently has a negative segment margin. Typical monthly statistics for the three product lines are shown in the chart below.

	Sportswear		*Athletic Shoes*		*Athletic Socks*	
	₹		₹		₹	
Sales	6,00,000	100%	3,50,000	100%	1,80,000	100%
Variable costs	2,58,000	43	2,62,500	75	90,000	50
Contribution margin	3,42,000	57	87,500	25	90,000	50
Traceable fixed costs	1,32,000	22	1,05,000	30	77,400	43
Segment margin	2,10,000	35%	(17,500)	(5%)	12,600	7%

Crimson is considering discontinuing the manufacture and sale of athletic shoes. All costs traceable to the product line would be eliminated if the product line is discontinued. Management estimates that the sale of athletic socks would decline 20 pcr cent from this decision because both products are sold to the same customers. Sportswear is sold to different customers, and sales are not anticipated to decline as a result of the decision.

Required:

A. 1. Prepare a schedule of operating data for Crimson Industries assuming that the athletic shoe line is discontinued.

2. What is the net effect on Crimson's segment margin?

3. Would you recommend that Crimson discontinue the athletic shoe product line?

B. Assume that Crimson Industries believes that a concentrated advertising effort of ₹ 10,000 for sportswear would increase sales of sportswear by 10 pcr cent if the athletic shoe line were discontinued.

1. What is the net effect on Crimson's segment margin?

2. Would this affect your decision in Requirement A.3.? (*M.Com. Delhi* 2004)

(*CMA, USA, Adapted with Permission*)

Solution:

A. 1. The schedule of operating data for Crimson Industries, assuming that the athletic shoe line is discontinued, is presented below.

	Sportswear ₹		*Socks** ₹	
Sales	6,00,000	100%	1,44,000	100%
Variable costs	2,58,000	43	72,000	50
Contribution margin	3,42,000	57	72,000	50
Traceable fixed cost	1,32,000	22	77,400	54
Segment margin	2,10,000	35	(5,400)	(4)

*Socks and variable costs decrease by 20%

2. The net effect on Crimson's segment margin is a decrease of ₹ 500, calculated as follows.

	₹	₹
With athletic shoes:		
Sportswear	2,10,000	
Athletic shoes	(17,500)	
Socks	12,600	2,05,100
Without athletic shoes:		
Sportswear	2,10,000	
Socks (Requirement A.1.)	(5,400)	2,04,600
Change in segment margin		(500)

3. It is recommended that Crimson's Industries should not discontinue the athletic shoes product line because the segment margin decreases by ₹ 500 if athletic shoes are eliminated.

B. 1. If a concentrated advertising effort of ₹ 10,000 is undertaken, the net effect on Crimson Industries segment margin would be an increase of ₹ 23,700 calculated as follows.

	Sportswear ₹		₹
Total segment margin with athletic shoes (From Requirement A.2.)			2,05,100
Sales (increase 10%)	6,60,000	100%	
Variable costs	2,83,800	43	
Contribution margin	3,76,200	57	
Traceable fixed costs (₹ 1,32,000 + ₹ 10,000 advertising)	1,42,000	22	
Segment margin sportswear	2,34,200	35	
Plus: Socks	(5,400)		
Total segment margin without athletic shoes			2,28,8 00
change in segment margin			23,700

2. Yes; it is recommended that the athletic shoes product line be discontinued. Crimson Industries' segment margin would increase by ₹ 23,700 as a result of eliminating the athletic shoes product line and expending ₹ 10,000 on concentrated advertising to increase sportswear sales by 10 percent.

Illustrative Problem 49 (Make or Buy Decision)

The HCL Technologies Ltd. manufactures an electronic component which is used in television. It reports the following cost information about the costs of making component in 2015 and the expected costs in 2016.

	Current Costs in 2015	*Expected Costs in 2016*
Variable manufacturing costs per component:		
Direct material cost per component	₹ 1,800	₹ 1,700
Direct manufacturing labor cost per component	500	450
Variable manufacturing cost per batch for setups, material handling, and quality control	16,000	15,000
Fixed manufacturing cost:		
Fixed manufacturing overhead costs that can be avoided if components are not made	32,00,000	32,00,000
Fixed manufacturing overhead costs of plant depreciation, insurance, and administration that can not be avoided even if components are not made	80,00,000	80,00,000

HCL manufactured 8,000 components in 2015 in 40 batches of 200 each. In 2016, HCL anticipates a requirement of 10,000 components. The components would be needed in 80 batches of 125 each.

The Tata Infocom has approached HCL about supplying components in 2016 at ₹ 3,000 per component on whatever delivery schedule HCL wants.

Required:

1. Calculate the total expected manufacturing cost per unit of making components in 2016.
2. Suppose the capacity currently used to make components will become idle if HCL purchases components from Tata. On the basis of financial considerations alone, should HCL make components or buy them from Tata? Show your calculations.
3. Now suppose that if HCL purchases components from Tata, its best alternative use of the capacity currently used for components is to make and sell special component to the Sony Corporation.

HCL estimates the following incremental revenues and costs for this special component.

Total incremental future costs	₹ 2,00,00,000
Total expected incremental future revenues	₹ 2,15,00,000

On the basis of financial considerations alone, should HCL make component or buy them from Tata? Show your calculations.

Solution:

1. The expected manufacturing cost per unit of components in 2016 is as follows:

	Total Manufacturing Costs of components (1)	Manufacturing Cost per Unit (2) = (1) ÷ 10,000
Direct materials ₹ 1,700 × 10,000	₹ 1,70,00,000	₹ 1,700
Direct manufacturing labor ₹ 450 × 10,000	45,00,000	450
Variable batch manufacturing costs ₹ 15,000 × 80	12,00,000	120
Fixed manufacturing costs:		
Avoidable fixed manufacturing costs	32,00,000	320
Unavoidable fixed manufacturing costs	80,00,000	800
Total manufacturing costs	₹ 3,39,00,000	₹ 3,390

2. The following table identifies the incremental costs in 2012 if HCL (*a*) made components and (*b*) purchased components from Tata.

Incremental Items	*Total Incremental Costs* Make	Buy	*Per-Unit Incremental Costs* Make	Buy
Cost of purchasing components from Tata		₹ 3,00,00,000		₹ 3,000
Direct materials	₹ 1,70,00,000		₹ 1,700	
Direct manufacturing labor	45,00,000		450	
Variable batch manufacturing costs	12,00,000		120	
Avoidable fixed manufacturing costs	32,00,000		320	
Total incremental costs	₹ 2,59,00,000	₹ 3,00,00,000	₹ 2,590	₹ 3,000
Difference in favor of making	₹ 41,00,000		₹ 410	

Note that the opportunity cost of using capacity to make components is zero since HCL would keep this capacity idle if it purchases components from Tata.

HCL should continue to manufacture the components internally since the incremental costs to manufacture are ₹ 2,590 per unit compared to the ₹ 3,000 per unit that Tata has quoted. Note that the unavoidable fixed manufacturing costs of ₹ 80,00,000 (₹ 800 per unit) will continue to be incurred whether HCL makes or buys. These are not incremental costs under either the make or the buy alternative and are, hence, irrelevant.

3. HCL should continue to make components. The simplest way to analyze this problem is to recognize that HCL would prefer to keep any excess capacity idle rather than use it to make special component for Sony. Why? Because expected incremental future revenues from special component, ₹ 2,00,00,000 are less than expected incremental future costs, ₹ 2,15,00,000. HCL keeps its capacity idle, we know from requirement 2 that it should make components rather than buy them.

In this case, an important point to be noted is that HCL loses no contribution by not being able to make and sell special component for Sony Corporation, the opportunity cost of using its facilities to make components is zero. Therefore, HCL is not foregoing any profits by using the capacity to manufacture components. If it does not produce components, HCL will prefer to keep capacity idle rather than go for manufacturing special components for Sony Corporation and thereby lose some money on it. HCL will keep capacity idle.

Alternatively, part (3) can be answered using total cost approach or opportunity cost analysis, as displayed below.

Alternatives for HCL

Relevant Items	*Make components and Do Not Make Special components*	*Buy components and Do Not Make Special components*	*Buy components and Make Special components*
Total-alternatives approach to make-or-buy decisions			
Total incremental costs of making/buying components (from requirement 2)	₹ 2,59,00,000	₹ 3,00,00,000	₹ 3,00,00,000
Excess of future costs over future revenues from special components	0	0	15,00,000
Total relevant costs	₹ 2,59,00,000	₹ 3,00,00,000	₹ 3,15,00,000
Decision: HCL will minimize manufacturing costs by making components			
Opportunity-cost approach to make-or-buy decisions			
Total incremental costs of making/buying components (from requirement 2)	₹ 2,59,00,000	₹ 3,00,00,000	₹ 3,00,00,000
Opportunity cost: profit contribution forgone because capacity will not be used to make special components	0*	0*	0
Total relevant costs	2,59,00,000	3,00,00,000	3,00,00,000

*Opportunity cost is 0 because HCL does not give up anything by not making special components. HCL is best off leaving the capacity idle (rather than manufacturing and selling special components for Sony Corporation).

REFERENCES

1. Sidney Davidson et al, *Managerial Accounting,* The Dryden Press, p. 410.
2. Lane K. Anderson and Harold M. SollenBerger, *Managerial Accounting,* South Western Publishing Co., 1992, p. 548.
3. Edward J. Blocher, Kung H. Chen, Gary Cokins and Thomas W. Lin, Cost Management, Tata McGraw Hill Publishing Co., 2006, p. 335.
4. Ronald W. Hilton, *Managerial Accounting,* Tata McGraw Hill Publishing Co., 2006, p. 587.
5. Ronald W. Hilton, Ibid, p. 586.
6. Wayne J. Morse, James R. Davis and Al L. Hartgraves, *Management Accounting,* Thomson, 2003, p. 128.
7. Ray H. Garrison and Eric W. Noreen, *Managerial Accounting,* Irwin McGraw Hill, 2000, p. 639.
8. Ronald W. Hilton, *Managerial Accounting, Ibid*, p. 608.
9. Charle, T. Horngreen, Srikant M. Datar and George Foster, *Cost Accounting, A Managerial Emphasis,* Pearson Education, New Delhi, p. 439.
10. Jesset T. Barfield, Cecily A. Raiborn and Michael R. Kinney, *Cost Accounting, Traditions and Innovations,* Thomson, 2003, p. 505.
11. Milton F. Usry and Lawrence H. Hammer, *Cost Accounting, Planning and Control,* South Western Publishing Co., 1991, p. 692.
12. Milton F. Usry, *Ibid*, p. 690.
13. Wayne J. Morse, James R. Davis and Al. L. Hartgraves, *Ibid*, p. 133.

CRITICAL ANALYSIS AND DISCUSSION QUESTIONS, SELF-ASSESSMENT QUESTIONS, MULTIPLE CHOICE QUESTIONS, PROBLEMS, AND CASES

CRITICAL ANALYSIS AND DISCUSSION QUESTIONS

1. Discuss the nature of short-run and long-run decisions.
2. What are the steps in a managerial decision-making process.
3. What do you mean by differential analysis? Explain the concept of differential revenue and differential costs.
4. What are relevant costs? What are its characteristics?
5. Explain how do qualitative factors influence a manager's decision. Give examples.
6. Explain the nature of the following differential analysis decisions:
   (*a*) Make or Buy
   (*b*) Add or drop a product
   (*c*) Sell or process further
   (*d*) Operate or shutdown
   (*e*) Special orders
   (*f*) Replace or retain
   Also, discuss what relevant information are used in making above decisions.
7. What is incremental cost? Does incremental cost mean the same thing as variable cost?
8. Give examples of how incremental costs are used in decision-making.
9. A departmental store is thinking of eliminating one of its departments because the accountant using the total cost basis to profitability analysis, says the department is operating at a loss. What should be investigated before the final decision is made?
10. Explain the basic characteristics of costs involved in decision-making.
11. How would you go about determining the point at which a manufacturing company that is facing a period of operating losses should shut down, assuming that profitability of operations is the only point to be considered?
12. Why is the contribution that a product makes towards the recovery of non-escapable costs a better measure of its profitability than the profit or loss reported on its sale after it has been charged with its fair share of all costs?
13. In the very long-run, all costs are differential. Explain. (*M.Com., Delhi*)
14. Explain the uses of differential accounting in decision-making. Give suitable illustrations in at least three areas of decision-making. (*M.Com., Delhi,*)
15. Distinguish between variable costs and differential costs and highlight the importance of differential costs in non-routine decisions. (*M.Com., Delhi*)
16. Describe the steps in the decision-making process. In which steps does the management accountant play major roles?
17. Rajan, owner of several small local businesses, said recently: "The general rule I follow in making short-run decision is that variable costs are almost always relevant and fixed costs are almost always irrelevant." Do you agree? why or why not?

18. In deciding to add or to delete a line of business, what version of profitability should be used? Explain.
19. Although a special order would have contributed ₹ 1,00,000 to profits and the company has excess capacity, management rejected the order. What are the possible reasons for management's action?
20. What do you mean by relevant costs and relevant revenue?
21. Explain why depreciation on an existing asset is always irrelevant?
22. Relevant costs always determine which alternative should be chosen. Do you agree?
23. "All future costs are relevant" Do you agree? why?
24. "Variable costs are always relevant and fixed costs are always irrelevant." Do you agree? Why?
25. "A branch or business segment that shows negative operating income should be shutdown." Do you agree? Explain briefly.
26. "Managers will always choose the alternative that maximises operating income or minimises costs in the decision model "Do you agree? Why?
27. Describe some potential problems or pitfalls that should be avoided in differential analysis.
28. Amit enters the departure area of Indigo Airline just before a flight to Banglore is to take off. The plane is about 80% full, and the regular fare for the flight is ₹ 10,000. Amit has neither a ticket nor a reservation for the flight but he offers to pay ₹ 4,000 to take the flight. Assume there are no variable costs associated with the number of passengers. Should the Indigo accept Amit's offer if it uses the incremental principle. Will the airline accept Amit's offer? Why or why not?
29. What are the characteristics of relevant cost? Why are future costs not always relevant?
30. Ramaswamy, owner of cafe at Delhi University is trying to decide whether to make Piza or buy them from a supplier, Super Narula, in Delhi. Ramaswamy has come to you for advice. What factors would you tell him to consider in making his choice?
31. You have an old stereo system. You have paid ₹ 5,000 for the stereo system. The current market value of the stereo is ₹ 1,500. A new stereo system of the same make and model could be purchased for ₹ 6,000. Which of these figures is relevant to your decision to sell or to keep the stereo system? If any figures are not relevant, explain why.
32. "Variable cost are irrelevant whenever they do not differ among the alternatives at hand". Explain.
33. Define outsourcing and explain how the relevant cost analysis is used in the outsourcing decision.
34. Explain why depreciation on an existing asset is always irrelevant?
35. Give an example of a future cost that is not relevant.
36. Give an example of a fixed cost that is relevant.
37. Discuss the importance of complementary effects in a keep-or-drop decision.
38. Why are fixed costs never relevant in a product mix decision?
39. Distinguish between the quantitative and qualitative aspects of decisions.
40. "Any future cost is relevant." Do you agree? Explain.
41. Explain the qualitative factors in Make/Buy decisions.

42. What criteria must be satisfied for information to be relevant?
43. Why might a manager inappropriately consider sunk costs when making a decision?
44. What considerations other than costs are relevant to outsourcing decision?
45. To go from New Delhi to Mumbai for a business meeting, Amitabh booked an Air India flight for ₹ 30,000 with a departure on Wednesday and a return on Friday of the same week. The travel agent told Amitabh that if he were to return on Sunday, the ticket price would fall to ₹ 15,000. What factor(s) did the Air India appear to focus on when setting its ticket prices?
46. A quantitative analysis enables a decision maker to put a "price" on the sum total of the qualitative characteristics in a decision situation. Explain this statement.
47. "A branch or segment that shows negative operating income should be shut down". Do you agree? Explain.
48. In considering a special order that will enable a company to make use of idle capacity, which of the following costs would probably not be differential.
    (*a*) Materials
    (*b*) Depreciation of buildings
    (*c*) Direct labour
    (*d*) Variable overhead
49. If you are considering buying a second car, what are the differential costs of that decision?
50. Suppose you are responsible for ordering a replacement for your office photocopy machine. Part of your job is to decide whether to buy it or lease it.

Required:

(*a*) Describe something that couldbe considered relevant information in this decision and explain why it is relevant.

(*b*) Describe something that could be considered irrelevant information in this decision and explain why it is irrelevant.

(*c*) Explain why it was important to distinguish between relevant and irrelevant information in this problem.

SELF-ASSESSMENT QUESTIONS

A. Fill in the blanks with the appropriate word given in the brackets:

1. The most beneficial decision that a business firm should make is the one with .... (lowest expense/largest revenue/greatest net profit).
2. Non-routine decisions are made .... (regularly/periodically).
3. Decisions relating to ordinary business activities are known as ....(recurring/nonrecurring).
4. Historical costs......................relevant costs (are/are not.)
5. Relevant costs are .... costs. (past/standard/controllable/future).
6. Decisions are made on the basis of......................costs associated with alternatives (all/difference in).
7. The decision maker should use..........................factors when there are no cost or revenue differences among different alternative (quantitative/qualitative).

8. The decision maker should consider..........................in case of limiting factor (s) to maximise the profit (sales/fixed cost/variable cost/contribution margin).

B. Listed below are a company's monthly unit costs to manufacture and market a particular product.

	₹
Manufacturing costs:	
Direct material	200
Direct labour	240
Variable indirect	160
Fixed indirect	100
Marketing costs:	
Variable	250
Fixed	150

The company must decide to continue making the product or buy it from an outside supplier. The supplier has offered to make the product at the same level of quality that the company can make it in-house. Fixed marketing costs would be unaffected, but variable marketing costs would be reduced by 30 pcr cent if the company were to accept the proposal. What is the maximum amount per unit that the company would pay the supplier without decreasing its operating income?

(*a*) ₹ 850 (*b*) ₹ 675 (*c*) ₹ 775
(*d*) ₹ 525 (*e*) ₹ 875

C. Kator Co. is a manufacturer of industrial components. One of their products that is used as a sub-component in auto manufacturing is KB-96. This product has the following financial structure per unit.

	₹
Selling price	150
Direct materials	20
Direct labour	15
Variable manufacturing overhead	12
Fixed manufacturing overhead	30
Shipping and handling	3
Fixed selling and administrative	10
Total costs	90

1. Kator Co. has received a special, one-time, order for 1,000 KB-96 parts. Assuming Kator has excess capacity, the minimum price that is acceptable for this one-time, special order is in excess of

(*a*) ₹ 47 (*b*) ₹ 50 (*c*) ₹ 60
(*d*) ₹ 77 (*e*) ₹ 90

2. During the next year, KB-96 sales are expected to be 10,000 units. All of the costs will remain the same except for fixed manufacturing overhead which will increase by 20 per cent and material which will increase by 10 percent. The selling price per unit for next year will be ₹ 160. Based on this data, the contribution margin from KB-96' for next year will be

(*a*) ₹ 6,20,000 (*b*) ₹ 7,50,000 (*c*) ₹ 10,80,000
(*d*) ₹ 11,00,000 (*e*) ₹ 11,10,000

3. Kator Co. has received a special, one-time, order for 1,000 KB-96 parts. Assume that Kator is operating at full capacity, and the next best alternative use of their capacity on existing equipment is LB-64 that would produce a contribution of ₹ 10,000. The minimum price that is acceptable, using the original data, for this one-time, special order is in excess of

   (a) ₹ 57 (b) ₹ 60 (c) ₹ 70
   (d) ₹ 87 (e) ₹ 100

D. Randall Corporation is a table manufacturing company that has the following cost structure for producing the table tops.

Unit Costs	
	₹
Direct materials	23.00
Direct labour	12.00
Variable manufacturing overhead	10.00
Fixed manufacturing overhead	17.00
Variable administrative costs	2.00
Fixed administrative costs	3.00
Total units costs	67.00

1. Recently, Randall Corporation received an offer from Blurr Corporation to supply the table tops to Randall. Randall is considering buying the table tops from Blurr instead of manufacturing them internally. Which one of the following statements is correct?
   (a) Randall should reject Blurr's offer if it is less than ₹ 47.00, and Randall has excess manufacturing capacity.
   (b) Randall should accept Blurr's offer if it is ₹ 50.00 or more, and Randall has excess manufacturing capacity.
   (c) Randall should accept Blurr's offer if it is less than ₹. 47.00, and Randall has excess manufacturing capacity.
   (d) Randall should reject Blurr's offer if it is ₹ 50.00 or more.
   (e) Randall should accept Blurr's offer if it is less than ₹ 64.00 and Blurr has excess manufacturing capacity.
2. Assume that Randall Corporation was operating at full capacity. If Randall had any additional capacity, they could manufacture chairs, which have costs per unit as follows.

Unit Costs	
	₹
Selling price	100.00
Direct materials	38.00
Direct labour	22.00
Variable manufacturing overhead	19.50
Fixed manufacturing overhead	4.75
Variable administrative costs	2.50
Fixed administrative costs	3.25
Operating margin	10.00

Using the above data, reconsider the offer that Randall received from Blurr Corporation to supply the table tops to Randall instead of Randall manufacturing them internally. What is the maximum price from Blurr that Randall would be willing to accept?

(*a*) ₹ 57.00 (*b*) ₹ 67.00 (*c*) ₹ 65.00
(*d*) ₹ 68.00 (*e*) ₹ 60.00

E. Condensed monthly operating income data for Korbin Co. for May 31, 2017, is presented below.

Korbin Co.
Combined Income Statement
May 31, 2017

	Urban Store ₹	***Suburban Store*** ₹	***Total*** ₹
Sales	80,000	1,20,000	2,00,000
Variable costs	32,000	84,000	1,16,000
Contribution margin	48,000	36,000	84,000
Direct fixed costs	20,000	40,000	60,000
Store segment margin	28,000	(4,000)	24,000
Common fixed cost	4,000	6,000	10,000
Operating income	24,000	(10,000)	14,000

Additional information regarding Korbin's operations follows.

- One-fourth of each store's direct fixed costs would continue if either store is closed.
- Korbin allocates common fixed costs to each store on the basis of sales volume.
- Management estimates that closing the Suburban Store would result in a ten per cent decrease in the Urban Store's sales, while closing the Urban Store would not affect the Suburban Store's sales.
- The operating results for May 2017 are representative of all months.

1. A decision by Korbin to close the Suburban Store would result in a monthly increase (decrease) in Korbin's operating income of

(*a*) ₹ (10,800) (*b*) ₹ (6,000) (*c*) ₹ (1,200)
(*d*) ₹ 4,000 (*e*) ₹ 10,000

2. Korbin is considering a promotional campaign at the Suburban Store that would not affect the Urban Store. Increasing annual promotional expense at the Suburban Store by ₹ 60,000 in order to increase this store's sales by ten per cent would result in a monthly increase (decrease) in Korbin's operating income during 2017 (rounded) of

(*a*) ₹ (5,000) (*b*) ₹ (1,400) (*c*) ₹ 487
(*d*) ₹ 7,000 (*e*) ₹ 12,000

3. One-half of the Suburban Store's sales are from items sold at variable cost to attract customers to the store. Korbin is considering the deletion of these items, a move that would reduce the Suburban Store's direct fixed expenses by 15 per cent and result in a 20 per cent loss of Suburban Store's remaining sales volume. This change would not affect the Urban Store. A decision by Korbin to eliminate the items sold at cost would result in a monthly increase (decrease) in Korbin's operating income during 2017 of

(*a*) ₹ (5,200) (*b*) ₹ (1,200) (*c*) ₹ (6,000)
(*d*) ₹ 2,000 (*e*) ₹ 6,000

(*CMA, USA, Adapted with permission*)

Answer to Self-Assessment Questions

B. (b)
C. 1. (b) 2. (c) 3. (b)
D. 1. (c) 2. (c)
E. 1. (a) 2. (b) 3. (b)

F. Listed below are a number of costs that may be relevant in decisions faced by the management of a manufacturing company.

Item
(*a*) Sales revenue ....
(*b*) Direct materials ....
(*c*) Direct labour ....
(*d*) Variable manufacturing overhead ....
(*e*) Depreciation—Model B100 machine ....
(*f*) Book value—Model B100 machine ....
(*g*) Disposal value—Model B100 machine ....
(*h*) Market value—Model B300 machine (cost)..
(*i*) Depreciation—Model B300 machine ....
(*j*) Fixed manufacturing overhead (general) ......
(*k*) Variable selling expense ....
(*l*) Fixed selling expense ....
(*m*) General administrative overhead ....

Required:

Indicate whether each item is relevant or not relevant in the following situations (requirement 1 relates to Case 1, and requirement 2 relates to Case 2):

1. Management is considering purchasing a Model B300 machine to use in addition to the company's present Model B100 machine. This will increase the company's production and sales. The increase in volume will be large enough to require increases in fixed selling expenses and in general administrative overhead, but not in the fixed manufacturing overhead.
2. Management is instead considering replacing its present Model B 100 machine with a new Model B300 machine. The Model B100 machine would be sold. This change will have no effect on production or sales, other than some savings in direct materials costs due to less waste.

Answer:

Item	Case 1 Relevant	Case 1 Not Relevant	Case 2 Relevant	Case 2 Not Relevant
(*a*) Sales revenue	X			X
(*b*) Direct materials	X		X	
(*c*) Direct labour	X			X
(*d*) Variable manufacturing overhead	X			X
(*e*) Depreciation— Model B100 machine		X		X
(*f*) Book value— Model B100 machine		X		X
(*g*) Disposal value—Model B100 machine		X	X	
(*h*) Market value— Model B300 machine (cost)	X		X	
(*i*) Depreciation—Model B300 machine	X		X	
(*j*) Fixed manufacturing overhead		X		X
(*k*) Variable selling expense	X			X
(*l*) Fixed selling expense	X			X
(*m*) General administrative overhead	X			X

MULTIPLE CHOICE QUESTIONS

Select the correct answer for the following multiple choice questions:

1. The type of costs presented to management for a non-routine decision should be limited to:
   (*a*) Relevant costs (*b*) Standard costs
   (*c*) Controllable costs (*d*) Conversion costs
2. Other things remaining the same, ideal product mix is determined in terms of:
   (*a*) Sales (*b*) Variable costs
   (*c*) Total costs (*d*) Conversion costs
3. In a make or buy decision:
   (*a*) Only variable costs are relevant
   (*b*) Fixed costs that can be avoided in the future are relevant.
   (*c*) Fixed costs that will continue regardless of the decision are relevant.
   (*d*) a and b
4. Relevant costs are:
   (*a*) Future costs (*b*) Standard costs
   (*c*) Controllable costs (*d*) Historical costs
5. The decision maker should consider in case of limiting factor (s) to maximise the profit:
   (*a*) Sales (*b*) Contribution margin
   (*c*) Variable cost (*d*) Fixed cost.

6. The measurable value of an alternative use of resources is referred to as a (an):
   (*a*) Opportunity cost (*b*) Imputed cost
   (*c*) Differential cost (*d*) Sunk cost
7. A manager of a company reported the total additional cost required for the proposed increased production level. The increase in total cost is known as:
   (*a*) Controllable cost (*b*) Incremental cost
   (*c*) Opportunity cost (*d*) Out-of-pocket cost
8. Which of the following is usually an incremental cost:
   (*a*) Conversion cost
   (*b*) Period cost
   (*c*) Manufacturing overhead cost
   (*d*) Direct product cost
9. A cost incurred in the past and hence irrelevant for current decision-making is a:
   (*a*) Fixed cost (*b*) Discretionary cost
   (*c*) Sunk cost (*d*) Direct cost
10. A cost that cannot be changed by any decision made now or in the future is a (an):
    (*a*) Indirect cost (*b*) Uncontrollable cost
    (*c*) Opportunity cost (*d*) Sunk cost
11. The amount of increase or decrease in cost that is expected from a particular course of action as compared with an alternative is referred to as:
    (*a*) Differential cost (*b*) Replacement cost
    (*c*) Opportunity cost (*d*) Sunk cost.
12. A company is considering the disposal of equipment that was originally purchased for ₹ 2,00,000 and has accumulated depreciation to date of ₹ 1,50,000. The same equipment would cost ₹ 3,10,000 to replace. What is sunk cost?
    (*a*) ₹ 50,000 (*b*) ₹ 1,50,000
    (*c*) ₹ 2,00,000 (*d*) none of the above.
13. In deciding whether to manufacture a part or buy if from an outside supplier, a cost that is not relevant to the short run decision is:
    (*a*) Direct labour
    (*b*) Variable overhead
    (*c*) Fixed overhead that will be avoided if the part is bought from an outside supplier.
    (*d*) Fixed overhead that will continue even if the part is bought from an outside supplier.
14. A shut down point represents the level of production and sales at which:
    (*a*) Operating loss equals the cost of being shut down
    (*b*) Contribution margin is less than the fixed cost
    (*c*) Contribution margin is equal to the fixed cost
    (*d*) Total sales is equal to total costs
    (*e*) Total sales is less than the total cost.
15. A company temporarily has excess production capacity. The idle plant facilities can be used to manufacture a low-margin item. The low-margin item should be produced if it can be sold for more than its:

(*a*) Fixed costs
(*b*) Variable costs
(*c*) Variable costs plus any opportunity cost of the idle facilities
(*d*) Indirect costs plus any opportunity cost of the idle facilities.

16. In considering a special order situation that will enable a company to make use of presently idle capacity, which of the following costs would be irrelevant?
(*a*) Materials (*b*) Depreciation
(*c*) Direct labour (*d*) Variable overhead.

17. In deciding which of two new machines to purchase to replace an old machine, the management of Ashworth Company should consider as relevant:
(*a*) Historical costs associated with the old machine.
(*b*) Future costs which will be classified as variable rather than fixed.
(*c*) Future costs which will be different under the two alternatives.
(*d*) Future costs which will be classified as fixed rather than variable.

18. A company manufactures two joint products at a joint cost of ₹ 1,000. These products can be sold when split off or when further processed at an additional cost and sold as higher quality items. The decision to sell at split-off or further process should be based on the
(*a*) Assumption that the ₹ 1,000 joint cost is irrelevant.
(*b*) Allocation of the ₹ 1,000 joint cost using the relative sales-value approach.
(*c*) Assumption that the ₹ 1,000 joint cost must be allocated using a physical measure approach.
(*d*) Allocation of the ₹ 1,000 joint cost using any equitable and rational allocation basis.

19. B. Co. is considering replacing an old machine with a new machine. Which of the following items is economically relevant to B's decision? (Ignore income tax considerations.)

	Carrying Amount of Old Machine	***Disposal Value of New Machine***
(*a*)	Yes	No
(*b*)	No	Yes
(*c*)	No	No
(*d*)	Yes	Yes

20. Jago Co. has two products that use the same manufacturing facilities and cannot be subcontracted. Each product has sufficient orders to utilize the entire manufacturing capacity. For short-run profit maximization, Jago should manufacture the product with the
(*a*) Lower total manufacturing costs for the manufacturing capacity.
(*b*) Lower total variable manufacturing costs for the manufacturing capacity.
(*c*) Greater gross profit per hour of manufacturing capacity.
(*d*) Greater contribution margin per hour of manufacturing capacity.

21. For the year ended December 31, 2017, Abel Co. incurred direct costs of ₹ 5,00,000 based on a particular course of action during the year. If a different course of action had been taken, direct costs would have been ₹ 4,00,000. In addition, Abel's 2017 fixed costs were ₹ 90,000. The incremental cost was
(*a*) ₹ 10,000 (*b*) ₹ 90,000
(*c*) ₹ 1,00,000 (*d*) ₹ 1,90,000

22. In a manufacturing environment, the best short-term profit-maximizing approach is to
    (*a*) Maximize unit gross profit times the number of units sold.
    (*b*) Minimize variable costs per unit times the number of units produced.
    (*c*) Minimize fixed overhead cost per unit by producing at full capacity.
    (*d*) Maximize contribution per unit times the number of units sold.
23. In equipment-replacement decisions, which one of the following does **not** affect the decision making process?
    (*a*) Current disposal price of the old equipment.
    (*b*) Operating costs of the old equipment.
    (*c*) Original fair market value of the old equipment.
    (*d*) Cost of the new equipment.
    (*e*) Operating costs of the new equipment.
24. An important concept in decision making is described as "the contribution to income that is foregone by not using a limited resource to its best alternative use." This concept is called
    (*a*) marginal cost (*b*) incremental cost
    (*c*) potential cost (*d*) opportunity cost
    (*e*) irrelevant cost
25. The relevance of a particular cost to a decision is determined by
    (*a*) riskiness of the decision. (*b*) number of decision variables.
    (*c*) amount of the cost. (*d*) potential effect on the decision.
    (*e*) accuracy of the cost.
26. In a make-versus-buy decision, the relevant costs include variable manufacturing costs as well as
    (*a*) factory management costs. (*b*) general office costs.
    (*c*) unavoidable costs. (*d*) avoidable fixed costs.
    (*e*) depreciation costs.
27. Which one of the following is most relevant to a manufacturing equipment replacement decision?
    (*a*) Original cost of the old equipment.
    (*b*) Disposal price of the old equipment.
    (*c*) Gain or loss on the disposal of the old equipment.
    (*d*) Original cost less depreciation of the old equipment.
    (*e*) A lump-sum write-off amount from the disposal of the old equipment.
28. When an organization decides on a course of action that is selected from a group of alternative courses of action, the benefit lost by not choosing the **best** alternative course of action is the
    (*a*) expected value. (*b*) incremental cost.
    (*c*) net realizable value. (*d*) avoidable cost.
    (*e*) opportunity cost.
29. Costs relevant to a make-or-buy decision include variable labour and variable materials as well as
    (*a*) unavoidable fixed costs. (*b*) depreciation.
    (*c*) factory management costs. (*d*) avoidable fixed costs.
    (*e*) property taxes.

30. When a multi-product plant operates at full capacity, quite often decisions must be made as to which products to emphasize. These decisions are frequently made with a short-run focus. In making such decisions, managers should select products with the
    (*a*) highest sales price per unit.
    (*b*) highest individual unit contribution margin.
    (*c*) highest sales volume potential.
    (*d*) highest contribution margin per unit of the constraining resource.
    (*e*) lowest variable cost per unit.
31. In a decision analysis situation, which one of the following costs is **not** likely to contain a variable cost component?
    (*a*) Labour (*b*) Overhead (*c*) Depreciation
    (*d*) Selling (*e*) Material
32. In a decision analysis situation, which one of the following costs is generally **not** relevant to the decision?
    (*a*) Incremental cost. (*b*) Differential cost. (*c*) Avoidable cost.
    (*d*) Historical cost (*e*) Opportunity cost.
33. In situations when management must decide on accepting or rejecting one-time-only special orders, where there is sufficient idle capacity, which one of the following is **not** relevant to the decision?
    (*a*) Absorption costs. (*b*) Differential costs. (*c*) Direct costs.
    (*d*) Variable costs. (*e*) Incremental costs.
34. Relevant or differential cost analysis
    (*a*) Takes all variable and fixed costs into account to analyze decision alternatives.
    (*b*) Considers only variable costs as they change with each decision alternative.
    (*c*) Considers the change in reported net income for each alternative to arrive at the optimum decision for the company.
    (*d*) Considers all variable and fixed costs as they change with each decision alternative.
35. The relevance of a particular cost to a decision is determined by the
    (*a*) Size of the cost.
    (*b*) Riskiness of the decision.
    (*c*) Potential effect on the decision.
    (*d*) Accuracy and verifiability of the cost.
36. Total unit costs are
    (*a*) Relevant for cost-volume-profit analysis.
    (*b*) Irrelevant in marginal analysis.
    (*c*) Independent of the cost system used to generate them.
    (*d*) Needed for determining product contribution.
37. The term relevant cost applies to all the following decision situations except the
    (*a*) Acceptance of a special order.
    (*b*) Determination of a product price.
    (*c*) Replacement of equipment.
    (*d*) Addition or deletion of a product line.

38. Which one of the following is most relevant to equipment replacement decision?
    (*a*) Original cost of the old equipment.
    (*b*) Disposal price of the old equipment.
    (*c*) Gain or Loss on the disposal of the old equipment.
    (*d*) A lump-sum write-off amount from the disposal of the old equipment.
39. Mili Co. plans to discontinue a division with ₹ 20,000 contribution margin. Overhead allocated to the division is ₹ 50,000, of which ₹ 5,000 cannot be eliminated. The effect of this discontinuance on Mili's pretax income would be an increase of
    (*a*) ₹ 5,000. (*b*) ₹ 20,000
    (*c*) ₹ 25,000. (*d*) ₹ 30,000
40. A company's approach to an insourcing *vs.* outsourcing decision
    (*a*) Depends on whether the company is operating at or below normal volume.
    (*b*) Involves an analysis of avoidable costs.
    (*c*) Should use absorption (full) costing.
    (*d*) Should use activity-based costing.
41. Costs relevant to an insourcing *vs.* outsourcing decision include variable manufacturing costs as well as
    (*a*) Avoidable fixed costs. (*b*) Factory depreciation.
    (*c*) Property taxes. (*d*) Factory management costs.
42. What is the opportunity cost of making a component part in a factory given no alternative use of the capacity?
    (*a*) The variable manufacturing cost of the component.
    (*b*) The total manufacturing cost of the component.
    (*c*) The total variable cost of the component.
    (*d*) Zero.
43. In an insourcing vs. outsourcing situation, which of the following qualitative factors is usually considered?
    (*a*) Special technology. (*b*) Skilled labor.
    (*c*) Special materials requirements. (*d*) All of the answers are correct.
44. In an insourcing vs. outsourcing decision, the decision process favors the use of total costs rather than unit costs. The reason is that
    (*a*) Unit cost may be calculated based on different volumes.
    (*b*) Irrelevant costs may be included in the unit amounts.
    (*c*) Allocated costs may be included in the unit.
    (*d*) All of the answers are correct.
45. Which of the following qualitative factors favors the buy choice in an insourcing vs. outsourcing decision?
    (*a*) Maintaining a long-run relationship with suppliers is desirable.
    (*b*) Quality control is critical.
    (*c*) Idle capacity is available.
    (*d*) All of the answers are correct.

(CMA, USA, Adapted with permission)

Answer to Multiple Choice Questions

1. (*a*)	2. (*a*)	3. (*d*)	4. (*a*)	5. (*b*)
6. (*a*)	7. (*b*)	8. (*d*)	9. (*c*)	10. (*d*)
11. (*a*)	12. (*c*)	13. (*d*)	14. (*a*)	15. (*c*)
16. (*b*)	17. (*c*)	18. (*a*)	19. (*b*)	20. (*d*)
21. (*c*)	22. (*d*)	23. (*c*)	24. (*d*)	25. (*d*)
26. (*d*)	27. (*b*)	28. (*e*)	29. (*d*)	30. (*d*)
31. (*c*)	32. (*d*)	33. (*a*)	34. (*d*)	35. (*c*)
36. (*b*)	37. (*b*)	38. (*b*)	39. (*c*)	40. (*b*)
41. (*a*)	42. (*d*)	43. (*d*)	44. (*d*)	45. (*b*)

PROBLEMS

1. Pooja Company manufactures cookware. Expected annual volume of 1,00,000 sets per year is well below its full capacity of 1,50,000. Normal selling price is ₹ 40/- per set. Manufacturing cost is ₹ 30/- per set (₹ 20 variable and ₹ 10 fixed). Total fixed manufacturing cost is ₹ 10,00,000. Selling and administrative expenses are expected to be ₹ 5,00,000 (₹ 3,00,000 fixed and ₹ 2,00,000 variable). A departmental store offers to buy 25,000 sets of ₹ 27/- per set. No extra selling and administrative costs would be caused by the order. Further, the acceptance of this order will not affect regular sales. Should the offer be accepted?

   You are to adopt Incremental Approach only for your decision making.

   Ans: Yes, operating income will increase by ₹ 1,75,000.

2. A company is considering replacing an old piece of machinery, which cost ₹ 6,00,000 and has ₹ 3,50,000 of accumulated depreciation to date, with a new machine that costs ₹ 4,50,000. The old equipment could be sold for ₹ 72,000. The annual variable production costs associated with the old machine are estimated to be ₹ 1,65,000 for eight years. The annual variable production costs for the new machine are estimated to be ₹ 1,12,750 for eight years.

   (*a*) Determine the total and annualized differential income or loss anticipated from replacing the old machine.

   (*b*) What is the sunk cost in this situation?

   Ans: (*a*) Annual differential income from new equipment ₹ 5,000.
   (*b*) ₹ 2,50,000 book value.

3. Overnight Express, an international couriers service, is considering eliminating operations in Eastern Europe. If the company dropped the East European Market, it would lose revenue of ₹ 10,00,000 annually. Management assign costs of ₹ 12,00,000 (₹ 8,00,000 variable and ₹ 4,00,000 fixed) to the East European Market. Therefore, the East European Market has an apparent annual loss of ₹ 2,00,000 per year (₹ 10,00,000 revenue minus ₹ 12,00,000 costs). Careful cost analysis reveals that if East European Operations were dropped, the reduction in costs would be only ₹ 8,00,000 of variable and ₹ 2,50,000 of fixed costs. The remaining ₹ 1,50,000 of fixed costs were general fixed costs the company allocated to the East European market. These costs would continue to be incurred and would not be saved by shutting down the East European market:

Required:

Should East European market operations be closed?

Ans: East European operation gives a differential loss of ₹ 50,000 and therefore should be closed.

4. A firm is selling X product, whose variable cost per unit is ₹ 10 and fixed cost is ₹ 6,000. It has sold 1,000 articles during one month at ₹ 20 per unit. Market research shows that there is a great demand for the product if the price can be reduced. If the price can be reduced to ₹ 12.50 per unit, it is expected that 5,000 articles can be sold in the expanded market. The firm has to take a decision whether to produce and sell 1,000 units at the rate of ₹ 20 or to produce and sell for the growing demand of 5,000 units at the rate of ₹ 12.50. Give your advice to the management in taking a decision.

Ans:

Profit (*a*) 1000 units, ₹ 4,000.

(*b*) 5000 units, ₹ 6,500.

Proposal to manufacture and sell 5000 units is preferable.

5. On November 1, Essence Stores is considering leasing a building and purchasing the necessary equipment to operate a retail store. Alternatively, the company could use the funds to invest in ₹ 1,40,000 of 5% govt. bonds that mature in 16 years. The bonds could be purchased at face value. The following data have been assembled.

Cost of store equipment	₹ 1,40,000
Life of store equipment	16 years
Estimated residual value of store equipment	₹ 15,000
Yearly costs to operate the store, excluding depreciation of store equipment	₹ 62,000
Yearly expected revenues—years 1-8	₹ 78,000
Yearly expected revenues—years 9-16	₹ 72,000

Required:

(*i*) Prepare a report as of November 1, 2017, presenting a differential analysis of the proposed operation of the store for the 16 years as compared with present conditions.

(*ii*) Based on the results disclosed by the differential analysis, should the proposal be accepted?

(*iii*) If the proposal is accepted, what would be the total estimated income from operations of the store for the 16 years?

Ans: (*i*) Differential loss ₹ 29,000

(*ii*) The proposal should be rejected.

(*iii*) Total estimated income from operating store ₹ 83,000.

6. A company is at present working at 90 per cent of its capacity and producing 13,500 units per annum. It operates a Flexible Budgetary Control System. The following figures are obtained from its budget:

	90% ₹	100% ₹
Sales	15,00,000	16,00,000
Fixed Expenses	3,00,500	3,00,600
Semi-Fixed Expenses	97,500	1,00,500
Variable Overhead Expenses	1,45,000	1,49,500
Units made	13,500	15,000

Labour and material cost per unit are constant under present conditions. Profit margin is 10 per cent.

(*a*) You are required to determine the differential cost of producing 1,500 units by increasing capacity to 100 per cent.

(*b*) What would you recommend for an export price for these 1,500 units taking into account that overseas prices are much lower than indigenous prices.

Ans: (*a*) Differential cost ₹ 97,267.

(*b*) Minimum price for export ₹ 64.84 per unit.

7. A factory is currently working at 50% capacity and produces 10,000 units of product P, the unit cost of which is ₹ 180 comprised as follows:

	₹	
Direct Material	100	
Direct labour	30	
Factory Overhead	30	(40% Fixed)
Administration Overhead	20	(50% Fixed)
The selling price per unit is ₹ 200.		

If the capacity is increased to 60%, the raw material cost will increase by 2% and selling price falls by 2%. At 80% capacity, raw material cost increases by 5% and selling price falls by 5%.

You are required to work out the total costs and profit for the three capacity levels and prepare a brief note for the management on the profitability at these levels of performance with your recommendation.

Ans: Profit at 50%, ₹, 2,00,000, at 60%, ₹ 2,12,000, at 80%, ₹ 2,12,000. It is advisable to run the factory at 60% capacity level. The total amount of profit at 60% and 80% capacity is the same. In fact, it will be preferable to use the surplus capacity over 60% for some other purpose.

8. J.P. stall owner is disturbed by the poor profit performance of his ice cream counter. He has prepared the following profit analysis for the month just ended:

	(₹)
Sales	45,000
Less: Cost of food	20,000
Gross profit	₹ 25,000
Less: Operating expenses:	
Wages of counter personnel	₹ 12,000

Paper products (*e.g.*, napkins)	4,000
Utilities (based on pcr cent of sales)	2,900
Depreciation of counter equipment and furnishings	3,000
Depreciation of building (based on percentage of sales)	5,000
Manager's salary (based on percentage of time spent on ice cream)	6,000
Total operating expenses	32,900
Income (loss) on ice cream counter	₹ (7,900)

Required:

(*a*) Revise the owner's analysis as you think appropriate. Justify your changes.

(*b*) Should the owner close the counter? What other factors should he consider before closing it?

Ans: (*a*) Closing the icecream centre is likely to decrease annual profits by ₹ 6,100

(*b*) Other factors to consider include whether ice cream sales are related to other sales.

9. The Hi-tech Manufacturing Company is presently evaluating two possible processes for the manufacture of a toy, and makes available to you the following information:

	Process A (₹)	***Process B*** (₹)
Variable cost per unit	12	14
Sales price per unit	20	20
Total fixed costs per year	30,00,000	21,00,000
Capacity (in units)	4,30,000	5,00,000
Anticipated sales (next years, in units)	4,00,000	4,00,000

You are required to suggest:

(*i*) Which process should be chosen? Substantiate your answer.

(*ii*) Would you change your answer as given above if you were informed that the capacities of the two processes are as follows: A, 6,00,000 units; B 5,00,000 units? Why? Substantiate your answer. (*M.Com., Delhi*)

Ans: (*i*) Process B may be chosen.

(*ii*) Process A may be chosen.

10. A Company manufactures three products A, B, C. There are no common process and the sale of one product does not affect price or volume of sales of any other.

The Company's budgeted profit/loss for 2017 has been abstracted as follows

	Total ₹	***A*** ₹	***B*** ₹	***C*** ₹
Sales	3,00,000	45,000	2,25,000	30,000
Production Cost: Variable	1,80,000	24,000	1,44,000	12,000
Fixed	60,000	3,000	48,000	9,000
Factory Cost	2,40,000	27,000	1,92,000	21,000

Selling and Administration Costs:				
Variable	24,000	8,100	8,100	7,800
Fixed	6,000	2,100	1,800	2,100
Total Cost	2,70,000	37,200	2,01,900	30,900
Profit	30,000	7,800	23,100	(–) 900

On the basis of the above, the Board had almost decided to eliminate product C, on which a loss was budgeted. Meanwhile, they have sought your opinion. As the company's Cost Accountant what would you advise? Give reasons for your answer.

Ans: P/V ratio, A 28.7%, B 32.4%, C 34%

It is found that product C, though has the highest P/V Ratio, seems to be non-profitable because it has to bear a higher percentage of fixed cost as compared to its total cost. The percentage comes to about 35.9% $\left(i.e., \frac{11,00}{30,900} \times 100\right)$ which in case of other products is too less. Since the surplus capacity generated by one product cannot be used for other products, there seems to be no justification for discontinuing product C till some new product is developed which will have a higher P/V ratio than product C. In the present circumstances. Since C has a higher P/V ratio, and if the sales continue to rise, C may start giving profit.

11. Cosmos Corporation manufactures toy cars in a plant that has theoretical capacity to produce 3,000 cars each month. Current monthly production is 80 per cent of practical capacity. The normal selling price is ₹ 360; unit-level costs and facility costs for the current activity level are as follows:

Unit-level costs	₹ 2,85,600
Facility-level costs:	
Manufacturing	9,60,000
Marketing	7,80,000
Total costs	₹ 20,25,600

Cosmos has just received a special order from a Japanese company for 1,100 cars at ₹ 310 each, with a target completion date in three months. Cosmos has never competed in the global marketplace. The company has hired a consultant for ₹ 55,000 each month of the contract to obtain advice on conducting business in Japan.

Required:

(*a*) Does Cosmos have sufficient productive capacity to accept the order? Explain.

(*b*) Is the order attractive from a financial perspective? Show computations to support your answer.

(*c*) Discuss any other considerations that Cosmos should include in analyzing the order.

(*d*) Is it beneficial for Cosmos to take a loss on this order if it desires to enter the Japanese market? Discuss briefly.

Ans: (*a*) Yes

(*b*) Accepting the order is profitable

(*c*) Cosmos should be concerned about effects on its future prices.

(*d*) Yes.

12. A company annually manufactures 10,000 units of a product at a cost of ₹ 400 per unit and there is home market for consuming the entire volume of production at the sale price of ₹ 425 per unit. In the year 2016, there is a fall in the demand for home market which can consume 10,000 units only at a sale price of ₹ 372 per unit. The analysis of the cost per 10,000 units is:

	₹
Materials	15,00,000
Wages	11,00,000
Fixed overheads	8,00,000
Variable overheads	6,00,000

The foreign market is explored and it is found that the market can consume 20,000 units of the product if offered at a sale price of ₹ 355 per unit. It is also discovered that for additional 10,000 units of the product (over initial 10,000 units) the fixed overhead will increase by 10 per cent. Is it worthwhile to try to capture the foreign market?

Ans: It is advisable to sell the goods in the foreign market.

13. Due to industrial depression, a plant is running, at present, at 50% of its capacity. The following details are available:

	Cost of Production per unit
	₹
Direct material	20
Direct labour	10
Variable overhead	30
Fixed overhead	20
	80
Production per month	20,000 units
Total cost of production	16,00,000
Sales price	14,00,000
Loss	(2,00,000)

An exporter offers to buy 5,000 units per month at the rate of ₹ 65 per unit and the company hesitates to accept the offer for fear of increasing its already large operating losses Advise.

Ans: The company should accept the offer since amount of loss will be reduced.

14. The budgeted results for X Co. include the following:

		₹ in lakhs	***Variable Cost as % of sales value***
Sales:	Product A	60	50%
	Product B	50	60%
	Product C	80	65%
	Product D	40	80%
	Product E	30	70%
		260	

Fixed overheads for the period ₹ 100 lakhs.

You are required to (*a*) prepare a statement showing the amount of loss expected, (*b*) assuming that the sales of only one product can be increased at a time, you are asked to recommend a change in the sales volume of each product which will eliminate the expected loss.

Ans: (*a*) Total loss ₹ 5,00,000.

Additional sales, required to break-even, assuming sales of only one product is increased at a time, to give the additional contribution of ₹ 5,00, 000, is calculated as follows:

$$\text{Sales required} = \frac{\text{Under – recovery of fixed overheads}}{\text{P/ V Ratio of the product}}$$

A	$\frac{5,00,000}{50\%}$	10,00,000
B	$\frac{5,00,000}{40\%}$	12,50,000
C	$\frac{5,00,000}{35\%}$	14,28,571
D	$\frac{5,00,000}{20\%}$	25,00,000
E	$\frac{5,00,000}{30\%}$	16,66,667

The company should utilise the spare capacity available for Product 'A' to achieve maximum profitability as its P/V Ratio is highest. Fixed costs remaining the same at every level of production, this combination will lead to maximum profitability.

15. A company follows the flexible budgeting system, and the position at 70% level of production, is as follows:

Production	40,000 units
Direct wages	₹ 60,00,000
Direct materials	80,00,000
Overhead:	
Fixed	84,00,000
Variable	42,00,000
	2,66,00,000

The selling price per unit is ₹ 865.

In the present market conditions there is hardly any chance for selling more locally. A special export order for 8,000 units at ₹ 650 per unit, is received.

(*a*) Would it be prudent for the company to accept the order at this price?

(*b*) What is the price beyond which it would be profitable to accept this order?

16. Able Company has plant capacity of 1,00,000 units per year, but the 2016 budget indicates that only 60,000 units will be produced and sold. The entire 2016 budget is as follows:

			₹
	Sales revenues (60,000 units at ₹ 400)		2,40,00,000
Less:	Cost of goods produced	₹	
	(based on production of 60,000 units):		
	Materials (Variable)	60,00,000	
	Labour (variable)	30,00,000	
	Variable manufacturing costs	45,00,000	
	Non-variable manufacturing costs	75,00,000	
	Total cost of goods produced		2,10,00,000
	Gross margin		30,00,000
Less:	Selling and administrative expenses:		
	Selling (10% of sales)	24,00,000	
	Administrative (non-variable)	36,00,000	
	Total selling and administrative expenses		60,00,000
	Loss from operations		(30,00,000)

Required:

(*a*) Given the budgeted selling price and cost data; how many units would Able have to produce and sell in order to break-even?

(*b*) Market research indicates that if Able were to drop its selling price to ₹ 380 per unit, it could sell 1,00,000 units in 2016. Would you recommend the drop in price? Indicate the new profit or loss figure.

17. Golden Printing Company is considering replacing a machine that has been used in its factory for four years. Relevant data associated with the operations of the old machine and the new machine, neither of which has any estimated residual value, are as follows:

Old Machine

Cost of machine, 10-year life	₹ 1,26,00,000
Annual depreciation (straight-line)	12,60,000
Annual manufacturing costs, excluding depreciation	42,50,000
Annual nonmanufacturing operating expenses	12,30,000
Annual revenue	95,00,000
Current estimated selling price of machine	32,40,000

New Machine

Cost of machine, six-year life	₹ 1,44,00,000
Annual depreciation (straight-line)	24,00,000
Estimated annual manufacturing costs, exclusive of depreciation	18,90,000

Annual nonmanufacturing operating expenses and revenue are not expected to be affected by purchase of the new machine.

Required:

(*i*) Prepare a differential analysis report, comparing operations utilizing the new machine with operations using the present equipment.

(*ii*) List other factors that should be considered before a final decision is reached.

Ans: (*i*) Differential income from replacement (six-year) total ₹ 30,00,000

18. The Midland Company published the following income statement for the year just ended:

	₹	₹	₹
Sales (15,000 units)			15,00,000
Cost of goods sold:			
Materials		4,50,000	
Labour		3,00,000	
Overhead:			
Fixed	2,00,000		
Variable	1,50,000	3,50,000	11,00,000
Gross profit on sales			4,00,000
Selling expenses		50,000	
Administrative expenses		1,00,000	1,50,000
Net profit			2,50,000

The High Point Company has offered to purchase 10,000 units for each of the next 10 years at a unit price of ₹ 90. This offer would have no effect on present sales. Present plant capacity is 20,000 units. The firm would have to buy new machinery in order to accept the offer and be able to continue producing the same quantity for its regular trade. The only machine available at the present time to do the job produces 20,000 units. It would cost the firm ₹ 10,00,000 and have a life of 10 years with no scrap value at that time.

Other fixed overhead is estimated to increase to ₹ 50,000 if the new offer is obtained. Variable overhead will increase proportionately to sales units. Labour costs will rise to ₹ 5 per unit according to a recent contract signed with the union. Suppliers of raw materials have indicated a 10% rise in prices in their latest price catalogues.

Selling and administrative expenses are expected to rise to ₹ 20,000 and ₹ 30,000 respectively.

Should the company accept the new offer or should it make a vigorous effort to use the present unused capacity at the present sales price and decline the High Point Company Business?

Ans: It is advisable for Midland Company to use the present unused capacity and decline the High Point Company business. Present profit ₹ 2,50,000, Unused capacity profit 1,10,000.

19. A manufacturer has planned his level of operation at 50% of his plant capacity of 30,000 units. His expenses are estimated as follows, if 50% of the plant capacity is utilized.

		₹
(*i*)	Direct Materials	8,28,000
(*ii*)	Direct Wages	11,16,000
(*iii*)	Variable and other Manufacturing Expenses	3,96,000
(*iv*)	Total Fixed Expenses irrespective of capacity utilisation	6,00,000

The expected selling price in the domestic market is ₹ 200 per unit. Recently, the manufacturer has received a trade enquiry from an overseas organisation interested in purchasing 6,000 units at a price of ₹ 145 per unit.

As a professional management accountant what would be your suggestion regarding acceptance or rejection of the offer? Support your suggestion with suitable quantitative information.

20. Alpha Company has the following budgeted figures for its various products for next year:

	Products		
	A	B	C
	(₹ '000)	(₹ '000)	(₹ '000)
Sales value	480	480	160
Variable costs	432	384	120
Fixed Costs (allocated)	24	36	50

The company is concerned about Product C and several alternatives are being considered:

Alternative 1

Cut C's selling price by 10%. It is estimated that this will increase C's unit sales by 40%

Alternative 2

Substitute a new product D for C. Estimated sales are ₹ 1,40,000 in the first year. Variable costs are estimated at 55% of sales. Fixed cost directly attributable to C of ₹ 10,000 will be eliminated but ₹ 16,000 additional fixed cost directly attributable to D will be incurred.

Alternative 3

Eliminate C entirely. This will reduce the fixed costs attributable to C by ₹ 10,000.

Alternative 4

Convert C into special finish by adding additional treatments, which will secure a price increase of 20%. The additional costs incurred will be 10% of the new increased price.

Management wants to know the effect of each alternative on the profit of the company and their ranking in order of preference.

Ans: The four alteratives have no relationship with products A and B. It can be assumed that these products will continue to make contribution whatever they are currently making. Therefore, there is no need to examine profitability of products A and B.

For Product C, the following ranking of alternatives is applicable:

Rank 1 — Alternative 2: Increase profit by ₹ 17,000
Rank 2 — Alternative 4: increase profit by ₹ 12,800
Rank 3 — Alternative 1: Increase profit by ₹ 9,600
Rank 4 — Alternative 3: Reduces profit by ₹ 30,000

21. The oriental Company's income statement at its present maximum capacity of 20,00,000 units per year shows the following:

Oriental Company

Income Statement for the Year Ending December 31, 2016

	₹	₹
Sales revenue 20,00,000 units @ ₹ 100		20,00,00,000
Cost of sales:		
Non-variable	5,00,00,000	
Variable	11,00,00,000	16,00,00,000
		4,00,00,000
Selling & Administrative expenses:		
Non-variable	2,00,00,000	
Variable	1,00,00,000	3,00,00,000
Net income		1,00,00,000

The Sales Manager states that sales could be increased to 25,00,000 units per year. Engineers estimate that the expanded volume could be obtained only through installation of additional facilities that would add ₹ 1,10,00,000 a year to the present non-variable factory cost. The Production Manager thinks the increased volume would reduce the present variable factory cost by ₹ 5 per unit. No change in the present structure of the selling and administrative expenses is anticipated.

The directors of the company are uncertain whether to go ahead and expand the present facilities.

Required:

Prepare data that would be useful to the directors in making their decision. Include in your report such data as the following (*a*) potential maximum profit with and without expansion; (*b*) break-even points before and after expansion; (*c*) sales volume needed to yield a profit of ₹ 1,00,00,000 if the expansion is carried out.

22. The Spring Manufacturing Company is considering accepting a special order for 50,000 mattresses which it received from a large chain of department stores. The order specified a price of ₹ 3000 per unit. This compared unfavourably to the company's regular price of ₹ 3300 per unit. The accounting department prepared the following analysis in an attempt to show that there would be cost saving resulting from the additional sales:

	Cost per unit without the Additional Sales (1,00,000 units) ₹	***Cost per unit with Additional Sales (1,50,000 units)*** ₹
Variable Costs	2000	2000
Fixed Cost	900	600
	2900	2600

No additional fixed costs would be incurred because there was excess capacity. In as much as the average cost per unit will be reduced from ₹ 2900 to ₹ 2600, the president of the firm believes he would be justified in reducing the price by ₹ 300 to sell to the department store chain.

Required:

Should the order for the 50,000 units at a price of ₹ 3000 be accepted? What factors not included in the accounting department's analysis should be considered in arriving at a decision?

23. A cycle tyre manufacturing company has been approached by a large shopkeeper that offers to buy 10,000 tyres at ₹ 3200. Delivery must be made within 30 days. The production capacity of the company is 64,000 units per month and there is inventory of 2,000 tyres. Expected sales at regular prices for the coming month are 60,000 tyres. It is estimated by the sales manager that about 50% of sales lost during the month would be made up in later months. Price and cost data per unit are as follows:

	₹	₹
Selling price		4800
Variable costs:		
Production	2400	
Selling	600	3000
Profit contribution		1800

The variable selling costs on the special order would be ₹ 100 per unit.

Required:

(*i*) Determine whether the offer should be accepted by the firm or not.

(*ii*) Determine the lowest price that the company could charge on the special order and not reduce its income.

(*iii*) Suppose now that the shopkeeper offers to buy 8,000 tyres per month at ₹ 3200 per tyre. The offer would be for an entire year. Expected sales are 60,000 tyres per month without accepting the special order. Assuming further that there is no beginning inventory and that sales lost during the year would not be made up in the following year, determine whether the offer should be accepted and determine the lowest price that company could accept. (*M.Com., Delhi,* 2008)

Ans: (*i*) Increase in profit ₹ 34,00,000. Offer should be accepted.
(*ii*) Lowest price ₹ 2,860.
(*iii*) Special order will reduce income by ₹ 16,00,000 p.m.
Lowest price per unit ₹ 3,400.

24. A company has prepared the following budget for the forthcoming year:

	₹ ***lakhs***
Sales	20.00
Direct materials	3.60
Direct labour	6.40
Factory overheads:	
Variable	2.20
Fixed	2.60
Administration overheads	1.80
Sales commission	1.00
Fixed selling overheads	0.40
Total costs	18.00
Profit	2.00

The policy of the company in fixing selling prices is to charge all overheads other than the prime costs on the basis of percentage of direct wages and to add a mark up of one-ninth of total costs for profit.

While the company is confident of achieving the budget drawn up as above, a new customer approached the company directly for execution of a special order. The direct materials and direct labour costs of the special order are estimated respectively at ₹ 36,000 and ₹ 64,000. This special order is in excess of the budgeted sales as envisaged above. The company submitted a quotation of ₹ 2,00,000 for the special order based on its policy. The new customer is willing to pay a price of ₹ 1,50,000 for the special order. The company is hesitant to accept the order below total cost as, according to the company management, it will lead to a loss.

You are required to state your arguments and advise the management on the acceptance of the special order.

Ans: The order is acceptable at a price of ₹ 1,50,000.

25. Paints Ltd. manufactures 2,00,000 tins of paint at normal capacity. It incurs the following manufacturing costs per unit:

	₹
Direct material	780
Direct labour	210
Variable overhead	250
Fixed overhead	400
Production cost / unit	1640

Each unit is sold for ₹ 2100, with an additional variable selling overhead incurred at ₹ 60 per unit.

During the next quarter, only 10,000 units can be produced and sold. Management plans to shut down the plant estimating that the fixed manufacturing cost can be reduced to ₹ 74,00,000 for the quarter.

When the plant is operating, the fixed overheads are incurred at a uniform rate throughout the year. Additional costs of plant shut down for the quarter are estimated at ₹ 14,00,000.

You are required:

(*i*) To advise whether it is more economical to shut down the plant during the quarter rather than operate the plant.

(*ii*) Calculate the shut down point for the quarter in terms of number of units.

Ans: It is better to shut down and save ₹ 32,00,000.

26. A multi product company has the following costs and output data for the last year.

	Product		
	X	***Y***	***Z***
Sales Mix	40%	35%	25%
	₹	₹	₹
Selling Price	20	25	30
Variable Cost per Unit	10	15	18
Total fixed Cost			1,50,000
Total sales			5,00,000

The Company proposes to replace product *Z* by product S. Estimated cost and output data are:

Sales Mix	50%	30%	20%
Selling Price	20	25	28
Variable Cost per unit	10	15	14
Total fixed costs			1,50,000
Total sales			5,00,000

Analyse the proposed change and suggest what decision the Company should take.

Ans: Profit will increase by ₹ 15,000 if produce *Z* is replaced by product *S*.

27. The management of Quinn Products Co. has been operating at below normal capacity, and there does not appear to be an opportunity to add a new product line that will increase profit.

The production manager suggests that a component, presently being purchased from Patrick Supply Company, can be produced by the Company. Normally, 1,50,000 units of this component are needed each year. The cost to manufacture 1,50,000 units has been estimated as follows:

	₹
Direct materials	11,25,000
Direct labour	6,75,000
Variable overhead	2,25,000
Additional fixed overhead if components are made	90,000
Allocated fixed overhead (100% of direct labour)	6,75,000
Total Cost	27,90,000

This component can be purchased from Patrick Supply Company at a price of ₹ 14.60 per unit. The sales manager objects to this plan, stating that Patrick Supply Company is also a customer and that the company sells 30,000 units of a finished product to the supplier and that these units add ₹ 30,000 to profit each year. This market will be lost if purchase are not made from the supplier. Furthermore, only 1,20,000 units of the component will be needed if the sales are lost, in as much as ₹ 30,000 units of this component are used to make the product sold to Patrick Supply Company.

Required:

Based upon the information given, should Quinn Products Co. make this component or purchase it from Patrick Supply Company. *(M. Com., Delhi)*

Ans: Net advantage in parts production ₹ 12,000. It is advisable to manufacture the parts.

28. Under normal operating conditions, the Beady Machine Company manufactures 6,000 units of a particular product in a six-month period. Each unit contributes ₹ 100 to fixed overhead costs and to profits. The fixed overhead costs for six months amount to ₹ 4,50,000. Strikes at other companies that buy this product have cut sales to a rate of 300 units a month. The company management is considering closing the plant for six months, anticipating that the market will be back to normal at the end of that time. The fixed overhead costs could be reduced to ₹ 2,50,000 for the six months the plant is closed, but the additional cost to protect the facilities and to start the plant up again have been estimated to total ₹ 50,000.

Required:

Should the plant be closed? If not, what is the lowest volume of sales for the next six months which would justify keeping the plant open? Show your workings also. (*M.Com. Delhi*)

Ans: The plant should not be closed. In case of shutdown, loss will be ₹ 3,00,000 which is more than operating loss of ₹ 2,70,000. Minimum sales required to keep the plant open is 1,500 units.

29. Modi Company purchases 10,000 items of a product annually from Bajaj Co. Because the price keeps increasing and reached ₹ 88 per unit last year, Modi's management has asked for a cost estimate to manufacture the items internally. Modi makes stampings and castings and has little experience with products that require assembly.

The engineering, manufacturing, and accounting departments have prepared a report for management that includes the following estimate for an assembly run of 10,000 items. To manufacture the items Modi will hire additional production employees but will need no additional equipment, space, or supervision. The report estimates that total costs for 10,000 units are estimated at ₹ 12,00,000, or ₹ 120 a unit. The current purchase price is ₹ 88 a unit, so the report recommends the continued purchase of the product. If the items are purchased, the currently unused space could be leased for ₹ 1,50,000 annually.

Components	₹ 270,000
Assembly labor*	290,000
Share of existing facility costs based on labor	640,000
Total costs	₹ 12,00,000

*Assembly labor consists of hourly production workers.

Required:

(*a*) Was the analysis prepared by Modi Company's engineering, manufacturing, and accounting departments and their recommendation to continue purchasing the items correct? Explain your answer and include any supporting calculations that you consider necessary.

(*b*) Present several benefits and problems of dealing with outside suppliers such as Bajaj Co.

Ans: Modi Co. should produce the item within the company.

Savings in costs in producing the item within the company, ₹ 1,70,000

30. Hansraj College is an undergaduate college located in New Delhi. It is evaluating its botany programme because the programme's tuition revenues and costs recently produced an ₹ 80,000 loss, which is typical of performance in the past few years. Tuition revenues earned totaled ₹ 320,000; operating expenses were faculty salaries, ₹ 215,000; supplies, ₹ 10,000; and other facility costs, ₹ 175,000. If the program is dropped, the following are expected:

- Some students will change programme, but overall college enrollment will decline as other students transfer to other universities. Total lost tuition revenue is estimated at ₹ 1,95,000.
- Temporary faculty members with combined salaries of ₹ 170,000 can be dismissed. The permanent faculty will transfer to the biology department. In addition, 75 per cent of the program's supplies cost can be saved.

- Other facility costs include ₹ 98,000 of general college overhead costs that are assigned to the programme and ₹ 77,000 of salaries earned by office and support personnel. One of these employees (annual salary, ₹ 22,000) will be transferred to the music department; other employees can be laid off.
- Equipment will be removed and transferred to the fine arts department at a cost of ₹ 1,100. The vacated space can be converted to a weight and physical conditioning facility for student atheletes. This new facility likely will help attract better athletes and make the college's athletic programs more competitive.

Required:

(*a*) Should Hansraj College drop the botany program? Show calculations.

(*b*) What other factors should be considered if the decision is made to drop the program?

(*c*) What options might be open to Hansraj College if it continues the program and the college's chairman mandates that "program losses must be eliminated within three years"?

Ans: (*a*) If the college drops the botany programme, its reduced expenses will exceed its lost revenues by ₹ 37,500.

31. Domestic political trouble in the country of an overseas supplier is causing concern in your company because it is not known when further supplies of raw material 'X' will be received. The current stock held of this particular raw material is 17,000 kgs., which costs ₹ 1,36,000. Based on raw material 'X', your company makes five different products and the expected demand for each of these, for the next three months, is given below together with other relevant information:

Product Code	*Kilogram of raw material 'X' / unit of finished product* (Kg.)	*Direct labour hours/unit of finished product* (Hrs.)	*Selling price/unit* (₹)	*Expected demand over three months* (units)
701	0.7	1.0	26	8,000
702	0.5	0.8	28	7,200
821	1.4	1.5	34	9,000
822	1.3	1.1	38	12,000
937	1.5	1.4	40	10,000

The direct wages rate/hour is ₹ 5 and production overhead is based on direct wages cost. The variable overhead absorption rate being 40% and the fixed overhead absorption rate being 60%. Variable selling costs, including sales commission are 15% of selling price. Budget fixed selling and administration costs are ₹ 3,00,000 per annum. Assume that the fixed production overhead incurred will equal the absorbed figure.

You are required to:

(*i*) Show what quantity of the raw material on hand ought to be allocated to which products in order to maximise profits for the forthcoming three months.

(*ii*) Present a brief statement showing contribution and profit for the forthcoming three months, if your suggestion in (*i*) is adopted.

Ans: (*i*) Product Ranking (Code), 702, 701, 822, 837, 821.

(*ii*) Total profit ₹ 1,27,360.

32. Ramnarayan, manager of an electronics division, was considering an offer by Manohar Swamy, manager of a sister division. Manohar's division was operating below capacity and had just been given an opportunity to produce 8,000 units of one of its products for a customer in a market not normally served. The opportunity involves a product that uses an electrical component produced by Ramnarayan's division. Each unit that Manohar's department produces requires two of the components. However, the price the customer is willing to pay is well below the price usually charged; to make a reasonable profit on the order, Manohar needs a price concession from Ramnarayan's division. Manohar had offered to pay full manufacturing cost for the parts. So that Ramnarayan would know that everything was aboveboard, Manohar had supplied the following unit-cost and price information concerning the special order, excluding the cost of the electrical component:

Selling price	₹ 320
Less Costs:	
Direct materials	(170)
Direct labor	(70)
Variable overhead	(20)
Fixed overhead	(3)
Operating profit	₹ 30

The normal selling price of the electrical component is ₹ 23 per unit. Its full manufacturing cost is ₹ 18.5, (₹ 10.5 variable and ₹ 8.0 fixed). Manohar had argued that paying ₹ 23 per component would wipe out the operating profit and result in division showing a loss. Ramnarayan was interested in the offer because his division was also operating below capacity (the order would not use all the excess capacity).

Required:

(*i*) Should Ram Narayan accept the order at a selling price of ₹ 18.5 per unit? By how much will his division's profits be changed if the order is accepted? By how much will the profits of Manohar division change if Ram agrees to supply the part at full cost?

(*ii*) Suppose that Ramnarayan offers to supply the component at ₹ 20. In offering the price, Ramnarayan says that it is a firm offer not subject to negotiation. Should Manohar accept this price and produce the special order? If Manohar accepts the price, what is the change in profits for Ramnarayan's division?

(*iii*) Assume that Ramnarayan's division is operating at full capacity and that he refuses to supply the part for less than the full price. Should Manohar still accept the special order? Explain.

Ans: (*i*) Order should be accepted at selling price of ₹ 18.5 as it will increase division's profit by ₹ 128,000.

(*ii*) Manohar should accept ₹ 20 price.

(*iii*) Yes.

33. Harish Aggarwal, a management accountant with the Maruti Udyog, is evaluating whether a particular component should continue to be manufactured by Maruti or purchased from Outside Vendor Company. Outside Vendor has submitted a bid to manufacture and supply the 32,000 units of the component that Maruti Udyog will need for 2016 at a selling price of ₹ 173.

Harish has gathered the following information regarding Maruti's costs to manufacture 30,000 units of component in 2015.

	₹
Direct materials	₹ 19,50,000
Direct manufacturing labor	12,00,000
Plant space rental	8,40,000
Equipment leasing	3,60,000
Other manufacturing overhead	22,50,000
Total manufacturing costs	66,00,000

Harish has also collected the following information related to manufacturing the components.

- Price of direct materials used in the production of the component are expected to increase by 8% in 2016.
- Maruti Udyog's direct manufacturing labor contract calls for a 5% increase in 2016.
- Maruti Udyog can withdraw from the plant space rental agreement without any penalty. Maruti Udyog will have no need for this space if component is not manufactured.
- The equipment lease can be terminated by paying ₹ 60,000.
- 40% of the other manufacturing overhead is considered variable. Variable overhead changes proportionately with the number of units produced. The fixed component of other manufacturing overhead costs is expected to remain the same whether or not component is manufactured.

Pradeep, plant manager at Maruti Udyog, indicates to Harish that the current performance of the plant can be significantly improved and that the cost increases he is assuming are unlikely to occur. Hence, the analysis should be done assuming costs will be considerably below current levels. Harish knows that Pradeep is concerned about outsourcing the component because it will mean that some of his close friends will be laid off.
Harish believes that it is unlikely that the plant will achieve the lower costs as Pradeep describes. He is very confident about the accuracy of the information he has collected, but he is also unhappy about laying off employees.

Required:

(*i*) On the basis of the financial information Harish has obtained, should Maruti Udyog make the component or buy it in 2016? Show your calculations.

(*ii*) What other factors should Maruti Udyog consider before making a decision?

(*M.Com, Delhi, 2013*)

Ans: Maruti Udyog should buy from outside vendor.

Savings in cost if purchased from outsider vendor, ₹ 1,54,400

34. Ramanuj, President and general manager of XYZ Company, was concerned about the future of one of the company's largest divisions. The division's most recent quarterly income statement follows:

		₹
	Sales	37,51,500
Less:	Cost of goods sold	27,22,400
	Gross profit	10,29,100
Less:	Selling and administrative expenses	11,00,000
	Operative income (loss)	(70,900)

Ramanuj is giving serious consideration to shutting down the division since this is the ninth consecutive quarter that it has shown a loss. To help him in his decision, the following additional information has been gathered:

- The division produces one product at a selling price of ₹ 100 to outside parties.
- The division sells 50 per cent of its output to another division within the company for ₹ 83 per unit (full manufacturing cost plus 25 percent). The internal price is set by company policy. If the division is shutdown, the user division would buy the part externally for ₹ 100 per unit.
- The fixed overhead assigned per unit is ₹ 20.
- There is no alternative use for the facilities if shut down. The facilities and equipment would be sold and the proceeds invested to produce an annuity of ₹ 1,00,000 per year.
- Of the fixed selling and administrative expenses, 30 per cent represent allocated expenses from corporate headquarters.
- Variable selling expenses are ₹ 5 per-unit sold for units sold externally. These expenses are avoided for internal sales. There are no variable administrative expenses.

Required:

(*a*) Prepare an income statement that more accurately reflects the division's profit performance.

(*b*) Should the president shutdown the division? What would be the effect on the company's profit if the division were closed?

(*M.Com., Delhi University, 2010*)

Ans:

	Outside	**Division within Co.**
(*a*) Net income	₹ 2,37,175	Loss (8825)
Total	₹ 2,28,350	

(*b*) In case of shutdown, the net loss associated with shutdown will be ₹ 18,41,750. Therefore, it is better to operate and not to shutdown.

35. Dronacharya Management Associates (DMA) operates a management consulting firm. It has just received an inquiry from a company as a prospective client about its prices for educational seminars for the prospective client's supervisors. The prospective client wants bids for three alternative activity levels: (1) one seminar with 25 participants (2) four seminars with 20 participants each (80 participants total), or (3) eight seminars with 144 participants in total. The consulting firm's accountants have provided the following differential cost estimates:

Startup Costs for the Entire job	₹ 60,000
Materials Costs per Participant (brouchures, handouts, etc.)	10,000
Differential Direct Labor Costs:	
One Seminar	1,20,000
Four Seminars	5,00,000
Eight Seminars	8,80,000

In addition to the preceding differential costs, DMA allocates fixed costs to jobs on a direct-labor-cost basis, at a rate of 75 per cent of direct labor costs (excluding setup costs). For example, if direct labor costs are ₹ 10,000, DMA would also charge the job ₹ 7,500 for fixed costs. DMA seeks to make a profit of 20 per cent above cost for each job. For this purpose, profit is revenue minus all costs assigned to the job, including allocated fixed costs. DMA has enough excess capacity to handle this job with ease.

Required:

(a) Assume DMA bases its bid on the average total cost, including fixed costs allocated to the job, plus the 20 per cent markup on cost. What should DMA bid for each of the three levels of activity?

(b) Compute the differential cost (including startup cost) and the contribution to profit for each of the three levels of activity.

(c) Assume the prospective client gives three options. It is willing to accept either of DMA's bids for the one-seminar or four-seminar activity levels, but the prospective client will pay only 88 pcr cent of the bid price for the eight-seminar package. DMA's Chief Operating Officer responds, "Taking the order for 12 per cent below our bid would wipe out our profit! Let's take the four-seminar option; we make the most profit on it." Do you agree? What would be the contribution to profit for each of the three options?

Ans:

	One Seminar	*Four seminars*	*Eight seminars*
(a) Bid Price (₹)	6,24,000	20,82,000	36,480
(b) Contribution margin (₹)	1,94,000	7,22,000	12,680

(c) One should disagree with Chief Operating Officer. Eight seminars will provide greater contribution to fixed costs and profit even with the lower price.

36. Jet Airways has leased a single jet aircraft that it operates between Delhi and Bangalore. Only economy class seats are available on this plane. An analyst has collected the following information.

Seating capacity per plane	360 passengers
Average number of passengers per flight	200 passengers
Average one-way fare	₹ 5,000
Variable fuel costs	₹ 1,40,000 per flight
Food and beverage service costs (no charge to passenger)	₹ 200 per passenger
Commission to travel agents paid by Jet Airways (all tickets are booked by travel agents)	8% of fare
Fixed annual lease costs allocated to each flight	₹ 5,30,000 per flight
Fixed ground-services (maintenance, check in, baggage handling)	₹ 70,000 per flight
Fixed flight-crew salaries allocated to each flight	₹ 40,000 per flight

For simplicity, assume that fuel costs are unaffected by the actual number of passengers on a flight

Required:

1. Calculate total contribution margin from passenger that Jet Airways earns on each one-way flight between Delhi and Bangalore.
2. The Market Research Department of Jet Airways indicates that lowering the average one-way fare to ₹ 4,800 will increase the average number of passenger per flight to 212. On the basis of financial considerations alone, should Jet Airways lower its fare? Show your calculations.
3. Travel International, a tour operator, approaches Jet Airways on the possibility of chartering its aircraft. The terms of charter are as follows:

(*a*) For each one-way flight. Travel International will pay Jet Airways ₹ 7,45,000 to charter the plane and to use its flight crew and ground-service staff

(*b*) Travel International will pay for fuel costs; and

(*c*) Travel International will pay for all food costs.

On the basis of financial considerations alone, should Jet Airways accept Travel International offer? Show your calculations. What other factors should Jet Airways consider in deciding whether to charter its plane to Travel International?

Ans: 1. ₹ 8,80,000

2. Total contribution margin ₹ 8,93,792 which is higher than ₹ 8,80,000

3. Jet Airways is better off not charting the plane and instead lowering its own fare.

37. Rohatagi consulting Co is a "head-hunting" firm that provides information about candidates for executive and mid-level positions. Major customers include companies and large size business firms.

The cost per billable hour of service at the company's normal volume of 5,000 billable hours per month is as follows. (A billable hour is one hour billed to a client.)

Average Cost per Hour Billed to Client:		
Variable Labor-Consultants	₹ 200	
Variable Overhead, Including Supplies and Clerical Support	40	
Fixed Overhead, Including Allowance for Unbilled Hours	160	
	₹ 400	
Marketing and Administrative Costs per Billable Hour (all fixed)		100
Total Hourly Cost		500

Treat each question independently. Unless given otherwise, the regular fee per hour is ₹ 600.

Required:

(*a*) How many hours must the firm bill per month to break even?

(*b*) Market research estimates that a fee increase to ₹ 750 per hour would decrease monthly volume to 4,000 hours. The accounting department estimates that fixed costs would be ₹ 10,00,000 while variable costs per hour would remain unchanged. How would a fee increase affect profits?

(*c*) Rohatagi Consulting is operating at its normal volume. It has received a special request from a corporate official to provide investigative services on a special-order basis. Because of the long-term nature of the contract (four months) and the magnitude (1,000 hours per month), the customer believes a fee reduction is in order. The company has a capacity limitation of 6,000 hours per month. Fixed costs will not change if the firm accepts the special order. What is the lowest fee Rohatagi Consulting would be willing to charge?

Ans: (*a*) 3611 hours

(*b*) Profit would increase by ₹ 5,40,000

(*c*) Minimum price will be higher than ₹ 240.

CASES

1. Rakesh was walking down the street on his way back from class when he spotted a beautiful ring in the jewellery store window. He immediately went inside and purchased the ring and had it packed for his new girl friend. When he arrived home, a phone message informed him that his new girl friend had just got engaged to another fellow and she was leaving the university. When he took the ring out of the box to look at it, the setting fell out of the ring. A trip to the jewellery store proved even more frustrating. The manager pointed to the "all sales final" sign and said they would not take it back, and since they were closing the store they no longer had a repair department that could reset the ring. Rakesh also learnt that when he charged the ring to his credit card, it had exceeded his credit limit and within a few days he began to get threatening notices and telephone calls from the bank. Unfortunately, he will not have any money to pay on his credit card bill until next term starts.

   In the light of decision making steps usually applied by decision makers, how these steps could have been used by Rakesh to achieve a more favourable result.?

2. Shalini is deciding where to live during her second year at university. During her first year, she lived in the university hostel. Recently, her friend Surabhi asked her to share an off-campus flat for the uncoming university year. Shalini likes the idea of living in a flat, but she is -concerned about how much it will cost.

   To help her decide what to do, Shalini collected information about costs. She would pay ₹ 4000 per month in rent. The minimum lease term on the apartment is six months. Shalini estimates that her share of the uility bills will be ₹ 750 per month. She also estimates that groceries will cost ₹ 2000 per month. Shalini spent ₹ 3500 on a new sofa over the summer. If she lives in the university hostel, she will put the sofa in storage at a cost of ₹ 350 per month. Shalini expects to spend ₹ 75,000 on university fees and ₹ 4500 on books each semester. Room and board on campus would cost Shalini ₹ 29,000 per semester (five months). This amount includes a food plan of 20 meals per week. This cost is non-refundable if the meals are not eaten.

Required:

(*a*) Use *only* the cost information collected by Shalini for the following tasks.

- (*i*) List all of the costs for each option.
- (*ii*) Review your lists and cross out the costs that are irrelevant to Shalini's decision. Explain why these costs are irrelevant.
- (*iii*) Calculate and compare the total *relevant* costs of each option.
- (*iv*) Given the cost comparison, which living arrangement is the better choice for Shalini? Explain.

(*b*) Identify uncertainties in the cost information collected by Shalini.

- (*i*) Determine whether each cost is likely to be (1) known for sure, (2) estimated with little uncertainty, or (3) estimated with moderate or high uncertainty.
- (*ii*) For each cost that is known for sure, explain where Shalini would obtain the information.
- (*iii*) For each cost that must be estimated, explain why the cost cannot be known.

(*c*) List additional information that might be relevant to Shalini's decision (list as many items as you can).

- (*i*) Costs not identified by Shalini
- (*ii*) Factors other than costs

(*d*) Explain why conducting a cost comparison is useful to Shalini, even if factors other than costs are important to her decision.

(*e*) Consider your own preferences for this problem. Do you expect Shalini's preferences to be the same as yours? How can you control for your biases as you give Shalini advice?

(*f*) Think about what Shalini's priorities might be for choosing a housing arrangement. How might different priorities lead to different choices?

(*g*) Describe how information that Shalini gains over this next year might affect her future housing arrangements.

3. A Banglore-based Stamping plant, was one of the largest and most modern steel plants in India. It began producing parts for Compro's model cars in 2012.

The Company's plant consisted of a series of processes. The first process cut sheets of metal to the desired size. Each subsequent process performed bending, punching or shaping operations. After the metal was passed through the last process in the line, it was bonderized and shipped to the different assembly plants.

The company had a large toolroom capable of producing smaller dies and many of the other tools and specially designed jigs and fixtures required by the extensive production equipment used in the plant. In the early part of 2017, the toolroom was operating at considerably less than capacity and this was a source of concern to the plant manager.

In March 2017, Mr. Ram, the plant manager, called a meeting to discuss what should be done about the toolroom. Attending the meeting were Shyam, the Controller, Ghanshym, the Manager of Purchasing, and Mohan, the Toolroom Manager.

Following is an edited version of the meeting.

Ram: It seems to me we have to develop a policy for deciding what tools and dies we should make ourselves and which ones we should buy. At the present time, we have a lot of excess capacity in the toolroom.

Ghanshyam: It seems to me that we should make those tools and dies on which we can make an adequate profit, say 10% over cost. If the purchase price of a die or tool is less than our cost plus 10%, we should buy it. Otherwise, we should make it, if we have capacity.

Mohan: If I had to meet the overhead costs in this plant, I'd never make anything. The other producers don't have the overhead that we have. They don't have our training programme, company newspapers, engineers, and accountants. Also, their pay scales are considerably less than ours. As a result, they can outbid me every time. I think we should make any tool or die as along as my variable costs are less than the purchase price.

Shyam: I can't agree with that position. All of your costs, except material, are fixed. If we follow your policy, we would decide all make-or-buy decisions in favour of making. We could fill the toolroom with parts on which we would be losing our shirts. It seems to me that we should produce nothing unless our total costs are less than the purchase price.

Ram: I would be a little worried about Mohan's suggestion too. How do we know that we are making the most profitable items? Also, what we do when the toolroom reaches capacity? Do we just fill the toolroom with everything until we use up its capacity and then buy everything else? If we did this, the decision as to whether we should make or buy an item would depend on the timing of the purchase order. Today, we have capacity, so we make it; tomorrow, our capacity is committed, so we buy it. How do we know that today's part isn't a lot more profitable than yesterday's?

Ghanshyam: I certainly disagree with Mohan. I have to keep our vendors reasonably happy; otherwise, we'll be in trouble when we need them.

Ram: We aren't getting anywhere here. We need to utilize our toolroom capacity. We need to produce the parts that earn us the most money. It would be better to have a proposed policy that will meet these two objectives.

Required:

Recommend a make-or-buy policy for the Banglore-based Stamping Plant. In this recommendation, be sure to include the following:

(*a*) The policy to be followed where excess capacity exists in the toolroom.

(*b*) The policy to be followed when there is no excess capacity in the toolroom.

(*c*) A workable definition of capacity-that is to say, if the policies for (*a*) and (*b*) are different, how can the Manager of Purchasing know whether capacity exists or not?

(*d*) Details as to what should be included in costs if the policy includes the use of cost data.

(*e*) An explanation telling why your policy will not result in filling the toolroom with unprofitable parts.

4. In the beginning of the year 2017, Prosoft Technology Ltd. developed and marketed business applications software for minicomputers, achieving a significant market share and a secure position in the industry. After maturing at this level of success, the company's mission became less clear. Further, software development for minicomputers was seen as costly with little value to the company, as the market for major business applications was saturated and the minor applications have limited markets.

In order to maintain Prosoft's market share, management decided to enter the growing personal computer field. While major programming would be required to make the company's existing software compatible with personal computers (PCs), management viewed the commitment of all personnel to this project as critical to the continued growth of Prosoft.

After weeks of executive strategy sessions regarding product specifications, management imposed the task deadlines and set the date for the introduction of its first PC product, an accounting package for general ledger, accounts payable, and accounts receivable applications. Three months prior to the introduction date, Prosoft began an advertising and dealer promotion campaign announcing the new product and setting the introduction date. Several technical problems arose during development, but the staff believed that a few time saving measures would enable them to complete the package in time to meet the announced date, Management felt considerable pressure to meet this date as Prosoft had previously missed an announced date and suffered the consequences. Two weeks before the announced date, Prosoft's marketing personnel learnt that an updated version of the PC operating software that Prosoft's new package was designed to interact with, was to be released shortly. The marketing staff knew that features could quickly be added to Prosoft's new product to take advantage of the new features in the operating software; however, there would not be time to field test the programme changes. The technical personnel warned the marketing staff of the dangers of releasing a product without proper field testing. But these warnings were not heeded. Management, with encouragement from the marketing staff, made the decision to incorporate the features necessary to take advantage of the new operating software and introduce the product on the scheduled date.

Not long after Prosoft despatched the first lots of its new software, customers began to complain about processing problems in the accounts payable and accounts receivables modules. Very quickly, it was determined that portions of Prosoft's new package were not compatible with the updated operating software. To correct the problem, the company had to rewrite the software and manuals and replace all existing products. The technical personnel were not dedicated to the development of the next PC product and this problem fragmented their efforts. The revised product was not available for three months, causing a loss of sales. The financial impact of the ₹ 5 crore error on the company with annual profits of ₹ 4 crore was devastating.

Required:

(*a*) Identify the steps in the general decision-making process.
(*b*) Using the steps identified in Requirement (*a*), describe the weaknesses in Prosoft's decision-making process.
(*c*) Recommend changes to correct the weaknesses identified in Requirement (*b*).

(*M.Com., Delhi,* 2002)

5. Sportway Inc, is a wholesale distributor supplying a wide range of moderately priced sporting equipment to large chain stores. About 60 per cent of Sportways's products are purchased from other companies, while the remainder of the products are manufactured by Sportway. The company's plastics department is currently manufacturing molded fishing tackle boxes. Sportway is able to manufacture and sell 8,000 tackle boxes annually, making full use of its direct labour capacity available at workstations. Following are the selling price and costs associated with Sportways's tackle boxes.

	(₹)	(₹)
Selling price per box		8600
Costs per box:		
Molded plastic	800	
Hinges, latches, handle	900	
Direct labour (₹ 1500/hour)	1875	
Manufacturing overhead	1250	
Selling and administrative expenses	1700	6525
Profit per box		2075

Because Sportway believes it could sell 12,000 tackle boxes if it had sufficient manufacturing capacity, the company has looked into the possibility of purchasing the tackle boxes for distribution. Maple Products, a steady supplier of quality products, would be able to provide up to 9,000 tackle boxes per year at a price of ₹ 6800 per box delivered to Sportway's facility.

Bart Johnson, Sportway's product manager, has suggested that the company could make better use of its plastic department by manufacturing skateboards. To support his position, Bart has a market study that indicates an expanding market for skateboards and a need for additional suppliers. He believes that Sportway could expect to sell 17,500 skateboards annually at a price of ₹ 4500 per skateboard. Bart's estimate of the costs to manufacture the skateboards follows:

	(₹)	(₹)
Selling price per skateboard		4500
Costs per skateboard:		
Molded plastic	550	
Wheels, hardware	700	
Direct labour (₹1500/hour)	750	
Manufacturing overhead	500	
Selling and administrative expenses	900	3400
Profit per skateboard		1100

In the plastics department, Sportway uses direct labour hours as the application base for manufacturing overhead. Included in the manufacturing overhead for the current year is ₹ 50,00,000 of factorywide, fixed manufacturing overhead that has been allocated to the plastics department. For each unit of product that Sportway sells, regardless of whether the product has been purchased or is manufactured by Sportway, an allocated ₹ 600 fixed overhead cost per unit for distribution is included in the selling and administrative expenses for all products. Total selling and administrative expenses for the purchased tackle boxes would be ₹ 1000 per unit.

Required:

(*a*) In order to maximize the company's profitability, prepare an analysis based on the data presented that will show which product or products Sportway, Inc. should manufacture and/ or purchase. It should also show the associated financial impact. Support your answer with appropriate calculations.

(*b*) Discuss some qualitative factors that might impact on Sportway's decision.

(*CMA, USA, Adapted with permission*)

Ans: (*a*) To maximize the company's profitability, Sportway should purchase 9,000 tackle boxes from Maple Products, manufacture 17,500 skateboards and 1,000 tackle boxes.

Improvement in total contribution margin ₹ 2,36,25,000.

6. Gian Auto Corporation manufactures automobiles, vans, and trucks. Among the various Gian Auto plants around the United States is the Denver Cover plant, where vinyl covers and upholstery fabric are sewn. These are used to cover interior seating and other surfaces of Gian Auto products.

Pam Vosilo is the plant manager for Denver Cover. The plant was the first Gian Auto plant in the region. As other area plants were opened, Pam, in recognition of her management ability, was given the responsibility of managing them. She functions as a regional manager although the budget for her and her staff is charged to the Denver plant.

Pam has just received a report indicating that GianAuto could purchase the entire annual output of Denver Cover from outside suppliers for ₹ 300 lakhs. Pam is astonished at the low outside price because the budget for Denver Cover's operating costs was set at ₹ 520 lakhs. She believes that Denver Cover will have to close down operations in order to realize the ₹ 220 lakhs in annual cost savings.

The budget (in thousands) for Denver Cover's operating costs for the coming year follows:

	(₹)	(₹)
Materials		12,000
Labour:		
Direct	13,000	
Supervision	3,000	
indirect plant	4,000	20,000
Overhead:		
Depreciation (equipment)	5,000	
Depreciation (building)	3,000	
Pension expenses	4,000	

Plant manager and staff	2,000	
Corporate allocation	6,000	20,000
Total budgeted costs		52,000

Additional facts regarding the plant's operations are as follows:

- Due to Denver Cover's commitment to use high-quality fabrics in all its products, the purchasing department was instructed to place blanket orders with major suppliers to ensure the receipt of sufficient materials for the coming year. If these orders are cancelled as a consequence of the plant closing, termination charges would amount to 15 per cent of the cost of direct materials.
- Approximately 700 plant employees will lose their jobs if the plant is closed. This includes all direct labourers and supervisors as well as the plumbers, electricians, and other skilled workers classified as indirect plant workers. Some would be able to find new jobs, but many others would have difficulty. All employees would have difficulty matching Denver Cover's base pay of ₹ 9.40 per hour, the highest in the area. A clause in Denver Cover's contract with the union may help some employees; the company must provide employment assistance to its former employees for 12 months after a plant closing. The estimated cost to administer this service would be ₹ 10 lakhs for the year.
- Some employees would probably elect early retirement because Denver Cover has an excellent pension plan. In fact, ₹ 30 lakhs of next year's pension expense would continue whether Denver Cover is open or not.
- Pam and her staff would not be affected by the closing of Denver Cover. They would still be responsible for administering three other area plants.
- Denver Cover considers equipment depreciation to be a variable cost and uses the units-of-production method to depreciate its equipment; Denver Cover is the only GianAuto plant to use this depreciation method. However, Denver Cover uses the customary straight-line method to depreciate its building.

Required:

1. Prepare a quantitative analysis to help in deciding whether or not to close the Denver Cover plant. Explain how you treated the nonrecurring relevant costs.
2. Consider the analysis in Requirement 1 and add to it the qualitative factors that you believe are important to the decision. What is your decision? Would you close the plant? Explain

(*CMA, USA, Adapted with permission*)

Ans:

	Make	**Buy**
First year	₹ 3,60,00,000	3,58,00,000
Subsequent years	₹ 3,60,00,000	3,30,00,000

Denver Cover Plant should be closed.

7. Ashwani Kumar is manager of the Delhi Public Schools in National Capital Region (NCR) of Delhi. He is preparing for the upcoming meeting of the D.P. School Board. In addition to presenting reports on the routine operations of schools in the NCR, Ashwini will be expected to make recommendations on two special agenda items. The first item addresses

the number of high school classroom teachers for the next school year; the second involves the inclusion of computer courses in the education programme. Both of these items have budget implications that must be addressed. Ashwini is responsible for developing the NCR budget under the direction of, and within the guidelines, established by the Delhi Public School Board. Once the board approves the budget, it is voted on by the citizens representatives in the NCR, i.e., the citizens accept or reject the budget.

Ashwini must determine the number of teachers that will be needed to teach classes 10, 11, and 12 at Delhi Public School next year. The salary line is always the largest single item in the school budget and will be the subject of intense discussion before it is voted on by the citizens representatives. To aid in making his recommendations, Ashwini has the following information available: the current high school enrollment, the current ninth class enrollment, historical data on students transferring in and out of the region, and statistics on the number of students that can be expected to drop out of Delhi Public School. The Delhi Public School has always maintained a teacher-student ratio that is at or above the state average.

The Principals at Delhi Public Schools have proposed that the computer facilities at the school be utilized in the evenings to conduct adult education courses to gain increased benefits from the investment in these facilities. Ashwini has been given little information about this programme although he has been told that additional materials would be required (e.g., additional software and training manual) which could be expensive. There is little formal information available about local interest in a programme of this nature, and Ashwini is not sure that the programme will generate enough revenue to defray the costs. Based on Ashwini's recommendation, a decision about this programme will be reached at the next meeting.

Required:

(*a*) Identify the steps in the general decision-making process under rational and objective conditions.

(*b*) Citing examples from the situation given above, identify the areas and steps which would require comprehensive investigation and decision in the decision-making process.

8. Prior to last year, Big Bazar Company had not kept departmental income statements. To achieve better management control, the company decided to install department-by-department accounts. At the end of last year, the new accounts showed that although the business as a whole was profitable, the Dry Fruits Department had shown a substantial loss. The income statement for the Dry Fruits Department, shown here, reports on operations for 2016.

Dry Fruits Department

Income Statement for the Year Ending 2016

Sales	₹ 2,50,00,000	
Cost of Goods Sold	1,87,50,000	
Gross Margin		₹ 62,50,000
Costs:		
Payroll, Direct Labor, and Supervision	₹ 16,50,000	
Commissions of Sales Staff[a]	15,00,000	

Rent[b]	13,00,000	
State govt. Taxes[c]	1,50,000	
Insurance on Inventory	2,00,000	
Depreciation[d]	3,50,000	
Administration and General Office[e]	11,00,000	
Interest for Inventory Carrying Costs[f]	2,50,000	
Total Costs		65,00,000
Loss before Income Taxes		₹ (2,50,000)

Additional Computations:

[a]All sales staff are compensated on straight commission at a uniform 6 per cent of all sales.

[b]Rent is charged to departments on a square-foot basis. The company rents an entire building, and the Dry Fruits Department occupies 15 per cent of the building.

[c]Assessed annually on the basis of average inventory on hand each month.

[d]5 per cent of cost of departmental equipment.

[e]Allocated on basis of departmental sales as a fraction of total company sales.

[f]Based on average inventory quantity multiplied by the company's borrowing rate for three-month loans.

Analysis of these results has led management to suggest that it close the Dry Fruits Department. Members of the management team agree that keeping the Dry Fruits Department is not essential to maintaining good customer relations and supporting the rest of the company's business. In other words, eliminating the Dry Fruits Department is not expected to affect the amount of business done by the other departments.

Required:

What action do you recommend to management of Big Bazar Company in the short run? Why?

Ans: Dry Fruits Department be continued as it makes ₹ 25,00,000 contribution to overhead.

(M.Com. Delhi, 2014)

9. Omex Builders has been offered a contract by Excel Ltd. to build for it five special Guest Houses for use by top management. Each Guest House will be an independent one. The contract will be for a period of one year and the offer price is ₹ One crore. In addition Excel Ltd. will also provide 2 grounds of land, free of cost, for the purpose of construction. The Chief Accountant of Omex Builders has prepared an estimate on the basis of which he has advised that the contract should not be accepted at the price offered. His estimate was as follows:

		₹ In lacs
Land (3 Ground at ₹ 20 lacs each)		60
Drawings and design		7
Registration		10
Materials:		
	Cement and Sand	6
	Bricks and Tiles	4
	Steel	10

	Others (including interior decoration)	10
Labour – Skilled		12
	– Unskilled	8
	– Supervisor's Salary	5
Overheads General		12
	Depreciation	6
	Total Cost	150

The Accountant also provides the following information:

Land: The total requirement of land is 3 grounds costing ₹ 20 lacs per ground Excel Ltd. will provide 2 grounds free of cost.

Drawing and Design: These have already been prepared and 50% of the cost has already been incurred.

Materials:

(*i*) Cement and sand are already in stock and are in regular use. If used for this contract, they have to be replaced at a cost of ₹ 8 lacks.

(*ii*) Bricks and tiles represent purchases made several months before for a different contract. They could be sold readily for a net ₹ 5 lacks after meeting all further expenses.

(*iii*) Others: Materials worth ₹ 2 lacs relating to interior decoration are in stock for which no alternative use is expected in the near future. However they can be sold for ₹ 1 lac.

Labour:

(*i*) Skilled workers will be transferred to this project from another 'project. The Project Manager claimed that if the men were returned to him, he could have earned the company an additional ₹ 2 lacs in terms of profits.

(*ii*) The supervisor undertakes various tasks in the sites and his pay and continuity of employment will not be affected by the new contract. If the contract is taken, he will devote half of his time.

Overheads:

(*i*) The equipment that would be used on the contract was bought one year before for ₹ 30 lacks and is expected to last for five years. It can also be used on other contracts and the current replacement price might be ₹ 32 lacs and in a year's time it will be ₹ 25 lacks.

(*ii*) The general overheads includes both specific and absorbed overheads. If the contract is not undertaken, ₹ 4 lacks of the same can be avoided.

Omex Builders has also on hand another project, which would not be executed if the contract from Excel Ltd. were to be accepted. The estimated profit on that project is ₹ 10 lacs.

In the light of information given above, you are required to indicate with reasons whether the contract from Excel Ltd. should be accepted or not.

Ans: Total relevant costs are ₹ 93 lakhs and the offer price is ₹ 1 crore. The offer should be accepted.

10. A Ltd., which is a good customer of B Ltd, has asked B to produce 400 units of a special variation of one of the standard products that it buys from B Ltd. The estimated full cost of producing each unit of the standard product is ₹ 900, of which ₹ 600 is variable cost and ₹ 300 is allocated fixed cost. The selling price is ₹ 1080 per unit. Although B is not geared to make the modifications required, it decides for 'customer relationship' reasons to agree to go ahead and supply the order. It will be possible to modify up to 100 of the special units each 40 hour week, without disrupting regular production, but special machinery will be required for the purpose. There are three alternative ways of obtaining this machinery. Details are as follows:

1. *Adapting existing machinery*

   The existing machinery which could be adapted is not being used at present, although it is envisaged that in approximately three months it will be required in its present form for a contract currently being negotiated. Costs of adapting this machinery would be ₹ 45,000, and after the order has been completed it would cost ₹ 54,000 to remove the adaptations and replace worn parts, etc., in order to return the machine to its current value. The machinery which could be adapted originally cost ₹ 3,00,000 five years ago and is being depreciated at ₹ 30,000 p.a. A special insurance policy would have to be held while it was operated in its adapted form, the fixed annual premium associated with this being 2% of the value of the machine when adapted. The current value of the machine is ₹ 90,000. Variable operating costs associated with using the adapted machinery would be; labour ₹ 90 per hour and maintenance ₹ 45 per hour.

2. *Hiring specialist machinery*

   The charge for hiring suitable machinery, which includes maintenance and insurance, but no labour costs, is ₹ 150 per production hour with a minimum hire charge of ₹ 9000 per week.

3. *Purchasing specialist machinery*

   To buy a new machine would cost ₹ 1,50,000. Operating, maintenance and insurance costs would be on the same basis as for the adapted one. The manufacturers of the machinery estimate that it loses value at the rate of ₹ 60 for every unit produced, and on this basis they are prepared to repurchase any machinery sold by them, after deducting a further 10% of the residual value to cover transaction expenses.

Required:

(*i*) Prepare a report to the managers of B Ltd, advising them which of the alternative courses of action would be most beneficial, based upon the given information. Indicate ways in which your recommendation might be further improved. In your report suggest a price to be charged to A Ltd. for the modified product, mentioning the factors which should be considered before a final decision is taken.

(*ii*) Suppose that A Ltd. was willing to place a continuing order for the modified product. In this new situation, broadly explain the alterations needed to produce a long-run cost analysis of the alternatives.

Ans: (*i*) Hiring specialist machinery would be beneficial. Price (a) when units would not otherwise have been manufactured, ₹ 4,92,480. (b) Units could otherwise have been sold, ₹ 5,64,480.

(*ii*) Costs of three alternative should be appraised and decision would be taken accordingly.

11. "At last, I can see some light at the end of the tunnel," said Chandrasekhar, president of Jaico Products. "Our losses have shrunk from over ₹ 75,000 a month at the beginning of the year to only ₹ 26,000 for March. If we can just isolate the remaining problems with products A and C, will be in the black by the first of next year."

The company's income statement for the latest month (March) is presented below (absorption costing basis):

Income Statement
For March

	Total Company	Product A	Product B	Product C
Sales	₹ 15,00,000	₹ 6,00,000	₹ 4,00,000	₹ 5,00,000
Less cost of goods sold	9,22,000	3,72,000	2,20,000	3,30,000
Gross margins	5,78,000	2,28,000	1,80,000	1,70,000
Less operating expenses:				
Selling	4,24,000	1,62,000	1,12,000	1,50,000
Administrative	1,80,000	72,000	48,000	60,000
Total operating expenses	6,04,000	2,34,000	1,60,000	2,10,000
Net income (loss)	₹ (26,000)	₹ (6,000)	₹ 20,000	₹ (40,000)

"What recommendations did that business consultant make?" asked Mr. Chandrasekhar. "We paid the guy ₹ 100 an hour, surely he found something wrong." "He says our problems are concealed by the way we make up our statements," replied Kavita, the executive vice president. "He left us some data on what he calls 'traceable' and 'common' costs that he says we should be isolating in our reports." The data to which Ms. Kavita was referring are shown below:

	Total Company	Product A	Product B	Product C
Variable costs:*				
Production (materials, labour, and variable overhead)	—	18%	32%	20%
Selling	—	10%	8%	10%
Traceable fixed costs:				
Production	₹ 376,00	₹ 180,000	₹ 36,000	₹ 160,000
Selling	282,000	102,000	80,000	100,000
Common fixed costs:				
Production	210,000	—	—	—
Administrative	180,000	—	—	—

*As a percentage of sales.

"I don't see anything wrong with our statements," said Mr. Chandrasekhar. "Raghav, our chief accountant, says that he has been using this format for over 30 years. He is also very careful to allocate all of our costs to the products."

"I'll admit that Raghav always seems to be on top of things," replied Ms. Kavita. "By the way, purchasing says that the X7 chips we use in products A and B are on back order and won't be available for several weeks. From the looks of March's income statement, we had better concentrate our remaining inventory of X7 chips on product B." (Two X7 chips are used in both product A and product B.)

The following additional information is available on the company:

(*a*) Work in process and finished goods inventories are negligible and can be ignored.

(*b*) Products A and B each sell for ₹ 250 per unit, and product C sells for ₹ 125 per unit. Strong market demand exists for all three products.

Required:

1. Prepare a new income statement for March, segmented by product and using the contribution approach. Show both Amount and per cent columns for the company in total and for each product.
2. Assume that Mr Chandrasekhar is considering the elimination of product C due to the losses it is incurring. Based on the statement you prepared in (1) above, what points would you make for or against elimination of product C?
3. Do you agree with the company's decision to concentrate the remaining inventory of X7 chips on product B? Why or why not?
4. Product C is sold in both a vending and a home market with sales and cost data as follows:

		Market	
	Total	**Vending**	**Home**
Sales	₹ 500,000	₹ 50,000	₹ 450,000
Variable costs:*			
Production	—	20%	20%
Selling	—	28%	8%
Traceable fixed costs:			
Selling	₹ 75,000	₹ 45,000	₹ 30,000

*As a percentage of sales.

The remainder of product C's fixed selling costs and all of product C's fixed production costs are common to the markets in which product C is sold.

(a) Prepare an income statement showing product C segmented by market. Use the contribution approach and show both Amount and per cent columns for the product in total and for each market.

(b) What points revealed by this statement would you be particularly anxious to bring to the attention of management?

Ans: 1. Total net loss ₹ 26,000

2. Product C should not be eliminated.
3. No, the company should concentrate its remaining inventory of X7 chips on Product A, not Product B.
4. (a) Product C margin ₹ 90,000.

12. The Midwest Division of the Paibec Corporation manufactures subassemblies used in Paibec's final products. Lynn Hard of Midwest's profit planning department has been assigned the task of determining whether Midwest should continue to manufacture a subassembly component, MTR-2000, or purchase it from Marley Company, an outside supplier. Marley has submitted a bid to manufacture and supply the 32,000 units of MTR-2000 that Paibec will need for 2017 at a unit price of ₹ 17.30. Marley has assured Paibec that the units will be delivered according to Paibec's production specifications and needs. The contract price of ₹ 17.30 is applicable only in 2017, but Marley is interested in entering into a long-term arrangement beyond 2017.

Lynn has submitted the following information regarding Midwest's cost to manufacture 30,000 units of MTR-2000 in 2016.

Direct material	₹ 195,000
Direct labor	120,000
Factory space rental	84,000
Equipment leasing costs	36,000
Other manufacturing costs	225,000
Total manufacturing costs	₹ 660,000

Lynn has collected the following information related to manufacturing MTR-2000:

- Equipment leasing costs represent special equipment used to manufacture MTR-2000. Midwest can terminate this lease by paying the equivalent of one month's lease payment for each of the two years left on its lease agreement.
- Forty per cent of the other manufacturing overhead is considered variable. Variable overhead changes with the number of units produced, and this rate per unit is not expected to change in 2017. The fixed manufacturing overhead costs are not expected to change whether Midwest manufactures or purchases MTR-2000. Midwest can use equipment other than the leased equipment in its other manufacturing operations.
- Direct material cost used in the production of MTR-2000 is expected to increase 8 per cent in 2017.
- Midwest's direct labor contract calls for a 5 per cent wage increase in 2017.
- The facilities used to manufacture MTR-2000 are rented under a month-to-month rental agreement. Midwest would have no need for this space if it does not manufacture MTR-2000. Thus, Midwest can withdraw from the rental agreement without any penalty.

John Porter, Midwest divisional manager, stopped by Lynn's office to voice his opinion regarding the outsourcing of MTR-2000. He commented, "I am really concerned about outsourcing MTR-2000. I have a son-in-law and a nephew, not to mention a member of our bowling team, who works on MTR-2000. They could lose their jobs if we buy that component from Marley. I really would appreciate anything you can do to make sure the cost analysis shows that we should continue making MTR-2000. Corporate is not aware of materials cost increase and may be you can leave out some of those fixed costs. I just think we should continue making MTR-2000."

Required:

1. Prepare a relevant cost analysis that shows whether the Midwest Division should make MTR-2000 or purchase it from Marley Company for 2017.
2. Identify and briefly discuss the strategic factors that Midwest should consider in this decision.
3. By referring to the specific ethical standards for management accountants, assess the ethical issues in John Porter's request of Lynn Hardt.(*CMA USA Adapted*)

Ans: 1. Midwest Division should purchase the parts for a saving of ₹ 15,440.

13. Atlas Manufacturing Co. produces exercise bicycles. The costs of manufacturing and marketing exercise bicycles at the company's normal volume of 3,000 units per month is as follows:

Atlas Manufacturing
Cost per Unit

Unit Manufacturing Costs:		
Variable Materials	₹ 100	
Variable Labor	150	
Variable Overhead	50	
Fixed Overhead	200	
Total Unit Manufacturing Costs		₹ 500
Unit Non-manufacturing Costs		
Variable	₹ 100	
Fixed	100	
Total Unit Non-manufacturing Costs		200
Total Unit Costs		₹ 700

Unless otherwise stated, assume that the situations described in the questions are not connected; treat each independently. Unless otherwise stated, assume a regular selling price of ₹ 1,000 per unit and a volume of 3,000 bicycles per month.

(a) Market research estimates that volume could be increased to 3,500 units, which is well within production capacity limitations if the price were cut from ₹ 1,000 to ₹ 900 per unit. Assuming that the cost behavior patterns implied by the data given above are correct, would you recommend taking this action? What would be the impact on monthly sales, costs, and income?

(b) On March 1, Jindal Co. offers Atlas a contract to supply 500 units to Jindal Co. hospitals for a March 31 delivery. Because of an unusually large number of rush orders from its regular customers, Atlas plans to produce 4,000 units during March, which will use all available capacity. If it accepts the Atlas order, it would lose 500 units normally sold to regular customers to a competitor. The Jindal contract would reimburse its "share of March manufacturing costs" plus pay a ₹ 50,000 fixed fee (profit). (No variable marketing costs would be incurred on the order's units). What impact would accepting the contract have on March income? (Part of your problem is to figure out the meaning of "share of March manufacturing costs").

(c) Atlas has an opportunity to enter a new market. An attraction of the new market is that its demand is higher when the domestic market's demand is quite low; thus, idle production facilities could be used without affecting normal business.

An order for 1,000 units is being sought at a below-normal price to enter this market. For this order, shipping costs will total ₹ 75 per unit; total (marketing) costs to obtain the contract will be ₹ 4,000. No other variable marketing costs would be required on this order, and it would not affect domestic business. What is the minimum unit price that Atlas should consider for this order of 1,000 units?

(d) An inventory of 200 units of an obsolete model of the exercise bicycle remains in the stockroom. These must be sold through regular channels (has incurring variable marketing costs) at reduced prices or the inventory will soon be valueless. What is the minimum acceptable selling price for these units?

(e) Atlas Manufacturing receives a proposal from an outside contractor who will make and ship 1,000 units per month directly to Atlas Manufacturing's customers.

The proposal would not affect Atlas Manufacturing's fixed non-manufacturing costs, but its variable non-manufacturing costs would decline by 20 per cent for these 1,000 units produced by the contractor. Atlas Manufacturing's plant would operate at two-thirds of its normal level. Total fixed manufacturing costs would decline by 30 percent. What in-house unit cost should the firm use to compare with the quotation received from the supplier? Should the firm accept the proposal for a price (that is, payment to the contractor) of ₹ 600 per unit?

(f) Assume the same facts as in part (e) except that the firm will use idle facilities to produce 800 low-impact bicycles per month that would be sold to people with injuries or other physical impairments. It can sell these low-impact bicycles for ₹ 1,200 each, while the costs of production would be ₹ 700 per unit variable manufacturing cost. Variable non-manufacturing costs would be ₹ 100 per unit. Fixed non-manufacturing and manufacturing costs will not change whether the firm manufactures the original 3,000 regular bicycles or the mix of 2,000 regular bicycles plus 800 low-impact bicycles. What is the maximum purchase price per unit that Atlas Manufacturing should be willing to pay the outside contractor? Should it accept the proposal for a price of ₹ 600 per unit?

Ans: (a) Lowering prices reduces operating profit to ₹ 8,50,000 from ₹ 9,00,000.

(b) Do not accept contract, Income with contract ₹ 13,25,000, Income without contract ₹ 15,00,000.

(c) Minimum price ₹ 379.

(d) Minimum price ₹ 100 (differential costs).

(e) ₹ 500 per unit maximum purchase price.

(f) Maximum purchase price ₹ 600.

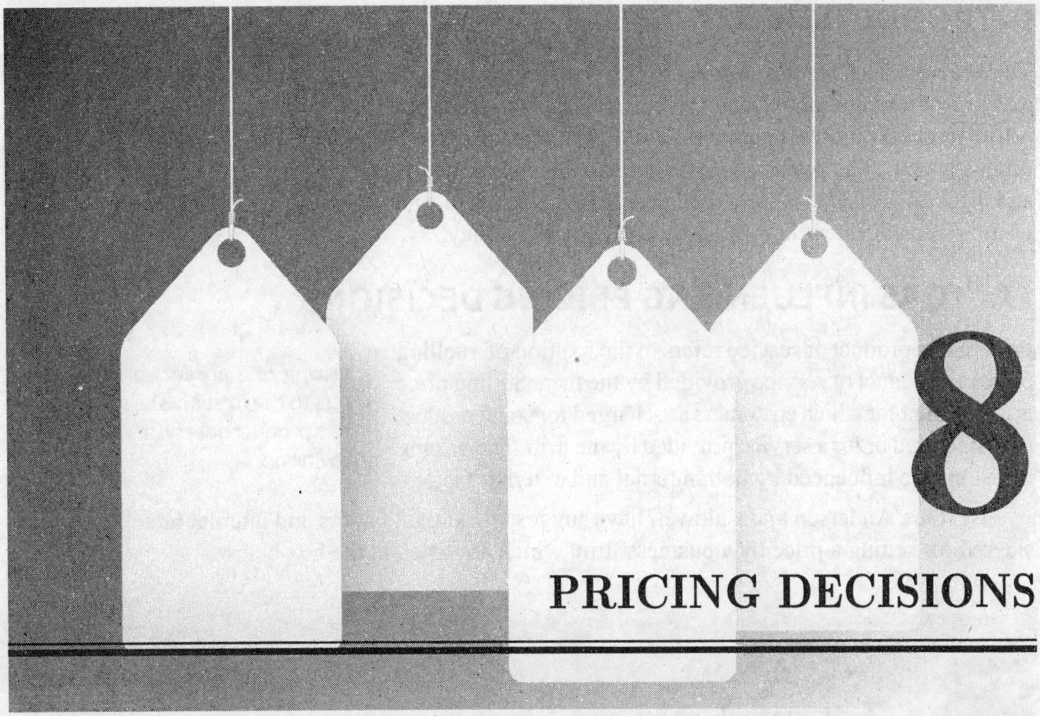

8

PRICING DECISIONS

LEARNING OBJECTIVES:

After reading this chapter, you should be able to:

- Explain the Factors Influencing Pricing Decisions
- Explain Different Methods of Pricing
- Understand Short-run and Long-run Pricing Decisions
- Explain the Concept of Competitive Pricing, Target Pricing, Pricing in Life cycle Product Costing, Pareto Analysis in Pricing Decisions, Economic Approach to Pricing
- Identify Price Indifference Point

INTRODUCTION

The previous chapter has discussed how relevant revenue and cost analysis help management in making various alternative choice decisions such as make or buy, add or drop product, product mix, sell or process further, operate or shutdown, replace or retain, buy or lease, special order, export proposals, etc. The present chapter discusses 'pricing decisions' which is one of the most crucial and difficult decisions which a business firm has to make, and analyses how cost information can be useful to management in framing suitable pricing policy.

FACTORS INFLUENCING PRICING DECISIONS

Pricing of a product or service refers to the fixation of a selling price to a product or service provided by the firm. Selling price is the amount for which customers are charged for some product manufactured or for a service provided by the firm. The pricing decisions are influenced by both internal and external factors.

Pricing of a product or service refers to the fixation of a selling price to a product or service provided by the firm.

Needles, Anderson and Caldwell have suggested external factors and internal factors to be considered for setting a price by a business firm, which are listed in the box below.

Factors in Setting a Price

External Factors:

Total demand for product or service and its elasticity
Number of competing products or services
Quality of competing products or services
Current prices of competing products or services
Customer's preferences for quality versus price
Sole source versus heavy competition (Number of suppliers in the market)
Seasonal demand or continual demand
Life of product or service
Economic and political climate and trends and likely changes in them in future.
Type of industry to which the product belongs and future outlook of the industry.
Governmental guidelines, if any.

Internal Factors:

Cost of product or service
— Variable costs
— Full absorption costs
— Total costs
— Replacements, Standard or any other cost base
Price geared toward return on investment
Loss leader or main product
Quality of materials and labour inputs
Labour intensive or automated process
Markup percentage updated
Usage of scarce resources
Firm's profit and other objectives
Pricing decision as a longrun decision or short term decision or a one time spare capacity decision

Source: Belverd E. Needles, Henry R. Anderson and James C. Caldwell, Financial and Managerial Accounting, Houghton Mifflin Company, 1988, p. 905.

Among the many factors influencing the pricing decisions, the three major influences are customers, competitors and costs.[1]

1. *Customers:* Managers examine pricing problems through the eyes of their customers. Increasing prices may cause the loss of a customer to a competitor or it may cause a customer to choose a less expensive substitute product.

2. *Competitors:* No business operates in a vacuum. Competitors' reactions also influence pricing decisions. A competitor's aggressive pricing may force a business to lower its prices to be competitive. On the other hand, a business without a competitor can set higher prices. A business with knowledge of its competitor's technology, plant capacity and operating policies is able to estimate its competitors' cost, which is valuable information in setting prices. Managers consider both their domestic and international competition in making pricing decisions. Firms with excess capacity because demand is low in domestic markets may price aggressively in their export markets.

3. *Costs:* Costs influence prices because they affect supply. The lower the cost relative to the price, the greater the quantity of product the company is willing to supply. A product that is consistently priced below its cost can drain large amounts of resources from an organisation.

In making pricing decisions, all the above three factors are important. However, when setting prices, companies weigh customers, competitors and costs differently. Companies selling homogeneous products in highly competitive markets must accept the market price. In less competitive markets, products are differentiated and managers have some discretion in setting prices. As competition further decreases, the key factor affecting pricing decisions is the customers' willingness to pay, not costs or competitors. Pricing strategy is now being accepted as a tool for providing customer satisfaction and continuous improvement of the product as well.

DIFFERENT METHODS OF PRICING

The different methods of pricing are discussed in detail below.

Total Cost Plus or Full Cost Plus Pricing

Total cost plus or full cost pricing involves all costs plus a profit margin.

Total cost plus or full cost plus pricing involves all costs plus a profit margin. It includes not only the product's direct costs but also the indirect costs incurred by the overall company which have to be allocated to different products. An obvious problem in this method is the determination of total costs. If multiple products are manufactured, the cost determination process is complex. In this situation, indirect or non-manufacturing costs have to be distributed among the different products in order to determine finally the full cost of different products. An example of price calculation using cost plus method is as follows:

		(₹)	(₹)
	Direct material		100
	Direct labour		200
	Factory Overheads:		
	Fixed	150	
	Variable	50	200
	Total manufacturing cost		500
	Non-manufacturing overheads:		
	Fixed	100	
	Variable	—	100
	Total Cost		600
Add:	Profit margin (25% on total cost)		150
	Selling price		750

Advantages

Full cost plus method has the following advantages:

- It is simple to operate if cost structures of products are known
- The pricing decision under full cost approach becomes standardised and such decisions can easily be delegated to lower management
- It ensures recovery of total costs and also provides a reasonable rate of return to the firm
- It helps a business firm to predict the selling prices of other competitive firms, especially of those firms who are having similar cost structures
- This pricing method is important in contracting industries where price of the contracts needs to be determined considering fixed costs also
- This method does not require estimating demand of products before fixing the selling prices. Instead, a standard profit margin on total cost can be used
- This brings stability in the pricing policy and selling price can be justified to customers. On the other hand, prices based on less than total cost such as marginal cost may prompt the customers to believe that the low price will prevail, in absence of which consumers will be dissatisfied and the firm can face serious problem
- Full cost pricing is consistent with absorption costing system
- If similar technologies and techniques are employed within an industry, such that there is likely to be broad comparability of cost structures between different firms operating in the industry, then widespread use of cost-plus methods can lead to a high degree of price stability

Disadvantages

Full cost method has the following disadvantages too:

- It ignores demand and competition and may result into under-pricing or over-pricing of products.
- Fixed costs are likely to be distributed on some arbitrary basis as there are different methods of apportionment and thus total costs of different products will be different depending on which apportionment method is used.
- In full cost pricing, the choice of volume or capacity base is very important. There are different concepts of capacity starting from maximum to normal or lower, or expected and different unit product costs will emerge under these concepts. It means selling prices will be subject to wider fluctuations.
- This method does not distinguish between relevant costs (e.g., variable costs and incremental fixed costs) and irrelevant costs (fixed costs).
- The proper treatment of fixed cost presents a problem in full costs pricing. As volume increases, the fixed cost and full cost per unit decreases. If price follows cost, price goes down and further spurs demand. Unfortunately, the opposite is more distressing. As volume decreases, full cost increases. As price goes up, demand falls and volume declines again — a downward spiral. Hence, any attempt to consider the demand situation in establishing the full cost of the product involves circular reasoning.
- This method cannot always shield the firm from a loss. When the product is priced higher, the unit cost (considering the fixed costs as well) and sales demand falls below the volume level used to calculate the fixed cost per unit, the total sales revenue will be inadequate to cover the total fixed costs. In other words, full cost pricing will ensure recovery of total costs and earning of target profit when sales volume is equal to or more than the volume or capacity level which has been used to estimate total unit costs.

Within full cost plus method, some other cost bases can be used for determining the selling price such as manufacturing cost plus or conversion cost plus.

Manufacturing Cost Plus Pricing

Manufacturing cost (or product cost) plus pricing includes cost incurred specifically for manufacturing the product plus a profit margin. The profit margin added to this cost must cover all operating expenses and generate a satisfactory level of profit. Using the information given in the earlier example, a cost of ₹ 500 will be used. To this cost, a higher profit margin needs to be added to cover non-manufacturing overheads as well as to provide a satisfactory level of profit to the firm. For example, selling price calculation may be as follows:

Total manufacturing costs	₹ 500
Add: Profit margin (50% on manufacturing cost)	₹ 250
Selling price	₹ 750

Conversion Cost Plus Pricing

Conversion cost plus pricing uses conversion cost for determining the selling price and to this cost a profit margin is added. This pricing method is generally followed when the customer provides the materials. This method depends on the assumption that greater profits can be realised if efforts are directed to products requiring less labour and overhead because more units can be produced and sold.

Rate of Return Pricing

Determination of return on capital employed is one of the most crucial aspects of price fixation process. In this process instead of arbitrarily adding a percentage on cost for profit, the firm determines an average markup on cost necessary to produce a desired rate of return on its investment. Under this method three issues arise:

(*a*) The basis on which the capital employed is computed

(*b*) Which items should be covered in the return on capital

(*c*) What rate of return can be regarded as fair

The rate of return to be earned by the firm or industry must depend on the risk involved. The desirability of earning adequate profits for the purpose of ploughing back into business should be kept in mind.

Situations Under which Full Cost Plus Pricing can be used

Most companies rely on full cost information reports when setting prices. There is economic justification for reliance on full costs for pricing decisions in three types of circumstances[2]:

1. Many contracts for the development and production of customised products and many contracts with government agencies specify that prices should equal full costs plus a markup. Prices set in regulated industries such as electric utilities also are based on full costs.
2. When a firm enters into a long-term contractual relationship with a customer to supply a product, most activity costs are likely to emerge and full costs become relevant for the long term pricing decisions.
3. The third situation is representative of many industries. When demand is low, firms adjust the prices downward to acquire additional business based on the lower incremental costs when surplus capacity is available. Conversely, when demand for products is high, firms adjust the prices upward based on the higher incremental costs when capacity is fully utilised.

Because demand conditions fluctuate overtime, prices also fluctuate overtime with demand conditions. Although the fluctuating short-term prices are based on the appropriate incremental costs, over the long run, their average tends to equal the price based on the full costs that will be recovered in a long-term contract. In other words, the price determined by adding on a markup to the full costs of a product serves as a bench mark or target price from which the firm can adjust prices up or down depending on demand conditions[3].

On the strengths and weaknesses of full cost-based prices, Decoster et al.[4] observe the following:

(*i*) Although the cost-based pricing formula is simple, it does not agree with economic theory, because it ignores the relationships between demand and price and between price and volume. The price determined by full cost plus a markup may be so high that there are no customers. If so, some of the volume potential of the firm will be idle. There is a circularity problem. Volume is used to determine price in the full cost based pricing formula, yet the number of units the company sells and therefore the firm's volume, may depend on price.

(*ii*) A principal reason (for the wider use of pricing policies based on full cost) is the inability of the decision maker to quantify the demand curve. This inability to apply economic theory leads the business manager to apply intuitive judgement coupled with trial-and-error methods. Many decision-makers begin with a full cost approach and then, on the basis of buyer's reaction, adjust the price. In this way, the full cost based price represents a first approximation — a target price whose markup must be adjusted to meet the actual market place.

(*iii*) Another reason for the adoption of full costs-based prices is the belief that theory represent a "floor" or "safe" price that will prevent losses. This safety factor is more illusory than real. Although the per-unit sales price will cover the per-unit full cost, losses may still be incurred if the sales volume is not achieved.

(*iv*) Perhaps the most convincing reason for the use of cost-based prices is that the costs of a particular firm are comparable with costs of other firms in the industry. One firm's costs are reasonable estimates of its competitors' costs, and hence its prices are likely to be comparable to those of its competitors. If most companies use similar facilities to perform similar activities, they will have similar full costs, and thus, similar prices if they produce at about the same volume level.

Marginal Cost Plus Pricing

This method, also known as contribution approach, uses only variable costs as the basis for pricing. Fixed costs are not added to the product, service or contract. This pricing method emphasizes the relationship between prices and costs that vary directly with sales. It ignores fixed costs altogether. However, fixed cost should be taken into account in determining the profit margin to be added to variable costs to arrive at the selling price.

Marginal cost approach helps a business firm to enter into new markets easily, to increase its competitive position in the existing markets, to survive during trade depressions, to utilise spare available capacity, to dispose off surplus or obsolete stock, to make profitable special order decisions.

Marginal cost-plus pricing also known as contribution approach uses only variable cost as the basis for pricing. It ignores fixed costs.

Marginal cost-plus pricing brings some disadvantages to the firm as well. For instance, recovery of fixed costs may be doubted. There is likely to be undesirable competition for cutting prices to a lower level. In case management decides to increase lower marginal cost pricing, it may face dissatisfaction from the consumers.

Using the information given in the earlier example, marginal costs of ₹ 350 can be used to set the selling price. Obviously, it indicates the cost below which the price should not fall, otherwise the company would have losses. Also, a higher profit margin can be added to marginal cost which may work as a long term selling price even for normal sales. For instance, if the profit margin of 100% is added to marginal costs of ₹ 350, the selling price will be ₹ 700.

Marginal cost plus method is useful in those situations where a firm has recovered its total fixed costs from sales in the normal market but is unable to increase its further sales in that market. If still spare capacity is available, the firm may attempt to sell to some other customers or markets at lower (marginal cost-plus) price which will provide some contribution towards fixed cost and thus profit will increase. For a long-term pricing policy, it is necessary that a higher profit margin should be added to marginal cost to recover both variable and fixed costs in the long run. A smaller profit margin will lead to low sales revenue which will not be sufficient to recover fixed costs.

Differential Cost Plus Pricing

This method involves adding a markup on differential cost which is the increase in total cost resulting from the production of additional units. Differential cost pricing differs from variable cost pricing in which a mark up on variable cost is added, whereas both variable costs and fixed costs are included in the differential costs on which a markup is determined. This method can be applied where some revenue above differential cost may be received rather than no revenue at all. Such additional revenue makes some contribution towards the recovery of fixed costs which are already incurred.

Standard Costs

Standard costs represent the costs that should be attained under efficient operating conditions at a normal capacity. The cost-based methods discussed earlier have some adverse implications and include costs due to inefficient manufacturing, wasteful operations, etc. That is, it is likely that unnecessary costs may be assigned to the product. On the other hand, standard costs use costs from efficient operations plus the agreed profit. Also, pricing can be done more quickly. However, before standards are used as a basis for pricing decisions, care should be taken to see that the standards established reflect current conditions. While using standard costs, variances must be controlled carefully to ensure that prices reflect realistic production costs. If standard costs differ from actual costs significantly, the standard costs should be modified to conform to real operating situations.

SHORT-RUN VS. LONG-RUN PRICING DECISIONS

The time horizon of the decision is critical in computing the relevant costs in a pricing decision. The two ends of the time horizon are: Short-Run and Long-Run.

Short-run Pricing Decisions

Short-run decisions include pricing for a one-time-only special order with no long-term implications. The time horizon is typically six months or less. Business firms can encounter situations where they are faced with the opportunity of bidding for a one-time special order in competition with other suppliers. In this situation, only the incremental costs of undertaking the order should be taken into account. It is likely that most of the resources required to fill the order have already been acquired and the cost of these resources will be incurred whether or not the bid is accepted by the customer. In manufacturing companies, incremental costs of one-time special order will include:

1. Additional materials required to comply with the order.
2. Additional labour, overtime and other labour costs.
3. Power, fuel and maintenance costs for the machinery and equipment required to fulfill the order.

In service companies, incremental costs of providing some additional services would be very less. For instance, the incremental cost of accepting one-time special business by a hotel would comprise the cost of additional meals, bathroom facilities and laundering.

In most situations, incremental costs to be incurred relate to unit-level activities. The companies have already resources incurred for batch, product and service-sustaining activities.

According to Colin Drury[5], any bid for one-time special orders that is based on covering only short-term incremental costs must meet all of the following conditions:

1. Sufficient capacity is available for all resources that are required to fulfil the order. If some resources are fully utilised, opportunity costs of scarce resources must be covered by the bid price.
2. The bid price will not affect the future selling prices and the customer will not expect repeat business to be priced to cover short term incremental costs.
3. The order will utilise unused capacity for only a short period and capacity will be released for use on more profitable opportunities. If more profitable opportunities do not exist and a short term focus is always adopted to utilise unused capacity, then the effect of pricing a series of special orders over several periods to cover incremental costs constitutes a long term decision. Thus, the situation arises whereby the decision to reduce capacity is continually deferred and short-term incremental costs are used for long-term decisions.

Long-run Pricing Decisions

Short-run pricing decisions are not appropriate for long-run pricing policy since short-run pricing policy is subject to short-run demand and supply conditions. Most firms use full cost information while setting long-run pricing decisions. In the long-run, firms can adjust the supply of virtually all of their activity resources. Therefore, a product or service should be priced to cover all of the resources that are committed to it. If a firm is unable to generate sufficient revenues to cover the long run costs of all its products and its business sustaining costs, then it will make losses and will not be able to survive. There is a need for determining accurately the long-run or full costs of individual products or services so that product pricing decisions for the long-run can be made satisfactorily.

In the previous section, full cost-based prices has already been discussed.

COMPETITIVE PRICING

When a business firm fixes its price mainly on the consideration of what its competitors are charging, its pricing policy under such a situation is called competitive pricing or competition-oriented pricing. It is not necessary under competitive pricing to charge the same price as charged by the firm's competitors. But under such a pricing, the firm may keep its prices lower or higher than its competitors by a certain percentage. A firm's *own costs or demand may* change, but it maintains its price because its competitors maintain their prices. Also, the firm may change its price when its competitors change their prices, even if its own costs or demand have not altered. Two types of competitive pricing are generally found:

> When a business firm fixes its price mainly on the consideration of what its competitors are charging, its pricing policy under such a situation is called **competitive pricing.**

(*i*) Going rate pricing
(*ii*) Sealed bid pricing

> **Going rate pricing** is a competitive pricing method under which a firm tries to keep its price at the average level charged by the industry.

Going Rate Pricing

Going rate pricing is a competitive pricing method under which a firm tries to keep its price at the average level charged by the industry. The use of such a practice of pricing is especially useful where it is difficult to measure costs. Adoption of going rate pricing may yield fair return and also would be least disruptive for industry's harmony.

Going rate pricing primarily reflects pricing practice in homogeneous product markets. The firm selling a homogeneous product in a highly competitive market has actually very little choice about the setting of its price. The firm which is going to charge more than the going rate would attract virtually no customers. The firm should not charge less because it can sell its output at the going rate. Going rate pricing generally applies to homogeneous products such as food, textiles, raw materials, etc.

Sealed bid-pricing

Competitive pricing is also found in those situations where firms compete on the basis of bids, such as original equipment manufacturer and defence contract work. The bid is the firm's offer, price which is the pricing based on expectations of how competitors will price rather than on a firm's own costs or demand. The objective of the firm in the bidding situation is to get the contract, and this means that it hopes to set its price lower than that set by any of the other bidding firms. In practice, however the firm does not ordinarily set its price below a certain level. If a firm is keen to get the contract with a view to keep its plant, manpower and other resources busy, still it cannot quote a price below its marginal cost. Further, if the firm quotes its price higher than marginal cost, it may provide profit to it but the firm has little chance of getting the contract.

TARGET PRICING

A target price is the estimated price for a product or service that potential customers will be willing to pay. This estimate is based on an understanding of customers' perceived value for a product and competitors' responses. The target price forms the basis for calculating target costs. A target cost is the estimated long-run cost of a product or service and when a product or service is sold, the target price enables the company to achieve targeted profit. Target cost is derived by subtracting the target profit from the target price. Developing target prices and target costs requires the following five steps:

> **Target price** is the estimated price for a product or service that potential customers will be willing to pay.

- Develop a product that satisfies the needs of potential customers
- Choose a target price based on customers' perceived value for the product and the prices competitors charge
- Derive a target cost by subtracting the desired profit margin from the target price
- Estimate the actual cost of the product
- If estimated actual cost exceeds the target cost, investigate ways of driving down the actual cost to the target cost

As stated earlier, managers generally use a cost-based approach for long-term pricing decision and in this cost-based approach, a markup is added to the cost base.

On cost-plus pricing and target price, Horngreen, Datar and Foster[5] make the following observation.

> The target pricing approach reduces the need to go back and forth among prospective cost-plus prices, customer reactions, and design modifications. Instead, the target-pricing approach first determines product characteristics and target price on the basis of customer preferences and expected competitor responses. Market considerations and the target price then serve to focus and motivate managers to reduce costs ("cost down") and achieve the target cost and the target operating income. Sometimes the target cost is not achieved. Managers must then redesign the product, or work with a smaller profit margin.

LIFE CYCLE PRODUCT COSTING AND PRICING

Business firms need to consider how to cost and price a product over a multiyear product life cycle. The product life cycle considers the time from initial research and development on a product to when customer servicing and support is no longer offered for that product. Life cycle costing tracks costs attributable to each product from start to finish. Life cycle costs provide important information for pricing. A product life cycle budget highlights to managers the importance of setting prices that will cover all life cycle costs. Life cycle budgeting is related closely to target pricing and target costing.

A different notion of life cycle costs is customer life cycle costs. Customer life cycle costs focus on the total costs incurred by a customer to acquire and use a product or service until it is replaced. Customer life cycle costs can be an important consideration in the pricing decision.

PARETO ANALYSIS IN PRICING DECISIONS

Vilfredo, an Italian economist, has propounded that 70% – 80% of value represents 20% – 30% of volume. This proposition can be noticed in many business areas such as the following :

- Stock Control
- Customer profitability
- Quality control
- Pricing of a product in a multiproduct situation
- Activity-Based Costing (20% cost drivers are responsible for 80% of total cost)

In pricing decisions, Pareto Analysis is very useful to a multiproduct company. Pareto Analysis may indicate that 80% of a firm's sales revenue come from 20% of its products. Such analysis helps the management to design appropriate pricing strategies for 80% of its product groups so that they can contribute more in overall sales revenue of the firm. Those products which constitute 20% of the total products may require a different pricing strategy. This may signal to the management to adopt a more sophisticated and competitive advantage pricing because these products are essential for the company survival. Further, attempts should be made by a firm to convert 80% products (which currently contribute poorly to total sales) into more profit making products.

ECONOMIC APPROACH TO PRICING

In many cases, cost information is of vital importance in pricing decisions. The discussion in the preceding sections has focussed on how pricing decisions are influenced by the cost of the product, actions of competitors and the extent to which customers value the product.

In economics, the basic assumption is that a firm will attempt to set the selling price at a level where profits are maximised. The firm has a profit maximising goal and known cost and revenue functions. Typically increase in sales quantities require reduction in selling prices, causing marginal revenue (the varying increment in total revenue derived from the sale of an additional unit) to decline as sales increase. Increase in production causes an increase in marginal cost (the varying amount in total cost required to produce and sell an additional unit of production). In economic theory, profits are maximised at the sales volume where marginal revenues equal marginal costs. Firms continue to produce as long as the marginal revenue derived from the sale of each additional unit exceeds the marginal cost of producing that unit. Economic theory provides a useful framework for thinking about pricing decisions. The ideal price is the one that will lead customers to purchase all the units a firm can provide up to the point where the last unit has a marginal cost exactly equal to its marginal revenue.

Economists argue that pricing should be set with a recognition of demand considerations, not just on costs. They show mathematically—after making appropriate assumptions—that firms in a somewhat monopolistic situation can maximize their profits at the price-output combination where marginal revenue equals marginal costs. In situations in which managers know the algebric form of both the demand and the cost curves, it is a simple computation to calculate the price-output combination that maximizes company profits.

In practice, however, managers rarely follow the economists' prescriptions. Two big factors have limited the applicability of the economists' pricing model:

1. Difficulty in estimating the demand curve
2. Difficulty in estimating the cost curve[6]

Economic theory is seldom used for pricing decisions. There are many difficulties such as the following:

Firstly, economic models assume that a firm can estimate a demand curve for its products. Most firms have hundreds of different products and varieties and it is therefore an extremely difficult task to estimate demand curves at the individual product level. The problem becomes even more complex when competitive reactions are taken into account since these are likely to impact the price/demand estimates that have been incorporated in the demand curve.

Secondly, economic theory assumes that only price influences the quantity demanded. However, in reality, demand of a product is influenced by many factors such as product quality, packaging, advertising and promotion, after-sales service etc. Therefore, any theory which uses only price factor to determine customer demand would not be able to measure it correctly.

Morse, Davis and Hartgraves observe[7]:

> Perfect competition and an indefinite time period are required to achieve equilibrium prices where marginal revenues equal marginal costs. In the short run, most for-profit organisations attempt to achieve a target profit rather than a maximum profit. One reason for this is an inability to determine the single set of actions that will lead to profit maximisation. Furthermore, managers are more apt to strive to satisfy a number of goals (such as profit for investors, job security for themselves and their employees, and being a good corporate citizen) than to strive for the maximization of a single profit goal. In any case, to maximise profits, a company's management would have to know the cost and revenue functions of every product the firm sells. For most firms, this information cannot be developed at a reasonable cost.

PRICE INDIFFERENCE POINT

> **Price Indifference Point** is the sales level at which a firm's net income is same between two pricing alternatives.

A price indifference point is the sales level at which a firm's net income is same between two pricing alternatives. The price indifference point indicates the volume of sales at which the new price gives a profit equal to the profit of old sales volume and price. In case, sales volume at new price is lower than sales volume at old price (when there is price indifference point), firm should reject the price increase since firm's profit will decrease. In contrary to this, if expected sales volume with price increase is greater than the price indifference point, profit will increase. Price indifference point's concept is very useful in short-term decision making situations.

Illustrative Problem 1 (Determining Minimum Price)

S Limited is engaged in manufacturing activities. It has received a request from one of its important customers to supply a product which will require conversion of material 'M', which is a non-moving item.

The following details are available:

Book value of material M	₹ 60
Realisable value of material M	₹ 80
Replacement cost of material M	₹ 100

It is estimated that conversion of one unit of 'M' into one unit of the finished product will require one labour hour. At present, labour is paid at the rate of ₹ 20 per hour. Other costs are as follows:

Out-of-pocket expenses	₹ 30 per unit
Allocated overheads	₹ 10 per unit

The labour will be re-deployed from other activities. It is estimated that the temporary redeployment will not result in loss of contribution. The employees to be re-deployed are permanent employees of the company.

Required:

Estimate the minimum price to be charged from the customer so that the company is not worse off by executing the order.

Solution:

Relevant costs of producing one unit of the finished product

	₹
Cost of material 'M' (realisable value)	80
Cost of labour (Being sunk cost)	0
Out-of-pocket expenses	30
	110

Allocated overhead is not relevant for the decision. The customer should be charged ₹ 110 per unit.

Illustrative Problem 2 (Return on Capital and Selling Price)

The cost structure of a product is :

Direct materials	₹ 6
Direct labour	₹ 2
Variable overheads	₹ 4
Fixed overhead	₹ 5,10,000

Sales 50,000 units per annum

The capital employed in fixed assets is ₹ 12 lakh and its current assets is 50% of sales. Determine the selling price per unit to earn a return of 20% on capital employed.

Solution:

Working Notes:

Current assets	= 50% of sales
Fixed assets	= ₹ 12,00,000

Let total sales be x

Capital employed

= Fixed assets + current assets

= 12,00,000 + 50% of sales

Return on Capital Employed

= 0.20 (12,00,000 + 0.50 x)

= 2,40,000 + 0.10 x

Calculation of Total Cost of 50,000 units

		(₹)
Direct material	@ ₹ 6	3,00,000
Direct labour	@ ₹ 2	1,00,000
Variable overheads	@ ₹ 4	2,00,000
Fixed overheads		5,10,000
Total cost		11,10,000

Sales = Total cost + Return on capital employed

x = 11,10,000 + (2,40,000 + 0.10x)

x = 13,50,000 + 0.10x

x – 0.10x = 13,50,000

0.90x = 13,50,000

x = 13,50,000 ÷ 0.90

∴ Sales = ₹ 15,00,000

Selling price per unit = ₹ 15,00,000 ÷ 50,000 units

= ₹ 30 per unit

Illustrative Problem 3 (Minimum Price Calculation)

R. Ltd. will produce 3,00,000 kgs of S and 6,00,000 kgs of Y from an input of 9,00,000 kgs of raw material Z. The selling price of S is ₹ 800 per kg and that of Y is a ₹ 600 per kg.

Processing costs amount to ₹ 54 crores per month as under:

		(₹)
Raw material Z	(9,00,000 kgs at ₹ 300 per kg)	27,00,00,000
Variable processing costs		18,00,00,000
Fixed processing costs		9,00,00,000
Total		54,00,00,000

There is an offer to purchase 60,000 kgs of Y additionally at a price of ₹ 400 per kg. The existing market for Y will not be affected by accepting the offer. But the price of S is likely to be decreased uniformly on all sales. Find the minimum reduced average price for S to sustain the increased sales.

Solution:

Since S and Y are produced simultaneously from an input of raw material Z, therefore, when additionally 60,000 kg of Y will be produced, then 30,000 kgs of S will also be produced simultaneously. The input of material Z required for these additional 60,000 kgs of Y and 30,000 kgs of S will be 90,000 kgs of material Z. Hence, the cost of processing 90,000 kgs of material will be as follows:

		(₹)
Cost of raw material Z	(90,000 kgs × ₹ 300)	2,70,00,000
Variable processing cost	(90,000 kgs × ₹ 200)	1,80,00,000
Total cost of processing		4,50,00,000
Less: Sales revenue from 60,000 kgs of Y	(60,000 kg × ₹ 400)	2,40,00,000
Balance cost to be recovered		2,10,00,000
Current sales revenue from the sale of 3,00,000 kgs of S	(3,00,000 kgs × ₹ 800)	24,00,00,000
Total sales revenue to be earned from the sale of S	(3,00,000 kgs + 30,000 kgs)	26,10,00,000
Hence, minimum reduced price per kg of S to recover ₹ 26,10,00,000 from the sale of 3,30,000 kgs of S (₹ 26,10,00,000 ÷ 3,30,000 kgs)		791

Illustrative Problem 4 (Selling Price to Earn Desired Profit)

Relevant particulars of a product are:

Direct material cost	50%
Direct wages cost	20%
Overheads	30%
Selling price	₹ 80,000

It is anticipated the next year the direct materials and direct labour costs will increase by 20% and 25% respectively. The effect of the increase in costs will cause a reduction of 25% in the amount of profit. Calculate the selling price required to be fixed for next year to earn the same percentage of profit on selling price as at present.

Solution:

Let the total cost = X

Profit = Y

X + Y = ₹ 80,000 (*i*)

After increase

	Current	*Increase*	*Revised*
Direct materials	50%	20%	60%
Direct labour	20%	25%	25%
Overheads	30%		30%
			115%

Profit = 0.75 Y

1.15*x* + 0.75Y = 80,000

Solving equations (i) and (ii)

we get X = 50,000 Y = 30,000

Increased cost $= ₹\ 50{,}000 \times \frac{115}{100} = ₹\ 57{,}500$

Profit % $= \frac{₹\ 30{,}000}{₹\ 80{,}000} \times 100 = 37.5\%$ of Cost

$= 62.50\%$

Increased selling price required $= \frac{₹\ 57{,}500}{₹\ 62.50} \times 100$

$= ₹\ 92{,}000$

Illustrative Problem 5 (Budgeted Profit and Selling Price)

The following figures are available from the records of the Bright Manufacturing Co. for the year ended 31-3-2017:

	(₹)
Sales (30,000 units)	4,50,000
Sales returns, discounts etc.	13,500
Cost of sales	3,06,000
Selling expenses	60,000
General expenses	30,000

The Budget Committee of the Company has estimated the following changes in the Income and Costs for the next year :

30% increase in the number of units sold

20% increase in material cost per unit

15% increase in direct labour cost per unit

10% increase in production overhead cost per unit

14% increase in selling expenses to attain higher volume

7% increase in general expenses

Inventory quantities are expected to remain fairly constant, hence, it is decided to ignore any change in inventory valuation. The composition of the cost of a unit of finished goods during the last year was in the ratio of 3 : 2 : 1 for material, direct labour and overheads respectively. No change is contemplated in the current year.

From the above data, you are required to compute the unit sale price at which the concern should sell the product in the current year to earn a budgeted profit of ₹ 60,000.

Solution:

Profitability statement for the year ended 31-3-2017

		(₹)
Sales		4,50,000
Less: Costs :		
Cost of sales	3,06,000	
Sales returns, discounts etc.	13,500	
Selling expenses	60,000	
General expenses	30,000	4,09,500
Profit		40,500

Budgeted profitability statement for the year ended 31-3-2018

		(₹)
Costs:		
Material	(1,53,000 × 130 ÷ 100 × 120 ÷ 100)	2,38,680
Direct labour	(1,02,000 × 130 ÷ 100 × 115 ÷ 100)	1,52,490
Overheads	(51,000 × 130 ÷ 100 × 100 ÷ 100)	72,930
Selling expenses	(60,000 × 114 ÷ 100)	68,400
General expenses	(30,000 × 107 ÷ 110)	32,100
Total budgeted cost		5,64,600
Add: Desired profit		60,000
Desired sales revenue		6,24,600

After considering sales returns @ 3%, the gross desired sales revenue is ₹ 6,24,600 × 100 ÷ 97 = ₹ 6,43,918.

Selling price to be fixed of the year ended 31-3-2018

$$= \frac{₹\,6,43,918}{39,000 \text{ units}} = ₹\,16.51 \text{ per unit}$$

Illustrative Problem 6 (Target Cost Pricing)

Hindustan Motor Corporation uses target costing. Assume that Hindustan marketing personnel estimate that the competitive selling price for the new model car in the upcoming year will need to be ₹ 2,20,000. Assume further that the Car's total unit cost for the upcoming year is estimated to be ₹ 1,81,000 and that Hindustan requires a 20% profit margin on selling price (which is equivalent to a 25% markup on total cost).

a. What price will Hindustan establish for the new model car for the upcoming year?

b. What impact will target costing have on Hindustan Motor Corporation, given the assumed information?

Solution:

a. The price will be set at the estimated market price required to remain competitive, or ₹ 2,20,000. Under the target cost concept, the market dictates the price, not the markup on cost.

b. The required profit margin of 20% of the estimated ₹ 2,20,000 price implies a ₹ 1,76,000 target product cost as follows:

Target Product Cost = ₹ 2,20,000 – (₹ 2,20,000 × 20%)

Target Product Cost = ₹ 2,20,000 – ₹ 44,000

Target Product Cost = ₹ 1,76,000

Since the estimated manufacturing cost of ₹ 1,81,000 exceeds the target cost of ₹ 1,76,000, Hindustan Motor Corporation will try to remove ₹ 5,000 from its total costs in order to maintain competitive pricing within its profit objectives.

Comments: Target costing provides pressure to keep costs competitive. The method assumes that the company may not be able to successfully add a markup to its costs because the resulting price may be too high in the market-place. For example, merely adding the 25% markup on the

₹ 1,81,000 product cost would result in an uncompetitive price of ₹ 2,26,250. The target cost concept moves backward by taking the price as given and then determining the cost that is required for a given profit objective.

Illustrative Problem 7 (Pricing Policy)

The budgeted cost data of a product manufactured by XYZ Co. Ltd. is furnished as below:

Budgeted units to be produced	2,00,000
Variable cost (₹)	32 per unit
Fixed cost (₹)	16 lacs

It is proposed to adopt cost plus pricing approach with a mark-up of 25% on full budgeted cost basis.

However, research by the marketing department indicates that demand of the product in the market is price sensitive. The likely market responses are as follows:

Selling price (₹ per unit)	44	48	50	56	60
Annual Demand (units)	1,68,000	1,52,000	1,40,000	1,28,000	1,08,000

Analyse the above situation and determine the best course of action.

(CA Final, Nov. 2015)

Solution:

Analysis of Cost plus Pricing Approach

The company has a plan to produce 2,00,000 units and it proposed to adopt Cost *plus* Pricing approach with a markup of 25% on full budgeted cost. To achieve this pricing policy, the company has to sell its product at the price calculated below:

Qty.	2,00,000 units
Variable Cost (2,00,000 units × ₹ 32)	64,00,000
Add: Fixed Cost	16,00,000
Total Budgeted Cost	80,00,000
Add: Profit (25% of ₹ 80,00,000)	20,00,000
Revenue (need to earn)	1,00,00,000
Selling Price per unit $\left(\frac{₹\,1,00,00,000}{2,00,000\text{ units}}\right)$	50 p.u.

However, at selling price ₹ 50 per unit, the company can sell 1,40,000 units only, which is 60,000 units less than the budgeted production units.

After analyzing the price-demand pattern in the market (which is price sensitive), to sell all the budgeted units, market price needs to be further lowered, which might be lower than the total cost of production.

Statement Showing "Profit at Different Demand & Price Levels"

	I	II	III	IV	Budgeted
Qty. (units)	1,68,000	1,52,000	1,40,000	1,28,000	1,08,000
	₹	₹	₹	₹	₹
Sales	73,92,000	72,96,000	70,00,000	71,68,000	64,80,000
Less: Variable Cost	53,76,000	48,64,000	44,80,000	40,96,000	34,56,000
Total Contribution	20,16,000	24,32,000	25,20,000	30,72,000	30,24,000
Less: Fixed Cost	16,00,000	16,00,000	16,00,000	16,00,000	16,00,000
Profit (₹)	4,16,000	8,32,000	9,20,000	14,72,000	14,24,000
Profit (% on total cost)	5.96	12.87	15.13	25.84%	28.10%

Determination of the Best Course of Action

(*i*) Taking the above calculation and analysis into account, the company should produce and sell 1,28,000 units at ₹ 56. At this price, company will not only be able to achieve its desired mark up of 25% on the total cost but can earn maximum contribution as compared to other even higher selling price.

(*ii*) If the company wants to uphold its proposed pricing approach with the budgeted quantity, it should try to reduce its variable cost per unit, for example, by asking its supplier to provide a quantity discount on the materials purchased.

Illustrative Problem 8 (Considering Opportunity Costs in Selling Price)

V Ltd. manufactures desks. The following information is provided:

	Per Unit
	(₹)
Material (3 kgs @ ₹ 20 per kg)	60
Labour	50
Variable overheads	40
Allocated fixed overheads	20

Material is currently used to make chairs which provide contribution of ₹ 50 per unit. 2 kg of material is required for each chair. What is the minimum price per desk if:

(*i*) material is plentiful

(*ii*) material is scarce

Solution:

The minimum price of a product is determined in different manners depending on different situations as listed below:

(*i*) When the product has been made, the minimum price will be whatever is recoverable subject to recovering any disposal costs. All costs incurred in manufacturing the product are sunk costs and therefore not relevant in pricing decisions.

(*ii*) When the product is to be made and there are no scarce resources. In this case, the minimum price will be equal to incremental costs of making the product.

(*iii*) When the product is to be made and there are scarce resources — In this case, the minimum price is calculated as follows:

Minimum price = Incremental costs of making product (external opportunity costs) + Opportunity costs of scarce resources (internal opportunity cost)

Using the above guidelines, the minimum price per desk will be as follows:

(*i*) Material is Plentiful

Minimum Price = Incremental cost of making desks

= 60 + 50 + 40 = ₹ 150 per desk.

(*ii*) Material is Scarce

Minimum Price = Incremental costs + internal opportunity

$$= ₹\,150 + \left(\frac{\text{Contribution}}{\text{Kg of material}} = \frac{₹\,50}{2\text{ Kg}} \times 3\text{ Kg}\right)$$

= 150 + 75

= ₹ 225 per desk.

Illustrative Problem 9 (Fixing Selling Price)

The Grasim is a washing machine produced by Progressive Sales Limited and sold exclusively by mail order. Last year 10,000 machines were produced and sold at a selling price of ₹ 19,000 each. The cost of each machine was:

	₹
Direct materials	6,000
Direct labour	6,000
Other direct costs	600
Variable overheads	800
Variable cost	13,400
Fixed overheads	2,400
	15,800

During the coming year it is expected that costs will increase by the following: direct material 30%, direct labour 15%, other direct costs 20%, variable overheads 10%, fixed overheads 5%.

Market research has shown that the company could increase the selling price of the machine to ₹ 21,000 and still sell 8,000 units; alternatively if the price was reduced to ₹ 17,500 it would be possible to double sales to 20,000 units.

You are required, for the coming year, to:

(*a*) Determine the selling price of the machine if the number sold and the annual profits are to remain unchanged.

(*b*) Determine how many machines the company would have to sell if it did not change the price charged but maintained the profit level achieved last year.

(*c*) Evaluate the market research information and give your advice on the price that should be charged for the Grasim in the coming year. In giving your advice, you should take into account the results of parts (*a*) and (*b*) above.

Solution:

Workings

	Last year (₹) (per unit)		Next year (₹) (per unit)
Selling price	19,000	10,000 units	
Material	6,000	+ 30%	7,800
Labour	6,000	+ 15%	6,900
Direct cost etc.	600	+ 20%	720
Variable overheads	800	+ 10%	880
	13,400		16,300
Contribution	5,600	5,60,00,000	
Fixed overheads	2,400	2,40,00,000	+ 5% ₹ 2,52,00,000
Profit	3,200	₹ 3,20,00,000	

		₹	
(*a*)	Profit required	3,20,00,000	
	Fixed costs to cover	2,52,00,000	
	Contribution required	5,72,00,000	
	Number of units	10,000	
	Contribution per unit	5,720	
	Variable cost	16,300	
	Selling price	22,020	
(*b*)	Selling price	19,000	
	Variable cost	16,300	
	Contribution per unit	2,700	
	Contribution required	5,72,00,000	
	At ₹ 2,700 per unit	21,185	units

		₹	₹
(*c*)	Selling price	21,000	17,500
	Variable cost	16,300	16,300
	Contribution per unit	4,700	1,200
	Units	8,000	20,000
	Contribution	3,76,00,000	2,40,00,000
	Fixed cost	2,52,00,000	2,52,00,000
	Profit	1,24,00,000	12,00,000

Data provided are incomplete as we do not know what happens at intermediate prices. However, it is clear that simply to maintain profit at last year's level, 10,000 units would need to be sold at ₹ 22,020. Could 10,000 units be sold at this price? In the light of the market research, part (*b*) presents an unrealistic option — 20,000 would be sold at ₹ 17,500. The best available result, therefore, comes from a price of ₹ 22,000, which gives a reduced profit.

Illustrative Problem 10 (Desired Profit and Selling Price)

ABC Company recently commenced production of a new product P which required the investment of ₹ 20,00,00,000 in assets. The costs of producing and selling 1,00,000 units of product P are estimated as follows:

		₹ (Per unit)
Variable Costs:		
Direct materials		240
Direct labour		650
Factory overhead		90
Selling and administrative expenses		20
Total:		1,000
Fixed Costs:		
Factory overhead	₹ 60,00,000	
Selling and administrative expenses	₹ 1,40,00,000	

ABC Company is currently considering the establishment of a selling price for product P. The Managing Director of the company has decided to use the cost plus approach to product pricing and has indicated that product P must earn an 18% rate of return on invested assets.

Required:

(*i*) Determine the amount of desired profit from the production and sale of product P.

(*ii*) Assuming that total cost concept is used, determine:

(*a*) cost per unit

(*b*) markup percentage and

(*c*) selling price of product P

(*iii*) Assuming that the product cost concept is used, determine

(*a*) cost per unit

(*b*) markup percentage

(*c*) selling price of product P

(*iv*) Assuming that the variable cost concept is used, determine (*a*) cost per unit (*b*) markup percentage (*c*) selling price of product P.

(*v*) Assuming that for the current year, the selling price of product P was ₹ 1,560 per unit. To date 80,000 units have been produced and sold and analysis of the domestic market indicates that 15,000 additional units are expected to be sold during the remainder of the year. Recently, ABC company received an offer from XYZ company for 4,000 units of product P at ₹ 1,150 each. XYZ company will market the units in Indonesia under its own brand name and no additional selling and administrative expenses associated with the sale will be incurred by ABC company. The additional business is not expected to affect the domestic sales of product P and the additional units could be produced during the current year, using existing capacity.

Required (*a*) prepare a differential analysis report of the proposed sale to XYZ company (*b*) based upon the differential analysis report in (*a*), should the proposal be accepted?

Solution:

(*i*) Amount of desired profit = ₹ 20,00,00,000 × 18% = ₹ 3,60,00,000

(*ii*) (*a*) Total Costs:

		₹
Variable costs (₹ 1,000 × 1,00,000 units)	=	10,00,00,000
Fixed Cost (₹ 60,00,000 + ₹ 1,40,00,000)	=	2,00,00,000
Total		12,00,00,000

$$\text{Cost per unit} = \frac{₹\ 12{,}00{,}00{,}000}{1{,}00{,}000\ \text{units}} = ₹\ 1{,}200$$

(*b*)
$$\text{Markup percentage} = \frac{\text{Desired profit}}{\text{Total costs}}$$
$$= \frac{₹\ 3{,}60{,}00{,}000}{₹\ 12{,}00{,}00{,}000} = 30\%$$

(*c*)

Cost per unit	₹ 1,200
Markup (₹ 1,200 × 30%)	360
Selling price	₹ 1,560

(*iii*) (*a*) Total manufacturing costs:

Variable (₹ 980 × 1,00,000 units) =	₹ 9,80,00,000
Fixed factory overhead	60,00,000
Total:	10,40,00,000

Cost per unit =

₹ 10,40,00,000 ÷ 1,00,000 units = ₹ 1,040

(*b*) Markup percentage =

$$\frac{\text{Desired profit + Total selling and administrative expenses}}{\text{Total manufacturing costs}}$$
$$= \frac{₹\ 3{,}60{,}00{,}000 + ₹\ 1{,}40{,}00{,}000 + (₹\ 20 \times 1{,}00{,}000\ \text{units})}{₹\ 10{,}40{,}00{,}000}$$
$$= \frac{3{,}60{,}00{,}000 + 1{,}40{,}00{,}000 + 20{,}00{,}000}{10{,}40{,}00{,}000}$$
$$= \frac{5{,}20{,}00{,}000}{10{,}40{,}00{,}000}$$

Markup percentage = 50%

(*c*)

Cost per unit	₹ 1,040
Markup (₹ 1040 × 50%)	520
Selling price	₹ 1,560

(*iv*) (*a*) Variable cost per unit ₹ 1,000

Total variable cost = ₹ 1000 × 1,00,000 units = ₹ 10,00,00,000

(*b*)
$$\text{Markup percentage} = \frac{\text{Desired profit + Total fixed costs}}{\text{Total variable costs}}$$
$$= \frac{₹\ 3{,}60{,}00{,}000 + ₹\ 60{,}00{,}000 + ₹\ 1{,}40{,}00{,}000}{₹\ 10{,}00{,}00{,}000}$$

Markup percentage = 56%

	(c) Cost per unit	₹ 1,000
	Markup (₹ 1,000 × 56%)	560
	Selling price	₹ 1,560
(v)	(a) Proposal to sell to XYZ Co.	
	Differential revenue from offer:	
	Revenue from sale of 4,000 additional units at ₹ 1,150	= ₹ 46,00,000
	Differential cost of acceptance of offer:	
	Variable costs of 4,000 additional units at ₹ 980	= 39,20,000
	Profit from offer	₹ 6,80,000
	(b) The proposal should be accepted.	

Illustrative Problem 11 (Pricing Policy)

Mr Sudhir runs a small printing business. Each job is undertaken according to special instructions from the customer. Mr Sudhir uses a system recommended by his trade association to fix the price he charges to his customers. He estimates what he paid for the paper used (he keeps large stocks of paper) and adds a standard percentage for 'consumables' (ink etc.). He estimates the number of labour hours required for the job and values them at the appropriate wage rate; he adds a standard percentage to cover fixed overhead costs. The sum of all these items gives a 'total cost' for the job and he adds 10% to total costs for his profit. The standard percentages are set equal to the actual percentage relationships between corresponding total costs during the previous month.

Actual results for last month are as follows:

	(₹)	(₹)
Sales		2,66,000
Cost of paper used	24,000	
Consumables	3,000	
Wages	1,20,000	
Fixed costs	96,000	
		2,43,000
Net profit		23,000

Last month, Mr Sudhir's employees were fully occupied. During the current month just ending, however, business has fallen by 15% — measured in labour hours required. No one has been laid off. Mr Sudhir has simply paid for idle time. Total wage costs for the current month and total fixed costs are the same as last month; cost of paper used is ₹ 22,000 and cost of consumables ₹ 2,250. No special prices have been charged on any jobs during the month. Mr Sudhir is surprised to find, however, that he has made a loss on his business even though each job has shown a satisfactory profit.

(a) Prepare a calculation showing the amount of the loss for the current month.

(b) Explain how the loss has arisen and comment critically on Mr Sudhir's pricing system.

Solution :

First, calculate sales revenue at 'cost-plus' prices:

	(₹)
Paper	22,000
Consumables $\left(\frac{3,000}{24,000} = 12\frac{1}{2}\% \text{ of paper cost}\right)$	2,750
Labour (85% of capacity ₹ 120,000)	1,02,000
Fixed overheads $\left(\frac{96,000}{1,20,000} = 80\% \text{ of labour}\right)$	81,600
'Total cost'	2,08,350
'Profit' (10% of total cost)	20,835
Sales revenue	2,29,185

Income statement for current month

	₹	₹
Sales revenue		2,29,185
Less Paper (given in question)	22,000	
Consumables (given in question)	2,250	
Wages (per last month)	1,20,000	
Fixed costs (per last month)	96,000	2,40,250
Loss for month		11,065

The loss has arisen because labour has been paid while 'idle' and because fixed overheads have not been fully 'recovered'.

Mr Sudhir's pricing system may be criticised because:

1. No account is taken of demand conditions.
2. Percentage relationships are set using historical rather than expected relationships.
3. Fixed costs are charged on an arbitrary basis to jobs.
4. Paper is charged out at historical, rather than current costs.
5. No account is taken of the existence of spare capacity. Additional jobs could possibly have been obtained at a price below 'full cost' but above incremental cost.

Illustrative Problem 12 (Cost-plus target Return on Investment Pricing)

John is the managing partner of a business that has just finished building a 60-room motel. John anticipates that he will rent these rooms for 16,000 nights next year (or 16,000 room-nights). All rooms are similar and will rent for the same price. John estimates the following operating costs for next year :

Variable operating costs	₹ 30 per room-night
Fixed costs	
Salaries and wages	₹ 17,50,000
Maintenance of building and pool	3,70,000
Other operating and administration costs	14,00,000
Total fixed costs	₹ 35,20,000

The capital invested in the motel is ₹ 96,00,000. The partnership's target return on investment is 25%. John expects demand for rooms to be uniform throughout the year. He plans to price the rooms at full cost plus a markup on full cost to earn the target return on investment.

Required :

(*a*) What price should John charge for a room-night? What is the markup as a percentage of the full cost of a room-night?

(*b*) John's market research indicates that if the price of a room-night determined in requirement (a) is reduced by 10%, the expected number of room-nights John could rent would increase by 10%. Should John reduce prices by 10%? Show your calculations.

Solution:

Cost-plus target return on Investment Pricing.

(*a*) Target operating income = Target return on investment × Invested capital

Target operating income (25% × ₹ 96,00,000)	₹ 24,00,000	
Total fixed costs	35,20,000	
Target contribution margin	₹ 59,20,000	
Target contribution margin per room, (₹ 59,20,000 ÷ 16,000)	₹ 370	
Add variable costs per room	30	
Price to be charged per room	₹ 400	
Proof:		
Total room revenues (₹ 400 × 16,000 rooms)		₹ 64,00,000
Total costs :		
Variable costs (₹ 30 × 16,000)	₹ 4,80,000	
Fixed costs	35,20,000	
Total costs		40,00,000
Operating income		₹ 24,00,000

The full cost of a room= variable cost per room + fixed cost per room

The full cost of a room = ₹ 30 + (₹ 35,20,000 ÷ 16,000) = ₹ 30 + ₹ 220 = ₹ 250

Markup per room = Rental price per room – Full cost of a room

= ₹ 400 – ₹ 250 = ₹ 150

Markup percentage as a fraction of full cost = ₹ 150 ÷ ₹ 250 = 60%

(*b*) If price is reduced by 10%, the number of rooms John could rent would increase by 10%.

The new price per room would be 90% × ₹ 400	₹ 360
The number of rooms John expects to rent is 110% of 16,000	17,600
The contribution margin per room would be ₹ 360 — ₹ 30	₹ 330
Contribution margin (₹ 330 × 17,600)	₹ 58,08,000

Because the contribution margin of ₹ 58,08,000 at the reduced price of ₹ 360 is less than the contribution margin of ₹ 59,20,000 at a price of ₹ 400, John should not reduce the price of the rooms. Note that the fixed costs of ₹ 35,20,000 will be the same under the ₹ 400 and the ₹ 360 price alternatives and are, hence, irrelevant to the analysis.

Illustrative Problem 13 (Pricing Based on Target Cost)

Raheja Co., manufactures color laser printers. Model A200 presently sells for ₹ 40,000 and has a total product cost of ₹ 32,000 as follows:

Direct materials	₹ 23,000
Direct labor	6,000
Factory overhead	3,000
Total	₹ 32,000

It is estimated that the competitive selling price for color laser printers of this type will drop to ₹ 38,000 next year. Raheja Co. has established a target cost to maintain its historical markup percentage on product cost. Engineers have provided the following cost reduction ideas:

1. Purchase a plastic printer cover with snap-on assembly. This will reduce the amount of direct labor by nine minutes per unit.
2. Add an inspection step that will add six minutes per unit of direct labor but reduce the materials cost by ₹ 800 per unit.
3. Decrease the cycle time of the injection molding machine from four minutes to three minutes per part. Thirty percent of the direct labor and 42% of the factory overhead is related to running injection molding machines.

The direct labour rate is ₹ 2500 per hour.

Required:

a. Determine the target cost for Model A200 assuming that the historical markup on product cost is maintained.

b. Determine the required cost reduction.

c. Evaluate the three engineering improvements to determine if the required cost reduction (drift) can be achieved.

Solution:

a. Historical markup percentage: $\frac{₹ 40{,}000 - ₹ 32{,}000}{₹ 32{,}000} = 25\%$

$\frac{₹ 8000}{₹ 40000} = 20\%$ markup on selling price

₹ 38,000 revised selling price × 20% markup = ₹ 7,600 amount of markup

₹ 38,000 selling price – ₹ 7,600 markup = ₹ 30,400 target cost

b. Required cost reduction: ₹ 32,000 – ₹ 30,400 = ₹ 1,600

c.

1. Direct labor reduction:	$\frac{9 \text{ min.}}{60 \text{ min.}} \times ₹ 2{,}500$	=		₹ 375
2. Additional inspection:	$\frac{6 \text{ min.}}{60 \text{ min.}} \times ₹ 2{,}500$	=	₹ (250)	
Direction material reduction:			800	550

3. Injection molding productivity improvement:

Direct labor improvement (25%* × 30% × ₹ 6000)	₹ 450	
Factory overhead improvement (25%* × 42% × ₹ 3000)	315	765
Total Savings		₹ 1,690

*Improving the cycle time from four minutes to three minutes is a 25% reduction.

The total savings exceeds the required target cost reduction by ₹ 90. Thus, these improvements are sufficient to meet the target cost.

Illustrative Problem 14 (Minimum Selling Price)

LMV Limited manufactures product Z in departments A and B which also manufacture other products using same plant and machinery. The information of product Z is as follows:

Items	Department A (₹)	Department B (₹)
Direct material per unit	30	25
Direct labour per unit (₹ 10 per hout)	30	40
Overhead rates:		
Fixed	8 per hour	4 per hour
Variable	6 per hour	3 per hour
Value of Plant and Machinery	25 lakhs	15 lakhs

Overheads are recovered on the basis of direct labour hours. Variable selling and distribution overheads relating to product Z are amounting to ₹ 30,000 per month. The product requires a working capital of ₹ 4,00,000 at the target volume of 1,500 units per month occupying 30 per cent of practical capacity.

You are required:

(*i*) To calculate the price of product Z to yield a contribution to cover 21 percent rate of return on investment.

(*ii*) Set the minimum selling price of the product if (a) the product is well established in the market; (b) the product is first time launched in the market.

Solution:

(*i*) Statement showing price of Product Z

			(₹)
Direct Material	Deptt. A	30	
	Deptt. B	25	55
Direct Labour	Deptt. A	30	
	Deptt. B	40	70
Variable overhead	Deptt. A 3 × 6	18	
	Deptt B 4 × 3	12	30
Variable selling and distribution overhead 30,000/1,500			20
Total Variable Cost per unit			175
Total hours required for a target of 1,500 units of product Z			
Deptt. A 1,500 × 3			4500 hours
Deptt. B 1,500 × 4			6000 hours
			10500 hours

10,500 hours represent 30% capacity

So total capacity per month 10,500/0.30 = 35,000 hours.

Yearly capacity is 35000 × 12 = 4,20,000 hours.

Fixed capital employed in both department = ₹ 40.00 Lakhs

(25 Lakhs + 15 Lakhs)

Expected return	= 0.21 × 40,00,000	= ₹ 8,40,000
Contribution per hour	= 8,40,000/4,20,000	= 2.00 per hour
Working Capital	= 0.21 × 4,00,000	= 84,000
Contribution per unit 84,000/18,000		= ₹ 4.67 per unit
Total contribution required		₹
To cover fixed cost 3 hours of A and 4 hours of B = 7 × 2		= 14.00
To working capital		= 4.67
		18.67

Fixed charges recovery is based on usage. Full capacity is not being used by product Z and departments are also producing other products using same plant and machinery.

Price of Product = Variable cost + contribution required = 175 + 18.67 = ₹ 193.67 per unit.

(*ii*) Price of product when product is well established in market:

Variable Cost	175
Fixed Cost (24 + 16)	40
Total price	215

The product is first time launched in the market, and then variable cost ₹ 175 should form the basis for price fixation.

Illustrative Problem 15 (Minimum Price)

XL Polymers, located in Sahibabad Industrial Area, manufactures high quality industrial products. AT Industries has asked XL Polymers for a special job that must be completed within one week.

Raw material R_1 (highly toxic) will be needed to complete the AT Industries' special job. XL Polymers purchased the R_1 two weeks ago for ₹ 7,500 for a job 'A' that recently was completed. The R_1 currently in stock is the excess from that job and XL Polymers had been planning to dispose of it. XL Polymers estimates that it would cost them ₹ 1,250 to dispose of the R_1. Current replacement cost of R_1 is ₹ 6,000.

Special job will require 250 hours of labour G_1 and 100 hours of labour G_2. XL Polymers pays their G_1 and G_2 employees ₹ 630 and ₹ 336 respectively for 42 hours of work per week. XL Polymers anticipates having excess capacity of 150 [G_1] and 200 [G_2] labour hours in the coming week. XL Polymers can also hire additional G_1 and G_2 labour on an hourly basis; these part-time employees are paid an hourly wage based on the wages paid to current employees.

Suppose that material and labour comprise XL Polymer's only costs for completing the special job.

Required:

Calculate the 'Minimum Price' that XL Polymers should bid on this job?

(*CA Final, Nov. 2015*)

Solution:

Opportunity Cost of Labour: G_2 labour has zero opportunity cost as there is no other use for the time already paid for and is available. However, XL Polymers needs to pay an additional amount for G_1 labour. This amount can be saved if the special job were not there.

G1 labour:	
Hours Required	250
Hours Available	150
Extra Hours Needed	100
Cost per hour (₹ 630/42 hrs)	₹ 15
Opportunity Cost	₹ 1,500

Thus, the 'Opportunity Cost of Labour' for completing the special job is ₹ 1,500.

Opportunity Cost of Material – XL Polymers has no alternative use for the R_1, they must dispose of it at a cost of ₹ 1,250. Thus, XL Polymers actually saves ₹ 1,250 by using the materials for the AT Industries' special job. Consequently, the 'Opportunity Cost of Material' is - ₹ 1,250 (i.e., the opportunity cost of this resource is negative).

The minimum price is the price at which XL Polymers just recovers its 'Opportunity Cost'. XL Polymer's 'Total Opportunity Cost' is ₹ 250 (₹ 1,500 – ₹ 1,250). Accordingly, minimum price for the special job is ₹ 250.

Illustrative Problem 16 (Pricing Decisions Under Bottleneck Operations)

Gemini Steel Company produces three grades of steel: high, good, and regular grade. Each of these products (grades) has high demand in the market, and Gemini is able to sell as much as it can produce of all three. The furnace operation is a bottleneck in the process and is running at 100% of capacity. Gemini wants to improve steel operation profitability. The variable conversion cost is ₹ 80 per process hour. The fixed cost is ₹ 41,00,000. In addition, the cost analyst was able to determine the following information about the three products:

	High Grade	Good Grade	Regular Grade
Budgeted units produced	5,000	5,000	5,000
Total process hours per unit	15	15	12
Furnace hours per unit	5	4	3
Unit selling price	₹ 2,700	₹ 2,500	₹ 2,100
Direct materials cost per unit	₹ 1,200	₹ 1,000	₹ 780

The furnace operation is part of the total process for each of these three products. Thus, for example, 5 of the 15 hours required to process High Grade steel are associated with the furnace.

Required:

(*i*) Determine the unit contribution margin for each product.

(*ii*) Provide an analysis to determine the relative product profitabilities, assuming that the furnace is a bottleneck.

(*iii*) Assume that management wishes to improve profitability by increasing prices on selected products. At what price would High and Good grades need to be offered in order to produce the same relative profitability as Regular Grade steel?

Solution:

(*i*)

	High Grade	Good Grade	Regular Grade
Selling price	₹ 2,700	₹ 2,500	₹ 2,100
Variable conversion cost per unit*	₹ 1,200	₹ 1,200	₹ 960
Direct materials cost per unit	1,200	1,000	780
	₹ 2,400	₹ 2,200	₹ 1,740
Contribution margin per unit	₹ 300	₹ 300	₹ 360

*₹ 80 × 15 process hours = ₹ 1200

₹ 80 × 12 process hours = ₹ 960

(*ii*) The contribution margin per unit may give false signals when an organization has production bottlenecks. Instead, Gemini should use the contribution margin per bottleneck hour to determine relative product profitability, as follows:

	High Grade	Good Grade	Regular Grade
Contribution margin per unit	₹ 300	₹ 300	₹ 360
Furnace (bottleneck) hours per unit	÷ 5	÷ 4	÷ 3
Contribution margin per furnace hour	₹ 60	₹ 75	₹ 120

The Regular Grade steel has the largest contribution margin per unit (₹ 360) and the largest contribution margin per furnace hour (₹ 120). Both Good Grade and High Grade have the same contribution margin per unit of ₹ 300. However, using production bottleneck analysis indicates that the Good Grade is actually more profitable at ₹ 75 contribution margin per furnace hour than High Grade's ₹ 60 contribution margin per furnace hour. Thus, the company would want to sell product in the following preference order:

(*a*) Regular Grade

(*b*) Good Grade

(*c*) High Grade

(*iii*) One way to revise the pricing would be to increase the price to the point where all three products produce profitability equal to the highest profit product. This would be determined as follows:

$$\frac{\text{Revised Price of High Grade Steel}}{\text{Unit Contribution Margin per Furnace Hour for Regular Grade}} = \frac{\text{Revised Price of High Grade} - \text{Unit Variable Cost}}{\text{Furnace Hours of High Grade per Unit}}$$

Regular Grade

₹ 120 = (Revised Price of High Grade – ₹ 2400)/ 5 hrs.

₹ 600 = (Revised Price of High Grade – ₹ 2400)

₹ 3000 = Revised Price of High Grade

High Grade steel would require a revised price of ₹ 3000 in order to deliver the same unit contribution margin per bottleneck hour as does Regular Grade steel.

$$\frac{\text{Revised Price of Good Grade Steel}}{\text{Contribution Margin per Furnace Hour for Regular Grade}} = \frac{\text{Revised Price of Good Grade} - \text{Unit Variable Cost}}{\text{Furnace Hours of Good Grade per Unit}}$$

₹ 120 = (Revised Price of Good Grade – ₹ 2,200)/ 4 hrs.

₹ 480 = (Revised Price of Good Grade – ₹ 2,200)

₹ 2,680 = Revised Price of Good Grade

Good Grade steel would require a revised price of ₹ 2,680 in order to deliver the same unit contribution margin per bottleneck hour as does Regular Grade steel.

Illustrative Problem 17 (Pricing Decision for Bidding)

Sri Ram Industries, is preparing to submit a bid for a ball-bearings order. Sandeep, controller of the Bearings Division of the company, has asked Rohan, the cost analyst, to prepare the bid. To determine price, Sri Ram's policy is to mark up the full costs of the product by 10%. Sandeep tells Rohan that he is keen on winning the bid and that the price he calculates should be competitive. Rohan prepares the following costs for the bid:

Direct materials		₹ 4,00,000
Direct manufacturing labor costs		1,00,000
Overhead costs :		
Design and parts administration	₹ 40,000	
Production-order	50,000	
Setup	55,000	
Materials-handling	65,000	
General and administration	90,000	
Total overhead costs		3,00,000
Full product costs		₹ 8,00,000

All direct costs and 30% of overhead costs are incremental costs of the order.

Sandeep reviews, the numbers and says, "Your costs are too high. You have allocated too much overhead costs to this job. You know our fixed overhead is not going to change if we win this order and manufacture the bearings. Rework your numbers. You have got to make the costs lower."

Rohan verifies that his numbers are correct. He knows that Sandeep wants this order because the additional revenues from the order would lead to a big bonus for Sandeep and the senior division managers. Rohan knows that if he does not come up with a lower bid, Sandeep will be very upset.

Required:

(*i*) Using Sri Ram's pricing policy and based on Rohan's estimates, calculate the price Sri Ram should bid for the ball-bearings order.

(*ii*) Calculate the incremental costs of the ball-bearing order. Why do you think Sri Ram Co. uses full costs of the product rather than incremental costs in its pricing decisions?

(*iii*) Evaluate whether Sandeep's suggestion to Rohan to use lower cost numbers is unethical. Would it be unethical for Rohan to change his analysis so that a lower cost can be calculated? What steps should Rohan take to resolve this situation?

(*M.Com. Delhi*)

Solution:

(*i*) Sri Ram prices at full product costs plus a mark-up of 10% = ₹ 8,00,000 + 10% of ₹ 8,00,000 = ₹ 8,00,000 + ₹ 80,000 = ₹ 8,80,000.

(*ii*) The incremental costs of the order are as follows:

Direct materials	₹ 4,00,000
Direct manufacturing labor	1,00,000
30% of overhead costs (30% × ₹ 3,00,000)	90,000
Incremental costs	₹ 5,90,000

Any bid above ₹ 5,90,000 will generate a positive contribution margin for Sri Ram Co. The company may prefer to use full product costs because it regards the new ball-bearings order as a long-term business relationship rather than a special order. For long-run pricing decisions, managers prefer to use full product costs because it indicates the bare minimum costs they need to recover to continue in business rather than shut down. For a business to be profitable in the long run, it needs to recover both its variable and its fixed product costs. Using only variable costs may tempt the manager to engage in excessive long-run price cutting as long as prices give a positive contribution margin. Using full product costs for pricing thereby prompts price stability.

(*iii*) Not using full product costs (including an allocation of fixed overhead) to price the order, particularly if it is in direct contradiction of company policy, may be unethical.

Rohan should indicate to Sandeep that the costs were correctly computed and that determining prices on the basis of full product costs plus a mark-up of 10% are required by company policy. If Sandeep still insists on making the changes and reducing the costs of the order, Rohan should raise the matter with Sandeep's superior. If, after taking all these steps, there is continued pressure to understate the costs, Rohan should consider resigning from the company, rather than engage in unethical behaviour.

Illustrative Problem 18

A hotel operated by a company has 180 single rooms and 60 double rooms. The rent of the double rooms is set at 160% of the rent of the single rooms. The operational costs per day per room are estimated as under:

	Single Rooms	Double Rooms
	₹	₹
Variable costs	300	500
Fixed costs	500	780

The average occupancy of both the single rooms and double rooms is expected to be 85% throughout a year of 365 days. In fixing the room rent, the company desires to earn a margin of safety of 20%. The hotel has to pay a tax of 20% on its tariff.

Required:

(*i*) Calculate the tariff per day per

(1) Single room and

(2) Double room.

(*ii*) The hotel intends to reserve the normal occupancy of 12 single rooms for one of its valued corporate customers at a discount (excluding tax) of 10% of the rent. What increase in the occupancy of the remaining single room days is required to compensate the loss arising form the discount.

Solution:

Working notes:

1. Single and Double rooms occupancy:

Single rooms occupancy days:	180 rooms × 365 days × 85%	55,845
Double rooms occupancy days:	60 rooms × 365 days × 85%	18,615

2. Total variable cost of single and double rooms occupancy days:

Variable cost of single rooms occupancy days: (₹)	55,845 × ₹ 300	1,67,53,500
Variable cost of double rooms occupancy days: (₹)	18,615 × ₹ 500	93,07,500
	Total variable costs: (₹)	2,60,61,000

3. Total Fixed cost of single and double rooms days:

Fixed cost of single room days	55,845 × ₹ 500	2,79,22,500
Fixed cost of double room days	18,615 × ₹ 780	1,45,19,700
	Total Fixed costs: (₹)	4,24,42,200

4. Computation of total desired revenue of the Hotel:

Since the margin of safely is 20% therefore break even point is 80%

At 80% that is at BEP the revenue (₹ 2,60,61,000 + ₹ 4,24,42,200)	6,85,03,200
Hence the total desired revenue (₹)	₹ 8,56,29,000

5. Computation of notional single room occupancy days:

The rent of each double room is 160% of the rent of the single room. To facilitate the task of determining the room rent of a double room per day, we convert the double room occupancy days as follows:

Double room occupancy days	18,615
Notional single room occupancy days (18,615 × 1.66)	29,784
Add: Single room occupancy days	55,845
Total notional single room occupancy days	85,629

(i) Computation of tariff per day:

Total desired revenue (₹): I (Refer to working note 4)	8,56,29,000
Total notional single room occupancy days: II (Refer to working note 5)	85,629
Rent per notional single room day ₹: (I / II)	1,000
Double room rent (₹ 1,000 × 1.6)	1,600

Tariff per day for single room (₹) (100/80 × ₹ 1000)	1,250
Tariff per day for double room (₹) (100/80 × ₹ 1000)	2,000

(ii) Computation of increase in the occupancy days of the remaining single rooms, so as to compensate 10% discount of the rent, given to a valued corporate customer:

No, of single rooms reserved for valued corporate customer	12
Occupancy days for reserved rooms (12 rooms × 365 days × 85%)	3,723
Discount given on the room rent per day (₹) (10% × ₹ 1,000)	100
Total amount of revenue lost due to discount (₹) (3,723 occupancy days × ₹ 100)	3,72,300
Contribution per day on a single room (₹) (₹ 1,000 – ₹ 300)	700
Increase in the occupancy days required in respect of single rooms (₹ 3,72,300 / ₹ 700)	531.86 or 532 days

REFERENCES

1. Charles T. Horngreen, Sri Kant M. Datar and George Foster, Cost Accounting, A Managerial Emphasis, Pearson Education, 2008, pp. 477-478.
2. Anthony A.At Kinson et al., Management Accounting, Prentice Hall International, 1997, p. 323.
3. Anthony A.At Kinson et al., *Ibid*, p. 349.
4. Don T. Decoster et al., Management Accounting, John Wiley and Sons, 1988, p. 349
5. Charles T. Horngreen, Sri Kant M. Datar, George Foster, *Ibid*, p. 438.
6. Roberts S. Kaplan and Anthony A. At Kinson, Advanced Management Accounting, Pearson, 1998, p. 152.
7. Wayne J. Morse, James R. Davis and Al. L. Hartgraves, Management Accounting, A Strategic Approach, South Western College, Publishing, 2000, p. 374.

CRITICAL ANALYSIS AND DISCUSSION QUESTIONS, SELF-ASSESSMENT QUESTIONS, MULTIPLE CHOICE QUESTIONS, PROBLEMS AND CASES

CRITICAL ANALYSIS AND DISCUSSION QUESTIONS

1. In the long run, selling price will tend to equal costs plus reasonable profits. Discuss.
2. List the factors taken into consideration in fixing the selling price by a business firm.
3. Discuss full cost plus and marginal cost plus methods of pricing. Which pricing method can be useful to a firm and under what situations.
4. In markup pricing, what elements must be covered by the markup when full costs are used? What elements must be covered when variable costs are used?
5. Explain how the treatment of fixed costs presents a problem in full cost pricing.
6. The marketing manager of Apollo Textiles company says that product prices should always be set by supply and demand in the market place to ensure high sales level. The Finance Manager says that product prices should always be based on cost to ensure profitability. Is either correct? Does a middle path exist?
7. In the long run, the normal selling price must be set high enough to cover what factors?
8. What are the three cost concepts commonly used in applying the cost plus approach to product pricing?
9. Although the cost plus approach to product pricing may be used by management as a general guideline, what are some examples of other factors that managers should also consider in setting product prices?
10. Define differential cost pricing and give an illustration of when it is in the company's best interest for management not to use this method.
11. Why do unit differential costs sometimes establish the minimum sales price in short-run pricing decisions?
12. Name some external and internal factors that influence the pricing decision.
13. "Prices must cover both variable and fixed costs of production". Do you agree with this statement? Explain.
14. Why is the evaluation of short term pricing and product mix decisions different from the evaluation of long-term pricing and product mix decisions.
15. What additional costs should a firm consider when making a short term pricing decision when surplus production capacity is not available and it must employ overtime, extra shifts, subcontracting or other means to augment the limited capacity?
16. State and explain the circumstances when using full costs for pricing decisions can be justified?
17. "Relevant costs for pricing decisions are full costs of the product." Explain.
18. How is activity-based costing useful for pricing decisions?
19. "Price setting generally requires a balance between market forces and cost considerations." Explain.

20. List the four common cost bases used in cost plus pricing. How can they all result in the same price?
21. Why is a focus on the customer such a key principle of target costing?
22. Distinguish between target costing and target pricing.
23. Peter Drucker argues that one of the seven deadly business sins is to base prices on costs, which means first measuring the current cost of a product or service and then "marking it up" by adding a profit margin. He blames the disappearance of many consumer electronics in the world in part on its practice of basing prices on costs. What is an alternative to basing prices on costs?
24. You enter the Departure Terminal of an airline at New Delhi just before a flight to Mumbai. The plane is about 80% full and the regular fare for the flight is ₹ 12,000. You do not have a ticket for the flight, but you offer to pay ₹ 5,000 to take the flight. Assume there are no variable costs associated with the number of passengers. Should the Airline accept your offer if it employs the incremental principle? Will the Airline accept your offer? Why or why not?
25. "In target costing, price determines costs rather than vice versa." Explain.
26. "Basing prices on only the variable costs of a job results in suicidal underpricing." Do you agree? Why?
27. In the longrun, the normal selling price must be set high enough to cover what factors?

SELF-ASSESSMENT QUESTIONS

A. Green Company produces product A which it sells for ₹ 1,800. The following cost data apply:

Type of cost	***Per unit*** (₹)
Direct materials (3 lbs.× ₹ 150)	450
Direct labour	645
Variable overhead	135
Fixed overhead	150
Variable selling expenses	110
Fixed selling expenses	220
	1,710

Green has thought of marketing a new product B with the same cost structure as product A except that the price will be ₹ 1,560. Green Company currently has the plant capacity necessary for this expansion. Because of the cost structure, Green Company will find the production and sale of product B in the short run to be:

(*a*) Not profitable unless the price can be raised to ₹ 1,710.

(*b*) Not profitable at any price.

(*c*) Not profitable at ₹ 1,560 because the fixed selling expense and fixed manufacturing overhead will not be covered by the price.

(*d*) Profitable to produce and sell product B in the short run at the price of ₹ 1,560.

B. Adly Company wishes to earn a 30 per cent return on its ₹ 1,00,00,000 investment in equipment used to produce product X. Based on estimated sales of 10,000 units of product X next year, the costs per unit would be as follows:

Variable manufacturing costs	₹ 500
Fixed selling and administrative costs	₹ 200
Fixed manufacturing costs	100

At how much per unit should product X be priced for sale?

(*a*) ₹ 500 (*b*) ₹ 800
(*c*) ₹ 1000 (*d*) ₹ 1100

C. State the most appropriate pricing policy to be adopted in the following independent situations:

(i) Modern patented drug entering the market.
(ii) The latest version of a mobile phone is being launched by an established, financially strong company.
(iii) An established company has recently entered the stationery market segment and launched good quality paper for printing at home and office.
(iv) A car manufacturer is launching an innovative, technologically advanced car in the highly priced segment.

(*CA Final, Nov. 2015*)

Answer:

Sl. No.	Pricing Policy
(i)	Skimming Pricing
(ii)	Penetration Pricing
(iii)	Market Price
(iv)	Skimming Pricing

MULTIPLE CHOICE QUESTIONS

Select the correct answer for the following multiple choice questions.

1. For which cost concept used in applying the cost plus approach to product pricing are fixed manufacturing costs, fixed selling, administrative expenses and desired profit allowed for in the determination of markup?
(*a*) Total cost (*b*) Product cost
(*c*) Variable cost (*d*) None of the above.
2. In the contribution margin approach to pricing, the price at which the income remains constant is equal to the price that covers
(*a*) Prime costs (*b*) Variable costs
(*c*) Fixed costs (*d*) Fixed and variable costs plus the desired profit.
3. A company wants to sell a product at a gross margin of 20 per cent. The cost of the product is ₹ 200. The selling price should be
(*a*) ₹ 160 (*b*) ₹ 210
(*c*) ₹ 240 (*d*) ₹ 250
4. ABC Company manufactures a product that has a variable cost of ₹ 50 per unit. Fixed costs total ₹ 10,00,000 allocated on the basis of the number of units produced. Selling price is computed by adding a 10 per cent markup to full cost. How much should the selling price be per unit for 1,00,000 units?

(*a*) ₹ 55 (*b*) ₹ 60
(*c*) ₹ 61 (*d*) ₹ 66

5. A company has always used the full cost of its product as the starting point in the pricing of that product. The price set by competitors and the demand for the company's only product, Purifier, has never been predictable. Recently, the market share has been increasing as it continues to lower its price, but total revenues have not changed significantly relative to the gain in sales volume. The likely reason for the stability of total revenue is:
   (*a*) The variable cost component of the full cost.
   (*b*) The unstable contribution margin.
   (*c*) The fixed cost component of the full cost.
   (*d*) The drop in the incremental cost of the units in the increased sales volume.
6. Several surveys point out that most managers use full product costs, including unit fixed costs and unit variable costs, in developing cost-based pricing. Which one of the following is **least** associated with cost-based pricing?
   (*a*) Simplicity. (*b*) Price stability.
   (*c*) Price justification. (*d*) Target pricing.
   (*e*) Fixed-cost recovery.
7. Narula Caterers quotes a price of ₹ 600 per person for a dinner party. This price includes the 6% sales tax and the 15% service charge. Sales tax is computed on the food plus the service charge. The service charge is computed on the food only. At what amount does Narula price the food?
   (*a*) ₹ 564 (*b*) ₹ 510
   (*c*) ₹ 492.2 (*d*) ₹ 474
8. Based on potential sales of 500 units per year, a new product has estimated traceable costs of ₹ 9,90,000. What is the target price to obtain a 15% profit margin on sales?
   (*a*) ₹ 2,329 (*b*) ₹ 2,277
   (*c*) ₹ 1,980 (*d*) ₹ 1,935
9. A company has developed and patented a new laser disc reading device that will be marketed internationally. Which of the following factors should the company consider in pricing the device?
   I. Quality of the new device.
   II. Life of the new device.
   III. Customers' relative preference for quality compared to price.
   (*a*) I and II only. (*b*) I and III only.
   (*c*) II and III only. (*d*) I, II and III.
10. Conversion cost pricing
    (*a*) places heavy emphasis on the cost of materials used in manufacturing a product.
    (*b*) places minimal emphasis on the cost of materials used in manufacturing a product.
    (*c*) could be used when the customer furnishes the material used in manufacturing a product.
    (*d*) places heavy emphasis on indirect costs and disregards consideration of direct costs.
    (*e*) places heavy emphasis on direct costs and disregards consideration of indirect costs.

Answer to Multiple Choice Questions:

1. (c)	2. (d)	3. (c)	4. (d)	5. (b)
6. (d)	7. (c)	8. (a)	9. (d)	10. (c)

PROBLEMS

1. An Electronics Company has the following costs structure for an electronic product:

	₹
Direct material	50
Direct labour	75
Variable overheads	30
Fixed overheads	45
Total unit cost	200

Fixed selling and administrative costs ₹ 6,00,000.

Additional information:

(*i*) Budgeted production and sale for the next year is 20,000 units.

(*ii*) The management feels that a minimum return of 20% is required on equity investments of ₹ 20,00,000.

What price should it charge for one unit of its output.

Ans: ₹ 250.

2. The marketing manager and the controller of a Company have been working closely together over the past few months to arrive at the most profitable price for the company's product. Based on their analysis and various market surveys, the following sales volumes at the various prices are forecasted:

28,000 units at ₹ 100 per unit
40,000 units at ₹ 90 per unit
48,000 units at ₹ 80 per unit
50,000 units at ₹ 75 per unit

Fixed costs of ₹ 5,00,000 would not change over the 28,000 units to 50,000 units capacities above; however, variable expense is projected to be the following per unit:

Direct material	₹ 25
Direct labour	₹ 20
Variable production	₹ 5
Variable marketing	₹ 10

Required:

Determine the selling price at which company income would be maximized.

3. A manufacturer produces a single product and has prepared its master budget for 2017 as follows:

	(000) ₹	(000) ₹
Sales		6,600

Direct materials	1,600	
Direct labour	800	
Variable overheads	600	
Total direct costs	3,000	
Factory overheads	1,000	
Factory cost	4,000	
Administration overheads	400	
Total cost		4,400
Profit		2,200

Towards the end of 2017, an enquiry is received from a potential customer. Direct costs have been estimated as follow:

Direct material	₹ 26,000
Direct labour	₹ 14,000
Variable overheads	₹ 8,000

Assume (*i*) the recovery of factory overheads and administration overheads in the same percentage as given in the 2017 budget and (*ii*) maintaining the 2017 profit margin percentage:

Find out what price should it quote to the customer?

Ans. Selling price ₹ 1,05,600.

4. Johnson Company produces two products A and B. Data on cost and production are as follows:

	Product A	***Product B***
Materials Cost per unit	₹ 350	₹ 160
Labour hours required per unit	3	2
Hourly labour rate	₹ 150	₹ 120
Planned production	20,000 units	40,000 units

Annual fixed overhead costs amount to ₹ 84,00,000.

Required:

Assuming the manager wants to set a price with a 10 per cent markup based on full cost, prepare an analysis showing what the selling price for each product would be if the fixed overhead costs were allocated using:

(*a*) Total number of planned production units.

(*b*) Total planned direct labour hours.

5. X Ltd. manufactures special purpose gauges to customer specifications. The highly skilled labour force is always working to full capacity and the budget for the next year shows:

	(₹)	(₹)
Sales		40,000
Direct Materials	4,000	
Direct Wages (3,200 hours @ ₹ 5)	16,000	
Fixed Overhead	10,000	30,000
Profit		10,000

An enquiry is received from XYZ Ltd. for a gauge which would use ₹ 60 of Direct materials and 40 labour hours.

(a) What is the minimum price to quote to XYZ Ltd?

(b) Would the minimum price be different if spare capacity were available but materials were subject to a quote of ₹ 4,000 per year?

Ans. (a) ₹ 510, (b) ₹ 560

6. The share of production and cost based fair price computed separately for a common product for each of the four divisions of a company are as follows:

	Divisions			
	A	B	C	D
Share of production %	40	25	20	15
Direct Materials (₹)	30	36	34	38
Direct Labour (₹)	20	24	28	32
Depreciation (₹)	60	40	32	20
Other Overheads (₹)	60	60	56	48
	170	160	150	138
20% return on Capital employed (₹)	126	86	70	46
Fair Price (₹)	296	246	220	184
Capital Employed per unit (₹) :				
Net Fixed Assets ₹ per unit	600	400	320	200
Working capital ₹ per unit	30	30	30	30
Total capital (₹ per unit)	630	430	350	230

The Company wants to fix an uniform price for the product. Advise the company.

Answer: Uniform price for the common product for each of the four companies is ₹ 251.50.

7. Somesh of Agra presently operates his plant at 80% of the normal capacity to manufacture a product only to meet the demand of Government of Tamil Nadu under a rate contract. He supplies the product for ₹ 4,00,000 and earns a profit margin of 20% on sales realisations. Direct cost of units is constant.

The indirect costs as per his budget projections are:

Indirect costs	*20,000 units (80% capacity)*	*22,500 units (90% capacity)*	₹ *25,000 units (100% capacity)*
Variable	80,000	90,000	1,00,000
Semi-variable	40,000	42,500	45,000
Fixed	80,000	80,000	80,000

He has received an export order for the product equal to 20% of its present operations. Additional packing charges on his order will be ₹ 1,000.

Arrive at the price to be quoted for the export order to give him a profit margin of 10% on the export price.

Answer: ₹ 12.50 per unit

8. HD Labs Co., situated at Hyderabad recently began production of a new product, flat panel displays, which required an investment of ₹ 15,00,000 in assets. The costs of producing and selling 12,000 units of flat panel displays are estimated as follows:

Variable costs per unit:		Fixed costs:	
Direct materials	₹ 140	Factory overhead	₹ 9,60,000
Direct labor	30	Selling and administrative expenses	4,80,000
Factory overhead	50		
Selling and administrative expenses	25		
Total	₹ 245		

HD Labs Co. is currently considering establishing a selling price for flat panel displays. The president of HD Labs has decided to use the cost-plus approach to product pricing and has indicated that the displays must earn a 20% rate of return on invested assets.

Required:

1. Determine the amount of desired profit from the production and sale of flat panel displays.
2. Assuming that the total costs concept is used, determine (a) the cost per unit, (b) the markup percentage and (c) the selling price of flat panel displays.
3. Assuming that the product cost concept is used, determine (a) the cost per unit, (b) the markup percentage, and (c) the selling price of flat panel displays.
4. Assuming that the variable cost concept is used, determine (a) the cost per unit, (b) the markup percentage, and (c) the selling price of flat panel displays.
5. Comment on any additional considerations that could influence establishing the selling price for flat panel displays.
6. Assume that as of August 1, 2017, 5,000 units of flat panel displays have been produced and sold during the current year. Analysis of the domestic market indicates that 4,000 additional units are expected to be sold during the remainder of the year at the normal product price determined under the total cost concept. On August 3, HD Labs received an offer from Vision Systems, Mumbai, for 1,500 units of flat panel displays at ₹ 235 each. Vision Systems will market the units in Thailand under its own brand name, and no selling and administrative expenses associated with the sale will be incurred by HD Labs Inc. The additional business is not expected to affect the domestic sales of flat panel displays, and the additional units could be produced using existing capacity.
   a. Prepare a differential analysis report of the proposed sale to Vision Systems.
   b. Based on the differential analysis report in part (a), should the proposal be accepted?

Answer:

1. ₹ 3,00,000
2. (a) ₹ 365 (b) 6.85% (c) Selling price ₹390
3. (a) ₹ 300 (b) 30% (c) ₹ 390
4. (a) ₹ 29,40,000 (b) 59.18% (c) ₹ 390
5. Other Considerations may include the price of competing products, general economic conditions of the market place, etc.
6. (a) Differential income ₹ 22,500
   (b) The proposal should be accepted.

CASES

1. Many businesses are offering their products and services over the Internet. Some of these companies are listed below:

Company Name	Product
Jet Air Lines	Airlines tickets
Amazon.com	Books
HP	Personal computers

Required:

(a) For each site, determine the following:
   1. A product (or service) description.
   2. A product price.
   3. A list of costs that are required to produce and sell the product selected in part (1).
   4. Whether the costs identified in part (a) (3) are fixed costs or variable costs.

(b) Which of the three products do you believe has the largest markup on variable cost?

2. The late-night receptionist of Kailash Hotel, New Delhi was told to lower the price of rooms for potential guests who were reluctant to pay the full price and who were considering going elsewhere. The minimum price to be charged for a room was ₹ 2,000 per night, which was above the variable cost of ₹ 1,000 per night for cleaning and maintenance. The full price for the room was ₹ 4,000 per night.

Required:

(*a*) What type of pricing decision rule should the hotel provide the night receptionist when almost all of the rooms are rented and more potential guests might arrive.

(*b*) How does this pricing rule differ from a long term pricing strategy?

M.Com. Delhi, 2004, 2008)

3. The Department of Commerce, University of Delhi is running three postgraduate programmes: Master in Commerce, Master in International Business, Master in Human Resource Development. The Vice-chancellor of the university is considering adding 75 students to these programmes, 25 in each entering class of each programme for the next five years. The Vice-Chancellor argues that since excess capacity exists in classes, no additional faculty will be required. Thus, the teaching costs of these 75 additional students is zero. Comment on the Vice-Chancellor's argument.

4. Assume that a person quotes a price of ₹ 7,000 for a room in Taj Hotel, New Delhi for Saturday with low expected room demand in New Delhi, so there is excess room capacity. The fully allocated cost per room per day is assumed from hotel records as follows:

Housekeeping labor cost*	₹ 3,400
Hotel depreciation expense	4,200
Cost of room supplies (soap, paper, etc.)	600
Laundry labor and material cost*	1,000
Cost of desk staff	500
Utility cost (mostly air conditioning)	400
Total cost per room per day	₹ 10,100

*Both housekeeping and laundry staff include many part-time workers, so that the workload is variable to demand.

Required:

Should Taj Hotel accept the customer bid for a night in New Delhi on December 17 at a price of ₹ 7,000?

5. The following conversation took place between Rahul, vice president of marketing, and Amit, controller of HP Computer Company:

Rahul: I am really excited about our new computer coming out. I think it will be a real market success.

Amit : I'am really glad you think so, I know that our success will be determined by our price. If our price is too high, our competitors will be the ones with the market success.

Rahul: Don't worry about it, We'll just mark out product cost up by 25% and it will all work out. I know we'll make money at those markups. By the way, what does the estimated product cost look like?

Amit: Well, there's the rub. The product cost look as if it's going to come in at around ₹ 12,000. With a 25% markup, that will give us a selling price of ₹ 15,000.

Rahul: I see your concern. That's a little high. Our research indicates that computer prices are dropping and that this type of computer should be selling for around ₹12,500 when we release it to the market.

Amit: I'm not sure what to do.

Rahul: Let me see if I can help. How much of the ₹ 12,000 is fixed cost?

Amit: About ₹ 2,000.

Rahul: There you go. The fixed cost is sunk. We don't need to consider it in our pricing decision. If we reduce the product cost by ₹ 2000, the new product with a 25% markup would be right at ₹ 12,500. Boy, I was really worried for a minute there. I knew something wasn't right.

Required:

(a) If you were Amit, how would you respond to Rahul's solution to the pricing problem?

(b) How might target costing be used to help solve this pricing dilemma?

PART

4

PLANNING, CONTROL AND PERFORMANCE MEASUREMENT

9

BUDGETING

LEARNING OBJECTIVES:

After reading this chapter, you should be able to:

- Define Budgeting, Budgetary Control and Distinguish Between Budgeting and Forecasting
- Explain the Relationship Between Planning and Control Process and Budgeting
- Explain Objectives and Functions of Budgeting, its Advantages and Limitations
- Understand Budgeting Procedure, Budget Committee, Budget Period, Budget Centres, Principal Budget Factor and Elements of a Successful Budgeting Plan
- Distinguish Between Planning Budgets and Control Budgets
- Explain Behavioural Dimensions of Budgeting
- Distinguish Between Fixed and Flexible Budgeting and Understand Advantages of Flexible Budgeting
- Explain Different Types of Functional and Financial Budgets and Concept of Master Budget and Revision of Budgets
- Explain Zero-Based Budgeting; Planning, Programming and Budgeting System (PPBS); Activity-Based Budgeting (ABB); Life Cycle Budget; Kaizen Budgeting and Government Budgeting

CONCEPT OF BUDGETING

One of the primary objectives of management accounting is to provide information to management for planning and control. Budgeting acts as a tool of both planning and control. Budgeting is a formal process of financial planning using estimated financial and accounting data. The Chartered Institute of Management Accountants (UK) defines a budget as:

> **Budgeting** is a formal process of financial planning using estimated financial and accounting data.

- *a financial and/or quantitative statement, prepared and approved prior to a defined period of time, of the policy to be pursued during that period for the purpose of attaining a given objective. It may include income, expenditure and the employment of capital.*

The National Association of Accountants (USA) (now Institute of Management Accountants) defines budgeting as:

- *the process of planning all flows of financial resources into, within, and from an entity during some specified future period.*

BUDGETING AND FORECASTING

Sometimes the terms 'budgeting' and 'forecasting' are used interchangeably. Both terms have some similarities. *For example*, both relate to future events and involve prediction of something. The basic difference between budgeting and forecasting lies in the degree of sophistication involved in the predictions used by them. According to the Institute of Management Accountants (USA):

- *forecasting is a process of predicting or estimating future happening.*

Forecasting is an essential part of the budgeting process. Forecasting is estimating future events and their effects on the budget. Forecasting comes to an end after mere estimating. Budgeting is a process of preparing budgets and further control aspects are involved in its procedure. Besides, forecasting can be made by a business for purposes other than budgeting, such as a forecast of general business conditions. Such forecasts are sometimes not used in budgeting.

> **Forecasting** is estimating future events and their effects on the budget.

Budgeting is not merely forecasting of a particular event. It is not simply an estimation or prediction; it is a plan. In simple terms, budgeting is an attempt, at the beginning of the year (or at any other period), to plan the profit and loss account for the year and to aim for a definite balance sheet at its end, instead of relying upon chance.

CONCEPT OF BUDGETARY CONTROL

Budgetary control is a control measure in which the actual state of affairs is compared with the budget so that appropriate action may be taken with regard to any deviations before it is too late. Budgeting is thus merely a part of budgetary control. The Chartered Institute of Management Accountants (UK) defines budgetary controls as:

- *the establishment of budgets relating the responsibilities of executives to the requirements of a policy and the continuous comparison of actual with budgeted results either to secure by individual action the objective of that policy or to provide a basis for its revision.*

Briefly, the use of a budget to control a firm's activities is known as budgetary control. Budgetary control has the following main objectives:

> **Budgetary control** is a control measure in which the actual state of affairs is compared with the budget so that appropriate action may be taken with regard to any deviations.

1. To provide an organised procedure for planning. It provides a detailed plan of action for a business over a definite period of time.
2. To coordinate all the activities of various departments of a business firm in such a manner that the maximum profit will be achieved for the minimum use of resources.
3. To provide a means of determining the responsibility for all deviations from the plan (budget), and to supply information on the basis of which necessary corrective action may be taken. Thus, budgetary control has the objective of controlling cost.

PLANNING AND CONTROL PROCESS AND BUDGETING

> **Planning** provides a framework which helps management to develop a plan of action.
>
> **Control** is the process of using feedback on actual performances and results.

Budgeting is a vital part in the planning and control process. Planning provides a framework which helps management to develop a plan of action, to estimate future revenues and costs, to anticipate future events, to reduce uncertainty about the future and to increase the chances of achieving the goals and objectives of the organisation through coordination of plans. Control is the process of using feedback on actual performances and results, comparing the actual results with the plans, measuring its deviations from plans and policies and finally taking corrective actions to bring all future activities in line with the plan (budget). If the deviation is a result of a plan that is unrealistic or incorrect, the plan (budget) may have to be revised and updated. Thus, planning and control process helps managers plan how to use resources, including people, to achieve particular goals and objectives and to control the use of resources to achieve those goals and objectives.

Furthermore, plans, as stated above, identify objectives and the actions needed to achieve them. Budgets are the quantitative expressions of these plans, expressed in either physical or financial terms or both. Budget is a plan showing how resources are to be acquired and used over a specific time period. Thus, a budget is a method for translating the goals and strategies of an organisation into operational terms. On the relationship between planning and budgeting, Anderson and Sollenberger[1] observe:

> Planning identifies a desired output while budgeting identifies inputs needed to achieve that output. Thus, management uses the planning process to establish programme, make basic policies and set goals and objectives for the overall organisation. Budgeting, as a part of the planning process, coordinates the details of the many activities needed to implement the programmes that meet the company's goals and objectives.

In the control process, budget, which is a plan of action, is used to control by comparing actual operations and performances as they happen with the planned (budgeted) operations. Figure 9.1 shows the relationship between planning and control and the role that budgets play in this overall process.

PLANNING BUDGETS AND CONTROL BUDGETS

As stated earlier, budget is a financial plan which is subsequently used for control purposes as well to ensure that company goals and policies are achieved. A single composite budget is used for both planning and control functions and it is not logical to have two types of budgets for these two functions. However, when used for planning and for control, the same budget becomes known as planning budget and control budget. The similarities and differences between planning and control budgets are as follows:[2]

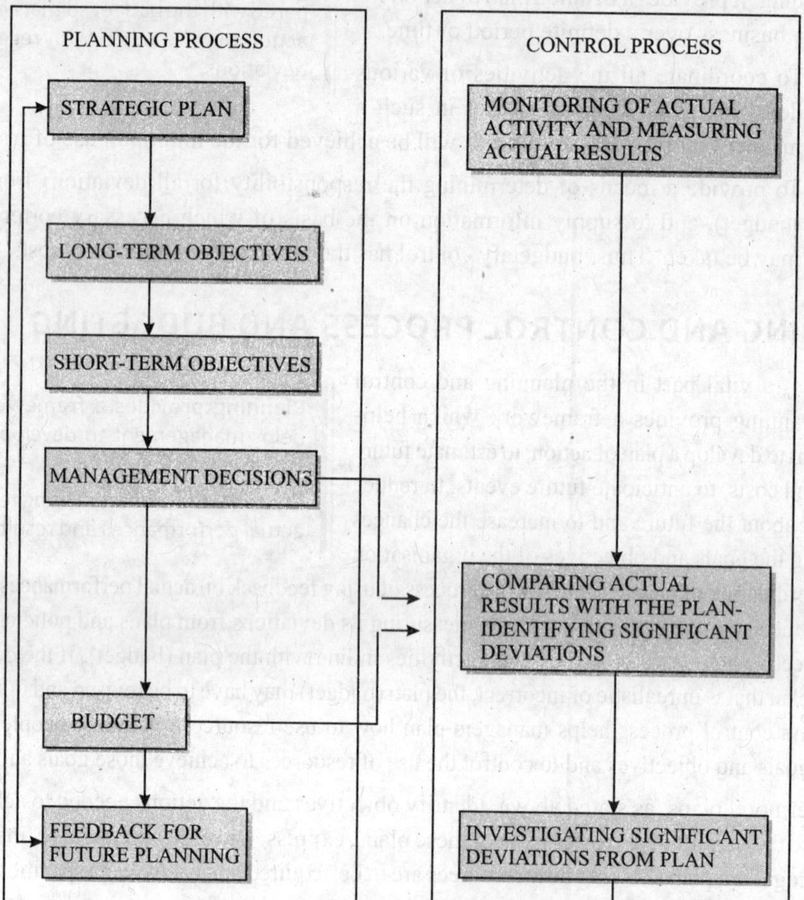

Figure 9.1: Planning, Control Process and Budgets

1. Both types of budgets must be flexible — planning budgets to change in circumstances and control budgets to change in activity levels.
2. They both need feedback in order to evaluate performance and to ensure that standards are up-to-date.

3. Control budgets analyse costs and revenues on a departmental basis, whereas planning budgets analyse costs and revenues on a product line basis.
4. Planning budgets are prepared for the whole firm whereas control budgets can be sectionalised.
5. Participation is encouraged in control budgets, but not in planning budgets.
6. In planning budgets, the standards reflect what management believes will happen, *i.e.*, planning budget reflects management's real beliefs. However, in control budgets, the standards are set to influence behaviour in a way which is beneficial to the organisation.

STRATEGIC PLANNING AND BUDGETING

Before a budget is formulated, an organisation should develop a strategic plan. A strategic plan identifies strategies for future activities and operations, defines goals, directions and resource needs involving a 3 to 5 year time duration or longer. For instance, a strategic plan includes long-range (generally 5 years or more) forecasts of markets, sales including new products, price policies, production and capacity requirements, aggregate level of costs, resource needs and financing requirements. Strategic plans also identify major capital investments required to maintain present facilities and production capacity, increase capacity or diversify to other products. In short, strategic plan states the long-range strategy for achieving organisational goals. After developing a strategic plan, planning and control process requires that this strategic plan should be translated into long-term and short-term objectives. In the light of these objectives, management makes decisions and formulates budgets. It is necessary that management should develop a perfect linkage between the budget and the strategic plan. In developing this linkage, however, management should take care that all attention is not focussed on the short-run. This is important because budgets, as one-period plans, are short-run in nature.[3] As the operations are carried out, they are monitored to ensure compliance with the budget.

> **Strategic plan** states the long-range strategy for achieving organisational goals.
>
> **Tactical planning** is concerned with determining specific objectives and means by which strategic plans will be achieved.

Strategic planning is not concerned with day-to-day operations, although the strategic plan is the foundation on which short-term planning is based. Managers engaging in strategic planning should identify key variables, believed to be the direct causes of the achievement or non-achievement of organizational goals and objectives. Key variables can be internal (under the control of management) or external (normally noncontrollable by management). Effective strategic planning requires that managers build plans and budgets that blend and harmonize external considerations and influences with the firm's internal factors.[4]

Strategic Planning and Tactical Planning

Strategic planning is different from tactical planning which is concerned with determining specific objectives and means by which strategic plans will be achieved. Some tactical plans, such as corporate policy statements, exist for the long term and address repetitive situations. Most tactical plans, however, are short term (1 to 18 months); they are considered 'single-use' plans and are developed to address a given set of circumstances or to cover a specific period of time.

The annual budget is an example of a single-use tactical plan. Although a budget is typically prepared for a one-year period, shorter period (quarterly and monthly) plans should also be included for the budget to work effectively. A well-prepared budget translates a company's strategic and tactical plans into usable guides for company activities. Table 9.1 illustrates the relationships among strategic planning, tactical planning, and budgeting.

Table 9.1: Relationships Among Planning Processes

Who?	What?	How?	Why?
Top management	Strategic planning	Statement of organizational mission, goals, and strategies; long range (5-10 years)	Establish a long-range vision of the organization and provide a sense of unity of and commitment to specified purposes
Top management and mid-management	Tactical planning	Statement of organizational plans; short range (1-18 months)	Provide direction for achievement of strategic plans; state strategic plans in terms on which managers can act; furnish a basis against which results can be measured
Top management, mid-management, and operational management	Budgeting	Quantitative and monetary statements that coordinate company activities for a year or less	Allocate resources effectively and efficiently; indicate a commitment to objectives; provide a monetary control device

Source: Jesset T. Barfield, Cecily A. Raiborn and Michael R. Kinney, Cost Accounting, Traditions and Innovations, Thomson, 2003, p. 555.

Both strategic and tactical planning require that the latest information regarding the economy, environment, technological developments, and available resources be incorporated into the setting of goals and objectives. This information is used to adjust the previously gathered historical information for any changes in the key variables for the planning period. The planning process also demands that, as activity takes place and plans are implemented, a monitoring system be in place to provide feedback so that the control function can be operationalized.[5]

OBJECTIVES AND FUNCTIONS OF BUDGETING

An effective budgeting system is vital to the success and survival of a business firm. Without a fully coordinated budgeting system, management cannot know the direction business is taking. Organisations that do not plan are likely to wander aimlessly and ultimately succumb to the swirl of current events. Budgeting helps management in the following ways.

Budgets Compel Planning

> **Budget** is a formal planning framework that provides specific deadlines to achieve departmental objectives and contributes towards the overall objectives of an organisation.

Almost all business activities require some planning to ensure efficient and maximum use of scarce resources. The first step in planning is defining a company's broad aims and objectives. After the broad objectives have been defined, strategies to achieve the desired goals are formulated and tentative schedules set up. The budget is a detailed schedule of the proposed combination of the various factors of production which is the most profitable for the ensuing period. It is a formal planning framework that provides specific deadlines to achieve departmental objectives and contributes towards the overall objectives of an organisation. A budget incorporates expected performance and present managerial targets. These targets guide the business operations and help in overcoming problem and analysing the future. Budgeting influences strategies which tend to change if conditions or managerial objective change such as changing product lines.

Budgeting moves an organisation from an informal, 'reactive' style to a formal 'proactive' style of management. As a result, less time is spent solving unanticipated problems and more time is spent on positive measures and preventive actions.

Budgets Improve Coordination

Coordination is a managerial function under which all factors of production and all departmental activities are balanced and integrated to achieve the objectives of the organisation. The budgeting process provides the basis for individuals in all parts of the organisation to exchange ideas on how best to achieve these objectives.

> **Coordination** is a managerial function under which all factors of production and all departmental activities are balanced and integrated to achieve the objectives of the organisation.

There is a need for coordination between the production and sales departments. A production manager should ensure adequate production to meet the anticipated demand of the sales department. In turn, the finance manager has to ensure adequate cash to meet greater output requirements. Purchasing and personnel managers must know the factory's material and labour requirements. Budgeting forces the managers of these diverse functions to communicate their plans and coordinate their activities. Budgets help management to coordinate in the following ways:

1. The existence of a well-laid plan is the major step towards achieving coordination. Executives are forced to think of the relationships among individual operations, and the company as a whole.
2. Budgets help to restrain the empire building efforts of executives. Budgets broaden individual thinking by helping to remove unconscious biases on the part of engineers, sales and production officers.
3. Budgets help to search out weaknesses in the organisational structure. The formulation and administration of budgets isolate problems of communication, of fixed responsibility, and of working relationships.

Budgeting ensures coordination in the absence of which different departments in an organisation may act in a manner which is beneficial only to their individual departments, but not to the firm's objectives as a whole. A sales department may sell more than the production department can produce or vice versa. The sales department may think only in terms of price, the production manager may be concerned only with quality, the purchasing manager may aim to buy in large quantities to avail of the advantage of discount, the finance manager has to take care of maturing obligations and make arrangements for funds to meet increasing business requirements. The budgeting process helps in removing inconsistencies among the goals and actions of each department and reconciles their differences so that each department contributes towards the overall objectives of the organisation.

Budgets Improve Communication

It is necessary in an efficient organisation that all people be informed about the objectives, policies, programmes and performances. They should have a clear understanding of the aims and objectives and the part that they are to play in goal attainment. This is made possible through their participation in the budgeting process. Budgets inform each manager of what others have agreed to do. They also inform managers of the resources available to achieve objectives and targets.

Budgets Provide a Basis of Control and Performance Evaluation

Budgeting enters into control at three points:

1. When a budget is being formulated, departments analyse their plans for the future and submit estimates as per their requirements, justifying each of their demands by demonstrating a need.

2. After budgets of different departments have been reviewed and approved they become targets that set desirable limits on spending.
3. At the end of the budget period, a comparison of actual expenditures with budget expenditure is made as a means of judging performances and fixing responsibility for deviations.

Budgets are the basis of performance evaluation in an organisation as they reflect realistic estimates of acceptable and expected performance. Most managers are interested to know what is expected of them so that they may monitor their own performance. It is more accurate, reliable and reasonable to measure current performance against a budget rather than against a vague expectation or against results of previous year when conditions might have changed. The sales department should be evaluated against what was reasonable to expect rather than against what was achieved in the previous year. As a basis for judging actual results, budgeted performance is generally considered a better criterion than past performance.

ADVANTAGES OF BUDGETING

Budgeting plays an important role in the effective use of resources and achieving overall organisational goals. It has the following advantages:

1. Budgeting compels and motivates management to make an early and timely study of its problems. It generates a sense of caution and care, and adequate study among managers before decisions are made by them.
2. Budgeting provides a valuable means of controlling income and expenditure of a business as it is a 'plan for spending.'
3. Budgeting provides a tool through which managerial policies and goals are periodically evaluated, tested and established as guidelines for the entire organisation.
4. Budgeting helps in directing capital and other resources into the most profitable channels.
5. Budgeting enables management to decentralise responsibility without losing control of the business. It reveals weaknesses, inefficiencies, deviations in the organisation very promptly which can be checked immediately to achieve a desired goal.
6. The use of budgeting in an organisation develops an attitude of 'cost consciousness', stimulates the effective use of resources, and creates an environment of profit-mindedness throughout the organisation. It emphasises how much should be spent to achieve a goal.
7. It provides a norm, basis or yardstick for measuring performance of departments and individuals working in organisations. Individual managers can evaluate their own decisions and achievements and take suitable steps to improve their performances.
8. Budgeting encourages productive competition, provides incentive to perform efficiently and gives a sense of purpose to each individual in the organisation. All these positive factors lead to higher output and increase employee productivity.
9. Budgeting provides a systematic and disciplined approach to the solution of problems in the organisation.
10. Budgeting, if executed in nearly every enterprise, helps the total national economy by providing stability of employment, economic use of resources and effective prevention of waste.

DISADVANTAGES OF BUDGETING

While budgeting performs many functions and has many advantages that are vital to an organisation, it has certain limitations which require careful consideration:

1. Planning, budgeting or forecasting is not an exact science; it uses approximations and judgement which may not be cent per cent accurate. At best, a budget is an estimate; no one knows precisely what will happen in the future.
2. The success and utility of budgeting depends on the cooperation and participation of all members of management. All persons should direct their efforts according to the plan. The top management also should adhere to the budget and provide cooperation. Many a time budgeting has failed because executive management has paid only lip service to its execution.
3. A budget is only a tool and neither eliminates nor takes over the place of management. A budget cannot be substituted for management but should only be used by management for accomplishing managerial functions. Executives generally feel 'circled in' by a budget and its related figures. They fail to understand that budget is meant to provide detailed information, goals and targets which may help them in achieving the company objectives.
4. The establishment of a budgeting process takes time. Also, sometimes too much is expected from a budget and in case expectations are not fulfilled, the blame is put on the budget. An efficient budgeting programme requires that responsible persons should understand the philosophy, objectives and essentials of budgeting.
5. Excessive emphasis on budgeting may result in attempts by lower level management and employees to buck the system by providing inaccurate estimates of future costs and revenues, and by failing to take advantage of changes in the environment because to do so would result in a deviation from plan, they would be considered as operating contrary to the budget. Under an unbalanced budget programme, employees will tend to overestimate costs and underestimate revenues, thus creating budget slack.
6. As the end of budget period approaches and employees realise that actual expenses have not been as great as allowed by the budget, there may be a temptation to spend excessive amounts in order to 'use up' the budget allowance. Such activities result in sub-optimal profits for the company.

Blocher, Chen, Cokins and Lin[6] comment:

> Spending the budget is another serious ethical issue in budgeting. Managers might believe that their future budgets will be reduced if they do not use up all the budgeted amounts. As a result, managers might resort to wasteful spending to exhaust the remaining budgeted amount before the end of the period. This wastes precious resources on activities that yield little or no benefit to the firm or acquire unnecessary assets to use up remaining funds. Furthermore, managers waste time on unproductive efforts in trying to exhaust the budgeted expenditure.

BUDGETING PROCEDURE

The budgeting procedure or programme varies widely from one organisation to another. Differences in management style, organisation objectives, structure of competition and similar factors affect the procedures companies adopt in budget preparations. However, there are a set of guidelines (procedures) which are used in the budgeting process by a large number of organisations. These common steps can be listed as follows:

1. ***Obtaining Estimates:*** Obtaining estimates of sales, production levels, expected costs, and availability of resources from each sub-unit/division/department: The departmental heads

or managers are required to provide estimates of future conditions and activities that will have an impact on the company. The discussion and participation may be in the form of informal discussions and/or detailed written reports of plans which will be submitted to the budget committee for approval.

2. ***Coordinating Estimates:*** In many organisations, the budget committee evaluates the different plans submitted by various organisational units to determine the potentiality of plans in the overall interest of the company and to estimate what resources are available and can be fairly allocated among the various units of the organisation.
3. ***Communicating Budget:*** Communicating the budget to responsible managers and the concerned departments: After individual budget plans have been approved in the light of organisational goals and availability of resources, the budgets should be communicated to departments and responsible managers. Changes and modifications incorporated in the final budget should be made known to managers to obtain their cooperation and support for the budgets. Budgeting requires effective communication to convince the departmental manager about changes in the budget.
4. ***Implementing Budget Plan:*** The final budget is presented to the managers concerned and adopted as the plan of operation for the coming budget period. The various service units in a business enterprise are required to provide the necessary materials, labour, facilities and other resources to carry out the budget.
5. ***Reporting Interim Progress towards Budgeted Objectives:*** As a feedback in the budgeting process, performance reports are prepared to inform departmental managers and top management about the performances achieved in terms of budgeted figures. Such an investigation may call for a need to revise the budget during the year. For example, it is advisable to reduce production when sales are low than to continue with high production levels. This feedback of information can also be used as a basis for preparing the next year's budget.

ORGANIZATION FOR BUDGETING (THE BUDGET COMMITTEE)

Responsibility for budget direction and execution is usually placed in the hands of a Budget Committee which reports directly to top management. In large companies, the budget committee is composed of executives incharge of major functions of the business and includes the sales manager, HRD manager, finance manager, production manager, chief engineer, treasurer and chief accounts officer. One member of the budget committee is the budget director who is in-charge of preparing a budget manual of instructions and accumulating the proposed budget data. In large companies, the position may be a full-time job; in smaller companies, the post may be assigned to the finance manager or chief accounts officer or some other officer who acts as budget director on a part-time basis.

The principal functions of the budget committee are to:

1. Decide the company's general policies and objectives
2. Receive and review individual budget estimates concerning different departments/units/divisions
3. Suggest changes, modifications in accordance with organisational objectives
4. Approve budgets which act as an authority/target for departmental action
5. Receive and analyse performance reports regarding the implementation of budgets
6. Suggest corrective action to improve efficiency and achieve budgetary goals

In performing these functions, the budget committee headed by the budget director becomes a management committee. It is a powerful force in coordinating and balancing the various activities of an organisation and exercising real control over business operations. Differences among members of the budget committee representing different departments may arise. However, these conflicts should be eliminated. It is true that every member will not get all what he asks for. But all members should be given a fair hearing by the committee and should not be left with the impression that there has been any discrimination.

The budget director himself is not expected to prepare the budget; his duty is merely to supervise and direct the budget programme. Obviously the budget director must have a sufficient high status in order to ensure that the budgeting programme will command respect and attention throughout the organisation. Often required to act as a mediator, a budget director needs the skill of a master politician who can avoid saying yes without flatly saying no. Also called for is a talent for selling the budget to the organisation.

BUDGET PERIOD

The budget period is an important factor in developing a comprehensive budgeting programme. This is the period for which forecasts can reasonably be made and budgets can be formulated. A business enterprise generally prepares a short-range budget, and a long-range budget.

> **Budget period** is the period for which forecasts can reasonably be made and budgets can be formulated.

Short-range Budget

Short-range budgets may cover periods of three, six or twelve months depending upon the nature of the business. Most manufacturing firms use one year as the planning period. Wholesale and retail firms usually employ a six-month budget which is related to their selling seasons. In determining the period of the short-range budget, the following factors should be considered:

1. The budget period should be long enough to cover complete production of various products
2. For business of a seasonal nature, the budget period should cover at least one entire seasonal cycle
3. The budget period should be long enough to allow for the financing of production well in advance of actual needs. It should provide adequate time to arrange the funds for production and other purposes
4. The budget period should coincide with the financial accounting period to compare actual results with budget estimates and thus to facilitate better interpretation of the performance

> **Short-range budgets** may cover periods of three, six or twelve months depending upon the nature of the business.
>
> **Long-range budgets** or plans are neither described in precise terms, nor are they expected to be completely coordinated future budgets.

Long-range Budget

A long-range budget or planning is defined as:

- *a systematic and formalised process for purposefully directing and controlling future operations toward a desired objective for periods extending beyond one year.*

Long-range budgets or plans are neither described in precise terms, nor are they expected to be completely coordinated future budgets. They cover specific areas, such as future sales, future production, long-term capital expenditures, extensive research and development programmes, financial requirements, profit forecast, etc. They evaluate the future implications associated with present decisions and help management in making present decisions and select the most profitable alternative. Long-range budgeting does not eliminate risk altogether; it only reduces the risk to a level which does not hamper the production and achievement of company objectives.

There are many factors which are duly considered while preparing long-term budgets, such as market trends, economic factors, growth of population, consumption pattern, industrial production, national income, government's economic and industrial policy. Quantitative sales can be budgeted for a three to five years period. After forecasting sales, a budgeted profit and loss account can be prepared relating anticipated sales to corresponding cost and thus net operating profit can be forecasted. Likewise, a balance sheet for many years can be prepared to forecast cash, inventory levels, accounts receivable, accounts payable, liabilities, etc. The forecasted profit and loss account and balance sheet for a long-range is a very useful tool in accomplishing the objectives of the organisation as a whole.

There are advantages and disadvantages in both long-term and short-term budgeting, and the choice must be made judiciously. Short-term budgeting has the advantage of accuracy in budgeted figures which relate to future activity. Long-term budgeting may be less reliable as predictions for a longer period are relatively inaccurate. On the other hand, short-term budgeting has some limitations. One of the objectives of budgeting is anticipating problems long before they appear so that sufficient time is available for satisfactory solutions. This objective is difficult to achieve in short-term budgeting. Therefore, it is necessary for a business firm to prepare both long-term and short-term budgets.

ELEMENTS OF A SUCCESSFUL BUDGETING PLAN

The success of the budgeting process in an organisation depends on the following essential elements:

1. ***Accurate Forecasting of Business Activities:*** Forecasting is a prerequisite in a budgeting process. It is not only the starting point, but is also critical to the development of an accurate budget.

2. ***Coordinating Business Activities:*** Budgeting needs to coordinate all the individual budgets into an integrated plan as each budget has certain implications for the other budgets. There must be coordination between sales, production, purchasing and personnel budgets.

3. ***Communicating the Budgets:*** The success of a comprehensive budgeting programme depends on communication of individual budgets to the different units in the organisation. The basic point is that the preparation of the budget is of no value unless it is known to the person for whom it is meant. Managers are not responsible for budget unless the budget is communicated clearly, concisely and in an authoritative manner to them.

4. ***Acceptance and Cooperation:*** Successful budgeting also requires that budgets should be accepted by the people who must execute them. Budgeting should have the active cooperation of the entire organisation from the top to the bottom. Cooperation for the budget can be achieved in a number of ways.

5. ***Reasonable Flexibility:*** The budgeting programme should contain reasonable flexibility if the situation so demands. However, it should be noted that too much flexibility and too much tightness are both undesirable. Too much flexibility will weaken the cost control and the budget will become inoperative. Similarly, too much rigidity not permitting reasonable deviations will create problems and restrictions in the implementation of the budget. If conditions have changed making the estimates and budgets inaccurate, the budgets should be revised.

6. ***Providing a Framework for Evaluation:*** Budgeting provides a basis to evaluate the performance of different departments. A comprehensive budget, properly developed, will contain initially organisational goals and expectations and subsequently can be used as an effective evaluation technique.

According to Shields,[7] the key to successful budgeting lies in basing its design not on financial budgets, but rather on an organisation's strategic goals, critical success factors and related performance measures. He has given five recommendations for the design of budgeting that is good for business, that is, ones that maximize the realized benefits from budgeting:

1. Measure output, not input:
   - A focus on inputs induces behavior that is myopic, inwardly directed, cost minimizing, and blaming.
   - Outputs include financial performance, quality, market share, customer satisfaction, and innovation.
   - Measure outputs in financial or non-financial metrics as appropriate.
2. Plan first, budget later:
   - Avoid extending last year's budget (e.g., next budget = last budget +/– ₹ *X*).
   - Sequentially develop a long-term plan, a long-term budget, a short-term plan, and finally a short-term — operating — budget.
   - Set discretionary programme expenses during the long-term planning process and don't change them during the short-term planning and budgeting process. For example, don't reduce them in tough times or when the aggregated total of sub-budgets is not consistent with desired organizationwide future performance.
   - Exclude some strategic resources from subunit budgets if there is pressure to reduce operating budgets or budgeted spending.
3. Budgeting is for managers, not accountants:
   - Don't base budgeting designs on financial accounting or tax regulations and practices.
   - Tie budgeting to strategic and operating planning, not financial and tax accounting.
4. Design against turf wars:
   - Budgets designed around functional departments such as marketing and manufacturing that link vertically with similar functional units leads to myopic behavior intended to protect the functional departments at the expense of the organization and its customers.
   - Organize budgets by customers, geography, products, technology, and business processes, to focus employees and budgets on customers.
5. Build budget busting into the system:
   - Develop contingency plans during budgeting to promote planning and fast reaction to changes in SWOT.
   - Allow budget revisions to include new products and processes after a budget is approved.

BUDGET CENTRES

An organisation is usually broken down into different budget centres for administrative and control purposes. A budget centre is the lowest level in an organisation for which detailed costs are budgeted, separately from those of other budget centres. The Chartered Institute of Management Accountants (U.K.) defines a budget centre as:

> A **budget centre** is the lowest level in an organisation for which detailed costs are budgeted, separately from those of other budget centres.

■■ *a section of the organisation of an undertaking defined for the purposes of budgetary control.*

The main factor in setting up budget centres is one of fixing responsibility for action and inaction. To ensure adequate cost control, the budget centres should fulfil the following conditions:

1. The budget of a particular budget centre should specify precisely the costs controllable by the person responsible for that centre.
2. Costs for which responsibility is joint, e.g., work carried out by a maintenance department should be kept separate from costs which can be controlled by one manager.
3. Costs that are apportioned between two or more budget centres should also be controlled and for such costs one person should be made responsible.

LIMITING OR PRINCIPAL BUDGET FACTOR

When budgets are made, there is invariably some factor which governs or sets a limit to the quantity which can be made or sold. This is known as the limiting or principal budget factor. The Chartered Institute of Management Accountant (UK) defines a principal budget factor as:

- *the factor the extent of whose influence must first be assessed in order to ensure that the functional budgets are reasonably capable of fulfillment.*

In the field of sales, the limiting factor is customer demand which is influenced by many factors, such as price and quality of the product, competition, the general purchasing power of the public, advertising, etc. In the field of production, the principal budget factor may be plant capacity, the supply of labour of the right quality, or the availability of scarce materials. Sometimes, management itself may impose limiting factors, e.g., management may control production to maintain a definite price level or management may not decide to purchase plant and machinery and thus to maintain the same plant capacity.

The limiting or principal budget factors must be carefully considered while preparing the budget. If not properly taken into account, budgets may not be realistic and become difficult to achieve. Coordination among different departments will be lacking. The principal budget factors can be eliminated by taking suitable measures, for example, the plant capacity can be increased by purchase of additional plant.

BEHAVIOURAL DIMENSION OF BUDGETING

The achievement of organisation's goals and objectives depend on the people who work in the organisation. Therefore, management should know the effects created by planning and control tools and techniques on the people within the organisation. A budget affects virtually everyone in an organization: those who prepare the budget, those who use the budget to facilitate decision making and those who are evaluated using the budget. Budgets are used to evaluate the manager's performances and to decide about their salary increases, bonuses, promotions, etc. Since a manager's financial status and career can be affected, budgets can have a significant behavioural effect. Similarly, budgets may motivate the workers to increase their level of activity and efficiency. Whether the effect of budget is positive or negative, depends to a large extent on how budgets are prepared and used. It is important, therefore, that management must know the effects of budgets on people and the effects of people on the budget. Herein, some behavioural implications of budgeting have been discussed.

Dysfunctional Behaviour

Budgets can bring positive behaviour among the people when the goals of individual managers are found in conformity with the goals of the organisation. The perfect matching (or near perfect matching) between the organisational and managerial goals is often referred to as goal congruence. The managers who participate in the budget making process may feel happy in producing a fair budget in terms of organisational goals and objectives. Such a budget may induce and motivate others to bring excellence in their performance. But sometimes, due to improper implementation of the budget and unrealistic management expectations, the reaction of subordinate managers are found to be negative, which in turn has adverse impact on achieving the organisational goals. Such a negative behaviour is known as dysfunctional behaviour which is defined as an individual behaviour that is in basic conflict with the goals of the organisation. Anderson and Sollenberger comment:

> **Dysfunctional behaviour** is an individual behaviour that is in basic conflict with the goals of the organisation.

> Management can create negative budgeting attitudes in several ways. One of these is using budgets or giving the impression they are being used, to squeeze every ounce of productivity out of employees, or solely to identify poor performers or as a means of restricting an employee's ability to perform. If budget variances are always viewed as 'bad news', subordinates will quickly adjust their behaviour to avoid negative evaluations. Necessary managerial actions may not be taken because of fear of penalties. Unless top management is willing to recognise the need for flexibility, reality and positive change, lower management support quickly dissipates.[8]

In order to create and promote a reasonable degree of positive behaviour among the people in an organisation, a budgeting system should possess the following important features or elements:[9]

1. Frequent feedback on performance
2. Flexible budgeting capabilities
3. Monetary and non-monetary incentives
4. Participation
5. Realistic standards
6. Controllability of costs (Non-controllable costs, if included in a budget, should be separated from controllable costs and labelled as non-controllable)

Participative Budgeting

Budgeting processes are either top down or bottom up. In a top-down budgeting process, top management prepares budgets for the entire organisation, including those for lower-level operations. This process often is referred to as authoritative budgeting. A participative budgeting process, on the other hand, is a botton-up approach that involves the people affected by the budget, including lower-level employees, in the budget preparation process. With a **bottom-up** or **participative budget,** managers at all levels—and in some cases, even non-managers—are involved in budget preparation. Budget proposals originate at the lowest level of management possible and are then integrated into the proposals for the next level, and so on, until the proposals reach the top level of management where the budget is completed.

> **Top-down budgeting process/Authoritative budgeting:** Top management prepares budget for entire organisation, including lower-level operations.
>
> **Bottom-up/Participative Budget:** Budget proposals originate at the lowest level and then integrated into the proposals for next level.

Participation by employees in the budget preparation can provide them the feeling that "this is our budget," rather than the feeling generally noticed among employees that "this is the budget imposed by the top on us."

Participation by the subordinate managers in preparing the budget is considered to increase employee motivation and reduce organisational conflict. One indication that an organisation encourages active employee participation is the existence of good superior-subordinate relationships fostered by (*i*) frequent person-to-person contact (*ii*) the use of results in performance appraisal (*iii*) the use of departmental meetings to review actual results and (*iv*) the creation of a 'game' spirit (margin for error, tolerance and slack).[10]

Participation helps ensure that important issues are considered and that employees understand the importance of their roles in meeting organizational goals. It also provides opportunities for problem solving and fosters employee commitment to agreed-upon goals. Hence, budget predictions are likely to be more accurate, and the people responsible for the budget are more likely to strive to accomplish its objectives. These self-imposed budgets or participative budgets reinforce the concept of participative management and should strengthen the overall budgeting process.[11]

Participative budgeting increases employee initiative, performance and morale. This budgeting communicates a sense of responsibility to subordinate managers and fosters creativity. Such budgeting process often gives top management a better grasp of the problems their employees face and provides the employees a better understanding of the dilemmas that the top management deals with. Since the subordinate manager creates the budget, it is more likely that the budget's goals will become the manager's personal goals, resulting in a higher degree of goal congruence. The increased responsibility and challenge inherent in the (participative budgeting) process provide non-monetary incentives that lead to a higher level of performance. Individuals involved in setting their own standards will work harder to achieve them. In addition to the behavioural benefits, participative budgeting has the advantage of involving individuals whose knowledge of local conditions may enhance the entire planning process.[12]

Participative budgeting has some problems and negative consequences which should be avoided. Firstly, when top management has total control of the budgeting process and simultaneously seeks superficial participation from lower level managers, pseudo participation exists in the budgeting process. Pseudo participation, which pretends to be participation but is not, is a form of deceit. The result can be a decrease in motivation. In such a situation, top management is only seeking formal acceptance of the budget from subordinate managers and is not seeking their real input.

Secondly, too much participation and discussion can lead to delay in budget making and can result into significant and irreconcilable differences among the members involved in the budgeting process. Thirdly, participative budgeting can lead to easy budget targets or targets which do not match with the organization's stategy and goals.

Excessive Pressure Created by Budgets

Budgets are used in to direct control and coordinate all activities in the organisation. In this task, budgets should not generate excessive pressure and stress on the subordinate managers, supervisors and the people working in the organisation. In order to eliminate undesirable pressure, the budget goals and standards should be set which are neither too high (tight) nor too low (loose). If the standards and the budgeted goals are too high, motivation becomes poor and failing to achieve them may frustrate the managers and in turn, this frustration can result in poorer performance. Similarly, if the goals and standards are too easily achieved, a manager may lose interest and his performance may decline. As goals and standards are tightened (but not made too tight), motivation will increase. In fact, the objective should be to get subordinate managers in a participative setting to set high but achievable goals and standards. This is one that is tight enough to motivate, yet still realistic. Supervisors and upper level managers must make careful judgements about how tight the budget goals and standards should be for each manager. Further, direct, clear feedback allows the employee to adjust aspiration levels and strive to achieve desired rewards.

It can be concluded that no budget can be successful as long as people are unwilling to accept it. The problem of motivating a company's personnel, however, is difficult to solve. Motivational requirements that have been suggested include the following:[13]

1. A compensation system that builds and maintains a clearly understood relationship between results and rewards.
2. A system for performance appraisal that employees understand with regard to their individual effectiveness and key results, their tasks and their responsibilities, their degree and span of influence in decision-making, as well as the time allowed to judge their results.
3. A system of communication that allows employees to query their superiors with trust and honest communication.
4. A system of promotion that generates and sustains employee faith in its validity and judgement.
5. A system of employee support through coaching, counseling, and career planning.
6. A system that not only considers company objectives, but also employees skills and capacities.
7. A system that will not settle for mediocrity, but which reaches for realistic and attainable standards, stressing improvement and providing an environment in which the concept of excellence can grow.

Budgetary Slack (Cushion)

Budgetary slack, also known as padding the budget, takes place when a manager deliberately underestimates revenues, overestimates costs and requests more funds than needed to support the budgeted level of activities. The difference between the revenue or cost projections that a person provides and a realistic estimate of the revenue or cost is called budgetary slack.

> **Budgetary slack** in the difference between the revenue or cost projections that a person provides and a realistic estimate of the revenue or cost.

In all organisations, there is a tendency to introduce slack or a cushion in the budget. For instance, subordinate managers can know on the basis of past experiences that their budget proposals will be cut by senior managers and therefore will be tempted to pad certain expenses or make low-revenue estimates. On the contrary, the senior managers knowing the padding habits of their subordinate managers, may be tempted to increase the level of expected revenues and reduce the budgeted expenses. Similarly, the sales managers underestimate their sales projections, the controller introduces slack by maintaining excessive cash balances, etc. The degree of slack tends to grow in good years, when satisfactory profits are easily attainable, in bad years slack is voluntarily decreased throughout the organisation.

Morse, Davis and Hartgraves[14] observe:

> While most managers have a natural inclination to be conservative in developing their budgets, at some level the blatant padding, or building slack into the budget, becomes unethical. In an extreme case, it might even be considered theft if an inordinate level of budgetary slack creates favorable performance variances that lead to significant bonuses or other financial gain for the manager. Another form of falsifying budgets occurs when managers include expense categories in their budgets that are not needed in their operations, and the funds are subsequently used to pad other budget categories. The deliberate falsifications of budgets is unethical behavior and is grounds for dismissal in most organizations.

According to Hilton,[15] there are three primary reasons for padding the budget or budgetary slack. Firstly, people often perceive that their performance will look better in their superiors' eyes if they can 'beat the budget.'

Secondly, budgetary stack often is used to cope with uncertainty. A departmental supervisor may feel confident in the cost projections for 10 cost items. However, the supervisor also may feel that some unforeseen event during the budgetary period could result in unanticipated costs. *For example*, an unexpected machine breakdown could occur. One way of dealing with that unforeseen event is to pad the budget. If nothing goes wrong, the supervisor can beat the cost budget. If some negative event does occur, the supervisor can use the budgetary slack to absorb the impact of the event and still meet the cost budget.

Thirdly, the reason why cost budgets are padded is that budgetary cost projections are often cut in the resource-allocation process. Thus, we have a vicious circle. Budgetary projections are padded because they will likely be cut, and they are cut because they are likely to have been padded.

In order to reduce excessive slack, top management may introduce strenuous cost-cutting measures and put too much pressure to decrease the slack. However, in reality, their attempts may create conflict in the organisation, may widen differences among managers, and top management can be looked upon as being arbitrary, and ignorant and insensitive of the needs of lower-level managers in their achieving budgetary goals. The solution lies in finding a level of slack that maintains efficiency and avoids the conflict caused by excessive pressure to reduce the slack. Further, top management should carefully review budgets proposed by subordinate managers and provide input, where needed, in order to decrease the effects of building slack into the budget. Also, managers can be given incentives not only to achieve budgetary projections but also to provide accurate projections. This can be done by asking managers to justify all or some of their projections and by rewarding managers who consistently provide accurate estimates.

Top Management Support

The attainment of budget goals and standards at the lower and middle level management depends to a large extent on the support, participation and cooperation extended by top management in the preparation and execution of budgets. Top managers by their actions should create an environment and give impression to the subordinate managers about their commitment and support to the budget goals and objectives. Otherwise, the planning and control function will be damaged in case subordinate managers think that their top managers are not sincere while preparing and using the budgets.

If a budget program is to be successful, it must have the complete acceptance and support of the persons who occupy key management positions. If lower or middle managers sense that top management is lukewarm about budgeting, or if they sense that top management simply tolerates budgeting as a necessary evil, then their own attitudes will reflect a similar lack of enthusiasm. Budgeting is hard work, and if top management is not enthusiastic about and committed to the budget program, then it is unlikely that anyone else in the organization will be either.

In administering the budget program, it is particularly important that top management does not use the budget to pressure or blame employees. Using budgets in such negative ways will breed hostility, tension, and mistrust rather than cooperation and productivity. Unfortunately, the budget is too often used as a pressure device and excessive emphasis is placed on 'meeting the budget' under all circumstances. Rather than being used as a weapon, the budget should be used as a positive instrument to assist in establishing goals, measuring operating results, and isolating areas that need attention.[16]

Anderson and Sollenberger[17] list the following four important ingredients to demonstrate the existence of top management support:

1. Top management must establish clearly delineated lines of authority and responsibility.
2. Appropriate goals and objectives that other management levels can easily translate into activities must be developed.

3. Top management must actively review and approve budgets and follow-up on budget variances. This conveys the importance they attach to budgeting.
4. Top management must exhibit a positive attitude toward involving lower management levels in the process.

Morse, Davis and Hartgraves[18] observe:

> It is important for management to understand that budgets are not perfect. Mistakes in prediction and judgement are made and unforeseen circumstances often develop, necessitating modification of the budget. Unless top management is willing to recognise when changes in the budget are needed, support for the budget at lower levels will quickly erode. If an organisation is to receive maximum benefit from the budget process, support for the budget at the top management level, as well as at lower levels, must be maintained. Achieving this support may be the most difficult challenge facing an organisation undertaking budget for the first time. Lower-level managers are not likely to respect the budget and the related performance reports if they perceive a lack of commitment by top management. Disregard for the budget by top management can quickly destroy the effectiveness of the budget throughout the organisation.

Inter-departmental Conflict

The budgeting process is rightly considered a technical and formal one. However, in reality, the budgeting process becomes most often an informal bargaining process or wherein managers of different departments compete for organisation scarce resources. According to Hopwood[19] this can lead to a dilution of original goals, as managers try (and fight) for power and recognition. Departmental conflict or conflict between the managers are also due to the fact that different departments are found blaming each other when they fail to achieve their targets. Further, a feeling of 'them' and 'us' exists between the budget staff, *i.e.*, accounts departments (them), and the other departments (us). This is because the budget staff's success is the other's failure, e.g., the accountant's success in finding an adverse variance identifies another employee's failure to achieve his budget.[20] To solve the problem of departmental conflict and to reduce resentment and distrust among subordinate managers, Argyris has suggested the following two measures:

1. Real participation and not pseudo-participation in the preparation of budgets by employees should be encouraged. Real participation involves people in the decision-making process whereas pseudo-participation pressurises people into budget acceptance. Real participation gives more responsibility to people, boosts their morale and has a motivational impact.
2. There should be training in human relations and improvements in communication systems.

To conclude, management should know and be concerned about the influence of the budgeting process on the people within the organisation and also how people in an organisation influence the budgeting process through their behaviour and perception. It can be rightly said that an ideal budgeting system is one which achieves complete goal congruence and simultaneously creates a drive in managers to achieve the organisational goals and objectives.

James L Piera[21] has made the following remarkable observations on behavioural function of budgeting.

> In the field of cost control, use the budget as a tool to be placed in the foreman's hands-not as a club to be held over their heads. To implement this rule, it may be a good idea to design an educational programme. Cost reduction must be placed on the basis of mutual effort toward a common aim. The creation of this atmosphere is an essential, definite step in budget practice.

He further observes:

> We are beginning to learn that no tool can be used effectively unless the hand that guides it is rightly motivated. Like all other techniques of business, the budget should be a door open to more satisfying and profitable work—not an instrument of torture.
>
> Then it will be known that what you can do without a budget you can do better with one. It will be seen that entire planning and control procedure is a device for freeing men to do their best work—not a machine of restriction and condemnation.
>
> Planning is but another word for vision that sees a creative achievement before it is manifest. Control is but a name for direction. The genius of management can not fail to turn the budget idea finally into positive channels, so that people individually as well as business leadership generally will reap the harvest that it promises.

FIXED AND FLEXIBLE BUDGETING

The concepts of fixed and flexible budgeting are discussed below.

Fixed Budgeting

The Chartered Institute of Management Accountants (UK) defines a fixed budget as:

- *the budget which is designed to remain unchanged irrespective of the level of activity actually attained.*

It is based on a single level of activity. A fixed budget performance report compares data from actual operations with the single level of activity reflected in the budget. It is based on the assumption that the company will work at some specified level of activity and that a stated production will be achieved. It suggests that the budget is not adjusted when production level changes.

> **Fixed Budget** is based on a single level of activity. **Flexible budget** is prepared for a range *i.e.*, for more than one level of activity.

However, in practice, fixed budgeting is rarely used. The main reason is that actual output is often significantly different from the budgeted output. In such a case, the budget cannot be used for the purpose of cost control. The performance report may be misleading and will not contain very useful information. For example, if actual production is 12,000 units in place of the budgeted 10,000 units, the costs incurred cannot be compared with the budget which relates to different levels of activity. Since, in fixed budgeting, units are overlooked, a cost to cost comparison without considering the units may give misleading results. The performance report prepared under fixed budgeting merely discloses whether actual costs were higher or lower than budgeted costs. The fact that costs and expenses are affected by fluctuations in volume limits the use of the fixed budget. If budgeted costs are compared with the actual costs at the end of the year, it will be difficult to infer how successful a business firm has been in keeping expenses within the allowed limits.

A fixed budget can be usefully employed when budgeted output is close enough to the actual output. It is also important to note that budget levels should be determined on the basis of what is likely to happen in the future rather than on the basis of what has happened in the past. Past information is useful in future planning. But budgeting on the basis of a rule of thumb such as "last year's figure plus 20%" is not beneficial. The most appropriate and logical approach is first to determine what needs to be done and then to decide how it is to be done. The budgeting process may then be adopted to estimate cost for the specific tasks that have been identified.

Flexible Budgeting

A flexible budget is defined in the terminology of cost accounting, issued by the Chartered Institute of Management Accountants (UK) as:

- *a budget which by recognising the difference between fixed, semi-fixed and variable costs, is designed to change in relation to the level of activity attained.*

> **Flexible budget** is also known by other names, such as variable budget, dynamic budget, sliding scale budget, step budget, expenses formula budget and expenses control budget.

A flexible budget is a budget that is prepared for a range, *i.e.*, for more than one level of activity. It is a set of alternative budgets to different expected levels of activity. The flexible budget is also known by other names, such as variable budget, dynamic budget, sliding scale budget, step budget, expenses formula budget and expenses control budget. The underlying principle of a flexible budget is that every business is dynamic, ever-changing, and never static. Thus, a flexible budget might be developed that would apply to a 'relevant range' of production, say 8,000 units to 12,000 units. Under this approach, if actual production slips to 9,000 units from a projected 10,000 units, the manager has a specific tool (*i.e.*, the flexible budget) that can be used to determine budgeted cost at 9,000 units of output. The flexible budget provides a reliable basis for comparison because it is automatically geared to changes in a production activity.

A flexible budget provides information to managers for multiple levels of output in case actual output is different from the expected level. The performance reports at the end of the accounting period are compared with a budget based on the actual output attained during the period. A flexible budget has the following important features:

1. It covers a range of activity (output).
2. It is flexible, *i.e.*, easy to change with variation in production levels.
3. It facilitates performance measurement and evaluation.

Planning or budgeting for a range of activity rather than for a single level of activity is always preferable due to the uncertainty involved in forecasting future events accurately. Flexible budgeting assumes that uncertainty is likely to bring in fluctuations in the activity level. This budgeting aims to provide information about the effects of changes in activity levels and thus helps managers in making more effective decisions. In flexible budgeting, that range of activity is selected which is likely to occur. Activity levels, not likely to occur, are not included. Most often, one activity level at each extreme of the activity range is selected, with one or more in between. Among different activity levels, the most likely activity level is made the basis for planning business operations. The flexibility involved in this budget makes a very useful decision-making tool for management. Perhaps the most important point in favour of flexible budgeting is that it provides the most accurate and reliable base for measuring performance and efficiency of the departments and individuals working in the organisation.

Steps in Flexible Budgeting

The following steps (stages) are involved in developing a flexible budget:

1. Deciding the range of activity to which the budget is to be prepared.
2. Determining the cost behaviour patterns (fixed, variable, semi-variable) for each element of cost to be included in the budget.
3. Selecting the activity levels (generally in terms of production) to prepare budgets at those levels.
4. Preparing the budget at each activity level selected by associating the activity level with corresponding costs. The corresponding costs to be attached with each activity level are determined in terms of their behaviour, *i.e.*, fixed, variable, semi-variable.

Advantages of Flexible Budgeting

Flexible budgeting is budgeting that is automatically tailored to any level of activity. Welsch[22] has listed three specific uses of the flexible budget.

1. To facilitate development of the departmental expense budgets for inclusion in the profit plan.
2. To provide expense goals for the managers of responsibility centres during the period covered by the profit plan.
3. To provide adjusted budget allowances for comparison purposes (against actual expenses) in the monthly performance reports.

In general, flexible budgeting has the following important advantages:

1. *Accurate Budgeting:* The use of flexible budgets may result in the preparation of more accurate budgets. Flexible budgeting techniques require that consideration is to be given to the output factor in budget preparation. Since all costs do not behave in the same manner (as some costs rise faster than others when production increase) a budget giving consideration to the volume (output) factor is bound to be more accurate than one where volume is not considered.

2. *Accurate Performance Measurement:* The flexible budgeting technique incorporates changes in activity level and compares actual results with the budget in terms of output achieved. This facilitates more meaningful comparison and evaluation between actual and budgeted data as comparable data are compared. The deviations resulting from the comparison are reliable and helpful to management in cost control and decision-making.

3. *Coordination:* Flexible budgeting results in coordination between all activities/departments of a business. Production is planned in relation to expected sales, materials and labour are acquired to meet expected production requirements. Facilities are provided to achieve budgetary goals, and funds are made available for the investments necessary to have higher output.

4. *Control Tool:* Flexible budgeting is an effective management control tool. Business operations are conducted more efficiently and losses are avoided or reduced. Comparison between the budgeted costs (at the actual production level) and actual costs form the basis for analysing cost variances and fixing responsibility for the same. In fact, managers themselves feel motivated in controlling costs for which they are responsible. The flexible budget provides cost goals or targets based on scheduled activity or output before the decision point, *i.e.*, before the cost is incurred. This contributes to cost control throughout the organisation.

TYPES OF BUDGETS

Budgets are the end product of the budgeting process. The numbers and types of budgets in a business enterprise depend on the size and nature of the business. However, in a manufacturing concern, the following budgets are generally prepared.

> **Budgets** are the end product of the budgeting process.

Operating/Functional Budgets

An operating/functional budget is expressed in both units and amount. When operating budgets relates to revenues, the units presented are expected to be sold and the stated amount reflect selling prices. On the contrary, when an operating budget relates to cost, the stated amount reflects costs and the input units presented are expected to be either transferred into output units or consumed. Operating budgets include the following budgets:

> An **operating/functional budget** is expressed in both units and amount.

1. Sales Budget
2. Production Budget
3. Production Cost Budget

(*i*) Direct Materials Budget
(*ii*) Direct Labour Budget
(*iii*) Factory Overhead Budget
4. Ending Inventories Budget
5. Cost of Goods Sold Budget
6. Selling Expense Budget
7. Administrative Expense Budget

Financial Budgets

Financial budgets are prepared from the monetary details available in operating budgets. Financial budgets indicate the funds to be generated or consumed during the budget period and are the ultimate focal points for top management. Financial budgets include the following budgets:

Financial budgets are prepared from the monetary details available in operating budgets.

1. Budgeted Income Statement
2. Capital Expenditure Budget
3. Research and Development Budget
4. Cash Budget
5. Budgeted Balance Sheet
6. Statement of Cash Flows

SALES BUDGET

The most important budget, which all other budgets are contingent upon, is the sales budget. All budgets, such as production budget, inventory budget, personnel budget, administration budget, selling and distribution budget and others are all affected by the sales budget and are dependent upon the revenue derived from sales. Therefore, the sales budget is the starting point in preparing other functional budgets. Developing a sales budget requires forecasting future sales levels. Exhibit 9.1 presents a specimen of a sales budget.

Sales budget is the starting point in preparing other functional budgets.

Exhibit 9.1: Sales Budget

ABC Company Ltd.
Sales Budget for the Year Ending December 31, 2016

Products	*Budget sales units*	*Budgeted sales price* (₹)	*Total*
A	70,000	80	56,00,000
B	80,000	120	96,00,000
	1,50,000		1,52,00,000

Forecasting Sales

The three main factors that should be considered by management in forecasting sales are: (*a*) information concerning past performance, (*b*) information about present conditions within the individual company and in each sales territory, (*c*) data concerning the industry and general business conditions.

The information about past performance is the starting point for sales forecasting. The sales record for past years, and particularly for the year just ending should be available to management in minute detail.

The second essential step in forecasting sales is the accumulation of data regarding conditions within the company and in each sales territory. The management can obtain a good picture of sales prospects through information sent to the head office by salesmen, dealers, and sales officers of different territories. A survey may be conducted in sales territories about sales possibilities prior to the beginning of the fiscal year. Also, regular reports, monthly or more frequently, regarding business conditions, may be obtained. The market analysis or survey covers three fields: products, markets, and methods of distribution. The survey about the product covers the information about characteristics, its present uses, the possibility of creating new demands, main selling centres, and suggestions as to improvements in the appearance of package, trade-mark, or the product itself.

Information about general business conditions are known as 'business barometers' and they should be considered in preparing a sales forecast. The following are important business indicators:

1. Gross national product, which is the total market value of output of goods and services produced in the entire economy
2. Personal income and purchasing power of the population
3. Unemployment conditions
4. Government crop reports
5. Steel, coal and oil production
6. Wholesale price indices
7. Business failures
8. Industrial production index
9. Government policies
10. Cyclical phases of the country's economy

Sales Analysis

After collecting all relevant information for a sale forecast, sales analysis or budget is prepared. The sales budget is usually prepared on the lines of (*i*) product, (*ii*) territory, and (*iii*) customer.

- ***Sales Budget by Product:*** This budget is prepared in terms of quantities of the various classes of products. This further helps in the preparation of the production budget which is always in terms of units to be manufactured by the production departments.
- ***Sales Budget by Territory or Area:*** Sometimes products are sold in different geographical areas or territories. This requires that the sales budget be prepared for each territory as a means of fixing separate targets for different salesmen representing different territories. The differences between sales targets and sales achievement for each may help in determining accountability and giving proper incentives for target performance. A sales budget by territory also helps in preparing the distribution cost budget for different areas.

Sales budgets (prepared both on product and territory basis) in terms of quantity and value are further broken down into monthly sales figures so that sales quotas can be fixed for salesmen. This also ensures coordination between production, sales, purchasing and stores departments.

- ***Sales Budget by Customer:*** A sales budget prepared on either basis may be further classified as to the type of customers. Customer classification will indicate sales to wholesalers, retailers, jobbers, institutions, government agencies, educational institutions, foreign business, etc. This analysis reveals the contribution of each type of customer to total sales of the business firm. This may also point out that certain potential customers are not being given proper attention by the sales manager.

PRODUCTION BUDGET

After preparing the sales budget, the production budget is prepared. A production budget is stated in physical units. It specifies the number of units of each product that must be produced to satisfy the sales forecasts and to achieve the desired level of closing finished goods inventory. Essentially, the production budget is the sales budget adjusted for inventory changes as follows:

Units to produce = Budgeted sales + Desired closing inventory of finished goods – Beginning inventory of finished goods.

A specimen production budget in given in Exhibit 9.2.

Exhibit 9.2: Production Budget

ABC Company
Total Production Budget for the Month of December, 2016

	Products	
	A	***B***
Budget sales (units)	70,000	80,000
Add: Desired closing finished goods inventory	20,000	30,000
	90,000	1,10,000
Less: Beginning finished goods inventory	40,000	50,000
Units to be produced	50,000	60,000

The production budget, like other budgets, is detailed by months or quarters along with a tentative annual budget. Further, budgets are prepared for every production centre for comparison with actual production. The production budget contributes to planning, coordination, and control. A production budget tends to reveal weaknesses and sources of potential trouble which can then be avoided by timely management action. The production budget is the primary basis for planning raw material requirements, labour needs, capital and cash requirements, and factory costs. Therefore, the production budget becomes the foundation for factory planning in general. It gives the factory executives something tangible upon which to base operational decisions.

PRODUCTION COST BUDGET

A production cost budget summarises the materials budget, labour budget, the factory overhead budget, and may be expressed and analysed by departments and/or products. A production cost budget, also known as a manufacturing budget is made up of three budgets:

1. Direct Materials Budget
2. Direct Labour Budget
3. Factory Overhead Budget

Production cost budget summarises the materials budget, labour budget, the factory overhead budget.

Direct Materials Budget

A direct materials budget indicates the expected amount of direct materials required to produce the budgeted units of finished goods. This budget specifies the cost of direct materials used and the cost of the direct

Direct materials budget indicates the expected amount of direct materials required to produce the budgeted units of finished goods.

materials purchased. Exhibit 9.3 explains the calculation of the direct materials budget. The usage part of the direct materials budget determines the cost of purchases of direct materials.

The direct materials budget is useful in the following ways:

1. It helps the purchasing department to prepare a schedule to ensure delivery of materials when needed.
2. It helps in fixing minimum and maximum levels of inventories in the stores department.
3. It helps the finance manager to determine the financial requirements to meet production targets.

The materials budget usually deals with direct materials only. Supplies and indirect materials are generally included in the factory overhead budget.

Exhibit 9.3: Direct Materials Budget

ABC Company
Direct Materials budget for the Year Ending December, 2016

A. Usage Budget

	Products		*Total*
	A	***B***	
Budgeted production in units	50,000	60,000	
Direct materials requirement			
Product A 5 kg per unit	× 5		
Product B 8 kg per unit		× 8	
Direct materials usage (kg)	2,50,000	4,80,000	
Cost per kg	₹1.00	1.50	
Cost of direct materials used	₹2,50,000	7,20,000	₹ 9,70,000

B. Purchase Budget

Direct Materials (in Kg)			***Total***
	A	***B***	
Direct Materials usage	2,50,000	4,80,000	
Budgeted closing direct materials inventory	+ 50,000	+75,000	
Total requirement	3,00,000	5,55,000	
Beginning direct materials inventory	70,000	1,00,000	
Purchase of direct materials	2,30,000	4,55,000	
Cost per kg	₹1.00	₹ 1.50	
Cost of purchase	2,30,000	₹ 6,82,000	₹ 9,12,000

Direct Labour Budget

> **Labour budget** estimates the labour, adequate in number and grades, to enable the production budget to be achieved.

The labour budget estimates the labour, adequate in number and grades, to enable the production budget to be achieved. It is generally preferable to prepare a separate direct labour budget and to include indirect labour in the factory overhead budget. The labour budget for direct and indirect labour helps the personnel or employment department in determining the number and types of workers needed. If additional workers are not needed, the task of the personnel department is easy. However, when workers are to be recruited, the personnel department has to make plans in advance. The labour budget prepared must disclose the following information: (*i*) the number of each type or grade of worker required in each period to achieve the budgeted output; (*ii*) budgeted cost of such labour in each period; (*iii*) period of training necessary for different types of workers.

Exhibit 9.4 illustrates the preparation of a direct labour budget.

Exhibit 9.4: Direct Labour Budget

ABC Company
Direct Labour Budget for the Year Ending December, 2016

	Products		
	A	***B***	***Total***
Budgeted production requirements	50,000	60,000	
Direct labour hours per unit	3	2	
Total direct labour hours	1,50,000	1,20,000	2,70,000
Direct labour cost per hour	₹ 5.00	₹ 5.00	₹ 5.00
Total direct labour cost (₹)	7,50,000	6,00,000	13,50,000

Factory Overhead Budget

The factory overhead budget is prepared on the basis of the chart of accounts which reflects different expense accounts and which properly classifies expense accounts and details the cost centres or departments. Although expenses can be classified in different manners such as natural classification, variability, the preparation of the factory overhead budget requires that expenses should be classified by departments since expenses are incurred by various departments. In this way, departmental heads should be held accountable for expenses incurred by their departments.

> **Factory overhead budget** is prepared on the basis of the chart of accounts which properly classifies expense accounts and details the cost centres or departments.

Exhibit 9.5 depicts the factory overhead budget wherein overhead costs have been classified into fixed and variable components.

Exhibit 9.5: Factory Overhead Budget

ABC Company
Factory Overhead Budget for the Year Ending December, 2016
(based on budgeted capacity of 2,70,000 direct labour)

Items	*Direct labour Hours*	*Rate per direct labour hour* (₹)	*Total cost* (₹)
A. Variable factory overhead:			
(*i*) Supplies	2,70,000	1.00	2,70,000
(*ii*) Repairs	2,70,000	0.50	1,35,000
(*iii*) Indirect labour	2,70,000	1.00	2,70,000
(*iv*) Other	2,70,000	0.40	1,08,000
Total variable factory overhead cost			7,83,000*

B. Fixed factory overhead cost:		
(*i*) Supervision	₹ 4,00,000	
(*ii*) Depreciation	5,50,000	
(*iii*) Property tax	2,50,000	
(*iv*) Others	1,77,000	
Total fixed factory overhead cost		13,77,000
Total factory overhead cost		21,60,000

Predetermined overhead rate $= \dfrac{₹\,21,60,000}{2,70,000 \text{ hours}}$

$= ₹\,8.00$ per direct labour hour

ENDING INVENTORIES BUDGET

An inventory budget can be prepared to find out the values of direct materials and finished goods inventory as shown in Exhibit 9.6.

Exhibit 9.6: Ending Inventories Budget

ABC Company
Ending Inventory Budget for the Year Ending December, 2016

	₹
Direct materials inventory	
Product A 50,000 kg × ₹ 1.00 per kg	50,000
Product B 75,000 kg × ₹ 1.50 per kg	1,12,500
	1,62,500
Finished goods inventory	
Product A 20,000 units × ₹ 25.00	5,00,000
Product B 30,000 units × ₹ 30.00	9,00,000
	14,00,000

Cost of Goods Sold Budget

After preparing direct materials, direct labour, factory overhead, and ending inventory budgets, the cost of goods sold budget can be prepared. The cost of goods sold budget summarises all the above budgets as shown in Exhibit 9.7.

Exhibit 9.7: Cost of Goods Sold Budget

ABC Company
Cost of Goods Sold Budget for the Year Ending December 31, 2016

Direct materials	₹	₹
Beginning inventory	2,00,000	
Purchase	9,12,500	
	11,12,500	
Less: Closing inventory	1,62,500	

Cost of direct materials used	9,50,000
Direct labour	13,50,000
Factory overhead	21,60,000
Total factory cost	44,60,000
Beginning finished goods inventory	25,00,000
Total goods available for sale	69,60,000
Closing finished goods inventory	14,00,000
Cost of goods sold	55,60,000

SELLING EXPENSE BUDGET

Selling and distribution cost budget shows the budgeted costs of promoting sales for the budget period.

Closely related with the sales budget is the selling and distribution cost budget which shows the budgeted costs of promoting sales for the budget period. It is also known as marketing expense budget. The selling cost budget is made up of a number of cost items, some of which are fixed and some variable. The principal fixed expenses are salaries and depreciation; the principal variable expenses are commissions, travel, advertising and bad debts. The variable expenses vary directly with sales. A selling expense budget consists mainly of the following major items:

1. Sales representative (salaries, commissions, entertainment and travelling)
2. Sales office (office supplies, salaries, postage, telephone, rent and rates)
3. Publicity office (salaries, office costs, press, journals, televisions, cinema, samples, sundries)
4. Warehousing, packing and despatch (salaries, packing wages, drivers' wages, vehicle costs, sundries)

Exhibit 9.8 exhibits an annual selling expense budget classified according to fixed and variable expenses. The annual budget should be broken down on a monthly basis so that actual expenses can be compared with the budget monthly. Also, separate budgets for each of these expenses may be prepared especially in the case of a large company.

Exhibit 9.8: Selling Expenses Budget

ABC Company
Selling Expense Budget for the Year Ending December 31, 2016

Items	*Costs* (₹)	*Total costs* (₹)
(A) Variable selling expenses:		
(*i*) Sales Commission	35,000	
(*ii*) Salary and wages	40,000	
(*iii*) Advertising	15,000	
(*iv*) Travelling	22,000	1,12,000
(B) Fixed selling expenses:		
(*i*) Warehousing	60,000	
(*ii*) Publicity expenses	30,000	
(*iii*) Marketing manager's salary	60,000	
(*iv*) Depreciation	27,000	1,77,000
Total selling expenses		2,89,000

ADMINISTRATIVE EXPENSE BUDGET

The administrative expense budget covers the administrative costs for non-manufacturing business activities. Budgeting administrative expense is often difficult. Perhaps the first difficulty is in classifying certain costs as production or administrative. For example, costs like purchasing, engineering, persónnel, research and development can be administrative as well as production. Unless such and other expenses are properly classified, their proper budgeting and subsequent control cannot be exercised. The second difficulty is in determining persons responsible for the incurrence and control of these costs. However, in order to accomplish the purpose of cost control in cost accounting, it is necessary that each item of cost should be under the jurisdiction and control of a responsible person who is accountable for incurring the cost.

> **Administrative expense budget** covers the administrative costs for non-manufacturing business activities.

Exhibit 9.9: Administrative Expense Budget

ABC Company
Administrative Expense Budget for the Year Ending December 31, 2016

Items	*Amount* (₹)	*Amount* (₹)
(A) Variable administrative expenses:		
(*i*) Supplies	35,000	
(*ii*) Clerical wages	60,000	
Total variable administrative expenses		95,000
(B) Fixed administrative expenses:		
(*i*) Directors remuneration	1,20,000	
(*ii*) Legal charge	20,000	
(*iii*) Depreciation	25,000	
(*iv*) Salaries	30,000	
(*v*) Rent	60,000	
(*vi*) Postage, telephone etc.	32,000	
Total fixed administrative expenses		2,87,000
Total administrative expenses		3,82,000

The administrative expenses budget contains expenses like directors' remuneration, legal charges, audit fees, salaries, rent, office expenses, interest, property taxes, postage, telephone, telegraph, etc. These expenses should be properly classified under different headings to determine the responsibility of cost incurrence and control. *For example*, these expenses can be classified into different categories such as company administration, general accounting, general office, etc. Exhibit 9.9 presents administrative expense budget.

BUDGETED INCOME STATEMENT

A budgeted income statement summarises all the individual budgets, *i.e.*, sales budget, cost of goods sold budget, selling budget, and administrative expense budget. No new estimates are made; figures are taken

> **Budgeted income statement** summarises all the individual budgets, *i.e.*, sales budget, cost of goods sold budget, selling budget, and administrative expense budget.

from budgets previously prepared. This budget determines income before taxes. If the tax rate is available, net income after taxes can also be computed. Exhibit 9.10 exhibits a budgeted or projected income statement.

Exhibit 9.10: Budgeted Income Statement

ABC Company
Budgeted Income Statement for the Year Ending December, 2016

		(₹)
Sales		1,52,00,000
Cost of goods sold		55,60,000
Gross profit		96,40,000
Selling expenses	2,89,000	
Administrative expenses	3,82,000	6,71,000
Income before taxes		89,69,000
Income taxes (assuming 50%)		44,84,500
Net income		44,84,500

CAPITAL EXPENDITURE BUDGET

> **Capital expenditure** is one of the most important areas of managerial decisions and are relatively large in comparison with operating expenditures and have a long-term impact on the organisation and the achievement of its goals.

The budgeting of capital expenditure is one of the most important areas of managerial decisions. Generally, capital expenditures are relatively large in comparison with operating expenditures and have a long-term impact on the organisation and the achievement of its goals. Therefore, any errors in this budgeting decision may prove very critical to the business firm. The capital expenditure budget aims at minimising errors while making capital expenditure decisions. It is necessary that business firms should establish definite procedures and methods for evaluating the merits of a project before funds are committed. The effective control of capital expenditures is exercised in advance by requiring that each proposed project be evaluated in terms of its merits. After alternative capital expenditure projects have been investigated regarding expected sales, manufacturing costs, marketing costs, etc., the most profitable alternative should be selected.

Capital expenditure budgets are prepared for both short and long-range projects depending on the requirements of the business firm. Short-range projects are implemented during the current accounting period; therefore, these provisions should be made in the current budget. Long-range projects are not executed in the current period, they are expressed only in general terms. They become budget commitments only when the time for their implementation approaches. Top management has the responsibility of translating long-term capital projects into budget commitments.

RESEARCH AND DEVELOPMENT BUDGET

Research has now become a continuous activity in many industries. Research and development programme should be identified and their corresponding cost should be budgeted. The Financial Accounting Standards Board of USA defines the two terms, 'research' and 'development', in the following manner:

1. Research is planned search or critical investigation aimed at discovery of new knowledge with the hope that such knowledge will be useful in developing a new product or service

(hereinafter 'product'), or a new process or technique (hereinafter 'process'), or in bringing about a significant improvement in an existing product or process.

2. Development is the translation of research findings or other knowledge into a plan or design for a new product or process or for a significant improvement to an existing product or process whether intended for sale or use. It includes the conceptual formulation, design, and testing of product alternatives, construction of prototypes, and operation of pilot product alternatives, plants. It does not include routine or periodic alterations to existing products, production lines, manufacturing processes, and other ongoing operations even though those alterations may represent improvements and it does not include market research or market testing activities.

Research and development budget is the most important tool for planning and controlling research and development cost.

The research and development budget is the most important tool for planning and controlling research and development cost. It compels management to think in advance about the fairness of these expenses both in total amounts and in each field of a research programme. It helps in coordination with the company's other plans and projects. Since the research and development programmes compete with other desirable activities in allocation of funds, coordination is needed to balance financially immediate and long-term company plans. Also this budget guides the research and development department to plan correctly the staff and equipment requirements and special facilities needed for the work.

Research projects should be planned and evaluated and then grouped into long-term and short-term projects. A short-term research programme is needed to earn a satisfactory rate of return on the funds invested. A long-term research programme is developed to ensure that the research programmes are in line with future market trends and demand and research costs are in conformity with budgeted financial position. Research and development is discretionary costs and therefore in case of decline in operating income and financial position of the business, some research programmes may be curtailed or postponed.

CASH BUDGET

Cash budget contains detailed estimates of cash receipts (cash inflows) and disbursements (cash outflows) for the budget period or some other specific period.

A cash budget contains detailed estimates of cash receipts (cash inflows) and disbursements (cash outflows) for the budget period or some other specific period. The preparation of a cash budget has the following objectives:

1. It indicates the effect on the cash position of seasonal requirements, large inventories, unusual receipts, and slowness in collecting receivables.
2. It indicates the cash requirements needed for a plant or equipment expansion programme.
3. It points up to the need for additional funds from sources such as bank loans or sale of securities and the time factors involved. In this connection it might also exert a cautionary influence on plans for plant expansion leading to a modification of capital expenditure decisions.
4. It indicates the availability of cash for taking advantage of discounts.
5. It assists in planning the financial requirements of bond retirements, income tax instalments, and payments to pensions and retirement funds.
6. It shows the availability of excess funds for short-term or long-term investments.
7. It indicates cash requirements for current operating activities.
8. It helps in focusing on cash usage priorities currently required and unavoidable versus postponable or permanently avoidable.

9. It serves as a basis for evaluating the actual cash management performance of responsible individuals, using measurement criteria such as the target average daily balance as compared with the actual average daily balance in each cash account.

Thus, a cash budget is a useful tool in the cash management of organisations as it reveals potential cash shortages as well as potential periods of excess cash. It brings equilibrium between available cash and the cash demanding activities–operations, capital expenditures, etc. A cash budget which reveals the cash position may indicate: (*i*) the need for additional financing to meet projected cash deficits or (*ii*) the need to put excess cash to profitable use not allowing it to lie idle in the cash account.

The cash budget is closely related to the sales budget and operating expenses budget. But these budgets themselves do not automatically determine an optimum cash position. This is because of the difference in the nature of the cash budget and other budgets. The cash budget is concerned with and determines the timing of cash inflows and outflows on cash basis whereas the other budgets are concerned with and determine the timing of the basic transaction on an accrual basis. A cash budget includes no accrual items.

Period of Cash Budget

The period of time covered by a cash budget depends on the type of business, management planning needs, and cash position. A cash budget may generally be related to the following time periods:

1. ***Operational Cash Planning:*** Cash budgets may be prepared monthly, weekly or even daily to meet informational requirements of management. This type of cash budgeting is primarily meant for dynamic control of cash balances to minimise interest cost on loans and opportunity cost deriving from idle cash in the business.
2. ***Short-range:*** Short-range cash budgeting is prepared annually and is in correspondence with the annual profit plan. It indicates cash inflows and outflows as generated by the annual profit plan. It helps in determining short-term credit needs and controlling cash during the year.
3. ***Long-range:*** Long-range budgeting does not disclose detailed estimates of revenue and expenses. Its purpose is to determine whether cash can be generated through working capital growth and at what times funds are needed. The effects of business expansion and long-term trends are incorporated in long-range cash budgeting. Long-range cash projection is in accord with (*i*) the timing of the capital expenditure projects, and (*ii*) the timing of the long-range profit plan (usually five years).

Projection of long-range cash inflows (primarily from sales and services) and long-range cash outflows (primarily from expenses and capital expenditures, including expansion projects) is vital for making financing decisions and developing long-term credit needs.

Preparation of a Cash Budget

A cash budget may be prepared by following either of three generally accepted procedures:

1. ***Receipts and Disbursements Method:*** In this method, all anticipated cash receipts are carefully forecasted such as cash sales, cash collections from debtors, dividends, interest on investments, proceeds from sale of assets, royalties, bank loans, etc. Likewise, cash disbursements for materials purchases, supplies, salaries, repayment of loans, dividends, taxes, expenses, purchase of plant or requirement are also determined. The preparation of a cash budget according to this method requires the use of the following budgets: (*a*) sales budget, (*b*) direct materials budget, (*c*) direct labour budget, (*d*) factory overhead, (*e*) selling and administrative expense budget, (*f*) capital expenditure budget, (*g*) research and development budget, (*h*) financial budget, regarding dividends, loans, income taxes, etc. This method is useful for short-range cash projection but is not appropriate for long-term cash budgeting. This method is in accord with the annual profit plan.

2. ***Adjusted Profit and Loss Method:*** The second approach is the profit and loss method or adjusted net income method. The starting point in this approach is budgeted profit reflected in the income statement. Basically, projected profit is converted from an accrual basis to a cash basis. That is, the budgeted profit of a period is adjusted for non-cash transactions and expected cash-oriented changes in asset and liability accounts not affected by profit calculations. Using the budgeted profit for a period as a starting point, various non-cash transactions are added back to net profit for the period. Non-cash items are depreciation, bad and doubtful acounts, expired insurance premiums, and income tax accruals. After this, anticipated decreases in assets or increase in liabilities are further added and anticipated increase in assets or decreases in liabilities are deducted. The budgeted cash at the end of a period is the cash balance at the beginning of the period plus the net cash increase (or minus the net cash decrease) as indicated in the analysis of the adjusted profit method. This method is especially appropriate for making long-range cash projections, but it is not useful in planning and control of cash as compared to the receipts and disbursement method. The reason is that the adjusted profit method does not contain detailed cash receipts and disbursement items; rather it shows only aggregate cash flows.

3. ***Balance Sheet Method:*** The third approach is the balance sheet method. In this approach closing balances of all (budgeted) balance sheet items except cash and bank balances are found and put in a budgeted balance sheet. If the total of liabilities side items is more than the total of asset side items, the balancing figure will be cash/bank balance. On the contrary, if the total of assets side items is more than the total of liabilities side items, the balancing figure will be bank overdraft or shortage in cash. Budgeted exhibits of closing balance sheet items can be found after adjusting the opening balance sheet items with the transactions anticipated for the year.

BUDGETED OR PROJECTED BALANCE SHEET

A projected balance sheet represents the expected financial position at a particular date. The projected balance sheet is prepared from the budgeted balance sheet at the beginning of the budget period and the expected changes in the account balances reflected in the operating budgets, capital expenditure budgets, and cash budget. If any of the accounts or relationships among the accounts appearing on the projected balance sheet are not according to management's requirements and objectives, the operating plan might have to be changed. *For example*, if a bank or financial institution requires a business firm to maintain a certain minimum current ratio and debt-equity ratio, the operating plan would have to be changed if these ratios are indeed too low. Furthermore, unfavourable ratios may decrease the value of company shares in the stock exchange and lower the credibility of the firm in the investment market. The projected balance sheet also automatically determines the arithmetical accuracy of other budgets since they are used in preparing the forecasted balance sheet.

STATEMENT OF CASH FLOWS

The projected statement of cash flows is usually prepared from data in the budgeted income statement and changes between the projected balance sheet at the beginning of the budget period and projected balance sheet at the end of the budget period. This projected statement is very useful to management in the financial planning process.

MASTER BUDGET (OR COMPREHENSIVE BUDGET)

> **Master budget** is the summary or total budget package for a business firm.

A master budget sometimes called a comprehensive budget, is the summary or total budget package for a business firm. A comprehensive budget is a set of financial statements and other schedules showing the expected or proforma results for a future period. A comprehensive budget normally contains an income statement, a balance sheet, a statement of cash receipts and disbursements and schedules of production, purchases and fixed asset acquisitions. The budget packages might have other components depending on the needs of the firm. A comprehensive budget is the end product of the budget-making process. A master budget is a tool for coordinating all the individual budgets of an organisation into an acceptable effective plan. It shows the budgeted profit and loss account for the budget period and the budgeted balance sheet at the end of the period. It reveals the top management's goals of revenues, expenses, net income, cash flows, and financial position. The other budgets prepared by a business firm are specific, *i.e.*, they deal with separate distinct activities of the organisation such as sales, production, selling and distribution and administrative activities. A master budget takes the macro (aggregate) view of the business enterprise and coordinates sales with production; raw materials, manpower, machinery and other resources with production targets, and the like. The coordination and cohesiveness among different budgets helps management in making better predictions of profitability, cash flow, financial position and the firm's capacity to overcome challenges. The master budget is an integrative tool that cuts across divisional boundaries in order to coordinate the firm's diverse activities. While master budgets provide plans for an entire system, operating budgets provide plans for the organisation's sub-system, that is, operating budgets constitute the building blocks used to complete the master budget.

Whether a business firm prepares specific operating budgets or a complete master budget depends on a number of factors. The primary reason is the need of management at a particular time. *For example*, management may be more concerned with a single or specific aspect at a time, such as adequacy of the cash position. If the cash budget reveals that all is well, it may be the only budget needed to be prepared for management's use. If the cash budget reveals an inadequate or poor cash position, then other budgets making up the master budget will have to be prepared. In this situation, new budgets or forecasts will continue to be prepared, unless management finds an acceptable set of budgets.

REVISION OF BUDGETS

As stated earlier in the chapter, successful budgets should have adequate flexibility to meet changing business conditions. Since budgets are used for planning, operation, coordination and control, they should be revised if changes occur in the environment. Revision of budgets may be necessary due to the following factors some of which might have been considered earlier in the development of budgets:

1. Errors committed in preparing the budgets which may subsequently be known.
2. Emergence of unforeseen and unanticipated situations which may cause the budget to be revised.
3. Changes in internal factors, e.g., production, forecast, sales forecast, capacity utilisation, etc.
4. Changes in external factors, e.g., market trends, nature of the economy, prices of inputs and resources, consumer tastes and fashions.

Changes in above factors do not affect a firm's budgets if they are of minor significance. Some changes, however, considerably affect budgets and in this situation, management is faced with two problems:

1. Whether only individual budgets should be changed;
2. Whether the master budget be changed

Regarding the first question, most business firms are in agreement and suggest that specific individual budgets should be changed. For instance, if there is likely to be a significant change in expected sales (increase or decrease), production and purchasing departments should be informed about this to avoid over-stocking or under-stocking. Failure to inform them would breakdown coordination and subsequently the budget goals.

A revision of the master budget is debatable and sometimes is opposed on two counts: (*i*) the master budget process is highly complex and expensive; (*ii*) the evaluation process may take care of these changes if the changes take place. The second argument is more or less on middle ground.

While it argues for revision when changes do occur, it focuses on actual effects rather than projected changes. It is felt that this avoids making small changes in the plan that are of little consequence and keeps management from trying to outguess random fluctuations in their forecast. Those who support the revision of the master budget argue that the revised budget is a better and more effective basis for performance evaluation and control. By revising budget, all members of the organisation come to know of the expectations and standards for which they will be accountable.

FLEXIBLE BUDGETS—ILLUSTRATIVE PROBLEMS

Illustrative Problem 1

The following data are available in a manufacturing company for a yearly period.

	₹ *(Lakhs)*
Fixed expenses:	
Wages and salaries	9.5
Rent, rates and taxes	6.6
Depreciation	7.4
Sundry administrative expenses	6.5
Semi-variable expenses (at 50% of capacity):	
Maintenance and repairs	3.5
Indirect labour	7.9
Sales department salaries, etc.	3.8
Sundry administrative salaries	2.8
Variable expenses (at 50% of capacity):	
Materials	21.7
Labour	20.4
Other expenses	7.9
	98.0

Assume that the fixed expenses remain constant for all levels of production: semi-variable expenses remain constant between 45% and 65 % of capacity, increasing by 10% between 65% and 80% capacity and by 20 % between 80 % and 100% capacity.

Sales at various levels are:	₹ *(Lakhs)*
50% capacity	100
60% capacity	120
75% capacity	150
90% capacity	180
100% capacity	200

Prepare a flexible budget for the year and forecast the profit at 60%, 75%, 90% and 100% capacity.

Solution:

Flexible Budget for the period

Capacity level	50%	60%	75%	90%	100%
Sales (₹ in lakhs)	100	120	150	180	200
Fixed expenses:					
Wages and salaries	9.5	9.5	9.5	9.5	9.5
Rent, Rates and taxes	6.6	6.6	6.6	6.6	6.6

Depreciation	7.4	7.4	7.4	7.4	7.4
Sundry administration expenses	6.5	6.5	6.5	6.5	6.5
(A) Total fixed cost	30.0	30.0	30.0	30.0	30.0
Semi - variable expenses:					
Maintenance and repair	3.5	3.5	3.8	4.2	4.2
Indirect labour	7.9	7.9	8.7	9.5	9.5
Sales department salaries	3.8	3.8	4.2	4.6	4.6
Sundry administrative expenses	2.8	2.8	3.1	3.3	3.3
(B) Total semi - variable costs	18.0	18.0	19.8	21.6	21.6
Variable expenses:					
Materials	21.7	26.0	32.5	39.0	43.4
Labour	20.4	24.5	30.6	36.7	40.8
Other expenses	7.9	9.5	11.9	14.3	15.8
(C) Total variable cost	50.0	60.0	75.0	90.0	100.0
(D) Total cost (A) + (B) + (C)	98.0	108.0	124.8	141.6	151.6
(E) Sales	100.0	120.0	150.0	180.0	200.0
(F) Profit (E – D)	20	12.0	25.2	38.4	48.4

Illustrative Problem 2

The budget manager of Jaypee Electricals Ltd. is preparing a flexible budget for the accounting year commencing from Ist April 2016. The company produces one product, component - Peekay, Direct material costs ₹ 7 per unit. Direct labour average ₹ 2.50 per hour and requires 1.60 hours to produce one unit of Peekay.

Salesmen are paid a commission of ₹ 1 per unit sold. Fixed selling and administration expenses amount to ₹ 85,000 per year.

Manufacturing overhead has been estimated in the following amounts under specified conditions of volume:

Volume of production (in units)	1,20,000	1,50,000
Expenses:	₹	₹
Indirect materials	2,64,000	3,30,000
Indirect labour	1,50,000	1,87,500
Inspection	90,000	1,12,500
Maintenance	84,000	1,02,000
Supervision	1,98,000	2,34,000
Depreciation — Plant & Equipment	90,000	90,000
Engineering services	94,000	94,000
Total manufacturing overhead	9,70,000	11,50,000

Normal capacity of production of the company is 1,25,000 units. Prepare a budget of total cost at 1,40,000 units of output.

Solution:

Flexible Budget for the year April 2016 to March 2017
Production Volume 1,40,000 units

Items of cost	*Fixed Costs (₹)*	*Variable Cost (₹) per unit*	*Variable Cost (₹) Total*	*Total Cost (₹)*
Direct materials	—	7.00	9,80,000	9,80,000
Indirect Labour	—	4.00	5,60,000	5,60,000
Indirect materials	—	2.20	3,08,000	3,08,000
Indirect labour	—	1.25	1,75,000	1,75,000
Inspection	—	0.75	1,05,000	1,05,000
Maintenance	12,000	0.60	84,000	96,000
Supervision	54,000	1.20	1,68,000	2,22,000
Depreciation — plant & Equipment	90,000	—	—	90,000
Engineering services	94,000	—	—	94,000
Sales commission	—	1.00	1,40,000	1,40,000
Fixed selling and distribution expenses	85,000	—	—	85,000
Total	3,35,000	18.00	25,20,000	28,55,000

Working Notes:

Segregation of semi-variable costs into fixed and variable components:

$$\text{Variable cost per unit} = \frac{\text{Difference in cost}}{\text{Difference in output}}$$

Fixed cost = Total cost – Variable cost

(*i*) Maintenance

$$\text{Variable cost per unit} = \frac{₹\ 1,02,000 - 84,000}{1,50,000 - 1,20,000}$$

$$= \frac{₹\ 18,000}{30,000\ \text{units}} = ₹\ 0.60\ \text{per unit}$$

$$\text{Fixed cost} = ₹\ 84,000 - (1,20,000 \times .60)$$

$$= 84,000 - 72,000$$

$$= ₹\ 12,000$$

$$\text{Variable cost} = 1,40,000\ \text{units} \times .60 = ₹\ 84,000$$

(*ii*) Supervision

$$\text{Variable cost per unit} = \frac{₹\ 2,34,000 - 1,98,000}{1,50,000 - 1,20,000}$$

$$= \frac{₹ 36,000}{30,000\ \text{units}}$$

$$= ₹\ 1.20\ \text{per unit}$$

Fixed cost	= ₹ 1,98,000 – (1,20,000 × 1.20)
	= 1,98,000 – 1,44,000
	= 54,000
Variable cost	= 1,40,000 units × ₹ 1.20
	= ₹ 1,68,000

(*iii*) Indirect materials, indirect labour, inspection are fully variable costs. This can be proved by taking these elements of costs and following the above method of segregation. For instance, as an example, indirect materials is taken.

Indirect materials

$$\text{Variable cost per unit} = \frac{₹\ 3,30,000-2,64,000}{1,50,000-1,20,000}$$

$$= \frac{₹\ 66,000}{30,000} = ₹\ 2.20 \text{ per unit}$$

Fixed cost	= ₹ 2,64,000 – (120,000 × 2.20)
	= 2,64,000 – 2,64,000
	= No. fixed cost

Illustrative Problem 3

The manufacturing overhead budget for Johnson Company contains the following items.

Variable costs:	
Indirect materials	₹ 25,000
Indirect labor	12,000
Maintenance expenses	10,000
Manufacturing supplies	6,000
Total variable	₹ 53,000
Fixed costs:	
Supervision	₹ 17,000
Inspection costs	1,000
Insurance expenses	2,000
Depreciation	15,000
Total fixed	₹ 35,000

The budget was based on an estimated 2,000 units being produced. During November, 1,500 units were produced, and the following costs incurred.

Variable costs	
Indirect materials	₹ 25,200
Indirect labor	13,500
Maintenance expenses	8,200
Manufacturing supplies	5,100
Total variable	₹ 52,000

Fixed costs	
Supervision	₹ 19,300
Inspection costs	1,200
Insurance expenses	2,200
Depreciation	14,700
Total fixed	₹ 37,400

Required:

(*a*) Determine which items would be controllable by the production manager. (Assume 'supervision' excludes production manager's own salary.)

(*b*) How much should have been spent during the month for the manufacture of the 1,500 units?

(*c*) Prepare a flexible manufacturing overhead budget report for the production manager.

(*d*) Prepare a responsibility report. Include only the costs that would have been controllable by production manager. Describe clearly the areas in which performance of production manager needs to be improved.

Solution:

(*a*) The production manager should be able to control all the variable costs and the fixed costs of supervision and inspection. Insurance and depreciation ordinarily are not the responsibility of the department manager.

(*b*) The total variable cost per unit is ₹ 26.50 (₹ 53,000 ÷ 2,000). The total budgeted cost during the month to manufacture 1,500 units is variable costs ₹ 39,750 (₹ 1,500 × ₹ 26.50) plus fixed costs (₹ 35,000), for a total of ₹ 74,750 (₹ 39,750 + ₹35,000).

(*c*)

Production Department
Manufacturing Overhead Budget Report (Flexible)
for the Month Ended November 30, 2016

	Budget at 1,500 Units	Actual at 1,500 Units	Difference Favourable F Unfavourable U
Variable costs			
Indirect materials (₹ 12.50)	₹ 18,750	₹ 25,200	₹ 6,450 U
Indirect labour (₹ 6)	9,000	13,500	5,500 U
Maintenance (₹ 5)	7,500	8,200	700 U
Maintenance supplies (₹ 3)	4,500	5,100	600 U
Total	39,750	52,000	12,250 U
Fixed costs			
Supervision	17,000	19,300	2,300 U
Inspection	1,000	1,200	200 U
Insurance	2,000	2,200	200 U
Depreciation	15,000	14,700	300 F
Total fixed	35,000	37,400	2,400 U
Total costs	₹ 74,750	₹ 89,400	₹ 14,650 U

(*d*) Because a production department is a cost center, the responsibility report should include only the costs that are controllable by the production manager. In this type of report, no distinction is made between variable and fixed costs. Budget data in the report should be based on the units actually produced.

Production Department
Manufacturing Overhead Responsibility Report
for the Month Ended November 30, 2016

Controllable Costs	Budget	Actual	Difference Favourable F Unfavourable U
Indirect materials	₹ 18,750	₹ 25,200	₹ 6,450 U
Indirect labour	9,000	13,500	4,500 U
Maintenance	7,500	8,200	700 U
Manufacturing supplies	4,500	5,100	600 U
Supervision	17,000	19,300	2,300 U
Inspection	1,000	1,200	200 U
Total	₹ 57,750	₹ 72,500	₹ 14,750 U

The performance of production manager in controlling costs that are his responsibility was very disappointing in the month of November. As indicated in the accompanying responsibility report, total costs were ₹ 14,750 over budget. On a percentage basis, costs were 26% over budget. As you can see, actual costs were over budget for every cost item. In three instances, costs were significantly over budget (indirect materials 34%, indirect labour 50%, and supervision 14%).

It is imperative that the production manager should find ways to implement more effective cost control measures.

Illustrative Problem 4

The financial controller of SG Ltd. has prepared the following estimates of working results for the year ending March 31, 2014:

Direct material per unit (₹)	16.00
Direct labour per unit (₹)	40.00
Variable overheads per unit (₹)	12.00
Selling price per unit (₹)	125.00
Fixed expenses (₹)	6,75,000 p.a.
Sales (₹)	25,00,000 p.a.

During the 2014-15, it it expected that the material prices and variable overheads will go up by 10% and 5% respectively. As a result of re-engineering of business processes, the overall direct labour efficiency will increase by 12%, but the wage rate will go up by 5%. The fixed overheads are also expected to increase by ₹ 1.25,000. The vice president-manufacturing states that the same level of output as obtained in 2013-14 should be maintained in 2014-15 also and efforts should be made to maintain the same level of profit by suitably increasing the selling price.

The vice-president-marketing states that the market will not absorb any increase in the selling price. On the other hand, he proposes that publicity involving advertisement expenses as given below will increase the quantity of sales as under:

Advertisement expenses (₹)	80,000	1,94,000	3,20,000	4,60,000
Additional units of sales	2,000	4,000	6,000	8,000

You have been appointed as a management Accountant in SG Ltd., and as a initial assignment during the training period, you have been requested to:

(*a*) Present an income statement for the year 2014-15

(*b*) Find the revised price and the percentage of increases in the price for 2014-15, if the views of the vice-president-manufacturing are accepted.

(*c*) Evaluate the four alternative proposals put forth by the vice-president-marketing. Determine the best output level to be budgeted and prepare an overall income statement for the year 2014-15 at that level of output. (workings should form part of your answer)

(*M.Com., Delhi,* 2014)

Solution:

Income Statement for the Year Ending 2013-14

	Particulars	*Price/unit*	*Amount* (₹)
	Sales $\left(\frac{₹\ 25,00,000}{125} = 20,000 \text{ units}\right)$	125	25,00,000
Less:	Direct Labour	40	(8,00,000)
	Direct Material	16	(3,20,000)
	Variable Overhead	12	(2,40,000)
	Gross Profit		11,40,000
Less:	Fixed Expenses		(6,75,000)
	Net Profit		4,65,000

(*a*) **Income Statement (2014-15)**

	Particulars	*Price/unit* (₹)	*Amount* (₹)
	Sales [20,000 units]	125	25,00,000
Less:	Direct Material (16 × 1.1)	17.6	(3,52,000)
	Direct Labour	37.5	(7,50,000)
	Variable Overhead (12 × 1.05)	12.6	(2,52,000)
	Gross Profit		11,46,000
Less:	Fixed Expenses		(8,00,000)
	Net Profit		3,46,000

Working Note:

$$\text{Labour cost} = 8,00,000 \times \frac{12}{112} \times 1.05 = ₹\ 7,50,000$$

(*b*) Decrease in level of profit = (₹ 4,65,000 – 3,46,000)

= ₹ 1,19,000

$$\therefore \text{Price should be increased by} = \frac{1,19,000}{20,000}$$

= ₹ 5.95

or

Output should be = 20,000 units

Profit should be = ₹ 4,65,000

Total cost (for 20,000 units) = VC + FC

= 13,54,000 + 8,00,000

= 21,54,000

Add: Profit 4,65,000

Desired sales ₹ 26,19,000

$$\text{Revised selling price} = \frac{\text{Sales}}{\text{Output}} = \frac{₹\ 26,19,000}{20,000} = ₹\ 130.95 \text{ per unit}$$

∴ New Price = ₹ 125 + 5.95

= ₹ 130.95 per unit

$$\text{Percentage increase in price} = \frac{5.95}{125} \times 100$$

= 4.76%

Income Statement for the Alternatives

	Particulars	*2000 units*	*4000 units*	*6000 units*	*8000 units*
		(₹)	(₹)	(₹)	(₹)
	Sales @ 125	27,50,000	30,00,000	32,50,000	35,00,000
Less:	Direct Material @ ₹ 176	(3,87,200)	(4,22,400)	(4,57,600)	(4,92,800)
	Direct labour @ ₹ 37.5	(8,25,000)	(9,00,000)	(9,75,000)	(10,50,000)
	Variable OH @ ₹ 12.6	(2,77,200)	(3,02,400)	(3,27,600)	(3,52,800)
	Advertisement expenses	(80,000)	(1,94,000)	(3,20,000)	(4,60,000)
	Gross Profit	11,80,600	11,81,200	11,69,800	11,44,400
Less:	Fixed exp.	(8,00,000)	(8,00,000)	(8,00,000)	(8,00,000)
	Net Income	3,80,600	3,81,200	3,69,800	3,44,400

Option 2 that is selling Additional 4000 units with advertisement expenses of ₹ 1,94,000 is the most profitable.

Illustrative Problem 5

The production supervisor of the Machining Department for Nell Company agreed to the following monthly static budget for the upcoming year:

Machining Department
Monthly Production Budget

Wages	₹ 5,40,000
Utilities	36,000
Depreciation	60,000
Total	₹ 6,36,000

The actual amount spent and the actual units produced in the first three months of 2016 in the Machining Department were as follows:

	Amount Spent	Units Produced
January	₹ 6,00,000	1,10,000
February	5,70,000	1,00,000
March	5,45,000	90,000

The Machining Department supervisor has been very pleased with this performance, since actual expenditures have been less than the monthly budget. However, the plant manager believes that the budget should not remain fixed for every month but should "flex" or adjust to the volume of work that is produced in the Machining Department. Additional budget information for the Machining Department is as follows:

Wages per hour	₹ 18.00
Utility cost per direct labour hour	₹ 1.20
Direct labour hours per unit	0.25
Planned unit production	120,000

Required:

(*a*) Prepare a flexible budget for the actual units produced for January, February, and March in the Machining Department. Assume depreciation is a fixed cost.

(*b*) Compare the flexible budget with the actual expenditures for the first three months. What does this comparison suggest?

Solution:

(*a*)

A	B	C	D
Machining Department			
Flexible Production Budget			
for the Three Months Ending March 31, 2016			
	January	***February***	***March***
Units of production	110,000	100,000	90,000
Wages	₹ 495,000	₹ 450,000	₹ 405,000

Utilities	33,000	30,000	27,000
Depreciation	60,000	60,000	60,000
Total	₹ 588,000	₹ 540,000	₹ 492,000
Supporting calculations:			
Units of production	110,000	100,000	90,000
Hours per unit	× 0.25	× 0.25	× 0.25
Total hours of production	27,500	25,000	22,500
Wages per hour	× ₹ 18.00	× ₹ 18.00	× ₹ 18.00
Total wages	₹ 495,000	₹ 450,000	₹ 405,000
Total hours of production	27,500	25,000	22,500
Utility cost per hour	× ₹ 1.20	× ₹ 1.20	× ₹ 1.20
Total utilities	₹ 33,000	₹ 30,000	₹ 27,000

Depreciation is a fixed cost, so it does not 'flex' with changes in production. Since it is the only fixed cost, the variable and fixed costs are not classified in the budget.

(b)

	January	**February**	**March**
Total flexible budget	₹ 588,000	₹ 540,000	₹ 492,000
Actual cost	600,000	570,000	545,000
Excess of actual cost over budget...	₹ (12,000)	₹ (30,000)	₹ (53,000)

The excess of actual cost over the flexible budget suggests that the Machining Department has not performed as well as originally thought. Indeed, the department is spending more than would be expected, and it's getting worse, given the level of production for the first three months.

Illustrative Problem 6

The Apollo Blood Bank, a private charity partly supported by government grants, is located at Hyderabad. The Blood Bank has just finished its operations for September, which was a particularly busy month due to a powerful hurricane that hit neighbouring states causing many injuries. Many residents willingly donated their blood to help people in other cities. As a consequence, the blood bank collected and processed over 20% more blood than had been originally planned for the month.

A report prepared by a government official comparing actual costs to budgeted costs for the Blood Bank appears below. Continued support from the government depends on the Blood Bank's ability to demonstrate control over their costs.

Apollo Blood Bank
Cost Control Report
for the Month Ended September 30, 2016

	Actual	**Budget**	**Variance**
Litres of blood collected	620	500	120 F

Variable costs:			
Medical supplies	₹ 9,350	₹ 7,500	₹ 1,850 U
Lab tests	6,180	6,000	180 U
Refreshments for donors	1,340	1,000	340 U
Administrative supplies	400	250	150 U
Total variable cost	17,270	14,750	2520 U
Fixed costs:			
Staff salaries	10,000	10,000	—
Equipment depreciation	2,800	2,500	300 U
Rent	1,000	1,000	—
Utilities	570	500	70 U
Total fixed cost	14,370	14,000	370 U
Total cost	₹ 31,640	₹ 28,750	₹ 2,890 U

The managing director of the Blood Bank was very unhappy with this report, claiming that his costs were higher than expected due to the emergency on the neighbouring cities. He also pointed out that the additional costs had been fully covered by payments from grateful recipients. The government official who prepared the report countered that all of the figures had been submitted by the Blood Bank to the government; he was just pointing out that actual costs were a lot higher than promised in the budget.

Required:

1. Prepare a new performance report for September using the flexible budget approach.
2. Do you think any of the variances in the report you prepared should be investigated? Why?

Solution:

1. The cost formulas in the flexible budget report below were obtained by dividing the costs on the static budget in the question by the budgeted level of activity (500 liters). The fixed costs are carried over from the static budget.

Apollo Blood Bank
Flexible Budget Performance Report
for the Month Ended September 30, 2016

Budgeted activity (in liters)	500
Actual activity (in liters)	620

Costs	Cost Formula (per litre)	Actual Costs Incurred for 620 Litres	Budget Based on 620 Litres	Variance
Variable costs:				
Medical supplies	₹ 15.00	₹ 9,350	₹ 9,300	₹ 50 U
Lab tests	12.00	6,180	7,440	1,260 F
Refreshments for donors	2.00	1,340	1,240	100 U

Administrative supplies	0.50	400	310	90 U
Total variable costs	₹ 29.50	17,270	18,290	1,020 F
Fixed costs:				
Staff salaries		10,000	10,000	–
Equipment depreciation		2,800	2,500	300 U
Rent		1,000	1,000	—
Utilities		570	500	70 U
Total fixed costs		14,370	14,000	370 U
Total costs:		₹ 31,640	₹ 32,290	₹ 650 F

2. The overall variance is favourable and none of the unfavourable variances is particularly large. Nevertheless, the large favourable variance for lab tests is worrisome. Perhaps the blood bank has not been doing all of the lab tests for HIV, hepatitis, and other blood-transmittable diseases that it should be doing. This is well worth investigating and points out that favourable variances may warrant attention as much as unfavourable variances.

   Some may wonder why there is a variance for depreciation. Fixed costs can change; they just don't vary with the level of activity. Depreciation may have increased because of the acquisition of new equipment or because of a loss on equipment that must be scrapped. (This assumes that the loss flows through the depreciation account on the performance report.)

Illustrative Problem 7

A company markets products X and Y which it makes by using its capacity to the extent of 50% on X and 30% on Y. Budget for 2016 is as given below:

		X	*Y*
Production units		5,000	4,500
Direct Material/unit	₹	300	200
Conversion cost/unit :			
Variable	₹	100	80
Fixed	₹	50	40
Selling price per unit	₹	500	350
Profit per unit	₹	50	30

For the next year's budget, the following factors are relevant:

Direct material cost will go up by 6%

Variable conversion cost will increase by 10%

Selling price will increase by :

Product X 4%, Product Y 6%

To utilize the idle capacity of 20%, three proposals as under were put forth :

(i) Product X and sell the output at the revised price. Production of X from the idle time, however, will be less by 10%

(ii) Product Y but the increased production will be sold at the existing price.

(iii) Utilize the idle capacity to produce a new product Z whose details are as under:

Production from idle capacity 2,000 units

Direct materials ₹ 400 per unit

Variable conversion cost ₹ 200 per unit

Selling price ₹ 700 per unit

Special publicity expense ₹ 20,000

The present allocation of 50% and 30% respectively on products X and Y cannot be changed.

Required:

You are required to prepare statements of profitability for 2016 and 2017.

Solution:

Budget 2016

Units	5000	4500	₹	₹	₹
Sales	500	350	25,00,000	15,75,000	40,75,000
Dir Materials	300	200	15,00,000	9,00,000	24,00,000
Conversion V :	100	80	5,00,000	3,60,000	8,60,000
F :	50	40	2,52,000	1,80,000	4,30,000
Total			22,50,000	14,40,000	36,90,000
Profit			2,50,000	1,35,000	3,85,000

Budget 2017:

(i) Product X:	50% capacity	= 5000 units	
	20% capacity	= 2000 units	
	Less 10%	1800 units	
	₹	Increase	₹
SP	500	4%	520
Less: Direct Material	300	6%	318
Conversion Variable	100	10%	110
			428
Contribution			92

Total contribution 1800 × 92 = ₹ 1,65,600

(ii) Product Y	30% capacity = 4500 units		
	20% capacity = 3000 units		
	₹	Increase	₹
Selling Price	350	—	350
D. Materials	200	6%	212
Conversion Variable	80	10%	88
			300
Contribution			50

Total Contribution 3000 × 50 = ₹ 1,50,000

(*iii*) Product Z : 2000 units

S. Price	700
D. Materials	400
Conversion Variable	200
	600
Contribution	100

	₹
Total Contribution 2000 × 100 =	2,00,000
Publicity Expenses	20,000
Profit	1,80,000

It is better to produce product Z : In that event selling price of Y can be increased to 350 × 1.06 = 371 per unit

Budget 2017 (₹)

	X	Y	Z	X	Y	Z	Total
Units	5000	4500	2000				
Per Unit: (₹)							
Sales	520	371	700	26,00,000	16,69,500	14,00,000	56,69,500
D. Mat.	318	212	400	15,90,000	9,54,000	8,00,000	33,44,000
Conversion (Variable)	110	88	200	5,50,000	3,96,000	4,00,000	13,46,000
Total				21,40,000	13,50,000	12,00,000	46,90,000
Contribution				4,60,000	3,19,500	2,00,000	9,79,500
Fixed Costs 4,30,000							
Publicity 20,000							4,50,000
						Profit	5,29,500

Illustrative Problem 8 (Flexible Budget for Selling Expenses)

Bajaj Company employs flexible budgeting techniques to evaluate the performance of several of its activities. The selling expenses flexible budgets for three representative monthly activity levels follow.

Representative Monthly Flexible Budgets for Selling Expenses

Activity measures:			
Unit sales volume	4,00,000	425,000	450,000
Sales volume	₹ 1,00,00,000	₹ 1,06,25,000	₹ 1,12,50,000
Number of orders	4,000	4,250	4,500
Number of salespersons	72	72	72
Monthly expenses:			
Advertising and promotion	₹ 12,00,000	₹ 12,00,000	₹ 12,00,000
Administrative salaries	57,000	57,000	57,000
Sales salaries	75,600	75,600	75,600

Sales commissions	3,00,000	318,750	337,500
Salesperson travel	1,70,000	175,000	180,000
Sales office expense	4,90,000	498,750	507,500
Shipping expense	6,75,000	712,500	750,000
Total	₹ 29,67,600	₹ 30,37,600	₹ 31,07,600

The following assumptions were used to develop the selling expenses flexible budgets:

(*a*) The average size of Bajaj's sales force during the year was planned to be 72 people.

(*b*) Salespersons are paid a monthly salary plus commission on gross sales.

(*c*) The travel costs are best characterized as a step-variable cost. The fixed portion is related to the number of salespersons, the variable portion tends to fluctuate with gross sales.

(*d*) Sales office expense is a mixed cost with the variable portion related to the number of orders processed.

(*e*) Shipping expense is a mixed cost with the vaiable portion related to the number of units sold.

A sales force of 80 persons generated a total of 4,300 orders resulting in a sales volume of 4,20,000 units during November. The gross sales amounted to ₹ 109 lakhs. The selling expenses incurred for November were as follows:

Advertising and promotion	₹ 13,50,000
Administrative salaries	57,000
Sales salaries	84,000
Sales commissions	3,27,000
Salesperson travel	1,85,000
Sales office expense	4,97,200
Shipping expense	7,30,000
Total	₹ 32,30,200

Required:

1. Explain why the selling expenses flexible budgets presented would not be appropriate for evaluate Bajaj Company's November selling expenses; indicate how the flexible budget would have to be revised.

2. Prepare a selling expenses report for November that Bajaj Company can use to evaluate its control over selling expenses. The report should have a line for each selling expense item showing the appropriate budgeted amount, the actual selling expense, and the monthly variation.

Solution:

1. The flexible budgets presented are based on three different activity levels, none of which coincide with the actual level of performance for November. The budget must be restated to a level of activity that matches the actual results. The fixed and variable components of the mixed costs must be segregated and a budgeted cost calculated for the level of activity attained.

2.

Bajaj Company
Selling Expenses Report
For the Month of November

Monthly Expenses	Budget	Actual	Variance
Advertising and promotion	₹ 12,00,000	₹ 13,50,000	₹ 150,000 U
Administrative salaries	57,000	57,000	0
Sales salaries[a]	84,000	84,000	0
Sales Commissions[b]	3,27,000	3,27,000	0
Salesperson travel[c]	1,87,200	1,85,000	2,200 F
Sales office expenses[d]	5,00,500	4,97,200	3,300 F
Shipping expensee	7,05,000	7,30,000	25,000 U
Total	₹ 30,60,700	₹ 32,30,200	₹ 169,500 U

[a](₹ 75,600/72) (80) = ₹ 84,000

[b](₹ 3,00,000/₹ 1,00,00,000) (₹ 1,09,00,000) = ₹ 3,27,000

[c]Change in cost: ₹ 1,75,000 – ₹ 1,70,000 = ₹ 5,000

Change in sales ₹ 1,06,25,000 – ₹ 1,00,00,000 = ₹ 6,25,000

Variable cost per Rupee of sales = Change in cost divided by change in activity level

₹ 5,000/₹ 6,25,000 = ₹ 0.008 per Rupee of sales

Fixed cost at 72-person level:

₹ 1,70,000 – (₹ 1,00,00,000 × 0.008) = ₹ 90,000

Fixed cost at 80-person level:

(₹ 90,000/72) × 80 = ₹ 100,000

Total travel budget:

₹ 1,00,000 fixed + (₹ 1,09,00,000 × 0.008) variable = ₹ 1,87,200

[d]Change in cost: ₹ 4,98,750 – ₹ 4,90,000 = ₹ 8,750

Change in number of orders: 4,250 – 4,000 = 250

Variable cost per order: ₹ 8,750/250 = ₹ 35

Fixed cost: ₹ 4,90,000 – (4,000 × ₹ 35) = ₹ 3,50,000

Total office expense budget:

₹ 3,50,000 + (4,300 × ₹ 35) = ₹ 5,00,500

[e]Change in cost: ₹ 7,12,500 – ₹ 6,75,000 = ₹ 37,500

Change in number of units: 4,25,000 – 4,00,000 = 25,000

Variable cost per unit: ₹ 37,500/25,000 = ₹ 1.50

Fixed cost: 6,75,000 – (4,00,000 × ₹ 1.50) = ₹ 75,000

Total shipping expense budget:

₹ 75,000 + (420,000 × ₹ 1.50) = ₹ 7,05,000

Illustrative Problem 9 (Flexible Budget and Performance Report)

Ashok Rajpurohit, finance manager for Maruti Manufacturing Company, Pune, prepared the following budget for manufacturing costs at two different levels of activity for 2016.

Diret Labor Hours

	Level of Activity	
	50,000	**100,000**
Diret materials	₹ 3,00,000	₹ 6,00,000
Direct labor	2,00,000	4,00,000
Depreciation (plant)	1,00,000	1,00,000
Subtotal	₹ 6,00,000	₹ 11,00,000

Machine Hours

	Level of Activity	
	200,000	**300,000**
Maintaining equipment	₹ 3,60,000	₹ 5,10,000
Machining	1,12,000	1,62,000
Subtotal	₹ 4,72,000	₹ 6,72,000

Material Moves

	Level of Activity	
	20,000	**40,000**
Matrials handling	₹ 1,65,000	₹ 2,90,000

Number of Batches Inspected

	Level of Activity	
	100	**200**
Inspections	₹ 1,25,000	₹ 2,25,000
Total	₹ 13,62,000	₹ 22,87,000

During 2016, Maruti worked a total of 80,000 direct labor hours, used 2,50,000 machine hours, made 32,000 moves, and performed 120 batch inspections. The following actual costs were incurred:

Direct materials	₹ 4,40,000
Direct labor	3,55,000
Depreciation	1,00,000
Maintenance	4,25,000
Machining	1,42,000
Materials handling	2,32,500
Inspectioins	1,60,000

Maruti applies overhead using rates based on direct labor hours, machine hours, number of moves, and number of batches. The second level of activity (the far right column in the preceding table) is the practical level of activity (the available activity for resources required in advance of usage) and is used to compute predetermined overhead pool rates.

Required:

1. Prepare a performance report for Maruti's manufacturing costs in 2016.
2. Assume that one of the products produced by Maruti is budgeted to use 10,0000 direct labor hours, 15,000 machine hours, and 500 moves and will be produced in five batches. A total of 10,000 units will be produced during the year. Calculate the budgeted unit manufacturing cost.
3. One of Maruti's managers said the following: "Budgeting at the activity level makes a lot of sense. It really helps us manage costs better. But the above budget really needs to provide more detailed information. For example, I know that the materials-handling activity involves the usage of forklifts and operators, and this information is lost with simply reporting the total cost of the activity for various levels of output. We have four forklifts, each capable of providing 10,000 moves per year. We lease these forklifts for five years, at ₹ 10,000 per year. Furthermore, for our two shifts, we need up to eight operators if we run all four forklifts. Each operators is paid a salary of ₹ 30,000 per year. Also, I know that fuel costs us about ₹ 0.25 per move."

   Based on these comments, explain how this additional information may help Maruti better manage its costs. Also, assuming that these are the only three items, expand the detail of the flexible budget for materials handling to reveal the cost of these three resource items for 20,000 moves and 40,000 moves, respectively. *(M.Com. Delhi)*

Solution:

1. **Performance Report**
   For the Year 2016

	Actual Costs	Budgeted Costs*	Budget Variance
Direct materials	₹ 4,40,000	₹ 4,80,000	₹ 40,000 F
Direct labor	3,55,000	3,20,000	35,000 U
Depreciation	1,00,000	1,00,000	0
Maintenance	4,25,000	4,35,000	10,000 F
Machining	1,42,000	1,37,000	5,000 U
Materials handling	2,32,500	2,40,000	7,500 F
Inspections	1,60,00	1,45,000	15,000 U
Total	₹ 18,54,500	₹ 18,57,000	₹ 2,500 F

* Budget formulas for each item can be computed by using the high-low method (using the appropriate cost driver for each method). Using this approach, the budgeted costs for the actual activity levels are computed as follows:

Direct materials: ₹ 6 × 80,000

Direct labor: ₹ 4 × 80,000

Depreciation: ₹ 1,00,000

Maintenance: ₹ 60,000 + ₹ 1.50 × 2,50,000)

Machining: ₹ 12,000 + (₹ 0.50 × 2,50,000)

Materials handling: ₹ 40,000 + (₹ 6.25 × 32,000)

Inspections: ₹ 25,000 + (₹ 1,000 × 120)

2. Pool rates: ₹ 11,00,000/1,00,000 = ₹ 11 per DLH
   ₹ 6,72,000/300,000 = ₹ 2.24 per MHr
   ₹ 2,90,000/40,000 = ₹ 7.25 per move
   ₹ 2,25,000/200 = ₹ 1,125 per batch
   Note: The first pool has material and labor costs included.

   Unit cost:

Pool 1: ₹ 11 × 10,000	=	₹ 1,10,000
Pool 2: ₹ 2.24 × 15,000	=	33,600
Pool 3: ₹ 7.25 × 500	=	3,625
Pool 4: ₹ 1,125 × 5	=	5,625
Total		₹ 1,52,850
Units		÷ 10,000
Unit cost		₹ 15.29*

   *Rounded

3. Knowing the resources consumed by activities and how the resource costs change with the activity driver should provide more insight into managing the activity and its associated costs. For example, if moves could be reduced to 20,000 from the expected 40,000, then costs can be reduced by not only eliminating the need for four operators, but by reducing the need to lease from four to two forklifts. However, in the short run, the cost of leasing forklifts may persist even though demand for their service is reduced.

	20,000 moves	40,000 moves
Materials handling:		
Forklifts	₹ 40,000	₹ 40,000
Operators	1,20,000	2,40,000
Fuel	5,000	10,000
Total	₹ 1,65,000	₹ 2,90,000

   The detail assumes that forklift leases must continue in the short run but that the number of operators may be reduced (assumes each operator can do 5,000 moves per year).

FUNCTIONAL BUDGETS – ILLUSTRATIVE PROBLEMS

Illustrative Problem 10 (Materials Requirement)

Bala company expects to sell 84,000 units of finished goods over the next 3-month period. The company currently has 44,000 units of finished goods on hand and wishes to have an inventory of 48,000 units at the end of the 3-months period. To produce 1 unit of finished goods, it requires 4 units of raw materials. The company currently has 2,00,000 units of raw materials on hand and wishes to have an inventory of 2,20,000 units of raw materials on hand at the end of the 3-month period.

How many units of raw materials must Bala Company purchase during the 3-month period?

Solution:

Material Requirements

$$\begin{pmatrix}\text{Finished Units}\\ \text{to be produced}\end{pmatrix} = \begin{pmatrix}84,000\text{ Units}\\ \text{to be sold}\end{pmatrix} + \begin{pmatrix}48,000\text{ Units in}\\ \text{Ending Inventory}\end{pmatrix} - \begin{pmatrix}44,000\text{ Units in}\\ \text{Beginning Inventory}\end{pmatrix}$$

Units to be Produced = 88,000

Units of Raw Materials to be used = 4 Units of Raw Materials per finished Unit × 88,000 Units

= 3,52,000

$$= \begin{pmatrix}\text{Units of Raw Materials}\\ \text{to be purchased}\end{pmatrix} = \begin{pmatrix}3,52,000\text{ Units}\\ \text{to be used}\end{pmatrix} + \begin{pmatrix}2,20,000\text{ Units desired}\\ \text{ending inventory}\end{pmatrix} - \begin{pmatrix}2,00,000\text{ Units in}\\ \text{beginning inventory}\end{pmatrix}$$

= 3,72,000 Units

Illustrative Problem 11 (Production Budget)

Gama Engineering Company Limited manufactures two products X and Y. An estimate of the number of units expected to be sold in the first seven months of 2016 is given below:

	Product X	***Product Y***
January	500	1,400
February	600	1,400
March	800	1,200
April	1,000	1,000
May	1,200	800
June	1,200	800
July	1,000	900

It is anticipated that:

1. there will be no work-in-progress at the end of any month; and
2. finished units equal to half the anticipated sales for the next month will be in stock at the end of each month (including December 2015). The budgeted production and production costs for the year ending 31st December, 2016 are as follows:

	Product X	***Product Y***
Production (units)	11,000	12,000
Direct materials per unit (₹)	12	19
Direct wages per unit (₹)	5	7
Other manufacturing charges apportionable to each type of product (₹)	33,000	48,000

You are required to prepare:

(*a*) A production budget showing the number of units to be manufactured each month.

(*b*) A summarised production costs budget for the six-month period January to June 2016.

Solution:

Gama Engineering Company Limited

(a) Production Budget (in units) for the Six months Ending 30th June, 2016

	Jan.	*Feb.*	*March*	*April*	*May*	*June*
Product X:						
Closing stock	300	400	500	600	600	500
Sales	500	600	800	1,000	1,200	1,200
	800	1000	1300	1600	1800	1700
Less: Opening stock	250	300	400	500	600	600
Production (in units)	550	700	900	1,100	1,200	1,100
Product Y:						
Closing stock	700	600	500	400	400	450
Sales	1,400	1,400	1,200	1,000	800	800
	2,100	2,000	1,700	1,400	1,200	1,250
Less: Opening stock	700	700	600	500	400	400
Production (in units)	1,400	1,300	1,100	900	800	850

(b) Summarised Production Cost Budget for the Six Months Ending 30th June 2016

Production (in units)		**5550**		**6350**
		X		***Y***
	Units cost	***Total cost***	***Unit cost***	***Total cost***
Direct Materials	₹ 12	₹ 66,600	₹ 19	₹1,20,650
Direct Wages	5	27,750	7	44,450
Manufacturing charges	3	16,650	4	25,400
	20	1,11,000	30	1,90,500

Note: Manufacturing charges have been presumed to be variable costs in the absence of any other information. They could, however, be presumed to be fixed charges also for the whole year. In such a case they will be taken as 50% of the annual charges for the first six months in each case.

Illustrative Problem 12 (Production and Materials Purchase Budget)

As a cost accountant of Modern Manufacturing Company, you are asked to prepare a quarterly production budget and direct materials purchase budget for the accounting year, Ist July, 2015 to 30 June, 2016.

The following information is relevant:

(*i*) The company manufactures only two products A and B

(*ii*) Sales volume forecast (in units):

2015-2016	***A***	***B***
Quarter I	1,500	2,000

Quarter II	1,000	2,500
Quarter III	1,000	2,000
Quarter IV	1,500	2,500
2016–2017		
Quarter I	1,500	2,500

(*iii*) Raw materials requirement forecast: The standard quantities of the two raw materials, X and Y which should be used in the manufacture of the two products and the prices of these raw materials have been estimated as follows:

Standard quantities:	Estimated costs:
Raw materials X–2 units for each unit of product A	Raw material X–₹ 10 for each unit of A
Raw materials Y–3 units for each unit of product B	Raw material Y–₹ 6 for each unit of B

Usage variance:

5% is provided to cover spoilage and scrap in the case of material X and 4% in the case of materials Y.

(*iv*) Stock forecast:

Estimated opening stock

Product A	750 units
Product B	1,250 units
Raw material X	1,578 units
Raw material Y	3,900 units

It is planned that the closing stock level at the end of each quarter should be maintained at a level equal to half the expected sales for the next quarter for both the products and the raw materials stock at the end of each quarter should be held accordingly.

Solution:

Production Budget

	Qr I		***Qr II***		***Qr III***		***Qr IV***		***Total***	
Units	**A**	**B**	**A**	**B**	**A**	**B**	**A**	**B**	**A**	**B**
Sales Forecast	1,500	2,000	1,000	2,500	1,000	2,000	1,500	2,500	5,000	9,000
(+) Closing stock	500	1,250	500	1,000	750	1,250	750	1,250	2,500	4,750
(–) Opening stock	750	1,250	500	1,250	500	1,000	750	1,250	2,500	4,750
Production Units	1,250	2,000	1,000	2,250	1,250	2,250	1,500	2,500	5,000	9,000

Material Purchase Budget

	Qr I		***Qr II***		***Qr III***		***Qr IV***		***Total***	
Units	**A**	**B**	**A**	**B**	**A**	**B**	**A**	**B**	**A**	**B**
Standard Consumption	2,500	6,000	2,000	6,750	2,750	6,750	3,000	7,500	10,000	27,000
(+)Usage variance	125	240	100	270	125	270	150	300	500	1,080
(+)Closing stock	1,000	3,750	1,000	3,000	1,500	3,750	1,500	3,750	5,250	14,820

(+)Spoilage (5%,4%)	50	150	50	120	75	150	75	150		
(–)Opening stock	1,575	3,900	1,050	3,900	1,050	3,120	1,575	3,900	5,250	14,820
Purchase	2,100	6,240	2,100	6,240	3,150	7,800	3,150	8,800	10,500	28,080
	X	X	X	X	X	X	X	X	X	X
	10	6	10	6	10	6	10	6	10	6
Purchase Value (₹)	21,000		21,000		31,500		31,500		1,50,000	
		37,440		37,440		46,800		52,800		1,68,480
Total Purchases (₹)		58,440		58,440		78,300		73,300		2,73,480

Illustrative Problem 13 (Production Budget and Direct Materials Purchase Budget)

JCL Corporation manufactures and sells two products RB and RD. Three types of materials, A, B and C are required for producing these products. Projected information for 2015-16 is given below:

Product	Projeced Sales for 2015-16 (units)	Inventory (in units) On 1-4-2015	On 31-3-2016	Direct Labour Required (Honours/Unit)
RB	75,000	25,000	31,250	4
RD	50,000	10,000	11,250	6

Raw material stock and usage are as follows:

Direct Material	Required per unit RB	RD	Inventory on 1-4-2015	Inventory on 31-3-2016
A	5.00 kg	5.00 kg	40,000 kg	45,000 kg
B	2.50 kg	3.00 kg	36,250 kg	40,000 kg
C	0	1:00 kg	7,500 kg	8,750 kg

You are required to prepare the following for 2015-16:

(*i*) Production budget (in units)

(*ii*) Direct material purchase budget in quantities for A, B and C.

(*iii*) After (*i*) and (*ii*), you are told that only 6,00,000 labour hours will be available for production. If there is no requirement to hold the stated level of finished goods closing inventory, what would be the principal budget factor? Substantiate your view with appropate figures.

(*CA Final, Nov. 2015*)

Solution:

(*i*) **Statement Showing "Production Budget"**

Particulars	'RB' (units)	'RD' (units)
Inventory (at the end of the year)	31,250	11,250
Add: Projected Sales	75,000	50,000
Total Requirements	1,06,250	61,250
Less: Beginning inventory	25,000	10,000
Production	81,250	51,250

(*ii*) **Statement Showing "Direct Material Purchase Budget"**

Particulars	Material 'A' (Kg.)	Material 'B' (Kg.)	Material 'C' (Kg.)
Requirement for Production 'RB'	4,06,250 (81,250 units × 5 Kg.)	2,03,125 (81,250 units × 2.50 Kg.)	—
Requirement for Production 'RD'	2,56,250 (51,250 units × 5 Kg.)	1,53,750 (51,250 units × 3 Kg.)	51,250 (51,250 units × 1 Kg.)
Total Requirement	6,62,500	3,56,875	51,250
Add: Closing invntory	45,000	40,000	8,750
Less: Beginning inventory	40,000	36,250	7,500
Purchase	6,67,500	3,60,625	52,500

(*iii*) **Statement Showing "Direct Labour Hours Required vs Available"**

Particulars	'RB' Units	'RD' Units	Total
Maximum Sales	75,000	50,000	
Less: From Stock	25,000	10,000	
Required Goods for Prdn.	50,000	40,000	
Direct Labour Requirement	2,00,000 (50,000 units × 4 hrs.)	2,40,000 (40,000 units × 6 hrs.)	4,40,000 hrs.
Direct Labour Available			6,00,000 hrs.

∵ Direct Labour Hrs. (Requirement) is < Direct Labour Hrs. (Availability)

∴ Principal Budget Factor is Sales (units)

Illustrative Problem 14 (Selling Expense Budget)

Medicare Ltd. sells pharmaceutical products to medical practitioners and chemists. Sales orders are obtained in two ways. Mostly the company's salesmen book orders directly when they call on customers. Others called Mail orders are directly placed by the chemists and doctors on the basis of the company's catalogue and price list left with them by the salesmen. Salesmen receive commission of 5% of sales they obtain personally and 2% of mail order sales received from their respective territories. Despatch and billing expenses average 4% of sales revenue, regardless of the source of the order.

Sales are budgeted as under for 2016

Quarter	*Total Sales* ₹	*Salesmen's Orders* ₹	*Mail Orders* ₹
First	5,00,000	80%	20%
Second	8,00,000	70%	30%
Third	10,00,000	60%	40%
Fourth	7,50,000	80%	20%

Fixed selling Expenses:	₹
Sales salaries	36,000
Advertising	1,00,000
Travel	40,000

Sales salaries and travelling expenses are paid out in a steady flow throughout the year. 50% of advertising is incurred in second quarter and the balance 30% and 20% are incurred in the third fourth quarters.

(a) Prepare a Budget of selling Expenses by quarter for 2016.

(b) It has been suggested that a 50% increase in budgeted advertising expenditure would double the proportion of mail order sales and would permit a 50 % reduction in budgeted travelling expenses. Would operations under this plant be more profitable? Support your answer with necessary computation.

Solution:

(a) Selling Expenses Budget

(₹)	*Quarter 1*	*Quarter 2*	*Quarter 3*	*Quarter 4*
Direct Sales	4,00,000	5,60,000	6,00,000	6,00,000
Mail order	1,00,000	2,40,000	4,00,000	1,50,000
	5,00,000	8,00,000	10,00,000	7,50,000
(b) Selling Exp. Budget Commission				
Direct sales 5%	20,000	28,000	30,000	30,000
Mail Order 2%	2,000	4,800	8,000	3,000
	22,000	32,800	38,000	33,000
Despatching & Billing 4%	20,000	32,000	40,000	30,000
Sales salaries	9,000	9,000	9,000	9,000
Advertising	—	50,000	30,000	20,000
Travel	10,000	10,000	10,000	10,000
	61,000	1,33,800	1,27,000	1,02,000

Direct Sales converted to Mail Order

	₹
Quarter 1 (20% of 5,00,000)	1,00,000
Quarter 2 (30% of 8,00,000)	2,40,000
Quarter 3 (40% of 10,00,000)	4,00,000
Quarter 4 (20% of 7,50,000)	1,50,000
	8,90,000
Sales Commission saved (5%–2%)	26,700
Travel Exp. saved (50%)	20,000
Total Savings	46,700
Increase in Advt. Cost (50%)	50,000
Net increase in Cost and Reduction of Profit	3,300

Operations under this plan would reduce the profit, and therefore, not recommended.

Illustrative Problem 15 (Marketing Expense Budget)

Mumbai Corporation has just received its marketing expense report for July, which follows.

Item	Amount
Sales Commissions	₹ 140,000
Sales Staff Salaries	60,000
Telephone and Mailing	16,000
Building Lease Payment	20,000
Heat, Light, and Water	5,000
Packaging and Delivery	28,000
Depreciation	15,000
Marketing Consultants	20,000

You have been asked to develop budgeted costs for July of next year. Here are additional data relevant to July of next year:

- Sales volume is expected to increase by 5 per cent.
- Sales prices are expected to increase by 10 per cent.
- Commission are based on a percentage of sales revenue.
- Sales staff salaries will increase 4 per cent next year regardless of sales volume.
- Telephone and mailing expenses are scheduled to increase by 8 per cent even with no change in sales volume. However, these costs are variable with the number of units sold, as are packaging and delivery costs.
- Building rent is based on a five-year lease that expires in three years.
- Heat, light, and water are scheduled to increase by 12 per cent regardless of sales volume.
- Packaging and delivery vary with the number of units sold.
- Depreciation includes furniture and fixtures used by the sales staff. The company has just acquired an additional ₹ 1,900 in furniture that will be received at the start of next year and will be depreciated over a 10-year life using the straight-line method.
- Marketing consultant expenses were for a special advertising campaign that runs from time to time. During the coming year, the costs are expected to average ₹ 35,000 per month.

Required:

Prepare a budget for marketing expenses for July in the coming year. Management hopes to keep the total marketing expense budget under ₹ 350,000 in Year 2. Based on your budget, are the expected marketing expenses for Year 2 under ₹ 350,000?

If not, which expenses are budgeted to increase the most?

Solution:

Item	July		Adjustments		Budgeted For Next July
Sales Commissions	₹ 140,000	×	1.05 × 1.10	=	₹ 161,700
Sales Staff Salaries	60,000	×	1.04	=	62,400
Telephone and Mailing	16,000		1.08 × 1.05	=	₹ 18,144

Building Lease	20,000	None	=	18,144
Heat, Light, and Water	5,000 ×	1.12	=	5,600
Packaging and Delivery	28,000 ×	1.05	=	29,400
Depreciation	15,000 +	(₹ 1,900/10 years)	=	16,900
Marketing Consultants	20,000	Not Applicable		35,000
Total Budgeted Costs				₹ 3,49,144

It appears that the company will barely achieve its goal of holding the total marketing expense budget under ₹ 3,50,000 for the year. The costs that increase the most are commissions. It might not be wise to cut sales commissions. The company should start looking at ways to cut telephone and mailing costs, perhaps with greater reliance on e-mail and the web.

Illustrative Problem 16

Bullen and Company makes and sells high-quality glare filters for microcomputer monitors. John Crane, controller, is responsible for preparing Bullen's master budget and has assembled the data below for 2016.

The direct labour rate includes wages and all employee-related benefits and the employer's share of FICA. Labour saving machinery will be fully operational by March. Also, as of March 1, the company's union contract calls for an increase in direct labour wages that is included in the direct labour rate.

Bullen expects to have 10,000 glare filters in inventory at December 2015, and has a policy of carrying 50 per cent of the following month's projected sales in inventory.

	2016			
	January	**February**	**March**	**April**
Estimated unit sales	**20,000**	**24,000**	**16,000**	**18,000**
Sales price per unit	₹ 80	₹ 80	₹ 75	₹ 75
Direct labour hours per unit	4.0	4.0	3.5	3.5
Direct labour hourly rate	₹ 15	₹ 15	₹ 16	₹ 16
Direction materials cost per unit	₹ 10	₹ 10	₹ 10	₹ 10

Required:

A. Prepare the following monthly budgets for Bullen and Company for the first quarter of 2016. Be sure to show supporting calculations.
1. Production budget in units
2. Direct labour budget in hours
3. Direct materials budget
4. Sales budget

B. Calculate the total budgeted contribution margin for Bullen and Company for the first quarter of 2016. Be sure to show supporting calculations.

C. Discuss at least three behavioural consideration in the profit-planning and budgeting process.

(*CMA, USA Adapted with permission*)

Solution:

A. Following are the monthly budgets for Bullen and Company for the first quarter of 2016

	January	February	March	Quarter
1. **Production budget (units)**				
Sales units	20,000	24,000	16,000	60,000
Plus: ending inventory	12,000	8,000	9,000	9,000
Total units required	32,000	32,000	25,000	69,000
Less: beginning inventory	10,000	12,000	8,000	10,000
Units to be produced	22,000	20,000	17,000	59,000
2. **Direct labour budget (hours)**				
Units to be produced	22,000	20,000	17,000	59,000
Direct labour hours per unit	4.0	4.0	3.5	
Total labour budget (hours)	88,000	80,000	59,500	227,500
3. **Direct materials budget (₹)**				
Units to be produced	22,000	20,000	17,000	59,000
Cost per unit	₹ 10	₹ 10	₹ 10	₹ 10
Total direct materials cost	₹ 220,000	₹ 200,000	₹ 170,000	₹ 590,000
4. Sales budget (₹)				
Sales units	20,000	24,000	16,000	60,000
Sales price per unit	₹ 80	₹ 80	₹ 75	
Total sales revenue budget	₹ 16,00,000	₹ 19,20,000	₹ 12,00,000	₹ 47,20,000

B. The total budgeted contribution margin for Bullen and Company for the first quarter of 2016 would be calculated as follows:

Bullen and Company
Budgeted Contribution Margin
First Quarter, 2016

	January	February	March	Quarter
Direct labour hours per unit	4.0	4.0	3.5	
Direct labour hourly rate	₹ 15	₹ 15	₹ 16	
Direct labour cost per unit	₹ 60	₹ 60	₹ 56	
Sales units	20,000	24,000	16,000	60,000
Sales revenue	₹ 16,00,000	₹ 19,20,000	₹ 12,00,000	₹ 47,20,000
Direct labour cost	12,00,000	14,40,000	8,96,000	35,36,000
Material cost	2,00,000	2,40,000	1,60,000	6,00,000
Contribution margin	₹ 2,00,000	₹ 2,40,000	₹ 1,44,000	₹ 58,400

C. At least three behavioural considerations in the profit-planning and budgeting process include the following.

- **Goal alignment is critical. The individual manager's goals may be conflicting with the firm's goals. Setting targets in a budget process helps focus and motivate a manager to achieve the firm's objectives.**
- **Participation from lower-level managers and other employees has two benefits. It uses information from those closest to the process, and the managers have a stronger commitment to the budget itself.**
- **The entire budget process is a form of communication. Feedback and other forms of improving communication are essential throughout the process.**

FINANCIAL BUDGETS — ILLUSTRATIVE PROBLEMS

Illustrative Problem 17 (Cash Receipts Budget)

A company normally collects cash from credit customers as follows: 50 per cent in the month of sale, 30 per cent in the first month after sale, 18 per cent in the second month after sale, and 2 per cent are never collected. Sales, all on credit, are expected to be as follows:

	₹
January	5,00,000
February	6,00,000
March	4,00,000
April	5,00,000

(*a*) Calculate the amount of cash expected to be received from customers during March.

(*b*) Calculate the amount of cash expected to be received from customers during April.

Solution:

	₹
(a) Budgeted cash collection in March:	
From January Sales (.18 × 5,00,000)	90,000
From February Sales (.30 × 6,00,000)	1,80,000
From March Sales (.50 × 4,00,000)	2,00,000
Total Budgeted Collections in March	4,70,000
(b) Budgeted cash collections in April:	
From February Sales (.18 × 6,00,000)	1,08,000
From March Sales (.30 × 4,00,000)	1,20,000
From April Sales (.50 × 5,00,000)	2,50,000
Total Budgeted Collection in April	4, 78,000

Illustrative Problem 18

Based on the following information, prepare a Cash Budget for ABC Ltd:

	1st Quarter (₹)	2nd Quarter (₹)	3rd Quarter (₹)	4th Quarter (₹)
Opening cash balance	10,000	—	—	—
Collection from customers	1,25,000	1,50,000	1,60,000	2,21,000

Payments:				
Purchase of material	20,000	35,000	35,000	17,000
Other expenses	25,000	20,000	20,000	17,000
Salary and wages	90,000	95,000	95,000	1,09,200
Income tax	5,000	—	—	—
Purchase of machinery	—	—	—	20,000

The company desires to maintain a cash balance of ₹ 15,000 at the end of each quarter. Cash can be borrowed or repaid in multiple of ₹ 500 at an interest of 10% per annum. Management does not want to borrow cash more than what is necessary and wants to repay as early as possible. In any event, loans cannot be extended beyond four quarters. Interests is computed and paid when the principal is repaid. Assume that borrowings take place at the beginning and repayments are made at the end of the quarters.

Solution:

Cash Budget for ABC Ltd.

Particulars	1st Quarter (₹)	2nd Quarter (₹)	3rd Quarter (₹)	4th Quarter (₹)
Opening Cash balance	10,000	15,000	15,000	15,325
Add: collection from customers	1,25,000	1,50,000	1,60,000	2,21,000
(A) Total cash available	1,35,000	1,65,000	1,75,000	2,36,325
Payments:				
Purchase of materials	20,000	35,000	35,000	17,000
Other expenses	25,000	20,000	20,000	17,000
Salary and wages	90,000	95,000	95,000	1,09,200
Income tax	5,000	—	—	—
Purchase of machinery	—	—	—	20,000
(B) Total cash payment	**1,40,000**	**1,50,000**	**1,50,000**	**1,63,200**
Minimum cash balance reqd.	15,000	15,000	15,000	15,000
(C) Total cash required	1,55,000	1,65,000	1,65,000	1,78,200
Excess (Deficit) A-C	(20,000)	—	10,000	58,125
Financing:				
Borrowing	20,000	—	—	—
Repayment	—	—	(9,000)	(11,000)
Interest Payment	—	—	(675)*	(1,100)*
(D) Total effect of financing	20,000	—	(9,675)	(12,100)
Cash balancing at the end of quarters (A + D – B)	15,000	15,000	15,325	61,025

*9,000 × 0.10 × 9/12 = ₹ 675. Similarly interest has been calculated for one year @ 10% per annum on ₹ 11,000.

Illustrative Problem 19 (Cash Budget)

Prepare cash budget for July-December from the following information:

(*i*) The estimated sales, expenses etc. are as follows:

(₹ in lacs)

	June	July	Aug.	Sept.	Oct.	Nov.	Dec.
Sales	34	40	40	50	50	60	65
Purchase	24	16	17	20	20	25	28
Wages and Salaries	12	14	14	18	18	20	22
Miscellaneous	5	6	6	6	7	7	7
Interest Received	2	—	—	2	—	—	2
Sales of Shares	—	—	20	—	—	—	—

(*ii*) 20% of the sales are on cash with 3% cash discount and the balance on credit.

(*iii*) 1% of he credit sales are returned by the customers. 2% of the net receivable constituted bad debt losses. 50% of the good accounts receivable are collected in the month following the sales with 1% cash discount, 30% of the good accounts receivable are collected in the 2nd month following the sales and the rest in the 3rd month following sales.

(*iv*) The time lag in the payment of misc. expenses and purchases is one month. Wages and salaries are paid fortnightly with a time lag of 15 days.

(*v*) The company keeps a minimum cash balance of ₹ 25.00 lakhs. Cash in excess of ₹ 27 lakhs is invested in 9% Govt. securities in the multiple of ₹ 1 lakh. Interest is receivable on montlhy basis. Shortfalls in the minimum cash balance are made good by borrowings from banks in multiple of ₹ 2 lakhs and also repaid by same amount. The rate of interest is 12% p.a. (compound interest)

(*vi*) The opening cash balance is ₹ 26 lacs.

(*vii*) Sales in the months April and May was ₹ 44 and 40 lacs respectively.

(*CA Final Nov. 2010, M.Com., Delhi, 2016*)

Solution:

***Working Note* 1:**

Let Sales	100	
Less: Cash sales	20	20 × 97% = 19.4% of Sale (monthly)
Debtors	80	
Less: Return 1%	0.08	
Net Receivable	79.2	
Less: Bad Debt (2%)	1.584	
Good Debtors	77.62	

Good Debtors 77.62 × 50% × 99% = 38.42% of Previous Month Sales.

Months Following Sales:

2nd Month *following sales* = 77.62 × 30% = 23.28% of 2nd Previous Month Sale (PMS)

3rd Month *following sales* = 77.62 × 20% = 15.53% of 3rd Previous Month Sale (PMS)

Collection Pattern

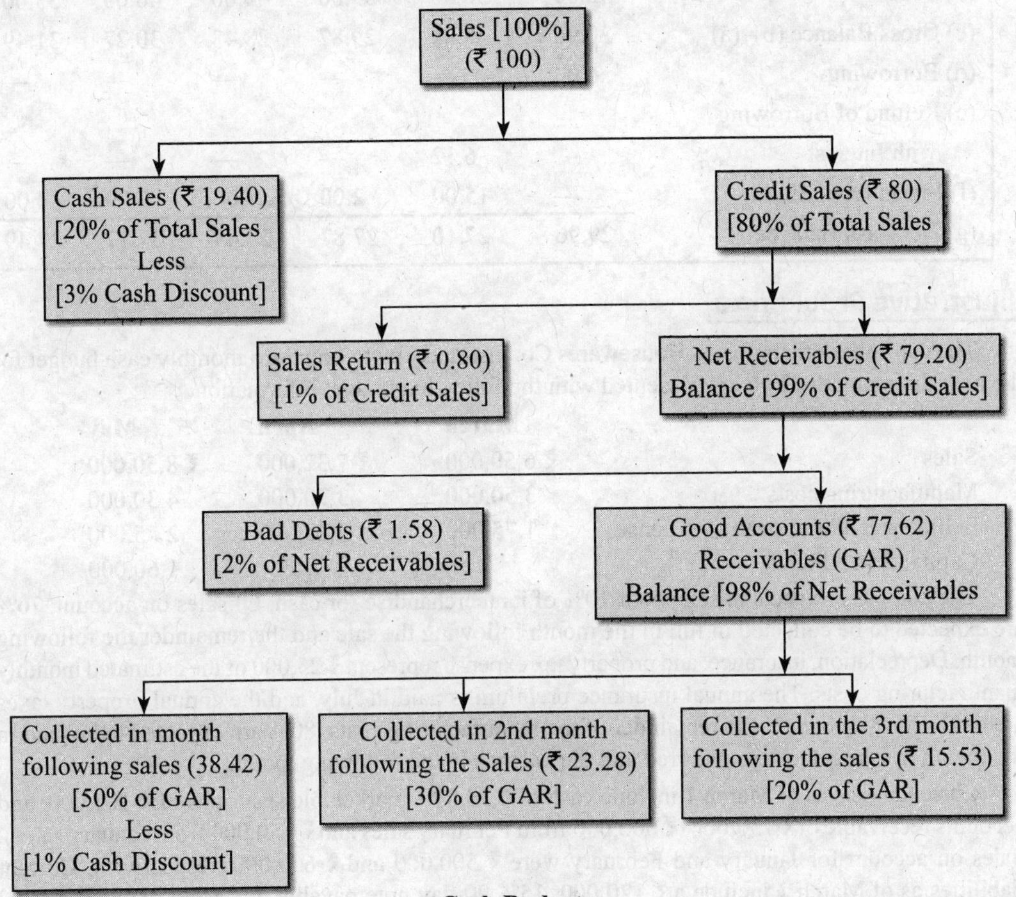

Cash Budget

	July	Aug.	Sept.	Oct.	Nov.	Dec.
Opening Balance	26.00	26.96	27.10	27.87	27.43	27.27
Collection from Sales:						
Cash sales 19.4% of Sales	7.76	7.76	9.70	9.70	11.64	12.61
Collection: 38.42% of PMS	13.06	15.37	15.37	19.21	19.21	23.05
23.28% of 2nd PMS	9.31	7.92	9.31	9.31	11.64	11.64
15.53% of 3rd PMS	6.83	6.21	5.28	6.21	6.21	7.76
Interest-Business	—	—	2.00	—	—	2.00
Govt. Bond	—	—	0.11	0.13	0.14	0.16
Sales of Shares	—	20.00	—	—	—	—
(a) Total	62.96	84.22	68.87	72.43	76.27	84.49
Payments p.m. [1 m lag]	24.00	16.00	17.00	20.00	20.00	25.00
– Misc Expenses [1 m lag]	5.00	6.00	6.00	6.00	7.00	7.00
– Wages and Salary [1/2 m lag]	7.00	7.00	9.00	9.00	10.00	11.00
[1/2 of previous month]	6.00	7.00	7.00	9.00	9.00	10.00

(b) Total	42.00	36.00	39.00	44.00	46.00	53.00
(c) Gross Balance (b)–(a)	20.96	48.22	29.87	28.43	30.27	31.49
(d) Borrowing	6.00	—	—	—	—	—
(e) Refund of Borrowing with Interest	—	6.12	—	—	—	—
(f) Inv. in Govt. Bond	—	15.00	2.00	1.00	3.00	4.00
(g) Net Cash Balance	29.96	27.10	27.87	27.43	27.27	27.49

Illustrative Problem 20

The controller of Hindustan Housewares Co. instructs you to prepare a monthly cash budget for the next three months. You are presented with the following budget information:

	March	April	May
Sales	₹ 6,50,000	₹ 7,32,000	₹ 8,50,000
Manufacturing costs	3,50,000	3,70,000	4,30,000
Selling and administrative expenses	1,75,000	2,25,000	2,45,000
Capital expenditures			1,60,000

The company expects to sell about 10% of its merchandise for cash. Of sales on account, 70% are expected to be collected in full in the month following the sale and the remainder the following month. Depreciation, insurance, and property tax expense represent ₹ 25,000 of the estimated monthly manufacturing costs. The annual insurance premium is paid in July, and the annual property taxes are paid in November. Of the remainder of the manufacturing costs, 80% are expected to be paid in the month in which they are incurred and the balance in the following month.

Current assets as of March 1 include cash of ₹ 30,000, marketable securities of ₹ 105,000, and accounts receivable of ₹ 750,000 (₹ 600,000 from February sales and ₹ 150,000 from January sales). Sales on account for January and February were ₹ 500,000 and ₹ 600,000, respectively. Current liabilities as of March 1 include a ₹ 120,000, 15% 90-day note payable due May 20 and ₹ 60,000 of accounts payable incurred in February for manufacturing costs. All selling and administrative expenses are paid in cash in the period they are incurred. It is expected that ₹ 1,800 in dividends will be received in March. An estimated income tax payment of ₹ 46,000 will be made in April. The regular quarterly dividend of ₹ 12,000 is expected to be declared in April and paid in May. Management desires to maintain a minimum cash balance of ₹ 40,000.

Required:

1. Prepare a monthly cash budget and supporting schedules for March, April, and May.
2. On the basis of the cash budget prepared in part (1), what recommendation should be made to the controller?

Solution:

1.

A	B	C	D

Cash Budget

For the Three Months Ending May 31, 2016

	March	April	May
Estimated cash receipts from:			

Cash sales	₹ 65,000	₹ 73,200	₹ 85,000
Collection of accounts receivable[a]	570,000	589,500	636,660
Dividends	1,800		
Total cash receipts	₹ 636,800	₹ 662,700	₹ 721,660
Estimated cash payments for:			
Manufacturing costs[b]	₹ 320,000	₹ 341,000	₹ 393,000
Selling and administrative expenses	175,000	225,000	245,000
Capital expenditures			1,60,000
Other purposes:			
Note payable (including interest)			124,500
Income tax		46,000	
Dividends			12,000
Total cash payments	₹ 495,000	₹ 612,000	₹ 934,500
Cash increase or (decrease)	₹ 141,800	₹ 50,700	₹ (212,840)
Cash balance at beginning of month	30,000	171,800	222,500
Cash balance at end of month	₹ 171,800	₹ 222,500	₹ 9,660
Minimum cash balance	40,000	40,000	40,000
Excess or (deficiency)	₹ 131,800	₹ 182,500	₹ (30,340)

Computations:

[a]**Collections of accounts receivable:**	**March**	**April**	**May**
January sales	₹ 150,000[1]		
February sales	420,000[2]	₹ 180,000[3]	
March sales		409,500[4]	₹ 175,500[5]
April sales			461,160[6]
Total	₹ 570,000	₹ 589,500	₹ 636,660

[1]₹ 500,000 × 30% = ₹ 150,000

[2]₹ 600,000 × 70% = ₹ 420,000

[3]₹600,000 × 30% = ₹ 180,000

[4]₹ 650,000 × 90% × 70% = ₹ 409,500

[5]₹ 650,000 × 90% × 30% = ₹ 175,500

[6]₹ 732,000 × 90% × 70% = ₹ 461,160

[b]**Payments for manufacturing costs:**	**March**	**April**	**May**
Payment of accounts payable, beginning of month balance[c]	₹ 60,000	₹ 65,000	₹ 69,000
Payment of current month's cost[d]	260,000	276,000	324,000
Total	₹ 320,000	₹ 341,000	₹ 393,000

Accounts payable, February 1 balance = ₹ 60,000

(₹ 350,000 – ₹ 25,000) × 20% = ₹ 65,000

(₹ 370,000 – ₹ 25,000) × 20% = ₹ 69,000

[d](₹ 350,000 – ₹ 25,000) × 80% = ₹ 260,000

(₹ 370,000 – ₹ 25,000) × 80% = ₹ 276,000

(₹ 430,000 – ₹ 25,000) × 80% = ₹ 324,000

2. The budget indicates that the minimum cash balance will not be maintained in May. This is due to the capital expenditures and note repayment requiring significant cash outflows during this month. This situation can be corrected by borrowing and/or by the sale of the marketable securities, if they are held for such purposes. At the end of March and April, the cash balance will exceed the minimum desired balance, and the excess could be considered for temporary investment.

Illustrative Problem 21

ABC Company is organized in three divisions, each with a division manager, a small office staff, and its own sales force. The various divisions sell different kinds of products and deal with different groups of customers.

The company's budget director has received the following proposals and estimates for next year from the division managers:

(₹ '000)

	Division A	Division B	Division C
Divisional marketing costs amounting to	₹ 150	₹ 500	₹ 300
Will produce revenues of	1,000	3,000	2,100
And cost of goods sold of	650	1,650	1,260
Administrative expenses to support these activities will total	150	300	200
Accounts receivable will increase by	10	200	50
Inventories will exceed this year's ending balances by	50	100	50
Accounts payable will increase by	15	50	80

The expenses of the company's central management are tentatively budgeted at ₹ 4,00,000 for the year to be paid in cash. Cash purchases of equipment amounting to ₹ 1,30,000 and cash dividends of ₹ 3,50,000 are also proposed. Of the equipment purchases, ₹ 60,000 is to replace existing equipment and ₹ 70,000 is for expansion. The expansion proposals, which management has approved in principle, will have no effect on next year's income statement.

Depreciation is included in the administrative expense figures above as follows: central management, ₹ 10,000, division A, ₹ 5,000 division B, ₹ 15,000 division C, ₹ 20,000.

Required:

(*a*) Prepare a tentative profit plan and cash budget for next year, on the assumption that all these proposals are approved.

(*b*) The company will start next year with a cash balance of ₹ 2,90,000 and an unused line of bank credit of ₹ 1,00,000. The minimum cash balance is 5 per cent of sales. Is the tentative plan feasible?

Solution:

	Division A	Division B	Division C	Total
				(₹ '000)
Profit Plan				
Sales revenues	₹ 1,000	₹ 3,000	₹ 2,100	₹ 6,100
Divisional expenses:				
Cost of goods sold	650	1,650	1,260	3,560
Marketing	150	500	300	950
Administrative	150	300	200	650
Total	950	2,450	1,760	5,160
Division margin	₹ 50	₹ 550	₹ 340	940
Headquarters expenses				400
Net income				₹ 540
Cash Budget				
Revenues	₹ 1,000	₹ 3,000	₹ 2,100	₹ 6,100
Less: Increase in receivables	10	200	50	260
Collections	990	2,800	2,050	5,840
Cost of goods sold	650	1,650	1,260	3,560
Add: inventory increase	50	100	50	200
Purchases	700	1,750	1,310	3,760
Less: Increases in payables	15	50	80	145
Payments to suppliers	685	1,700	1,230	3,615
Division marketing costs	150	500	300	950
Division administration (expense less depreciation)	145	285	180	610
Total divisional disbursements	980	2,485	1,710	5,175
Division cash flow	₹ 10	₹ 315	₹ 340	665
Head-office disbursements:				
Central administration				390
Equipment				130
Dividends				350
Total head-office disbursements				870
Net decrease in cash				₹ (205)

(*b*)

Anticipated cash balance ₹ 2,90,000 – ₹ 2,05,000	₹ 85,000
Minimum cash balance: 5% × ₹ 61,00,000	3,05,000
Cash shortage	₹ 2,20,000

Since the company has only a ₹ 100,000 line of credit, the proposed plan is not financially feasible.

Illustrative Problem 22 (Cash Budget)

SM Ltd. Furnishes the following forecast for the quarter ending 31st March. 2016

Sales: January	₹ 12,00,000
February	₹ 11,00,000
March	₹ 14,00,000

During the month of December 2015 the company made a sale of ₹ 10,00,000 and computed the cost of sales as under:

Raw material	₹ 3,50,000
Wages (variable)	₹ 1,75,000
Overheads (variable)	₹ 1,75,000
Overheads (fixed)	₹ 1,50,000

The fixed overheads include depreciation of ₹ 40,000.

One–fifth of sales is for cash on which a cash discount of 1.5% is allowed. Of the remaining portion 50% is collected in the same month and the balance in the next month. Raw material suppliers allow a credit of one month. Wages are paid on the last working day of the month to which they relate. While variable overheads are paid in the next month, fixed overhead expenses are met in the same month.

The percentage of contribution to sales as obtained in December 2015 is expected to be maintained during the forthcoming quarter also. The cash balance on 1st January, 2016 is ₹ 50,000. The company has to pay ₹ 3,50,000 as interest on term loan in January 2016 and a sum of ₹ 60,000 as instalment of arrears of wages in March 2016 and the bank will debit quarterly interest of ₹ 4,00,000 on drawing in March 2016.

Prepare a cash budget showing the cash position for each of the three months of the quarter ending March 2016. (*M. Com. Delhi, 2007*)

Solution:

Sales:	*Dec. 2015*	*Jan. 2016*	*Feb. 2016*	*Mar. 2016*
Cash sales	2,00,000	2,40,000	2,20,000	2,80,000
Credit sales	8,00,000	9,60,000	8,80,000	11,20,000
Total sales	10,00,000	12,00,000	11,00,000	14,00,000
Cost of sales:				
Raw materials	3,50,000	4,20,000	3,85,000	4,90,000
Wages	1,75,000	2,10,000	1,95,000	2,45,000
Overheads variable	1,75,000	2,10,000	1,92,000	2,45,000
Depreciation	40,000	40,000	40,000	40,000
Overheads fixed	1,10,000	1,10,000	1,10,000	1,10,000

Cash Budget

	January 2016	*February* 2016	*March* 2016
	₹	₹	₹
Receipts:			
Opening balance	50,000	(–)28,600	1,75,600

Debtors (for last month)	4,00,000	4,80,000	4,40,000
Debtors (for this month)	4,80,000	4,40,000	5,60,000
Cash sales less discount	2,36,400	2,16,700	2,75,800
Total	11,66,400	11,08,100	14,51,400
Payments:			
Raw Materials	3,50,000	4,20,000	3,85,000
Wages	2,10,000	1,92,500	2,45,000
Overheads variable	1,75,000	2,10,000	1,92,500
Overheads fixed	1,10,000	1,10,000	1,10,000
Arrears of Wages	—	—	60,000
Interest on term loan	3,50,000	—	—
Bank interest	—	—	4,00,000
Total	11,95,000	9,32,500	13,92,500
Deficit (carried over) (to be met by loan or overdraft)	28,600	—	—
Surplus carried over (after liquidation of Loan or overdraft)	—	1,75,600	58,900

In framing the cash budget, a provision should be made for meeting the deficit in January 2016 to the extent of ₹28,600 by loan or overdraft. If we assume that the loan/draft is paid back in February 2016, the closing balances at the end of February and March 2016, will be ₹ 1,75,600 and ₹ 58,900 respectively.

Illustrative Problem 23 (Cash Budget)

The management accountant of Jay Engineering Company is gathering data to prepare the cash budget for July 2016. He plans to develop the budget from the following information:

(*a*) Of all sales, 30 per cent are cash sales.

(*b*) Of credit sales, 60 per cent are collected within the month of sale. Half of the credit sales, collected within the month receive a 2 per cent cash discount (for accounts paid within 10 days). Twenty per cent of credit sales are collected in the following month; remaining credit sales are collected the month thereafter. There are virtually no bad debts.

(*c*) Sales for the second two quarters of the year follow. (The first three months are actual sales, and the last three months are estimated sales.)

Sales	
April	₹ 4,60,000
May	6,00,000
June	10,00,000
July	11,40,000
August	12,00,000
September	11,34,000

(*d*) The company sells all that it produces each month. The cost of raw materials equals 24 per cent of each sales. The company requires a monthly ending inventory equal to the coming month's production requirements. Of raw materials purchases, 50 per cent are paid for in the month of purchase. The remaining 50 per cent are paid for in the following month.

(*e*) Wages total ₹ 1,10,000 each month and are paid in the month incurred.

(*f*) Budgeted monthly operating expenses total ₹ 3,36,000, of which ₹ 50,000 is depreciation and ₹ 6,000 is expiration of prepaid insurance. (The annual premium of ₹ 72,000 is paid on January 1.)

(*g*) Dividends of ₹ 140,000, declared on June 30, will be paid on July 15.

(*h*) Old equipment will be sold for ₹ 25,200 on July 4.

(*i*) On July 13, new equipment will be purchased for ₹ 1,68,000.

(*j*) The company maintains a minimum cash balance of ₹ 20,000.

(*k*) The cash balance on July 1 is ₹ 27,000.

Required:

Prepare a cash budget for July. Give a supporting schedule that details the cash collections from sales.

Solution:

Jay Engineering Company

Cash Budget For the Month of July 2016

Beginning cash balance	₹ 27,000
Collections:	
Cash sales (0.3 × ₹ 11,40,000)	3,42,000
Credit sales:	
July:	
With discount[a]	2,34,612
Without discount[b]	2,39,400
June[c]	1,40,000
May[d]	84,000
Sale of old equipment	25,200
Total cash available	₹ 10,92,212
Less disbursements:	
Raw materials:	
July[e]	₹ 1,44,000
June[f]	1,36,800
Direct labour	1,10,000
Operating expenses	2,80,000
Dividents	1,40,000
Equipment	1,68,000
Total disbursements	₹ 9,78,800
Minimum cash balance	20,000
Total cash needs	₹ 9,98,800
Excess of cash available over needs	₹ 93,412
Ending cash balance	₹ 1,13,412

Supporting schedule:

[a](0.7 × ₹ 11,40,000) × 0.6 × 0.5 × 0.98

[b](0.7 × ₹ 11,40,000) × 0.6 × 0.5

[c](0.7 × ₹ 10,00,000) × 0.2

[d](0.7 × ₹ 6,00,000) × 0.2

[e]July requirements (0.24 × ₹ 11,40,000)	₹ 2,73,600
Desired ending inventory (0.24 × ₹ 12,00,000)	2,88,000
Total requirements	₹ 5,61,600
Less: Beginning inventory	2,73,600
Purchases	₹ 2,88,000

July payment: ₹ 2,88,000/2 = ₹ 1,44,000

[f]₹ 2,73,600/2 = ₹ 1,36,800 (June purchases are computed as shown for July.)

Illustrative Problem 24

Kinsman, a retailer, provides the following data for 2015 and 2016:

	December 31, 2015	*December* 31, 2016
Cash	₹ 2,00,000	—
Trade account receivable	84,000	₹ 78,000
Merchandise inventory	1,50,000	1,40,000
Accounts payable—merchandise	(95,000)	(98,000)

Budgeted sales for 2016 are ₹ 12,00,000; sales for 2015 were ₹ 11,00,000. Cash sales average 20 per cent of total sales each year. Cost of goods sold for 2016 is estimated to be ₹ 8,40,000. Budgeted 2016 variable operating expenses are ₹ 1,20,000. They vary in proportion to sales and are paid 50 per cent in the year incurred and 50 per cent the following year. Unpaid variable expenses are not included in accounts payable above.

Fixed operating expenses, including ₹ 35,000 depreciation and ₹ 5,000 uncollectible accounts expense, total ₹ 1,00,000 per year. Such expenses involving cash payments are paid 80 per cent in the year incurred and 20 per cent the following year. Unpaid fixed expenses are not included in accounts payable above.

Prepare a cash budget for 2016 with supporting computations on cash collection from credit sales and cash disbursements for purchases of merchandise and operating expenses.

(*M.Com, Delhi, 2013*)

Solution:

Cash Budget
For the Year 2016 (₹)

Beginning balance	2,00,000
Collections (*a*)	12,01,000
Total	14,01,000
Disbursements:	
Purchases of merchandise (*b*)	8,27,000
Operating expenses (c)	1,75,000
Total disbursements	10,02,000
Ending balance	3,99,000

Supporting computations:

(*a*) Cash collection in 2016:

Trade accounts receivable, December 31, 2015, collected in 2016		₹ 84,000
Budgeted 2016 cash sales (₹ 12,00,000 × 20%)		2,40,000
Budgeted 2016 credit sales (₹ 12,00,000 × 80%)		9,60,000
Less: Uncollectible accounts expense	₹ (5,000)	
Trade accounts receivable, December 31, 2016	(78,000)	(83,000)
Cash collected in 2016		₹ 12,01,000

(*b*) Cash disbursements for purchases of merchandise:

	(₹)
Cost of goods sold, 2016	₹ 8,40,000
Inventory, December 31, 2015	1,40,000
Cost of goods available for sale	9,80,000
Inventory, December 31, 2015	1,50,000
Purchases, 2016	8,30,000
Increases in accounts payable-merchandise	3,000
Cash disbursed in 2016 for purchases of merchandise	8,27,000

(*c*) Cash disbursement for operating expenses:

Variable operating expenses:		
2016 expenses of ₹ 1,20,000, 50% paid in 2016	₹ 60,000	
2015 expenses of ₹ 1,10,000 (10% of sales ₹ 11,00,000), 50% paid in 2016	55,000	
		₹ 1,15,000
Fixed operating expenses:		
Total for each year	1,00,000	
Less: Depreciation and uncollectible accounts expenses	40,000	
Fixed operating expenses involving cash payments each year	₹ 60,000	
2015 paid in 2016 (₹ 60,000 × 20%)	12,000	
2016 paid in 2016 (₹ 60,000 × 80%)	48,000	60,000
Cash disbursed in 2016 for variable and fixed operating expenses		1,75,000

Illustrative Problem 25

Friendly Freddle's is an independently owned major appliance and electronics discount chain with seven stores located in a Midwest metropolitan area. Rapid expansion has created the need for careful planning of cash requirements to ensure that the chain is able to replenish stock adequately and meet payment schedules to creditors. Fred Ferguson, founder of the chain, has established a banking relationship that provides a ₹ 2,00,000 line of credit to Friendly Freddie's. The bank requires that a minimum balance of ₹ 8,200 be kept in the chain's bank account at the end of each month. When the balance goes below ₹ 8,200, the bank automatically extends the line of credit in multiples of ₹ 1,000 so that the bank account balance is at least ₹ 8,200 at month-end.

Friendly Freddie's attempts to borrow as little as possible and repays the loans quickly in multiples of ₹ 1,000 plus 2 per cent monthly interest on the entire loan balance. Interest payments and any principal payments are paid at the end of the month following the loan. The chain currently has no outstanding loans.

The following cash receipts and disbursements data apply to the fourth quarter of the current calendar year.

Estimated beginning cash balance	₹ 8,800
Estimated cash sales:	
October	14,000
November	29,000
December	44,000
Sales on account:	
July (actual)	1,30,000
August (actual)	1,04,000
September (actual)	1,28,000
October (estimated)	1,35,000
November (estimated)	1,42,000
December (estimated)	1,88,000

Projected cash collection of sales on account is estimated to be 70 per cent in the month following the sale, 20 per cent in the second month following the sale, and 6 per cent in the third month following the sale. The 4 per cent beyond the third month following the sale is determined to be uncollectible. In addition, the chain is scheduled to receive ₹ 13,000 cash on a note receivable in October.

All inventory purchases are made on account as the chain has excellent credit with all vendors because of a strong payment history. The following information regarding inventory purchases is available.

Inventory Purchases	
September (actual)	₹ 1,20,000
October (estimated)	1,12,000
November (estimated)	1,28,000
December (estimated)	95,000

Cash disbursements for inventory are made in the month following purchase using an average cash discount of 3 per cent for timely payment. Monthly cash disbursements for operating expenses during October, November, and December are estimated to be ₹ 38,000, ₹ 41,000, and ₹ 46,000 respectively.

Required:

Prepare Friendly Freddic's cash budget for the months of October, November and December showing all receipts, disbursements, and credit line activity, where applicable.

(CMA, USA Adapted)

Solution:

Cash Budget
October through December

	October	November	December
Beginning cash balance	₹ 8,800	₹ 8,600	₹ 9,120
Receipts:			
Cash sales	₹ 14,000	₹ 29,000	₹ 44,000
Collections of sales on account[1]	118,200	126,340	134,080
Note receivable repayment	13,000		

Total cash receipts	₹ 145,200	₹ 155,340	₹ 178,080
Cash available	₹ 154,000	₹ 163,940	₹ 187,200
Disbursements:			
Payments of inventory purchases[2]	₹ 116,400	₹ 108,640	₹ 124,160
Operating expenses	38,000	41,000	46,000
Loan repayment		5,000	4,000
Interest[3]		180	80
Total disbursements	₹ 154,400	₹ 154,820	₹ 174,240
Cash balance	₹ (400)	₹ 9,120	₹ 12,960
Bank loan[4]	9,000		
Adjusted cash balance	₹ 8,600	₹ 9,120	₹ 12,960

[1]Collections of sales on account:

		October	November	December
July	6% of ₹ 130,000	₹ 7,800		
August	20% of ₹ 104,000	20,800		
	6% of ₹ 104,000		₹ 6,240	
September	70% of ₹ 128,000	89,600		
	20% of ₹ 128,000		25,600	
	6% of ₹ 128,000			₹ 7,680
October	70% of ₹ 135,000		94,500	
	20% of ₹ 135,000			27,000
November	70% of ₹ 142,000			99,400
December	0			
Total		₹ 118,200	₹ 126,340	₹ 134,080

[2]Payments for inventory purchases:

	October	November	December
September pruchases (97% of ₹ 120,000)	₹ 116,400		
October purchases (97% of ₹ 112,000)		₹ 108,640	
November purchases (97% of ₹ 128,000)			₹ 124,160

[3]Total collections:

November—2% of ₹ 9,000

December—2% of ₹ 4,000

[4]Loans must be taken out and repaid in multiples of ₹ 1,000.

Illustrative Problem 26 (Cash Budget)

Bajaj Products, Ltd., is planning its cash needs for July. Since the company will be buying some new equipment during the month, the treasurer is sure that some borrowing will be needed, but he is uncertain how much. The following data have been assembled to assist the treasurer in preparing a cash budget for the month:

(*a*) Equipment will be purchased during July for cash at a cost of ₹ 45,000.

(*b*) Selling and administrative expenses will be:

Advertising	₹ 110,000
Sales salaries	50,000
Administrative salaries	35,000
Shipping	2,100

(*c*) Sales are budgeted at ₹ 800,000 for July, Customers are allowed a 2½% cash discount on accounts paid within 10 days after the end of the month of sale. Only 50% of the payments made in the month following sale fall within the discount period (All of the company's sales are on account).

(*d*) On June 30, the company will have the following accounts receivable outstanding:

Month	Sales	Accounts Receivable at June 30	Percentage of Sales Uncollected at June 30	Percentage to Be Collected in July
March	₹ 4,30,000	₹ 6,450	1½%	?
April	5,90,000	35,400	6%	?
May	6,40,000	1,28,000	20%	?
June	7,20,000	7,20,000	100%	?

Bad debts are negligible. All March receivables shown above will have been collected by the end of July, and the collection pattern implicit in the schedule above will be the same in July as in pervious months.

(*e*) Production costs are budgeted as follows for July:

Prime costs:		
Raw materials to be used in production		₹ 3,42,000
Direct labour		95,000
Overhead costs:		
Indirect labour	₹ 36,000	
Utilities	1,900	
Payroll benefits	14,800	
Depreciation	28,000	
Property taxes	1,100	
Fire insurance	1,700	
Amortization of patents	3,500	
Scrapping of absolute goods	2,600	89,600
Total production costs		₹ 5,26,600

(*f*) The raw materials inventory is budgeted to increase by ₹ 18,000 during July; other inventories will not change.

(*g*) Half of the raw materials purchased each month is paid for in the month of purchase; the other half is paid for in the following month. Accounts payable at June 30 for raw materials purchases will be ₹ 1,72,000.

(*h*) All July payroll amounts will be paid for within the month of July.

(*i*) Utilities costs are paid for within the month.

(*j*) The ₹ 14,800 monthly charge above for 'Payroll benefits' includes the following items:

Company pension plan, including $\frac{1}{12}$ of a ₹ 9,600 special adjustment that was paid in April	₹ 7,000
Group insurance (payable semiannually, with the last payment having been made in January)	900
Unemployment insurance (payable monthly)	1,300
Vacation pay, which represents $\frac{1}{12}$ of the annual cost (July's vacations will require ₹ 14,100)	5,600

(*k*) Property taxes are paid in June of each year.

(*l*) Fire insurance premiums were paid in January, in advance.

(*m*) The company has an open line of credit with the State Bank. All borrowing from the bank must be in round ₹ 1,000 amounts.

(*n*) The cash balance on June 30 will be ₹ 78,000; the company must maintain a cash balance of at least ₹ 75,000 at all times.

Required:

1. Prepare a schedule showing expected cash collections for July.
2. Compute (*a*) budgeted cash disbursements for raw materials purchases, and (*b*) budgeted cash disbursements for overheat for July.
3. Prepare a cash budget for July.
4. A member of the board of directors of Bajaj Products stated, "The monthly cash budget shows the company's cash surplus or deficiency and assures us that an un unexpected cash shortage will not occur." Comment on this statement.

Solution:

1. Collection pattern:

	Percentage of Sales Uncollected at June 30*	Percentage to be Collected in July
a. March	1½%	1½%
b. April	6%	(b) – (a) = 4½%
c. May	20%	(c) – (b) = 14%
d. June	100%	(d) – (c) = 80%

*Given.

Schedule of expected cash collections:

From March sales (1½% × ₹ 430,000)	₹ 6,450
From April sales (4½% × ₹ 590,000)	26,550
From May sales (14½% × ₹ 640,000)	89,600
From June sales (80% × ₹ 720,000)	5,76,000
Total	6,98,600
Less cash discounts (₹ 576,000 × 50% × 2½%)	7,200
Net cash collections	₹ 6,91,400

2. (*a*) Budgeted cash payments for raw materials purchases:

Accounts payable, June 30		₹ 1,72,000
July purchases: ½ (₹ 342,000 + ₹ 18,000)		1,80,000
Total cash payments		₹ 3,52,000

(*b*) Budgeted cash payments for overhead:

Indirect labour		₹ 36,000
Utilities		1,900
Payroll benefits:		
Company pension plan (₹ 7,000 – ₹ 800)	₹ 6,200	
Group insurance (6 × ₹ 900)	5,400	
Unemployment insurance	1,300	
Vacation pay	14,100	27,000
Total cash payments		₹ 64,900

3. **Cash Budget**

July

Cash balance, beginning		₹ 78,000
Add collections from customers		6,91,400
Total cash available		7,69,400
Less disbursements:		
Raw material purchases (above)	₹ 3,52,000	
Direct labour	95,000	
Overhead (above)	64,900	
Advertising	1,10,000	
Sales salaries	50,000	
Administrative salaries	35,000	
Shipping	2,100	
Equipment purcheses	45,000	7,54,000
Excess (deficiency) of cash		15,400
Financing:		
Borrowing		60,000
Repayments		—
Interest		
Total effects		60,000
Cash balance, ending		₹ 75,400

4. The statement is incorrect. Even though the cash budget shows that there is an overall excess of cash during the month, there is no assurance that shortages will not develop on a day-to-day basis *during* the month. For example, cash receipts may come later in the month than cash payments—resulting in temporary cash shortages. Unless cash receipts and payments occur uniformly over time, cash budgeting may need to be done on a weekly or daily basis. In addition, unexpected events can create a cash shortage.

Illustrative Problem 27 (Cash Budget)

The Managing Director of Ceat Tyre Co. asks you to prepare a monthly cash budget for the next three months. You are presented with the following budget information:

	June	July	August
Sales	₹ 1,20,000	₹ 1,50,000	₹ 2,00,000
Manufacturing costs	50,000	65,000	72,000
Selling and administrative expenses	35,000	40,000	45,000
Capital expenditures	—	—	48,000

The company expects to sell about 10% of its merchandise for cash. Of sales on account, 60% are expected to be collected in full in the month following the sale and the remainder the following month. Depreciation, insurance, and property tax expence represent ₹ 8,000 of the estimated monthly manufacturing costs. The annual insurance premium is paid in February, and the annual property taxes are paid in November. Of the remainder of the manufacturing costs, 80% are expected to be paid in the month in which they are incurred and the balance in the following month.

Current assents as of June 1 include cash of ₹ 45,000, marketable securities of ₹ 65,000, and account receivable of ₹ 1,43,000 (₹ 1,05,000 from May sales and ₹ 38,400 from April sales). Sales on account in April and May were ₹ 96,000 and ₹ 1,05,000 respectively. Current liabilities as of June 1 include a ₹ 60,000, 12%, 90-day note payable due August 20 and ₹ 8,000 of accounts payable incurred in May for manufacturing costs. All selling and administrative expenses are paid in cash in the period they are incurred. It is expected that ₹ 3,500 in dividends will be received in June. An estimated income tax payment of ₹ 18,000 will be made in July. The regular quarterly dividend of ₹ 8,000 is expected to be declared in July and paid in August. Management desires to maintain a minimum cash balance of ₹ 35,000.

Required:

1. Prepare a monthly cash budget and supporting schedules for June, July, and August 2016.
2. On the basis of the cash budget prepared in part (1), what recommendation should be made to the Managing Director?

Solution:

1.

Ceat Tyre Co.
Cash Budget
For the Three Months June, July, August 2016

	June	July	August
Estimates cash receipts from:			
Cash sales	₹ 12,000	₹ 15,000	₹ 20,000
Collection of accounts receivable[a]	1,01,400	1,06,800	1,24,200
Dividends	3,500		
Total cash receipts	₹ 1,16,900	₹ 1,21,800	₹ 1,44,200
Estimated cash payments for:			
Manufacturing costs[b]	₹ 41,600	₹ 54,000	₹ 62,600
Selling and administrative expenses	35,000	40,000	45,000
Capital expenditures			48,000

	June	July	August
Other purposes:			
Note payable (including interest)			61,800
Income tax		18,000	
Dividends			8,000
Total cash payments	₹ 76,600	₹ 1,12,000	₹ 2,25,400
Cash increase or (decrease)	₹ 40,300	₹ 9,800	₹ (81,200)
Cash balance at beginning of month	45,000	85,300	95,100
Cash balance at end of month	₹ 85,300	₹ 95,100	₹ 13,900
Minimum cash balance	35,000	35,000	35,000
Excess or (deficiency)	₹ 50,300	₹ 60,100	₹ (21,100)

Working Notes:

[a] Collections of accounts receivable:	June	July	August
April sales	₹ 38,400[1]		
May sales	63,000[2]	₹ 42,000[3]	
June sales		64,800[4]	₹ 43,200[5]
July sales			81,000[6]
Total	₹ 1,01,400	₹ 1,06,800	₹ 1,24,200

[1] ₹ 96,000 × 40% = ₹ 38,400

[2] ₹ 1,05,000 × 60% = ₹ 63,000

[3] ₹ 1,05,000 × 40% = ₹ 42,000

[4] ₹ 1,20,000 × 90% × 60% = ₹ 64,800

[5] ₹ 1,20,000 × 90% × 40% = ₹ 43,200

[6] ₹ 1,50,000 × 90% × 60% = ₹ 81,000

[b] Payments for manufacturing costs:	June	July	August
Payment of accounts payable, beginning of month balance[c]	₹ 8,000	₹ 8,400	₹ 11,400
Payment of current month's cost[d]	33,600	45,600	51,200
Total	₹ 41,600	₹ 54,000	₹ 62,600

[c] Accounts payable, June 1 balance = ₹ 8,000

(₹ 50,000 – ₹ 8,000) × 20% = ₹ 8,400

(₹ 65,000 – ₹ 8,000) × 20% = ₹ 11,400

[d] (₹ 50,000 – ₹ 8,000) × 80% = ₹ 33,600

(₹ 65,000 – ₹ 8,000) × 80% = ₹ 45,600

(₹ 72,000 – ₹ 8,000) × 80% = ₹ 51,200

2. The cash budget shows that the minimum cash balance will not be maintained in August. This is due to the capital expenditures and note repayment requiring significant cash payments during this month. This situation can be corrected by borrowing and/or by the sale of the marketable securities, if they are held for such purposes. At the end of June and July, the cash balance will exceed the minimum desired balance, and the excess could be considered for temporary investment.

MASTER BUDGET- ILLUSTRATED PROBLEMS

Illustrative Problem 28 (Budgeted Income Statement)

A glass manufacturing company requires you to calculate and present the budget for the next year from the following information:

Sales:	
Toughened glass	₹ 3,00,00,000
Bent toughened glass	₹ 5,00,00,000
Direct material cost	60% of sales
Direct wages	20 workers @ ₹ 15000 per month
Factory overheads:	
Indirect labour:	
Works manager ₹ 50,000 per month	
Foreman ₹ 40,000 per month	
Stores and spares	2½ % on sales
Depreciation on machinery	₹ 12,60,000
Light and power	₹ 5,00,000
Repairs and maintenance	₹ 8,00,000
Other sundries	10% on direct wages
Administration, selling and distribution expenses	₹ 14,00,000 per year

Solution:

Budgeted Income Statement for the Period Ending on...

				₹
Sales (as per sales budget)				
	Toughened glass... units @ ₹...			3,00,00,000
	Bent toughened glass...units @ ₹			5,00,00,000
				8,00,00,000
Less:	Cost of production (as per cost of production budget)		₹4,80,00,000	
	Direct materials (...units @ ₹....)		36,00,000	
	Prime cost		5,16,00,000	
	Factory overhead:			
	Variable:			
	Stores and spares (2½ % of sales)	20,00,000		
	Light and power	5,00,000		
	Repairs and maintenance	8,00,000	33,00,000	
	Fixed:			
	Works manager's salary	6,00,000		

	Foreman's salary	4,80,000		
	Depreciation	12,60,000		
	Sundries	3,60,000	27,00,000	
	Works cost			5,76,00,000
	Gross profit			2,24,00,000
Less:	Administration, selling and distribution overheads			14,00,000
	Net profit			2,10,00,000

Illustrative Problem 29

Super Drive, a computer disk storage and backup company, uses accrual accounting. The company's Statement of Financial Position for the year ended December, 2016 is as follows:

Statement of Financial Position
December, 2016

Assets	
Cash	52,000
Accounts Receivable, net	1,50,000
Inventory	3,15,000
Property, plant and equipment	10,00,000
Total assets	**15,17,000**
Liabilities	
Accounts Payable	1,75,000
Common equity	9,00,000
Retained earnings	442,000
Total liabilities	**15,17,000**

Additional information regarding Super Drive's operations include the following:

- Sales are budgeted at ₹ 5,20,000 for January, 2017 and ₹ 5,00,000 for February, 2017.
- Collections are expected to be 60% in the month of sale and 40% in the month following the sale.
- 80% of the disk drive components are purchased in the month prior to the month of sale, and 20% are purchased in the month of sale. Purchased components are 40% of the cost of goods sold.
- Payment for the components is made in the month following the purchase.
- Cost of goods sold is 80% of sales.

(CMS, USA, Adapted with permission)

Required:

(*i*) The budgeted cash collections for the month of January 2017 are

(a) ₹ 2,08,000

(b) ₹ 5,20,000

(c) ₹ 4,02,000

(d) ₹ 4,62,000

(ii) **The projected balance in accounts payable on January, 2017 is**

(a) ₹ 1,61,280

(b) ₹ 1,66,400

(c) ₹ 4,16,000

(d) ₹ 2,01,600

(iii) **Refer to the information preceding question (*i*). The projected gross profit for the month ending January, 2017 is**

(a) ₹ 4,16,000

(b) ₹ 1,04,000

(c) ₹ 5,36,000

(d) ₹ 0

Solution:

(*i*) The correct answer is (d) Collections are expected to be 60% in the month of sale and 40% in the month following the sale. Thus, collections in January consist of the ₹ 1,50,000 of receivables at November 30, plus 60% of January sales. Total collections are therefore ₹4,62,000 [₹1,50,000 + (60% × ₹5,20,000)].

Answer (a) is incorrect because ₹2,08,000 equals 40% of January sales. Answer (b) is incorrect because total sales are not collected in the month of sale. Answer (C) is incorrect because 100% of receivable will be collected, not 60%.

(*ii*) The correct answer is (a): payment are made in the month following purchase. The balance in accounts payable on December 31, is ₹ 1,75,000; this amount will be paid in December. The account is credited for purchases of a portion of components to be used for sales in January (20% of January components) and a portion for sales in February (80% Components). Cost of goods sold is 80% of sales, and components are 40% of cost of goods sold. Thus January component needs are ₹ 1,66,400 (40% × 80% × ₹ 5,20,000 sales) and February component needs are ₹ 1,60,000 (40% × 80% × ₹ 5,00,000 sales). The January purchases of January component needs equals ₹33,280 (20% × ₹1,66,400). January purchases of February component needs are ₹ 1,28,000 (80% × ₹ 1,60,000). Hence, the total of January purchases (ending balance in accounts payable) equals ₹1,61,280 (₹33,280 + ₹1,28,000).

Answer (b) is incorrect because ₹ 1,66,400 equals January component needs. Answer (C) is incorrect because ₹4,16,000 equals cost of sales for January. Answer (d) is incorrect because ₹2,01,600 assumes that purchased components are 40% of sales.

(*iii*) The correct answer is (b): Given that cost of goods sold is 80% of sales, gross profit is 20% of sales. Consequently, proforma gross profit is ₹ 1,04,000 (20% × ₹ 5,20,000). Answer (a) is incorrect because ₹4,16,000 is cost of goods sold (80% of sales). Answer (C) is incorrect because gross profit cannot be greater than sales. Answer (d) is incorrect because gross profit is earned when cost of goods sold is less than 100% of sales.

Illustrative Problem 30 (Budgeted Income Statement and Balance Sheet)

The balance sheet of ABC Ltd at 1 January 2016 is expected to be as follows:

Capital and liabilities			*Assets*		
	(₹)	(₹)		(₹)	(₹)
Ownership interest			Fixed assets, at cost		870,000
Share capital		5,00,000	*Less* Accumulated depreciation		210,000
Reserves		135,000			660,000
		6,35,000	Current assets:		
8% loan stock		200,000	Stock	150,000	
			Trade debtors	70,000	
			Cash	55,000	275,000
Current liabilities:					
Dividend due	40,000				
Trade creditors	60,000	100,000			
		935,000			935,000

The following is a summary of the transactions expected by the company during the year ending 31 December 2016.

1. Sales are expected to amount to ₹ 800,000. All sales are on credit and ABC Ltd expects that 12% of the annual sales will not have been paid for at 31 December 2016.
2. All purchases of stock are on credit and are expected to amount to ₹ 650,000. The company expects to owe its suppliers ₹ 65,000 at 31 December 2016. It expects to have stocks on hand at that date of ₹ 250,000 at cost price.
3. New fixed assets are expected to be purchased for cash during the year, costing ₹ 150,000. No fixed assets will be sold. Depreciation is to be provided on all fixed assets (including those bought during the year` at the rate of 10% on cost.
4. Interest on the loan stock is payable annually in arrears on 31 December.
5. Operating expenses for the year (other than those mentioned above) are expected to amount to ₹ 65,000, payable as they are incurred.
6. The dividend due at 1 January 2016 will be paid during the year, and the company intends to provide for a dividend of a similar amount at 31 December 2016.

Required:

(*a*) Prepare a budgeted income statement for the year ending 31 December 2016, and a budgeted balance sheet as at that date.

(*b*) Comment on the figures revealed by your budgets.

Solution:

(*a*) ABC Ltd budgeted income statement for the year ending 31 December 2016

	₹ '000	₹ '000
Sales		800
Less: Cost of goods sold (150 + 650 – 250)		550
Gross profit		250
Less: Depreciation (10% × [870 + 150])	102	
Loan interest	16	
Operating expenses	65	183
Income		67
Less: Dividend		40
Add to reserves		27

ABC Ltd budgeted balance sheet at 31 December 2016	₹ '000	₹ '000
Fixed assets, at cost (870 + 150)	1,020	
Less: Accumulated depreciation (210 + 102)	312	708
Current assets		
Stock	250	
Trade debtors (12% × 800)	96	346
		1,054
Less: Current liabilities		
Dividend due	40	
Trade creditors	65	
Bank overdraft (see below)	87	192
		862
Represented by Share capital		500
Reserves (135 + 27)		162
8% loan stock		200
		862

Note:

Cash budget for 2016

	₹000	₹000
Cash in hand at 1 January		55
Add: Receipts from customers (70 + 800 – 96)		774
		829
Less: Payments to suppliers (60 + 650 – 65)	645	
Purchase of fixed assets	150	
Loan interest paid	16	

Operating expenses paid	65	
Dividend paid	40	916
Cash deficit at 31 December		87

(*b*) The figures reveal that, although the company expects an income of ₹ 67,000 during 2016 (more than enough to cover the proposed dividend), the cash balance of ₹ 55,000 will become a deficit of ₹ 87,000. This reduction in cash is due primarily to the purchase of fixed assets and the increased credit granted to customers. The company will need to make arrangements to acquire the required finance if it is to survive the year ahead. The figures provide the opportunity to discuss the relationship between accounting income and changes in cash balances.

Illustrative Problem 31 (Budgeted Income Statement and Balance Sheet)

ABC Ltd. has the following (summarised) balance sheet as at 30 April 2016

	₹000	₹000
Share capital		1,000
Revenue reserve (undistributed profit)		754
		1,754
4% debenture stock (long-term loan)		300
Current liabilities:		
Trade creditors	1,200	
Inland revenue (for tax)	30	
Bank overdraft	300	1,530
		3,584
Freehold land and buildings at cost		320
Manufacturing equipment, tools, dies, etc.		560
		880
Current assets:		
Stock of raw materials, work in progress and finished goods at cost or under		1,300
Trade debtors		1,404
		3,584

Estimates prepared in the accounting department for the following three months are as follows:

	₹000
Sales on credit, spread equally over the three months (sales are on deferred terms: the debtors will pay in 12 equal instalments, the first falling in the month in which the debt is incurred)	576
Purchase of raw materials, spread equally over the three months (purchases will all be for cash, as suppliers will not give any more credit)	114
Manufacturing wages (payable in cash weekly); total for three months	228
Other expenses (non-manufacturing wages and salaries, insurance, heating and lighting, rates, etc.) (These will be payable in cash and arise evenly over the three months.)	237

It is estimated that it will be possible to collect in each month about $\frac{1}{6}$ of the debts due to the company at 30 April	
It is expected that $\frac{1}{3}$ of the trade creditors at 30 April will have to be paid in each of the three months	
The tax is payable immediately	
The expected sales will absorb finished goods at a book value (based on manufacturing labour and materials only) of	342
The bank overdraft limit (*i.e.* the maximum advance allowed) is	600
one quarter's interest on the debenture must be paid in July	

Required:

(a) Prepare a clear statement for the directors of the company showing, month by month, the estimated cash receipts and payments of the company for the next three months.

(b) Prepare an estimated income statement for the period and an end-period balance sheet. (Write ₹ 14,000 off equipment for depreciation.)

(c) Comment on the situation revealed by these statements.

Solution:

(a) Cash Budgets, May–July 2016

	May ₹000	*June* ₹000	*July* ₹000	*Total* ₹000
Receipts				
Collections from old debtors				
($\frac{1}{6}$ × 1,404)	234	234	234	702
Collections from new debtors				
($\frac{1}{12}$ × 1/3 × 576)	16			
($\frac{1}{12}$ × 1/3 × 576 × 2)		32		
($\frac{1}{12}$ × 1/3 × 576 × 3)			48	96
	250	266	282	798
Payments				
Suppliers for old debts ($\frac{1}{3}$ × 1,200)	400	400	400	1,200
Suppliers for new purchases (1/3 × 114)	38	38	38	114
Manufacturing wages ($\frac{1}{3}$ × 228)	76	76	76	228
Other expenses ($\frac{1}{3}$ × 237)	79	79	79	237
Inland revenue	30			30
Debenture interest ($\frac{1}{4}$ × 4% × 300)			3	3
	623	593	596	1,812
Surplus/(deficit) for the month	(373)	(327)	(314)	(1,014)
Balance at start of month	(300)	(673)	(1,000)	(300)
Surplus/(deficit) at end of month	(673)	(1,000)	(1,314)	(1,314)

(*b*) Budgeted Income Statement, May–July 2016

	₹000	₹000
Sales		576
Less: Manufacturing labour and materials	342	
Other expenses	237	
Debenture interest	3	
Depreciation	14	596
Loss for the period		20

Budgeted Balance Sheet at 31 July 2016

	₹000	₹000
Share capital		1,000
Revenue reserve (754–20)		734
		1,734
4% debenture		300
Current liabilities:		
Trade creditors	0	
Bank overdraft (limit)	600	600
Additional finance required (1,314 – 600)		714
		₹ 3,348
Freehold land and buildings, at cost		320
Manufacturing equipment, net of depreciation (560–14)		546
		866
Current assets:		
Stocks	1,300	
Trade debtors (1,404 + 576 – 798)	1,182	2,482
		₹ 3,348

(*c*) The budgeted loss for the period is ₹ 20,000. However, the finance required increases from ₹ 3,00,000 to ₹ 13,14,000 due primarily to the harsh terms imposed by creditors and the generous terms allowed to customers. The main short-term problem is to find the ₹ 7,14,000 finance required over and above the current overdraft limit. In the longer term, the company should realise that, despite the extremely generous credit terms allowed to customers, a contribution sufficient to cover costs is not being earned (particularly when account is taken of the interest which will have to be paid on new finance).

Illustrative Problem 32

ABC Ltd., a company with two divisions, has recently installed a budgetary control system which is intended to help appraise managerial efficiency. The budget performance report for last month is:

		Division A	Division B
Sales in units:	Actual	7,500	5,000
	Budget	6,000	7,000
Price per unit (₹):	Actual	15	30
	Budget	20	35
Total variable costs (₹)*			
Material (₹):	Actual	40,000	25,000
	Budget	24,000	28,000
Labour (₹):	Actual	22,500	30,000
	Budget	16,000	28,000
Total contribution to fixed overhead and profits (₹)	Actual	50,000	95,000
	Budget	80,000	189,000

*Budget figures are based on budgeted sales.

Additional information, covering all the factors which affected performance during the month, is given:

1. The firm produces to order and keeps no stocks. The demand conditions assumed in the budget for division A did in fact apply during the month. It was, however, expected that the sales of division B would be 2,500 units under the original budget at the budget price because of a temporary decline in the market. This shortfall in volume is expected to be recouped at the budgeted price in the next month by working exceptional overtime at a cost of ₹ 10,000. The sales manager of division B was able partially to offset the temporary decline in sales by cutting the price to below the budget figure.
2. Both divisions use the same raw material, but each employs its own purchasing officer. Because of conditions in the world market, the price of the material rose at the beginning of the month by 50% over the budgeted price. The buyer in division B persuaded suppliers to pass on only half of this increase.
3. The production manager of division A has been able to cut material wastage by employing more skilled labour, costing ₹ 2,500 more than expected. A new factory has recently been built near division B, and by offering higher wage rates has attracted most of B's best workers. ABC Co. has, as yet, not increased its wage rate, and the personnel manager of B has been forced to empty workers who can achieve only 50% of the budgeted output per hour.

Required:

Prepare a statement explaining the difference between budgeted and actual performance during the month, in the way you think will best enable management to trace and eliminate inefficiency. As far as possible, try to include information which will enable management to appraise the performance of each of the executives mentioned. Such information may alternatively be given as a brief commentary to your statement.

Solution:

Accounts for last month run as follows:

	Division A				Division B			
		Actual (₹)		*Budget* (₹)		*Actual* (₹)		*Budget* (₹)
Sales	7,500 @ ₹ 15	112,500	6,000 @ ₹ 20	120,000	5,000 @ ₹ 30	150,000	7,000 @ ₹ 35	245,000
Materials		40,000		24,000		25,000		28,000
Labour		22,500		16,000		30,000		28,000
		62,500		40,000		55,000		56,000
Contribution		50,000		80,000		95,000		189,000
Contribution per unit				₹ 13 1/3				₹ 27

Results may helpfully be analysed as follows:

Division A				*Responsibility of*
Budget profit			₹ 80,000	
Less: Loss from selecting wrong point on demand curve $7{,}500\ (15 - 6\frac{2}{3}) - 6{,}000\ (20 - 6\frac{2}{3})$			₹ 17,500	Executive who set price
			₹ 62,500	
Materials price variance $(\frac{1}{3} \times ₹\ 40{,}000)$		₹ 13,333(U)		Market conditions
Gain from economy of material $₹\ 24{,}000 \times \dfrac{7{,}500}{6{,}000} - ₹\ (40{,}000 - 13{,}333)$, ₹ 3,333				
Offset by extra labour cost	₹ 2.500	₹ 833(F)	₹ 12,500	Production manager
Actual Profit			₹ 50,000	

Division B		*Responsibility of*
Budgeted profit	₹ 189,000	
Less: Loss from fall in market conditions 2,500 (35 – 8)	₹ 67,500	Market conditions
	₹ 1,21,500	Make up next period but for ₹ 10,000 of extra cost

Less: Loss from selecting new point on demand curve 5,000 (30 – 8) minus 4,500(35 – 8)		₹ 11,500	Sales manager
		₹ 110,000	
Materials price variance 5,000 × ₹ 4 × 50%	₹ 10,000		Market conditions
Offset by special negotiation ½× ₹ 10,000	₹ 5,000		Buyer gets credit
	₹ 5,000(U)		
Labour efficiency (5,000 × ₹ 4 – ₹ 30,000)	₹ 10,000(U)	₹ 15,000	Whoever sets wage
Actual profit		₹ 95,000	rates – not production manager

This example rests on two important principles of analysis:

1. Where a decision affects volume, the gain or loss should be measured in terms of changes in contribution.
2. It is important to separate uncontrollable variances due to external factors from those attributable to internal actions.

Illustrative Problem 33 (Master Budget Profit Plan)

Sri Ram Piston Co. has the following data from Year 1 operations, which are to be used for developing Year 2 budget estimates:

Revenues (1,00,000 units)		₹ 7,46,000
Manufacturing Costs:		
Materials	₹ 1,33,000	
Variabls Costs	1,80,900	
Fixed Costs (excluding depreciation)	72,000	
Depreciation (fixed)	89,000	4,74,900
Marketing and Administrative Costs:		
Marketing (variable)	₹ 95,000	
Depreciation of Marketing Building and Equipment	22,600	
Administrative (fixed) (excluding depreciation)	90,110	
Depreciation of Administrative Building and Equipment	8,400	2,16,110
Total Costs		6,91,010
Operating Profits		₹ 54,990

All depreciation costs are fixed. Sales volume and prices are expected to increase by 12 per cent and 6 percent, respectively. On a per-unit basis, expectations are that materials costs will increase by 10 per cent and variable manufacturing costs will decrease by 4 percent. Fixed manufacturing costs are expected to decrease by 7 percent.

Variable marketing costs will change with volume. Administrative cash costs are expected to increase by 8 percent.

Prepare a master budget profit plan for Year 2. Management wants to increase operating profits by 20 per cent over Year 1's ₹ 54,990 expected profits. Based on your budget for Year 2, are profits expected to increase by 20 percent? Why or why not?

Solution:

Sri Ram Piston Co.

Master Budget Plan for Year 2

		Calculation
Sales	₹ 8,85,651	₹ 7,46,000 × 1.12 × 1.06
Less: Variable Costs:		
Materials	1,63,856	₹ 1,33,000 × 1.12 × 1.10
Other Manufacturing	1,94,504	₹ 1,80,900 × 1.12 × .96
Marketing	1,06,400	₹ 95,000 × 1.12
Contribution Margin	₹ 4,20,891	
Less: Fixed Costs:		
Manufacturing Depreciation	89,000	Unchanged
Other Manufacturing	66,960	₹ 72,000 × .93
Marketing Depreciation	22,600	Unchanged
Administrative Depreciation	8,400	Unchanged
Administrative	97,319	₹ 90,110 × 1.08
Operating Profit	₹ 1,36,612	

The projected operating profit will be more than the double of the operating profit for year 1. Revenue increases more than 18% while total variable costs increase considerably less and total fixed costs increase very little.

Illustrative Problem 34 (Cash Budget, Budgeted Profit and Loss A/C, Budgeted B/S)

On 31 December, the summary balance sheet of Bookland booksellers, was as follows:

	₹		₹
Capital	10,00,000	Shop equipment	3,75,000
Creditors	5,00,000	Stock of books	6,00,000
Proposed dividends	75,000	Debtors	3,75,000
		Cash in bank	2,25,000
	15,75,000		15,75,000

The following transactions are anticipated for the next three months:

	Credit Sales (₹)	*Cash Sales* (₹)	*Credit Purchase* (₹)	*Cash Purchase* (₹)
January	3,75,000	3,50,000	6,00,000	50,000
February	4,50,000	1,25,000	5,75,000	25,000
March	5,00,000	3,00,000	6,75,000	25,000

Additionally, you are informed:

Wages paid will be ₹ 25,000 per month.

Postage and packing is to be 20 % of credit sales, and paid in the month on sale.

Debtors normally pay one month after books are sold to them.

Creditors are paid one month after receipts of books.

Shop equipments will be replaced on 1 January. The new equipment will cost ₹ 6,00,000 and payment will be made in equal installments in February, March and April. The old equipment will realize ₹ 2,00,000 in February.

Depreciation of the new equipment will be 10% p.a. and charged to accounts monthly.

Half the dividends proposed will be paid in March, half in July next.

The company expects a gross profit of 1/3 on selling price.

Required:

(*i*) A cash budget for the three separate months ending 31 March.

(*ii*) A forecast trading and profit and loss account for the same three months in total only.

(*iii*) A forecast balance sheet as at 31 March.

Solution:

(i) Cash Budget for three Months Ending 31st March

	January	February	March
Receipts:	(₹)	(₹)	(₹)
Sales: Credit	3,75,000	3,75,000	4,50,000
Cash	3,50,000	1,25,000	3,00,000
Equipment		2,00,000	
	7,25,000	7,00,000	7,50,000
Payments:			
Purchase: Credit	5,00,000	6,00,000	5,75,000
Cash	50,000	25,000	25,000
Wages	25,000	25,000	25,000
Postage & packing	75,000	90,000	1,00,000
Dividends			37,500
Equipment		2,00,000	2,00,000
	6,50,000	9,40,000	9,62,500
Cash flow	75,000	(2,40,000)	(2,12,500)
Opening balance	2,25,000	3,00,000	60,000
Closing balance	3,00,000	60,000	(1,52,500)

(ii) Forecast Trading and Profit & Loss Account for Three Months Ending 31st March

	₹	₹	₹
Sales (credit 13,25,000 + cash 7,75,000)			21,00,000
Less: Stock at 1st January	6,00,000		
Add: Purchases (18,50,000 + 10,00,000)	19,50,000		
		25,50,000	
Less : Stock at 31 March		11,50,000	
			14,00,000
Gross Profit (33.3% on sales)			7,00,000
Less: *Wages*		75,000	
Postage and packing		2,65,000	
Loss on sale of equipment		1,75,000	
Depreciation		15,000	
			5,30,000
Net profit			1,70,000

(iii) Forecast Balance Sheet as at 31st March

	₹	₹	₹
Fixed assets:			
Equipment, at cost		6,00,000	
Less: Depreciation		15,000	
			5,85,000
Current assets:			
Stock		11,50,000	
Debtors		5,00,000	
		16,50,000	
Less: Current liabilities:			
Creditors	8,75,000		
Bank overdraft	1,52,500		
Dividends due	37,500	10,65,000	
			5,85,000
			11,70,000
Represented by:			
Capital		10,00,000	
Net Profit		1,70,000	11,70,000

Illustrative Problem 35 (Cash Budget)

Alpha-Tech, a rapidly growing distribution of electronic components, is formulating its plans for 2016. Carol Jones, the firm's marketing director, has completed the sales forecast presented below.

Alpha-Tech
2016 Forecast Sales
(in thousands)

Month	*Sales* (₹)	*Month*	*Sales* (₹)
January	9,000	July	15,000
February	10,000	August	15,000
March	9,000	September	16,000
April	11,500	October	16,000
May	12,500	November	15,000
June	14,000	December	17,000

Philip Smith, an accountant in the Planning and Budgeting Department, is responsible for preparing the cash flow projection.

- Alpha-Tech's excellent record in accounts receivable collection is expected to continue. Sixty per cent of billings are collected the month after the sale and the remaining 40 per cent two months after.
- The purchase of electronic components is Alpha –Tech's largest expenditure and is estimated to be 40 per cent of sales. Seventy per cent of the parts are received by Alpha-Tech one month prior to sale and 30 per cent are received during the month of sale.
- Historically, 75 per cent of accounts payable have been paid one month after receipt of the purchased components, and the remaining 25 per cent is paid two months after receipt.
- Hourly wages and fringe benefits, estimated to be 30 per cent of the current month's sales, are paid in the month incurred.
- General and administrative expenses are projected to be ₹ 1,56,20,000 for the year. The breakdown of these expenses is presented at the top of the next column. All expenditures are paid uniformly throughout the year, except the property taxes which are paid at the end of each quarter in four equal installments.

2016 Forecasted General and Administrative Costs
(in thousands)

	(₹)
Salaries and fringe benefits	3,200
Promotion	3,800
Property taxes	1,360
Insurance	2,000
Utilities	1,800
Depreciation	3,460
Total	₹ 15,620

- Income tax payments are made at the beginning of each calendar quarter based on the income of the prior quarter. Alpha-Tech is subject to an effective income tax rate of 40 per cent. Alpha-Tech's operating income for the first quarter of 2016 is projected to be ₹ 32,00,000. The company pays 100 per cent of the estimated tax payment.
- Alpha-Tech maintains a minimums cash balance of ₹ 5,00,000. If the cash balance is less than ₹ 5,00,000 at the end of each month, the company borrows amounts necessary to maintain this balance. All amounts borrowed are repaid out of subsequent positive cash flow. The projected April 1, 2016 opening balance is ₹ 5,00,000.
- Alpha-Tech has no short-term debt as of April 1, 2016.
- Alpha-Tech uses a calendar year for both financial reporting and tax purposes.

Required:

A. Prepare a cash budget for Alpha-Tech by month for the second quarter of 2016. Ignore any interest expense associated with borrowing.

B. Discuss why cash budgeting is important for Alpha-Tech.

(CMA, USA, Adapted with permission)

Solution:

A. The proforma cash budget for Alpha-Tech for the second quarter of 2016 is presented below. Supporting calculation are presented later.

Alpha-Tech
Cash Budget
for the Second Quarter 2016

	April (₹)	*May* (₹)	*June* (₹)
Beginning balance	5,00,000	5,00,000	12,30,000
Collections[1]			
February sales	40,00,000		
March sales	54,00,000	36,00,000	
April sales		69,00,000	46,00,000
May sales			75,00,000
Total receipts	94,00,000	1,05,00,000	1,21,00,000
Total cash available	99,00,000	1,10,00,000	1,33,30,000
Disbursements:			
Accounts payable	41,55,000	47,35,000	52,85,000
Wages[2]	34,50,000	37,50,000	42,00,000
General & Administrative[3]	9,00,000	9,00,000	9,00,000
Property taxes			3,40,000
Income taxes[4]	12,80,000		
Total disbursements	97,85,000	93,85,000	1,07,25,000

Cash balance	1,15,000	16,15,000	26,05,000
Cash borrowed	3,85,000		
Cash repaid		(3,85,000)	
Ending balance	5,00,000	12,30,000	26,05,000

[1]60% of sales in first month; 40% of sales in second month

[2]30% of current month sales

[3]Total less property taxes and depreciation ÷ 12

[4]40% × ₹ 32,00,000

B. Cash budgeting is important for Alpha-Tech because as sales grow so will expenditure for input factors. Since these expenditures generally precede cash receipts, the company must plan for possible financing to cover the gap between payments and receipts. The cash budget shows the probable cash position at certain points in time, allowing the company to plan for borrowing, as Alpha-Tech must do in April.

Cash budgeting also facilitates the control of excess cash. The company may be losing investment opportunities, if excess cash is left idle. The cash budget alerts management to periods when there will be excess cash available for investment, thus facilitating financial planning and cash control.

Supporting Calculations

Accounts payable–parts received:

Cost of goods sold

Month	*40% of sales* (₹)	*Timing*	*February* (₹)	*March* (₹)	*April* (₹)	*May* (₹)	*June* (₹)
February	40,00,000	.30	12,00,000				
March	36,00,000	.70	25,20,000				
March	36,00,000	.30		10,80,000			
April	46,00,000	.70		32,20,000			
April	46,00,000	.30			13,80,000		
May	50,00,000	.70			35,00,000		
May	50,00,000	.30				15,00,000	
June	56,00,000	.70				39,20,000	
			37,20,000	43,00,000	48,80,000	54,20,000	
Payments:							
February	37,20,000	.25			9,30,000		
March	43,00,000	.75			32,25,000		
March	43,00,000	.25				10,75,000	
April	48,80,000	.75				36,60,000	
April	48,80,000	.25					12,20,000
May	54,20,000	.75					40,65,000
			0	0	41,55,000	47,35,000	52,85,000

Illustrative Problem 36 (Cash Budget and Balance Sheet)

Tarun Desai, controller for Reliance Retailers, has assembled the following data to assist in the preparation of a cash budget for the third quarter of 2016.

(*a*) Sales:

May (actual)	₹ 1,00,000
June (actual)	1,20,000
July (estimated)	90,000
August (estimated)	1,00,000
September (estimated)	1,35,000
October (estimated)	1,10,000

(*b*) Each month, 30 per cent of sales are for cash and 70 per cent are on cedit. The collection pattern for credit sales is 20 per cent in the month of sale, 50 per cent in the following month, and 30 per cent in the second month following the sale.

(*c*) Each month, the ending inventory exactly equals 50 per cent of the cost of next month's sales. The markup on goods is 25 per cent of cost.

(*d*) Inventory purchases are paid for in the month following the purchase.

(*e*) Recurring monthly expenses are as follows:

Salaries and wages	₹ 10,000
Depreciation on plant and equipment	4,000
Utilities	1,000
Other	1,700

(*f*) Property taxes of ₹ 15,000 are due and payable on July 15, 2016.

(*g*) Advertising fees of ₹ 6,000 must be paid on August 20, 2016.

(*h*) A lease on a new storage facility is scheduled to begin on September 2, 2016. Monthly payments are ₹ 5,000.

(*i*) The company has a policy to maintain a minimum cash balance of ₹ 10,000. If necessary, it will borrow to meet its short-term needs. All borrowing is doen at the beginning of the month. All payments on principal and interest are made at the end of a month. The annual interest rate is 9 percent. The company must borrow in multiples of ₹ 1,000.

(*j*) A partially completed balance sheet as of June 30, 2016, follows. (Accounts payable is for inventory purchases only.)

Cash	₹ ?	
Accounts receivable	?	
Inventory	?	
Plant and equipment	4,25,000	
Accounts payable		₹ ?
Common equity		2,10,000
Retained earnings		2,68,750
Total	₹ ?	₹ ?

Required:

1. Complete the balance sheet given in (j).
2. Prepare a cash budget for each month in the third quarter and for the quarter in total. (The third quarter begins on July 1.) Provide a supporting schedule of cash collections.
3. Prepare a pro forma balance sheet as of September 30, 2016.

Solution:

1. To determine accounts payable as of June 30, a schedule of purchases will be constructed. This schedule will also be used to build the cash budget.

Let X = Cost of sales, and sales = 1.00.

If X + 0.25X = 1.00, then X = 0.80.

	June	July	August	September
Cost of sales	₹ 96,000	₹ 72,000	₹ 80,000	₹ 108,000
Desired end. inventory*	36,000	40,000	54,000	44,000
Total requirements	₹ 1,32,000	₹ 1,12,000	₹ 1,34,000	₹ 1,52,000
Less: Beginning inventory	48,000	36,000	40,000	54,000
Purchases	₹ 84,000	₹ 76,000	₹ 94,000	₹ 98,000

*0.50 × Next month's cost of sales

Since purchases are paid for in the following month, accounts payable at the end of June is ₹ 84,000. Inventory for June 30 is ₹ 36,000.

Accounts receivable for June 30 is computed as follows:

From June:	0.7 × ₹ 120,000 × 0.8* =	₹ 67,200
From May:	0.7 × ₹ 100,000 × 0.3* =	21,000
Total		₹ 88,200

*By June 30, 20% of June credit sales and 70% of May credit sales have been collected, leaving 80% and 30%, respectively, to be collected.

Given accounts payable, the total liabilities plus shareholder's equity must equal ₹ 5,62,750 (₹ 84,000 + ₹ 2,10,000 + ₹ 2,68,750). Cash is the difference between total assets and all other assets except cash (₹ 5,62,750 – ₹ 4,25,000 – ₹ 36,000 – ₹ 88,200). This difference is ₹ 13,550.

	Assets	Liabilities and Shareholders' Equity
Cash	₹ 13,550	
Accounts receivable	88,200	
Inventory	36,000	
Plant and equipment	4,25,000	
Accounts payable		₹ 84,000
Common equity		2,10,000
Retained earnings		2,68,750
Total	₹ 5,62,750	₹ 5,62,750

2. **Reliance Retailers**

Cash Budget

For the Quarter Ending September 30, 2016

	July	August	September	Total
Beginning cash balance	₹ 13,550	₹ 10,450	₹ 10,405	₹ 13,550
Cash collections*	102,600	100,700	113,300	316,600
Total cash available	₹ 116,150	₹ 111,150	₹ 123,705	₹ 330,150
Cash disbursements:				
Purchases**	₹ 84,000	₹ 76,000	₹ 94,000	₹ 254,000
Salaries and wages	10,000	10,000	10,000	30,000
Utilities	1,000	1,000	1,000	3,000
Other	1,700	1,700	1,700	5,100
Property taxes	15,000			15,000
Advertising fees		6,000		6,000
Lease			5,000	5,000
Total disbursement	₹ 111,700	₹ 94,700	₹ 111,700	₹ 318,100
Minimum cash balance	10,000	10,000	10,000	10,000
Total cash needs	₹ 121,700	₹ 104,700	₹ 121,700	₹ 328,100
Excess (deficiency)	₹ (5,550)	₹ 6,450	₹ 2,005	₹ 2,050
Financing:				
Borrowing	₹ 6,000			₹ 6,000
Repayments		₹ (6,000)		(6,000)
Interest***		(45)	₹ 0	(45)
Total financing	₹ 6,000	₹ (6,045)	₹ 0	₹ (45)
Ending cash balance	₹ 10,450	₹ 10,405	₹ 12,005	₹ 12,005
*Cash collections:				
Cash sales	₹ 27,000	₹ 30,000	₹ 40,500	₹ 97,500
Credit sales:				
Current month	12,600	14,000	18,900	45,500
Prior month	42,000	31,500	35,000	108,500
From two months ago	21,000	25,200	18,900	65,100
Total collections	₹ 1,02,600	₹ 1,00,700	₹ 1,13,300	₹ 316,600

**Taken from the purchases schedule developed in Requirement 1.

***₹ 6,000 × 0.09/12

2. **Reliance Retailers**

Pro Forma Balance Sheet

September 30, 2016

	Assets	Liabilities and Shareholders' Equity
Cash	₹ 12,005	
Accounts receivable[a]	96,600	
Inventory[b]	44,000	
Plant and equipment[c]	4,13,000	
Accounts payable[b]		₹ 98,000
Common equity		2,10,000
Retained earnings[d]		2,57,605
Total	₹ 5,65,605	₹ 5,65,605

[a](0.7 × ₹ 1,35,000 × 0.8) + (0.7 × ₹ 1,00,000 × 0.3).

[b]From purchases schedule prepared in Requirement 1.

[c][₹ 4,25,000 – 3(₹ 4,000)].

[d]If total assets equal ₹ 5,65,605, then liabilities plus shareholders' equity must also equal that amount. Subtracting accounts payable and common equity from total liabilities and shareholders' equity gives retained earnings of ₹ 2,57,605.

BUDGETING IN INTERNATIONAL PERSPECTIVE

Multinational Companies (MNCs) have specific problems of preparing budgets for their international operations. Budgeting is complex for MNCs because of fluctuations in foreign currency exchange rates, the high inflation rates found in some countries, local economic conditions and governmental policies affecting business practices, costs structure and marketing practices.

Fluctuations in foreign currency exchange rates may make the budgeting task difficult. Indian exporters may be able to forecast with some accuracy their sales in the local foreign currency such as USA or UK. However, the amounts the exporters will ultimately receive in their own currency depends on currency exchange rates prevailing at that time. The exporters will receive less money than expected if the exchange rates are found to be less favourable.

Companies that are heavily involved in export operations often hedge their exposure to exchange rate fluctuations by buying and selling sophisticated financial contracts. These hedges ensure that if the company loses money in its exporting operations because of exchange rate fluctuations, it will make up that loss with gains on its financial contracts. When an MNC uses hedging operations, the costs of these activities should be budgeted along with other expenses.

Some MNCs have operations in countries with very high inflation rates—sometimes exceeding 100% a year. Such high inflation rates—called *hyperinflation*—can render a budget obsolete very quickly. A common budgeting tactic in such countries is to reduce the lead time for preparing the budget and to revise the budget frequently throughout the year in the light of the actual inflation experienced to date.

In addition to problems with exchange rates and inflation, MNCs must be sensitive to government policies in the countries in which they operate that might affect labour costs, equipment purchases, cash management, or other budget items.[23]

ZERO-BASED BUDGETING (ZBB)

> **Zero-Based Budgeting (ZBB)** is a method of budgeting whereby all activities are evaluated each time a budget is formulated and every item of expenditure in the budget is fully justified.

Zero-Based Budgeting (ZBB) is a method of budgeting whereby all activities are evaluated each time a budget is formulated and every item of expenditure in the budget is fully justified. That is, ZBB involves starting from scratch or zero.

In traditional budgeting, departmental managers need justify only increases over the prior year's budget (known as incremental budgeting). This implies that what is already being spent is automatically sanctioned. Under the ZBB concept each department's functions are reviewed completely and all expenditures, rather than only the increases, must be approved. Also, in some departments, ascertainment of budgets costs is easier than other departments. For example, in production departments, it is easier to determine costs of inputs to achieve a level of budgeted output. But, in other departments such as accounts, personnel, research and development, it is difficult to even identify the output, and therefore equally greater difficult to determine the cost of input to sustain (unidentifiable) output. Consequently, the budgets of previous year tend to be subjectively increased as the next year's budgeted expenditure. However, the previous year's budgets may be inefficient and adjusting merely next year's budgets to the previous year's budget may result in wastages. ZBB overcomes this problem, to a certain extent. ZBB rejects the traditional view of annual budgeting as an incremental process which takes into account current expenditure plus an estimate of next year's expenditure to arrive at the next budget. Instead, the projected expenditure for existing programmes should start from base zero with each year's budgets being compiled as if the programmes were being launched for the first time.

Some basic differences between traditional budgeting and zero-based budgeting are shown in Exhibit 9.11.

Exhibit 9.11: Differences between Traditional Budgeting and Zero-Base Budgeting

Traditional Budgeting	Zero-Based Budgeting
Starts with last year's funding appropriation	Starts with a minimal (or zero) figure for funding
Focuses on money	Focuses on goals and objectives
Does not systematically consider alternatives to current operations	Directly examines alternative approaches to achieve similar results
Produces a single level of appropriation for an activity	Produces alternative levels of funding based on fund availability and desired results

Application of ZBB

ZBB involves the following stages (steps):

1. Each separate activity of the organisation is identified and called a decision package. A decision package is a document that identifies and describes a specific activity in such a manner that management can (*i*) evaluate it and rank it against other activities competing for limited resources, and (*ii*) decide whether to approve or disapprove it.
2. Each decision package must be justified, *i.e.*, it should be enquired into whether a decision package promotes the goals of an enterprise.
3. If justified, then the cost of minimum efforts needed to sustain each decision package is determined.
4. Alternatives for each decision package are considered in order to select better and cheaper options for the package.

5. Incremental decision packages are also justified and costed in the above manner. These incremental packages describe the costs and benefits of additional work that could be done above that required by the base package for the minimum amount of work needed to carry out the activity.
6. Managers rank their decision package in order of priority for resource allocation.
7. Resources are allocated to the packages.

Advantages of ZBB

Listed below are the advantages of ZBB

1. It represents a move towards allocation of resources by need and benefit and thus results in more efficient allocation of resources.
2. It identifies and eliminates wastages and obsolete operations.
3. It ensures that the best possible methods of performing jobs are used and that new ideas emerge.
4. It creates a questioning attitude rather than one which accepts that current practices represent value for money.
5. It leads to increased staff involvement which may lead to improved motivation and greater interest in the job.
6. It increases communication and coordination within the organisation.
7. Managers become more aware of the costs of inputs which helps them to identify priorities.
8. The documentation of decision packages provides management with a deep, coordinated knowledge of all organisation's activities.
9. It is useful specially for service departments where it can be difficult to identify output.

Disadvantages of ZBB

Listed below are the disadvantages of ZBB

1. The costs involved in preparing a vast number of decision packages in a large firm are very high.
2. It is very time-consuming and a large amount of additional paper work is involved.
3. Managers develop fear and feel threatened by ZBB and therefore may oppose new ideas and changes.
4. The ranking of decision packages and allocation of resources is subjective to a certain degree, which can result in departmental conflict.
5. Administration and communication of ZBB process may become critical problems because more managers become involved in this process than in most budgeting and planning procedures and these problems are further compounded in large organisations.

Garrison and Noreen[24] have observed on the utility and applicability of zero-base budgeting in the following manner:

> Nearly everyone would agree that zero-base budgeting is a good idea. The only issue is the frequency with which a zero-base review is carried out. Under zero-base budgeting, the review is performed every year. Critics of zero-base budgeting charge that properly executed zero-base budgeting is too time-consuming and too costly to justify on an annual basis. In addition, it is argued that annual reviews soon become mechanical and that the whole purpose of zero-base budgeting is then lost.

Whether or not a company should use an annual review is a matter of judgment. In some situations, annual zero-base reviews may be justified; in other situations, they may not because of the time and cost involved. However, most managers would at least agree that on occasion zero-base reviews can be very helpful."

PLANNING, PROGRAMMING AND BUDGETING SYSTEM (PPBS)

Planning, Programming and Budgeting System (PPBS) is used in governmental, non-profit or non-commercial organisations to enable them to make more informed decisions about resources allocation. These organisations' activities produce results that are often difficult to measure in monetary terms or that may take several years to be measured (although the related activities must continue to be funded annually). Thus, relating outputs to inputs is often extremely difficult.

> **PPBS** are prepared on the basis of programmes, *i.e.*, planned activities that have specified objectives.

PPBS differs from traditional non-profit and non-manufacturing budgets in the sense that the later are prepared as line item budgets whereas the former (PPBS) are prepared on the basis of programmes, *i.e.*, planned activities that have specified objectives. In PPBS, budgets for line/functional items for whole department are not presented. Instead, the expenses associated with specific programmes are detailed. For instance, a railway authority may have the programme of total computerisation of its booking system, a municipal authority may have programmes of providing drinking water or providing health facilities in the city. Such programmes require greater coordination among several departments to make a specific programme successful.

PPBS is taken by extending the planning period beyond the one-year budget period. PPBS is the counterpart of the long-term planning process which is operated in profit oriented organisations. PPBS is based on a rational model of decision-making and involves the following stages:

1. Identify and define the objectives of programme.
2. Select performance or output measures to assess the effectiveness of the programme.
3. Identify and evaluate alternative methods of achieving the objectives laid down for each specific programme. For this, costs and benefits associated with each alternative course of action should be detailed.
4. Select the appropriate programmes on the basis of cost benefit analysis as done in (3).
5. Implement the selected alternative and monitor its performance to ensure that the objectives of the programmes are achieved given the resources allocated to those programmes.

Barfield, Raiborn and Kinney[25] state that programme budgeting requires the use of detailed surrogate measures of output and necessitates answers to the following questions:

1. When should results be measured? Because many not-for-profit programs are effective only after some period of time, multiple measurements are necessary to determine effectiveness. When should these measures begin to be made and how often should they be made thereafter?
2. What results should be chosen as output measures? Many not-for-profit programs have multiple results. For example, the institution of reading programs for illiterate adults can reduce unemployment rates, overall crime statistics, welfare provided, and so forth. Should a determination be made of which results are more important than others or should all results be given equal weight?
3. What program actually caused the result? There are questions about the legitimacy of cause-and-effect relationships when measuring the results of not-for-profit programs. *For example*, did an adult literacy program reduce the unemployment statistics or was that reduction more appropriately deemed a result of money spent for job placement programs?

4. Did the program actually affect the target population? An adult literacy program may be aimed at the unemployed. If the majority of persons who attended the program already had jobs, the program had no impact on the target group. However, the program could still be considered effective if the participants increased their job skills and employment levels.

Advantages of PPBS

PPBS is useful in government and not-for-profit organizations as well as for service activities in for-profit businesses. This process can help managers evaluate and control discretionary costs, avoid excessive cost expenditures, and makes certain that expenditures are used for programmes and activities that generate the most beneficial results.

PPBS has certain advantages compared to traditional departmental/functional budgets:

1. PPBS leads to a more effective allocation of resources by cutting across departmental barriers, providing to managers specific information related to the activities and by co-ordinating scarce resources and skilled personnel located in different departments on a particular programme or project.
2. PPBS compels management to identify and evaluate the activities, functions or programmes which are carried out in terms of their objectives, efficiency and effectiveness.
3. Programme budgeting provides adequate information which will enable management to assess the effectiveness of its plans and to focus on the organisation's outputs (the objectives to be achieved).
4. PPBS enables management to long-term perspective and commitments in certain programmes while preparing the annual budget. For instance, an education programme may involve capital expenditure for a ten-year period. In this situation, the decision makers will have to keep in mind future commitments and resources availability while constructing the annual programme budget. In this way, the annual budget is placed in the long-term context and becomes a part of long-term programme.

ACTIVITY-BASED BUDGETING (ABB)

> **ABB** is a planning approach applying activity drivers to estimate the levels and costs of activities necessary to provide budgeted quantity and quality of production.

Activity-based budgeting applies activity-based costing principles to budgeting. It focuses on the numerous activities necessary to produce and market goods and services. ABB is a planning approach applying activity drivers to estimate the levels and costs of activities necessary to provide the budgeted quantity and quality of production. ABB can be applied to nearly any activity and is useful for managing product and period costs. ABB is typically used in the course of an annual budgeting process that begins with the preparation of a sales budget followed by a production budget. These budgets establish expected output targets for sales, distribution, and manufacturing. Using these documents as basic inputs, the following subsequent steps are taken under ABB.

ABB Steps:

1. Select a function for which costs are to be estimated, *i.e.*, distribution, marketing, finance, accounting.
2. Identify all activities necessary to execute the selected function.
3. Identify the activity driver for each activity.
4. Estimate the necessary volume of each activity driver to meet output objectives, *i.e.*, sales and production levels specified in the master budget.
5. Identify the resources consumed by each activity.
6. Estimate the cost of providing each resource.

ABC and ABB

ABC uses a two-stage cost allocation process. First, overheads are assigned to cost pools that reflect the activities constituting the production process. Then, cost drivers are ascertained that are suitable for each activity cost pool. Second, in the stage II, overhead costs are allocated from each activity cost pool to cost objects (e.g. products, services, customers) in proportion to the amount of activity consumed.

In ABB, first, products or services to be produced and the customers to be served are identified. Then the activities that are necessary to produce these products and services are determined. Finally, the resources necessary to perform the specified activities are quantified. Conceptually, ABB takes the ABC model and reverses the flow of the analysis. ABC assigns resource costs to activities, and then it assigns activity costs to products and services produced and customers served. ABB, on the other hand, begins by forecasting the demand for products and services as well as the customers to be served. These forecasts then are used to plan the activities for the budget period and budget the resources necessary to carry out the activities.

The difference between ABC and ABB, as explained here in, is displayed in Figure 9.2.

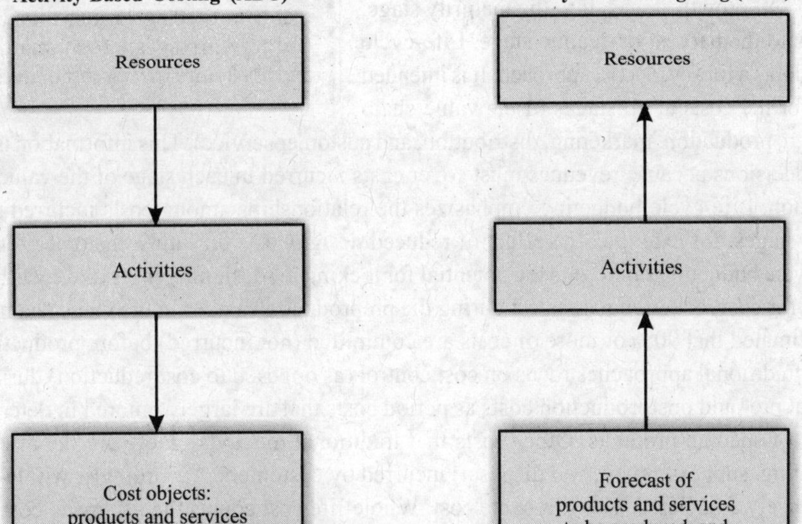

**Source*: Robert S. Kaplan and Robin Cooper, *Cost and Effect*, (Harvard Business School Press, 1998), pp. 303.

Figure 9.2: Activity-based Costing vs. Activity-based Budgeting

Advantages of ABB

Activity-based budgeting is an useful anticipatory control because it estimates the usage and costing rates of drivers before costs are locked in. After operations, it is useful for comparing actual costing rates and driver usage with the amounts budgeted.

With ABB data, costs can be managed by changing the level of specific activities and the impact on the objective function will be more easily understood. Also, the activity-based budget leads to more interesting questions about cost incurrence and cost management opportunities. *For example*, why are we processing 55,000 transactions per year? Can we recontract with our vendors under long-term supply agreements to reduce the number of transactions? If activity-based budgeting is effectively implemented, the result should be an increase in profits and cash flows.

Activity-based budgeting is a planning and control system which seeks to support the objective of continuous improvement. It helps in the understanding and management of costs. It establishes a clear link with strategic objectives and planning. It stimulates a focused, participative approach by all levels in the organisation to guide and sustain continuous improvement.

According to Kolb and Donnelly,[26] "By using ABB information, the user can arguably effect a change in the process before the process takes place. This is very important concept because after the activity has been performed and the cost has been totaled, there is nothing that can be done to change the cost incurred; it is done. Taking a preemptive position with the activities, costs can result in a more favourable outcome."

LIFE-CYCLE BUDGET

> **Life-cycle budget** estimates a product's revenues and expenses over its entire life cycle beginning with research and development, proceeding through the introduction and growth stages, into the maturity stage, and finally into the harvest or decline stage.

A life-cycle budget estimates a product's revenues and expenses over its entire life cycle beginning with research and development, proceeding through the introduction and growth stages, into the maturity stage, and finally into the harvest or decline stage. Life-cycle budgeting adopts a life-cycle cost approach. It is intended to account for the costs at all stages of the value chain (R&D, design, production, marketing, distribution, and customer service). This information is important for pricing decisions because revenues must cover costs incurred in each stage of the value chain, not just production. Life-cycle budgeting emphasizes the relationships among costs incurred at different value-chain stages, for example, the effect of reduced design costs on future customer-service costs. Thus, life-cycle budgeting highlights the potential for locking in (designing in) future costs because the opportunity for cost reduction is greatest during the preproduction stages in the value chain. Indeed, it has been estimated that 90% or more of costs are committed (not incurred) before production begins. In contrast, traditional approaches focus on cost control (as opposed to cost reduction) during production and treat pre- and postproduction costs as period costs that are largely ignored in determining the profitability of specific products. Other costs that traditional methods ignore are the after-purchase costs (operating, support, repair, and disposal) incurred by customers. Accordingly, **whole-life cost** is a concept closely associated with life-cycle cost. Whole-life cost equals the life-cycle cost plus after-purchase costs. Attention to the reduction of all whole-life costs through analysis and management of all value-chain activities is a powerful competitive tool because of the potential for increasing customer satisfaction. Life-cycle and whole-life cost concepts are associated with target costing and target pricing. A firm may determine that market conditions require that a product sell at a given **target price.** Hence, a **target cost** can be determined by subtracting the desired unit profit margin from the target price. The cost reduction objectives of life-cycle and whole-life cost management can therefore be determined using target costing.

KAIZEN BUDGETING

The Japanese term 'kaizen' means continuous improvement, and 'kaizen budgeting' assumes the continuous improvement of products and processes, usually by way of many small innovations rather than major changes. It requires estimates of the effects of improvements and the costs of their implementation. Accordingly, kaizen budgeting is based not on the existing system but on changes yet to be made, and budget targets can not be reached unless those improvements occur. Kaizen budget estimates may be based on learning curves, that is, expected reductions in labour time during the early stages of production as experience is gained. A kaizen budget may also relate to the product life cycle concept. The greatest improvements should occur during the early phases of the cycle, for example, during R&D and design, before costs are locked in.

GOVERNMENT BUDGETING

Governmental budgeting differs from private-sector budgeting. A governmental budget is not only a financial plan and a basis for evaluating performance but also an expression of public policy and a form of control having the force of law. Thus, a governmental budget is a legal document adopted in accordance with procedures specified by applicable laws. A governmental budget must be complied with by the administrators of the governmental unit for which the budget is prepared. By law, the administrators can not exceed the budget without a formally approved budget amendment. Moreover, because the effectiveness and efficiency of governmental efforts are difficult to measure in the absence of the profit-centreed activity that characterizes business operations, the use of budgets in the appropriation process is of major importance. Accordingly, budgetary accounts may be incorporated into the formal accounting systems of governments, and a budgetary comparison statement can be issued.

REFERENCES

1. Lane K. Anderson and Harold M. Sollenberger, *Managerial Accounting,* South Western Publishing Co., 1992, p. 304.
2. Colin Biggs and David Benjamin, *Management Accounting Techniques*, Heinenmann Professional Publishing, 1989, p. 141.
3. Don R. Hansen and Maryanne M. Mowen, *Management Accounting,* South Western Publishing Co., 2000, p. 667.
4. Jesset T. Barfield, Ceacily A. Raiborn and Michael R. Kinney, Cost Accounting, Traditions and Innovations, Thomson, 2003, pp. 553-554.
5. Jesset T. Barfield, Cecily A. Raiborn and Michael R. Kinney, *Ibid*, p. 555.
6. Edward J. Blocher, Kung H. Chen, Gary Cokins and Thomas W. Lin, Cost Management, Tata, McGraw Hill Publishing Co., 2006, p. 306.
7. Micheal D. Shields, "Operating Budgets and Budgeting-Benefits and Costs" in Roman L-Weil, and Micheal W. Maher (Eds), Handbook of Cost Management, John Wiley and Sons, 2005, pp. 571-572.
8. Lane K. Anderson and Harold M. Sollenberger, *Ibid*, p. 330.
9. Don R. Hansen and Maryanne M. Mawen, *Management Accounting*, South Western Publishing Co., 2000, p. 294.
10. Don T. DeCoster, *Management Accounting. A Decision Emphasis,* John Wiley and Sons. 1988, p. 567.
11. Wayne J. Morse, James R. Davis and Al L. Hartgraves, *Management Accounting, A Strategic Approach*, South Western College Publishing, 2000. pp. 493.
12. Don. R. Hansen and Maryanne M. Mowen, *Management Accounting,* South Western Publishing Co., 2000, p. 694.
13. Mitton F. Usry and Lawrence H. Hammer, Cost Accounting, Planning and Control, South Western Publishing Co. Cinncinati, pp. 478-479.
14. Wayne J. Morse, James R. Davis, and Al L. Hartgrasses, *Management Accounting*, A Strategic Approach *Ibid*, p. 495.
15. Ronald W. Hilton, *Managerial Accounting*, Tata McGraw Hill Publishing Co., 2006, pp. 375-376.

16. Ray H. Garrison, Eric W. Noreen and Peter C. Brewer, *Managerial Accounting* 13th Edition, McGraw Hill Education (India) Pvt. Ltd, 2011, p. 372.
17. Lane K. Anderson and Harold M. Sollenberger, *Managerial Accounting*, *Ibid*, p. 329.
18. Wayne J. Morse, James R. Davis and Al L. Hartgraves, *Management Accounting*, A Strategic Approach, South Western College Publishing, 2000, p. 495-496.
19. A.G. Hopwood, Accounting and Organisational Behaviour in B. Carsberg and A. Hope (Eds.), Current Issues in Accounting, Philip Allen.
20. Argyris, Integrating the Individual and the Organisation, John Wiley and Sons, 1964.
21. James L. Pierce, "The Budget Comes of Age" Harvard Business Review.
22. Glenn A. Welsch, Budgeting, Profit Planning and Control, p. 22.
23. Ray H. Garrison and Eric W. Noreen, *Managerial Accounting*, Irwin McGraw Hill, 2000, p. 403.
24. Ray H. Garrison and Eric W. Noreen, *Managerial Accounting*, *Ibid*, p. 403.
25. Jesset T. Barfield, Cecily A. Raiborn and Michael R. Kinney, *Cost Accounting, Traditions and Innovations*, Thomson, 2003, p. 688.
26. Mathew W. Kolb and Joseph P. Donnelly, "Best Practices in Activity-Based Management", in Steve Player, Roberto Lacerda (Ed) Arthur Anderson's Global Lessions in Activity-Based Management, John Wiley & Sons, 1999, p. 29.

CRITICAL ANALYSIS AND DISCUSSION QUESTIONS, SELF-ASSESSMENT QUESTIONS, MULTIPLE CHOICE QUESTIONS, PROBLEMS AND CASES

CRITICAL ANALYSIS AND DISCUSSION QUESTIONS

1. Define budget and budgetary control.
2. Explain the relationship between planning and control process and budgeting.
3. List the major components of a planning and control process.
4. Explain how an organisation can benefit from budgeting? (*M. Com. Delhi, 2015*)
5. What is the meaning of an operating budget, financial budget and a master budget?
6. Explain the role of a sales forecast in budgeting. What is the difference between a sales forecast and a sales budget.
7. What is participative budgeting? How does it help in creating positive behaviour among the people in an organisation?
8. Discuss the differences between fixed and flexible budgeting. Why are flexible budgets considered superior to fixed budget?
9. How important is for the management of an organisation to know the behavioural dimensions of the budgeting process? Identify some behavioural implications of the budgeting.
(*M. Com. Delhi, 2005, 2008, 2012, 2014*)
10. What is budgetary slack? Is it good? Why or why not?
11. How does budgeting help management in the discharge of their functions?
12. What is a cash budget? How is it prepared?
13. How does budgeting serve as an instrument of control?
14. What are the advantages arising out of the budgetary system? What do you think are the essentials of an effective budgetary control system?
15. Discuss the objectives and limitations of budgeting.
16. Define budgeting and discuss the objectives of introducing a budgetary system in an organisation.
17. Explain the difference between a forecast and a budget. Give examples to illustrate the differences between:
    (*a*) Fixed budget
    (*b*) Flexible budget
    (*c*) Functional budget
18. What are functional budgets? Which functional budgets are most commonly used by management?
19. Define budgetary control and distinguish it from standard costing. Discuss the inter-relationship between budgetary control and the standard costing system.
20. Discuss briefly the procedure for the preparation of a sales budget.
21. Describe briefly the fundamental functions of business budgets. (*M. Com., Delhi, 2009*)

22. Explain the concept of a flexible budget. How is it prepared?
23. Point out the benefits that may be derived from budgetary control by a manufacturing concern.
24. What is zero-based budgeting (ZBB)? What are the steps in ZBB?
25. Discuss the advantages and disadvantages of Zero-Based Budgeting.
26. Explain Planning, Programming and Budgeting System (PPBS).
27. Enumerate the procedure of Planning, Programming and Budgeting System (PPBS).
28. What are the advantages of PPBS as compared to traditional system?
29. A student develops a spending plan for a year. In this budgeting. Why?
30. "The flexible budget is a poor bench mark. You should develop a budget and stay with it." Comment.
31. "Budgeted performance is a better criterion than past performance for judging managers". Do you agree? Explain.
32. "Production managers and marketing managers are like oil and water. They just do not mix. "How can a budget assist in reducing traditional battles between these two areas?
33. Explain behavioural dimensions of budgeting. *(M. Com., Delhi University, 2011)*
34. How does zero-based budgeting differ from traditional budgeting?
35. How are budgets used as both planning and control tools?
36. "Budgeting is an unnecessary burden on many managers. It takes time away from important day-to-day problems." Do you agree? Explain.
37. "The sales forecast is the corner stone for budgeting." Why?
38. Define the following:
    (*a*) Zero base budgeting
    (*b*) Activity-Based budgeting
    (*c*) Life cycle budgeting
    (*d*) Kaizen budgeting
39. Why should motivational considerations be a part of budget planning and utilization? List several ways to motivate employees with budgets.
40. How important are the behavioural aspects of a budgetary control system? Explain.
41. All budgets depends on the sales budget. Is this true? Explain.
42. Discuss the differences between static and flexible budgets. Why are flexible budgets superior to static budgets for performance reporting?
43. What is participative budgeting? Discuss some of its advantages.
44. A budget too easily achieved will lead to diminished performance. Do you agree? Explain.
45. Explain how an activity-based budget is prepared.
46. What are the main differences between functional and activity-based budgets?
47. Briefly describe the type of human behaviour problems that might arise if budget goals are set too tightly.
48. What behavioural problems are associated with setting a budget too losely?
49. How would management evaluate performance without a budget?

50. The Chief Executive Officer of Reliance Home Appliances Co. remarked to a Colleague, "I do not understand why other companies waste so much time in the budgeting process. I set our company goals and everyone strives to meet them. What is wrong with that approach?" Comment on the executive's remark.

51. Ragini Kamath, controller of Digital Data Systems Ltd., believes that effective budgeting greatly assists in meeting the goals and objectives of the organisation. She argues that the budget serves as a blueprint for the operating activities during each reporting period, making it an important control device. She believes that sound management evaluations can be based on the comparisons of performance and budgetary schedules and that employees respond more favourably when they participate in the budgetary process.

    Ashok, Finance Manager, agrees that budgeting is essential for overall organisational success, but he argues that human resources are too valuable to spend much time planning and preparing the budgetary process. He thinks that the roles people play in budgetary preparation are not important in the final analysis of a budget's effectiveness.

Required:

Contrast the participative versus imposed budgeting concepts and indicate how the ideas of Ragini and Ashok fit the two categories.

52. Praveen was having dinner with one of his friends at a restaurant in New Delhi. His friend, Rajnish, a local manager of a courier mail service told Praveen that he consistently overstated the amount of resources needed in his budget requests for his division. He also told Praveen that year after year he was able to obtain the budget requested. When Praveen asked him why he did this, Rajnish replied, "It is a dog-eat-dog world out there. If I am going to succeed and move up the ladder, I have got to perform well. Having those extra resources really helps".

Required:

Discuss Rajnish's point of view relating to budgeting. Is he justified in this approach. Explain.

53. The owner of a small clothing store says, "I run a small operation. I know my employees well. They are very loyal to me. I also know my business well. I know what to do to generate revenues and how to control costs. I don't need formal budgets." Do you agree with this statement? Why or why not?

54. "In large organizations, formal budgets are perhaps the only effective means for organization-wide communication." Comment on this statement.

55. Actual events rarely unfold exactly as expected, particularly in complex scenarios. Thus, budget assumptions are likely to be proven wrong as actual events unfold. What then is the value of a budget?

56. Firms use budgets as a benchmark for performance evaluation, especially in large organizations. Since close supervision may not be possible in such organizations, is this role of budgets simply a substitute for close-supervision? Comment.

57. "Budgets are only as good as the forecasts upon which they are based." In some industries, it is very difficult to forecast demand accurately, while in other industries demand conditions are relatively stable. Discuss the role of budgeting in these two settings.

58. What are the similarities and differences between the cash budget and the cash flow statement that we find in firms' financial reports?

59. Do you believe that budgets lead organization to place too much emphasis on financial performance and not enough emphasis on the qualitative and nonfinancial aspects of performance ? Why or why not?

60. Some experts argue that budgets have to be "loose" and "flexible" for companies that are in their growth phase. Other experts believe that good planning and control through well-formulated budgets can never hurt. Which line of reasoning do you agree with? Are these two arguments necessarily inconsistent?

61. Participative, or bottom-up,budgeting is a time-consuming process in large organizations. Yet, it is perhaps most beneficial to these companies. Discuss the advantages and disadvantages of participative budgeting in large organizations.

62. When would a top-down budgeting be preferable to bottom-up or participative budgeting?

63. A criticism of budget lapsing is that it forces decision makers to find ways to spend the money allocated to them in the budget, even when there is no real need. Do you agree with this criticism? Can you think of situations where budget lapsing would actually be beneficial to an organization?

SELF-ASSESSMENT QUESTIONS

A. Orion Corporation is preparing a cash budget for the six months beginning January 1, 2016. Shown below are the company's historical collection pattern and the budgeted credit sales for the period.

65 per cent collected in month of sale

20 per cent collected in the first month after sale

10 per cent collected in the second month after sale

4 per cent collected in the third month after sale

1 per cent uncollectible

	(₹)
January	1,60,000
February	1,85,000
March	1,90,000
April	1,70,000
May	2,00,000
June	1,80,000

The estimated total cash collections during April from accounts receivable would be

(*a*) ₹ 1,54,900

(*b*) ₹ 1,67,000

(*c*) ₹ 1,71,666

(*d*) ₹ 1,73,400

(*e*) ₹ 1,76,200

B. ABC Company, a small retail store, had the following results of operations for May 2016. The budget for June and July 2016 are also given.

	May (₹)	*June* (₹)	*July* (₹)
Sales	42,000	40,000	45,000
Cost of sales	21,000	20,000	22,500
Gross margin	21,000	20,000	22,500
Other cash expenses	20,000	20,000	20,000
Operating income	1,000	0	2,500

Sales are collected 80 per cent in the month of the sale and the balance in the month following the sale. The goods contained in cost of sales were purchased in the month prior to the month of sale, and vendor payment is in the month following the sale. All other cash expenses are paid in the month of the sale.

1. The amount of cash collected during the month of June 2016 will be
   (*a*) ₹ 32,000
   (*b*) ₹ 40,000
   (*c*) ₹ 40,400
   (*d*) ₹ 41,000
   (*e*) ₹ 41,600
2. Cash disbursements for ABC Company for the month of June 2016 will be
   (*a*) ₹ 20,000
   (*b*) ₹ 21,000
   (*c*) ₹ 40,000
   (*d*) ₹ 41,000
   (*e*) ₹ 42,500

C. Himalaya Furnishing Co. is a manufacturer of tables sold to schools, restaurants, hotels, and other institutions. The table tops are manufactured, but the table legs are purchased from an outside supplier. The Assembly Department takes a manufactured table top and attaches the four purchased table legs. It takes 20 minutes of labour to assemble a table. The company follows a policy of producing enough tables to insure that 40 per cent of next month's sales are in the finished goods inventory. The Co. also purchases sufficient raw materials to insure that raw materials inventory is 60 per cent of the following month's scheduled production. Himalaya's sales budget in units for the next quarter is as follows.

July	2,300
August	2,500
September	2,100

Himalaya's ending inventories in units for June 30, 2016 are

Finished goods	1,900
Raw materials (legs)	4,000

1. The number of tables to be produced during August 2016 is
   (a) 1,400 tables
   (b) 2,340 tables
   (c) 1,440 tables
   (d) 1,600 tables
   (e) 2,380 tables
2. Disregarding your response to Item 1, assume the required production for August and September is 1,600 and 1,800 units, respectively, and the July 31, 2016, raw materials inventory is 4,200 units. The number of table legs to be purchased in August is
   (a) 6,520 legs
   (b) 9,400 legs
   (c) 5,080 legs
   (d) 6,400 legs
   (e) 6,840 legs
3. Assume that Himalaya Co. will produce 1,800 units in the month of September 2016. How many employees will be required for the Assembly Department?
   (Fractional employees are acceptable since employees can be hired on a part-time basis. Assume a 40-hour week and a 4-week month.)
   (a) 15 employees
   (b) 3.75 employees
   (c) 60 employees
   (d) 600 employees
   (e) 1.5 employees

(CMA, USA, Adapted with permission)

Answers to Self-assessment Questions

A. (d)

B. 1. (c) 2. (d)

C. 1. (b) 2. (a) 3. (b)

MULTIPLE CHOICE QUESTIONS

Select the correct answer for the following multiple choice questions:

1. Information to prepare a flexible budget includes
   (a) Total fixed costs, total variable costs
   (b) Total fixed costs, total variable costs and capacity base
   (c) Unit fixed costs and unit variable costs
   (d) Total fixed costs, variable costs per unit, several levels of activity
2. The scarce factor of production is known as
   (a) Key factor
   (b) Limiting factor
   (c) Critical factor
   (d) All of the above

3. Which of the following is a budget designated to furnish budgeted costs for any level of activity actually attained:
   (*a*) Fixed budget
   (*b*) Flexible budget
   (*c*) Master budget
   (*d*) Production budget
4. Flexible budgets are useful for
   (*a*) Planning purposes only
   (*b*) Planning, performance evaluation and feedback control
   (*c*) Control of performance only
   (*d*) Nothing at all
5. The budget that summarise future plans for acquisition of plant facilities and equipment is the:
   (*a*) Cash budget
   (*b*) Sales budget
   (*c*) Capital expenditure budget
   (*d*) None of the above
6. A report comparing actual results with the budget figures is called a
   (*a*) Budget report
   (*b*) Budget performance report
   (*c*) Flexible budget report
   (*d*) None of the above
7. The system that "builds in" the effect of fluctuations in volume of activity into the various budgets is termed:
   (*a*) Budget performance reporting
   (*b*) Continuous budgeting
   (*c*) Flexible budgeting
   (*d*) None of the above
8. A fixed budget
   (*a*) Drops the current month or quarter and adds a future month or a future quarter as the current month or quarter is completed.
   (*b*) Presents a statement of expectations for a period of time but does not present a firm commitment.
   (*c*) Presents the plan for only one level of activity and does not adjust to change in the level of activity.
   (*d*) Divides the activities of individual responsibility centres.
9. The Chief Executive Officer of a company believes that budgetary controls should not be used because they stifle entrepreneurship and threaten the pervading atmosphere of the company. Your position is
   (*a*) Total agreement because budgets are known to destroy initiative and motivation.
   (*b*) Total disagreement because budgets are the only tool that can give effective guidance to a company in meeting objectives.

(c) Total agreement because all budgets are known to be used by top management to manipulate people as well as results.

(d) Neither agreement nor disagreement because the procedures used to create and operate a budget can cause the budget stifle initiative and create threatening environment in the company.

10. When an organisation prepares a forecast, it

(a) Present a statement of expectations for a period of time but does not present a firm commitment.

(b) Consolidates the plans of the separate requests into one overall plan.

(c) Presents the plan for a range of activity so that the plan can be adjusted for changes in activity levels.

(d) Classifies budget requests by activity and estimates the benefits arising from each activity.

(e) Divides the activities of individual responsibility centres into a series of packages that are ranked ordinarily.

11. A flexible budget

(a) Classifies budget requests by activity and estimates the benefits arising from each activity.

(b) Presents a statement of expectations for a period of time but does not present a firm commitment.

(c) Presents the plan for only one level of activity and does not adjust to changes in the level of activity.

(d) Presents the plan for a range of activity so the plan can be adjusted for changes in activity levels.

(e) Divides the activities of individual responsibility centres into a series of package that are ranked ordinarily.

12. The primary difference between a fixed budget and a variable (flexible) budget is that a fixed budget

(a) Includes only fixed costs, while a variable budget includes only variable costs.

(b) Is concerned only with future acquisitions of fixed assets, while a variable budget is concerned with expenses which vary with sales.

(c) Cannot be changed after the period begins, while a variable budget can be changed after the period begins.

(d) Is a plan for a single level of sales (or other measure of activity), while a variable budget consists of several plans, one for each of several levels of sales (or other measure of activity).

13. The purpose of a flexible budget is to

(a) Allow management some latitude in meeting goals

(b) Eliminate cyclical fluctuations in production reports by ignoring variable costs

(c) Compare actual and budgeted results at virtually any level of production

(d) Reduce the total time in preparing the annual budget

14. Flexible budgeting is a reporting system wherein the

(a) Budget standards may be adjusted at will

(b) Planned level of activity is adjusted to the actual level of activity before the budget comparison report is prepared.

(*c*) Reporting dates vary according to the levels of activity reported upon
(*d*) Statements included in the budget report vary from period to period

15. When using a flexible budget what will occur to fixed costs (on a per unit basis) as production increases within the relevant range?
(*a*) Fixed costs per unit will decrease
(*b*) Fixed costs per unit will remain unchanged
(*c*) Fixed costs per unit will increase
(*d*) Fixed costs are not considered in flexible budgeting

16. When production levels are expected to decline within a relevant range, and a flexible budget is used, what effects would be anticipated with respect to each of the following?

	Fixed costs per unit	***Variable costs per unit***
(*a*)	Increase	Increase
(*b*)	Increase	No change
(*c*)	No change	No change
(*d*)	No change	Increase

17. A flexible budget is appropriate for a

	Direct labour budget	***Marketing budget***
(*a*)	No	No
(*b*)	No	Yes
(*c*)	Yes	No
(*d*)	Yes	Yes

18. A flexible budget is appropriate for a (an)

	Administrative budget	***Direct material budget***
(*a*)	Yes	No
(*b*)	Yes	Yes
(*c*)	No	Yes
(*d*)	No	No

19. When a flexible budget is used, a decrease in production levels within a relevant range would
(*a*) Decrease variable cost per unit
(*b*) Decrease total costs
(*c*) Increase total fixed costs
(*d*) Increase variable cost per unit

20. The flexible budget for a producing department may include

	Direct labour	***Factory overhead***
(*a*)	No	Yes
(*b*)	No	No
(*c*)	Yes	No
(*d*)	Yes	Yes

21. A flexible budget is
    (*a*) Not appropriate when costs and expenses are affected by fluctuations in volume limits.
    (*b*) Appropriate for any relevant level of activity
    (*c*) Appropriate for control of factory overhead but not for control of direct materials and direct labour.
    (*d*) Appropriate for control of direct materials and direct labour but not for control of factory overhead.
22. The two most appropriate factors for budgeting manufacturing overhead expenses would be
    (*a*) Management judgement and sales
    (*b*) Sales volume and production volume
    (*c*) Machine-hours and production volume
    (*d*) Management judgement and contribution margin
    (*e*) Management judgement and production volume
23. Where goods are to be sold on which customers are given three months' credit, goods sold on credit in June would be included in the cash budget for:
    (*a*) June (*b*) August
    (*c*) September (*d*) October
24. New equipment is expected to be purchased by cheque in June of the forthcoming period, details of which are as follows:

    Cost : ₹ 16,000

    Life : five years

    Scrap value at the end of its life: ₹ 4,000

    Depreciation using the straight-line basis (*i.e.*, a percentage of cost per year/month)

    The amount of depreciation which will be included in the cash budget for the month of June will be:
    (*a*) Nil (*b*) 200
    (*c*) 266 (*d*) 12,000
    (*e*) 16,000
25. Which of the following statements regarding budgets is false?
    (*a*) They are formal documents that quantify a company's plans
    (*b*) They enhance communication and coordination
    (*c*) They are useful in planning but not in control
    (*d*) They provide a basis for evaluating performance
26. Which of the following is false ?
    (*a*) Including some non-monetary measures of performance in a budget is not likely to be advantageous.
    (*b*) If a key aspect of a company's success is high quality, defect free products, it may be useful to budget the number of defects and the number of customer complaints at levels consistent with high quality.
    (*c*) Actual number of defects and complaints can be compared with the budgeted quantity to evaluate performance.
    (*d*) If a company is experiencing problems with employee absenteeism, it may be useful to budget an acceptable number of days missed and compare actual days missed with the target.

27. The basic difference between a master budget and a flexible budget is that a master budget is

    (*a*) Only used before and during the budget period and a flexible budget is only used after the budget period.

    (*b*) For an entire production facility and a flexible budget is applicable to single departments only.

    (*c*) Based on one specific level of production and a flexible budget can be prepared for any production level within a relevant range.

    (*d*) Based on a fixed standard and a flexible budget allows management latitude in meeting goals.

28. The use of standard costs in the budgeting process signifies that an organization has most likely implemented a

    (*a*) Flexible budget
    (*b*) Capital budget
    (*c*) Zero-base budget
    (*d*) Static budget
    (*e*) Strategic budget

29. An advantage of incremental budgeting when compared to zero-based budgeting is that incremental budgeting

    (*a*) Encourages adopting new projects quickly
    (*b*) Accepts the existing base as being satisfactory
    (*c*) Eliminates functions and duties that have outlived their usefulness
    (*d*) Makes it easy to discontinue outdated functions
    (*e*) Eliminates the need to periodically review all functions to obtain optimum utilization of resources

30. Which one of the following items would have to be included for a company preparing a schedule of cash receipts and disbursements for the calendar year 2016?

    (*a*) The annual depreciation for 2016
    (*b*) A purchase order issued in December 2015 for items to be delivered in February 2016
    (*c*) Dividends declared in November 2016 to be paid in January 2017 to shareholders of record as of December 2016
    (*d*) The amount of uncollectible customer accounts for 2016
    (*e*) Borrowing funds from a bank on a note payable taken out in June 2016 and agreeing to pay the principal and interest in June 2017.

31. Individual budget schedules are prepared to develop an annual comprehensive or master budget. The budget schedule that would provide the necessary input data for the Direct Labour Budget would be the

    (*a*) Sales forecast
    (*b*) Raw materials purchases budget
    (*c*) Schedule of cash receipts and disbursements
    (*d*) Schedule of manufacturing overhead
    (*e*) Production budget

32. Which one of the following statements regarding the difference between a flexible budget and a static budget is correct?
    (*a*) A flexible budget primarily is prepared for planning purposes while a static budget is prepared for performance evaluation
    (*b*) A flexible budget provides cost allowances for different levels of activity whereas a static budget provides costs for one level of activity
    (*c*) A flexible budget includes only variable costs whereas a static budget includes only fixed costs
    (*d*) A flexible budget is established by operating management while a static budget is determined by top management
    (*e*) Variances will always be larger with a flexible budget than with a static budget
33. The process of creating a formal plan and translating goals into a quantitative format is
    (*a*) Process costing (*b*) Activity-based costing
    (*c*) Job order costing (*d*) Budgeting
    (*e*) Variance analysis
34. When budgets are used for performance evaluation and to set limits on spending, the process will often result in departments adding something "extra" to insure the budgets will be met. This "extra" is
    (*a*) Management by objectives (*b*) Strategic planning
    (*c*) Continuous budgeting (*d*) Tactical planning
    (*e*) Budgetary slack
35. The financial budget process includes
    (*a*) The cash budget (*b*) The capital budget
    (*c*) The budgeted statement of cash flows (*d*) The budgeted balance sheet
    (*e*) All of the above
36. The master budget process usually begins with the
    (*a*) Production budget (*b*) Operating budget
    (*c*) Financial budget (*d*) Capital budget
    (*e*) Sales budget
37. The production budget process usually begins with the
    (*a*) Direct labour budget (*b*) Direct materials budget
    (*c*) Manufacturing overhead budget (*d*) Sales budget
    (*e*) Ending inventory budget
38. A continuous (rolling) budget
    (*a*) Presents the plan for only one level of activity and does not adjust to changes in the level of activity
    (*b*) Presents the plan for a range of activity so the plan can be adjusted for changes in activity
    (*c*) Is a plan that is revised monthly or quarterly, dropping one period and adding another
    (*d*) Is one of the budgets that is part of a long-range strategic plan, unchanged unless the strategy of the company changes
    (*e*) Works best for a company that can reliably forecast its sales revenue and expenses.

39. A method of budgeting where the cost of each programme must be justified, starting with the one most vital to the company is

(*a*) Flexible budgeting (*b*) Zero-based budgeting
(*c*) Continuous budgeting (*d*) Probabilistic budgeting
(*e*) Incremental budgeting

40. Which one of the following reasons is not a significant reason for planning in an organization?

(*a*) Promoting coordination among operating units
(*b*) Forcing managers to consider expected future trends and conditions
(*c*) Developing a basis for controlling operations
(*d*) Progressing toward the objectives of the organisation
(*e*) Monitoring profitable operations

41. The budgeting process should be one that motivates managers and employees to work toward organisational goals. Which one of the following is least likely to motivate managers?

(*a*) Participation by subordinates in the budgetary process
(*b*) Having top management set budget levels
(*c*) Use of management by exception
(*d*) Holding subordinates accountable for the items they control
(*e*) Setting budget targets at attainable levels

42. Which one of the following items should be done first when developing a comprehensive budget for a manufacturing company?

(*a*) Determination of the advertising budget
(*b*) Development of a sales budget
(*c*) Development of the capital budget
(*d*) Determination of equipment acquisitions
(*e*) Preparation of a proforma income statement

43. Flexible budgets

(*a*) Provide for external factors affecting company profitability
(*b*) Are used to evaluate capacity utilization
(*c*) Are budgets that project costs based on anticipated future improvements
(*d*) Accommodate changes in activity levels
(*e*) Accommodate changes in the inflation rate

44. Which one of the following items is the last schedule to be prepared in the normal budget preparation process?

(*a*) Cash budget (*b*) Cost of goods sold budget
(*c*) Direct labour budget (*d*) Manufacturing overhead budget
(*e*) Selling expense budget

45. Comparing actual results with a budget based on achieved volume is possible with the use of a

(*a*) Step budget (*b*) Monthly budget
(*c*) Master budget (*d*) Rolling budget
(*e*) flexible budget

46. The process of developing plans for a company's expected operations and controlling the operations to help carry out those plans is known as
    (*a*) Preparing a period budget
    (*b*) Preparing a master budget
    (*c*) Budgetary control
    (*d*) Preparing a fixed budget
    (*e*) Participative budgeting
47. The cash receipts budget includes
    (*a*) Funded depreciation
    (*b*) Operating supplies
    (*c*) Extinguishment of debt
    (*d*) Interest expense
    (*e*) Loan proceeds
48. The cash budget must be prepared before you can complete the
    (*a*) Capital expenditure budget
    (*b*) Sales budget
    (*c*) Forecasted balance sheet
    (*d*) Production budget
    (*e*) Forecasted income statement
49. The budgeting tool or process where estimates of revenues and expenses are prepared for each product beginning with the product's research and development phase and traced through to its customer support phase is a (n)
    (*a*) Master budget
    (*b*) Activity-based budget
    (*c*) Zero-based budget
    (*d*) Life-cycle budget
    (*e*) Incremental budget
50. In planning and controlling capital expenditures, the most logical sequence is to begin with
    (*a*) Analyzing capital addition proposals
    (*b*) Making capital expenditure decisions
    (*c*) Analyzing and evaluating all promising alternatives
    (*d*) Identifying capital addition projects and other capital needs
    (*e*) Developing capital budgets
51. The first step in the sales planning process is to
    (*a*) Assemble all the data that are relevant in developing a comprehensive sales plan
    (*b*) Develop management guidelines specific to sales planning, including the sales planning process and planning responsibilities
    (*c*) Prepare a sales forecast consistent with specified forecasting guidelines, including assumptions
    (*d*) Apply management evaluation and judgment to develop a comprehensive sales plan
    (*e*) Secure managerial commitment to attain the goals specified in the comprehensive sales plan
52. Which one of the following is the best characteristic concerning the capital budget? The capital budget is a (n)
    (*a*) Plan to insure that there are sufficient funds available for the operating needs of the company
    (*b*) Exercise that sets the long-range goals of the company including the consideration of external influences caused by others in the market
    (*c*) Plan that results in the cash requirements during the operating cycle
    (*d*) Plan that coordinates and communicates a company's plan for the coming year to all departments and divisions
    (*e*) Plan that assesses the long-term needs of the company for plant and equipment purchases

53. There are various budgets within the master budget cycle. One of the these budgets is the production budget. Which one of the following **best** describes the production budget?
    (*a*) It summarizes all discretionary costs
    (*b*) It includes required direct labour hours
    (*c*) It includes required material purchases
    (*d*) It aggregates the monetary details of the operating budget
    (*e*) It is calculated from the desired ending inventory and the sales forecast
54. A difference between standard costs used for cost control and budgeted costs
    (*a*) Can exist because standard costs must be determined after the budget is completed
    (*b*) Can exist because standard costs represent what costs should be, whereas budgeted costs represent expected actual costs
    (*c*) Can exist because budgeted costs are historical costs, whereas standard costs are based on engineering studies
    (*d*) Cannot exist because they should be the same amounts
55. A flexible budget is appropriate for
    (*a*) Control of direct materials and direct labour but not selling and administrative expenses.
    (*b*) Any level of activity
    (*c*) Control of direct labour and direct materials but not fixed factory overhead
    (*d*) Control of selling and administrative expenses but not factory overhead
56. A systemized approach known as Zero-base budgeting (ZBB)
    (*a*) Presents planned activities for a period of time but does not present a firm commitment
    (*b*) Divides the activities of individual responsibility centres into a series of packages that are prioritized
    (*c*) Classifies the budget by the prior year's activity and estimates the benefits arising from each activity
    (*d*) Commences with the current level of spending
57. When preparing a performance report for a cost centre using flexible budgeting techniques, the planned cost column should be based on the
    (*a*) Budgeted amount in the original budget prepared before the beginning of the year
    (*b*) Actual amount for the same period in the preceding year
    (*c*) Budget adjusted to the actual level of activity for the period being reported
    (*d*) Budget adjusted to the planned level of activity for the period being reported
58. The difference between the actual amounts and the flexible budget amounts for the actual output achieved is the
    (*a*) Production volume variance
    (*b*) Flexible budget variance
    (*c*) Sales volume variance
    (*d*) Standard cost variance
59. Which one of the following budgeting methodologies would be most appropriate for a firm facing a significant level of uncertainty in unit sales volumes for next year?
    (*a*) Top-down budgeting
    (*b*) Life-cycle budgeting
    (*c*) Static budgeting
    (*d*) Flexible budgeting

60. Proforma financial statements are part of the budgeting process. Normally, the last proforma statement prepared is the
    (*a*) Income statement
    (*b*) Statement of cost of goods sold
    (*c*) Statement of cash flows
    (*d*) Statement of manufacturing costs
61. A Manufacturing company currently uses the company budget as a planning tool only. Management has decided to use budgets for control purposes also. To implement this change, the management accountant must
    (*a*) Organize a budget committee and appoint a budget director
    (*b*) Report daily to operating management all deviations from plan
    (*c*) Synchronize the budgeting and accounting system with the organizational structure
    (*d*) Develop forecasting procedures
62. Which one of the following organizational policies is most likely to result in undesirable managerial behavior?
    (*a*) Joe Walk, the chief executive officer of Eagle Rock Brewery, wrote a memorandum to his executives stating, "Operating plans are contracts, and they should be met without fail"
    (*b*) The budgeting process at Madsen Manufacturing starts with operating managers providing goals for their respective departments
    (*c*) Fullbright Lighting holds quarterly meetings of departmental managers to consider possible changes in the budgeted targets due to changing conditions
    (*d*) At Fargo Transportation, managers are expected to provide explanations for variances from the budget in their departments
63. Various budgets are included in the master budget cycle. One of these budgets is the production budget. Which one of the following best describes the production budget?
    (*a*) It includes required direct labour hours
    (*b*) It includes required material purchases
    (*c*) It aggregates the monetary details of the operating budget
    (*d*) It is calculated from the desired ending inventory and the sales forecast
64. A budget manual, which enhances the operation of a budget system, is most likely to include
    (*a*) A chart of accounts
    (*b*) Distribution instructions for budget schedules
    (*c*) Documentation of the accounting system software
    (*d*) Company policies regarding the authorization of transactions
65. The goals and objectives upon which an annual profit plan is most effectively based are
    (*a*) Financial measures such as net income, return on investment, and earnings per share
    (*b*) Quantitative measures such as growth in unit sales, number of employees, and manufacturing capacity
    (*c*) Qualitative measures of organizational activity such as product innovation leadership, product quality levels, and product safety
    (*d*) A combination of financial, quantitative, and qualitative measures

66. The use of budgetary slack does not allow the preparer to
    (*a*) Be flexible under unexpected circumstances
    (*b*) Increase the probability of achieving budgeted performance
    (*c*) Use the budget to control subordinate performance
    (*d*) Blend personal goals with organisational goals
67. From the perspective of corporate management, the use of budgetary slack
    (*a*) Increases the effectiveness of the corporate planning process
    (*b*) Increases the ability to identify potential budget weaknesses
    (*c*) Encourages the use of effective corrective actions
    (*d*) Increases the likelihood of inefficient resource allocation
68. A planning calendar in budgeting is the
    (*a*) Calender period covered by the budget
    (*b*) Schedule of activities for the development and adoption of the budget
    (*c*) Sales forecast by months in the annual budget period
    (*d*) Schedule of dates at which goals are to be met
69. Which one of the following is not considered to be a benefit of participative budgeting?
    (*a*) Individuals at all organisational levels are recognised as being part of the team; this results in greater support of the organisation
    (*b*) The budget estimates are prepared by those in direct contact with various activities.
    (*c*) Managers are held responsible for reaching their goals, and they can not shift their responsibility by blaming the unrealistic goals demanded by the budget
    (*d*) When managers set the final targets for the budget, top management need not be concerned with the overall profitability of current operations
70. The budget that describes the long-term position, goals, and objectives of an entity within its environment is the
    (*a*) Capital budget
    (*b*) Operating budget
    (*c*) Cash management budget
    (*d*) Strategic budget
71. Budgetary slack can best be described as
    (*a*) The elimination of certain expenses to enhance budgeted income
    (*b*) The planned overestimation of budgeted expenses
    (*c*) A plug number used to achieve a preset level of operating income
    (*d*) The planned underestimation of budgeted expenses

(CMA, USA, Adapted with permission)

Answer to Multiple Choice Questions

1. (*d*)	2. (*a*)	3. (*b*)	4. (*b*)	5. (*c*)
6. (*b*)	7. (*c*)	8. (*c*)	9. (*b*)	10. (*a*)
11. (*d*)	12. (*d*)	13. (*c*)	14. (*b*)	15. (*a*)
16. (*b*)	17. (*c*)	18. (*c*)	19. (*b*)	20. (*d*)
21. (*b*)	22. (*c*)	23. (*c*)	24. (*a*)	25. (*c*)
26. (*a*)	27. (*c*)	28. (*a*)	29. (*b*)	30. (*e*)
31. (*e*)	32. (*b*)	33. (*d*)	34. (*e*)	35. (*e*)

36. (*e*)	37. (*d*)	38. (*c*)	39. (*b*)	40. (*e*)
41. (*b*)	42. (*b*)	43. (*d*)	44. (*a*)	45. (*e*)
46. (*c*)	47. (*e*)	48. (*c*)	49. (*d*)	50. (*d*)
51. (*b*)	52. (*e*)	53. (*e*)	54. (*b*)	55. (*c*)
56. (*b*)	57. (*c*)	58. (*b*)	59. (*d*)	60. (*c*)
61. (*c*)	62. (*a*)	63. (*d*)	64. (*b*)	65. (*d*)
66. (*c*)	67. (*d*)	68. (*b*)	69. (*d*)	70. (*d*)
71. (*b*)				

PROBLEMS

1. **Prepare a flexible budget for overheads on the basis of data given below. Ascertain the overhead rates at 50, 60 and 70 per cent capacity.**

	At 50% *Capacity*	At 60% *Capacity*	At 70% *Capacity*
Variable Overheads:	₹	₹	₹
Indirect material		6,000	
Indirect labour		18,000	
Semi-variable overheads:			
Electricity (40% fixed, 60% variable)		30,000	
Repairs and maintenance (80% fixed, 20% variable)		3,000	
Fixed Overheads:			
Depreciation		16,500	
Insurance		4,500	
Salaries		15,000	
Total overheads		93,000	

Estimated direct labour hours— 1,860

Answer:

Overheads rates

Capacity level 50% = ₹ 55

Capacity level 60% = ₹ 50

Capacity level 70% = ₹ 46.

2. **The profitability statement of Gourmat Co. Ltd. has been summarised as follows:**

	₹	₹
Sales		15,00,000
Direct Materials	4,50,000	
Direct Wages	3,00,000	
Variable Overheads	1,20,000	
Fixed Overheads	4,40,000	13,10,000
Profit		1,90,000

The budgeted capacity of the company is ₹ 20,00,000 but the key factor is sales demand. It is proposed that in order to utilise the existing capacity the selling price of this only product manufactured by the company should be reduced by 5%.

You are required to prepare a forecast statement which should show the effect of the proposed reduction in selling price and included any changes in costs expected during the coming year. The following additional information is given:

(*i*) Sales forecast ₹ 19,00,000 (after reduction)
(*ii*) Direct Materials price are expected to increases by 2%
(*iii*) Direct wages rates are expected to increases by 5% per unit
(*iv*) Variable overheads are expected to increases by 5% per unit
(*v*) Fixed overheads will increase by ₹ 20,000

Answer: Profit ₹ 2,40,000.

3. The budgeted cost of a factory specialising in the production of a single product at the optimum capacity of 6,400 units per annum amounts ₹ 1,76,048 as detailed below:

Fixed cost		₹ 20,688
Variable cost:		
Power	₹ 1,440	
Repairs etc.	₹ 1,700	
Miscellaneous	₹ 540	
Direct material	₹ 49,280	
Direct labour	₹ 1,02,400	1,55,360
		1,76,048

Having regard to possible impact on sales turnover by market trends the company decided to have a flexible budget with a production target of 3,200 and 4,800 units (the actual quantity proposed to be produced being left to a later date before commencement of the budget period). Prepare a flexible budget for production levels at 50% and 75% capacity.

Assume selling price per unit is maintained at ₹ 40 as at present, indicate the effect on net profit.

Administration, selling and distribution expenses continue at ₹ 3,600.

Answer: Net Profit (*a*) 100%, ₹ 75,352
(*b*) 75% ₹ 51,192
(*c*) 50% ₹ 26,032.

4. A company produces and sells four types of dolls for children. It also produces and sells a set of dress kit for the dolls.

The company has worked out the following estimates for the next year:

Doll	Estimated Demand	Standard Material Cost (₹)	Standard Labour Cost (₹)	Estimated Sales Price Per Unit (₹)
A	50,000	20	15	60
B	40,000	25	15	80

C	35,000	32	18	100
D	30,000	50	20	120
Dress Kit	2,00,000	15	5	50

To encourage the sale of dress kits, a discount of 20% in its price is offered if it were to be purchased along with the doll. It is expected that all the customer,~ buying dolls will also buy the dress kit.

The company's factory has effective capacity of 2,00,000 labour hours per annum on a single-shift basis and it produces all the products on that basis. The labour hour rate is ₹ 15. Overtime of labour has to be paid at double the normal rate.

Variable cost works out to 40% of direct labour cost. Fixed costs are ₹ 30 lakhs per annum. There will be no inventory at the end of the year.

You are to draw a conservative estimate of the year's profitability.

Answer: Profit ₹ 55,38,000.

5. Draw a material procurement budget (quantitative) from the following informations:

Estimated sales of a product 40,000 units. Each unit of the product requires 3 units of material A and 5 units of material B.

Estimated opening balances at the commencement of the next year:

Finished product	5,000	units
Material A	12,000	units
Material B	20,000	units
Material on order:		
Material A	7,000	units
Material B	11,000	units

The desirable closing balances at the end of the next year:

Finished product	7,000	units
Material A	15,000	units
Material B	25,000	units
Material on order:		
Material A	8,000	units
Material B	10,000	units

Answer: Units to be procured A 1,30,000; B 2,14,000.

6. From the following information relating to 2016 and conditions expected to prevail in 2017, prepare a budget for 2017.

State the assumptions you have made.

2016 Actuals

	₹	
Sales	1,00,00,000	(40,000 units)
Raw materials	53,00,000	
Wages	11,00,000	
Variable overheads	16,00,000	
Fixed overheads	10,00,000	

2017 Prospects

Sales		1,50,00,000	(60,000 units)
Raw materials	5%	Price increase	
Wages	10%	Increase in wage rate	
Additional plant	5%	Increase in productivity	
		One lathe, ₹ 25,00,000	
		One drill, ₹ 12,00,000	

Answer: Budget for 2017 : ₹ 11,53,900.

7. Prepare a production budget for each month and a summarised production cost budget for the six-month period ending 31st December, 2016 from the following data of product X.

   (*i*) The units to be sold for different months are as follows:

July 2016	1,100
August	1,100
September	1,700
October	1,900
November	2,500
December	2,300
January 2017	2,000

   (*ii*) There will be no work-in-progress at the end of any month.

   (*iii*) Finished units equal to half the sales for the next month will be in stock at the end of each month (including June 2016).

   (*iv*) Budgeted production and production cost for the year ending 31st December, 2016 are as follows:

Production (units)	22,000
Direct material per unit	₹ 10.00
Direct wages per unit	₹ 4.00
Total factory overhead apportioned to product	88,000

   Answer: Total production cost ₹ 1,98,900.

8. The cost of an article at a capacity level of 10,000 units is given under A below. For a variation in capacity above or below this level, the individual expenses vary as indicated in B below:

	A (₹)	***B***	
Material cost	5,00,000	100%	varying
Labour cost	3,00,000	100%	varying
Power	30,000	80%	"
Repairs and maintenance	35,000	80%	"
Stores	20,000	80%	"
Inspection	8,000	25%	"
Depreciation	1,00,000	100%	"
Administrative overhead	36,000	25%	"
Selling overhead	45,000	50%	
Total	10,74,000		
Cost per unit	107.4		

Find out the unit cost of the product under each individual expense at production levels of 8,000 units and 12,000 units.

Answer: Cost per unit ₹ 109.1, ₹ 106.26.

9. The expenses budgeted for the production of 10,000 units in a factory are as under:

	Per unit (₹)		Per unit (₹)
Materials	700	Variable expense (direct)	50
Labour	250	Selling expenses (10% fixed)	130
Variable overheads	200	Distribution expenses (fixed)	70
Fixed overheads (₹ 10,00,000)	100	Administrative expenses	50
			1550

Prepare a budget for production of:

(*i*) 8,000 units

(*ii*) 6,000 units

Administration overheads are fixed for all levels.

10. A company is manufacturing two products X and Y. A forecast about the number of units to be sold in the first seven months is given below:

Month	***Product X***	***Product Y***
January	10,000	28,000
February	12,000	28,000
March	16,000	24,000
April	20,000	20,000
May	24,000	26,000
June	24,000	16,000
July	20,000	18,000

It is anticipated that:

(*i*) There will be no work-in-progress at the end of any month.

(*ii*) Finished units equal to half the sales for the next month will be in stock at the end of each month (including December of previous year).

Budgeted production and production costs for the year ending 31st December are as follows:

	Product X	***Product Y***
Production (Units)	2,20,000	2,40,000
Direct materials per unit	12.5	19
Direct wages per unit (₹)	4.5	7
Total factory overheads to each type of product (₹)	66,000	96,000

Prepare for six months ending 30th June, production budget and a summarised cost of production budget.

Answer: Production Budget total = 2,38,000 units; Total cost of production = ₹ 1,16,00,000.

11. Rokar Corporation is a manufacturer of tables sold to schools, restaurants, hotels, and other institutions. The table tops are manufactured by Rokar, but the table legs are purchased from an outside supplier. The Assembly Department takes a manufactured table top and attaches the four purchased table legs. It takes 20 minutes of labour to assemble a table. The company follows a policy of producing enough table to ensure that 40 per cent of next month's sales are in the finished goods inventory. Rokar also purchases sufficient materials to ensure that materials inventory is 60 per cent of the following month's scheduled production. Rokar's sales budget in units for the next quarter is as follows:

July	2,300
August	2,500
September	2,100

Rokar's ending inventories in units for June 30, 2016, are as follows:

Finished goods	1,900
Materials (legs)	4,000

Required:

1. Calculate the number of tables to be produced during August 2016.
2. Disregarding your response to Requirement 1, assume the required production units for August and September are 1,600 and 1,800, respectively, and the July 31, 2016, materials inventory is 4,200 units. Compute the number of table legs to be purchased in August.
3. Assume that Rokar Corporation will produce 1,800 units in September 2016. How many employees will be required for the Assembly Department in September? (Fractional employees are acceptable since employees can be hired on a part-time basis. Assume a 40-hour week and a 4-week month.) *(CMA USA adapted)*

Answer: 1. 2340 tables 2. 6520 3. No. of employees 3.75

12. Historically, Assam Wood Products has had no significant bad debt experience with its customers. Cash sales have accounted for 10 per cent of total sales, and payments for credit sales have been received as follows:

40 per cent of credit sales in the month of the sale.

30 per cent of credit sales in the first subsequent month.

25 per cent of credit sales in the second subsequent month.

5 per cent of credit sales in the third subsequent month.

The forecast for both cash and credit sales is as follows:

January	₹ 95,000
February	65,000
March	70,000
April	80,000
May	85,000

Required:

1. What is the forecasted cash inflow for Assam Wood Produce for May?
2. Due to deteriorating economic conditions. Assam Wood Products has now decided that its cash forecast should include a bad debt adjustment of 2 per cent of credit sales, beginning with sales for the month of April. Because of this policy change, what will happen to the total expected cash inflow related to sales made in April?

Answer: 1. ₹ 70,875 2. Decrease in cash from credit sales ₹ 1440.

13. Prepare a cash budget in respect of 6 months from July to December from the information given in the table as under:

Month	Credit Sales '000 ₹	Material '000 ₹	Wages '000 ₹	Overheads: Production '000 ₹	Overheads: Administration ₹	Overheads: Selling ₹	Overheads: Distribution ₹	Overheads: Research and Development ₹
April	100	40	10.0	4.4	3,000	1,600	800	1,000
May	120	60	11.2	4.8	2,900	1,700	900	1,000
June	80	40	8.0	5.6	3,000	1,500	700	1,200
July	100	60	8.0	4.6	2,900	1,400	900	1,200
August	120	70	10.0	5.6	3,000	1,900	1,100	1,200
September	140	80	10.0	5.4	3,000	2,000	1,200	1,400
October	160	90	10.0	5.8	3,100	2,250	1,250	1,600
November	180	100	11.0	6.0	3,100	2,150	1,250	1,500
December	200	110	11.6	6.4	2,200	2,300	1,500	1,600

Cash balance on July 1 was expected to be ₹ 1,50,000.

Expected Capital Expenditure:

Plant and Machinery to be installed in August at a cost of ₹ 40,000 will be payable on September 1. Extension to Research and Development Department amounting to ₹ 10,000 will be completed on August 1, payable ₹ 2,000 per month from completion date. Under a hire-purchase agreement ₹ 4,000 is to be paid each month.

Cash sales of ₹ 2,000 per month are expected. No commission is payable.

A sales commission of 5 per cent on (credit) sales is to be paid within the month following the sales.

Period of credit allowed by suppliers	3 months
Period of credit allowed to customers	2 months
Delay in payment of overheads	1 month
Delay in payment of wages	1 month

Income-tax of ₹ 1,00,000 is due to be paid October 1. Preference share dividend of 10 per cent on ₹ 2,00,000 is to be paid on November 1.

Ten per cent calls on ordinary share capital of ₹ 4,00,000 is due on July 1 and September 1.

Dividend from investments amounting to ₹ 30,000 expected on November 1.

Answer: Balance July ₹ 2,44,000; Aug. ₹ 2,36,000; September ₹ 2,63,000; October ₹ 1,89,000; November ₹ 2,33,000; Dec. ₹ 2,75,000.

14. A newly started company wishes to prepare cash budget from January. Prepare a cash budget for the first six months from the following estimated revenues and expenses:

Months	Total sales	Materials	Wages	Production	₹ Selling & distribution
January	20,00,000	20,00,000	4,00,000	3,20,000	80,000
February	22,00,000	14,00,000	4,40,000	3,30,000	90,000
March	24,00,000	14,00,000	4,60,000	3,30,000	80,000
April	26,00,000	14,00,000	4,60,000	3,40,000	90,000
May	28,00,000	12,00,000	4,80,000	3,50,000	90,000
June	30,00,000	16,00,000	4,80,000	3,60,000	1,00,000

Cash balance on 1st January was ₹ 10,00,000. A new machine is to be a installed at ₹ 30,00,000 on credit to be repaid by two installments in March and April.

Sales commission @ 5 % on total is to be paid within the month following actual sales.

₹ 10,00,000 being the amount of 2nd call may be received in March. Share premium amounting to ₹ 2,00,000 is also obtainable with 2nd call.

Period of credit allowed by suppliers—2 months

Period of credit allowed to customer —1 months

Delay in payment of overhead —1 month

Delay in payment of wages —1/2 month

Assume cash sales to be 50% of total sales.

Answer: Balance Jan ₹ 18,00,000; Feb ₹ 29,80,000; March ₹ 20,000; April ₹ 6,10,000; May ₹ 8,80,000; June ₹ 15,20,000.

15. From the information given below, prepare a cash budget of the Jaipur Refrigerators (P) Ltd. for the quarter January-March 2017:

	Dec' 2016	*Jan'* 2017	*Feb'* 2017	*March'* 2017	*April'* 2017
(*a*) Sales budget (units)	60	60	65	75	80
(*b*) Selling price per unit ₹	1,000	1,000	1,000	1,000	1,000
(*c*) Off-season discount	20%	20%	10%	—	—
(*d*) End of month inventory units	10	12	15	25	25

(*e*) Half the sales proceeds are collected in the month of sale and the other half in the month following.

(*f*) Materials amounting to ₹ 300 per unit manufactured are purchased one month in advance of manufacture and paid for in cash, earning 5% cash discount on half of the material purchased.

(*g*) Direct labour budget was ₹ 50 per unit and variable overhead ₹ 100 per unit.

(*h*) Indirect labour budget was ₹ 6,000 per month.

(*i*) Depreciation was provided uniformly at ₹ 3,000 per month.

(*j*) The fixed overheads budget was ₹ 6,000 per month during off season and ₹ 7,000 during the season. Out of this, the quarterly premium for fire insurance amounting to ₹ 600 was payable in the first month of each quarter.

(*k*) Dividends for the year 2016, amounting to ₹ 20,000 were expected to be declared in March 2017 and payments were to be spread between March and April.

(*l*) A machine was sold for ₹ 10,000 in December 2016 on 3 month' credit.

(*m*) The company had overdraft with the State Bank of Jaipur and Bikaner up to ₹ 50,000.

Answer: Balance January ₹ 6,410, February ₹ 12,797.50, March ₹ 30,597.50.

16. Some key figures from the budget of Moore Company for the first quarter of operations for 2017 are shown below:

	January	*February*	*March*
Credit sales	₹ 80,000	₹ 70,000	₹ 86,000
Credit purchases	34,000	32,000	40,000
Cash disbursements:			
Wages and salaries	4,000	3,500	4,200
Rent	1,500	1,500	1,500
Equipment purchases	25,000	—	2,000

The company estimates that 10 per cent of its credit sales will never be collected. Of those that will be collected, one-half will be collected in the month of sale and the remainder will be collected in the following month. Purchases on account will all be paid for in the month following purchase. December 2016 sales were ₹ 90,000. The beginning cash balance is ₹ 1,00,000.

Using the information given above, prepare a cash budget.

Answer: Ending cash balance, January ₹ 1,46,000, February ₹ 1,74,500, March ₹ 2,05,000

17. Based on the following information prepare a Cash budget for ABC Ltd.

	1st Qtr. ₹	*2nd Qtr.* ₹	*3rd Qtr.* ₹	*4th Qtr.* ₹
Opening Cash balance	10,00,000			
Collections from Customers	1,25,00,000	1,50,00,000	1,60,00,000	2,21,00,000
Payment:				
Purchase of Materials	20,00,000	35,00,000	35,00,000	54,20,000
Other Expenses	25,00,000	20,00,000	20,00,000	17,00,000
Salary and Wages	90,00,000	95,00,000	95,00,000	1,09,20,000
Income Tax	5,00,000	—	—	—
Purchase of machinery	—	—	—	20,00,000

The company desired to maintain a cash balance of ₹ 15,00,000 at the end of each quarter. Cash can be borrowed or repaid in multiples of ₹ 50,000 at an interest of 10% per annum. Management does not want to borrow cash more than what is necessary and wants to repay as early as possible. In any event, loans can not be extended beyond four quarters. Interest is computed and paid when the principal is repaid. Assume that borrowings take place at the beginning and repayments are made at the end of the quarters.

Answer: Closing Cash Balance, Ist Quarter ₹ 15,00,000, 2nd Quarter ₹ 15,00,000, 3rd Quarter ₹ 15,32,500, 4th Quarter ₹ 23,82,500

18. ABC Co. wished to arrange overdraft facilities with its bankers during the period April to June 2017 when it will be manufacturing mostly for stock. Prepare a Cash Budget for the above period from the following data, indicating the extent of the bank facilities the company will require at the end of the each month:

(*a*)	*Sales* ₹	*Purchases* ₹	*Wages* ₹
February	18,00,000	12,48,000	1,20,000

March	19,20,000	14,40,000	1,40,000
April	10,80,000	24,30,000	1,10,000
May	17,40,000	24,60,000	1,00,000
June	12,60,000	26,80,000	1,50,000

(*b*) 50 per cent of the credit sales are realised in the month following the sales and the remaining 50 per cent in the second month following. Creditors are paid in the month of purchase.

(*c*) Cash at Bank 1.4.2017 (estimated) ₹ 2,50,000

Answer: Overdraft required

May ₹ 4,70,000 June ₹ 16,70,000

19. The January 1 cash balance of the Jay Company is ₹ 5,000. Sales of the first four months of the first year are expected to be as follows: January, ₹ 65,000; February, ₹ 54,000; March, ₹ 66,000; and April, ₹ 63,000. On January 1, collected amounts for November and December of the previous year are ₹ 13,500 and ₹ 39,150, respectively; collections from customers follow this pattern; 55% in the month of sale, 30% in the month following the sale, 13% in the second month following the sale, and 2% uncollectible.

    Materials purchases for December were ₹ 10,000. Forecast purchases for the coming year are: January ₹ 12,500; February, ₹ 16,500; March, ₹ 13,000; and April, ₹ 14,000. Purchases are usually paid by the 10th of the month following the month of purchase. Other cash expenditure of ₹ 41,000 are forecasted for each month.

Calculate:

(*i*) Expected cash collection during February

(*ii*) Expected cash balance, February 1

(*iii*) Expected cash balance, February 28.

Answer: Cash collection February ₹ 60,510, Cash balance-February 1, ₹ 27,550, Cash balance-February 28, ₹ 34,560

20. The management of Crammore Manufacturing Company at the beginning of 2017 anticipated (1) a decrease in sales as compared with 2016 because of production time lost in converting to new products, and (2) a considerably smaller profit margin due to higher material and labour costs. The controller was asked to prepare a cash budget based on estimated 2017 sales of ₹ 24 lakhs (a decrease of ₹ 3,00,000) and, in particular, to forecast the cash position at the close of 2017.

    The treasure's forecast of certain balance sheet and other items was as follows:

Accounts receivable (net)	₹ 35,000	decrease
Accounts payable	20,000	decrease
Inventories	17,000	increase
Additions to plant (gross)	125,000	
Addition to retained earnings	25,000	
Income for 2017 (after depreciation but before income taxes)	95,000	
Depreciation expense, 2017	48,000	
Income taxes for 2017 (payable in 2018)	45,000	
Dividend payments (at 2016 rates)	30,000	

The cash balance on January 1, 2017 was ₹ 54,000 and the tax liability on that date, arising from 2016 taxable income, amounted to ₹ 93,000.

(*a*) Assuming that any balance sheet items not listed above would be unchanged, prepare a schedule of forecast cash receipts and cash disbursements for 2017 and determine the expected cash balance as on December 31, 2017.

(*b*) What action would you expect management to take when it sees the cash flow estimates for the year? (*M.Com., Delhi University, 2011*)

Answer: Hint

(*a*) Expected disbursements:		(₹)
Sales		24,00,000
Net income before taxes		95,000
Total expenses		23,05,000
Depreciation		48,000
Cash expenses		22,57,000
Accounts payable decrease		20,000
Inventory increase		17,000
Income taxes		93,000
Dividends		30,000
Additions to plant		1,25,000
Total expected disbursements		25,42,000
Expected collections:		
Sales	24,00,000	
Accounts receivable decrease	35,000	
Total expected collections		24,35,000
Expected excess of disbursements over collections		1,07,000
Cash balance, January 1, 2017		54,000
Expected cash deficit, December 31, 2017		₹ 53,000

(*b*) management might seek ways of improving the current profit margin. Because material and labour costs are rising, competitors' costs may be increasing too, and a price increase might be feasible. Significant cost reductions or changes in product mix, however, probably can not be realised soon enough to do much for the 2017 cash flow, except possible as mentioned below:

Other than a possible price increase, management would seem to have two main options: (1) reduce "discretionary" expenditures on such items as plant and equipment, dividends, or special programmes now included under expenses; or (2) obtain additional cash by borrowing. The planned capital expenditure programme is very large, but may be entirely necessary to effect the planned changeover in product lines. Stock sales may be difficult to make because reported income is now low, so the choice is really between borrowing and cutting back.

Unless the capital budget has a good deal of slack in it, the company would seem to be ripe for some kind of borrowings. One possible source is to increase accounts payable instead of reducing them — inventories are increasing, after all — but this will provide only ₹ 37,000, even if the entire increase in inventory can be financed this way. The cash balance cannot be reduced to zero, either, and the company would seem to need at least ₹ 50,000 in funds. Passing the dividend would yield only ₹ 30,000 of this.

21. (Budgeted Income Statement). ABC company is a manufacturer of video-conferencing products. Regular units are manufactured to meet marketing projections and specialized units are made after an order is received. Maintaining the video-conferencing equipment is an important area of customer satisfaction. Due to slowdown in the computer industry, the video-conferencing equipment segment has suffered leading to a decline in company's financial performance. The following income statement shows results for the year 2017.

Income Statement for the year ending December 2017

		(₹ '000)
Revenues :	(₹)	(₹)
Equipment	60,000	
Maintenance contracts	18,000	
Total revenues		78,000
Cost of goods sold		46,000
Gross margin		32,000
Operating costs :		
Marketing	6000	
Distribution	1500	
Customer maintenance	10,000	
Administration	9000	
Total Operating costs		26,500
Operating income		5,500

The company's management team is in process of preparing the 2018 budget and is studying the following information :

(*i*) Selling prices of equipment are expected to increase by 10% as the economic recovery begins. The selling price of each maintenance contract is unchanged from 2017.

(*ii*) Equipment sales in units are expected to increase by 6% with a corresponding 6% growth in units of maintenance contracts.

(*iii*) Cost of each unit sold is expected to increase by 3% to pay for the necessary technology and quality improvements.

(*iv*) Marketing costs are expected to increase by ₹ 25,00,000 but administration costs are expected to remain at 2017 level.

(*v*) Distribution costs very in proportion to the number of units of equipment sold.

(*vi*) Two maintenance techniques are to be added at a total cost of ₹ 13,00,000 which covers salaries and related travel costs. The objective is to improve customer service and shorten response time.

(*vii*) There is no beginning or ending inventory of equipment.

Required:

Prepare a budgeted income statement for 2018.

22. Assam Boards, Co., a manufacturer of snow boards, decided in October Year 1 that it needed cash to continue operations. It began negotiating for a one-month bank loan of ₹ 100,000 starting November 1 Year 1. The bank would charge interest at the rate of 1 per cent per month and require the company to repay interest and principal on November 30 Year 1. In considering the loan, the bank requested a projected income statement and cash budget for November:

The following information is available:

- The company budgeted sales at 2,000 units per month in October Year 1, December Year 1, and January Year 2, and at 3,000 units in November Year 1. The selling price to distributors is ₹ 100 per unit.
- The inventory of finished goods on October 1 was 24,000 units. The number of units of finished goods inventory at the end of each month equals 20 per cent of unit sales anticipated for the following month. There is no work in process.
- The company purchases materials, so it has no raw materials inventory.
- Selling expenses are 10 per cent of gross sales. Administrative expenses, which include depreciation of ₹ 500 per month on office furniture and fixtures, total ₹ 33,000 per month.
- The manufacturing budget for snow boards on normal production of 2,000 units per month, follows:

Materials	₹ 80,000
Labor	20,000
Variable Overhead	10,000
Fixed Overhead (includes depreciation of ₹ 4,000)	60,000
Total	₹ 170,000

Required:

(a) How much is the expected production in units for October, November, and December?

(b) Prepare a projected income statement for November.

Answer: (a) With 24,000 units of inventory on hand, the company has sufficient inventory to support production. No inventory needs to be produced and no raw materials need be purchased.

(b) Operating profit ₹ 11,000.

23. The following information is available for Year 1 for Reliance Products:

Revenues (100,000 units)		₹ 7,25,000
Manufacturing Costs:		
Materials	₹ 42,000	
Variable Costs	35,600	
Fixed Costs (excluding depreciation)	81,900	
Depreciation (fixed)	2,49,750	4,09,250
Marketing and Administrative Costs:		
Marketing (variable)	₹ 1,05,600	
Depreciation of Marketing Buildings and Equipment	37,400	
Administrative (fixed) (excluding depreciation)	1,27,300	

Administrative Depreciation	18,700	2,89,000
Total Costs		6,98,250
Operating Profits		₹ 26,750

All depreciation costs are fixed and are expected to remain the same for Year 2. Sales volume is expected to increase by 20 percent, and prices are expected to increase by 5 percent. Materials costs are expected to decrease by 8 per cent per unit. Variable manufacturing costs are expected to decrease by 2 per cent per unit. Fixed manufacturing costs, other than depreciation, are expected to increase by 5 percent.

Variable marketing costs change with volume. Administrative costs are expected to increase by 10 percent.

Prepare a master budget profit plan for Year 2. Management wants to increase profits by 20 per cent over Year 1's budget of ₹ 26,750. According to budget, are profits expected to increase by 20 percent? Why or why not?

Answer: Operating profit in year 2, ₹ 1,66,671.

24. The following tentative trial balance as of December 31, 2015, is prepared by the Accounting Department of Himalaya Publishing Co., Mumbai.

Cash	₹ 1,18,600	
Accounts Receivable	2,32,400	
Finished Goods	1,48,900	
Work in Process	32,700	
Materials	52,500	
Prepaid Expenses	4,000	
Plant and Equipment	5,80,000	
Accumulated Depreciation—Plant and Equipment		₹ 2,51,000
Accounts Payable		1,82,500
Equity ₹ 15 per share		4,50,000
Retained Earning		2,85,600
	₹ 11,69,100	₹ 11,69,100

Factory output and sales for 2016 are expected to total 32,000 units of product, which are to be sold at ₹ 100 per unit. The quantities and costs of the inventories at December 31, 2016, are expected to remain unchanged from the balances at the beginning of the year.

Budget estimates of manufacturing costs and operating expenses for the year are summarized as follows:

	Estimated Costs and Expenses	
	Fixed (Total for Year)	**Variable (Per Unit Sold)**
Costs of goods manufactured and sold:		
Direct materials	—	₹ 25.00
Direct labor	—	7.80

Factory overhead:		
Depreciation of plant and equipment	₹ 32,000	—
Other factory overhead	10,000	4.50
Selling expenses:		
Sales salaries and commissions	1,15,000	12.80
Advertising	1,12,400	—
Miscellaneous selling expense	8,400	2.00
Administrative expenses:		
Office and officers salaries	75,400	6.25
Supplies	3,900	1.00
Miscellaneous administrative expense	2,000	1.50

Balances of accounts receivable, prepaid expenses, and accounts payable at the end of the year are not expected to differ significantly from the beginning balances. The income tax of ₹ 2,80,000 on 2016 taxable income will be paid during 2016. Regular quarterly cash dividends of ₹ 1.50 a share are expected to be declared and paid in March, June, September, and December on 30,000 shares of common equity outstanding. It is anticipated that fixed assets will be purchased for ₹ 1,70,000 cash in May.

Required:

1. Prepare a budgeted income statement for 2016.
2. Prepare a budgeted balance sheet as of December 31, 2016, with supporting calculations.

Answer:

1. Net income ₹ 6,13,700
2. Balance sheet total ₹ 13,51,800

CASES

1. Kalawati Hospital in New Delhi, introduced a new budgeting method that allowed the hospital's annual plan to be updated for changes in operating plans. For example, if the budget was based on 400 patient-days (number of patients × number of days in the hospital) and the actual count rose to 450 patient-days, the variable costs of staffing, lab work, and medication costs could be adjusted to reflect this change. The budget manager stated, "I work with hospital directors to turn data into meaningful information and effect change before the month ends."

Required:

(a) What budgeting methods are being used under the new approach?

(b) Why are these methods superior to the former approaches?

2. Raghvendra is the controller of Banglore Laboratories, a manufacturer and distributor of generic prescription pharmaceuticals. He is currently in the process of preparing the annual budget and reviewing the current business plan. The business unit managers of Banglore prepare and assemble the detailed operating budgets with technical assistance from the corporate accounting staff. The final budgets are then presented by the business unit

managers to the corporate executive committee for approval. The corporate accounting staff reviews the budgets for adherence to corporate accounting policies, but no detailed review for reasonableness of the line items within the budget is done.

Raghvendra is aware that the upcoming year for the company may be a difficult one due to the expiration of a major patent and the loss of a licensing agreement for another product line. He also knows that during the budgeting process, "budgetary slack" is created in varying degrees throughout the organisation. Raghvendra believes this slack has a negative effect on the overall business objectives of Banglore Laboratories and should be eliminated where possible.

Required:

(a) Define budgetary slack.

(b) Explain the advantages and disadvantages of budgetary slack from the point of view of each of the following:

(i) The business unit manager who must achieve the budget.

(ii) Corporate management.

(c) Raghvendra is considering implementing zero-based budgeting at Banglore Laboratories.

(i) Define zero-based budgeting.

(ii) Describe how zero-based budgeting could be advantageous to Banglore Laboratories in controlling budgetary slack.

(iii) Discuss the disadvantages Banglore Laboratories might encounter from using zero-based budgeting. *(CMA, USA, Adapted with permission)*

3. An effective budget converts the objectives and goals of management into quantified plans. If done correctly, it can serve as a motivating force within the company as well the basis of control and performance evaluation. Creating a budget is essential to the operation of a company. The manner in which it is prepared and the roles of accountable employees in that preparation have an impact on the effectiveness of the budget as a tool for planning, communicating, and controlling.

Two different approaches to preparing a budget are the imposed budget and the participative budget. The imposed budget is created by top management with minimal input from those individuals who are accountable for budgetary results. The participative budget, in contrast, encourages input, and accountable individuals directly participate in the budgeting process along with top management.

Required:

(a) Discuss the behavioural implications of the imposed budgetary approach.

(b) (i) Describe at least three benefits that an organisation can derive from a participative budgetary approach.

(ii) Describe at least three potential problems to the organisation of participative budgeting.

(c) Discuss the behavioural impact on operational management employees of participative budgeting. *(CMA, USA, Adapted with permission)*

4. A bank manager of State Bank of India, Delhi University uses the managerial accounting system to track the costs of operating the various departments within the bank. The departments include Cash Management, Commercial Loans, Mortgage Loans, Operations, Credit Card, and Branch Services. The budget and actual results for the Operations Department are as follows for December 2016.

Resources	Budget	Actual
Salaries	₹ 2,00,000	₹ 2,00,000
Benefits	30,000	30,000
Supplies	45,000	42,000
Travel	20,000	30,000
Training	25,000	35,000
Overtime	25,000	20,000
Total	₹ 3,45,000	₹ 3,57,000

Required:

(a) What information is provided by the budget? Specifically, what questions can the bank manager ask of the Operations Department manager?

(b) What information does the budget fail to provide? Specifically, could the budget information be presented differently to provide even more insight for the bank manager?

5. HEL Company is a large multidivision firm with several plants in each division. A comprehensive budgeting system is used for planning operations and measuring performance. The annual budgeting process starts in August, five months prior to the beginning of the fiscal year starting January next year. At this time, the division managers submit proposed budgets for sales, production and inventory levels, and expenses. Capital expenditure requests also are formalized at this time. The expense budgets include direct labour and all overhead items that are separated into fixed and variable components. Direct materials are budgeted separately in developing the production and inventory schedules.

The expense budgets for each division are developed from its plants' results, as measured by the percentage variation from an adjusted budget in the first six months of the current year and a target expense reduction percentage established by the corporation.

To determine plant percentages, the plant budget for the just completed half-year period is revised to recognize changes in operating procedures and costs outside the control of plant management (e.g., labour wage rate changes, product style changes, and so forth). The difference between this revised budget and the actual expenses is the controllable variance and is expressed as a percentage of the actual expenses. This percentage is added (if unfavorable) to the corporate target expense reduction percentage. A favorable plant variance percentage is subtracted from the corporate target. If a plant had a 2% unfavorable controllable variance and the corporate target reduction was 4%, the plant's budget for the next year should reflect costs approximately 6% below this year's actual costs.

Next year's final budgets for the company, the divisions, and the plants are adopted after corporate analysis of the proposed budgets and a careful review with each division manager of the changes made by corporate management. Division profit budgets include allocated corporate costs, and plant profit budgets include allocated division and corporate costs.

Return on assets is used to measure the performance of divisions and plants. The asset base for a division consists of all assets assigned to the division, including its working capital, and an allocated share of corporate assets. For plants, the asset base includes the assets assigned to the plant plus an allocated portion of the division and corporate assets. Recommendations for promotions and salary increases for the executives of the divisions and plants are influenced by how well actual return on assets compares with the budgeted return on assets.

The plant managers exercise control only over the cost portion of the plant profit budget because the divisions are responsible for sales. Only limited control over the plant assets is exercised at the plant level.

The manager of the Chennai, a major plant in the Southern Division, carefully controls his costs during the first six months so that any improvement appears after the target reduction of expenses is established. He accomplishes this by careful planning and timing of his discretionary expenditures.

During 2016, the property adjacent to the Chennai Plant was purchased by HEL Company. This expenditure was not included in the 2016 capital budget. Corporate management decided to divert funds from a project at another plant since the property appeared to be better long-term investment.

Also during 2016, HEL Company experienced depressed sales. In an attempt to achieve budgeted profit, corporate management announced in August that all plants were to cut their annual expenses by 6%. In order to accomplish this expense reduction, the Chennai Plant manager reduced preventive maintenance and postponed needed major repairs. Employees who quit were not replaced unless absolutely necessary. Employee training was postponed whenever possible. The raw materials, supplies, and finished goods inventories were reduced below normal levels.

Required:

(a) Evaluate the budget procedure of HEL Company with respect to its effectiveness for planning and controlling operations.

(b) Is the HEL Company's use of return on assets to evaluate the performance of the Chennai Plant appropriate? Explain your answer.

(c) Analyze and explain the Chennai Plant manager's behaviour during 2016.

(CMA, USA, Adapted with permission)

6. Nitin, the Finance Manager in New Delhi Manufacturing Company (NDMC), New Delhi recognizes the importance of the budgetary process for planning, control, and motivation purposes. He believes that a properly implemented participative budgeting process for planning purposes, and a management by exception reporting procedure based on that budget will motivate his subordinates to improve productivity within their particular departments. Based on this philosophy, Nitin has implemented the following budget procedures.

- An appropriation target figure is given to each department manager. This amount is the maximum funding that each department can expect to receive in the next fiscal year.
- Department managers develop their individual budgets within the following spending constraints as directed by the Finance Manager's staff.

(i) Expenditure requests cannot exceed the appropriation target.

(ii) All fixed expenditures should be included in the budget. Fixed expenditures would include such items as contracts and salaries at current levels.

(iii) All projects directed by higher authority should be included in the budget in their entirety.

- The Finance Manager consolidates the departmental budget requests from the various departments into one budget that is to be submitted for the entire division.
- Upon final budget approval by the NDMC, the Finance Manager's staff allocates the appropriation to the various departments on instructions from the division manager. However, a specified percentage of each department's appropriation is held back in anticipation of potential budget cuts and special funding needs. The amount and use of this contingency fund are left to the discretion of the division manager.
- Each department is allowed to adjust its budget when necessary to operate within the reduced appropriation level. However, as stated in the original directive, specific projects authorized by higher authority must remain intact.
- The final budget is used as the basis of control for a management by exception form of reporting. Excessive expenditures by account for each department are highlighted on a monthly basis. Department managers are expected to account for all expenditures over budget. Fiscal responsibility is an important factor in the overall performance evaluation of department managers.

Nitin believes his policy of allowing the department managers to participate in the budget process and then holding them accountable for their performance is essential, especially during these times of limited resources. He further believes that department managers will be positively motivated to increase the efficiency and effectiveness of their departments because they have provided input into the initial budgetary process and required to justify any unfavorable performances.

Required :

(a) Explain the operational and behavioural benefits that generally are attributed to a participative budgeting process.

(b) Identify deficiencies in Nitin's participative budgetary policy for planning and performance evaluation purposes. For each deficiency identified, recommend how the deficiency can be corrected. *(CMA, USA, Adapted with permission)*

7. Hindustan Machine Tools (HMT) is a manufacturer of small industrial tools with annual sales of approximately ₹ 350 lakhs. Sales growth has been steady during the year, and there is no evidence of cyclical demand. Production has increased gradually during the year and has been evenly distributed throughout each month. The company has a sequential processing system. The four manufacturing departments—Casting, Machining, Finishing, and Packaging—are all located in the same building. Fixed overhead is assigned using a plantwide rate.

HMT has always been able to compare with other manufacturers of small tools. However, its market has expanded only in response to product innovation. Thus, research and developement are very important and have helped HMT to expand as well as maintain demand.

Sekhar Pillai, controller, has designed and implemented a new budget system in response to concerns voiced by Rahul Bajaj, president. Sekhar prepared an annual budget that has been divided into 12 equal segments; this budget can be used to assist in the timely evaluation of monthly performance. Rahul Bajaj was visibly upset upon receiving the May performance report for the Machining Department as given below. Rahul Bajaj exclaimed, "How can they be efficient enough to produce nine extra units every working day and still miss the budget by ₹ 3,000 per day?" Rajat, supervisor of the Machining Department, could not understand "all the red ink" when he knew that the department had operated more efficiently in May than it had in months. Rajat stated, 'I was expecting a pat on the back, and instead, the boss tore me apart. What's more, I don't even know why!'

HMT Co.
Machining Department Performance Report
For the Month Ended May 31, 2016

	Budgeted	**Actual**	**Variance**
Volume in units	3,000	3,185	185
Variable manufacturing costs:			
Direct materials	₹ 2,40,000	₹ 2,48,430	₹ 8,430
Direct labor	2,77,500	2,93,020	15,520
Variable overhead	3,33,000	3,50,350	17,350
Total variable costs	₹ 8,50,500	₹ 8,91,800	₹ 41,300
Fixed manufacturing costs:			
Indirect labor	₹ 33,000	₹ 33,340	₹ 340
Depreciation	15,000	15,000	—
Taxes	3,000	3,000	—
Insurance	2,400	2,400	—
Other	9,300	10,270	970
Total fixed costs	₹ 62,700	₹ 64,010	₹ 1,310
Corporate costs:			
Research and development	₹ 24,000	₹ 37,280	₹ 13,280
Selling and administrative	36,000	40,750	4,750
Total corporate costs	₹ 60,000	₹ 78,030	₹ 18,030
Total costs	₹ 9,73,200	₹ 10,33,840	₹ 60,640

Required:

(i) Review the May performance report. Use the information given in the report and elsewhere.

(a) Discuss the strengths and weaknesses of the new budgetary system.

(b) Identify the weaknesses of the performance report, and explain how it should be revised to eliminate each weakness.

(ii) Prepare a revised report for the Machining Department using the May data.

(iii) What other changes would you make to improve HMT's budgetary system?

(CMA, USA adapted with permission)

Answer: *(ii)* Total costs, Budget ₹ 96,565; Actual ₹ 95,581, Variance 984 F

8. TabComp Inc. is a retail distributor for MZB-33 computer hardware and related software and support services. TabComp prepares annual sales forecasts of which the first six months for 2016 are presented below.

Cash sales account for 25 per cent of TabComp's total sales, 30 per cent of the total sales are paid by bank credit card, and the remaining 45 per cent are on open account (TabComp's own charge accounts). The cash and bank credit card sales are received in the month of the sale. Bank credit card sales are subject to a four-per cent discount deducted at the time of the daily deposit, The cash receipts for sales on open account are 70 per cent in the month following the sale, 28 per cent in the second month following the sale, and the remaining are estimated to be uncollectible.

TabComp Inc.
Sales Forecast
Six Months - 2016

	Hardware Sales		Software	Total
	Units	(₹)	Sales and Support	Sales
January	130	3,90,000	₹ 1,60,000	₹ 5,50,000
February	120	3,60,000	1,40,000	5,00,000
March	110	3,30,000	1,50,000	4,80,000
April	90	2,70,000	1,30,000	4,00,000
May	100	3,00,000	1,25,000	4,25,000
June	125	3,75,000	2,25,000	6,00,000
Total	675	20,25,000	9,30,000	29,55,000

TabComp's month-end inventory requirements for computer hardware units are 30 per cent of the next month's sales. A one-month lead time is required for delivery from the manufacturer; thus, orders for computer hardware units are placed on the 25th of each month to assure that they will be in the store by the first day of the month needed. The computer hardware units are purchased under terms of n/45 measured from the time the units are delivered to TabComp. TabComp's purchase price for the computer units is 60 per cent of the selling price.

Required:

A. Calculate the cash that TabComp can expect to collect during April 2016. Be sure to show all of your calculations.

B. TabComp is determining the MZB-33 computer hardware units that will be ordered on January 25, 2016.

(*i*) Determine the projected number of computer hardware units that will be ordered.

(*ii*) Calculate the value of the order that TabComp will place for these computer hardware units.

(*iii*) In which month will TabComp pay for these computer hardware units?

C. As part of the annual budget process, TabComp prepares a cash budget by month for the entire year. Explain why a company such as TabComp prepares a cash budget by month for the entire year. (*CMA, USA, Adapted with permission*)

Answer: (A) Total collections ₹ 4,29,400.

(B) (i) 104 (ii) ₹ 1,87,200 is value of order (iii) Payment will be made on the last day of the 45-day discount period.

(C) Monthly cash budgets are prepared in order to plan for cash needs.

9. Raghav is the dean of a business school at Banglore International University, India. The university is under strong financial pressures, and the university president has asked all the deans to cut costs. Raghav is wondering how he should respond to this request.

The university receives its operating funds from three sources: (1) tuition (60%), (2) government grants–(25%), and (3) gifts and endowment income (15%). The money flows into the university's general operating fund. A management committee consisting of the university president, the three vice presidents, and the nine deans allocates funds to the individual schools. The university's charter requires that it operate with a balanced budget.

The initial allocation of funds reflects (1) committed costs that cannot be avoided, primarily the employment costs of tenured faculty and (2) committed costs relating to overhead items, such as staff, building maintenance, and other operations costs. The balance of funds is allocated to discretionary activities, such as scholarships, program changes or additions, and sports.

The various deans compare their respective funding levels. The basis of comparison is to divide total university expenditures by the number of full-time students to get an average cost per student. Then the average cost per student is multiplied by the number of full-time students to get the target funding for each school. On average, the actual funding for the business school has been about 70% of the target funding, which is the second lowest in the university. (The lowest is the arts faculty.)

Because of the rapid growth of committed and administrative costs, the amount of funds allocated to discretionary activities has been declining from a historic level of about 10%. Thus year, the projected revenues will not even cover the projected committed costs. In response to this development, the president has called on all deans to do your best to reduce the level of expenditures.

The president's request has been met with skepticism by many deans, who are notorious for digging in their heels, ignoring requests for spending cuts, and then being bailed out by funds released from other activities or raised to meet the budget short-fall. Many deans believe that the departments that sacrificed and reduced their budgets would only create funds that would be used by the university to support other schools that had made little or no effort to reduce their budgets. Then these schools would be asked to make even more cuts to make up for the lack of cuts in schools that made little progress in cost reduction. On the other hand, the deans also believe that if there were no reaction to the president's initial request for cost-reductions, arbitrary cutbacks would be imposed on the individual schools.

In response to this situation, Raghav is wondering what to do. He knows that by increasing class sizes slightly, using some part-time teachers, and eliminating some optional courses that seldom attract many students, he can trim about ₹ 8,00,000 from his operating budget of ₹ 11,000,000. However, making these changes would create hardships for both the students and faculty in the business school and, given the historic relationship of the school's average funding to its target funding, Raghav is wondering whether the business school should be asked to make additional sacrifices.

Raghav knows that he has several alternatives:

- Do nothing, arguing that the business school is already cost effective relative to others and it is the time for others to reduce their cost structures.
- Make the cuts that he has identified but stretch them out over a number of years and stop making them if other schools are not doing their share in cutting costs.
- Make the cuts unilaterally and advise the administration that the business school budget can be reduced by about ₹ 800,000.

Required:

Explain what you would do if you were Raghav and why. Your explanation should include your analysis of the motivation of all schools to cut costs in an environment that traditionally has taken advantage of those that cooperate.

10. Dr. Pranav Goswami, a dental practitioner in New Delhi has been facing financial difficulties caused by the absence of proper planning and control. He realises that budgetary control is surely needed. You have been hired by Dr. Goswami to act as a consultant and to prepare a plan of action that will help his dental practice regain financial stability. Dr. Goswami has made available the following finanial information for a typical month.

	Revenues		
	Average Free		Quantity
Fillings	₹ 500		90
Crowns	3000		19
Root canals	1700		8
Bridges	5000		7
Extractions	450		30
Cleaning	250		108
X-rays	150		150
	Costs		
Salaries:			
Two dental assistants		₹ 19,000	
Receptionist/bookkeeper		15,000	
Hygienist		18,000	
Public relations (Mrs. Goswami)		10,000	
Personal salary		65,000	
Total salaries			₹ 1,27,000
Benefits			13,440
Building lease			15,000
Dental supplies			12,000
Janitorial			3,000
Utilities			4,000
Phone			1,500

Offrice supplies	1,000
Lab fees	50,000
Loan payments	5,700
Interest payments	5,000
Miscellaneous	5,000
Depreciation	7,000
Total costs	₹ 2,49,640

Benefits include Dr. Goswami's share of social security and a health insurance premium for all employees. Although all revenues billed in a month are not collected, the cash flowing into the business is approximately equal to the month's billings because of collections from prior months. The dental office is open Monday through Thursday from 8:30 a.m. to 4:00 p.m. and on Friday from 8:30 a.m. to 12:30 p.m. A total of 32 hours are worked each week. Additional hours could be worked, but Dr. Goswami is reluctant to do so because of other personal endeavors that he enjoys.

Dr. Goswami has noted that the two dental assistants and the receptionist are not fully utilized. He estimates that they are busy about 65 to 70 per cent of the time. Dr. Goswami's wife spends about five hours each week on a monthly newsletter that is sent to all patients; she also maintains a birthday list and sends cards to the patients on their birthdays.

Dr. Goswami spends about ₹ 24,000 yearly on informational seminars. These seminars, targeted especially for dentists, teach them how to increase their revenues. It is from one of these seminars that Dr. Goswami decided to invest on promotion and public relations (the newsletter and the birthday list).

Required:

1. Prepare a monthly cash budget for Dr. Goswami. Does Dr. Goswami have a significant cash flow problem? How would you use the budget to show Dr. Goswami why he is having financial difficulties?
2. Using the cash budget prepared in Requirement 1 and the information given in the case, recommend actions to solve Dr. Goswami's financial problems. Prepare a cash budget that reflects these recommendations and demonstrates to Dr. Goswami that the problems can be corrected. Do you think that Dr. Goswami will accept your recommendations?

Answer:

1. Total cash needs ₹ 2,42,640 Deficiency of cash ₹ 29,040.
2. Dr. Goswami must either increase revenues to make up the deficiency or cut costs or do both. Based on these recommendations, a revised cash budget can beprepared which will show excess cash available over needs.

11. Ashok Leyland Automobile Co. manufactures an automobile safety seat for children that it sells through several retail chains. The cost of manufacturing and marketing children's automobile safety seats at the company's forecasted volume of 15,000 units per month follows:

Variable Materials	₹ 3,00,000
Variable Labor	1,50,000
Variable Overhead	30,000
Fixed Overhead	1,80,200

Total Manufacturing Costs		₹ 6,60,200
Variable Non-manufacturing Costs		₹ 75,000
Fixed Non-manufacturing Costs		1,05,000
Total Non-manufacturing Costs		₹ 1,80,000
Total Costs		₹ 8,40,200

Selling price is ₹ 70 per unit unless otherwise stated. Ignore income taxes.

The planned production and sales for each month of the year is 15,000 units per month.

However, 1,08,000 units were produced and sold in the first six months of this year, and the income statement for the six months was as follows.

Sales Revenue		₹ 70,20,000
Manufacturing Costs:		
Variable Materials	₹ 21,60,000	
Variable Labor	11,34,000	
Variable Overhead	3,24,000	
Fixed Overhead	10,26,000	46,44,000
Gross Margin		₹ 23,76,000
Marketing Costs:		
Variable Marketing	₹ 6,48,000	
Fixed Marketing	6,50,000	12,98,000
Operating Profit		₹ 10,78,000

Early in July, the senior management of Ashok Leyland Automobile Co. met to evaluate the company performance for the first half of the year. The following conversation took place.

Ajit Doval (president): "Our performance for the first half of this year leaves much to be desired. Despite higher unit sales than forecast, our actual profits are lower than what we expected."

Amit Dhawan (sales manager): "I suspect production needs to shape up" (he said smugly). "We in sales have pursued an aggressive marketing strategy and the three-quarters of 10 lakhs sales revenue higher than forecast is proof enough of our improved performance."

Sharad (production manager): "Wait a minute, now! We managed to bring down unit costs from ₹ 44.00 to ₹ 43.00 with no help from sales, I must add! What's the use of production plans when sales can change them anytime it likes? In February,Amit wanted a rush order for 4,000. In March, it was 8,000 units. Then in April he said to hold off on production; then in June he wanted 6,000. You know what I think..."

Ajit Doval: "Hold on, now! I refuse to let this degenerate into a witch hunt. We have to examine this problem with more objectivity." (He turned to his secretary and asked does he have any ideas.)

Required:

Suppose you are a consultant hired by Ashok Leyland Automobile Co. Write a report to the president analyzing the company's performance. Include a comparison of the actual results to the flexible budget and to the master budget.

Answer:

Operating profits (1,08,000 units) ₹ 10,78,000
Flexibile budget 1,08,000 units, Operating profit ₹ 18,52,800
Operating profits 90,000 units ₹ 12,58,800

10

STANDARD COSTING AND VARIANCE ANALYSIS

LEARNING OBJECTIVES:

After reading this chapter, you should be able to:

- Explain Historical Cost and its Limitations
- Define Standard Cost and Standard Costing
- Distinguish between Standard Costs and Estimated Costs, Standard Costs and Budgets, and Explain the Advantages of Standard Costing
- Describe Different Types of Standards and Aspects of Setting Standards
- Explain the Methods of Computing Material Cost Variances, Labour Cost Variances, Overhead Cost Variances, Sales Variances
- Understand Managerial Uses of Variances, Variance Analysis and Performance Evaluation and Qualities of Variance Reports
- Identify Uses of Standard Costing in Service Industry Firms
- Understand Limitations of Standard Costing

CONTROL OF COST: AN INTRODUCTION

Control of cost is one of the most important objectives of cost and management accounting and cannot be achieved without some standard against which actual can be compared. The use of standard costs increases cost consciousness among management and employees and can improve business profits by providing a base for performance evaluation. This chapter introduces the concept and basic procedures of standard costing and also explains the techniques used in standard cost variance analysis. However, before discussing standard costing, it will be appropriate to evaluate briefly historical cost accounting and its limitations.

HISTORICAL COST AND ITS LIMITATIONS

Historical cost systems are principally associated with recording of historical, or as they are commonly called, actual costs. Historical costing is the ascertainment of costs after they have been incurred. The recording of historical costs is useful as it determines the cost of resources used towards achieving organisational objectives. Historical costs, however, have the following limitations:

1. Historical costs are collected after they have been incurred and therefore are ineffective in cost control. The costs have been incurred, they cannot be undone and no steps can be taken to correct inefficiencies.
2. Historical costs are not helpful in cost reduction since they contain no standards or goals towards which employees can work.
3. Historical costs do not provide reliable guides to management in the tasks of budgeting, planning and decision-making. Historical costs reflect a situation in a previous period. But the company, in fact, may be working under conditions different from those prevailing during that previous period. Therefore, historical costs are not useful in budget making, performance evaluation, detecting above or below—standard performance.

STANDARD COST AND STANDARD COSTING: DEFINITIONS

> **Standard cost** is a planned cost for a unit of product or service rendered.

A standard cost is a planned cost for a unit of product or service rendered. Standard costs are highly detailed, scientifically predetermined costs of material, labour and overhead chargeable to a product or service. Standard costs represent excellent target costs that should be obtained. The Chartered Institute of Management Accountants (U.K.) defines standard costs as:

- *a predetermined cost which is calculated from management's standards of efficient operation and the relevant necessary expenditure. It may be used as a basis for price fixing and for cost control through variance analysis.*

The term 'standard', has been called by different names in accounting, *e.g.*, 'a norm', 'a model or example or comparison', 'a measure of comparison', 'a criterion of excellence', 'a yardstick', 'a benchmark', 'an index of waste or potential saving', 'a sea level from which to measure cost altitudes', 'a gauge.' A standard may be a norm or a measure of comparison in terms of specific items such as pounds or kilograms of materials, labour hours required, hours of plant capacity used.

Standard costing is the setting of predetermined cost estimates in order to provide a basis for comparison with actual costs. The Chartered Institute of Management Accountants (UK) defines standard costing as:

- *the preparation and use of standard cost, their comparison with actual cost and the analysis of variance to their causes and points of incidence.*

STANDARD COSTS AND ESTIMATED COSTS

The term 'standard' costs should not be confused with 'estimated costs.' Standards cost and estimated costs differ in the following respects:

Firstly, estimated costs are frequently less accurately determined. Estimated costs are developed from projections using averages of past data regarding performance. Standard costs are predetermined realistically and much more scientifically through the use of time and motion studies, engineering estimates and specifications, selected measures of plant capacity, cost behaviour patterns.

Secondly, estimated costs are not helpful to management in accomplishing managerial functions as they are not scientifically predetermined costs. But standard costs involve more sophistication, operation analysis and evaluation and comprehensive review of internal and external factors. They become reliable measures for product costing, product pricing, planning, coordination and cost control purposes.

Thirdly, estimated cost emphasises on actual cost with which it is compared at the end of the accounting period. If the estimated costs are found higher or lower than actual costs they are revised for use in the next accounting period. In standard costing, the emphasis is on standard costs, *i.e.*, what costs of material, labour and overhead should be incurred if the factory is to be operated as a highly efficient unit with each manager, foreman, worker, plant and machine functioning as an efficient part of the production process. Under standard costing, actual costs are ascertained only to facilitate their comparison with standard costs.

STANDARD COSTS AND BUDGETS

Standard costs and budgets are both vital tools in planning, operation and control of a business enterprise. Both differ in the following respects:

1. A standard costing system can operate without any comprehensive budgeting system. But budgets in absence of standard costs will only be fair estimates and cannot provide a reasonable base against which the actual results can be compared.

2. The objectives of budgeting are different from standard costing. A budget is a profit plan reflecting anticipated financial inflows and outflows. It is comprehensive in nature and covers several business activities, such as production, purchase, selling and distribution, research and development. Budgets include both income and expenditure, but standards are set usually for expenses only. Standard costs are developed only for the production and related manufacturing cost.

3. Budgets project the volume of business and levels of costs which should be maintained. That is, they reflect cost ceilings which should not be exceeded if the budgeted profit is to be attained. Standard costs emphasise the cost levels to which cost should be reduced. If costs reach this level, profit will be increased. Standards are minimum targets which are to be attained by actual performance at specific efficiency.

4. Budgets covering the entire business present the forecasted profit and loss account and sometimes balance sheet also. Therefore, budgets act as guides for operating the business on a definite course of action. Standards are frequently used only in labour operation and do not represent expected costs but the cost that should be in a certain assumed conditions of performance.

5. The term 'standard' is a unit concept and the term 'budgeted cost' is a total concept. It may be helpful to think of a standard as a budget for the production of a single unit of output.

6. Budgets if achieved by the organisation do not usually involve much variance analysis. The achievement of budget targets point out the efficiency attained and therefore no analysis on a large scale is needed unless circumstances have considerably changed. Under standard costing, detailed variance analysis is carried out to find out deviations so that corrective action may be taken.

7. Review and revision of budgets is more frequently based on the changing circumstances than those of standard costs. Standard costs are more static and subject to less change.

8. Budgets are equally important for planning, organisation, coordination and control functions of management. Standard costs contribute relatively more to the control function than other managerial function although standards are used for all business functions.

9. Budgeting may be applied in such businesses which are of a jobbing nature, but standard costing is difficult to apply because of the dissimilar nature of different jobs. Jobs are better controlled through predetermined budget and cost for different jobs are ascertained historically. In those businesses where manufacturing is done under conditions of continuous processing or under mass production methods, standard costing is applied.

SIMILARITIES BETWEEN STANDARD COSTING AND BUDGETING

In spite of the above differences, there are some similarities between standard costing and budgeting. Both have in common the establishment of predetermined measures of performance and the comparison of actual and planned performance so as to disclose deviations which are used for the purpose of cost control. Both have the same objective of managerial control and are therefore interrelated and cannot function independently. Both help in the preparation of reports which compare actual costs and predetermined costs for management planning and control. Standards are almost indispensable to the work of establishing and operating a budget. A study made by the National Association of Accountants (USA) (now Institute of Management Accounts) concludes that standard costs are especially valuable in developing the cost side of the budget because they provide a reliable and convenient source of data for converting the budgeted production schedule into requirements for raw materials, labour and services.

ADVANTAGES OF STANDARD COSTING

Standard costing is a system of cost accounting which facilitates the performance of the entire managerial process—planning, organisation, coordination and control. Among the many advantages generally attributed to standard costing, the most important may be listed as follows:

1. ***Managerial Planning:*** Planning is a process of using all resources in such a manner that maximises business profits. Management must plan for efficient and economic operations for standard costs to be effective. The standard costs, carefully determined, will disclose inefficiencies in operations, which can be thoroughly investigated and remedial action taken. Standard costs are more convenient than actual costs for budget preparation because the standard costs at different production levels and for different product mixes are readily built up into total costs as required by the budget.

2. ***Coordination:*** The establishment of standards coordinates all functions—manufacturing, marketing, engineering, research and accounting towards the achievement of a common goal. Setting standards involves defining and communicating targets so that they can work towards the attainment of the goal.

3. ***Cost Control:*** Cost control and cost reduction are probably the most important aims of any costing system; and standard costing gives due recognition to this fact. Cost control has the objective of production of the required quality at the lowest cost attainable under existing conditions. Effective control requires detailed standards, to show how much of each material should be used, how much labour should be required for each operation, and what facilities and services will be needed. Standards enable management to make periodic comparison of actual costs with standard costs in order to measure performance and to take action to maintain control over costs. Standard costs help management in cost control through the principle of exception, *i.e.*, highlighting only those activities which fail to come up to standard or which exceed standard. Standards help develop cost conscious attitudes, because it makes cost variances clearly observable by management.

4. ***Economical Means of Costing and Record-keeping:*** The use of standard costs can reduce clerical labour and expense by avoiding detailed record-keeping which is necessary when actual costs alone are used. The following benefits are derived which reduce the cost of record-keeping:

(*i*) By carrying inventory at standard cost, store ledgers can be kept in terms of quantities only.

(*ii*) When standard costs are used, requisition or bills for materials to be put into production can be written and priced more rapidly than when the goods must be priced at actual cost.

(*iii*) The standard cost of goods finished can be obtained immediately upon completion since it is necessary to multiply the quantity by the unit standard cost.

(*iv*) The time required to prepare reports which are used by management can be reduced.

(*v*) The time which must be devoted by management to the study and analysis of cost reports is much reduced when standard costs are used.

(*vi*) The time required to assemble cost data for budget preparation or special cost studies such as pricing is reduced because it is not necessary to devote so much time to the analysis and collection of past actual costs.

5. ***Formulating Price and Production Policies:*** Standard costs as compared to actual costs can be used for estimating selling prices. When standard unit costs are available, expected costs and sales prices can be computed on the basis of standard costs. Standard costs are predetermined costs which help management in the decision process by providing standard unit costs for various levels of activity. Standard costs are thus useful to management in determining price policies, preparing bids for prospective orders, planning production of new product and new methods, and furnishing cost estimates in all managerial decisions.

Actual costs, on the other hand, may reflect excessive usage of material, abnormal labour times or an inequitable charge for overhead. Actual overhead cost per unit at any given time may be so influenced by temporary fluctuations in production levels as to make actual cost entirely unusable for pricing.

Necessary adjustments in standards to incorporate changing conditions can be done without any difficulty whenever required. Standard overhead rates are determined upon a normal production or activity level and therefore, provide an acceptable base for determining product prices which will recover full overhead costs in the long run.

6. ***Standards as Incentives to Employees:*** If standards are reasonable and attainable they act as incentives to employees to improve their performances and to maintain the quality of the product. Each worker performs his job with advance knowledge of the standard set for the particular job; he knows that if his work is less than the standard, he is responsible for the variance. Standards motivate workers, supervisors and foremen to work more efficiently in the accomplishment of their respective standards. Many incentives like cash bonus, individual and group bonus, prizes, vacation time, and promotions can be given for equalling or surpassing standards. Similarly, management can decide upon action to be taken for below standard performance.

The focus on using a standard costing system should be an influencing behaviour through positive reinforcement and appropriate motivation. Seldom does long-term success result from penalties and punishments[1].

DIFFERENT TYPES OF STANDARDS

The two principal considerations affecting the classification of standards are: (*i*) attainability of standards, that is, the ease with which it is possible to achieve the standards, and (*ii*) frequency with which the standards are revised. On the basis of these two factors, it is possible to classify standards as ideal, normal, basic, current or expected actual standards.

1. ***Ideal, Perfect, Maximum Efficiency or Theoretic Standards:*** Ideal standards (costs) are the standards which can be attained under the most favourable conditions possible. The level of performance under ideal standards would be achieved through the best possible combination of factors — the most favourable prices for materials and labour, highest output with best equipment and layout, and maximum efficiency in the utilisation of the production resources—in other words, maximum output at minimum cost. Such standards reflect only goals or targets without any hope of performance being currently achieved. These standards are extremely tight and do not provide for waste and inefficiency in any form; no material is wasted; no units are spoiled; there are no idle hours; operators work at predetermined speeds; the available capacity is fully utilised. The ideal standard represents the ultimate goal to strive for, but its attainment is impossible over sustained periods. It sets its sights on the stars.

2. ***Normal Standards:*** Normal standards are the average standards which (it is anticipated) can be attained during a future period of time, preferably long enough to cover one business cycle. Standards are set on a normal capacity basis which represent a volume that averages out the company's peak and slack periods. Constant unit costs are employed throughout the cycle, regardless of changes in current costs or selling prices. These standards are not revised until the cycle has run its full course. This generally results in an incorrect valuation of inventories and consequent errors in the profit disclosed as the inventories are understated in periods of high prices, and overstated when prices are low. Since these standards do not reflect the goals to be attained, they are not often used.

3. ***Basic Standards:*** The Chartered Institute of Management Accountants (UK) defines a basic standard as the standard which is established for use unaltered for an indefinite period which may be a long period of time. Basic standards are seldom revised or updated to reflect current operating costs and price level changes. Basic standards representing a fixed base are used primarily to measure trends in operating performance. Although useful, basic standards must be adjusted before they can be used for performance evaluation purposes. They can be based upon any capacity level that is selected initially to develop the standards.

4. ***Currently Attainable or Expected Actual Standards:*** Current standards are standards which are established for use over a short period of time, and are related to current conditions. They represent current costs to be expected from efficient operations. These standards do not anticipate ideal performance; they are difficult, but possible to achieve. Currently attainable standards are formulated after making allowance for the cost of normal spoilage, cost of idle time due to machine breakdowns, and the cost of other events which are unavoidable in normal efficient operations. They take the place of actual cost and are recorded in account books and financial statements. Any deviation from these standards reflect inefficiencies in the production activities, unless the variances have occurred due to uncontrollable factors. Currently attainable standards are revised to reflect changes in methods and prices. Much effort and costs are involved in developing these standards. Based on engineering estimates, currently attainable standards are most expensive of the four types of standards. But these standards are most accurate and very useful to management in product costing, inventory valuations, estimates, analyses, performance evaluation, planning, employee motivation, and for managerial decision-making and external financial reporting.

HOW TIGHT SHOULD STANDARDS BE

The establishment of standards or standard cost is decided by the use to be made of them. It can be rightly said that a single standard may not be suitable for all purposes. For the purposes of cost control, tight standards need to be established. The attainable (good) performance standards are useful for purposes of inventory valuation, product costing and income determination. Realistic standards are needed for pricing decisions and capital expenditure decisions.

High Standards

A high standard helps in cost reduction and motivating employees to try to reach the targets established. High standards represent the best possible performance and, if achieved, raise the levels of performance and efficiency as compared to poor or loose standards. High standards being unattainable in practice may not be good for the employees. Employees may not seriously accept them because they know that they are unattainable and impossible to achieve. Employees will always have an opportunity to explain away or excuse the failure to reach them. High standards are also not realistic and therefore cannot be used in product costing, inventory valuation, financial statement, planning and capital investment decisions.

Low (Loose) Standards

A standard which is low or loose can be attained by poor performance. However, it defeats the purpose of standard costing and fails to disclose inefficiencies. Similarly, standards set in terms of average past performance expect too little. Since jobs on which performance is poor are likely to be more numerous than are jobs on which performance is exceptionally good, average past performance standards are usually considerably looser. Such standards do not help management in cost control as they are not accurate measures to compare actual results.

In conclusion, it can be said that accountants generally seem to favour currently attainable standards which are most appropriate for performance appraisal, accounting purposes, cost control and decision-making. Such standards produce good performance, promote employee motivation and include unavoidable elements, such as spoilage, lost time, capacity not utilised in setting standards.

DEVELOPING OR SETTING STANDARDS

The success of a standard cost system depends upon the reliability and accuracy of the physical standards as well as the standard costs. All factors related with standard-setting should be considered in the establishment of standards. Whatever method is used, standards must be established for a definite period of time so that they can be effective in performance evaluation, control and analysis of costs. Standards are usually set for a six or twelve month period. Sometimes a longer period is used but rarely a shorter period. Standards are developed for:

1. Materials
2. Labour
3. Overhead

Materials Standards

Two standards must be developed for materials:

1. Material quantity (usage) standard
2. Material price standard

Materials Quantity Standard

Materials quantity standard specify what kind, what quantity of materials should be used to make a product desired. The development of materials quantity standard is the task of the engineering department or the design department which specifies how the product is to be produced. There are three methods generally used for setting materials quantity standards:

1. Engineering studies to determine the kind and quality specifications, assembly specifications of materials, spoilage allowance, expected yield, quantity specification.
2. Analysis of past experience in usage of materials for the same or similar products. This provides that past performance should be averaged or the standards should be based on jobs or periods which are selected as typical. Such standards include past spoilage and excess usage, if any. This method does not contain the best combination of quantity, methods and product quality as does the engineering study method. However, this method is less costly and quite satisfactory in setting standards for minor items of cost and for developing standards for a brief period.
3. Test-runs under controlled conditions : Under this method, the raw materials specifications are determined on a formula basis. A quantity of materials or units are put into process and the results carefully noted and studied. Results obtained which are further used to determine standards in this manner are usually somewhat artificial because workers become too much sensitive about the results, give undue attention to the test lots and use greater than ordinary care in using the materials.

The materials quantity standard should be developed after taking into account allowance for acceptable levels of spoilage, shrinkage, evaporation, leakage, etc. In such cases, the standard quantity is increased to include these elements. The determination of the percentage of spoilage should be based on the findings that emerge after experimental and development stages of the product have been passed.

Materials Price Standard

A materials price standard is defined as a pre-established measure, expressed in monetary terms of the price of material. Setting materials price standards is often quite difficult because materials prices are influenced more by external factors than internal factors.

Price standards permit: (*i*) checking the performance of the purchasing department, and (*ii*) measuring the effect of price increases or decreases on business profits. The purchasing department may take some measures to control the cost of materials such as buying in economical quantities, using the cheapest methods of transportation, taking discount facilities through prompt and timely payment, purchasing less costly materials, etc.

Materials price variances for the purpose of control should be calculated at the time of purchase of materials and should not be delayed till the time materials are issued for production. If computation of price variance is delayed, useful information for cost control is withheld and it might be too late for remedial action to be taken.

Labour Standards

As in the case of direct materials, labour standards are also established for both rate and quantity (efficiency). For standard cost purpose, direct labour is treated separately from indirect labour, which is included in the factory overhead. Two standards are usually developed for labour costs:

1. Labour usage (or efficiency) standard.
2. Labour cost (or rate) standard.

Labour Usage (or Efficiency) Standard

The process of determining labour time standards is quite similar to setting material's quantity standards. Establishing standard time requires determination of time needed to complete each operation in product manufacture when working under standard conditions. Specific prerequisites to effective labour time standards are:

1. Efficient plant layout with modern equipment to provide maximum production at minimum cost.
2. Development of a planning, routing, scheduling and despatching staff to provide a smooth flow of production without undue delay and confusion.
3. Provision for the careful purchase of materials to flow into production at the proper time, when workmen and machines are available.
4. Standardisation of labour operations and methods, with adequate instructions to and training of workers so that manufacturing can be performed under the best possible conditions.

Labour time standards can be developed using any one of the following methods:

1. Determining the average of past performance of previous periods.
2. Using experimental test runs of the manufacturing operations under expected normal conditions.
3. Using time and motion studies of the various labour operations under expected normal conditions. This helps in determining the standard time to be taken to complete a job or to produce a product.
4. Making a reasonable estimate in advance, based upon a thorough study of the situation, experience, knowledge of the manufacturing operations and the product.

Labour time standards should be established after reasonable allowances are made for fatigue, personal needs of workers and unavoidable delays. Some business enterprises prefer to include other items, such as allowance for set-up time, change over, machine breakdown, waiting time of operations, rework and paid vacation time. However, it is better to include costs relating to these items in the overhead budget instead of in the direct labour standards. These costs are not related to the efficiency of the workers and therefore, can be best controlled through the overhead budget.

Labour Rate (or Cost) Standard

A labour rate standard is defined as:

■■ *a pre-established measure expressed in monetary terms of the price of labour.*

Standard cost rates for each type of direct labour may be determined on the basis of current labour rates. However, other factors such as union negotiations and experience of the workers are properly considered before setting labour rate standards. If labour rate standards are kept up-to-date, the resulting variances should be relatively small. Labour rate variances usually arise from: (*i*) the use of a worker with a wrong rate for a specific operation; (*ii*) use of excess workers per machine; or (*iii*) paying higher (expensive) hourly rates instead of prescribed rates because of low productivity. Labour rate variances are usually not large and therefore receive lesser managerial attention than labour quantity variances.

FACTORY OVERHEAD COST STANDARDS

The concept can be understood broadly as follows.

Complex Nature of Overhead Costs

Factory overhead cost standards are much more complex than those of direct material and direct labour. By nature, direct material and direct labour costs are variable costs, whereas factory overheads are partly fixed and partly variable. Direct materials and direct labour standards can be determined per unit without determining in advance the number of units to be manufactured. But because of some fixed factory overhead costs, it is difficult to say that overhead cost will be ₹ X per unit. An "if" question is involved in this, *i.e.*, overhead costs will be ₹ X per unit, if, and only if, a certain production level is achieved.

Setting Overhead Standards

Setting standard overhead costs requires the determination of: (1) standard capacity and (2) standard overhead costs for this capacity. The standard overhead costs can be computed using theoretical ideal capacity, normal capacity or expected actual capacity. The ideal capacity is attainable only under ideal conditions and therefore is never used. The normal or expected actual aims at a production level according to an existing set of conditions. This capacity does not require complete utilisation of all available facilities but is based on the efficient utilisation of resources and operations.

After standard capacity is determined, overhead—variable and fixed—to be incurred at that capacity is prepared. The standard overhead rate is found by dividing the standard or budgeted overhead at standard capacity by the volume selected to represent standard capacity. Volume may be measured in units of product, standard productive hour (labour or machine) or some standard cost, such as direct labour cost.

$$\text{Standard overhead rate} = \frac{\text{Standard overhead}}{\text{Standard production}}$$

REVISION OF STANDARDS

The question of whether standards should be revised is a difficult one. Some argue that many revisions in standards only destroy the effectiveness and increase operational details. In contrast, standards, if not revised, destroy its utility as means of inventory valuation and cost control. Therefore, standard costs require continuous review and, at time, frequent change. Changing prices, technological advances, new personnel, new machinery, changing quality of materials and new labour negotiations, all influence standards and make them obsolete resulting in unrealistic budgets, poor cost control, and unreasonable unit cost for inventory valuation and income determination.

A company should establish a programme to revise standards whenever required so that standards can be set at a currently attainable level. Labour rate standards should be revised for any change in labour rates; material quantity standards for any change in type, quality of material or method of production. If a new machine is purchased to replace an old machine, labour time standards and material quantity standards should be updated. In addition to these obvious revisions, in every business firm there should be a system for revising standards for adequacy and suitability at least once a year. A periodic review of standards is desirable to accomplish the objectives of standard costing. Standards through an annual review programme will become currently attainable standards or at least closer to such standards.

VARIANCE ANALYSIS

The function of standards in cost accounting is to reveal variances between standard costs which are allowed and actual costs which have been recorded. The Chartered Institute of Management Accountants (UK) defines variances as:

- *the difference between a standard cost and the comparable actual cost incurred during a period.*

Variance analysis can be defined as:

- *the process of computing the amount of, and isolating the cause of variances between actual costs and standard costs.*

Variance analysis involves two phases:

1. Computation of individual variances, and 2. Determination of Cause (s) of each variance.

First, we concentrate on the computation of material, labour and factory overhead variances. Analysis of causes, reporting variances to managers, and accounting disposition of variances conclude the study of standard costing.

MATERIAL VARIANCE

The following variances constitute material variances:

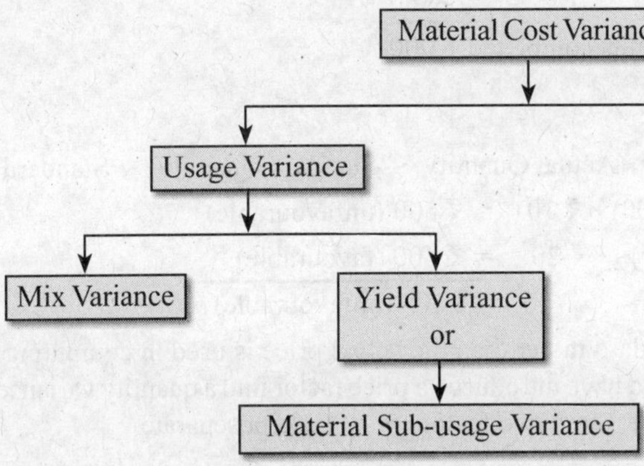

Figure 10.1: Material Variance

Material Cost Variance

Material cost variance is the difference between the actual cost of direct material used and standard cost of direct materials specified for the output achieved. This variance results from differences between quantities consumed and quantities of materials allowed for production and from differences between prices paid and prices predetermined. This can be computed by using the following formula:

> **Material cost variance** is the difference between the actual cost of direct material used and standard cost of direct materials specified for the output achieved.

Material cost variance = (AQ × AP) – (SQ × SP)

Where AQ = Actual quantity

AP = Actual price

SQ = Standard quantity for the actual output

SP = Standard price

Material Usage Variance

The material quantity or usage variance results when actual quantities of raw materials used in production differ from standard quantities that should have been used to produce the output achieved. It is that portion of the direct materials cost variance which is due to the difference between the actual quantity used and standard quantity specified. As a formula, this variance is shown as:

> **Material quantity** or **usage variance** results when actual quantities of raw materials used in production differ from standard quantities that should have been used to produce the output achieved.

Materials quantity variance = (Actual Quantity – Standard Quantity) × Standard Price

A material usage variance is favourable when the total actual quantity of direct materials used is less than the total standard quantity allowed for the actual output.

Example:

Compute the materials usage variance from the following information:

Standard material cost per unit			Materials issued
Material A — 2 pieces @ ₹ 10	=	20	Material A 2,050 pieces
Material B — 3 pieces @ ₹ 20	=	60	Material B 2,980 pieces
		₹ 80	

Units completed 1,000

Solution:

Materials usage variance = (Actual Quantity – Standard Quantity) × Standard Price

Material A = (2,050 – 2,000) × ₹ 10	= ₹ 500 (unfavourable)
Material B = (2980 – 3000) × ₹ 20	= ₹ 400 (favourable)
Total	= ₹ 100 (unfavourable)

It should be noted that the standard rather than the actual price is used in computing the usage variance. Use of an actual price would have introduced a price factor into a quantity variance. Because different departments are responsible, these two factors must be kept separate.

Material Price Variance

A materials price variance occurs when raw materials are purchased at a price different from standard price. It is that portion of the direct materials which is due to the difference between actual price paid and standard price specified and cost variance multiplied by the actual quantity. Expressed as a formula,

Materials price variance = (Actual price – Standard price) × Actual quantity

Materials price variance is unfavourable when the actual price paid exceeds the predetermined standard price. It is advisable that materials price variance should be calculated for materials purchased rather than materials used. Purchase of materials is an earlier event than the use of materials. Therefore, a variance based on quantity purchased is basically an earlier report than a variance based on quantity actually used. This is quite beneficial from the viewpoint of performance measurement and corrective action. An early report will help the management in measuring the performance so that poor performance can be corrected or good performance can be expanded at an early date.

> **Materials price** is that portion of the direct materials which is due to the difference between actual price paid and standard price specified and cost variance multiplied by the actual quantity.

Recognizing material price variances at the time of purchase lets the firm carry all units of the same materials at one price—the standard cost of the material, even if the firm did not purchase all units of the materials at the same price. Using one price for the same materials facilitates management control and simplifies accounting work.

If a direct materials price variance is not recorded until the materials are issued to production, the direct materials are carried on the books at their actual purchase prices. Deviations of actual purchase prices from the standard price may not be known until the direct materials are issued to production.

Example:

Assuming in Example 1 that material A was purchased at the rate of ₹ 10 and material B was purchased at the rate of ₹ 21, the material price variance will be as follows:

Materials price variance = (Actual Price – Standard Price) × Actual Quantity

Material A = (10 – 10) × 2,050 = Zero

Material B = (21 – 20) × 2,980 = 2980 (unfavourable)

Total material price variance = ₹ 2980 (unfavourable)

The total of materials usage variance and price variance is equal to materials cost variance.

Materials Mix Variance

The materials usage or quantity variance can be separated into mix variance and yield variance.

For certain products and processing operations, material mix is an important operating variable, specific grades of materials and quantity are determined before production begins. A mix variance will result when materials are not actually placed into production in the same ratio as the standard formula. For instance, if a product is produced by adding 100 kg of raw material A and 200 kg of raw material B, the standard material mix ratio is 1:2. Actual raw materials used must be in this 1:2 ratio, otherwise a materials mix variance will be found. Material mix variance is usually found in industries, such as textiles, rubber and chemicals, etc. A mix variance may arise because of attempts to achieve cost savings, effective resources utilisation and when the needed raw materials quantities may not be available at the required time.

> **Materials mix variance** is that portion of the materials quantity variance which is due to the difference between the actual composition of a mixture and the standard mixture.

Materials mix variance is that portion of the materials quantity variance which is due to the difference between the actual composition of a mixture and the standard mixture. It can be computed by using the following formula:

Materials mix variance = (Standard cost of actual quantity of the actual mixture – Standard cost of actual quantity of the standard mixture)

Or

Materials mix variance = (Actual mix – Revised standard mix of actual input) × Standard price

Revised standard mix or proportion is calculated as follows:

$$\frac{\text{Standard mix of a particular material}}{\text{Total standard quantity}} \times \text{Actual input}$$

Example:

A product is made from two raw materials, material A and material B. One unit of finished product requires 10 kg of material. The following is standard mix:

Material A –	20% –	2 kg @ ₹ 20	=	₹ 40
Material B –	80% –	8 kg @ ₹ 10	=	₹ 80
	100% –	10 kg @ ₹ 12	=	₹ 120

During a period one unit of product was produced at the following costs:

Material A –	8 kg @ ₹ 20	=	₹ 160
Material B –	4 kg @ ₹ 12.5	=	₹ 50
	12 kg @ ₹ 17.5	=	₹ 210

Compute the materials mix variance.

Solution:

Materials mix variance = (Actual proportion – Revised standard proportion of actual input) × Standard price.

Revised standard proportion =

$$\frac{\text{Standard proportion of a particular mix}}{\text{Total standard quantity}} \times \text{Actual input}$$

Revised standard proportion:

Material A = 2/10 × 12 = 2.40 kg

Material B = 8/10 × 12 = 9.60 kg

Materials mix variance:

Material A = (8 kg – 2.40 kg) × 20

= 5.60 × 20 = ₹ 112.0 (unfavourable)

Material B = (4 kg – 9.60) × 1.00

= 5.60 × 10 = ₹ 56 (favourable)

Total mix variance = ₹ 56 (unfavourable)

Materials Yield Variance

> **Materials yield variance** occurs when the output of the final product does not correspond with the output that could have been obtained by using the actual inputs.

Materials yield variance explains the remaining portion of the total materials quantity variance. It is that portion of materials usage variance which is due to the difference between the actual yield obtained and standard yield specified (in terms of actual inputs). In other words, yield variance occurs when the output of the final product does not correspond with the output that could have been obtained by using the actual inputs. In some industries like sugar, chemicals, steel, etc. actual yield may differ from expected yield based on actual input resulting into yield variance.

The total of materials mix variance and materials yield variance equals materials quantity or usage variance. When there is no materials mix variance, the materials yield variance equals the total materials quantity variance. Accordingly, mix and yield variances explain distinct parts of the total materials usage variance and are additive. The formula for computing yield variance is as follows:

Yield Variance = (Actual yield – Standard Yield specified) × Standard cost per unit

Example:

Standard input = 100 kg, standard yield = 90 kg, standard cost per kg of output = ₹ 200
Actual input 200 kg, actual yield 182 kg. Compute the yield variance.

Solution:

Standard yield for the actual input = $\frac{90}{100}$ × 200 = 180 kg

Yield variance = (Actual yield – Standard yield for the actual input) × Standard cost per unit (per kg)

= 182 – 180 × ₹ 200

= 2 × 200 = ₹ 400 (favourable)

The above yield variance can be computed by using another formula also, *e.g.*,

Yield Variance = (Actual Loss–Standard Loss on Actual Input)×Standard Cost per unit

= (18 kg – 20 kg) × ₹ 200

= ₹ 400 (favourable)

In this example, there is no mix variance and therefore, the materials usage variance will be equal to the materials yield variance.

The above formula uses output or loss as the basis of computing the yield variance. Yield variance can also be computed on the basis of input factors only. The fact is that loss in inputs equals loss in output. A lower yield simply means that a higher quantity of inputs have been used and the anticipated or standard output (based on actual inputs) has not been achieved. Yield, in such a case, is known as sub-usage variance (or revised usage variance) which can be computed by using the following formula:

Sub-usage or revised usage variance = (Revised Standard Proportion of Actual Input – Standard quantity) × Standard Cost per unit of input

Example:

Standard material and standard price for manufacturing one unit of a product is given below:

	Standard material	Standard price
Material A	5 kg	@ ₹ 40
Material B	3 kg	@ ₹ 60

The actual production of the product is 400 units.

The actual material A 2,500 kg @ ₹ 39

B 1,000 kg @ ₹ 62.5

Calculate the materials sub-usage variance.

Solution:

Revised standard proportion of actual input:

Material A = 5/8 × 3,500 = 2,187.5 kg

Material B = 3/8 × 3,500 = 1,312.5 kg

Material sub-usage variance:

(Revised standard proportion of actual input – Standard quantity) × SP

Material A = (2,187.5 – 2,000) × 40

= 187.5 × 40 = ₹ 7,500 (unfavourable)

Material B = (1,312.5 – 1,200) × 60

= 112.5 × 60 = ₹ 6,750 (unfavourable)

Total materials sub-usage variance = ₹ 14,250 (unfavourable)

Or

$$(3{,}500 - 3{,}200) \times \frac{₹\ 1{,}52{,}000}{3{,}200}$$

$$= 300 \times \frac{1{,}52{,}000}{3{,}200} = ₹\ 41{,}250 \text{ (unfavourable)}$$

Materials yield variance always equals sub-usage variance. The difference lies only in terms of calculation. The former considers the output or loss in output and the latter considers standard inputs and actual input used for the actual output. Mix and yield variance both provide useful information for production control, performance evaluation and review of operating efficiency.

Illustrative Problem 1

The standard materials cost to produce a tonne of chemical X is:

300 kg of material A @ ₹ 10 per kg

400 kg of material B @ ₹ 5 per kg

500 kg of material C @ ₹ 6 per kg

During a period, 100 tonnes of mixture X was produced from the usage of:

35 tonnes of material A at a cost of ₹ 9,000 per tonne

42 tonnes of material B at a cost of ₹ 6,000 per tonne

53 tonnes of material C at a cost of ₹ 7,000 per tonne

Calculate the price, usage and mix variances.

Solution:

Material	*Standard*			*Actual*		
	Qty. (kg)	*Rate (₹)*	*Amount (₹)*	*Qty (kg)*	*Rate (₹)*	*Amount (₹)*
A	30,000	10	3,00,000	35,000	9	3,15,000
B	40,000	5	2,00,000	42,000	6	2,52,000
C	50,000	6	3,00,000	53,000	7	3,71,000
	1,20,000		8,00,000	1,30,000		9,38,000

Materials cost variance = Actual cost – Standard cost for actual output

= ₹ 9,38,000 – ₹ 8,00,000

= ₹ 1,38,000 (Adverse)

Materials price variance = Actual quantity × (Actual price – Standard price)

A = 35,000 × (9 – 10) = ₹ 35,000 (F)

B = 42,000 × (6 – 5) = ₹ 42,000 (A)

C = 53,000 × (7 – 6) = ₹ 53,000 (A)

Total: ₹ 60,000 (A)

Material usage variance = Standard price × (Actual quantity – Standard quantity for actual output)

A = ₹ 10 × (35,000 – 30,000) = ₹ 50,000 (A)

B = 5 × (42,000 – 40,000) = ₹ 10,000 (A)

C = 6 × (53,000 – 50,000) = ₹ 18,000 (A)

Total: ₹ 78,000 (A)

Materials mix variance = Standard price × (Actual qty. – Revised std. qty.)

A = ₹ 10 × (35,000 – 32,500)

= 10 × 2,500 = ₹ 25,000 (A)

$$B = 5 \times \left(42{,}000 - \frac{1{,}30{,}000}{3}\right)$$

$$= 5 \times \frac{4,000}{3} = ₹\,6,667\ (F)$$

$$C = 6 \times \left(53,000 - \left(53,000 - \frac{1,62,500}{3}\right)\right)$$

$$= 6 \times \frac{3,500}{3} = 7,000\ (F)$$

Total = 11,333 (A)

Working notes

1. Revised standard quantity $= \dfrac{\text{Std. quantity of a mix} \times \text{Total actual quantity}}{\text{Total std. quantity of mixture}}$

$$A = \frac{30,000}{1,20,000} \times 1,30,000 = 32,500 \text{ kg}$$

$$B = \frac{40,000}{1,20,000} \times 1,30,000 = \frac{1,30,000 \text{ kg}}{3}$$

$$C = \frac{50,000}{1,20,000} \times 1,30,000 = \frac{1,62,500 \text{ kg}}{3}$$

2. Std. cost per unit of output $= \dfrac{\text{Total standard cost}}{\text{Total standard output}}$

$$= \frac{₹\,8,00,000}{100} = ₹\,8,000 \text{ per tonne}$$

3. Std. output for actual mix $= \dfrac{\text{Std. output}}{\text{Standard mix}} \times \text{Actual mix}$

$$= \frac{100}{1,20,000} \times 1,30,000$$

$$= \frac{1,300}{12} \text{ tonnes}$$

Materials yield variance although not asked for in the question would be calculated as follows:

Materials yield variance = (Actual output – Standard output for actual mixture) × Standard cost per unit of output

$$= \left(100 - \frac{1,300}{12}\right) \times ₹\,8,000$$

$$= 100/12 \times ₹\,8,000$$

$$= ₹\,66,667 \text{ (Adverse)}$$

Illustrative Problem 2

In a manufacturing process, the following standards apply :

Standard prices : Raw material A ₹ 10 per kg

B ₹ 50 per kg

Standard mix : 75% A and 25% B (by weight)

Standard output (weight of product as a percentage of weight of raw material) – 90%

In a particular period actual costs, usages and output were as follows:

4,400 kgs of A costing ₹ 46,500

1,600 kgs of B costing ₹ 78,500

Output 5,670 kgs of product.

The budgeted output for the period was 7,200 kgs.

Compute the material cost variances.

Solution:

Standard yield from 6,000 kgs (4,400 kgs + 1600 kgs) of input is

			₹
Material A (75%)	4,500 kg @ ₹ 10	=	45,000
Material B (25%)	1,500 kg @ ₹ 50	=	75,000
	6,000 kg		1,20,000
Less:			
Normal loss @ 10%	600 kg		
Std. output	5,400 kg		

Std. cost of actual output of 5,670 kg $= \frac{1,20,000}{5,400} \times 5,670$

$= ₹\ 1,26,000$

Actual cost of actual output of 5,670 kg

		₹
	4,400 kg × ₹ 10.568 =	46,500
	1,600 kg × ₹ 49.063 =	78,500
	6,000 kg	1,25,000
Less actual loss	330 kg	
Actual output	5,670 kg	

Material cost variance = 1,26,000 – 1,25,000 = ₹ 1,000 (F)

Material price variance :

A (10 – 10.568) × 4,400	= 2499.20 (A)
B (50 – 49.063) × 1,600	= 1499.20 (F)
	1000.0 (A)

Material usage variance: ₹

A $\left(\frac{4,500 \times 5,670}{5,400} - 4,400\right) \times 10 = 3,250\ (F)$

B $\left(\frac{1,500 \times 5,670}{5,400} - 1,600\right) \times 50 = 1,250\ (A)$

2,000 (F)

Material mix variance:

A (4,500 – 4,400) × 10 = 1,000 (F)

B (1,500 – 1,600) × 50 = 5,000 (A)

4,000 (A)

Yield variance = $(5{,}400 - 5{,}670) \times \frac{1{,}20{,}000}{5{,}400} = 6{,}000\ (F)$

Illustrative Problem 3

A company manufacturing 'distempers' operates a costing system. The standard cost of one of the products of the company shows the following standards:

Materials	*Quantity*	*Standard price per kg* ₹	*Total* ₹
A	40 kg	75	3,000
B	10 kg	50	500
C	50 kg	20	1,000
Material cost per unit (Total)			4,500

The standard input mix is 100 kg and the standard output of the finished product is 90 kg

The actual results for period are:

Material used

A = 2,40,000 kg @ ₹ 80/kg

B = 40,000 kg @ ₹ 52/kg

C = 2,20,000 kg @ ₹ 21/kg

Actual output of the finished product = 4,20,000 kg

You are required to calculate the material price, mix and yield variance.

Solution:

	Standard			*Actual*		
Material	*Qty/kg*	*Rate (₹)*	*Amount (₹)*	*Qty/kg*	*Rate (₹)*	*Amount (₹)*
A	2,00,000	75	1,50,00,000	2,40,000	80	1,92,00,000
B	50,000	50	25,00,000	40,000	52	20,80,000
C	2,50,000	20	50,00,000	2,20,000	21	46,20,000
	5,00,000		2,25,00,000	5,00,000		2,59,00,000

Standard output = 4,50,000 kg

Actual output = 4,20,000 kg

Material cost variance = (Actual cost – std. cost of actual output)

= 2,59,00,000 – 4,20,000 × 50

= ₹ 49,00,000 (A)

Material price variance = Actual qty. × (Actual rate – standard rate)

A = 2,40,000 × (80 – 75) = 12,00,000 (A)

B = 40,000 × (52 – 50) = 80,000 (A)

C = 2,20,000 × (21– 20) = 2,20,000 (A)

15,00,000 (A)

Materials usage variance = Standard rate × (Actual qty. – Standard qty. for actual output)

A = 75 × (2,40,000 – 2,00,000 × 42/45) = 40,00,000 (A)

B = 50 × (40,000 – 50,000 × 42/45) = 3,33,333 (F)

C = 20 × (2,20,000 – 2,50,000 × 42/45) = 2,66,667 (F)

34,00,000 (A)

Material Mix Variance = Standard rate × (Actual qty. – Revised std. qty.)

A = 75 (2,40,000 – 2,00,000) = 30,00,000 (A)

B = 50 (40,000 – 50,000) = 5,00,000 (F)

C = 20 (2,20,000 – 2,50,000) = 6,00,000 (F)

19,00,000 (A)

Material yield variance = Standard cost per unit × (Actual output—Standard output for actual mix)

= 50 (4,20,000 – 4,50,000)

= ₹ 15,00,000 (A)

Illustrative Problem 4

SV. Ltd. manufactures BXE by mixing three raw materials. For every batch of 100 kgs of BXE, 125 kgs of raw materials are used. In February 2017, 60 batches were prepared to produce an output of 5,600 kg of BXE. The standard and actual particulars for February 2017 are as under:

Raw material	***Mix %***	***Standard price per kg ₹***	***Mix %***	***Actual price per kg ₹***	***Quantity of Raw Materials purchased kg***
A	50	20	60	21	5,000
B	30	10	20	8	2,000
C	20	5	20	6	1,200

Calculate:

(*i*) Material Cost Variance (*ii*) Material Price Variance (*iii*) Material Mix Variance (*iv*) Material Yield Variance.

Solution:

Raw Material	***Standard*** kg ₹	***rate*** ₹	***Amount***	***Actual*** kg	***rate*** ₹	***Amount*** ₹
A	3,750	20	75,000	4,500	21	94,500
B	2,250	10	22,500	1,500	8	12,000
C	1,500	5	7,500	1,500	6	9,000
	7,500		1,05,000	7,500		1,15,500

Material cost variance = (Actual cost – Standard cost for actual output)

$$= 1,15,500 - \frac{1,05,000}{6,000} \times 5,600$$

$$= 1,15,500 - 98,000 = 17,500 \text{ (A)}$$

Material price variance = Actual qty. × (AR – SR)

A = 4,500 × (21 – 20) = 4,500 (A)
B = 1,500 × (8 – 10) = 3000 (F)
C = 1,500 × (6 – 5) = 1,500 (A)
Total 3,000 (A)

Material usage variance = Standard rate × Std. Qty. for actual output)

$$A = 20 \times 4,500 - \left(\frac{3,750}{6,000} \times 5,600\right)$$

$$= 20 \times (4,500 - 3,500) = 20,000 \text{ (A)}$$

$$B = 10 \times \left(1,500 - \frac{2,250}{6,000} \times 5,600\right)$$

$$= 10 \times (1,500 - 2,100) = 6,000 \text{ (F)}$$

$$C = 5 \times \left(1,500 - \frac{1,500}{6,000} \times 5,000\right)$$

$$= 5 \times (1,500 - 1,400) = 500 \text{ (A)}$$

Total 14,500 (A)

Material mix variance = Standard Rate × (Actual Qty – Revised Std. Qty.)

A = 20 × (4,500 – 3,750) = 15,000 (A)
B = 10 × (1,500 – 2,250) = 7,500 (F)
C = 5 × (1,500 – 1,500) = 0
Total 7,500 (A)

Since the Standard Mix and Actual Mix are the same, the Standard Quantity and Revised Standard Quantity will also be the same.

Material yield variance = Standard cost per unit × (Actual output – Standard output for actual mix)

$$= \frac{1,05,000}{6,000} \times (5,600 - 6,000)$$

= 17.5 × 400 = 7,000 (A)

The Material Yield Variance is equal to Material Sub-usage Variance calculated as follows:

Material Sub-usage variance = SR × (Revised St. Qty. – St. Qty. for actual output)

A = 20 × (3,750 – 3,500) = 5,000 (A)
B = 10 × (2250 – 2100) = 1,500 (A)
C = 5 × (1500 – 1400) = 500 (A)
Total 7,000 (A)

Note: The question gives quantity of raw materials purchased and not quantity actually used. It has been presumed that total quantity used was 7,500 kg. In case of material C purchase amounts to 1,200 kgs. only and hence opening stock has been presumed of 300 units at ₹ 6 per unit.

Alternative Solution: In case quantity purchased is taken as quantity actually used, the various variances will be as follows:

(*i*) Material price variable = Actual quantity × (Actual Rate – Standard Rate)

A =	5,000 × (21 – 20)	= 5,000 (A)
B =	2,000 × (8 – 10)	= 4,000 (F)
C =	1,200 × (6 – 5)	= 1,200 (A)
Total		2,200 (A)

(*ii*) Material usage variance = Standard rate × (actual qty. – standard quantity for actual output)

$$A = 20 \times \left(5{,}000 - \frac{3{,}750}{6{,}000} \times 5{,}600\right)$$

$$= 20 \times (5{,}000 - 3{,}500)$$

$$= 20 \times 1500 = 30{,}000 \text{ (A)}$$

$$B = 10 \times \left(2{,}000 - \frac{2{,}250}{6{,}000} \times 5{,}600\right)$$

$$= 10 \times (2{,}000 - 2{,}100)$$

$$= 10 \times 100 = 1{,}000 \text{ (F)}$$

$$C = 5 \times \left(1{,}200 - \frac{1{,}500}{6{,}000} \times 5{,}600\right)$$

$$= 5 \times (1{,}200 - 1{,}400)$$

$$= 5 \times 200 \qquad = 1{,}000 \text{ (F)}$$

Total: 28,000 (A)

Material mix variance = Standard rate × (Actual quantity – Revised standard quantity)

$$\text{Revised Std. Qty.} = \frac{\text{Actual total mix}}{\text{Standard mix}} \times \text{Standard Quantity}$$

$$A = \frac{8{,}200}{7{,}500} \times 3{,}750 = 4{,}100$$

$$B = \frac{8{,}200}{7{,}500} \times 2{,}250 = 2{,}460$$

$$C = \frac{8{,}200}{7{,}500} \times 1{,}500 = 1{,}640$$

A = 20 (5,000 – 4,100)	= 18,000 (A)
B = 10 × (2,000 – 2,460)	= 4,600 (F)
C = 5 (1,200 – 1,640)	= 2,200 (F)
Total:	11,200 (A)

Material yield variance = Standard cost per unit × (Actual output – Standard output for actual mix)

$$= \frac{1,05,000}{6,000} \times \left(5,600 - \frac{6,000}{7,500} \times 8,200\right)$$

$$= 17.5 \times (5,600 - 6,560)$$

$$= 16,800 \text{ (A)}$$

Material yield variance is equal to material sub-usage variance which can be ascertained as follows:

Material sub-usage variance = Standard rate × (Revised standard quantity – Standard quantity for actual output)

A = 20 × (4,100 – 3,500)	= 20 × 600	=	12,000 (A)
B = 10 × (2,460 – 2,100)	= 10 × 360	=	3,600 (A)
C = 5 × (1,640 – 1,400)	= 5 × 240	=	1,200 (A)
Total:			16,800 (A)

Illustrative Problem 5

Vinak Ltd. produces an article by blending two raw materials. It operates a standard costing system and the following standards have been set for raw materials:

Materials	Standard mix	Standard price per kg
A	40%	₹ 4.00
B	60%	₹ 3.00

The standard loss in processing is 15%.

During April 2017 the company produced 1,700 kg of finished output. The position of stocks and purchases for the month of April 2017 is under:

Material	***Stock on* 1.4.2017 *(kg)***	***Stock on* 30.4.2017 *(kg)***	***Purchased during April* 2017 *(kg)***	***Cost* (₹)**
A	35	5	800	3,400
B	40	50	1,200	3,000

Calculate the following variances:

(*i*) Materials price variance

(*ii*) Materials usage variance

(*iii*) Materials yield variance

(*iv*) Materials mix variance

(*v*) Total materials cost variance

Solution:

Standard cost of standard mix:

Type of material	*Standard quantity of materials required*	*Standard price per kg*	*Standard quantity*
A	800	₹ 4	₹ 3,200
B	1,200	₹ 3	₹ 3,600
Total	2,000		6,800

Notes:

1. The loss being 15% to produce 85 kg of an article, the standard quantity of material required is 100 kg. Therefore, to produce 1,700 kg of the article the standard quantity of material required is $\frac{100}{85} \times 1{,}700$ kg or 2,000 kg.
2. Out of 2,000 kg of material used, 40% is type A and 60% is type B, *i.e.*, 800 kg of A and 1,200 kg of B are the standard quantities.

Actual costs

Types of material kg	*Actual quantity of material used kg*	*Actual price per ₹*	*Actual quantity × actual price*
A	830	4.25	3,518.75*
B	1,190	2.50	2,995.00*
Total	2,020		6,513.75

* Actual quantity of material A is 830 kg; out of this 35 kg is available at the standard price of ₹ 4 per kg and remaining 795 kg at ₹ 4.25 per kg.

Actual quantity of material B used is 1,190 kg; out of this 40 kg is available at the standard price of ₹ 3 per kg and remaining 1,150 kg at ₹ 2.50.

(*i*) Materials price variance = Actual quantity × (Actual price – Standard price)

A. Standard price of 830 units @ 4		3,320.00
Actual price of 35 units @ ₹ 4	140.00	
795 units @ ₹ 4.25	3,378.75	
		3,518.75
		198.75 (A)
B. Standard price of 1,190 units @ ₹ 3		3,570.00
Actual price of 40 units @ ₹ 3	120.00	
1,150 units @ ₹ 2.50	2,875.00	
		2,995.00
		575.00 (F)
		376.25 (F)

(*ii*) Material (Total) usage variance = Standard price × (Actual quantity – Standard quantity)

A : 4 × (830 – 800)	120.00 (A)
B : 3 × (1,190 – 1,200)	30.00 (F)
	90.00 (A)

(*iii*) Materials (yield variance = Standard rate × (Actual yield – standard yield)

$$\text{Standard rate} = \frac{\text{Total standard cost}}{\text{Yield}} = \frac{₹\,6{,}800}{1{,}700} = ₹\,4 \text{ per kg}$$

Yield variance = 4 (1,700 – 1,717*) or ₹ 68 (A)

* By using 2,000 kg of material, standard yield is 1,700 kg.

Therefore, the standard yield by using 2,020 kg of material will be (1,700/2,000) × 2,020 or 1,717 kg.

(*iv*) Material mix variance = Actual quantity × (per unit standard cost of standard mix – per unit standard cost of actual mix)

$$= 2{,}020\left(\frac{6{,}800}{2{,}000} - \frac{6{,}890}{2{,}020}\right)$$

= 2,020 (3.4 – 3.410) or ₹ 22 (A)

(*v*) Materials cost variance = (Actual cost – Standard cost)

= ₹ 6,513.75 – 6,800

= ₹ 286.25 (F)

Illustrative Problem 6

JS Limited used a full standard cost system with raw material inventory carried at standard. The following data were taken from the records of the company for the year ended 31.12.2016:

Opening raw materials inventory	₹ 300
Closing raw materials inventory	250
Net purchases	410
Material price variance	10 A
Material usage variance	20 A
Direct labour cost (actuals)	900
Direct labour cost (standard)	840
Actual overhead cost incurred	875
Overheads cost variance	45 F
Opening Work-in-Progress inventory	120
Closing Work-in-Progress inventory	140
Opening finished goods inventory	360
Cost of goods sold reported	2,240

***Note*:** F denotes favourable and 'A' denotes adverse. You are required to compute:

1. Raw material purchases at standard
2. Raw materials consumed at actuals
3. Raw materials consumed at standard
4. Labour cost variance
5. Standard overhead costs

6. Total manufacturing cost at standard
7. Cost of goods manufactured
8. Cost of product sold to customers
9. Closing finished goods inventory

Solution:

1.	Raw material purchases at standard:	
	Net purchases at actual	₹ 410
Less:	Material price variance (A)	10
		400
2.	Raw materials consumed at actual:	
	Raw materials consumed at standard (as per 3 below)	₹ 450
Add:	Materials usage variance (A)	₹ 20
		₹ 470
3.	Raw materials consumed at standard:	
	Opening stock at standard	₹ 300
Add:	Purchases at standard (as per 1)	₹ 400
		₹ 700
Less:	Closing stock at standard	₹ 250
		₹ 450
4.	Labour Cost Variance:	
	Direct Labour Cost of standard	₹ 840
Less:	Actual Direct Labour Cost	₹ 900
		₹ 60 (A)
5.	Standard Overhead Cost:	
	Actual Overheads	₹ 875
Add:	Overhead Cost Variance	₹ 45 (F)
		₹ 920
6.	Total (or Gross) Manufacturing Cost at Standard:	
	Standard Raw Material Cost	₹ 450
	Standard Direct Labour Cost	₹ 840
	Standard Overhead Cost	₹ 920
		₹ 2,210
7.	Cost of goods manufactured (at standard):	
	Opening WIP (at standard)	₹ 120
Add:	Total or Gross Cost of Goods manufactured	₹ 2,210
		₹ 2,330
Less:	Closing WIP (at standard)	140
		₹ 2,190

8.	Cost of products sold to customers (at standard)	
	Cost of goods sold reported	₹ 2,240
Less:	Adverse variances:	
	Material cost variance – price variance	10 (A)
	Usage variance	20 (A)
		30 (A)
	Direct labour cost variance	60 (A)
		90 (A)
		₹ 2,150
Add:	Overhead cost variance	45 (F)
		₹ 2,195
9.	Closing stock of finished goods inventory at standard:	
	Opening finished goods inventory at standard	₹ 360
Add:	Cost of goods manufactured at standard	₹ 2,190
		₹ 2,550
Less:	Cost of products sold to customers at standard	₹ 2,195
		₹ 355

LABOUR VARIANCES

Direct labour variances arise when actual labour costs are different from standard labour costs. In analysis of labour costs, the emphasis is on labour rates and labour hours. Labour variances constitute the following:

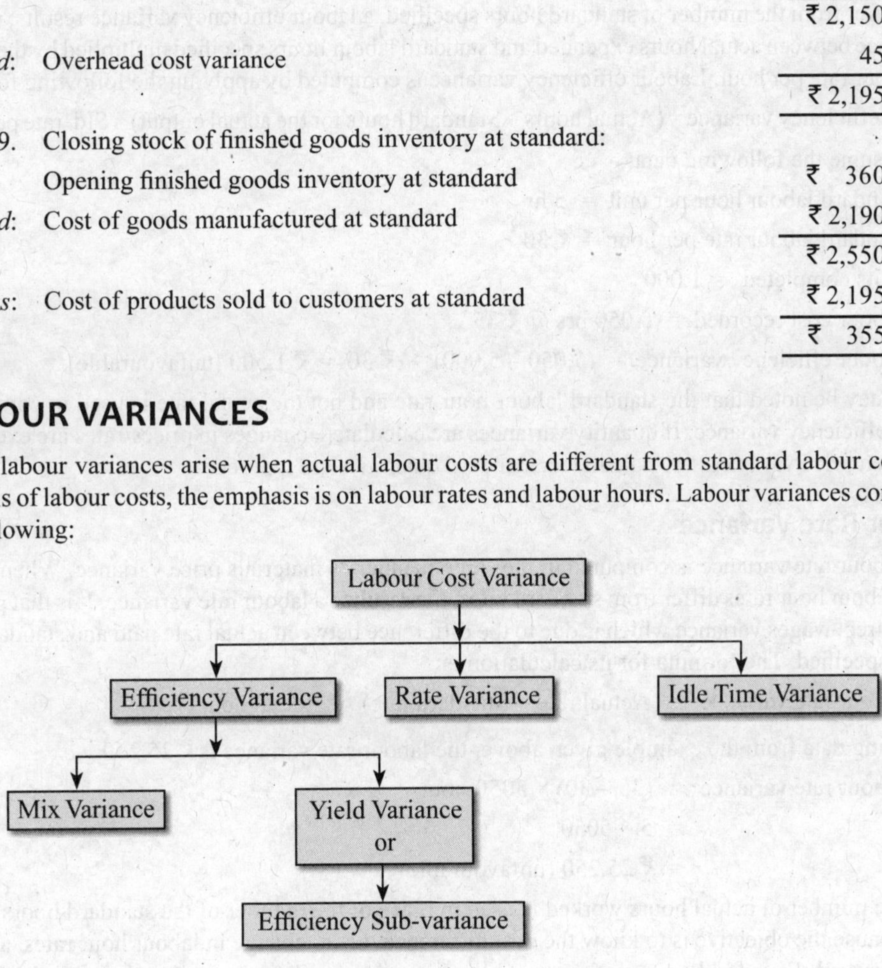

Figure 10.2: Labour Cost Variance

Labour Cost Variance

Labour cost variance denotes the difference between the actual direct wages paid and the standard direct wages specified for the output achieved. This variance is calculated by using the following formula:

Labour cost variance = (AH × AR) – (SH × SR)

Where AH = Actual hours

AR = Actual rate

SH = Standard hours

SR = Standard rate

Labour Efficiency Variance

The calculation of labour efficiency or usage variance follows the same pattern as the computation of materials usage variance. Labour efficiency variance occurs when labour operations are more efficient or less efficient than standard performance. If actual direct labour hours required to complete a job differ from the number of standard hours specified, a labour efficiency variance results; it is the difference between actual hours expended and standard labour hours specified multiplied by the standard labour rate per hour. Labour efficiency variance is computed by applying the following formula:

Labour efficiency variance = (Actual hours – Standard hours for the actual output) × Std. rate per hour.

Assume the following data:

Standard labour hour per unit = 5 hr

Standard labour rate per hour = ₹ 30

Units completed = 1,000

Labour cost recorded = 5,050 hrs @ ₹ 35

Labour efficiency variance = (5,050 – 5,000) × ₹ 30 = ₹ 1,500 (unfavourable)

It may be noted that the standard labour hour rate and not the actual rate is used in computing labour efficiency variance. If quantity variances are calculated, changes in prices/rates are excluded, and when price variances are calculated, standard quantities are ignored.

Labour Rate Variance

Labour rate variance is computed in the same manner as materials price variance. When actual direct labour hour rates differ from standard rates, the result is a labour rate variance. It is that portion of the direct wages variance which is due to the difference between actual rate paid and standard rate of pay specified. The formula for its calculation is:

Labour rate variance = (Actual rate – Standard rate) × Actual hours

Using data from the example given above, the labour rate variance is ₹ 25,250, *i.e.*,

Labour rate variance = (35 – 30) × 5050 hours

= 5 × 5050

= ₹ 25,250 (unfavourable)

The number of actual hours worked is used in place of the number of the standard hours specified because the objective is to know the cost difference due to change in labour hour rates, and not hours worked. Favourable rate variances arise whenever actual rates are less than standard rates; unfavourable variances occur when actual rates exceed standard rates.

Labour Mix Variance

Labour mix variance is computed in the same manner as materials mix variance. Manufacturing or completing a job requires different types or grades of workers and production will be complete if labour is mixed according to standard proportion. Standard labour mix may not be adhered to under some circumstances and substitution will have to be made. There may be changes in the wage rates of some workers; there may be a need to use more skilled or expensive types of labour, *e.g.*, employment of men instead of women; sometimes workers and operators may be absent. These lead to the emergence of a labour mix variance which is calculated by using the following formula:

Labour mix variance = (Actual labour mix – Revised standard labour mix in terms of actual total hours) × Standard rate per hour

To take an example, suppose the following were the standard labour cost data per unit in a factory:

Class	Proportion				
A	50%	3 hours @	₹ 40	=	₹ 120
B	50%	3 hours @	₹ 20	=	₹ 60
	100%	6 hours	₹ 30		₹ 180

In a period, many class B workers were absent and it was necessary to substitute class B workers. Since the class A workers were less experienced with the job, more labour hours were used. The recorded costs of a unit were:

Class	Proportion			Costs
A	75%	6 hours @	₹ 40	₹ 240
B	25%	2 hours @	₹ 20	₹ 40
	100%	8 hours	₹ 35	₹ 280

Labour mix variance will be calculated as follows:

Labour mix variance = (Actual proportion – Revised standard proportion of actual total hours) × standard rate per hour

Revised standard proportion:

$$\text{Class A} = \frac{3}{6} \times 8 = 4 \text{ hours}$$

$$\text{Class B} = \frac{3}{6} \times 8 = 4 \text{ hours}$$

Applying the formula:

Class A =(6 – 4) × ₹ 40 = ₹ 80 (unfavourable)

Class B =(2 – 4) × ₹ 20 = ₹ 40 (favourable)

Total labour mix variance = ₹ 40 (unfavourable)

Labour Yield Variance

The final product cost contains not only material cost but also labour cost. Therefore, gain or loss (higher or lower output than the standard output) should take into account labour yield variance also. A lower output simply means that final output does not correspond with the production units that should have been produced from the hours expended on the inputs. It can be computed by applying the following formula:

Labour yield variance = (Actual output – Standard output based on actual hours) × Av. Std. Labour Rate per unit of output.

Or

Labour yield variance = (Actual loss – Standard loss on actual hours) × Average standard labour rate per unit of output

Labour yield variance is also known as labour efficiency sub-variance which is computed in terms of inputs, *i.e.*, standard labour hours and revised labour hours mix (in terms of actual hours). Labour efficiency sub-variance is computed by using the following formula:

Labour efficiency sub-variance = (Revised standard mix – standard mix) × Standard rate

Idle Time Variance

Idle time variance occurs when workers are not able to do the work due to some reason during the hours for which they are paid. Idle time can be divided according to causes responsible for creating idle time, *e.g.*, idle time due to breakdown, lack of materials or power failures. Idle time variance will be equivalent to the standard labour cost of the hours during which no work has been done but for which workers have been paid for unproductive time. Suppose, in a factory 2,000 workers were idle because of a power failure. As a result of this, a loss of production of 4,000 units of product A and 8,000 units of product B occurred. Each employee was paid his normal wage (a rate of ₹ 20 per hour). A single standard hour is needed to manufacture four units of product A and eight units of product B. Idle time variance will be computed in the following manner:

Standard hours lost:

$$\text{Product A} = \frac{4{,}000}{4} = 1{,}000 \text{ hr.}$$

$$\text{Product B} = \frac{8{,}000}{8} = 1{,}000 \text{ hr.}$$

Total hours lost = 2,000 hr.

Idle time variance (power failure)

2,000 hours @ ₹ 20 per hour = ₹ 40,000 (Adverse)

Illustrative Problem 7

Standard hours for manufacturing two products M and N are 15 hours per unit and 20 hours per unit respectively. Both products require identical kind of labour and the standard wage rates per hour is ₹ 5. In the year 2016, 10,000 units of M and 15,000 units of N were manufactured. The total of labour hours actually worked were 4,50,500 and the actual wage bill came to ₹ 23,00,000. This include 12,000 hours paid for @ ₹ 7 per hour and 9,400 hours paid for @ ₹ 7.50 per hour, the balance having been paid at ₹ 5 per hour. You are required to compute the labour variances.

Solution:

Labour cost variance = (Actual labour cost – Standard labour cost for actual output)

Standard cost:

For product M = 10,000 × 15 × 5 = 7,50,000

For product N = 15,000 × 20 × 5 = 15,00,000

Total standard cost = 22,50,000

Total actual labour cost = ₹ 23,00,000

Labour cost variance = ₹ 23,00,000 – ₹ 22,50,000

= ₹ 50,000 (Adverse)

Labour rate variance = Actual hours × (Actual rate – Std. rate)

= 12,000 × (₹ 7 – ₹ 5) = ₹ 24,000 (A)

= 9,400 × (₹ 7.50 – ₹ 5) = ₹ 23,500 (A)

= 4,29,100 × (₹ 5 – ₹ 5) = –

Total: ₹ 47,500 (A)

Labour efficiency variance = Std. rate × (Actual time – Std. time)

= ₹ 5 × (4,50,500 – 4,50,000)

= ₹ 2,500 (Adverse)

Illustrative Problem 8

The standard labour component and the actual labour component engaged in a week for a job are as under:

		Skilled workers	***Semi-skilled workers***	***Unskilled workers***
(A)	Standard number of workers in the gang	32	12	6
(B)	Standard wage rate per hour (₹)	30	20	10
(C)	Actual number of workers employed in the gang during the week	28	18	4
(D)	Actual wage rate per hour (₹)	40	30	20

During the 40 hours working week, the gang produced 1,800 standard labour hours of work.

Calculate:

(*i*) Labour efficiency variance

(*ii*) Labour mix variance

(*iii*) Rate of wages variance

(*iv*) Total labour cost variance

Solution:

	Standard			***Actual***		
Category of workers	***Hrs.***	***Rate (₹)***	***Amount (₹)***	***Hrs.***	***Rate (₹)***	***Amount (₹)***
Skilled	1,280	30	38,400	1,120	40	44,800
Semi-skilled	480	20	9,600	720	30	21,600
Unskilled	240	10	2,400	160	20	3,200
	2,000		50,400	2,000		69,600

Labour cost variance = Actual cost – Standard cost for actual output

= ₹ 69,600 – ₹ 45,360

= ₹ 24,240 (Adverse)

Labour rate variance = Actual time × (Actual rate – Standard rate)

Skilled = ₹ 1,120 × (40 – 30)

= ₹ 11,200 (A)

Semi-skilled = ₹ 720 × (30 – 20)

= ₹ 7,200 (A)

Unskilled = ₹ 160 × (20 – 10)

= ₹ 1,600 (A)

Total = ₹ 11,200 (A) + ₹ 7,200 (A) + ₹ 1,600(A)

= 20,000 (Adverse)

Labour efficiency variance = Standard rate × (Actual time – Standard time for actual output)

Skilled = 30 × (1,120 – 1,152)

= ₹ 960 (F)

Semi-skilled = 20 × (720 – 432)

= ₹ 5,760 (A)

Unskilled = 10 × (160 – 216)

= ₹ 560 (F)

Total = ₹ 960 (F) + ₹ 5,760 (A) + ₹ 560 (F)

= ₹ 4,240 (A)

Labour mix variance = Standard rate × (Actual time – Revised standard time)

Skilled = 30 × (1,120 – 1,280)

= ₹ 4,800 (F)

Semi-skilled = 20 × (720 – 480)

= ₹ 4,800 (A)

Unskilled = 10 × (160 – 240)

= ₹ 800 (F)

Total = ₹ 4,800 (F) + ₹ 4,800 (A) + ₹ 800 (F)

= ₹ 800 (Favourable)

Labour yield variance = Standard cost per hour of work × (Actual output – Standard output for actual mix)

= 25.2 × (1,800 – 2,000)

= ₹ 5,040 (Adverse)

Working Notes

1. Standard cost for actual output $= ₹ \frac{50,400}{2,000} \times 1,800$

$= ₹ 45,360$

2. Standard time for actual output:

Skilled $= \frac{1,800}{2,000} \times 1,280 = 1,152$ hrs

Semi-skilled $= \frac{1,800}{2,000} \times 480 = 432$ hrs

Unskilled $= \frac{1,800}{2,000} \times 240 = 216$ hrs

3. Revised standard time $= \frac{\text{Actual mix}}{\text{Standard mix}} \times \text{Standard time}$

Since, Standard Mix and Actual Mix are the same, the Standard Time will also be the Revised Standard Time.

Standard Cost per hour of standard work

$$= \frac{\text{Total Standard cost}}{\text{Total Standard hours of work}}$$

$$= \frac{50{,}400}{2{,}000}$$

$$= ₹\ 25.2$$

Illustrative Problem 9

A building can be constructed by engaging a gang of workers as per details given below for 100 working days of eight hours each.

Standard data:

	Skilled	Semi-skilled	Unskilled
No. of workers in the gang	6	8	6
Standard rate of wages/hr.	₹ 25	₹ 20	₹ 16

Actual completion of the work however took 104 days of eight hours each. This includes 16 hours of stoppages due to heavy rains. The actual number of workers engaged and the actual rates paid are given below:

	Skilled	Semi-skilled	Unskilled
No. engaged	8	6	6
Actual rate/hr.	₹ 30	₹ 24	₹ 16

Calculate the following variances :

(a) Labour cost variances
(b) Labour rate variance
(c) Labour efficiency variance
(d) Labour mix variance
(e) Idle time variance

Solution:

(i) Standard labour cost:

			Days hrs.		
Skilled workers	=	6 nos. @ ₹ 25 for	100 × 8	=	₹ 1,20,000
Semi-skilled workers	=	8 nos. @ ₹ 20 for	100 × 8	=	₹ 1,28,000
Unskilled workers	=	6 nos. @ ₹ 16 for	100 × 8	=	₹ 76,000
					₹ 3,24,800

Standard gang time	=	800 hours.		
Standard gang rate/hr.	=	₹ 3,24,800 ÷ 800	=	₹ 406/hr.

(ii) Actual labour cost:

		Nos.	days	hr/day		rate		₹
Skilled workers	=	8 ×	104 ×	8	×	₹ 30	=	₹ 1,99,680
Semi-skilled workers	=	6 ×	104 ×	8	×	₹ 24	=	₹ 1,19,808
Unskilled workers	=	6 ×	104 ×	8	×	₹ 16	=	₹ 79,872
								₹ 3,99,360

(iii) Standard labour cost for actual hours of actual gang:

			Days hrs.		
Skilled workers	=	8 nos. @ ₹ 25 for	104 × 8	=	₹ 1,66,400
Semi-skilled workers	=	6 nos. @ ₹ 20 for	104 × 8	=	₹ 99,840
Unskilled workers	=	6 nos. @ ₹ 16 for	104 × 8	=	₹ 79,872
					₹ 3,46,112

(iv) Standard labour cost for actual hours of standard gang:

			Days hrs.		
Skilled workers	=	6 nos. @ ₹ 25 for	104 × 8	=	₹ 1,24,800
Semi-skilled workers	=	8 nos. @ ₹ 20 for	104 × 8	=	₹ 1,33,120
Unskilled workers	=	6 nos. @ ₹ 16 for	104 × 8	=	₹ 79,872
					₹ 3,37,792

(v) Standard labour cost for actual hours utilised for completion of the work.

(104 × 8 – 16) × ₹ 406 = ₹ 3,31,296

Calculation of variances:

(a) Labour Cost Variance:

(Actual labour cost – Std. Cost of Actual hours utilised for completion of the work):

(3,99,360 – 3,31,296) = ₹ 68,064 (Adv.)

(b) Labour Rate Variance:

(Actual labour cost – Std. L. Cost for Actual hours of Actual gang):

(3,99,360 – 3,46,112) = ₹ 53,248 (Adv.)

(c) Labour Efficiency Variance: (Std. L. Cost of Actual hrs – Std. Labour Cost of Actual hrs. utilised for completion of the work):

= (3,46,112 – 3,31,269) = ₹ 14,816 (Adv.)

(d) Labour Mix Variance: (Std. L. Cost of Actual hours – Std. Lab. Cost of Actual hrs in Std Mix)

= (3,46,112 – 3,37,792) = ₹ 8,320 (Adv.)

(e) Idle time Variance = Idle time × Std. Rate = 16 × 406 = ₹ 6,496 (Adv.)

Illustrative Problem 10

The Radiology Department provides imaging services for Parkside Medical Centre. One important activity in the Radiology Department is transcribing digitally recorded analyses of images into a written report. The manger of the Radiology Department determined that the average transcriptionist could type 750 lines of a report in an hour. The plan for the first week in May called for 60,000 typed lines to be written. The Radiology Department has two transcriptionists. Each transcriptionist is hired form an employment firm that requires temporary employees to be hired for a minimum of a 40-hour week. Transcriptionists are paid ₹ 16.000 per hour. The manager offered a bonus if the department could type more than 65,000 lines for the week, without overtime. Due to high service demands, the transcriptionists typed more lines in the first week of May than planned. The actual amount of lines typed in the first week of May was 72,000 lines, without overtime. As a result, the bonus caused the average transcriptionist hourly rate to increase to ₹ 19.000 per hour during the first week in May.

Required:

(i) If the department typed 60,000 lines according to the original plan, what have been the labour time variance?

(ii) What was the labour time variance as a result of typing 72,000 lines?

(iii) What was the labour rate variance as a result of the bonus?

(iv) The manager is trying to determine if a better decision would have been to hire a temporary transcriptionist to meet the higher typing demands in the first week of May, rather than paying out the bonus. If another employee was hired from the employment firm, what would have been the laour time variance in the first week?

(v) Which decision is better, paying the bonus or hiring another transcriptionist?

(vi) Are there any performance-related issues that the labour time and rate variances fail to consider? Explain.

Solution:

(i) Actual hours provided (2 × 40 hrs)	80
Standard hours required for the original plan	80*
Labour time difference	0
standard labour rate	× ₹ 16.00
Direct labour time variance	₹ 0.00

$$* \frac{60,000 \text{ lines}}{750 \text{ lines per hour}} = 80 \text{ hrs.}$$

(ii) Actual hours provided (2 × 40 hrs)	80
Standard hours required for the actual results	96*
Labour time difference	– 16
Standard labour rate	× ₹ 16.00
Direct labour time variance—favourable	– ₹ 256.00

$$* \frac{72,000 \text{ lines}}{750 \text{ lines per hr.}} = 96 \text{ hrs.}$$

(iii) Actual labour rate	19.00
Standard labour rate	16.00
Difference	₹ 3.00
Actual hours provided (2 × 40 hrs.)	80
Direct labour rate variance—unfavourable	₹ 240.00

The labour cost variance is ₹ 16 favourable (– ₹ 256 favourable time variance + 240 unfavourable rate variance).

(iv)

Actual hours provided (3 × 40 hrs.)	120
Standard hours required for the actual results	96
Labour time difference	24
Standard labour rate	× ₹ 16.00
Direct labour time variance—unfavourable	₹ 384.00

(v) The bonus is the better approach by ₹ 400. The cost variance for paying the bonus was ₹ 16 favourable which is the sum of the time variance and rate variance from (ii) and (iii) above (₹ – 256 F + ₹ 240 U). The cost variance that would result form hiring another employee would have been ₹ 384 unfavourable from (iv) above. Thus, the net benefit for paying the bonus over hiring another employee is ₹ 400 (₹ 16 F + ₹ 384 U).

(vi) The labour rate and time variances fail to consider the number of errors in the report from typist fatigue. A report that has many errors will require significant time for correction at a later date. In addition, report errors can cause doctors to draw incorrect conclusions from the test analyses. Thus, managers should consider not only the efficiency of doing the work but also the quality of the work.

Illustrative Problem 11

From the following data of A Co. Ltd. relating to budgeted and actual performance for the month of March, 2016, compute the Direct Material and Direct Labour Cost Variances.

Budgeted data for March:

Units to be manufactured	1,50,000
Units of direct material required (based on std. rates)	4,95,000
Planned purchase of raw materials (Units)	5,40,000
Average unit cost of direct material	₹ 8
Direct labour hours per unit of finished goods 3/4 hr	
Direct labour cost (Total)	₹ 29,92,500

Actual data at the end of March

Units actually manufactured	1,60,000
Direct material cost (purchase cost based on units actually issued)	₹ 43,41,900
Direct material cost (purchase cost based on units actually purchased)	₹ 45,10,000
Average unit cost of direct material	₹ 8.20
Total direct labour hours for March	1,25,000
Total direct labour cost for March	₹ 33,75,000

Solution:

Direct Material Variances

MCV = Actual material cost – Std. material cost of actual output
= 43,41,900 – 1,60,000 × 3.3 × 8
= 43,41,900 – 42,24,000
= 1,17,900 (Adverse)

MPV = Actual Qty. × (Actual Rate – Std. Rate)
= 5,29,500 × (8.20 – 8)
= ₹ 1,05,900 (Adverse)

MUV = Std. Rate × (Actual Qty. – Std. Qty. for actual output)
= 8 × (5,29,500 – 1,60,000 × 3.30)
= 8 × (5,29,500 – 5,28,000)
= ₹ 12,000 (Adverse)

Direct Labour Variances

LCV = Actual labour cost – Std. labour cost for actual output
= 33,75,000 – 1,60,000 × 3/4 × 26.60
= 33,75,000 – 31,92,000
= ₹ 1,83,000 (Adverse)

LRV = Actual time × (Actual Rate – Std. Rate)
= 1,25,000 × (27 – 26.60)
= ₹ 50,000 (Adverse)

LEF = Std. Rate × (Actual time – Std. time for actual output)
= 26.60 × (1,25,000 – 1,60,000 × 3/4)
= 26.60 × (1,25,000 – 1,20,000)
= ₹ 1,33,000 (Adverse)

Working Notes

(*i*) Standard Units of Direct Material required per unit of output

$$= \frac{4,95,000}{1,50,000} = 3.30 \text{ units}$$

(*ii*) Total Actual Quantity of Direct Material used

$$= \frac{43,41,900}{8.20} = 5,29,500 \text{ units}$$

(*iii*) Standard Direct Labour Cost per hour

$$= \frac{29,92,500}{1,50,000 \times 3/4} = \frac{29,92,500}{1,12,500} = ₹\ 26.60$$

(*iv*) Actual Direct Labour Cost per hour

$$= \frac{33,75,000}{1,25,000} = ₹\ 27$$

OVERHEAD VARIANCES

The analysis of factory overhead variances is more complex than variance analysis for direct materials and direct labour. There is no standardisation of the terms or methods used for calculating overhead variances. For this reason, it is necessary to be familiar with the different approaches which can be applied in overhead variances. Generally, the computation of the following overhead variances are suggested:

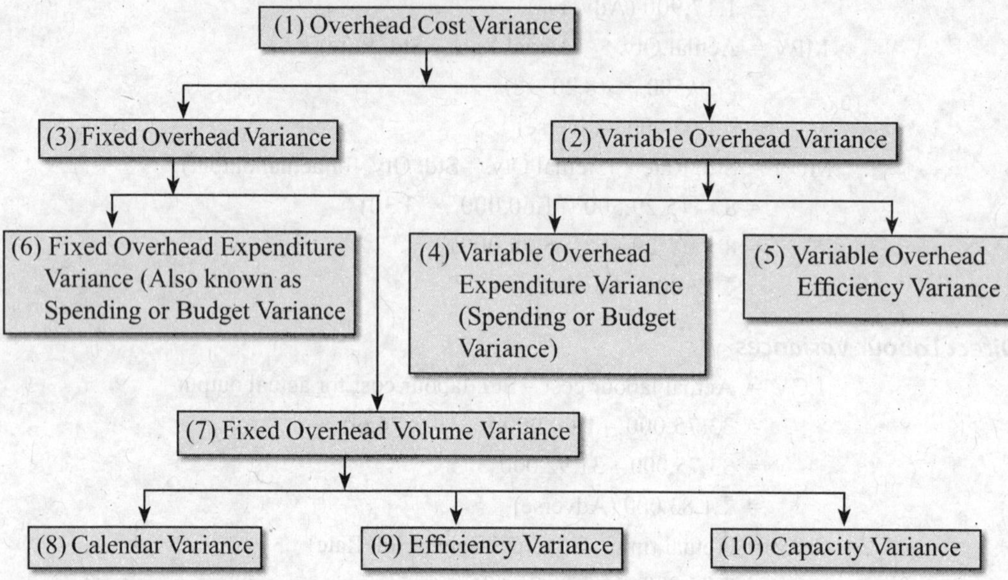

Figure 10.3: Overhead Variance

1. *Total Overhead Cost Variance:* This overall overhead variance is the difference between the actual overhead cost incurred and the standard cost of overhead for the output achieved. This can be computed by applying the following formula:

(Actual overhead incurred) – (Standard hours for the actual output × Standard overhead rate per hour)

Or

(Actual overhead incurred) – (Actual output × Standard overhead rate per unit)

To illustrate the overall overhead variance, assume that the actual overhead for a department amounts to ₹ 1,00,000 for the month of January and standard (or allowed) hours for work performed total 4,500 hours, while actual hours used are 5,000. If overhead rate is ₹ 20 per hour, the overall overhead variance will be the following:

Actual department overhead	₹ 1,00,000
Overhead charged to production (4,500 hr × ₹ 20)	₹ 90,000
Overall or net overhead variance (Unfavourable)	₹ 10,000

2. *Variable Overhead Variance:* It is the difference between actual variable overhead cost and standard variable overhead allowed for the actual output achieved. The formula for computing this variance is as follows:

(Actual Variable Overhead Cost) – (Actual Output × Variable Overhead rate per unit)

Or

(Actual Variable Overhead Cost) – (Std. hours for actual output × Std. Variable overhead rate per hour)

3. *Fixed Overhead Variance:* This variance indicates the difference between the actual fixed overhead cost and standard fixed overhead cost allowed for the actual output. This variance is found by using the following formula:

Fixed Overhead Variance = (Actual Fixed Overhead Cost – Fixed Overhead absorbed)

Or

(Actual Fixed Overhead Cost) – (Actual Output × Fixed Overhead rate per unit)

Or

(Actual fixed overhead cost) – (Std. hours for actual output × Std. fixed overhead rate per hour)

4. *Variable Overhead Expenditure (Spending or Budget) Variance:* This variance indicates the difference between actual variable overhead and budgeted variable overhead based on actual hours worked. This variance is found by using the following:

(Actual variable overhead – Budgeted variable overhead)

5. *Variable Overhead Efficiency Variance:* This variance is like labour efficiency variance and arises when actual hours worked differ from standard hours required for good units produced. The actual quantity produced and standard quantity fixed might be different because of higher or lower efficiency of workers employed in the manufacturing of goods. This variance is found by using the following formula:

(Actual hours – Standard hours for actual output) × Standard variable overhead rate per hour

6. *Fixed Overhead Expenditure (Spending or Budget) Variance:* This variance indicates the difference between actual fixed overhead and budgeted fixed overhead. The formula for computing this variance is as follows:

(Actual fixed overhead – Budgeted fixed overhead)

If actual fixed overhead costs are greater than budgeted fixed costs, an unfavourable variance results because actual costs exceed the budget. Actual overhead costs seldom equal budgeted costs because property tax rates may change, insurance premiums may increase or equipment changes may affect depreciation rates. As an illustration, assume that a company completed 36,000 units (equal to 18,000 standard production hours) in 18,500 hours at the recorded fixed cost of ₹ 7,51,000. The standard fixed cost rate per hour is ₹ 40. Therefore,

Expenditure variance = (Actual fixed overhead costs – Budgeted fixed overhead costs)

That is, = 7,51,000 – (18,500 × 40)

= 7,51,000 – 7,40,000

= ₹ 11,000 (Unfavourable)

The expenditure or budget variance provides management with information which helps in controlling costs. The budget variance is usually prepared on a departmental basis and the factors that cause the budget variances are, therefore, controllable by departmental managers.

7. *Fixed Overhead Volume Variance:* Volume variance relates to only fixed overhead. This variance arises due to the difference between the standard fixed overhead cost allowed (absorbed) for the actual output and the budgeted fixed overhead based on standard hours allowed for actual output achieved during the period. The variance shows the over-or-under-absorption of fixed overheads during a particular period. If the actual output is more than the standard output, there is over-absorption and variance is favourable. If actual output is less than the standard output, the volume variance is unfavourable. The formula for computing this variance is as follows:

(Budgeted fixed overhead applied to actual output – Budgeted fixed overhead based on standard hours allowed for actual output)

Or

(Actual production – Budgeted production) × Std. fixed overhead rate per unit

Volume variance is further sub-divided into three variances:

8. *Fixed Overhead Calendar Variance:* It is that portion of volume variance which is due to the difference between the number of actual working days in the period to which the budget is applicable and budgeted number of days in the budget period.

If actual working days is more than the budgeted working days, the variance is favourable as work has been done on days more than budgeted or allowed and vice-versa. The formula is as follows:

(No. of actual working days – No. of budgeted working days) × Std. fixed overhead rate per day.

Calendar variance can be computed based on hours or output. Then the formulae are:

Hours Basis

Calendar Variance = (Revised Budget Capacity hours – Budget Hours) × Std. Fixed Overhead rate per hour

If revised budgeted capacity hours are more than the budgeted hours, the variance will be favourable. In the reverse situation, the variance will be unfavourable.

Output Basis

Calendar Variance = (Revised budgeted quantity in terms of actual number of days worked – Budgeted quantity) × Standard fixed overhead rate per unit

If revised budgeted quantity is more than the budgeted quantity; the variance is favourable; if revised budgeted quantity is less, the variance will be unfavourable.

9. *Fixed Overhead Efficiency Variance:* It is that portion of volume variance which arises when actual hours of production used for actual output differ from the standard hours specified for that output. If actual hours worked are less than the standard hours, the variance is favourable and when actual hours are more than the standard hours, the variance is unfavourable. The formula is:

Fixed Overhead Efficiency Variance = (Actual hours – Standard hours for actual production) × Fixed overhead rate per hour

Fixed Overhead Efficiency Variance = (Actual production – Standard production as per actual time available) × Fixed overhead rate per unit

10. *Fixed Overhead Capacity Variance:* It is that part of fixed overhead volume variance which is due to the difference between the actual capacity (in hours) worked during a given period and the budgeted capacity (expressed in hours). The formula is

Capacity Variance = (Actual Capacity Hours – Budgeted Capacity) × Standard fixed overhead rate per hour

This variance represents idle time also. If actual capacity hours are more than the budgeted capacity hours, the variance is favourable and if actual capacity hours are less than the budgeted capacity hours, the variance will be unfavourable.

In case actual number of days and budgeted number of days are also given, then budgeted capacity hours will be calculated in terms of actual number of days and it will be known as revised budgeted capacity hours, *i.e.*, budgeted hours in actual days worked. In this situation, the formula for calculating capacity variance will be as follows:

Capacity Variance = (Actual Capacity hours – Revised Budgeted Capacity hours) × Standard fixed overhead rate per hr.

In the above formula, the variance will be favourable if actual capacity hours are more than the revised budgeted hours. However, if actual capacity hours are lesser than the revised budgeted hours, the variance will be adverse as lesser hours means that lesser actual hours have been worked taking the actual days utilised into account.

Two-way, Three-way and Four-way Variance Analysis

The above overhead variances are also classified as Two-way, Three-way and Four-way variance. The different variances under these categories are listed below. The formula for computing these variances are similar to as explained in the preceding section.

1. ***Two-way Variance Analysis:*** The two-way analysis computes two variances: budget variance (sometimes called flexible budget or controllable variance) and volume variance, which means:

   (*i*) Budget variance = Variable spending variance + Fixed spending (budget Variance + Variable efficiency variance

   (*ii*) Volume variance = Fixed volume variance

2. ***Three-way Variance Analysis:*** The three-way analysis computes three variances: spending, efficiency and volume variances. Therefore,

   (*i*) Spending variance = Variable spending variance + Fixed spending (budget) variance

   (*ii*) Efficiency variance = Variable efficiency variance

   (*iii*) Volume variance = Fixed volume variance

3. ***Four-way Variance Analysis:*** The four-way analysis includes

   (*i*) Variable spending variance

   (*ii*) Fixed spending (budget) variance

   (*iii*) Variable efficiency variance

   (*iv*) Fixed volume variance.

Illustrative Problem 12

Budgeted hours for month of March	= 180 hours
Standard rate of article produced per hour	= 50 units
Budgeted fixed overhead	= ₹ 27,000
Actual Production	= 9,200 units
Actual hours for Production	= 175 hours
Actual fixed Overhead Costs	= ₹ 28,000

Calculate Overhead Cost Variances.

Solution:

1. **Overhead Cost Variance**

(Actual Overhead Cost – Standard Overhead of actual output)

(₹ 28,000 – 9,200 units × 3)

₹ 28,000 – 27,600 = ₹ 400 (unfavourable)

$$\text{Standard Overhead rate per unit} = \frac{₹\ 27{,}000}{180\text{ hrs} \times 50} = \frac{27{,}000}{9{,}000} = ₹\ 3$$

2. **Overhead Expenditure Variance**

(Actual Overhead – Budgeted Overhead)

(₹ 28,000 – 27,000) = ₹ 1,000 (unfavourable)

3. **Overhead Volume Variance**

(Budgeted Overhead for actual output – Budgeted fixed overhead)

(₹ 3 × 9,200 units – 2,700)

(27,600 – 27,000) = ₹ 600 (favourable)

It can be calculated in the following manner also:

(Actual Production – Budgeted Production) × Std. rate per unit

(9,200 – 9,000) × ₹ 3 = ₹ 600 (favourable)

Or

(Budgeted hrs for actual production – Budgeted hours) × Std. rate per hour

(*184 hrs – 180) × ₹ 150

4 × 150 = ₹ 600 (favourable)

For 9,000 units standard hours required = 180 hrs.

$$\text{For 9,200 units standard hours} = \frac{9{,}200 \times 180}{9{,}000} = 184\text{ hrs.}$$

Illustrative Problem 13

From the following data, calculate overhead variances:

	Budgeted	***Actual***
Output	15,000 units	16,000 units
No. of working days	25	27
Fixed overheads	₹ 3,00,000	₹ 3,05,000
Variable overheads	₹ 4,50,000	₹ 4,70,000

There was an increase of 5% in capacity.

Solution:

1. ***Total Overhead Cost Variance:***

(Actual overhead cost – Actual units × Std. Rate)

(₹ 3,05,000 + 4,70,000 – 16,000 × ₹ 50)

₹ 7,75,000 – ₹ 8,00,000 = ₹ 25,000 (favourable)

$$\text{Standard rate} = \frac{\text{Standard Overhead}}{\text{Standard Output}}$$

2. ***Variable Overheads Variance***

   (Actual variable cost – Actual units × Std. Rate)

   (4,70,000 – 16,000 × ₹ 30)

   ₹ 4,70,000 – ₹ 4,80,000 = ₹ 10,000 (favourable)

3. ***Fixed Overhead Variance***

   Actual fixed overhead cost – (Actual units × Std. Rate of fixed overhead)

   3,05,000 – (16,000 × 20)

   3,05,000 – 3,20,000 = ₹ 15,000 (favourable)

4. ***Volume Variance***

   Actual units × St. rate – Budgeted fixed overheads

   16,000 × ₹ 20 – ₹ 3,00,000 = ₹ 20,000 (favourable)

5. ***Expenditure Variance***

   Actual fixed overheads – Budgeted fixed overheads

   ₹ 3,05,000 – ₹ 3,00,000 = ₹ 5,000 (unfavourable)

6. ***Capacity Variance***

   Std. Rate × (Revised budget units – Budgeted units)

   Revised budgeted units = Budgeted units + Increase in capacity

   $= 15{,}000 + \frac{5}{100} \times 15{,}000 = 15{,}750$ units

   = Capacity variance

   = ₹ 20 (15,750 units – 15,000 units)

   = ₹ 20 × 750 = ₹ 15,000 (favourable)

7. ***Calendar Variance***

   Increase or decrease in production due to more or less working days × Std. rate per unit within 25 days, standard production with increased capacity = 15,750 units within 2 days

   (27 – 25), production will be increased by = $\frac{15{,}750 \times 2}{25} = 1{,}260$ units

   Calendar variance = 1,260 units × ₹ 20

   = ₹ 25,200 (favourable)

8. ***Efficiency Variance***

   Std. rate × (Actual production – Std. production)

   Standard production:

   Budgeted production = 15,000 units

   Production increased due to increase in capacity 5% = 750 units

   Now budgeted production = 15,000 + 750 = 15,750 units

   Production increased due to 2 more working days

   Units for 2 days = $\frac{15{,}750 \times 2}{25 \text{ days}} = 1{,}260$ units

   Total units = 15,750 + 1,260

   = 17,010 units

   Efficiency Variance = ₹ 20 (16,000 units – 17,010 units)

   ₹ 20 (– 1,010 units) = ₹ 20,200 (unfavourable)

Illustrative Problem 14

In department A, the following data is submitted for the week ending 31st October:

Standard output for 40 hours per week	1,400 units
Standard fixed overhead	₹ 1,40,000
Actual output	1,200 units
Actual hours worked	32 hrs
Actual fixed overhead	₹ 150,000

Prepare a statement of variances

Solution:

Basic calculations:

Budgeted overhead	₹ 1,40,000
Actual overhead	₹ 1,50,000
Standard output (in units)	1,400
Actual output (in units)	1,200
Standard hours	40
Actual hours	32

1. Standard production per standard hour $= \dfrac{\text{Standard output}}{\text{Standard hours}}$

$$= \frac{1,400}{40} = 35 \text{ units}$$

2. Standard fixed overhead rate per unit $= \dfrac{\text{Standard fixed overhead}}{\text{Standard units produced}}$

$$= \frac{₹\,1,40,000}{1,400} = ₹\,100$$

3. Standard fixed overhead rate per hour $= \dfrac{\text{Standard fixed overhead}}{\text{Standard hours worked}}$

$$= \frac{₹\,1,40,000}{40} = ₹\,3,500$$

Statement of fixed overhead variances of department A:

A. Expenditure variance:

(Actual overhead – Budgeted overhead)

₹ 1,50,000 – ₹ 1,40,000 = ₹ 10,000 (Adverse)

B. Volume variance:

Std. fixed overhead rate per unit × (Actual output – Budgeted output)

₹ 100 (1,200 – 1,400) = ₹ 20,000 (Adverse)

C. Total overhead cost variance

(Actual overhead – Overhead recovered by actual output)

₹ 1,50,000 – ₹ 1,20,000 = ₹ 30,000 (Adverse)

(*a*) Efficiency variance:

Std. fixed overhead rate per unit × (Actual production – Std. production for actual hours)
₹ 100 (1200 – 32 × 35) = ₹ 8000 (Favourable)

(*b*) Capacity variance:
Std. fixed overhead rate per hour (Actual hours – Standard hours)
₹ 3,500 (32 – 40) = ₹ 28,000 (Adverse)

Illustrative Problem 15

A Cost Accountant of a company was given the following information regarding the overheads for February, 2016:

(*a*) Overheads cost variance ₹ 1,400 adverse.
(*b*) Overheads volume variance ₹ 1,000 adverse.
(*c*) Budgeted hours for February 2016, 1,200 hours.
(*d*) Budgeted overheads for February 2016, ₹ 6,000.
(*e*) Actual rate of recovery of overheads ₹ 8 per hour.

You are required to assist him in computing the following for February, 2016:

(1) Overheads expenditure variance.
(2) Actual overheads incurred.
(3) Actual hours for actual production.
(4) Overheads capacity variance.
(5) Overheads efficiency variance.
(6) Standard hours for actual production. (*M.Com., Delhi* 2004, 2011)

Solution:

Computation of Required Variances

(1) Overheads Expenditure Variance
= Overheads Cost Variance – Overheads Volume Variance
= ₹ 1,400 (A) – ₹ 1,000 (A)
= ₹ 400 (A)

(2) Actual Overheads incurred
= Budgeted Overheads + Overhead Expenditure Variance
= ₹ 6,000 + ₹ 400 (A)
= 6,400

(3) Actual hours for actual production

$$= \frac{\text{Actual overheads incurred}}{\text{Actual rate of recovery of overheads per hour}}$$

$$= \frac{₹\ 6{,}400}{8} = 800 \text{ hours}$$

(4) Overheads Capacity Variance
= Standard Overhead × (Actual Hours – Budgeted Hours)
= 5 × (800 hours – 1,200 hours)

= ₹ 2,000 (A)

$$= \text{Standard Rate of Overhead} = \frac{\text{Budgeted overheads}}{\text{Budgeted hours}}$$

$$= \frac{₹\ 6{,}000}{1{,}200} = ₹\ 5 \text{ per hour}$$

(5) Overhead Efficiency Variance

= Overheads Volume variance – Overhead Capacity variance

= ₹ 1,000 (A) – ₹ 2,000 (F)

= ₹ 1,000 (F)

(6) Standard Hours for Actual Production

Volume Variance

= Standard Overheads Rate × (Standard hours for Actual Production – Budgeted Hours)

or 1,000 (A) = 5 (x – 1,200)

or 1,000 (A) = 5 x – 6,000

or –5 x = – 5,000

or x = 1,000 hours

Illustrative Problem 16

New India Company uses a standard costing system. The company prepared its budget for 2016 at 10,00,000 machine hours for the year. Total budgeted overhead costs is ₹ 12,50,00,000. The variable overhead rate is ₹ 100 per machine hour (₹ 200 per unit). Actual results for 2016 are as follows:

Machine hours	9,60,000 hrs.
Output	4,98,000 units
Variable overhead	₹ 10,08,00,000
Fixed overhead Spending variance	₹ 60,00,000 A

Required:

(I) Compute for the fixed overhead

(*a*) Budgeted amount

(*b*) Budgeted cost per machine hour

(*c*) Actual cost

(*d*) Volume variance

(II) Compute variable overhead spending variance and variable overhead efficiency variance.

(*M. Com., Delhi University,* 2009, 2010)

Solution:

(I) For Fixed Overhead

(*a*) ***Budgeted Amount***

	Total budgeted overhead	=	₹ 12,50,00,000
Less:	Budgeted variable overhead		
	(10,00,000 machine hrs × ₹ 100	=	10,00,00,000

budgeted rate per machine hour)

Budgeted fixed overhead 2,50,00,000

(b) *Budgeted (fixed) Cost per Machine Hour*

$$= \frac{₹\ 2,50,00,000 \text{ budgeted amount}}{10,00,000 \text{ budgeted machine hours}}$$

= ₹ 25 per machine hour

(c) *Actual Cost (fixed)*

It is calculated through fixed overhead spending variance.

Fixed overhead spending variance = Actual cost incurred – Budgeted amount

∴ Actual cost = Budgeted amount + Unfavourable spending variance

= 2,50,00,000 + 60,00,000 A

= ₹ 3,10,00,000

Because fixed overhead spending variance is unfavourable, the amount of actual costs is higher than the budgeted amount.

(d) *Production Volume Variance*

Budgeted variable overhead per unit = ₹ 200

Budgeted variable overhead rate = ₹ 100 per machine hour

Therefore budgeted machine hours allowed per unit = ₹ 200/₹ 100

= 2 machine hours

Formula

Budgeted fixed overhead – Fixed overhead absorbed or allowed for actual output units

= ₹ 2,50,00,000 – (₹ 25 per machine hour × 2 machine hours per unit × 4,98,000 units)

= ₹ 2,50,00,000 – ₹ 2,49,00,000 (absorbed fixed overhead)

= ₹ 1,00,000 Adverse

Or

Another Formula

(St hrs for actual production – Budgeted hrs) × St. fixed overhead rate per hr

= (2 × 4,98,000) – (10,00,000 hrs) × ₹ 25

= (9,96,000 hrs – 10,00,000 hrs) × ₹ 25

= ₹ 1,00,000 Adverse

Or

Another Formula

(Budgeted production – Actual production) × St. fixed overhead rate per unit

$$\text{Standard fixed overhead rate per unit} = \frac{\text{Budgeted fixed overhead}}{\text{Budgeted units}}$$

$$= \frac{₹\ 2,50,00,000}{5,00,000 \text{ units}}$$

= ₹ 50 per unit

Budgeted units = 2 machine hour needed for 1 unit

∴ In 10,00,000 machine hours, units produced will be

$$= \frac{10,00,000}{2} = 5,00,000 \text{ units}$$

Now, applying the formula

(5,00,000 units – 4,98,000 units) × ₹ 50

= 2,000 units × ₹ 50 = ₹ 1,00,000 Adverse

(II) For Variable Overhead

(*a*) ***Variable Overhead Spending Variance***

(Budgeted Variable ovehead cost – Actual Variable overhead)

Budgeted variable overhead cost = Actual hrs works × St. Variable overhead rate per hour

= 9,60,000 hrs × ₹ 100

= ₹ 9,60,00,000

Now, applying the formula

= (₹ 9,60,00,000 – ₹ 10,08,00,000)

= ₹ 48,00,000 Adverse

Or

Another Formula

(St. machine hr rate – Actual machine hr rate) × Actual hrs worked

$$= \left(₹ 100 - \frac{₹ 10,08,00,000}{9,00,000 \text{ hrs}}\right) \times 9,60,000 \text{ hrs}$$

= (₹ 100 – ₹ 105) × 9,60,000 hrs

= ₹ 48,00,000 Adverse

(*b*) ***Variable Overhead Efficiency Variance***

(St. hours for actual output – Actual hrs) × St. Variable overhead rate per hour

= ((4,98,000 units × 2 hrs) – 9,60,000 hrs) × ₹ 100

= (9,96,000 hrs – 9,60,000 hrs) × ₹ 100

= 36,000 hours × ₹ 100

= ₹ 36,00,000 Favourable

Note: The other variances, although not asked in the question, have been computed as below.

(III) For Fixed Overhead

Calender Variance, Efficiency Variance, Capacity Variance.

(*a*) ***Fixed Overhead Calendar Variance***

= (Budgeted hrs – Revised budgeted Capacity hrs) × St. fixed overhead rate per hour

= (10,00,000 hrs – 2 hrs × 4,98,000 units) × ₹ 25

= (10,00,000 hrs – 9,96,000 hrs) × ₹ 25

= 4,000 hrs × 25 = ₹ 1,00,000 Adverse

Variance is adverse because of lesser use of hours available.

(*b*) ***Fixed Overhead Efficiency Variance***

(st. hr for actual production – Actual hrs) × Fixed overhead rate per hour

= (2 hrs × 4,98,000 units) – 9,60,000 hrs) × 25

= (9,96,000 hrs – 9,60,000 hrs) × 25

= 36,000 hrs × ₹ 25

= ₹ 9,00,000 F

It is favourable because actual hrs are less than standard hours.

(*c*) ***Fixed Overhead Capacity Variance***

(Budgeted Capacity hrs – Actual Capacity hours) × St. fixed overhead rate per hr

= (9,96,000 hrs – 9,60,000 hrs) × ₹ 25

= 36,000 hrs × ₹ 25

= ₹ 9,00,000 Adverse

Since actual hours are less than budgeted hours, in terms of capacity utilisation, it indicates Adverse Variance

Fixed Overhead Expenditure Variance (also known as Spending or Budget Variance)

(Budgeted fixed overhead – Actual fixed overhead)

= ₹ 2,50,00,000 – ₹ 3,10,00,000

= ₹ 60,00,000 Adverse

This is already given in the question.

Fixed Overhead Variance

(Budgeted fixed overhead cost – Actual fixed overhead cost)

Budgeted fixed overhead cost =

(*i*) Actual output units × St. fixed overhead rate per unit

Or

(*ii*) St. hours for actual output × St. fixed overhead rate per hour

Applying the formula

(*i*) (4,98,000 units × ₹ 50 per unit) – ₹ 3,10,00,000

= 2,49,00,000 – 3,10,00,000

= ₹ 61,00,000 Adverse

Or

(*ii*) (9,96,000 hrs × ₹ 25 per hr) – ₹ 3,10,00,000

= ₹ 2,49,00,000 – ₹ 3,10,00,000

= ₹ 61,00,000 Adverse

Verification

Fixed overhead Variance = Fixed overhead expenditure variance + Fixed overhead volume variance

₹ 61,00,000 A = ₹ 60,00,000 A + ₹ 1,00,000 A

Variable Overhead Variance

(Budgeted variable overhead cost – Actual variable overhead cost)

Budgeted variable overhead cost =

(*i*) Actual output units × St. variable overhead rate per unit

Or

(*ii*) St. hours for actual output × St. variable overhead rate per hour

Applying the Formula

(*i*) (4,98,000 units × ₹ 200 per unit) – ₹ 10,08,00,000
= ₹ 9,96,00,000 – ₹ 10,08,00,000
= ₹ 12,00,000 Adverse

Or

(*ii*) (9,96,000 hrs × ₹ 100) – ₹ 10,08,00,000
= ₹ 9,96,00,000 – ₹ 10,08,00,000
= ₹ 12,00,000 Adverse

Verification

Variable overhead variance = Variable overhead expenditure variance + Variable overhead efficiency variance

₹ 12,00,000 A = ₹ 48,00,000 A + ₹ 36,00,000 F

₹ 12,00,000 A = ₹ 12,00,000 A

Total Overhead Cost Variance

(Budgeted overhead cost – Actual overhead cost)

Budgeted overhead cost =

(*i*) Actual output units × St. overhead rate per unit

Or

(*ii*) St. hours for actual output × St. overhead rate per hour

Applying the Formula

St. overhead rate per unit = Variable overhead rate + Fixed overhead rate
= ₹ 200 + ₹ 50 = ₹ 250

Or

St. overhead rate per hour = Variable overhead rate per hour + Fixed overhead rate per hour
= ₹ 100 + ₹ 25 = ₹ 125

(*i*) (4,98,000 units × ₹ 250) – (₹ 3,10,00,000 + ₹ 10,08,00,000)
= ₹ 12,45,00,000 – ₹ 13,18,00,000
= ₹ 73,00,000 Adverse

Or

(*ii*) (9,96,000 hrs × ₹ 125) – (₹ 3,10,00,000 + ₹ 10,08,00,000)
= ₹ 12,45,00,000 – ₹ 13,18,00,000
= ₹ 73,00,000 Adverse

Verification

Total overhead cost variance = Fixed overhead cost variance + Variable overhead cost variance

₹ 73,00,000 A = ₹ 61,00,000 A + ₹ 12,00,000 A

₹ 73,00,000 A = ₹ 73,00,000 A

Illustrative Problem 17

The following information has been extracted from the books of Goru Enterprises which is using standard costing system:

Actual output = 9,000 units

Direct wages paid = 1,10,000 hours at ₹ 22 per hour, of which 5,000 hour, being idle time, were not recorded in production

Standard hours = 10 hours per unit

Labour efficiency variance = ₹ 3,75,000 (A)

Standard variable Overhead = ₹ 150 per unit

Actual variable Overhead = ₹ 16,00,000

You are required to calculate:

(*i*) Idle time variance

(*ii*) Total variable overhead variance

(*iii*) Variable overhead expenditure variance

(*iv*) Variable overhead efficiency variance.

Solution:

Actual output = 9,000 units

Idle time = 5,000 hours

Production time (Actual) = 1,05,000 hours

Standard hours for actual production = 10 hours / unit × 9,000 units = 90,000 hours.

Labour efficiency variance = ₹ 3,75,000 (A)

i.e. Standard rate × (Standard Production time – Actual production time) = ₹ 3,75,000 (A).

SR (90,000 – 1,05,000) = – 3,75,000

$$SR = \frac{-3,75,000}{-15,000} = ₹ 25$$

(*i*) Idle time variance = 5,000 hours × 25 ₹ / hour = ₹ 1,25,000. (A)

(*ii*) Standard Variable Overhead = ₹ 150 / unit

Standard hours = 10 hours / unit

Standard Variable Overhead rate / hour = 150 / 10 = ₹ 15 / hour

Total Variable Overhead variance = Standard Variable Overhead – Actual Variable Overhead

= Standard Rate × Standard hours – Actual rate × Actual hours

= (15) × (10 × 9,000) – 16,00,000

= 13,50,000 – 16,00,000

Total Variable Overhead Variance = 2,50,000 (A)

(*iii*) Variable Overhead Expenditure Variance = (Standard Rate × Actual Hours) – (Actual Rate × Actual Hours)

= (15 × 1,05,000) – 16,00,000

= 15,75,000 – 16,00,000

= ₹ 25,000 (A)

(*iv*) Variable Overhead Efficiency Variance = Standard Rate × (Standard Hours for actual output – Actual hours for Actual output)

= 15 (90,000 – 1,05,000)

= 15 (– 15,000)

= ₹ 2,25,000 (A)

Alternative Solution

Actual Outpur = 9,000 Units

Idle time = 5,000 hrs

Direct Wages Paid = 1,10,000 hours @ ₹ 22 output of which 5,000 hours being idle, were not recorded in production.

Standard hours = 10 per unit.

Labour efficiency variance = ₹ 3,75,000 (A)

Or

Standard Rate (Standard Time – Actual Time) = – 3,75,000

$$\text{Or } (90{,}000 - 1{,}05{,}000) = \frac{-3{,}75{,}000}{\text{Standard Rate}}$$

Or Standard Rate = ₹ 25/-

(*i*) Idle time variance = Standard Rate × Idle time

= 25 × 5,000 = ₹ 1,25,000 (A)

(*ii*) Standard Variable Overhead / unit = 150

$$\text{Standard Rate} = \frac{150}{10} = ₹\ 15/\text{hour}$$

Standard Quantity = 10 hours

Actual Variable Overhead = 16,00,000

Standard Variable Overhead = 150 × 9,000	= 13,50,000
Actual Variable Overhead	= 16,00,000
Total Variable Overhead Variance	= 2,50,000 (A)

(*iii*) Variable Overhead expenditure Variance = Standard Variable Overhead for actual hours – Actual Variable Overhead

= (150 × 1,05,000) – 16,00,000

= 15,75,000 – 16,00,000

= 25,000 (A)

(*iv*) Variable overhead efficiency variance = (Standard Variable Overhead for actual output – Standard Variable Overhead for Actual hours)

= 15 (10 hours × 90,000 units – 1,05,000)

= 15 (90,000 – 1,05,000)

= 15 (– 15,000)
= 2,25,000 (A)

Illustrative Problem 18

The Norkhill Furniture Company has the following standard cost per unit of furniture:

	₹
Direct material (50 feet of lumber @ ₹ 400 per 100 feet)	200
Direct labour (3 hours @ ₹ 100)	300
Variable overhead (3 direct labour hours @ ₹ 50)	150
Fixed Overhead (₹ 3,00,000 per month/3,000 monthly direct labour hours) × 3 direct labour hours	300
	950

For July 2016, when 1100 units of furniture were produced, the following information is available:

Lumber purchased: 50,000 feet at ₹ 390 per 100 feet
Lumber used: 56,000 feet
Direct labour: 3,100 hours @ ₹ 105
Variable overhead: ₹ 1,55,000
Fixed Overhead: ₹ 2,90,000

Any materials price variance is assigned to the purchasing department at the time of purchase.

You are required to:

(*a*) Prepare a flexible budget for the actual level of activity.

(*b*) Prepare a complete analysis of all variances, including a three-way analysis of overhead variances.

Solution:

(*a*) Flexible Budget

	***Flexible Budget* Am. (₹)**	***Actual* (₹)**	***Variance* (₹)**
Material (₹ 200 × 1,100)	2,20,000	2,18,400	1,600 (F)
Labour (₹ 300 × 1,100)	3,30,000	3,25,500	4,500 (F)
Variable (₹ 150 × 1,100)	1,65,000	1,55,000	10,000 (F)
Total	7,15,000	6,98,900	16,100 (F)
Fixed overhead costs	3,00,000	2,90,000	10,000 (F)
Total manufacturing costs	10,15,000	9,88,900	26,100

(*b*) Variances

(*i*) Material Price Variance = (AP – SP) × AQ
= (₹ 390 – 400) × 560
= ₹ 5,600 (F)

(*ii*) Material Usage Variance = (AQ – SQ) × SP
= (560 – 550) × ₹ 400
= ₹ 4,000 (A)

(*iii*) Labour rate variance = (AR – SR) × AH
= (₹ 105 – 100) × 3,100
= ₹ 15,500 (A)

(*iv*) Labour efficiency variance = (AH – SH) × SR
= (3,100 – 3,300) × ₹ 100
= ₹ 20,000 (F)

Three-way Analysis of Overhead Variances

(*i*) Spending variance = (Actual Overhead costs – Budgeted overhead Costs based on actual hours)
= 4,45,000 – (₹ 3,00,000 + 100 × 33,100 hours)
= 4,45,000 – 4,55,000
= ₹ 10,000 (F)

(*ii*) Efficiency variance
= (Budgeted overhead costs based on actual hours – Budgeted overhead costs based on Std. hours)
= (₹ 4,55,000 – (₹ 3,00,000 + ₹ 50 × 3300 hrs)
= 4,55,0000 – 4,65,000
= ₹ 10,000 (F)

(*iii*) Volume variance
= (Budgeted overhead Costs based on Std. hours in terms of actual units – Applied over head costs)
= (₹ 150 × 3300 hrs) – (₹ 150 × 3100 hrs)
= ₹ 4,95,000 – 4,65,000
= ₹ 30,000 (F)

Illustrative Problem 19

Following is the standard cost of a component:

Materials	2 Units at ₹ 15	₹ 30
Labour	3 Hours at ₹ 20	₹ 60
Total over heads	3 Hours at ₹ 10	₹ 30

During a particular month 10,000 units of the component were produced and the same was found to be at 60% capacity of the budget. In preparing the variance report for the month, the cost accountant gathered the following information:

Labour	₹ 6,50,000
Variable overheads	₹ 2,00,000
Fixed overheads	₹ 3,00,000
Material price variance	₹ 70,000 (A)
Material cost variance	₹ 50,000 (A)
Labour rate variance	₹ 50,000 (F)
Fixed overhead expenditure variance	₹ 50,000 (A)

You are required to prepare form the above details:

(1) Actual material cost incurred

(2) Standard cost of materials actually consumed

(3) Labour efficiency variance

(4) Variable OH efficiency variance

(5) Variance OH expenditure variance

(6) Fixed OH efficiency variance

(7) Fixed OH capacity variance

(8) Fixed OH volume variance

Solution:

1. Actual material cost incurred

Material cost variance = Standard cost of material of actual output – Actual material cost incurred

Or

$$\text{Actual material cost incurred} = \left\{\begin{matrix}\text{Standard cost of material} \\ \text{of actual output}\end{matrix} - \begin{matrix}\text{Material cost} \\ \text{variance}\end{matrix}\right\}$$

= {10,000 units × 2 units × ₹ 15 + ₹ 50,000}

= 3,00,000 + ₹ 50,000

= ₹ 3,50,000

2. Standard coat of materials actually consumed

Material price variance = (Standard cost – Actual cost) Actual quantity consumed.

Or

$$\text{Standard cost of materials actually consumed} = \left\{\begin{matrix}\text{Actual material} \\ \text{cost incurred}\end{matrix} + \begin{matrix}\text{Material price} \\ \text{variance}\end{matrix}\right\}$$

= ₹ 3,50,000 – ₹ 70,000 = ₹ 2,80,000

3. Labour efficiency variance (Refer to working note 1)

$$= \left\{\begin{matrix}\text{Standard hours} \\ \text{for actual output}\end{matrix} - \begin{matrix}\text{Actual hours} \\ \text{worked}\end{matrix}\right\}\begin{matrix}\text{Standard rate} \\ \text{per hour}\end{matrix}$$

= {10,000 units × 3 hours – 35,000 hours} ₹ 20.

= {₹ 6,00,000 – ₹ 7,00,000} = ₹ 1,00,000 (Adv.)

4. Variable OH efficiency variance (Refer to working note 2)

$$= \text{Standard variable overhead rate per hour}\left\{\begin{matrix}\text{Standard} \\ \text{hours}\end{matrix} - \begin{matrix}\text{Actual} \\ \text{hours}\end{matrix}\right\}$$

= ₹ 5 {30,000 hours – 35,000 hours} = ₹ 25,000 (Adv.)

5. Variable OH expenditure variance (Refer to working note 1)

$$= \left\{\begin{matrix}\text{Budgeted variable overhead} \\ \text{for acrtual hours}\end{matrix} - \begin{matrix}\text{Actual variable} \\ \text{overhead}\end{matrix}\right\}$$

= {₹ 5 × 35,000 hours – ₹ 2,00,000} = ₹ 25,000 (Adv.)

6. Fixed OH efficiency variance (Refer to working notes 1and 2)

$$= \text{Standard fixed overhead rate per hour}\left\{\begin{matrix}\text{Standard hours for} \\ \text{actual output}\end{matrix} - \begin{matrix}\text{Actual} \\ \text{hours}\end{matrix}\right\}$$

= ₹ 5 {30,000 hours – 35,000 hours} = ₹ 25,000 (Adv.)

7. Fixed OH capacity variance (Refer to-working notes 1and 2)

$$= \frac{\text{Standard variable overhead}}{\text{rate per hour}} \left\{ \text{Actual capacity hours} - \text{Budgeted capacity hours} \right\}$$

= ₹ 5 {35,000 hours – 50,000 hours}= ₹ 75,000 (Adv.)

8. Fixed OH volume variance (Refer to working note 3)

$$= \frac{\text{Standard variable overhed}}{\text{rate per hour}} \left\{ \text{Actual output} - \text{Budgeted output} \right\}$$

$$= ₹\ 15 \left\{ 10{,}000 \text{ units} - \frac{50{,}000 \text{ hours}}{3 \text{ hours}} \right\}$$

= 1,50,000 – 2,50,000 = 1,00,000 (Adv.)

Working Notes

1. Labour rate variance:

   = {Standard rate per hour - Actual rate per hour} Actual hours

   = Or ₹ 50,000 = 20 × ₹ 6,50,000

   = Or x = 35,000 hours

2. Standard hours = 10,000 units × 3 hours = 30,000 hours

   $$\text{Budgeted hours} = \left\{ \frac{30{,}000 \text{ hours} \times 100}{60} \right\} = 50{,}000 \text{ hours}$$

   Budgeted fixed overhead = Actual fixed overhead + Expenditure variance

   = ₹ 3,00,000 – ₹ 50,000 = ₹ 2,50,000

   $$\left\{ \begin{array}{l} \text{Standard fixed overhead} \\ \text{rcovery rate per hour} \end{array} \right\} = \frac{₹\ 2{,}50{,}000}{50{,}000 \text{ hours}} = ₹\ 5 \text{ per hour}$$

   Total overhead rate per hour = ₹ 10

   Variable overhead rate per hour = ₹ 5

   {₹ 10 – ₹ 5}

3. Standard fixed overhead per unit = ₹ 15

   {3 hours × ₹ 5}

Illustrative Problem 20

Reddy Labouratories, produce various chemical compounds for industrial use. One compound, called Fludex, is prepared by means of an elaborate distilling process. The company has developed standard costs for one unit Fludex, as follows:

	Standard Quantity	***Standard Price or Rate***	***Standard Cost***
Direct materials	2.5 Kg.	₹ 20.00 per Kg.	₹ 50.00
Direct labour	1.4 hours	12.50 per hour	₹ 17.50
Variable manufacturing over head	1.4 hours	3.50 per hour	₹ 4.90
			₹ 72.40

During November the following activity was recorded by the company relative to production of Fludex.

a. Materials purchased, 12,000 kilograms at a cost of ₹ 2,25,000.

b. There was no beginning inventory of materials on hand to start the month; at the end of the month, 2,500 kilograms of material remained in the warehouse unused.

c. The company employs 35 lab technicians to work on the production of Fludex, During November, each worked an average of 160 hours at an average rate of ₹12 per hour.

d. Variable manufacturing overhead is assigned to Fludex on the basis of direct labour- hours. Variable manufacturing overhead costs during November totalled ₹ 18,200.

e. During November, 3,750 good units of Fludex were produced.

The company's management is anxious to determine the efficiency of the activities surrounding the production of Fludex.

Required:

1. For materials used in the production of Fludex:
   a. Compute the price and quantity variances.
   b. The materials were purchased from a new supplier who is anxious to enter into a long-term purchase contact. Would you recommend that the company sign the contract? Explain.
2. For direct labour employed in the production of Fludes:
   a. Compute the rate and efficiency variances.
   b. In the past, the 35 technicians employed in the production of Fludex consisted of 20 senior technicians and 15 assistants. During November, the company experimented with only 15 senior technicians and 20 assistant in order to save costs. Would you recommend that the new labour mix be continued? Explain.
3. Compute the variable overhead spending and efficiency variances. What relationship can you see between this efficiency variance and the labour efficiency variance?

Solution:

1. a. In the solution below, the materials price variance is computed on the entire amount of materials purchased whereas the materials quantity variance is computed only on the amount of materials used in production:

Actual Quantity of Inputs, at Actual Price	Actual Quantity of Inputs, at Standard Price	Standard Quantity Allowed for Output, at Standard Price
(AQ × AP)	(AQ × SP)	(SQ × SP)
₹ 225,000	12,000 kgs × ₹ 20.00 per kg = ₹ 240,000	9,375 kgs* × ₹ 20.00 per kg = ₹ 187,500

Price Variance,
₹ 15,000 F

9,500 kgs. × ₹ 20.00 per kg
= ₹ 1,90,000

Quantity Variance,
₹ 2,500 U

*3,750 units × 2.5 kgs. per unit = 9,375 kgs.

Alternatively:

Materials price variance = AQ (AP – SP)

12,000 kgs. (₹ 18.75 per kg.* – ₹ 20.00 per kg.) = ₹ 15,000 F

₹ 2,25,000 ÷ 12,000 kgs. = ₹ 18.75 per kg.

Materials quantity variance = SP (AQ – SQ)

₹ 20.00 per kg. (9,500 kgs. – 9,375 kgs.) = ₹ 2,500 U

b. Yes, the contract probably should be signed. The new price of ₹ 18.75 per kg is substantially lower than the old price of ₹ 20.00 per kg, resulting in a favourable price variance of ₹ 15,000 for the month. Moreover, the material from the new supplier appears to cause little or no problem in production as shown by the small materials quantity variance for the month.

2. a

Actual Hours of Inputs, at the Actual Rate (AH × AR)	Actual Hours of Inputs, at the Standard Rate (AH × SR)	Standard Hours Allowed for Output, at the Standard Price (SH × SR)
5,600 hrs.	5,600 hrs.	5,250 hrs.**
× ₹ 12.00 per hr.	× ₹ 12.50 per hr.	× ₹ 12.50 per hr.
= ₹ 67, 200	= ₹ 70,000	= ₹ 65,625

Rate Variance, ₹ 2,800 F

Efficiency Variance, ₹ 4,375 U

Total Variance, ₹ 1,575 U

*35 technicians × 160 hrs. per technician = 5,600 hrs.

** 3,750 units × 1.4 hrs. per technician = 5,250 hrs.

Alternatively:

Labour rate variance = AH (AR – SR)

5,600 hrs. (₹ 12.00 per hr. – ₹ 12.50 per hr.) = ₹ 2,800 F

Labour efficiency variance = SR (AH – SH)

₹ 12.50 per hr. (5,600 hrs. – 5,250 hrs.) = ₹ 4,375 U

b. No, the new labour mix probably should not be continued. Although it decreases the average hourly labour cost form ₹ 12.50 to ₹ 12.00, thereby causing a ₹ 2,800 favourable labour rate variance, this savings is more than offset by a large unfavourable labour efficiency variance for the month. Thus, the new labour mix increases overall labour costs.

3.

Actual Hours of Inputs, at the Actual Rate (AH × AR)	Actual Hours of Input, at the Standard Rate (AH × SR)	Standard Hours Allowed for Output, at the Standard Price (SH × SR)
₹ 18,200	5,600 hrs.*	5,250 hrs.**
	× ₹ 3.50 per hr.	× ₹ 3.50 per hr.

= ₹ 19,600 = ₹ 18,375

Spending Variance, ₹ 1,400 F | Efficiency Variance, ₹ 1,225 U

Total Variance, ₹ 175 U

*Based on direct labour hours: 35 technicians × 160 hours per technician = 5,600 hrs.

** 3,750 units × 1.4 hrs. per unit = 5,250 hrs.

Alternatively:

Variable overhead spending variance = AH (AR – SR)

5,600 hrs. (₹ 3.25 per hr.* – ₹ 3.50 per hr.) = ₹ 1,400 F

₹ 18,200 ÷ 5,600 hrs. = ₹ 3.25 per hr.

Variable overhead efficiency variance = SR (AH – SH)

₹ 3.50 per hr. (5,600 hrs. – 5,200 hrs.) = ₹ 1,225 U

Both the labour efficiency variance and the variable overhead efficiency variance are computed by comparing actual labour-hours to standard labour-hours. Thus, if the labour efficiency variance is unfavourable, then the variable overhead efficiency variance will be unfavourable as well.

Illustrative Problem 21

Sunglow Limited manufactures and sells a single product. From the records of the company, the following information is available for November:

The standard cost comprises the following

Direct material	Unit	₹
X	8	320
Y	24	1,680
Z	16	400
		2,400
Direct wages (₹ 40 per hour)		1,600
Variable overhead (25% of direct wages)		400
Fixed overhead (based on budgeted production of		600
10,000 units of the final product per month)		5,000

The budgeted selling price is ₹ 700 each and the budgeted sales for the month were 14,000 units.

The following were the transactions for the month:

Direct material	Units	Purchased Price per unit	Issued unit
X	44,000	42	82,400
Y	1,40,000	71	2,46,400
Z	60,000	24	1,64,000
Direct Wages:		₹ 90,00,000 (3,98,000 hours)	
Overheads:			
Variable		₹ 2,00,000	

Fixed	₹ 3,00,000
Production:	11,000 units
Sales:	9,000 units at ₹ 700 each and
	3,500 units at ₹ 750 each

Required:

Calculate (*i*) Material price variance; (*ii*) Material mix variance; (*iii*) Labour rate variance (*iv*) Labour efficiency variance (*v*) Variable overhead efficiency variance; and (*vi*) Fixed overhead efficiency variance. (*CA Final Nov. 2012*)

Solution:

(*i*) **Material Price Variance** = Actual Quantity × Std. Price – Actual Cost

Material 'X' = (82,400 Units × ₹ 40) – (44,000 × ₹ 42) = ₹ 88,000 (A)

Material 'Y' = (2,46,400 Units × ₹ 70) – [(1,40,000 × ₹ 71) + (1,06,400 × ₹ 70)] = ₹ 1,40,000 (A)

Material 'Z' = (1,64,000 Units × ₹ 25 – [(60,000 × ₹ 24) + (1,04,000 × ₹ 25)] = ₹ 60,000 (F)

Total = ₹ 88,000 (A) + ₹ 1,40,000 (A) + ₹ 60,000 (F) = ₹ 1,68,000 (A)

(*ii*) **Material Mix Variance** = Std. Price × (Revised Actual Quantity – Actual Quantity)

Material 'X' = ₹ 40 × (82,133 units – 82,400 units) = ₹ 10,680 (A)

Material 'Y' = ₹ 70 × (2,46,400 units – 2,46,000 units) = ₹ 0

Material 'Z' = ₹ 25 × (1,64,267 units – 1,64,000 units) = 6,675 (F)

Total = ₹ 10,680 (A) + ₹ 0 + ₹ 6,675 (F) = ₹ 4,005 (A)

(*iii*) **Labour Rate Variance** = Actual hours × (Std. Rate – Actual Rate)

= 3,98,000 hrs × (₹ 40 – ₹ 22.613) = ₹ 69,20,000 (F)

Note: Actual Rate = ₹ 90,00,000/3,98,000 = ₹ 22.613

(*iv*) **Labour Efficiency Variance** = Std. Rate × (Standard hours – Actual hours)

= ₹ 40 × (4,40,000 hrs. – 3,98,000 hrs.) = ₹16,80,000 (F)

(*v*) **Variance Overhead Efficiency Variance**

= Std. Rate per Hour × (Standard Hours for Actual Production – Actual Hours)

= (₹ 400/40 hrs.) × [(11,000 units × 40 hrs.) – 3,98,000 hrs.)]

= ₹ 4,20,000 (F)

(*vi*) **Fixed Overhead Efficiency Variance**

= Std. Rate per Hour × (Standard Hours for Actual Production – Actual Hours)

= (₹ 600/40 hrs.) × [(11,000 units × 40 hrs.) – 3,98,000 hrs.)]

= ₹ 6,30,000 (F)

Working Notes:

1. Opening Inventory is valued at Standard Cost.

2. **Standard Cost and ₹ Actual Cost of Material**

Material	SQ	SR	SQ × SR	AQ	AR	AQ × AR	RQ
X	88,000 Units (11,000 × 8)	₹ 40 (320/8)	₹ 35,20,000	44,000 Units 38,400 Units	₹ 42 ₹ 40	₹ 33,84,000	82,133 Units [4,92,800/5,28,000 × 88,000]
Y	2,64,000 Units (11,000 × 24)	₹ 70 (1,680/24)	₹ 1,84,80,000	1,40,000 Units 1,06,400 Units	₹ 71 ₹ 70	₹ 1,73,88,000	2,46,400 Units [4,92,800/5,28,000 × 2,64,000]
Z	1,76,000 Units (11,000 × 16)	₹ 25 (400/16)	₹ 44,00,000	60,000 Units 1,04,000 Units	₹ 24 ₹ 25	₹ 40,40,000	1,64,267 Units [4,92,800/5,28,000 × 1,76,000]
Total	5,28,000 Units		₹ 2,64,00,000	4,92,800 Units		₹ 2,48,12,000	4,92,800 Units

Illustrative Problem 22

A company is engaged in manufacturing of several products. The following data have been obtained from the record of a machine shop for an average month:

Budgeted:

No. of working days	24
Working hours per day	8
No. of direct workers	150
Efficiency	One standard hour per clock hour
Down time	10%
Overheads:	
Fixed	₹ 75,400
Variable	₹ 90,720

The actual data for the month of August 2013 are as follows:

Overheads	
Fixed	₹ 78,800
Variable	₹ 70,870
Net operator hours worked	20,500
Standard hours produced	22,550

There was a special holiday in August 2013.

Required:

(*i*) Calculate all the relevant fixed overhead variances.

(*ii*) Calculate variable overheads expenditure and efficiency variance. (*CA Final*)

Solution:

Basic Workings

Maximum Hours	(24 Days × 8 Hours × 150 Workers)	28,800 Hours
Budgeted Hours	(28,800 Hours less 10%)	25,920 Hours

Actual Hours (given)	20,500 Hours
Standard Hours (produced)	22,550 Hours
Budgeted Working Days	24 Days
Actual Working Days	23 Days
Standard Rate (Fixed Overheads) per hour $\left(\frac{₹\ 75,400}{25,920\ hrs.}\right)$	₹ 2.908...
Standard Rate (Variable Overheads) per hour $\left(\frac{₹\ 90,720}{25,920\ hrs.}\right)$	₹ 3.5

Computation of Variances:

(*i*) **Fixed Overhead Variances**

Absorbed Fixed Overheads [SH × SR]	Budgeted Fixed Overheads [BH × SR]	Actual Fixed Overheads [AH × AR]	Budgeted Overheads for Actual Hours [SR × AH]	Possible Fixed Overheads
₹ 2.908... × 22,550 hrs.	25,920 hrs. × ₹ 2.908...	20,500 hrs × ₹ 3.84... *	₹ 2.908... × 20,500 Hrs	₹75,400 × $\frac{23\ Days}{24\ Days}$
₹ 65,597	₹ 75,400	₹ 78,800	₹ 59,633	₹ 72,258

* ₹ 78,800/20,500 hrs.

Note:

SR = Standard Rate per Hour

SH = Standard Hours = Expected Time for Actual Output

BH = Budgeted Hours = Expected Time for Budgeted Output

AR = Actual Rate per Hour

AH = Actual Hours

Fixed Overhead Cost Variance = Absorbed Fixed Overheads – Actual Fixed Overheads
= ₹ 65,597 – ₹ 78,800
= ₹ 13,203 (A)

Fixed Overhead Expenditure Variance = Budgeted Fixed Overheads – Actual Fixed Overheads
= ₹ 75,400 – ₹ 78,800
= ₹ 3,400 (A)

Fixed Overhead Volume Variance = Absorbed Fixed Overheads – Budgeted Fixed Overheads
= ₹ 65,597 – ₹ 75,400
= ₹ 9,803 (A)

Fixed Overhead Capacity Variance = Budgeted Fixed Overheads for Actual Hours – Possible Fixed Overheads
= ₹ 59,633 – ₹ 72,258
= ₹ 12,625 (A)

Fixed Overhead Calendar Variance = Possible Fixed Overheads – Budgeted Fixed Overheads

= ₹ 72,258 – ₹ 75,400

= ₹ 3,142 (A)

Fixed Overhead Efficiency Variance = Absorbed Fixed Overheads – Budgeted Fixed Overheads for Actual hours

= ₹ 65,597 – ₹ 59,633

= ₹ 5,964 (F)

(*ii*) **Variable Overhead Variances**

Standard Variable Overheads [SR × SH]	Actual Variable Overheads [AH × AR]	Budgeted Variable Overheads for Actual Hours [SR × AH]
₹ 3.5 × 22,550 hrs.	20,500 hrs. × ₹ 3.45...*	₹ 3.5 × 20,500 hrs.
₹ 78,925	₹ 70,870	₹ 71,750

* ₹ 70,870/20,500 hrs.

Note:

SR = Standard Rate per hour

SH = Standard Hours = Expected Time for Actual Output

AR = Actual Rate per hour

AH = Actual Hours

Variable Overhead Cost Variance = Standard Variable Overheads for Production – Actual Variable Overheads

= ₹ 78,925 – ₹ 70,870

= ₹ 8,055 (F)

Variable Overhead Expenditure Variance = Budgeted Variable Overheads for Actual Hours – Actual Variable Overheads

= ₹ 71,750 – 70,870

= ₹ 880 (F)

Variable Overhead Efficiency Variance = Standard Variable Oveheads for Production – Budgeted Variable Overheads for Actual hours

= ₹ 78,925 – ₹ 71,750

= ₹ 7,175 (F)

Illustrative Problem 23

Eastern Company manufactures special electrical equipment and parts. The firm uses a standard cost system with separate standards established for each product.

The transformer department manufactures a special transformer. This department measures production volume in direct labor-hour and uses a flexible budget system to plan and control department overhead.

Standard costs for the special transformer are determined annually in September for the coming year. The standard cost of a transformer at its Kolkata plant for the year just completed is ₹ 67 per unit, as shown here:

Direct materials		
Iron	5 sheets × ₹ 2	₹ 10
Copper	3 spools × ₹ 3	9
Direct labor	4 hours × ₹ 7	28
Variable overhead	4 hours × ₹ 3	12
Fixed overhead	4 hours × ₹ 2	8
Total		₹ 67

Overhead rates were based on normal and expected monthly capacity for the year, both of which were 4,000 direct labor-hours. Practical capacity for this department is 5,000 direct labor-hours per month. Variable overhead costs are expected to vary with the number of direct labor-hours actually used.

During October, the plant produced 800 transformers. This number was below expectations because a work stoppage occurred during labor contract negotiations. When the contract was settled, the department scheduled overtime in an attempt to reach expected production levels.

The following costs were incurred in October:

Direct Material	
Iron	Purchased 5,000 sheets at ₹ 2.00/sheet and used 3,900 sheets
Copper	Purchased 2,200 spools at ₹ 3.10/spool and used 2,600 spools
Direct Labor	
Regular time:	2,000 hours at ₹ 7.00 and 1,400 hours at ₹ 7.20
Overtime:	600 of the 1,400 hours were subject to overtime premium. The total overtime premium of ₹ 2,160 is included in variable overhead in accordance with company accounting practices.
Factory Overhead	
Variable	₹ 12,000
Fixed	₹ 8,800

Required:

1. What is the most appropriate time to record any variance of actual materials prices from standard?
2. What is the direct labor rate (price) variance?
3. What is the direct labor efficiency variance?
4. What is the total direct materials price variance?
5. What is the total direct materials usage variance?
6. What is the variable overhead spending variance?
7. What is the variable overhead efficiency variance?
8. What is the budget (spending) variance for fixed overhead?
9. What is the factory overhead production volume variance?

Solution:

1. At the time of purchase.

2.

Total actual direct labor cost	2,000 ₹ 7 + 1,400 × ₹ 7.20 =	₹ 24,080
Total actual hours at the standard hourly rate	3,400 × ₹ 7 =	23,800
Direct labor rate (price) variance		₹ 280 U

3.

Total actual direct labor hours at standard wage rates	3,400 × ₹ 7 =	₹ 23,800
Total standard direct labor cost for units manufactured	800 × 4 × ₹ 7 =	22,400
Direct labor efficiency variance		₹ 1,400 U

4.

	Quantity Price Purchased	Price: Actual	Standard	Difference	Variance
Iron	5,000	₹ 2	₹ 2	- 0 -	- 0 -
Copper	2,200	₹ 3.10	₹ 3	₹ 0.10	₹ 220 U
Material price variance					₹ 220 U

5.

	Quantity Used	Standard Allowed	Standard Difference	Usage Price	Variance
Iron	3,900	800 × 5 = 4,000	100 F	₹ 2	₹ 200 F
Copper	2,600	800 × 3 = 2,400	200 U	₹ 3	600 U
Material quantity (usage) variance					₹ 400 U

6.

Actual variable overhead		₹ 12,000
Standard variable overhead applied to total hours worked	3,400 × ₹ 3 =	10,200
Variable overhead spending variance		₹ 1,800 U

7.

Standard variable overhead applied to total hours worked		₹ 10,200
Total standard variable overhead for units manufactured	800 × 4 × ₹ 3 =	9,600
Variable overhead efficiency variance		₹ 600 U

8.

Actual fixed overhead		₹ 8,800
Budgeted fixed overhead	4,000 × ₹ 2	= 8,000
Fixed overhead budget (spending) variance		₹ 800 U

9.

Budgeted fixed overhead		₹ 8,000
Fixed overhead applied to units manufactured	800 × 4 × ₹ 2	= 6,400
Fixed overhead production volume variance		₹ 1,600 U

SALES VARIANCES

Sales variance is the difference between the actual value of sales achieved in a given period and budgeted value of sales. There are many reasons for the difference in actual sales and budgeted sales such as selling price, sales volume, sales mix. Sales variances can be calculated by using any one of the following two methods.

> **Sales variance** is the difference between the actual value of sales achieved in a given period and budged value of sales.

A. Sales variance based on turnover

B. Sales variances based on margin (*i.e.*, contribution margin or profit).

The first approach *i.e.*, sales variance based on turnover, accounts for difference in actual sales and budgeted sales. The sales variances using margin approach accounts for differences in actual profit and budgeted profit. In the margin method, it is assumed that cost of production is constant, *i.e.*, no difference is assumed between actual cost of production and standard cost of production. The reason for this assumption is that cost variances are calculated separately to analyse the difference between actual cost and standard cost of production. Therefore, cost side of the sales variance is assumed constant under the margin method. Sales variances computed under these two methods show different amounts of variance.

The different sales variances under these two approaches and their formula are given below:

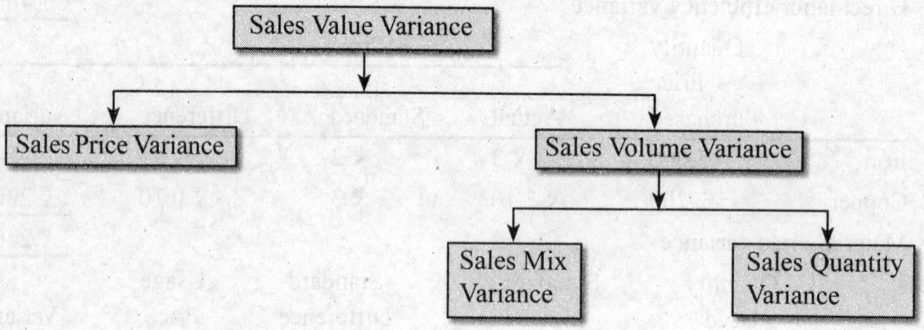

Figure 10.4: Sales Variances based on Turnover

1. *Sales Value Variance:* Also known as sales variance, this variance shows the difference between actual sales value and budgeted sales value. The formula is

Sales Value Variance = (Actual value of sales – Budgeted value of sales)

Actual sales = Actual quantity sold × Actual selling price

Budgeted sales = Standard quantity × Standard selling price

Or

Sales value variance = (Actual quantity × Actual selling price) – (Standard quantity × Standard selling price)

If actual sales are more than the budgeted sales, there is favourable variance and if actual sales are less than the budgeted sales, unfavourable variance arises.

2. *Sales Price Variance:* This variance is due to the difference between actual selling price and standard or budgeted selling price. The formula is:

Sales price variance = (Actual selling price – Budgeted selling price) × Actual quantity

If actual selling price is less than the budgeted selling price, variance is unfavourable and if actual selling price is more than the budgeted selling price, there will be favourable sales price variance.

3. *Sales Volume Variance:* Sales volume variance arises when the actual quantity sold is different from the budgeted quantity. If actual sales quantity exceeds the budgeted sales quantity, there is a favourable sales volume variance and if actual quantity sold is less than the budgeted quantity, the variance is unfavourable. The formula is

Sales volume variance = (Actual quantity – Budgeted quantity) × Budgeted selling price

Sales volume variance is divided into two variances:

(*i*) Sales mix variance (*ii*) Sales quantity variance

(i) *Sales Mix Variance:* Sales mix variance is one part of overall sales volume variance. This variance shows the difference between actual mix of goods sold and budgeted mix of goods sold. The formula is:

Sales Mix Variance = (Actual Mix of quantity sold – Actual quantity in standard proportion) × Standard selling price

Or

Sales Mix Variance = (Budgeted price per unit of actual mix – Budgeted price per unit of budgeted mix) × Total actual quantity.

If actual sales mix are more than the mix in standard or budgeted proportion, the variance is favourable and if actual mix sales are less than the standard mix (of actual sales), the variance is unfavourable. Similarly, if budgeted price per unit of actual mix is more than the budgeted price per unit of budgeted mix, favourable variance will arise. In the reverse situation, variance will be unfavourable.

(ii) *Sales Quantity Variance:* This variance is also a part of overall volume variance. This variance shows the difference between total actual sales quantity and total budgeted sales quantity. If total actual quantity is more than the total budgeted quantity, variance will be favourable and if total actual quantity is less than the total budgeted quantity, there will be unfavourable sales quantity variance. The formula is

Sales quantity variance = (Total actual quantity – Total budgeted quantity) × Budgeted price per unit of budgeted mix

The total of sales mix variance and sales quantity variance will be equal to sales volume variance.

Sales Variances Based on Margin (Contribution Margin or Profit)

As stated earlier, the sales variances using margin approach show the difference in actual profit and budgeted profit only, whereas sales variances based on turnover show the difference between total actual sales and total budgeted sales.

The following sales variances are calculated if margin or profit is the basis of calculation:

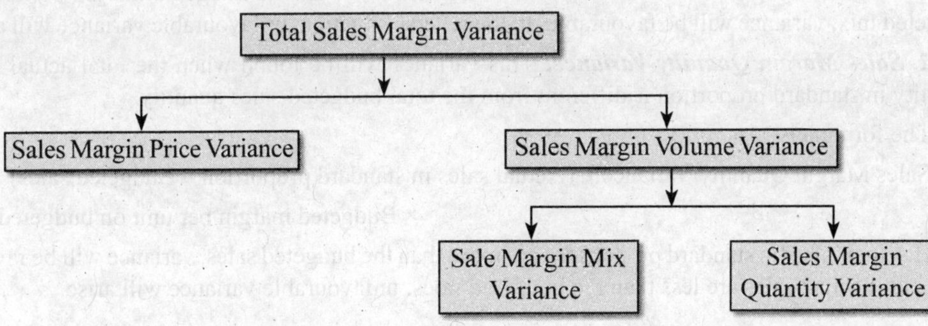

Figure 10.5: Sales Variances based on Margin or Profit

1. *Total Sales Margin Variance:* This variance indicates the aggregate or total variance under the margin method. This variance shows the difference between actual profit and budgeted profit. The formula is:

Total sales margin variance = Actual Profit – Budgeted profit

If actual profit is more than the budgeted profit, variance will be favourable and if actual profit is less than the budgeted profit, unfavourable variance will arise.

2. *Sales Margin Price Variance:* This variance is one part of total sales margin variance and arises due to the difference between actual margin per unit and budgeted margin per unit. It is significant to note that, assuming cost of production being constant, the difference in the actual margin and budgeted margin will only be because of the difference between actual selling price and budgeted selling price. The formula for calculating sales margin price variance is

Sales Margin Price Variance = (Actual Margin per unit – Budgeted Margin per unit) × Actual quantity

If actual margin per unit is more than the budgeted margin per unit, favourable variance will be found and if actual margin is less than the budgeted margin, variance will be unfavourable.

3. *Sales Margin Volume Variance:* This variance shows the difference between actual sales units and budgeted sales units.

The formula is:

Sales Margin Volume Variance = (Actual quantity – Budgeted quantity) × Budgeted Margin per unit.

If actual sales units are more than the budgeted sales units, variance will be favourable and if actual sales units are less than the budgeted sales units, unfavourable variance will arise.

Sales margin volume variance can be calculated using another formula which is:

Sales margin volume variance = (Standard profit on actual quantity of sales – Budgeted profit)

If standard profit exceeds budgeted profit, variance will be favourable and if standard profit is less than the budgeted profit, unfavourable variance will emerge.

Sales margin volume variance consists of (*i*) sales margin mix variance and (*ii*) sales margin quantity variance.

1. *Sales Margin Mix Variance:* This variance shows the difference between actual mix of goods and budgeted (standard) mix of goods sold. The formula is

Sales Margin Mix Variance = (Actual sales mix – Standard proportion of actual sales mix) × Budgeted margin per unit.

If budgeted margin per unit on actual sales mix is more than the budgeted margin per unit on budgeted mix, variance will be favourable. In the reverse situation, unfavourable variance will arise.

2. *Sales Margin Quantity Variance:* This variance will be found when the total actual sales quantity in standard proportion is different from the total budgeted sales quantity.

The formula is

Sales Margin Quantity Variance = (Actual sales in standard proportion – Budgeted sales) × Budgeted margin per unit on budgeted mix

If actual sales (in standard proportion) are more than the budgeted sales, variance will be favourable and if actual sales are less than the budgeted sales, unfavourable variance will arise.

Illustrative Problem 24

Jumbo Food Products Ltd. Operates a system of standard costing and in respect of one of its products which is manufactured within a single cost centre, data for one week have been analysed as follows:

Standard Cost Data	*(Per unit)*	₹
Direct Materials	10 kgs of ₹ 1.5	15.00
Direct Wages	5 hours at ₹ 4.00	20.00

Production Overheads	5 hours at ₹ 5.00	25.00
		60.00

Other overheads may be ignored.

Profit Margin is 20% of sale price.

Budgeted Sales are ₹ 60,000 per week.

Actual Data:	₹
Sales	59,760
Direct materials	12,870
Direct Wages	16,324

Analysis of variances:

		Adverse	*Favourable*
Direct Materials:	Price	1170	—
	Usage	—	750
Direct Labour:	Rate	—	636
	Efficiency	360	—
Production Overhead:	Expenditure	—	400
	Volume	—	750

The production and sales achieved resulted in no changes of stock. You are required to compute:

(*i*) The actual output;

(*ii*) Actual profit;

(*iii*) Actual price per kg of material;

(*iv*) Actual rate per labour hour;

(*v*) Amount of production overhead incurred;

(*vi*) Amount of production overhead absorbed;

(*vii*) Production overhead efficiency variance;

(*viii*) Selling price variance;

(*ix*) Sales volume profit variance.

Solution:

Jumbo Food Products Ltd.

(*i*) *Actual Output:*

Actual Direct Wage Cost:	₹ 16,324
Less: Adverse labour Efficiency Variance (Adv)	₹ 360
	₹ 15,964
Add: Labour Rate Variance (Fav)	₹ 636
Total Standard direct wage cost	₹ 16,600

Output = Total standard direct wages cost ÷ Standard direct wages per unit = ₹ 16,600 ÷ ₹ 20 = 830 units.

Alternatively,

	₹
Actual direct materials :	12,870
Less: Adverse material price variance	1,170
	11,700
Add: Favourable material usage variance	750
Total standard material cost	12,450

(Output = 12,450 /15 = 830 units)

(ii) *Actual Profit:*

Actual sales		59,760
Less: Direct Material		(12,870)
Direct wages		(16,324)
Production Overhead (830 × 25)	20,750	
Less: Favourable O.H. variances		
Expenditure	(400)	
Volume	(750)	19,600
Actual Profit		10,966

(iii) *The Actual Price per kg of Material:*

	₹
Direct materials	12,870
Less: Adverse price variance	1,170
Total standard material cost	11,700

Total Standard material cost ÷ Standard price per kg = 11,700 ÷ 1.50 = 7,800 kg.

Actual price per kg of material = 12,870 ÷ 7,800 = ₹ 1.65

(iv) *Actual Rate per Labour Hour:*

	₹
Actual direct wages	16,324
Add: Favourable labour rate variance	636
Total standard wages cost	16,960

Actual hours worked

= Standard wages ÷ Std. wages / unit

= 16,960 ÷ 20 × 5 hours = 4,240 hours

Actual rate per labour hour : ₹ 16,324/4,240 = ₹ 3.85

(v) *The Amount of Production Overhead Incurred:*

Standard production overhead (830 × 25) =		₹ 20,750
Less: Favourable O.H. Variance:		
Expenditure	400	
Volume	750	₹ 1,150
		₹ 19,600

(vi) The Amount of Production Overhead Absorbed:

Units produced × standard overhead absorption rate = 830 × ₹ 25 = ₹ 20,750

(vii) Production Overhead Efficiency Variance:

(Standard production overhead for actual hours worked – Standard production overhead for actual production)

= (4,240 hours × ₹ 5 – 830 units × ₹ 25)

= ₹ 21,200 – ₹ 20,750 = ₹ 450 (Adv)

(viii) Selling Price Variance:

(Actual sales value realised – Standard value of Actual sales)

= (₹ 59,760 [given] – 830 units × 60 × 1.25 ÷ 1.00)

(20% on sales price *i.e.* ₹ 255 on cost)

= (₹ 59,760 – ₹ 62,250) = ₹ 2,490 (Adv)

(ix) Sales Volume Profit Variance:

(Standard sales margin on actual sales – standard sales margin as per standard cost data)

= (830 units × ₹ 15 – 800 units × ₹ 15)

= ₹ 12,450 – ₹ 12,000 = ₹450 (Fav)

[Standard sales margin = (₹ 75 – ₹ 60) = ₹ 15]

Illustrative Problem 25

The budgeted and actual sales of a concern manufacturing and marketing a single product are furnished below:

Budgeted sales	10,000 units at ₹ 40 per unit
Actual sales	5,000 units at ₹ 35 per unit
	8,000 units at ₹ 40 per unit

Calculate: (*a*) Sales price variance (*b*) Sales volume variance

Solution:

(*a*)	Sales price variance	=	Actual sales – Standard sales
	Standard sales	=	Standard price × Actual quantity
		=	₹ 40 × 13,000
		=	₹ 5,20,000
	Actual sales	=	Actual price × Actual quantity
		=	₹ 35 × 5,000 + ₹ 40 × 8,000
		=	₹ 1,75,000 + ₹ 3,20,000
		=	₹ 4,95,000
	Sales price variance	=	₹ 4,95,000 – ₹ 5,20,000
		=	₹ 25,000 (Adverse)
(*b*)	Sales volume variance	=	Standard sales – Budgeted sales
		=	₹ 5,20,000 – 4,00,000
		=	₹ 120,000 (Favourable)
	Sales value variance	=	Actual sales – Budgeted sales

= ₹ 4,95,000 – ₹ 4,00,000

= ₹ 95,000 (Favourable)

Illustrative Problem 26

Alplha Ltd. uses standard costing system for manufacturing its single product 'APS'. Standard cost card is as follows:

	Per unit (₹)
Selling Price	120
Direct Material (1 kg per unit)	20
Direct Labour (6 hrs @ ₹ 8 per hour)	48
Variable Overheads	24
Contribution	28

Actual and budgeted activity levels in units for the month of September are:

	Budget	Actual
Sales	50,000	51,200
Production	50,000	52,000

Actual sales revenue and variable costs for the month of September are given as under:

Sales	₹ 61,33,760
Direct Material	10,65,600
Direct Labour (3,00,000 hrs)	24,42,000
Variable Overheads	12,28,000

Calculate:

(*i*) Direct Labour Rate Variance

(*ii*) Direct Labour Efficiency Variance

(*iii*) Sales Volume Variance

(*iv*) Sales Price Vaiance

(*v*) Comment on your findings in (*i*) and (*ii*) above. (*CA Final, Nov. 2015*)

Solution:

(*i*) **Labour Rate Variance** = Standard Cost of Actual Time – Actual Cost

= (SR × AH) – (AR × AH)

Or

= (SR – AR) × AH

= (₹ 8.00 – ₹ 8.14) × 3,00,000 hrs.

= ₹ 42,000 (A)

Working

$$\text{Actual Labour Rate per hour} = \frac{\text{Actual Paid}}{\text{Actual Hours}}$$

$$= \frac{₹\ 24,42,000}{3,00,000 \text{ hrs.}}$$

= ₹ 8.14

(*ii*) **Labour Efficiency Variance** = Standard Cost of Standard Time for Actual Production – Standard Cost of Actual Time

= (SH × SR) – (AH × SR)

Or

= (SH – AH) × SR

= (3,12,000 hrs. – 3,00,000 hrs.) × ₹ 8.00

= ₹ 96,000 (F)

Working

Standard Hours = Actual Production × Std. hrs. per unit

= 52,000 units × 6 hrs.

= 3,12,000 hrs.

(*iii*) **Sales Volume Variance** = Standard Sales – Budgeted Sales

Or

= Budgeted Price × (Actual Quantity – Budgeted Quantity)

= ₹ 120 × (51,200 units – 50,000 units)

= ₹ 1,44,000 (F)

(*iv*) **Sales Price Variance** = Actual Sales – Standard Sales

Or

= Actual Quantity × (Actual Price – Budgeted Price)

= 51,200 units × (₹ 119.80 – ₹ 120)

= ₹ 10,240 (A)

Working

Actual Sales Price = $\frac{\text{Actual Sales}}{\text{Actual Qty.}}$

= $\frac{₹\ 61,33,760}{51,200 \text{ units}}$

= ₹ 119.80

(*v*) **Comment**

Direct Labour Rate Variance

Adverse labour rate variance indicates that the labour rate per hour paid is more than the set standard. The reasons may include among other things such as:

(1) While setting standard, the current/future market conditions like pending labour negotiation/cases, has not been considered (or predicted) correctly.

(2) The labour may have been told that their wage rate will be raised or bonus will be paid if they work efficiently.

Direct Labour Efficiency Variance

It indicates that the workers have produced actual production quantity in less time than the time allowed. The reason for favourable labour efficiency variance may include among other things the following:

(1) While setting standard, workers efficiency could not be estimated properly, this may happen due to non-observance of time and motion study.

(2) The workers may be new in the factory, hence, efficiency could not be predicted properly.

(3) The foreman or personnel manager responsible for labour efficiency, while providing his/her input at the time of budget/standard, has adopted conservative approach.

(4) The increase in the labour rate might have encouraged the labours to do work more efficiently.

In this particular case, it may have happened that since labour payment has been increased, labour efficiency has also increased. In a nutshell, because of additional labour rate (Adverse), labour efficiency has gone up (Favourable).

Illustrative Problem 27

Japan Products Ltd. had drawn up the following Sales budget for August 2013:

'B' Product	5,000 units at ₹ 100 each
'C' Product	4,000 units at ₹ 200 each
'S' Product	6,000 units at ₹ 180 each

The actual sales for August, 2013 were:

'B' Product	5,750 units at ₹ 120 each
'C' Product	4,850 units at ₹ 180 each
'S' Product	5,000 units at ₹ 165 each

The cost per unit of B, C and S Product were ₹ 90, ₹ 170 and ₹ 130 respectively. Analyse the Sales Variance to show the effects on turnover and the effects on Profit. (CA Final)

Solution:

A. **BASED ON SALES MARGIN**

BASIC CALCULATIONS

Statement Showing Budgeted Margin, Actual Margin and Standard Margin

Product Quantity (units)	Budgeted (units)	Budgeted Margin per unit (₹)	Budeted Margin (₹)	Actual Quantity (units)	Actual Margin per unit (₹)	Actual Margin (₹)	Std. Margin (₹)
1	2	3	4	5	6	7	8 = 3 × 5
B	5,000	10	50,000	5,750	30	1,72,500	57,500
C	4,000	30	1,20,000	4,850	10	48,500	1,45,500
S	6,000	50	3,00,000	5,000	35	1,75,000	2,50,000
Total	15,000		4,70,000	15,600		3,96,000	4,53,000

COMPUTATION OF VARIANCE

Sales Margin Variance = Actual Margin – Budeted Margin

= AQ × AM – BQ × BM

For Product B	=	₹ 1,72,500 – ₹ 50,000
	=	₹ 1,22,500 (F)
For Product C	=	₹ 48,500 – ₹ 1,20,000
	=	₹ 71,500 (A)
For Product S	=	₹ 1,75,000 – ₹ 3,00,000
	=	₹ 1,25,000 (A)
Total (B + C + S)	=	₹ 1,22,500 (F) + ₹ 71,500 (A) + ₹ 1,25,000 (A)
	=	₹ 74,000 (A)
Sales Margin Price Variance	=	Actual Margin – Standard Margin
	=	AQ × AM – BQ × BM Or AQ × (AM – BM)
For Product B	=	₹ 1,72,500 – ₹ 57,500
	=	₹ 1,15,000 (F)
For Product C	=	₹ 48,500 – ₹ 1,45,500
	=	₹ 97,000 (A)
For Product S	=	₹ 1,75,000 – ₹ 2,50,000
	=	₹ 75,000 (A)
Total (B + C + S)	=	₹ 1,15,000 (F) + ₹ 97,000 (A) + ₹ 75,000 (A)
	=	₹ 57,000 (A)
Sales Margin Volume Variance	=	Standard Margin – Budeted Margin
	=	AQ × BM – BQ × BM Or BM × (AQ – BQ)
For Product B	=	₹ 57,500 – ₹ 50,000
	=	₹ 7,500 (F)
For Product C	=	₹ 1,45,500 – ₹ 1,20,000
	=	₹ 25,500 (F)
For Product S	=	₹ 2,50,000 – ₹ 3,00,000
	=	₹ 50,000 (A)
Total (B + C + S)	=	₹ 7,500 (F) + ₹ 25,500 (F) + ₹ 50,000 (A)
	=	₹ 17,000 (A)
Sales Margin Mix Variance	=	Total Actual Quantity (units) × (*Average* Budgeted Margin *per unit* of Actual Mix – *Average* Budgeted Margin *per unit* of Budgeted Mix)

$$= 15{,}600 \text{ units} \times \left(\frac{₹\ 4{,}53{,}000}{15{,}600 \text{ units}} - \frac{₹\ 4{,}70{,}000}{15{,}000 \text{ units}} \right)$$

= 35,800 (A)

Sales Margin Quantity Variance = *Average* Budgeted Margin *per unit* of Budgeted Mix × [Total Actual Quantity (units) – Total Budgeted Quatity (units)]

$$= \left(\frac{₹\ 4,70,000}{15,000 \text{ units}}\right) \times (15,600 \text{ Units} - 15,000 \text{ Units})$$

= 18,800 (F)

B. **BASED ON SALES VALUE**

BASIC CALCULATIONS

Statement Showing Budgeted Sales, Actual Sales and Standard Sales

Product Quantity (units)	Budgeted (units)	Budgeted Price per unit (₹)	Budgeted Sales (₹)	Actual Quantity (units)	Actual Price per unit (₹)	Actual Sales (₹)	Std. Sales (₹)
1	2	3	4	5	6	7	8 = 3 × 5
B	5,000	100	5,00,000	5,750	120	6,90,000	5,75,000
C	4,000	200	8,00,000	4,850	180	8,73,000	9,70,000
S	6,000	180	10,80,000	5,000	165	8,25,000	9,00,000
Total	15,000		23,80,000	15,600		23,88,000	24,45,000

COMPUTATION OF VARIANCE

Sales Value Variance = Actual Sales – Budgeted Sales

= AP × AQ – BP × BQ

For Product B = ₹ 6,90,000 – ₹ 5,00,000 = ₹ 1,90,000 (F)

For Product C = ₹ 8,73,000 – ₹ 8,00,000 = ₹ 73,000 (F)

For Product S = ₹ 8,25,000 – ₹ 10,80,000 = ₹ 2,55,000 (A)

Total = ₹ 1,90,000 (F) + ₹ 73,000 (F) + ₹ 2,55,000 (A)

= ₹ 8,000 (F)

Sales Price Variance = Actual Sales – Standard Sales

= AP × AQ – BP × AQ

Or

AQ × (AP – BP)

For Product B = 5,750 Units × (₹ 120.00 – ₹ 100.00) = ₹ 1,15,000 (F)

For Product C = 4,850 Units × (₹ 180.00 – ₹ 200.00) = ₹ 97,000 (A)

For Product S = 5,000 Units × (₹ 165.00 – ₹ 180.00) = ₹ 75,000 (A)

Total = ₹ 1,15,000 (F) + ₹ 97,000 (A) + ₹ 75,000 (A)

= ₹ 57,000 (A)

Sales Volume Variance = Standard Sales – Budgeted Sales

= BP × AQ – BP × BQ

Or

= BP × (AQ – BQ)

For Product B	=	₹ 100 × (5,750 Units – 5,000 Units) = ₹ 75,000 (F)
For Product C	=	₹ 200 × (4,850 Units – 4,000 Units) = ₹ 1,70,000 (F)
For Product S	=	₹ 180 × (5,000 Units – 6,000 Units) = ₹ 1,80,000 (A)
Total	=	₹ 75,000 (F) + ₹ 1,70,000 (F) + ₹ 1,80,000 (A)
	=	₹ 65,000 (F)

Sales Mix Variance = Total Actual Qty (units) × (*Average* Budgeted Price *per unit* of Actual Mix – *Average* Budgeted Price *per unit* of Budgeted Mix)

$$= 15{,}6000 \text{ Units} \times \left[\left(\frac{₹\,24{,}45{,}000}{15{,}600\,\text{Units}}\right) - \left(\frac{₹\,23{,}80{,}000}{15{,}000\,\text{Units}}\right)\right]$$

= 30,200 (A)

Sales Quantity Variance = Average Budgeted Price per unit of Budgeted Mix × [Total Actual Qty (units) – Total Budgeted Qty (units)]

$$= \left(\frac{₹\,23{,}80{,}000}{15{,}000\text{ Units}}\right) \times (15{,}600 \text{ Units} - 15{,}000 \text{ Units})$$

= ₹ 95,200 (F)

Illustrative Problem 28

The following data relates to a company for a period.

	Standard			*Actual*		
	Qty.	***Sale price*** ₹	***Total*** ₹	***Qty.***	***Sales price*** ₹	***Total*** ₹
Product X	500	50	25,000	500	50	25,000
Product Y	400	60	24,000	600	62.5	37,500
Product Z	300	70	21,000	400	67.5	27,000

Calculate: (*i*) sales value variance, (*ii*) sales price variance, (*iii*) sales mix variance, and (*iv*) sales sub-volume variance.

Solution:

(*i*) ***Sales value variance:***

	₹
Formula: (Actual quantity × AP) – (SQ × SP)	
Product X (500 × 50) – (500 × 50)	Nil
Product Y (600 × 62.5) – (400 × 60)	
₹ 37,500 – 24,000	= 13,500 (F)
Product Z (400 × 67.5) – (300 × 70)	
27,000 – 21,000	6,000 (F)
Total sales value variance	19,500 (F)

(*ii*) ***Sales price variance:***

Formula: (AP – SP) × Actual Quantity

Product X (₹ 50 – 50) × 500	Nil
Product Y (62.5 – 60) × 600	1,500 (F)
Product Z (₹ 67.5 – 70) × 400	1,000 (A)
Total sales price variance	500 (F)

(*iii*) ***Sales mix variance:***

Formula (Actual proportion – Revised standard mix of actual total sale) × SP

Product X (500 – 625) × 50	6,250 (A)
Product Y (600 – 500) × 60	6,000 (F)
Product Z (400 – 375) × 70	1,750 (F)
Total sales mix variance ₹	1,500 (F)

(*iv*) ***Sale sub-volume variance:***

Formula: (Revised standard mix – Standard mix) × SP

Product X (625 – 500) × 50	6,250 (F)
Product Y (500 – 400) × 60	6,000 (F)
Product Z (375 – 300) × 70	5,250 (F)
Total sale sub-volume variance ₹	17,500 (F)

Check:

Sale price variance + Sales mix variance + Sales sub usage = Sales value variance

₹ 500 (F) + ₹ 1,500 (F) + ₹ 17,500 (F) = ₹ 19,500 (F)

Working Notes

Revised Standard Mix

If 1,200 units are total sales, product A sold = 500

Product A, If 1,500 $= \frac{\text{Standard units of product}}{\text{Total standard units}} \times \text{AQ}$

$= \frac{500}{1,200} \times 1,500 = 625 \text{ units}$

Product B $= \frac{400}{1,200} \times 1,500 = 500 \text{ units}$

Product C $= \frac{300}{1,200} \times 1,500 = 375 \text{ units}$

Illustrative Problem 29

Compute the sales variances (total, price and volume) from the following figures:

Product	*Budgeted quantity*	*Budgeted Price per Unit (₹)*	*Actual quantity*	*Actual Price per unit (₹)*
P	4000	25	4800	30
Q	3000	50	2800	45
R	2000	75	2400	70
S	1000	100	800	105

Solution:

Working Notes

Product	*Budgeted Price* (₹)	*Actual Price* (₹)	*Budgeted Qty.*	*Actual Qty.*	*Budgeted Sales* (₹)	*Standard Sales (Actual Sales at Budgeted price)* (₹)	*Actual sales* (₹)
	a	**b**	**c**	**d**	**e = a × c**	**f = a × d**	**g = b × d**
P	25	30	4,000	4,800	1,00,000	1,20,000	1,44,000
Q	50	45	3,000	2,800	1,50,000	1,40,000	1,26,000
R	75	70	2,000	2,400	1,50,000	1,80,000	1,68,000
S	100	105	1,000	800	1,00,000	80,000	84,000
					5,00,000	5,20,000	5,22,000

Calculation of Variances:

Sale Price Variance = Actual Quantity (Actual Price – Budgeted Price)
= Actual Sales – Standard Sales
= 5,22,000 – 5,20,000 = ₹ 20,000 (Favourable)

Sales Volume Variance = Budgeted Price (Actual Quantity – Budgeted Quantity)
= Standard Sales (Actual Sales at Standard Price) – Budgeted Sales
= 5,20,000 – 5,00,000 = ₹ 20,000 (Favourable)

Total Sales Variance = Actual Sales – Budgeted Sales
= 5,22,000 – 5,00,000 = ₹ 22,000 (Favourable)

Verification: Total Sales Variance (₹ 20,000/- Favourable) = Sales Price Variance (₹ 2,000/- Favourable) + Sales Volume Variance (₹ 20,000 Favourable)

Illustrative Problem 30

Despite increase in the sales price of its sole product to the extent of 20%, a company finds that it has incurred loss during the year 2012 to the extent of ₹ 3.40 lakhs as against the profit of ₹ 5 lakhs in 2011. The adverse situation is attributed mainly due to increase in variable cost and fixed cost, the increase over the previous years being on an average 15% and 12% respectively. The following figures are extracted from the books of the company.

	2011	2012
	(₹ in lakhs)	
Sales	120	129.60
Variable cost	100	115.00
Fixed cost	15	18.00

You are required to analyse the variances relating to sales, fixed and variable overheads over the year in order to bring out the reasons for the fall in profit. *(CA Final)*

Solution:

(*i*) ***Sales Variances*** (In lakhs of Rupees)

Sales during 2012 at 2011 prices	= 129.60 × 100/120 = 108
Sales price variance	= 129.60 – 108.00 = 21.60 (Favourable) ...(*i*)
Decrease in sales	= 120 – 108
	= 12 or 10% over 2011 sales
PV Ratio in 2011, 20/120 × 100	= 16.6%

Loss of contribution during 2012 due to lower volume of sales

= 12/6 × 100 × 1/100 = 2.0 ... (*ii*)

(*ii*) ***Variable Cost Variance***

Variable cost of 2012 at 2011 price level

= 115 × 100/115 = 100

Expenditure variance = 115 – 100 = 15 (Adverse) ... (*iii*)

Sales Volume in 2012 has increased by 10%

The variable cost should therefore be 100 – 10 = 90

Hence efficiency variance 90 – 100 = 10 (Adverse) ... (*iv*)

(*iii*) ***Fixed Cost Variances***

Fixed cost of 2012 at 2011 costs	= 18 × 100/112 = 16.07
Expenditure variance 18.00 – 16.07	= 1.93 (Adverse) ... (*v*)
Volume variance = 15 – 16.07	= 1.07 (Adverse) ...(*vi*)

Reconciliation Statement (***₹ in lakhs***)

		+	–
	Profit during 2011	5.00	
(*i*)	Sales price variance	21.60	
(*ii*)	Loss of contribution due to lower sales		2.00
(*iii*)	Variable cost expenditure variance		15.00
(*iv*)	Variable cost efficiency variance		10.00
(*v*)	Fixed cost expenditure variance		1.93
(*vi*)	Fixed cost volume variance		1.07
	Loss during 2012	3.40	
		30.00	30.00

Illustrative Problem 31

The following information has been extracted from the books of a company using standard costing system for November 2016.

Direct materials:

800 kgs. of materials were consumed. The purchase cost thereof is ₹ 49,600. Standard price per kg. of direct material is ₹ 60. The expected output is 8 units per kg. of direct material.

Direct Labour:

Budget for a 5-day week of 40 hours:

Grade A labour 8,000 hours @ ₹ 5 per hour.

Grade B labour 8,000 hours @ ₹ 4 per hour.

During November 2016, due to shortage of labour, the mix was changed as under:

Grade A labour 6,000 hours @ ₹ 5 per hour.

Grade B labour 10,000 hours @ ₹ 4 per hour.

Analysis of working revealed:

Grade A labour 6,600 hours @ ₹ 5.20 per hour.

Grade B labour 11,000 hours @ ₹ 3.90 per hour.

There were 21 days in November 2016, out of which one day was holiday leaving 20 working days. In fact, the company actually worked 21 days in November 2016. However, power failure, machine breakdown, etc. resulted in 240 idle hours of Grade A labour.

Variable overheads:

Standard cost per unit ₹ 2.50.

Actual overheads ₹ 15,750 for November 2016

Fixed overheads:

Budget ₹ 4,40,000 per annum.

Budget production 62,500 units per annum.

Actual overheads for November 2016 ₹ 35,000.

Other data:

Budgeted weeks 50 in a year.

Actual production in November 2016, 6,000 units.

Sales:

Budget 6,000 units @ ₹ 60 each.

Actual 4,800 units @ ₹ 62 each.

Required:

Analyse the variances in as much detail as possible.

(*M.Com., Delhi, 2015*)

Solution:

I. Direct Material Variances

Output	= 6,000 units	
Standard quantity	= 6,000/8	= 750 kgs.

I. **Direct Material Cost Variance**

(Std. units × Std. price) – (Actual units × Actual price)

= (750 × 60) – (800 × 62)

= 45,000 – 49,600 = 4,600 (A)

2. **Direct Material Price Variance**

Actual Qty. (Std. price per kg. – Actual price per kg.)

= 800 (60 – 62) = 1,600 (A)

3. Direct Material Usage Variance

Std. price per kg. (Std. Qty. – Actual Qty.)

= 60 (750 – 800) = 3000 (A)

Verification

Price variance + Usage variance = Cost variance

= ₹ 1,600 (A) + ₹ 3,000 (A) = ₹ 4,600 (A)

II. **Direct Labour Variance**

Budget no. of days

= 50 weeks × 5 days/per week = 250 days

Budgeted production = 62,500 units

Production per day (62,500 units/250 days) = 250 units

Production for 20 days

= 250 units × 20 days = 5000 units

Std. Time per unit

= 16,000 hrs./5,000 units = 3.2 hrs.

Std. hrs. for actual production

= 6,000 units x 3.2 hrs. = 19,200 hrs.

Std. Hours

Grade A	9,600
Grade B	9,600
Total	19,200

Revised Std. hours

Grade A	7,200
Grade B	12,000
Total	19,200

Actual hrs. on job in revised Std. ratio

Grade A	6,510
Grade B	10,850
Total	17,360

Actual hrs. on job

Grade A	6,360
Grade B	11,000
Total	17,360

Actual hrs.

Grade A	6,600
Grade B	11,000
Total	17,600

1. Direct Labour Cost Variance

(Std. hrs × Std. price) – (Actual hrs. × Actual rate)

Grade A = (9,600 hrs. × ₹ 5) – (6,600 hrs. × ₹ 5.20)

= ₹ 48,000 – ₹ 34,320 = ₹ 13,680 (F)

Grade B = (9,600 hrs. × ₹ 4) – (11,000 hrs. × ₹ 3.90)

= ₹ 38,400 – ₹ 42,900 = ₹ 4,500 (A) = ₹ 9,180 (F)

2. Direct Labour Rate Variance

Actual time (Std. rate – Actual rate)

Grade A = 6,600 (5 – 5.20) = 1,320 (A)

Grade B = 11,000 (4 – 3.90) = 1,100 (F) = 220 (A)

3. Direct Labour Efficiency Variance

Std. rate (Std. time for actual output – Actual time)

Grade A = 5 (7,200 – 6,360) = 4,200 (F)

Grade B = 4,(12,000 – 11,000) = 4,000 (F) = 8,200 (F)

4. Direct Labour Mix Variance

Std. rate (Revised Std. time – Actual time)

Grade A = 5 (6,510 – 6,360) = 750 (F)

Grade B = 4 (10,850 – 11,000) = 600 (A) = 150 (F)

5. Direct Labour Yield Variance

Std. rate (Revised Std. hours – Actual hrs. on Job in revised Std. ratio)

Grade A = 5 (7,200 – 6,510) = 3,450 (F)

Grade B = 4 (12,000 – 10,850) = 4,600 (F) = 8,050 (F)

6. Idle Time Variance

Std. Rate (Actual hours on Job – Actual hours)

Grade A = 5 (6,360 – 6,600) = 1,200 (F)

Grade B = 4 (11,000 – 11,000) = (*Nil*) = 1,200 (A)

7. Direct Labour Revision Variance

Std. rate (Std. hrs. – Revised Std. hrs.)

Grade A = 5 (9,600 – 7,200) = 12,000 (F)

Grade B = 4 (9,600 – 12,000) = 9,600 (A) = 2,400 (F)

III. Variable Overhead Variance

Std. variable overhead rate per hour = ₹ 2.50/3.2 hr.

= Re. 0.78125 per hr.

1. Variable Overhead Cost Variance

$$\left(\begin{array}{c}\text{Std. hrs. for}\\ \text{actual output}\end{array} \times \begin{array}{c}\text{Std. variable}\\ \text{overhead rate per hour}\end{array}\right) - \text{Actual overhead}$$

= (19,200 × 0.78125) – 15,750

= 15,000 – 15,750 = 750 (A)

2. Variable Overhead Expenditure Variance

$$\left(\begin{array}{c}\text{Actual hrs. for}\\ \text{actual output}\end{array} \times \begin{array}{c}\text{Std. variable}\\ \text{overhead rate per hour}\end{array}\right) - \text{Actual overhead}$$

= (17,360 × 0.78125) – 15,750

= 13,563 – 15,750 = 2,187 (A)

3. Variable Overhead Efficiency Variance

$$= \left(\text{Std. hours} \times \begin{matrix}\text{Std. variable} \\ \text{overhead rate per hour}\end{matrix}\right) - \left(\begin{matrix}\text{Actual hrs.} \\ \text{on the job}\end{matrix} \times \begin{matrix}\text{Std. variable} \\ \text{overhead rate per hour}\end{matrix}\right)$$

= (19,200 × 0.78125) – (17,360 × 0.78125)

= 15,000 – 13,563 = 1,437 (F)

IV. **Fixed Overhead Variance**

Std. Fixed overhead

= 62,500 units × 3.2 hrs. = 2,00,000 hrs.

Std. Fixed oerhead rate per hour

= ₹ 4,40,000/2,00,000 hrs. = ₹ 2.20 per hour

Budgeted hours in actual days

$$= \frac{16{,}000}{20 \text{ days}} \times 21 \text{ days} = 16{,}800 \text{ hrs.}$$

1. Fixed Overhead Cost Variance

$$\left(\begin{matrix}\text{Std. hrs. for} \\ \text{actual production}\end{matrix} \times \begin{matrix}\text{Std. fixed} \\ \text{overhead rate}\end{matrix}\right) - \text{Actual fixed overheads}$$

= (19,200 × 2.20) – 35,000

= 42,240 – 35,000 = 7,240 (F)

2. Fixed Overhead Expenditure Variance

Budgeted overheads – Actual overheads

= (16,000 × 2.2) – 35,000

= 35,200 – 35,000 = 200 (F)

3. Fixed Overhead Volume Variance

Std. rate per hour (Std. hrs. – Budgeted hrs.)

2.20 (19,200 – 16,000) = 7,040 (F)

V. **Sales Variance**

Standard Quantity = 6,000 units

Actual Quantity = 4,800 units

Selling price per unit = 60

1. Sales Value Variance

(Std. Qty. × Std. Selling price) – (Actual Qty. × Actual Selling Price)

= (6,000 × 60) – (4,800 × 62)

= 3,60,000 – 2,97,600 = 62,400 (A)

2. Sales Price Variance

Actual Qty. (Std. selling price – Actual selling price)

= 4,800 (60 – 62) = 9,600 (F)

3. Sales Volume Variance

Std. Selling Price (Std. Qty. – Actual Qty.)

= 60 (6,000 – 4,800) = 72,000 (A)

Summary of Variance

Particulars	Variances Favourable	Adverse	Total
1. Direct Material			
(a) Price	—	1,600	
(b) Usage	—	3,000	
	—	4,600	
Direct Material Cost Variance			4,600 (A)
2. Direct Labour			
(a) Rate	—	220	
(b) Efficiency			
- Mix	150	—	
- Yield	8,050	—	
- Idle time	—	1,200	
- Revision	2,400	—	
	10,600	1,420	
Direct Labour Cost Variance			9,180 (F)
3. Variable Overhead			
(a) Expendiure	—	2,187	
(b) Efficiency	1,437	—	
	1,437	2,187	
Variable Overhead Cost Variance			750 (A)
4. Fixed Overhead			
(a) Expenditure	200	—	
(b) Volume	7,040	—	
	7,240	—	
Fixed Overhead Cost Variance			7,240 (F)
5. Sales Variances			
(a) Price	9,600	—	
(b) Volume	—	72,000	
	9,600	72,000	
Sales Value Variance			62,400 (A)

Illustrative Problem 32

RST Ltd. has provided the following summarized results for two years:

	Year ended (₹ in lacs) 31-03-2014	31-3-2015
Sales	3,000	3,277.50
Material	2,000	2,357.50

Variable overheads	500	525.00
Fixed overheads	300	367.50
Profit	200	27.50

During the year ended 31-3-2015, sale price has increased by 15% whereas material and overhead prices have increased by 15% and 5% respectively. You are required to analyse the variances of revenue and each element of cost over the year in order to bring out the reasons for the change in profit. Present a profit reconcilation statement starting from profits in 2013-2014 showing the factors responsible for the change in profits in 2014-2015. (*CA Final May 2014*)

Solution:

Reconciliation Between Budgeted Profit and Actual Profit

Particulars	**(₹ in lacs)**	**(₹ in lacs)**
Budgeted Profit		200.00
Sales Margin Variances:		
Price	427.50 (F)	
Volume	10.00 (A)	417.50 (F)
Direct Material Variances:		
Price	307.50 (A)	
Usage	150.00 (A)	457.50 (A)
Variable Overheads Variances:		
Expenditure	25.00 (A)	
Efficiency	25.00 (A)	50.00 (A)
Fixed Overhead Variances:		
Expenditure	67.50 (A)	
Volume	15.00 (A)	82.50 (A)
Actual Profit		27.50

Computation of Varianes (In Lacs)

Sales Variances

Price Variance = Actual Sales – Standard Sales
= ₹ 3,277.50 – ₹ 2,850.00 = ₹ 427.50 (F)

Volume Variance = Standard Sales – Budgeted Sales
= ₹ 2,850 – ₹ 3,000 = ₹ 150 (A)

Sales Margin Variances

Sales Margin Price Variance = Sales Price Variance
= ₹ 427.50 (F)

Sales Margin Volume Variance = Sales Volume Variance × Budgeted Net Profit Ratio
= ₹ 150 (A) × [₹ 200/3,000] = ₹ 10 (A)

Material Variances

Material Price Variance = Standard Cost of Actual Quantity – Actual Cost
= ₹ 2,050.00 – ₹ 2,357.50 = ₹ 307.50 (A)

Material Usage Variance	=	Standard Cost of Standard Quantity for Actual Output – Standard Cost of Actual Quantity
	=	₹ 1,900 – ₹ 2,050 = ₹ 150 (A)

Variable Overhead Variance

Expenditure Variance	=	Budgeted Variable Overheads for Actual Hours – Actual Variable overheads
		Or
	=	Std. Rate per unit × Expected Output for Actual Hours Worked – Actual Variable Overheads
	=	₹ 500 – ₹ 525 = ₹ 25 (A)
Efficiency Variance	=	Standard Variable Overheads for Production – Budgeted Variable Overheads for Actual Hours
		Or
	=	Std. Rate per unit × Actual Output – Std. Rate unit × Expected Output for Actual Hours Worked
	=	₹ 475 – ₹ 500 = ₹ 25 (A)

Fixed Overhead Variances

Expenditure Variance	=	Budgeted Fixed Overheads – Actual Fixed Overheads.
	=	₹ 300 – ₹ 367.50 = ₹ 67.50 (A)
Volume Variance	=	Absorbed Fixed Overheads – Budgeted Fixed Overheads
	=	₹ 285 – ₹ 300 = ₹ 15 (A)

Working Notes (₹ in lacs)

Note 1:

Sales in current years (C.Y.)	
Less: Increase due to price rise [₹ 3,277.50 lacs × 15/115]	427.50
Sales in C.Y. at previous year P.Y. Prices [Standard Sales]	2,850.00
Sales in P.Y.	3,000.00
Fall in Sales in C.Y. [₹ 3,000 lacs – ₹ 2,850 lacs]	150.00
Percentage fall	5%

Note 2:

Material Cost in P.Y.	2,000.00
Less: 5% for Decrease in Volume	100.00
'Standard Material Usage' at P.Y. Prices	
(Standard Cost of Standard Quantity for Actual output)	1,900.00
Actual Material Cost C.Y.	2,357.50
Less: 15% Increase in Prices [₹ 2,357.50 lakhs × 15/115]	307.50
Actual Materials Used, at P.Y. Prices (Standard Cost of Actual Quantity)	2,050.00

Note 3:

Variable Overheads Cost in P.Y.	500.00

Less: 5% due to fall in Volume of Sales in C.Y.	25.00
"Standard Overheads for Production" in C.Y.	475.00
Actual Variable Overheads Incurred in C.Y.	525.00
Less: 5% for Inrease in Price [₹ 525 lacs × 5/105]	25.00
Amount Spent in C.Y. at P.Y. Prices (Budgeted Variable Overheads for Actual Hours)	500.00

Note 4:

Fixed Overheads Cost in P.Y.	300.00
Less: 5% due to fall in Volume of Sales in C.Y.	15.00
"Standard Overheads for Production" in C.Y. (Absorbed Fixed Overheads)	285.00

Illustrative Problem 33

The budgeted output of a single product manufacturing company for the year ending 31st March was 5,000 units. The financial results in respect of the actual output of 4,800 units achieved during the year were as under:

	₹
Direct material	29,700
Direct wages	44,700
Variable overheads	72,750
Fixed overheads	39,000
Profit	36,600
Sales	2,22,750

The standard wage rate is ₹ 4.50 per hour and the standard variable overhead rate is ₹ 7.50 per hour.

The cost accounts recorded the following variances for the year:

Variances	Favourable ₹	Adverse ₹
Material price		300
Material usage	—	600
Wage rate	750	0
Labour efficiency	—	2,250
Variable overhead expenses	3,000	—
Variable overhead efficiency	—	3,750
Fixed overhead expense	—	1,500
Spelling price	6,750	—

Required:

(*i*) Prepare a statement showing the original budget.

(*ii*) Prepare the standard product cost sheet per unit.

(*iii*) Prepare a statement showing the reconciliation of originally budgeted profit and the actual profit.

Solution:

Basic Calculations:

			₹
(*a*)	Actual Sales		2,22,750
	Less: Price Variance (Favourable)		6,750
	Standard Sales		2,16,000
	Units Sold		4,800

Budgeted Price per Unit: $= \dfrac{₹\,2,16,000}{4,800 \text{ units}} = ₹\,45$

		₹	₹
(*b*)	Material Used		29,700
	Less: Price Variance (Adverse)	300	
	Usage Variance (Adverse)	600	900
	Standard Cost		28,800

Standard Material Cost per Unit $= \dfrac{₹\,28,800}{4,800 \text{ units}} = ₹\,6$

			₹
(*c*)	Direct Wages Spent		44,700
	Add: Wage Rate Variance (Favourable)		750
			45,450
	Less: Efficiency Variance (Adverse)		2,250
	Standard Wages		43,200

Standard Wage Rate per Unit $= \dfrac{₹\,43,200}{4,800 \text{ units}} = ₹\,9$

(*d*) Standard Direct Wage Rate is ₹ 4.50 per Hour

Hence Standard Time per Unit: ₹ 9 ÷ 4.50 Hour = 2 Hours

(*e*) Variable Overheads:

Standard Rate ₹ 7.50 per Hour

Variable Overhead per Unit: 2 hrs. × 7.50 = ₹ 15

(**Note:** Alternatively, this may be calculated by adjusting variances as in other cases)

			₹
(*f*)	Fixed Overhead Spent		39,000
	Less: Fixed Overhead Expense Variance (Adverse)		1,500
	Budgeted Overheads		37,500

Std. Fixed Overhead Rate per Unit: $\dfrac{₹\,37,500}{5,000 \text{ units}} = ₹\,7.50$

(*g*) Fixed Overhead Recovered: 4,800 Units × ₹ 7.50 = ₹ 36,000 (Absorbed)

(*h*) Fixed Overhead Volume Variance

(Absorbed Overheads – Budgeted Overheads) = ₹ 36,000 – ₹ 37,500

= ₹ 1,500 (Adverse)

(*i*) Budgeted Sales: 5,000 units × ₹ 45 = ₹ 2,25,000

(*j*) Actual Sales = ₹ 2,22,750

(*k*) Sale Volume Variance ₹ 45 × (4,800 Units – 5,000 Units)

[Budgeted Price × (Actual Qty. – Budgeted Qty.)] = ₹ 9,000 (A)

(*i*) Statement Showing the Original Budget:

		₹
Budgeted Sales	(5,000 units × ₹ 45)	2,25,000
Less: Budgeted Costs:		
Direct Material	(5,000 units × ₹ 6)	30,000
Direct Wages	(5,000 units × ₹ 9)	45,000
Variable Overheads	(5,000 units × ₹ 15)	75,000
Fixed Overheads	(5,000 units × ₹ 7.50)	37,500
Profit:		37,500

(*ii*) Statement Showing Standard Product Cost Sheet per Unit:

	₹
Budgeted Sales	6.00
Direct Wages	9.00
Prime Cost	15.00
Variable Overheads	15.00
Fixed Overheads	7.50
Total Cost	37.50
Profit	7.50
Selling Price	45.00

(*iii*) Statement Showing Reconciliation of the Original Budgeted Profit and the Actual Profit

Particulars	₹	₹
Budgeted Profit:		37,500.00
(Budgeted Quantity × Budgeted Margin)		
Sales Margin Variances:		
Sales Margin Volume Variance*		(1,500.00)
Standard Profit		36,000.00
Effect of Other Variances		
Material Cost Variances:		
Material Price Variance	(300.00)	
Material Usage Variance	(600.00)	(900.00)
Labour Cost Variances:		
Labour Rate Variance	750.00	
Labour Efficiency Variance	(2,250.00)	(1,500.00)
Variable Overhead Cost Variances:		
Variable Overhead Expenditure Variance	3,000.00	
Variable Overhead Efficiency Variance	(3,750.00)	(750.00)

Fixed Overhead Cost Variances:			
Fixed Overhead Expenditure Variance	(1,500.00)		
Fixed Overhead Volume Variance	(1,500.00)	(3,000.00)	
Sales Margin Variances:			
Sales Margin Price Variance		6,750.00	600.00
Actual Profit for the Month			36,600.00

Adverse Shown by (-) Symbol

*Sales Margin Volume Variance = Sales Volume Variance × Budgeted Net Profit Ratio

= ₹ 9,000 (A) × [₹ 7.50/₹ 45 × 100)% = 1,500 (A)

Illustrative Problem 34

The CEO of your company has been given the following statement showing the results for a recent month:

Particulars	*Master Budget*	*Actual*
Units produced & sold	10,000	9,000
	₹	₹
Sales	8,00,000	7,00,000
Direct material	2,00,000	1,84,000
Direct Wages	3,00,000	2,62,000
Variable overhead	1,00,000	94,000
Fixed overhead	1,00,000	98,000
Total Cost	7,00,000	6,38,000
Net Surplus	1,00,000	62,000

The standard cost of the product is as follows:

Direct material (1 kg @ ₹ 20/kg) ₹ 20.00 per unit

Direct labour (1 hour @ ₹ 30/hour) ₹ 30.00 per unit

Variable overhead (1 hour @ ₹ 10/hour) ₹ 10.00 per unit

Actual results for the month revealed that 9,800 kg. of material was used and 8,800 labour hours were recorded.

(*i*) Prepare a flexible budget for the month and compare with the actual results.

(*ii*) Calculate material volume and variable overhead efficiency variances.

Solution:

(*i*)

Particular	*Master Buget*		*Flexible Budget*	*Actual*	*Variance*
Units	10,000		9,000	9,000	
	(₹) Total	(₹) Per unit	(₹)	(₹)	
Sales	8,00,000	80	7,20,000	7,00,000	20,000 (A)

Direct Material	2,00,000	20	1,80,000	1,84,000	4,000 (A)
Direct Wages	3,00,000	30	2,70,000	2,62,000	8,000 (F)
Variable Overhead	1,00,000	10	90,000	94,000	4,000 (A)
Total Variable Cost	6,00,000	60	5,40,000	5,40,000	-
Contribution	2,00,000	20	1,80,000	1,60,000	20,000 (A)
Fixed Overhead	1,00,000	10	1,00,000	98,000	2,000 (F)
Net Profit	1,00,000	10	80,000	62,000	18,000 (A)

(*ii*) ***Calculation of Variances:***

Material Volume Variance: SP (SQ – AQ) = 20 (9,000 – 9,800) = 16,000 (A)

Variable Overhead efficiency variance SR (SH – AR) = 10 (9,000 – 8,800) = 2,000 (F)

Illustrative Problem 35

A company producing a single product anticipated certain profits on an expected production and sale of 80,000 units, but found on actual working that the profits turned out to be much below expectation. From the following particulars, you are required to draw up a reconciliation between the company's actual and budgeted profits explaining the variations and their various causes. You are also required to determine in particular the material price variances, wage rate variance and sales price and volume variance:

	Anticipated	*Actual*
Units	80,000	70,000
Net selling price per unit	₹ 40	₹ 42
Material per unit	4 kg	4 kg
Rate of material per kg	₹ 4	₹ 4.50
Labour hours per unit	5 hours	4.50
Rate per labour hour	Re. 1	₹ 1.20
Variable overhead per labour hour	₹ 1.60	₹ 2.00
Fixed overhead per unit	₹ 2.00	₹ 2.40

Solution:

Statement of Anticipated and Actual Profits

Particulars	*Anticipated*		*Actual*	
	Per unit	*Total*	*Per unit*	*Total*
Units produced and sold		80,000		70,000
Direct material cost	₹ 16	12,80,000	₹ 18	12,60,000
Direct labour cost	₹ 5	4,00,000	₹ 5.40	3,78,000
Variable overheads	₹ 8	6,40,000	₹ 9	6,30,000
Fixed overheads	₹ 2	1,60,000	₹ 2.40	1,68,000
Total cost of sales	₹ 31	24,80,000	₹ 34.80	24,36,000
Sales	₹ 40	32,00,000	₹ 42	29,40,000
Profit	₹ 9	7,20,000	₹ 7.20	5,04,000

Difference in profit = ₹ 7,20,000 – 5,04,000
= ₹ 2,16,000

Analysis of variance is done as follows:

(*i*) Materials price variance
= Actual quantity × (Actual price – Standard price)
= 70,000 × 4 (₹ 4.50 – ₹ 4.00)
= ₹ 1,40,000 (Adverse)

(*ii*) Material usage variance is nil since actual usage 4 kg per unit is in line with anticipated usage.

(*iii*) Wages rate variance
= Actual quantity × (Actual price – Standard price)
= 70,000 × 4.50 (1.20 – 1.00)
= ₹ 63,000 (A)

(*iv*) Labour efficiency variance
= Standard rate per hour × (Actual hours – Standard hours)
= 1.00 (70,000 × 4.50 – 70,000 × 5.00)
= ₹ 35,000 (Favourable)

(*v*) Variable overheads expenditure variance
= Actual expenditure – Standard recovery
= ₹ 2.00 × 70,000 × 4.50 – ₹ 1.60 × 70,000 × 5.00
= 70,000 (Adverse)

(*vi*) Fixed overhead volume variance
= Standard recovery – Budgeted allowance
= 70,000 × 2.00 – 80,000 × ₹ 2.00
= ₹ 20,000 (Adverse)

(*vii*) Fixed overheads expenditure variance
= Actual expenditure – Budget allowance
= 70,000 × ₹ 2.40 – 80,000 × ₹ 2.00
= ₹ 8,000 (Adverse)

(*viii*) Selling price variance
= Actual sales quantity × (Actual price – Standard price)
= 70,000 (₹ 42 – ₹ 40)
= 1,40,000 (Favourable)

(*ix*) Sales volume variance
= Standard profit per unit × (Actual quantity – Budgeted quantity)
= ₹ 9 (70,000 – 80,000)
= ₹ 90,000 (Adverse)

Summary of Variance (₹)

	Favourable	*Adverse*
Materials price variance		1,40,000
Wages rate variance		63,000
Labour efficiency variance	35,000	
Variance overheads expenditure variance		70,000
Fixed overheads volume variance		20,000
Selling price variance	1,40,000	
Fixed overhead expenditure variance		8,000
Sales volume variance		90,000
Total	1,75,000	3,91,000

Net variance = ₹ 3,91,000 (A) – ₹ 1,75,000 (F) = 2,16,000 (adverse). This explains the profit shortage of ₹ 2,16,000 due to various causes.

REVISION VARIANCE

When a budget is revised, but where, as a matter of policy, the change is not incorporated in the standard cost rate, a variance will arise termed as a Revision Variance. Revision variance is the difference between the basic standard cost and the revised standard cost.

DISPOSITION OF VARIANCE

Variances may be disposed of in either of the following ways:

(1) Inventories and the cost of goods sold may be adjusted to reflect the actual costs.

(2) Variances may be transferred to the profit and loss account.

Under the first method, all variances are allocated between the inventory accounts and cost of goods sold account.

This method, in fact, converts the accounts balances from standard costs to actual historical costs. The following arguments are given in support of this method:

1. Only actual costs should be recorded in the cost of goods sold account and inventory accounts. The supporters of this method do not favour standard costs as true costs or costs suitable for use in the profit and loss account but as merely guides in factory management. Actual costs are facts and therefore, should be used in the financial statements.
2. Variances from the standard are costs and not losses and therefore, should be reflected in the inventory valuations and cost of goods sold.
3. If the variances are large, standard costs do not represent the actual costs and therefore, are not good measures to determine the costs of goods sold and inventory.

Under the second method, the variances are considered as profit or loss items in the period in which they occurred. The work-in-process, finished goods inventory, and cost of goods sold are stated at standard costs. Unfavourable cost variances are deducted from the gross profit at standard costs. Favourable cost variances are added to the gross profit calculated at standard cost. The treatment of the cost variances under this method is shown on the income statement as given below:

ABC Company
Income Statement for the Year Ending December 31, ...

	₹	₹
Sales revenue		5,00,000
Cost of sales (Standard)	3,00,000	
Selling and administrative expenses (Standard)	1,50,000	4,50,000
Net Income (Standard)		50,000
Deduct unfavourable variance from standard profit:		
Material price	200	
Material usage	800	
Labour efficiency	900	
Overhead:		
Volume	2,000	
Budget	1,100	5,000
Net income (actual)		45,000

The second method has the following arguments in its favour:

1. Standard costs helps in the preparation of statements at an early date; actual cost delays the determination of inventory costs and cost of goods sold.
2. Standard costs avoid the inclusion of costs due to wastage, losses, inefficiencies, excessive overheads from low production volume. Standard cost represents normal costs and therefore inventory figures are conservative and acceptable for income determination and other purposes.
3. In a multi-product company, it may be difficult to determine accurately how much variance should be distributed to each product.
4. In taking corrective action, managers may find it more useful when variances are depicted in the profit and loss account. Managerial attention is usually hampered when variances are combined with cost of goods manufactured.

It is difficult to suggest which method should be followed in accounting for variances. If the variances are large and significant, the first method, *i.e.*, distribution of variances to the respective accounts appears to be appropriate for financial reporting, tax and job and contract pricing purposes. The second method may be preferable when the variances are insignificant. Thus, the treatment of variances depends on many factors such as (*i*) size of variance, (*ii*) accuracy of standard costs, (*iii*) causes of variances such as incorrect standard costs, (*iv*) timing of variances, *e.g.*, caused by seasonal fluctuation, (*v*) type of variance — material, labour, and overhead.

MANAGERIAL USES OF VARIANCES

Determination of variances is only the first step in the process of standard cost variance analysis. Mere computation of material, labour and overhead variances is useless for cost control and performance evaluation. The final objective of variance analysis is to determine the person(s) responsible for each variance and to pinpoint the cause(s) for incurrence of these variances. Properly used standard cost variances are useful tools in achieving effective cost control. That is, before management can take effective action for improving control over costs, it needs to know not only the amount of variances, but also where the variance originated, who was responsible for them, and what caused them to arise. Analysis of standard cost variances is, therefore, necessary by responsibilities and causes.

Analysis of Variances by Responsibilities

Control over cost must be applied at the place and time where the cost originates. Variances must be identified with the manager responsible for the costs incurred, who should be held responsible for the cost. The cost factors which are directly controllable by operating supervisors must be separated from those cost factors for which executive management is responsible.

Specific titles of individuals who are responsible for each type of variance differ among business enterprises. Generally speaking, the following personnel are held accountable for variances noted against them:

Responsibility for Cost Variances

Variance	*Personnel Responsible*
• Materials price variance	Purchasing agent or purchasing manager
• Materials quantity variance	Plant superintendent, departmental supervisors, machine operators, quality control department and material handlers
• Labour rate standard	Personnel (employment) department manager, departmental supervisor and plant superintendent.
• Labour efficiency variance	Plant superintendent, departmental supervisors, production scheduling department, quality control department, material handlers and machine operators.
• Overhead expenditure variance	Variable portion is the responsibility of the individual foreman or supervisor, they are expected to keep actual expenses within the budget. Fixed portion is the responsibility of top management.
• Overhead efficiency variance	Same personnel who are responsible for labour efficiency variance.
• Overhead volume variance	Top management and production schedules.

Analysis of Variances by Causes

Variances reflect the effect on costs which certain events or conditions have produced. Before management can decide whether or not action is called for and, if so, what should be done, it is necessary to know what caused the variance to arise. Reasons for the variance should be determined and plans for necessary corrective action made either by discussing possible causes with the supervisors or by examining underlying data and records. The analysis of variances by causes is, therefore, an important aspect of the use of standard costs to attain effective cost control. For any standard cost variance, there are many possible causes. The following list is not all inclusive but does indicate causes responsible for variances.

Possible Causes of Standard Cost Variances

Materials Price Variance

- Recent changes in purchase price of materials.
- Failure to purchase anticipated quantities when standards were established resulting in higher prices owing to non-availability of quantity purchase discounts.

- Not taking cash discounts anticipated at the time of setting standards resulting in higher prices.
- Substituting raw material differing from original materials specifications.
- Freight cost changes and changes in purchasing and storekeeping costs, if these are debited to the materials cost.

Materials Quantity Variance

- Poor material handling.
- Inferior workmanship by machine operator.
- Faulty equipment.
- Cheaper, defective raw material causing excessive scrap.
- Inferior quality control inspection.
- Pilferage.
- Wastage due to inefficient production method.

Labour Rate Variance

- Recent labour rate change within industry.
- Employing a man of a grade different from the one laid down in the standard.
- Labour strike leading to utilisation of unskilled help.
- Labour layoff causing skilled labour to be retained at higher rates, so as to prevent resignations and job switching.
- Employee sickness and vacation time.
- Paying a higher overtime allowance than provided for in the standard.

Labour Efficiency Variance

- Machine breakdown, use of defective machinery and equipment
- Inferior raw materials
- Poor supervision
- Lack of timely material handling
- Poor employee performance
- Inefficient production scheduling — delays in routine work, materials, tools and instructions
- Inferior engineering specifications
- New inexperienced employees
- Insufficient training of workers
- Poor working conditions — inadequate or excessive heating, lighting, ventilation, etc.

Overhead Volume Variance (Factors causing either Idle Time or overtime of Plant and Facilities)

- Failure to utilise normal capacity
- Lack of sales order
- Too much idle capacity
- Inefficient or efficient utilisation of existing capacity
- Machine breakdown

- Defective materials
- Labour troubles
- Power failures

Overhead Efficiency Variance

They include all causes which are listed under labour efficiency variance.

Analysis of Variances by Products

Since management usually wants current true costs when decisions are to be made with respect to pricing and related questions, variances are often analysed by products in order to arrive at correct product costs. Companies producing non-standard goods according to customer's specification may also help analyse variances by job orders. The analysis of variances by causes is useful in deciding whether or not cost variances should be allocated to products in arriving at product costs for pricing. Standard product costs should be reviewed periodically and revised when it is found that the standard product costs in use are no longer useful for the purpose.

VARIANCE ANALYSIS AND PERFORMANCE EVALUATION

A key use of variance analysis is in performance evaluation. Two attributes of performance are commonly measured.[2]

- ***Effectiveness:*** The degree to which a predetermined objective or target is met — for example, sales, customer satisfaction, etc.
- ***Efficiency:*** The relative amount of inputs used to achieve a given level of output — the smaller the quantity of inputs used to make a given number of output units or the greater output units made from a given quantity of input, the greater the efficiency.

Horngreen, Datar and Foster[3] have mentioned a few precautions for managers while using variance analysis for evaluating the performance of their subordinates:

1. Managers should not automatically interpret a favourable variance as 'good news'.
2. Managers benefit from variance analysis because it highlights individual aspects of performance.

   If any single performance measure (for example, a labour efficiency variance or a consumer rating report) receives excessive emphasis, managers tend to make decisions that maximise their own reported performance in terms of that single performance measure. In turn, managers' actions may conflict with the organisation achieving its overall goals. This faulty perspective on performance arises because top management has designed a performance measurement and reward system that does not adequately emphasize total organisation objectives.
3. The goal of variance analysis is for managers to understand why variances arise, to learn, and to improve future performance. For instance, to reduce unfavourable direct materials usage (quantity) variance, we may seek improvements in product design, in the quality of supplied materials, in the commitment of the manufacturing labour force to do the job right the first time, and so on. Variance analysis should not be a tool to "play the blame game" (that is, for every unfavourable variance a person is sought to blame or even punish). Rather, it should help the company learn about what happened and how to perform better in future.

4. An over-emphasis on performance evaluation may cause managers to take actions to achieve the budget and avoid an unfavourable variance, even if such actions could hurt the company in the long run. For example, the manufacturing manager may push workers to produce jackets within the time allowed, even if this action could lead to poorer quality jackets being produced, which could later hurt revenues. Such negative impacts are less likely to occur if variance analysis is seen as a way of promoting organisational learning.
5. Managers can also use variance analysis to create a virtuous cycle of continuous improvement. How? by repeatedly identifying causes of variances, initiating corrective actions, and evaluating results of actions.
6. Almost all companies use a combination of financial and non-financial performance measures for planning and control rather than relying exclusively on either type of measure. Managers excise control by observing workers and by focusing on non-financial measures, say, number of square yards of cloth used to produce 1000 jacket.

Standards perceived to be unreasonable exert excessive pressure, are inflexible, or viewed as part of an unfair or uneven performance evaluation and reward systems. Managers or employees with negative perceptions often are discouraged and adopt protective or defensive behavior. Some may even try to sabotage the system using tactics such as padding the budget, decreasing product and service quality, increasing absenteeism, having lackadaisical attitudes, and decreased initiative, among others. On the other hand, managers and other employees who have positive perceptions of a standard cost system show enthusiasm, creativity, and productivity.[4]

PROBLEMS WITH THE USE OF STANDARD COSTS IN TODAY'S MANUFACTURING ENVIRONMENT

There are some problems associated with the use of standard costs in an advanced manufacturing setting, JIT production methods, global competitive environment, quality driven demand and continuous process improvement. These problems or limitations are as follows:

1. Standard costing variance reports may not be useful if they are prepared on a monthly basis and released many days after the period.
2. Standard cost variances are too aggregate and are not related to specific product lines, production batches. This makes it difficult to determine the causes of variances and persons responsible for the variances.
3. Standard costing encourages the employees to cover up unfavourable variances. Traditional standard costing pays undue importance to direct labour, which is rapidly becoming a relatively unimportant factor of production.
4. Standard costing tends to measure performances in terms of difference between the actual and standards. But other non-financial measures such as maintaining and improving quality, ontime delivery, customer satisfaction and the like are equally important in performance evaluation.
5. Products may have shorter life cycles which means that standards are relevant for only a short time.
6. Mere accomplishing standards is not sufficient, continuous improvement may be necessary to survive in the current competitive environment.
7. Too much emphasis on meeting the standards may overshadow other important objectives such as maintaining and improving quality, on-time delivery, and customer satisfaction. This tendency can be reduced by using supplemental performance measures that focus on these other objectives.

According to Blocher, Chen, Cokins and Lin[5]:

> Recent advances in manufacturing concepts and technologies have greatly impacted manufacturing processes, costing methods, and standard costing systems. With the introduction of just-in-time (JIT), automation, manufacturing cells, total quality management, throughput time, supply-chain management, and other modern manufacturing concepts and technologies, many firms have changed their focuses of cost control and management. No distinction between units purchased and units used is necessary in determining direct materials variances for firms that maintain a minimal inventory or that use a JIT system. For these firms, the quantity purchased in a period is almost the same as the amount used or needed during the period.
>
> Furthermore, firms using JIT systems or supply-chain management often have less interest in materials purchase price variances. These firms often purchase materials from suppliers under long-term contracts to ensure deliveries of quality materials as scheduled or needed. These firms emphasize the total cost of their materials procurements, not just materials purchase costs. Factors such as quality, reliability, and availability often outweigh the purchase cost.
>
> The arrival of new manufacturing technologies such as automation, flexible manufacturing system, and cluster or cell manufacturing has deemphasized the importance of direct labour variances. Firms that use automated manufacturing system use little or no direct labour and attach little importance to labour rate and efficiency variances.

STANDARD COSTING IN SERVICE INDUSTRY FIRMS

Standard costing system plays a vital role in the cost management of a manufacturing enterprise. However, standards can be set in service industry firms for many activities undertaken by them. For example, Air India can set standards for fuel and maintenance costs. Standard cost can be used in non-profit organisations, governmental units, hospitals, banks and other service enterprises for budgeting, cost control and performance evaluation in the same manner as manufacturing firms use standards and standard costing.

CHARACTERISTICS OF VARIANCE REPORTS

Variance reports basically aim to inform managers responsible for the operation when actual performance differs from the standards. Control of production and costs is a matter of timing; the effectiveness of the control is often in direct proportion to the speed with which variances are reported. Timely reporting often requires daily and weekly reporting of performance information. Therefore, it is important to focus managerial attention on off-standard conditions immediately following each shift, day or week, rather than to accumulate and summarise variances from standards each month. A month, and generally even a week, is too long a period for many off-standard conditions to remain unchecked and uncorrected, because the time interval may prevent positive identification of employees who are responsible for the unsatisfactory work. Prompt review of variances can disclose conditions needing managerial attention and can also provide management with information which contributes to the making of sounder decisions with respect to the future.

Variance analysis reports are primarily control reports. In developing and reporting the variances it should be remembered that the results must (*i*) deal with relevant distinctions, (*ii*) be understandable, (*iii*) measure with reasonable accuracy what they are supposed to measure, (*iv*) be presented and explained concisely, (*v*) be timely, and (*vi*) provide the amount of details needed by different persons at each level of management.

LIMITATIONS OF STANDARD COSTING

Standard costs are not without their shortcomings.

The first limitation is regarding the predetermined nature of standard costs. The accuracy of standard costs is bounded by the knowledge and skill of the people who created them and they contain the prejudices of their makers. Such badly conceived standard costs do not enjoy the confidence of the users of the system.

Secondly, it is difficult to select a type of standard (ideal, currently attainable, normal, etc.) which can help in cost control and achieve other managerial purposes. If standards are too low, they defeat the objective of standard costing and bring the operating efficiency down. If they are too high, they can create ill-will and encourage employees to beat the system by fair means or foul. There is also a dispute as to what level of standards should be used for external financial reporting, and internal management purposes.

Thirdly, a good programme of standard costing requires that both management and operating personnel should have full confidence in it and standards should be fair and workable. Educating employees is necessary in this regard. However, lack of acceptability, education and communication is a major difficulty in operating a standard costing system. There is the problem of human relation to add to the problems of setting up and operating the system, and sometimes this aspect is more involved in standard costing than the mechanics of the system itself.

Fourthly, the variances calculated under standard costing are at too aggregate a level and come too late to be useful. Some managerial accountants argue that traditional standard costing is out of step with the philosophy of cost management systems and activity-based management. A production process comprises many activities. These activities result in costs. By focusing on the activities that cause costs to be incurred, by eliminating non-value-added activities, and by continually improving performance in value-added activities, costs will be minimized and profit maximized.What is needed are performance measures that focus directly on performance in the activities that management wants to improve. For example, such activities could include product quality, processing time and delivery performance.[6]

Fifthly, these days products are having shorter product life cycles and therefore standards have utility only for a shorter duration. When new products are designed and developed, new standards would also be needed.

In spite of the above limitations, standard costing has developed into an extraordinary and very useful tool and has contributed much in providing different kinds of cost data for so many different purposes.

REFERENCES

1. Edward J. Blocher, Kung H. Chen, Gary Cokins, Thomas W. Lin, *Cost Management,* Tata Mc Graw Hill Publishing Co, 2006, p. 535.
2. Charles T. Horngreen, Sri Kant M. Datar and George Foster, *Cost Accounting,* A *Management Emphasis,* Pearson. Education, 2008, p. 262
3. Charles T. Horngreen, Sri Kant M. Datar and George Foster, *Ibid,* pp. 262-263
4. Edward J. Blocher, Kung H-Chen, Gary Cokins, Thomas W. Lin, Ibid, P. 535
5. Edward J. Blocher et at, *Ibid,* p. 534
6. Ronald W. Hilton, *Managerial Accounting,* Tata Mc Graw Hill Publishing Co., 2006, pp. 424-425.

CRITICAL ANALYSIS AND DISCUSSION QUESTIONS, SELF-ASSESSMENT QUESTIONS, MULTIPLE CHOICE QUESTIONS, PROBLEMS AND CASES

CRITICAL ANALYSIS AND DISCUSSION QUESTIONS

1. Identify the role of standard costs in the budgetary control process.
2. Discuss briefly the use of standard costs in the following management activities: cost reductions, operating performance evaluation, product pricing decisions and providing incentives.
3. Compare and contrast the usefulness of ideal standards, basic standards and currently attainable standards.
4. "Standard costs are bases for a proper managerial control of manufacturing operation." Define standard cost and explain the above statement.
5. What is standard costing and how would you distinguish it from budgetary control?
6. What are the points of similarity and difference between budgeted and standard costs?
7. "Variance analysis is an integral part of standard cost accounting." Explain this statement.
8. By purchasing low-grade materials, a company reports favorable material price variance, but it consistently experience unfavorable material quantity variances. What relationship may exist between these conditions? Is the price variance really favorable?
9. What are shortcomings of historical costs for managerial uses?
10. What is the difference between an estimated cost and a standard cost?
11. Describe briefly how standard costs are set for *(a)* material *(b)* labour.
12. Briefly explain the meaning of each of the following variances: material prices, material usages, labour efficiency and labour rate.
13. Discuss some of the problems that might be created by standards which are set too high and by standards which are too loose.
14. What are the advantages and limitations of standard costing?
15. Discuss briefly some of the limitations of standard costs.
16. Explain why overhead variances are generally treated as period costs.
17. Discuss the information which a well-designed cost report should give to management from the point of view of production and control. How should such information be given?
18. How does standard costing improve the control function?
19. Explain why the materials price variance is often computed at the point of purchase rather than at the point of issuance.
20. A standard cost sheet is a key component of a standard cost system. Describe a standard cost sheet and explain why it is significant.
21. Explain the significance of overhead variances with suitable illustrations. *(M. Com., Delhi)*
22. The variance analysis, the key element in standards costing, essentially consists of the application of the principle of management by exception." Elucidate. *(M. Com., Delhi)*
23. Which type of standards do you believe will better motivate employees, ideal or practical?, Why?

24. Do favorable variances always represent good performance? Do unfavorably variances always represent bad performance.
25. The budget variance for variable production costs is broken down into quantity and price variances. Explain why the quantity variance is more useful for control purposes than the price variance.
26. What is the cause of an unfavorable volume variance? Does the volume variance convey any meaningful information to managers?
27. Which do you think is more important for control of fixed overhead costs: spending variance or volume variance? Explain.
28. "Overhead variances should be viewed as interdependent rather than independent." Comment.
29. "Managers should be rewarded for favorable variances and punished for unfavorable variances." Do you agree? Explain.
30. What are some common causes of usage variances?
31. In a service environment with no inventories, is variance analysis useful? Why or why not?
32. Which manager is usually in the best position to influence the direct material quantity variance.
33. Explain why the quantity purchased is used in computing the direct material price variance, but the actual quantity consumed is used in computing the direct material quantity variance.

SELF-ASSESSMENT QUESTIONS

A. Fill in the blanks with the appropriate word given in the brackets:

1. .... costs are not useful in cost control (estimated/historical/standard).
2. Standard costs represent the.................... costs in a given set of circumstances (ideal/real).
3. ....standards are the standards which can be attained under the most favorable conditions possible (ideal/normal/currently attainable).
4. Normal standards are set on a .... capacity basis. (ideal/average/currently attainable).
5. An unfavorable material quantity variance means that .... direct materials were used than expected (more/less).
6. Material price variance is regarded unfavorable when .... price for materials exceeds .... the price (standard, actual).
7. A .... is responsible for materials price variance (purchasing manager/plant superintendent).

B. You are provided with the following data:

Standard hours:	Standard hours for actual level of activity:	Actual hours:
2,750	2,400	2,650

The standard wage rate per hour was ₹ 6.50. The actual wage rate per hour was ₹ 7.00.

1. The adverse labour rate variance amounts to:

   (*a*) ₹ 1,200 (*b*) ₹ 1,325 (*c*) ₹ 1,375

2. The labour efficiency variance is
(*a*) ₹ 650 favorable (*b*) ₹ 1,625 favorable
(*c*) ₹ 650 adverse (*d*) ₹ 1,625 adverse

C. You have been supplied with the following data:

	Standard	***Actual***	***Standard for Actual level***
Usage (units)	5,000	6,400	6,000
Cost of materials:	(at ₹ 4.50)	(at ₹ 4.25)	(at ₹ 4.50)
	₹ 22,500	₹ 27,200	₹ 27,000

The material cost variance can be divided into:

	Price variance of	Usage variance of:
(*a*)	₹ 1,500 favorable	₹ 1,800 adverse
(*b*)	₹ 1,600 favorable	₹ 1,700 adverse
(*c*)	₹ 1,500 favorable	₹ 1,700 adverse
(*d*)	₹ 1,600 favorable	₹ 1,800 adverse

D. Super store uses a standard costing system in the manufacture of its single product. The 35,000 units of raw material in inventory were purchased for ₹ 1,05,000 and two units of raw material are required to produce one unit of final product. In November, the company produced 12,000 units of product. The standard allowed for material was ` 60,000, and there was an unfavorable quantity variance of ₹ 2,500.

1. Super store's standard price for one unit of material is
(*a*) ₹ 2.00. (*b*) ₹ 2.50. (*c*) ₹ 3.00.
(*d*) ₹ 5.00. (*e*) ₹ 6.00.

2. The units of material used to produce November output totalled
(*a*) 12,000 units. (*b*) 12,500 units. (*c*) 23,000 units.
(*d*) 24,000 units. (*e*) 25,000 units.

3. The materials price variance for the units used in November was
(*a*) ₹ 2,500 unfavorable. (*b*) ₹ 11,000 unfavorable.
(*c*) ₹ 12,500 unfavorable. (*d*) ₹ 3,500 unfavorable.
(*e*) ₹ 2,500 favorable.

E. Blaster Co., a manufacturer of portable radios, purchases the components from subcontractors to use to assemble into a complete radio. Each radio requires three units each of Part XBEZ52 which has a standard cost of ₹ 145 per unit. During May 2016, Blaster experienced the following with respect to part XBEZ52.

	Units
Purchases (₹ 18,00,000)	12,000
Consumed in manufacturing	10,000
Radios manufactured	3,000

1. During May 2016, Blaster Inc. incurred a purchase price variance of
(*a*) ₹ 45,000 unfavorable (*b*) ₹ 45,000 favorable
(*c*) ₹ 50,000 favorable. (*d*) ₹ 60,000 unfavorable.
(*e*) ₹ 60,000 favorable.

2. During May 2016, Blaster Co. incurred a material efficiency variance of
   (a) ₹ 1,45,000 unfavorably. (b) ₹ 1,45,000 favorable.
   (c) ₹ 4,35,000 unfavorable. (d) ₹ 4,35,000 favorable.
   (e) ₹ 4,50,000 unfavorable.
   (CMA, USA, Adapted with permission)

Ans: D 1. (b) 2. (e) 3. (c)

Ans: E 1. (d) 2. (a)

MULTIPLE CHOICE QUESTIONS

Select the Correct Answer for the following Multiple Choice Questions:

1. The difference between the standard hours for the actual output and actual hours is:
   (a) Labour rate variance (b) Overhead cost variance
   (c) Labour efficiency variance (d) Overhead volume variance
2. Cost variance include all but one of the following:
   (a) Direct material variance (b) Direct labour variance
   (c) Variable overhead variance (d) Sales variance
3. A Standard cost system may be used in:
   (a) Either job order costing or process costing
   (b) Job order costing but not process costing
   (c) Process costing but not job order costing
   (d) Neither process costing nor job costing
4. If actual hours worked exceed the standard hours allowed, what type of variance will occur:
   (a) Favorable labour usage (efficiency) variance
   (b) Favorable labour rate variance
   (c) Unfavorable labour usage (efficiency) variance
   (d) Unfavorable labour rate variance
5. An unfavorable materials price variance occurs because of
   (a) Price increase in raw materials
   (b) Price decrease in raw materials
   (c) Less than anticipated normal wastage in the manufacturing process
   (d) More than anticipated normal wastage in the manufacturing process
6. Which of the following is a purpose of standard costing?
   (a) Determine a break-even production level
   (b) Control costs
   (c) Allocate cost with more accuracy
   (d) Eliminate the need for subjective decisions by management
7. When calculating variances from standard costs, the difference between actual and standard price multiplied by actual quantity gives a:
   (a) Total price and quantity variance (b) Price variance
   (c) Volume variance (d) Mix variance

8. If a company follows a practice of isolating variances at the earliest point in time, what would be the appropriate time to isolate and calculate a material price variance?
   (*a*) When material is issued
   (*b*) When material is purchased
   (*c*) When material is used in production
   (*d*) When purchase order is originated
9. In a standard cost system, the materials price variance is obtained by multiplying the:
   (*a*) Actual price by the difference between actual quantity purchased and standard quantity used
   (*b*) Actual quantity purchased by the difference between actual price and standard price
   (*c*) Standard price by the difference between standard quantity purchased and standard quantity used
   (*d*) Standard quantity purchased by the difference between actual price and standard price
10. How is a labour rate variance computed?
   (*a*) Difference between standard and actual rate multiplied by standard hours
   (*b*) Difference between standard and actual hours multiplied by actual rate
   (*c*) Difference between standard and actual rate multiplied by actual hours
   (*d*) Difference between standard and actual hours multiplied by the difference between standard and actual rate
11. Materials usage variance is normally chargeable to which department?
   (*a*) Production (*b*) Purchasing
   (*c*) Finished goods (*d*) Material storage
12. The absolute minimum cost that would be possible under the best conceivable operating conditions is a description of which type of standard cost?
   (*a*) Currently attainable (expected) (*b*) Ideal
   (*c*) Normal (*d*) Practical
13. The concept of "management by exception" refers to management's:
   (*a*) consideration of only those items which vary materially from plans
   (*b*) consideration of only rare events
   (*c*) consideration of items selected at and on
   (*d*) lack of a predetermined plan
14. Which of the following terms is best identified with a system of standard costs?
   (*a*) Marginal costing (*b*) Contribution approach
   (*c*) Management by exception (*d*) Standardised accounting system
15. What is the normal year end treatment of material variance recognized in a cost accounting system utilizing standards?
   (*a*) Reclassified to deferred charges until all related production is sold
   (*b*) Allocated among cost of goods manufactured and ending work-in-process inventory
   (*c*) Closed to cost of goods sold in the period in which they arose
   (*d*) Capitalised as a cost of ending finished goods inventory
16. Which of the following is one of the purposes of standard cost?
   (*a*) To simplify costing procedures and expedite cost reports

(*b*) To replace budgets and budgeting

(*c*) To use them as a basis for product costing for external reporting purposes

(*d*) To eliminate having to account for under-applied or over-applied factory overhead at the end of the period

17. When using full absorption costing, what costs attendant to an element of production (material, labour or overhead) are used in order to compute variances from standard amounts?

(*a*) Total costs (*b*) Variable costs

(*c*) Fixed costs (*d*) Controllable costs

18. A company employing very tight (high) standards in a standard-cost system should expect that:

(*a*) No incentive bonus will be paid

(*b*) Most variances will be unfavourable

(*c*) Employees will be strongly motivated to attain the standards

(*d*) Costs will be controlled better than if lower standards were used

19. Listed below are four names for different kind of standards associated with a standard cost system. Which of these describes the labour costs that should be incurred under forthcoming efficient operating conditions?

(*a*) Ideal (*b*) Basic

(*c*) Maximum-efficiency (*d*) Currently attainable

20. When performing input-output variance analysis in standard costing, "standard hours allowed" is a means of measuring

(*a*) Standard output at standard hours (*b*) Actual output at standard hours

(*c*) Standard output at actual hours (*d*) Actual output at actual hours

21. Which of the following standard costing variances would be least controllable by a production supervisor?

(*a*) Overhead volume (*b*) Overhead efficiency

(*c*) Labour efficiency (*d*) Material usage

22. What type of direct material variances for price and usage will arise if the actual number of pounds of materials used exceeds standard pounds allowed but actual cost was less than standard cost?

	Usage	***Price***
(*a*)	Unfavourable	Favourable
(*b*)	Favourable	Favourable
(*c*)	Favourable	Unfavourable
(*d*)	Unfavourable	Unfavourable

23. If the total materials variance (actual cost of materials used compared with the standard cost of the standard amount of materials required) for a given operation is favourable, why must this variance be further evaluated as to price and usage?

(*a*) There is no need to further evaluate the total material variance if it is favourable

(*b*) Generally accepted accounting principles require that variances be analyzed in three stages

(*c*) All variances must appear in the annual report to equity owners for proper disclosure

(*d*) To allow management to evaluate the efficiency of the purchasing and production functions

24. If a company uses a predetermined rate for absorbing manufacturing overhead, the volume variance is the:

(*a*) Under-applied or over-applied fixed cost element of overhead
(*b*) Under-applied or over-applied variable cost element of overhead
(*c*) Difference in budgeted costs and actual cost of fixed overhead items
(*d*) Difference in budgeted costs and actual costs of variable overhead items

25. Excess direct labour wages resulting from overtime premium will be disclosed in which type of variance?

(*a*) Yield (*b*) Quantity
(*c*) Labour efficiency (*d*) Labour rate

26. Given below are the notations and their respective meanings:

AH = Actual hours
SHA = Standard hours allowed for actual production
AR = Actual rate
SR = Standard rate

Which formula represents the calculation of the labour-efficiency variance?

(*a*) SR (AH – SHA) (*b*) AR (AH – SHA)
(*c*) AH (AR – SR) (*d*) SHA (AR – SR)

27. A debit balance in the labour-efficiency variance indicates that:

(*a*) Standard hours exceed actual hours
(*b*) Actual hours exceed standard hours
(*c*) Standard rate and standard hours exceed actual rate and actual hours
(*d*) Actual rate and actual hours exceed standard rate and standard hours

28. A labour efficiency debit balance indicates that:

(*a*) The wage rate paid to production workers was below the standard
(*b*) Wage rate paid to production workers was above the standard
(*c*) Less time was spent on production than was called for by the standard
(*d*) More time was spent on production than was called for by the standard

29. What does a credit balance in direct-labour efficiency variance account indicate?

(*a*) The average wage rate paid to direct-labour employees was less than the standard rate
(*b*) The standard hours allowed for the units produced were greater than actual direct-labour hours used.
(*c*) Actual total direct-labour costs incurred were less than standard direct-labour costs allowed for the units produced
(*d*) The number of units produced was less than the number of units budgeted for the period

30. Which of the following is the most probable reason a company would experience an unfavourable labour rate variance and a favourable labour efficiency variance?

(*a*) The mix of workers assigned to the particular job was heavily weighted towards the use of higher paid experienced individuals

(*b*) The mix of workers assigned to the particular job was heavily weighted towards the use of new relatively low paid unskilled workers

(*c*) Because of the production schedule workers from other production areas were assigned to assist this particular process

(*d*) Defective materials caused more labour to be used in order to produce a standard unit

31. A spending variance for variable overhead based on direct labour hours is the difference between actual variable overhead cost and variable overhead cost that should have been incurred for the actual hours worked and results from:

(*a*) Price and quantity differences for overhead costs

(*b*) Price differences for overhead costs

(*c*) Quantity differences for overhead costs

(*d*) Differences caused by variations in production volume

32. Price variances and efficiency variances can be key to the performance measurement within a company. In evaluating the performance within a company, a material efficiency variance can be caused by all of the following except the

(*a*) performance of the workers using the material

(*b*) actions of the purchasing department

(*c*) design of the product

(*d*) skill level of the labour force

(e) sales volume of the product

33. Over-applied factory overhead would result if

(*a*) The plant was operated at less than normal capacity

(*b*) Factory overhead costs incurred were less than costs charged to production

(*c*) Factory overhead costs incurred were unreasonably large in relation to units produced

(*d*) Factory overhead costs incurred were greater than costs charged to production

34. The fixed overhead application rate is a function of a predetermined "normal" activity level. If standard hours allowed for good output equal this "normal" activity level for a given period, the volume variance will be:

(*a*) Zero

(*b*) Favourable

(*c*) Unfavourable

(*d*) Either favourable or unfavourable depending on the budgeted overhead

35. In analyzing factory overhead variances, the volume variance is the difference between the:

(*a*) Amount shown in the flexible budget and the amount shown in the master budget

(*b*) Master budget application rate and the flexible budget application rate multiplied by actual hours worked

(c) Budget allowance based on standard hours allowed for actual production for the period and the amount applied during the period

(d) Actual amount spent for overhead items during the period and the amount applied during the period

36. What standard cost variance represents the difference between actual factory overhead incurred and budgeted factory overhead based on actual hours worked?
(*a*) Volume variance (*b*) Spending variance
(*c*) Efficiency variance (*d*) Quantity variance

37. Standard costing will produce the same financial statement results as actual or conventional costing when standard cost variances are distributed to:
(*a*) Cost of goods sold (*b*) An income or expense account
(*c*) Cost of goods sold and inventory (*d*) A balance sheet account

38. How should a usage variance that is significant in amount be treated at the end of an accounting period?
(*a*) Reported as a deferred charge or credit
(*b*) Allocated among work-in-process inventory, finished goods inventory, and cost of goods sold
(*c*) Charged or credited to cost of goods manufactured
(*d*) Allocated among cost of goods manufactured, finished goods inventory, and cost of goods sold

39. Preferably, under-applied overhead resulting from unanticipated price increase should be written off by:
(*a*) Decreasing cost of goods sold
(*b*) Increasing cost of goods sold
(*c*) Decreasing cost of goods sold, work-in-process inventory, and finished goods inventory
(*d*) Increasing cost of goods sold, work-in-process inventory, and finished goods inventory

40. Which standard would be preferably used in practice?
(*a*) The basic standard (*b*) The normal standard
(*c*) The expected standard (*d*) The ideal standard

41. The direct material cost variance can be divided between:
(*a*) A usage and a price variance (*b*) A mix and a yield variance
(*c*) A usage and a rate variance (*d*) An efficiency and a mix variance

42. Companies in what type of industry may use a standard cost system for cost control?

	Mass Production Industry	**Service Industry**
(*a*)	Yes	Yes
(*b*)	Yes	No
(*c*)	No	No
(*d*)	No	Yes

43. Carr Co. had an unfavourable materials usage variance of ₹ 900. What amounts of this variance should be charged to each department?

	Purchasing	***Warehousing***	***Manufacturing***
(*a*)	Re. 0	Re. 0	₹ 900
(*b*)	Re. 0	₹ 900	Re. 0
(*c*)	₹ 300	₹ 300	₹ 300
(*d*)	₹ 900	Re. 0	Re. 0

44. Which of the following variances would be useful in calling attention to a possible short term problem in control of overhead costs?

	Spending variance	Volume variance
(*a*)	No	No
(*b*)	No	Yes
(*c*)	Yes	No
(*d*)	Yes	Yes

45. Which one of the following is least likely to be involved in establishing standard costs for evaluation purposes?
    (*a*) Budgetary accountants (*b*) Industrial engineers
    (*c*) Top management (*d*) Quality control personnel
    (*e*) Line management
46. Under a standard cost system, the material price variances are usually the responsibility of the
    (*a*) production manager (*b*) cost accounting manager
    (*c*) sales manager (*d*) purchasing manager
    (*e*) industrial engineering manager
47. Under a standard cost system, the material efficiency variances are the responsibility of
    (*a*) production and industrial engineering
    (*b*) purchasing and industrial engineering
    (*c*) purchasing and sales
    (*d*) sales and industrial engineering
    (*e*) production and inventory control
48. Under a standard cost system, labour price variances are usually **not** attributable to
    (*a*) union contracts approved before the budgeting cycle
    (*b*) labour rate predictions
    (*c*) the use of a single average standard rate
    (*d*) the assignment of different skill levels of workers than planned
    (*e*) the payment of hourly rates instead of prescribed piecework rates
49. A favourable material price variance coupled with an unfavourable material usage variance would **most** likely result from
    (*a*) machine efficiency problems
    (*b*) product mix production changes
    (*c*) the purchase and use of higher than standard quality material
    (*d*) labour efficiency problems
    (*e*) the purchase of lower than standard quality material
50. The appropriate method for the disposition of under-applied or over-applied factory overhead
    (*a*) is to cost of goods sold only
    (*b*) is to finished goods inventory only

(*c*) is apportioned to cost of goods sold and finished goods inventory

(*d*) depends on the significance of the amount

(*e*) is to miscellaneous expense

51. A standard costing system is **most** often used by a firm in conjunction with

(*a*) management by objectives (*b*) target (hurdle) rates of return

(*c*) participative management programmes (*d*) flexible budgets

(*e*) job order cost systems

52. The variance that arises solely because the quantity actually sold differs from the quantity budgeted to be sold is

(*a*) static budget variance (*b*) master budget increment

(*c*) sales mix variance (*d*) sales volume variance

(*e*) flexible budget variance

53. Variable overhead is applied on the basis of standard direct labour hours. If for a given period, the direct labour efficiency variance is unfavourable, the variable overhead efficiency variance will be

(*a*) favourable (*b*) unfavourable

(*c*) zero (*d*) the same amount as the labour efficiency variance

(*e*) indeterminable since it is not related to the labour efficiency variance

54. The difference between the actual amounts and the flexible budget amounts for the actual output achieved is the

(*a*) production volume variance (*b*) flexible budget variance

(*c*) sales volume variance (*d*) standard cost variance

(*e*) budget variance

55. The variance in an absorption costing system that measures the departure from the denominator level of activity that was used to set the fixed overhead rate is the

(*a*) spending variance (*b*) efficiency variance

(*c*) sales volume variance (*d*) production volume variance

(*e*) flexible budget variance

56. The efficiency variance for either labour or material can be sub-divided into

(*a*) spending variance and yield variance (*b*) yield variance and price variance

(*c*) volume variance and mix variance (*d*) mix variance and price variance

(*e*) yield variance and mix variance

57. Which one of the following variances is **most** controllable by the production control supervisor?

(*a*) Material price variance (*b*) Material usage variance

(*c*) Variable overhead spending variance (*d*) Fixed overhead budget variance

(*e*) Fixed overhead volume variance

58. For a company that produces more than one product, the sales volume variance can be divided into which two of the following additional variances?
    (*a*) Sales price variance and flexible budget variance
    (*b*) Sales mix variance and sales price variance
    (*c*) Sales efficiency variance and sales price variance
    (*d*) Sales quantity variance and sales mix variance
    (*e*) Sales mix variance and production volume variance
59. The production volume variance is due to
    (*a*) inefficient or efficient use of direct labour hours
    (*b*) efficient or inefficient use of variable overhead
    (*c*) difference from the planned level of the base used for overhead allocation and the actual level achieved
    (*d*) excessive application of direct labour hours over the standard amounts for the output level actually achieved
    (*e*) a significant shift in the mix and yield of direct labour relative to the static budget
60. David Rogers, purchasing manager at Fairway Manufacturing Corporation, was able to acquire a large quantity of raw material from a new supplier at a discounted price. Marion Corner, inventory supervisor, is concerned because the warehouse has become crowded and some things had to be rearranged. Brian Jones, vice-president of production, is concerned about the quality of the discounted material. However, the engineering department had tested the new raw material and indicated that it is of acceptable quality. At the end of the month, Fairway experienced a favourable material usage variance, a favourable labour usage variance, and a favourable material price variance. The usage variances were solely the result of a higher yield from the new raw material. The favourable material price variance would be considered the responsibility of the
    (*a*) purchasing manager (*b*) inventory supervisor
    (*c*) vice-president of production (*d*) engineering manager
    (*e*) production manager
61. The purpose of identifying manufacturing variances and assigning their responsibility to a person/department should be to
    (*a*) use the knowledge about the variances to promote learning and continuous improvement in the manufacturing operations
    (*b*) trace the variances to finished goods so that the inventory can be properly valued at year end
    (*c*) determine the proper cost of the products produced so that selling prices can be adjusted accordingly
    (*d*) pinpoint fault for operating problems in the organisation
    (*e*) assure an accurate accounting of all costs
62. The inventory control supervisor at Wilson Manufacturing Corporation reported that a large quantity of a part purchased for a special order that was never completed remains in stock. The order was not completed because the customer defaulted on the order. The

part is not used in any of Wilson's regular products. After consulting with Wilson's engineers, the vice-president of production approved the substitution of the purchased part for a regular part in a new product. Wilson's engineers indicated that the purchased part could be substituted provided it was modified. The units manufactured using the substituted part required additional direct labour hours resulting in an unfavourble direct labour efficiency variance in the production department. The unfavourable direct labour efficiency variance resulting from the substitution of the purchased part in inventory would **best** be assigned to the

(*a*) sales manager (*b*) inventory supervisor
(*c*) engineering manager (*d*) production manager
(*e*) vice-president of production *(CMA, USA Adapted with permission)*

Answer to Multiple Choice Questions

1. (c)	2. (d)	3. (c)	4. (c)	5. (a)
6. (b)	7. (b)	8. (b)	9. (b)	10. (a)
11. (a)	12. (a)	13. (a)	14. (c)	15. (c)
16. (a)	17. (a)	18. (b)	19. (d)	20. (b)
21. (a)	22. (a)	23. (d)	24. (a)	25. (d)
26. (a)	27. (b)	28. (d)	29. (b)	30. (a)
31. (d)	32. (e)	33. (b)	34. (a)	35. (c)
36. (b)	37. (c)	38. (b)	39. (b)	40. (c)
41. (a)	42. (a)	43. (a)	44. (c)	45. (c)
46. (d)	47. (a)	48. (a)	49. (e)	50. (d)
51. (d)	52. (d)	53. (b)	54. (b)	55. (d)
56. (e)	57. (b)	58. (d)	59. (c)	60. (a)
61. (a)	62. (e)			

PROBLEMS

1. From the data given below, calculate the materials price variance, the materials usage variance and materials mix variance. Consumption per 100 units of product:

Raw material	***Standard***	***Actual***
A	40 units @ ₹ 50 per unit	50 units @ ₹ 50 per unit
B	60 units @ ₹ 40 per unit	60 units @ ₹ 45 per unit

(***Answer:*** Material price variance ₹ 300 (A); Mix variance ₹ 60 (A); Usage variance ₹ 500 (A).

2. The standard material cost for 100 kg of chemical D is made up of:

Chemical A — 30 kg @ ₹ 4 per kg

Chemical B — 40 kg @ ₹ 5 per kg

Chemical C — 80 kg @ ₹ 6 per kg

In a batch, 500 kg of chemical D was produced from a mix of:

Chemical A — 140 kg at a cost of ₹ 588

Chemical B — 220 kg at a cost of ₹ 1,056

Chemical C — 440 kg at a cost of ₹ 2,860

How do the yield, mix and price factors contribute to the variance in the actual cost per 100 kg of chemical D over the standard cost?

(***Answer:*** Material cost variance ₹ 100.80 (A): Material price variance ₹ 40.80 (A); Material mix variance ₹ 6.67 (A); Material sub-usage variance ₹ 53.33 (A); Material usage variance ₹ 60 (A).

3. XY Ltd., manufacturers of product P, use a standard cost system. Standard product and cost specifications for 1,000 kg of product P are as follows:

Ingredients	***Quantity (kg)***	***Price ₹ per kg***	***Cost (₹)***
A	800	2.50	2,000
B	200	4.00	800
C	200	1.00	200
Input	1,200		3,000 = ₹ 2.50 per kg
Output	1,000		3,000 = ₹ 3.00 per kg

Materials records indicate:	Consumption in January
A	1,57,000 kg @ ₹ 2.40
B	38,000 kg @ ₹ 4.20
C	36,000 kg @ ₹ 1.10

Actual finished production for the month of January is 2,00,000 kg. Calculate:

(*i*) Materials price variance; (*ii*) Materials mix variance; (*iii*) Materials yield variance

(***Answer:*** ₹ 4,500 (F); ₹ 3,000 (A); ₹ 22,500 (F).

4. The following standard and actual data relate to a manufacturer:

	Standard			***Actual***		
Material	***Qty. (Kg)***	***Price (₹)***	***Total (₹)***	***Qty. (Kg)***	***Price (₹)***	***Total (₹)***
A	500	6	3,000	400	6	2,400
B	400	3.75	1,500	500	3.60	1,800
C	300	3.00	900	400	2.80	1,120
	1,200			1,300		
Less:			Actual loss	220		
10% loss	120					
	1,080		5,400	1,080		₹ 5,320

Calculate: (*i*) Materials cost variance; (*ii*) Materials price variance; (*iii*) Materials mix variance; (*iv*) Materials yield variance; (*v*) Total material usage variance.

(***Answer:*** (*i*) ₹ 80 (F) (*ii*) ₹ 155 (F) (*iii*) ₹ 375 (F) (*iv*) ₹ 450 (A) (*v*) ₹ 75 (A)).

5. The standard cost of a certain chemical mixture is:

   40% material A at ₹ 200 per tonne

   60% material B at ₹ 300 per tonne

   A standard loss of 10% is expected in production. During a period materials used are:

   90 tonnes material A at the cost of ₹ 180 per tonne

   110 tonnes material B at the cost of ₹ 340 per tonne

   The weight produced is 182 tonnes of good production

   Calculate and present:

   (*i*) Materials price variance; (*ii*) Materials usage variance; (*iii*) Materials mix variance; (*iv*) Materials yield variance.

(***Answer:*** (*i*) ₹ 2,600 (A) (*ii*) ₹ 1,577.77 (F) (*iii*) ₹ 1,000 (F) (*iv*) ₹ 577.77 (F)

Hint:

1. Standard quantity of input of actual production:

   Material A, if 90 tonnes is output, standard material A = 40 tonnes, if 182 tonnes is output,
   standard material is:

   $$\text{Material A} = \frac{40}{90} \times 182 = \frac{728}{9}$$

   $$\text{Material B} = \frac{60 \times 182}{90} = \frac{364}{3} \text{ tonnes}$$

2. Standard loss on actual input:

   200 × 10/100 = 20 tonnes

3. Average standard price:

40 tonnes of Material A @ 200 per tonne	₹ 8,000
60 tonnes of Material B @ 300 per tonne	18,000
100 tonnes	26,000
Less: Normal loss 10	
90 tonnes	

   $$\text{Average standard price per tonne} = ₹\ \frac{26,000}{90} = \frac{2,600}{9}$$

6. The standard cost of a certain chemical mixture is; 40% material A @ ₹ 20 per unit, 60% material B @ ₹ 30 per unit. A standard loss of 10% is expected in production. During a period of one month 90 units of material A @ ₹ 18 per unit and 110 units of material B @ ₹ 34 per unit were used to produce 182 units of good production.

   Calculate the (*a*) material price variance (*b*) material mix variance and (*c*) material yield variance.

(***Answer:*** (*a*) ₹ 260 (A); (*b*) ₹ 100 (F); (*c*) ₹ 57.78 (F)).

7. The standard quantity of material required is 4 kgs. per unit of actual output. The relevant figures are as under:

Material	A	B	C	D
Standard mix %	30%	40%	20%	10%
Price per kg. (₹)	1.25	1.50	3.50	3.00
Actual qty. used (Kg.)	1,180	1,580	830	440
Actual price per kg. (₹)	1.30	1.80	3.40	3.00
Actual output: 1,000 units				

Calculate price variance, mix variance, sub-usage variance and total material cost variance.

Answer:

Material cost variance ₹ 620 (A)

Material price vaiance ₹ 450 (A)

Material usage vaiance ₹ 170 (A)

Material mix variance ₹ 110.75 (A)

Material yield variane ₹ 59.25 (A)

8. The details regarding composition and the weekly wage rates of labour force engaged on a job scheduled to be computed in 30 weeks are as follows:

Category of workers	Standard		Actual	
	No. of Labourers	Weekly wage Rate (₹)	No. of Labourers	Weekly wage rate (₹)
Skilled	75	60	70	70
Semi-skilled	45	40	30	50
Unskilled	60	30	80	20

The work is actually completed in 32 weeks. Calculate the various labour variances.

(***Answer:*** Labour cost variance ₹ 13,000 (A), Rate variance ₹ 6,400 (A), Labour efficiency 6,600 (A), Mix variance ₹ 9,600 (F), Labour sub-efficiency ₹ 16,200 (A)).

9. The following information is available from the cost records of Vatika & Co. for the month of August, 2016:

Material purchased 24,000 kg ₹ 1,05,600

Material consumed 22,800 kg

Actual wages paid for 5,940 hours ₹ 29,700

Unit produced 2160 units.

Standard rates and prices are:

Direct material rate is ₹ 4.00 per unit

Direct labour rate is ₹ 4.00 per hour

Standard input is 10 kg. for one unit

Standard requirement is 2.5 hours per unit.

Calculate all material and labour variances for the month of August, 2016.

Answer:

(*i*) Material cost variance ₹ 13,920 (A)

(*ii*) Master price variance ₹ 9,120 (A)

(*iii*) Master usage variance ₹ 4,800 (A)

(*iv*) Labour cost variance ₹ 8,100 (A)

(*v*) Labour rate variance ₹ 5,940 (A)

(*vi*) Labour efficiency variance ₹ 2,160 (A)

10. The following data are given about a company for a month.

	Standard	Actual
No. of working days	20	22
Man hours per day	8,000	8,400
Output per man hour in unit	1.0	0.9
Overhead cost (₹)	1,60,000	1,68,000

Calculate overhead variances such as:

(*i*) Overhead cost variance, (*ii*) Overhead efficiency variance, (*iii*) Overhead capacity variance, (*iv*) Overhead calendar variance.

(***Answer:*** (*i*) ₹ 1,680 (A) (*ii*) ₹ 18,480 (A) (*iii*) ₹ 24,800 (F) (*iv*) ₹ 16,000 (F).

11. Vinak Ltd. has furnished you the following information for the month of August:

	Budget	***Actual***
Output (Units)	30,000	32,500
Hours	30,000	33,000
Fixed overhead	₹ 45,000	50,000
Variable overhead	₹ 60,000	68,000
Working days	25	26

Calculate the variances. (M. Com., Delhi, 2014)

(***Answer:*** Total overhead cost variance ₹ 4,250 (A), Variable overhead cost variance ₹ 3,000 (A), Fixed overhead cost variance ₹ 1,250 (A), Expenditure variance ₹ 5,000 (A), Efficiency variance ₹ 750 (A), Capacity variance ₹ 4,500 (F), Calendar variance ₹ 1,800 (F).

12. From the following data for a factory for the month of January, compute overhead variances under four-way analysis:

	Standard	***Actual***
Number of units produced	15,000	8,000
Capacity (hours)	30,000	17,000
Variable overheads	30,000	15,500
Fixed overheads	45,000	46,300

(*M.Com., Delhi*)

Answer: (*i*) Spending variance ₹ 200 (F), (*ii*) Variable efficiency ₹ 13,000 (F), (*iii*) Fixed efficiency ₹ 19,500 (A), (*iv*) Idle capacity ₹ 19,500 (A), (*v*) Net variance ₹ 13,200 (F).

13. Alliance Franchise Ltd. operates a small business with wide seasonal fluctuation. Budgeted overhead is ₹ 12,000 per month plus ₹ 2 per direct labour hour at the normal volume of 1,000 units. The standard labour cost per unit of production is 3 hours at ₹ 5 per hour. During March 2016, 800 units were produced which required 2,500 direct labour hours at a total labour cost of ₹ 12,000. Actual overhead amounted to ₹ 17,200, of which ₹ 5,500 were variable.

Compute the following variances:

(*i*) Labour efficiency variance, (*ii*) Variable overhead efficiency variance, (*iii*) Variable overhead spending variance, (*iv*) Fixed overhead spending variance, (*v*) Fixed overhead volume variance. (*M. Com., Delhi*)

Answer: (*i*) ₹ 500 (A) (*ii*) ₹ 200 (A) (*iii*) ₹ 500 (A) (*iv*) ₹, 1,700 (A) (*v*) ₹ 2,400 (A).

14. The Tejas Manufacturing Company employs a standard cost accounting system. The standard factory overhead rate was computed based on normal capacity.

	₹
Budgeted variable expenses	12,000
Budgeted fixed expenses	8,000
Total	20,000

Factory overhead rate: ₹ 20,000/20,000 hours = Re. 1.00 per direct labour hour.
Two labour hours are required to manufacture each finished unit. During the month 8,750 units were completed. There were no beginning or ending work-in-process inventories. 18,400 labour hours were worked and actual factory overhead was ₹ 18,250.

Required:

Prepare an analysis of factory overhead using two, three and four-variance method.

(*M.Com., Delhi*)

15. From the following information (supposing production of 1,56,000 units) prepare an analysis of variances:

Standard direct-labour hours allowed per unit produced	0.25
Standard direct-labour rate per hour	₹ 6.00
Actual direct-labour hours of input	42,000
Actual direct-labour rate per hour	₹ 6.10
Variable manufacturing overhead actually incurred	₹ 34,000
Fixed manufacturing overhead actual incurred	₹ 1,55,000

(*M.Com., Delhi*)

16. The cost department informed the shop foreman that 1,000 hours were allowed for the completion of job No. 436. Overhead is applied on the basis of direct labour hours with the rate based on a total overhead of ₹ 50,000 for 1,00,000 direct labour hours; 60% of the overhead is considered variable. When the job was completed, job time tickets indicated a total of 1,500 hours worked. The cost department charged ₹ 900 actual expenses to the job. You are required to make an analysis of the overheads applicable to job 436 using (*a*) three-variance method and (*b*) two-variance method. (*M. Com., Delhi*)

Answer: Total overhead variance ₹ 400 (A) (*i*) spending variance ₹ 150 (A), efficiency variance ₹ 250 (A), (*ii*) controllable variance ₹ 400 (A), capacity variance cannot be calculated in this question as it is calculated for the total firm, whereas herein information is given for a particular cost centre.

17. B Ltd. started trading on 1st November 2016, manufacturing and selling one product. The standard cost per unit was:

    Direct material: Standard price ₹ 10 per kilogram.
    Standard quantity : 20 kilogram per unit
    Direct labour: Standard rate of pay ₹ 5.50 per hour.
    Standard time allowance: 12 hours per unit

Production overhead costs, all classified as fixed, were budgeted at ₹ 9,00,000 per annum. The standard time for producing one unit is 12 machine hours and normal capacity is 60,000 machine hours per annum. Production overhead is absorbed on machine hours.

For the year ended 31st October 2017, the costs incurred and other relevant information are given below:

Direct material used	1,00,000 kilograms at a cost of ` 10,50,000
Direct wages paid	₹ 3,10,000 for 62,000 hours
Production overhead	₹ 9,26,000
Machine capacity used	60,000 hours
Actual output	4,800 units

Assuming no stocks of work-in-progress or finished goods at year end.

You are required to :

(a) Show the standard product cost for one unit.

(b) Calculate variances for material (usage and price), labour (rate and efficiency) and overhead. *(M.Com., Delhi, 2014)*

Answer:

(a) ₹ 446

(b)	Material usage variance	₹ 40,000 (A)
	Material price variance	₹ 50,000 (A)
	Labour rate variance	₹ 31,000 (F)
	Labour efficiency varince	₹ 24,200 (A)
	Fixed overhead volume variance	₹ 36,000 (A)
	Overhead expenditure variance	₹ 26,000 (A)

18. Walenhorst Company's machining department prepared its 2016 budget based on the following data:

Maximum capacity	50,000 units
Machine-hours per unit	2
Variable factory overhead	₹ 3.00 per hour
Fixed factory overhead	₹ 3,60,000

At the time when the department prepared its budget, it expected to oprate at 80 percent of the maximum capacity. The department uses machine-hours to apply factory overhead. In 2016, the firm spent 85,000 machine-hours and ₹ 625,000 in manufacturing overhead to manufacture 42,000 units.

Required:

Determine for the year

1. The factory overhead application rate.
2. The total flexible budget factory overhead for operation in 2016.
3. The production volume variance.
4. The factory overhead spending variance.
5. The factory overhead efficiency variance.
6. The variable and fixed factory overhead spending variances if the actual fixed factory overhead for the year was ₹ 375,000.

Answer:

1. ₹ 7.50
2. ₹ 6,12,000
3. ₹ 18000 (F)
4. ₹ 10,000 (A)
5. ₹ 3000 (A)
6. The firm needs to know the amount of variable and fixed factory overhead incurred in order to do a four variance analysis.

19. Ice Box Gourmet, produces containers of frozen food. During April. The company produced 725 cases of food and incurred the following actual costs.

Variable overhead	₹ 5,500
Fixed overhead	13,000
Actual labor cost (4,000 direct-labor hours)	75,600
Actual material cost (15,000 pounds purchased and used)	33,000

Standard cost and annual budget information are as follows:

Standard Costs per Case

Direct labor (5 hours at ₹ 18)	₹ 90.00
Direct material (20 pounds at ₹ 2)	40.00
Variable overhead (5 hours at ₹ 1.50)	7.50
Fixed overhead (5 hours at ₹ 3)	15.00
Total	₹ 152.50

Annual Budget Information

Variable overhead	₹ 75,000
Fixed overhead	₹ 150,00
Planned activity for year	50,000 direct-labor hours

Required:

Prepared a complete analysis of cost variances as is possible from the available data.

20. The following information is available in respect of Y Ltd. for a week:

(*a*) 400 kg of raw material were actually used in producing product 'EXE'. The purchase cost thereof being ₹ 24,800. The standard price per kg of raw material is ₹ 60. The expected output is 12 units of product 'EXE' from each kg of raw material. Raw material price variance and usage variance as computed by cost accountant are ₹ 800 (adverse) and ₹ 600 (adverse) respectively.

(*b*) The week is of 40 hours. The standard time to produce one unit of 'EXE' is 30 minutes. The standard wage rate is ₹ 5 per labour hour. The company employs 60 workers who have been paid hourly wage rate as under:

Number of workers	6	8	46
Hourly wage rate (₹)	4.80	5.20	5.00

(*c*) Budgeted overheads for a four-weekly period is ₹ 81,600. The actual fixed overheads spent during the said week are ₹ 19,800.

(*d*) Entire output of 'EXE' has been sold at its standard selling price of ₹ 15 per unit.

You are required to:

(*i*) Compute the variances relating to labour and overheads.

(*ii*) Prepare a statement showing total standard costs, standard profit and actual profit for the week. (*CA Final*)

Answer:

I. Labour variances, cost variance ₹ 316 (A), Rate variance ₹ 16 (A), Efficiency ₹ 300 (A)

II. Fixed overhead variances, cost variance ₹ 90 (F), Volume variance ₹ 510 (A), Expenditure ₹ 600 (F), Actual profit ₹ 13,584

21. In a manufacturing co. the standard units of production of the year were fixed at 1,20,000 units and overhead expenditures were estimated to be:

Fixed	₹ 12,000	Variable	₹ 6,000
Semi-Variable	₹ 1,800		

Actual production during April of the year was 8,000 units. Each month has 20 working days.

During the month in question there was one statutory holiday. The actual overheads amounted to:

Fixed	₹ 1,190	Variable	₹ 480
Semi-Variable	₹ 192		

Semi-variable charges are considered to include 60 per cent expenses of fixed nature and 40 per cent of variable character.

Find out the

(*a*) Overhead Cost Variance

(*b*) Fixed Overhead Cost Variance

(*c*) Variable Overhead Cost Variance

(*d*) Fixed Overhead Volume Variance

(*e*) Fixed Overhead Expenditure Variance

(*f*) Calendar Variance.

Answer:

(*a*) ₹ 542 (A)

(*b*) ₹ 433.20 (A)

(*c*) ₹ 108.80 (A)

(*d*) ₹ 218 (A)

(*e*) ₹ 215.20 (A)

(*f*) ₹ 54.50 (A)

22. The details regarding a product manufactured by ZED and Co. for the last one week are as follows:

Standard Cost (for one unit)		₹
Direct Materials	(10 unit @ ₹ 1.50)	15
Direct Wages	(5 hours @ ₹ 8.00)	40
Production Overheads	(5 hours @ ₹ 10.00)	50
		105

Actual (for whole activity)	₹
Direct Materials	6,435
Direct Wages	10,324
Direct Materials	
Price	585 (A)
Usage	375 (F)
Direct Wages	
Rate	636 (F)
Usage	360 (A)
Production Overheads:	
Expenditure	400 (F)
Volume	750 (F)

You are required to calculate:

(*i*) Actual output units

(*ii*) Actual price of material per unit

(*iii*) Actual wage rate per labour hour

(*iv*) Amount of production overhead incurred

(*v*) Production overhead efficiency variance

Answer:

(*i*) 3900 units

(*ii*) ₹ 1.65 per unit

(*iii*) ₹ 7.7 per hour

(*iv*) ₹ 19,600

(*v*) ₹ 450 (A)

23. The Standard Cost Card of producing one unit of Item 'Q' is as under:

			₹
Direct material—	A—	12 Kg. @ ₹ 10/-	120
	B—	5 Kg. @ ₹ 6/-	30
Direct wages—		5 Hrs. @ ₹ 3/-	15
Fixed production overheads			35
Total standard cost			200

Fixed Production overhead is absorbed on expected annual output of 13,200 units. Actual result for the month of September, 2016 are as under:

Actual production: 1,000 units

		₹
Direct material A	11,000 Kg.	1,21,000
B	5,200 Kg.	28,600
Direct wages	5,500 Hrs.	17,500
Fixed Overheads		39,000

You are required to calculate all variances.

Answer:

I. Material variances: Cost ₹ 400 (F), Price ₹ 8,400 (A), Usage ₹ 8800 (F), Mix ₹ 1740 (F), Yield ₹ 7060 (F)

II. Labour variances: Cost ₹ 2500 (A), Rate ₹ 1000 (A), Efficiency ₹ 1500 (A)

III. Fixed overhead variances: Cost ₹ 4000 (A), Expenditure ₹ 500 (A), Volume ₹ 3500 (A), Capacity NIL, Efficiency ₹ 3500 (A).

24. The budgeted sales for one month and the actual results achieved are as under:

Product	***Budget***			***Actual***		
	Quantity Nos.	***Rate ₹***	***Amount ₹***	***Quantity Nos.***	***Rate ₹***	***Amount ₹***
A	1,000	100	1,00,000	1,200	125	1,50,000
B	700	200	1,40,000	800	150	1,20,000
C	500	300	1,50,000	600	300	1,80,000
D	300	500	1,50,000	400	600	2,40,000
	2,500		5,40,000	3,000		6,90,000

Calculate in respect of each product, the sales variances.

(***Answer:*** Sales value ₹ 1,50,000 (F): Sales price ₹ 30,000 (F); Sales volume ₹ 1,20,000 (F)

25. PH Ltd. furnishes the following information relating to budgeted sales and actual sales for April 2016.

	Product	***Sales Quantity (units)***	***Selling price per unit (₹)***
Budgeted Sales	A	1,200	15
	B	800	20
	C	2,000	40
Actual sales	A	880	18
	B	880	20
	C	2,640	38

Calculate the following variances:

(*i*) Sales quantity variance, (*ii*) Sales mix variance, (*iii*) Total sales variance.

(***Answer:*** ₹ 22,400 (F); ₹ 11,000 (F); ₹ 2,640 (A), ₹ 19,760 (F).

26. The Sales Manager of a company engaged in the manufacture and sale of three products K, L and M gives you the following information for the month of October 2016:

Budgeted Sales:

Product	Units Sold	Selling Price per unit	Standard Contribution Margin per unit
K	2,000	₹ 12	₹ 6
L	2,000	₹ 8	₹ 4
M	2,000	₹ 5	₹ 1

Actual Sales:

K	1,500 units for ₹ 15,000
L	2,500 units for ₹ 17,500
M	3,500 units for ₹ 21,000

You are required to calculate Sales Variances

Answer:

I. Based on Sales Margin

Sales margin ₹ 1500 (A), Price ₹ 2000 (A), Volume ₹ 500 (F), Mix ₹ 5000 (A), Quantity ₹ 5500 (F)

II. Based on Sales Value

Sales value variance ₹ 3500 (F), Price ₹ 2000 (A), Volume ₹ 5500 (F), Mix ₹ 7000 (A), Quantity ₹ 12,500 (F)

27. The following information relates to a manufacturing concern:

Standard	₹
Material A 24,000 kgs @ ₹ 3 per kg	72,000
Material B 12,000 kgs @ ₹ 4 per kg	48,000
Wages 60,000 hours @ ₹ 4 per hour	2,40,000
Variable Overheads 60,000 hours @ ₹ 1 per hour	60,000
Fixed Overheads 60,000 hours @ ₹ 2 per hour	1,20,000
Total Cost	5,40,000
Budgeted Profit	60,000
Budgeted Sales	6,00,000
Budgeted Production (units)	12,000
Actual	
Sales (9,000 units)	4,57,500
Material A Consumed 22,275 kgs.	62,370
Material B Consumed 10,890 kgs.	44,649
Wages Paid (48,000 hours)	1,91,250
Fixed Overhead	1,20,900
Variable Overhead	45,000
Labour Hours Worked	47,700
Closing (Work in Progress)	900 units
Degree of Completion	
Material A and B	100%
Wage and Overheads	50%

You are required to calculate all variances.

Answer:

I. Material variance: Cost ₹ 8019 (A), Price ₹ 3,366 (F), Usage ₹ 11,385 (A), Mix ₹ 165 (F), Yield ₹ 11,550 (A).

II. Labour variance: Cost ₹ 2250 (A), Rate ₹ 750 (F), Efficiency ₹ 1,800 (A), Idle time ₹ 1,200 (A)

III. Variable overhead variances: Cost ₹ 2250 (F), Expendiure ₹ 2700 (F), Efficiency ₹ 450 (A).

IV. Fixed overhead variances: Cost ₹ 26,400 (A), Expenditure ₹ 900 (A), Volume ₹ 22,500 (A), Efficiency ₹ 900 (A), Capacity ₹ 24,600 (A).

V. Sales varainces: Value ₹ 1,42,500 (A), Price ₹ 7,500 (F), Volume ₹ 1,50,000 (A), Sales margin price ₹ 7500 (F), Sales volume ₹ 15,000 (A), Margin ₹ 7500 (A)

28. A company operating on a standard costing system, for a given four-week period budgeted for sales of 10,000 units at ₹ 50 per unit, actual sales were 9,000 units at ₹ 51.25 per unit. Costs relating to that period were as follows:

	Standard (₹)	***Actual*** (₹)
Materials	2,50,000	2,57,000
Wages	75,000	70,870
Fixed overhead	20,000	18,810
Variable overhead	10,000	9,250
Semi-variable overhead	2,700	2,430
Standard hours	50,000	
Actual hours	40,500	

(*i*) The standard material content of each unit is estimated at 25 kg at ₹ 1 per kg. Actual figures were 26 kg at ₹ 1.10 per kg.

(*ii*) The standard wages per unit are 5 hours at ₹ 1.50 per hour, actual wages were 4.5 hours at ₹ 1.75.

(*iii*) Semi-variable overhead consists of five-ninths fixed expenses and four-ninths variable.

(*iv*) There were no opening stocks and the whole production for the period was sold.

(*v*) The four week period was a normal period.

You are required:

(*a*) to compute the variances in sales, materials, labour and overheads due to all possible causes; and

(*b*) with the help of such a computation, draw a statement reconciling the actual profit for the period with the standard profit.

Answer:

Standard profit ₹ 1,42,300

Actual profit ₹ 1,02,485

CASES

1. Himalayan Drugs Ltd., a manufacturer of health-care equipment, has been in business for 15 years. Last year, in an effort to better control the costs of their products, the management accountant implemented a standard cost system. Reports are issued monthly for tracking performance, and any negative variances are further investigated.

The production manager complained that the standards are unrealistic, stifle motivation by concentrating only on negative variances, and are out of date too quickly. He noted that his recent switch to a new equipment for the wheelchairs has resulted in higher material costs but decreased labour times. The net result was no increase in the total cost of producing the wheelchair. The monthly reports continue to show a negative material variance and a positive labour variance, despite the fact that there are indications that the workers are slowing down.

(*a*) Describe several ways that a standard cost system strengthens management in cost control.

(*b*) Describe at least two reasons why a standard cost system may negatively impact the motivation of production employees. (*CMA, USA, Adapted with permission*)

2. Indian Motors Ltd. has been experiencing declining profit margins and has been looking for ways to increase operating income. It cannot raise selling prices for fear of losing business to its competitors. It must either cut costs or improve productivity. The Co. uses a standard cost system to evaluate the performance of the assembly department. All negative variances at the end of the month are investigated. The assembly department rarely completes the operations in less time than the standard allows (which would result in a positive variance). Most months, the variance is zero or slightly negative. Reasoning that the application of lower standard costs to the products manufactured will result in improved profit margins, the production manager had recommended that all standard times for assembly operations be drastically reduced. The production manager has informed the assembly personnel that he expects them to meet these new standards.

   Will the lowering of the standard costs (by reducing the time of the assembly operations) result in improved profit margins and increased productivity? (*CMA, USA, Adapted with permission*)

3. Crunchy Chips India (CCI) Ltd., is a specially frozen-food processor located in Punjab in India. Since its founding in 2009, CCI has enjoyed a loyal clientele that is willing to pay premium prices for the high-quality frozen food it prepares from specialised recipes. In the last two years, the company has experienced rapid sales growth in its operating region and had many enquiries about supplying its products on a national basis. To meet this growth, CCI expanded its processing capabilities which resulted in increased production and distribution costs. Furthermore, CCI has been encountering pricing pressures from competitors outside its normal marketing region.

   Because CCI desires to continue its expansion, Raghvendra, Chief Executive Officer, has engaged a consulting firm to assist CCI in determining its best course of action. The consulting firm recommended instituting a standard costing system that would also facilitate a flexible budgeting system to better accommodate the changes in demand that can be expected when serving an expanding market area. Raghvendra met with his management team and explained the consulting firm's recommendations. Raghvendra then assigned the task of establishing standard costs to his management team. After discussing the situation with the respective staffs, the management team met to review the matter.

   Rakesh, purchasing manager, advised that meeting expanded production would necessitate obtaining basic food supplies from other than CCI's traditional sources. This would entail increased raw material and other costs and might result in lower quality supplies. Consequently, these increased costs would need to be made up by the processing department if current costs are to be maintained or reduced.

   Ramesh, processing manager, countered that the need to accelerate processing cycles to increase production, coupled with the possibility of receiving lower grade supplies, could be expected to result in a slip in quality and a greater product rejection rate. Under these circumstances, per unit labour utilisation could not be maintained or reduced and forecasting future unit labour content would become very difficult.

Rajiv, production engineer, advised that if equipment is not properly maintained and thoroughly cleaned at prescribed daily intervals, the quality and unique taste of the frozen-food products would probably be affected.

Johnson, Vice-President of Sales, stated that if quality could not be maintained, CCI could not expect to increase sales to the levels projected.

When Raghvendra was apprised of the problems encountered by his management team, he advised them that if agreement could not be reached on the appropriate standards, he would arrange to have them set by the consulting firm and everyone would have to live with the results.

Required:

(I) List the major advantages of using a standard costing system.

(II) Identify those who should participate in setting standards, and describe the benefits of their participation in the standard setting process.

(III) What could be the consequences if Raghvendra, Chief Executive Officer, has the standards set by an outside consulting firm? (*M. Com., Delhi 2001*)

4. Vikas Mohan is production manager of the Equipment Division of BHEL Ltd. Equipment Division has limited contact with outside customers and no sales staff. Most of its customers are other divisions of BHEL. All sales and purchases with outside customers are handled by other corporate divisions. Therefore, Equipment Division is treated as a cost centre for reporting and evaluation purposes, rather than as a revenue or profit centre.

Vikas perceives accounting as an historical number generating process that provides little useful information for conducting his job. Consequently, the entire accounting process is regarded as a negative motivational device that does not reflect how hard or how effectively he works as a production manager. Vikas tried to discuss these perceptions and concerns with Manish, the controller for the Equipment Division. Vikas told Manish, "I think the cost report is misleading. I know I've had better production over a number of operating periods, but the cost report still says I have excessive costs. Look, I'm not an accountant; I'm a production manager. I know how to get a good quality product out. Over a number of years, I've even cut the raw materials used to do it. But the cost report doesn't show any of this. Basically, it's always negative, no matter what I do. There's no way you can win with accounting or the people at corporate headquarters who use those reports."

Manish gave Vikas little consolation. "The accounting system and the cost reports generated by headquarters," Manish stated, "are just part of the corporate game and almost impossible for an individual to change. Although, these accounting reports are pretty much the basis for evaluating the efficiency of your division and the means corporate management uses to determine whether you have done the job they want, you shouldn't worry too much. You haven't been fired yet! Besides, these cost reports have been used by BHEL for the last twenty-five years."

Vikas perceived (from talking to the production manager of the Zinc Division) that most of what Manish said was probably true. However, some minor cost reporting changes for Zinc had been agreed to by corporate headquarters. Vikas also knew from the trade grapevine that the turnover of production managers was considered high at BHEL, even though relatively few were fired. Most seemed to end up quitting, usually in disgust, because of beliefs that they were not being evaluated fairly. Typical comments of production managers who have left BHEL are:

- "Corporate headquarters doesn't really listen to us. All they consider are those misleading cost reports. They don't want them changed, and they don't want any supplemental information."
- "The accountants may be quick with numbers, but they don't know anything about production. As it was, I either had to ignore the cost reports entirely or pretend they are important even though they didn't tell how good a job I had done. No matter what they say about not firing people, negative reports mean negative evaluations. I'm better off working for another company."

A recent copy of the cost report prepared by corporate headquarters for the Equipment Division is shown below. Vikas does not like this report because he believes it fails to properly reflect the division's operations, thereby resulting in an unfair evaluation of performance.

Equipment Division
Cost Report
for the Month of April 2016

	Original Budget (₹)	Actual Cost (₹)	Excess Cost (₹)
Aluminum.............	4,00,000	4,37,000	37,000
Labour..................	5,60,000	5,40,000	
Overhead.............	1,00,000	1,34,000	34,000
Total......................	10,60,000	11,11,000	71,000

Required:

(*a*) Comment on Vikas's perceptions of Manish (the controller); corporate headquarters; the cost report; and himself as a production manager. Discuss how his perceptions affect his behaviour and probable performance as a production manager and employee of BHEL.

(*b*) Identify and explain three changes that could be made in the cost information presented to the production managers that would make the information more meaningful and less threatening to them. (*M.Com., Delhi, 2003*)

5. Krishnamurthy is the manufacturing supervisor of the Atlas Manufacturing Company, which produces a variety of plastic products. Some of these products are standard items that are listed in the company's catalogue, while others are made to customer specification. Each month, Krishnamurthy receives a performance report displaying the budget for the month, the actual activity for the period, and the variance between budget and actual. Part of Krishnamurthy's annual performance evaluation is based on his department's performance against budget. Atlas's purchasing manager, Ramaswamy, also receives monthly performance reports and is evaluated in part on the basis of these reports.

   Last month's reports have just been distributed on the 21st of this month, when Krishnamurthy met Ramaswamy in the hallway outside their offices. Scowling, Krishnamurthy began the conversation, "I see we have another set of monthly performance reports hand-delivered by that not very nice junior employee in the budget office. He seemed pleased to tell me that I was in trouble with my performance again."

Ramaswamy: "I got the same treatment. All I ever hear about are the things I haven't done right. Now, I'll have to spend a lot of time reviewing the report and preparing explanations. The worst part is that the information is almost a month old, and we spend all this time on history."

Krishnamurthy: "My biggest gripe is that our production activity varies a lot from month to month, but we're given an annual budget that's written in stone. Last month, we were shut down for three days when a strike delayed delivery of the basic ingredient used in our plastic formulation, and we had already exhausted our inventory. You know about that, of course, since we asked you to call all over the country to find an alternate source of supply. When we got what we needed on a rush basis, we had to pay more than we normally do."

Ramaswamy : "I expect problems like that to prop up from time to time — that's part of my job — but now we'll both have to take a careful look at the report to see where charges are reflected for that rush order. Every month, I spend more time making sure I should be charged for each item reported than I do making plans for my department's daily work. It's really frustrating to see charges for things I have no control over."

Krishnamurthy: "The way we get information doesn't help either. I don't get copies of the reports you get, yet a lot of what I do is affected by your department and by most of the other departments we have. Why do the budget and accounting people assume that I should only be told about my operations even though the president regularly gives us pep talks about how we all need to work together as a team."

Ramaswamy: "I seem to get more reports than I need, and I am never asked to comment until top management calls me on the carpet about my department's shortcomings. Do you ever hear comments when your department shines?"

Krishnamurthy: "I guess they don't have time to review the good news. One of my problems is that all the reports are in Rupees. I work with people, machines, and materials. I need information to help me this month solve this month's problems — not another report of the rupees expended last month or the month before."

Required:

(*a*) Based upon the conversation between Krishnamurthy and Ramaswamy, describe the likely motivation and behavior of these two employees resulting from Atlas Manufacturing Company's variance reporting system.

(*b*) Both employees and companies should benefit from properly implemented variance reporting systems.

(i) Describe the benefits that can be realized from using a variance reporting system.

(ii) Based on the situation presented above, recommend ways for Atlas Manufacturing Company to improve its variance reporting system so as to increase employee motivation.

(CMA, USA adapted with permission)

6. As part of its cost control program, Tata Motors Company uses a standard costing system for all manufactured items. The standard cost for each item is established at the beginning of the fiscal year, and the standards are not revised until the beginning of the next fiscal

year. Changes in costs, caused during the year by changes in material or labour inputs or by changes in the manufacturing process, are recognized as they occur by the inclusion of planned variances in Tata's monthly operating budgets.

Following is the labour standard that was established for one of Tata's products effective April 1, 2016, the beginning of the fiscal year:

Assembler A labour (5 hrs. @ ₹ 100)	₹ 500
Assembler B labour (3 hrs. @ ₹ 110)	330
Machinist labour (2 hrs. @ ₹ 150)	300
Standard cost per 100 units	₹ 1,130

The standard was based on the labour being performed by a team consisting of five persons with assembler A skills, three persons with assembler B skills, and two persons with machinist skills; this team represents the most efficient use of the company's skilled employees. The standard also assumed that the quality of materials that had been used in prior years would be available for the coming year.

For the first seven months of the fiscal year, actual manufacturing costs at Tata have been within the standards established. However, the company has received a significant increase in orders, and there is an insufficient number of skilled workers to meet the increased production. Therefore, beginning in April, the production teams will consit of eight persons with assembler A skills, one person with assember B skills, and one person with machinist skills. The reorganized teams will work more slowly than the normal teams; as a result, only 80 units will be produced in the same time period in which 100 units would normally be produced. Faulty work has never been a cause for units to be rejected in the final inspection process, and it is not expected to be a cause for rejection with the reoganized teams.

Furthermore, Tata has been notified by its material supplier that lower-quality materials will be supplied beginning April 1. Normally, one unit of materials is required for each good unit produced, and no units are lost due to defective material. Tata estimates that 10 per cent of the units manufactured after April 1 will be rejected in the final inspection process due to defective material.

Required:

I. Determine the number of units of lower-quality matarial that Tata Company must enter into production in order to produce 54,000 good finished units.

II. How many hours of each class of labour must be used to manufacture 54,000 good finished units?

III. Determine the amount that should be included in Tata's April operating budget for the planned labour variance caused by the reorganization of the labour teams and the lower-quality material. *(M. Com., Delhi, 2012)*

Answer:

I. 60,000 Units

II. Assembler A = 6,000 hours

Assembler B = 750 hours

Assembler C = 750 hours

III. ₹ 1,84,800

7. Sound Sensation Co. is a small manufacturer of electronic musical instruments. The plant manager received the following variable factory overhead report for the period:

	Actual	Budgeted Variable Factory Overhead at Actual Production	Controllable Variance
Supplies	₹ 28,000	₹ 26,520	₹ 1,480 U
Power and light	35,000	33,990	1,010 U
Indirect factory wages	26,112	20,400	5,712 U
Total	₹ 89,112	₹ 80,910	₹ 8,202U

Actual units produced: 10,200 (85% of practical capacity)

The plant manager is not pleased with the ₹ 8,202 unfavorable variable factory overhead controllable variance and has come to discuss the matter with the controller. The following discussion occurred:

Plant Manager: I just received this factory report for the latest month of operation. I'm not very pleased with these figures. Before these numbers go to headquarters, you and I will need to reach an understanding.

Controller: Go ahead, what's the problem?

Plant Manager: What's the problem? Well, everything. Look at the variance. It's too large. If I understand the accounting approach being used here, you are assuming that my costs are variable to the units produced. Thus, as the production volume declines, so should these costs. Well, I don't believe that these costs are variable at all. I think they are fixed costs. As a result , when we operate below capacity, the costs really don't go down at all. I'm being penalized for costs I have no control over at all. I need this report to be redone to reflect this fact. If anything, the difference between actual and budget is essentially a volume variance. Listen, I know that you're a team player. You really need to reconsider your assumptions on this one.

Required:

If you were in the controller's position, how would you respond to the plant manager?

8. Amcor Inc, is a large manufacturing company, which runs its own electrical power plant form the excess steam produced in its manufacturing process. Power is provided to two production departments. Department A and Department B. The capacity of the power plant was originally determined by the expected peak demands of the two production departments. The expected average usage and peak demands are, respectively, 60 per cent and 6,60,00,000 kilowatt hours (kwh) for Department A, and 40 per cent and 4,40,00,000 kwh for Department B.

The budgeted monthly costs of producing power, based on normal usage of 10,00,00,000 kwh, are ₹ 3,00,00,000 in fixed costs and ₹ 75,00,000 in variable costs. For the month of November, the actual kwh used was 6,00,00,000 by Department A and 2,00,00,000 by Department B. Actual fixed costs were ₹ 3,00,00,000 and actual variable costs were ₹ 75,00,000.

Sam McNeil, cost accountant, prepared the monthly actual report shown below. McNeil fully allocated all power plant costs on the basis of actual kwh used by each production department. This report will be submitted to the divisional controller and the two production department operating mangers.

Amcoe Inc.
Monthly Allocation Report
November 2016

Power plant usage	8,00,00,000 kwh
Actual costs:	
Fixed	₹ 3,00,00,000
Variable	75,00,000
Total	₹ 3,75,00,000
Rate per kwh (₹ 3,75,00,000 ÷ 80,000,000 kwh)	₹ 0.46875
Allocations:	
To Department A(6,00,00,000 kwh × ₹ 0. 46875)	₹ 2,81,25,000
To Department B(2,00,00,000 kwh × ₹ 0. 46875)	₹ 93,75,000
Total allocated	₹ 3,75,00,000

Required:

A. 1. Discuss at least two problems with the monthly allocation report prepared by Sam MC Neil for November 2016 at Amcor Inc.

2. Prepare a revised monthly allocation report for November 2016 using a flexiable budget approach.

B. 1. For November 2016 analyze the efficiency of Amcor Inc's power plant by using variance analysis.

2. Discuss the meaning of this variance and identify who should be held responsible for it.

3. Should Amcor Inc, change the cost allocation method used, and if so, how should the cost allocation method be changed?

C. Discuss the behavioral implications of Sam McNeil's monthly allocation report for November 2016 on the production managers of Department A and Department B at Amcor Inc.

(CMA, USA, Adapted with permission).

Answer:

A. 1. At least two problems with Amcor Inc.'s November 2016 monthly allocation report prepared by Sam McNeil include the following:

- The cost charged to the production departments is dependent on factors which the operating managers can-not directly control. The price and efficiency of the power plant is controlled by the Service Department.
- A single application rate is used when separate rates for fixed and variable costs should have been used. Fixed costs were assigned as if they were variable costs.

2. Total allocation, Fixed ₹ 3,00,00,000

Variable ₹ 60,00,000

B. 1. Efficiency Variance ₹ 15,00,000 (A)

2. This unfavorable variance means that the efficiency of the power plant was below expectations and the power plant manger should be held responsible; the production department managers have no control over power plant operations.

3. Amcor Inc, should change its cost allocation method to a fixed-fee based on planned capacity, with a standard rate for variable costs based on an efficient level of operations.

That is, a dual rate method, as described in Requirement A.2., should be used. This method insulates users against the inefficiencies of the Service Department's management and charges users only for actual services used, regardless of usage levels by other departments.

C. The behavioral implications of Sam MC Neil's monthly allocation report for November 2016 on the production managers of Departments A and B at Amcor Inc, will be negative. The production manager of Department A will feel frustrated and demotivated. Because Department B's volume was down and the power plant was inefficient, Department A bears a higher percentage of the power plant costs, something that the manager of Department. A has no control over. Department B's allocation includes the power plant inefficiencies.

9. Smylan Company employs a standard costing system using absorption costing. The standards for manufacturing overhead are established at the beginning of each year by estimating the total variable and fixed manufacturing overhead costs for the year and then dividing the costs by the estimated activity base. Smylan has a fairly automated manufacturing operation, and the variable overhead closely follows machine hour usage. Thus, machine hours are used to apply both variable and fixed manufacturing overhead.

The standard manufacturing overhead application rates shown below were based on an estimated manufacturing overhead for the coming year of ₹ 40,80,000 of which ₹ 14,40,000 is variable and ₹ 26,40,000 is fixed. These costs were expected to be incurred uniformly throughout the year. The total machine hours (MH) for the expected annual output, also expected to be uniform throughout the year, were estimated at 1,20,000 MH.

Standard Manufacturing Overhead Application Rates

Variable	₹ 12 per MH
Fixed	22 per MH
Total	₹ 34 per MH

Smylan has reduced production in the past three months because orders have been down. In fact, manufacturing activity for the current month was 80 per cent of what was expected. This reduced level of demand for Symlan's products is expected to continue for at least the next three months.

Sara Edwards, cost, accountant, has prepared some preliminary figures on manufacturing overhead for the current month at the request of Frank Paige, vice president-production, and these amounts are presented below.

Manufacturing Overhead
Preliminary Figures for the Month

Actual machine hours for the month		8,050
Standard machine hours allowed for actual output produced		8,000
Total applied manufacturing overhead		₹ 2,72,000
Actual manufacturing overhead:		
Variable	₹ 95,800	
Fixed	2,11,200	3,07,000
Total manufacturing overhead variance		₹ 35,000 U

Edwards and Paige had the following conversation about this analysis.

Paige: "I just don't understand these number. I have tried to control my costs with the production cut back. I figured that my budget for one month should be about

₹ 340,000, which would give me a ₹ 33,000 favorable variance, yet you show that I have a ₹ 35,000 unfavorable variance."

Edwards: "Well, you may have done a pretty good job in controlling your costs. You really cannot take one-twelfth of your annual estimated costs to get the monthly budget for comparing to your actual costs. A detailed variance analysis of manufacturing overhead would shed more light on your performance. The largest component is probably your fixed manufacturing overhead volume variance."

Paige: "Can you do that detailed variance analysis for me? What do I have to do to reduce or eliminate that fixed manufacturing overhead volume variance?"

Edwards: "Sure, we can do the detailed variance analysis. I would have done it for you, but we just go these figures together now. The fixed manufacturing overhead volume variance is not that important. I'm not sure that you really can or want to reduce it under our present economic situation."

Required:

A. Sara Edwards indicated that Frank Paige should not take one-twelfth of the annual estimated costs to get a monthly budget figure for comparing to the actual costs for the month. Explain what Edwards meant by this comment.

B. Prepare a detailed variance analysis of the manufacturing overhead for Smylan Company for the current month by calculating the following variances.

1. Overhead spending variancne.
2. Variable overhead efficiency variance.
3. Fixed overhead volume variance.

C. Sara Edwards also commented that the fixed manufacturing overhead volume variance is not that important and Frank Paige might not really be able to or want to reduce the fixed overhead volume variance for the month.

1. Explain what the fixed overhead volume variance measures.
2. Explain how Paige could eliminate the fixed overhead volume variance.
3. Under the present economic conditions, would it be to Paige's **best** interest to eliminate the fixed overhead volume variance? Explain your answer.

D. Discuss how Smylan Company can benefit by having Frank Paige participate more in the budgeting process.

(CMA, USA, Adapted with permission)

Answer:

A. While the costs and activity were planned to be evenly distributed throughout the year, Smylan's actual activity was less than estimated. Thus, the actual variable manufacturing costs should be compared to a flexible budget set at the actual activity levels.

B. 1. Total overhead spending variance ₹ 9600 (F)

2. Variable overhead efficiency variance ₹ 600 (A)

3. Fixed overhead volume variance ₹ 44,000 (A)

C. 1. The fixed overhead volume variance (some-times referred to as the fixed overhead denominator variance) measures how well a company uses its fixed manufacturing capacity as measured by the activity base selected.

2. Frank Paige can eliminate the fixed overhead volume variance by increasing Smylan Company's production up to the expected activity level for the month.
3. Increasing production would not necessarily be in he best interest of Frank Paige and Smylan Company. The only way to reduce he fixed overhead volume variance would be to increase production and produce more units, which would increase Smylan's inventory of finished goods at a time of reduced demand. This would result in an increased investment in inventory plus additional inventory storage costs.

D. If Frank Paige were to participate more in the budgeting process, Smylan Company would benefit in the following ways:

- Paige would have a better understanding of the variances, thus enabling him to more effectively mange his operation.
- The participation will increase Paige's motivation as he will feel more in control. He will had the opportunity to help determine many of the numbers, thus meeting his needs for self-determination and competence.
- The budget should be more accurate since it will incorporate the input of the person closest to the process.

10. Techno Arcade, Inc, manufactures video game machines. Market saturation and technological innovations have caused pricing pressures that have resulted in declining profits. To stem the slide in profits until new products can be introduced, top management has turned its attention to both manufacturing economies and increased production. To realize these objectives, an incentive program has been developed to reward production managers who contribute to an increase in the number of units produced and achieve cost reductions, In addition, a just- in-time purchasing program has been implemented, and raw materials are purchased on an as-needed basis.

The production managers have responded to the pressure to improve manufacturing performance in several ways that have resulted in an increased number of completed units over normal production levels. The video game machines put together by the Assembly Group require parts from both the Printed Circuit Boards (PCB) and the Reading Heads (RH) groups. To attain increased production levels, the PCB and RH group started rejecting parts that previously would have been tested and modified to meet manufacturing standards. Preventive maintenance on machines used in the production of these parts has been postponed with only emergency repair work being performed to keep production lines moving. The Maintenance Department is concerned that there will be serious breakdowns and unsafe operating conditions.

The more aggressive Assembly Group production supervisors have pressured maintenance personnel to attend to their machines at the expense of other groups. This has resulted in machine downtime in the PCB and RH groups which, when coupled with demands for accelerated parts delivery by the Assembly Group, has led to more frequent part rejections and increased friction among departments. Techno Arcade operates under a standard-costing system. The standard costs are as follows:

Standard Cost per unit

	Standard Cost Per Unit		
	Quantity	***Cost***	***Total***
Direct material:			
Housing unit	1 unit	₹ 20	₹ 20
Printed circuit boards	2 boards	15	30
Reading heads	4 heads	10	40

Direct labour:			
Assembly group	2.0 hour	8	16
PCB group	1.0 hour	9	9
RH group	1.5 hour	10	15
Total	4.5 hours		
Variable overhead*		2	9
Total standard cost per unit			₹ 139

*Applied on the basis of direct labour: 4.5 direct-labour hours at ₹ 2 per hour.

Techno Arcade prepares monthly performance reports based on standard costs. the following table shows the contribution report for May, when production and sales both reached 2,200 units. The budgeted and actual unit sales price in May were the same at ₹ 200.

Techno Arcade, Inc.
Contribution Report
for the Month of May

	Actual	***Budgeted***	***Variance***
Units	2,200	2,000	200 F
Revenue	₹ 4,40,000	₹ 4,00,000	₹ 40,000 F
Variable costs:			
Direct material	₹ 2,20,400	₹ 1,80,000	₹ 40,400 U
Direct labour	93,460	80,000	13,460 U
Variable overhead	18,800	18,000	800 U
Total variable costs	₹ 3,32,660	₹ 2,78,000	₹ 54,660 U
Contribution margin	₹ 1,07,340	₹ 1,22,000	₹ 14,660 U

Techno Arcade's top management was surprised by the unfavorable contribution-margin variance in spite of the increased sales in May, Jack Rath, director of cost management, was assigned to report on the reasons for the unfavorable contribution results as well as the individuals or groups responsible.

After a thorough review of the data, Rath prepared the following usage report.

Techno Arcade, Inc.
Usage Report
for the Month of May

Cost item	***Actual Quantity***	***Actual Cost***
Direct material:		
Housing units	2,200 units	₹ 44,000
Printed circuit boards	4,700 boards	75,200
Reading heads	9,200 heads	101,200

Direct labour:		
Assembly	3,900 hours	31,200
Printed circuit boards	2,400 hours	23,760
Reading heads	3,500 hours	38,500
Total	9,800 hours	
Variable overhead		18,800
Total variable cost		₹ 3,32,660

Rath reported that the PCB and RH groups supported the increased production levels but experienced abnormal machine downtime, causing idle personnel. This required the use of overtime to keep up with the accelerated demand for parts. The idle time was charged to direct labour. Rath also reported that the production managers of these two groups resorted to parts rejections as opposed to testing and modifying procedures formerly applied. Rath determined that the Assembly Group met management's objectives by increasing production while utilizing lower than standard hours.

Required:

a. Calculate the following variances, and explain the ₹ 14,660 unfavorable variance between the budgeted and actual contribution margin during May. Assume that all raw material purchased during May was placed into production.

1. Direct labour rate variance.
2. Direct labour efficiency variance.
3. Direct material price variance.
4. Direct material quantity variance.
5. Variable overhead spending variance.
6. Variable overhead efficiency variance.
7. Sales price variance.
8. Contribution margin sales volume variance.

b. 1. Identify and briefly explain the behavioural factors that could promote friction among the production managers and between the production managers and the maintenance manager.

2. Evaluate Rath's analysis of the unfavourable contribution results in terms of its completeness and its effect on the behaviour of the production groups.

(CMA adapted with permission)

Answer:

a. 1. Direct labour rate variance	₹ 5660 (A)
2. Direct labour efficiency variance	₹ 200 (F)
3. Direct material price variance	₹ 13,900 (A)
4. Direct material quantity variance	₹ 8,500 (A)
5. Variable overhead spending variance	₹ 800 (F)
6. Variable overhead efficiency variance	₹ 200 (F)
7. Sales price variance	NIL
8. Contribution margin sales volume variance	₹ 14,660 (A)

b 1. Behavioral factors that may promote friction among the production managers and between the production managers and the maintenance manager include the following:

- The managers of the PCB and RH groups will be dissatisfied with the maintenance manager because equipment downtime has caused them to incur additional overtime costs.
- The Assembly Group is dependent on the input of the other production departments. In order to increase production, the managers of the Assembly Group are likely to pressure the other managers. This type of pressure is most probably the reason why the PCB and RH groups began rejecting parts that would normally have been modified and used.

2. Jack Rath's report is incomplete since he has not identified the real causes of the unfavorable results and has left management to draw its own conclusions. In addition, Rath has only addressed the labour issues and has failed to account for the material variances or mention the maintenance problems that resulted in downtime for some departments. The department managers are likely to view the report as incomplete and unfair.

11. Raymond Company manufactures shirts sold to customers for embossing with various slogans and emblems. Ashish Shanker, manufacturing supervisor, recently received the following November production report; the November budget is based on the manufacture of 80,000 shirts.

November 2016 Production Report

Cost Item	Standard	Actual	Variance
Direct material	₹ 1,60,000	₹ 1,62,000	₹ (2,000)
Direct labor	2,40,000	2,46,000	(6,000)
Factory overhead	20,0,000	2,41,900	(41,900)

Ashish was extremely upset by the negative variances in the November report because he had worked very closely with his people for the past two months to improve productivity and to ensure that all workers are paid their standard wage rates. He immediately asked to meet with his boss, Raghav Desai. Also disturbed by the November results, Raghav suggested that Ashish meet with Amit the Co's controller, to see if he can gain further insight into the production problems. Amit was extremely helpful and provided Ashish with additional information on the annual budget and these actual amounts for November.

Variable Overhead Expenditures

	Annual	Per Unit	November
Indirect material	₹ 4,50,000	₹ 0.45	₹ 36,000
Indirect labor	3,00,000	0.30	33,700
Equipment repair	2,00,000	0.20	16,400
Equipment power	50,000	0.05	12,300
Total	₹ 10,00,000	₹ 1.00	₹ 98,400

Fixed Overhead Expenditures

	Annual	November
Supervisory salaries	₹ 2,60,000	₹ 22,000
Insurance	3,50,000	29,500

Property taxes	80,000	6,500
Depreciation	3,20,000	34,000
Heat, light, telephone	2,10,000	21,600
Quality inspection	2,20,000	29,900
Total	₹ 14,40,000	₹ 1,43,500

- Factory overhead at Raymond includes both variable and fixed components and is applied on the basis of direct labor-hours. The company's 2016 budget includes the manufacture of 10 lakhs shirts and the expenditure of 2,50,000 direct labor-hours.
- The standard labor rate is ₹ 12 per hour and the stanard materials cost per shirt is ₹ 2.
- Actual production for November was 82,000 shirts.

With these data, Amit and Ashish analyzed the November variances, paying particular attention to the factory overhead variance because of its significance. Amit knows that part of the problem is that Raymond does not use flexible budgeting, and he will try to explain this to Ashish as they analyze the data.

Required:

1. By calculating the following four variances, explain the ₹ 41,900 unfavorable variance between budgeted and actual factory overhead during the month of November 2016.
   (*a*) Variable factory overhead sales volume variance.
   (*b*) Variable overhead efficiency variance.
   (*c*) Variable overhead spending variance.
   (*d*) Fixed overhead spending variance.
2. Describe the likely behavioral impact of the information provided by the calculations in Requirement 1 on Ashish Shanker. Be sure to make specific reference to the variances calculated, indicating his responsibility in each case. *(CMA USA Adated)*

Answer:

(*a*) Sales volume variance ₹ 2000 (A)
(*b*) Variable overhead efficiency ₹ NIL
(*c*) Variable overhead spending ₹ 16,400 (A)
(*d*) Fixed overhead spending ₹ 23,500 (A)

11

PERFORMANCE MEASUREMENT IN DIVISIONALISED COMPANIES

LEARNING OBJECTIVES:

After reading this chapter, you should be able to:

- Define Decentralisation/Divisionalisation and Explain the Advantages, Disadvantages and Degree of Decentralisation
- Understand Functional Organisational structure
- Explain Responsibility Centre, Types of Responsibility Centre — Cost Centre, Revenue Centre, Profit Centre, Investment Centre
- Define Responsibility Accounting and Identify the Relationship between Responsibility Accounting and Controllability
- Know what is Responsibility Performance Reporting and Explain its Preparation for Cost Centre and Profit Centre
- Explain Different Measures of Financial Performance — Variance Analysis, Division Contribution Margin, Division Net Profit, ROI, RI, Economic Value Added
- Identify Non-financial Measures of Performance
- Distinguish Between Evaluating a Division and Manager of a Division
- Understand Performance Measurement in Multinational Companies

DECENTRALISATION/DIVISIONALISATION

> **Decentralisation** is the process of delegating decision authority and responsibility in an organisation.

In small organisations, decision-making and management of the business are often done by a single individual. However, in a large organisation, especially organisation engaged in manufacturing/undertaking multiple products and activities, successful management of it by the top management becomes more difficult. In order to overcome this difficulty, the large organisation may be decentralised or divisionalised. The process of delegating decision authority and responsibility in an organisation is known as decentralisation. In any organisation, in fact, some authority can be found delegated to lower level management. In this way, almost every organisation can be said to be 'decentralised.' However, decentralisation or divisionalisation is found in case of companies producing multiple products. Divisions in companies mean different things in different companies. In some companies, divisions are organised on the basis of product lines whereas in some decentralised companies, divisions may be created on the basis of geographical areas. Also, the term 'decentralisation' or 'divisionalisation' refers to those situations where individual managers of decentralised sub-units are given responsibility for profit and not just costs or revenues. In decentralised organisations, top management handles broad corporate policies, establishes long range plans, raises capital and conducts other coordinating activities.

An example of divisionalised (decentralised) organisational structure is displayed in Figure 11.1. It can be noticed that different divisions have been created in terms of products made in each division in this particular decentralised company and these divisions are responsible for all the operations relating to their respective products. Divisional managers will have decision-making authority for their divisions and thus may be free to set selling prices, choose which market to sell in, make product mix and output decisions, make purchasing decisions. Some functions (activities) like research and development, industrial relations, general administration may be centralised with the top management which may have a responsibility for providing services to all of the divisions.

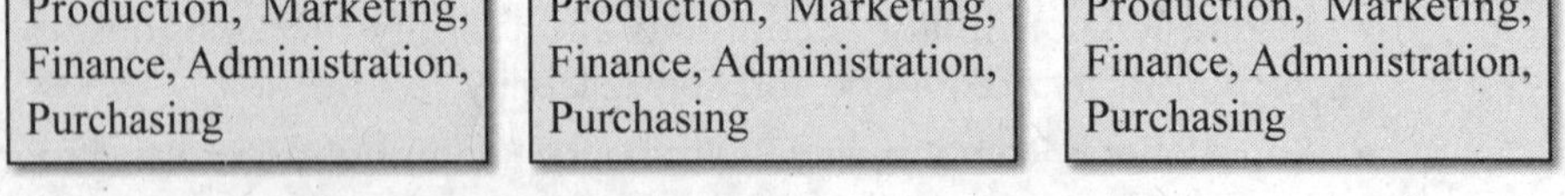

Figure 11.1: Divisionalised Organisational Structure

Advantages of Divisionalisation

Divisionalisation/decentralisation features several advantages for an organisation which include:

1. Top management becomes free from detailed involvement in day-to-day operations and enables them to devote their time and efforts to strategic planning, policy formulation, overall coordination and direction.
2. It improves the decision-making process and leads to more informed decisions in the organisation because the managers who are directly involved in the day-to-day running of business and are familiar with the situation, make decision.

3. Speedier decisions can be made as decisions can be taken on the spot by the manager without any need of sending to/getting information from top management.
4. Managers can rapidly respond to changes in the market, competition, opportunities available, due to non-existence of administrative bottlenecks in their organisation which can increase the profitability of the overall company.
5. Experience of decision-making at the divisional level provides the divisional managers better career training.
6. Decentralisation enhances the motivation and efficiency of the divisional managers as they find their status increased with wider responsibilities and greater freedom to manage their activities and more control over the factors which determine their performances.
7. Divisionalisation may be more helpful in building good labour-management relations as the divisional managers will be able to maintain personalised contact with the employees.

Disadvantages of Divisionalisation

There are some disadvantages of divisionalisation. They are listed as follows:

1. Different divisions are likely to compete unreasonably and they may take action which may increase their profits but only at the expense of other divisions. This may adversely affect cooperation and harmony between divisions and in turn, the profitability of entire company may suffer. For example, two managers competing in a common product market may engage in price cutting to win customers. As a result, the overall company profits may be less than the profits that could have been if the price cutting has not occurred.
2. There will be duplication of various assets and costs in the different operating divisions. For example, each division might have separate sales force and administrative office staff, but centralisation of these personnel could save money. Further, the costs of gathering and processing information in a divisionalised organisation might be greater than if such information were gathered and processed centrally. If top management of a decentralised company are going for divisionalisation, it is important that they assess whether the additional benefits will exceed the additional costs.
3. A further argument against divisionalisation is that top management loses some control by delegating decision-making to divisional managers. It is argued that a series of control reports is not as effective as detailed knowledge of a company's activities. However, with a good system of performance evaluation together with appropriate control information, top management should be able to control operations just as effectively.[1]

Degree of Decentralisation

In a decentralised organisation, divisions are organised on the basis of product lines and are differentiated by the type of goods or services produced and responsibility for planning and controlling their operations are given to divisional managers. These divisional managers have the authority to make decisions without first seeking the approval of top management.

The degree or level of decentralisation varies significantly among divisionalised companies and there is no one best level of decentralisation which can be suggested for all decentralised companies. In some companies for example, a divisional manager may have authority over all plant operations, including plant asset acquisitions and replacement. In other decentralised companies, however, a divisional manager may only have authority for scheduling production and for controlling the cost of direct materials, direct labour and factory overhead. The most appropriate quantum or level of decentralisation for a divisionalised company can be determined on the basis of benefits and disadvantages of divisionalisation as they apply to a company's specific, unique circumstances.

Anderson and Sollenberger[2] suggest that the top management must resolve the following three problems associated with decentralisation to realise the full benefits or advantages:

1. ***Competent People:*** Without competent people, the best policies break down and a lack of control reduces the efficiency and effectiveness of operations.
2. ***Measurement System:*** The same measurement system must be implemented and maintained for all sub-units. Top management must develop policies that provide consistency in reporting periods, methods of reporting and methods of data collection.
3. ***Suboptimisation:*** Left to themselves, division managers will work for their own interests without consideration of benefits to the entire organisation. Top management needs to focus all managers' efforts on corporate goals through planning and creative systems.

FUNCTIONAL ORGANISATIONAL STRUCTURE

A functional organisational structure is one in which all functions of a similar type within an organisation are placed under the control of a departmental head or manager. Such departmental managers have responsibility to perform only a part of the overall functions. An example of a functional organisational structure is shown in Figure 11.2. In this Figure 11.2, it is shown that the company has five separate departments, *e.g.*, production, marketing, purchasing, accounts and administration, research and development. In this manufacturing company, manager of each department (or activity) is a part of the process of purchasing the raw materials, using raw materials to make finished products, selling finished products to customers, administering accounts and administration, and finally supervising research and development activities. For example, the purchasing department is responsible for purchasing raw materials and supplies for all products at a minimum cost, reasonable quality and within proper time so that production requirements can be fulfilled without any difficulty.

A **functional organisational structure** is one in which all functions of a similar type within an organisation are placed under the control of a departmental head or manager.

The production department has the responsibility for the manufacture of all products and the marketing department performs the selling function and is responsible for creating sales revenue for the company. In a functional or centralised organisation, all decisions such as pricing, production, product mix are made by the top management and therefore functional managers or departmental heads in a centralised organisation enjoy far less independence and autonomy than the divisional managers in a decentralised or divisionalised organisation. For example, the production managers in a functional organisation (Figure 11.2) has no control over sources of supply, selling prices and does not make production and product mix decisions.

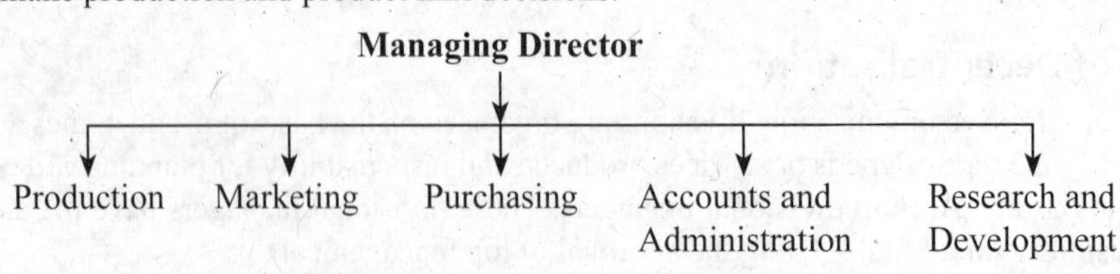

Figure 11.2: Functional Organisational Structure

RESPONSIBILITY CENTRE

A responsibility centre may be defined as:

- *an area of responsibility which is controlled by an individual. A responsibility centre is an activity such as department over which a manager exercises responsibility.*

Responsibility areas may be departments (drilling or maintenance department), product lines (chemicals or fertilizers), territories (North or South) or any other type of identifiable unit or combination of units. The specific types of responsibility areas depend on the nature of the firm and its activities. A plant manager is in charge of a plant and is usually responsible for producing budgeted quantities of specific products within budgeted cost limits. A sales manager is responsible for getting orders from customers, and so on. In most cases, it is relatively easy to identify activities with specific managers. However, in some cases it is not a simple task to isolate the responsibilities of managers.

It should be noted that effective planning and control systems are structured around the implicit or explicit areas of responsibility within the organisation. Further, to be held accountable for performance, managers must have clearly defined areas of responsibility—activities they control.

TYPES OF RESPONSIBILITY CENTRES

Responsibility centres can be classified by the scope of responsibility assigned and decision-making authority given to individual managers. The following are the four common types of responsibility centres.

Cost Centre

A cost or expense centre is a segment of an organisation in which the managers are held responsible for the cost incurred in that segment but not for revenues. Responsibility in a cost centre is restricted to cost. For planning purposes, the budget estimates are cost estimates; for control purposes, performance evaluation is guided by a cost variance equal to the difference between the actual and budgeted costs for a given period. Cost centre managers have control over some or all of the costs in their segment of business, but not over revenues. Cost centres are widely used forms of responsibility centres. In manufacturing organisations, the production and service departments are classified as cost centre. Also, a marketing department, a sales region or a single sales representative can be defined as a cost centre. Cost centre may vary in size from a small department with a few employees to an entire manufacturing plant. In addition, cost centres may exist within other cost centres. For example, a manager of a manufacturing plant organised as a cost centre may treat individual departments within the plant as separate cost centres, with the department managers reporting directly to plant manager. Similarly, in University of Delhi, the entire university or departments within the university or each college could be viewed as cost centre. Further, within a college, each department could also be a cost centre. Cost centre managers are responsible for the costs that are controllable by them and their subordinates. However, which costs should be charged to cost centres, is an important question in evaluating cost centre managers.

> A **cost or expense centre** is a segment of an organisation in which the managers are held responsible for the cost incurred in that segment but not for revenues.

Revenue Centre

A revenue centre is a segment of the organisation which is primarily responsible for generating sales revenue. A revenue centre manager does not possess control over cost, investment in assets, but usually has control over some of the expense of the marketing department. The performance of a revenue centre is evaluated by comparing the actual revenue with budgeted revenue, and actual marketing expenses with budgeted marketing expenses. The Marketing Manager of a product line, or an individual sales representative are examples of revenue centres.

> A **revenue centre** is a segment of the organisation which is primarily responsible for generating sales revenue.

Profit Centre

A profit centre is a segment of an organisation whose manager is responsible for both revenues and costs. In a profit centre, the manager has the responsibility and the authority to make decisions that affect both costs

> A **profit centre** is a segment of an organisation whose manager is responsible for both revenues and costs.

and revenues (and thus profits) for the department or division. The main purpose of a profit centre is to earn profit. Profit centre managers aim at both the production and marketing of a product. The performance of the profit centre is evaluated in terms of whether the centre has achieved its budgeted profit. A division of the company which produces and markets the products may be called a profit centre. Such a divisional manager determines the selling price, marketing programmes and production policies. Profit centres make managers more concerned with finding ways to increase the centre's revenue by increasing production or improving distribution methods. The manager of a profit centre does not make decisions concerning the plant assets available to the centre. *For example*, the manager of the sporting goods department does not make the decisions to expand the available floor space for the department.

Mostly profit centres are created in an organisation in which they (profit divisions) sell products or services outside the company. In some cases, profit centres may be selling products or services within the company. For example, repairs and maintenance department in a company can be treated as a profit centre if it is allowed to bill other production departments for the services provided to them. Similarly, the data processing department may bill each of company's administrative and operating departments for providing computer-related services.

An example of profit centres in a super market having different retail departments is displayed in Figure 11.3.

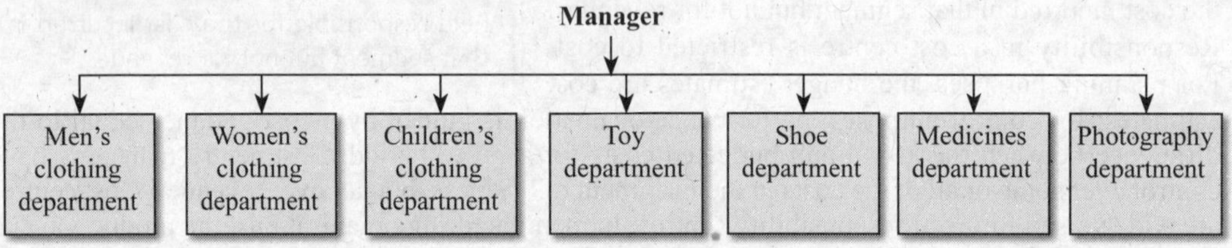

Figure 11.3: Profit Centre

In profit centres, managers are encouraged to take important decisions regarding the activities and operations of their divisions. Profit centres are generally created in terms of product or process which has grown in size and has profit responsibility. In some organizations, profit centres are given complete autonomy on sourcing supplies and making sales. However, in other organisations, such independence may not be found. Top management does not allow profit centre divisions to buy from outside sources if there is idle capacity within the firm. Also, the top management may be hesitant to part with designs and other specifications to maintain quality and safety of the product and due to fear of losing the market that the firm has already created for its products.

Benefits of Creating Profit Centres

The creation of profit centres in a diversified or divisionalized firm has many benefits.

1. ***Better Planning and Decision Making:*** Profit centres managers are independent in managing the activities and are responsible for profit and success of their business units. This encourages them to make better planning, profitable decisions and exercise control. It creates a sense of accountability among the profit centre managers.

2. ***Participation in Organizational Plans and Policies:*** Although profit centre managers are independent in the management of their business units, they function within the umbrella of overall organization. They get opportunities to participate in the discussion of plans and policies at the firm level. This widens their perspective and inculcates the habit of taking an integrated and macro view of activities in place of a narrow division specific view. In this process, profit centres managers can get trained to be the senior managers of their companies or other firms in the future.

3. ***Beneficial Competitive Environment:*** All profit centres managers target success and profit by managing costs and aiming higher revenues. This creates a competitive environment among the managers managing their respective business units which is not only beneficial for them but also contributes in achieving the overall objectives of the firm and in maximizing the firm profit.

Essentials of a Profit Centre

The basic requirements of a profit centre are as follows[3]:

1. ***Operational Autonomy:*** Business unit managers should have sufficient freedom to take operating decisions on a profit-oriented basis ***for example***, regarding purchase, product mix, pricing and inventory. Unless they have sufficient autonomy to take decisions in respect of the above, the very purpose of delegating authority and treating profit as a measure of divisional performance would be defeated. Top management, therefore, must not impose its decisions on business unit managers. However, the decision taken by these divisional managers must be conducive to the achievement of the organisational objectives and policies.
2. ***Sourcing Inputs and Markets for Products:*** Business unit managers must have authority to source supply and markets to make profitable and sound make-or-buy decisions. Even if they are not permitted to actually purchase from external suppliers or from parties outside the organisation, they should be able to gain full information regarding demand and supply conditions and the prevailing and expected price trend in the industry.
3. ***Measurable Costs and Revenues of Different Profit Centres:*** The inputs and the outputs of the profit centres should be capable of separate measurement. By this, the need for apportionment of common input and output is minimised if not altogether eliminated. This makes it essential that the boundaries of different profit centres/divisions be clearly demarcated to preclude overlapping of activities. In the absence of well-defined boundaries and consequent overlapping of operations, unit managers may tend to take credit for everything that goes well and blame the other division for whatever goes wrong. Also, it would be necessary not to include the corporate office and other administration costs, over which the business unit/divisional manager has no control, in the divisional profit performance reports. When the boundaries of the responsibility centres have a lot of overlapping operations/activities, managers are not adequately motivated to take decisions from the point of view of the likely impact on the profit of their unit.
4. ***Using Profit as a Measure of Performance:*** Although the contribution of a profit centre can not be measured solely by the amount of profit contributed by it, profit must be treated as the main measure of a business unit's performance by the top management. If the top management does not give weightage to this, the divisional manager will tend to show less concern for this vital aspect of performance. Since the business unit manager can boost profit by ignoring the need for repairs to plant and machinery or by deliberately reducing certain expenses, it would be necessary to use three or four non-profit measures of performance, for example, sales per employee, and production hours lost as a result of breakdown of machinery for evaluation.
5. ***Size of Profit Centre:*** Unless the division is large enough, it should not be treated as a profit centre. A small workshop or a section of a department, for instance, can not be regarded as a profit centre. There should be a sizeable amount of work being performed in the business unit for it to be under the charge of a senior executive such as a general manager or divisional manager who could be given decision-making powers and the responsibility for all its activities, including profit performance.

Investment Centre

> **Investment centre** is responsible for both profits and investments.

An investment centre is responsible for both profits and investments. The investment centre manager has control over revenues, expenses and the amounts invested in the centre's assets. He also formulates the credit policy which has a direct influence on debt collection, and the inventory policy which determines the investment in inventory. The manager of an investment centre has more authority and responsibility than the manager of either a cost centre or a profit centre. Besides controlling costs and revenues, he has investment responsibility too. 'Investment on asset' responsibility means the authority to buy, sell and use divisional assets.

Exhibit. 11.1: Summary of Cost, Profit and Investment Centres

	Decision Rights	*Typically Used When*
Cost centre	Input mix (labour, materials, supplies)	• Central manager can measure output, knows the cost functions, and can set the optimal quantity and appropriate rewards • Central manager can observe the quality of the cost centre's output • Cost centre manager has knowledge of the optimal input mix
Profit centre	• Input mix • Product mix • Selling prices (or output quantities)	• Profit centre manager has the knowledge to select the correct price/quantity • Profit centre manager has the knowledge to select the optimal product mix
Investment centre	• Input mix • Product mix • Selling prices (or output quantities) • Capital invested in centre	• Investment centre manager had the knowledge to select the correct price/quantity • Investment centre manager has the knowledge to select the optimal product mix • Investment centre manager has the knowledge about investment opportunities

RESPONSIBILITY ACCOUNTING

> **Responsibility Accounting** refers to the accounting process that reports how well managers (of responsibility centres) have fulfilled their responsibility.
>
> **Responsibility Accounting System** is an information system that personalises control reports by accumulating and reporting cost and revenue information according to defined responsibility centres within a company.

The term 'responsibility accounting' refers to the accounting process that reports how well managers (of responsibility centres) have fulfilled their responsibility. It is a system that measures the plans (by budgets) and actions (by actual results) of each responsibility centre. Also known as activity or profitability accounting, it is an information system that personalises control reports by accumulating and reporting cost and revenue information according to defined responsibility centres within a company. Responsibility accounting systems are tailored to the organisation structure so that revenue and costs are accumulated and reported by centres of responsibility within the organisation. The responsibility accounting system makes the following important assumptions:

1. The areas of responsibility are defined for which managers should be held responsible.
2. Managers are only charged with the items and responsibility over which they can exercise a significant degree of direct control.

3. Managers should actively participate in establishing the goals or budgets against which their performance is measured.
4. Goals defined for each area of responsibility should be attainable with efficient and effective performance.
5. Control (performance) reports should contain significant information related to each area of responsibility.
6. Responsibility centre managers should try to accomplish the budgets and objectives established for their respective areas of responsibility.

Hilton[4] observes:

> The proper focus of a responsibility-accounting system is *information*. The system should identify the individual in the organization who is in the best position to explain each particular event or financial result. The emphasis should be on providing that individual and higher-level managers with information to help them understand the reasons behind the organization's performance. When properly used, a responsibility-accounting system *does not emphasize blame.* If managers feel they are beaten over the head with criticism and rebukes when unfavourable variances occur, they are unlikely to respond in a positive way. Instead, they will tend to undermine the system and view it with skepticism. But when the responsibility-accounting system emphasizes its informational role, managers tend to react constructively, and strive for improved performance.
>
> Managerial accountants often use the responsibility-accounting system to motivate actions considered desirable by upper-level management. Sometimes the responsibility-accounting system can solve behavioural problems as well.

RESPONSIBILITY ACCOUNTING AND CONTROLLABILITY

> **Controllability** is the degree of influence that a specific manager has over costs, revenues, or other items in question.

Responsibility accounting is closely related with the goal of controllability. Controllability is the degree of influence that a specific manager has over costs, revenues, or other items in question. Accordingly, in responsibility accounting those elements in a certain area of activity are identified which are controllable and then a person is given the responsibility for managing such elements. Responsibility accounting implies that individuals in an organisation can not be responsible for those items which they can not control. They should also not claim any authority over those revenues which are not the result of their actions and performances. For instance, a foreman in a production department can be held responsible only for direct material and direct labour costs, because these are the costs which are controllable by him. On the other hand, divisional manager of the production division can be held accountable for all direct and indirect costs incurred in his division. Generally, those decision makers who are placed higher in the authority hierarchy, are held responsible for a greater number of activities and financial elements. In the long run, however, all costs are controllable by someone in the organisation.

Horngreen, Datar and Foster[5] advise:

> Managers should avoid overemphasising controllability. Responsibility accounting is more far-reaching. It focuses on information and knowledge, not control. The key question is, who is the best informed? Put another way, who is the person who can tell us the most about the specific item in question regardless of that person's ability to exert personal control? For instance, purchasing managers may be held accountable for total purchase costs, not because of their ability to affect market prices, but because of their ability to predict

uncontrollable prices and explain uncontrollable price changes— performance reports for responsibility centres also may include uncontrollable items because this approach could change behaviour in the direction top management desires. A cost centre manager may emphasise production efficiency and deemphasise the pleas of sales personnel for faster service and rush orders. In a profit centre, the manager is responsible for both costs and revenues. Thus, even though the manager still has no control over sales personnel, the manager will now more likely weigh the impact of his or her decisions on costs and revenues, rather than solely on costs.

Example:

The printing department of a large company informs the marketing department that the price of printing 100,000 colour flyers will be ₹ 60,00,000. The marketing department submits the material for the flyer two weeks later than originally planned and tells the printing department that the scheduled date of completion has been advanced two weeks. In order to achieve the new schedule, the printing department incurs an additional production cost of ₹ 15,00,000.

1. In an organisation using responsibility accounting, where would the additional costs be assigned? Would these costs be considered controllable costs? What effect might this have on future printing orders from the marketing department?
2. In an organisation that does not use responsibility accounting, where would the various costs be assigned? What effect might this have on future printing orders from the marketing department?

Solution:

1. In an organisation using responsibility accounting, the originally quoted price of ₹ 60,00,000 plus the additional cost of ₹ 15,00,000 would be assigned to the marketing department. This would be considered a controllable cost. The long-range effect might be that the marketing department will become more cost-conscious and will plan activities better.
2. In an organisation that does not employ responsibility accounting, the additional production costs most probably would be assigned to the printing department. There would be no motivation by the marketing department to adhere to scheduled dates or to plan printing needs in a better fashion.

RESPONSIBILITY PERFORMANCE REPORTING

Responsibility performance reporting implies the reporting phase of responsibility accounting. Responsibility reporting has two purposes:

- To determine the degree of performance in the area of responsibility for which the responsibility manager is directly responsible.
- To formulate measures to improve the performance of the responsibility centre manager.

The responsibility reporting should be suitable and relevant with respect to content, frequency of reporting and level of details required. In order to provide relevant contents in the report, only those items that are controlled by the particular responsibility centre manager should be reported. Frequency of reporting and the quantum of details in the report can be decided in terms of requirements. Generally in a production department of a manufacturing enterprise, detailed data on production, direct costs, indirect costs needs to be gathered and reported to foreman quite frequently. However, the same data is reported to senior management in a summarised form and at less frequent intervals. The difference in the frequency of reporting in this situation is due to the fact that the foreman has direct responsibility whereas senior managers have overall responsibility for long-term and strategic decisions: Usry and Hammer[6] have mentioned the following as characteristics of responsibility reporting:

1. Reports should fit the organisation chart, that is, the report should be addressed to the individual responsible for the items covered by it, who, in turn will be able to control those costs under his jurisdiction. Managers must be educated to use the results of the reporting system.
2. Report should be prompt and timely. Prompt issuance of a report requires that cost records be organised so that information is available when it is needed.
3. Reports should be issued with regularity. Promptness and regularity are closely tied up with the mechanical aids used to assemble and issue reports.
4. Reports should be easy to understand. Often they contain accounting terminology that managers with little or no accounting training find difficult to understand, and vital information may be incorrectly communicated. Therefore, accounting terms should be explained or modified to fit the user. Top management should have some knowledge of the kind of items chargeable to an account as well as the methods used to compute overhead rates, make cost allocations and analyse variances.
5. Reports should convey sufficient but not excessive details. The amount and nature of the details depend largely on the management level receiving the report. Reports to management should neither be flooded with immaterial facts or so condensed that management lacks vital information essential to carrying out its responsibilities.
6. Reports should give comparative figures, *i.e.*, a comparison of actual with budgeted figures or of predetermined standards with actual results and the isolation of variances.
7. Reports should be analytical. Analysis of underlying papers, such as time tickets, scrap tickets, work orders, and materials requisitions, provide reasons for poor performance which might have been due to power failure, machine breakdown, an inefficient operator, poor quality of materials, or many other similar factors.
8. Reports for operating management should, if possible, be stated in physical units as well as in terms of money since monetary information may give a foreman not trained in the language of the accountant a certain amount of difficulty.
9. Reports may tend to highlight departmental efficiencies and inefficiencies, results achieved, future goals or targets.

Responsibility reports help each successively higher level of management in evaluating the performances of subordinate managers and their respective organisation units. The reports should be tailored to fit the planning, controlling and decision making needs of subordinate managers and should include both monetary and non-monetary information.

RESPONSIBILITY REPORTING FOR COST CENTRES

A specimen of responsibility performance reporting for cost centres is given in Exhibit 11.2 which has been designed to provide relevant cost information to three levels of responsibility centres in a manufacturing enterprise — Foreman, Production Manager, General Manager.

Exhibit 11.2: Cost Centres Responsibility Report

Responsibility Report for Cost Centres

(A) Foreman (Paint Section)

Item	*Actual Cost (₹)*	*Budgeted Cost (₹)*	*Variance (₹)*
Direct materials	50,000	48,400	(–) 1,600
Direct labour	31,000	34,000	(+) 3,000
Indirect labour	12,000	12,000	—
Supplies	1,000	1,600	(+) 600
	94,000	96,000	(+) 2,000

(B) Production Manager

Item	*Actual Cost (₹)*	*Budgeted Cost (₹)*	*Variance (₹)*
Paint section	94,000	96,000	(+)2,000
Cleaning section	1,20,000	1,21,000	(+) 1,000
Assembly section	1,61,000	1,58,000	(–) 3,000
	3,75,000	3,75,000	0

(C) General Manager

Item	*Actual Cost (₹)*	*Budgeted Cost (₹)*	*Variance (₹)*
Production department	3,75,000	3,75,000	(–)
Sales department	3,74,000	3,80,000	(+) 6,000
Office administration	1,10,000	1,12,000	(+) 2,000
Interest on loans	15,000	15,000	—
	8,74,000	8,82,000	(+) 8,000

From Exhibit 11.2, it can be found that each responsibility report contains items and information which are required by the concerned responsibility centre manager and which are within his responsibility area. For example, in the foreman's report, relevant production cost information is given. In the responsibility report prepared for the production manager, information on different sections of his department is included in aggregated manner and for the general manager, the responsibility report contains information for different departments. It can be further noticed that responsibility reporting goes on aggregating information as the reports are prepared for higher level managers in the organisational hierarchy. That is, the amount of detail decreases as reports reach higher and higher levels of management. Managers cannot make effective use of information that is too detailed and voluminous. Departmental managers do not routinely receive reports detailing all of the costs of the work centres. Managers who want such detailed information can get it and might well seek it if they were concerned about some particular elements of cost.

RESPONSIBILITY REPORTING FOR PROFIT CENTRES

Responsibility accounting reports for profit centres are normally in the form of income statements. The principle of controllability also applies to responsibility reporting for profit centres. Exhibit 11.3 gives a sample of responsibility report for profit centres organised on the basis of product lines and geographical areas. Managers at the lowest level of profit centre are responsible for product lines. They are subordinate to the managers of the geographical areas, who are, in turn, responsible to the Managing Director of the company.

Profit centre reporting can be prepared in a different manner to provide more detail on individual components of the appliance segment in the particular region. Exhibit 11.4 shows an alternative responsibility reporting format giving information on different categories of appliances. For simplicity, budgeted figures are omitted. The critical point in responsibility reporting is conveying the best information: the selection of the elements to include and the format are secondary.[7]

Exhibit 11.3: Profit Centres Responsibility Reports

Responsibility Reports for Profit Centres (Thousands of Rupees)

	Current Month		Year to Date	
	***Budget* (₹)**	***Over (Under)* (₹)**	***Budget* (₹)**	***Over (Under)* (₹)**
Report to Product Manager —				
Appliances, Asian Region				
Sales	122.00	1.5	387.0	3.2
Variable costs:				
Production	47.5	2.8	150.7	5.9
Selling and administrative	12.2	1.8	38.7	1.9
Total variable costs	59.7	4.6	189.4	7.8
Contribution margin	62.3	(3.1)	197.6	(4.6)
Direct fixed costs	(36.0)	(1.2)	98.5	(3.1)
Product margin	26.3	(1.9)	99.1	(1.5)
Report to Manager — Asian Region				
Product margins:				
Appliances	26.3	(1.9)	99.1	(1.5)
Industrial equipment	37.4	3.2	134.5	7.3
Tools	18.3	1.1	59.1	(2.0)
Total Product margins	82.0	2.4	292.7	3.8
Regional expenses (common to all product lines)	18.5	0.8	61.2	(1.3)
Regional margin	63.5	1.6	231.5	5.1
Report to Executive Vice-President				
Regional margins:				
Asian	63.5	1.6	231.5	5.1
European	78.1	(4.3)	289.4	(8.2)
USA	211.8	(3.2)	612.4	(9.6)
Total regional margins	353.4	(5.9)	1,133.3	(12.7)
Corporate expenses (common to all regions)	87.1	1.4	268.5	3.1
Corporate profit	266.3	(7.3)	864.8	(15.8)

Exhibit 11.4: Responsibility Reports for Individual Products

Alternative Responsibility Reporting Format
Report to Product Manager – Appliances, Asian Region (thousands of Rupees)

	Total (₹)	*Small Home Appliances* (₹)	*Large Home Appliances* (₹)	*Commercial Appliances* (₹)
Sales	122.0	39.0	34.2	48.8
Variable costs:				
Production	47.5	12.1	9.4	26.0
Selling and administrative	12.2	3.9	3.4	4.9
Total variable costs	59.7	16.0	12.8	30.9
Contribution margin	62.3	23.0	21.4	17.9
Direct fixed costs	27.5	4.2	15.2	8.1
Margin	34.8	18.8	6.2	9.8
Costs common to products in the appliance line	8.5			
Product margin	26.3			

Illustrative Problem 1

Nicefit manufactures ready-made garments by a simple process of cutting the clothes in various shapes and sewing the corresponding pieces together to form the finished products.

The Sewing Department and the Cutting Department report to the Production Manager who along with Engineering Manager reports to the Director — Manufacturing. The Sales Manager, Publicity Manager and the Credit Manager report to the Managing Director of the Company

The Accounts Department reports the following for the last quarter of 2016:

	Budgeted (₹)	*Actual* (₹)
Bad Debt Losses	5,000	3,000
Cloth used	31,000	36,000
Advertising	4,000	4,000
Audit Fees	7,500	7,500
Credit Reports	1,200	1,050
Sales Representative :		
Travelling Expenses	9,000	10,200
Sales Commission	7,000	7,000
Cutting Labour	6,000	6,600
Thread	500	450
Sewing Labour	17,000	18,400
Credit Dept. Salaries	8,000	8,000
Cutting Utilities	800	700
Sewing Utilities	900	950
Director, Marketing:		
Salaries & Admn. Exp.	20,000	21,400

Production Engineering Expenses	13,000	12,200
Sales Management Office Expenses	16,000	15,700
Production Manager Office Expenses	18,000	17,000
Director — Manufacturing Salaries & Admn. Expenses	21,000	20,100

Using the above data, prepare responsibility accounting reports for the Director – Marketing, the Director — Manufacturing and the production Manager.

Solution:

Responsibility Accounting Reports

	***Budgeted* (₹)**	***Actual* (₹)**	***Variance* (₹)**	
For the Production Manager				
Cutting Department:				
Cloth	31,000	36,000	5,000	(Unfavourable)
Cutting labour	6,000	6,600	600	(Unfavourable)
Cutting Utilities	800	700	100	(Favourable)
Total, Cutting Dept (A)	37,800	43,300	5,500	(Unfavourable)
Sewing Department:				
Thread	500	450	50	(Favourable)
Sewing Labour	17,000	18,400	1,400	(Unfavourable)
Sewing Utilities	900	950	50	(Unfavourable)
Total Sewing Dept (B)	18,400	19,800	1,400	(Unfavourable)
Total (A + B)	56,200	63,100	6,900	(Unfavourable)
For the Director – Manufacturing				
Production Department*	56,200	63,100	6,900	(Unfavourable)
Production Engineering Expenses	13,000	12,200	800	(Favourable)
Production Manager – Office Expenses	18,000	17,000	1,000	(Favourable)
Total	87,200	92,300	5,100	(Unfavourable)

(* As per Responsibility Accounting Report for the Production Manager)

For the Director — Marketing

	₹	₹	₹	
Sales Representative:				
Travelling Expenses	9,000	10,200	1200	(Unfavourable)
Sales Commission	7,000	7,000	—	
Total (A)	16,000	17,200	1,200	(Unfavourable)
Sales Management:				
Office Expenses (B)	16,000	15,700	300	(Favourable)
Advertising (C)	4,000	4,000	—	
Credit Department :				
Salaries	8,000	8,000	—	
Credit Reports	1,200	1,050	150	(Favourable)

Bad Debt Losses	5,000	3,000	2,000	(Favourable)
	14,200	12,050	2,150	
Total (A + B + C + D)	50,200	48,950	1,250	(Favourable)

Illustrative Problem 2

A manufacturing company has five plants A,B,C,D and E. Each plant has a forming, cleaning and packing department.

Each level of management has responsibility over costs incurred at its level.

The budget for the current year has been set up as follows:

Plant	*Budgeted cost* (₹)
A	67,500
B	61,250
C	54,200
D	67,500
E	67,500

Budgeted information for Plant C is as follows:

Plant Manager's office	₹ 1,175
Forming department	₹ 15,000
Cleaning department	27,725
Packing department	10,300

Budgeted information for Plant C forming department is as follows:

Direct materials	4,167
Direct labour	7,500
Factory overhead	3,333

The following additional budgeted data are available:

President Office	8,125
Vice-President, Marketing	10,000
Vice-President, Manufacturing Office	2,084

The following actual costs are incurred during the year:

Plant	*Actual Cost*
A	63,825
B	62,150
C	54,238
D	65,550
E	68,400

The actual cost for Plant C (Forming Department) were as follows:

Direct materials	₹ 167	under-budget
Direct labour	2,000	under-budget
Factory overhead	167	over-budget

Actual costs for Plant C (Plant Manager) were:

Plant Manager's Office	1,238
Cleaning department	28,750
Packing department	11,250
Forming department	13,000

Actual costs for the President's level were:

President, Office	8,188
Vice-President, Marketing	14,900
Vice-President, Manufacturing	3,16,658

Prepare a responsibility report for the year showing the details of the budgeted, actual and variance amounts for the following areas:

Level 1 Forming department, Plant C
Level 2 Plant Manager, Plant C
Level 3 Vice-President, Manufacturing
Level 4 President

Solution:

Responsibility Report

	Budgeted (₹)	***Actual*** (₹)	***Variance*** (₹)
President (level 4)	8,125	8,188	63
President's office	10,000	14,900	4,900
Vice-President, Manufacturing	3,20,034	3,16,658	(3,376)
Total controllable costs	3,38,159	3,39,746	1,587
Vice-President, Manufacturing: (level 3)			
Vice-President, Manufacturing Office	2,084	2,495	411
Plant A	67,500	63,825	(3,675)
Plant B	61,250	62,150	900
Plant C	54,200	54,238	(38)
Plant D	67,500	65,550	(1,950)
Plant E	67,500	68,400	900
Total controllable costs	3,20,034	3,16,658	(3,376)
Plant Manager, Plant C (level 2)			
Plant Manager's office	1,175	1,238	63
Forming department	15,000	13,000	(2,000)
Cleaning department	27,725	28,750	1,025
Packing department	10,300	11,250	950
Total controllable costs	54,200	54,238	38
Forming department, Plant C (level 1)			
Direct materials	4,167	4,000	(167)

Direct labour	7,500	5,500	(2,000)
Factory overhead	3,333	3,500	167
Total controllable costs	15,000	13,000	(2,000)

MEASURING DIVISIONAL PERFORMANCE

Performance measurement is aimed in respect of all responsibility centres. Whether dealing with a cost, profit or investment centre, performance can only be evaluated by comparing results with something. Probably the best way to encourage managers to act in the firm's best interests is to measure their performance in relation to budgeted results. The following requisites are noticeworthy for selection of measures of performance:

1. Performance measurement criteria must be clear. This will help the divisional managers to decide on which items they should concentrate their efforts and resources.
2. The targets or objectives contained in the performance measures should be attainable with reasonable efforts. If targets are too high, they will undermine the effectiveness of divisionalised control system. Targets should be established jointly by the performance manager and coordinating manager to promote acceptance of organisational goals by the responsibility centre manager.
3. Divisional performance measures are not confined to quantitative measurements. There are many departments such as legal department, personnel department, fire safety department, etc. for which quantitative parameters are not appropriate. Therefore, such measures should be selected which can help in making a judgement of the level of activity performed by a responsibility centre.
4. Performance measures selected should help in making a realistic assessment of the effectiveness and efficiency of a responsibility centre. Effectiveness requires measuring achievement of a division in terms of parameters or criteria that measure its final benefits or ultimate output. Efficiency focuses on measuring achievements in terms of yardsticks or norms that measure output or intermediate output related to the use of resources. Efficiency, thus, focuses on the relationship of output to inputs, whereas, effectiveness implies contribution to the achievement of ultimate goals of the responsibility centre, division or department.
5. Performance measures should be competent enough to evaluate both short-term and long-term performance of a division. In fact, there is a need of using not one goal but multiple goals to assess a division. Multiple measures enhances goal congruence and reduces sub-optimisation. Concentrating on a single goal or measure, say, profits, can be useful in the short-run as it can result into maximisation of profit. However, it may work against the overall objectives and interests of an organisation. Multiple measures or goals include productivity, profitability, human resource development, employee attitudes, market share, customer relations, contribution to social responsibility. It is argued that too many goals sometimes may confuse the divisional managers. Therefore, adequate as well as manageable measures, say four to five, can be preferably used.

DIFFERENT MEASURES OF FINANCIAL PERFORMANCE

The following financial measures are generally used to evaluate a division's performance.

1. ***Variance Analysis:*** Variance analysis may be (*i*) cost variance analysis and (*ii*) revenue variance analysis. As stated earlier, performance of a cost centre can be evaluated using cost variance analysis, *i.e.*, by comparing the actual costs with the standard costs. Standard

costs display the costs–the cost centre should have incurred, given their actual activity. Any variance between the actual costs and standard costs require corrective action by the management. On measuring the performance (in terms of incurrence of costs) attempts are made to minimise the costs of cost centre.

Measuring the performance of cost centre only in terms of cost incurred without relating to benefits achieved by the centre is not considered fair by many companies. Therefore, most companies use both financial (cost) data and non-financial measures (units produced, number of customers attended, etc.) in performance measurement.

Decoster *et al.*[8] observe:

> It is difficult to assess the effectiveness and efficiency of a cost centre, even with a budget, because the financial impact of decisions is measured only by costs. There is no corresponding financial measure of what the cost centre accomplished. If not done carefully, the analysis of a cost centre may lead to the assumption that the best cost centre is the one that spreads the least. This attitude ignores benefits contributed by the cost centre to the overall firm.

Revenue variance analysis can be used in evaluating the performance of a revenue centre. If actual sales (revenues) are different from budgeted sales, they become the primary focus of management attention. While evaluating the performance of a revenue centre, costs incurred are not used as a yardstick.

2. ***Division Contribution Margin:*** Division contribution margin is defined as:

■■ *the total division revenue less the direct costs of the division.*

This measure of performance emphasises the contribution of each division to overall company profit. In this measure, all revenues and costs traceable to the division are included and all common, indirect costs of the company are excluded. The reason is that operating expenses directly traceable to or incurred for the sole benefit of a specific division are generally subject to the control of the divisional manager. Indirect costs are incurred for the benefit of the entire company and are thus not subject to the control of individual division managers.

The direct contribution margin is the most useful profit measure for comparing divisional performances, for making resource allocation decisions and for overall corporate planning and policy decisions. Top management of the company often use the direct contribution margin to decide in which divisions additional investments should be made and in this decision will surely prefer those divisions which are giving greatest contribution margin.

The contribution margin analysis can also be used to decide the discontinuance of a division or a certain operation. If a specific division or department provides a contribution margin, the division should not be eliminated but retained, although the allocation of indirect costs results in a net loss for that division.

3. ***Division Net Profit:*** The division net profit is the most appropriate profit measure for evaluation of a division's performance. This analysis can be used to judge the performance of a profit centre as both cost and revenue data measured in financial terms are available. Division net profit is obtained after considering related revenues, direct costs and a part of indirect costs incurred for the benefit of the division. Direct costs are easily identified with and traced to the division benefited. Indirect costs like salaries of company executives, officers, office staff, accounts staff are not identifiable with specific division and therefore should be allocated using an equitable and reasonable basis of allocation of indirect costs. There are many methods of cost allocation available and no single method can be considered superior under all circumstances. Hence the determination of divisional profit, that is, its performance, can itself be unreliable if it includes a part of indirect costs.

The division net profit criterion is useful in the sense that a division manager becomes aware of the full costs incurred for the entire company and allocated full costs to the specific division. This may inspire the division manager to take measures to control costs and to improve the profitability of the division.

4. ***Controllable Profit:*** It is claimed that while measuring the performance of a profit division, it is better to use a measure of divisional revenue less divisional costs and a divisional revenue less divisional controllable costs should be used to measure the performance of divisional manager. When fixed costs are considered and allocated to divisions, the resulting direct profit figure is more a measure of the division's performance rather than the divisional manager's performance.

   On the contrary, controllable profit (divisional revenue — divisional controllable costs) is a much better measure of divisional manager's performance as it considers all costs — fixed or variable — which are within his control. The full cost can be suitable to measure a division's performance but not the performance of a divisional manager because then he is held responsible for some costs (allocated fixed costs) which is not controllable by him and which he cannot influence directly or indirectly.

   Roland Fox *et*[9] *al.* observe:

   > If the performance of the manager is being assessed, then it would seem reasonable to base that assessment only on costs and revenues that are controllable by him. Thus, apart from those service costs that are clearly identifiable with the activities of an individual division, the expenses of the central head office should not be included, even if the absence of an administrative centre would cause additional expenses in the division. The vast majority of central expenses are uncontrollable by divisional management and their joint nature makes any allocation arbitrary and unfair. However, if the performance of the division is being evaluated, then it is perfectly reasonable to allocate all the operating expenses of the head office, together with the cost of say short-term financing undertaken by it, although the usual caveats regarding the decision value of such indirect costs should be observed by top management.

5. ***Return on Investment (ROI):*** This measure expresses divisional profit as a percentage of the firm's investment in the division and is similar to the widely accepted 'return on capital employed' measure used in the external analysis and interpretation of accounts. This is calculated as:

$$\text{ROI} = \frac{\text{Divisional Profit}}{\text{Divisional Investment}}$$

$$= \frac{\text{Net Profit}}{\text{Sales}} \times \frac{\text{Sales}}{\text{Investment}}$$

$$\downarrow \qquad \downarrow$$

$$= \text{(Net Profit margin) (Asset Turnover)}$$

The ROI ratio can be divided into other ratios such as net profit margin and the asset turnover as shown above. The net profit margin is the result of firm's pricing policy and its cost control. It is a measure of the relationships among sales, expenses, volume and profit.

The asset turnover shows the amount of sales generated by the assets available and whether a division has over- or under-utilised its assets. Thus, for analysis purposes, the basic formula of ROI is broken down into the product of return on sales and investment turnover and will appear as follows:

$$\text{ROI} = \frac{\text{Divisional Profit}}{\text{Divisional Investment}} = \underbrace{\frac{\text{Divisional Net Profit}}{\text{Divisional Sales}}}_{\text{(Net Profit margin)}} \times \underbrace{\frac{\text{Divisional Sales}}{\text{Divisional Investment}}}_{\text{(Asset Turnover)}}$$

The above formula for computing ROI is also known as DuPont formula. The above expanded version will produce the same ROI because divisional sales cancels out both the denominator in the first factor and the numerator in the second factor. The DuPont formula is useful in evaluating divisions. This is because the profit margin and the investment turnover reflect the following underlying operating relationships of each division:

- Profit margin indicates *operating profitability* by computing the rate of profit earned on each sales Rupee.
- Investment turnover indicates *operating efficiency* by computing the number of sales Rupees generated by each amount of invested assets.

If a division's profit margin increases, and all other factors remain the same, the division's rate of return on investment will increase. For example, a division might add more profitable products to its sales mix and, thus, increase its operating profit, profit margin, and rate of return on investment.

If a division's investment turnover increases, and all other factors remain the same, the division's rate of return on investment will increase. *For example*, a division might attempt to increase sales through special sales promotions and thus increase operating efficiency, investment turnover, and rate of return on investment.

The rate of return on investment, profit margin, and investment turnover operate in relationship to one another. Specifically, more income can be earned by either increasing the investment turnover, increasing the profit margin, or both.

Figure 11.4 traces the origin of du pont formula of ROI.

In the early 1900s, the E.I. Du Pont de Nemours Powder Company was the leading firm manufacturing high explosives and was later to grow into one of the world's largest chemical companies. To control and evaluate its operations, Du Pont managers developed the concept of *return on investment*.

The financial staff traced the cost and revenues for each product produced. This gave management accurate information on profits, which provided a more precise way of evaluating financial performance. However, managers found product-line profits to be an incomplete measure of performance because these did not indicate the rate of return on capital invested. One manager said, "The true test of whether the profit is too great or too small is the rate of return on the money invested in the business and not the per cent of profit on the cost."

Developing a rate of return on each segment of business required accurate data on investment. Du Pont undertook a careful valuation of each of its plants, properties, and inventories by product line. These data, along with profits, allowed management to track ROI by product line. In addition, Du Pont managers decomposed ROI (Profits ÷ Investment) into its component parts to understand the underlying changes in ROI. Figure 11.4 illustrates this decomposition.

ROI is the product of sales turnover (Sales ÷ Total investment) and return on sales (Earnings ÷ Sales). Given these data, managers could detemine the causes of a product's change in ROI. Du Pont managers used these data to evaluate new capital appropriations tby establishing the policy that there "be no expenditures for additions to the earnings equipment if the same amount of money could be applied to some better purpose in another branch of the company's business."

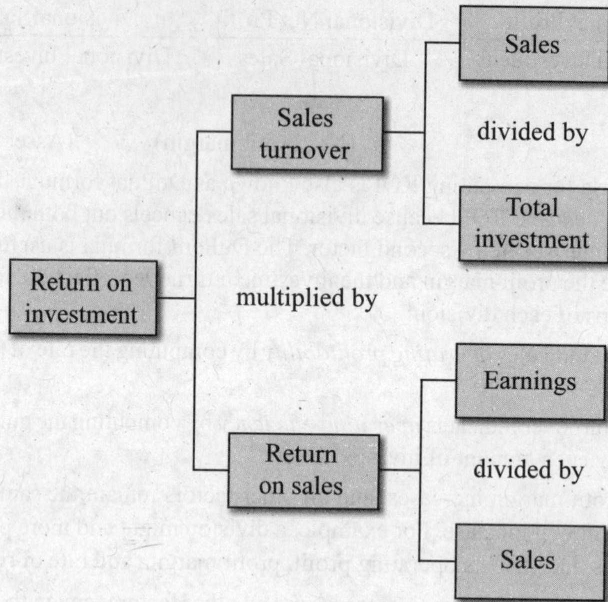

Figure 11.4: Du Pont Company ROI Method

Example:

A merchandising firm sells its goods through department stores and discount houses which it has setup for operating the sales. The ROI of both businesses is 20 per cent and has the following data:

	Department Stores (₹)	***Discount Warehouses*** (₹)
Divisional profit	20,000	32,000
Divisional investment	1,00,000	1,60,000
Divisional sales	2,00,000	4,80,000

Calculation:

Department Stores

$$\text{Overall ROI} = \frac{\text{Divisional Profit}}{\text{Divisional Investment}}$$

$$= \frac{₹\ 20{,}000}{₹\ 1{,}00{,}000}$$

$$= 20\%$$

$$\text{Expanded ROI} = \frac{\text{Divisional Profit}}{\text{Divisional Sales}} \times \frac{\text{Divisional Sales}}{\text{Divisional Investment}}$$

$$= \frac{₹\ 20{,}000}{₹\ 2{,}00{,}000} \times \frac{₹\ 2{,}00{,}000}{₹\ 1{,}00{,}000}$$

$$= 10\ \% \times 2$$

$$= 20\ \%$$

Discount Warehouses

$$\text{Overall ROI} = \frac{\text{Divisional Profit}}{\text{Divisional Investment}}$$

$$= \frac{₹\ 32{,}000}{₹\ 1{,}60{,}000}$$

$$= 20\%$$

$$\text{Expanded ROI} = \frac{\text{Divisional Profit}}{\text{Divisional Sales}} \times \frac{\text{Divisional Sales}}{\text{Divisional Investment}}$$

$$= \frac{₹\ 32{,}000}{₹\ 4{,}80{,}000} \times \frac{₹\ 4{,}80{,}000}{₹\ 1{,}60{,}000}$$

$$= 6.67\% \times 3$$

$$= 20\%$$

It can be observed that the Department Stores earns higher profit per Rupee of sales but only turns over capital (assets) employed only twice. In case of Discount Houses, the sales volume generated is thrice of the assets invested therein and thus capital turnover is 3. However, profit earned per rupee of sales is lower which is only 6.67 % as compared to 10% of Department Stores.

The ROI formula recognises that the absolute size of divisional operating profit alone does not provide a basis for measuring its performance, but rather the relation between the division's net income and the assets used in the generation of that income. For example, the fact that division A has net income of ₹ 50,000 does not necessarily mean that it was more successful than Division B which has profit of ₹ 40,000. The difference between these profit levels could be attributable entirely to a difference in the investment size of divisions. In such a situation, ROI proves to be a good measure of performance of a division. For example, assuming that the investments in Division A and B are ₹ 2,00,000 and ₹ 1,00,000 respectively, the ROI can better indicate their comparative performances.

$$\text{ROI} = \frac{\text{Divisional Profit}}{\text{Divisional Investment}}$$

$$\text{Division A} = \frac{₹\ 50{,}000}{₹\ 2{,}00{,}000} = 25\%$$

$$\text{Division B} = \frac{₹\ 40{,}000}{₹\ 1{,}00{,}000} = 40\%$$

Thus, using ROI it is proved that Division B is more efficient and has made more profit than Division A.

ROI can be increased by any of the following actions, all other factors being held constant:

(1) An increase in sales price or sales volume.

(2) A decrease in operating costs (fixed or variable).

(3) A reduction in divisional investment.

USE OF ROI

For ROI to be useful, income and investment must be determined consistently and fairly:

1. Income and investment must be measured in the same way for each division. For example, all business units must use the same inventory cost flow assumption (FIFO or LIFO) and the same depreciation method.
2. The measurement method must be reasonable and fair for all divisions. For example, if some units have much older assets than other units have, the use of historical cost-based net book value for assets can significantly bias the ROI measures in favor of the older units.[10]

ACCOUNTING POLICIES AND ROI

Accounting policies followed by business firms on measurement of income, valuation of inventory, size of investment influence ROI.

1. ***Income Determination:*** Accounting policies regarding revenue and expense recognition affect net income determination. Recognition of revenues and expenses affect ROI by determining when a sale is recognized as revenue and when an expenditure is recognized as an expense. Any difference in revenue and expense recognition policies of different divisions will result into significant variation in their ROIs due to mere differences in the accounting policies.

   Besides the revenue and expense policies, the income may be affected by other factors as well such as the following:

   (*i*) ***Treatment of Nonrecurring Items:*** Income can be affected by nonrecurring charges or revenues and then would not be comparable to income of prior periods or of other business divisions or units. For example, the high advertisement costs for introducing a new product might significantly distort net income in the period involved.

   (*ii*) ***Income Taxes:*** Income taxes can differentially affect the various units, with the result that after-tax net income may not be comparable. This could be true, for example, if the business units operate in different countries with different tax rates and tax treaties.

   (*iii*) ***Foreign Exchange Rate Fluctuations:*** Business units that operate in foreign countries are subject to foreign exchange rate fluctuations that can affect the income and the value of investments of these units.

   (*iv*) ***Allocation of Common Cost:*** When the different business units share a common facility or cost, such as the personnel department or data processing cost, that common cost is often allocated to the units on some fair-share basis. Different allocation methods result in different costs for each division, and therefore they affect the divisions income.

2. ***Valuation of Inventory:*** There are different methods of inventory valuation such as FIFO, LIFO, Weighted Average Cost etc. Similary for valuation of inventory, absorption costing or variable costing method can be used. Each method produces different figures for cost of goods sold and inventory which, in turn, influences net income and finally ROI of different business units.

3. ***Valuation of Assets or Invested Capital:*** Assets or invested capital determine the size of investment which is used for computing ROI. There can be different concepts of assets such as the following:

   (*i*) *Total Assets:* This includes all assets, tangible assets, intangible assets, fictitious assets.

   (*ii*) *Total Tangible Assets:* This excludes intangible assets, fictitious assets from the total assets.

   (*iii*) *Gross Book Value:* This is the acquisition cost of the assets.

   (*iv*) *Net Book Value:* The net book value is the acquisition cost less accumulated depreciation.

   (*v*) *Total Assets Less Current Liabilities:* This approach encourages investment centre managers to minimize resources tied up in assets and maximize the use of short term credit to finance operation.

   (*vi*) *Current Values:* In some cases, the long-lived assets are a significant portion of total investment because most long-lived assets are stated at historical cost, and the historical cost figures will become irrelevant and misleading in case of price changes.

   If historical cost value is used for investment in ROI, the result is that *ROI can be significantly overstated* relative to ROI determined with the current value of the assets. The consequence is that the use of historical cost ROI can mislead managers, since the inflated ROI figures can create an illusion of profitability. The illusion is removed when the assets are replaced later at their current value, and the amount of income might not have been sufficient to support the replacement of the asset at the current higher value.

(*vii*) *Allocation of shared assets:* When shared facilities, such as a common maintenance facilities are involved, management must determine a fair sharing arrangement. Top management should trace the assets to the business units that used them and allocate the assets that can not be traced on a basis which is as close to actual usage as possible. For example, the investment in a vehicle maintenance facility might be allocated on the basis of the number of vehicles used in each unit or on their total value in each unit.

Alternatively, the required capacity and therefore the investment in the joint facility are sometimes large because the user units require high levels of service at periods of high demand. The assets should be allocated according to the *peak demand* by each individual unit; units with higher peak-load requirements that cause the need for capacity then receive a relatively larger portion of the investment. For example, a computer services department might require a high level of computer capacity because certain users require a large amount of service at certain times.[11]

Besides the above interpretations of assets/investment, depreciation policy and capitalization policy adopted by a firm influence income as well as the size of investment. Larger depreciation amount reduces ROI. Similarly, if an item is expensed, and not capitalized, it will also reduce ROI.

WHICH ASSETS (INVESTMENT) TO USE TO CALCULATE ROI

Generally speaking, for computing ROI, investment is defined in terms of net book value of assets plus working capital. A key principle in deciding the investment for ROI is to know the degree of control, the manager of investment centre has over making investments in assets. For example, investment centre managers many not have control over their divisions' cash balance, debtors, inventory or may control only a fraction of these items. Accordingly, that portion of these items or similar other items should be included in the investment which are within the control of investment centre managers.

Blocher, Chen, Cokins and Lin[12] make the following suggestions on deciding the asset for calculating ROI.

1. Long-lived assets commonly are included in investment if they are traceable to the unit. Management problems arise, however, if the long-lived assets are leased or if some significant portion of them is idle. Leasing requires a clear firmwide policy regarding how to treat leases in determining ROI so that unit managers are properly motivated to lease or not to lease, as is the firm's policy. In general, the leased assets should be included as investments since they represent assets used to generate income, and the failure to include them can cause a significant overstatement of ROI.

2. For idle assets, the main issue is again controllability. If the idle assets have an alternative use or are readily saleable, they should be included in the investment amount for ROI. Also, if top management wants to encourage the divestment of idle assets, including idle assets in ROI would motivate the desired action since divestment would reduce investment and increase ROI. Alternatively, if top management sees a potential strategic advantage to holding the idle assets, excluding idle assets from ROI would provide the most effective motivation since holding idle assets would not reduce ROI.

3. The use of historical costs of assets may produce higher ROI. But replacement cost, if higher than historical cost, will result into lower ROI. A proper strategic approach is to use an investment value in ROI that considers replacing the assets at their current market value so that decisions are made on the basis of the current and future profitability of the firm's products and services, not on the basis of their past profitability alone.

4. In addition to its strategic value, the use of current value helps to reduce the unfairness of historical cost net book value when comparing among busness units with *different aged assets.* Units with older assets under the net book value method have significantly higher ROIs than units with newer assets because of the effect of price changes and of accumulating depreciation over the life of the assets. If the old and new assets are contributing equivalent service, the bias in favor of the unit with older assets is unfair to the manager of a unit with newer assets. The difference is also misleading for strategic decision makers. The use of current values helps to reduce this bias since current values are not affected as strongly by age of assets as are historical cost-based net book values. The use of current values improves the use of ROI both as a measure of the performance of the manager and of the economic performance of the unit itself; current values make the ROI calculation both more relevant and comparable.
5. Grossbook value is preferred by those who value the objectivity of a historical cost number; purchase cost is a reliable, verifiable number. In contrast, replacement cost is preferred when ROI is used to evaluate the manager or the unit as a continuing enterprise because the use of replacement cost is consistent with the idea that the assets will be replaced at the current cost and the business will continue. On the other hand, the liquidation value is most useful when top management is using ROI to evaluate the business unit for potential disposal, and the relevant current cost is the sales value of the assets, or liquidation value.

ADVANTAGES OF ROI

ROI has the following advantages:

1. ***Better Measure of Profitability:*** It relates net income to investments made in a division giving a better measure of divisional profitability. All divisional managers know that their performance will be judged in terms of how they have utilized assets to earn profit, this will encourage them to make optimum use of assets. Also, it ensures that assets are acquired only when they are sure to give returns in consonance with the organisation's policy. Thus, the major focus of ROI is on the required level of investment. For a given business unit at a given point of time, there is an optimum level of investment in each asset that helps maximise earnings. A cost-benefit analysis of this kind helps managers find out the rate of return that can be expected from different investment proposals. This allows them to choose an investment that will enhance both divisional and organisational profit performance as well as enable effective utilisation of existing investments.
2. ***Achieving Goal Congruence:*** ROI ensures goal congruence between the different divisions and the firm. Any increase in divisional ROI will bring improvement in overall ROI of the entire organization.
3. ***Comparative Analysis:*** ROI helps in making comparison between different business units in terms of profitability and asset utilization. It may be used for inter-firm comparisons, provided that the firms whose results are being compared are of comparable size and of the same industry. ROI is a good measure because it can be easily compared with the related cost of capital to decide the selection of investment opportunities.
4. ***Performance of Investment Division:*** ROI is significant in measuring the performance of investment division which focuses on earning maximum profit and making appropriate decisions regarding acquisition and disposal of capital assets. Performance of investment centre manager can also be assessed advantageously with ROI.
5. ***ROI as Indicator of other Performance Ingredients:*** ROI is considered the single most important measure of performance of an investment division and it includes other performance aspects of a business unit. A better ROI means that an investment centre has

satisfactory results in other fields of performance such as cost management, effective asset utilization, selling price strategy, marketing and promotional strategy etc.

6. ***Matching with Accounting Measurements:*** ROI is based on financial accounting measurements accepted in traditional accounting. It does not require a new accounting measurement to generate information for calculating ROI. All the numbers required for calculating ROI are easily available in financial statements prepared in conventional accounting system. Some adjustments in existing accounting numbers may be necessary to compute ROI, but this does not pose any problem in calculating ROI.

DISADVANTAGES OF ROI

ROI has the following limitations:

1. ***Varying Concept of Profit and Investment:*** Satisfactory definition of profit and investment are difficult to find. Profit has many concepts such as profit before interest and tax, profit after interest and tax, controllable profit, profit after deducting all allocated fixed costs. Similarly, the term investment may have many connotations such as gross book value, net book value, historical cost of assets, current cost of assets, assets including or excluding intangible assets.
2. ***Need to use Similar Accounting Policies:*** While comparing ROI of different companies, it is necessary that the companies use similar accounting policies and methods in respect of valuation of stocks, valuation of fixed assets, apportionment of overheads, treatment of research and development expenditure, etc.
3. ***Sub-optimal Decisions by Divisions :*** ROI may influence a divisional manager to select only investments with high rates of return (*i.e.*, rates which are in line or above his target ROI). Other investments that would reduce the division's ROI but could increase the value of the business may be rejected by the divisional manager. It is likely that another division may invest the available funds in a project that might improve its existing ROI (which may be lower than a division's ROI which has rejected the investment) but which will not contribute as much to the enterprise as a whole. These types of decisions are sub-optimal and can distort an enterprise's overall allocation of resources and can motivate a manager to make underinvesting in order to preserve its existing ROI. A good or satisfactory return is defined as an ROI in excess of some minimum desired rate of return, usually based on the firm's cost of capital.

   Business units having higher ROI and some other units having lower ROI are impacted differently by using ROI as investment selection criteria, ROI evaluation provides disincentive to the best division (having higher ROI) to grow, whereas the division with the lowest ROI will have an incentive to invest in new projects to improve their ROI. In this situation, the most profitable units are demotivated to invest in a project that does not exceed their current ROI, although the project would give a good return. This may be in conflict with goal congruence and interests of the firm as a whole.

   Suppose a division's ROI is 25%

   $$\text{ROI} = \frac{\text{Profit ₹ 1,00,000}}{\text{Investment ₹ 4,00,000}} \times 100$$

   Assume, further, there is an opportunity to make additional investment of ₹2,00,000 which will give 20% ROI. This investment is acceptable to the company because the company requires a minimum 15% ROI for this type of investment. This investment lowers the division's ROI to 23.3% calculated as follows:

$$\text{New ROI} = \frac{₹\ 1,00,000 + ₹\ 40,000}{₹\ 4,00,000 + ₹\ 2,00,000} \times 100$$

$$= 23.3\ \%$$

A comparison of old ROI (25%) with the new ROI (23.3%) would imply that performance has declined. Consequently, a divisional manager might decide not to make such an investment.

4. ***Short-term Focus:*** ROI provides focus on short term results and profitability; long term profitability focus is ignored. ROI considers current period's revenue and cost and do not pay attention to those expenditures and investments that will increase long term profitability of a business unit. Based on ROI, the managers tend to avoid the new investments and expenditure due to returns being uncertain or return may not be realized for sometime. Managers using ROI may cut spending on employee training, productivity improvements, advertising, research and development with the narrow objective of improving the current ROI. However, these decisions may impact long term profitability negatively. Therefore, it is advisable for the investment division or business unit to use ROI as only one parameter of an overall evaluation criteria to decide the acceptance/rejection of new investment.
5. ***Managers' Attitude to Influence ROI:*** Investment Centre managers can influence (manipulate) ROI by changing accounting policies, determination of investment size or asset, treatment of certain items as revenue or capital. Sometimes, managers may reduce the investment base by scrapping old machines that still earn a positive return but less than others. Thus, the practice of abandoning old machines that are still serviceable may be used by managers to increase their ROI and a series of such actions may be harmful to the organisation as a whole.
6. ***Residual Income (RI):***

Residual income can be defined as:

- *the net income of a division, less the 'imputed' capital charge on the assets used by the division.*

The capital charge is the minimum acceptable rate of return and is calculated by applying this required (or target) rate of return to the division's investment base. Theoretically, rate of return should be the division's cost of capital; in most cases, however it is a cut-off rate based on the firm's objectives and strategies and will be somewhat higher than the divisional cost of capital. RI is calculated as

RI = Divisional profit – (Per cent capital charge × Divisional Investment)

The 'divisional profit' and 'divisional investment' are as they are defined in ROI. Using the data given in the above example, *i.e.*, divisional profit ₹ 1,00,000, investment ₹ 4,00,000 and further assuming capital charge of 15%, the RI will be ₹ 40,000 calculated as follows:

RI = ₹ 1,00,000 – (15% × ₹ 4,00,000)

= 1,00,000 – 60,000

= ₹ 40,000

Residual income from the additional investment of ₹ 2,00,000 will be

RI = ₹ 40,000 – (15% × ₹ 2,00,000)

= ₹ 10,000

Therefore, after making additional investment, the total residual income of the division will be ₹ 50,000, *i.e.*,

RI = Profits 1,00,000 + 40,000 – (15% × (₹ 4,00,000 + 2,00,000))
= (1,40,000 – 90,000)
= ₹ 50,000

Thus, the additional investment increases residual income, appropriately improving the measure of performance, whereas the use of ROI has worsened the measure of performance as it gives an overall lower ROI.

RI has the following advantages:

1. It avoids suboptimal decisions as investments are not rejected merely because they lower the divisional manger's ROI.
2. It maximizes growth of the company and increases shareholders' wealth by accepting opportunities which earn a rate of return in excess of the cost of capital.
3. The cost of capital charge on divisional investments ensures that divisional managers are aware of the opportunity cost of funds.
4. Charging each division with the company's cost of capital ensures that decisions taken by different divisions are compatible with the interests of the organisation as a whole.

The following are the weaknesses of RI:

1. Like ROI, it is difficult to have satisfactory definition of 'divisional profit' and 'divisional investment.'
2. It may be difficult to calculate an accurate cost of capital. Also decision has to be taken to use company's cost of capital or specific divisional cost of capital. The former enhances divisional goal congruency and the later reflects each division's level of risk.
3. Identifying controllable and uncontrollable factors at divisional level may be difficult.

7. ***Economic Value Added (EVA):*** Economic Value added can be used for evaluating the performance of a division or segment. Economic value added, like residual income, charges an investment centre or division for the cost of their investments in long term assets and working capital. Economic value added is generated only if after-tax operating income exceeds the cost of investing the capital.

The EVA as defined by Stern Stewart & Co. is expressed as follows:

$$\text{Economic Value Added} = \left(\begin{array}{c}\text{Investment}\\ \text{centre's after tax}\\ \text{operating income}\end{array}\right) - \left(\begin{array}{c}\text{Investment}\\ \text{Centre's total}\\ \text{assets}\end{array} - \begin{array}{c}\text{Investment}\\ \text{centre's current}\\ \text{liabilities}\end{array}\right) \times \begin{array}{c}\text{Weighted}\\ \text{average cost}\\ \text{of capital}\end{array}$$

EVA is fairly similar to residual income. One may think of EVA as residual income based on actual weighted average cost of capital rather than on management's required minimum rate of return. Like residual income, the economic value added is expressed in amount. However, it differes from residual income in two important ways. First, an investment centre's current liabilities are subtracted from its total assets. Second, the weighted-average cost of capital is used in the EVA calculation. Why does using the actual weighted-average cost of capital matter? If the required minimum rate of return differs from the weighted average cost of capital, the amount of income required to cover the cost of the investment will also differ.

The weighted-average cost of capital (WACC) is defined as follows:

$$\text{Weighted average cost of capital} = \frac{\left(\begin{array}{c}\text{After tax}\\ \text{cost of debt capital}\end{array}\right)\left(\begin{array}{c}\text{Market value}\\ \text{of debt}\end{array}\right) + \left(\begin{array}{c}\text{Cost of}\\ \text{equity capital}\end{array}\right)\left(\begin{array}{c}\text{Market}\\ \text{value of equity}\end{array}\right)}{\text{Market value of debt} + \text{Market value of equity}}$$

EVA calculation has four steps:

Step 1: Calculating Net Operating Profit

The first step in calculating EVA is to determine the net operating profit, which is operating income minus income taxes. This amount is sometimes referred to as net operating profit after taxes, or NOPAT. One of the goals of EVA is to remove what some people view as income distortions created by the application of Generally Accepted Accounting Principles (GAAP). For example, many companies incur research and development costs to provide an ongoing stream of viable products. GAAP requires that these costs be expensed as they are incurred, even though the research and development effort provides future benefits. EVA adjusts operating income to recognize the future benefits of these costs. Some EVA models make over 150 such adjustments to operating income.

Stern Stewart makes specific adjustments to after-tax operating income and invested capital. These adjustments convert after-tax operating income into a closer approximation of cash income and invested capital into a closer approximation of the cash invested in the economic resources the company uses to create value.

Some of these adjustments include:

1. Focusing on economic substance over legal form in financial reporting of assets *e.g.*, capitalised leases, sale and lease back, factoring of receivables.
2. Capturing goodwill *e.g.*, brand equity, human capital and add back amortised goodwill to after tax operating income.
3. Writing back of provisions for deferred taxes and provision for inventory obsolescence.
4. Capitalise research and development expenses.
5. Use taxes paid rather than tax expense.
6. Use FIFO for inventory valuation.
7. If a company deducts any interest expense in computing operating income, it must add this (after-tax) interest expense to its after-tax operating income.

Step 2: Calculating Invested Capital

The amount of invested capital is the total assets minus current liabilities.

$$\text{Invested capital} = \text{Total assets} - \text{Current liabilities}$$

Why are current liabilities subtracted from total assets? Current liabilities, such as accounts payable, really do not qualify as "invested capital," since the company has received no cash from them. Being allowed to pay a bill 30 or 60 days after the purchase does not require an investment of capital by the creditor.

Some companies make adjustments to invested capital similar to those made to net operating profit. For instance, many companies add the value of "off-balance sheet" assets such as operating leases that carry a long-term commitment. The goal of these adjustments is to determine the most accurate measure possible of invested capital.

Step 3: Calculating the Weighted-Average Cost of Capital

Creditors and investors provide the capital necessary to conduct business and earn a profit. Needless to say, they do not provide their capital for free; they expect to earn a return on their investment. Finance theory says that the rate of return required by creditors is different from the return required by investors. The weighted-average cost of capital (WACC) is the combined rate of return required by all capital providers. The WAAC is calculated for the company as a whole and then used in divisional calculations.

To calculate the weighted-average cost of capital, we need to know the relative percentage of capital provided by each source, as well as the required rate of return.

Step 4: Calculating EVA

Once we have determined the net operating profit, invested capital, and the weighted-average cost of capital, we can calculate EVA as per the following formula:

EVA = Net operating profit – [Invested capital × Weighted average cost of capital]

Positive EVA indicates that a company surpassed the expectations of its shareholders. On the other hand, if the EVA is zero, this should be treated as sufficient achievement because the shareholders have earned a return that compensates the risk. The concept of EVA is based on common accounting items like interest-bearing debt, equity capital and net operating profit. It differs from traditional measures mainly in that it takes into account the cost of equity.

EVA overcomes some of the limitations associated with ROI and other measures of performance. It considers incremental wealth that a particular investment division creates or destroys. EVA provides more useful information to the managers for making correct decisions. Investment centre managers are encouraged to use EVA as a tool of performance measurement to take decisions and formulate strategies that enhances EVA.

To improve EVA, managers must earn more after-tax operating income with the same capital, use less capital to earn the same after-tax operating income, or invest capital in high-return projects. Divisional managers find EVA particularly helpful because it allows them to incorporate the cost of capital which is generally only available at the company wide level, into decisions at the division level. Comparing the actual EVA achieved to the projected EVA is useful for evaluating performance and providing feedback. If EVA is positive, the company is creating wealth. If it is negative, then the company is destroying capital. In the long run, only those companies creating capital or wealth can survive.

How to Increase EVA

EVA can be enhanced through taking the following measures:

1. Increasing operating profits without adding further capital in the business.
2. Ensuring that ROI on additional funds invested is more than weighted average cost of capital.
3. Liquidating non-productive capital by releasing capital from those activities that do not cover even the cost of capital.

Joel Stern[13], originator of EVA observes:

> If the increasingly competitive business environment warrants consistently outperforming your peers, adopting the EVA framework is the way to go. EVA is a corporate performance measure that aligns employment incentives with shareholder interests. It is based on measuring economic profits as opposed to accounting profits. EVA requires alignment of the entire organisation, right from board to shop floor, with a mindset focused on creating wealth. EVA can be enhanced by either of two measures. You can grow the business and thereby increase net assets, or manage the existing capital and try to improve the rate of return on net assets. Employees behave like owners because the key to ownership is having significant money at risk — in this compensation — and act as value — change agents.

Table 11.1 gives a summary of different financial measures for divisional performance evaluation.

Table 11.1: Examples of Responsibility Centres and Performance Measures

Responsibility Centres	*Examples*	*Performance Measures Used*
Cost centres	Manufacturing departments Service production departments, such as road maintenance for a city Support department, such as accounting and billing departments in a hospital Discretionary cost centres, such as marketing and research and development	Cost budgets and variances Comparisons to benchmark cost per unit or service Efficiency measures (days to close, number of new products) Industry benchmarks (*e.g.* R&D as a percentage of sales)
Revenue centres	Travel agencies Sales departments for manufactures	Revenue budgets and variances Growth in revenues Customer satisfaction
Profit centres	Retail sales outlets for clothing, books, or restaurants Corporate divisions and departments responsible for revenues and costs	Revenue and cost budgets and variances Accounting earnings such as operating income, or earnings before or after taxes
Investment centres	Corporate divisions and business segments responsible for investment decisions	Return on investment (ROI) Residual income Economic value added (EVA)

Example:

Videocon reported the following information for the year just ended:

	Segment A	Segment B	Segment C
Pre-tax operating income	₹ 40,00,000	₹ 20,00,000	₹ 30,00,000
Current assets	40,00,000	30,00,000	40,00,000
Long-term assets	1,60,00,000	1,30,00,000	80,00,000
Current liabilities	20,00,000	10,00,000	15,00,000

If the applicable income tax rate and after-tax weighted average cost of capital for each segment are 30% and 10%, respectively, the segment with the highest economic value added (EVA) is

(*a*) Segment A.

(*b*) Segment B.

(*c*) Segment C.

(*d*) Not determinable from this information.

Solution: The correct answer is (C)

EVA equals after-tax operating income minus the product of the after-tax weighted-average cost of capital and an investment base equal to total assets minus current liabilities. Thus, the EVA for Segment C is ₹10,50,000 {30,00,000 × (1.0 – .3)} – {.10 × (₹ 40,00,000 + 80,00,000 – 15,00,000)}.

Answer (a) is incorrect because the EVA for Segment A is ₹ 10,00,000.

Answer (b) is incorrect because the EVA for Segment B is minus ₹ 1,00,000.

Answer (d) is incorrect because the EVAs are determinable.

NON-FINANCIAL MEASURES OF PERFORMANCE

ROI and RI both are recognised as important measures for evaluating the performance of a division. However, these and other financial measures are not considered fully adequate to evaluate the performance of a responsibility centre. Also, these techniques are short-term measures and division managers may be tempted, therefore, to derive short-term benefits (through using these measures) at the expense of long-term benefit of the company. Hence, it has been argued that additional non-financial measures should be used to evaluate a division's performance besides using ROI and RI techniques.

A nonfinancial performance measure expresses performance in a measure other than money. For example, airlines use on-time performance, per cent of bags lost, and number of customer complaints as nonfinancial performance measures. Such measures are often used to evaluate the time, quality or quantity of a business activity.

Johnson and Kaplan[14] have emphasised the importance of non-financial measures and comment in the following manner:

"More important than attempting to measure monthly or quarterly profits is measuring and reporting a variety of non-financial indicators. The indicators should be based on the company's strategy and include key measures of manufacturing, marketing and R and D systems. For example, a company emphasising quality could measure internal failure indicators – scrap, network, part-per-million defect rates, unscheduled machine down-time and external failure indicators – customer complaints, warranty expenses and service calls. Rather than attempting to extract such information from a system designed primarily to satisfy external reporting and auditing requirements, we should design systems consistent with the technology of the organisation, its product strategy and its organisation structure."

Colin Drury[15] also advises considering other measures of performance in the following words:

> ROI and Residual income cannot stand alone as a measure of divisional performance. Short-run profitability is only one of the factors contributing to a company's long-run objectives. Return on investment and residual income are short-run concepts that deal only with the past year, whereas managerial performance measures should focus on future results that can be expected because of present actions. Divisional performance measurement should also measure those other factors that are critical to the success of the organisation. In particular, the performance measure should support the corporate objectives and the competitive strategies of the organisation.

Non-financial measures are often linked to either the inputs or outputs of an activity or process. A process is a sequence of activities for performing a task. To illustrate, the counter sevice activity of a fast-food restaurant such as McDonald is used. The following inputs/outputs could be identified for providing customer service:

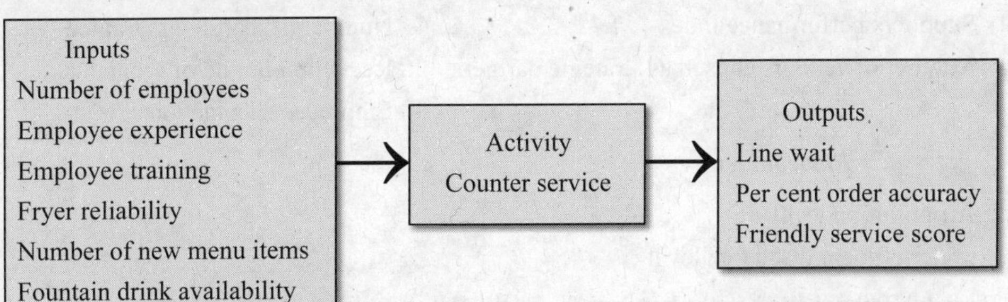

The customer service outputs of the counter service activity include the following:

1. Line wait for the customer
2. Per cent order accuracy in serving the customer
3. Friendly service experience for the custormer

Some of the inputs that impact the customer service outputs include the following:

1. Number of employees
2. Employee experience
3. Employee training
4. Fryer (and other cooking equipment) reliability
5. Number of new menu items
6. Fountain drink availability

A fast-food restaurant can develop a set of linked nonfinancial performance measures across inputs and outputs. The output measures tell management how the activity is performing, such as keeping the line wait to a minimum. The input measures are used to improve the output measures. For example, if the customer line wait is too long, then improving employee training or hiring more employees could improve the output (decrease customer line wait).

The additional non-financial measures or multiple measures of performance are market share, customers' complaints, personnel turnover ratios, personnel training and development, product or service quality, delivery reliability, minimisation of wastages and losses etc. A brief list of non-financial measures of performance is given in Table 11.2.

Table 11.2: Non-finance Measures of Performance

Customers	***Operations***
1. Customer retention ratio	1. Number of new products introduced
2. Customer satisfaction index	2. Time to develop new products
3. Percentage of delivery compliance on time	3. Reduction in operation cycle time
4. Number of customer complaints	4. Turnover per rupee of wage
5. Average time for complaint resolution	5. Productivity
6. Time between a customer order and product delivery	6. Scrap feed per production run
7. Customer preference ranking	7. Overtime
	8. Throughput time
	9. Inventory turnover
Suppliers	***HR and Safety***
1. Suppliers performance index	1. Number of man-hours trained
2. Number of vendors chosen as strategic partners	2. Reduction in rate of accidents.
	3. Employee satisfaction
Environment	
1. Air pollution level	
2. Water effluent discharge level	

Barfield, Raiborn and Kinney have suggested the following important non-monetary information to be given in responsibility reports.

- Departmental/divisional throughput
- Number of defects (by product, product line, supplier)

- Number of orders backlogged (by date, quantity, cost and selling price)
- Number of customer complaints (by type and product); method of complaint resolution
- Percentage of orders delivered on time
- Manufacturing (or service) cycle efficiency
- Percentage of reduction of non-value-added time from previous reporting period (broken down by idle time, storage time, move time, and quality control time)
- Number and percentage of employee suggestions considered significant and practical
- Number and percentage of employee suggestions implemented
- Number of unplanned production interruptions
- Number of schedule changes
- Number of engineering change orders; percentage change from previous period
- Number of safety violations; percentage change from previous period
- Number of days of employee absences; percentage change from previous period

Source: Jesset T. Barfield, Cecily A. Raiborn and Michael R. Kinney, Cost Accounting, Traditions and Innovations, Thomson, 2003, p. 800

The non-financial measures are vital to the success of a division and also to the overall success of a firm. Also, financial and non-financial goals and targets are often included as a part of a divisional manager's plan and responsibility. By informing the lower-level managers about the significance of non-financial measures and goals, and long-run factors as well, top management can duly minimise the tendency to overemphasise ROI and RI. It is rightly claimed that any financial measures like ROI and RI have drawbacks while evaluating divisional performance, since it is virtually impossible to capture in one financial measure all the variables that measure the success of a division. For example, two divisional managers having equal amounts of investments in their respective divisions, may also have similar ROI and RI. However, this does not surely mean that their performances are also equal. For example, one division might have provided excellent customer service and thereby has created customer goodwill and reputation for the company. The other division might have done very poorly in the area of customer service. Likewise, a specific division may have invested on providing training, education, job enrichment and development, whereas some other division might have totally neglected these activities. Obviously, difference in the different divisions on account of non-performance of these and similar activities will not enter into ROI and RI calculated for different divisions.

Use of Multiple Measures

A progessively designed performance measurement system should encompass various types of measures, especially those that track factors considered necessary for world-class status. The "performance pyramid" (Exhibit 11.5) summarizes the types of measures needed at different organizational levels and for different purposes. Within the pyramid are measures that consider both long-term and short-term organizational objectives. These measures can be financial and nonfinancial.

Although internal measures of performance are used, the true measure of performance is judged by a company's customers. Good performance is typically defined as providing a product or service that equals or exceeds a customer's quality, price, and delivery expectations. Such a definition of good performance is totally unrelated to internal measurements such as standerd cost variances or capacity utilization. Thus, nonfinancial measures that detect the degree to which customer desires are being met are becoming more important. Companies that cannot meet quality, price, and delivery expectations will find themselves without customers and without any need for financial measures of performance[16].

Exhibit 11.5: The Performance Pyramid

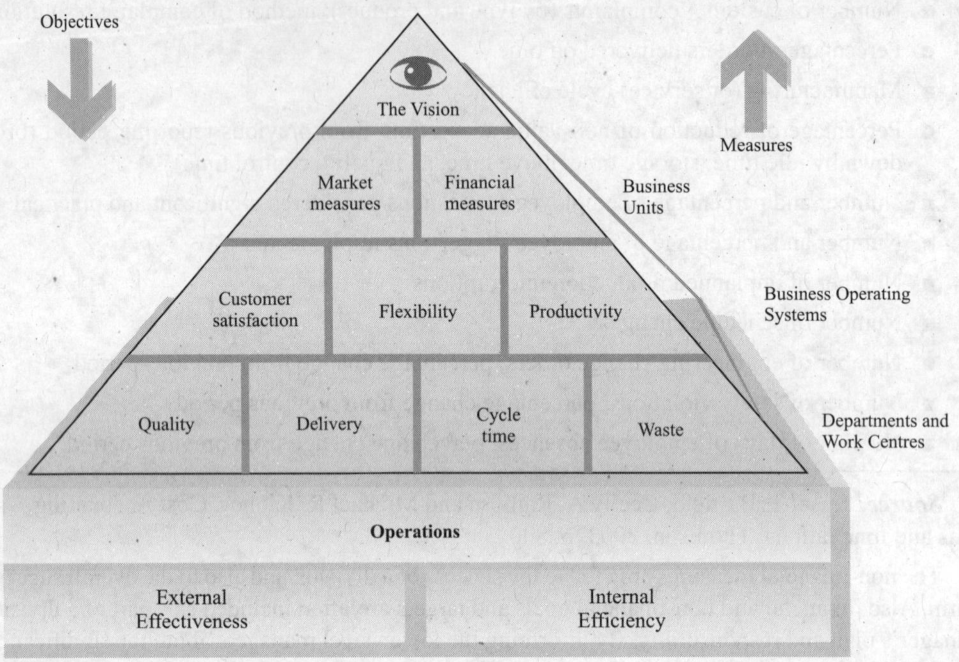

Source: C.J. McNair, Richard L. Lynch and Kelvin F. Cross, "Do Financial and Nonfinancial Measures of Perfomance Have to Agree?" Management Accounting (November 1990). Institute of Management Accountants, Montvale, N.J., USA., p.30

EVALUATING A DIVISION VS EVALUATING A DIVISION'S MANAGER

Most often a distinction is (or should be) made while measuring the performance of a division and that of evaluating a division manager's performance while using ROI and RI tools. It is said that it is advisable to discriminate between the measure of a division's performance and that of a division's manager. ROI and RI give clues to where an organisation might be wise to increase, maintain or reduce investment and other things being equal, higher ROI and RI are desirable. However, for evaluating the managers of divisions, both ROI and RI have drawbacks, depending on how the results for a division are interpreted. Many a times managers are found performing well despite the poor performance by the division (as per its ROI and RI) due to factors outside the manager's control. Thus, the evaluation of a manager is not necessarily identical to the evaluation of the cost, revenue, profit or investment division.

The vital issue in the subject of evaluation — division or manager — is the standard or norms which should be used for comparison. There are several bases which can be used for comparison and evaluation such as:

- Comparison with budgets and targets
- Comparison among different divisions within the firm
- Comparison with historical results
- Comparison with industry averages

1. ***Comparison with Budgets and Targets:*** Budgets and targets are useful tools for assessing the performance of division managers when managers participate and commit themselves to

meeting budgeted goals or targets. Comparison of actual and budgeted results are considered the best possible comparison for judging a manager's performance. If the manager meets or exceeds his targets or budgets, he would be rewarded. However, it may be that even with the best management, a division can not be turned around. Thus, it is entirely possible that the division or the centre would be disbanded even though the manager had received a highly positive evaluation.

It is conceivable that there would be conflicts in the outcomes of an evaluation based on targeted performance with the results of an evaluation based on opportunity costs. This merely implies that the objectives for evaluating managers are different from the objectives of evaluating a division. Top management would like to reward the manager that performs well in an adverse situation but, conversely, should be willing to bail out of a bad operation if better use can be made of company resources.[17]

2. ***Comparison Among Different Divisions within the Firm:*** Comparison among different divisions within a business enterprise can be made and subsequently divisions can be ranked in terms of relative profitability. The ranking given to divisions will highlight the relative contributions of the different divisions. However, such a ranking should not be used to decide the ranking of the managers of different divisions, because different divisions should be expected to have different ROIs. For example, ROI is generally higher for units (divisions or firms) operating in consumer markets than for those selling mostly to other industrial firms. Both ROI and RI should be higher for divisions taking on higher risks. The performance of a particular division manager must not be obscured by intra-firm comparisons that ignore the nature of the divisions. A mediocre manager might be able to earn a respectable ROI in a division operating in a growing industry. On the other hand, an excellent manager might be doing a great job to maintain an ROI of 5% in a division operating in a declining industry.[18]
3. ***Comparison with Historical Results:*** Comparing current performances of a division with the historical (or previous) performances of the same division is a preferable evaluative tool. This comparison removes the weaknesses which are found from comparing divisions in different industries. Historical comparisons will show relative improvement or poor results. However, comparison of the current results with the previous results should be used with precaution for evaluating a manager's performance. The reason is that measurement of a division's performance may be subject to accounting measurements, policies, and methods which may influence the profit measurement during different periods of time. It is difficult to say, therefore, whether historical results are good or bad.
4. ***Comparison with Industry Averages:*** Comparing divisional results with industry averages can be useful because differences among divisions resulting from differences in industry do not influence the comparison. A division (and its manager) can be seen as better or worse than the firms with which it competes. Such comparisons present their own problems, however, because a division should be expected to earn a higher ROI than an entire firm operating in the same industry. A division benefits from being part of a larger organisation. As the trend to diversification continues, it becomes increasingly difficult to find companies to which the performance of a single division can be compared.[19]

Maciariello[20] makes the following significant observations on the question of evaluating a divisional manager's performance:

1. Often it is argued that the division or manager being evaluated should only be held accountable for those items that can be controlled by the manager or the centre. Thus, if central management decides that a particular operating division will sell a given number

of units of output at a given price, the division manager has no control over that decision, and hence should not be evaluated based on the results of operations as that decision affects the results. The various operating divisions and managers would probably best be evaluated by comparing actual costs with budgeted costs and not evaluated on some measure of divisional profits. In other words, the managers and divisions would be evaluated based on the factors that they can control, namely, costs.

2. An interesting problem arises in implementing this concept in an ongoing problem, *e.g.*, how to evaluate the performance of a manager who takes over an existing division where the assets, operating structure, and markets are established prior to the manager's arrival at the helm. The new manager can not control the facts before he joins the organisation. The new manager can be evaluated on the basis of results of his own plan and targets that he sets and works for their achievements. In short, the longer the manager is at the division, the more responsibility the manager takes for the success of the division.

PERFORMANCE MEASUREMENT IN MULTINATIONAL COMPANIES

A multinational company is one that does business in more than one country in such a volume that its well-being and growth rest in more than one country. Multinational companies may be either (*i*) a large decentralised firm having a corporate head office and many divisions or (*ii*) a parent company and a number of subsidiaries.

There are some additional problems[21] in measuring and comparing the performance of divisions of a multinational company, such as the following:

1. Economic, legal, political, social and cultural environments differ significantly across countries.
2. Governments in some countries may impose controls and limit selling prices of a company's product. For example, some developing countries impose tarifts and custom duties to restrict the import of certain goods.
3. Availability of materials and skilled labour as well as costs of materials, labour and infrastructure (power, transportation and communication) may also differ significantly across countries.
4. Divisions operating in different countries keep score of their performance in different currencies. Issues of inflation and fluctuations in foreign currency exchange rates affect performance measures greatly.

With respect to evaluation, multinational companies should take into account changes in exchange rates, which are the relationships of foreign currencies to domestic currency. One problem for performance evaluation is that the local — the one in a foreign country does business in the foreign currency, but the multinational cares about the results in its home currency (say Rupees for Indian multinationals). The trouble is that the local manager and the division can look good or bad in foreign currency (say dollar or pound) simply because of changes in exchange rates, even though he or she is not responsible for exchange rate fluctuations.

Suppose, an Indian multinational has a division in USA and income statement of the division for July 2016 is as follows:

Sales	\$. 3,00,000
Expenses	\$. 2,00,000
Income	\$. 1,00,000

If dollar is worth ₹ 60, the division would show income of ₹ 60,00,000 for the month of July 2016. But suppose next month the division does exactly the same business and has the same income statement but the value of dollar increases to ₹ 70. Then the division shows ₹ 70,00,000, a 16.66% increase from the last month even though it did the same business. Alternatively, if the value of dollar drops to ₹55, then the division would show income of ₹ 55,00,000 a 8.33% drop from last month although it did the same business. Evaluating the manager's (or the division's) performance in terms of reports using home currency gives undue credit to him when the exchange rate rises and penalises him for a decline in the exchange rate.

The issue of restating foreign divisions income and / or subsidiaries income into home currency also affects the preparation of financial statements. This restatement can result in gain and loss opportunities on the revaluation of foreign currencies and can impact a subsidiary's financial statements and the related ROI and residual income measures. The potential for gain or loss on currency revaluation is particularly relevant for countries whose currencies are volatile - and depreciating vis-a-vis the home country's currency.

Activity-Based Responsibility Accounting

Responsibility accounting systems under the traditional accounting attempt to measure financial performance of different responsibility centres such as expense, revenue, profit. Activity-based costing/management (ABC/M) measures costs incurred on activities that are responsible for the incurrence of costs. Therefore, under ABC/M, responsibility accounting systems are activity-based, Under this approach, management considers not only the costs but activities as well. Responsibility-based accounting systems helps managers in many decisions such as which activities add value to the product or service of the firm? Which activities do not add value and therefore not necessary? What improvements can be made in the activities being performed? How costs of activities can be made effective and optimal? In this way, activity-based responsibility accounting makes activity analysis, separates value added and non-value added activities, eliminates non-value added activities and manages both the costs and activities.

Illustrative Problem 3

A bank considers acquiring new computer equipment. The computer will cost ₹ 160,000 and result in a cash savings of ₹ 70,000 per year (excluding depreciation) for each of the five years of the asset's life. It will have no salvage value after five years. Assume straight-line depreciation (depreciation expensed evenly over the life of the asset). The company's tax rate is 15 per cent, and there are no current liabilities associated with this investment.

Required:

(*a*) What is the ROI for each year of the asset's life if the division uses beginning-of-year net book value asset balances for the computation?

(*b*) What is the economic value added each year if the weighted-average cost of capital is 25 percent?

Solution:

$$\text{Annual Income} = ₹\ 70,000 - \frac{₹\ 1,60,000}{5\ \text{Years}} = ₹\ 38,000$$

Year	Investment Base	a. ROI ₹ 38,000 ÷ Base	b. EVA [₹ 38,000 × (1 – .15)] – [(Base – ₹ 0) × .25]
1	₹ 1,60,000	23.8%	(₹ 7,700)
2	1,28,000	29.7%	300
3	96,000	39.6%	8,300
4	64,000	59.4%	16,300
5	32,000	118.8%	24,300

Note: Base decreases by annual depreciation of ₹ 32,000.

Illustrative Problem 4

Indigo Airlines, has two divisions organized as profit centres, the Passenger Division and the Cargo Division. The following divisional income statements were prepared:

Divisional Income Statements For the Year Ended June 30, 2016

	Passenger Division		*Cargo Division*	
Revenues		₹ 14,00,000		₹ 14,00,000
Operating expenses		9,50,000		12,00,000
Income from operations before service department charge:		₹ 4,50,000		₹ 2,00,000
Less service department charges:				
Training	₹ 80,000		₹ 80,000	
Flight scheduling	75,000		75,000	
Reservations	1,05,000	2,60,000	105,000	2,60,000
Income from operations		₹ 1,90,000		₹ (60,000)

The service department charge rate for the service department costs was based on revenues. Since the revenues of the two divisons were the same, the service department charges to each division were also the same.

The following additional information is available:

	Passenger Division	*Cargo Division*	*Total*
Number of personnel trained	200	50	250
Number of flights	250	350	600
Number of reservations requested	14,000	0	14,000

Required:

(*a*) Does the income from operations for the two divisions accurately measure performance?

(*b*) Correct the divisional income statements, using the activity bases provided above in revising the service department charges.

Solution:

(a) The reported income from operations does not accurately measure performance because the service department charges are based on revenues. Revenues are not associated with the profit centre manager's use of the service department services. For example, the Reservations Department serves only the Passenger Division. Thus, by charging this cost on the basis of revenues, these costs are incorrectly charged to the Cargo Division. Additionally, the Passenger Division requires personnel. Since these personnel must be trained, the training costs assigned to the Passenger Division should be greater than the Cargo Division.

(*b*)

Indigo Airlines,
Divisional Income Statements for the Year Ended June 30, 2016

	Passenger Division		*Cargo Division*	
Revenues		₹ 14,00,000		₹ 14,00,000
Operating expenses		9,50,000		12,00,000
Income from operations before service department charges		₹ 4,50,000		₹ 2,00,000
Less service department charges:				
Training (Note 1)	₹ 1,28,000		₹ 32,000	
Flight scheduling (Note 2)	62,500		87,500	
Reservations (Note 3)	2,10,000	4,00,500	—	1,19,500
Income from operations		₹ 49,500		₹ 80,500

Note 1: Passenger Division, (₹ 1,60,000/250 personnel trained) × 200
Cargo Division, (₹ 1,60,000/250 personnel trained) × 50

Note 2: Passenger Division, (₹ 1,50,000/600 flights) × 250
Cargo Division, (₹ 1,50,000/600 flights) × 350

Note 3: Passenger Division, (₹ 2,10,000/14,000 reservations) × 14,000
Cargo Division, (₹ 2,10,000/14,000 reservations) × 0

Illustrative Problem 5

Indian Coffee House operates coffeehouses on university campuses in three districts. The operating performance for each district follows.

	District		
	Delhi	*Mumbai*	*Pune*
Sales	₹ 19,00,000	₹ 85,00,000	₹ 1,00,00,000
Operating Profit	2,00,000	5,00,000	10,00,000
Investment	20,00,000	62,50,000	80,00,000

Required:

(*a*) Using the operating profit margin percentage as the criterion, which is the most profitable district?

(*b*) Using the rate of return on investment as the criterion, which is the most profitable district?

(*c*) Which of the two measures better indicates operating performance? Explain your reasoning.

Solution:

The return on investment (ROI), profit margin percentage, and asset turnover ratio of the three divisions are as follows. All amounts are in thousands of Rupees (000 omitted).

	Return on Investment	=	Profit Margin Percentage	×	Asset Turnover Ratio
Delhi District:	₹ 200/₹ 2,000	=	₹ 200/₹ 1,900	×	₹ 1,900/₹ 2,000
	10%	=	10.53%	×	.95
Mumbai District:	₹ 500/₹ 6,250	=	₹ 500/₹ 8,500	×	₹ 8,500/₹ 6,250
	8%	=	5.88%	×	1.36
Pune District:	₹ 1,000/₹ 8,000	=	₹ 1,000/₹ 10,000	×	₹ 10,000/₹ 8,000
	12.5%	=	10%	×	1.25

(*a*) Using the profit margin percentage, the ranking of the districts is Delhi, Pune, Mumbai.

(*b*) Using ROI, the ranking of districts is Pune, Delhi, and then Mumbai.

(*c*) The ROI is a better measure of overall performance because it relates profits to the investment, or capital, required to generate those profits. Delhi had the largest profit margin percentage. However, it required more capital to generate sales than did Pune. Thus, its overall profitability is less. Note that Mumbai had the largest asset turnover ratio. However, it generated the smallest amount of operating profit per Rupee of sales, resulting in the lowest ROI of the three districts.

Illustrative Problem 6

Division A and B are both considering an outlay on new investment projects.

	Division A	*Division B*
Investment outlay	₹ 1,00,000	₹ 1,00,000
Net return on the new investment	₹ 16,000	₹ 11,000
Current ROI	18%	11%

The company's cost of capital is 13%. Should the project be accepted or rejected?

Solution:

(*i*) Using ROI

$$\text{ROI on New investment} = \frac{\text{Net Return}}{\text{New investment}}$$

$$\text{Division A} = \frac{₹\ 16{,}000}{₹\ 1{,}00{,}000} \times 100 = 16\%$$

$$\text{Division B} = \frac{₹\ 11{,}000}{₹\ 1{,}00{,}000} \times 100 = 11\%$$

Division A should reject the new investment as its ROI is 16% which is less than the current ROI of 18%. Division B can accept the investment as its current ROI of 11% is equal to new ROI on new investments.

(ii) **Using RI**	***Division A***	***Division B***
Investment	₹ 1,00,000	₹ 1,00,000
Net Income on new Investment	16,000	11,000
Less: Imputed Cost of capital 13%	13,000	13,000
Residual Income	3,000	(2,000)

Division A should accept the investment as it will make RI of ₹ 3,000 and Division B should reject it because it will give a loss of ₹ 2,000.

Illustrative Problem 7

The following information relates to budgeted operation of Division X of a manufacturing company.

	(₹)
Sales: (50,000 units of ₹ 8)	4,00,000
Less: Variable costs @ ₹ 6 per unit	3,00,000
Contribution margin	1,00,000
Less: Fixed costs	75,000
Divisional profit	25,000

The amount of divisional investment is ₹ 1,50,000 and the minimum desired rate of return on the investment is the cost of capital of 20%.

Required:

(*i*) Calculate divisional expected ROI

(*ii*) Calculate divisional expected RI

(*iii*) Comment on the results of (i) and (ii)

(*iv*) The divisional manager has the opportunity to sell 10,000 units at ₹ 7.50 per unit. Variable cost per unit would be the same as budgeted, but fixed costs would increase by ₹ 5,000. Additional investment of ₹ 20,000 would also be required. If the manager accepts the special order, by how much and in what direction would his residual income change?

Solution:

(*i*) $$\text{ROI} = \frac{₹\ 25{,}000}{₹\ 1{,}50{,}000} \times 100\% = 16.7\ \%$$

(*ii*) $$\begin{aligned}\text{RI} &= \text{Divisional profit} - \text{Minimum desired rate of return}\\ &= ₹\ 25{,}000 - (20\% \times ₹\ 1{,}50{,}000)\\ &= 25{,}000 - 30{,}000\\ \text{RI} &= (₹\ 5000)\end{aligned}$$

(*iii*) The desired rate of return is 20% but the division X is expecting to achieve an ROI of 16.7%. The expected profit of ₹ 25,000 is less than the ₹ 30,000 minimum return required, resulting in the negative of ₹ 5,000 residual income.

(*iv*) Opportunity to sell additional 10,000 unit

	Original budget ₹	*Additional budget* ₹	*Total* ₹
Sales	4,00,000	75,000	4,75,000
Less: Variable cost	3,00,000	60,000	3,60,000
Contribution	1,00,000	15,000	1,15,000
Less: Fixed costs	75,000	5,000	80,000
Divisional profit	25,000	10,000	35,000
Less: Cost of capital (20%)	30,000	4,000	34,000
Residual Income	(5000)	6000	1000

The target residual income changes from a negative balance of ₹ 5,000 to a positive one of ₹ 1,000 as a result of the new opportunity to sell 10,000 units. This is due to the fact that ₹ 10,000 expected profit from additional order is offset by a further ₹ 4,000 cost of capital, thereby increasing residual income by ₹ 6,000.

Illustrative Problem 8

The vice president of operations of Ranbaxy Co. is evaluating the performance of two divisions organized as investment centres. Invested assets and condensed income statement data for the past year for each division are as follows:

	Network Equipment Division	*Personal Computing Division*
Sales	₹ 14,00,000	₹ 11,20,000
Cost of goods sold	8,45,000	6,90,000
Operating expenses	3,45,000	2,06,000
Invested assets	10,00,000	14,00,000

Required:

1. Prepare condensed divisional income statements for the year ended December 31, 2016, assuming that there were no service departmen charges.
2. Using the DuPont formula for rate of return on investment, determine the profit margin, investment turnover, and rate of return on investment for each division.
3. If management's minimum acceptable rate of return is 14%, determine the residual income for each division.
4. Discuss the evaluation of the two divisions, using the performance measures determined in parts (1), (2) and (3).

Solution :

1.

Ranbaxy Co.
Divisional Income Statements
For the Year Ended December 31, 2016

	Network Equipment Division	Personal Computing Division
Sales	₹ 14,00,000	₹ 11,20,000
Cost of goods sold	8,45,000	6,90,000
Gross profit	₹ 5,55,000	₹ 4,30,000
Operating expenses	3,45,000	2,06,000
Income from operations	₹ 2,10,000	₹ 2,24,000

2. Rate of Return on Investment = Profit Margin × Investment Turnover

$$\text{Rate of Return on Investment} = \frac{\text{Income from Operations}}{\text{Sales}} \times \frac{\text{Sales}}{\text{Invested Assets}}$$

$$\text{Network Equipment Division: ROI} = \frac{₹2,10,000}{₹14,00,000} \times \frac{₹14,00,000}{₹10,00,000}$$

$$\text{ROI} = 15\% \times 1.4$$

$$\text{ROI} = 21\%$$

$$\text{Personal Computing Division: ROI} = \frac{₹224,000}{₹11,20,000} \times \frac{₹1,120,000}{₹14,00,000}$$

$$\text{ROI} = 20\% \times 0.8$$

$$\text{ROI} = 16\%$$

3. Network Equipment Division: ₹ 70,000 [₹ 2,10,000 – (₹ 10,00,000 × 14%)]
   Personal Computing Division: ₹ 28,000 [₹ 2,24,000 – (₹ 14,00,000 × 14%)]

4. On the basis of income from operations, the Personal Computing Division generated ₹ 14,000 more income from operations than did the Network Equipment Division. However, income from operations does not consider the amount of invested assets in each division. On the basis of the rate of return on investment, the Network Equipment Division earned 21% on invested assets, while the Personal Computing Division earned only 16% on invested assets. Although the Personal Computing Division has a higher profit margin than the Network Equipment Division (20% vs. 15%), the Network Equipment Division has a higher investment turnover (1.4 vs. 0.8), which generated its higher rate of return on investment. Residual income can be viewed as a combination of the preceding two performance measures. Residual invome considers the absolute amount of income from operations generated by each division and also considers a minimum rate of return to be earned by each division. On the basis of residual income, the Network Equipment Division is the more profitable of the two divisions.

Illustrative Problem 9

Mumbai Sporting Goods Co. operates two divisions—the Action Sports Division and the Team Sports Division. The following income and expense accounts were provided from the trial balance as of June 30, 2016, the end of the current fiscal year, after all adjustments, including those for inventories, were recorded and posted:

Sales—Action Sports (AS) Divison	₹ 1,45,00,000
Sales—Team Sports (TS) Division	1,76,00,000
Cost of Goods Sold—Action Sports (AS) Division	87,00,000
Cost of Goods Sold—Team Sports (TS) Division	1,02,08,000
Sales Expense—Action Sports (TS) Division	23,20,000
Sales Expense—Team Sports (TS) Division	24,64,000
Administrative Expense—Action Sports (AS) Division	14,50,000
Administrative Expense—Team Sports (TS) Division	15,66,400
Advertising Expense	₹ 6,42,000
Transportation Expense	3,14,960
Accounts Receivable Collection Expense	2,01,750
Warehouse Expense	16,00,000

The bases to be used in allocating expenses, together with other essential information, are as follows:

a. Advertising expense—incurred at headquarters, charged back to divisions on the basis of usage: Action Sports Division, ₹ 256,800; Team Sports Division, ₹ 385,200.

b. Transportation expense—charged back to divisions at a charge rate of ₹ 12.40 per bill of lading: Action Sports Division, 12,000 bills of lading; Team Sports Division, 13,400 bills of lading.

c. Accounts receivable collection expense—incurred at headquarters, charged back to divisions at a charge rate of ₹ 7.50 per invoice: Action Sports Division, 12,400 sales invoices; Team Sports Division, 14,500 sales invoices.

d. Warehouse expense—charged back to divisions on the basis of floor space used in storing division products: Action Sports Division, 120,000 square feet; Team Sports Division, 80,000 square feet.

Required:

Prepare a divisional income statement: Action Sports Division and Team Sports Division. Provide supporting schedules for determining service department charges.

Solution:

Mumbai Sporting Goods Co.

Divisional Income Statements for the Year Ended June 30, 2016

	Action Sports Division	Team Sports Division
Sales	₹ 1,45,00,000	₹ 1,76,00,000
Cost of goods sold	87,00,000	1,02,08,000
Gross profit	₹ 58,00,000	₹ 73,92,000

Divisional selling expenses	₹ 23,20,000	₹ 24,64,000
Divisional administrative expenses	14,50,000	15,66,400
	₹ 37,70,000	₹ 40,30,400
Income from operations before service department charges	₹ 20,30,000	₹ 33,61,600
Less service department charges:		
Advertising expense	₹ 2,56,800	₹ 3,85,200
Transportation expense	1,48,800	1,66,160
Accounts receivable collection expense	93,000	1,08,750
Warehouse expense	9,60,000	6,40,000
Total	₹ 14,58,600	₹ 13,00,110
Income from operations	₹ 5,71,400	₹ 20,61,490

Supporting Schedule:

Service Department Charges

	Action Sports Division	Team Sports Division	Total
Advertising expense	₹ 2,56,800	₹ 3,85,200	₹ 6,42,000
Transportation rate per bill of lading	₹ 12.40	₹ 12.40	
Number of bills of lading	× 12,000	× 13,400	
Transportation expense	₹ 1,48,800	₹ 1,66,160	₹ 3,14,960
Accounts receivable collection rate	₹ 7.50	₹ 7.50	
Number of sales invoices	× 12,400	× 14,500	
Accounts receivable collection expense	₹ 93,000	₹ 1,08,750	₹ 2,01,750
Warehouse rate per sq. ft. (₹ 16,00,000/2,00,000 sq. ft.)	₹ 8.00	₹ 8.00	
Number of square feet	× 1,20,000	× 80,000	
Warehouse expense	₹ 9,60,000	₹ 6,40,000	₹ 16,00,000

Illustrative Problem 10

Dr. Reddy Labouratories, has the following data available for two of its divisions for last year:

	Divison X	*Division Z*
Sales	₹ 2,00,000	₹ 5,00,000
Contribution Margin	80,000	2,20,000
Operating Income	50,000	90,000
Average Operating Assets	1,80,000	3,60,000
Average Current Liabilities	30,000	50,000
Werighted Average Cost of Capital	12%	12%

The tax rate for the company is 40 percent.

Required:

a. Compute the following for each division:

(1) Sales margin

(2) ROI

(3) EVA

b. Briefly discuss which division appears most successful and why.

c. Assume a prospective project for Division X has operating income of ₹ 10,000, average operating assets of ₹ 60,000, average current liabilities of ₹ 4,000, and has a positive net present value. Assume the manager of Division X is evaluated based on ROI for merit pay and promotion. Would that manager want to go ahead with this prospective project? Would your answer change if the manager were evaluated based on EVA? If so, how and why would your answer change?

Solution:

The problem does not specify pre-tax or after-tax results. We generally accept either, but point out that many companies use the after-tax result for sales margin and ROI. EVA routinely uses after-tax amounts. In addressing requirement c, one should use after-tax amounts for ROI to make the measures comparable to EVA.

a. Division X Sales margin = ₹ 50,000(1 – .40)/₹ 2,00,000 = 15%

(or ₹ 50,000/₹ 2,00,000 = 25% before tax)

Division Z Sales margin = ₹ 90,000(1 – .40)/₹ 5,00,000 = 10.08%

(or ₹ 90,000/₹ 5,00,000 = 18.00% before tax)

Division X ROI = ₹ 50,000(1 – .40)/₹ 1,80,000 = 16.67%

(or Rs. 50,000/₹ 1,80,000 = 27.78% before tax)

Division Z ROI = ₹ 90,000(1 – .40)/₹ 3,60,000 = 15%

(or ₹ 90,000/₹ 3,60,000 = 25% before tax)

Division X EVA = ₹ 50,000(1 – .40) – .12(₹ 1,80,000 – ₹ 30,000)

= ₹ 30,000 – ₹ 18,000 = ₹ 12,000

Division Z EVA = ₹ 90,000(1 – .40) – .12(₹ 3,60,000 – ₹ 50,000)

= ₹ 54,000 – ₹ 37,200 = ₹ 16,800

b. Division X has the higher ROI, implying that it uses its assets more efficiently. However, Division Z is also generating more economic profit than Division X because it is larger. If one could invest in only one or the other division, then the investor would choose Division Z because it generates more economic value than Division X.

c. ROI: New Division ROI using the same approach as in requirement a.

Division X, new ROI = (₹ 50,000 + ₹ 10,000)(1 – .40) / (₹ 1,80,000 + ₹ 60,000)

= 15%. Compare to 16.67% in requirement a.

Division X, new EVA = (₹ 50,000 + ₹ 10,000)(1 – .40) – .12(₹ 1,80,000 + ₹ 60,000 – ₹ 30,000 – ₹ 4,000)

= ₹ 36,000 – ₹ 24,720

= ₹ 11,280. Compare to ₹ 12,000 in requirement a.

ROI would drop. EVA would decrease very little. Using the ROI performance measure creates a conflict for the manager. Taking the project would be good for company value because it has a positive NPV, but the manager would look worse because divisional ROI would decrease. Using EVA, the division's performance would look worse, but not by as much.

Illustrative Problem 11

XYZ company has three divisions whose income statements and balance sheets are summarised below:

	Division X	*Division Y*	*Division Z*
Sales (₹)	5,00,000	(*d*)	(*g*)
Operating income (₹)	25,000	30,000	(*h*)
Operating assets (₹)	1,00,000	(*e*)	2,50,000
Turnover	(*a*)	(*f*)	0.4
Margin	(*b*)	0.4%	5%
ROI	(*c*)	2%	(*i*)

Required:

(1) Supply by the missing data in the table above and summarise the results.

(2) Comment on the relative performance of each division. What questions can be raised as a result of their performance?

Solution:

1. Return of Investment (ROI)

$$\frac{\text{Operating income}}{\text{Operating assets}} = \frac{\text{Operating income}}{\text{Sales}} \times \frac{\text{Sales}}{\text{Operating assets}}$$

$$= \text{Margin} \times \text{Turnover}$$

(*a*) Division × Turnover $= \frac{5,00,000}{1,00,000} = 5 \text{ times}$

(*b*) Division × Margin $= \frac{25,000}{5,00,000} = 5\%$

(*c*) Division × ROI $= \text{Turnover} \times \text{Margin}$

$$= 5 \text{ times} \times 5\%$$

$$= 25\%$$

(*d*) Division Y Sales

$$\text{Margin} = 0.4\% = 0.004 = \frac{30,000}{\text{Sales d}}$$

$$\text{d} = \frac{30,000}{.004} = ₹\ 75,00,000$$

(*e*) Division Y operating assets

$$\text{ROI} = \frac{\text{Operating income}}{\text{Operating assets}}$$

$$2\% = \frac{30{,}000}{\text{Operating assets}}$$

$$e = \frac{30{,}000}{.02} = ₹15{,}00{,}000$$

(*f*) Division Y Turnover

$$= \frac{\text{Sales}}{\text{Operating assets}}$$

$$= \frac{75{,}00{,}000}{15{,}00{,}000} = 5 \text{ times}$$

(*g*) Division Z Sales

$$\text{Turnover} = \frac{\text{Sales}}{\text{Operating assets}}$$

$$0.4 = \frac{\text{Sales g}}{2{,}50{,}000}$$

$$g = .4 \times 2{,}50{,}000 = ₹\ 1{,}00{,}000$$

(*h*) Division Z operating income

$$\text{Margin} = \frac{\text{Operating income}}{\text{Sales}}$$

$$5\% = \frac{h}{1{,}00{,}000}$$

$$h = 1{,}00{,}000 \times 5\% = ₹\ 5{,}000$$

(*i*) EOI Division Z = Turnover × Margin

$$= 0.4 \times 5\%$$

$$= 2\% \text{ or } \frac{5{,}000}{2{,}50{,}000} = 2\%$$

Summarising the results:

	Div. X	*Div. Y*	*Div. Z*
Turnover	5 times	5 times	0.4 times
Margin	5%	0.4%	5%
ROI	25%	2%	2%

2. Division X performed best. It appears that Divisions Y and Z are in trouble. Division Y turns over its assets as often as Division X, but Y's margin on sales is much lower. Thus, Division Y must work on improving its margin. The following questions are raised about Division Y. Is the low margin due to inefficiency? Is it due to excessive material, labour and /or overhead costs?

Division Z, on the other hand, does just as well as Division X in terms of profit margin — both divisions earn 5% on sales. But Division Z has a much lower turnover of capital than Division X. Therefore, Division Z should take a close look at its investments. Is it too much tied up in inventories and receivables ? Are there unused fixed assets? Is there idle cash sitting around?

Illustrative Problem 12

A division of a large group company has prepared the following summarised budget for the ensuing year:

	₹ (lac)
Profit	660
Net current assets (average for the year)	750
Fixed assets (at cost)	3,000
Accumulated depreciation	1,440

The group financial controller has proposed the following non-routine transaction:

At the beginning of the year, the division will buy a plant for ₹360 lac to achieve a reduction of ₹ 105 lac in revenue expenses. This plant will have a life of 5 years with no salvage value at the end of the 5th year.

The divisional manager asks you to evaluate the Financial Controller's proposal from the point of view of performance of the division. Ignore taxation.

Solution:

Performance will be judged by comparing (i) the return on capital employed as per budget and (ii) the return on capital employed which will include the proposed new plant.

(i)	Budgeted ROCE:	Current assets		750
		Fixed assets	3,000	
		(less) Accumulated depreciation	(1,440)	1,560
		Capital employed		2,310

ROCE = (660/2,310) × 100 = 28.57%.

		₹ (lac)
(ii)	ROCE with new plant:	
	Cost of new plant	360
	(Less) Depreciation for the budgeted year (1/5)	(72)
	Year-end value	288
	Revised capital employed (2,310 + 288)	2,598
		₹ (lac)
	Profit as per budget	660
	Add for reduction in revenue expenses	105
	(Less) Depreciation on new plant	(72)
	Revised profit	693

Revised ROCE = (693/2,598) × 100 = 26.67%.

Since existing ROCE 28.5% is more than the revised ROCE (26.67%), the proposal, if implemented will be harmful and divisional manager may not welcome it.

Illustrative Problem 13

Financial data for ABC Company for last year appear below:

ABC Company
Statements of Financial Position

	Beginning Balance	*Ending Balance*
Assets:		
Cash	₹ 1,20,000	₹ 1,60,000
Accounts receivable	1,10,000	1,00,000
Inventory	50,000	60,000
Plant and equipment (net)	1,80,000	1,60,000
Investment in XYZ, Company	50,000	60,000
Land (undeveloped)	1,20,000	1,20,000
Total assets	₹ 6,30,000	₹ 6,60,000
Liabilities and owner's equity:		
Accounts payable	₹ 70,000	₹ 90,000
Long-term debt	5,00,000	5,00,000
Owners' equity	60,000	70,000
Total liabilities and owner's equity	6,30,000	6,60,000

ABC Company
Income Statement

Sales		₹ 12,22,000
Less operating expenses		10,99,800
Net operating income		1,22,200
Less interest and taxes:		
Interest expense	₹ 60,000	
Tax expense	20,000	80,000
Net income		₹ 42,200

The company paid dividends of ₹ 32,200 last year. The "Investment in XYZ Company" on the statement of financial position represents an investment in the shares of another company.

Required:

a. Computer the company's margin, turnover, and return on investment for last year.

b. The Board of Directors of ABC has set a minimum required return of 25%. What was the company's residual income last year?

Solution:

a. Operating assets do not include investments in other companies or in undeveloped land.

	Beginning Balance	*Ending Balance*
Cash	₹ 1,20,000	₹ 1,60,000
Accounts receivable	1,10,000	1,00,000
Inventory	50,000	60,000
Plant and equipment (net)	1,80,000	1,60,000
Total operating assets	₹ 4,60,000	₹ 4,80,000

Average operating assets = (₹ 4,60,000 + ₹ 4,80,000) ÷ 2 = ₹ 4,70,000

Margin = Net operating income ÷ Sales = ₹ 1,22,000 ÷ ₹ 12,22,000 = 10%

Turnover = Sales ÷ Average operating assets = ₹ 12,22,000 ÷ ₹ 4,70,000 = 2.6

ROI = Margin × Turnover = 10% × 2.6 = 26%

b.		
	Net operating income	₹ 1,22,200
	Minimum required return (25% × ₹ 4,70,000)......	1,17,500
	Residual income	₹ 4,700

Illustrative Problem 14

Auto India Company Limited (AICL) is engaged in manufacturing automobile parts. The following particulars for 2016–2017 are available from the records of AICL:

	₹
Sales	50,00,000
Less: Variable Cost	33,25,000
Contribution	16,75,000
Less: Fixed Cost	9,00,000
Net Income	7,75,000

Following additional information concerning the performance of 3 departments has been given below:

(Figure in ₹)

Particular	**Departments**		
	P	**Q**	**R**
Sales	21,40,000	17,90,000	10,70,000
Variable Cost	14,23,000	11,90,000	7,12,000
Direct Fixed Cost	2,80,000	2,45,000	1,75,000

(i) Rank the three departments on the basis of their proportionate measure of relative profitability.

(ii) Corporate Marketing Department of AICL proposes to increase advertisement expenses by ₹ 1,25,000 with an expectation of 10% increase in sales in all three departments.

Analyse the effect of this proposal on the Company as a whole and on each department and give your suitable recommendation.

Solution:

Auto India Company Limited

Performance Evaluation Report for 2016–2017 (*Figures in Rupees*)

Particulars	Departments			
	P	**Q**	**R**	**Total**
Sales Revenue	21,40,000	17,90,000	10,70,000	50,00,000
Less: Controllable Variable cost	14,23,000	11,90,000	7,12,000	33,25,000
Controllable Contribution Margin	7,17,000	6,00,000	3,58,000	16,75,000
Less: Controllable direct fixed cost	2,80,000	2,45,000	1,75,000	7,00,000
Segment Profit Contribution	4,37,000	3,55,000	1,83,000	9,75,000
Less: Common company wide cost	—	—	—	2,00,000
Net Income	—	—	—	7,75,000
Segment Profit Contribution as % of Sales	20.42%	19.83%	17.10%	—
Ranking	I	II	III	

Performance Evaluation Report

(Impact of enhancement of Advertisement Expenses) (*Figures in Rupees*)

Particulars	Departments			
	P	**Q**	**R**	**Total**
Sales Revenue	23,54,000	19,69,000	11,77,000	55,00,000
Less: Controllable Variable cost	15,65,300	13,09,000	7,83,200	36,57,500
Controllable Contribution Margin	7,88,700	6,60,000	3,93,800	18,42,500
Less: Controllable direct fixed cost (given)	2,80,000	2,45,000	1,75,000	7,00,000
Less: Advertising cost (allocated on the basis of sales ratio)	53,500	44,750	26,750	1,25,000
Segment Profit Contribution	4,55,200	3,70,250	1,92,050	10,17,500
Less: Common company wide cost	—	—	—	2,00,000
Net Income	—	—	—	8,17,500
Segment Profit Contribution as % of Sales	19.34%	18.80%	16.32%	—
Ranking	I	II	III	—

Recommendation: Although there has been a decline in the segment profit contribution as a percentage of sales for all three departments, total segment profit contribution as a result of advertisement campaign, has shown a rise.

The company's Net Income thus increased from ₹ 7,75,000 to ₹ 8,17,500.

Illustrative Problem 15

The pupils' Book Co. has two book selling outlets: Kalidas Book House and Tulsidas Book House. Each store has a manager who has a great deal of decision authority over the individual stores. A central office however, handles advertising, marketing research, acquisition of books, legal services, and other staff functions. The Pupils' Book Co's current accounting system allocates all costs to the stores.

Results for 2016–17 were:

Amount in ₹

Item	Total Company	Kalidas Book House	Tulsidas Book House
Sales Revenue	7,00,000	3,50,000	3,50,000
Cost of merchandise sold	4,50,000	2,25,000	2,25,000
Gross Margin	2,50,000	1,25,000	1,25,000
Operating Expenses:			
Salaries and wages	63,000	30,000	33,000
Supplies	45,000	22,500	22,500
Rent and Utilities	60,000	40,000	20,000
Depreciation	15,000	7,000	8,000
Allocated staff cost	60,000	30,000	30,000
Total operating expenses	2,43,000	1,29,500	1,13,500
Operating income (Loss)	7,000	(4,500)	11,500

Each bookstore manager makes decisions that affect salaries and wages, supplies and depreciation. In contrast, rent and utilities are beyond the managers' control because the managers did not choose the location or size of the store.

Supplies are variable costs. Variable salaries and wages are equal to 8% of the cost of merchandise sold; the remainder of salaries and wages is a fixed cost. Rent, utilities and depreciation are also fixed costs. Allocated staff costs are unaffected by any events at the bookstores, but they are allocated as a proportion of sales revenue.

Required:

(i) Using the contribution approach, prepare a performance report that distinguishes the performance of each bookstore from that of the bookstore manager.

(ii) Evaluate the performance of each bookstore.

(iii) Evaluate the performance of each manager.

Solution:

(i) Performance Report of Kalidas Book House & Tulsidas Book House

Amount in ₹

Item	**Total Company**	**Kalidas Book House**	**Tulsidas Book House**
Sales Revenue	7,00,000	3,50,000	3,50,000
Variable Cost:			
Cost of merchandise sold	4,50,000	2,25,000	2,25,000
Salaries & Wages	36,000	18,000	18,000

Supplies	45,000	22,500	22,500
Total Variable Cost	5,31,000	2,65,500	2,65,000
Contribution Margin	**1,69,000**	**84,500**	**84,500**
Less: Fixed Cost controllable by book-store managers:			
Salaries and Wages	27,000	12,000	15,000
Depreciation	15,000	7,000	8,000
Controllable Fixed Cost	42,000	19,000	23,000
Contribution controllable by managers	1,27,000	65,500	61,500
Less: Fixed Cost controllable by others :			
Rent & Utilities	60,000	40,000	20,000
Contribution by book-store	**67,000**	**25,500**	**41,500**
Unallocated cost	60,000		
Operating Income	7,000		

(ii) The financial performance of the bookstores is best evaluated under the line "*Contribution by bookstores*". Tulsidas has a substantially higher contribution, despite equal level of sales revenues in the two stores.

The major reason for this performance is the lower rent and utilities paid by Tulsidas.

(iii) The financial performance by the managers is best judged by the line "*contribution controllable by managers*". By this measure, the performance of Kalidas's manager is better than that of Tulsidas's. The contribution margin is the same for each store but Tulsidas's manager paid ₹4,000 more in controllable fixed cost than did Kalidas's manager. Of course, this decision could be beneficial in the long run. What is missing from each of this segment report is the concerned Master budget and a Flexible budget, which would be the best benchmark for evaluating both bookstore and bookstore manager.

Illustrative Problem 16

ABC is a diversified company producing and distributing different products. Product X division within the company handles a specific product and would like to earn a long run rate of return of 20%. Product X division will charge its unit selling price as necessary to provide this return. The following data are available on the division and its products:

Variable cost per unit	₹ 200
Total annual fixed costs	₹ 12,20,000
Long run normal demand	10,000 units each year
Average operating assets owned by the division	₹ 14,00,000

Required:

1. Compute the per unit selling price that will provide the desired rate of return.
2. Assume that actual sales fluctuate from 8,500 units to 11,500 units. Compute the margin, turnover and ROI that would be realised on sales at 8,500 units, 10,000 units and 11,500 units levels of activity (use the selling price computed in part 1 for your computations).
3. Explain what your computations in part 2 suggest to you in so far as applying the rate of return formula to divisions subject to cyclical movement in the economy.

Solution:

$$\text{ROI} = \frac{\text{Operating Income}}{\text{Sales}} \times \frac{\text{Sales}}{\text{Assets}}$$

↓ Margin ↓ Turnover

1. Total sales Value of 10,000 units

Variable cost (₹ 200 × 10,000) = ₹ 20,00,000

Fixed cost = 12,20,000

Return @ 20%

$$(14,00,000 \times \frac{20}{100}) = 2,80,000$$

Total sales value 35,00,000

$$\text{Selling price per unit} = \frac{35,00,000}{10,000 \text{ units}} = ₹\ 350$$

2. Calculation of Margin, Turnover and ROI at 8,500 units

Operating income = (8,500 units × ₹ 350) – (8,500 × ₹ 200) – ₹ 12,20,000

= 29,75,000 – 17,00,000 – 12,20,000

= ₹ 55,000

$$\text{Margin} = \frac{55,000}{29,75,000} \times 100 = 1.85\%$$

$$\text{Turnover} = \frac{29,75,000}{14,00,000} = 2.125$$

ROI = Margin × Turnover

ROI = 1.85% × 2.125 = 3.93%

Or

$$\frac{55,000}{14,00,000} \times 100 = 3.93\%$$

At 10,000 units level

Operating income = (10,000 × 350) – (10,000 × 200) – 12,20,000

= 35,00,000 – 20,00,000 – 12,20,000

= ₹ 2,80,000

$$\text{Margin} = \frac{2,80,000}{35,00,000} \times 100 = 8\%$$

$$\text{Turnover} = \frac{35,00,000}{14,00,000} = 2.5$$

ROI = 8% × 2.5 = 20%

At 11,500 units

Operating income = (11,500 × 350) – (11,500 × 200) – 12,20,000

$$= 40{,}25{,}000 - 23{,}00{,}000 - 12{,}20{,}000$$

$$= 5{,}05{,}000$$

$$\text{Margin} = \frac{5{,}05{,}000}{40{,}25{,}000} \times 100 = 12.55\%$$

$$\text{Turnover} = \frac{40{,}25{,}000}{14{,}00{,}000} = 2.875$$

$$\text{ROI} = 12.55 \times 2.875 = 36.08\%$$

Summary of calculations

Sales in units	*Margin*	*Capital Turnover*	*ROI*
8,500	1.85%	2.125	3.93%
10,000	8%	2.5	20%
11,500	12.55%	2.875	36.08%

3. The computations in part 2 suggest the following with regard to product X Division' subject to cyclical movements in the economy.

(*a*) ROI as a measurement of performance has some limitations. When unit sales were increased from 8,500 to 10,000 units (an increase of 17.6%), ROI increased more than 400%. When unit sales were 11,500 instead of 8,500 (an increase of 35.3%), ROI increased 818%. In other words, ROI fluctuates greatly for changes in sales. This does not suggest that ROI should not be used for divisions that are subject to cyclical movements in the economy. Rather, managements should be aware of how greatly ROI can fluctuate compared to changes in sales. For example, management can set target ROI to vary depending on the part of a cycle the economy is in or perhaps set an ROI range rather than one ROI value.

(*b*) The division manager has no (or very little) control over sales, which are affected greatly by outside economic forces. Therefore, top management should exercise caution in using ROI as a measure of divisional performance in this type of business.

Illustrative Problem 17

PIC is a multinational company specialising in the production and sale of biscuits and chocolates. The Divisional profit statement for biscuits division for the month of December 2016 is:

	(₹)	(₹)	***Budget*** (₹)
Sales (50% on credit terms)		11,40,000	12,00,000
Divisional expenses:			
Materials	8,00,000		
Manufacturing costs	70,000		
Marketing	93,000		
Divisional administration	58,000	10,21,000	10,00,000
Divisional contribution		1,19,000	2,00,000
Proportion of head office expenses		1,00,000	1,00,000
Net profit		19,000	1,00,000

The balance sheet for the division analyses the divisional net investment as follows:

Traceable assets:		
Premises	6,00,000	
Plant	5,10,000	
Vehicles	30,000	
		11,40,000
Stocks:		
Materials	9,00,000	
Finished goods	1,60,000	
Debtors	9,00,000	
Current liabilities	(3,20,000)	16,40,000
Net traceable assets		27,80,000
Proportion of centrally administered assets:		
Cash	10,000	
Other	60,000	70,000
Divisional net investment		₹ 28,50,000

The biscuit industry does not experience seasonal fluctuations. The month of December is typical of all the other months in the year so far as performance is concerned. The cost of capital for the group is 15%.

Required:

(*a*) Evaluate the performance of the management of the biscuits division using four methods. Comment on the limitations of the methods you have employed.

(*b*) How would your method of evaluation of the performance of this division differ if the evaluation were made to check economic rather than managerial performance?

Solution:

(*a*) Evaluation of managerial performance should include all elements in the division that management can control. The degree of autonomy enjoyed by a division will determine the control that managers maintain over pricing, investment and other factors that affect profit.

(*i*) Profit Contribution

The division has contributed ₹ 1,19,000 to the central costs and profit of the group, but this is well below budget. The responsibility of management for this deficit depends on the influence that divisional managers can exercise over sales, marketing and costs, and whether the budget used as a yardstick was attainable in realistic terms. Contribution does not take into account the assets under the control of divisional management and can not comment on the return on investment needed to earn that return.

(*ii*) Net Income

This measure of performance shows only a small net profit for the division. As a performance evaluator, it fails to set return against investment and also includes head office charges, which, presumably, are outside the control of divisional management.

***(iii)* Return on Investment (ROI)**

$$\frac{\text{Net income}}{\text{Investment}} = \frac{12 \times ₹\ 19{,}000}{₹\ 28{,}50{,}000} \times \frac{100}{1} = 8\%$$

Whether this performance is good or bad depends on the expected return and the cost of capital for the group (15%). It certainly sets the return against investment, but for evaluation of managerial performance perhaps centrally administered assets and allocated head office costs should not be included in the analysis. Perhaps, the following could be used as an alternative:

$$\frac{₹\ 1{,}19{,}000 \times 12}{₹\ 27{,}80{,}000} \times \frac{100}{1} = 51\%$$

The measurement of profit and investment may be made in ways that lead to unreliable conclusions from ROI, *e.g.*, historic cost of assets set against current cost revenue. Decisions that maximise divisional ROI may not necessarily be best for the group as a whole.

***(iv)* Residual Income**

Residual income is the income remaining after deducting a charge for the use of funds invested in the division based on the cost of capital.

Net profit	₹ 19,000
Less (28,50,000 × 0.15 ÷ 12) Investment charges	₹ 35,625
Residual income	₹ (16,625)

Management is not making sufficient return to service group funds allocated to the division at the group cost of capital. However, if head office expense and centrally administered assets are excluded, a divisional residual income can be calculated relating to factors that divisional managers can influence. Residual income can be calculated as follows:

Net profit		1,19,000
Less investment charge	27,80,000 × 0.15 ÷ 12	34,750
Residual income	₹	84,250

Other measures of managerial performance:

Stock control

$$\frac{\text{Closing stock materials}}{\text{Usage of materials}} = \frac{₹\ 9{,}00{,}000}{₹\ 8{,}00{,}000 \times 12} \times \frac{365}{1} = 34\ \text{days}$$

Debtor control

$$\frac{\text{Debtors}}{\text{Credit sales}} = \frac{₹\ 9{,}00{,}000}{(1/2 \times 11{,}40{,}000)} \times \frac{365}{1} = 576\ \text{days}$$

(b) *Economic Performance:* This is to decide whether the division produces enough income to support the capital invested in it. Does invested capital produce more than it costs? To this end, all costs of the division, whether controllable by divisional management or not, and all traceable and centrally administered assets also should be taken into account. All divisions are compared according to a single standard.

Illustrative Problem 18

Compro Electronics is facing stiff competition from imported goods. Its operating income margin has been declining steadily for the past several years; the company has been forced to lower prices so that it can maintain its market share. The operating results for the past three years are as follows:

	Year 1	Year 2	Year 3
Sales	₹ 1,00,00,000	₹ 95,00,000	₹ 90,00,000
Net operating income	12,00,000	10,45,000	9,45,000
Average assets	1,50,00,000	1,50,00,000	1,50,00,000

For the coming year, Compro's CEO plans to install a JIT purchasing and manufacturing system. He estimates that inventories will be reduced by 70 per cent during the first year of operations, producing a 20 per cent reduction in the average operating assets of the company, which would remain unchanged without the JIT system. He also estimates that sales and operating income will be restored to Year 1 levels because of simultaneous reductions in operating expenses and selling prices. Lower selling prices will allow Compro to expand its market share.

Required:

(*i*) Compute the ROI, margin, and turnover for Years 1, 2 and 3.

(*ii*) Suppose that in Year 4 the sales and operating income were achieved as expected but inventories remained at the same level as in Year 3. Compute the expected ROI, margin, and turnover. Explain why the ROI increased over the Year 3 level.

(*iii*) Suppose that the sales and net operating income for Year 4 remained the same as in Year 3 but inventory reductions were achieved as projected. Compute the ROI, margin, and turnover. Explain why the ROI exceeded the Year 3 level.

(*iv*) Assume that all expectations for Year 4 were realised. Compute the expected ROI, margin and turnover. Explain why the ROI increased over the Year 3 level.

Solution:

	Year 1	Year 2	Year 3
(*i*) ROI	$= \dfrac{₹\ 12,00,000}{₹\ 1,50,00,000} \times 100 = 8.00\%$	$\dfrac{₹\ 10,45,000}{₹\ 1,50,00,000} \times 100 = 6.97\%$	$\dfrac{₹\ 9,45,000}{₹\ 1,50,00,000} \times 100 = 6.30\%$
Margin	$= \dfrac{₹\ 12,00,000}{₹\ 1,00,00,000} \times 100 = 12.00\%$	$\dfrac{₹\ 10,45,000}{₹\ 95,00,000} \times 100 = 11.00\%$	$\dfrac{₹\ 9,45,000}{₹\ 90,00,000} \times 100 = 10.50\%$
Turnover	$= \dfrac{₹\ 1,00,00,000}{₹\ 1,50,00,000} \times 100 = 0.67$	$\dfrac{₹\ 95,00,000}{₹\ 1,50,00,000} \times 100 = 0.63$	$\dfrac{₹\ 90,00,000}{₹\ 1,50,00,000} \times 100 = 0.60$

(*ii*) ROI $= \dfrac{₹\ 12,00,000}{₹\ 1,50,00,000} \times 100 = 8\%$

Margin $= \dfrac{₹\ 12,00,000}{₹\ 1,00,00,000} \times 100 = 12\%$

Turnover $= \dfrac{₹\ 1,00,00,000}{₹\ 1,50,00,000} \times 100 = 0.67$

The ROI increased because expenses decreased and assets turned over at a higher rate (sales increased).

(*iii*) Operating assets = ₹ 1,50,00,000 × 80% = ₹ 1,20,00,000

	ROI	= ₹ 9,45,000/₹ 1,20,00,000	= 7.88%
	Margin	= ₹ 9,45,000/₹ 90,00,000	= 10.5%
	Turnover	= ₹ 90,00,000/₹ 1,20,00,000	= 0.75

The ROI increased because assets decreased.

(*iv*)	ROI	= ₹ 12,00,000/₹ 1,20,00,000	= 10%
	Margin	= ₹ 12,00,000/₹1,00,00,000	= 12%
	Turnover	= ₹ 1,00,00,000/₹1,20,00,000	= 0.83

The ROI increased because expenses decreased and assets turned over at a higher rate (sales increased and the amount of assets decreased). Both margin and turnover increased.

Illustrative Problem 19

The following data have been collected relating to W division of the MACRO group.

Data for W Division

		₹
Sales Revenue	External customers	6,00,000
	Internal transfers	3,50,000
Variable operating costs	Labour	95,000
	Materials	1,60,000
	Overheads	42,500
Fixed operating costs	Controllable by division	78,000
	Controllable centrally	41,000
Divisional management cost	Controllable centrally	26,500
Fixed Assets (at cost)	Divisional purchases	4,50,000
	Central purchases	2,50,000

Total central administration and management cost 6,84,210

(These are apportioned on the basis of sales revenue which was ₹ 52 lakhs for the group as a whole)

The group's weighted average cost of capital is estimated at 15% and it is the group policy to calculate depreciation on a straight line basis at 25% and to impute interest on a gross investment basis

Prepare from the above data, a divisional performance statement on

(i) Profit centre approach

(ii) Investment centre approach.

Solution:

Divisional Performance Statement

Divisional Revenue			9,50,000
(Less) Variable Cost :			
	Labour	95,000	
	Materials	1,60,000	
	Overheads	42,500	(2,97,500)
Divisional contribution			6,52,500
(Less) Controllable fixed overhead			(78,000)

(Less) Controllable depreciation [4,50,000 × 25%]		(1,12,500)
Controllable profit		₹ 4,62,000
(i) **Profit Centre Approach**		
Controllable Profit, as worked above		4,62,000
(Less) Non-controllable fixed operating costs		
	41,000 + 26,500 = 67,500	
Non-controllable depreciation	= 62,500	(1,30,000)
(Less) Apportioned Central charges		
	(6,84,210/52,00,000) × 9,50,000 =	(1,25,000)
Net Profit before tax		₹ 2,07,000
(ii) **Investment Centre Approach**		
Net profit before tax (same as in Profit Centre Approach)		₹ 2,07,000
(Less) 15% Cost of Capital		
(being imputed interest on gross investment in		
fixed assets : — Controllable	67,500	
— Non-controllable	37,500 =	(1,05,000)
Net Residual Income before tax		₹ 1,02,000

Illustrative Problem 20

Jaipur Golden Transport Co. has three regional divisions organized as profit centres. The chief executive officer (CEO) evaluates divisional performance, using income from operations as a per cent of revenues. The following quarterly income and expense accounts were provided from the trial balance as of December 31, 2016.

Revenues—East Division	₹ 6,00,000
Revenues—West Division	7,10,000
Revenues—Metro Division	9,80,000
Operating Expenses—East Division	3,62,400
Operating Expenses—West Division	3,93,540
Operating Expenses—Metro Division	5,27,760
Corporate Expenses—Shareholder Relations	87,500
Corporate Expenses—Customer Support	3,00,000
Corporate Expenses—Legal	1,22,400
General Corporate Officers' Salaries	2,04,000

The company operates three service departments: Shareholder Relations, Customer Support, and Legal. The Shareholder Relations Department conducts a variety of services for shareholders of the company. The Customer Support Department is the company's point of contact for new service, complaints, and requests for repair. The department believes that the number of customer contacts is an activity base for this work. The Legal Department provides legal services for division management. The department believes that the number of hours billed is an activity base for this work. The following additional information has been gathered:

	East	West	Metro
Number of customer contacts	3,750	4,500	6,750
Number of hours billed	850	1,360	1,190

Required:

1. Prepare quarterly income staements showing income from operations for the three divisions.
2. Identify the most successful division according to the profit margin.
3. Provide a recommendation to the CEO for a better method for evaluating the performance of the divisions. In your recommendation, identify the major weakness of the present method.

Solution:

1.

Jaipur Golden Transport Co.
Divisional Income Statements For the Quarter Ended December 31, 2016

	East	West	Metro
Revenues	₹ 6,00,000	₹ 7,10,000	₹ 9,80,000
Operating expenses	3,62,400	3,93,540	5,27,760
Income from operations before service department charges	₹ 2,37,600	₹ 3,16,460	₹ 4,52,240
Less service department charges:			
Customer support (₹ 20 × customer contacts)	₹ 75,000	₹ 90,000	₹ 1,35,000
Legal (₹ 36 × number of hours billed)	30,600	48,960	42,840
	₹ 1,05,600	₹ 1,38,960	₹ 1,77,840
Income from operations	₹ 1,32,000	₹ 1,77,500	₹ 2,74,400

Supporting schedules:

Service department charge rates for the two service department, Customer Support and Legal, are determined as follows:

	East	West	Metro	Total
Number of customer contacts	3,750	4,500	6,750	15,000
Number of hours billed	850	1,360	1,190	3,400

	Service Cost	÷	Output	=	Rate
Customer contact rate	₹ 3,00,000	÷	15,000	=	₹ 20 per contact
Legal billing rate	1,22,400	÷	3,400	=	36 per hour

Note: The Shareholder Relations Department and general corporate officers' salaries are not controllable by division management and thus are not included in determining division income from operations.

2. The CEO evaluates the three divisions using income from operations as a per cent of revenues (profit margin). This measure is calculated for the three divisions as follows:

   East Division: 22% (₹ 1,32,000/₹ 6,00,000)

   West Division: 25% (₹ 1,77,500/₹ 7,10,000)

   Metro Division: 28% (₹ 2,74,400/₹ 9,80,000)

According to the CEO's measure, the Metro Division has the highest performance.

3. The method used to evaluate the performance of the divisions should be revaluated. The present method identifies the amount of income from operations per Rupee of earned revenue. However, this company requires a significant investment in fixed assets, for research, development, production, and distribution facilities. In addition, the amount of assets may not be related to the revenue earned. For example, some divisions are able to concentrate assets in a densely populated regional area and service a large population over those assets (*e.g.*, Metro Division). Other regions, however, have widely distributed assets over sparsely populated areas that use less services over those assets. The present measure fails to incorporate these differences in asset utilization into the measure. Naturally, the amount of assets used by a division in earning a return is a very important consideration in evaluating divisional performance. Therefore, a better divisional performance measure would be either (a) rate of return on investment (income from operations divided by divisional assets) or (b) residual income (income from operations less a minimal return on divisional assets). Both measures incorporate the assets used by the divisions.

Illustrative Problem 21

Hudco Ltd. requires its various operating divisions to meet the company's target return of 15% on investment, as specified by the board. Besides the ROI of 15%, the board also requires an annual positive cash flow. The Steady Division has achieved the 15% target for many years. Steady's assets are mainly plant and equipment (its property rented), plus net current assets. The average age of its assets has increased by 10 months per year over the last four years. A recent benchmarking exercise has shown that Steady's productivity is below that of its competitors, although its financial performance appears very good. The divisional operations director has recently presented a proposal for a major investment in new plant and machinery. He argued that without substantial investment Steady would not be able to compete on either quantity or delivery time. The divisional sales director agreed that these factors had become the two most important features in winning new orders. The budgeted financial figures for 2016 are shown here:

Steady Division - 2012

	(₹ *Crore*)
Sales	168.60
Operating profit before depreciation	22.20
Depreciation	3.00
Operating profit	19.20
Interest payable	1.80
Divisional net profit before tax	17.4[illegible]
Plant and equipment	[illegible]
Net current assets	[illegible]0
Total divisional assets	[illegible]

The proposals for new investment would lead to a net increas[illegible] equipment of ₹ 36 crore and a reduction in net current assets of ₹ 12 crore. Steady ex[illegible] new assets would lead to an increase in operating profit before depreciation of ₹ 8.4 [illegible] increase in depreciation of ₹ 4.8 crore. Hudco charges 12% on all funds used by di[illegible]

3. The method used to evaluate the performance of the divisions should be revaluated. The present method identifies the amount of income from operations per Rupee of earned revenue. However, this company requires a significant investment in fixed assets, for research, development, production, and distribution facilities. In addition, the amount of assets may not be related to the revenue earned. For example, some divisions are able to concentrate assets in a densely populated regional area and service a large population over those assets (*e.g.*, Metro Division). Other regions, however, have widely distributed assets over sparsely populated areas that use less services over those assets. The present measure fails to incorporate these differences in asset utilization into the measure. Naturally, the amount of assets used by a division in earning a return is a very important consideration in evaluating divisional performance. Therefore, a better divisional performance measure would be either (a) rate of return on investment (income from operations divided by divisional assets) or (b) residual income (income from operations less a minimal return on divisional assets). Both measures incorporate the assets used by the divisions.

Illustrative Problem 21

Hudco Ltd. requires its various operating divisions to meet the company's target return of 15% on investment, as specified by the board. Besides the ROI of 15%, the board also requires an annual positive cash flow. The Steady Division has achieved the 15% target for many years. Steady's assets are mainly plant and equipment (its property rented), plus net current assets. The average age of its assets has increased by 10 months per year over the last four years. A recent benchmarking exercise has shown that Steady's productivity is below that of its competitors, although its financial performance appears very good. The divisional operations director has recently presented a proposal for a major investment in new plant and machinery. He argued that without substantial investment Steady would not be able to compete on either quantity or delivery time. The divisional sales director agreed that these factors had become the two most important features in winning new orders. The budgeted financial figures for 2016 are shown here:

Steady Division - 2012

	(₹ *Crore*)
Sales	168.60
Operating profit before depreciation	22.20
Depreciation	3.00
Operating profit	19.20
Interest payable	1.80
Divisional net profit before tax	17.40
Plant and equipment	60.00
Net current assets	36.00
Total divisional assets	96.00

The proposals for new investment would lead to a net increase in plant and equipment of ₹ 36 crore and a reduction in net current assets of ₹ 12 crore. Steady expects that the new assets would lead to an increase in operating profit before depreciation of ₹ 8.4 crore and a net increase in depreciation of ₹ 4.8 crore. Hudco charges 12% on all funds used by divisions.

You are required to —

(a) Calculate the return on investment for Steady Division for 2016, with and without the new investment proposal. Briefly comment on the expected performance of Steady Division for each option.

(b) Calculate the Residual Income (RI) for Steady Division for 2016, with or without the new investment proposal. Briefly comment on whether using RI would improve the measurement of Steady's performance.

(c) Outline the major features of Economic Value Added (EVA) and briefly discuss whether its use could improve divisional performance measurement for Hudco.

Solution:

(a)

Hudco Ltd. - Steady Division

Return on Investment (ROI)

	Without investment		**With investment**
	₹ *Cr.*		₹ *Cr.*
PBIT	19.20	(+ 8.4 – 4.8)	22.80
Total Assets	96.00	(+ 36.00 – 12.00)	120.00
ROI	20%		19%

Comments:

Steady's return is more than the company's target. However, the information of poor productivity and aged assets makes a discerning accountant wonder if the apparent better results were the products of low asset values rather than production efficiency.

With new additional investment, the ROI is reduced. This might discourage the Steady management to undertake the proposed investment, though this will mean that the division remains a weak link in respect of productivity, quality of goods and service in its market.

This measure, ROI, obstructs a clear vision of the merit of a project at times.

(b)

Residual Income (RI)

	Without investment		**With investment**
	₹ *Cr.*		₹ *Cr.*
PBIT	19.20		22.80
Imputed interest charge			
@ 12% (on 96.00)	(11.52)	(on 120.00)	(14.40)
RI	7.68		8.40

Comments:

As in ROI, RI also shows better results as the imputed interest on older assets gets smaller.

However, the RI measure here will encourage new investment. As against the current return, a target return is decided with a view to long term objective of the corporate management. Sometimes the target rate of return is used as the imputed interest charge; a positive RI in this case will indicate a project that earns in excess of the target ROI.

Performance measures must be designed to reward decisions that are optimum for the company as a whole.

3. The method used to evaluate the performance of the divisions should be revaluated. The present method identifies the amount of income from operations per Rupee of earned revenue. However, this company requires a significant investment in fixed assets, for research, development, production, and distribution facilities. In addition, the amount of assets may not be related to the revenue earned. For example, some divisions are able to concentrate assets in a densely populated regional area and service a large population over those assets (*e.g.*, Metro Division). Other regions, however, have widely distributed assets over sparsely populated areas that use less services over those assets. The present measure fails to incorporate these differences in asset utilization into the measure. Naturally, the amount of assets used by a division in earning a return is a very important consideration in evaluating divisional performance. Therefore, a better divisional performance measure would be either (a) rate of return on investment (income from operations divided by divisional assets) or (b) residual income (income from operations less a minimal return on divisional assets). Both measures incorporate the assets used by the divisions.

Illustrative Problem 21

Hudco Ltd. requires its various operating divisions to meet the company's target return of 15% on investment, as specified by the board. Besides the ROI of 15%, the board also requires an annual positive cash flow. The Steady Division has achieved the 15% target for many years. Steady's assets are mainly plant and equipment (its property rented), plus net current assets. The average age of its assets has increased by 10 months per year over the last four years. A recent benchmarking exercise has shown that Steady's productivity is below that of its competitors, although its financial performance appears very good. The divisional operations director has recently presented a proposal for a major investment in new plant and machinery. He argued that without substantial investment Steady would not be able to compete on either quantity or delivery time. The divisional sales director agreed that these factors had become the two most important features in winning new orders. The budgeted financial figures for 2016 are shown here:

Steady Division - 2012

	(₹ *Crore*)
Sales	168.60
Operating profit before depreciation	22.20
Depreciation	3.00
Operating profit	19.20
Interest payable	1.80
Divisional net profit before tax	17.40
Plant and equipment	60.00
Net current assets	36.00
Total divisional assets	96.00

The proposals for new investment would lead to a net increase in plant and equipment of ₹ 36 crore and a reduction in net current assets of ₹ 12 crore. Steady expects that the new assets would lead to an increase in operating profit before depreciation of ₹ 8.4 crore and a net increase in depreciation of ₹ 4.8 crore. Hudco charges 12% on all funds used by divisions.

You are required to —

(a) Calculate the return on investment for Steady Division for 2016, with and without the new investment proposal. Briefly comment on the expected performance of Steady Division for each option.

(b) Calculate the Residual Income (RI) for Steady Division for 2016, with or without the new investment proposal. Briefly comment on whether using RI would improve the measurement of Steady's performance.

(c) Outline the major features of Economic Value Added (EVA) and briefly discuss whether its use could improve divisional performance measurement for Hudco.

Solution:

(a) **Hudco Ltd. - Steady Division**

Return on Investment (ROI)

	Without investment		**With investment**
	₹ *Cr.*		₹ *Cr.*
PBIT	19.20	(+ 8.4 – 4.8)	22.80
Total Assets	96.00	(+ 36.00 – 12.00)	120.00
ROI	20%		19%

Comments:

Steady's return is more than the company's target. However, the information of poor productivity and aged assets makes a discerning accountant wonder if the apparent better results were the products of low asset values rather than production efficiency.

With new additional investment, the ROI is reduced. This might discourage the Steady management to undertake the proposed investment, though this will mean that the division remains a weak link in respect of productivity, quality of goods and service in its market.

This measure, ROI, obstructs a clear vision of the merit of a project at times.

(b) **Residual Income (RI)**

	Without investment		**With investment**
	₹ *Cr.*		₹ *Cr.*
PBIT	19.20		22.80
Imputed interest charge			
@ 12% (on 96.00)	(11.52)	(on 120.00)	(14.40)
RI	7.68		8.40

Comments:

As in ROI, RI also shows better results as the imputed interest on older assets gets smaller.

However, the RI measure here will encourage new investment. As against the current return, a target return is decided with a view to long term objective of the corporate management. Sometimes the target rate of return is used as the imputed interest charge; a positive RI in this case will indicate a project that earns in excess of the target ROI.

Performance measures must be designed to reward decisions that are optimum for the company as a whole.

(c) **Economic Value Added (EVA)**

EVA, as a measure, follows the same principle as RI. Value addition by a project is measured by EVA. However, this measure looks at the impact on economic value of the business by the project. This requires a procedure which may deviate from the conventional accounting principles. For example, fully written off goodwill, research and development may be reinstated at their economic values with corresponding adjustments to the reported profit. The use of all the assets to generate economic benefits is thus highlighted. The emphasis on measuring value creating in the EVA should encourage managers to make decisions that are compatible with the objectives of the business as a whole.

Indeed, assets are often measured on a current cost basis within the EVA, which will eliminate the misleading benefit that appears to be gained from holding assets for longer than their economic value warrants.

Divisional bonus schemes may be based on EVA for motivation of managers, which will attain corporate goal congruence at the same time.

Illustrative Problem 22

Laxmi Shiv Bhagwati (LSB) Ltd. is a chain restaurant operating in South India. The company has two sources of long-term capital: debt and equity. LSB's cost of issuing debt is the after-tax cost of the interest payments on the debt, considering the fact that the interest payments are tax deductible. LSB's cost of equity capital is the investment opportunity rate of LSB's investors, that is, the rate they could earn on investments of risk similar to that of investing in LSB. The interest rate on LSB's ₹80,00,00,000 of long-term debt is 9 percent, and the company's tax rate is 40 percent. LSB's cost of equity capital is 14 percent. Moreover, the market value (and book value) of LSB's equity is ₹ 12,00,00,000.

The company consists of two divisions: properties division and food service division. The divisions' total assets, current liabilities, and before-tax operating income for the most recent year are as follows:

Division	Before-Tax Operating Income	Total Assets	Current Liabilities
Properties	₹ 2,90,00,000	₹ 1,45,000,000	₹ 30,00,000
Food Service	1,50,00,000	6,40,00,000	60,00,000

Required:

a. Calculate the weighted-average cost of capital for Laxmi Shiv Bhagwati Ltd.

b. Calculate the economic value added (EVA) for each of LSB's divisions.

Solution:

Weighted-average Cost of Capital and EVA

a. The weighted-average cost of capital (WACC) is defined as follows:

$$\text{Weighted-average cost of capital} = \frac{\left(\begin{array}{c}\text{After-tax cost}\\ \text{of debt capital}\end{array}\right)\left(\begin{array}{c}\text{Market}\\ \text{value of debt}\end{array}\right)+\left(\begin{array}{c}\text{Cost of}\\ \text{equity capital}\end{array}\right)\left(\begin{array}{c}\text{Market value}\\ \text{of equity}\end{array}\right)}{\begin{array}{c}\text{Market value}\\ \text{of debt}\end{array}+\begin{array}{c}\text{Market value}\\ \text{of equity}\end{array}}$$

The interest rate on LSB's ₹ 8,00,00,000 debt is 9 percent, and the company's tax rate is 40 percent. Therefore, the after-tax cost of debt is 5.4 per cent [9% × (1–40%)]. The cost of LSB's equity capital is 14 percent. Moreover, the market value of the company's equity is ₹ 12,00,00,000. The following calculation shows that LSB's WACC is 10.56 percent.

$$\text{Weighted-average cost of capital} = \frac{(.054)(₹\ 8,00,00,000) + (.14)(₹\ 12,00,00,000)}{₹\ 8,00,00,000 + ₹\ 12,00,00,000} = .1056$$

b. The economic value added (EVA) is defined as follows :

$$\text{Economic value added} = \text{Investment centre's after-tax operating income} - \left[\left(\text{Investment center's total assets} - \text{Investment center's current liabilities}\right) \times \text{Weighted-average cost of capital}\right]$$

We have the following calculations of EVA for each of the company's divisions.

Division	After-Tax Operating Income (in lakhs)		Total Assets (in lakhs)		Current Liabilities (in lakhs)		WACC		Economic Value Added (in lakhs)
Properties	₹ 290 (1–.40)	–	₹ 1450	–	₹ 30	×	.1056	=	₹ 24.048
Food Service	₹ 150 (1–.40)	–	₹ 640	–	₹ 60	×	.1056	=	₹ 28.752

Illustrative Problem 23

The three divisions of Godrej Foods are Snack Goods, Cereal, and Frozen Foods. The divisions are structured as investment centres. The following responsibility reports were prepared for the three divisions for the prior year:

	Snack Goods	**Cereal**	**Frozen Foods**
Revenues	₹ 15,00,000	₹ 24,00,000	₹ 13,50,000
Operating expenses	6,84,600	11,79,000	4,83,000
Income from operations before service department charges	₹ 8,15,400	₹ 12,21,000	₹ 8,67,000
Service department charges:			
Promotion	₹ 2,10,000	₹ 4,15,000	₹ 3,25,000
Legal	95,400	86,000	1,64,000
	₹ 3,05,400	₹ 5,01,000	₹ 4,89,000
Income from operations	₹ 5,10,000	₹ 7,20,000	₹ 3,78,000
Invested assets	₹ 25,00,000	₹ 48,00,000	₹ 18,00,000

Required:

1. Which division is making the best use of invested assets and thus should be given priority for future capital investments?
2. Assuming that the minimum acceptable rate of return on new projects is 12%, would all investments that produce a return in excess of 12% be accepted by the divisions?
3. Can you identify opportunities for improving the company's financial performance?

Solution:

1. The rate of return on invested assets is computed as follows:

	Snack Goods	Cereal	Frozen Foods
Income from operations	₹ 5,10,000	₹ 7,20,000	₹ 3,78,000

Invested assets	÷ ₹ 25,00,000	÷ ₹ 48,00,000	÷ ₹ 18,00,000
ROI	20.4%	15.0%	21.0%

The Frozen Foods Division appears to be making the best use of invested assets, since its ROI is the highest.

2. Not all projects that have greater than a 12% rate of return would be accepted. This is because all three divisions have an ROI that is greater than 12%. Thus, any project that is accepted between the 12% minimum and their existing ROI would cause their ROI to drop. This is true because of averaging. There would be little incentive to accept such projects if the divisions know they are competing against each other on the basis of ROI.
3. There are two approaches to improving ROI: (1) improving the profit margin or (2) improving the investment turnover. For all three divisions, the profit margin is excellent:

Snack Goods	34% (₹ 5,10,000/₹ 15,00,000)
Cereal	30% rounded (₹ 7,20,000/₹ 24,00,000)
Frozen Foods	28% (₹ 3,78,000/₹ 13,50,000)

However, the investment turnover is slow in all three divisions. The company doesn't return many sales Rupees per Rupee invested in assets, as shown below.

Snack Goods	0.60 (₹ 15,00,000/₹ 25,00,000)
Cereal	0.50 (₹ 24,00,000/₹ 48,00,000)
Froze Foods	0.75 (₹ 13,50,000/₹ 18,00,000)

The divisions need to work on increasing revenues or reducing invested assets in order to improve ROI.

Illustrative Problem 24

Atlas Industries produces tool and dye machinery for manufacturers. The company expanded vertically in 2016 by acquiring one of its suppliers of alloy steel plates, Jindal Steel Company. To manage the two separate businesses, the operations of Jindal are reported separately as an investment centre.

Atlas monitors its divisions on the basis of both unit contribution and return on average investment (ROI), with investment defined as average operating assets employed. Management bonuses are determined on ROI. The average cost of capital is 11 per cent of operating investment.

Jindal's cost of goods sold is considered to be entirely variable, while the division's administrative expenses are not dependent on volume. Selling expenses are a mixed cost with 40 per cent attributed to sales volume. Jindal contemplated a capital acquisition with an estimated ROI of 11.5 percent; however, divisional management decided against the investment because it believed that the investment would decrease Jindal's overall ROI. The 2016 operating statement for Jindal follows. The division's operating assets employed were ₹ 1,57,50,000 at November 30, 2016, a 5 per cent increase over the 2015 year-end balance.

Jindal Steel Division

Operating Statement for the Year Ended December 31, 2016 (₹ '000 omitted)

Sales revenue		₹ 25,000
Less expenses;		
Cost of goods sold	₹ 16,500	
Administrative expenses	3,955	
Selling expenses	2,700	23,155
Income from operations before income taxes		₹ 1,845

Required:

(*a*) Calculate the unit contribution margin for Jindal Steel Division if 14,84,000 units were produced and sold during the year ended December 31, 2016.

(*b*) Calculate the following performance measures for 2016 for the Jindal Steel Division:

(*i*) Pretax return on average investment in operating assets employed (ROI).

(*ii*) EVA calculated on the basis of average operating assets employed.

(*c*) Explain why the management of the Jindal Steel Division would have been more likely to accept the contemplated capital acquisition if EVA rather than ROI had been used as a performance measure.

(*d*) The Jindal Steel Division is a separate investment centre within Atlas Industries. Identify several items that Jindal should control if it is to be evaluated fairly by either the ROI or EVA performance measures.

(*CMA, USA, adapted with permission, M. Com. Delhi University, 2010*)

Solution:

(*a*) Sales	₹ 2,50,00,000
Less: Cost of goods sold	(1,65,00,000)
Selling expenses (₹ 2,700 × 40%)	(10,80,000)
Total contribution margin	₹ 74,20,000

Unit contribution margin = ₹ 74,20,000/14,84,000

= ₹ 5

(*b*) (*i*) ROI = Income before taxes/Average operating assets

= ₹ 18,45,000/₹ 1,53,75,000

= 12%

Average operating assets =

= (₹ 1,57,50,000 + ₹ 1,50,00,000 *) / 2

= ₹ 1,53,75,000

* November 30, 2015, operating assets = $\frac{₹\ 1{,}57{,}50{,}000}{1.05}$

= ₹ 1,50,00,000

(*ii*) EVA = ₹ 18,45,000 – (0.11) (₹ 1,53,75,000)

= ₹ 18,45,000 – ₹ 16,91,250

= ₹ 1,53,750

(*c*) The management of Jindal Steel would have preferred to accept capital acquisition if EVA was used as the performance measure because the investment would have increased both the division's wealth and the management bonuses. In case ROI is used as a performance measure, the management of Jindal is likely to reject any investment that would lower the overall ROI (12 per cent in 2016), even though the return is higher than the required minimum, because this would reduce bonuses.

(*d*) Jindal steel must be able to control all items related to profits and investment if it is to be evaluated fairly as an investment centre using ROI or EVA as performance measures. Jindal must control all elements of the business except the cost of invested capital, that being controlled by Atlas Industries.

Illustrative Problem 25

Performance measures are an essential component of a management control system and often play a vital role in determining business outcomes. The following situations come from unrelated companies.

Triton Industries

The operating divisions of Triton Industries are evaluated on several performance measures, one of which is operating income. Triton's corporate overhead is allocated to the divisions on the basis of each division's revenue, and this allocation is included in the calculation of operating income. The information given in the chart below is available for the first quarter of 2016.

Triton Industries First Quarter 2016

	Bicknell Division	*Norton Division*	*Driscoll Division*	*Total*
Revenues	₹ 23,04,000	₹ 32,40,000	₹16,56,000	₹ 72,00,000
Cost of goods sold	8,64,000	16,84,800	8,10,000	33,58,800
Gross margin	14,40,000	15,55,200	8,46,000	38,41,200
Division overhead	2,20,000	4,30,000	1,90,000	8,40,000
Corporate overhead	5,12,000	7,20,000	3,68,000	16,00,000
Division operating income	7,08,000	4,05,200	2,88,000	14,01,200

The manager of the Norton Division has been carrying a line of products that are marginally profitable but use facilities that would otherwise be idle. This product line is scheduled to be replaced over the next two years: but, in view of the first quarter's results, the manager is considering dropping the line immediately. The first quarter accounting data for this product line are as follows.

Revenues	₹ 6,00,000
Cost of goods sold	5,00,000
Avoidable division overhead	1,00,000

Rite Auto Shops

The owners of Rite Auto Shops stress customer satisfaction and speedy repairs. The mechanics are paid a base hourly wage of ₹25 plus piece-work incentives based on standard times and the type of job. For example a brake adjustment is estimated to take 90 minutes and has a work incentive of ₹ 10 if the adjustment is completed within 90 minutes. The company has recently started measuring customer satisfaction through the use of surveys and the monitoring of customer complaints.

Ashton Corporation

Ashton Corporation recently announced a bonus plan to award the manager of the most profitable division. The three division managers are to choose whether return on investment (ROI) or residual income (RI) will be used to measure profitability. In addition, they must decide whether investment will be measured using gross book value or net book value. The following information is available for the year just ended.

Division	*Gross Book Value of Assets*	*Division Operating Income*
Bristol	₹ 8,00,000	₹ 95,000
Darden	7,60,000	92,000
Gregory	5,00,000	61,600

All assets were purchased four years ago and have four years of useful life remaining. Ashton uses straight-line depreciation with no salvage value and an imputed interest charge for calculating residual income of 10 per cent of investment.

Required:

A. 1. Prepare a revised operating income statement for Triton Industries assuming that the manager of the Norton Division had stopped the sale and production of the marginally profitable product line at the beginning of the quarter, and

2. Discuss whether or not Triton Industries' measure of division profitability is encouraging behaviour that is beneficial to all parties.

B. Evaluate the mechanics compensation plan at Rite Auto Shops by

1. Describing the likely behaviour of the mechanics.
2. Recommending improvements to the plan.

C. Each division manager of Ashton Corporation has selected a method of bonus calculation that places his or her division in first place. Identify the method for calculating profitability that each manager selected, supporting your answer with appropriate calculations.

(CMA, USA, Adapted with Permission, M. Com. Delhi University, 2009)

Solution:

A. 1. A revised income statement for Triton Industries, prepared on the assumption that the manager of Norton Industries had discontinued the sale and production of the marginally profitable product line at the beginning of the quarter, is presented below.

Triton Industries
Statement of Income for the Quarter Ended March 31, 2016

	Bicknell Division	*Norton Division*	*Driscoll Division*	*Total*
Revenues	₹ 23,04,000	₹ 26,40,000(2)	₹ 16,56,000	₹ 66,00,000
Cost of goods sold	8,64,000	11,84,800(2)	8,10,000	28,58,800
Gross margin	14,40,000	14,55,200	8,46,000	37,41,200
Division overhead	2,20,000	3,30,000(2)	1,90,000	7,40,000
Corporate overhead(1)	5,60,000	6,40,000	4,00,000	16,00,000
Division operating Income	6,60,000	4,85,200	2,56,000	14,01,200

Notes:

(1) Reallocation of corporate overhead based on the percentages to total revenue assuming discontinuance of Norton Division marginal product line.

₹ 23,04,000 ÷ 66,00,000 = 35% × ₹ 16,00,000 = ₹ 5,60,000

₹ 26,40,000 ÷ 66,00,000 = 40% × ₹ 16,00,000 = ₹ 6,40,000

₹ 16,56,000 ÷ 66,00,000 = 25% × ₹ 16,00,000 = ₹ 4,00,000

(2) Restatement of Norton Division financial data assuming discontinuance of marginal product line.

Revenue	₹ 32,40,000	-	₹ 6,00,000	=	₹ 26,40,000
Cost of goods sold	₹ 16,84,800	-	₹ 5,00,000	=	₹ 11,84,800
Division overhead	₹ 4,30,000	-	₹ 1,00,000	=	₹ 3,30,000

2. Triton Industries' measure of division profitability is not encouraging behaviour that is beneficial to all parties for the following reasons.
   - The measure is dysfunctional since the divisions are being penalised for increasing revenues. Managers will be demotivated and behave in a manner that will not benefit the firm over time.
   - The allocation of corporate overhead on the basis of division revenues is inappropriate since revenues are not the drivers of corporate overheads.

B. 1. Rite Auto Shops current compensation plan encourages mechanics to complete the job in less than the standard amount of time. In order to earn the incentive, mechanics are in effect being encouraged to ignore job quality, take short cuts by not performing all specified functions, and focus on time only. Their behaviour will likely be to work rapidly to outperform the standard time per job without regard to quality or customer satisfaction.

2. A more congruent plan would be to base the compensation on customer satisfaction and quality as well as timeliness of job completion. While quality and customer satisfaction are difficult to measure precisely, they can be determined through customer surveys, customer complaints, quality inspections by supervisors, etc.

C. The calculations of the several bonus plans being evaluated at Ashton Corporation and the plans that the respective division managers would select to place their division in first place are presented below:

ASTHON CORPORATION

Calculation of Residual Income (RI) and Return on Investment (ROI) for Each Corporate Division (₹ in thousands)

Residual income (RI) calculations

Gross Book Value

Division	*Operating Income*	*Gross Book Value*	*Capital Charge @ 10%*	*Residual Income GBV*
Bristol	₹ 95.0	₹ 800.0	₹ 80.0	₹ 15.0
Darden	92.0	760.0	76.0	16.0(1)
Gregory	61.6	500.0	50.0	11.6

Net Book Value

Division	*Operating Income*	*Net Book Value*	*Capital Charge @ 10%*	*Residual Income NBV*
Bristol	₹ 95.0	₹ 400.0	₹ 40.0	₹ 55.0(2)
Darden	92.0	380.0	38.0	54.0
Gregory	61.6	250.0	25.0	36.6

Return on investment (ROI) calculations.

Gross Book Value

Division	*Operating Income*	*Gross Book Value*	*Return on Investment GBV*
Bristol	₹ 95.0	₹ 800.0	11.88%
Darden	92.0	760.0	12.11%
Gregory	61.6	500.0	12.32%(3)

Net Book Value

Division	*Operating Income*	*Gross Book Value*	*Accumulated Depreciation*	*Net Book Value*	*Return on Investment NBV*
Bristol	₹ 95.0	₹ 800.0	₹ 400.0	₹ 400.0	23.75%
Darden	92.0	760.0	380.0	380.0	24.21%
Gregory	61.6	500.0	250.0	250.0	24.64%(3)

Notes:

(1) The Darden Division selected the residual income [RI] method based on gross book value (GBV) as it placed the division first with an RI of ₹ 16,000.

(2) The Bristol Division selected the RI method based on net book value (NBV) as it placed the division first with RI of ₹ 55,000.

(3) The Gregory Division selected the return on investment (ROI) method based on either GBV or NBV as both methods placed the division in first place.

Illustrative Problem 26

A condensed income statement for the Water Sports Division of Apollo Sports Co. for the year ended March 31, 2016, is as follows:

Sales	₹ 6,00,000
Cost of goods sold	2,36,000
Gross profit	₹ 3,64,000
Operating expenses	2,74,000
Income from operations	₹ 90,000
Invested assets	₹ 5,00,000

Assume that the Water Sports Division received no charges from service departments.

The president of Apollo Sports has indicated that the division's rate of return on a ₹ 5,00,000 investment must be increased to at least 22% by the end of the next year if operations are to continue. The division manager is considering the following three proposals:

Proposal 1: Transfer equipment with a book value of ₹ 1,00,000 to other divisions at no gain or loss and lease similar equipment. The annual lease payments would be less than the amount of depreciation expense on the old equipment by ₹ 18,000. This decrease in expense would be included as part of the cost of goods sold. Sales would remain unchanged.

Proposal 2: Reduce invested assets by discontinuing a product line. This action would eliminate sales of ₹ 75,000, cost of goods sold of ₹ 26,600, and operating expenses of ₹ 21,400. Assets of ₹ 1,50,000 would be transferred to other divisions at no gain or loss.

Proposal 3: Purchase new and more efficient machinery and thereby reduce the cost of goods sold by ₹ 30,000. Sales would remain unchanged, and the old machinery, which has no remaining book value, would be scrapped at no gain or loss. The new machinery would increase invested assets by ₹ 2,50,000 for the year.

Required:

(*i*) Using the DuPont formula for rate of return on investment, determine the profit margin, investment turnover, and rate of return on investment for the Water Sports Division for the past year.

(*ii*) Prepare condensed estimated income statements and compute the invested assets for each proposal.

(*iii*) Using the DuPont formula for rate of return on investment, determine the profit margin, investment trunover, and rate of return on investment for each proposal.

(*iv*) Which of the three proposals would meet the required 22% rate of return on investment?

(*v*) If the Water Sports Division were in an industry where the profit margin could not be increased, how much would the investment turnover have to increase to meet the president's required 22% rate of return on investment? (*M. Com., Delhi University, 2012*)

Solution:

(i) Rate of Return on Investment = Profit Margin × Investment Turnover

$$\text{Rate of Return on Investment} = \frac{\text{Income from Operations}}{\text{Sales}} \times \frac{\text{Sales}}{\text{Invested Assets}}$$

$$\text{Water Sports Division: ROI} = \frac{₹90{,}000}{₹6{,}00{,}000} \times \frac{₹6{,}00{,}000}{₹5{,}00{,}000}$$

$$\text{ROI} = 15\% \times 1.2$$

$$\text{ROI} = 18\%$$

(*ii*)

Apollo Sports Co. — Water Sports Division
Estimated Income Statements
For the Year Ended March 31, 2016

	Proposal 1	**Proposal 2**	**Proposal 3**
Sales	₹ 6,00,000	₹ 5,25,000	₹ 6,00,000
Cost of goods sold	2,18,000	2,09,400	2,06,000
Gross profit	₹ 3,82,000	₹ 3,15,600	₹ 3,94,000
Operating expenses	2,74,000	2,52,600	2,74,000
Income from operations	₹ 1,08,000	₹ 63,000	₹ 1,20,000
Invested assets	₹ 4,00,000	₹ 3,50,000	₹ 7,50,000

(*iii*) Rate of Return on Investment = Profit Margin × Investment Turnover

$$\text{Rate of Return on Investment} = \frac{\text{Income from Operations}}{\text{Sales}} \times \frac{\text{Sales}}{\text{Invested Assets}}$$

$$\text{Proposal 1:} \quad \text{ROI} = \frac{₹1{,}08{,}000}{₹6{,}00{,}000} \times \frac{₹6{,}00{,}000}{₹4{,}00{,}000}$$

$$\text{ROI} = 18\% \times 1.5$$

$$\text{ROI} = 27\%$$

Proposal 2: $$\text{ROI} = \frac{₹63,000}{₹5,25,000} \times \frac{₹5,25,000}{₹3,50,000}$$

$$\text{ROI} = 12\% \times 1.5$$

$$\text{ROI} = 18\%$$

Proposal 3: $$\text{ROI} = \frac{₹1,20,000}{₹6,00,000} \times \frac{₹6,00,000}{₹7,50,000}$$

$$\text{ROI} = 20\% \times 0.8$$

$$\text{ROI} = 16\%$$

(*iv*) Proposal 1 would yield a rate of return on investment of 27%.

(*v*) Rate of Return on Investment = Profit Margin × Rquired Investment Turnover

22% = 15% × Required Investment Turnover

Required Investment Turnover = 1.47 (22%/15%)

Current Investment Turnover = 1.20

Increase in Investment Turnover = 0.27

or

22.5% Increase (0.27/1.20)

Illustrative Problem 27

J. K. Company is a privately held diversified company with five separate divisions organized as investment centres. A condensed income statement for the Apparel Division for the past year, assuming no service department charges, is as follows:

Apparel Division
Income Statement
for the Year Ended December 31, 2015

Sales	₹ 2,25,00,000
Cost of goods sold	1,68,70,000
Gross profit	₹ 56,30,000
Operating expenses	11,30,000
Income from operations	₹ 45,00,000
Invested assets	₹ 3,00,00,000

The manager of the Apparel Division was recently presented with the opportunity to add an addtional product line, which would require invested assets of ₹ 1,50,00,000. A projected income statement for the new product line is as follows:

New Product Line
Projected Income Statement
for the Year Ended December 31, 2016

Sales	₹ 90,00,000
Cost of goods sold	52,00,000

Gross profit	₹ 38,00,000
Operating expenses	24,50,000
Income from operations	₹ 13,50,000

The Apparel Division currently has ₹ 3,00,00,000 in invested assets, and the company's overall rate of return on investment, including all divisions, is 8%. Each division manager is evaluated on the basis of divisional rate of return on investment, and a bonus equal to ₹ 9,000 for each percentage point by which the division's rate of return on investment exceeds the company average is awarded each year.

The president is concerned that the manager of the Apparel Division rejected the addition of the new product line, when all estimates indicated that the product line would be profitable and would increase overall company income. You have been asked to analyze the possible reasons why the Apparel Division manager rejected the new product line.

Required:

1. Determine the rate of return on investment for the Apparel Division for the past year.
2. Determine the Apparel Division manager' bonus for the past year.
3. Determine the estimated rate of return on investment for the new product line.
4. Why might the manager of the Apparel Division decide to reject the new product line? Support your answer by determining the prjected rate of retun on investment for 2016, assuming that the new product line was launched in the Apparel Division, and 2016 actual operating results were similar to those of 2015.
5. Can you suggest an alternative performance measure for motivating division managers to accept new investment opportunities that would increase the overall company income and rate of return on investment?

Solution:

1. $\text{Rate of Return on Investment} = \dfrac{\text{Income from Operations}}{\text{Invested Assets}}$

$$\text{ROI} = \frac{₹45,00,000}{₹3,00,00,000}$$

$$\text{ROI} = 15\%$$

or

$$\text{Rate of Return on Investment} = \frac{\text{Income from Operations}}{\text{Sales}} \times \frac{\text{Sales}}{\text{Invested Assets}}$$

$$\text{ROI} = \frac{₹45,00,000}{₹2,25,00,000} \times \frac{₹2,25,00,000}{₹3,00,00,000}$$

$$\text{ROI} = 20\% \times 0.75$$

$$\text{ROI} = 15\%$$

2. ₹ 63,000 (7 × ₹ 9,000 = ₹ 63,000, where 7 = 15% – 8%)

3. $\text{Rate of Return on Investment} = \dfrac{\text{Income from Operations}}{\text{Invested Assets}}$

$$\text{ROI} = \frac{₹13{,}50{,}000}{₹1{,}50{,}00{,}000}$$

$$\text{ROI} = 9\%$$

or

$$\text{Rate of Return on Investment} = \frac{\text{Income from Operations}}{\text{Sales}} \times \frac{\text{Sales}}{\text{Invested Assets}}$$

$$\text{ROI} = \frac{₹13{,}50{,}000}{₹90{,}00{,}000} \times \frac{₹9{,}000{,}000}{₹1{,}50{,}00{,}000}$$

$$\text{ROI} = 15\% \times 0.60$$

$$\text{ROI} = 9\%$$

4. Even though the addition of the new product line would increase the overall company rate of return on investment, its addition would decrease the Apparel Divison's rate of return on investment from 15% to 13% (₹ 58,50,000/₹ 4,50,00,000). This decrease could negatively influence management's evaluation of the division manager. In addition, this decrease in the division's rate of return on investmert would also decrease the division manager's bonus by approximately ₹ 18,000 (2 × ₹ 9,000, where, 2 = 15% – 13%).

5. Use of residual income as a performance measure and as the basis for granting bonuses would motivate division managers to accept investment opportunities that exceed a minimum rate of return. If the minimum rate of return was set at 8%, any investment opportunity whose rate exceeded 8% would be viewed as acceptable. If this performance measure had been used, the Appreal Division manager would have increased the division's residual income by ₹ 1,50,000 through the addition of the new product line, as shown below.

Projected income from operations of new product line	₹ 13,50,000
Minimum amount of desired income from operations (₹1,50,00,000 × 8%)...	12,00,000
Residual income from new product line	₹ 1,50,000

The manager's bonus could then be calculated as a per cent of residual income. In this case, a bonus equal to 3% of residual income would achieve a bonus similar to the initial plan:

Income from operations	₹ 45,00,000
Minimum desired income (8% × ₹ 3,00,00,000)	24,00,000
Residual income	₹ 21,00,000
× Bonus percentage	× 3%
Bonus	₹ 63,000

The new project would add ₹ 4,500 (₹ 1,50,000 × 3%) to the bonus.

In addition, nonfinancial performance indicators about product quality and customer satisfaction can be used to supplement the financial numbers.

REFERENCES

1. Colin Drury, Management and Cost Accounting, Thomson Learning, 2000, p. 795.
2. Lane K. Anderson and Harold M. Sollenberger, Managerial Accounting, South Western publishing Co., 1992 p. 699.
3. Mohinder N. Kaura, Management Control and Reporting System, Sage Publications, 2002, pp. 98-100.

4. Ronald W. Hilton, Managerial Accounting, Tata McGraw Hill, 2005, p. 510.
5. Charles T. Horngreen, Sri Kant M. Datar and George Foster, Cost Accounting, A Managerial Emphasis, Pearson Education, 2008, p. 219.
6. Milton E. Usry and Lawrence H. Hammer, Cost Accounting, Planning and Control, South Western Publishing Co., 1991, pp. 452–453.
7. Joseph G. Louderback III and Jay S. Holmen, Managerial Accounting, Thomson, 2003, p. 373.
8. Don T. Decoster *et al*, Management Accounting, A Decision Emphasis, John Wiley and Sons, 1988, p. 547.
9. Roland Fox, Decision Making A Managerial Accounting Perspective, Butterworth Heinemun, 1990, p. 349.
10. Edward J. Blocher, Kung H. Chen, Gary Cokins, Thomas W. Lin., Cost Management, A Strategic Emphasis, Tata McGraw Hill Publishing Co., 2005, p. 770.
11. Edward J. Blocher, Kung H. Chen Gary Cokins, Thomas W. Lin, *Ibid*, p. 773.
12. Edward J. Blocher et al., *Ibid* p. 773–777.
13. Speech by Joel Stern at a seminar organized by India Times Mindscape of the Times of India, February 25, 2005.
14. H. T. Johnson and R. S. Kaplan, Relevance Lost – The Rise and Fall of Management Accounting, Harvard Business School Press, 1987.
15. Colin Drury, Management and Cost Accounting, Chapman and Hall, 1992, p. 743.
16. Jesset T. Barfield, Cecily A. Raiborn and Michal R. Kinnery, Cost Accounting, Traditions and Innovations, Thomson, p. 907
17. Joseph A. Maciariello, Management Control Systems, Prentice Hall, 1984.
18. Geraldine F. Dominiak and Joseph G. Louderback III, Managerial Accounting, PWS Kent publishing Co., 1991, p. 447.
19. Joseph G. Louderback III and Jay S. Holman, Managerial Accounting, p. 433.
20. Joseph A. Maciariello, *Ibid.*
21. M. Z. Iqbal, International Accounting, A Global Perspective, South Western College Publishing, 2000.

CRITICAL ANALYSIS AND DISCUSSION QUESTIONS, SELF-ASSESSMENT QUESTIONS, MULTIPLE CHOICE QUESTIONS, PROBLEMS, AND CASES

CRITICAL ANALYSIS AND DISCUSSION QUESTIONS

1. What is decentralisation? What are the advantages of decentralisation?
2. Explain the concept of responsibility centres.
3. How will you measure the performance of cost and revenue division?
4. Describe and compare the main performance measures that have been suggested to measure the divisional performance.
5. Profit, Return on Investment and Residual Income have stood the test of time and are widely used for measuring the performance of a division. Describe the strengths and weaknesses of these measures of performance.
6. Outline problems in defining and measuring capital employed in a division.
7. Explain the rationale of using an interest charge while measuring the performance of a division.
8. "In ROI, there is lack of consensus on the definition of numerator and denominator both." Explain.
9. Distinguish between a cost centre, a profit centre and an investment centre.
10. How is performance generally measured in cost centre, profit centre and investment centre. *(M.Com., Delhi, 2004)*
11. Explain the advantages and disadvantages of ROI for divisional performance measurtment, what is the importance of non-financial measures of performance. *(M. Com, Delhi, 2015)*
12. When comparing various divisions, why is it important that the divisions have the same or similar accounting methods?
13. List the components of ROI equation, tell how they are related and identify an action a manager can take regarding each component to improve ROI.
14. How is residual income defined? What is the major advantage of using residual income in performance evaluation versus ROI.
15. What are net profit margin and asset turnover? Explain how these concepts can improve the evaluation of an investment centre.
16. What advantages and disadvantages are shared by ROI and Residual Income? What can be done to overcome this problem? *(M.Com., Delhi, 2003, 2011)*
17. Name three performance measures useful in evaluating investment centres.
18. What are two ways of expressing ROI?
19. In a decentralised company in which the divisions are organised as investment centres, how could a division be considered the least profitable, even though it earned the largest amount of operating income?
20. "The ROI measure may be based in favour of divisions with older plant and equipment." Explain.
21. "Evaluation of a division's performance is different from evaluating the performance of divisional manager." Explain this statement, giving reasons. *(M.Com., Delhi, 2006)*
22. "In computing ROI, there are problems both with regard to numerator and the denominator." Point out these problems and give your considered views thereon.
23. "It may be desirable to use a different ROI measure for evaluating the performance of a division and the performance of the division's manager." Explain.

24. What are margin and turnover? Explain how these concepts can improve the evaluation of an investment centre.
25. What special problems arise when evaluating performance in multinational companies?
26. Why is it important to distinguish between the performance of a manager and the performance of the organisation subunit for which the manager is responsible?
27. What are the benefits of ROI? Explain how each can lead to improved profitability.
28. What are disadvantages of ROI? Explain how each can lead to decreased profitability.
29. What are the measurement issues to consider when using return or investment ?
30. What are the advantages and limitations of residual income?
31. "Always try to distinguish between the performance of a segment and its managers." Why?
32. "The essence of decentralization is the use of profit centres." Explain.
33. What problems do you see in establishing and evaluating responsibility centres in the following:
    (a) University of Delhi
    (b) Colleges within university of Delhi
    (c) Departments within university of Delhi
    (d) Departments within colleges of university of Delhi.
34. Why do some companies use gross book value instead of net book value to measure a division's invested capital.
35. For what decisions is the manager of a cost centre not responsible?
36. In a decentralised company in which the divisions are organized as investment centres, how could a division be considered the least profitable even though it earned the largest amount of income from operations?
37. Discuss the impact of accounting policies on ROI.
38. Which assets should be used to compute ROI.
39. Discuss the advantages and disadvantages of ROI as a performance measure.
40. Organizational experts say that decentralization "co-locates knowledge and decision rights." What does this statement mean? Is decentralization always beneficial? What are the costs associated with delegating decision making to lower levels of an organization?
41. Some argue that decentralization results in maximizing profit division by division. It may not lead to profit maximization at the overall firm level. Do you agree? Why or why not?
42. In choosing a performance measure, many argue that controllability is the operative principle in that a manager should be able to influence the metric. Some argue for informativeness, which says that any metric that provides insight into the manager's performance (whether controllable or not) is a good measure. Discuss, providing an example of an informative measure that is not controllable.
43. "Why not simply evaluate the performance of all divisional managers based on the entire firm's profit? That way, we do not have to worry about dividional managers not acting in the firm's best interests." Is this a reasonable argument? Why or why not?
44. Consider each of the following scenarios.
    A. Ashok Dhawan, plant manager for the laser printer factory of Compugear Co. brushed his hair back and sighed. December had been a bad month; two machines had broken down, and some direct labourers (all on salary) were idled for part of the month. Materials prices increased, and insurance premiums on the factory increased. No way out of it—costs were going up. He hoped that the marketing VP would be able to push through some price increases, but that really wasn't his department.

B. Ms. Jyoti Reddy was delighted to see that her ROI figures had increased for the third straight year. She was sure that her campaign to lower costs and use machinery more efficiently (enabling her factories to sell several older machines) was the reason why she planned to take full credit for the improvements at her semiannual performance review.

C. Rajnish, sales manager for ABC Co., was not pleased with a memo from headquarters detailing the recent cost increases for the laser printer line. Headquarters suggested raising prices. "Great," thought Rajnish, " An increase in price will kill sales—and revenue will go down. Why can't the plant shape up and cut costs like every other company in India is doing? Why turn this into my problem?"

D. Ms Sonam, looked at the quarterly profit/loss statement with disgust. Revenue was down and cost was up—what a combination! Then, she had an idea. If she cut back on maintenance of equipment and let a product engineer go, expenses would decrease—perhaps enough to reverse the trend in operating income.

E. Ms Nidhi, had just been hired to improve the fortunes of the Southern Division of ABC Co. She met with top staff and hammered out a three-year plan to improve the situation. A centrepiece of the plan is the retiring of obsolete equipment and the purchasing of state-of-the-art, computer-assisted machinery. The new machinery would take time for the workers to learn to use, but once that was done, waste would be virtually eliminated.

Required:

For each of the above independent scenarios, indicate the type of responsibility centre involved (cost, revenue, profit, or investment) and the accounting numbers on which performance evaluation is likely based.

Answer: Cost centre – Total cost

Profit centre – Operating Income

Revenue Centre – Sales

Investment centre – Return on Investment

45. The senior management of Calvin Company has proposed the following three performance measures for the company:
    1. New income as a per cent of shareholder's equity
    2. Revenue growth
    3. Employee satisfaction

Management believes these three measures combine both financial and nonfinancial meeasures and are thus superior to using just financial measures.

What advice would you give Calvin Company for improving its performance measurement system?

Self-Assessment Questions

A. REB Service Co. is a computer service centre. For the month of May 2016, REB had the following operating statistics.

Sales	₹ 4,50,000
Operating income	25,000
Net profit after taxes	8,000
Total assets	5,00,000
Shareholders' equity	2,00,000
Cost of capital	6%

Based on the above information, which one of the following statements is correct? REB has a

(*a*) return on investment of 4 percent.

(*b*) residual income of ₹ (5000).

(*c*) return on investment of 1.6 percent.

(*d*) residual income of ₹ (22,000).

(*e*) residual income of ₹ 13,000.

B. The following information pertains to Bala Co. for the year ended December 31, 2016:

Sales	₹ 6,00,000
Income	1,00,000
Capital Investment	4,00,000

Which of the following equations should be used to compute Bala's return on investment?

(*a*) (4/6) × (6/1) = ROI (*b*) (6/4) × (1/6) = ROI

(*c*) (4/6) × (1/6) = ROI (*d*) (6/4) × (6/1) = ROI

C. The following information pertains to Quest Co.'s Gold Division for the current year:

Sales	₹ 3,11,000
Variable cost	2,50,000
Traceable fixed costs	50,000
Average invested capital	40,000
Imputed interest rate	10%

Quest's return on investment was

(*a*) 10.00% (*b*) 13.33%

(*c*) 27.50% (*d*) 30.00%

D. Listed below is selected financial information for the Western Division of the ABC Company for the last year.

Account	***Amount (thousands)***
Average working capital	₹ 625
General and administrative expenses	75
Net sales	4,000
Average plant and equipment	1,775
Cost of goods sold	3,525

If ABC treats the Western Division as an investment centre for performance measurement purposes, what is the before-tax return on investment (ROI) for last year?

(*a*) 34.78%

(*b*) 22.54%

(*c*) 19.79%

(*d*) 16.67%

E. Ramesh is the general manager of the Industrial Product Division, and his performance is measured using the residual income method. Ramesh is reviewing the following forecasted information for his division for next year:

Category	*Amount (thousands)*
Working capital	₹ 1,800
Revenue	30,000
Plant and equipment	17,200

If the imputed interest charge is 15% and Ramesh wants to achieve a residual income target of ₹ 20,00,000, what will costs have to be in order to achieve the target?

(*a*) ₹ 90,00,000 (*b*) ₹ 1,08,00,000
(*c*) ₹ 2,51,50,000 (*d*) ₹ 2,56,90,000

F. The following selected data pertain to a Division of Eagle Co. for 2016:

Sales	₹ 4,00,000
Operating income	40,000
Capital turnover	4
Imputed interest rate	10%

What was Division's residual income?

(*a*) ₹ 0 (*b*) ₹ 4,000
(*c*) ₹ 10,000 (*d*) ₹ 30,000

G. The following is a summarised income statement of a profit centre in ABC Company for March 2016:

Contribution margin		₹ 70,000
Period expenses:		
Manager's salary	₹ 20,000	
Facility depreciation	8,000	
Corporate expense allocation	5,000	33,000
Profit centre income		37,000

Which of the following amounts would most likely be subject to the control of the profit centre's manager?

(*a*) ₹ 70,000
(*b*) ₹ 50,000
(*c*) ₹ 37,000
(*d*) ₹ 33,000

(CMA, USA, Adapted with permission)

Answer to self-Assessment Questions

A. (b) B. (b) C. (c) D. (d) E. (c)
F. (d) G. (a)

MULTIPLE CHOICE QUESTIONS

Select the correct answer for the following multiple choice questions:

1. When the manager has the responsibility for and authority to make decisions that affect costs and revenues, but no responsibility for or authority over assets invested in the department, the department is referred to as:
   (*a*) Cost centre (*b*) Profit centre
   (*c*) Investment centre (*d*) None of the above
2. The term used to describe the excess of departmental gross profit over direct departmental expenses is:
   (*a*) Income from operations (*b*) Net income
   (*c*) Departmental margin (*d*) None of the above
3. What term identifies an accounting system in which the operations of business are broken down into cost centres and the control function of a foreman, sales manager, or supervisor is emphasised?
   (*a*) Responsibility accounting (*b*) Operations - research accounting.
   (*c*) Control accounting (*d*) Budgetary accounting
4. Internal reports prepared under the responsibility-accounting approach should be limited to which of the following costs?
   (*a*) Only variable costs of production
   (*b*) Only conversion costs
   (*c*) Only controllable costs
   (*d*) Only costs properly allocable to the cost centre under generally accepted accounting principles.
5. The most desirable measure of departmental performance for evaluating the performance of the department manager is departmental:
   (*a*) Revenue less controllable departmental expenses.
   (*b*) Net income.
   (*c*) Contribution to indirect expenses.
   (*d*) Revenue less departmental variable expenses.
6. Which of the following items of cost would be least likely to appear in a performance report based on responsibility accounting techniques for the supervisor of an assembly line in a large manufacturing situation?
   (*a*) Supervisor's salary (*b*) Materials
   (*c*) Repairs and maintenance (*d*) Direct labour.
7. When used for performance evaluation, periodic internal reports based on a responsibility accounting system should not
   (*a*) Be related to the organisation chart.
   (*b*) Include allocated fixed overhead.
   (*c*) Include variances between actual and budget controllable costs.
   (*d*) Distinguish between controllable and non-controllable costs.

8. The budget for a given cost during a given period was ₹ 80,000. The actual cost for the period was ₹ 72,000. Considering these facts, it can be said that the plant manager has done a better than expected job in controlling the cost if.
   (*a*) The cost is variable and actual production was 90% of budgeted production.
   (*b*) The cost is variable and actual production equalled budgeted production.
   (*c*) The cost is variable and actual production was 80% of budgeted production.
   (*d*) The cost is a discretionary fixed cost and actual production equalled budgeted production.
9. What is the most appropriate base to use in computing a rate of return for a business segment?
   (*a*) Total segment assets employed.
   (*b*) Total segment assets employed less allocated liabilities of the company.
   (*c*) Current assets of the segment.
   (*d*) Current assets less current liabilities of the segment.
10. Assuming that sales and net income remain the same, a company's return on investment would
   (*a*) Increase if the invested capital — employed turnover rate decreases.
   (*b*) Increase if the invested capital — employed turnover rate increases.
   (*c*) Increase if invested capital increases.
   (*d*) Decrease if invested capital decreases.
11. A company's return on investment (ROI) would generally increase when
   (*a*) Assets increase
   (*b*) Selling prices decrease
   (*c*) Costs decrease
   (*d*) Costs increase
12. A company's rate of return on investment is the
   (*a*) Percentage of profit to sales divided by the capital — employed turnover rate.
   (*b*) Percentage of profit to sales multiplied by the capital — employed turnover rate.
   (*c*) Investment capital divided by the capital — employed turnover rate.
   (*d*) Investment capital multiplied by the capital — employed turnover rate.
13. Rate of return on assets can be calculated by multiplying profit margin by
   (*a*) Net income (*b*) Net sales
   (*c*) Inventory turnover (*d*) Asset turnover
   (*e*) Average total assets
14. Division A of Kron Co. has sales of ₹ 3,50,000, cost of goods sold of ₹ 2,00,000 and operating expenses of ₹ 30,000 and invested assets of ₹ 6,00,000. What is the ROI for Division A?
   (*a*) 20% (*b*) 25%
   (*c*) 40% (*d*) None of the above
15. Division A of a company has ROI of 24% and an investment turnover of 1.6. What is the profit margin?
   (*a*) 6% (*b*) 15%
   (*c*) 24% (*d*) None of the above

16. The basic objective of the RI approach of performance measurement and evaluation is to have a division maximise its.
    (*a*) ROI rate
    (*b*) Imputed interest rate charge
    (*c*) Cash flows
    (*d*) Cash flows in excess of a desired minimum amount
    (*e*) Income in excess of a desired minimum return
17. The imputed interest rate used in the RI approach for performance measurement and evaluation can best be characterised as the
    (*a*) historical weighted average cost of capital for the company.
    (*b*) marginal after-tax cost of new equity capital.
    (*c*) average return on investment that has been earned by the company over a particular time period.
    (*d*) target ROI set by management.
    (*e*) average prime lending rate for the year being evaluated.
18. Which of the following items would most likely not be incorporated into the calculation of a division's investment base when using the RI approach for performance measurement and evaluation?
    (*a*) Fixed assets employed in divisional operations.
    (*b*) Vacant land being held by the division as a potential site for a new plant.
    (*c*) Divisional inventories when division management exercises control over the inventory levels.
    (*d*) Divisional accounts payable when division management exercises control over the amount of short-term credit utilised.
    (*e*) Divisional accounts receivable when division management exercises control over credit policy and credit terms.
19. A segment of an organisation is referred to as a profit centre if it has the
    (*a*) authority to make decisions affecting the major determinants of profit including the power to choose its markets and sources of supply.
    (*b*) authority to make decisions affecting the major determinants of profit including the power to choose its market and sources of supply and significant control over the amount of invested capital.
    (*c*) authority to make decisions over the most significant cost of operations including the power to choose the sources of supply.
    (*d*) authority to provide specialised support to other units within the organisation.
    (e) responsibility for combining the raw materials, direct labour, and other factors of production into a final output.
20. A segment of an organisation is referred to as an investment centre if it has the:
    (*a*) authority to make decisions affecting the major determinants of profit including the power to choose its markets and sources of supply.

(*b*) authority to make decisions affecting the major determinants of profit including the power to choose its market and sources of supply and significant control over the amount of invested capital.

(*c*) authority to make decisions over the most significant costs of operations including the power to choose the sources of supply.

(*d*) authority to provide specialised support to other units within the organisation.

(*e*) responsibility for developing markets for and selling of the output of the organisation.

21. A segment of an organisation is referred to as a service centre if it has the

(*a*) responsibility for developing markets for and selling of the output of the organisation.

(*b*) responsibility for combining the raw materials, direct labour, and other factors of production into a final output.

(*c*) authority to make decisions affecting the major determinants of profit including the power to choose its markets and sources of supply.

(*d*) authority to provide specialised support to other units within the organisation.

(*e*) authority to make decisions over the most significant costs of operations including the power to choose the sources of supply.

22. A segment of an organisation is referred to as an expense centre if it has the

(*a*) responsibility for developing markets for and selling of the output of the organisation.

(*b*) authority to make decisions affecting the major determinants of profit including the power to choose its markets and sources of supply.

(*c*) authority to make decisions over the most significant costs of operations including the power to choose the sources of supply.

(*d*) authority to provide specialised support to other units within the organisation.

(*e*) responsibility for combining the raw materials, direct labour, and other factors of production into a final output.

23. Controllable revenue would be included in a performance report for a

	Profit centre	***Cost centre***
(*a*)	No	No
(*b*)	No	Yes
(*c*)	Yes	No
(*d*)	Yes	Yes

24. Division A is considering a project that will earn a rate of return which is greater than the imputed interest charge for invested capital, but less than the division's historical return on invested capital. Division B is considering a project that will earn a rate of return that is greater than the division's historical return on invested capital, but less than the imputed interest charge for invested capital. If the objective is to maximise residual income, should these divisions accept or reject their projects ?

	A	***B***
(*a*)	Accept	Accept
(*b*)	Reject	Accept

(*c*)	Reject	Reject
(*d*)	Accept	Reject

25. Which combination of changes in asset turnover and income as a percentage of sales will maximise the return on investment?

	Asset turnover	***Income as a percentage of sales***
(*a*)	Increase	Decrease
(*b*)	Increase	Increase
(*c*)	Decrease	Increase
(*d*)	Decrease	Decrease

26. Which one of the following will not occur in an organisation that gives managers throughout the organisation maximum freedom to make decisions?
    (*a*) Individual managers regarding the managers of other segments as they do external parties.
    (*b*) Two divisions of the organisation having competing models that aim for the same market segments.
    (*c*) Delays in securing approval for the introduction of new products.
    (*d*) Greater knowledge of the marketplace and improved service to customers.
27. The least complex segment or area of responsibility for which costs are allocated is a (n)
    (*a*) Profit centre. (*b*) Investment centre.
    (*c*) Contribution centre. (*d*) Cost centre.
28. The segment margin of an investment centre after deducting the imputed interest on the assets used by the investment centre is known as
    (*a*) return on investment. (*b*) residual income.
    (*c*) operating income. (*d*) return on assets.
    (*e*) return on assets committed.
29. In responsibility accounting, a centre's performance is measured by those costs which are controllable. Controllable costs are **best** described as including
    (*a*) direct material and direct labour only.
    (*b*) only those costs that the manager can influence in the current time period.
    (*c*) only discretionary costs.
    (*d*) those costs about which the manager is knowledgeable and informed.
    (*e*) incremental and fixed costs.
30. The budgeting process which uses management by objectives and input from the individual manager is an example of the application of
    (*a*) flexible budgeting.
    (*b*) human resource management.
    (*c*) responsibility accounting.
    (*d*) capital budgeting.
    (*e*) crisis management.

31. A successful responsibility accounting and reporting system is dependent upon
    (*a*) the correct allocation of controllable variable costs.
    (*b*) identification of the management level at which all costs are controllable.
    (*c*) the proper delegation of responsibility and authority.
    (*d*) a reasonable separation of costs into their fixed and variable components since fixed costs are not controllable and must be eliminated from the responsibility report.
    (*e*) the cost of maintaining and operating the responsibility accounting system.
32. The Stonebrook Company uses a performance reporting system that reflects the company's decentralisation of decision making. The departmental performance reports show actual costs incurred during the period against budgeted costs. Any variances from the budget are assigned to the individual department manager who controls the costs. Stonebrook is using a type of system called.
    (*a*) transfer-pricing accounting. (*b*) flexible budgeting.
    (*c*) contribution accounting. (*d*) responsibility accounting.
    (*e*) activity-based budgeting.
33. Digital Tech uses an accounting system that charges costs to the manager who has the authority to make decisions incurring the costs. For example, if a sales manager authorises a rush order that results in additional manufacturing costs, then these additional costs are charged to the sales manager. This type of accounting system is known as
    (*a*) responsibility accounting. (*b*) functional accounting.
    (*c*) transfer-pricing accounting. (*d*) contribution accounting.
    (*e*) programme budgeting.
34. One approach to measuring divisional performance is return on investment. Return on investment is expressed as operating income
    (*a*) divided by the current year's capital expenditures plus cost of capital.
    (*b*) minus imputed interest charged for invested capital.
    (*c*) divided by fixed assets.
    (*d*) divided by current assets.
    (*e*) divided by total assets.
35. Decentralised firms can delegate authority and yet retain control and monitor managers performance by structuring the organisation into responsibility centres. Which one of the following organisational segments is most likely an independent business?
    (*a*) Revenue centre. (*b*) Profit centre.
    (*c*) Cost centre. (*d*) Investment centre.
    (*e*) Activity centre.
36. Which denominator used in the return on investment (ROI) formula is criticised because it combines the effects of operating decisions made at one level of the organisation with financing decisions made at another organisational level?
    (*a*) Working capital. (*b*) Total assets employed.
    (*c*) Shareholder's equity. (*d*) Working capital plus other assets.
    (*e*) Total assets available.

37. The segment margin of the Wire Division of Reliance Company should not include
    (*a*) Net sales of the Wire Division
    (*b*) Fixed selling expenses of the Wire Division.
    (*c*) Variable selling expenses of the Wire Division.
    (*d*) The Wire Division's fair share of the salary of Reliance Company's president.
38. The basic purpose of a responsibility accounting system is
    (*a*) Budgeting. (*b*) Motivation.
    (*c*) Authority. (*d*) Variance analysis.
39. A major problem in comparing profitability measures among companies is the
    (*a*) Lack of general agreement over which profitability measure is best.
    (*b*) Differences in the size of the companies.
    (*c*) Differences in the accounting methods used by the companies.
    (*d*) Differences in the dividend policies of the companies.
40. Most firms use return on investment (ROI) to evaluate the performance of investment centre managers. If top management wishes division managers to use all assets without regard to financing, the denominator in the ROI calculation will be
    (*a*) Total assets available. (*b*) Total assets employed.
    (*c*) Working capital plus other assets. (*d*) Shareholders equity.
41. Which denominator used in the return on investment (ROI) formula is criticized because it combines the effects of operating decisions made at one organisational level with financing decisions made at another organisation level?
    (*a*) Total assets employed. (*b*) Shareholders equity.
    (*c*) Working capital plus other assets. (*d*) Total assets available.
42. A large company allocates the costs of its headquarters staff to its decentralised divisions. The best reason for this allocation is to
    (*a*) More accurately measure divisional operating results.
    (*b*) Improve divisional managements' morale.
    (*c*) Remind divisional managers that common costs exist.
    (*d*) Discourage any use of central support services.
43. A firm earning a profit can increase its return on investment by
    (*a*) Increasing sales revenue and operating expenses by the same amount.
    (*b*) Decreasing sales revenues and operating expenses by the same percentage.
    (*c*) Increasing investment and operating expenses by the same amount.
    (*d*) Increasing sales revenues and operating expenses by the same percentage.
44. Which one of the following statements pertaining to the return on investment (ROI) as a performance measurement is incorrect?
    (*a*) When the average age of assets differs substantially across segments of a business, the use of ROI may not be appropriate.
    (*b*) ROI relies on financial measures that are capable of being independently verified, while other forms of performance measures are subject to manipulation.

(*c*) The use of ROI may lead managers to reject capital investment projects that can be justified by using discounted cash flow models.

(*d*) The use of ROI can make it undesirable for a skillful manager to take on troubleshooting assignments such as those involving turning around unprofitable divisions.

45. Residual income is a performance evaluation that is used in conjunction with, or instead of, return on investment (ROI). In many cases, residual income is preferred to ROI because

(*a*) Residual income is a measure over time, while ROI represents the results for one period.

(*b*) Residual income concentrates on maximising absolute income rather than a percentage return as with ROI.

(*c*) The imputed interest rate used in calculating residual income is more easily derived than the target rate that is compared to the calculated ROI.

(*d*) Average investment is employed with residual income while year-end investment is employed with ROI.

46. Residual income is a better measure for performance evaluation of an investment centre manager than return on investment because

(*a*) The problems associated with measuring the asset base are eliminated.

(*b*) Desirable investment decisions will not be neglected by high-return divisions.

(*c*) Only the gross book value of assets needs to be calculated.

(*d*) The arguments about the implicit cost of interest are eliminated.

(*CMA, USA, Adapted with permission*)

Answer to Multiple Choice Questions

1. (b)	2. (c)	3. (a)	4. (c)	5. (a)
6. (a)	7. (a)	8. (b)	9. (a)	10. (b)
11. (c)	12. (b)	13. (d)	14. (a)	15. (b)
16. (e)	17. (d)	18. (b)	19. (a)	20. (b)
21. (d)	22. (e)	23. (c)	24. (d)	25. (b)
26. (c)	27. (d)	28. (b)	29. (b)	30. (c)
31. (c)	32. (d)	33. (a)	34. (e)	35. (d)
36. (c)	37. (d)	38. (b)	39. (c)	40. (a)
41. (b)	42. (c)	43. (d)	44. (b)	45. (b)
46. (b)				

PROBLEMS

1. Rahul Gambhir is responsible for the Finishing Activity Centre at Delite Plumbing Fixtures. A budget for the centre for July, 2016 is as follows:

	(₹)
Materials and supplies	9,64,000
Labour	7,32,000
Supervision	3,00,000

Fuel	1,68,000
Telephone	43,000
Postage	26,000
Taxes and insurance	1,75,000
Heat and light	1,54,000
Repairs and maintenance	1,87,000
Depreciation — equipment	90,000
Other allocated plant costs	3,40,000
Total	31,79,000

The actual cost of materials and supplies for the month was ₹ 9,57,000, labour, ₹ 7,48,000 and fuel, ₹ 1,71,000. Telephone amounted to ₹ 48,000. Repairs and maintenance cost was ₹ 1,85,000. Heat and light cost was ₹ 1,60,000 and the other allocated plant costs were ₹ 5,70,000. All other costs were in agreement with the budget.

The cost of supervision, taxes and insurance, heat and light, depreciation of equipment, and other allocated plant costs are not controllable by Rahul Gambhir.

Required:

Prepare a responsibility report showing a comparison of the actual and budgeted costs for July. Separate the controllable costs from the uncontrollable costs in the report.

Answer:

	Actual	***Budget***
Controllable costs ₹	21,35,000	21,20,000
Non controllable costs	12,95,000	10,59,000

2. Yonex India Ltd. is segmented into three divisions A,B and C. All were formed in the same year and now all assets have left exactly one-half of their expected life. Top management is attempting to determine which of the division is the most profitable. The following data have been prepared for your analysis:

	Division		
	A ***(₹)***	***B*** ***(₹)***	***C*** ***(₹)***
Net income before taxes	78,000	90,000	96,000
Investment base-gross book value	3,90,000	5,00,000	6,00,000
Investment base-net book value	1,95,000	2,50,000	3,00,000

Prepare rankings of the three divisions using ROI and RI with a capital charge of 12.5% that each division manager might use to assert that here is the most profitable division. (*M.Com., Delhi*)

Answer:

Ranking

ROI	**RI (Gross Book Value)**	**RI (Net Value)**
A	A	B
B	B	C
C	C	A

3. A company has two divisions, X and Y and evaluates its managers on the ROI criterion. Budget for the next year are as follows:

	X (₹)	*Y* (₹)	*Total* (₹)
Investment	12,00,000	10,00,000	22,00,000
Revenue	6,00,000	3,00,000	9,00,000
Operating expenses	(3,00,000)	(2,00,000)	(5,00,000)
Profit	3,00,000	1,00,000	4,00,000

A new investment opportunity has arisen and could be adopted by either division. It requires an investment of ₹ 2,00,000 and promises annual operating profits of ₹ 40,000.

Required:

(*i*) Which division (X or Y) would accept the new project? Why?

(*ii*) If an RI criterion with minimum ROI of 18% were in use, which division (X or Y) would accept the new project? Why?

(*iii*) With minimum ROI of 18% should the new project be adopted from the viewpoint of the company as a whole ? Why?

4. The Chocolate Division of the International Confection Company had a rate of return on investment (ROI) of 12 per cent (=₹ 12,00,000/₹ 1,00,00,000) during Year 7, based on sales of ₹ 2,00,00,000. In an effort to improve its performance during Year 8, the company instituted several cost-saving programs, including the substitution of automatic equipment for work previously done by workers and the purchase of raw materials in large quantities to obtain quantity discounts. Despite these cost-saving programs, the company's ROI for Year 8 was 10 per cent (= ₹ 11,00,000/₹ 1,10,00,000), based on sales of ₹ 2,00,00,000.

Required:

a. Break down the ROI for Year 7 and Year 8 into profit margin and investment turnover ratios.

b. Explain the reason for the decrease in ROI between the two years using the results from part a.

Answer:

a.	ROI	Profit margin	Investment turnover
Year 7	12%	6%	2.0
Year 8	10%	5.5%	1.82

b. Sales remain the same. However, investment increased due to larger amounts of inventory and fixed assets.

5. The following information relates to the operating performance of two divisions of Sony Electronics, for last year.

	Europe Division	Asia Pacific Division
Operating Profits	₹ 30,00,000	₹ 40,00,000
Total Assets (at gross acquisition cost)	2,00,00,000	5,00,00,000
Total Assets (net of accumulated depreciation)	1,50,00,000	1,50,00,000

Required:

a. Compute the return on investment (ROI) of each division, using total assets at gross book value as the investment base.

b. Compute the ROI of each division, using total assets net of accumulated depreciation (net book value) as the investment base.

c. Which of the two measures do you think gives the better indication of operating performance? Explain your reasoning.

Answer:

	Europe Division	Asia Pacific Division
a. ROI	15%	8%
b. ROI	20%	26.67%

6. The following information relates to the operating performance of three divisions of a company for last year.

	Easten Division	Central Division	Western Division
Operating Profit	₹ 4,00,000	₹ 30,00,000	₹ 40,00,000
Investment	50,00,000	90,00,000	1,80,00,000

Required:

a. Compute the rate of return on investment (ROI) of each division for last year.

b. Assume that the firm levies a charge on each division for the use of funds. The charge is 10 per cent on investment, and the accounting system deducts it in measuring divisional net income. Recalculate ROI using divisional net income after deduction of the use-of-funds charge in the numerator.

c. Which of these two measures do you think gives the better indication of operating performance? Explain your reasoning.

Answer:

	Eastern Division	Central Division	Western Division
a. ROI	8.0%	33.33%	22.22%
b. ROI	– 2%	23.33%	12.22%

7. A company has two department stores, which are organised as divisions. One store is at Kanpur where business activity is declining. The other store is in Bengaluru, located in an area of the city that is expanding rapidly. Results of operations for each store for 2016 are shown as follows:

	Bengaluru **(₹)**	***Kanpur*** **(₹)**
Sales	₹ 39,00,000	₹ 17,50,000
Total costs	₹ 27,62,000	₹ 15,70,000
Average current assets	₹ 5,87,500	₹ 1,65,000
Average long-term assets (net)	₹ 40,62,500	₹ 9,62,000
Minimum desired rate of return	15%	10%

Required:

(i) ROI for each division

(a) Compute the return on sales

(b) Compute the asset turnover

(c) Compute the ROI

(ii) Residual income for each division

(a) Compute residual income

(b) Compute the residual income percentage

8. ABC Company has two divisions A and B. Invested assets and condensed income statement data for each division for the past year ended December 31 are as follows:

	Division A (₹)	**Division B** (₹)
Sales	31,25,000	51,00,000
Cost of goods sold	25,00,000	40,00,000
Operating expenses	1,50,000	5,90,000
Invested assets	25,00,000	30,00,000

Required:

(i) Prepare condensed income statements for the past year for each division.

(ii) Using the expanded expression, determine the profit margin, investment turnover, and rate of return on investment for each division.

(iii) If management desires a minimum rate of return of 12%, determine the residual income for each division.

9. The following information relates to the operating performance of two divisions of a company:

	Division A (₹)	**Division B** (₹)
Operating Profit	4,00,000	6,00,000
Total Assets (based on acquisition cost)	40,00,000	75,00,000
Total Assets (based on current replacement cost)	60,00,000	80,00,000

Required:

(a) Compute the return on investment (ROI) of each division, using total assets stated at acquisition cost as the investment base.

(b) Compute the ROI of each division, using total assets based on current replacement cost as the investment base.

(c) Which of the two measures do you think gives the better indication of operating performance? Explain your reasoning.

10. The Bella Vista Woodwork Company uses return on investment and economic value added as performance evaluation measures for its division managers. The company's weighted-

average cost of capital is 10 percent. Assume a tax rate of 20 percent. Financial data for the company's three divisions follow.

	U.S. Division	***Asia Division***	***Europe Division***
Sales	₹ 3,00,000	₹ 3,75,000	₹ 4,50,000
Operating Income	25,500	28,000	29,500
Assets	1,50,000	1,25,000	1,75,000
Current Liabilities	10,000	5,000	15,000

Required:

a. Compute the return on investment for each division.

b. Compute the economic value added amount for each division.

c. Which division's manager is performing the best using ROI? Which division's manager is performing the best using economic value added? Explain your results.

Answer:

	U.S. Division	**Asia Division**	**Europe Division**
a. ROI	17%	22.4%	16.9%
b. EVA (₹)	6,400	10,400	7,600

11. The following information relates to the operating of three divisions of a company for 2016.

	Division A ₹	***Division B*** ₹	***Division C*** ₹
Divisional contribution to Central Corporate Expenses	5,00,000	5,00,000	5,00,000
Divisional Investment	40,00,000	50,00,000	60,00,000
Divisional Sales	2,40,00,000	2,00,00,000	1,60,00,000
Divisional Employees (No.)	22,500	12,000	10,500

The company evaluates divisional performance using rate of return on investment (ROI) after allocating a portion of the central corporate expenses to each division. Central corporate expenses for 2016 were ₹ 9,00,000.

Required:

(*a*) Compute the ROI of each division before allocation of central corporate expenses.

(*b*) Compute the ROI of each division assuming central corporate expenses are allocated based on divisional investments (that is, allocate 4/15 to Division A, 5/15 to Division B, and 6/15 to Division C).

(*c*) Repeat part (b), assuming that central corporate expenses are allocated based on divisional sales. (*M.Com., Delhi, 2008*)

12. The following information relates to the operating performance of three divisions of Johnson Co.

	Division A	***Division B***	***Division C***
Operating profit (₹)	6,40,000	30,00,000	60,00,000
Investment (₹)	80,00,000	1,50,00,000	3,75,00,000

Required:

(*a*) Compute the rate of return on investment (ROI) of each division.

(*b*) Assume that a charge is levied on each division for the use of capital. The charge is 10 per cent on investment, and it is deducted in measuring divisional net income. Recalculate ROI using divisional net income after deduction of the use-of-capital charge in the numerator.

(*c*) Which of these two measures do you think gives the better indication of operating performance? Explain your reasoning.

13. Supply the missing data in the following table.

	Division A	***Division B***	***Division C***
Sales (₹)	60,000	75,000	1,00,000
Operating income	(a)	₹25,000	(e)
Operating assets	₹ 30,000	(c)	₹50,000
ROI	15%	10%	20%
Minimum required rate of return	10%	(d)	(f)
Residual income (RI)	(b)	₹ 5,000	0

Answer:

(*a*) ₹ 4,500, (*b*) ₹ 1,500, (*c*) ₹ 2,50,000
(*d*) 8% (*e*) ₹ 10,000 (*f*) 20%

14. The manager of a division that produces add-on products for the automobile industry has just been presented the opportunity to invest in two independent projects. The first is an air conditioner for the back seats of vans and mini vans. The second is a turbocharger. Without the investments, the division will have average assets for the coming year of ₹ 2,56,00,000 and expected operating income of ₹ 35,84,000. The outlay required for each investment and the expected operating incomes are as follows:

	Air Conditioner	***Turbocharger***
Outlay	₹ 7,50,000	₹ 5,40,000
Operating income	67,500	54,000

Corporate headquarters will borrow up to ₹ 13,00,000 for the automotive add on division for further investments. The amount borrowed will be through unsecured bonds at a rate of 9 percent. The marginal tax rate is 35 percent.

Required:

(*i*) Compute the ROI for each investment project.

(*ii*) Compute the budgeted *divisional* ROI for each of the following four alternatives:

(*a*) The air conditioner investment is made.

(*b*) The turbocharger investment is made.

(*c*) Both investments are made.

(*d*) Neither additional investment is made.

Assuming that divisional managers are evaluated and rewarded on the basis of ROI performance, which alternative do you think the divisional manager will choose?

(*iii*) Suppose that the borrowing must be for the entire ₹13,00,000. Calculate the EVA of the two investments taken as a package. Based on EVA, are the investments profitable?

Answer:

(*i*) ROI, Air conditioner 9%, Turbocharger 10%

(*ii*) (*a*) 13,86%, (*b*) 13.92%, (*c*) 13.78%, (*d*) 14.00%

The manager will choose neither of the additional investments.

(*iii*) EVA ₹ 45,450. The two investments increase the wealth of the division as EVA is positive. Therefore, investments are profitable.

15. Performance Financial Services Co. is a diversified investment company with three operating divisions organized as investment centres. Condensed data taken from the records of the three divisions for the year ended June 30, 2016, are as follows:

	Retail Division	***Electronic Brokerage Division***	***Investment Banking Division***
Fee revenue	₹ 25,00,000	₹ 14,00,000	₹ 32,50,000
Operating expenses	16,00,000	13,02,000	26,00,000
Invested assets	50,00,000	3,50,000	40,62,500

The management of Performance Financial Services Co. is evaluating each division as a basis for planning a future expansion of operations.

Required:

(*i*) Prepare condensed divisional income statements for the three divisions, assuming that there were no service department charges.

(*ii*) Using the DuPont formula for rate of return on investment, compute the profit margin, investment turnover, and rate of return on investment for each division.

(*iii*) If available funds permit the expansion of operations of only one division, which of the divisions would you recommend for expansion, based on parts (i) and (ii)? Explain.

Answer:

	Retail Division	***Electronic Division***	***Banking Division***
(*i*) Income (₹)	9,00,000	98,000	6,50,000
(*ii*) ROI	18%	28%	16%

(*iii*) Electronics division.

16. A condensed income statement for the Snowboard Division of Jindal Co. for the year ended December 31, 2016, is as follows:

Sales	₹ 12,00,000
Cost of goods sold	8,26,000
Gross profit	₹ 3,74,000
Operating expenses	2,30,000
Income from operations	₹ 1,44,000
Invested assets	₹ 10,00,000

Assume that the Snowboard Division received no charges from service departments. The president of Jindal Co. has indicated that the division's rate of return on a ₹ 10,00,000 investment must be increased to at least 18% by the end of the next year if operations are to continue. The division manager is considering the following three proposals:

Proposal 1: Transfer equipment with a book value of ₹ 40,000 to other divisions at no gain or loss and lease similar equipment. The annual lease payments would exceed the amount of depreciation expense on the old equipment by ₹ 24,000. This increase in expense would be included as part of the cost of goods sold. Sales would remain unchanged.

Proposal 2: Purchase new and more efficient machining equipment and thereby reduce the cost of goods sold by ₹ 1,20,000. Sales would remain unchanged, and the old equipment, which has no remaining book value, would be scrapped at no gain or loss. The new epuipment would increase invested assets by an additional ₹ 6,00,000 for the year.

Proposal 3: Reduce invested assets by discontinuing an engine line. This action would eliminate sales of ₹ 3,30,000, cost of goods sold of ₹ 2,86,300, and operating expenses of ₹ 65,000. Assets of ₹ 4,20,000 would be transferred to other divisions at no gain or loss.

Required:

1. Using the DuPont formula for rate of return on investment, determine the profit margin, investment turnover, and rate of return on investment for the Snowboard Division for the past year.
2. Prepare condensed estimated income statements and compute the invested assets for each proposal.
3. Using the DuPont formula for rate of return on investment, determine the profit margin, investment turnover, and rate of return on investment for each proposal.
4. Which of the three proposals would meet the required 18% rate of return on investment?
5. If the Snowboard Division were in an industry where the profit margin could not be increased, how much would the investment turnover have to increase to meet the president's required 18% rate of return on investment?

Answer:

1. ROI	14.4%		
	Proposal 1	***Proposal 2***	***Proposal 3***
2. Income (₹)	1,20,000	2,64,000	1,65,300
3. ROI	12.5%	16.5%	28.5%

4. Proposal 3.

5. 25% increase.

17. ABC Company's income statement for last month is given below:

Vulgan Company

Income Statement For the Month Ended June 30

Sales	₹ 7,50,000
Less variable expenses	3,36,000
Contribution margin	4,14,000
Less fixed expenses	3,78,000
Net income	₹ 36,000

Management is disappointed with the company's performance and is wondering what can be done to improve profits. By examining sales and cost records, you have determined the following:

a. The company is divided into two sales territories—Northern and Southern. The Northern territory recorded ₹ 3,00,000 in sales and ₹ 1,56,000 in variable expenses during June;

the remaining sales and variable expenses were recorded in the Southern territory. Fixed expenses of ₹ 1,20,000 and ₹ 1,08,000 are traceable to the Northern and Southern territories, respectively. The rest of the fixed expenses are common to the two territories.

b. The company sells two products—A and B. Sales of A and B totalled ₹ 50,000 and ₹ 2,50,000, respectively, in the Northern territory during June. Variable expenses are 22% of the selling price for A and 58% for B. Cost records show that ₹ 30,000 of the Northern territory's fixed expenses are traceable to A and ₹ 40,000 to B, with the remainder common to the two products.

Required:

1. Prepare segmented income statements first showing the total company broken down between sales territories and then showing the Northern territory broken down by product line. Show both Amount and per cent columns for the company in total and for each segment.
2. Look at the statement you have prepared showing the total company segmented by sales territory. What points revealed by this statement should be brought to the attention of management?
3. Look at the statement you have prepared showing the Northern territory segmented by product lines. What points revealed by this statement should be brought to the attention of management?

Answer:

1. Sales territories, Segment margin, Northern ₹ 24,000; Southern ₹ 1,62,000 Total company ₹ 36,000 Product Line Product A, ₹ 9,000 Product B, ₹ 65,000.

CASES

1. The CEO of Future Company has returned from an executive management programme. He sees you in the office lounge and says: "As I read and hear more and more on valuing assets, I am increasingly surprised by the 'language of accounting.' Yes, I understand historical cost and its problems. But you accountants also mix and match terms like market value, replacement value, economic value, present value, opportunity value, disposal value, entry value, and more values! May be you could help clear up this confusion for me by writing a memo that lays out how these terms can help to make decisions about divisional performance and about keeping or selling these assets and to inform our shareholders about our performance."

   Prepare a memo for CEO as suggested above.

2. Punjab National Bank set up an independent planning department at corporate headquarters. This department is responsible for most aspects of budgeting (revenue and expense forecasting, profit planning, capital investment). Planning department personel are responsible to the vice-president for administration. The resulting budgets are incorporated into the control system that the controller's department designed and administered.

   Outline an effective control system for the planning department's activities (that is, how the bank should evaluate the performance of the planning department).

3. Harrison Furniture Company is orgnized into two divisions, Assembling and Finishing. The Assembling Division combines raw materials into a semifinished product. The product then goes to the Finishing Division for painting, polishing, and packing.

   During May, the Assembling Division had significantly higher raw materials costs than expected because poor-quality raw materials required extensive rework. As a result of the rework, Assembly transferred fewer units than expected to the Finishing Division. The Finishing Division incurred higher labour costs per unit of finished product because workers had substantial idle time. The president of the company is upset about these events.

Required:

a. Whom should the firm hold responsible for the raw materials variance in the Assembling Division? Explain.

b. Whom should the firm hold responsible for the labour (idle time) variance in the Finishing Division? Explain.

4. The Customer Service Department of Reliance Industries asked the Publications Department to prepare a brochure for its training program. The Publications Department delivered the brochures and charged the Customer Service Department a rate that was 25% higher than could be obtained from an outside printing company. The policy of the company required the Customer Service Department to use the internal publications group for brochures. The Publications Department claimed that it had a drop in demand for its services during the fiscal year, so it had to charge higher prices in order to recover its payroll and fixed costs.

Required:

Should the cost of the brochure be transferred to the Customer Service Department in order to hold the department head accountable for the cost of the brochure? What changes in policy would you recommend?

5. Cadbury India Ltd. uses rate of return on investment (ROI) as a basis for determining the annual bonus of divisional managers. The firm allocates central corporate expenses to the divisions based on total sales. The calculation of ROI for 2016 for two of its divisions follows:

	Light Chocolate Division	***Dark Chocolate Division***
Division Contribution to Central Corporate Expenses and Operating Profit	₹ 1,00,000	₹ 5,00,000
Share of Central Corporate Expenses	(10,000)	(25,000)
Divisional Operating Profit	₹ 90,000	₹ 4,75,000
Divisional Investment (assets)	₹ 6,00,000	₹ 47,50,000
ROI	15 Per cent	10 Per cent

Indicate several factors that, if present, would bias the ROI measure as Cadbury India Ltd., has calculated it and lead to possible inequities in determining the annual bonus.

6. Allyn Company has two divisions, the Semiconductor Division and the PC Division. The PC Division may purchase semiconductors from the Semiconductor Division or from outside suppliers. The Semiconductor Division sells semiconductor products both internally and externally. The Market price for semiconductors is ₹ 15,000 per 100 semiconductors. Dinesh is the controller of the PC Division and Ritesh is the controller of the Semiconductor Division. The following conversation took place between Dinesh and Ritesh.

Dinesh: I hear you are having problems selling semiconductors out of your division. Maybe I can help.

Ritesh: You've got that right. We're producing and selling at about 80% of our capacity to outsiders. Last year we were selling 100% of capacity. Would it be possible for your division to pick up some of our excess capacity? After all, we are part of the same company.

Dinesh: What kind of price could you give me?

Ritesh: Well, you know as well as I that we are under strict profit responsibility in our divisions, so I would expect to get market price, Rs. 15,000 for 100 semiconductors.

Dinesh: I'm not so sure we can swing that. I was expecting a price break from a sister division.

Ritesh: Hey, I can only take this "sister" stuff so far. If I give you a price break, our profits will fall from last year's levels. I don't think I could explain that. I'm sorry, but I must remain firm—market price. After all, it's only fair—that's what you would have to pay from an external supplier.

Dinesh: Fair or not, I think we'll pass. Sorry we couldn't have helped.

Required:

Was Dinesh behaving ethically by trying to force the Semiconductor Division into a price break? Comment on Ritesh's reactions.

Answer:

Dinesh is not behaving unethically by attempting to get a good price from the Semiconductor Division.

7. Harry Klein, inventor, formed Peerless Load Levelers Company in 2011 to produce a simple three-piece device for automatically leveling loads on industrial conveyer belts. As the business grew and prospered. Klein expanded the factory and added employees, but he continued to control every aspect of the enterprise himself. Klein only hired individuals who would follow his orders unquestioningly. Over the years, the product mix was expanded to include several products, all variants of the original design.

Klein had no need to develop a human resource function, accounting systems, or computerised business systems. He also felt that he did not need a budget process. "I know exactly how well we are doing." he would repeatedly assert. "Why do I need some new budgeting idea to tell me what I already know?"

In 2016, Peerless reached a level of 180 production employees, 3 managers (who reported directly to Klein), and 20 clerical people. The three managers are: John Richards, Shaping and Forming Department; Karl Willis, Assembly Department; and Susan Lyle, Finishing Department. Each manager is responsible for all aspects of his/her department's product manufacturing including purchasing, production, inspection, and customer complaints.

In 2016, Klein passed away unexpectedly. The situation at Peerless turned to chaos as only Klein had the complete view of the company. Eileen Klein-Robb, Klein's daughter and current president, had never been involved in the business and needed help quickly. She has engaged Robert Snider, consultant, to determine what Peerless needs to do to bring sense and structure to the operation.

Snider, after studying the operation, has suggested that Peerless needs a method of evaluating, monitoring, and controlling performance, especially at the production level. Snider's recommendation has not changed the reporting relationship of Richards, Willis, and Lyle. However, the functions of the three managers have changed as follows.

- Richards will be the purchasing manager and handle all vendor relationships and raw materials inventories.
- Willis will be the production manager and oversee three newly promoted supervisors of the Shaping and Forming Department, the Assembly Department and the Finishing Department.

- Lyle will be the quality manager and oversee product quality, inspection, customer relations and engineering changes.

Snider has also suggested installing a responsibility accounting and budgeting system to control performance at the various levels of production and management. Klein-Robb, although interested in this system, is uncertain and wants more information about responsibility accounting.

Required:

A. List four characteristics and requirements for a responsibility accounting system.

B. Describe the following centres and define their missions when used with a responsibility accounting system.

1. Cost centres.
2. Profit centres.
3. Investment centres.

C. 1. Identify at least three advantages that may be gained from a responsibility accounting system.

2. Identify at least one major-risk when using a responsibility accounting system.

D. If Eileen Klein-Robb were to incorporate Robert Snider's functional recommendations at Peerless Load Levelers Company, identify at least two specific operational performance measures that Klein-Robb should implement for

- John Richards, purchasing manager.
- Karl Willis, production manager.
- Susan Lyle, quality manager. (*CMA, USA, Adapted with permission*)

8. The Texon Company is organised into autonomous divisions along regional market lines. Each division manager is responsible for sales, cost of operations, acquisition and financing of divisional assets, and working capital management.

The vice-president of general operations for the company will retire in September 2016, and a replacement is being sought. A review of the performance, attitudes, and skills of several management employees has been undertaken. Interviews have also been held with qualified outside candidates. The selection committee has narrowed the choice to the managers of divisions A and F.

Both candidates were appointed division managers in late 2012. The manager of division A had been the assistant manager of that division for the preceding five years. The manager of division F had served as assistant division manager of division B before being appointed to his present post. He took over division F, a division newly formed in 2011, when its first manager left to join a competitor. The financial results of their performance in the past three years are reported below.

(*i*) Determine ROI for each year for each manager.

(*ii*) Texon Company measures the performance of the divisions and the division managers on the basis of their return on investment (ROI). Is this an appropriate measurement for the division managers? Explain.

(*iii*) Many believe that a single measure, such as ROI, is inadequate to fully evaluate performance. What additional measure (s) could be used for performance evaluation? Give reasons for each measure listed.

(*iv*) Per year, which manager performed better.

(*v*) On the basis of the information given, which manager would you recommend for vice-president of general operations? Present reasons to support your answer.

(₹ *000*)

	Division A			*Division F*		
	2013	**2014**	**2015**	**2013**	**2014**	**2015**
Estimated industry sales—	10,000	12,000	13,000	5,000	6,000	6,500
Division sales	1,000	1,100	1,210	450	600	750
Variable costs	300	320	345	135	175	210
Discretionary costs	400	405	420	170	200	230
Committed costs	275	325	350	140	200	250
Total costs	975	1,050	1,115	445	575	690
Net income	25	50	95	5	25	60
Assets employed	330	340	360	170	240	300
Liabilities	103	105	115	47	100	130
Net investment	227	235	245	123	140	170

(*CMA, USA, Adapted with permission*) (M.Com. Delhi 2004)

Answer:

Manager of Division F has better sales growth (as compared to industry) and greater income growth rate. Division F manager is better qualified than the manager of Division A.

9. Amit was recently appointed as vice-president of operations for Reliance company. Amit has a manufacturing background and previously served as operations manager of Reliance's Tractor Division. The business segments of Reliance include the manufacture of heavy equipment, food processing, and financial services.

In a recent conversation with Pradeep, Reliance's chief financial officer, Amit suggested that segment managers be evaluated on the basis of the segment data appearing in Reliance annual financial report. This report presents revenues, earnings, identifiable assets, and depreciation for each segment for a five-year period. Amit believes that evaluating segment managers by criteria similar to those used to evaluate the company's top management would be appropriate. Pradeep expressed his reservations about using segment information from the annual financial report for this purpose and suggested that Amit consider other ways to evaluate the performance of segment managers.

Required:

(*i*) Explain why the segment information prepared for public reporting purposes may not be appropriate for the evaluation of segment management performance.

(*ii*) Describe the possible behavioural impact on Reliance Company's segment managers if their performance is evaluated on the basis of the information in the annual financial report.

(*iii*) Identify and describe several types of financial information that would be more appropriate for Amit to review when evaluating the performance of segment managers.

(*M.Com. Delhi, 2008, 2011 & CMA, USA, Adapted with permission*)

10. Domi Products, a multi-divisional manufacturing company, measures performance and awards bonuses to division managers based upon divisional operating income. Under the current bonus plan, common company-wide operating expenses are allocated evenly to all five of its divisions. For example, if rent were ₹ 50,000, each division would be charged ₹ 10,000. In planning next year's budget, corporate management has requested that the division managers recommend how common expenses should be distributed to the divisions. The division managers met and jointly developed an incentive plan that would more equitably distribute common expenses on the basis of resources used and measure each division manager's performance based on return on assets (ROA), with divisional bonuses based on a target ROA. They jointly presented their recommendation to corporate management.

Required:

A. Describe at least three problems that Domi Products could encounter when using return on assets (ROA) as the basis of performance measurement.

B. 1. Define the residual income approach to segment performance measurement.

2. Determine if Domi Products should implement this approach instead of the ROA approach.

C. Discuss the behavioural implications of

1. the division managers' involvement in the corporate budgeting process, and
2. the decision to more equitably allocate common costs.

(CMA, USA, Adapted with permission)

11. Building Services Co. (BSC) was started a number of years ago by Jim and Joan Forge to provide cleaning services to both large and small businesses in their home city. Over the years, as local businesses reduced underutilised building maintenance staffs, more and more cleaning services were subcontracted to BSC. BSC also expanded into other building services such as painting and local moving.

BSC maintains a pool of skilled workers who are contracted to perform the non-cleaning services because these services do not recur on a day-to-day basis for the individual buildings. Many of BSC's full-time employees have been with the firm for a number of years. Five zone managers are each responsible for furnishing recurring nightly cleaning services to several businesses. In addition, the zone manager sells and schedules non-cleaning service jobs for the company's central pool of skilled employees. Informal meetings are held periodically to discuss BSC's performance, personnel allocations, and scheduling problems. BSC's budgeting and planning has been done by the Forges, who also manage variations from budgets.

The Forges recently decided to retire and sold the business to Commercial Maintenance Inc. (CMI), which provides similar services in a number of metropolitan locations that surround BSC's business area. After news of the sale, several of BSC's long-term employees appeared resentful of the change in ownership and did not know what to expect.

CMI's senior management met with BSC's managers and announced that George Fowler would become president of BSC and that BSC would continue to operate as a separate subsidiary of CMI. Furthermore, in accordance with CMI's management philosophy, a responsibility accounting system is to be implemented at BSC. Also, in line with other CMI subsidiaries, a goal-oriented performance system and participatory budgeting process are being considered; however, no decision will be made until an evaluation of BSC's existing policies, operational culture, and management is completed. In view of the significant change in management philosophy, CMI has taken considerable time in explaining how each system operates and assuring BSC's managers that they are expected and encouraged to participate in both the planning and implementation of any of the systems that are to be adopted.

Required:

For each of the following systems at Building Services Co. (BSC),

- responsibility centre system,
- goal-oriented performance system,
- participatory budgeting system,

(*i*) identify at least two behavioural advantages that could arise.

(*ii*) identify at least two potential problems that could arise.

(*iii*) discuss the likelihood that the system will contribute to the alignment of organisational and personal goals. (*CMA, USA, Adapted with permission*)

12. Gigantic Corporation's division managers have been expressing growing dissatisfaction with the methods Gigantic uses to measure division performance. Division operations are evaluated every quarter by comparison with the master budget prepared during the prior year. Division managers claim that many factors are completely out of their control but are included in this comparison, resulting in an unfair and misleading performance evaluation.

The managers have been particularly critical of the process used to establish standards and budgets. The annual budget, stated by quarters, is prepared six months prior to the beginning of the operating year. Pressure by top management to reflect increased earnings has often caused divisional managers to overstate revenues and/or understate expenses. In addition, once the budget is established, divisions must "live with the budget." Frequently, external factors such as the state of the economy, changes in consumer preferences, and actions of competitors have not been recognised in the budgets that top management supplied to the divisions. The credibility of the performance review is curtailed when the budget cannot be adjusted to incorporate these changes.

Recognising these problems, top management agreed to establish a committee to review the situation and to make recommendations for a new performance evaluation system. The committee consisted of each division manager, the corporate controller, and the executive vice-president. At the first meeting, one division manager outlined an achievement of objectives system (AOS). In this performance evaluation system, division managers are evaluated according to three criteria :

- *Doing better than last year.* Various measures are compared to the same measures of the prior year.
- *Planning realistically.* Actual performance for the current year is compared to realistic plans and /or goals.
- *Managing current assets.* Various measures are used to evaluate division management's achievements and reactions to changing business and economic conditions.

One division manager believed that this system would overcome many of the current system's inconsistencies because divisions could be evaluated from three different viewpoints. In addition, managers would have the opportunity to show how they would react and account for changes in uncontrollable external factors.

Another manager cautioned that the success of a new performance evaluation system would be limited unless it had the complete support of top management.

Required:

a. Explain whether the proposed AOS would improve Gigantic Corporation's evaluation of division performance.

b. Develop specific performance measures for each of the three criteria in the proposed AOS that could be used to evaluate division managers.

c. Discuss the motivational and behavioural aspects of the proposed performance measurement system. Also recommend specific programs that could be instituted to promote morale and give incentives to divisional management. (*CMA, USA, Adapted with permission*)

13. The Truck Division of Mahindra & Mahindra Co. has been experiencing revenue and profit growth during the years 2015-2017. The divisional income statements are provided below.

Mahindra & Mahindra Co.
Divisional Income Statements, Truck Division
for the Years Ended December 31, 2015-2017

	2015	2016	2017
Sales	₹ 8,40,000	₹ 12,00,000	₹ 14,00,000
Cost of goods sold	6,05,000	8,56,000	9,87,000
Gross profit	₹ 2,35,000	₹ 3,44,000	₹ 4,13,000
Operating expenses	1,09,000	1,28,000	1,33,000
Income from operations	₹ 1,26,000	₹ 2,16,000	₹ 2,80,000

Assume that there are no charges from service departments. The vice president of the division, Gyan Murthy, is proud of his division's performance over the last three years. The president of the company, Sameer Nanda, is discussing the division's performance with Gyan, as follows:

Gyan: As you can see, we've had a successful three years in the Truck Division.

Sameer : I'm not too sure.

Gyan: What do you mean? Look at our results. Our income from operations has more than doubled, while our profit margins are improving.

Sameer: I am looking at your results. However, your income statements fail to include one very important piece of information; namely, the invested assets. You have been investing a great deal of assets into the division. You had ₹ 4,20,000 in invested assets in 2015, ₹ 8,00,000 in 2016, and ₹ 17,50,000 in 2017.

Gyan: You are right. I've needed the assets in order to upgrade our technologies and expand our operations. The additional assets are one reason we have been able to grow and improve our profit margins. I don't see that this is a problem.

Sameer: The problem is that we must maintain a 20% rate of return on invested assets.

Required:

1. Determine the profit margins for the Truck Division for 2015-2017.
2. Compute the investment turnover for the Truck Division for 2015-2017.
3. Compute the rate of return on investment for the Truck Division for 2015-2017.
4. Evaluate the division's performance over the 2015-2017 time period. Why was Sameer concerned about the performance? (*M. Com., Delhi University 2014*)

Answer:

	2015	2016	2017
1. Profit margin	15%	18%	20%
2. Investment turnover	2.0	1.5	0.8
3. ROI	30%	27%	16%

14. The Birla Group Company at Kolkata manages several divisions in India. The head office staff of The Birla Group evaluates managers of the divisions by keeping track of the rate of

return each division earns on the average level of assets invested at the division. The head office staff considers 20 per cent, which is The Birla's Group's after-tax cost of capital, to be the minimum acceptable annual rate of return on average investment. When a division's rate of return drops below 20 per cent, division management can expect an unpleasant investigation by the head office and perhaps some firings. When the rate of retun exceeds 20 per cent and grows through time, the head office staff is invariably pleased and rewards division management. When the rate of return exceeds 20 per cent but declines over time, the head office staff sends out unpleasant memoranda and cuts the profit-sharing bonuses of the division managers.

In Division A, average assets employed during the year amount to ₹ 60,00,000. Division A has been earning 40 per cent per year on its average investment for several years. Management of Division A is proud of its extraordinary record—earning a steady 40 per cent per year.

In Division B, average assets employed during the year also amount to ₹ 60,00,000. Division B has been earnign 25 per cent per year on its average investment. In the preceding three years, the rate of return on investment was 20 per cent, 22 per cent, and 23 per cent, respectively. Management of Division B is proud of its record of steadily boosting earnings.

New investment opportunities have arisen at both Division A and Division B. In both cases, the new investment opportunity will require a cash outlay today of ₹ 30,00,000 and will provide a rate of return on investment of 30 per cent for each of the next eight years. The average amount of assets invested in the project will be ₹ 30,00,000 for each of the next eight years. Both new investment opportunities have positive net present value when the discount rate is 20 per cent per year (the after-tax cost of capital of The Birla Group).

When word of the new opportunities reached the head office staff, the prospects of the two new investments pleased the staff, because both investments would yield a better-than-average return for The Birla Group.

Management of Division A computed its rate of return on investment both with and without the new investment project and decided not to undertake the project. Management of Division B computed its rate of return on investment both with and without the new investment project and decided to undertake it.

When word of the two divisions' actions reached the head office staff, it was perplexed. Why did Division A's management turn down such a good opportunity? What in the behavior of the head office staff induced Division A's management to reject the new project? Is management of Division B doing a better job than management of Division A? What may the head office do to give Division A an incentive to act in a way more consistent with the well-being of The Birla Group?

Answer:

		Division A
	Without New Project	**With New Project**
ROI	40%	36.7%
Income in excess of company minimum	12,00,000	15,00,000
		Division B
ROI	25%	26.7%
Income in excess of company minimum	3,00,000	6,00,000

(*M. Com., Delhi University 2014*)

15. Music Teachers, India., is an educational association for music teachers that has 20,000 members The association operates from a central headquarters but has local membership chapters throughout India. Monthly meetings are held by the local chapters to discuss recent developments on topics of interest to music teachers. The association's journal, Teachers' Forum, is issued monthly with features about recent developments in the field. The association publishes books and reports and also sponsors professional courses that qualify for continuing professional education credit. The association's statement of revenues and expenses for the current year is presented below.

Music Teachers, India.

Statement of Revenues and Expenses

For the Year Ended March 31, 2016

Revenues	₹ 32,75,000
Less expenses:	
Salaries	9,20,000
Personnel costs	2,30,000
Occupancy costs	2,80,000
Reimbursement of member costs to local chapters	6,00,000
Other membership services	5,00,000
Printing and paper	3,20,000
Postage and shipping	1,76,000
Instructors' fees	80,000
General and administrative	38,000
Total expenses	31,44,000
Excess of revenues over expenses	₹ 1,31,000

The board of directors of Music Teachers, India, has requested that a segmented statement of operations be prepared showing the contribution of each profit centre to the association. The association has four profit centres: Membership Division, Magazine Subsciptions Division, Books and Reports Division, and Continuing Education Division. Raman Pandit has been assigned reponsibility for preparing the segmented statement, and he has gathered the following data prior to its preparation.

a. Membership dues are ₹ 100 per year, of which ₹ 20 is considered to cover a one-year subscription to the association's journal. Other benefits include membership in the association and chapter affiliation. The portion of the dues covering the magazine subsciption (₹ 20) should be assigned to the Magazine Subscription Division.

b. One-year subscriptions to Teachers' Forum were sold to nonmembers and libraries at ₹ 30 per subscription. A total of 2,500 of these subscriptions were sold last year. In addition to subscriptions, the magazine generated ₹ 1,00,000 in advertising revenues. The costs per magazine subscription were ₹ 7 for printing and paper and ₹ 4 for postage and shipping.

c. A total of 28,000 technical reports and professional texts were sold by the Books and Reports Division at an average unit selling price of ₹ 25. Average costs per publication were ₹ 4 for printing and paper and ₹ 2 for postage and shipping.

d. The association offers a variety of continuing education courses to both members and non-members. The one-day courses had a tuiting cost of ₹ 75 each and were attended by 2,400 students. A total of 1,760 students took two-day courses at a tuition cost of ₹125 for each student. Outside instructors were paid to teach some courses.

e. Salary costs and space occupied by division follow:

	Salaries	SpaceOccupied (square feet)
Membership	₹ 2,10,000	2,000
Magazine Subsciptions	1,50,000	2,000
Books and Reports	3,00,000	3,000
Continuing Education	1,80,000	2,000
Corporate staff	80,000	1,000
Total	₹ 9,20,000	10,000

Personnel costs are 25% of salaries in the separate divisions as well as for the corporate staff. The ₹ 2,80,000 in occupancy costs includes ₹ 50,000 in rental cost for a warehouse used by the Books and Reports Division for storage purposes.

f. Printing and paper costs other than for magazine subscriptions and for books and reports relate to the Continuing Education Division.

g. General and administrative expenses include costs relating to overall administration of the association as a whole. The company's corporate staff does some mailing of materials for general administrative purposes.

The expenses that can be traced or assigned to the corporate staff, as well as any other expenses that are not traceable to the profit centres, well be treated as common costs. It is not necessary to distinguish between variable and fixed costs.

Required:

1. Prepare a segmented statement of revenues and expenses for Music Teachers, India. This statement should show the segment margin for each division as well as results for the association as a whole.
2. Give arguments for and against allocating all costs of the association to the four divisions.

(CMA, USA. adapted with permission)

Answer:

1. Division segment margin, Mambership ₹ 1,91,500, Magazine ₹ 94,000, Books & Reports ₹ 38,000, Continuing Education Loss ₹ 1,500.

   Excess of revemes over expensts Total ₹ 1,31,000.
2. There are arguments for and against allocation of all costs to the four divisions.

12

TRANSFER PRICING

LEARNING OBJECTIVES:

After reading this chapter, you should be able to:

- Explain the Concept of Transfer Pricing, its Objectives and Requisites of a Sound Transfer Pricing System
- Explain the Different Methods of Transfer Pricing – Market Prices, Cost-based Prices, Negotiated Prices and Dual Prices
- Understand Activity-based Costs for Transfer Pricing
- Identify Disadvantages of Tansfer Pricing and Guidelines for an Optimum Transfer Pricing System
- Explain Transfer Pricing in Multinational Companies

CONCEPT OF TRANSFER PRICING

A transfer price is that notional value at which goods and services are transferred between divisions in a decentralised organisation. In divisionalised companies, where profit or investment centres are created, there is likely to be interdivisional transfers of goods, or services and this internal transfers create the problem of transfer pricing. In such companies, a satisfactory system of transfer pricing is necessary for measuring the performance of divisions. Transfer prices are normally set for intermediate products which are goods and services that are supplied by the selling division to the buying division. The goods that are produced by the buying division and sold to the outside world are known as final products.

> **Transfer price** is that notional value at which goods and services are transferred between divisions in a decentralised organisation.

It can be said that the problem of suitable transfer prices arises only when divisions do business with one another. One way to eliminate the need to establish transfer prices is to eliminate all transactions among divisions. The problem with this solution is that it would forgo for the company and the divisions the very substantial scale economies that come as a result of being able to centralise certain corporate functions while simultaneously achieving the benefits of decentralisation. On the other hand, the greater the number of transfer relative to the volume of a division's operations, the less independent it becomes and the more meaningless it is to establish separate divisions with profit and investment responsibilities.

OBJECTIVES IN SOUND TRANSFER PRICING SYSTEM

A question arises as to how the transfer of goods and services between divisions should be priced. The price charged to the interdivisional transfer of goods and services is revenue to the selling division and cost to the buying division. Therefore the price charged will affect the profit of both divisions; benefit (revenue) to one division can be created only at the expense of the other division. For example, the selling division will benefit from charging higher prices for such transfers of goods and services. However, for the buying division, this will result into higher costs. The transfer prices, thus, can have impact on the evaluation of each division's performance and measures applied for such measurements of performance. While determining transfer prices a number of criteria (objectives) should be fulfilled.

> **Objectives of Sound Transfer Pricing System** include:
> - Accurate measurement of divisional performance
> - Motivation to managers to maximise profitability
> - Ensure divisional autonomy and authority
> - Goal congruence
> - Benefits to multinational companies

1. Transfer prices should help in the accurate measurement of divisional performance (profitability).
2. Transfer prices should motivate the divisional managers into maximising the profitability of their divisions and making decisions that are in the best interests of the organisations as a whole.
3. Transfer prices should ensure that divisional autonomy and authority is preserved. The main purpose of decentralisation is to enable divisional managers to exercise greater autonomy and to measure the overall results achieved on a profit centre or investment centre. It is, therefore, not proper to give divisional managers authority by one hand by placing them in charge of divisional operations and to remove that authority by dictating transfer prices that affect the performance of the division.

4. Transfer prices should allow goal congruence to take place, which in effect means that the objectives of divisional managers are compatible with the objectives of overall company.
5. A transfer pricing system, if properly established, can check multinational companies and international groups which may try to manipulate transfer prices between countries in order to minimise the overall tax burden.

Transfer pricing attempts to create external market conditions within an organisation. In fact, all managers rightly feel concerned about profit and profitability which act as motivators for them. Transfer pricing should not be merely viewed through accounting mirrors. But it should be filtered through economic considerations, marketing impact and behavioural effects as well. Therefore, transfer pricing decisions should attempt to blend, judiciously and optimally, accounting, marketing and behavioural aspects.

Transfer pricing decisions should attempt to blend, judiciously and optimally, accounting, marketing and behavioural aspects.

The important relationships between transfer pricing practices and other variables are shown in Figure 12.1. At the centre of the diagram are transfer pricing practices—the phenomenon to be explained both descriptively (what is done) and prescriptively (what should be done). The prescriptive findings are obtained by separating the described practices into situations in which transfer pricing was managed effectively and situations in which it was not.

Figure 12.1 shows that there are two principal determinants of transfer pricing practices: strategy and administrative process. Transfer pricing practices affect economic decisions, which in turn affect corporate performance. Transfer pricing practices also affect performance measurement, evaluation, and reward, which in turn affect perceptions of fairness by individual managers. Figure 12.1 also shows that strategy and administrative process each directly affect economic decisions; corporate performance; performance measurement, evaluation, and reward; and individual fairness. The fundamental difficulty in managing transfer pricing involves establishing practices that will lead to decisions that enhance corporate performance, while at the same time measuring, evaluating, and rewarding performance in light of these practices in a way that managers perceive as fair.

Two principal determinants of **transfer pricing practices:** strategy and administrative process.

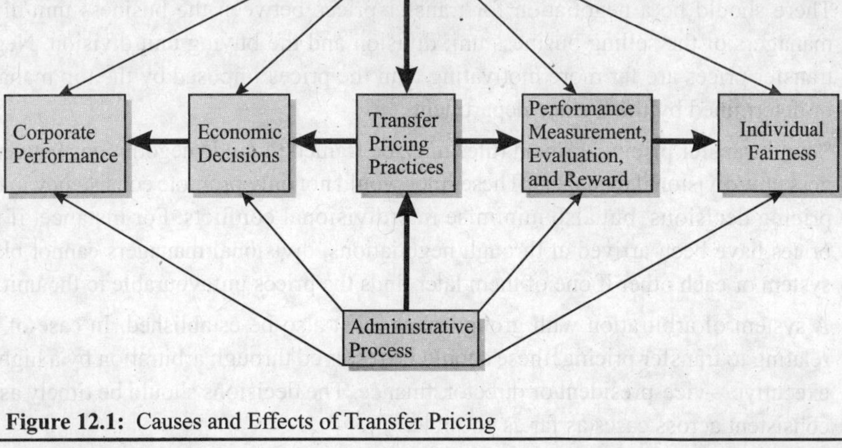

Figure 12.1: Causes and Effects of Transfer Pricing

Source: Robert G. Eccles, The Transfer Pricing Problem, A Theory for Practice, Lexington Books, 1985, P. 7.

Barfield, Raiborn and Kinney[1] observe:

> The determination of the type of transfer pricing system to use should reflect the organizational units' characteristics as well as corporate goals. No single method of setting a transfer price is best in all instances. Also, transfer prices are not intended to be permanent; they are frequently revised in relation to changes in costs, supply, demand, competitive forces, and other factors. Flexibility by the selling segment to increase a transfer price when reduced productive capacity is present and to increase a transfer price when excess productive capacity exists is a strong management lever. Regardless of what method is used, a thoughtfully set transfer price will provide an appropriate basis for the calculation and evaluation of segment performance, the rational acquisition or use of goods and services between corporate divisions, the flexibility to respond to changes in demand or market conditions, and a means of motivation to encourage and reward goal congruence by managers in decentralized operations.

REQUISITES OF A SOUND TRANSFER PRICING SYSTEM

The requisites of a sound transfer pricing system are as follows[2]:

1. It should be simple to understand and easy to operate.
2. It should enable fixation of fair transfer prices for the output transferred or service rendered. A divisional manager who considers the transfer price to be unfair to the division would be demotivated.
3. Ideally, the business unit/divisional manager must be given autonomy and freedom to sell in the open market. This does not, however, mean that without complete autonomy, a system of transfer pricing and evaluation of divisions on the basis of profits contributed by them cannot exist. Frequently, divisional managers will have restrictions in this regard. Even when there are compulsions to sell the products or provide services tó an internal division, it is profitable to allow the divisional managers to sell a small quantity (5–10 percent) to customers outside the organisation or to buy small quantities from sources outside it.
4. The business unit/divisions should have free access to various sources of market information.
5. There should be a negotiation for transfer prices between the business unit/divisional managers of the selling business unit/division and the buying unit/division. Negotiated transfer prices are far more motivating than the prices imposed by the top management or determined by the finance department.
6. Sound transfer pricing ground rules must be framed to guide negotiations between business unit/divisional managers. These rules would not only promote consistency in transfer pricing decisions, but also minimise interdivisional conflicts. For instance, if transfer prices have been arrived at through negotiations, divisional managers cannot blame the system or each other if one of them later finds the prices unfavourable to the unit.
7. A system of arbitration with ground rules must also be established. In case of failures relating to transfer pricing, these should be resolved through arbitration by a higher level executive—vice-president or director, finance. The decisions should be timely as well as consistent across cases as far as possible.
8. Top management should discourage prolonged arguments between business unit/divisional managers.

9. Transfer prices can be reviewed annually or as dictated by the demand and supply conditions in the market. Transfer pricing guidelines must state the circumstance under which a revision of transfer prices can be made during the year.
10. When transfer prices are based on market price, long-run competitive/normal prices must be considered.
11. Transfer pricing and arbitration ground rules can be reviewed once in four years or earlier if there is a major change in business conditions.

Fox, Kennedy and Sugden[3] suggest that ideally, a transfer price should be:

1. Simple to calculate
2. Robust (not requiring frequent adjustment)
3. Fair (hence motivating to both parties)
4. Profit maximising (for the company as a whole)

METHODS OF TRANSFER PRICING

The different methods of transfer pricing are discussed in length below.

General Transfer-Pricing Rule

Management's objective in setting a transfer price is to encourage goal congruence among the division managers involved in the transfer. A general rule that will ensure goal congruence is given below.

$$\text{Transfer price} = \begin{array}{c}\text{Additional } \textit{outlay cost} \\ \text{per unit incurred because} \\ \text{goods are transferred}\end{array} + \begin{array}{c}\textit{Opportunity cost} \text{ per unit} \\ \text{to the organisation} \\ \text{because of the transfer}\end{array}$$

The general rule specifies the transfer price as the sum of two cost components. The first component is the outlay cost incurred by the division that produces the goods or services to be transferred. Outlay costs will include the direct variable costs of the product or service and any other outlay costs that are incurred only as a result of the transfer. The second component in the general transfer-pricing rule is the opportunity cost incurred by the organization as a whole because of the transfer. An *opportunity cost* is a benefit that is forgone as a result of taking a particular action.

> **Transfer price** is the sum of two cost components.
> - Outlay Cost
> - Opportunity Cost

> **Opportunity cost** is a benefit that is forgone as a result of taking a particular action.

Broadly, there are four bases available for determining transfer prices, but many options are also available within each base. These methods are:

1. Market based Prices.
2. Cost-based Prices
   (*i*) Variable cost
   (*ii*) Actual full cost
   (*iii*) Full cost plus profit margin
   (*iv*) Standard full cost
3. Negotiated Prices
4. Dual prices

Market-based Prices

> **Market price** refers to a price in an intermediate market between independent buyers and sellers.

Market price refers to a price in an intermediate market between independent buyers and sellers. When there is a competitive external market for the transferred product, market prices work well as transfer prices. When transferred goods are recorded at market prices, divisional performance is more likely to represent the real economic contribution of the division to total company profits. If the goods cannot be bought from a division within the company, the intermediate product would have to be purchased at the current market price from the outside market. Divisional profits are therefore likely to be similar to the profits that would be calculated if the divisions were separate organisations. Consequently, divisional profitability can be compared directly with the profitability of similar companies operating in the same type of business. Managers of both buying and selling divisions are indifferent between trading with each other or with outsiders. No division can benefit at the expense of another division. In the market price situation, top management will not be tempted to intervene.

> **Market-based prices** are based on opportunity costs concepts.

Market-based prices are based on opportunity costs concepts. The opportunity cost approach signals that the correct transfer price is the market price. Since the selling division can sell all that it produces at the market price, transferring internally at a lower price would make the division worse off. Similarly the buying division can always acquire the intermediate goods at the market price, so it would be unwilling to pay more for an internally transferred goods. Since the minimum transfer price for the selling division is the market price and the maximum price for the buying division is also the market price, the only possible transfer price is the market price[4].

The market price can be used to resolve conflicts among the buying and selling divisions. From the company viewpoint, market price is the optimal so long as the selling division is operating at full capacity. The market price does not allow any gains or losses in efficiency of the selling division. It saves administrative costs as the use of competitive market prices are free from any dispute, argument and bias.

However, there are some problems in using the market price approach.

1. ***Appropriate Market Price may not exist:*** Firstly, finding a competitive market price may be difficult if such a market does not exist. Catalogue price may only vaguely relate to actual sales prices. Market prices may change often. Also, internal selling expenses may be less than would be incurred if the products were sold to outsiders. Further, the fact that two responsibility centres are parts of one company indicates that there may be some advantages from being part of one company and not being two separate companies dealing with each other in the market. For example, there may be more certainty about the internal division's product quality or delivery reliability. Or the selling division may make a specialised product for which there are not substitutes in the market. Hence, it may not be possible to use market prices.

2. ***Excess Production Capacity:*** Another problem with market prices can occur when a selling division is not operating at full capacity and cannot sell all its products. To illustrate this point, assume that material used by Division A in a company are being purchased from outside market at ₹ 200 per unit. The same materials are produced by Division B. If Division B is operating at full capacity, say of 80,000 units and can sell all its products to either Division A or to outside buyers, then the use of transfer price of ₹ 200 per unit (market price) has no effect on Division B's income or total company profit. Division B will earn revenue of ₹ 200 per unit on all its production and sales, regardless of who buys its product and Division A will pay ₹ 200 per unit, regardless of whether it purchases the materials from Division B or from an outside supplier. In this situation, the use of market price as the transfer price is appropriate.

However, if Division B is not operating at full capacity and unused capacity exists in that division, the use of market price may not lead to maximisation of total company profit. To illustrate this point, assume that Division B has unused capacity of 30,000 units and it can continue to sell only 50,000 units to outside buyers. In this situation, the transfer price should be set to motivate the manager of Division A to purchase from Division B if the variable cost per unit of product of Division B is less than the market price. If the variable costs are less than ₹ 200 per unit but the transfer price is set equal to the market price of ₹ 200, then the manager of Division A is indifferent as to whether materials are purchased from Division B or from outside suppliers, since the cost per unit to Division B would be the same, ₹ 200. However, Division A's purchase of 20,000 units of materials from outside suppliers at a cost of ₹ 200 per unit would not maximise overall company profit, since this market price per unit is greater than the unit variable cost of Division B, say ₹ 100. Hence, the intracompany transfer could save the company the difference between the market price per unit and Division B's unit variable expenses. This savings of ₹ 100 per unit would add ₹ 20,00,000 (20,000 units X ₹ 100) to overall company profit.

Transfer prices based on market prices are consistent with the responsibility accounting concept of profit centres and investment centres. In addition to encouraging division managers to focus on divisional profitability, market-based transfer prices help to show the contribution of each division to overall company profit. When aggregate divisional profits are determined for the year, and ROI and RI are computed, the use of a market based transfer price helps to assess the contributions of each division to overall corporate profits.

Hilton[5] sums up difficulty associated with general rule of transfer pricing in the following words:

1. *Difficulting in Measuring Opportunity Costs:* The general transfer-pricing rule will always promote goal-congruent decision making if the rule can be implemented. However, the rule is often difficult or impossible to implement due to the difficulty of measuring opportunity costs. Such a cost-measurement problem can arise for a number of reasons. One reason is that the external market may not be perfectly competitive. Under **perfect competition**, the market price does not depend on the quantity sold by any one producer. Under **imperfect competition**, a single producer or group of producers can affect the market price by varying the amount of product available in the market. In such cases, the external market price depends on the production decisions of the producer. This in turn means that the opportunity cost incurred by the company as a result of internal transfers depends on the quantity sold externally. These interactions may make it impossible to measure accurately the opportunity cost caused by a product transfer.

2. *Nature of Transferred Goods:* Other reasons for difficulty in measuring the opportunity cost associated with a product transfer include uniqueness of the transferred goods or services, a need for the producing division to invest in special equipment in order to produce the transferred goods, and interdependencies among several transferred products or services. For example, the producing division may provide design services as well as production of the goods for a buying division. What is the opportunity cost associated with each of these related outputs of the producing division? In many such cases it is difficult to sort out the opportunity costs.

3. *Distress Market Prices:* Occasionally an industry will experience a period of significant excess capacity and extremely low prices. For example, when oil prices soared due to a foreign oil embargo, the market prices for recreational vehicles and power boats fell temporarily to very low levels.

Under such extreme conditions, basing transfer prices on market prices can lead to decisions that are not in the best interests of the overall company. Basing transfer prices on artificially *low distress market prices* could lead the producing division to sell or close the productive resources devoted to producing the product for transfer. Under distress market prices, the producing division manager might prefer to move the division into a more profitable product line. While such a decision might improve the division's profit in the short run, it could be contrary to the best interests of the company overall. It might be better for the company as a whole to avoid divesting itself of any productive resources and to ride out the period of market distress. To encourage an autonomous division manager to act in this fashion, some companies set the transfer price equal to the long-run average external market price, rather than the current (possibily depressed) market price[6].

Cost-based Prices

When external markets do not exist or are not available to the company or when information about external market prices is not readily available, companies may decide to use some forms of cost-based transfer pricing system.

As stated earlier, cost-based transfer prices may be in different forms such as variable cost, actual full cost, full cost plus profit margin and standard full cost.

> **Cost-based transfer prices** may be in different forms such as variable cost, actual full cost, full cost plus profit margin and standard full cost.

1. ***Variable Cost:*** Variable cost-based pricing approach is useful when the selling division is operating below capacity. The manager of the selling division will generally not like this transfer price because it yields no profit to that division. In this pricing system, only variable production costs are transferred. These costs are direct materials, direct labour and variable factory overhead. Variable cost has the major advantage of encouraging maximum profits for the entire firm.. By passing only variable costs alone to the next division, production and pricing decisions are based on cost-volume-profit relationships for the firm as a whole. The obvious problem is that selling division is left holding all its fixed costs and operating expenses. That division is now a loss division, no where near a profit centre[7].

2. ***Actual Full Cost:*** In actual full cost approach, transfer price is based on the total product cost per unit which will include direct materials, direct labour and factory overhead. When full cost is used for transfer pricing, the selling division can not realise a profit on the goods transferred. This may be disincentive to the selling division. Further, full cost transfer pricing can provide perverse incentives and distort performance measures. A full cost transfer price would have shutdown the chances of any negotiation between divisions about selling at transfer prices.

3. ***Full Cost Plus Profit Margin:*** Full cost plus mark up (or profit margin) overcomes the weaknesses of full cost basis transfer pricing system. The full cost plus price include the allowed cost of the item plus a mark up or other profit allowance. With such a system, the selling division obtains a profit contribution on units transferred and hence, benefits if performance is measured on the basis of divisional operating profits. However, the manager of the buying division would naturally object that his costs (and hence reported performance) are adversely affected.

The basic question in full cost plus mark up is 'what should be the percentage of mark up.' It can be suggested that the mark up percentage should cover operating expenses and provide a target return on sales or assets.

4. ***Standard Costs:*** In actual cost approaches, there is a problem of measuring cost. Actual cost does not provide any incentive to the selling division to control cost. All product costs are transfered to the buying division. While transferring actual costs, any variances or inefficiencies in the selling division are passed along to the buying division. The problem of isolating the variances that have been transferred to subsequent buyer division becomes extremely complex. To promote responsibility in the selling division and to isolate variances within divisions, standard costs are usually used as a basis for transfer pricing in cost-based systems.

Whether transferring at differential costs or full costs, standard costs, where available, are often used as the basis for the transfer. This encourages efficiency in the selling division because inefficiencies are not passed onto the buying division. Otherwise, the selling division can transfer cost inefficiencies to the buying division. Use of standard cost reduces risk to the buyer. The buyer knows that standard costs will be transferred and avoids being charged with suppliers's cost overruns.[8]

Negotiated Prices

> **Negotiated prices** are middle solutions between market prices and cost-based prices—a price arrived at by buying and selling divisions.

Negotiated prices are generally preferred as a middle solution between market prices and cost-based prices. Under negotiated prices, the managers involved act much the same as the managers of independent companies. Negotiation strategies may be similar to those employed when trading with outside markets. If both divisions are free to deal either with each other or in the external market, the negotiated price will likely be close to the external market price. If all of a selling division's output can not be sold in the external market (that is, a portion must be sold to the buying division), the negotiated price will likely be less than the market price and the total margin will be shared by the divisions.

The conditions under which a negotiated transfer price will be successful include[9]:

1. ***Some Form of Outside Market for the Intermediate Product:*** This avoids a bilateral monopoly situation in which the final price could vary over too large a range, depending on the strength and skill of each negotiator.
2. ***Sharing of all Market Information among the Negotiators:*** This should enable the negotiated price to be close to the opportunity cost of one or preferably both divisions.
3. ***Freedom to Buy or Sell Outside:*** This provides the necessary discipline to the bargaining process.
4. ***Support and Occasional Involvement of Top Management:*** The parties must be urged to settle most disputes by themselves, otherwise the benefits of decentrallzation will be lost. Top management must be available to mediate the occasional unresolvable dispute or to intervene when it sees that the bargaining process is clearly leading to suboptimal decisions. But such involvement must be done with restraint and tact if it is not to undermine the negotiating process.

Negotiated price avoids mistrusts, bad feelings and undesirable bargaining interests among divisional managers. Also, it provides an opportunity to achieve the objectives of goal congruence, autonomy and accurate performance evaluation. The overall company is beneficiary if selling and buying divisions can agree upon some mutually transfer prices. Negotiated transfer price is considered as a vital integrating tool among divisions of a company which is necessary to achieve goal congruence. If negotiations help ensure goal congruence, top management has little temptation to intervene between divisions. The agreed prices also can be used for performance measurement without creating any friction. The use of negotiated prices is consistent with the concept of decentralised decision-making in the divisionalised firms.

However, negotiated prices have the following disadvantages:

- A great deal of management effort, time and resources can be consumed in the negotiating process.
- The final emerging negotiated price may depend more on the divisional manager's ability and skill to negotiate than on the other factors. Thus, performance measures will be distorted leading to incorrect evaluation of divisional performance.
- One divisional manager having some private information may take advantage of another divisional manager.
- It is time-consuming for the managers involved.
- It leads to conflicts between divisions.
- It may lead to a suboptimal level of output if the negotiated price is above the opportunity cost of supplying the transferred goods.

Garrison and Noreen[10] observe:

> The difficulty is that not all managers understand their own businesses and not all managers are cooperative. As a result, negotiations often break down even when it would be in the manager's own best interest to come to an agreement. Sometimes that is the fault of the way managers are evaluated.
>
> If managers are pitted against each other, rather than against their own past performance or reasonable bench-marks, a non-cooperative atmosphere is almost guaranteed. Nevertheless, it must be admitted that even with the best performance evaluation system, some people by nature are not cooperative.

Dual Prices

Under dual prices of transfer pricing, selling division sells the transferred goods at a (*i*) market or negotiated market price or (*ii*) cost plus some profit margin. But the transfer price for the buying division is a cost-based amount (preferably the variable costs of the selling division). The difference in transfer prices for the two divisions could be accounted for by special centralised account. This system would preserve cost data for subsequent buyer departments, and would encourage internal transfers by providing a profit on such transfers for the selling divisions.

> **Under Dual prices of transfer pricing,** selling division sells the transferred goods at a (i) market or negotiated market price or (ii) cost plus some profit margin.

Dual prices give motivation and incentive to selling divisions as goods are transferred at market price and this arrangement provides a minimal cost to the buying division as well. Market price can be considered as the most appropriate base for the selling division. Thus dual pricing system has the function of motivating both the selling division and buying division to make decisions that are consistent with the overall goals of decentralisation—goal congruence, accurate performance measurement, autonomy, adequate motivation to divisional manager.

Table 12.1 summarizes the advantages and disadvantages of each method of transfer pricing.

Table 12.1: Advantages and Disadvantages of Common Transfer Pricing Methods

Method	Advantages	Disadvantages
Market-based transfer prices	• Objective • Less subject to manipulation • Often leads to correct long-run make/buy decisions	• Might not exist for speciality items • Might not capture interdependencies among divisions
Variable-cost transfer prices	• Can approximate the opportunity cost of transferring one more unit • Gives the buying division incentive to purchase the correct number of units if selling division has excess capacity	• Does not allow the selling division to recover its fixed costs • Variable cost might vary with output • Selling division has incentive to classify fixed costs as variable costs
Full-cost transfer prices	• Avoids disputes over which costs are fixed and which are variable • Simplicity	• Selling division can export its inefficiencies to the buying division • Buying division purchases too few units

(*Contd.*)

Method	Advantages	Disadvantages
Negotiated transfer prices	• Both selling and buying divisions have incentives to transfer the number of units that maximize their combined profits	• Time-consuming • Depends on the relative negotiating skills of the two divisions
Dual prices	• Eliminates costly disputes over transfer pricing, incentive to both selling and buying divisions	• Reduces the benefits from having two decentralized responsibility centres

Source: Jarold L. Zimmerman, Accounting for Decision Making and Control, Vth Edition, McGraw Hill, Irwin, 2006, P. 225.

SUMMARY VIEW

Transfer pricing policy aims to drive the divisions, who are more inclined to act in their individual self interest and consider their own costs, prices and market opportunities, toward behaviour that is best for the organization. Economies of scale, synergies and saving transaction costs motivate divisional managers to conduct transactions within the company rather than using market-based transactions with external supplier and customers.

> **Transfer pricing policy** aims to drive the divisions, who are more inclined to act in their individual self interest and consider their own costs, prices and market opportunities, toward behaviour that is best for the organization.

In reality, no particular transfer pricing system can be suggested for all decentralised companies as no one transfer price will be helpful to them in achieving all their goals and objectives. The divisionalised companies should first determine their goals and priorities before selecting a transfer pricing. Therefore, the transfer pricing methods selected by a particular business enterprise must reflect the requirements and characteristics of that enterprise and must ultimately be judged by the decision making behaviour that it motivates. Anderson and Sollenberger have presented their evaluation of different transfer pricing approaches as displayed in Table 12.2.

Table 12.2: Different Transfer Pricing Approaches

	Goal Congruence	Performance evaluation	Autonomy	Administrative cost
1. Market Prices	Good	Very strong	Very strong	Low, if available
2. *Cost-based prices:*				
(*i*) Actual full cost	Poor	Poor	Poor	Very low
(*ii*) Full cost plus a profit percentage	Poor	Average	Average	Low
(*iii*) Variable cost	Strong	Very poor	Poor	often low
3. Negotiated prices	Strong	Strong	Strong to Poor	High
4. Dual prices	Strong (Variable Cost)	Strong (Market price)	Poor	High

Source: Lane K. Anderson and Harold M. Sollenberger, Managerial Accounting, South Western Publishing Co., 1992, P. 720.

Kaplan and Atkinson[11] have given the following recommendations in choosing a transfer pricing practice.

1. Where a competitive market exists for the intermediate product, the market price, less selling, distribution, and collection expenses for outside customers, represents an excellent transfer price.
2. Where an outside market exists for the intermediate product but is not perfectly competitive and where a small number of different products are transferred, a negotiated transfer price system will probably work best, since the outside market price can serve as an approximation of the opportunity cost. At least occasional transactions with outside suppliers and customers must occur if both divisions are to have credibility in the negotiating process and if reliable quotes from external firms are to be obtained.
3. When no external market exists for the intermediate product, transfers should occur at the long-run marginal cost of production. This cost will facilitate the decision making of the purchasing division by providing the stability needed for long-run planning but at the same time exposing the cost structure so that short-run improvements and adjustments can be made. A periodic fixed fee based on capacity reserved for the buying division is incorporated in the marginal cost calculation. The fixed fee, ideally based on product and facility-sustaining costs from an ABC model, should allocate the capacity-related costs of the facility in proportion to each user's planned use of the facility's resources. The fixed fee forces the purchasing division to recognize the full cost of the resources required to produce the intermediate product internally, and it provides a motivation for the producing divisions to cooperate in choosing the proper level of productive capacity to acquire.
4. A transfer price based on fully allocated costs per unit (using present, that is, non-ABC, methods of allocation) or full cost plus markup has no discernible desirable properties. Although the full-cost transfer price, has limited economic validity, it remains widely used. The marginal cost calculated from an ABC model does provide the capability for managers to use a full-cost approach that is consistent with economic theory.

SETTING TRANSFER PRICES IN DIFFERENT SITUATIONS

The company uses transfer prices to transfer goods and services between divisions while allowing them to retain their autonomy. The transfer price can motivate managers to act in the best interest of the company.

To help explain the issues involved with transfer pricing, we will discuss four transfer pricing situations:

1. No outside suppliers are available
2. Outside suppliers are available, but the selling division is below capacity
3. Outside suppliers are available, and the selling division is at capacity
4. Outside suppliers are available, the selling division is below capacity, and alternative facility uses exist

Each example requires a differential revenue/cost analysis

Case I: No Outside Suppliers

If a company evaluates division managers on division profit measures, they will consider transfer price important. The company as a whole, however, will receive the same operating profit regardless of the transfer price, assuming that it can not purchase the part from another company (externally).

For example, assume that HCL Technologies Ltd. has two decentralized divisions, Hardware and Computers. Computers division has always purchased certain units from Hardware division at ₹ 50 per unit, but Hardware might raise the price to ₹ 70 per unit (the current market price). Hardware has variable costs per unit of ₹ 50 and monthly fixed costs of ₹ 10,000. The Computers division bundles the units with other products and sells them for ₹ 100 each. Computers Division incurs no additional variable costs, and monthly fixed costs total ₹ 5,000, Computer Division produces 1,500 units per month. Given this information, which transfer price will provide the highest operating profit? As Exhibit 12.1 shows the transfer price will not affect overall company operating profit.

Clearly, a change in transfer prices does not change the total company operating profit, but does affect division performance. Hardware division would likely prefer the higher transfer price because its operating profit increases from a loss of ₹ 10,000 to a profit of ₹ 20,000, especially if the company evaluates the division on its operating profit. Computers division, however, would prefer the lower transfer price.

Exhibit 12.1: Profit Calculation with No Outside Suppliers

Transfer Price of ₹ 50 per unit

	Hardware	Computers
Sales		
₹ 50 × 1,500	₹ 75,000	
₹ 100 × 1,500		₹ 1,50,000
Variable costs		
₹ 50 × 1,500	75,000	
₹ 50 × 1,500		₹ 75,000
Fixed Costs	10,000	5,000
Operating profit	₹ (10,000)	₹ 70,000
Total company operating profit	₹ 60,000	

Transfer Price of ₹ 70 per unit

	Hardware	Computers
Sales		
₹ 70 × 1,500	₹ 1,05,000	
₹ 100 × 1,500		₹ 1,50,000
Variable costs		
₹ 50 × 1,500	75,000	
₹ 70 × 1,500		₹ 105,000
Fixed Costs	10,000	5,000
Operating profit	₹ 20,000	₹ 40,000
Total company operating profit	₹ 60,000	

Case II: Transfer Pricing When Outside Suppliers are Available (Selling Division Below Capacity)

Using the same data as in Case 1 for HCL Technologies Ltd. let's add an additional option for Computers division: purchasing units from an outside supplier for ₹ 60 (the outside supplier offers a good deal to get Computers' business). If Computers division buys from an outside supplier, the facilities that Hardware division uses to manufacture these units would remain idle. Which option yields the highest total company operating profit for HCL Technologies (transfer from Hardware or purchase from outside supplier)?

As Exhibit 12.2 shows, purchasing units from an outside supplier will result in a loss in company wide operating profit of ₹ 15,000, the additional cost to the company of purchasing the units externally for ₹ 60 versus purchasing the units internally for ₹ 50 (₹ 15,000 = [₹ 60 – ₹ 50] × 1,500 units).

The general economic transfer pricing rule when the seller is operating below capacity (with idle capacity) states that the seller should set the transfer price at the variable cost per unit (or the differential cost of production). Thus, in this example, the seller should set the transfer price at its variable cost (₹ 50 per unit) to maximize overall company operating profits and to send the correct signal from the Hardware Division to the Computers Division that the variable cost of producing the item is ₹ 50.

Exhibit 12.2: Profit Calculation with Outside Suppliers Available, Selling Division Below Capacity

Transfer Price of ₹ 50 per unit

	Hardware	Computers
Sales		
50 × 1,500	₹ 75,000	
100 × 1,500		1,50,000
Variable costs		
50 × 1,500	75,000	
50 × 1,500		75,000
Fixed Costs	10.000	5,000
Operating profit	(10,000)	70,000
Total company operating profit	60,000	

Purchase Externally for ₹ 60 per unit

	Hardware	Computers
Sales		
70 × 0	0	
100 × 1,500		1,50,000
Variable costs		
50 × 0	0	
60 × 1,500		₹ 90,000
Fixed Costs	10,000	5,000
Operating profit	(10,000)	₹ 55,000
Total company operating profit	45,000	

Case III: Transfer Pricing When Outside Suppliers are Available (Selling Division at Capacity)

Using data as in Case II for HCL Technologies Ltd., we change one assumption. Assume that Hardware does not have idle capacity if Computers division buys from an outside supplier. Instead, if Computers buys from an outside supplier, Hardware division can sell all of its units to the outside at the market price of ₹ 70 (*i.e.* Hardware is operating at capacity). Which option yields the highest total company operating profit for HCL Products (transfer from Hardware or purchase from outside supplier)?

As Exhibit 12.3 shows that purchasing units from an outside supplier results in a gain in company wide operating profit of ₹ 15,000, which is the savings for Computers division of purchasing the units externally for ₹ 60, versus purchasing the units internally for ₹ 70 ([₹ 70 – ₹ 60] × 1,500 units = ₹ 15,000).

The general economic transfer pricing rule when the seller is operating at capacity is that the seller should transfer at the market price. Thus, with this example, the seller should set the transfer price at its market price (₹ 70 per unit) to maximize overall company operating profits.

Exhibit 12.3. Profit Calculation with Outside Suppliers Available, Selling Division at Capacity

Transfer Price of ₹ 70 per unit

	Hardware	Computers
Sales		
70 × 1,500	₹ 1,05,000	
100 × 1,500		1,50,000
Variable costs		
50 × 1,500	75,000	
70 × 1,500		1,05,000
Fixed Costs	10,000	5,000
Operating profit	20,000	40,000
Total company operating profit	60,000	

Purchase Externally for ₹ 60 per unit

	Hardware	Computers
Sales		
70 × 1,500	1,05,000	
100 × 1,500		1,50,000
Variable costs		
50 × 1,500	75,000	
60 × 1,500		₹ 90,000
Fixed Costs	10,000	5,000
Operating profit	20,000	₹ 55,000
Total company operating profit	75,000	

Case IV: Transfer Pricing When Outside Suppliers are Available (Selling Division Below Capacity with Alternative Facility Utilisation)

Using the same data as in Case I for HCL Technologies Ltd., we make additional changes in our assumptions. Assume that Hardware division has idle capacity if Computers division buys from an outside supplier for ₹ 60 per unit. However, if Computers Division buys from an outside supplier, the firm can use the Hardware idle capacity for other purposes, resulting in cash operating saving of ₹ 35,000. Which option yields the highest total company operating profit for HCL Technologies (transfer from Hardware or purchase from outside supplier)?

As Exhibit 12.4 shows, purchasing units from an outside supplier results in a gain in company wide operating profit of ₹ 20,000 the operating savings (₹ 35,000) less the additional cost of purchasing the units externally ([₹ 60 – ₹ 50] × 1,500 units = ₹ 15,000).

Exhibit 12.4: Outside Suppliers are Available (Selling Division Below Capacity with Alternative Facility Utilisation)

Transfer Price of ₹ 50 per unit

	Hardware	Computers
Sales		
50 × 1,500	₹ 75,000	
100 × 1,500		1,50,000
Variable costs		
50 × 1,500	75,000	
50 × 1,500		75,000
Fixed Costs	10,000	5,000
Operating profit	(10,000)	70,000
Total company operating profit	60,000	

Purchase Externally for ₹ 60 per unit

	Hardware	Computers
Sales		
70 × 0	0	
100 × 1,500		1,50,000
Variable costs		
50 × 0	0	
60 × 1,500		₹ 90,000
Fixed Costs	10,000	5,000
Operating savings	35,000	0
Operating profit	25,000	₹ 55,000
Total company operating profit	80,000	

The preceding examples demonstrate the two rules for establishing a transfer price:

1. If the selling division is operating at capacity, the transfer price should be the market price.
2. If the selling division has idle capacity, and the division can not use the idle facilities for other purposes, the transfer price should be at least the variable costs incurred to produce the goods.

ACTIVITY-BASED COSTS (ABC) AND TRANSFER PRICING

When activity-based costs are used for transfer prices, the buying division is charged for the unit-related and batch-related costs associated with the transferred products, plus an annual fixed fee, calculated from the product-related and facility-sustaining Costs. Under ABC, the producing division has the opportunity to recover all its costs, including its capacity-related costs. The inclusion of product and facility-sustaining costs in the transfer price represents a reservation price that the buying division pays to acquire the intermediate product at short-run marginal cost–defined as the unit and batch costs associated with the production of incremental units.

Kaplan and Atkinson[12] comment about the implications of assigning product and facility-sustaining costs to the transfer prices.

> Assigning product and facility-sustaining costs as a fixed annual fee raises some interesting motivational and control issues. Suppose that the fixed fee assigned to each user is based on that user's planned (or long-run average) use of the product and facility. For example, if a division uses 20% of the average capacity, the division is assigned 20% of the fixed costs of the facility. The prepaid capacity would be reserved for the user paying for that capacity. This scheme has two desirable economic traits. First, in the short run, transfers will take place at short-run marginal (unit plus batch) cost, as economic theory dictates. Second, people will tend to be more honest in the capacity acquisition stage. If they overstate their expected requirements, perhaps to ensure adequate capacity for their own use, they will pay a higher fixed fee in later years. If they understate their expected requirements, to avoid the fixed fee for capacity, they may not have sufficient capacity for their needs as capacity either is not acquired or is reserved for others who have expressed a willingness to pay the fixed fee for that capacity.

DISADVANTAGES OF TRANSFER PRICING

There are some disadvantages to be given due consideration before setting transfer prices. These disadvantages are:

1. There can be disagreement among organisational divisional managers as to how the transfer price should be set.
2. Additional costs, time and manpower will be required to execute transfer prices and design the accounting system.
3. For some departments or divisions, for example service departments, transfer prices do not work equally well because these departments do not provide measurable benefits.
4. Transfer prices may cause dysfunctional behaviour among managers of organisational units.
5. The issue of transfer prices in multinational companies is highly complicated.

Besides the above, each type of transfer prices have their own merits and demerits.

GUIDELINES FOR AN OPTIMUM TRANSFER PRICING SYSTEM

Kaura[13] in his study of Indian companies practices on transfer pricing has suggested the following rules for a successful transfer pricing system:

1. Negotiated transfer prices are likely to have greater appeal to managers because of the dynamic business environment in which rapid responses and flexibility provide a definite edge.
2. If market prices are used as a base for evolving transfer prices through negotiations, long-run competitive market prices should be used.
3. If divisional managers are allowed to buy or sell a small quantity (5-10 percent) outside the company, it gives them an awareness of the supply and demand conditions of the market, which facilitates negotiation of transfer prices by them.
4. Interdivisional disputes should be referred to a transfer pricing coordinator/arbitrator. The latter should resolve these disputes with the involvement of divisional managers.
5. If outside sourcing is proposed, this should be reviewed by the corporate controller's office based on the financial data presented by the supplying and the buying divisions. The controller must then make a recommendation on sourcing and pricing to the operating management group (a cluster of divisions formed into a group under the charge of a vice-president in each organisation) or to the corporate management.
6. Corporate/group management must consciously avoid spending inordinate time listening to business unit/divisional manager's explanations which often seek to blame other divisions for their own inefficiencies.
7. Heavy emphasis should be placed on operating profitability, working together and developing skills for performing in an open and competitive market.

Managers at different levels in a firm attempt to achieve different objectives through their transfer pricing policies. Kaplan[14] observes that corporate managers, divisional managers and financial staffs may desire the following:

Corporate Managers Want Transfer Prices to

- Encourage division managers to make decisions that maximize the long-run profitability of the overall firm.
- Provide information so that managers can make good short-term decisions (such as bids for orders) and long-term decisions (e.g., adding or deleting product lines).

Division Managers Want Transfer Prices to

- Represent fairly the financial performance of their division
- Reflect the impact of good business decisions within their division (e.g., product mix and improved efficiency)
- Require downstream division managers to include the full costs associated with the products they are receiving from upstream divisions.

Financial Staffs Want Transfer Prices That

- Are simple and credible, so that they will be used and are useful for division managers.
- Are easy to use and easy to explain

TRANSFERS BETWEEN DIVISIONS IN DIFFERENT COUNTRIES

The creation of foreign subsidiaries and bases of operation for cross border flow of products, services, trademarks, funding and technology is having a significant impact on the issue of transfer pricing in today's international business scenario. The transfer pricing problem for multinationals is of great significance. There are different income tax rates in different countries. So, it becomes desirable from the view point of overall corporate strategy to show higher profits in low-tax countries and lower profits in high-tax countries. One way to do so is through transfer prices.

There are two basic issues relating to transfer prices in case of multinational companies having divisions in different countries.

1. ***Income Tax Rates:*** Multinational companies always consider domestic and foreign income tax rates while setting transfer prices. For instance, suppose an Indian company based in

India has a division in Australia. The Indian division manufactures a component which is transferred to Australian division for assembly and sale of the final product. Assume, the income tax rate in India is higher than the income tax rate in Australia. The different income tax rates will influence the transfer price for the component.

Suppose, the management of the company sets a lower transfer price for the component, this will result in lower profits for the Indian division because transfer prices become revenue for this Indian division. However, the lower transfer prices will produce high income for the Australian division because transfer prices will be cost for the Australian division. Since the tax rate is lower in Australia, the overall company will save on income tax. The company, by setting a low transfer price, tends to shift a portion of its income to a country having lower tax rate. In some countries, there are regulations and laws prohibiting such transfer pricing practices.

2. ***Import Duties:*** Transfer pricing policies followed by multinational companies are affected by import duties or tariffs. These are the fees charged to an importer generally on the basis of the reported value of the goods being imported. Consider the above example again of a multination firm with divisions in India and Australia. If Australia imposes an import duty on goods transferred in from the Indian division, the company has an incentive to set a relatively low transfer price on the transferred goods. This will reduce the duty to be paid and maximize the overall profit for the company as a whole. Like income taxes, countries sometimes make laws to restrict multinational firms' flexibility in setting transfer prices to minimize import duties payable by them.

Factors Affecting Multinational Transfer Prices

The following considerations are used by multinational companies for deciding transfer pricing policy.

1. ***Transfer Prices as a Tool to Minimize Worldwide Taxes, Duties and Tariffs:*** Transfer prices may be set between two subsidiaries of a holding company and/or two units of a corporate body in such a way to minimize the taxes, duties and tariffs on their overall profit. For example, suppose, tax rate on profit in country X is lower than in country Y. The subsidiary in Y will then underinvoice its export to the subsidiary in X. The profit at the latter subsidiary will be inflated, but that will bear a lower tax burden.
2. ***Avoidance of Financial Restrictions on Profit Repatriation Imposed by Government:*** When in a country, financial restrictions on profit repatriation is imposed by Government, transfer prices is set among two subsidiaries by overinvoicing its imports. In some countries there may be restriction on repatriation of income and dividend/profits. Goods are sought to be transferred to subsidiaries in these countries at more than the price otherwise settled at arm's length.
3. ***Avoidance of Divisional Conflicts:*** Transfer prices are set among the units in such a way that general co-ordination between units are promoted, the implementation of appropriate procedures to ensure, as far as possible, uniformity in the classification and application of costs are maintained and divisional conflicts among different units are reduced.
4. ***Overall Goal Congruence:*** Transfer prices should help achieve overall goal congruence with regard to profit/income and customer satisfaction.
5. ***Inflation:*** If a country hosting a subsidiary, has a high rate of inflation, early repatriation of fund is done by overcharging goods, exported to it so that money may not be tied up in a currency that depreciates. However, the tax and fiscal authorities of the host countries are vigilant. They impose penalty for manipulated evasion of taxation or import duties. To safeguard the position, the taxpayer may enter into an advanced pricing agreement with the related two tax authorities.

Besides the above considerations, multinational companies have different internal and external objectives of transfer pricing policies, as displayed in Figure 12.2.

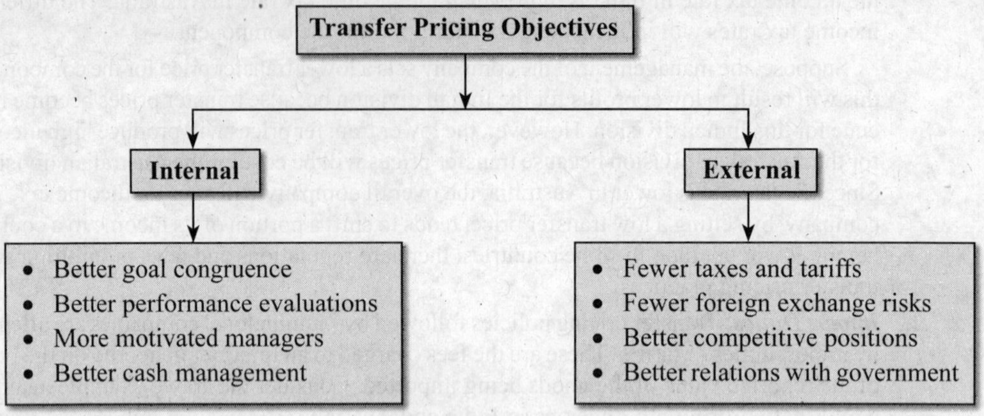

Figure 12.2: Multinational Company Transfer Pricing Objectives.

Source: Jesset T. Barfield, Cecily A. Raiborn and Michal R. Kinney, Cost Accounting, Traditions and Innovations, Thomson, 2003, P. 819.

Example:

Suppose that Division A buys a product from Division B. The divisions are in different countries. The tax rate in Division A's country is 20% and Division B's country 60%. Both use the same currency to prepare income statements. Some data about the two divisions are as follows:

Division A

Selling price of Division A's product	100
Variable cost, excluding transfer price	20
Tax rate in Division A's country	20%

Division B

Variable cost of division B's product	30
Tax rate in Division B's country	60%

Assume, Division B transfers 1000 units to Division A at 30 and 60. The effect of this transfer and income tax effect are displayed in the income statements prepared below.

		***Transfer at* 30**	
		Division A	***Division B***
Sales	(1000 × 100)	1,00,000	—
	(1000 × 30)	—	30,000
Less:	Variable Cost:		
	(1000 × (20 + 30)	50,000	—
	(1000 × 30)	—	30,000
	Contribution margin	50,000	0
	Income tax at 20% and 60%	10,000	0

			Transfer at 60
Sales	(1000 × 100)	1,00,000	—
	(1000 × 60)	—	60,000
Less:	Variable Costs:		
	(1000 × (20 + 60)	80,000	
	(1000 × 30)	—	30,000
	Contribution margin	20,000	30,000
	Income tax at 20% and 60%	4,000	18,000

Note: As identical currency has been used by both the divisions, in the above income statements, currency is not indicated. Any currency can be assumed.

The above income statements show that total income taxes are only 10,000 when Division B transfers its product at 30 *i.e.* at the lower price. At higher price, total income taxes are 22,000. The company minimises its total taxes if Division B gives the product to Division A. However, the government and tax authorities in Division B's country would not be inclined to allow this. If the company compells Division B to sell at a low price, it saves considerable tax, but penalises the performance of Division B and its manager. Also, suggesting a low transfer price would enhance the performance of Division A and its managers.

There are similar problems with regard to import duties, tariffs which are based on values reported for incoming goods. If a division is transferring goods to another division located in a high-tariff country, a low transfer price reduces the tariff. Similarly, with high export duties, it is appropriate to have a low transfer price.

Another area where income-shifting is tempting is in management fees and allocations of corporate costs. A company can shift income from a division (foreign country) to itself (home country) by charging a management fee. If the fee is based on sales or assets, it is really just a cost allocation. But the more cost charged to a division or subsidiary in a high-tax country and the less charged to those in low-tax countries, the lower the multinational's total tax bill. Here again, the reported performance of the local managers is influenced by corporate policies.

Besides the problems associated with portraying performance, some of the practices described above, if arbitrarily imposed, are unethical and in some countries illegal. Various authorities such as those responsible for collecting income taxes in the various countries will try to ensure that artificially high or low transfer prices are disallowed and that corporate charges reflect the services provided at the corporate level.[15]

To check transfer-pricing manipulations, it can be suggested to develop a standardised transfer pricing policy and procedures to be implemented globally. A second suggestion is to mandate increased disclosures about the magnitude and effects of transfer-pricing on subsidiary income and tax liabilities in the financial reports of transnational corporations engaged in cross-border transactions. The third suggestion would be to institute an electronics-based transfer-pricing enforcement mechanism in accordance with its unique position as a global information technology superpower.

However, as long as some countries continue to operate as tax havens, income shifting by MNCs is tacitly encouraged and will continue unabated. Concurrent with globally acceptable standards must be the gradual elimination of tax rate differentials that contribute to income-shifting and the inevitable misallocation of tax revenues.

Illustrative Problem 1

A company has two divisions, Division A and Division B. Division A normally purchases its parts from Division B of the same company. Division A has learned that Division B is increasing its price to ₹ 110 per unit. As a result, Division A manager has decided to purchase the parts from an outside supplier at a unit cost of ₹ 100, ₹ 10 less than it would cost to purchase the same part from Division B. The Division B manager has explained that inflation is the cause of the price increase and that the loss of parts normally transferred to Division A will hurt the division as well as the company profits. The Division B manager feels that the company as a whole would benefit from the sale of parts to Division A. The following costs and unit purchases represent the normal annual transaction.

	₹
Units purchased	1,000
Division B's variable cost per unit	95
Division B's fixed cost per unit	10

Required:

1. Will the company as a whole benefit if Division A purchases the unit from the outside supplier for ₹ 100 per unit. Assume that there are no alternative uses for Division B's facilities.
2. What would be the effect if the outside selling price decreases by ₹ 8 per unit, assuming that Divisions B remains idle.
3. If Division B's facilities could be put into production for other sales at an annual cost saving of ₹ 14,500, should Division A still purchase from the outside?

Solution:

The comparative income statement approach has been used to solve the questions:

1. **Division A's action to purchase at ₹ 100**

	Buy Outside ₹	***Buy Inside*** ₹
Total purchase costs	1,00,000	—
Total outlay costs	—	95,000
Net cash outflow to the company as a whole.	1,00,000	95,000

The company as a whole will benefit if Division A buys inside.

	Buy Outside ₹	***Buy Inside*** ₹
2. Total purchase costs	92,000	—
Total outlay costs	—	95,000
Net cash outflow to the company as a whole.	92,000	95,000

The company as a whole will benefit if Division A buy from the outside supplier at ₹ 92 per unit.

	Buy Outside ₹	Buy Inside ₹
3. Total purchase costs	1,00,000	—
Total outlay costs	—	95,000.
Revenue (or cost savings)		
from using Division B's facilities	14,500	
Net cash outflow to the company as a whole	85,500	95,000

In this case, the company as a whole will be better off if Division A buys outside and Division B's facilities are utilised elsewhere.

Alternative Solution:

Using opportunity cost concept, the question can be analysed as follows:

	1	2	3
(*a*) Total purchase costs	1,00,000	92,000	1,00,000
Total outlay costs if purchased inside	95,000	95,000	95,000
Total opportunity costs if purchased inside	—	—	14,500
(*b*) Total relevant costs	95,000	95,000	1,09,500
Net advantage (disadvantage) to company as a whole (a-b)	5,000	(3000)	(9,500)

Illustrative Problem 2

A company is a multidivisional company and its managers have been delegated full profit responsibility and complex autonomy to accept or reject transfers from other divisions.

Division A produces a sub-assembly with a ready competitive market. This sub-assembly is currently used by Division B for a final product that is sold outside at ₹ 1,200. Division A charges Division B market price for the sub-assembly which is ₹ 700 per unit. Variable costs are ₹ 520 and ₹ 600 for Divisions A and B respectively.

The manager of Division B feels that Division A should transfer the subassembly, at a lower price than market because at this price, Division B is unable to make a profit.

Required:

1. Compute Division B's profit contribution if transfers are made at the market price and also the total contribution to profit for the company.
2. Assume that Division A can sell all its production in the open market. Should Division A transfer goods to Division B? If so, at what price.
3. Assume that Division A can sell in the open market only 500 units at ₹ 700 per unit out of 1,000 units that it can produce every month and that a 20 percent reduction in price is necessary to sell full capacity. Should transfers be made? If so, how many units should it transfer and at what prices? Submit a schedule showing comparisons of contribution margins under three different alternatives to support your decision.

Solution:

Division B's contribution Margin		₹
1. Selling Price of Final Product	₹	1,200
Less: Division B's variable cost	600	
Division B's purchase cost	700	1,300
Division B's loss		(100)
Company's contribution Margin		
Selling price of final product		1,200
	₹	₹
Less: Division B's variable cost	600	
Division A's variable cost	520	1,120
Company's Contribution margin		80
2. Selling price of sub-assembly		700
Less: Division A's variable cost		520
Company's contribution margin		180

The company contribution is ₹ 100 greater if the sub-assembly is sold on the intermediate market rather than to Division B. Thus, it should be sold in the intermediate market. *The market price would be the appropriate transfer price if transfers were made:*

3. Alternative 1: Transfer 1000 units to Division B

   Alternative 2: Sell 500 units in the intermediate market at ₹ 700 and transfer 500 units to Division B.

   Alternative 3: Sell 1,000 units on the intermediate market at 20% reduced price.

***Alternative* 1:**

		₹
Company sales (1000 units × ₹ 1200)		12,00,000
Less: Variable costs		11,20,000
Contribution margin		80,000
Variable costs = 1000 units @ ₹ 520	5,20,000	
1,000 units @ ₹ 600	6,00,000	
	11,20,000	

***Alternative* 2:**

	₹
Company sales	9,50,000
(500 units @ ₹ 700)	
(500 units @ ₹ 1200)	
Variable costs	
(1000 units @ ₹ 520)	
(500 units @ ₹ 600)	8,20,000
Contribution margin	1,30,000

***Alternative* 3:**

	₹
Company sales	
1000 units @ ₹ 560 (700 – 140)	5,60,000
Variable costs	
1000 units @ ₹ 520	5,20,000
	40,000

Decision: Transfers should be made, 500 units should be transferred to Division B. The transfer price should be set at a price greater than the variable cost of Division A (₹ 520) and less than the marginal revenue to Division B (₹ 600). Division B's marginal revenue will be ₹ 600 (₹ 1200 market price–division B's own variable cost ₹ 600).

Illustrative Problem 3

The BPL Ltd. manufactures and sells television sets. The Assembly Division assembles the television sets. It buys the screens for the television sets from the Screen Division. The Screen Division is operating at capacity. The incremental cost of manufacturing the screens is ₹ 700 per unit. The Screen Division can sell as many screens as it wants in the outside market at a price of ₹ 1,100 per screen. If it sells screens in the outside market, the Screen Division will incur variable marketing and distribution costs of ₹ 40 per unit. Similarly, if the Assembly Division purchases screens from outside suppliers, it will incur variable purchasing costs of ₹ 20 per screen.

Required:

(*i*) Using the general guideline on transfer pricing, what is the minimum transfer price at which the Screen Division will sell screens to the Assembly Division?

(*ii*) Suppose division managers act automously to maximize their own division's operating income, either by transacting internally or buying and selling in the market. If the two division managers were to negotiate a transfer price, what is the range of acceptable transfer prices?

Solution:

(*i*) If the Screen Division sells screens in the outside market, it will receive, for each screen, the market price of the screen minus variable marketing and distribution costs per screen = ₹ 1,100 – ₹ 40 = ₹ 1,060. The incremental cost of manufacturing each screen is ₹ 700. The Screen Division is operating at capacity. Hence, the opportunity cost per screen of selling the screen to the Assembly Division rather than in the outside market is the contribution margin the Screen Division would forgo if it transferred screens internally rather than sold them in the outside market.

Contribution margin per screen = ₹ 1,060 – ₹ 700 = ₹ 360.

Minimum transfer price per screen = Incremental costs per screen up to the point of transfer + Opportunity costs per screen to the selling division

That is,

Minimum transfer price per screen = ₹ 700 + ₹ 360 = ₹ 1,060

(*ii*) If the two division managers were to negotiate a transfer price, the range of possible transfer prices is between ₹ 1,060 and ₹ 1,120 per screen. As calculated in requirement (*i*), the Screen Division will be willing to supply screens to the Assembly Division only if the transfer price equals or exceeds ₹ 1,060 per screen.

If the Assembly Division were to purchase the screens in the outside market, it will incur a cost of ₹ 1,120, the cost of the screen equal to ₹ 1,100 plus variable purchasing costs of ₹ 20 per screen. Hence, the Assembly Division will be willing to buy screens from the Screen Division only if the price does not exceed ₹ 1,120 per screen. Within the price range of ₹ 1,060 and ₹ 1,120 per screen, each division will be willing to transact with the other. The exact transfer price between ₹ 1,060 and ₹ 1,120 will depend on the bargaining strengths of the two divisions.

Illustrative Problem 4

Division Z is a profit centre which produces four products A, B, C and D. Each product is sold in the external market also. Data for the period is:

	A	*B*	*C*	*D*
Market price per unit (₹)	150	146	140	130
Variable cost of production Per unit (₹)	130	100	90	85
Labour hours required per unit	3	4	2	3

Product *D* can be transferred to division *Y*, but the maximum quantity that may be required for transfer is 2,500 units of *D*.

The maximum sales in the external market are:

A	2,800 units
B	2,500 units
C	2,300 units
D	1,600 units

Division *Y* can purchase the same product at a price of ₹ 125 per unit from outside instead of receiving transfer of product *D* from Division *Z*.

What should be the transfer price for each unit for 2,500 units of *D*, if the total labour hours available in division *Z* are 20,000 hours?

Solution:

Ranking of products when availability of time is the key factor

Products	*A*	*B*	*C*	*D*
Market price	150	146	140	130
Less: Variable cost	130	100	90	85
Contribution p.u. (₹)	20	46	50	45
Labour hours p.u.	3	4	2	3
Contribution/labour hour	6.66	11.5	25	15
Ranking	IV	III	I	II
Maximum demand (units)	2,800	2,500	2,300	1,600
Total No. of hours	8,400	10,000	4,600	4,800
Allocation of 20,000 hours on the basis of ranking	600*	10,000	4,600	4,800

***Balancing figure**

Note: Time required meeting the demand of 2,500 units of product *D* for division *Y* is 7,500 hours. This requirement of time viz., 7,500 hours for providing 2,500 units of product *D* for division *Y* can be met by sacrificing 600 hours of Product *A* (200 units) and 6,900 hours of Product B (1,725 units).

Transfer Price = Variable cost + Opportunity cost

$$\textbf{Or} \quad ₹\,85+\frac{(₹\,6,900\times 11.5+600\times 6.66)}{2,500} = ₹\,85+\frac{(79,350+4,000)}{2500}$$

$$= ₹\,(85+33.34) = ₹\,118.34$$

Illustrative Problem 5

AB Ltd. makes component 'C' and billing machines. Division A makes component 'C' that is used in the final assembly of the machine in Division B.

(One unit of Component 'C' is used per machine). Component C has an outside market also. A and B operate as profit centres and each can take its own decisions. The following data is given in the existing scenario for Divisions A and B, under which Division A has enough special and external demand to use its capacity and hence is offering B rates of 800 ₹/Unit for quantity up to 750 units and 900 ₹/unit for more than 750 units, so that its outside contribution is not affected by transfers to B. A and B can sell any quantity up to the maximum indicated under ₹units sold', without affecting their future demands.

	Division A		***Division B***	
		Exernal market (normal sales)	*Special sales*	*External Market (normal sales)*
Selling Price (₹/u)	1,000	800	4,000	85
Variable manufacturing cost (₹/u)	600	600	1,500	(*excluding) component C)
Variable selling cost (₹/u)	100**	**	200**	(** Not incurred on into division transfers)
Total variable cost (₹/unit)	700	600	1,700*	(* excluding component c)
Contribution (₹/unit)	300	200		
Units Sold	1,250	750	900	
Production capacity	2,000 units		900 units	

For the next period, A requires for its own use in its selling outlets, 50 units of billing machines produced by B. B's manager proposes as follows:

Option 1: B will supply 50 machines to A on its variable manufacturing cost basis provided A supplies to B, 500 units of Component C at A's variable manufacturing cost basis.

Option II: Both A and B resort to total variable cost per unit basis applicable to normal external sale, though neither A nor B incurs any selling cost on inter division transfer. A will be given 50 machines for its use. A will have to supply B all the 900 units that B requires.

Option III: Both A and B use the external market selling price (i.e. 1,000 and 4,000 ₹/Unit for 900 units of Component 'C' and 50 machines respectively).

From a financial perspective, advise Division A's manager what he should chose. Support your advise with relevant figures.

What is the change in the rate of discount per unit given by B to A (based on unit transfer price to market price ratio) from option I to option II ? **[CA Final, May 2012]**

Solution:

The basis strategy for division A is to first divert the Special Sales and then the Normal Sales in the external market to minimize the opportunity loss.

	Option 1	Option 2	Option 3
Opportunity Lost (Units)			
Special Sales	500	750	750
External Market	-	150	150
Agreed Selling Price by Division A	600	700	1,000
Agreed Selling Price by Division B	2,100	2,400	4,000
(Including the Transfer price of Division A)			
Contribution (Lost)/Gain ? per unit			
Special Sales	(200)	(100)	200
External Market	-	(200)	100
Total Contribution (Lost)/Gain (?)			
Special Sales	(1,00,000)	(75,000)	1,50,000
External Market	-	(30,000)	15,000
Total	(1,00,000)	(1,05,000)	1,65,000
Contribution gain per unit by buying from B (?/u)	1,900	1,600	-
Total Contribution Gained (50 Machines) ?	95,000	80,000	-
Net Contribution Gained (50 Machines) ?	(5,000)	(25,00)	
			165,000

Decision: Option 3 is preferred.

Rate of change in discount (1900 -1600)/4000 = 7.5%

Illustrative Problem 6

An engineering company operates on profit centre basis. Each divisional head has full authority on all decisions regarding sales of the products and services of his division.

Division M buys a component X from Division K. Division K has fixed the price of X with effect from Ist July, 2016 @ ₹ 20 per unit whereas Division M proposes to purchase the component at ₹ 18 from the market. Division M requires 15,000 units of X annually. The cost of Division K for producing X is ₹ 17 variable cost per unit and ₹ 2 fixed cost per unit. Head of Division K approached the Managing director to persuade Division M to purchase the component from Division K and that the cost increase is due to installation of a new machinery utilised in the manufacture of component X resulting in higher depreciation charges. If division M does not buy from Division K, then the latter can put the facilities to alternative uses resulting in a saving of ₹ 20,000 per annum.

You are required to comment on the following:

1. Will the company as a whole benefit if Division M purchases the component from the market instead of from Division K;

   (*a*) if alternative use for the facilities of division K exists, and

   (*b*) if such use does not exist.

2. What are the effect of the alternatives open to division M?

Solution:

1. The problem involves a make or buy decision for the company.

   (*a*) If alternative use for the facilities of division K exists, the decision to purchase the component from the market will have the following effect:

		₹
	Purchase price ₹ 18 × 15,000 =	2,70,000
Add:	Fixed cost unrecovered	30,000
Less:	Savings from alternative use	(20,000)
	Total cost involved	2,80,000
	Cost of manufacture ₹ 19 × 15,000	2,85,000
	Saving to the company on purchase	5,000

   (*b*) If no alternative facility exists, saving of ₹ 20,000 will not come forth and in that case the company will lose ₹ 15,000 (₹ 20,000 – ₹ 5,000) if it goes in for the purchase of the component.

2. The alternative open to M are either to continue buying from K at the new price of ₹ 20 per unit or purchase the component from the market at ₹ 18 per unit. The effect of the alternative decision on Division M and K will be as follows:

   For Division M

   Purchase from K will involve a loss of ₹ 2 (₹ 20 – ₹ 18) per unit to this division totalling ₹ 30,000 per annum.

For Division K

Purchase by Division M will result in a profit of ₹ 1 (₹ 20 – ₹ 19) per unit, equal to ₹ 15,000 per annum for Division K. If Division M decides not to purchase from division K, the loss to the latter division will be:

(*i*) if alternative use of the facilities exist

		₹
	Fixed cost @ ₹ 2 per unit	= 30,000
Less:	Saving from alternative use	= 20,000
	Net loss	10,000

(*ii*) If alternative use of the facilities does not exist, the loss will be ₹ 30,000 due to the fixed costs.

In addition to the loss incurred as shown at (*i*) and (*ii*) above, Division K will lose the notional profit of ₹ 15,000 per annum which it would have earned on the sale to Division M.

Illustrative Problem 7

Metflow Division is a part of the AKG Group. Metflow Division produces a single product for which it has an external market which utilizes 80% of its production capacity.

Akali Division which is also a part of the AKG Group, requires units of the product available from Metflow as input to a product which will be sold outside the Group. Akali Division's requirements are equal to 40% of Metflow Division's production capacity.

Akali Division has a potential source of supply from outside the AKG Group. This outside supplier can supply 75% of Akali Division's requirements. The outside source may wish to quote a higher price if Akali Division only intends to take up part of its product availability.

Required:

Discuss aspects of transfer pricing principles and information availability which will affect the likely achievement of group profit maximization from the sourcing decision made by Akali Division in the above situation.

Solution:

The Metflow Division—Akali Division situation may be studied from a number of viewpoints:

(*i*) Where Metflow Division has an external market for its product (80% of its capacity), the transfer price should be set at market price in order to comply with the general rule:

TP = marginal cost + opportunity cost to the supplying division.

In this way any external supply available to Akali Division at less than the market price of Metflow Division's product will increase group profit.

(*ii*) Inter-divisional transfers may be effected with less packing costs and less delivery costs (say, using group vehicles). In this case the opportunity foregone by the group must be adjusted by the external costs that have been avoided. In this way Metflow Division will earn the same profit as from external sales and Akali Division will reject supplier quotes which are in excess of the adjusted market price quoted by Metflow Division.

(*iii*) For the 20% spare capacity, it appears Metflow Division has no external market. So, the opportunity cost is zero. Metflow Division can offer the product to Akali Division at marginal cost. Outside supplier quotes in excess of the marginal cost of Metflow Division must be rejected in this case.

(*iv*) The question states that the external supplier can supply 75% of Akali Division's requirement. This is equivalent to 30% of the capacity of Metflow. Since Metflow Division's spare capacity is only 20%, the balance 10% must be outsourced by Akali Division. The price of this balance quantity should not exceed the market price of Metflow Division's external sales.

It will be useful for Metflow Division to indicate the quantities which it is willing to supply at different prices, viz. 20% capacity at marginal cost and 10% capacity at adjusted market price. In this way Akali Division can evaluate this offer from the external source taking into account the probability that external source may require a higher price for a part order.

Illustrative Problem 8

Akash Industries Ltd. has two divisions — P (Production) and S (Selling). P-Division produces an intermediate product for which there is no external market. Using this intermediate, S-Division turns it to finished product — FM and sells in the market. Each unit of finished product consumes one unit of intermediate. The sales quantity is sensitive to the price charged and S (selling) Division has developed the following sales schedule:

Selling Price per unit (₹):	500	450	400	350	300	250
Sales Units (No.) :	1000	2000	3000	4000	5000	6000

The cost details are as follows:

	P-Division	S-Division
Variable Cost per unit (₹):	55	35
Fixed Cost per annum (₹):	3,00,000	4,50,000

The transfer price is ₹ 175 based on the full-cost basis.

Required:

(*i*) Prepare a profit statement showing the profits of both the departments separately and the Company as a whole.

(*ii*) Determine the selling price that will maximize the S-Division's profit and the price that will maximize the Company's profit.

Solution:

(*i*)

Akash Industries Ltd.

Profit Statement for Divisions — P & S and Company as a whole (₹ *in thousand*)

S-Division					P-Division			Company as a whole
Sales (units)	**Revenue**	**Variable cost**	**Transfer Price**	**Profit**	**Revenue**	**Variable cost**	**Profit**	**Profit**
1000	500	35	175	290	175	55	120	410
2000	900	70	350	480	350	110	240	720
3000	1200	105	525	570*	525	165	360	930
4000	1400	140	700	560	700	220	480	1040
5000	1500	175	875	450	875	275	600	1050**
6000	1500	210	1050	240	1050	330	720	960

(*ii*) It reveals from the exhibited profit statement that Division-S (Selling) has the maximum profit at a volume of sales at 3,000 units @ ₹ 400 per unit and whereas overall company's profit is maximum at 5,000 units @ ₹ 300 per unit.

Illustrative Problem 9

During the current year International Business Company's Asian Division incurred differential production costs of ₹ 60 lakhs for parts that are transferred to its European Division. Asian Division has substantial excess capacity. European Division uses those parts to produce the final product. In addition to the costs of the units transferred from Asian Division, European Division incurred differential costs of ₹ 80 lakh to produce the final product in addition to the costs of parts shipped to it from the Asian Division. Sales revenue for the final product sold by European Division is ₹ 300 lakhs. Other companies in the same country import similar parts as European Division at a cost of ₹ 70 lakhs. International Business Company has set its transfer price at ₹ 140 lakhs. The tax rate in the country where Asian Division is located is 40% while the tax rate for the country in which European Division is located is 70%.

Required:

(*a*) What would International Business Company's total tax liability for both divisions be if it used the ₹ 70 lakhs transfer price?

(*b*) What would the liability be if it used the ₹ 140 lakhs transfer price?

(*c*) What is the optimal transfer price from an incentive point of view, ignoring taxes? What would be each division's operating profit if this optimal incentive transfer price were used.

Solution:

(*a*) Use ₹ 70 lakh transfer price

	Asian	*European*
Revenue	₹ 70,00,000	₹ 3,00,00,000
Third-party costs	(60,00,000)	(80,00,000)
Transferred goods costs		(70,00,000)
Taxable income	₹ 10,00,000	₹ 1,50,00,0000
Tax rate	× 40%	× 70%
Tax liability	₹ 4,00,000	₹ 1,05,00,000
Total tax liability	₹ 1,09,00,000	(₹ 4,00,000 + ₹ 1,05,00,000)

(*b*) Use 140 lakhs transfer price

	Asian	*European*
Revenue	₹ 1,40,00,000	₹ 3,00,00,000
Third-party costs	(60,00,000)	(80,00,000)
Transferred goods costs		(1,40,00,000)
Taxable income	₹ 80,00,000	₹ 80,00,000
Tax rate	× 40%	× 70%
Tax liability	₹ 32,00,000	₹ 56,00,000
Total tax liability	₹ 88,00,000	(₹ 32,00,000 + ₹ 56,00,000)

(*c*) The optimal price for incentive purposes is ₹ 60 lakhs. Using ₹ 60 lakhs as the transfer price:

	Asian	*European*
Revenue	₹ 60,00,000	₹ 3,00,00,000
Third-party costs	(60,00,000)	(80,00,000)
Transferred goods costs		(60,00,000)
Taxable income	0	₹ 1,60,00,000
Tax rate	× 40%	× 70%
Tax liability	0	₹ 1,12,00,000
Total tax liability	₹ 1,12,00,000	

Illustrative Problem 10

A company has two manufacturing divisions, A and C. Each division operates as an independent profit centre. Division A, which produces two components 'Bright' and 'Light', has a capacity of 1,00,000 hours per annum. The annual fixed costs of A amount to ₹ 20 lacs.

The product cost data is as under:

	Bright	*Light*
Direct material/unit	₹ 10	₹ 5
Direct labour and variable overheads @ ₹ 35/labour hour	₹ 140	₹ 35

Division A has a permanent customer for the purchase of 15,000 units of 'Bright' per annum at a selling price of ₹ 300 per unit. The balance capacity is devoted to the production of 'Light', for which there is an unlimited sales potential at a price of ₹ 60 per unit.

Division C assembles 'Tight' by using imported component. The annual fixed costs of division C amount to ₹ 4,00,000.

The product cost data is as under:

	₹
Imported component	300
Direct Materials	40
Direct labour & variable overheads @ ₹ 25/hr	250
Selling price	700

With a view to minimizing dependence on imported components, the possibility of using 'Bright' was explored. It was found that the .import substitution was possible with slight modification, which will take two extra hours per unit of 'Tight' in Division C. The production of 'Tight' is estimated at 5,000 units per annum.

You are requested to present the division-wise profit statement and the company's profit as a whole on the basis of the following conditions:

(*i*) Division C imports 5,000 components for producing 'Tight'.

(*ii*) Division C substitutes 'Tight' by drawing 'Bright' from Division A at ₹ 300 per unit.

(*iii*) Same condition as in (*ii*) above but Division A supplies 'Bright' at ₹ 250 per unit.

Solution:

Workings for basic data:

Marginal contribution from products	*Bright*	*Light*	*Tight*
Selling price	300	60	700
Variable costs	150	40	590
Marginal contribution	150	20	110
Production time required per unit [hours]	4	1	

(*i*)

Contribution from	*Division A* ₹	*Division C* ₹	*Company* ₹
15,000 Bright units	22,50,000		
40,000 Light units	8,00,000		
5,000 Tight units		5,50,000	
Less: Fixed costs	(20,00,000)	(4,00,000)	
Profit	10,50,000	1,50,000	12,00,000

(*ii*)

Contribution from			
15,000 Bright (for sale outside)	22,50,000		
5,000 Bright (for supply to C)	7,50,000		
20,000 Light [using balance hours]	4,00,000		
5,000 Tight [contbn. at ₹ 60/unit]*		3,00,000	
Less: Fixed costs	(20,00,000)	(4,00,000)	
Profit + / Loss –	+ 14,00,000	–1,00,000	+ 13,00,000

• [₹ 110 as per working above less cost of two extra hours of machining @ ₹ 25/hour].

(*iii*) Since the transfer price is ₹ 50 less than in the case (*ii*) above, Division A's profit will reduce by ₹ 50 × 5,000 or ₹ 2,50,000 to ₹ 11,50,000 and Division C's profit will be ₹ 1,50,000 – making the Company's profit of ₹ 13,00,000.

Illustrative Problem 11

Division K is a profit centre which produces three products L, M & N. Each product has an external market:

Products	*L*	*M*	*N*
External Market price per unit (₹)	48	46	40
Variable Cost of production in Division K (₹)	33	24	28
Labour Hours required per unit in Division K	3	4	2

Product M can be transferred to J but the maximum quantity that might be required for transfer is 300 units of M.

Products	*L*	*M*	*N*
The maximum External Sales are (units)	800	500	300

Instead of receiving transfers of Product M from Divsion K, Division J could buy similar product in the open market at a slightly cheaper price of ₹ 45 per unit.

Required:

What should be the transfer price for each units of M, if the total labour hours available in Division K are:

(*i*) 3,800 hours;

(*ii*) 5,600 hours.

Solution:

Computation of Contribution per labour hour from external sales:

Products	*L*	*M*	*N*
External Market Price per unit (₹)	48	46	40
Variable Cost of Production in Division K (₹)	33	24	28
Contribution (₹)	15	22	12
Labour Hours required per unit in Division K	3	4	2
Contribution per labour Hour (₹)	5	5.50	6
Ranking	III	II	I

Computation of Transfer Price when the capacity is 3800 hours:

Hours required of N	=	300 × 2	=	600
Hours required for M	=	500 × 4	=	2000
				2600
Hours required for L	=	800 × 3	=	2400
				5000

The existing capacity is not sufficient to produce the units to meet the external sales. In order to transfer 300 units of M, 1200 hours are required in which division K will give up the production of L to this extent:

Variable Cost of M	₹ 24
(+) Contribution lost by giving up the production of L to the extent of 1200 hours = 1200 × ₹ 5 = 6000	
Opportunity Cost per unit (₹ 6000 ÷ 300 units)	₹ 20
Required Transfer Price	₹ 44

Computation of Transfer Price when the capacity is 5600 hours:

Variable Cost of M	₹ 24
(+) Contribution lost by giving up the production of L to the extent of 600 hours = 600 × ₹ 5 = 3000	
Opportunity Cost per unit (₹ 3000 ÷ 300 units)	₹ 10
Required Transfer Price	₹ 34

Illustrative Problem 12

Novelty Ltd. has two divisions – division DA and division DB. Division DA is currently operating at full capacity. It has been asked to supply its product to division DB. Division DA sells its product to its regular customers for ₹ 60 each. Division DB, currently operating at 50 percent capacity, is willing to pay ₹ 40 each for the component produced by Division DA (this represents the full absorption cost per component at division DA). The components will be used by division DB in supplementing its main product to conform to the need of special order. As per the contract terms of sale, the buyer calls for reimbursement of full cost to division DB, plus 10 percent.

Division DA has a variable cost of ₹ 34 per component. The cost per unit of division DB : subsequent to buying part from division DA is estimated as follows:

	₹
Purchased parts – outside vendors	180
Purchased component from division DA	40
Other variable costs	100
Fixed overheads including administration	80
	400

The company uses return on investment (ROI) in the measurement of division and Division managers' performance.

Required:

(*i*) As Manager of division DA would you recommend sales of your product to division DB at the stipulated price of ₹ 40?

(*ii*) Would it be in the overall interest of the company for Division DA to sell its product to Division DB.

(*iii*) Suggest an alternative transfer price and show how could it lead to goal congruence.

Solution:

Novelty Ltd.

(*i*) As Manager of Division DA. I would not recommend Sales at ₹ 40 per unit to Division – DB. Division – DA is already operating at its full capacity and the market is presumably absorbing all its products (output) at ₹ 60 per unit. The internal transfer made to Division DB, hence, would reduce its profit (by ₹ 60 – ₹ 40 = ₹ 20 per unit) as well as the Return on Investment (ROI).

(*ii*) Decision Analysis:

– Whether to transfer component from DA to DB at ₹ 40 per unit or not.

(*Figures in Rupees*)

Particulars	**Sold Externally**	**Transferred to Division DB**
Sale price (Division – DA)	60.00	
Sales price (Division – DB) (₹ 400 + 10%)		440.00
Less: Relevant / Incremental cost.		
For component of Division DA	34.00	34.00
Purchased parts from outside	—	180.00
Other variable cost	—	100.00
Profit per unit	26.00	126.00

Decision:

Yes, it will be in the overall interest of the Company that the transfer takes place, as it would augment the company's profit by ₹ 100 per unit.

(*iii*) Dual price basis of effecting transfer is the most appropriate. This will enhance co-operation between divisions, prevent sub-optimization by Managers, encourage the transferring Division to maximize income and provide the purchasing Division with cost information.

In this case, the relevant transfer price will be ₹ 60 (sale) so far as Division – DA is concerned and ₹ 40 (purchase) so far as Division DB is concerned. It will keep the profits of both the divisions unaffected and will facilitate the utilization of the idle capacity of Division – DB and it will also increase its profit.

	₹
Sale price (₹ 420 + 10 percent)	462.00
Less: costs (₹ 180 + ₹ 60 + ₹ 100)	340.00
	122.00

Illustrative Problem 13

A company has two divisions, Division 'A and Division 'B'. Division 'A' has a budget of selling 2,00,000 nos. of a particular component 'X' to fetch a return of 20% on the average assets employed.

The following particulars of Division 'A' are also known:

Fixed Overhead	:	₹ 5 lakhs
Variable Cost	:	Re. 1 per unit
Average Assets:		
Sundry Debtors	:	₹ 2 lakhs
Inventories	:	₹ 5 lakhs
Plant & Equipments	:	₹ 5 lakhs

However, there are certain constraints in marketing and only 1,50,000 units of the component 'X' can be directly sold to the market at the proposed price. It has been gathered that the balance 50,000 units of component 'X' can be taken up by Division 'B'. Division 'A' wants a price of ₹ 4 per unit of 'X' but Division 'B' is prepared to pay ₹ 2 per unit of 'X'.

Division 'A' has another option on hand, which is to produce only 1,50,000 units of component 'X'. This will reduce the holding of assets by ₹ 2 lakhs and fixed overhead by ₹ 25,000.

You are required to advise the most profitable course of action for Division 'A'.

Solution:

(*i*) Profit = 20% on average assets employed

= 20% × ₹ 2.00 lakhs + ₹ 5.00 lakhs + ₹ 5.00 lakhs) = ₹ 2,40,000

(*ii*) Desired revenue (on sale of 2,00,000 units of component of 'X')

= Fixed Cost + Variable Cost + Profit

= ₹ 5,00,000 + (Re. 1 × 2,00,000) + ₹ 2,40,000

= ₹ 9,40,000

(*iii*) Selling price per unit

Sales ÷ No. of Components

9,40,000 ÷ 2,00,000 = ₹ 4.70 per unit

Statement Showing the Most Profitable Course of Action for Division 'A'

Details	Option-1 Sell 1,50,000 units in market and transfer 50,000 units to Division 'B'	Option-2 Sell only 1,50,000 units in market
Sales Revenue of 1,50,000 units of Product 'X' sold @ ₹ 4.70 per unit (Working Note 3)	₹ 7,05,000	₹ 7,05,000
50,000 units of 'X' transferred to Division 'B' @ ₹ 2 per unit	₹ 1,00,000	—
Total revenue (A)	₹ 8,05,000	₹ 7,05,000
Cost Incurred:		
Fixed Costs (₹)	₹ 5,00,000	₹ 4,75,000
Variable Cost @ Re. 1/unit	₹ 2,00,000	₹ 1,50,000
Total Costs (₹)	₹ 7,00,000	₹ 6,25,000
Profit (C)	₹ 1,05,000	₹ 80,000
Capital employed (D)	₹ 12,00,000	₹ 10,00,000*
Return on capital employed (C)/(D) × 1 00	8.75%	8.00%

* Holding of assets gets reduced by ₹ 2,00,000 *i.e.*, capital employed gets reduced

Advise: Option 1 is better of the two options. It gives a better return on capital employed Recourse to option 1 will yield extra profit of ₹ **25,000** (*i.e.* ₹ 1 ,05,000 – ₹ 80,000)

Illustrative Problem 14

Escorts Co, manufacturer of tractors and other heavy farm equipment, is organised along decentralised lines, with each manufacturing division operating as a separate profit centre. Each division head has been delegated full authority on all decisions involving the sale of the division's output, both to outsiders and to other divisions of Escorts Co. Division C has in the past always purchased its requirement of a particular tractor-engine component from division A. However, when informed that division A was increasing its price to ₹ 15,000, division C's management decided to purchase the engine component from outside suppliers.

The component can be purchased by C for ₹ 13,500 on the open market. Division A insists that, owing to the recent installation of some highly specialised equipment and the resulting high depreciation charges, it would not be able to make an adequate profit on its investment unless it raised its price. A's management appealed to the top management of Escorts Co. for support in its dispute with C and supplied the following operating data:

C's annual purchase of tractor-engine component (units)	1,000
A's variable costs per unit of tractor-engine component	₹ 12,000
A's fixed costs per unit of tractor-engine component	2,000

Required:

(*a*) Assume that there are no alternative uses for internal facilities. Determine whether the company as a whole will benefit if C purchases the component from outside suppliers for ₹ 13,500 per unit.

(*b*) Assume that internal facilities of A would not otherwise be idle. By not producing the 1,000 units for C, A's equipment and other facilities would be assigned to other production operations, and would result in annual cash operating savings of ₹ 18,00,000. Should C purchase from outsiders?

(*c*) Assume that there are no alternative uses for A's internal facilities, and that the price of outsiders drops by ₹ 2,000. Should C purchase from outsiders?

(*d*) Assume that A could sell the 1,000 units to other customers at ₹ 15,500 per unit with variable selling costs of ₹ 500 per unit. Should C purchase the 1,000 components from outsiders at ₹ 13,500 per unit?

Solution:

(*a*) The company as a whole will not benefit if division C buys on the outside:

	₹
Purchase costs from outsider, 1,000 units @ ₹ 13,500	1,35,00,000
Less: Savings in variable costs by reducing division A output, 1,000 units @ ₹ 12,000	1,20,00,000
Disadvantage to the company as a whole	15,00,000

(*b*) The company will benefit if C purchases from the outsider:

	₹
Purchase costs from outsider, 1,000 units @ ₹ 13,500	1,35,00,000
Less: Savings in variable and fixed costs, 1,000 units @ ₹ 13,800 $\left[₹\,12{,}000 + ₹\,1{,}800\left(\dfrac{₹\,18{,}00{,}000}{1{,}000 \text{ units}}\right)\right]$	1,38,00,000
Advantage to the company as a whole	3,00,000

(*c*) The company will benefit it C purchases from the outside supplier:

	₹
Purchase costs from outsider, 1,000 units @ ₹ 11,500	1,15,00,000
Less: Savings in variable costs by reducing division A output, 1,000 units @ ₹ 12,000	1,20,00,000
Advantage to the company as a whole	5,00,000

(*d*) The company as whole would benefit in this situation if C purchased from outsiders, since the ₹ 15,00,000 disadvantage to the company as a whole by purchasing from the outside supplier would be more than covered by the ₹ 30,00,000 contribution margin of A's sale of the 1,000 units to other customers.

	₹
Purchase costs from outsider, 1,000 units @ ₹ 13,500	1,35,00,000
Less: Variable cost savings, 1,000 units @ 12,000	1,20,00,000
Disadvantage to the company as a whole	15,00,000
A's sales to other customers, 1,000 units @ ₹ 15,500	1,55,00,000
Less: Variable costs, 1,000 units @ ₹ 12,500	1,25,00,000
Contribution margin	30,00,000

Illustrative Problem 15

Videodays company manufactures stereo-receivers, televisions and VCR in its four divisions—Receiver, TV, VCR and Components. The components division produces electronic Components that can be used by the other three divisions. All the components this division produces can be sold to outside customers. However, from the beginning, about 70 percent of its output has been used internally. The current policy requires that all internal transfers of components be transferred at full cost.

Recently, Deepak Kumar, the new chief executive officer of Videodays, decided to investigate the transfer pricing policy. He was concerned that the current method of pricing internal transfers might force decisions by divisional managers that would be suboptimal for the firm. As part of his enquiry, he gathered some information concerning Component 12F, used by the Receiver Division in its production of a product, Model 357 K.

The Receiver Division sells 1,00,000 units of Model 357 K each year at a unit price of ₹ 21. Given current market situations, this is the maximum price that the Division can charge for Model 357K. The cost of manufacturing the product, Model 357K follows:

	₹
Component 12F	6.50
Direct materials	5.50
Direct labour	4.00
Variable overhead	1.00
Fixed overhead	2.00
Total unit cost	19.00

The Model 357 K is produced efficiently and no further reduction in manufacturing costs is possible.

The Manager of Components Division indicated that he could sell 1,00,000 units (the division's capacity for this part) of Component 12F to outside buyers at ₹ 12 per unit. The Receiver Division could also buy the part for ₹ 12 from external suppliers. He supplied the following details on the manufacturing cost of the component:

	₹
Direct materials	2.50
Direct labour	0.50
Variable overhead	1.50
Fixed overhead	2.00
Total unit cost	6.50

Required:

1. Compute the contribution margin earned by each division and the firmwide contribution margin associated with Component 12 F and Model 357 K.
2. Suppose that Deepak Kumar abolishes the current transfer pricing policy and gives divisional autonomy in setting transfer prices. Can you predict what transfer price the manager of components Division Manager will set? What should be the minimum and maximum transfer price for this part?
3. Given the new transfer price, predict how this will affect the production decision for Model 357 K of the Receiver Division Manager. How many units of component 12F will the manager of the Receiver Division purchase, either internally or externally.

4. Given the new transfer price set by the components Division and your answer to Requirement 3, how many units of 12F will be sold externally?
5. Given your answers to Requirements 3 and 4, compute the firmwide contribution margin. Was Deepak Kumar's decision to grant additional autonomy good or bad?

(*M.Com., Delhi* 2001)

Solution:

1.		*Component 12F*	*Model 357K*	*Company*
		₹	₹	₹
	Sales (1,00,000 units)	6,50,000	21,00,000	27,50,000
Less:	Variable expenses	4,50,000	17,00,000	21,50,000
	Contribution margin	2,00,000	4,00,000	6,00,000

Component 12F variable expenses =

Direct Material	₹ 2.50
Direct labour	.50
Variable overhead	1.50
	4.50

Model 357 K variable expenses =

Component 12 F	₹ 6.50
Direct material	5.50
Direct labour	4.00
Variable overhead	1.00
	17.00

2. The transfer price should be the market price of ₹ 12. This is the minimum price for the component Division (Selling Division) and the maximum price for the Receiver Division; (Buying Division).

Or

The manager of components division will set his transfer price as follows:

Transfer price = Marginal costs + F. costs + Profit foregone as not sold to outsiders

= (2.50 + 0.50 + 1.50 + 2.0) + (12 – 6.50)

= 6.50 + 5.50

= ₹ 12.

3. At a transfer price of ₹ 12 the cost of producing the radio will increase from ₹ 19 to ₹ 24.50 which is greater than the current selling price.

Unless the Receiver Division is able to increase the price of model 357K, the manager of the Receiver Division will discontinue production and will not purchase any unit of component 12 F.

4. All 1,00,000 units of 12F will be sold externally at the market price of ₹ 12 per unit.

5. Firmwide Contribution Margin

	₹
Sales	12,00,000
Variable expenses	4,50,000
Contribution margin	7,50,000

The contribution to profits increases by ₹ 1,50,000 (from ₹ 6,00,000 to ₹ 7,50,000). The CEO made the correct decision.

Illustrative Problem 16

ABC Company has a decentralized organization with a divisional structure. Each divisional manager is evaluated on the basis of ROI.

The Plastics Division produces a plastic container that the Chemical Division can use. Plastics can produce up to 1,00,000 of these containers per year. The variable costs of manufacturing the plastic containers are ₹ 450. The Chemical Division labels the plastic containers and uses them to store an important industrial chemical, which is sold to outside customers for ₹ 5,000 per container. The division's capacity is 20,000 units. The variable costs of processing the chemical (in addition to the cost of the container itself) are ₹ 2,600.

Required:

Assume each requirement is independent, unless otherwise indicated.

(*i*) Assume that all of the plastic containers produced can be sold to external customers for ₹ 1,200 each. The Chemical Division wants to buy 20,000 containers per year. What should the transfer price be?

(*ii*) Refer to Requirement 1. Assume ₹ 200 of avoidable distribution costs. Identify the maximum and minimum transfer prices. Identify the actual transfer price, assuming that negotiation splits the difference.

(*iii*) Assume that the Plastics Division is operating at 75 percent of capacity. The Chemical Division is currently buying 20,000 containers from an outside supplier for ₹ 950 each. Assume that any joint benefit will be split evenly between the two divisions. What is the expected transfer price? How much will the profits of the firm increase under this arrangement? How much will the profits of the Plastics Division increase, assuming that it sells the extra 20,000 containers internally?

(*iv*) Assume that both divisions have excess capacity. Currently 15,000 containers are being transferred between divisions at a price of ₹ 800. The Chemical Division has an opportunity to take a special order for 5,000 containers of chemical at a price of ₹ 3,375 per container. The manager of the Chemical Division approached the manager of the Plastics Division and offered to buy an additional 5,000 plastic containers for ₹ 500 each. Assuming that the Plastics Division has excess capacity totaling at least 5,000 units, should the manager take the offer? What is the minimum transfer price? The maximuim? Assume that the Plastics Division manager counters with a price of ₹ 550. Would the Chemical Division manager be interested?

Solution:

(*i*) ₹ 1,200

		₹
(*ii*)	Minimum transfer price	1,000
	Maximum Transfer Price	1,200
	Actual transfer price	1,100
(*iii*)	₹ 950 + ₹ 450	1,400/2
		700
Plastic Division		
	Additional Revenue (₹ 700 × 20,000) =	1,40,00,000
	Additional expenses (₹ 450 × 20,000) =	90,00,000
	Addition to profit	50,00,000
Chemical Division		
	Reduction of costs (₹ 950 – 700) × 20,000	50,00,000
	Total addition to firm profit	1,00,00,000
(*iv*)	Minimum Price	₹ 450
	Maximum Price	₹ 775 (₹ 3,375 – 2,600)

Although the offered price ₹ 500 would bring a contribution margin of ₹ 50, the joint benefit is ₹, 325 (775–450) per unit. The ₹ 50 contribution is not a fair share and so further negotiation might improve the outcome. Certainly, the manager of Chemical Division should be interested in the ₹ 550 price. The Division would capture more than half the joint benefit.

Illustrative Problem 17

The Industrial Machine Division has requested a specially designed subassembly from the Metal Fabricating Division. Because the subassembly is specially designed, there is no outside market price that can serve as a reference point for establishing an internal transfer price. The estimated cost of manufacturing the subassembly follows:

	₹
Direct material	100
Direct labour	25
Variable overhead	50
Fixed overhead*	30
Total unit cost	205

*Representing an allocation of existing fixed overhead. The total fixed overhead is the same regardless of whether the Metal Fabricating Division produces the subassembly.

The Industrial Machine Division will use 10,000 of the subassemblies per year.

Required:

(*i*) Assume that producing the special subassembly displaces other potential jobs. How should the manager of the Metal Fabricating Division set the transfer price for the custom-made subassembly?

(*ii*) Assume that two potential jobs will be displaced by the special subassembly. The expected revenue and costs of these jobs are as follows:

	Job 1	Job 2
	₹	₹
Revenues	26,00,000	15,00,000
Variable manufacturing	19,50,000	10,50,000
Fixed overhead	2,00,000	3,00,000

Compute the minimum price the Metal Fabricating Division should charge.

(*iii*) Now assume that the Metal Fabricating Division can produce the special sub-assembly without displacing any work for outside customers. What is the minimum transfer price that should be charged for the subassembly?

(*iv*) Refer to Requirement (*iii*). The manager of the Metal Fabricating Division has offered to supply the subassembly for full cost plus the division's average mark up. Assuming that the average markup is 35 percent, compute the offered transfer price. What do you think of the pricing scheme suggested by the manager of the selling division?

(*v*) Refer to Requirement (*iv*). The manager of the Industrial Machine Division refuses to pay the average markup. He indicates that an outside supplier has offered to produce the subassembly for ₹ 200 per unit. He offers to pay variable costs plus a lump sum of ₹ 1,25,000 to help cover fixed costs and provide some profit. Do you think the manager of the Metal Fabricating Division should accept this last offer? Would he be tempted to do so? Explain.

(*M. Com., Delhi,* 2003, 2010)

Solution:

(*i*) The Metal Fabricating Division should set a price equal to variable cost plus the contribution margin lost from displaced jobs.

(*ii*) **Calculation of contribution Margin lost**

		Job 1	Job 2
	Revenues	₹ 26,00,000	₹ 15,00,000
Less:	variable manufacturing	19,50,000	10,50,000
	Contribution	6,50,000	4,50,000

Total contribution margin lost = 6,50,000 + 4,50,000

= ₹ 11,00,000

$$\text{Contribution margin per unit lost} = \frac{11,00,000}{10,000}$$

= ₹ 110

Minimum transfer price to be set

Contribution margin lost = 110

Variable manufacturing cost = 175

= 285

(*iii*) Variable cost = ₹ 175

(*iv*) Full cost = ₹ 205

Add 35% = 71.75

Total 276.75

This approach is reasonable provided that there is no displacement of outside jobs. If outside jobs are displaced, then the approach taken in requirement no. (*ii*) is better.

(*v*) Suggested Transfer Price:

	₹
Direct Materials	100
Direct labour	25
Variable overhead	50
Lumpsum, per unit (1,25,000/10,000)	12.50
	187.50

The buying Division has offered to pay ₹ 187.50 per unit. This would add to profits because this price is above variable costs. However, this price is well below the normal mark up price and should be accepted only if there is excess capacity and no better use for the resources is available.

Illustrative Problem 18

Hero Cycles has two divisions, A and B, which manufacture expensive bicycles. Division A produces the bicycle frame and Division B assembles the rest of the bicycle onto the frame. There is market for both the subassembly and the final product. Each division has been designated as a profit centre. The transfer price for the subassembly has been set at the long run average market price. The following data are available for each division.

Selling price for final product	₹ 3,000
Long run average selling price for intermediate product	₹ 2000
Incremental costs for completion in division B	₹ 1,500
Incremental costs in division A	₹ 1,200

The manager of division B has made the following calculation:

Selling price for final product	₹ 3,000
Transferred-in-costs	(2,000)
Incremental costs for completion	(1,500)
Contribution (loss) on product	(500)

Required:

(*i*) Should transfer be made to division B if there is no unused capacity in division A. Is the market price the correct transfer price? Show your computations.

(*ii*) Assume that division A's maximum capacity for this product is 1000 units per month, and sales to the intermediate market are now 800 units. Should 200 units be transferred to division B? At what transfer price? Assume that for a variety of reasons, division A will maintain ₹ 2000 selling price indefinitely. That is, division A is not considering lowering the price to outsiders even if idle capacity exists.

(*iii*) Suppose division A quoted a transfer price of ₹ 1500 for upto 200 units. What would be the contribution to the company as a whole if a transfer were made. As manager of division B, would you be inclined to buy at ₹ 1,500. Explain.

(*M. Com., Delhi University,* 2011)

Solution:

(*i*) No, transfers should not be made to Division B if there is no excess capacity in Division A.

An incremental (outlay) cost approach shows a positive contribution for the company as a whole.

Selling price of final product		₹ 3,000
Incremental costs in Division A	₹ 1,200	
Incremental costs in Division B	1,500	2,700
Contribution		₹ 300

However, if there is no excess capacity in Division A, any transfer will result in diverting products from the market for the intermediate product. Sales in this market results in a greater contribution for the company as a whole. Division B should not assemble the bicycle since the incremental revenue Hero Cycles can earn, ₹ 1,000 per unit (₹ 3,000 from selling the final product—₹ 2,000 from selling the intermediate product) is less than the incremental costs of ₹ 1,500 to assemble the bicycle in Division B. Alternatively put, Hero Cycles's contribution margin from selling the intermediate product exceeds Hero Cycle's contribution margin from selling the final product.

Selling price of intermediate product	₹ 2,000
Incremental (outlay) costs in Division A	1,200
Contribution	₹ 800

Minimum transfer price

$$= \left(\begin{array}{c}\text{Additional incremental costs per unit}\\ \text{incurred up to the point of transfer}\end{array}\right) + \left(\begin{array}{c}\text{Opportunity costs per unit to the}\\ \text{supplying division}\end{array}\right)$$

= ₹ 1,200 + (₹ 2,000 – ₹ 1,200)

= ₹ 2,000, which is the market price

The market price is the transfer price that leads to the correct decision, that is, do not transfer to Division B unless there are compelling circumstances for continuing to market the final product. Therefore, B must either drop the product or reduce the incremental costs of assembly from ₹ 1,500 per bicycle to less than ₹ 1,000.

(*ii*) If (*a*) A has excess capacity, (*b*) there is intermediate external demand for only 800 units at ₹ 2,000, and (*c*) the ₹ 2,000 price is to be maintained, then the opportunity costs per unit to the supplying division are ₹ 0. The general guideline indicates a minimum transfer price of: ₹ 1,200 + ₹ 0 = ₹ 1,200, which is the incremental or outlay costs for the first 200 units. B would buy 200 units from A at a transfer price of ₹ 1,200 because B can earn a contribution of ₹ 300 per unit [₹ 3,000 – (₹ 1,200 + ₹ ₹ 1,500)]. In fact, B would be willing to buy units from A at any price up to ₹ 1,500 per unit because any transfers at a price of up to ₹ 1,500 will still yield B a positive contribution margin.

Note, however, that if B wants more than 200 units, the minimum transfer price will be ₹ 2,000 as computed in requirement (*i*) because A will incur an opportunity cost in the form of lost contribution of ₹ 800 (market price, ₹ 2,000 – outlay costs of ₹ 1,200) for every unit above 200 units that are transferred to B.

The following schedule summarizes the transfer prices for units transferred from A to B:

Units	***Transfer Price***
0 – 200	₹ 1,200 – ₹ 1500
200 – 1,000	₹ 2,000

(*iii*) Division B would show zero contribution, but the company as a whole generate a contribution of ₹ 300 per unit on the 200 units transferred. Any price between ₹ 1,200 and ₹ 1,500 would induce the transfer that would be desirable for the company as a whole. A motivational problem may arise regarding how to split the ₹ 300 contribution between Division A and B. Unless the price is below ₹ 1,500, B would have little incentive to buy.

Note: The transfer price that may appear optimal in an economic analysis may, in fact, be totally unacceptable from the viewpoints of (1) preserving autonomy of the managers, and (2) evaluating the performance of the divisions as economic units. For instance, to take an example, assume there is idle capacity and the ₹ 2,000 intermediate price is to be maintained. To direct that A should sell to B at A's available cost of ₹ 1,200 may be desirable from the viewpoint of B and the company as a whole. However, the autonomy (independence) of the manager of A is eroded. Division A will earn nothing, although it could argue that it is contributing to the earning of income on the final product.

If the manager of A wants a portion of the total company contribution of ₹ 300 per unit, the question is: How is an appropriate amount determined? This is a difficult question in practice. The price can be negotiated upward to somewhere between ₹ 1,200 and ₹ 1,500 so that some "equitable" split is achieved. A dual transfer-pricing scheme has also been suggested, whereby the supplier gets credit for the full intermediate market price and the buyer is charged with only variable or incremental costs. In any event, when there is heavy interdependence between divisions, such as in this case, some system of subsidies may be needed to deal with the three problems of goal congruence, management effort, and subunit autonomy. Of course, where heavy subsidies are needed, a question can be raised as to whether the existing degree of decentralization is optimal.

Illustrative Problem 19

TCS Company produces computers and computer components. The company is organized into several divisions that operate essentially as autonomous companies. The firm permits division managers to make investment and production-level decisions. The division managers can also decide whether to sell to other divisions or to outside customers.

Networks Division produces a critical component for computers manufactured by Computers Division. It has been selling this component to Computers for ₹ 20,000 per unit. Networks recently purchased new equipment for producing the component. To offset its higher depreciation charges, Networks increased its price to ₹ 22,000 per unit. The manager of Networks has asked the president to instruct Computers to purchase the component for the ₹ 22,000 price rather than to permit Computers to purchase externally for ₹ 20,000 per unit. The following information is obtained from the company's records: Computers annual purchases of the component, 400 units; Networks' variable costs per unit, ₹ 14,000. Networks' fixed costs per unit, ₹ 4,000.

Required:

(*a*) Assume that the firm has no alternative uses for Networks' idle capacity. Will the company as a whole benefit if Computers purchases the component externally for ₹ 20,000? Explain.

(*b*) Assume that the firm can use the idle capacity of Networks for other purposes, resulting in cash operating savings of ₹ 15,00,000. Will the company as a whole benefit if Computers purchases the component externally for ₹ 20000? Explain.

(*c*) Assume the same facts as in part (*b*), except that the outside market price drops to ₹ 18,000 per unit. Will the company as a whole benefit if Computers purchases the component externally for ₹ 18,000? Explain.

(*d*) As president, how would you respond to the manager of Networks? Discuss each scenario described in parts (*a*), (*b*), and (*c*). (*M. Com, Delhi,* 2013)

Solution:

(*a*) Incremental Cash Outflow of the Computers Divisions	
(₹ 20,000 × 400 Units)	₹ 80,00,000
Incremental Cash Savings of the Networks Division	
(₹ 14,000 × 400 Units)	(56,00,000)
Net Incremental Cash Outflow	₹ 24,00,000

The company will be worse off by ₹ 24,00,000 if the Computers Division purchases the component externally.

(*b*) Net Incremental Cash Outflow from Part (*a*)	₹ 24,00,000
Incremental Cash savings of the Networks Division	(15,00,000)
Net Incremental Cash Outflow	₹ 9,00,000

The company will be worse off by ₹ 9,00,000 if the Computers Division purchases the component externally.

(*c*) Incremental Cash Outflow of the Computers Division	
(₹ 18,000 × 400 Units)	₹ 72,00,000
Incremental Cash Savings of the Networks Division:	
Variable Costs (₹ 14,000 × 400)	(56,00,000)
Operating Savings	(15,00,000)
Net Incremenatal Cash Outflow	₹ 10,0000

The company will be worse off by ₹ 1,00,000 if the Computers Division purchases the component externally.

(*d*) Before responding, the president should raise three questions. First, which of the three conditions in Parts (*a*), to (*c*) is most likely to occur? The president should only consider interceding (on behalf of Computers Division) if the Computers Division's action will be detrimental to the company. Second, will the conditions expected to occur be short-lived or continually recurring? The president may permit the Computers Division to purchase the component externally if it is anticipated that the outside market price will soon increase to ₹ 22,000 or higher. In this way, divisional decision making autonomy is maintained. If the president intercedes, division managers may react negatively and harm the decentralized organization structure. The third, and perhaps most critical, question then is the effect of intercession (pleading on behalf of another) on divisional performance.

Illustrative Problem 20

Zesleen Ltd. has two manufacturing divisions. Each division operates as an independent profit centre. Division A is the only source of a component that is used in Division B in manufacturing of a final product, EUREKA. For each unit of EUREKA, one component manufactured by Division A is used. Demand for EUREKA is not steady. Division B can increase sale of Eureka by spending more on sales promotion and / or by reducing selling price. The Manager of Division B has prepared the following forecast:

Sales in units per day	1000	2000	3000	4000	5000	6000
Average selling price per unit of EUREKA (₹)	52.50	39.80	33.00	27.80	24.00	20.10

The manufacturing cost of EUREKA in Division B is ₹ 37,500 on first 1000 units and additional ₹ 7.50 per unit for every additional 1000 components manufactured.

Division A incurs a total cost of ₹ 15,000 per day for an output to 1000 components and the total costs will increase by ₹ 9,000 per day for every additional 1000 components manufactured.

Manager of Division A states that operating results of his Division will be optimized if the transfer price is set at ₹ 12 per component and accordingly he has set the above transfer price,

Required:

(*a*) Prepare a profitability statement at each level of Division A and Division B.

(*b*) Work out the profitability of company as a whole at the output level,

(*i*) When the net profit of Division A is maximum.

(*ii*) When the net profit of division B is maximum.

Solution:

(*a*) Statement Showing Profitability of Division —A (Under different Levels)

Sale per day (units)	*Rate ₹*	*Total Value ₹*	*Total Cost*	*Profit/(Loss) ₹*
1000	12.00	12000	15000	(3000)
2000	12.00	24000	24000	–
3000	12.00	36000	33000	3000
4000	12.00	48000	42000	6000
5000	12.00	60000	51000	9000
6000	12.00	72000	60000	12000

Statement Showing Profitability of Division —B (Under different Levels)

No of Units	*Selling Price*	*Sale Value*	*Transfer Price ₹*	*Other Mfg Cost ₹*	*Total Cost ₹*	*Profit/Loss ₹*
1000	52.50	52500	12000	37500	49500	3000
2000	39.80	79600	24000	45000	69000	10600
3000	33.00	99000	36000	52500	88500	10500
4000	27.80	111200	48000	60000	108000	3200
5000	24.00	120000	60000	67500	127500	(7500)
6000	20.10	120600	72000	75000	147000	(26400)

(*b*) (*i*) Profitability of the Company at the output Level where Division A's Net Profit is maximum:

	₹
Profit of Division A at 6000 Units	12,000
Profit of Division B at 6000 Units	(26,400)
Profit/Loss	(14,400)

(*ii*) Profitability of the company at the output level where division B's Net Profit is maximum:

	₹
Profit of Division B at 2000 Units	10,600
Profit of Division A at 2000 Units	—
Profit/(Loss)	10,600

(*iii*) When the Company is not Organized on Profit Centre Basis:

Profit At Different Levels of Output

Units	*Division-A* ₹	*Division-B* ₹	*Total Profit / (Loss)* ₹
1000	(3000)	3000	Nil
2000	—	10600	10600
3000	3000	10500	13500
4000	6000	3200	9200
5000	9000	(7500)	1500
6000	12000	(26400)	(14400)

Best Output Level for maximization of profit is 3000 units.

Illustrative Problem 21

Assam Lumber has a Raw Lumber Division and a Finished Lumber Division. The variable costs are

- Raw Lumber Division: ₹ 1,000 per 100 board-feet of raw lumber
- Finished Lumber Division ₹ 1,250 per 100 board-feet of finished lumber

Assume that there is no board-feet loss in processing raw lumber into finished lumber. Raw lumber can be sold at ₹ 2,000 per 100 board-feet. Finished lumber can be sold at ₹ 2,750 per 100 board-feet.

Required:

1. Should Assam Lumber process raw lumber into its finished form? Show your computations.
2. Assume that internal transfers are made at 110% of variable costs. Will each division maximize its division operating income contribution by adopting the action that is in the best interest of Assam Lumber? Explain.
3. Assume that internal transfers are made at market prices. Will each division maximize its division operating income contribution by adopting the action that is in the best interest of Assam Lumber? Explain.

Solution:

1. **Alternative 1:** Sell as raw lumber for ₹ 2,000 per 100 board feet:

Revenue	₹ 2,000	
Variable costs	1,000	
Contribution margin	₹ 1,000	per 100 board feet

Alternative 2: Sell as finished lumber for ₹ 2,750 per 100 board feet:

Revenue		₹ 2,750	
Variable costs:			
Raw lumber	₹ 1,000		
Finished lumber	1,250	2,250	
Contribution margin		₹ 500	per 100 board feet

Assam Lumber will maximize its total contribution margin by selling lumber in its raw form.

An alternative approach is to evaluate the incremental revenues and incremental costs in the Finished Lumber Division:

Incremental revenues, ₹ 2,750 – ₹ 2,000	₹ 750	
Incremental costs	1,250	
Incremental loss	₹ (500)	per 100 board feet

2. Transfer price at 110% of variable costs:

= ₹ 1,000 + (₹ 1,000 × 0.10)

= ₹ 1,100 per 100 board feet

	Sell as Raw Lumber	***Sell as Finished Lumber***
Raw Lumber Division		
Division revenues	₹ 2,000	₹ 1,100
Division variable costs	1,000	1,000
Division operating income	₹ 1,000	₹ 100
Finished Lumber Division		
Division revenues	₹ 0	₹ 2,750
Transferred-in costs	—	1,100
Division variable costs	—	1,250
Division operating income	₹ 0	₹ 400

The Raw Lumber Division will maximize reported division operating by selling raw lumber, which is the action preferred by the company as a whole. The Finished Lumber Division will maximize division operating income by selling finished lumber, which is contrary to the action preferred by the company as a whole.

3. Transfer price at market price = ₹ 2,000 per 100 board feet.

	Sell as Raw Lumber	***Sell as Finished Lumber***
Raw Lumber Division		
Division revenues	₹ 2,000	₹ 2,000
Division variable costs	1,000	1,000
Division operating income	₹ 1,000	₹ 1,000
Finished Lumber Division		
Division revenues	₹ 0	₹ 2,750
Transferred-in-costs	—	2,000
Division variable costs	—	1,250
Division operating income	₹ 0	₹ (500)

The Raw Lumber Division will maximize division operating income by selling raw lumber, which is the action preferred by the company as a whole. Finished Lumber Division will maximize division operating income by not further processing raw lumber, not further processing is preferred by the company as a whole.

Illustrative Problem 22

A management consultancy firm has two divisions – consultancy and data Processing. The two divisions provide services to each other, as per exigencies, apart from carrying out jobs independently.

During the month of November 2016, the consultancy division handled only one assignment for a total fee of ₹ 5,50,000. The cost incurred in consultancy division was ₹ 3,75,000 for the month. Further, the work involved 200 hours of data processing work. Although the consultancy division had the option of getting the data processing job done from outside, it decided to get the same done from the firm's data processing division, as they had spare hours in that month.

The budgeted cost of data processing division for 12 months ending 31.03.2016 were as under:

	₹
Variable costs:	
Skilled operator (6,000 hrs work)	12,00,000
Semi-skilled operator	7,20,000
Other costs	6,00,000
Fixed costs	24,00,000

The costs are incurred uniformly over the 12 months.

These entire costs are recovered on the basis of chargeable skilled operator hours, which for this purpose are taken as 90% of the hours worked. For taking up external assignments, the pricing policy of the data processing division is to add 40% of budgeted cost per chargeable hour as mark up.

During November 2016 actual operator cost, both skilled and semi-skilled, increased by 10% but the other costs decreased by 10%.

Calculate for the month of November 2016 —

(*a*) Transfer price to be charged by data processing division for 200 hrs of work to consultancy division on the basis of

(*i*) actual variable cost based on chargeable hours

(*ii*) standard variable cost plus 40% mark up.

(*iii*) market price based on total cost.

(*b*) The operating result for data processing division and the consultancy division separately on the basis of the three pricing policies as mentioned in (*a*) above.

Solution:

(*a*) Data processing division: Variable Cost

	Budget For the year ₹	***Budget*** For November 2016	***Increase (+) / Decrease (–)*** ₹	***Actual*** ₹
Skilled operator	12,00,000	1,00,000	(+) 10%	1,10,000
Semi-skilled opr.	7,20,000	60,000	(+) 10%	66,000
Other costs	6,00,000	50,000	(–) 10%	45,000
	25,20,000	2,10,000		2,21,000

Transfer price to be charged:

(*i*) Chargeable hours = (90% of 6,000 hrs.)/12 = 450 effective hours per month. For 200 hours of work. TP = (₹ 2,21,000/450) × 200 = ₹ 98,200.

(*ii*) Standard variable cost per hour = (₹ 2,10,000/450) = ₹ 467.

Total fee for 200 hours @ ₹ 467 = ₹ 93,400

₹ 93,400 + 40% of 93,400 = ₹ 1,30,760.

(*iii*) Market price based on total cost:

	₹/hour
Budgeted variable cost	467
Budgeted fixed cost, ₹ 2,00,000/450	444
	911
Add 40% mark-up	364
	₹ 1,275

For 200 hours = ₹ 1,275 × 200 hrs. = ₹ 2,55,000

(*b*) Operating result for November 2016 : on the basis of transfer price

	(*i*) ₹	**(*ii*)** ₹	**(*iii*)** ₹
Data processing Division:			
Sales – External 250 hrs × 1,275/-	3,18,750	3,18,750	3,18,750
Internal	98,200	1,30,760	2,55,000
	4,16,950	4,49,510	5,73,750
Variable cost	2,21,000	2,21,000	2,21,000
	1,95,950	2,28,510	3,52,750
Fixed cost	2,00,000	2,00,000	2,00,000
Profit/(Loss)	(4,050)	28,510	1,52,750
Consultancy Division:			
Fee	5,50,000	5,50,000	5,50,000
Direct cost of Division	3,75,000	3,75,000	3,75,000
Transfer price of DP Division	98,200	1,30,760	2,55,000
Total cost	4,73,200	5,45,760	6,30,000
Profit/(loss)	76,800	44,240	(80,000)

Illustrative Problem 23

Magatron Ltd. is having production shops which are cost centres. Each shop charges other shops for materials supplied and services rendered.

The shops are motivated through goal congruence, autonomy and management efforts. Megatron Ltd. is having a welding shop and painting shop. The welding shop welds annually 7,50,000 purchased items with other 15,00,000 shop made parts into 1,20,000 assemblies.

The assemblies are having variable cost of ₹ 19 each and are sold in the market at ₹ 24 per assembly. Out of the total production, 80% is diverted to painting shop at same price ruling in the market. Welding shop incurs a fixed cost of ₹ 5,00,000 per annum.

The painting shop is having a fixed cost of ₹ 6,00,000 and its cost of painting including transfered price from welding shop comes to ₹ 40 per unit. The painting shop sells all units transfered to it by welding shop at ₹ 50 per assembly.

Required:

(*i*) Find out profit of individual cost centres and overall profitability of the company.

(*ii*) Recommend course of action, if painting shop wishes to purchase its full requirement either from open market (@ ₹ 20 per assembly) or from welding shop at ₹ 20 per assembly.

Give reasons for your recommendations.

Solution:

Megatron Ltd

(*i*) Present Profitability of Individual Shops and Overall Profitability:

Particulars	*Welding Shop*			*Painting Shop*		
	Qty. Unit	*Rate (₹)*	*Value (₹)*	*Qty. Unit*	*Rate (₹)*	*Value (₹)*
Sale in Open market	24000	24.00	576000	96000	50.00	4800000
Transfer to Painting Shop	96000	24.00	2304000	—	—	—
Total Sales (A)	120000		2880000	96000		4800000
Less: Variable Cost (B): (120000×19)			2280000	(96000×40)		3840000
Contribution (A – B)			600000			960000
Less: Fixed Cost			500000			600000
PROFIT			100000			360000

Overall profit for the company = ₹ 460000, (100000 + 360000)

(*ii*) (*a*) When Painting Shop purchases all its requirement from Open Market at a Price of ₹ 20 per unit:

Particulars	*Welding Shop*			*Painting Shop*		
	Qty. Unit	*Rate (₹)*	*Value (₹)*	*Qty. Unit*	*Rate (₹)*	*Value (₹)*
Sale	24000	24.00	576000	96000	50.00	4800000
Less: Variable Cost	24000	19.00	456000	96000	36.00	3456000
Contribution			120000			1344000
Less: Fixed Cost			500000			600000
Profit/(Loss)			(380000)			744000

— Overall Profit for the Company = ₹ 364000 (744000 – 380000)

* Total Variable Cost of the unit of Painting Shop:

(Purchase Price from the market + own Variable Cost)

= ₹ 20 + (40 – Transfer price from welding shop) = 20 + (40 – 24) = ₹ 36.00

(*ii*) (*b*) *When all the requirements of Painting Shop is met*

By transfer from Welding Shop at a transfer price of ₹ 20 per unit:

Particulars	Welding Shop			Painting Shop		
	Qty unit	Rate (₹)	Value (₹)	Qty unit	Rate (₹)	Value (₹)
Sale in the open market	24000	24.00	576000	96000	50.00	4800000
Transfer to Painting Shop	96000	20.00	1920000	—	—	—
Total Sales	120000		2496000	96000		4800000
Less: Variable Cost	(120000×19)		2280000	(96000×36)		3456000
Contribution			216000			1344000
Less: Fixed Cost			500000			600000
Profit/(Loss)			(284000)			744000

Overall profit of the Company = ₹ 460000 (744000 – 284000)

The results of the three alternatives are summarized below:

(Fig. in ₹)

	Welding Shop	Painting Shop
Profit under alternative (*i*)	100000	360000
Profit/(Loss) under alternative (*ii*)(*a*)	(380000)	744000
Profit/(Loss) under alternative (*ii*)(*b*)	(284000)	744000

	₹
Overall Profit of the Company under alternative (*i*)	460000
under alternative (*ii*) (*a*)	364000
under alternative (*ii*) (*b*)	460000

Recommendation

After analyzing the summarized results of three alternatives pertaining to Individual Shops and Overall Company, we may recommend to accept the alternative (ii) (b). (requirements of painting shop to be met by transfer from Welding Shop at a T. P. of ₹ 20 per unit) due to the following reasons:

(A) It gives a maximum overall profit of ₹ 460000.

(B) Each shop is treated as a separate Cost Centre and not a profit centre.

(C) The policy of overall goal congruence of the company is followed.

Illustrative Problem 24

Bharat Dynamics Ltd. (BDL) has two divisions. The Mining Division makes toldine, which is then transferred to the Metals Division. The toldine is further processed by the Metals Division and is sold to customers at a price of ₹ 1,500 per unit. The Mining Division is currently required by BDL to transfer its total yearly output of 4,00,000 units of toldine to the Metals Division at 110% of full manufacturing cost. Unlimited quantities of toldine can be purchased and sold on the outside market at ₹ 900 per unit:

The following table gives the manufacturing costs per unit in the Mining and Metals divisions for 2016:

	Mining Division	*Metals Division*
Direct materials	₹ 120	₹ 60
Direct manufacturing labour costs	160	200
Manufacturing overhead costs	320[a]	250[b]
Total manufacturing costs per unit	₹ 600	₹ 510

[a]Manufacturing overhead costs in the Mining Division are 25% fixed and 75% variable.

[b]Manufacturing overhead costs in the Metals Division are 60% fixed and 40% variable.

Required:

(*a*) Calculate the operating incomes for the Mining and Metals divisions for the 4,00,000 units of toldine transferred under the following transfer-pricing methods: (a) market price and (b) 110% of full manufacturing costs.

(*b*) Suppose BDL rewards each division manager with a bonus, calculated as 1 % of division operating income (if positive). What is the amount of bonus that will be paid to each division manager under the transfer-pricing methods in requirement (*a*)? Which transfer-pricing method will each division manager prefer to use?

(*c*) What arguments would Amit, manager of the Mining Division, make to support the transfer-pricing method that he prefers?

Solution:

Effect of alternative transfer-pricing methods on division operating Income

	Internal Transfers at Market Prices Method A	***Internal Transfers at 110% of Full Costs/Method B***
(*a*) **Mining Division**		
Revenues		
₹ 900, ₹ 660[1] × 4,00,000 units	₹ 36,00,00,000	₹ 26,40,00,000
Deduct		
Division variable costs:		
₹ 520[2] × 4,00,000 units	20,80,00,000	20,80,00,000
Division fixed costs		
₹ 80[3] × 4,00,000 units	3,20,00,000	3,20,00,000
Division operating income	₹ 12,00,00,000	₹ 2,40,00,000
Metals Division		
Revenues		
₹ 1,500 × 4,00,000 units	₹ 60,00,00,000	₹ 60,00,00,000

Deduct		
Transferred-in costs		
₹ 900, ₹ 660 × 4,00,000 units	36,00,00,000	26,40,00,000
Division variable costs		
₹ 360[4] × 4,00,000 units	14,40,00,000	14,40,00,000
Division fixed costs		
₹ 150[5] × 4,00,000 units	6,00,00,000	6,00,00,000
Division operating income	₹ 3,60,00,000	₹ 13,20,00,000

[1]₹ 660 = ₹ 600 × 110%

[2]Variable cost per unit in Mining Division = Direct materials + Direct manufacturing labour + 75% of Manufacturing overhead = ₹ 120 + ₹ 160 + 75% × ₹ 320 = ₹ 520

[3]Fixed cost per unit = 25% of Manufacturing overhead = 25% × ₹ 320 = ₹ 80

[4]Variable cost per unit in Metals Division = Direct materials + Direct manufacturing labour + 40% of Manufacturing overhead = ₹ 60 + ₹ 200 + 40% × ₹ 250 = ₹ 360

[5]Fixed cost per unit in Metals Division = 60% of Manufacturing overhead = 60% × ₹ 250 = ₹ 150

(*b*) Bonus paid to division managers at 1 % of division operating income will be as follows:

	Method A ***Internal Transfers at Market Prices***	***Method B*** ***Transfers at 110% of Full Costs***
Mining Division manager's bonus		
(1% × ₹ 12,00,00,000; 1% × ₹ 2,40,00,000)	₹ 12,00,000	₹ 2,40,000
Metals Division manager's bonus		
(1% × ₹ 3,60,00,000; 1% × ₹ 13,20,00,000)	3,60,000	13,20,000

The Mining Division manager will prefer Method A (transfer at market prices) because this method gives ₹ 12,00,000 of bonus rather than ₹ 2,40,000 under Method B (transfers at 110% of full costs). The Metals Division manager will prefer Method B because this method gives ₹ 13,20,000 of bonus rather than ₹ 3,60,000 under Method A.

(*c*) Amit, the manager of the Mining Division, will appeal to the existence of a competitive market to price transfers at market prices. Using market prices for transfers in these conditions leads to goal congruence. Division managers acting in their own best interests make decisions that are also in the best interests of the company as a whole. Further, setting transfer prices based on cost will cause the Mining Division to pay no attention to controlling costs since all costs incurred will be recovered from the Metals Division at 110% of full costs.

Illustrative Problem 25

Hardware Ltd. Manufactures computer hardware products in different divisions which operate as profit centres. Printer Division makes and sells printers. The Printer Division's budgeted income statement, based on a sales volume of 15,000 units is given below. The Printer Division's Manager believes that sales can be increased by 2,400 units, if the selling price is reduced by ₹ 20 per unit from the present price of ₹ 400 per unit, and that, for this additional volume, no additional fixed costs will be incurred.

Printer Division presently uses a component purchased from an outside supplier at ₹ 70 per unit. A similar component is being produced by the Components Division of Hardware Ltd. and sold outside at a price of ₹ 100 per unit. Components Division can make this component for the Printer Division with a small modification in the specification, which would mean a reduction in the Direct Material cost for the Components Division by ₹ 1.5 per unit. Further, the Component Division will not incur variable selling cost on units transferred to the Printer Division. The Printer Division's Manager has offered the Component Division's Manager a price of ₹ 50 per unit of the component.

Component Division has the capacity to produce 75,000 units, of which only 64,000 units can be absorbed by the outside market.

The current budgeted income statement for Components Division is based on a volume of 64,000 units considering all of it as sold outside.

	Printer Division	*Component Division*
	₹ '000	**₹ '000**
Sales revenue	6,000	6,400
Manufacturing cost:		
Component	1,050	—
Other direct materials, direct labour		
And variable OH	1,680	1,920
Fixed OH	480	704
Total manufacturing cost	3,210	2,624
Gross margin	2,790	3,776
Variable marketing costs	270	384
Fixed marketing and Admn. OH	855	704
Non-manufacturing cost	1,125	1,088
Operating profit	1,665	2,688

Required:

(*i*) Should the Printer Division reduce the price by ₹ 20 per unit even if it is not able to procure the components from the Component Division at ₹ 50 per unit?

(*ii*) Without prejudice to your answer to part (*i*) above, assume that Printer Division needs 17,400 units and that, either it takes all its requirements from Component Division or all of it from outside source. Should the Component Division be willing to supply the Printer Division at ₹ 50 per unit?

(*iii*) Without prejudice to your answer to part (*i*) above, assume that Printer Division needs 17,400 units. Would it be in the best interest of Hardware Ltd. for the Components Division to supply the components to the Printer Division at ₹ 50?

Support each of your conclusions with appropriate calculations.

Solution:

(₹)

Particulars	*Printer Division* Existing price	Reduction in selling price	If component is purchased internally	*Components Division* Existing	If transfer is effected
Selling price	400	380	380	100	50
Component cost	70	70	50		
Other direct materials, labour and Variable overhead	112	112	112	30	28.50
Variable marketing cost	18	18	18	6	
Contribution	200	180	200	64	21.50
Volume units	15,000	17,400	17,400	64,000	17,400
Total contribution ('000)	3,000	3,132	3,480	4,096	374.10
Volume lost in the market (units)					6,400
Contribution lost					6 400 × 64 = 4,09,600

(*i*) Yes, Printer Division should institute the ₹ 20 price reduction on its printer units because net income would increase by ₹ 1,32,000 (₹ 31,32,000 – ₹ 30,00,000).

Alternatively by incremental approach the net increase can be computed as follows:

	₹
Contribution margin of sales increase (₹ 180 × 2,400)	4,32,000
Loss in contribution margin on original volume arising from decrease in selling price (15,000 × ₹ 20)	3,00,000
Increase in operating profit	1,32,000

(*ii*) No, the Component Division should not sell all 17,400 units to Printer Division for ₹ 50. If the Component Division does sell all 17,400 units to Printer, Component Division will only be able to sell 57,600 units to outside customers instead of 64,000 units due to the capacity restrictions. This would decrease Component Division's profit before taxes by ₹ 35,500. Supporting calculations are as follows:

	₹
Contribution from sales to printer (₹ 21.50 × 17,000)	3,74,100
Loss in contribution from loss of sales to outsiders (₹ 64 × 6,400)	4,09,600
Decrease in operating profit	35,500

(*iii*) Yes, it would be in the best interest of Hardware Ltd. for the Component Division to sell the units to the Printer division at ₹ 50 each. The net advantage to the Hardware Ltd. is ₹ 3,12,500 as shown below. The net advantage is the result of the cost savings from purchasing the Component unit internally and the contribution margin lost from 6,400 units that the Component Division otherwise would sell to outsiders.

	Total Company ₹ '000s
Incremental contribution – if the component is transferred within (3,480 – 3,132)	348.00
Contribution to the Component Division	374.10
Total incremental contribution	722.10
Less: Contribution lost by the Component Division	409.60
Net contribution gain	312.50

Illustrative Problem 26

A company is organized on decentralized lines, with each manufacturing division operating as a separate profit centre. Each division manager has full authority to decide on sale of division's output to outsiders or to other divisions. Division AB manufactures a single standardized product. Some output is sold externally and remaining is transferred to division XY where it is a subassembly in the manufacture of the division product. The unit cost of division AB product and division XY is as follows:

	Division AB **(₹)**	***Division XY*** **(₹)**
Transfer from division AB to XY	—	42.00
Direct Material	6.00	35.00
Direct Labour	3.00	4.50
Direct expenses	3.00	—
Variable manufacturing overheads	3.00	18.00
Fixed manufacturing overheads	6.00	18.00
Variable selling and packing expenses	3.00	2.50
	24.00	120.00

Division AB sold 40,000 units annually at the standard price of ₹ 45 in external market. In additions to the external sales, 10,000 units are transferred annually to division XY at internal price of ₹ 42 per unit. Variable selling and packing expenses are not incurred by supplying division- for the internal transfer of the product. Division XY incorporates the transferred goods into more advance product. The manager of division XY disagrees with the basis used to set the transfer price. He argues that transfer price should be made at variable cost since he claims that his division is taking output that division AB should be unable to sell at price ₹ 45.

He also submitted a report of the relationship between selling price and demand to support his disagreement. The report of customer demand at various selling prices for division AB and for division XY is as follows:

Division AB			
Selling price per unit (₹)	30	45	60
Demand (Units)	60,000	40,000	20,000
Division XY			
Selling price per unit (₹)	120	135	150
Demand (Units)	15,000	10,000	5,000

The company has sufficient capacity to meet demand at various selling prices. Internal transfer demanded units will be decided by XY division.

Required:

(*i*) To calculate divisional profitability and overall profitability of company if division AB transfers demanded units to XY at price of ₹ 42.

(*ii*) To calculate divisional profitability and overall profitability of company if division AB transfers demanded units to XY at variable cost.

(*iii*) In place of internal transfers, AB division can sell 10,000 units of their product in new external market without effecting existing market, at price ₹ 32 per unit and XY division can purchase these units at the rate of ₹ 31 in open market. Calculate company's profit by following above strategies.

Solution:

(*i*) **AB sells product at external market**

Selling price (₹)	30	45	60
Less Variable cost	18	18	18
Contribution (per unit)	12	27	42
Demands (units)	60,000	40,000	20,000
Total contribution	7,20,000	10,80,000	8,40,000

Optimal output is 40,000 units at a selling price of ₹ 45.

AB transfer at ₹ 42 to XY division then contribution of XY

Selling price (₹)	120	135	150
Less Variable cost VC + TP (42 + 60)	102	102	102
Contribution (per unit)	18	33	48
Demands (units)	15,000	10,000	5,000
Total contribution	2,70,000	3,30,000	2,40,000

Manager will choose output level 10,000 units at a selling price of ₹ 135.

Overall profit when transfer made at ₹ 42

Division AB contribution on 10,000 units [42 – (18 – 3)]	= 2,70,000
Division XY contribution 10,000 (135 – 102)	= 3,30,000
Total contribution	= 6,00,000
Division AB contribution from external market sale	= 10,80,000
Total profit	16,80,000

(*ii*) **AB transfer at variable cost**

Selling price (₹)	120	135	150
Less Variable cost (15 + 60)	75	75	75
Contribution (per unit)	46	60	75
Demands (units)	15,000	10,000	5,000
Total contribution	6,75,000	6,00,000	3,75,000

Optimal is 15,000 units at the rate of 120 per unit.

If AB transfer at Variable cost (₹ 15) then no contribution will be generated by AB division

XY division choose 15,000 units level contribution 15,000 × 45	=	6,75,000
Division AB contribution from external market sale	=	10,80,000
Total contribution		17,55,000

(*iii*) **Contribution AB division by selling 10,000 units to new external market at ₹ 32 and XY division purchasing at ₹ 31.**

Contribution (32 – 18) × 10,000	=	1,40,000
XY contribution [135 – (31 + 60)]	=	4,40,000
Division AB contribution from external market sale	=	10,80,000
Total contribution	=	16,60,000

Illustrative Problem 27

ABC Company's Cabinet Division manufactures a standard cabinet for television sets. The cost per cabinet is:

Variable cost per cabinet	₹ 700
Fixed cost per cabinet	300*
Total cost per cabinet	₹ 100

* Based on a capacity of 10,000 cabinets per year.

Part of the Cabinet Division's output is sold to outside manufacturers of television sets and part is sold to ABC Company's Quark Division, which produces a TV set under its own name. The Cabinet Division charges ₹ 1400 per cabinet for all sales.

The costs, revenue, and net income associated with the Quark Division's TV set is given below:

Selling price per TV set		₹ 4800
Less variable cost per TV set:		
Cost of cabinet	₹ 1400	
Variable cost of electronic parts	2100	
Total variable cost		3500
Contribution margin		1300
Less fixed costs per TV set		800*
Net income per TV set		₹ 500

* Based on a capacity of 3,000 sets per year.

The Quark Division has an order from an overseas source for 1,000 TV sets. The overseas source wants to pay only ₹ 3400 per set.

Required:

1. Assume that the Quark Division has enough idle capacity to fill the 1,000-set order. Is the division likely to accept the ₹ 3400 price or to reject it? Explain.
2. Assume that both the Cabinet Division and the Quark Division have idle capacity. Under these conditions, would it be an advantage or a disadvantage to the company as a whole for the Quark Division to reject the ₹ 3400 price? Show computations to support your answer.
3. Assume that the Quark Division has idle capacity but that the Cabinet Division is operating at capacity and could sell all of its cabinets to outside manufacturers. Compute the advantage or disadvantage of the Quark Division accepting the 1,000-set order at the ₹ 3400 unit price.
4. What conclusions do you draw concerning the use of market price as a transfer price in intracompany transactions? *(M-Com., Delhi, 2015)*

Solution:

1. The Quark Division will probably reject the ₹ 3400 price. This is because the price is below the Quark Division's "variable costs" of ₹ 3500 per set. Although these 'variable' costs contain a ₹ 1400 transfer price from the Cabinet Division, which in turn includes ₹ 300 per unit in fixed costs, from the perspective of the Quark Division the ₹ 1400 purchase price from the Cabinet Divison is a variable cost. Thus, it will reject the ₹ 3400 price offered.
2. If both the Cabinet Division and the Quark Division have idle capacity, then from the perspective of the entire company the ₹ 3400 offer should be accepted. By rejecting the ₹ 3400 price, the company will lose ₹ 600 in potential contribution margin per set:

Price offered per set		₹ 3400
Less variable costs per set:		
Cabinet Division	₹ 700	
Quark Division	2100	2800
Potential contribution margin per set		₹ 600

3. If the Cabinet Division is operating at capacity, any cabinets transferred to the Quark Division to fill the overseas order will have to be diverted from outside customers. Whether a cabinet is dold to outside customers or is transferred to the Quark Division, its production cost is the same. However, if a set is diverted from outside sales, the Cabinet Division (and the entire company) loses the ₹ 1400 in revenue. As a consequence, as shown below, there would be a net loss of ₹ 100 on each TV set sold for ₹ 3400.

Price offered per set		₹ 3400
Less:		
Lost revenue from sales of cabinets to outsiders	₹ 1400	
Variable cost of Quark Division	2100	3500
Net loss per TV		₹ (100)

4. When the selling division has no idle capacity, as in part (3), market price works very well as a transfer price. The cost to the company of a transfer when there is no idle capacity is

the lost revenue from sales to outsiders. If the market price is used as the transfer price, the purchasing division will view the market price of the transferred item as its cost—which is appropriate since that is the cost to the company. As a consequence, the manager of the purchasing division should be motivated to make decisions that are in the best interests of the company.

When the selling division has idle capacity, the cost to the company of the transfer is just the vriable cost of producing the item. If the market price is used as the transfer price, the manager of the purchasing division will view that as his/her cost rather than the real cost to the company which is just variable cost. Hence, the manager will have the wrong cost information for making decisions as we observed in parts (1) and (2).

Illustrative Problem 28

Tycon Ltd. has two manufacturing departments organized into separate profit centres known as Textile unit and Process House. The Textile unit has a production capacity of 5 lacs metres cloth per month, but at present its sales is limited to 50% to outside market and 30% to process house.

The transfer price for the year 2016 was agreed at ₹ 6 per metre. This price has been fixed in line with the extrnal wholesale trade price on 1st January, 2016. However, the price of yarn declined, which was the raw material of textile unit, with effect, that wholesale trade price reduced to ₹ 5.60 per metre with effect from 1st June, 2016. This price was however not made applicable to the sales made to the processing house of the company. The textile unit turned down the processing house request for revision of price.

The Process house refines the cloth the packs the output known as brand Rayon in bundles of 100 metres each. The selling price of the Rayon is ₹ 825 per bundle. The process house has a potential of selling a further quantity of 1,000 bundles of Rayon provided the overall prices is reduced to ₹ 725 per bundle. In that event it can buy the additional 1,00,000 metres of cloth from textile unit, whose capacity can be fully utilised. The outside market has no further scope.

The cost data relevant to the operations are:

	Textile unit	Proces house
	₹	₹
Raw material (per metre) on 1st June, 2016	3.00	Transfer price
Variable cost	1.20 (per metre)	80 (per bundle)
Fixed cost (per month)	4,12,000	1,00,000

You are required to:

(*i*) Prepare statement showing the estimated profitability for June, 2016 for Textile unit and Process house and company as a whole on the following basis:

(*a*) At 80% and 100% capacity utilisation of the Textile unit at the market price and the transfer price to the Processing house of ₹ 6 per metre.

(*b*) At 80% capacity utilisation of the Textile unit at the market price of ₹ 5.60 per metre and the transfer price to the Processing house of ₹ 6 per metre.

(*c*) At 100% capacity utilisation of the Textile unit at the market price of ₹ 5.60 per metre and the transfer price to the Processing house of ₹ 5.60 per metre.

(*ii*) Comment on the effect of the company's transfer pricing policy on the profitability of Processing house.

Solution:

(*i*) (a) *At 80% level* (in ₹)

Textile unit		**Process house**	
Sales (4,00,000 × 6)	24,00,000	Sales (1,50,000/100) × 825	12,37,500
Less		Less	
Raw material (4,00,000 × 3)	12,00,000	Transfer price (1,50,000 × 6)	9,00,000
Variable cost (4,00,000 × 1.2)	4,80,000	Variable cost (1,500 × 80)	1,20,000
Fixed cost	4,12,000	Fixed cost	1,00,000
Profit	3,08,000	Profit	1,17,500

Overall profit = 3,08,000 + 1,17,500 = ₹ 4,25,500

At 100% level

Sales (5,00,000 × 6)	30,00,000	Sales (2,50,000/100) × 725	18,12,500
Less		Less	
Raw material (5,00,000 × 3)	15,00,000	Transfer Price (2,50,000 × 6)	15,00,000
Variable cost (5,00,000 × 1.2)	6,00,000	Variable cost	2,00,000
Fixed cost	4,12,000	Fixed cost	1,00,000
Profit	4,88,000	Profit	12,500

Overall profit = 4,88,000 + 12,500 = ₹ 5,00,500

(b) *At 80% level* (market price 5.60 and transfer price 6/-) (in ₹)

Textile unit		Process house	
Sale (2,50,000 × 5.6)	1400000		
(1,50,000 × 6.0)	900000		
	23,00,000		
Less			
Raw material (4,00,000 × 3)	12,00,000		
Variable cost (4,00,000 × 1.2)	4,80,000		
Fixed cost	4,12,000		
Profit	2,08,000	Profit	1,17,500

(c) *Sales 100% level at* (5.60) (in ₹)

Sale (5,00,000 × 5.6)	28,00,000	Sales (2,50,000 × 725)	18,12,500
Less		Less	
Raw material (5,00,000 × 3)	15,00,000	Transfer Profit (2,50,000 × 5.6)	14,00,000
Variable cost (5,00,000 × 1.20)	6,00,000	Variable cost (2,500 × 80)	2,00,000
Fixed cost	4,12,000	Fixed cost	1,00,000
Profit	2,88,000	Profit	1,12,500

Overall profit = 2,88,000 + 1,12,500 = 4,00,500

(*ii*) Comment on the profitability of processing units:

	Transfer price (₹)	Profit (₹)
(a) 80% capacity	6.00	1,17,500
100% capacity	6.00	12,500
(b) 80% capacity	6.00	1,17,500
(c) 100% capacity	5.60	1,12,500

Processing house will not be interested to buy more than 1,50,000 meters from textile units.

Illustrative Problem 29

Harrison Co. operates a Pulp Division that manufactures wood pulp for use in the production of various paper goods. Revenue and costs associated with tonnes of pulp follow:

Selling price		₹ 7000
Less expenses:		
Variable	₹ 4200	
Fixed (based on a capacity of 50,000 tonnes per year)	1800	6000
Net income		1000

Harrison has just acquired a small company that manufactures paper cartons. This company will be treated as a division of Harrison with full profit responsibility. The newly formed Carton Division is currently purchasing 5,000 tonnes of pulp per year from a supplier at a cost of ₹7000 per tonne, less a 10% quantity discount. Harrison's president is anxious for the Carton Division to begin purchasing its pulp from the Pulp Division if an acceptable transfer price can be worked out.

Required:

For (1) and (2) below, assume that the Pulp Division can sell all of its pulp to outside customers at the normal ₹ 7000 price.

1. Are the managers of the Carton and Pulp Divisions likely to agree to a transfer price for 5,000 tonnes of pulp next year? Why or why not?
2. If the Pulp Division meets the price that the Carton Division is currently paying to its supplier and sells 5,000 tonnes of pulp to the Carton Division each year, what will be the effect on the profits of the Pulp Division, the Carton Division, and the company as a whole?

For (3) – (6) below, assume that the Pulp Division is currently selling only 30,000 tonnes of pulp each year to outside customers at the stated ₹ 7,000 price.

3. Are the managers of the Carton and Pulp Divisions likely to agree to a transfer price for 5,000 tonnes of pulp next year? Why or why not?
4. Suppose that the Carton Divisions outside supplier drops its price (net of the quantity discount) to only ₹ 5,900 per tonne. Should the Pulp Division meet this price? Explain. If the Pulp Division does not meet the ₹ 5,900 price, what will be the effect on the profits of the company as a whole?
5. Refer to (4) above. If the Pulp Division refuses to meet the ₹ 5,900 price, should the Carton Division be required to purchase from the Pulp Division at a higher price for the good of the company as a whole?
6. Refer to (4) above. Assume that due to inflexible management policies, the Carton Division is required to purchase 5,000 tonnes of pulp each year from the Pulp Division at ₹ 7,000 per tonne. What will be the effect on the profit of the company as a whole?

Solution:

1. The lowest acceptable transfer price from the perspective of the selling division is given by the following formula:

$$\text{Transfer price} \geq \text{Variable cost per unit} + \frac{\text{Total contribution margin on lost sales}}{\text{Number of units transferred}}$$

There is no idle capacity, so transfers from the Pulp Division to the Carton Division would cut directly into normal sales of pulp to outsiders. Since the costs are the same whether the pulp is transferred internally or sold to outsiders, the only relevant cost is the lost revenue of ₹ 7000 per tonnes from the pulp that could be sold to outsiders. This is confirmed in the following calculation:

$$\text{Transfer price} \geq ₹\ 4{,}200 + \frac{(₹\ 7{,}000 - ₹\ 4{,}200) \times 5{,}000}{5{,}000} = ₹\ 4{,}200 + (₹\ 7{,}000 - ₹\ 4{,}200)$$

$= ₹\ 7{,}000$

Therefore, the Pulp Division will refuse to transfer at a price less than ₹ 7,000 a tonne.

The Carton Division can buy pulp from an outside supplier for ₹ 7,000 a tonne, less a 10% quantity discount of ₹ 7,000 or ₹ 6,300 a tonne. Therefore, the Division would be unwilling to pay more than ₹ 6,300 per tonne.

Transfer price ≤ Cost of buying from outside supplier = ₹ 6,300

The requirements of the two divisions are incompatible. The Carton Division won't pay more than ₹ 6,300 and the Pulp Division will not accept less than ₹ 7,000. Thus, there will be no mutually agreeable transfer price and not transfer will take place.

2. The price being paid to the outside supplier, net of the quantity discount, is only ₹ 6,300. If this price is met by the Pulp Division, then profits in the Pulp Division and in the company as a whole will drop by ₹ 35,00,000 per year:

Lost revenue per tonne	₹ 7,000
Outside supplier's price	6,300
Loss in contribution margin per tonne	700
Number of tonnes per year	× 5,000
Total loss in profits	₹ 35,00,000

Profits in the Carton Division will remain unchanged, since it will be paying the same price internally as it is now paying externally.

3. There is idle capacity, so transfers from the Pulp Division to the Carton Division do not cut into normal sales of pulp to outsiders. In this case, the minimum price as far as the Carton Division is concerned is the variable cost per tonne of ₹ 4,200. This is confirmed in the following calculation:

$$\text{Transfer price} \geq 4{,}200 + \frac{₹\ 000}{5{,}000} = ₹\ 4{,}200$$

The Carton Division can buy pulp from an outside supplier for ₹ 6,300 a tonne and would be unwilling to pay more than that for pulp in an internal transfer. If the managers understand their own businesses and are reasonably cooperative, they should agree to a transfer and should settle on a transfer price within the range:

₹ 4,200 ≤ Transfer price ≤ ₹ 6,300

4. Yes, since the ₹ 5,900 figure represents a bona fide outside price. Even though ₹ 5,900 is less than the Pulp Division's ₹ 6,000 "full cost" per unit, it is within the range given in Part 3 and therefore will provide some contribution to the Pulp Division.

   If the Pulp Division does not meet the ₹ 5,900 price, it will lose ₹ 85,00,000 in potential profits:

Price per tonne	₹ 5,900
Less variable costs	4,200
Contribution margin per tonne	₹ 1,700

   5,000 tonnes × ₹ 1,700 = ₹ 85,00,000 potential increased profits

   This ₹ 85,00,000 in potential profits applies to the Pulp Divison and to the company as a whole.

5. No, the Carton Division should probably be free to go outside and get the best price it can. Even though this would result in suboptimization for the company as a whole, the purchasing division should probably not be forced to buy inside if better prices are available outside.

6. The Pulp Division will have an increase in profits:

Selling price	₹ 7,000
Less variable costs	4,200
Contribution margin per tonne	₹ 2,800

   5,000 tonnes × ₹ 2,800 = ₹ 1,40,00,000 increased profits

   The Carton Division will have a decrease in profits:

Inside purchase price	₹ 7,000
Outside purchase price	5,900
Increased cost per tonne	₹ 1,100

   5,000 tonnes × ₹ 1,100 = ₹ 55,00,000 decreased profits

   The company as a whole will have an increase in profits:

Increased contribution margin in the Pulp Division	₹ 2,800
Decreased contribution margin in the Carton Division	1,100
Increased contribution margin per ton	₹ 1,700

   5,000 tonnes × ₹ 1,700 = ₹ 85,00,000 increased profits

   So long as the selling division has idle capacity and the transfer price is greater than the selling division's variable costs, profits in the company as a whole will increase if internal transfers are made. However, there is a question of fairness as to how these profits should be split between the selling and buying divisions. The inflexibility of management in this situation causes damage to the profits of the Carton Division and greatly enhances the profits of the Pulp Division.

Illustrative Problem 30

A Company has two manufacturing divisions X and Y, X has a capacity of 96000 hours per annum. It manufactures two products. Gear and 'Engines' as per the following details.

	Gears	*Engines*
Direct Materials	240	64
Variable costs at 64/hour	256	64
Selling price in the outside market	640	128

Division 'Y' produces product `Wheels' as per the following details:

	₹/unit
Imported components	640
Direct Materials	96
Variable cost at ₹40 per hour	320
Selling price in the outside market	1,16

The fixed overheads for X and Y are ₹ 24 lakhs and ₹ 6 lakhs respectively. With a view to minimizing dependence on the imported component, the company has explored a possibility of Division Y using product 'Gears' instead of the imported component. This is possible provided Division Y spends 2 machine hours entailing an additional expenditure of ₹ 64 per component on modification of product 'Gears' to fit into 'wheels'. Production and sales of 'Wheels' in Division Y is limited to 5000 units per annum.

(*i*) What will be maximum transfer price per unit that Y will offer?

(*ii*) In each of the following independent situations, state with supporting calculations, the minimum transfer price per unit that X will demand from Y, if 5000 units are required by Y.

(*iii*) In which of the above situations in (ii) will the Management step in and compel X to sell to Y in the interest of overall company's profits? [*CA Final, May 2011]*

Solution:

(*i*) Y will pay only a maximum of (₹ 640 – ₹ 64) = ₹ 576 so that its outside purchase cost is matched, i.e. Maximum Transfer price by Y = 576 ₹ per unit.

	Gears (no. of units)	*Engines (no. of units)*
Market demand is limited to	20,000	20,000
Market demand is limited to	15,000	10,000
Market demand is limited to	18,000	24,000

	Gears	*Engines*	*Total*
Hours per unit	4	1	
Hours available			96,000
Units possible	24,000		
	or	96,000	
(ii) (a) Outside Demand	20,000	20,000	
Hours required	80,000	20,000	
Units required by Y	5,000		

Hours required	20,000	
Contribution per hour	36	30
Maximise Sales so that hours =	80,000	16,000
Hours used for Y	4,000	16,000
Contribution per unit of Y required	1,000	4,000

Contribution on units transferred to Y = (30 × 16,000) + (36 × 4000) = ₹ 6,24,000

Contribution per unit = 6,24,000/5,000 = ₹ 124.80

Minimum Transfer price per unit = Contribution + Variable Cost

= 124.8 + 240 + 256 = ₹ 620.80

(b)

	Gears	*Eng.*
Market Demand	15,000	10,000
Hours required per unit	4	1
Hours required	60,000	10,000
Spare capacity available =		26,000
Units of Gears possible = 26,000 per unit =		6,500
Required For transfer =		5,000

Since spare capacity is used, minimum transfer

Price = variable cost of manufacturing = 240 + 256 = 496

X will agree to anything above ₹ 496 per unit

(c) Market Demand

Units	18,000	24,000
Hours per unit	4	1
Hours required	72,000	24,000
Hours required for Y's demand		20,000

This will be need by sacrificing production of 'Engines'. Hence contribution per hours for transferred Units must be atleast.

Contribution Required on 5000 units = 20,000 × 30 = 6,00,000

Contribution Required per unit $= \dfrac{6,00,000}{5,000} = 120$ ₹

Minimum Transfer Price = Contribution per unit + Variable Cost

= 120 + 240 + 256

= ₹ 616 per unit

Gears and Engines earn a contribution.

Variable Cost of in house manufacturing of imported Components = 240 + 256 + 64 = 560

Production Outside = ₹ 640

₹ 80/- per unit is being paid for outside purchase

Contribution Lost per unit of facility X = 80/4 = 20 hrs.

Since X is earning higher contribution per hours 36 & 30 for each product, the management will not have to interfere in situation (a) & (c) where full production capacity is used for outside sales.

In (i) (b) Management need not interfere since it is a win-win situation. Departments can negotiable in the relevant range between 496 and 576.

Illustrative Problem 31

B Ltd. makes three products X, Y and Z in Divisions X, Y and Z respectively. The following information is given:

	X	Y	Z
Direct Material (₹/Unit) (excluding material X for Divisions Y and Z)	8	22	40
Direct Labour (₹/Unit)	4	6	8
Variable Overhead (₹/Unit)	2	2	2
Selling price to outside customers (₹/Unit)	25	65	90
Existing capacity (no. of units)	6,000	3,000	3,000
Maximum external Market demand (no of units)	5,000	5,500	5,000
Additional fixed cost that would be incurred to install additional capacity (₹)	45,000	9,000	23,100
Maximum additional units that can be produced by additional capacity	6,000	2,000	2,250

Y and Z need material X as their input. Material X is available in the market at ₹ 23 per unit. Defectives can be returned to suppliers at their cost. Division X supplies the material free from defects and hence is able to sell at ₹ 25 per unit. Each unit of Y and Z require one unit of X as input with slight modification.

If Y purchases from outside at ₹ 23 per unit, it has to incur ₹ 3 per unit as modification and inspection cost. If Y purchases from Division X, it has to incur, in addition to the transfer price, ₹ 2 per unit to modify it.

If Z gets the material from Division X, it can use it after incurring a modification cost, of ₹ 1 per unit. If Z buys material X from outside, it has to either inspect and modify it at its own shop floor at ₹ 5 per unit or use idle labour from Division X at ₹ 3 per unit. Division X will lend its idle labour as per Z's requirement even if Z purchases the material from outside.

The transfer prices are at the discretion of the Divisional Managers and will remain confidential. Assume no restriction on quantities of inter-division transfers or purchases.

Discuss with relevant figures the best strategy for each division and for the company as a whole.

[CA. Final, Nov. 2013]

Solution:

CONTRIBUTION PER UNIT

(₹)

Particulars	*Division X*			*Division Y*		*Division Z*
	Sale to	*Internal Transfer to*		*Purchase from*	*Transfer from*	*Transfer from*
	Outside	*Y*	*Z*	*Outside*	*X*	*X*
Selling Price	25.00	—	—	65.00	65.00	90.00
Transfer Price	—	24.00*	25.00	—	—	—
Direct Material (Excluding Material 'X')	8.00	8.00	8.00	22.00	22.00	40.00

Direct Labour	4.00	4.00	4.00	6.00	6.00	8.00
Variable Overhead	2.00	2.00	2.00	2.00	2.00	2.00
Purchase Price 'X'	—	—	—	23.00	—	—
Transfer Price 'X'	—	—	—	—	24.00	25.00
Modification Cost	—	—	—	3.00	2.00	1.00
Contribution	11.00	10.00	11.00	9.00	9.00	14.00

(*) Division 'Y' will not pay Division 'X' anything more than ₹ 24, because at 24, it will incur additional cost of ₹ 2 per unit to modify it, ₹ 23 + ₹ 3 = ₹ 26, the outside cost.

(#) To purchase material X from outside is costly for division 'Z' as after modification at own shop floor, cost of the same comes to Division 'Z' is ₹ 28 (₹ 23 + ₹ 5).

If Division 'X' goes to utilize its full capacity in that case labour would not be available for modification to Department 'Z'.

Accordingly Division 'Z' may purchase material X at ₹ 25 from Division 'X' i.e. market price to outsiders.

INTERNAL TRANSFER DECISION (UNITS)

Particulars		X	Y	Z
Existing Capacity	...(A),	6,000 units	3,000 units	3,000 units
Maximum Capacity *that can be added*	...(B)	6,000 units	2,000 units	2,250 units
Total Maximum that *can be produced*	...(C)=(A)+(B)	12,000 units	5,000 units	5,250 units
Maximum External Demand	...(D)	5,000 units	5,000 units	5,000 units
Balance	...(C)-(D)	7,000 units	—	250 units
Internal Transfer to Other Divisions		5,000 units to Z* 2,000 units to Y	N.A.	N.A.
Internal transfer from Other Divisions		N.A.	2,000 units transfer from X (material X)	5,000 units transfer from X (material X)

(*) Division 'X' will supply its production to Division 'Z' 'first (after meeting its external requirement) as contribution from product Z is high.

DECISION WHETHER TO EXPAND OR NOT

Particulars	*X*	*Y*	*Z*
Additional Fixed Cost on Expansion	₹ 45,000	₹ 9,000	₹ 23,100
Contribution that can be earned by expansion	(4,000 units × ₹11) + 2,000 units × ₹ TO)	(2,000 units × ₹ 9)	(2,000* units × ₹ 14)
Net Benefit from Expansion	₹ 19,000	₹ 9,000	₹ 4,900
Division	Expansion	Expansion	Expansion

(*) As maximum demand of product Z is 5,000 units which Division 'Z' first complete with existing capacity of 3,000 units. Balance 2,000 units from expansion.

NET REVENUE ADDITION (₹)

Particulars	*X*	*Y*	*Z*	*Total*
Contribution – External Sales	55,000 (5,000 units × ₹ 11)	45,000 (5,000 units × ₹ 9)	70,000 (5,000 units × ₹ 14)	1,70,000
Contribution – Internal Transfer	75,000 (2,000 units × ₹ 10) + 5,000 units × ₹ 11)	—	—	75,000
Additional Fixed Cost	45,000	9,000	23,100	77,100
Net Revenue Addition				1,67,900

Strategy for Company & Divisions:

(i) Division 'X' will transfer maximum possible material to Division 'Z' as Division 'Z' is offering maximum transfer price to Division 'X'. At the same time Division 'Z' is fetching maximum contribution for the organisation so it is beneficial for both the Divisions as well as organisation as a whole.

(ii) As shown above all the three Divisions are getting net benefit when they are taking decision to expand and hence, all the three divisions should expand their activity by incurring additional fixed cost on expansion.

REFERENCES

1. Jesset T. Barfield. Cecily A. Raiborn and Michael R. Kinney, *Cost Accounting, Traditions and Innovations*, Thomson, 2003, p. 818.
2. Mohinder N. Kaura, *Management Control and Reporting Systems*, Sage Publications, 2002, pp. 63-65. Readers are advised to go through this study for detailed study of transfer pricing followed by Indian companies.
3. Roland Fox, Alison Kennedy and Keith Sugden, *Decision Making, A Management Accounting Perspective*, CIMA, UK, 1990, p. 273.
4. Don R. Hansen and Maryamne. M. Mowen, *Management Accounting*, Thomson, 2005, p. 546.
5. Ronald W. Hilton, *Managerial Accounting*, McGraw Hill Education, 2006, p. 560.
6. Ronald W. Hilton. *Managerial Accounting Ibid*, p. 561.
7. Lane K. Anderson and Harold M. Sollenberger, *Management Accounting*. South-Western Publishing Co. 1992, p. 174.
8. Sidney Davidson *et al*. *Managerial Accounting*, The Dryden Press, 1988, p. 683.
9. Robert S. Kaplan and Anthony A. Atkinson, *Advanced Management Accounting*, III Edition, Pearson Education. 1998, p. 461.
10. Ray H. Garrison and EricW Noreen, *Managerial Accounting*, Irwin McGraw Hill, 2000, p. 585.
11. Robert S. Kaplan and Anthony A. Atkinson, *Advanced Management Accounting*, Pearson Education, 1998, p. 262.
12. Robert S. Kaplan and Anthony A. Atkinson, *Ibid*, p. 457.
13. Mohinder N. Kaura, *Ibid*, pp. 75-76.
14. Robert S. Kaplan, Danweiss and Eyal Desheh, "Transfer Pricing with ABC", *Management Accounting* (May 1997), pp. 20-28.
15. Joseph G. Louderback III and Jay S. Holmen, *Managerial Accounting*, Thomson, 2003, p. 442.

CRITICAL ANALYSIS AND DISCUSSION QUESTIONS, SELF-ASSESSMENT QUESTIONS, MULTIPLE CHOICE QUESTIONS, PROBLEMS AND CASES

CRITICAL ANALYSIS AND DISCUSSION QUESTIONS

1. What is a transfer price? Under what conditions are transfer prices necessary?
2. Using the criteria for evaluating transfer prices, evaluate each of the following transfer prices.
   (*i*) Market prices
   (*ii*) Full Cost
   (*iii*) Full cost plus mark up
   (*iv*) Opportunity Cost
   (*v*) Negotiated price
3. Explain a dual transfer price. What are the advantages and disadvantages of using such a pricing system?
4. What is the disadvantage of negotiated transfer prices when no intermediate market exists for the producing division?
5. Explain the opportunity cost approach to transfer pricing.
6. Identify three cost-based transfer prices. What are the disadvantages of cost-based transfer prices? When might it be appropriate to use cost-based transfer prices? (*M. Com. Delhi*, 2002)
7. When is the negotiated pricing preferred over the market price approach in setting transfer prices?
8. When using negotiated pricing approach to transfer pricing, within what range should the transfer price be established?
9. Why are market-based transfer prices considered optimal under many circumstances?
10. Why do companies often use prices other than market prices for interdivisional transfers?
11. Division A has no external markets. It produces a product that is used by Division B. Division B cannot purchase this product from any other source. What transfer pricing system would you recommend for the interdivisional sale of the product? Why?
12. "The use of market prices for transfer pricing may lead to dysfunctional decisions by some employees." Why? (*M. Com., Delhi*)
13. Many firms use cost plus negotiated transfer prices even though they do not lead to optimal results for individual products. Why? (*M. Com., Delhi*)
14. What properties should transfer pricing policies have?
15. Under what conditions is a market-based transfer price optimal?
16. "Under the general guidelines for transfer pricing, the minimum transfer price will vary depending on whether the supplying division has idle capacity or not." Do you agree? Explain.
17. What are the objectives of transfer pricing? What are the requisites of a sound transfer pricing system?
18. Discuss the essential guidelines for the success of transfer pricing system.
19. Write a note on transfer pricing in multinational companies.
20. Write explanatory notes on 'Cost-based and market-based transfer prices'. (*M. Com., Delhi* 2005, 2008)

21. What are the objectives of transfer pricing? Under what conditions are market-based prices and negotiated prices optimal? (*M. Com., Delhi*, 2003)
22. What are the advantages and disadvantages of top management's direct intervention in a transfer pricing dispute?
23. What is the general transfer-pricing rule?
24. Explain the effect of import duties, or tariffs, on the transfer-pricing policies of multinational companies.
25. What are some goals of a transfer pricing system in a decentralized organisation?
26. "In setting transfer prices for multinational companies, tax considerations can be the tail that wags the dog." Explain.
27. "Variable-cost transfer prices ensure that we make no dysfunctional decisions". Comment.
28. "Under the general guideline for transfer pricing, the minimum transfer price will vary depending on whether the selling division has idle capacity or not." Do you agree? Explain.
29. What are the objectives of sound transfer pricing system? How do market-based prices and negotiated prices help in achieving these objectives?
30. "Transfer pricing is confined to profit centres." Do you agree? Explain.
31. Why might income tax laws affect the transfer pricing policies of multinational companies?
32. What are the limitations to market-based transfer prices?
33. How does the choice of a transfer price affect the operating profits of both divisions involved in an intracompany transfer?
34. Discuss the advantages and disadvantages of negotiated transfer prices.
35. Examine the opportunity cost approach to transfer pricing.
36. "An action that is optimal for a division may not be optimal for the company as a whole." Explain.
37. What is transfer price? Explain the relevance of market prices, cost-based prices and negotiated prices under transfer pricing policy. (*M.Com., Delhi*, 2015)

SELF-ASSESSMENT QUESTIONS

A. An appropriate transfer price between two divisions of the Stark Company can be determined from the following data.

Fabricating Division	₹
Market price of subassembly	5,000
Variable cost of subassembly	2,000
Excess capacity (in units)	1,000
Assembling Division	
Number of units needed	900

What is the natural bargaining range for the two divisions?

(*a*) Between ₹ 2,000 and ₹ 5,000
(*b*) Between ₹ 5,000 and ₹ 7,000
(c) Any amount less than ₹ 5,000
(*d*) ₹ 5,000 is the only acceptable price.
(e) ₹ 2,000 is the only acceptable price.

B. Ajax Division of Carlyle Corporation produces electric motors, 20% of which are sold to Bradley Division of Carlyle and the remainder to outside customers. Carlyle treats its divisions as profit centres and allows division managers to choose their sources of sale and supply. Corporate policy requires that all interdivisional sales and purchases be recorded at variable cost as a transfer price. Ajax Division's estimated sales and standard cost data for the year ending December 31, 2016, based on the full capacity of 1,00,000 units, are as follows :

	Bradley ₹	***Outsiders*** ₹
Sales	9,00,000	80,00,000
Variable costs	(9,00,000)	(36,00,000)
Fixed costs	(3,00,000)	(12,00,000)
Gross margin	(3,00,000)	32,00,000
Unit sales	20,000	80,000

Ajax has an opportunity to sell the above 20,000 units to an outside customer at a price of ₹ 75 per unit during 2016 on a continuing basis. Bradley can purchase its requirements from an outside supplier at a price of ₹ 85 per unit.

Assuming that Ajax Division desires to maximize its gross margin, should Ajax take on the new customer and drop its sales to Bradley for 2016, and why?

(*a*) No, because the gross margin of the corporation as a whole would decrease by ₹ 2,00,000.

(*b*) Yes, because Ajax Division's gross margin would increase by ₹ 3,00,000.

(*c*) Yes, because Ajax Divisions's gross margin would increase by ₹ 6,00,000.

(*d*) No, because Bradley Division's gross margin would decrease by ₹ 8,00,000.

C. The management of James Corporation has decided to implement a transfer pricing system. James's MIS department is currently negotiating a transfer price for its services with the four producing divisions of the company as well as the marketing department. Charges will be assessed based on number of reports (assume that all reports require the same amount of time and resources to produce). The cost to operate the MIS department at its full capacity of 1,000 reports per year is budgeted at ₹ 45,00,000. The user subunits expect to request 250 reports each this year. The cost of temporary labour and additional facilities used to produce reports beyond capacity is budgeted at ₹ 4,800 per report. James could purchase the same services from an external Information Services firm for ₹ 70,00,000. What amounts should be used as the ceiling and the floor in determining the negotiated transfer price?

(*a*) Floor ₹ 3,600; Ceiling ₹ 5,600

(*b*) Floor ₹ 4,560; Ceiling ₹ 5,600

(*c*) Floor ₹ 4,800; Ceiling ₹ 7,000

(*d*) Floor ₹ 5,700; Ceiling ₹ 8,200.

D. Parkside Inc. has several divisions that operate as decentralized profit centres. Parkside's Entertainment Division manufactures video arcade equipment using the products of two of Parkside's other divisions. The Plastics Division manufactures plastic components, one type that is made exclusively for the Entertainment Division, while other less complex components are sold to outside markets. The products of the Video Cards Division are sold in a competitive market: however, one video card model is also used by the Entertainment Division. The actual costs per unit used by the Entertainment Division are presented below.

	Plastic Components ₹	Video Cards ₹
Direct materials	125	240
Direct labour	235	300
Variable overhead	100	150
Fixed overhead	40	225
Total Cost	500	915

The Plastics Division sells its commercial products at full cost plus a 25 percent markup and believes the proprietary plastic component made for the Entertainment Division would sell for ₹ 625 per unit on the open market. The market price of the video card used by the Entertainment Division is ₹ 1098 per unit.

1. A per-unit transfer price from the Video Cards Division to the Entertainment Division at full cost, ₹ 915 would
   (*a*) allow evaluation of both divisions on a competitive basis.
   (*b*) satisfy the Video Cards Division's profit desire by allowing recovery of opportunity costs.
   (*c*) demotivate the Entertainment Division and cause mediocre performance.
   (*d*) provide no profit incentive for the Video Cards division to control or reduce costs.
   (*e*) encourage the Entertainment Division to purchase video cards from an outside source.
2. Assume that the Entertainment Division is able to purchase a large quantity of video cards from an outside source at ₹ 870 per unit. The Video Cards Division, having excess capacity, agrees to lower its transfer price to ₹ 870 per unit. This action would
   (*a*) optimize the profit goals of the Entertainment Division while subverting the profit goals of Parkside Inc.
   (*b*) allow evaluation of both divisions on the same basis.
   (*c*) subvert the profit goals of the Video Cards Division while optimizing the profit goals of the Entertainment Division.
   (*d*) cause mediocre behaviour in the Video Cards Division as lost opportunity costs increase.
   (*e*) optimize the overall profit goals of Parkside Inc.
3. Assume that the Plastic Division has excess capacity and it has negotiated a transfer price of ₹ 560 per plastic component with the Entertainment Division. This price will
   (*a*) cause the Plastics Division to reduce the number of commercial plastic components it manufactures.
   (*b*) motivate both divisions as estimated profits are shared.
   (*c*) encourage the Entertainment Division to seek an outside source for plastic components.
   (*d*) demotivate the Plastics Division causing mediocre performance.
   (*e*) motivate the Plastic Division to increase the portion of its manufacturing devoted to the Entertainment Division. (*CMA, USA Adapted with permission*)

Answer to Self-Assessment Questions

A (*a*) B (*c*) C (*b*) D 1. (*d*) 2. (*e*) 3. (*b*)

MULTIPLE CHOICE QUESTIONS

Select the correct answer for the following multiple choice questions.

1. Which approach to transfer pricing uses the price at which the product or service transferred could be sold to outside buyers?
   (*a*) Cost price approach (*b*) Negotiated price approach
   (*c*) Market price approach (*d*) None of the above
2. In a decentralised company in which divisions may buy goods from one another, the transfer-pricing system should be designed primarily to
   (*a*) Increase the consolidated value of inventory.
   (*b*) Allow division managers to buy from outsiders.
   (*c*) Minimise the degree of autonomy of division managers.
   (*d*) Aid in the appraisal and motivation of managerial performance.
3. An internal report for a decentralised organisation reports transfers between segments. For this internal report, transfer prices charged for a product with a determinable market price would usually be based on
   (*a*) Cost or market, whichever is lower (*b*) Market price
   (*c*) Historical cost (*d*) Variable cost
4. Given a competitive outside market for identical intermediate goods, what is the best transfer price, assuming all relevant information is readily available?
   (*a*) Average cost of production.
   (*b*) Average cost of production, plus average production department allocated profit.
   (*c*) Market price of the intermediate goods.
   (*d*) Market price of the intermediate goods, less average production department allocated profit.
5. Transfer prices based on actual costs of the selling division as opposed to standard costs.
   (*a*) Are preferred by purchasing division
   (*b*) Often fail to provide the selling division with incentives to control costs.
   (*c*) Often encourage the selling division to control costs.
   (*d*) Often encourage the purchasing division to control costs.
6. The most fundamental responsibility centre affected by the use of market-based transfer prices is a (n)
   (*a*) Production centre (*b*) Investment centre
   (*c*) Cost centre (*d*) Profit centre
7. Transfer pricing should encourage goal congruence and managerial effort. In a decentralized organization, it should also encourage autonomous decision making. Managerial effort is
   (*a*) The desire and the commitment to achieve a specific goal.
   (*b*) The sharing of goals by supervisors and subordinates.
   (*c*) The extent to which individuals have the authority to make decisions.
   (*d*) The extent of the attempt to accomplish a specific goal.

8. A proposed transfer price may be based upon the outlay cost. Outlay cost plus opportunity cost is
   (*a*) The retail price.
   (*b*) The price representing the cash outflows of the supplying division plus the contribution to the supplying division from an outside sale.
   (*c*) The price usually set by an absorption-costing calculation.
   (*d*) The price set by charging for variable costs plus a lump sum or an additional markup, but less than full markup.
9. A proposed transfer price may be a cost-plus price. Variable-cost-plus price is
   (*a*) The price on the open market.
   (*b*) The price representing the cash outflows of the supplying division plus the contribution to the supplying division from an outside sale.
   (*c*) The price usually set by an absorption-costing calculation.
   (*d*) The price set by charging for variable costs plus a lump sum or an additional mark up, but less than full markup.
10. A proposed transfer price may be based upon the full-cost price. Full-cost price is
   (*a*) The price on the open market.
   (*b*) The price representing the cash outflows of the supplying division plus the contribution to the supplying division from an outside sale.
   (*c*) The price usually set by an absorption-costing calculation.
   (*d*) The price set by charging for variable costs plus a lump sum or an additional markup, but less than full markup.
11. A limitation of transfer prices based on actual cost is that they
   (*a*) Charge inefficiencies to the department that is transferring the goods.
   (*b*) Can lead to suboptimal decisions for the company as a whole.
   (*c*) Must be adjusted by some markup.
   (*d*) Lack clarity and administrative convenience.
12. Brent Co. has intracompany service transfers from Division Core, a cost centre, to Division Pro, a profit centre. Under stable economic conditions, which of the following transfer prices is likely to be most conducive to evaluating whether both divisions have met their responsibilities?
   (*a*) Actual cost (*b*) Standard variable cost
   (*c*) Actual cost plus markup (*d*) Negotiated price
13. A large manufacturing company has several autonomous divisions that sell their products in perfectly competitive external markets as well as internally to the other divisions of the company. Top management expects each of its divisional managers to take actions that will maximize the organization's goals as well as their own goals. Top management also promotes a sustained level of management effort of all of its divisional manager. Under these circumstances, for products exchanged between divisions, the transfer price that will generally lead to optimal decisions for the manufacturing company would be a transfer price equal to the
   (*a*) Full cost of the product.
   (*b*) Full cost of the product plus a markup.

(c) Variable cost of the product plus a markup.

(d) Market price of the product.

14. The Eastern division sells goods internally to the Western division of the same company. The quoted external price in industry publications from a supplier near Eastern is ₹ 200 per ton plus transportation. It costs ₹ 20 per Kg. to transport the goods to Western. Eastern's actual market cost per Kg. to buy the direct materials to make the transferred product is ₹ 100. Actual per Kg. direct labour is ₹ 50. Other actual costs of storage and handling are ₹ 40. The company president selects a ₹ 220 transfer price. This is an example of

(a) Market-based transfer pricing (b) Cost-based transfer pricing

(c) Negotiated transfer pricing (d) Cost plus 20% transfer pricing

15. Which of the following is the most significant disadvantage of a cost-based transfer price?

(a) Requires internally developed information.

(b) Imposes market effects on company operations.

(c) Requires externally developed information.

(d) May not promote long-term efficiencies.

16. Which of the following is not true about international transfer prices for a multinational firm?

(a) Allows firms to attempt to minimize worldwide taxes.

(b) Allows the firm to evaluate each division.

(c) Provides each division with a profit-making orientation.

(d) Allows firms to correctly price products in each country in which it operates.

17. In theory, the optimal method for establishing a transfer price is

(a) Flexible budget cost (b) Incremental cost

(c) Budgeted cost with or without a markup (d) Market price

(e) Actual cost with or without a markup

18. The price that one division of a company charges another division for goods or services provided is called the

(a) Market price (b) Transfer price

(c) Outlay price (d) Distress price

19. Which of the following statements regarding transfer pricing is false?

(a) When idle capacity exists, there is no opportunity cost to producing intermediate products for another division.

(b) Market-based transfer prices should be reduced by any costs avoided by selling internally rather than externally.

(c) No contribution margin is generated by the transferring division when variable cost-based transfer prices are used.

(d) The goal of transfer pricing is to provide segment managers with incentive to maximize the profits of their divisions. (CMA, USA, Adapted with permission)

Answer to Multiple Choice Questions

1. (c)	2. (d)	3. (b)	4. (c)	5. (b)
6. (d)	7. (d)	8. (b)	9. (d)	10. (c)
11. (b)	12. (b)	13. (d)	14. (a)	15. (d)
16. (d)	17. (d)	18. (b)	19. (d)	

PROBLEMS

1. HCL's Computer Parts has two decentralized divisions. Hardware and Pre-Fab. Pre-Fab has always purchased certain units from Hardware at ₹ 2300 per unit. Because Hardware plans to raise the price to ₹ 2600 per unit, Pre-Fab desires to purchase these units from outside suppliers for ₹ 2300 per unit. Hardware's costs follow: variable costs per unit, ₹ 2,000; annual fixed costs, ₹ 3,00,000. Annual production of these units for Pre-Fab is 1,500 units.

   If Pre-Fab buys from an outside supplier, the facilities Hardware uses to manufacture these units would remain idle. What would be the result if HCL's Computer Parts' management enforces a transfer price of ₹ 2600 per unit between Hardware and Pre-Fab?

   Answers:

   It would cost the company ₹ 4,50,000 if Pre-Fab purchased units from the outside supplier for ₹ 2300 each. If management enforced ₹ 2600 transfer price, then the overall company profits would not be affected by the transfer price increase.

2. The Hillman Enterprises has two divisions, A and B. Division A produces a computer circuit that is used in the finished product of Division B. The cost of producing the circuit are variable costs of ₹ 4,000 per circuit and fixed costs of ₹ 1,000 per circuit. The part is sold in the highly competitive computer market for ₹ 7,000 per circuit.

   Uptil now Division B bought 60% of the output of Division A at a negotiated price of ₹ 6,500 per circuit. But because of overemphasis on divisional welfare rather than company welfare, a new transfer pricing method must be developed. The suggestion was to add 35% to the total cost of the circuit when transferring to Division B. Another suggestion was to use the variable costs of ₹ 4,000 per circuit in arriving at a transfer price.

   You are required, using the above information and suggestions to determine the gross profit per finished unit for Division B according to the five principal transfer pricing methods. Pertinent data of Division B, in addition to the transfer price of the circuit, there are additional processing and marketing costs of ₹ 10,000 per unit. The selling price of the finished product of Division B is ₹ 20,000 per unit.

3. The Domino Company has two decentralized divisions, A and B. Division A has always purchased certain units from Division B at ₹ 7,500 per unit. Because Division B plans to raise the price to ₹ 10,000 per unit, Division A desires to purchase these units from outside suppliers for ₹ 7,500 per unit. Division B's costs follow:

	₹
Division B's variable costs per unit	7,000
Division B's annual fixed costs	15,00,000
Division A's purchase	1,000 units

   If Division A buys from an outside supplier, the facilities Division B uses to manufacture these units will remain idle. Would it be more profitable for the company to enforce the ₹ 10,000 transfer price than to allow Division A to buy from outside suppliers at ₹ 7,500 per unit.

   Answers:

   It would be profitable for the company to enforce ₹ 10,000 transfer price.

4. The shuttle division of the Zenith Company produces circuit boards which are sold to the transistor radio division of the company, as well as to outside buyers. The income statement (in contribution format) for the past year for the shuttle division is given below.

	To the Transistor Radio Division ₹	To Outside Buyers ₹
Sales:		
20,000 units at ₹ 300	60,00,000	
30,000 units at ₹ 400		1,20,00,000
Variable expenses:		
₹ 100	20,00,000	
₹ 200		60,00,000
Contribution margin	40,00,000	60,00,000
Fixed costs	15,00,000	30,00,000
Net income	25,00,000	30,00,000

An outside supplier has just offered the manager of the transistor radio division to supply the circuit boards at ₹ 175 each. The manager of the shuttle division would not meet this price, arguing that it costs him ₹ 175 to manufacture and sell each unit of a circuit board. Assume that no additional sales can be made to outside buyers. Answer the following:

(*i*) How did the shuttle division come up with the ₹ 175 unit cost figure?

(*ii*) Is the shuttle division required to meet the outside price of ₹ 175 for transistor radio sales?

(*iii*) Would you meet the ₹ 175 outside price if you were the manager of the shuttle division?

Answers:

(*ii*) No.

(*iii*) Shuttle Division should sell at ₹ 175 as it will help in recovering the fixed costs of ₹ 15,00,000.

5. A company fixes the inter-divisional transfer prices for its products on the basis of cost plus an estimated return on investment in its divisions. The relevant portion of the budget for the Division A for the year 2016-17 is given below:

Fixed assets	₹ 5,00,000
Current assets (other than debtors)	3,00,000
Debtors	2,00,000
Annual fixed cost of the division	8,00,000
Variable cost per unit of product	10
Budgeted volume of production per year (units)	4,00,000
Desired return on investment	28%

You are required to determine the transfer price for the Division A.

Answers:

Transfer price ₹ 12.70.

6. The A Division of Samtel Industries manufactures component R47, which it transfers to the B Division at 200% of variable costs. The variable cost of R47 is ₹ 140 per unit. Vikas. the management accountant of the A Division, calls Sonal, his assistant, into his office. Vikas

says, "I am not sure about the fixed- and variable-cost distinctions you are making. I think the variable cost is higher than ₹ 140 per unit."

Sonal knows that showing higher variable costs will increase the A Division's profits and lead to higher bonuses for the division employees. However, Sonal is uncomfortable about making any changes because he has used the same method to classify costs as either variable or fixed over the last few years. Nevertheless, Sonal recognizes that fixed- and variable-cost distinctions are not always clear-cut.

(*i*) Calculate A Division's contribution margin from transferring 10,000 units of R47 (*a*) if variable cost is ₹ 140 per unit, and (*b*) if variable cost is ₹ 160 per unit.

(*ii*) Evaluate whether Vikas's suggestion to Sonal regarding variable costs is ethical. Would it be ethical for Sonal to revise the variable cost per unit? What steps should Sonal take to resolve this situation?

Answers:

(*i*)

	VC (₹ 140)	VC(₹ 160)
Contribution margin (₹)	14,00,000	16,00,000

(*ii*) Sonal should raise the mattter with Vikas's superior, if there is continued pressure to increase the variable cost.

7. The components division produces a part that is used by the Goods Division. The cost of manufacturing the part is given below:

	₹
Direct materials	10
Direct labour	2
Variable overhead	3
Fixed overhead	5
Total cost	20

Fixed overhead is based on a practical volume at 2,00,000 parts

Other costs incurred by the Components Division are as follows:

	₹
Fixed selling and administrative	5,00,000
Variable Selling	₹ 1/unit

The part usually sells for between ₹ 28 and ₹ 30 in the external market. Currently, the Components Division is selling it to external customers for ₹ 29. The division is capable of producing 200,000 units of the part per year; however, because of a weak economy, only 150,000 parts are expected to be sold during the coming year. The variable selling expenses are avoidable if the part is sold internally.

The Goods division has been buying the same part from an external supplier for ₹ 28. It expects to use 50,000 units of the part during the coming year. The manager of the Goods Division has offered to buy 50,000 units from the Components Division for ₹ 18 per unit.

Required:

(*a*) Determine the minimum transfer price that the Components Division would accept.

(*b*) Determine the maximum transfer price that the manager of the goods division would pay.

(*c*) Should an internal transfer take place? Why? If you were the manager of the components Division, would you sell the 50,000 components for ₹ 18 each? Explain.

(*d*) Suppose that the average operating assets of the Components Division total ₹ 100 lakhs, Compute the ROI for the coming year, assuming that the 50,000 units are transferred to the Goods Division for ₹ 21 each. (*M. Com., Delhi*, 2014)

Answers:

(*a*) ₹ 15

(*b*) ₹ 28

(*c*) Yes, internal transfer will take place because Components Division would earn additional ₹ 1,50,000 profit (₹ 3 × 50,000). The total joint benefit is ₹ 6,50,000 (₹ 13 × 50,000).

(*d*) ROI 7.5%.

8. Green World company is a nursery products firm. It has three divisions that grow and sell plants: Western Division, Southern Division and Northern Division. Recently, the Southern Division of the company acquired a plastics factory that manufactures green plastic pots. These pots can be sold both externally and internally. Company policy permits each manager to decide whether to buy or sell internally. Each divisional manager is evaluated on the basis of return on investment.

The Western Division had bought its plastic pots in lots of 100 from a variety of vendors. The average price paid was ₹ 750 per box of 100 pots. However, the acquisition made Rohan, manager of the Western Division, wonder whether or not a more favourable price could be arranged. He decided to approach John Mathew, manager of the Southern Division, to see if he wanted to offer a better price for an internal transfer. Rohan suggested a transfer of 3,500 boxes at ₹ 700 per box.

John Mathew gathered the following information regarding the cost of a box of 100 pots:

	₹
Direct materials	350
Direct labour	80
Variable overhead	100
Fixed overhead	100
(based on ₹ 20,00,000/20,000 boxes)	
Total unit cost	630
Selling price	750
Production capacity	20,000 boxes.

Required:

(*i*) Suppose that the plastics factory is producing at capacity and can sell all that it produces to outside customers. How should John Mathew respond to Rohan's request for a lower transfer price?

(*ii*) Now Assume that the plastics factory is currently selling 16,000 boxes. What are the minimum and maximum transfer prices? Should John Mathew consider the transfer at ₹ 700 per box?

(*iii*) Suppose that Green World's policy is that all transfer prices be set at full cost plus 20 percent. Would the transfer take place? Why? or why not? (*M. Com. Delhi*, 2002)

Answers:

(*i*) John Mathew should not reduce the price charged to Rohan if he can sell all he produces.

(*ii*) Minimum transfer price ₹ 530

Maximum transfer price ₹ 750.

(*iii*) Transfer price ₹ 756. No, transfer will not take place.

9. The Parts Division supplies Part 678 to the Medical Products Division, which uses it in manufacturing a heart monitor. The Medical Products Division is currently operating below capacity (by 10,000 units) while the Parts Division is operating at capacity. Part 678 sells externally for ₹ 5,000. The costs of producing the heart monitor follows:

	(₹)
Part 678	5,000
Direct materials	10,000
Direct labour	2,000
Variable overhead	3,000
Fixed overhead	4,000
Total unit cost	24,000

The Medical Products Division has received an order for 1,000 heart monitors from a wholesaler, with an offering price of ₹ 23,000. Since company policy prohibits selling any product below full cost, the divisional manager requested a price concession from the Parts Division. When that manager refused the request, the manager of the Medical Products Division filed an appeal with higher-level management, arguing that a transfer price of full cost should be used so that pricing decisions in his division would not be distorted.

Required:

(*i*) Assume that the full cost of Part 678 is ₹ 3,000. Will the firm as a whole benefit if the part is transferred at ₹ 3,000. Should top management intervene?

(*ii*) Is anything wrong with the company policy that a division's selling price cannot be below full cost?

(*iii*) Compute the minimum and maximum transfer prices. Is an internal transfer indicated? If a transfer were to take place, what should the transfer price be?

Answers:

(*i*) Yes, the firm as a whole will benefit. The parts division will lose ₹ 2,000 (₹ 5,000 – 3,000) per unit but the Medical division will gain ₹ 5,000 per unit.

(*ii*) The company may not make profit when a division is operating below capacity

(*iii*) Minimum ₹ 5,000; Maximum ₹ 5,000. Transfer price should be ₹ 5,000.

10. The Film Division of Photolife, produces 35 mm film that can be sold externally or internally to Photolife's School Photography Division. Sales and cost data per roll of 35 mm film follow:

Unit selling price	₹ 295
Unit variable cost	140
Unit product fixed cost*	120
Practical capacity	5,00,000 units

Note: Unit product fixed costs has been calculated as follows = ₹ 6,00,00,000/5,00,000 units

During the coming year, the Film Division expects to sell 3,50,000 rolls of this film. The School Photography division currently plans to buy 1,50,000 rolls of the film on the outside market for ₹ 295 each. Anita Mathur, manager of the Film Division, has approached Kajol, manager of the School Photography Division, and offered to sell the 1,50,000 rolls for ₹ 294 each. Anita explained to Kajol that she can avoid selling costs of ₹ 2 per film roll and that she would split the savings by offering a Re. 1 discount on the usual price.

Required:

(*i*) What is the minimum transfer price that the Film Division would be willing to accept? What is the maximum transfer price that the School Photography division would be willing to pay? Should an internal transfer take place? What would be the benefit (or loss) to the firm as a whole if the internal transfer takes place?

(*ii*) Suppose Kajol knows that the Film Division has idle capacity. Do you think that she would agree to the transfer price of ₹ 294. Suppose she counters with an offer to pay ₹ 285. If you were Anita Mathur, would you be interested in this price? Explain with supporting computations.

(*iii*) Suppose that Photolife's policy is that all internal transfers take place at full manufacturing cost. What would the transfer price be? Would the transfer take place?

(*M. Com., Delhi University,* 2009)

Answers:

(*i*) Minimum Price ₹ 138, Maximum price ₹ 295, Yes, the transfer should take place.

(*ii*) Kajol may negotiate for a lower price.

(*iii*) Full cost transfer price ₹ 258. Yes, the transfer will take place.

11. ITC Company has a number of divisions including a furniture division and a motel division. The Motel Division owns and operates a line of budget motels located along major highways. Each year, the Motel Division purchases furniture for the motel rooms. Currently, it purchases a basic dresser from an outside supplier for ₹ 42. Raghuraj, manager of the Furniture Division, has approached George Mathew, manager of the Motel Division, about selling dressers to the Motel Division. Raghuraj has researched the dresser costs and determined the following costs:

Direct materials	₹ 8
Direct labour	4
Variable overhead	3
Fixed overhead	12
Total manufacturing cost	₹ 27

Currently, the Furniture Division has capacity to produce 75,000 dressers but is producing 60,000. The Motel Division needs 10,000 dressers per year.

Required:

(*i*) What is the maximum transfer price? The minimum transfer price? Should the transfer occur?

(*ii*) Suppose that Raghuraj and George Mathew agree on a transfer price of ₹ 30. What is the benefit to each division? What is the benefit to the company as a whole?

(*iii*) Suppose that the Furniture Division were operating at capacity. What would be the maximum transfer price? The minimum transfer price? Should the transfer take place in this case? Why or why not? (*M. Com., Delhi University,* 2012)

Answers:

(*i*) Maximum transfer price ₹ 42 Minimum transfer price ₹ 15.

(*ii*) Benefit to furniture division ₹ 1,50,000.
Benefit to Motel division ₹ 1,20,000

(*iii*) Maximum transfer price ₹ 42
Minimum transfer price ₹ 42.

It does not matter whether or not the transfer takes place.

12. Bajaj Company's Small Motor Division produces a variety of small motors that are used in various household and office appliances. Bajaj's Kitchen Products Division manufactures appliances such as blenders, juicers, coffee grinders, and so on. The most frequently used motor is Model A28, which can be purchased from a number of outside suppliers for ₹ 2300 each. The manager of the Kitchen Products Division has approached the manager of the Small Motor Division and offered to buy 1,50,000 Model A28 small motors. The Small Motor Division currently is producing at capacity and produces and sells 2,00,000 Model A28 motors to outside customers for ₹ 2,300 each.

Required:

(*i*) What is the minimum transfer price for the Small Motor Division? What is the maximum transfer price for the Kitchen Products Division? Is it important that transfers take place internally? If transfers do take place, what should the transfer price be?

(*ii*) Now assume that the Small Motor Division incurs selling costs of ₹ 200 per motor that could be avoided if the motors are sold internally. Identify the minimum transfer price for the Small Motor Division and the maximum transfer price for the Kitchen Products Division. Should internal transfers take place? If so, what is the benefit to the firm as a whole?

(*iii*) Suppose you are the manager of the Small Motor Division. Selling costs of ₹ 200 per motor are avoidable if they are sold internally. Would you accept an offer of ₹ 2200 from the manager of the other division? How much better off (or worse off) would your division be if this price is accepted?

Answers:

(*i*) Minimum and Maximum transfer price ₹ 2300.

(*ii*) Minimum transfer price ₹ 2100
Maximum transfer price ₹ 2300

(*iii*) Offer should be accepted.

13. Pfizer Industries is a vertically integrated firm with several divisions that operate as decentralized profit centres. Pfizer System Division manufactures scientific instruments and uses the products of two other divisions. The Board Division manufactures printed circuit boards (PCBs). One PCB model is made exclusively for the Systems Division using proprietary designs, while less complex models are sold in outside markets. The products of the Transistor Division are sold in a well-developed competitive market: however, one transistor model is also used by the System buying Division. The costs per unit of the products used by the System Division follow:

	PCB	***Transistor***
		₹
Direct material	2,500	800
Direct labour	4,500	1,000
Variable overhead	2,000	500
Fixed overhead	800	750
Total cost	9,800	3,050

The Board Division sells its commercial product at full cost plus a 25 percent markup and believes the proprietary board made for the Systems Division would sell for ₹ 12,250 per unit on the open market. The market price of the transistor used by the Systems Division is ₹ 3,700 per unit.

Required :

(*i*) What is the minimum transfer price for the Transistor Division? What is the maximum transfer price of the transistor for the System Division?

(*ii*) Assume the Systems Division is able to purchase a large quantity of transistors from an outside source at ₹ 2,900 per unit Further assume that the Transistor Division has excess capacity. Can the Transistor Division meet this price?

(*iii*) The Board Division and Systems Divisions have negotiated a transfer price of ₹ 11,000 per printed circuit board. Discuss the impact this transfer price will have on each division (*CMA, USA, Adapted with permission*), (*M. Com., Delhi,* 2007)

Answers:

(*i*) Minimum transfer price ₹ 3,700.

Maximum transfer price ₹ 3,700.

(*ii*) Yes, because the variable cost of the transistor is ₹ 2,300.

(*iii*) Negotiated price of ₹ 11,000 will give Board Division a profit of ₹ 1,200 per board and will reduce cost of Systems Division by ₹ 1,250.

14. Haryana Dairy Company has two divisions: the Milk Division and the Dairy Products Division. Divisional managers are evaluated on the basis of return on investment. The Milk Division has the capability to produce 5,00,000 litres of milk per day. The Dairy Products Division uses milk to produce ice cream, cheese, and cottage cheese. The following data are available for the Milk Division:

	₹
Selling price per litre	22.5
Variable production cost	5.0
Fixed production cost*	10.00

*Based on 5,00,000 litres of output

The Dairy Products Division uses 6,00,000 litres of milk per day when it is operating at capacity.

Required:

(Unless otherwise indicated, assume that the requirements are independent of each other.)

(*i*) Assume that the Milk division can sell all that it produces. The Dairy Products Division is operating at 90 percent of capacity. It can buy all the milk that it needs for ₹ 23.5 per litre from outside suppliers. What are the minimum and maximum transfer prices? What transfer price would you recommend? How many litres of milk will the Dairy Products Division buy internally, assuming that it is operating at 90 percent of capacity?

(*ii*) Refer to Requirement 1. How would your answers differ if the Milk Division can avoid distribution costs of ₹ 1.5 per litre if the milk is sold internally?

(*iii*) The manager of the Milk Division realizes that excess capacity will exist for the next six months of the current year. He is reluctant to sell any of the milk cows to reduce production because he expects the market to rebound in the coming year. Accordingly, the cows will continue to be milked, creating excess production of 40,000 litres. Unless a market for the excess milk can be found, it will simply be dumped. Discouraged with the possibility of finding any new outside customers, the manager of the Milk Division approaches the manager of the Dairy Products Division to see if a deal for internal sales can be arranged. The Dairy Products Division has been buying all of its milk from outside suppliers at ₹ 20 per litre. Assume that production of milk is spread evenly over the year and that milk sold externally is sold for the normal price. Under these conditions, identify the minimum and maximum transfer prices. Assume that the managers split the difference between the two prices. How many litres will be transferred internally? By how much will the profits of the firm and each division increase?

(*iv*) Refer to Requirement (*iii*). Now assume that the Milk Division has an offer to sell the 40,000 litres of extra milk to a government agency for conversion into powdered milk. The offering price is ₹ 10 per litre. How does this change your answers to Requirement (*iii*)?

Answers:

(*i*) Minimum price ₹ 22.5; Maximum price ₹ 23.5.

(*ii*) The transfer price will be between ₹ 21 and ₹ 23.5.

(*iii*) Minimum transfer price ₹ 5; Maximum transfer price ₹ 20. 40,000 litres of milk will be transferred internally.

(*iv*) Minimum ₹ 10; Maximum ₹ 20. The price will be ₹ 15 for the excess 40,000 litres.

15. Bearings Ltd. makes three products, A, B and C in Divisions A, B and C respectively. The following information is given:

	A	***B***	***C***	
Direct Materials (excluding material A for Divisions B and C)	4	15	20	₹/u
Direct Labour	2	3	4	₹/u
Variable overhead	1	1	1	₹/u
Selling price to outside customers	15	40	50	₹/u
Existing Capacity	5,000	2,500	2,500	(No. of units)
Maximum External demand	3,750	5,000	4,000	(No. of units)
Additional fixed costs that would be incurred to install additional capacity (₹)	24,000	6,000	18,700	
Maximum Additional units that can be produced by additional capacity (units)	5,000	1,250	2,250	

B and C need material A as their input. Material A is available outside at ₹ 15 per unit. Division A supplies the material free from defects. Each unit of B and C requires one unit of A as the input material.

If B purchases from outside, it has to pay ₹ 15 per unit. If B purchases from A, it has to incur in addition to the transfer price, ₹ 2 per unit as variable cost to modify it.

B has sufficient idle capacity to inspect its inputs without additional costs.

If C gets material from A, it can use it directly, but if it gets material from outside, which is at ₹ 15, it has to do one of the following:

(*i*) Inspect it at its own shop floor at ₹ 3 per unit

Or

(*ii*) Get the supplier to supply inspected products and pay the supplier ₹ 2 p.u. as inspection charges.

Or

(*iii*) A has enough idle labour, which it can lend to C to inspect at ₹ 1 p.u. even though C purchases from outside.

A has to fix a uniform transfer price for both B and C. The transfer price will not be known to outsiders and is at the discretion of the Divisional Managers.

What is the best strategy for each division and the company as a whole?

Answers:

Individual strategy is the company's best strategy.

16. Four products P, Q R and S are produced by profit centre Division A. Each product is sold in the external market also. Data for the period are as follows:

	P	*Q*	*R*	*S*
Market price per unit (₹)	70	69	56	46
Variable cost of production per unit (₹)	66	59	36	37
Labour hours per unit	3	2	2	3
Specific fixed costs (₹) per 10,000 units of product	2,500	12,600	15,000	18,000

Product S can be tranferred to Division B but the maximum quantity that might be required for transfer is 20,000 units of S. The specific fixed costs given above are avoidable if a product is not made. They are incurred for every 10,000 units.

The maximum sales (units) in the external market are:

P	30,000
Q	31,000
R	28,000
P	18,000

Division *B* can purchase the same product at a slightly cheaper price of ₹ 45 unit instead of receiving transfers of product *S* from division *A* without any extra transport/inspection costs. *B* can also take partial supplies from *A*.

(i) What is A's optimal product mix and the corresponding contribution net of specific fixed costs?

(ii) How many units should *A* transfer to *B* and at what price?

(iii) Is it in the company's interest to transfer 20,000 units of *S* to *B*?

(*CA, Final, Nov.* 2015)

Answers:

(*i*) Optimal product mixunits P 7333.33 units, Q 30,000 units, R 28,000 units, S 18,000 units Total profit ₹ 9,30,033,32

(*ii*) 7,333.33 units

(*iii*). Netgain from transfer of 20,000 units of S to B, ₹ 11.66.68. Since net gain is negligible, the company should consider other factors also.

17. Phoenix Co., a cellular communication company, has multiple divisions. Each division's managements compensated based on the division's operating income. Division A currently purchases callular equipment from outside markets and uses it to produce communication systems. Division B produces similar cellular equipment that it sells to outside customers but not to division A at this time. Division A's manager approaches division B's manager with a proposal to buy the equipment form division B. If it produces the cellular equipment that division A desires, B would incur variable manufacturing costs of ₹60 per unit.

Relevant Information about Division B

Sells 50,000 units of equipment to outside customers at ₹130 per unit.

Operating capacity is currently 80 percent, the division can perform at 100 percent.

Variable manufacturing costs are ₹ 70 per unit.

Variable marketing costs are ₹ 8 per unit.

Fixed manufacturing costs are ₹ 580,000.

Income per Unint for Division A (assuming parts purchased outside, not from division B)

Sales revenue		₹ 320
Manufacturing costs		
Cellular equipment	80	
Other materials	10	
Fixed costs	40	
Total manufacturing costs		130
		190
Gross margin		
Marketing costs		
Variable	35	
Fixed	15	
Total marketing costs		50
Operating income		₹ 140

Required:

1. Division A wants to buy 25,000 units from division B at ₹ 75 per unit. Should division B accept or reject the proposal? How would your answer differ if (a) Division A requires all 25,000 units in the order to be shipped by the same supplier, or (b) Division A would accept partial shipment form Division B?
2. What range will the managers of division A and B agree is the best price for each division?

Answers:

1. Division B manager should reject the proposal because it reduces division B's operating income by ₹ 2,75,000. The decision of division B not to sell inside is best for the firm as a whole.
2. Transfer price range ₹ 60 to ₹ 80.

CASES

1. Phillips India manufactures and sells lighting products. Phillips's sales and marketing divisions are organized along product lines-wall sconces, recessed lights, track lights, and so on. The Manufacturing Division produces lighting products for all the sales and marketing divisions

During the planning process, each sales and marketing division specifies the quantity of each style of light to be manufactured. Senior management then assigns the task of manufacturing the lights to different plants in the Manufacturing Division. Because manufacturing capacity is limited, some of the production is also outsourced. Senior management determines the manufacturing schedule on the basis of detailed studies that have been done to measure the time and cost of manufacturing different types of lighting products. Manufacturing managers are evaluated based on achieving target output within budgeted costs.

Required:

(*i*) Are the manufacturing plants in the Manufacturing Division cost centres or profit centres? Explain.

(*ii*) Phillips India is considering decentralizing its marketing and manufacturing decisions by letting manufacturing and marketing managers directly negotiate the prices for manufacturing various products.

(*a*) How should Phillips evaluate manufacturing plant managers under this proposal?

(*b*) Would you recommend that Phillips India decentralize its marketing and manufacturing decisions? Explain.

2. The XYZ Company manufactures and sells 10,000 boom boxes per year. The Assembly Division assembles the boom boxes. It buys the cassette deck for the boom box from the Cassette Deck Division. The Cassette Deck Division can manufacture at most 12,000 cassette decks. The demand for cassette decks is strong. Any cassette deck not sold to the Assembly Division can be sold in the outside market for ₹ 350 per unit. The Cassette Deck Divisioin currently sells 10,000 cassette decks to the Assembly Division and 2,000 cassette decks in the outside market. The incremental cost of manufacturing the cassette deck is ₹ 250 per unit.

A crucial component for producing high-quality cassette decks is the (cassette) head mechanism. The Cassette Deck Division manufactures the head mechanism for its cassette decks. Many outside suppliers have offered to supply cassette decks to XYZ Company. To ensure quality, XYZ Company requires that any outside supplier wanting to supply cassette decks to XYZ Company must purchase the head mechanism from the Cassette Deck Division. The Cassette Deck Division will charge ₹ 180 per unit for the head mechanism. The incremental cost of manufacturing the head mechanism is ₹ 120 per unit out of the total incremental costs of ₹ 250 per unit to manufacture the cassette deck. The Cassette Deck Division has unused capacity for manufacturing the head mechanism. That is, even if the Cassette Deck Division manufactures the head mechanism for outside suppliers, it will still be able to manufacture 12,000 cassette decks for sale in the outside market at ₹ 350 per unit.

An outside supplier is currently negotiating to supply 10,000 cassette decks to the Assembly Division for a price in the range of ₹ 370 to ₹ 430. If the outside supplier gets the business, it will buy the head mechanism from the Cassette Deck Division for ₹ 180 per unit.

Required:

Consider each question independently.

I. From the standpoint of XYZ Company as a whole, should the Assembly Divsion accept outside vendor's offer (*a*) at a price of ₹ 370 per cassette deck? (*b*) at a price of ₹ 430 per cassette deck? Show your computations.

II. What transfer price for cassette decks will result in the Cassette Deck Division and the Assembly Division taking actions that are optimal for XYZ Company as a whole? Explain your answer. *(M. Com., Delhi, 2014)*

Answers:

I. (*a*) At a price of ₹ 370, XYZ Company should outsource to the outside vender.

(*b*) At a price of ₹ 430, XYZ Company should reject the outside supplier's offer.

II. Transfer price at ₹ 410.

3. Supreme Industries Ltd. started as a single plant that produced the major components of electric motors, the company's main product, and then assembled them. Supreme later expanded by developing outside markets for some of the components used in its motors.

Eventually, Supreme reorganized into four manufacturing divisions: Bearing, Casing, Switch, and Motor. Each of the four manufacturing divisions operates as an autonomous unit, and divisional performance is the basis for year-ended bonuses.

Supreme's transfer pricing policy permits the manufacturing divisions to sell externally to outside customers as well as internally to the other divisions. The price for goods transferred between divisions is to be negotiated between the buying and selling divisions without any interference from top management.

Supreme's profits have dropped for the current year even though sales have increased, and the drop in profits can be traced almost entirely to the Motor Division. Ashok, chief financial officer, has determined that the Motor Division has purchased switches for its motors from an outside supplier during the current year rather than buying them from the Switch Division. The Switch Division is at capacity and has refused to sell the switches to the Motor Division because it can sell them to outside customers at a price higher than the actual full (absorption) manufacturing cost that has always been negotiated in the past with the Motor Division. When the Motor Division refused to meet the price the Switch Division was receiving from its outside buyer, the Motor Division had to purchase the switches from an outside supplier at an even higher price.

Ashok is reviewing Supreme's transfer pricing policy because he believes that suboptimization has occurred. While the Switch Division made the correct decision to maximize its divisional profit by not transferring the switches at actual full manufacturing cost, this decision was not necessarily in the best interest of the company. The Motor Division paid more for the switches than the selling price the Switch Division charged its outside customers. The Motor Division has always been Supreme's largest division and has tended to dominate the smaller divisions. Ashok has learned that the Casing and Bearing Divisions are also resisting the Motor Division's desires to continue using actual full manufacturing cost as the negotiated price.

Ashok has requested that the corporate accounting department study alternative transfer pricing methods that would promote overall goal congruence, motivate divisional management performance, and optimize overall company performance. Three of the transfer pricing methods being considered follow. If one of these methods is selected, it will be applied uniformly across all divisions:

(*a*) Standard full manufacturing costs plus markup.

(*b*) Market selling price of the products being transferred.

(*c*) Outlay (out-of-pocket) costs incurred to the point of transfer plus opportunity cost per unit.

Required:

(*i*) (*a*) Discuss both the positive and negative behavioural implications that can arise from employing a negotiated transfer price system for goods that are exchanged between divisions.

(*b*) Explain the behavioural problems that can arise from using actual full (absorption) manufacturing costs as a transfer price.

(*ii*) Discuss the behavioural problems that could arise if Supreme Industries decides to change from its current policy covering the transfer of goods between divisions to a revised transfer pricing policy that would apply uniformily to all divisions.

(*iii*) Discuss the likely behaviour of both 'buying' and 'selling' divisional managers for each of the three transfer pricing methods being considered by Supreme Industries.

(*a*) Standard full manufacturing costs plus markup.

(*b*) Market selling price of the products being transferred.

(*c*) Outlay (out-of-pocket) costs incurred to the point of transfer plus opportunity cost per unit. *(CMA, USA, adapted with permission)*

4. ABC Company consists of three divisions that formerly were three independent manufacturing companies. Bombay Automobiles and Calcutta Motors merged in 2015, and the merged company acquired Ashok Leyland in 2016. The name of the Company was subsequently changed to ABC Company and each company became a separate division retaining the name of its former company.

The three divisions have operated as if they were still independent companies. Each division has its own sales force and production facilities. Each division management is responsible for sales, cost of operations, acquisition and financing of divisional assets, working capital management. The corporate management of ABC evaluates the performance of the divisions and division managers on the basis of return on investment.

Ashok Leyland Division has just been awarded a contract for a product that uses a component manufactured by the Calcutta Division, as well as by outside suppliers. ABC used a cost figure of ₹ 3,800 for the component manufactured by Calcutta in preparing its bid for the new product. This cost figure was supplied by Calcutta Division in response to Ashok Division's request for the average variable cost of the component; it represents the standard variable manufacturing cost and variable selling and distribution expenses.

Calcutta Division has an active sales force that is continually soliciting new prospects. Calcutta's regular selling price for the component Ashok Division needs for the new product is ₹ 6,500. Sales of this component are expected to increase. However, the Calcutta management has indicated that it could supply Ashok Division with the required quantities of the component at the regular selling price less variable selling and distribution expenses. Ashok Division's management has responded by offering to pay standard variable manufacturing cost plus 20 percent.

The two divisions have been unable to agree on a transfer price. Corporate management has never established a transfer-pricing policy because interdivisional transactions have never occurred. As a compromise, the corporate vice president of finance suggested a price equal to the standard full manufacturing cost (*i.e.* no selling and distribution expenses) plus a 15 percent markup. This price has also been rejected by the two division managers because each considered it grossly unfair.

The unit cost structure for the Calcutta Division's component and the three suggested prices are shown below.

	₹
Standard variable manufacturing cost	3,200
Standard fixed manufacturing cost	1,200
Variable selling and distribution expenses	600
	5,000
Regular selling price less variable selling and distribution expenses (₹ 6,500 – ₹ 6,00)..	5,900
Standard full manufacturing cost plus 15% (₹ 4,400 × 1.15)..............	5,060
Variable manufacturing cost plus 20% (₹ 3,200 × 1.20)......................	3,840

Required:

(*a*) What should be the attitude of the Calcutta Division's management toward the three proposed prices?

(*b*) Is the negotiation of a price between the Ashok Division and Calcutta Division a satisfactory method of solving the transfer pricing problem? Explain your answer.

(*c*) Should the corporate management of ABC become involved in this transfer price controversy? Explain your answer.

(*CMA, USA, Adapated with permission, M. Com., Delhi,* 2004)

5. Hindustan Lever Ltd. (HLL), manufactures a line of men's perfumes and after-shave lotions. The manufacturing process is basically a series of mixing operations with the addition of certain aromatic and colouring ingredients. The finished product is packaged in a company-produced glass bottle and packed in cases containing six bottles.

HLL feels that the sale of its product is heavily influenced by the appearance and appeal of the bottle and has, therefore, devoted considerable managerial effort to the bottle production process. This has resulted in the development of certain unique bottle production processes in which management takes considerable pride.

The two areas (*i.e.* perfume production and bottle manufacture) have evolved over the years in an almost independent manner. In fact, a rivalry has developed between management personnel as to which division is more important to HLL. This attitude is probably intensified because the bottle manufacturing plant was purchased intact 10 years ago and no real interchange of management personnel or ideas (except at the top corporate level) has taken place.

Since the acquisition, all bottle production has been absorbed by the perfume manufacturing plant. Each area is considered a separate profit centre and evaluated as such. As the new corporate controller, you are responsible for the definition of a proper transfer value to use in crediting the bottle production profit centre and in debiting the packaging profit centre.

At your request, the bottle division general manager has asked certain other bottle manufacturers to quote a price for the quantity and sizes (other suppliers) demanded by the perfume division. These competitive prices are:

Volume (Equivalent Cases)*	*Total Price (₹ in lakhs)*	*Price per Case (₹)*
20 lakhs	40	200
40 lakhs	70	175
60 lakhs	100	167

* An "equivalent case" represents six bottles each.

A cost analysis of the internal bottle plant indicates that they can produce bottles at these costs:

Volume (Equivalent Cases)	*Total Price (₹ in lakhs)*	*Price per Case (₹)*
20 lakhs	32	160
40 lakhs	52	130
60 lakhs	72	120

(Your cost analysts point out that these costs represent fixed costs of ₹ 12 lakhs and variable costs of ₹ 10 per equivalent case.)

These figures have given rise to considerable corporate discussion as to the proper value to use in the transfer of bottles to the perfume division. This interest is heightened because a significant portion of a division manager's income is an incentive bonus based on profit centre results.

The perfume production division has the following costs in addition to the bottle costs:

Volume (Cases)	*Total Cost (₹ in lakhs)*	*Cost per Case (₹)*
20 lakhs	164	820
40 lakhs	324	810
60 lakhs	484	807

After considerable analysis, the marketing research department has furnished you with the following price-demand relationship for the finished product:

Sales Volume (Cases)	*Total Revenue (₹ in lakhs)*	*Price per Case (₹)*
20 lakhs	250	1,250
40 lakhs	456	1,140
60 lakhs	639	1,065

(*i*) The HLL has used market price transfer prices in the past. Using the current market prices and costs, and assuming a volume of 60 lakhs cases, calculate the income for

(*a*) The bottle division

(*b*) The perfume division

(*c*) The company

(*ii*) Is this production and sales level the most profitable volume for

(*a*) The bottle division?

(*b*) The perfume division

(*c*) The company

Explain your answer.

(*iii*) HLL uses the profit centre concept for divisional operation.

(*a*) What conditions should exist for a profit centre to be established?

(*b*) Should the two divisions of the HLL Company be organized as profit conters?

(*CMA, USA adapted with permission*)

Answers:

	Bottle Div.	Perfume Div.	Company
(*i*) Income at a volume of 60 lakhs cases (₹ in lakhs)	28	55	83
(*ii*) Production and sales level giving the most profitable volume (in lakhs)	60	40	60

(*iii*) (*b*) Bottle division should not be organized as a profit centre. Perfume division could be treated as a profit centre.

6. Hindustan Aeronautics Ltd. (HAL) is a diversified aerospace company, including two operating divisions, Specialized Semiconductors and Navigational Systems divisions Condensed divisional income statements, which involve no intracompany transfers and which include a breakdown of expenses into variable and fixed components, are as follows:

Divisional Income Statements for the Year Ended December 31, 2016

	Specialized Semi-conductors Division	*Navigational Systems Division*	*Total*
Sales:			
1,600 units @ ₹ 825 per unit	₹ 13,20,000		₹ 13,20,000
2,500 units @ ₹ 1,240 per unit		₹ 31,00,000	31,00,000
	₹ 13,20,000	₹ 31,00,000	₹ 44,20,000
Expenses:			
Variable:			
1,600 units @ ₹ 485 per unit	₹ 7,76,000		₹ 7,76,000
2,500 units @ ₹ 975* per unit		₹ 24,37,500	24,37,500
Fixed	4,88,000	6,36,000	11,24,000
Total expenses	₹ 12,64,000	₹ 30,73,500	₹ 43,37,500
Income from operations	₹ 56,000	₹ 26,500	₹ 82,500

*₹ 825 of the ₹ 975 per unit represents materials costs, and the remaining ₹ 150 per unit represents other variable conversion expenses incurred within the Navigational System Division.

The Specialized Semiconductors Division is presently producing 1,600 units out of a total capacity of 2,000 units. Materials used in producing the Navigational Systems Division's product are currently purchased from outside suppliers at a price of ₹ 825 per unit. The Specialized Semiconductors Division is able to produce the components used by the Navigational Systems Division. Except for the possible transfer of materials between divisions, no changes are expected in sales and expenses.

Required:

I. Would the market price of ₹ 825 per unit be an appropriate transfer price for HAL? Explain.

II. If the Navigational Systems Division purchases 400 units from the Specialized Semiconductors Division, rather than externally, at a negotiated transfer price of ₹ 625 per unit, how much would the income from operations of each division and total company income from operations increase?

III. Prepare condensed divisional income statements for HAL, based on the data in part (II).

IV. If a transfer price of ₹ 700 per unit is negotiated, how much would be the income from operations of each division and total company income from operations increase?

V. (*a*) What is the range of possible negotiated transfer prices that would be acceptable for HAL?

(*b*) Assuming that the managers of the two divisions can not agree on a transfer price, what price would you suggest as the transfer price?

Answers:

I. No.

II. The Semiconductor Division earns ₹ 140 per unit. The Navigational Systems Division saves ₹ 200 per unit on its purchases.

III. Income from Operations	***Semiconductor***	***Navigation Systems***
	₹ 1,12,000	1,06,500

IV. The increase in total company income from operations is also equal to the sum of the increases in the division incomes from operations.

V. If the division managers cannot agree on a transfer price, a price of ₹ 655 would be the best compromise.

7. PEXX is a manufacturing company of which division PQR manufactures a single standardized product. Some of the output is sold externally whilst the remainder is transferred to division RPQ where it is a subassembly in the manufacture of that division's product. PQR has the capacity (annual) to produce 30,000 units of the product. The unit costs of division PQR's product are as under:

	₹
Direct material	40
Direct labour	20
Direct expenses	20
Variable manufacturing overheads	20
Fixed manufacturing overheads	40
Sells and packaging expenses-variable	10
	150

Annually 20,000 units of the product are sold externally at the standard price of ₹ 300 per unit.

In addition to the external sales, 10,000 units are transferred annually to division RPQ at an internal transfer price of ₹ 290 per unit. This transfer price is obtained by deducting variable selling and packing expenses from the external price since those expenses are not incurred for internal transfers.

Division RPQ incorporates the transferred-in goods into a more advanced product. The unit costs of this product are as follows:

	₹
Transferred-in-item (from division PQR)	290
Direct material and components	230
Direct labour	30
Variable overheads	120
Fixed overheads	120
Selling and packaging expenses-variable	10
	800

Division RPQ's manager disagrees with the basis used to set the transfer price. He argues that the transfers should be made at variable cost plus an agreed (minimal) mark up because his division is taking output that division PQR would be unable to sell at the price of ₹ 300.

Partly because of this disagreement, a study of the relationship between selling price and demand has recently been carried out for each division by the company's sales director. the study has brought out the following demand schedule:

Division PQR

Selling price (₹)	200	300	400
Demand (units)	30,000	20,000	10,000

Division RPQ

Selling price (₹)	800	900	1,000
Demand (units)	14,400	10,000	5,600

The manager of the division RPQ claims that this study supports his case. He suggests that a transfer price of ₹ 120 would give division PQR a reasonable contribution to its fixed overheads while allowing division RPQ to earn a reasonable profit. He also believes that it would lead to an increase of output and an improvement in the overall level of company profits.

Required:

(*i*) Calculate the effect of the transfer price of ₹ 290 per unit on company's operating profit. Calculate the optimal product mix.

(*ii*) Advise the company on whether the transfer price should be revised to ₹ 120 per unit.

(*CA Final Nov. 2012*)

Answer:

(*i*) Transfer price ₹ 290 optimal product mix, External sales 20,000 units, Transfer to RPQ 10,000 units, Total company profit ₹ 55,00,000.

(*ii*) The revision of transfer price has no impact on the overall profitability of the company. However, it will alter the profitability of the Divisions.

8. City Instrument Company (CIC) consists of Semi-conductor Division and the Mini-computer Division each of which operates as an independent profit centre. Semi-conductor Division employs craftsmen, who produce two different electronic components, the new-high performance Super-chip and an older product called Okay-chip. These two products have the following cost characteristics:

	Super-chip		Okay-chip	
Material	Parts	₹ 20	Parts	₹ 10
Labour	2 hours × ₹ 140	₹ 280	1/2 hour × ₹ 140	₹ 70

Annual Overhead in Semi-conductor Division is ₹ 40,00,000 all fixed. Owing to high skill level necessary for the craftsmen, the Semi-conductor Division's capacity is set at 50,000 hours per year.

To date, only one customer has developed a product utilising super-chip, and this customer orders a maximum of 15,000 super-chips per year at a price of ₹ 600 per chip. If CIC cannot meet his entire demand, the customer curtails his own production. The rest of the semi-conductor's capacity is devoted to Okay-chips, for which there is unlimited demand at ₹ 120 per chip.

The Mini-computer Division produces only one product, a process control unit, which requires a complex circuit board imported at a price of ₹ 600. The control unit's costs are:

	Control Unit	
Material	Circuit board	₹ 600
	Other parts	80
Labour	5 hours @ ₹ 100	500

The Mini-Computer Division composed of only a small assembly plant and all overhead is fixed at a total of ₹ 8,00,000 per year. The current market price for the control unit is ₹ 1,400 per unit.

A joint research project has just revealed that with minor modifications, a single super-chip could be substituted for the circuit board currently used by the Mini-computer division. The modification would require an extra one hour of labour by Mini-computer's staff, for a total of 6 hours per control unit. Mini-computer has therefore asked Semi-conductor division to declare a transfer price at which Semi-conductro division would sell super-chip internally.

Required:

(*i*) Mini-computer expects to sell 5,000 control units this year. From the overall view point of CIC, how many super-chips should be transferred to Mini-computer Division to replace circuit boards?

(*ii*) If the demand for the control unit is sure to be 5,000 units, but its price is uncertain, what should be the transfer price of super-chip to ensure proper decisions? (All other data unchanged).

(*iii*) If demand for the control unit rises to 12,0000 units at a price of ₹ 1,400 per unit, how many of 12,000 units should be built using Super-chip? (All other data unchanged.)

(*CA Final, Nov. 2009*)

Answer:

(*i*) The entire requirement of 5000 units of Super-chips be produced and transferred to Mini Computer Division.

(*ii*) ₹ 460

(*iii*) 10,000 units of Super-chips can be made.

9. Supreme Products Co. is a divisionalized furniture manufacturer. The divisions are autonomous segments, with each being responsible for its own sales, costs of operations, working capital management, and equipment acquisition. Each division serves a different market in the furniture industry. Because the markets and products of the divisions are so different, there have never been many transfers between divisions.

   The Commercial Division manufactures equipment and furniture that is purchased by the restaurant industry. The division plans to introduce a new line of counter and chair units that feature a cushioned seat for the counter chairs. Sameer, the divisional manager, has discussed the manufacture of the cushioned seat with Rajan of the Office Division. They both believe a cushioned seat currently made by the Office Division for use on its deluxe office stool could be modified for use on the new counter chair. Consequently, Sameer has asked Rajan for a price for 100 unit lots of the cushioned seat. The following conversation took place about the price to be charged for the cushioned seats.

   Rajan: "Sameer, we can make the necessary modifications to the cushoined seat easily. The materials used in your seat are slightly different and should cost about 10 per cent more than those used in our deluxe office stool. However, the labor time (0.5 DLH) should be the same because the seat fabrication operation basically is the same. I would price the seat at our regular rate—full cost plus 30 percent markup."

   Sameer: "That's higher than I expected, I was thinking that a good price would be your variable manufacturing costs. After all, your capacity costs will be incurred regardless of this job."

   Rajan: "Sameer, I'm at capacity. By making the cushion seats for you. I'll have to cut my production of deluxe office stools. Of course, I can increase my production of economy office stools. The labor time freed by not having to fabricate the frame or assemble the deluxe stool can be shifted to the frame fabrication and assembly of the economy office stool. Fortunately, I can switch my labor force between these two models of stools without any loss of efficiency. As you know, overtime is not a feasible alternative in our community. I'd like to sell it to you at variable cost, but I have excess demand for both products. I don't mind changing my product mix to the economy model if I get a good return on the seats I make for you. Here are my standard costs for the two stools and a schedule of my manufacturing overheads."

Office Division
Standard Costs and Prices

	Deluxe Office Stool	**Economy Office Stool**
Materials, framing	₹ 8.15	₹ 9.76
Cushioned seat, padding	2.40	—
Vinyl	4.00	—
Molded seat (purchased)	—	6.00
Direct labor:		
1.5 DLH @ ₹ 7.50	11.25	
0.8 DLH @ ₹ 7.50		6.00
Manufacturing overhead:		
1.5 DLH @ ₹ 12.80	19.20	
0.8 DLH @ ₹ 12.80		10.24
Total standard cost	₹ 45,00	₹ 32.00
Selling price (30% markup)	₹ 58.50	₹ 41.60

Office Division
Manufacturing Overhead Budget

Overhead Item	Nature	Amount
Supplies	Variable—at current market price	₹ 420,000
Indirect labor	Variable	3,75,000
Supervision	Non-variable	2,50,000
Power	Use varies with activity; rates are fixed	1,80,000
Heat and light	Non-variable—light is fixed regardless of production while heat/air conditioning varies with fuel charges	1,40,000
Property tax and insurance	Non-variable—any change in amounts/rates is independent of production	2,00,000
Depreciation	Fixed dollar total	1,700,000
Employee benefits	20% of supervision, direct and indirect labor	5,75,000
Total overhead		₹ 3,8,40,000
Capacity in DLH		300,000
Overhead rate/DLH		₹ 12.80

Sameer: "I guess I see your point, Rajan, but I don't want to price myself out of the market. Maybe we should talk to corporate management to see if it can give us any guidance."

Required:

1. Sameer and Rajan did ask the Company's corporate management for guidance on an approprite transfer price. Corporate management suggested that they consider using a transfer price based upon variable manufacturing cost plus opportunity cost. Calculate a transfer price for the cushioned seat based upon variable manufacturing cost plus opportunity cost.
2. Which alternative transfer pricing system—full cost, variable manufacturing cost, or variable manufacturing cost plus opportunity cost—would be best as the underlying concept for an intracompany transfer pricing policy? Explain your answer. (*CMA, USA adapted*)

Answer:

1. ₹ 1,869 for a 100 unit lot or ₹ 18.69 per seat variable cost per 100 unit lot ₹ 1,329, Opportunity cost of shifting production to the economy office stool ₹ 540 (₹ 2520 – ₹ 1,980).

13

PERFORMANCE MEASUREMENT – BALANCED SCORECARD

LEARNING OBJECTIVES:

After reading this chapter, you should be able to:

- Understand the Concept of Performance Measurement
- Explain Traditional Performance Measurement Techniques
- Discuss Limitations of Traditional Performance Measurement Techniques
- Discuss Strategic Measurement Model
- Understand the Meaning of Balanced Scorecard
- Discuss Four Perspectives of Balanced Scorecard — Financial, Customer, Internal Business Process, Learning and Growth
- Explain Weighting Performance Measures, Characteristics of Good Balanced Scorecards, Requisites of Balanced Scorecards

PERFORMANCE MEASUREMENT: CONCEPT

Performance measurement is defined as the

- *systematic assignment of numbers to the performances and results in organisations.*

> **Performance measurement** is the systematic assignment of numbers to the performances and results in organisations.

Measurements are the yardsticks that tell us how we have done and motivate us to perform. Measurement is about recording human activity and providing a stimulus for action with the view of doing better all the time. Performance measurement is geared towards embracing change that help organisations achieve competitive supremacy. The question of measurement, although appearing as simple and straight forward, is found to be difficult in practice. D.S. Sink[1] in his article 'Achieving World Class Quality and Productivity Management; the Role of Measurement' comments:

> *'Measurement is a mystery'. Most people who attack the task of developing measurement systems eventually come to this conclusion. Even those who are considered experts readily admit that measurement is complex and still an unresolved mystery. Measurement is complex, frustrating, difficult, challenging, important, abused and misused.*

TRADITIONAL PERFORMANCE MEASUREMENT TECHNIQUES

The traditional approach to performance is based on information and techniques available in financial accounting, cost accounting, management accounting. The traditional techniques used by organisations are primarily financial measures such as contribution margin, ROI, RI, net profit, EPS, etc. The traditional techniques are backward looking. That is, they focus on past financial performance rather than on what managers are doing to create future shareholder value.

Limitations of Traditional Performance Measurement

The concern about the limitations of existing performance measurement system has been felt in both academic circles and in most organisations.

The following are the drawbacks of traditional performance measures:

1. All measures are short-term focused. Many organisations collect information which are only financial and operational. In all organisations, one can find all sorts of financial and operational statistics. The organisation can tell you its overhead expense, income, profit, and any other figure from the accounting system. Focusing only on the short term is one of the reasons that organisations struggle to survive over the long haul. These organisations often do well for a year or two, but end up failing in the long run. Long-term measures that any organisation must consider include the following:
   - Customer satisfaction
   - Employee satisfaction
   - Product/service quality
   - Public responsibility measures
2. All traditional measures are often based on outdated and irrelevant principles and lack relevance to the demands of the modern business environment.
3. Performance measures focus more on cost and revenue data and less on the process. Most of the time, it provides irrelevant or

> **Traditional Performance Measurement** drawbacks:
> - Short-term focused
> - Outdated and irrelevant principles
> - Focus on cost and revenue data, less on process
> - Lack activity and process analysis
> - Based on tracking single dimensions of performance
> - Encourage Competition and discourage teamwork.

misleading information. Performance measures which contain bottom line financial results are too late to take up useful corrective action.

4. Performance measures are without activity and process analysis which are essential to decide the value-added and non-value added activity and process. Business organisations have to analyze which processes are capable of fulfilling customer requirements time and time again.
5. Performance measures are based on tracking single dimensions of performance and they do not provide an integrated or holistic view of performance. Since performance is measured in specific areas only, managers tend to find themselves unable to assess whether they have implemented their strategies effectively.
6. Traditional performance measures encourage competition and discourage teamwork. Performance reports often compare one business unit with another's performance, rather than comparing each to its own performance and goals. This is a subtle form of discouraging teamwork. Whoever is number one likes being there and does not want to share secrets with the other business units or locations. The biggest danger comes in telling employees where they stand relative to their peers. Whether you are number one or number fifteen, learning how you rank against others is devastating to teamwork.

   Most performance appraisal systems also include measures that promote competition and discourage teams of employees to work together. Individuals are assessed, not teams in most systems. Individuals also get promotions and raises, not teams. Focusing exclusively on measures of individual performance is a common but detrimental practice in an organisation that is attempting to foster a spirit of cooperation and sharing.[2]

Johnson and Kaplan (1987)[3] have voiced their concern as follows:

> *Today's management accounting information, driven by the procedures and cycle of the organisation's financial reporting system, is too late, too aggregated, and too distorted to be relevant for managers' planning and control decisions.*

Later, Kaplan referring specifically to modern business environments which employ principles such as TQM, JIT, design for manufacture (DFM) and flexible manufacturing systems (FMS) concluded:

> *Existing systems for cost and performance measurement provided little motivation to support companies' attempts to incorportate TQM, JIT, DFM and FMS concepts into on-going, continuous improvement activities. In some instances, the traditional financial performance measures actually inhibited the improvement activities.*

This concern indicates the urgent need for looking at new ways of tracking down progress wherever it is made without necessarily having to quantify any output in financial terms.

Some characteristics of this new approach to measuring organisational performance are concepts such as the following:[4]

- Fewer are better – concentrate on measuring the vital few key variables rather than the trivial many
- Measures should be linked to the factors needed for success: key business drivers
- Measures should be a mix of past, present, and future to ensure that the organisation is concerned with all three perspectives
- Measures should be based around the needs of customers, shareholders, and other key stakeholders

- Measures should start at the top and flow down to all levels of employees in the organisation
- Multiple indices can be combined into a single index to give a better overall assessment of performance
- Measures should be changed or at least adjusted as the environment and strategy changes
- Measures need to have targets or goals established that are based on research rather than arbitrary numbers

Exhibit 13.1: Companies Innovate, Go beyond the Fixed Script on Appraisals

Traditional processes are in makeover mode as organisations such as InMobi, Godrej Industries, KPMG and RPG Group revamp and redesign their existing performance appraisal systems to make them more transparent, more inclusive and more agile. Over the past year, these companies, among others, have been overhauling their appraisal processes, looking to drive better performance and engagement among employees.

Mobile network firm InMobi opted for changes when it started feeling that the quarterly reviews just weren't doing enough. 'What are individuals passionate about? What will give them that 10x multiplier? Those conversations just weren't happening.' said, vice president, HR, at InMobi.

So, appraisal templates were done away with and meaningful conversations were encouraged instead, with an annual meeting to streamline them all, For every employee in a non-sales function, InMobi converted the variable pay to fixed pay to do away with the carrot-and-stick approach. Employees discussed their aspirations and 'big opportunity' goals with their managers, and were encouraged to become the drivers of their own growth and development. At the end of the year, each manager had to deliver a one-page report on the employee that encompassed everything from their contribution to areas that didn't work well and the manager's growth plan for the individual.

'Excitement levels have gone up, employees know the organisation is genuinely invested in their development. People are energised, they are driving the development agenda themselves'. 'It's driving a behavioural change, a culture change.'

A Gallup analysis of more than 50,000 Indian employees working in 10 major industry sectors in 22 global companies shows more than half of the employees (54%) feel that their company's Performance Management System (PMS) is not effective. According to them, an effective performance management system starts with a thorough goal setting process, followed by regular feedback and reviews/appraisals. It also identifies employees' developmental needs, includes robust reward and recognition practices and encourages collaboration, teamwork and communication.

Given that negative perception about performance appraisal process can breed demotivation, feelings of anguish and frustration that can ultimately impact performance, companies are trying to change the way performance appraisals are done. While the process itself is important in the PMS, the human element is the most important component in whether the employees perceive the system as effective or not,' says Paresh Rajgarhia, senior consultant, Gallup India.

Employees expectations have changed and today's performance management needs to be more developmental, coaching-based and agile. In line with that, organisations now expect managers to provide guidance, balanced constructive feedback at regular intervals and outline a vision plan for the employee.

Not surprisingly, organisations are spending time training both managers and employees on having these performance-related conversations. KPMG, for instance, has come up with a training module called 'having difficult conversations' for its performance managers.

"Vague phrases like 'your performance is not up-to-the mark' don't work. You need to give granular feedback, define the benchmark," says, head (people), performance and culture, KPMG in India. The company, which follows a 5-point ratings system, with 1 being the highest, has introduced a performance improvement plan for those getting a 4 rating.

Another change at KPMG has been in the performance tool itself. Called MyPD, it has been launched globally and provides for a lot more qualitative feedback. For a particular business or team, it links goals and priorities to targets and cascades them to different levels. "the new system also alows spontaneous feedback throughout the year as opposed to HR-driven checkpoints from both performance and engagement managers as well as colleagues on particular projects.

In some organisations, the most critical changes are happening at the senior leadership level. Last year, Godrej Industries introduced the People Asset Scorecard, applicable to all Godrej Leadership Forum (GLF) members, who are vice-presidents and above across businesses. It is designed to measure how well each leader is managing people processes applicable to his or her team.

"We use a 5-point scale. Ensuring base levels are met on people processes counts as a 3. You become eligible to be rated a 4 or a 5 if you play a larger and more active role in building the talent pipeline or as a brand ambassador for Godjej," explains, head group HR and corporate services, Godrej Industries and Associate Companies.

"When people down the order see senior leaders take a lot more interest in the overall process, it has a trickle-down effect in terms of overall engagement. We plan to cascade it down one level in the coming year,".

The RPG Group last year introduced a system when the company goals become the goals of the MD/CEO and his means to achieve the goals become the goals of his next level. The system advises employees to have a minimum of five and a maximum of seven goals with the weightage of each at a minimum of 10 and maximum of 40 out of 100. One goal must be on people development. The idea is to have clear focussed goals and adequate weightage in each goal.

HCL, on its part, has substantially differentiated in the distribution of the reward by staggering the quantum and the timing of reward. This aims at bringing about greater ownership among employees to know their goals, define performance standards and strive higher. Based on periodic feedback, HCL works with individuals rated lower in performance in shaping a development and improvement plan over the next performance period.

sreeradha.basu@timesgroup.com

Source: The Economic Times, New Delhi, April 11, 2014, p. 8.

STRATEGIC MEASUREMENT MODEL

In performance measurement, what is difficult is measuring the right things and learning to ignore other interesting data that do not help us become more successful. As one can see in the model in Figure 13.1, we begin by defining what an organisation does and what is the vision for the future. Next, an organisation should identify the strategies and the key success factors it needs to concentrate on to differentiate itself from competitors. During this phase, the organisation also identifies important business fundamentals on which it must focus to maintain its success. Business fundamentals tend to be issues that all organisations in the industry need to concentrate on, such as profitability, growth, or regulation. Selecting

Business fundamentals refers to issues an organisation needs to concentrate on such as profitability, growth or regulation.

the key success factors for an organisation is a major part of a business strategy, because then the organisations can concentrate on the selected areas of performance. These could be strengths they will continue to exploit or weaknesses that need to be corrected. From the key success factors and business fundamentals come the measures, or metrics. Once the organisation has defined all of the important measures on its scorecard, specific goals or objectives need to be set for each metric. Goals are based upon research and should help the organisation to achieve its overall vision. Care must be taken to make sure that all the goals link up well with each other, so that improved performance on one measure does not cause deterioration of performance on another measure. Once the goals or objectives have been identified, action plans need to be identified that will allow to achieve them. Finally, performance and activities are to be monitored and supervised to ensure their compliance with the goals and objectives. Performance reports and follow up reports are also required to be prepared with relevant and useful contents.

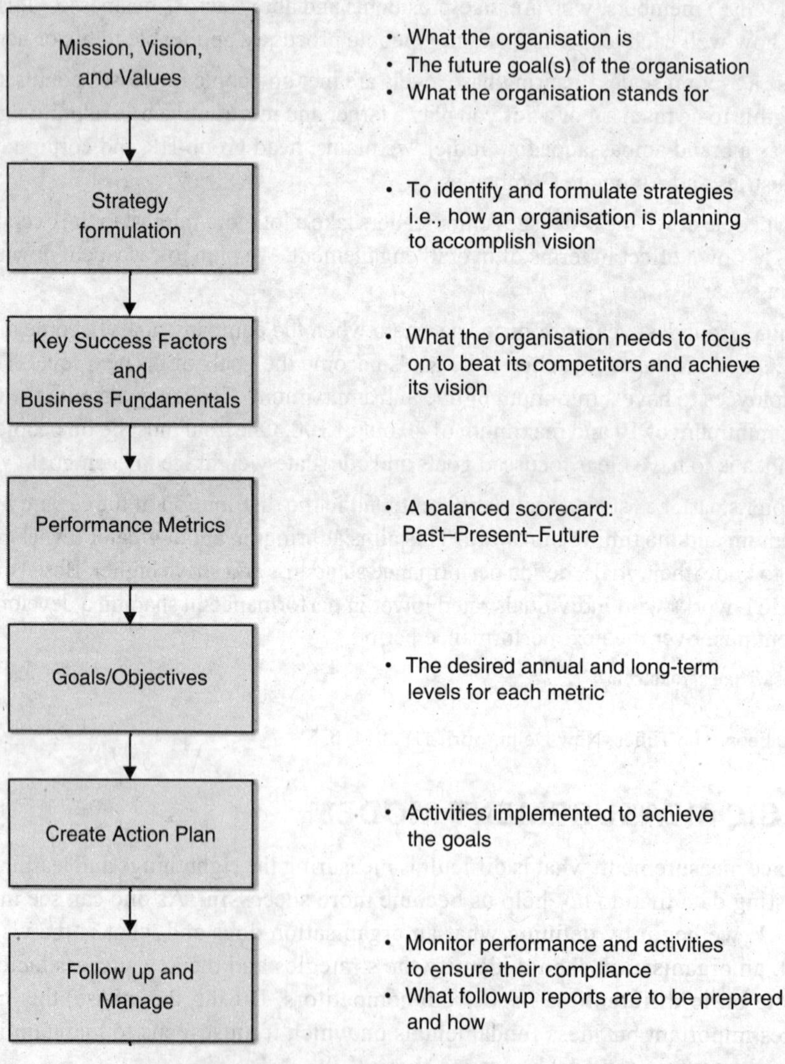

Figure 13.1: Strategic Measurement Model

BALANCED SCORECARD

Balanced Scorecard* is a technique of performance measurement developed by Robert Kaplan, a Harvard Professor and David Norton, a consultant.

Kaplan and Norton[5] comment on Balanced Scorecard (BSC) as follows:

> *The Balanced Scorecard (BSC) provides managers with the instrumentation they need to navigate to future competitive success. The Balanced Scorecard translates an organisation's mission and strategy into a comprehensive set of performance measures that provides the framework for a strategic measurement and management system. The balanced scorecard retains an emphasis on achieving financial objectives, but also includes the performance drivers of these financial objectives. The scorecard measures organisational performance across four balanced perspectives: financial, customers, internal business processes and learning and growth. The BSC enables companies to track financial results while simultaneously monitoring progress in building the capabilities and acquiring the intangible assets they need for future growth.*

MEANING OF BALANCE IN BALANCED SCORECARD

According to Atkinson, Banker, Kaplan and Mark Young[6], to be balanced, performance measurement systems must meet two requirements:

1. They should reflect the organisation's understanding of causes of successful performance on the organisation's primary objectives – that is, the performance measurement system should monitor both the organisation's performance and what management believes are the drivers of performance on the organisation's primary objectives. This is the depth requirement of being balanced.

> **Balanced Scorecard** is a technique of performance measurement developed by Robert Kaplan, a Harvard Professor and David Norton, a consultant.

2. The performance measurement system should measure the most critical aspects or differentiators of organisation performance. These aspects give the organisation its unique abilities to achieve its primary objective. This is the breadth requirement of being balanced.

The focus of the balanced scorecard is a system of performance measurements that organisations use to track performance on its primary and secondary objectives. In this sense, the organisation's planning and strategy, which defines what relationships the organisation must develop with its employees, its suppliers, and the community to be successful with its targeted customers, defines the focus and scope of the balanced scorecard.

---

*Adapted from

(*a*) R.S. Kaplan and D.P. Norton. The Balanced Scorecard: Translating Strategy into Action. Harvard Business School Publishing, Boston, 1996.

(*b*) Michael W. Maher, "The Balanced Scorecard and Non-financial Performance Measures", in Roman L. Weil and Michael W. Maher (Eds.), Handbook of Cost Management, John Wiley & Sons. 2005, pp. 657–668.

(*c*) Mark Graham Brown, Keeping Score, Using the Right Metrics to Drive World Class Performance, Quality Resources, New York, 1996.

(*d*) Robert Simon, Performance Measurement and Control Systems for Implementing Strategy, Prentice Hall, 2000.

(*e*) Charles T. Horngreen, George Foster and Sri Kant M. Datar, Cost Accounting, A Managerial Emphasis, Prentice Hall, 2010.

(*f*) Anthony A. Atkinson, Rajiv D. Banker, Robert S. Kaplan and S. Mark Young, Management Accounting, Prentice Hall International, New Jersey, 1997.

PERSPECTIVES (FACTORS) IN BALANCED SCORECARD

The balanced scorecard is a set of performance targets and results relating to four dimensions of performance – financial, customer, internal process and innovation. It recognises that organisations are responsible to different stakeholder groups such as employees, suppliers, customers, community and shareholders. The balanced scorecard shows an organisation's performance in meeting its objectives relating to stakeholders. Sometimes different stakeholders have different wants. For example, employees depend on an organisation for their employment. Shareholders depend on an organisation to maintain their investment. The organisation must balance those competing wants. Hence, the concept of a balanced scorecard is to measure how well the organisation is doing in view of competing stakeholder wants.

> **Balanced Scorecard** is a set of performance targets and results relating to four dimensions of performance – financial, customer, internal process and innovation.

Most organisations use four perspectives or four categories of performance measures as shown in Figure 13.2. The financial perspective indicates whether the company's strategy and operations add value to shareholders. For organisations that do not have shareholders, the financial perspective indicates how well the strategy and operations contribute to improving the organisation's financial health. The customer perspective indicates how the company's strategy and operations add value to customers. The internal business and production process perspective indicates the ability of the internal business processes to add value to customers and to improve shareholder wealth. Finally, the learning and growth perspective indicates the strength of the infrastructure for innovation and long-term growth. The balanced scorecard framework derives its power by providing a holistic view of business value through its four perspectives.

> **Four perspectives of performance measures:**
> - Financial perspective
> - Customer perspective
> - Internal business and production perspective
> - Learning and growth perspective

These four perspectives have been briefly discussed below.

Financial Perspective

The balanced scorecard uses financial performance measures, such as net income and return on investment, because all for-profit organisations use them. Financial performance measures provide a common language for analysing and comparing companies. People who provide funds to companies, such as financial institutions and shareholders, rely heavily on financial performance measures in deciding whether to lend or invest funds. Properly designed financial measures can provide an aggregate view of an organisation's success.

> **Financial perspective** assesses net income and return on investment.

Financial measures by themselves do not provide incentives for success. Financial measures tell a story about the past, but not the future; they have importance, but will not guide performance in creating value.

According to Brown,[7] a sound approach to financial measurement is to make sure that your data base includes three types of information:

1. *Historical Data:* How did we do last month, last week, this year, last year, and so on?
2. *Current Data:* How are we doing right now, today?
3. *Future Data:* How will we be doing in the next few months or years?

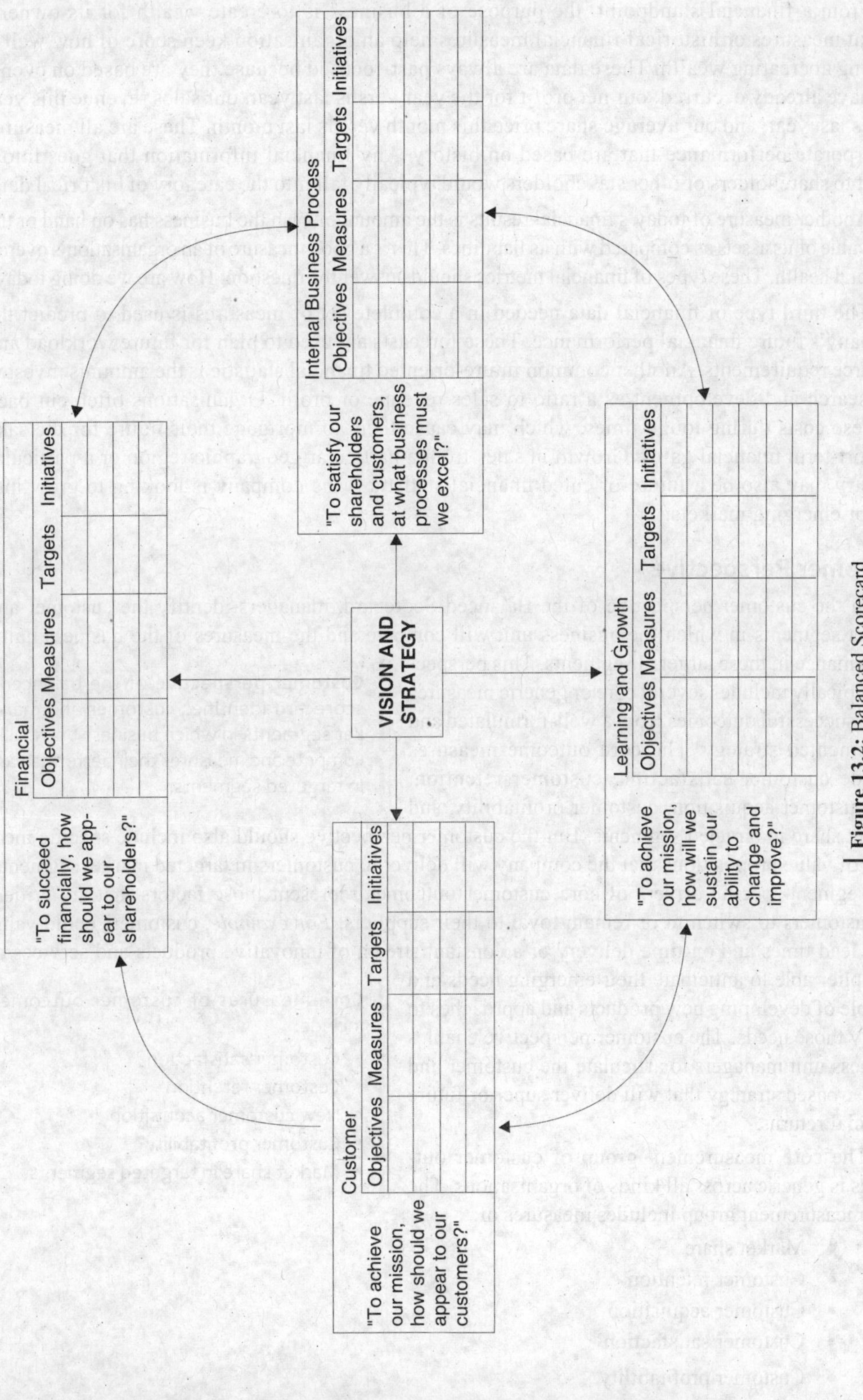

Figure 13.2: Balanced Scorecard

Source: R.S. Kaplan and D.P. Norton, "Using the Balanced Scorecard as a Strategic Management System," Harvard Business Review, Jan-Feb, 1996., p. 9

From a financial standpoint, the purpose of a business is to create wealth for its owners. Output measures or historical financial measures help an organisation keep score of how well it is doing at creating wealth. These data are always past-focused because they are based on events that have already occurred: our net profit for the year versus last year, our sales revenue this year versus last year, and our average share price this month versus last month. These are all measures of corporate performance that are based on history. Any financial information that goes into a report to shareholders or other stakeholders would typically fall into the category of historical data.

Another measure of today's financial results is the amount of cash the business has on hand or the total value of its assets as compared with its liabilities. This is a good measure of an organisation's overall financial health. These types of financial metrics should answer the question: How are we doing today?

The third type of financial data needed in a complete set of measures is used to predict the company's future financial performance. These forecasts are used to plan for future workload and resource requirements. Another common future-oriented financial statistic is the amounts invested in research and development as a ratio to sales revenue or profit. Organisations often cut back on these costs during tough times, which may cause them to mortgage their future for the sake of short-term financial gains. Growth in sales from a particular geographic region or a particular industry may also be a future-oriented financial statistic if the company is looking to grow into new or emerging markets.

Customer Perspective

In the customer perspective of the Balanced Scorecard, managers identify the customer and market segments in which the business unit will compete and the measures of the business unit's performance in these targeted segments. This perspective typically includes several core or generic measures of the successful outcomes from a well-formulated and implemented strategy. The core outcome measures include customer satisfaction, customer retention, new customer acquisition, customer profitability, and market share in targeted segments. But the customer perspective should also include specific measures of value propositions that the company will deliver to customers in targeted market segments. The segment-specific drivers of core customer outcomes represent those factors that are critical for customers to switch to or remain loyal to their suppliers. *For example*, customers could value short lead times and on-time delivery or a constant stream of innovative products and services or a supplier able to anticipate their emerging needs and capable of developing new products and approaches to satisfy those needs. The customer perspective enables business unit managers to articulate the customer and market-based strategy that will deliver superior future financial returns.

> **Customer perspective** of the balanced scorecard identifies customer and market segments in which business units will compete and measures their performance in targeted segments.

> **Core** measures of customer outcome include:
> - Customer satisfaction
> - Customer retention
> - New customer acquisition
> - Customer profitability
> - Market share in targeted segments

The core measurement group of customer outcomes is generic across all kinds of organisations. The core measurement group includes measures of:

- Market share
- Customer retention
- Customer acquisition
- Customer satisfaction
- Customer profitability

These core measures can be grouped in a chain of relationships causal as displayed in Figure 13.3.

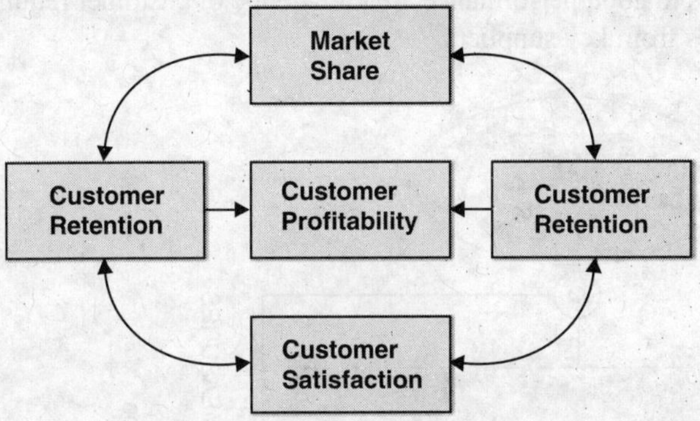

Market Share	Reflects the proportion of business in a given market (in terms of number of customers, amount spent, or unit volume sold) that a business unit sells.
Customer Acquisition	Measures, in absolute or relative terms, the rate at which a business unit attracts or wins new customers or business.
Customer Retention	Tracks, in absolute or relative terms, the rate at which a business unit retains or maintains ongoing relationships with its customers.
Customer Satisfaction	Assesses the satisfaction level of customers along specific performance criteria within the value proposition.
Customer Profitability	Measures the net profit of a customer, or a segment, after allowing for the unique expenses required to support that customer.

Figure 13.3: The Customer Perspective–Core Measures

Source: Robert S. Kaplan and David P. Norton, *Ibid.*

Internal Business Process Perspective

In the internal business process perspective, managers identify the critical internal processes in which the organisation must excel. These processes enable the business organisations to:

> **Internal business process perspective** identifies critical internal processes in which organisation needs to excel.

- Deliver the value propositions that will attract and retain customers in targeted market segments, and
- Satisfy shareholder expectations of excellent financial returns.

The key to excellence in any organisation is control of its processes to produce reliable and consistent products and services. Performing the right processes in the right manner leads to consistent levels of product and service quality. The difficulty lies in finding the right process variables to measure and setting the standards appropriate to performance levels of each of the process measures. Process and operational measures are leading-edge measures that are more short-term-focused. These are the measures that are typically monitored every day or at least every week. Some process variables are even monitored continuously to ensure the production and delivery of high-quality products and services. Achieving good performance levels on process or operational measures leads to high-quality products and services, which, in turn, lead to satisfied or delighted customers, which lead to repeat business and promote an organisation's long-term survival and success[8]. Figure 13.4 depicts this graphically.

In order to achieve consistently high performance, an organisation must control its inputs. The two most important inputs to good performance are knowledge of customer requirements and high-quality goods and services from key suppliers.

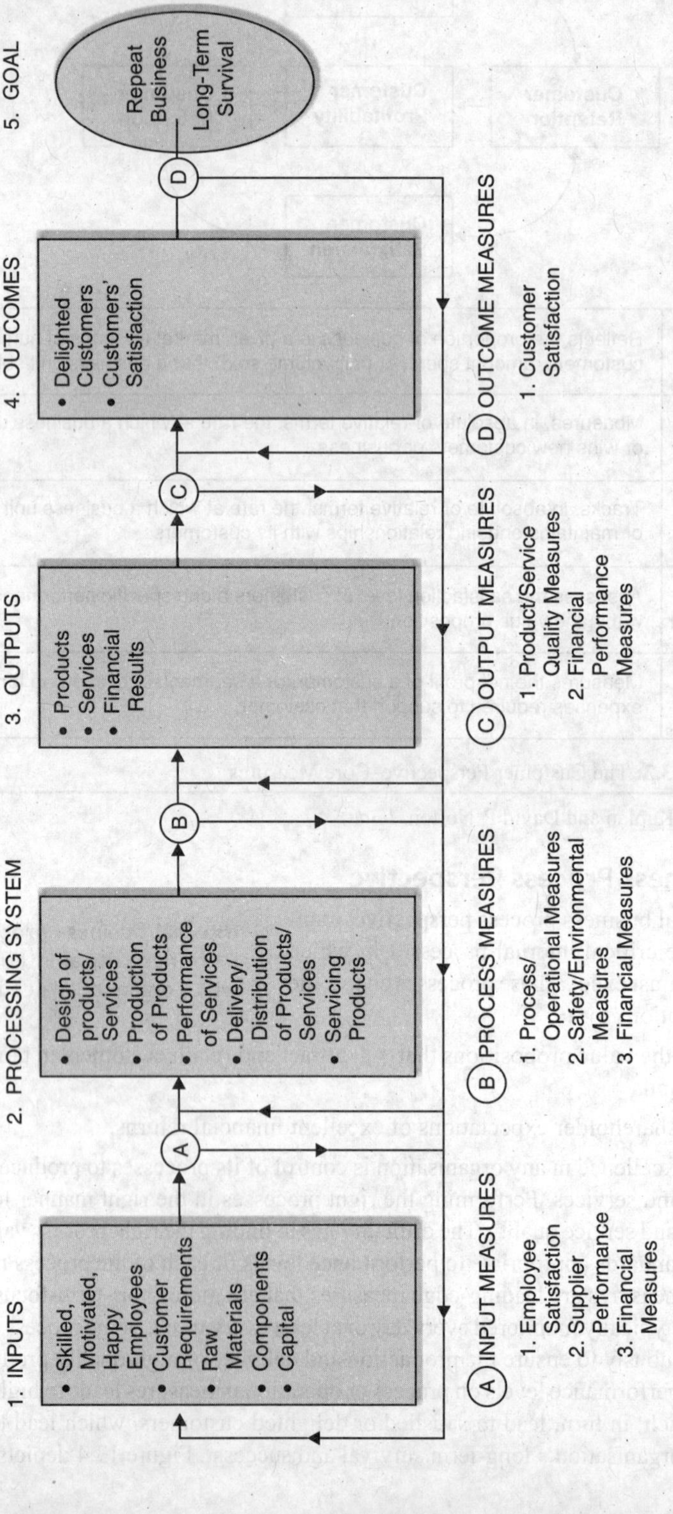

Figure 13.4: Macro Process Model of an Organisation

Source: Mark Graham Brown, Keeping Score, Using the Right Metrics to Drive World Class Performance, Quality Resources, New York, 1996, p. 96.

Process measures provide with the data needed to predict and control the quality of products and services. When a problem occurs with a product or service, the cause is usually found by looking at the process data. Results and outcomes are important for all organisations. In fact, they may be the most important thing. But how those results are achieved—the process measures—is also very important.

> Two most **important inputs to good performance** are:
>
> ☐ Knowledge of customer requirement
> ☐ High quality goods and services

Brown[9] finds that excellent organisations measure processes and operational results in the following manner

- Cycle time for all key processes is measured
- Rework time and/or costs are tracked for key production and service delivery processes
- Key measures of productivity are identified and tracked for major processes in the organisation
- Key processes have been identified in each unit, function, and department of the organisation, and process measures have been defined for each key process

> **Process measures** provide with the data needed to predict and control the quality of products and services.

- Process measures are correlated directly with product/service characteristics or performance factors that are of prime importance to customers
- Standards or goals are set for all key process measures, and those standards are based upon benchmark organisations and customer requirements
- Process measures promote a preventive approach to achieving consistently high quality products and services
- The organisation has developed an overall safety index that is tracked at least once a month, and consists of several output measures like lost-time accidents, as well as a number of preventive or behavioral measures
- A few future-oriented process measures are tracked that will help ensure long-term survival and success

Learning and Growth Perspective

For incentive purposes, the learning and growth perspective focuses on the capabilities of people. Managers would be responsible for developing employee capabilities. Key measures for evaluating managers' performance would be employee satisfaction, employee retention, and employee productivity.

> **Learning and growth perspective** focuses on the capabilities of people.

1. ***Employee Satisfaction:*** Employee satisfaction recognises the importance of employee morale for improving productivity, quality, customer satisfaction and responsiveness to situations. Managers can measure employee satisfaction by sending surveys, interviewing employees, or observing employees at work.
2. ***Employee Retention:*** Firms committed to retaining employees recognise that employees develop organisation-specific intellectual capital and provide a valuable non-financial asset to the company. Furthermore, firms incur costs when they must find and hire good talent to replace people who leave. Firms measure employee retention as the inverse of employee turnover–the per cent of people who leave each year.
3. ***Employee Productivity:*** Employee productivity recognises the importance of output per employee. Employees create physical output (*i.e.*, miles driven, pages produced, or lawns mowed), or financial output (*i.e.*, revenue per employee or profits per employee). The number of loans processed per loan officer per month would provide a simple measure of productivity for loan officers at a bank.

Within this core, the employee satisfaction objective is generally considered the driver of the other two measures, viz., employee retention and employee productivity (Figure 13.5).

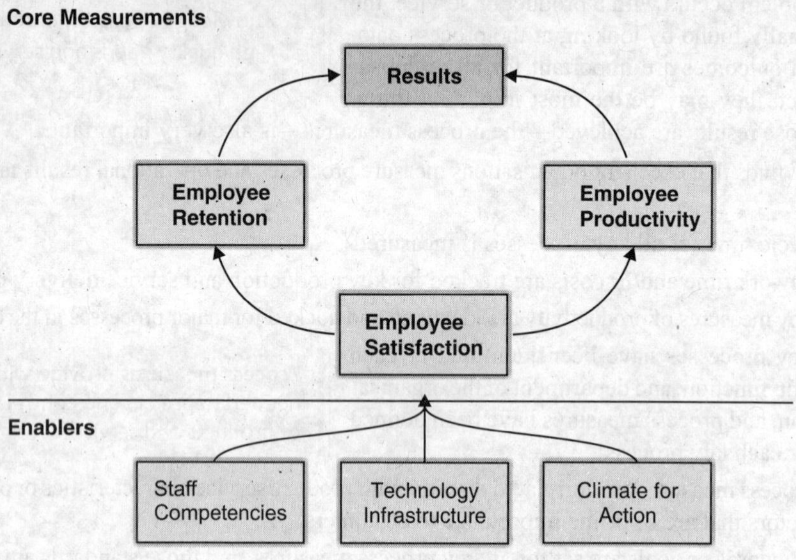

Figure 13.5: Learning and Growth Measurement Framework

Source: Robert S. Kaplan and David P. Norton, The Balanced Scorecard, Harvard Business School Press, 1996, p. 129.

A good incentive system rewards managers who promote high employee satisfaction, low employee turnover, and high employee productivity. An environment that supports employees provides greater opportunities for improving internal business processes, discussed earlier.

PERFORMANCE DRIVERS

A good balanced scorecard should have a mix of outcome measures and performance drivers. Outcome measures without performance drivers do not communicate how the outcomes are to be achieved. They also do not provide an early indication about whether the strategy is being implemented successfully. Conversely, performance drivers–such as cycle times and Part-Per-Million (PPM) defect rates—without outcome measures may enable the business unit to achieve short-term operational improvements, but will fail to reveal whether the operational improvements have been translated into expanded business with existing and new customers, and, eventually, to enhanced financial performance. A good Balanced Scorecard should have an appropriate mix of outcomes (lagging indicators) and performance drivers (leading indicators) of the business unit's strategy.

> A good balanced scorecard should have a mix of outcome measures and performance drivers.

Four Perspectives: Are they Sufficient

The four perspectives of the balanced scorecard should be considered as a template, not a straitjacket. No mathematical theorem exists to prove that four perspectives are both necessary and sufficient. The owners and capital contributors to the organisation appear on every scorecard through goals and measures in the financial perspective. Customer measures also appear on every scorecard (in the customer perspective) because customers are essential for meeting the financial goals. Goals and measures for employees appear on the balanced scorecard when outstanding performance along this dimension will lead to breakthrough performance for customers and shareholders.

Companies rarely use fewer than four perspectives but, depending on industry circumstances and a business unit's strategy, one or more additional perspectives may be needed. *For example*, some managers incorporate the interests of other important stakeholders, such as suppliers and the community. When strong supplier relationships are part of the strategy leading to breakthrough customer and/or financial performance, then outcome and performance driver measures for supplier relationships should be incorporated within the organisation's internal business process perspective. When outstanding environmental and community performance is a central part of a company's strategy, then objectives and measures for that perspective also become an integral part of a company's scorecard.[10]

WEIGHTING PERFORMANCE MEASURES

A company using a balanced scorecard will develop three to five performance measures for each of four perspectives or dimensions and the measures are tied to the company's strategy for success. The method of weighting various performance measures presents a problem for designers of balanced scorecards. Assigning a particular weight to each performance measure (e.g., customer satisfaction will count 15 per cent of the total performance score) does not allow for flexibility in assessing performance and for recognition of unforeseen problems arising during the performance period. For example, assume the designers assigned a weight of 15 per cent to customer satisfaction, but a particular division did superb work in improving customer satisfaction. Senior management might want to reward such performance more than implied by the 15 per cent weighting. Research has shown that the use of flexibility, such as assigning weights to performance measures after the performance period and incorporating subjective performance evaluations, results in complaints about favouritism. Some potential measures for each dimension are illustrated in Exhibit 13.2.

Hansen and Mowen[11] have referred to balanced scorecard as 'strategic-based responsibility accounting system' which translates the mission and strategy of an organisation into operational objectives and measures for four different perspectives: the financial perspective, the customer perspective, the process perspective and the infrastructure (learning and growth) perspective.

A more descriptive balanced scorecard is displayed in Exhibit 13.3.

Exhibit. 13.2: Some Examples of Measures for the Four Perspectives of a Balanced Scorecard

Perspectives	*Critical Success Factor*	*Measures*
Financial	Is the company achieving its financial goals? • Profitability • Liquidity • Sales • Market value	Operating income Return on assets Sales growth Cash flow from operations Reduction of administrative expense
Customer	Is the company meeting customer expectations? • Customer satisfaction • Dealer and distributor • Marketing and selling • Timeliness of delivery • Quality	Customer satisfaction Customer retention New customer acquisition Market share On time delivery Time to fill orders
Internal Processes	Is the company improving critical internal processes? • Quality • Productivity	Defect rate Lead time Number of suppliers Material turnover

Perspectives	Critical Success Factor	Measures
	• Flexibility • Equipment readiness • Safety	Per cent of practical capacity
Innovation	Is the company improving its ability to innovate • Product innovation • Timeliness of new product • Skill development • Employee morale • Competence	Amount spent on employee training Employee satisfaction Employee retention Number of new products New product sales as a per cent of total sales Number of patents

BALANCED SCORECARD EXAMPLE

Strategy: To be the leading organisation in our industry through constant innovation and adaptation to our environment. We will measure success in terms of value creation for our shareholders and customers, by the learning and growth of our employees, and by our good corporate citizenship.

Exhibit 13.3: Balanced Scorecard Example

Objectives	*Initiatives*	*Performance Measure*	*Target*
Financial Perspective			
Increase share-holder wealth	Develop new products	Return on assets	25%
Provide growth	Increase online sales	Percentage growth in sales	30%
Customer Perspective			
Increase market share	Increase advertising	Percentage market share	10%
Increase customer satisfaction	Increase postsales service	Percentage satisfied through survey	99%
Internal Business Process Perspective			
Reduce through-put time	Reduce non-value-added activities	Average throughput time	4 hours
Provide on-time delivery	Streamline delivery process	Percentage on-time delivery	90%
Reduce defects	Develop employee quality teams	Percentage defects	0.01%
Learning and Growth Perspective			
Develop a multiskilled workforce	Provide employee training	Percentage of employees with multiple skills	80%
Improve information systems	Hire new employees in computing	Number of employees in computing	20
Reduce employee turnover	Pay higher salaries	Percentage annual turnover	10%

Source: Cheryl S. Mcwatters, Dale C. Morse and Jerold L. Zimmerman, Management Accounting, McGraw Hill, Irwin, 2001, p. 442.

CHARACTERISTICS OF GOOD BALANCED SCORECARDS

Balanced scorecards to be effective and useful should have the following charateristics[12]:

1. Balanced scorecards should highlight a company's strategy by focusing on cause-and-effect relationship. Assume, Hindustan Unilever Ltd. aims to be a low-cost manufacturer and accelerate growth. The balanced scorecards should pinpoint specific objectives and measures in 'learning and growth perspective' which could improve internal business processes. These, in turn, would result into greater customer satisfaction, larger market share, higher operating income and shareholder wealth.
2. Balanced scorecards should help in communicating the strategy formulated to all members of an organisation by translating the strategy into a coherent and linked set of understandable and measurable operational targets. Subsequently, managers and employees take actions, based on scorecard, to achieve the firm's strategy. To facilitate decisions and actions in accordance with scorecards, it is preferable to develop scorecards at the division and department levels.

> Characteristics of Good Balanced Scorecards:
> - Focus on cause and effect relationship
> - Strategy translated to coherent and linked set of understandable and measurable operational targets
> - Emphasis on financial objectives and measures
> - Critical measures only
> - Suboptimal trade offs

3. In profit-seeking companies, the balanced scorecard gives strong emphasis on financial objectives and measures. Sometimes managers give too much importance to innovation, quality and customer satisfaction though they may not produce tangible benefits. A good balanced scorecard considers non-financial measures as a part of a strategy or programme to achieve and improve future financial performance. When financial and non-financial performance measures are properly linked in balanced scorecards, many non-financial measures serve as leading indicators of future financial performance.
4. The balanced scorecard limits the number of measures used by identifying only the most critical ones. Avoiding a proliferation of measures focuses management's attention on those that are key to the implementation of strategy.
5. The scorecard highlights suboptimal tradeoffs that managers may make when they fail to consider operational and financial measures together. For example, a company for which innovation is key, could achieve superior short-run financial performance by reducing spending on R&D. A good balanced scorecard would signal that the short-run financial performance may have been achieved by taking actions that hurt future financial performance because a leading indicator of that performance, R&D spending and R&D output, has declined.[13]

REQUISITES OF BALANCED SCORECARDS

Balanced scorecard requires an adequate planning system and understanding of organisation processes to fit the organisation's primary objectives. However, developing and using balanced scorecards for performance measurements are difficult tasks. The following are the requirements which should be satisfied by organisations before adopting balanced scorecard.[14]

1. *Management must define the organisation's primary objectives.* This is usually well done because most profit-seeking organisations have a narrow primary objective, namely, to increase shareholder wealth. In profit-seeking organisations that have primary objectives that include both social and owner wealth objectives, management must stipulate how decision-makers should weigh each of these objectives. In not-for-profit organisations like governments, management must state its objectives precisely.

2. *The organisation must understand how stakeholders and processes contribute to its primary objectives.* Many managers admit that this is problematic. For example, the organisation behaviour literature is unclear about whether increased employee motivation necessarily translates into improved employee and profit performance. Many organisations, despite implementing massive quality programs, really do not understand the effect of quality on performance and prefer to speak in platitudes when they say, *for example*, "quality is not an issue, you have to have quality just to be in the game."
3. *The organisation must develop a set of secondary objectives that are the drivers of performance on primary objectives.* This step is perhaps the most challenging and important in implementing the balanced scorecard. Accomplishing this task requires that processes and results come together. The organisation must invest resources to back the strategies that it feels will produce results. This task seeks answers to questions like how much should be invested in employee training, a customer satisfaction system, a quality improvement system, or an improved logistical system? Such decisions should be based on an understanding of how increased spending improves process results, such as improved customer satisfaction, which in turn results in improved performance on the organisation's primary objectives.
4. *The organisation must develop a set of measures to monitor performance on both primary and secondary objectives.* This is the conventional role for management accounting. This step raises issues about how to measure the variable of interest. For example, how does the organisation measure employee motivation or commitment to the organisation? These performance measures are important because they translate strategy into focus, since the measures that people are told to manage will drive their performance. If the organisation chooses the wrong set of measures, it will motivate inappropriate performance. Suppose, for example, that the organisation, lacking an ability to measure motivation, equates motivation with lavish incentive compensation and measures motivation by the amount of incentive compensation that it distributes to employees. However, incentive compensation actually may have little incremental effect on motivation.
5. *The organisation must develop a set of processes with their attendant implicit and explicit contracts with stakeholders to achieve those primary objectives.* Although this management requirement is well understood, the implied level of complexity required by the balanced scorecard is much deeper than what is done in normal practice. For example, based on 1980s experience, many managers developed the motto of "quality at any cost." Under the balanced scorecard, managers would asses the costs and benefits of schemes to improve quality.
6. *The organisation must make specific and therefore public statements about its beliefs concerning how processes create results.* Public statements and specific commitments to courses of action and expected results provide a basis for accountability. Therefore, they represent an element of management risk since management can be questioned more accurately about its failures. Many senior managers may find this level of risk distasteful. However, owners may find such public statements illuminating.

REFERENCES

1. D.S. Sink, "Achieving World Class Quality and Productivity Management: The Role of Measurement".
2. Mark Graham Brown, Keeping Score, Using the Right Metrics to Drive World Class Performance, Quality Resources, New York, 1996, p. 26.
3. Robert S. Kaplan and Thomas Johnson, Relevance Lost, The Rise and Fall of Management Accounting, Harvard Business School Press, 1987.
4. Mark Graham Brown, *Ibid*, pp.3-4.
5. Robert S. Kaplan and David P. Norton, The Balanced Scorecard, Harvard Business School Press, 1996.
6. Anthony A. Atkinson, Rajiv D. Banker, Robert S. Kaplan and S. Mark Young, Management Accounting, Prentice Hall International, New Jersey, 1997, PP. 532-533.
7. Mark Graham Brown, *Ibid*, pp. 50-52.
8. Mark Graham Brown, *Ibid*, p. 95.
9. Mark Graham Brown, *Ibid*, pp. 109-110.
10. Robert Simon, Performance Measurement and Control Systems for Implementing Strategy, Prentice Hall, 2000, p. 203.
11. Don R. Hansen and Maryanne M. Mowen, Management Accounting, South Western College Publishing, 2000, p. 379.
12. Charles T. Horngreen, George Foster and Sri Kant M. Datar Cost Accounting, A Managerial Emphasis, Prentice Hall, 2000, pp. 467-468.
13. Anthony A. Atkinson, Rajiv D. Banker, Robert S. Kaplan and S. Mark Young, Management Accounting, *Ibid*, pp. 533-534.
14. Charles T. Horngreen, George Foster and Sri Kant M. Datar, Cost Accounting, A Managerial Emphasis, Prentice Hall, 2000, pp. 469-470.

CRITICAL ANALYSIS AND DISCUSSION QUESTIONS, SELF-ASSESSMENT QUESTIONS, AND CASES

CRITICAL ANALYSIS AND DISCUSSION QUESTIONS

1. What is the meaning of performance measurement?
2. Explain traditional performance measurement techniques.
3. What are the shortcoming of traditional performance measures?
4. Define balanced scorecard. Explain characteristics of a good balanced scorecard.
5. Discuss the following perspectives of a balanced scorecard.
   (*a*) Financial (*b*) Customer
   (*c*) Internal business process (*d*) Learning and growth
6. How are performance measures weighted?
7. In what way customer perspective is important in balanced scorecard?
8. Explain the importance of learning and growth perspective.
9. Give some suggestions to be followed while using balanced scorecard.
10. Organisations in the public and non-profit sector, such as government agencies and social service entities, have financial systems that budget expenses and monitor and control actual spending. Identify why these organisations should consider developing a balanced scorecard of measurements to monitor and report on their performance. What should be the various perspectives in such a balanced scorecard of measurements?
11. Should top managers be responsible for delivering excellent financial performance to shareholders, leaving the details of customer relations, engineering design, and manufacturing operations to the mid-level managers of these various departments? Explain.
12. Are financial measures alone sufficient to measure the performance of an organisation during a period and to use as a basis for compensating the senior executives of an organisation? Why or why not?
13. What problems arise if any, from monitoring and rewarding senior executives by a combination of financial and non-financial measures?
14. What is strategic measurement model? Explain the important components of a strategic measurement model.
15. Explain the prerequisites for adopting balanced scorecard in an organisation.
16. Discuss the importance of balanced scorecard for a not-for-profit organisation.
17. Explain the differences between financial and non-financial performance measures and give two examples of each.
18. Identify four potential perspectives for a balanced scorecard and explain how they are related.
19. Mahindra and Mahindra Trucking moves produce from farms to markets. Its managers decided to implement a balanced scorecard around the entity's vision statement: 'We aim to be the industry leader in cost-effective and timely delivery of produce.' Provide two potential performance measures for each of the four perspectives for the balanced scorecard for Mahindra & Mahindra Trucking.
20. Suppose that a car dealership decided it would no longer compensate employees with sales commissions, but instead pay a salary with a bonus for high customer satisfaction ratings. What problems would you foresee from the dealership's financial perspective?

21. Describe the implementation process for the balanced scorecard.
22. What is strategic decision making? What role does it play in the balanced scorecard?
23. When implementing balanced scorecard, why do some managers use a different term to describe it?
24. What is meant balanced measures?
25. Why are non financial measures important in a strategic performance management system?
26. The 'Balanced Scorecard' approach aims to provide information to management to assist strategic policy formulation and achievement. It emphasises the need to procide the user with a set of information which addresses all relevant areas of performance in an objective and unbiased fashion.

Requirements:

(*i*) Discuss in general terms the main type of information which would be required by a manager to implement this approach to measuring performance;

(*ii*) Comment on three specific example of performance measures which could be used in a company in a service industry, *for example*, a firm of consultants.

SELF-ASSESSMENT QUESTIONS

1. Match each of the following performance measures to one or more of the four perspectives of the balanced scorecard. Note that a performance measure could measure performance for more than one perspective.

Performance Measures

- Employee productivity
- Employee satisfaction
- Return on investment
- Customer satisfaction
- Employee turnover
- On-time delivery performance from suppliers
- Percentage of customers who are repeat customers
- On-time delivery performance to customers
- Product quality

Balanced Scorecard Perspectives

- Learning and growth
- Internal business
- Customer
- Financial

2. Match each of the following performance measures to one or more of the four perspectives of the balanced scorecard. Note that a peformance measure could measure performance for more than one perspective.

Performance Measures

- Throughput time
- Economic value added
- Percentage of sales amount invested in employee training
- Ratings of supplier performance
- Increase in market share
- Employee retention

Balanced Scorecard Perspectives

- Learning and growth
- Internal business
- Customer
- Financial

EXERCISES

1. The following comment was made by the CEO of a company that recently implemented the Balanced Scorecard: " Responsibility in a strategic-based performance management system differs on the three D's: Direction, Dimension, and Diffusion."

Required:

Explain how this comment describes differences in responsibility between an activity-based and a strategic-based performance management system.

2. "A Balanced Scorecard expresses the complete story of a company's strategy through an integrated set of financial and nonfinancial measures that are both predictive and historical and which may be measured subjectively or objectively."

Required:

(*i*) Using the above statement about scorecard measures, explain how scorecard measurement differs from that of an activity-based management system.

(*ii*) Explain what is meant by historical and predictive measures. Why are both types important for describing a company's strategy?

3. The Balanced Scorecard is an approach that has the objective of driving change. Performance evaluation is an integral part of this effort. Performance evaluation within the Balanced Scorecard framework is also concerned with the effectiveness and viability of the organisation strategy.

Required:

(*i*) Describe how the Balanced Scorecard is used to drive organisational change.

(*ii*) Explain how performance evalution is used to assess the effectiveness and viability of an organisation's strategy.

4. Rastogi & Co. is a law firm in New Delhi. The firm has had a very loose and relaxed management style that has served it well in the past. However, more aggressive law firms have been winning new clients faster than Rastogi & Co. has. Thus, the managing partner, Mahesh, recently attended a seminar on performance measurement in law firms, where he learned about the balanced scorecard. He thought it might be a good tool for Rastogi & Co., one that would allow the firm to keep its culture yet still more aggressively seek new clients.

   Mahesh identified the following strategic objectives that fit with the firm's score values and provide a framework for assessing progress toward the firm's goals:

Financial

(*a*) To steadily increase the firm's revenues and profits.

Customer

(*a*) To understand the firm's customers and their needs.

(*b*) To value customer service over self-interest.

Internal Business Process

(*a*) Encourage knowledge sharing among the legal staff.

(*b*) To communicate with each other openly, honestly, and often.

(*c*) To empower staff to make decisions that benefit their clients.

Organisation Learning

(*a*) To maintain an open and collaborative environment that attracts and retains the best legal staff.

(*b*) To seek staff diversity.

Required:

(*i*) Develop at least one measure for each of the strategic objectives listed.

(*ii*) Explain how Rastogi & Co. can use this balanced scorecard to evaluate staff performance.

(*iii*) Should staff compensation be tied to the scorecard performance measures? Why or why not?

5. The following strategic objectives have been derived from a strategy that seeks to improve asset utilization by more careful development and use of its human assets and internal processes:

(*a*) Increase revenue from new products

(*b*) Increase implementation of employee suggestions

(*c*) Decrease operating expenses

(*d*) Decrease cycle time for the development of new products

(*e*) Decrease rework

(*f*) Increase employee morale

(*g*) Increase customer satisfaction

(*h*) Increase access of key employees to customer and product information

(*i*) Increase customer acquisition

(*j*) Increase return on investment (ROI)

(*k*) Increase employee productivity

(*l*) Decrease the collection period for accounts receivable

(*m*) Increase employee skills

The heart of the strategy is developing the company's human resources. Management is convinced that empowering employees will lead to an increase in economic returns. Studies have shown that there is a positive relationship between employee morale and customer satisfaction. Furthermore, the more satisifed customers pay their bills more quickly. It was hypothesized that as employees became more involved and more productive their morale inprove. Thus, the strategy incorporated key objectives that would lead to an increase in productivity and involvement.

Required:

Classify the objectives by perspective, and suggest a measure for each objective.

6. Hero Honda Bikes (HHB) wants to implement a balanced scorecard. Its mission statement reads, 'We build high-quality, reliable bikes at competitive prices.' The entity's competitive strategy is to continuously improve the functionality, reliability and quality of its bikes while holding prives at levels similar to competitors. The entity operates three subunits organised around the product lines for the three types of mountain bikes it currently produces A fourth bike line in development includes a finished design, with engineers currently working on the plans for the manufacturing process. HHB sells directly to bike shops and operates an Internet site that allows bike shops to place orders for customised products.

Required:

(*a*) Describe the implementation cycle for the balanced scorecard at HHB.

(*b*) Describe the four perspectives of the balanced scorecard, and list one or more performance objectives for each perspective that are likely to be important for HHB.

(*c*) Pick one performance objective for each perspective in part (*b*) and identify two or more potential measures. Explain how each measure would link to improved financial performance.

(*d*) Describe the pros and cons of implementing a balanced scorecard for HHB.

CASES

1. Ashok Dhawan, division manager of the Household Products Division, a maker of kitchen dishwashers, has just seen the balanced scorecard for his division for 2016. He immediately calls Amit, the division's management accountant, into his office for a meeting. "I think the employee-satisfaction and customer-satisfaction numbers are too low. These numbers are based on a random sample of subjective assessments made by individual managers and customer representatives. My own experience indicates that we are doing well on both these dimensions. Until we do a formal survey of employees and customers sometime next year, I think we are doing a disservice to ourselves and this company by reporting such low scores for employee and customer satisfaction. These scores will be an embarrassment for us at the division managers' meeting next month. We need to get these numbers up."

   Amit knows that the employee-and customer-satisfaction scores are subjective, but the procedure he used this year is identical to the procedures he has used in the past. He knows from the comments he had asked for that the scores represent the unhappiness of employees with the latest work rules and the unhappiness of customers with late deliveries. He also knows that these problems will be corrected in time.

   Required:

   1. Do you think that the Household Products Division should include subjective measures of employee satisfaction and customer satisfaction in its balanced scorecard? Explain.
   2. What should Amit do?

2. A business manager makes the following statement, "The financial perspective of the balanced scorecard indicates how the organisation adds value to shareholders. I am involved with two organisations: a small business that is a partnership, so it has no shareholders, and a temple trust that has no shareholders. While the balanced scorecard makes a lot of sense to me, the financial perspective is clearly irrelevant for these two organisations." How would you respond to this statement?

3. Some years back, State Bank of India (SBI) felt that the Internet was going to change the bank dealings with customers and would require SBI to become a more nimble and customer-focused organisation. As a result, SBI replaced its old measurement system, which was 90% oriented toward financial performance, with a balanced scorecard. The scorecard emphasized three "point of arrival" measures, which were:

   (*i*) Customer satisfaction index—a measure of customer satisfaction.

   (*ii*) Employee relations index—a measure of employee sentiment and morale.

   (*iii*) Competitive position—delivery performance relative to competition.

Required:

Why did SBI introduce a balanced scorecard and nonfinancial measures in its new performance measurement system?

4. At the beginning of the last quarter of 2015, Hindustan Unilіever Ltd. (HUL), a consumer products firm, hired Ritesh to take over one of its division. The division manufactured small home appliances and was struggling to survive in a very competitive market. Ritesh immediately requested a projected income statement for 2015. In response, the controller provided the following statement:

Sales	₹ 25,000,000
Variable expenses	20,000,000
Contribution margin	₹ 5,000,000
Fixed expenses	6,000,000
Projected loss	₹ (1,000,000)

After some investigation, Ritesh soon realized that the products being produced had a serious problem with quality. He once again requested a special study by the controller's office to supply a report on the level of quality costs. By the middle of November 2015 Ritesh received the following report from the controller:

Inspection costs, finished product	₹ 4,00,000
Rework costs	20,00,000
Scrapped units	6,00,000
Warranty costs	30,00,000
Sales returns (quality-related)	10,00,000
Customer complaint department	5,00,000
Total estimated quality costs	₹ 75,00,000

Ritesh was surprised at the level of quality costs. They represented 30 per cent of sales, certainly excessive. He knew that the division had to produce high-quality products to survive. The number of defective units produced needed to be reduced dramatically. Thus, Ritesh decided to pursue a quality-driven turnaround strategy. Revenue growth and cost reduction could both be achieved if quality could be improved. By growing revenues and decreasing costs, profitability could be increased.

After meeting with the managers of Production, Marketing, Purchasing, and Human Resources, Ritesh made the following decisions, effective immediately (end of November 2015):

(i) More will be invested in employee training. Workers will be trained to detect quality problems and empowered to make improvements. Workers will be allowed a bonus of 10 per cent of any cost savings produced by their suggested improvements.

(ii) Two design engineers will be hired immediately, with expectations of hiring one or two more within a year. These engineers will be in charge of redesigning processes and products with the objective of improving quality. They will also be given the responsibility of working with selected suppliers to help improve the quality of their products and processes. Design engineers were considered a strategic necessity.

(iii) Implement a new process: evaluation and selection of suppliers. This new process has the objective of selecting a group of suppliers that are willing and capable of providing nondefective components.

(iv) Effective immediately, the division will begin inspecting purchased components. According to Production, many of the quality problems are caused by defective components purchased from outside suppliers. Incoming inspection is viewed as a transitional activity. Once the division has developed a group of suppliers capable of delivering nondefective components, this activity will be eliminated.

(v) Within three years, the goal is to produce products with a defect rate less than 0.10 per cent. By reducing the defect rate to this level, Marketing is confident that market share will increase by at least 50 per cent (as a consequence of increased customer satisfaction). Products with better quality will help establish an improved product image and reputation, allowing the division to capture new customers and increase market share.

(vi) Accounting will be given the charge to install a quality information reporting system. Daily reports on operational quality data (e.g., percentage of defective units), weekly updates of trend graphs (posted throughout the division), and quarterly cost reports are the types of information required.

(vii) To help direct the improvements in quality activities, kaizen costing is to be implemented. For example, for the year 2015, a kaizen standard of 6 per cent of the selling price per unit was set for rework costs, a 25 per cent reduction from the current actual cost.

To ensure that the quality improvements were directed and translated into concrete financial outcomes, Ritesh also began to implement a Balanced Scorecard for the division. By the end of 2016, progress was being made. Sales had increased to ₹ 2,60,00,000, and the kaizen improvements were meeting or beating expectations. For example, reword costs had dropped to ₹ 15,00,000.

At the end of 2017, two years after the turnaround quality strategy was implemented, Ritesh received the following quality cost report:

Quality training	₹ 5,00,000
Supplier evaluation	2,30,000
Incoming inspection costs	4,00,000
Inspection costs, finished product	3,00,000
Rework costs	10,00,000
Scrapped units	2,00,000
Warranty costs	7,50,000
Sales returns (quality-related)	4,35,000
Customer complaint department	3,25,000
Total estimated quality costs	₹ 41,40,000

Ritesh also received an income statement for 2017:

Sales	₹ 3,00,00,000
Variable expenses	2,20,00,000
Contribution margin	₹ 80,00,000
Fixed expenses	58,00,000
Income for operations	₹ 22,00,000

Ritesh was pleased with the outcomes. Revenues had grown, and costs had been reduced by at least as much as the had projected for the two-year period. Growth next year should be even greater as he was beginning to observe a favorable effect from the higher-quality products. Also, further quality cost reductions should materialize as incoming inspection were showing much higher-quality purchased components.

Required:

1. Identify the strategic objectives, classified by Balanced Scorecard perspective.

   Next, suggest measures for each objective.
2. Using the results from Requirement 1, describe Ritesh's strategy using a series of if-then statements.
3. Explain how you would evaluate the success of the quality-driven turnaround strategy. What additional information would you like to have for this evaluation?
4. Explain why Ritesh felt that the Balanced Scorecard would increase the likelihood that the turnaround strategy would actually produce good financial outcomes.
5. Advise Ritesh on how to encourage his employees to align their actions and behavior with the turnaround strategy.

14

STRATEGIC MANAGEMENT ACCOUNTING

LEARNING OBJECTIVES:

After reading this chapter, you should be able to:

1. Define the Term 'Strategic Management Accounting'
2. Understand Some Techniques of Strategic Management Accounting such as Target Costing, Kaizen Costing, Life-cycle Costing, Theory of Constraints (TOC), Bench Marking, Activity-based Management (ABM), Just-In-Time (JIT) Method

STRATEGIC MANAGEMENT ACCOUNTING–CONCEPT AND DEFINITIONS

Management accounting aims at providing internal data pertaining to internal activities to take remedial action and maximise earnings.

Management accounting has been used by business enterprises since the time they realised that financial accounting information is not sufficient for planning, control, decision making and other managerial uses. Management accounting, in order to help management in different functions, has been able to develop techniques, methods and tools which have been used by managers and practitioners to solve their problems and decide managerial policies. The focus of management accounting traditionally has been internal *i.e.* to supply data regarding internal activities to evaluate them and to take remedial action to maximise the earnings of a business firm.

However, now, a business firm's environment has changed, has been highly competitive, is greatly affected by information technology and complex managerial problems. The focus has now shifted from traditional management accounting to strategic management accounting. The recent literature in developed countries such as USA, UK, Japan and others on management accounting has advised the application of strategic management accounting to achieve an organisation's missions. In late 1980s, the Chartered Institute of Management Accountants of UK commissioned an investigation to review state of development of management accounting. The findings of the enquiry was published in 1989 in a report entitled 'Management Accounting: Evolution not Revolution', authored by Bromwich and Bhimani. In this report and the other follow-up report entitled as 'Management Accounting: Pathways to Progress', Bromwich and Bhimani found strategic management accounting, a potential area for future development. In the US literature also, many researchers and authors have, in their studies and writings, given attention to this vital emerging area. This chapter aims to investigate strategic management accounting and some measures, tools and techniques being advocated for use by managements in this area.

Definitions of Strategic Management Accounting

What is strategic management accounting, what are its scope? Such questions have not yet been answered precisely by the accounting researchers, teachers and others. There is no comprehensive framework available on strategic management accounting. Some attempts have been made to define strategic management accounting. Simmonds[1] views strategic management accounting as the provision and analysis of management accounting data about a business and its competitors which is of use in the development and monitoring of the strategy of that business. Cooper and Kaplan[2] state that strategic accounting techniques are designed to support the overall competitive strategy of the organisation, principally by the power of using information technology to develop more refined product and service costs.

Bromwich[3] has given the following definition of strategic management accounting:

- *provision and analysis of financial information on the firm's product markets and competitors' costs and cost structures and the monitoring of the enterprise's strategies and those of its competitors in these markets over a number of periods.*

Innes[4] defines strategic management accounting as:

- *The provision of information to support the strategic decisions in the organisations. Strategic decisions usually involve the longer term, have a significant effect on the organisation and, although they may have an internal element, they also have an external element.*

Lord[5] has identified the following components of strategic management accounting:

1. Extension of traditional management accounting's internal focus to include external information about competitors

2. Relationship between the strategic position chosen by a firm and the expected emphasis on management accounting (*i.e.* accounting in relation to strategic positioning)
3. Gaining competitive advantage by analysing ways to decrease costs and/or enhance the differentiation of a firm's products, through exploiting linkages in the value chain and optimising cost drivers

TECHNIQUES OF STRATEGIC MANAGEMENT ACCOUNTING

There are many things which fall within the jurisdiction of strategic management accounting. Strategic management accounting uses different approaches/techniques to achieve strategy execution, to develop integrated approaches to performance measurement. Some of the important strategic tools for performance measurement, strategic planning and decision making have been discussed in previous chapters of the book such as Activity-Based Costing (ABC), balanced scorecard. Some other strategic tools have been covered in this chapter, which include:

1. Target Costing
2. Kaizen Costing
3. Life Cycle Costing
4. Theory of Constraints (TOC)
5. Bench Marking
6. Activity-Based Management (ABM)
7. Just-In-Time Method (JIT)

All of the above are discussed in great detail in the following sections.

TARGET COSTING

> **Target costing** is a systematic approach to establishing product cost goals based on market driven standards.

Target costing is a systematic approach to establishing product cost goals based on market driven standards. It is a strategic management process for reducing costs at the early stages of product planning and design. Target costing begins with identifying customer needs and calculating an acceptable target sales price for the product. Working backward from the sales price, companies establish an acceptable target profit and calculate the target cost as follows:

Target Cost = Expected selling price – Desired profit

Target Costing is different from standard costing. While target costs are determined by market driven standards (target sales price – target profit = target cost), standard costs are determined by design – driven standards with less emphasis on what the market will pay (engineered costs + desired markup = desired sales price).

The target cost is normally less than the current cost. Thus, managers must try to reduce costs from the design and manufacture of the product. The planned cost reduction is sometimes referred to as the cost 'drift.' Costs can be reduced in a variety of ways such as the following:

1. Simplifying the design
2. Reducing the cost of direct materials
3. Reducing the direct labour costs
4. Eliminating waste

Target costing tries to reduce costs as shown in Figure 14.1. The bar at the left in Figure 14.1 shows the actual cost and profit that can be earned during the current period. The bar at the right shows that the market price is expected to decline in the future. The target cost is estimated as the difference between the expected market price and the desired profit.

To reduce costs in target costing, the following analysis needs to be made. (*i*) reverse engineering (*ii*) value analysis, and (*iii*) process improvement. Reverse engineering tears down the competitors products with the objective of discovering more design features that create cost reductions. Value analysis attempts to assess the value placed on various product functions by customers. If the price customers are willing to pay for a particular function is less than its cost, the function is a candidate for elimination. Another possibility is to find ways to reduce cost of providing the function, e.g. using common components. Both reverse engineering and value analysis focus on product design to achieve cost reductions. The processes used to produce and market the product are also sources of potential cost reduction. Thus, redesigning processes to improve their efficiency can also contribute to achieving the needed cost reductions[6].

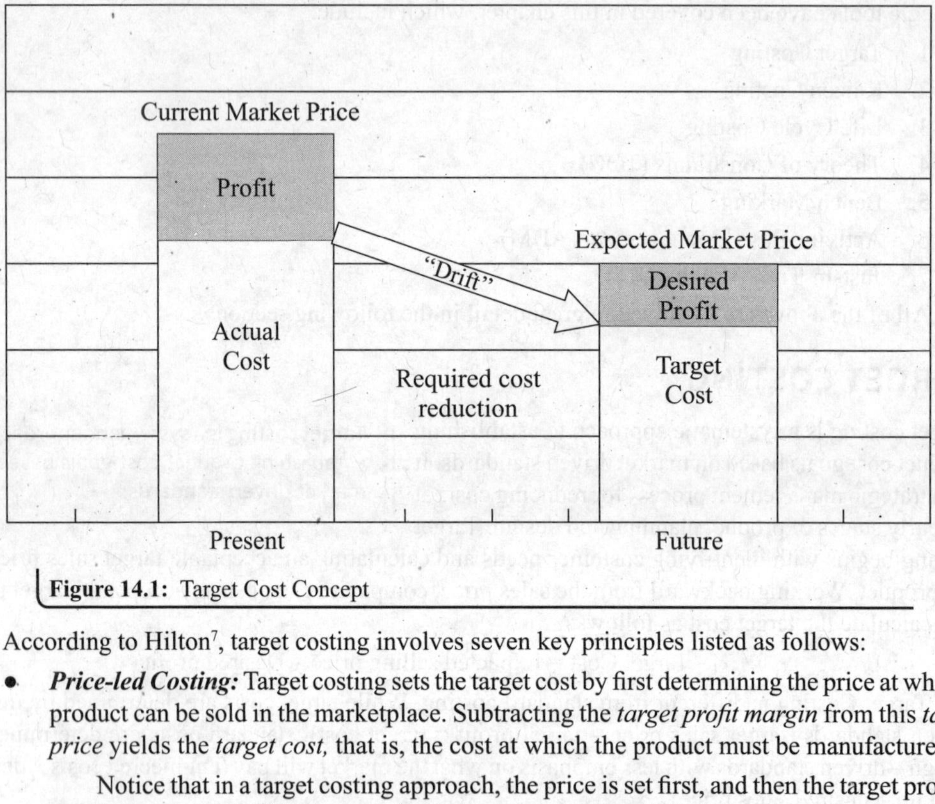

Figure 14.1: Target Cost Concept

According to Hilton[7], target costing involves seven key principles listed as follows:

- ***Price-led Costing:*** Target costing sets the target cost by first determining the price at which a product can be sold in the marketplace. Subtracting the *target profit margin* from this *target price* yields the *target cost,* that is, the cost at which the product must be manufactured.

  Notice that in a target costing approach, the price is set first, and then the target product cost is determined. This is opposite from the order in which the product cost and selling price are determined under traditional cost-plus pricing.
- ***Focus on the Customer:*** To be successful at target costing, management must listen to the company's customers. What products do they want? What features are important? How much are they willing to pay for a certain level of product quality? Management needs to aggressively seek customer feedback, and then products must be designed to satisfy customer demand and be sold at a price they are willing to pay. In short, the target costing approach is market driven.
- ***Focus on Product Design:*** Design engineering is a key element in target costing. Engineers must design a product from the ground up so that it can be produced at its target cost. This design activity includes specifying the raw materials and components to be used as well

as the labour, machinery, and other elements of the production process. In short, a product must be designed for manufacturability.

- ***Focus on Process Design:*** Every aspect of the production process must be examined to make sure that the product is produced as efficiently as possible. The use of touch labour, technology, global sourcing in procurement, and every aspect of the production process must be designed with the product's target cost in mind.
- ***Cross-functional Teams:*** Manufacturing a product at or below its target cost requires the involvement of people from many different functions in an organisation: market research, sales, design engineering, procurement, production engineering, production scheduling, material handling and cost management. Individuals from all these diverse areas of expertise can make key contributions to the target costing process. Moreover, a cross-functional team is not a set of specialists who contribute their expertise and then leave; they are responsible for the entire product.
- ***Life-cycle Costs:*** In specifying a product's target cost, analysts must be careful to incorporate all of the product's life-cycle costs. These include the costs of product planning and concept design, preliminary design, detailed design and testing, production, distribution and customer service. Traditional cost-accounting systems have tended to focus only on the production phase and have not paid enough attention to the product's other life-cycle costs.
- ***Value-chain Orientation:*** Sometimes the projected cost of a new product is above the target cost. Then efforts are made to eliminate *non-value-added costs* to bring the projected cost down. In some cases, a close look at the company's entire *value chain* can help managers identify opportunities for cost reduction.

Target costing is a common practice in Japan where markets are extremely competitive. The market determines the price of products and there is a little opportunity for the individual organisations to set prices. Therefore, controlling cost is extremely important.

The following are the advantages and disadvantages of target costing.

Advantages

- Takes proactive approach to cost management
- Orients organization toward customer
- Breaks down barriers between departments
- Enhances employee awareness and empowerment
- Fosters partnerships with suppliers
- Minimizes non-value-added activities
- Encourages selection of lowest-cost value-added activities
- Reduces time to market

Disadvantages

- To be effective, requires the development of detailed cost data
- Requires willingness to cooperate
- Requires many meetings for coordination

KAIZEN COSTING

Kaizen Costing, also referred as continuous improvement costing, is a mechanism for reducing and managing costs. Kaizen is the Japanese term for making

> **Kaizen costing** is a mechanism for reducing and managing costs.

continuous improvements in relatively small activities rather than major innovative improvement. The major difference between target and Kaizen costing is that target costing is applied during the design stage where as Kaizen costing is applied during the manufacturing stage of a product's life.

The objective of Kaizen costing is to reduce actual costs to manufacture a product below the standard cost. Standard cost system generally aims to achieve the cost standards set by management while Kaizen costing systems are more concerned with reducing actual costs below standard costs. The potential cost reductions are smaller with Kaizen costing because the products are already in the manufacturing stage of their life cycles and a significant proportion of costs will have become locked-in.

Kaizen costing tracks the cost reduction plans on a monthly basis. The Kaizen costing targets are expressed in the physical resources terms. If the head of a group fails to achieve the Kaizen costing target by 1 per cent, review by senior will start. Resource consumption is tightly controlled in many Japanese firms. Thus, the planned cost reductions are planned and monitored through Kaizen cost targets in terms of physical resources.

While implementing the concept of Kaizen, following few rules are to be observed:

- Identify your own problems
- Grade your problems like minor, difficult and major
- Select the smallest minor problem and start with it. After tackling this, move on to the next graded problem and so on
- Always ensure that improvement is a part of daily routine
- Never accept status quo
- Never reject any idea before trying it
- Share the experiments with colleagues
- Eliminate already tried but failed experiments, while sharing the problems with your colleagues
- Never hide problems, always highlight them

Table 14.1 Compares target costing and Kaizen costing.

Table 14.1: Target Costing Vs Kaizen Costing

	Target Costing	**Kaizen Costing**
What?	A procedural approach to determining a maximum allowable cost for an identifiable, proposed product assuming a given target profit margin	A mandate to reduce costs, increase product quality, and/or improve production processes through continuous improvement efforts
Used for?	New products	Existing products
When?	Development stage (includes design)	Primary production stages (introduction and growth; possibly, but not probably, maturity)
How?	Works best through aiming at a specified cost reduction objective; used to set original production standards	Works best through aiming at a specified cost reduction objective; reductions are integrated into original production standards to sustain improvements and provide new challenges
Why?	Extremely large potential for cost reduction because 80% to 90% of a product's lifelong costs are embedded in the product during the design and development stages	Limited potential for reducing cost of existing products, but may provide useful information for future target costing efforts

	Target Costing	Kaizen Costing
Focus?	All product inputs (material, labour, and overhead elements) as well as production processes and supplier components	Depends on where efforts will be most effective in reducing production costs; generally begins with the most costly component and (in the more mature companies) ends with overhead components

Source: Jesset T. Barfield, Cecily A. Raiborn and Michael R. Kinney, Cost Accounting, Traditions and Innovations, Thomson, 2003, p. 721.

LIFE-CYCLE COSTING

Life-cycle costs are all the costs associated with the product for its entire life cycle. Product life cycle costing traces costs and revenues of each product over several calendar periods throughout their entire life cycle.

Life-cycle costs are all the costs associated with the product for its entire life cycle.

The costs are included in different stages of the product life cycle:

- Development phase – R & D cost/Design cost
- Introduction phase – Promotional cost/Capacity costs
- Growth phase/Maturity – Manufacturing cost/Distribution costs/Product support cost
- Decline/Replacement phase – Plants reused/sold/scrapped/related costs

Manufacturers would base life cycle costing expense allocations on an expected number of units to be sold over the product's life. Each period's internal income statement using life cycle costing would show revenues on a life-to-date basis along with total cost of goods sold, total R and D project costs and total distribution and other marketing costs.

The following are the benefits of product life cycle costing:

1. It results in earlier actions to generate revenue or to lower costs than otherwise might be considered
2. It ensures better decision from a more accurate and realistic assessment of revenues and costs, atleast within a particular life cycle stage
3. It promotes long-term rewarding
4. It provides an overall framework for considering total incremental costs over the life span of the product

Life cycle costing helps companies to be aware of where their products are in their life cycles, because in addition to the sales effects, the life-cycle stage may have a tremendous impact on costs and profits. The life-cycle impact on each of these items is shown in Table 14.2.

Table 14.2: Effects of Product Life Cycles on Costs, Sales, and Profits

Stage	Costs	Approach to Costing	Sales	Profits
Development	No production costs, but R&D costs very high	Target costing	None	None; large loss on product due to expensing of R&D costs
Introduction	Production cost per unit; probably engineering change costs; high advertising cost	Kaizen costing	Very low unit sales; selling price may be high (for early profits) or low (for gaining market share)	Typically losses are incurred partially due to expensing of advertising

Stage	Costs	Approach to Costing	Sales	Profits
Growth	Production cost per unit decreases (due to learning curve and spreading fixed overhead over many units)	Kaizen costing	Rising unit sales; selling price is adjusted to meet competition	High
Maturity	Production cost per unit stable; costs of increasing product mix begin to rise	Standard costing	Peak unit sales; reduced selling price	Falling
Decline	Production cost per unit increases (due to fixed overhead being spread over a lower volume)	Standard costing	Falling unit sales; selling price may be increased in an attempt to raise profits or lowered in an attempt to raise volume	May return to losses

Source: Jesset T. Barfield, Cecily A. Raiborn and Michael R. Kinney, Cost Accounting, Traditions and Innovations, Thomson, 2003, p. 718.

THEORY OF CONSTRAINTS (TOC)

> **Theory of constraints** (TOC) is a manufacturing strategy that focuses on reducing the influence of bottlenecks on production processes.

> **Production bottleneck** is a point in the manufacturing process where the demand for the company's product exceeds the ability to produce the product.

The theory of constraints is a newly developed management method for dealing with constraints or bottlenecks. All business firms face limited resources and limited demand for their products. These limitations are called constraints. A production bottleneck (or *constraint*) is a point in the manufacturing process where the demand for the company's product exceeds the ability to produce the product. The Theory of Constraints (TOC) is a manufacturing strategy that focuses on reducing the influence of bottlenecks on production processes. The TOC assumes that the performance of a firm is adversely affected by its constraints. The TOC then develops a specific approach to manage constraints to maximise operating income and continuous improvement.

Profits can be increased by effectively managing the organization's constraints. One aspect of managing constraints is to decide how to best utilize them. If the constraint is a bottleneck in the production process, the manager should select the product mix that maximizes the total contribution margin. In additon, the manager should take an active role in managing the constraint himself. Management should focus efforts on increasing the efficiency of the bottleneck operation and on increasing its capacity. Such efforts directly increase the output of finished goods and will often pay off in an almost immediate increase in profits.

In a production bottleneck operation, the best measure of profitability is the unit contribution margin per production bottleneck constraint. For example, assume the production bottleneck constraint is process hours.

Therefore, the unit contribution margin per bottleneck constraint is expressed as follows:

$$\text{Unit Contribution Margin per Production Bottleneck Hour} = \frac{\text{Unit Contribution Margin}}{\text{Process hours per Unit}}$$

When a company has a production bottleneck, the unit contribution margin per bottleneck hour is a measure of each product's profitability. This measure can be used to adjust product prices to reflect the product's use of the bottleneck.

When a manager effectively increases the capacity of bottlenecks, it is called **relaxing (or elevating) the constraint.**

It is often possible for a manager to effectively increase the capacity of the bottleneck, which is called relaxing (or elevating) the constraint. For example, the stitching machine operator could be asked to work overtime. This would result in more available stitching time and hence more finished goods that can be sold. The benefits from relaxing the constraint in such a manner are often enormous and can be easily quantified. The implications are clear. Managers should focus much of their attention on managing bottlenecks. Managers should emphasize products that most profitably utilize the constrained resource. They should also make sure that products are processed smoothly through the bottlenecks, with minimal lost time due to breakdowns and setups. And they should try to find ways to increase the capacity at the bottlenecks.

The capacity of a bottleneck can be effectively increased in a number of ways including:

- Working overtime on the bottleneck
- Subcontracting some of the processing that would be done at the bottleneck
- Investing in additional machines at the bottleneck
- Shifting workers from processes that are not bottlenecks to the process that is a bottleneck
- Focusing business process improvement efforts such as TQM and Business Process Re-engineering on the bottleneck
- Reducing defective units. Each defective unit that is processed through the bottleneck and subsequently scrapped takes the place of a good unit that could be sold

The last three methods of increasing the capacity of the bottleneck are particularly attractive, since they are essentially free and may even yield additional cost savings.[8]

The theory of constraints focuses on three factors:

1. ***Throughput Contribution:*** This is equal to revenues minus direct material costs of goods sold.
2. ***Investments:*** It is the sum of direct materials cost, work-in-progress and finished goods inventories, R&D costs and costs of plant, equipment and buildings.
3. ***Operating Costs:*** This is equal to all operating costs other than direct materials. These costs are incurred to earn throughput contribution and include salaries and wages that are fixed costs, rent, utilities and depreciation.

The TOC has the objective of maximising throughput contribution while minimising investments and operating costs. It assumes a short-run time horizon and considers that operating costs are fixed. The following steps are required under TOC to manage bottleneck operations:

1. Recognise that the bottleneck operation determines throughput contribution of the plant as a whole.
2. Find the bottleneck operation by identifying operations with large quantities of inventory waiting to be worked on.
3. Keep the bottleneck operation busy and subordinate all non-bottleneck operations to the bottleneck operation. That is, the needs of the bottleneck operation determine the production schedule of non-bottleneck operations.

4. Increase bottleneck efficiency and capacity. The objective is to increase throughput contribution minus the differential cost of taking such action such as leasing another car and hiring another driver.

   The management accountant plays a key role in step (4) by calculating throughput contribution, identifying relevant and irrelevant costs and doing cost—benefit analysis of alternative actions.

5. Repeat steps (1) to (2) for new bottleneck.

The theory of constraints emphasises the management of bottleneck operations as the key to improving the performance of the production system as a whole. It focuses on the short-run maximisation of throughput contribution — revenue minus materials costs. Because TOC regards operating costs as difficult to change in the short-run, it does not identify individual activities and drivers of costs. TOC is therefore less useful for the long-run management of costs. Activity-based costing (ABC) systems, on the other hand, has a longer-run perspective focused on improving processes, by eliminating non-value added activities and reducing the costs of performing value-added activities. ABC systems are therefore more useful for long-run pricing, long-run cost control and profit planning and capacity management. The short-run TOC emphasis on maximising throughput contribution by managing bottlenecks complements the long-run strategic cost management focus of ABC.[9]

The TOC has several implications[10] for management.

- Management should identify the bottleneck. This is often difficult when several different products are produced in a facility containing many different production activities. One approach is to walk around and observe where inventory is building up in front of work stations. The bottleneck will likely have the largest piles of work that have been waiting for the longest time.
- Management should schedule production to maximise the efficient use of the bottleneck resource. Efficiently using the bottleneck resource might necessitate inspecting all units before they reach the bottleneck rather than after the units are completed. The bottleneck resource is too valuable to waste on units that may already be defective.
- Management should schedule production to avoid a buildup of inventory. Reducing inventory lowers the cost of inventory investments and the cost of carrying inventory. It also assists in improving quality by making it easier to identify quality problems that might otherwise be hidden in large piles of inventory. Reducing inventory will require a change in the attitude of managers who like to see machines and people constantly working. To avoid a buildup of inventory in front of the bottleneck, it may be necessary for people and equipment to remain idle until the bottleneck resource calls for additional input.
- Management should work to eliminate the bottleneck, perhaps by increasing the capacity of the bottleneck resource, redesigning products so they can be produced with less use of the bottleneck resource, rescheduling production procedures to substitute nonbottleneck resources, or outsourcing work performed by bottleneck resources.

BENCHMARKING

Benchmarking is the continuous process of measuring one's own product, services and activities against the best level of performance. These best levels of performance may be found either inside one's own organisation or in other competing organisations or in organisations having similar processes.

> **Benchmarking** is the continuous process of measuring one's own product, services and activities against the best level of performance.

Benchmarking uses best practices as the standard for evaluating activity performance. Within an organisation, different units (*for example*, different plant sites) that perform the same activities are compared. The unit with the best performance for a given activity sets the standard. Other units then have a target to meet or exceed. Further, the best practices unit can share information with other units on how it has achieved its superior results. Although benchmarking can focus on anything of interest, it typically deals with target costs for a product, service or operation, customer satisfaction, quality, inventory levels, inventory turnover, cycle time and productivity. In the beginning, bench marking was used for studying competitors. However, now-a-days benchmarking is widely used for all activities and services. According to Camp[11]:

> Although you must focus strongly on the competition, if that is the sole objective, playing catchup is the best you can do. Watching the competition does not tell you how to outdistance them. The mix of our bench mark activities have changed 180 degrees. In the early days, we spent 80 per cent of our benchmark time looking at the competition. Today we spend 80 per cent of that time outside our industry, because we have found innovative ideas from businesses in other industries.

Types of Benchmarking

The different types of benchmarking are:

1. ***Product Benchmarking (Reverse Engineering):*** It is an age old practice of product-oriented reverse engineering. Every organization buys its rival's products and tears down to find out how the features and performances etc., compare with its products. This could be the starting point for improvement.
2. ***Competitive Benchmarking:*** Corporate benchmarking has moved beyond product-oriented comparisons to include comparisons of process with those of competitors. In this type, the process studies may include marketing, finance, HR, R&D etc.
3. ***Process Benchmarking:*** This is the activity of measuring discrete performance and functionality against organization through performance in excellent analoguous business processes.
4. ***Internal Benchmarking:*** It is an application of process benchmarking, within an organization by comparing the performance of similar business units or business processes.
5. ***Strategic Benchmarking:*** It differs from operational benchmarking in its scope. It helps to develop a vision of the changed organizations. It will develop core competencies that will help sustained competitive advantage.
6. ***Global Benchmarking:*** It is extension of Strategic Benchmarking to include benchmarking partners on a global scale. eg., Ford Co. of USA benchmarked its Accounts Payable functions with that of Mazda in Japan and found to its surprise that the enitre function was managed by 5 persons as against 500 in Ford.

Benchmarking, to be effective and to lead to successful performance has to reflect the following elements[12]:

- ***Overall Impact on Customer Satisfaction:*** Benchmarking is about external focus and it is essential that all exercises seek to enhance the delivery of quality levels to the end customer.
- ***The Extent of Contribution to Raising Competitive Standards:*** Benchmarking is a strategic competitive tool and as such it seeks to achieve standards of performance in the market place and to raise the internal standards of effectiveness, making them more competitive.

- ***Opportunity to Create the Learning Organisation:*** Benchmarking makes organisations seek to establish standards way beyond meeting basic requirements and to work towards a continuous surge for new ideas, new methods and new ways of working.
- ***Inspirations from Best-In-Class Companies:*** Benchmarking gives organizations the impetus and the desire to follow those organisations which are top of the league and which pioneer new change and new innovations.
- ***Strengthening Weaker Processes:*** Benchmarking helps organisations focus on weaknesses and strengthen them. It also enables them to protect areas of strength and ensure that they sustain high levels of competitiveness.
- ***Enhancing Knowledge Pool:*** Benchmarking is a practice which encourages individuals to learn continuously and to ensure that their knowledge, skills and areas of expertise are never obsolete.
- ***Bringing in State-Of-The-Art Practices:*** Benchmarking, if introduced in a direct fashion, will always ensure that organisations are not lagging behind and they are always pioneering the latest practices that the market demands.
- ***Keeping the Organisation Externally Focused:*** Benchmarking reminds people to focus continuously and constantly on the end customer and on market demands, and as such, it changes the culture from internal focus to an external one.
- ***Extending Employees' Creative Contributions:*** Benchmarking encourages people to work smarter rather than harder, through constantly asking questions related to the practices, their jobs and tasks and to ask why the outputs are lower or higher than those of competitors and other organisations.

ACTIVITY-BASED MANAGEMENT (ABM)

Activity-based management (ABM) is a systematic, integrated approach that describes management decisions that use activity-based costing information to satisfy customers and improve profitability. ABM broadly includes aspects like pricing and product mix decisions, cost reduction and process improvement decisions and product design decisions.

> **Activity-based Management** (ABM) is a systematic, integrated approach that describes management decisions that use activity-based costing information to satisfy customers and improve profitability.

Activity-based management follow this premise: products consume activities; activities consume resources. If managers want their products to be competitive, they must know both (*i*) the activities that go into making the goods or providing the services and (*ii*) the cost of those activities. To reduce a product's cost, managers will likely have to change the activities the product consumes. A manager who announces, "I want across-the-board cuts—everyone reduce costs by 20 per cent," rarely gets the desired results. To make significant cost reduction people must first identify the activities that a product consumes. Then they must figure out how to rework those activities to improve production efficiency[13].

Activity-based Costing and Activity-based Management

The consortium for Advanced Manufacturing International (CAM-I) (USA) defines both the terms as follows:

Activity-based costing is defined as:

- *a methodology that measures the cost and performance of activities, resources and cost objects.*

Specially, resources are assigned to activities based upon consumption rates and activities are assigned to cost objects, again based on consumption. ABC recognises the causal relationships of cost driver to activities.

Activity-based management is defined as:

- *a discipline that focuses on the management of activities as the route to improving the value received by the customer and the profit achieved by providing this value. ABM includes cost driver analysis, activity analysis, and performance measurement, drawing on ABC as its major source of data.*

In simple terms, ABC is used to answer the question "what do things cost?" While ABM, using a process view, is concerned with what factors cause costs to occur. Using ABC data, ABM focuses on how to redirect and improve the use of resources to increase the value created for customers and other stakeholders.

Importance of ABM

ABM focuses on accountability for activities rather than costs and emphasises the maximisation of system wide performance instead of individual performance. ABM control recognizes that maximizing the efficiency of individual subunits does not necessarily lead to maximum efficiency for the system as a whole. The functional-based management control assigns costs to organisational units and then holds the organizational unit manager responsible for controlling the assigned costs. Performance is measured by comparing actual outcomes with standards or budgets. The emphasis is on financial measures of performance; non-financial measures are usually ignored. The functional based management traces costs to individuals who are responsible for incurring costs. The reward system is used to motivate managers to manage costs by increasing the operating efficiency of their organisational units. This approach assumes that maximising the performance of overall organisation is achieved by maximising the performance of individual organisational subunits.

In ABM, both financial and non-financial measures of performance are important. Table 14.3 compares the characteristics of functional-based and activity-based management.

Table 14.3: Functional and Activity-based Management Systems

Functional-Based Management	Activity-Based Management
1. Unit-based drivers	1. Unit- and non-unit-based drivers
2. Allocation-intensive	2. Tracing-intensive
3. Narrow and rigid product costing	3. Broad and flexible product costing
4. Focus on managing costs	4. Focus on managing activities
5. Sparse activity information	5. Detailed activity information
6. Maximisation of individual unit performance	6. System wide performance maximisation
7. Use of financial measures of performance	7. Use of both financial and non-financial measures of performance

Source: Don R. Hansen and Maryanne, Management Accounting, Thomson South-Western, 2005, p. 49.

Plowman[14] comments on the importance of ABM in the following words:

> Overhead costs are the black hole in conventional management information systems. ABM shines light into the hole. Knowledge of a business at the level of activities is the basic building block upon which new understanding can be built of where profits are being made and where they are being eroded.

By making visible what was previously invisible, ABM throws a spotlight on those aspects of a business where action can directly improve business performance. Because it deals with 'financial numbers', ABM is often seen as the preserve of the finance function. In fact, its real strength lies in providing genuinely, useful information for all functions in an organisation. Managers throughout the business need the right information to understand and address two key issues:

- How the company can position itself better in the market — for which accurate product and customer profitability information is vital
- How it can improve its internal capability and lower unit costs — for this, it needs to understand and change the procedures, systems and processes that create products and deliver services to customers

Areas in which ABM can be used

ABM can be used by companies in the following areas:

1. ***Developing Corporate Strategy:*** ABM can help the firms to develop appropriate company strategy, long-term plans and competitive advantage by focusing on and managing activities. Some firms have competitive advantage by providing a low-cost product or manage actitivities to reduce costs. To reduce costs generally requires changes in activities. Anyone can cut costs—if the operation is closed, costs will be reduced. However, ABM has the objective of cutting costs while maintaining quality and quantity of output.
2. ***Making Activity Analysis:*** ABM aims to achieve continuous improvement by making activity analysis *i.e.* by classifying each activity as value-added or non-value added. A value-added activity is an activity that adds value to a product or service from the view point of the customer. A non-value-added activity is an activity that does not add value to a product or service from the viewpoint of the customer. The value-added activities make up value-chain. The value chain is a linked set of value-creating activities leading from raw material sources to the ultimate end use of the goods or services produced. Value chain analysis is an ongoing process in which activities are constantly being classified, eliminated and improved.

Non-value added activities merely add to costs which can be eliminated without reducing product quality, performance or value. In a manufacturing firm, the following are examples of non-value added activities:

(*i*) ***Movement:*** Time spent for transfer around the factory floor where value-added activities are performed.

(*ii*) ***Waiting:*** Idle time does not add value to products. Reducing the time spent between value-added activities reduces cost of idle time.

(*iii*) ***Set up:*** Time spent preparing to perform a value-added activity.

(*iv*) ***Inspection:*** Time spent verifying that a value-added activity was done correctly.

(*v*) ***Storage:*** Storage of materials, work-in-process, or finished goods inventory is a non-value added activity.

The above non-value added activities are found in manufacturing organisations. In other organisations such as government departments, hospitals, universities, colleges, fast-food restaurants, utilities one may find a large number of non-value added activities.

3. Reducing customer response time—ABM helps to reduce customer response time by identifying activities that consume the most resources in value and time. ABM also helps in reducing customer response time by identifying and eliminating non-value added

activities. This way the customer response time and cost will decline. Customers also appreciate a quick response time to their orders which is facilitated through activity-based management.

JUST-IN-TIME (JIT) METHOD

Just-In-Time (JIT) is a purchasing and inventory control method in which materials are obtained just-in-time for production to provide finished goods just-in-time for sale. JIT is a demand-pull system. Demand for customer output (not plans for using input resources) triggers production. Production activities are "pulled" not "pushed" into action. As philosophy, JIT targets inventory as an evil presence that obscures problems that should be solved, and declares that, by contributing significantly to costs, target inventories keep a company from being as competitive or profitable as it otherwise might be. A just-in-time manufacturing system requires making goods or service only when the customer, internal or external, requires it. JIT requires better coordination with suppliers so that materials arrive immediately prior to their use. It reduces or eliminates inventory and the costs associated with carrying the inventory. It emphasises that workers immediately correct the system making defective units because they have no inventory. With no inventory to draw from for delivery to customers, just-in-time relies on high quality materials and production. It is required that the companies that use just-in-time manufacturing must eliminate all the sources of failure in the system. Production people must be better trained so that they can carry out their works without errors. Suppliers must be able to produce and deliver defect free materials or components just when they are required, and equipment must be maintained so that machine failures are eliminated.

JIT aims to achieve the following objectives:

- Zero inventory
- Zero breakdowns
- 100% on time delivery service
- Elimination of non-value added activities
- Zero defects.

The major differences between JIT manufacturing and traditional manufacturing are as shown in Table 14.4:

Table 14.4: Difference between JIT Manufacturing and Traditional Manufacturing

JIT	Traditional
Pull system	Push system
Insignificant or zero inventories	Significant inventories
Manufacturing cells (work centres)	Process structure
Multifunction labour	Specialised labour
Total quality management (TQM)	Acceptable quality level (AQL)
Simple cost accounting	Complex cost acconting

JIT applies to raw materials inventory as well as to work-in-process inventory. The goals are that both raw materials and work-in-process inventory are held to absolute minimums. JIT is used to complement other materials planning and control tools, such as EOQ and safety stock levels. In JIT system, production of an item does not commence until the organisation receives an order. When an order is received for a finished product, productions people give orders for raw materials. As soon as production is complete to fill the order, production ends. In theory, in JIT, there is no need for inventories because no production takes place until the organisation knows that it will sell them. In practice, however, companies using just-in-time inventory generally have a backlog of orders or stable demand for their products to assure continued production.

The fundamental objective of JIT is to produce and deliver what is needed, when it is needed, at all stages of the production process–just-in-time to be fabricated, subassembled, assembled, and dispatched to the customer. Although in practice there are no such perfect plans, JIT is an ideal and therefore a worthy goal. The benefits are low inventory, high manufacturing cycle rates, high output per employee, minimum floor space requirements, minimum indirect labour, and perfect in-process control. An associated requirement of a successful JIT operation is the pursuit of perfect quality in order to reduce, to an absolute minimum, delays caused by defective product units[15].

CASES

CASE 1

Eastern Switching Co. (ESC) produces telecommunications equipment. In recent years, the company has lost considerable market share to foreign competition and to several new domestic companies. Product quality is the primary factor that gives one company a competitive advantage over another. A reputation for reliability and for meeting customer specifications is often the determining factor in a sale, even when the price is higher.

Charles Laurent, ESC's president, decided to implement a company-wide quality improvement programme. He believes that the company's survival depends on improving product quality, and that the way to accomplish this is to adopt the philosophy and techniques of total quality management (TQM). Laurent's goal is to make ESC a world-class manufacturer and to become the best in the industry in terms of product quality and service.

Philip Larkin, ESC's vice president of operations, is concerned that the attempt to implement this programme will cause productivity to decline and costs to increase. He views "quality" as an abstract idea without measurable characteristics. To him, quality programmes are just executive slogans that lead to employee discussion groups and that slow down production.

Required:

A. In general, identify and discuss at least three factors that will help an organisation to successfully implement a quality improvement program.

B. Define and briefly discuss the following quality related terms.

1. Total quality management (TQM).
2. Employee involvement.
3. Competitive benchmaking.

C. Discuss Philip Larkin's concern at Eastern Switching Co. that quality programmes only decrease productivity and increase costs. *(CMA, USA, Adapted with permission)*

Solution:

A. At least three factors that will help an organisation to successfully implement a quality programme include

- Resource commitments to help increase employee empowerment. If the funds and personnel are not committed, the programme will probably fail.

- An accounting system that identifies quality costs. Knowing the costs of poor quality motivates change and provides a means for measuring improvement.
- An organisational culture change as the entire company needs to be focused on the customer.

B. 1. Total quality management (TQM) is a strategic commitment by top management to completely focus the company's efforts toward continuously improving level of quality to the customer throughout the company's business processes and practices.

2. Employee involvement is a process for empowering employees to take an active role in the company's quality improvement activities. Employee involvement focuses on using the creativity and problem-solving skills of all employees.

3. Competitive benchmarking is a continuous process of measuring a company's own products, services, processes, and practices against the best company in their class.

C. Underlying Larkin's concern is the assumption that productivity can only be increased by decreasing quality. Larkin's concern is shortsighted as he is only considering the short-term costs and not the long-term benefits. The initial implementation of a quality programme will temporarily result in lost production time as employees are trained and become more involved in production problem-solving, but these costs prove to be sound investments in the long term. Internal and external failure costs decline and customer satisfaction increases. Experience has shown that quality leads to a decrease in the number of defects, which in turn leads to a decrease in the resources dedicated to rework and inspection. Customer returns, warranty costs and customer lawsuits all decline. Moreover, the cost of future lost sales due to poor quality should decrease substantially.

CASE 2

Eileen Kunselman, president of Phoenix Electronics (PE), is concerned about the prospects of one of its major products. The president has been reviewing a marketing report with Jeff Keller, marketing product manager, for their 10-disk car compact disk (CD) changer. The report indicates another price reduction is needed to meet anticipated competitors' reduction in sales price. The current selling price for their 10-disk car CD changers is ₹ 3,500 per unit. It is expected that within three months PE's two major competitors will be selling their 10-disk car CD changers for ₹ 3,000 per unit. This concerns Kunselman because their current cost of producing the CD changers is ₹ 3,150 which yields a ₹ 350 profit on each unit sold.

The situation is especially disturbing because PE had implemented an activity based costing (ABC) system about two years ago. The ABC system helped them better identify costs, cost pools, cost drivers and reduce costs. Changes made when adopting ABC reduced costs on this product by approximately 15 per cent during the last two years. Now it appears cost will need to be reduced considerably more to remain competitive and to earn a profit on the 10-disk car CD changers. Total costs to produce, sell, and service the CD changer unit are as follows.

10-disk Car CD Changer

		Per Unit
Materials:	Purchased components	₹ 1,100
	All other materials	400
Labour:	Manufacturing, direct	650
	Setups	90
	Material handling	180
	Inspection	230
Machining:	Cutting, shaping and drilling	210
	Bending and finishing	140
Other:	Finished goods warehousing	50
	Warranty	100
	Total unit cost	3,150

Kunselman has decided to hire Donald Collins, a consultant, to help decide how to proceed. After two weeks of review, discussion, and value engineering analysis, Collins suggested that PE adopt a just-in-time (JIT) cell manufacturing process to help reduce costs. He also suggested that using target costing would help in meeting the new target price.

By changing to a JIT cell manufacturing system, PE expects that manufacturing direct labour will increase by ₹ 150 per finished unit. However, setup, material handling, inspection, and finished goods warehousing will all be eliminated. Machine costs will be reduced from ₹ 350 to ₹ 300 per unit, and warranty costs are expected to be reduced by 40 per cent.

Required:

A. 1. Define "target costing."

2. Define "value engineering."

B. Determine Phoenix Electronics' unit target cost at the ₹ 3,000 competitive sales price while maintaining the same percentage of profit on sales as is earned on the current ₹ 3,500 sales price.

C. If the just-in-time (JIT) cell manufacturing process is implemented with the changes in costs noted above, will Phoenix Electronics meet the unit target cost you determined in requirement B above? Prepare a schedule detailing cost reductions and the unit cost under the proposed JIT cell manufacturing process. (*CMA, USA, Adapted with permission*)

Solution:

A. 1. Target costing is a method of determining the allowable cost of a product or service. The allowable cost or target cost is an estimated long-run cost of a product or service that when sold will yield a target profit. Normally, the target sales price is determined first; this is generally equal to or less than the competitive market price of the product or service. The target profit is then deducted, leaving the target cost of production to earn the desired (normal) profit.

2. Value engineering is a systematic evaluation of all aspects of the cost structure of a product or service, including research and development, design of products and processes, production, marketing, distribution and customer service, with the objective of reducing costs while satisfying customer needs. It differs from traditional approaches to cost reduction and cost control in that its focus is on the elimination of non-value-added activities (e.g., waste) from the process.

Value engineering focuses on improving those qualities that the customer desires, while reducing or eliminating unnecessary moves, queues, setups, and other such activities that the customer will not pay for. The process is reengineered to eliminate non-value-added work and thereby enhance the value of the process to the customer.

B. Phoenix Electronics' current profit on sales is 10 per cent [(₹ 3,500 – ₹ 3,150)/₹ 3,500]. Therefore, the target cost for the new product must be ₹ 3,000 less 10 per cent, or ₹ 2,700 [₹ 3,000 – (₹ 3,000 × 10%)]

C. The proposed changes to the just-in-time (JIT) cell manufacturing process at Phoenix Electronics will bring costs down to ₹ 2,660 per unit, which is below the ₹ 2,700 target cost limit. Adjusted costs under the JIT cell manufacturing process are calculated below.

	Current	***(Increase /Decrease)***	***Revised***
Materials			
Purchased components	₹ 1,100		₹ 1,100
All other	400		400
Labour			
Manufacturing direct	650	₹ 150	800
Setups	90	(90)	00
Material handling	180	(180)	00
Inspection	230	(230)	00
Machining			
All	350	(50)	300
Other			
Finished goods warehousing	50	(50)	00
Warranty*	100	(40)	60
Total JIT Cost	3,150	(490)	2,660

*40% reduction

REFERENCES

1. K. Simmonds. Strategic Management Accounting for Pricing, A Case Example, Accounting & Business Research, 1982, pp. 206–214.
2. R. Cooper and R.S. Kaplan. "Measure Costs Right: Make the Right Decisions, Harvard Business Review. (Sept-October 1988). pp. 96-103.
3. M. Bromwich, "The Case for Strategic Management Accounting: the Role of Accounting Information for Strategy in Competitive Markets", Accounting, Organisations and Society, No. 1 (1990), pp. 27-46.
4. J. Innes. Strategic Management Accounting in J. Innes, (Ed.) Handbook of Management Accounting.
5. B. R. Lord, 'Strategic Management Accounting: the Emperor's New Clothes?', Management Accounting Research 7(3), 1996, pp. 347-366.

6. Don R. Hansen and Maryanne M. Mowen, Management Accounting, South Western College Publishing, 2000, pp. 394-395.
7. Ronald W. Hilton, Managerial Accounting, McGraw Hill Education, 2006, pp. 649-650.
8. Ray H. Garrison, and Eric W. Noreen, Managerial Accounting, Irwin McGraw Hill, 2000, p. 635.
9. Charles T. Horngreen, George Foster and Sri Kant M. Datar, Cost Accounting, a Managerial Emphasis, Prentice Hall of India Pvt. Ltd. p. 695.
10. Wayne J. Morse, James R. Davis and A1. L. Hartgraves, Management Accounting, Thomson, 2003, pp. 141-142.
11. Robert Camp, "A Bible for Benchmarking by Xeros" Financial Executives (July-August 1993), p. 24.
12. Mohamed Zairi, Measuring Performance for Business Results, Chapman & Hall, London, 1994, p. 67.
13. Michael W. Maher, Clyde P. Stickney, Roman L. Weil, Managerial Accounting, The Dryden Press, 1997, p. 149.
14. Brian Plowman, Activity-Based Management, Gower, Hamphshire, 2001, pp. 4-5.
15. Milton F. Usry and Lawrence H. Hammer, Cost Accounting, Planning and Control, South Western Publishing Co., 1999, p. 257.

CRITICAL ANALYSIS AND DISCUSSION QUESTIONS, AND MULTIPLE CHOICE QUESTIONS

CRITICAL ANALYSIS AND DISCUSSION QUESTIONS

1. What is strategic management accounting? Explain how strategic management accounting can provide information to senior managers in achieving their corporate objectives.
2. Define strategic management accounting. What aspects have been focussed in such accounting system?
3. Distinguish between traditional management accounting and modern management accounting.
4. Distinguish between value-added and non-value-added activities.
5. What is the relationship between target costing and continuous improvement costing?
6. What is competitive benchmarking? Why firms should have reliable suppliers when using just-in-time methods?
7. What are the dimensions of activity-based management (ABM)?
8. What is activity-analysis? How is this approach compatible with the goal of continuous improvement?
9. Distinguish between activity-base costing and activity-based management.
10. Explain how benchmarking can be used to improve activity performance.
11. Describe the benefits of life-cycle costing.
12. What is target costing? Describe how costs are reduced so that the target cost can be met?
13. What are the four key perspectives in the balanced scorecard?
14. "There is no trade-off between customer response time and on time performance". Do you agree? Explain.
15. Describe the three main measures used in the theory of constraints.
16. Describe just-in-time (JIT) method. What are the main features in a JIT production system?
17. Distinguish between traditional costing and target costing.
18. What is target costing? What principles are involved in it?
19. What is Kaizen costing?
20. Distinguish between target costing and Kaizen costing.
21. Discuss the Theory of Constraints (TOC).
22. How does TOC help management in improving profitability?
23. Discuss the considerations in benchmarking.
24. What are the uses of ABM?
25. Distinguish between JIT and traditional manufacturing.
26. What are the advantages of JIT?

27. What is a just-in-time manufacturing system? Why would organisations choose to adopt it?
28. Explain the similarities and differences among target costing, kaizen costing and life cycle costing.
29. Identify three products for which target costing and kaizen costing could be used. Identify three products for which target costing and kaizen costing would be inappropriate.
30. Explain the target costing cycle, and discuss the decision criteria used to determine whether a product will be manufactured using a target costing approach.
31. List some common advantages and disadvantages for target and kaizen costing.
32. You have recently been hired as an accountant for a start-up entity in the computer peripherals industry. The owners have developed and are manufacturing several wireless devices to enhance user mobility, such as a small electronic notebook. They want to become more competitive in this market and also develop several other products. They have asked you for ideas about ways to control costs and determine whether proposed new products will be profitable.

Required:

Write a presentation to the owners describing how they could use target costing and kaizen costing.

MULTIPLE CHOICE QUESTIONS

Select the correct answer for the following multiple choice questions.

1. The budgeting tool or process in which estimates of revenues and expenses are prepared for each product beginning with the product's research and development phase and traced through to its customer support phase is a (n)
   (*a*) Master budget
   (*b*) Activity-based budget
   (*c*) Zero-base budget
   (*d*) Life-cycle budget
2. Companies that adopt just-in-time purchasing systems often experience
   (*a*) A reduction in the number of suppliers
   (*b*) Fewer deliveries from suppliers
   (*c*) A greater need for inspection of goods as the goods arrive
   (*d*) Less need for linkage with a vendor's computerised order entry system
3. In target costing
   (*a*) the market price of the product is taken as a given
   (*b*) only raw materials, labour, and variable overhead cannot exceed a threshold target
   (*c*) only raw materials cannot exceed a threshold target
   (*d*) raw materials are recorded directly to cost of goods sold
   (*e*) both labour and manufacturing overhead are charged directly to conversion costs
4. The series of activities in which customer usefulness is added to the product is the definition of
   (*a*) a value chain
   (*b*) process value analysis
   (*c*) integrated manufacturing
   (*d*) activity-based costing
   (*e*) a cost measurement system

5. Life-cycle costing
   (*a*) is often used in financial and income tax reporting
   (*b*) is sometimes used as a basis for cost planning and product pricing
   (*c*) includes only manufacturing costs incurred over the life of the product
   (*d*) includes only manufacturing cost, selling expense, and distribution expense
   (*e*) emphasises cost savings opportunities during the manufacturing cycle
6. Companies that adopt just-in-time purchasing systems often experience
   (*a*) an increase in carrying costs
   (*b*) a reduction in the number of suppliers
   (*c*) fewer deliveries from suppliers
   (*d*) a greater need for inspection of goods
   (*e*) an increase in safety stock
7. Indian Airlines reducing the airfare on the Delhi-Mumbai sector following the introduction of the no frills airlines would be an example of:
   (*a*) Cost leadership (*b*) Price leadership
   (*c*) Product leadership (*d*) Focus
8. Benchmarking is:
   (*a*) The Analytical tool to identify high cost activities based on the 'Pareto Analysis'
   (*b*) The search of industries best practices that lead to superior performance
   (*c*) The simulation of cost reduction schemes that help to build commitment and improvement of actions
   (*d*) The framework that earmarks a linkage with suppliers and customers
9. Which of the following parameters are covered in Balanced Score Card?
   (*a*) Customers' Perspective (*b*) Financial Perspective
   (*c*) Suppliers' Perspective (*d*) Learning and growth

   Options:
   (*a*) (*a*) and (*b*) (*b*) (*b*) and (*d*)
   (*c*) (*a*) and (*c*) (*d*) (*a*), (*b*), (*c*) and (*d*)
10. In a TQM environment, external benchmarking is preferred to standard costing as a performance measurement technique because:
    (*a*) Standard Costs is applicable in a traditional mass-production industry
    (*b*) TQM refers to a pre-determined internal standard and emphasizes continuous imporvement
    (*c*) Concept of Standard Costing is alien to the emphasis given on employee-empowerment in TQM
    (*d*) Standard Costs become obsolete quickly
11. The idea of value chain was first suggested by:
    (*a*) Michael Porter (*b*) Joseph Juran
    (*c*) Goldratt and Core (*d*) John Shank

12. The concept of Target Costing originated in:

    a) USA (*b*) UK

    (*c*) Japan (*d*) Germany

Answer to Multiple Choice Questions

1. (*d*)	2. (*a*)	3. (*a*)	4. (*a*)	5. (*b*)
6. (*b*)	7. (*b*)	8. (*b*)	9. (*d*)	10. (*b*)
11. (*a*)	12. (*c*)			

15

MANAGEMENT CONTROL SYSTEM (MCS)

LEARNING OBJECTIVES:

After reading this chapter, you should be able to:

- Define Management Control System, Formal and Informal Control System; Identify Characteristics of MCS and Explain the Factors Influencing Management Control Systems
- Discuss Steps in Management Control System Such as Strategy Formulation, Management Control, Task or Operational Control
- Understand Simon's 4 P's of Strategy
- Distinguish between Strategy Formulation and Management Control; between Operational Control and Management Control
- Explain Management Control Structure and Process

MANAGEMENT CONTROL SYSTEM: DEFINITION AND NATURE

Horngreen, Datar and Foster[1] define management control system as:

- *A means of gathering and using information to aid and coordinate the process of making, planning, and control decisions throughout the organisation and to guide the behaviour of its managers and employees. The goal of management control system is to improve the collective decisions within an organisation in an economically feasible way.*

Different managers perform different responsibilities in an organisation and therefore different kinds of information are needed by them to manage the activities in their respective areas. Management control system should be able to develop, gather and communicate information to management at different levels in the organisation. Also, management control system should aim to provide financial as well as non-financial information as needed by different managers. Some examples of financial information are material costs, labour costs, net profit, investments made, etc. Non-financial data are those which are not in monetary terms such as production units per worker, labour hours, machine hours, time taken to comply with the customer's orders, absenteeism. Some information gathered under management control system may emerge from internal data maintained within the firm. Some other information required by managers may be gathered from external sources such as information about competitors' product. As stated earlier, different types of information are needed by persons working at different levels in the organisation. *For example*, top managers may require internal as well as external financial and non-financial data as their responsibilities relate to total organisation. However, a production manager would be more interested in internally generated financial and non-financial data.

MANAGEMENT CONTROL SYSTEM: FORMAL AND INFORMAL

> **Management Control System** includes formal and informal control system needed to guide, direct, motivate managers and other employees and coordinate their behaviours to achieve organisational goals.

Management control system includes both formal control system and informal control system. A formal control system requires that an organisation should have clear-cut rules, procedures, guidelines, plans relating to different managerial aspects. Such things are needed to guide, direct, motivate the managers and other employees and coordinate their behaviour to achieve organisational goals. In an organisation, many formal control systems may exist such as cost accounting system, management accounting system, production engineering systems, human resource system, quality maintenance system, etc. Informal management control systems are always unwritten and implicit. However, they contribute greatly in the implementation of business goals and strategies and help the organisation to attain high degree of motivation and goal congruence. Examples of informal management control systems are unwritten norms about good behaviour of managers and employees, loyalties, shared values, organisational culture and ethics, mutual commitments among managers and employees.

A major objective of management control is to encourage goal congruence, which means that as people work to achieve their own goals, they also work to achieve the goals of the company. People must have incentives to work towards the company's goals. To accomplish that objective, managers must assign responsibilities and develop performance evaluation criteria that motivate employees to work towards the company's goals.

A management control system is most effective when it establishes evaluation criteria that encourage goal-congruent behaviour and is implemented through a responsibility accounting system that employees trust to report their performance[2].

CHARACTERISTICS OF MANAGEMENT CONTROL SYSTEMS

Management control systems designed in an organisation should fulfil the following characteristics[3]:

1. Management control systems should be closely aligned to an organisation's strategies and goals.
2. Management control systems should be designed to fit the organisation's structure and the decision-making responsibility of individual managers.
3. Effective management control systems should motivate managers and employees to exert efforts toward attaining organisation goals through a variety of rewards tied to the achievement of those goals.

FACTORS INFLUENCING MANAGEMENT CONTROL SYSTEMS

Factors influencing the design of Management Control Systems are as follows[4]:

1. ***Size and Spread of the Enterprise:*** The size and spread of a large firm is bound to be different compared with that of a small firm. This would certainly determine the content and nature of the control system for each organisation.
2. ***Organisational Structure, Delegation and Decentralisation:*** Statutes and conventions govern organisational structure, and the extent of decentralisation and delegation in all enterprises. For example, the management philosophy of the State Bank of India is bound to be different from that of the State Trading Corporation. Also, within an enterprise, the degree of decentralisation and delegation changes from one point of time to another to meet changed environmental challenges and the opportunities that these may present. All these influence management control systems practiced in organisations.
3. ***Nature of Operations and Divisibility:*** Nature of operations and their divisibility affect management control systems. For example, in the oil industry, for instance, sub-units can not be formed on the basis of products. In many large trading companies, however, divisions can be created on the basis of products. Again, in the paper industry, the different stages in pulp making can not be subdivided for the purposes of management control, though pulp making as a whole can be regarded as a division.
4. ***Types of Responsibility Centres:*** Different control systems are needed for the various responsibility centres or sub-systems within an organisation. Whether the performance of a responsibility centre should be measured in terms of expenses or profitability or return on investment depends on the type of responsibility centre. For example, a bank may apply different performance measures to measure performance of its different branches. There are transactional differences between branches; some are deposit heavy or advance heavy, some are with or without safe deposit facilities or foreign exchange transaction. It is, therefore, not possible to have profit as the sole criteria for performance evaluation of all branches. Hence, control systems with different criteria of performance should be used for different sub-units.
5. ***People and their Perceptions:*** Perceptions of people in the organisation about the likely effects of the control system on their work life, job satisfaction, job security, promotion and general well-being could differ across organisations. These considerations will significantly influence the nature and content of the management control system needed in the organisation and must be duly considered while designing management control systems.

STEPS IN MANAGEMENT CONTROL SYSTEMS

Management control systems involve the entire planning and control systems of an organisation. Management control system has the following steps (also known as processes or phases) which occur in a sequence.

1. Strategy Formulation
2. Management Control
3. Task Control or Operational Control

The above three processes cannot be totally separated from each other; one does influence the other. However, at the same time, they are treated as distinct from each other for the purpose of designing a suitable planning and control system. It is necessary that organisations should be aware about the similarities and differences among them before developing planning and control system. Infact, strategic planning sets the guidelines for management control and management control sets the guidelines for task control.

Further, one should not think that each of the above three processes — strategy formulation management control and task control — includes either planning activity or controlling activity. Each process has a combination of both — planning and control.

In the following sections, the above three processes have been discussed in detail.

STRATEGY FORMULATION

> **Strategy** is an activity, goal or objective which is of great importance to an enterprise and will have vital impact on the achievement of an organisation's objectives.

The word 'strategy' indicates something like an activity, goal, objectives which are of great importance to an enterprise and which have vital impact on the achievement of an organisation's objectives. Strategy describes how an organisation matches its own capabilities with the opportunities in the market place in order to accomplish its overall objectives. Strategy determines enterprise policy and priorities for many organisational activities like research and development, marketing, financing, plant expansion. A strategy which is formulated by top management, should ensure integration of all activities and all aspects of organisation functions to achieve long range goals.

According to Shank and Govindrajan[5], strategy is:

- *the process by which managers, using a three-to five-year time horizon, evaluate external environmental opportunities as well as internal strengths and resources in order to decide on goals as well as a set of action plans to accomplish these goals. Thus, a business unit's strategy depends upon two interrelated aspects: (1) its mission or goals, and (2) the way the business unit chooses to compete in its industry to accomplish its goals — the business unit's competitive advantage.*

Strategy looks ahead to several years into the future. Strategies are concerned with the organisation's major products and services and related aspects of marketing, manufacturing, service delivery, and research and development. Strategic decisions almost invariably result in long-term financial costs and benefits and may require significant investment.

Strategy can also be defined as:

- *the art of creating value. It provides the intellectual frameworks, conceptual models, and governing ideas that allow a company's managers to identify opportunities for bringing value to customers and for delivering value at a profit. In this respect, strategy is the way a company defines its business and links together the only two resources that really matter in today's economy: knowledge and relationships or an organisation's competencies and its customers*[6]

According to Horngreen, Foster and Datar[7], in formulating its strategy, an organisation must thoroughly understand the industry in which it operates. Industry analysis focuses on five forces: (*a*) competitors, (*b*) potential entrants into the market (*c*) equivalent products (*d*) bargaining power of customers, and (*e*) bargaining power of input suppliers. The collective effect of these forces shapes an organisation's profit potential. In general, profit potential decreases with greater competition, stronger potential entrants, products that are similar and tougher customers and suppliers. To be successful, a company must both formulate an effective strategy and implement it vigorously. The management accountant has an important role to play in the implementation of strategy. This role takes the form of designing reports to help managers track progress in implementing strategy. Balanced scorecard is an approach used by many organisations to manage the implementation of their strategies.

The terms 'strategy' and 'policy' are often used interchangeably as are the terms goals and objectives. Strategy and policies as well as goals and objectives are constraints which should be considered in the design and operations of management control systems. Maciariello[8] highlights the complex relationship between strategy and policy in the following manner:

> Strategies are concerned with meeting the threats and opportunities presented by the environment external to the organisation. Policies, on the other hand, are an elaboration of strategy so as to apply effectively internal resources and thereby achieve objectives and goals. In still other words, constraints imposed by management upon the operations of the firm vis-a-vis the external environment represent its strategy, whereas the major internal constraints, those that it places on the internal operations of the firm, are referred to as "policies." Again, it should be noted that goals and objectives are also self-imposed internal constraints.

Hamel and Prahlad[9] in their popular book *Competing for the Futures* have described many facts of strategy, as listed below, which may be quite different from what prevails in many companies.

> It is a view of strategy that recognizes that a firm must unlearn much of its past before it can find the future. It is a view of strategy that recognizes it is not enough to optimally position a company within existing markets; the challenge is to pierce the fog of uncertainty and develop great *foresight* into the whereabouts of tomorrow's markets. It is a view of strategy that recognizes the need for more than an incrementalist, annual planning rain dance; what is needed is a *strategic architecture* that provides a blueprint for building the competencies needed to dominate future markets.
>
> It is a view of strategy that is less concerned with ensuring a tight fit between goals and resources and is more concerned with creating *stretch goals* that challenge employees to accomplish the seemingly impossible. It is a view of strategy as more than the allocation of scarce resources across competing projects; strategy is the quest to overcome resource constraints through a creative and unending pursuit of better resource leverage.
>
> It is a view of strategy that recognizes that companies not only compete within the boundaries of existing industries, they compete to *shape the structure* of future industries. It is a view of strategy that recognizes that competition for *core competence* leadership precedes competition for product leadership, and that conceives of the corporation as a portfolio of competencies as well as a portfolio of businesses. It is a view of strategy that recognizes that competition often takes place within and between *coalitions* of companies, and not only between individual businesses.
>
> It is a view of strategy that recognizes that product failures are often inevitable, but nevertheless provide the opportunity to learn more about just where the mother lode of future demand may lie. It is a view of strategy that recognizes that to capitalize on foresight and core competence leadership, a company must ultimately preempt competitors in critical global markets; that the issue is not so much time to market, but time to *global preemption*."

These are the themes in *Competing for the Future*: (Exhibit 15.1)

Exhibit 15.1: Strategy Paradigm

The New Strategy Paradigm	
Not Only	**But Also**
The Competitive Challenge	
Reengineering processes	Regenerating strategies
Organisational transformation	Industry transformation
Competing for market share	Competing for opportunity share
Finding the Future	
Strategy as learning	Strategy as forgetting
Strategy as positioning	Strategy as foresight
Strategic plans	Strategic architecture
Mobilizing for the Future	
Strategy as fit	Strategy as stretch
Strategy as resource allocation	Strategy as resource accumulation and leverage
Getting to the Future First	
Competing within an existing industry structure	Competing to shape future industry structure
Competing for product leadership	Competing for core competence leadership
Competing as a single entity	Competing as a coalition
Maximizing the ratio of new product "hits"	Maximizing the rate of new market learning
Minimizing time-to-market	Minimizing time to global preemption

Source: Gary Hamel and C.K. Prahlad, *Competing for the Future*, Harvard Business School Press, 1994, P. 26.

An organisation's strategy tries to match its internal skills and resources to the opportunities found in the external environment. Small organisations may have a single strategy, while large organisations often have an overall entity strategy as well as individual strategies for each business unit (such as a division). The business units' strategies should flow from the overall strategy to ensure that effective and efficient resource allocations are made, an overriding corporate culture is developed, and organisational direction is enhanced.

VISION, MISSION, GOALS

Vision

Designing a company vision statement is an essential step in the management process and functions to perform well in the future. A vision statement aims to provide a conceptual view of an organisation's future that is better than its present. The statement should provide a unifying focus on which all company personnel can base their decisions and activities. Thus, all employees will be working for the same long-term results.

> **Vision** is the core purpose and ideology of the organisation.
>
> **Mission Statement** is an organisational road map.

The vision is the core purpose and ideology of the organisation, which guides the organisation's overall direction and approaches towards its various stakeholder groups such as owners, employees, customers/clients, suppliers government, community, society and others.

Mission

Mission is what we do. A mission is a brief statement of what a business does or stands for. An organisation's mission is the basic purpose toward which its activities are directed. A mission statement is an organisational road map. It should (*i*) clearly state what the organisation wants to accomplish and (*ii*) express how that organisation uniquely meets its targeted customers needs with its products and services. Based on its mission, management sets a number of long- and short-range goals. Translating the organisation's mission into specific activities and resources needed for achievement is called planning.

A mission, by itself, may not seem all that profound, but when combined with a set of core values, these two concepts together can transform a workplace into something that employees believe in and are proud of. Many consulting firms as well as academic researchers have proposed the following three missions that a business unit can adopt[10]:

1. ***Build***: This mission implies a goal of increased market share, even at the expense of short-term earnings and cash flow. A business unit following this mission is expected to be a net user of cash in that the cash throw off from its current operations would usually be insufficient to meet its capital investment needs. Business units with low market share in high-growth industries typically pursue a build mission.
2. ***Hold***: This strategic mission is geared to the protection of the business unit's market share and competitive position. The cash outflows for a business unit following this mission would usually be more or less equal to cash inflows. Businesses with high market share in high-growth industries typically pursue a hold mission.
3. ***Harvest***: This mission implies a goal of maximizing short-term earnings and cash flow even at the expense of market share. A business unit following such a mission would be a net supplier of cash. Businesses with high market share in low-growth industries typically pursue a harvest mission.

Competitive Advantage

In terms of competitive advantage, Porter[11] proposed the following two generic ways in which businesses can develop sustainable competitive advantage:

1. ***Low Cost***: The primary focus of this strategy is to achieve low cost relative to competitors. Cost leadership can be achieved through approaches such as economies of scale of production, learning curve effects, tight cost control and cost minimisation in areas such as R&D, service, sales force or advertising.
2. ***Differentiation:*** The primary focus of this strategy is to differentiate the product offering of the business unit, creating something that is perceived by customers as being unique. Approaches to product differentiation include brand loyalty, superior customer service dealer network, product design and product features and/or product technology.

Goals

Goal is a definable, measurable objective.

Value Statement is a summary of the beliefs that define the organisation's culture.

Core Competency is any critical function or activity in which one organisation has a higher proficiency than its competitors.

A goal is a definable, measurable objective. Based on the organisation's mission, management sets a number of goals. The mission of a paper mill located in a small town is to provide quality paper products in order to earn a profit for its owners. The paper mill's goals might include earning an annual profit equal to

10 per cent of average total assets, maintaining annual dividends of ₹ 2 per share of common equity, developing a customer reputation for above-average quality and service, providing steady employment for area residents, and meeting or exceeding environmental standards.

A clear statement of mission and well-defined goals provide an organisation with an identity and unifying purpose, thereby ensuring that all employees are heading in the same direction. Having developed a mission and a set of goals, employees are more apt to make decisions that move the organisation toward its defined purpose.

Values Statement

A **value statement** can be generated that reflects the organisation's culture by identifying fundamental beliefs about what is important to the organisation. These values may be objective (such as profitability and increased market share) or subjective (such as ethical behaviour and respect for individuals).

A core value statement is a summary of the beliefs that define the organisation's culture.

Core Competencies

A **core competency** is any critical function or activity in which one organisation has a higher proficiency than its competitors. Core competencies are the roots of competitiveness and competitive advantage. **Organisational core competencies** are the organisation's strengths relative to competitors. To create value for stakeholders, an organisation must have strengths relative to competitors. The vision should build on existing and achievable strengths. Core competencies are different for every organisation; they are, so to speak, part of an organisation's personality. Technological innovation, engineering, product development, and after-sale service are some examples of core competencies. Organisations are likely to be more successful when their core competencies and strategies are well aligned.

Exhibit 15.2 presents many different potential areas of organisational strength.

Exhibit 15.2: Organisational Core Competencies

Strengths Relative to Competitors:

• Productivity	• Physical resources	• Legal rights
• Skills	• Customer/supplier relationships	• Regulatory advantages
• Knowledge	• Reputation	• Financial resources
• Technologies	• Growth opportunities	

Exhibit 15.3 displays an Indian Company's Vision and Mission.

Exhibit 15.3: Cement Corporation of India Ltd.

Vision

To emerge as a leading cement company committed to contribute to the economy and to enhance value for the stakeholders.

Mission

To augment the wealth creation for the company, deliver superior product and sustain market value.

Source: Cement Corporation of India Ltd., Annual Report 2014 – 15, p. 2

Exhibits 15.4 and 15.5 show corporate objectives and purpose as stated by two Indian Companies in their annual reports.

Exhibit 15.4: Corporate Objectives of NTPC

Corporate Objectives

To realise the vision and mission, eight key corporate objectives have been identified. These objectives would provide the link between the defined mission and the functional strategies:

■ **Business Portfolio Growth**

- To further consolidate NTPC's position as the leading thermal power generation company in India and establish a presence in hydro power segment.
- To broad base the generation mix by evaluating conventional and non-conventional sources of energy to ensure long run competitiveness and mitigate fuel risks.
- To diversify across the power value chain in India by considering backward and forward integration into areas such as power trading, transmission, distribution, coal mining, coal beneficiation, etc.
- To develop a portfolio of generation assets in international markets.
- To establish a strong services brand in the domestic and international markets.

■ **Customer Focus**

- To foster a collaborative style of working with customers, growing to be a preferred brand for supply of quality power.
- To expand the relationship with existing customers by offering a bouquet of services in addition to supply of power - e.g., trading, energy consulting, distribution consulting, management practices.
- To expand the future customer portfolio through profitable diversification into downstream businesses, inter alia retail distribution and direct supply.
- To ensure rapid commercial decision making, using customer specific information, with adequate concern for the interests of the customer.

■ **Agile Corporation**

- To ensure effectiveness in business decisions and responsiveness to changes in the business environment by:
  - Adopting a portfolio approach to new business development.
  - Continuous and co-ordinated assessment of the business environment to identify and respond to opportunities and threats.
- To develop a learning organisation having knowledge-based competitive edge in current and future businesses.
- To effectively leverage Information Technology to ensure speedy decision making across the organisation.

■ **Performance Leadership**

- To continuously improve on project execution time and cost in order to sustain long run competitiveness in generation.
- To operate & maintain NTPC stations at par with the best-run utilities in the world with respect to availability, reliability, efficiency, productivity and costs.

- To effectively leverase Information Technology to drive process efficiencies.
  - To aim for performance excellence in the diversification businesses.
  - To embed quality in all systems and processes.

■ **Human Resource Development**

- To enhance organisational performance by institutionalising an objective and open performance management system.
- To align individual and organisational needs and develop business leaders by implementing a career development system.
- To enhance commitment of employees by recognising and rewarding high performance.
- To build and sustain a learning organisation of competent world-class professionals.
- To institutionalise core values and create a culture of team-building, empowerment, equity, innovation and openness which would motivate employees and enable achievement of strategic objectives.

■ **Financial Soundness**

- To maintain and improve the financial soundness of NTPC by prudent management of the financial resources.
- To continuously strive to reduce the cost of capital through prudent management of deployed funds, leveraging opportunities in domestic and international financial markets.
- To develop appropriate commercial policies and processes which would ensure remunerative tariffs and minimize receivables.
- To continuously strive for reduction in cost of power generation by improving operating practices.

■ **Sustainable Power Development**

- To contribute to sustainable power development by discharging corporate social responsibilities.
- To lead the sector in the areas of resettlement and rehabilitation and environment protection including effective ash-utilisation, peripheral development and energy conservation practices.
- To lead development efforts in the Indian power sector through efforts at policy advocacy, assisting customers in reforms, disseminating best practices in the operations and management of power plants etc.

■ **Research and Development**

- To pioneer the adoption of reliable, efficient and cost-effective technologies by carrying out fundamental and applied research in alternate fuels and technologies.
- To carry out research and development of breakthrough techniques in power plant construction and operation that can lead to more efficient, reliable and environment friendly operation of power plants in the country.

Source: NTPC, 39th Annual Report 2014–15, p. 1

Exhibit 15.5: Hindustan Unilever

Our Purpose

Our clear Purpose helps us to remain distinct in the eyes of consumers, retailers and suppliers. It also means we can set an ambitious Vision – to double the size of the business whilst reducing our environmental footprint and increasing our positive social impact. To meet our growth ambition we invest in people whose talent will help us win through our brands and innovation, unrivalled execution in the market place and a relentless focus on continuous improvement for greater efficiency. Our environmental and social ambitions are driven through the Unilever Sustainable Living Plan (USLP), which has economic benefits and operates across all our brands, markets and our entire value chain. Even when markets are tough we cannot ignore sustainability. If we did, this would diminish the future resilience of Hindustan Unilever Limited (HUL) for its long-term shareholders. We would miss out on the growing consumer preference for goods that do not damage the environment or exploit people. Our entire business would rely on increasingly rare and expensive raw materials, pushing up our costs. Without more efficient use of energy our production costs would increase while we would miss considerable savings from more sustainable packaging and less waste. We would also risk the disapproval of governments, regulators and NGO's and our brands could suffer reputational damage, representing serious economic loss to the business. That's way sustainability is at the heart of everything we do to ensure we have a viable long-term business that is attractive to investors.

Source: Hindustan Unilever Ltd., Annual Accounts and Reports, 2014–15

Corporate Strategy and Business Strategy

Simons[12] has used the term strategy of two types — corporate strategy and business strategy.

"Corporate strategy defines the way that a firm attempts to maximise the value of the resources it controls. Corporate strategy decisions focus on where corporate resources will be invested.

Business strategy, by contrast, is concerned with how to compete in defined product markets."

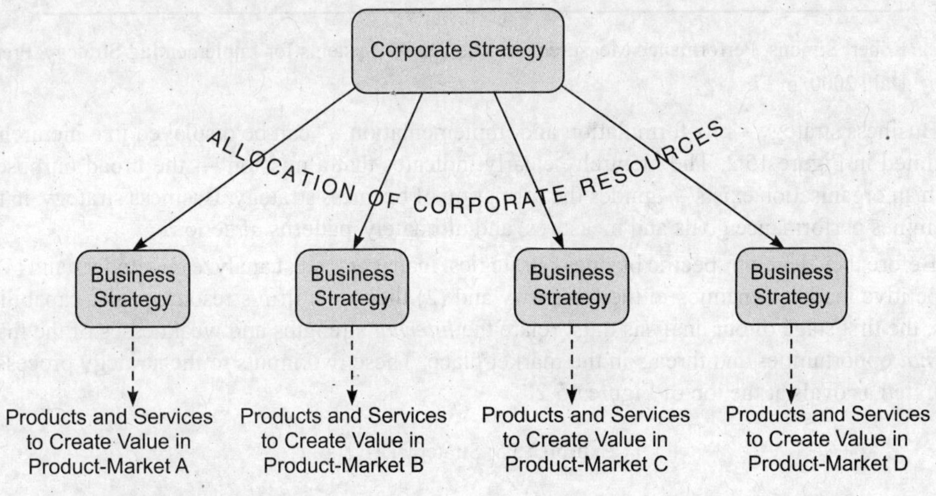

Figure 15.1: Corporate and Business Strategy

Corporate-level strategy results in decisions involving businesses to add, to retain, to emphasise, to deemphasise and businesses to divest. This strategy is about being in the right mix of businesses. Business strategy deal with how to create and maintain competitive advantage in each of the industries in which a company has chosen to participate. Competition between diversified firms is not seen at the corporate level. In fact, a business unit in one company generally competes with a business unit in another company. Business strategy formulation takes into account two factors (*i*) Mission of the business unit and (*ii*) its competitive advantage.

Figure 15.1 illustrates the distinction between corporate strategy and business strategy.

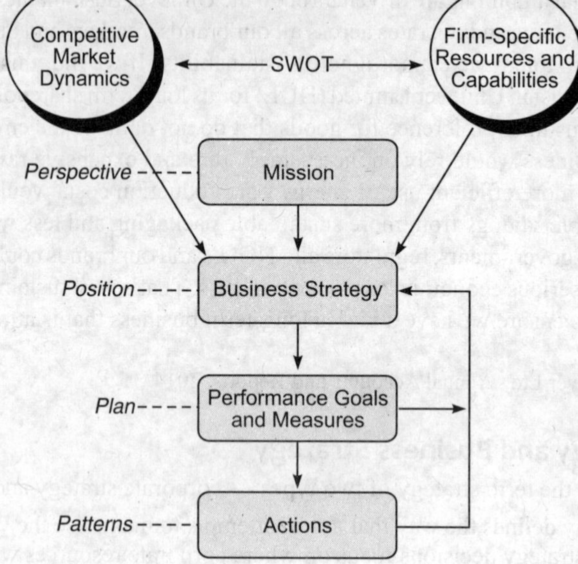

Figure 15.2: Hierarchy of Business Strategy

Source: Robert Simons, Performance Measurement and Control Systems for Implementing Strategy, Prentice Hall, 2000, p. 17.

Business strategy — its formulation and implementation — can be displayed in a hierarchy as illustrated in Figure 15.2. The hierarchy clearly indicates that a mission — the broad purpose for which an organisation exists — guides the formation of business strategy. Business strategy, in turn, determines performance goals and measures, and ultimately, patterns of action.

Before they develop specific business strategies, managers, must analyze and understand (1) the competitive market dynamics in their industry and (2) their own firm's resources and capabilities. Thus, the first stage of our analysis must relate the *internal* strengths and weaknesses of the firm to *external* opportunities and threats in the market place. These two inputs to the strategy process are illustrated as ovals at the top of Figure 15.2.

Exhibit 15.6: Strategy Drivers

Art of Seeing Trees Without Missing the Forest

The Drivers of Strategy

Robert S. Kaplan's proposal is commonsensical: corporate strategy ought to be aligned with strategies of individual business units. But, be points out, there are some basic thumb rules to be followed.

"The more diversified a corporation, the better it is for the strategy to develop first at the business unit level and then percolate up to the top. This would be a good idea for a well-diversified business house like the Tata group."

"But if the company is vertically integrated, or is like a hotel chain where you have identical units in many parts of the country, it is better for the strategy to come from the top. You can't have 1,000 different retail outlets, each one developing its own strategy. That would be chaos."

In cases where the strategy is top driven, it often meets with huge amounts of internal resistance. And as Kaplan puts it, it is first met with denial and then goes into 'medicinal stage' where it is seen as compulsory and people abide by it, but people don't necessarily understand why it is important. How do you tackle this?

Unless you have completely homogeneous retail outlets — such as restaurants and hotel chains — you cannot impose the strategy on all business units.

"Corporate strategy must be articulated and then communicated down to the business units. And then each business unit must develop a strategy that will be effective for them in their markets and their context.

But that will also have to reflect the corporate priorities," says Kaplan. Crafting a local strategy consistent with the corporate strategy creates the buy–in and integrates the business units.

"Asking the business units to accept the corporate strategy and also develop their own strategy creates a sort of 'dual citizenship'. Integrating this corporate strategy at the business unit level pushes the initiative to the business units and it becomes their strategy," says Kaplan.

The best example of dual citizenship is the Royal Canadian Mounted Police (RCMP) which is Canada's national policing force and also provides contract policing services at the regional level. "The wanted the local policing operations to focus not just on the day-to-day local operations, but also contribute to some national policing themes," says Kaplan.

Which is why, RCMP introduced 'dual citizenship'. "The idea is that an employee has to work very effectively for the local organisation (*i.e.*, the local police force), and also contribute to national themes." So a senior team in the RCMP defined a strategy and cascaded it down the ranks. The local units, in turn, considered the relevance of the national priorities for their divisions and then tailored them to fit their situation. Apparently, it works very well. And that really is Kaplan's theme.

Source: The Times of India, New Delhi, Saturday September 2, 2006, p. 18.

SIMON'S 4 P'S STRATEGY

Robert Simon[13] has analysed strategy from four different angles for formulating and implementing strategy effectively. These four different angles are:

Simon's 4 P's Strategy:
- Strategy as Perspective
- Strategy as Position
- Strategy as Plan
- Strategy as Patterns of Actions

1. *Creating a Mission — Strategy as Perspective:* Mission is the starting point for analysis of the formulation and implementation of business strategy. Good missions supply both inspiration and a sense of direction for the future. Missions are often written down in formal documents known as **mission statements** that are circulated widely throughout a firm.

A firm's mission provides an overarching *perspective* to all its activities. Rooted in a business's history, its culture, and the values of its senior managers, a mission statement provides the guideposts that allow all employees to understand how the firm responds to the opportunities that surround it.

2. *Choosing How to Compete — Strategy as Position*: With the mission of the business providing overall perspective — a backdrop for formulating strategy — the next step is to focus on two key questions about the **position of a business** in its competitive marketplace: (1) How do we create value for our customers? and (2) how do we differentiate our products and services from those of our competitors?

Managers of competing firms might answer these questions in very different ways. Some firms may choose to create value by offering their goods and services at *low cost*, hoping to draw customers who are price sensitive; other firms may compete by *differentiating* their products and services in a way that adds unique benefits for customers, or by *customising* product offerings to respond to the specialised needs of specific customer segments.

3. ***Setting Performance Goals — Strategy as Plan:*** After determining the mission and desired strategic position for the business (by analysing competitive dynamics and resources and capabilities), the preparation of plans and goals represents the formal means by which managers (*a*) communicate a business's strategy to the organisation and (*b*) coordinate the internal resources to ensure that the strategy can be achieved. When managers are asked, "What is your strategy?", they will often refer to their strategic plans — the documents where strategy is written down.

Goals as mentioned in the profit plans and operating plans are the ends or results that an organisation and its management want to achieve in implementing the business strategy. However, goals become actionable and more important when they are mentioned alongwith their respective time frames and quantitative indicators or targets. Without these, managers can not monitor progress and evaluate their success in achieving goals. For example, in case of a supermarket or retailer, the goals and their time frames and quantitative targets are displayed in Exhibit. 15.7.

Exhibit 15.7: Goals, Quantitative Targets, Time Schedules

Goals	*Quantitative Targets*	*Time Schedules*
1. Increase market share	1. By 5%	1. Within 12 months
2. Open new stores	2. Five new stores	2. During next year
3. Launch a new product line	3. Two new product lines	3. By January 1
4. Reduce expenses	4. By 7%	4. Over the next two years
5. Develop information – technology capabilities	5. Install new PCs and automated inventory system	5. In next one year
6. Improve customer satisfaction	6. By 15%	6. Within six months.

4. ***Feedback and Adjustment — Strategy as Patterns in Action***: Not all successful strategies are planned. Many emerge spontaneously. Strategies may arise from lower -or middle -level managers, from local experimentation and replication. The importance of sudden or emergent strategy and learning is as true in life in general as it is in business. Therefore, strategy can be systematically formulated or planned, as discussed earlier, or it can also originate in unexpected and unanticipated ways. It can be initiated by mid-level managers and operations or field people who are making day-to-day decisions aimed at maximising the value of scarce production capacity. Therefore, if new strategies are to emerge in unexpected ways, managers should be continuously aware of changing patterns of action in their businesses. Also, top managers should be ready to learn and be alert for changing patterns in the business so that they are able to embrace the new strategy when it becomes evident from the actions of lower-level employees that this new approach could pay a profitable pathway to the future[14].

To capture the benefits of emerging strategy, managers must foster **organisational learning**—the ability of an organisation to monitor changes in its environment and adjust its processes, products, and services to capitalise on those changes. They must use their performance measurement and control systems to encourage employees to constantly innovate and search for signs of change in the business. Managers must encourage employees to experiment, to find new opportunities, and test new ideas. And, perhaps most importantly, they must ensure that performance measurement and control systems create effective communication channels to move this information up the line from employees to senior managers at headquarters. Feedback becomes critical for learning: it allows managers to fine-tune and, sometimes, radically change their business strategies[15].

MANAGEMENT CONTROL

Management control refers to the evaluation by upper-level managers of the performance of mid-level managers. Management control is part of overall planning and control activities used by an organisation. Management Control is an activity between strategy formulation and task control. Management Control is a process by which management attempts to direct the efforts of an organisation to achieve the planned goals and objectives. According to Anthony and Govindrajan[16]:

- *Management Control is the process by which managers influence other members of the organisation to implement the organisation's strategies.*

Management control ensures that actual results match or even improve upon planned objectives, budgets or standards. Control includes the following steps:

> **Management Control** is a process by which management attempts to direct the efforts of an organisation to achieve the planned goals and objectives.

1. Determination of objectives, plans and standards
2. Measurement of actual performances
3. Comparing actual performance with the plans and standards
4. Identifying differences from the plans and standards (especially those differences which are significant and undesirable)
5. Taking corrective actions to bring outcomes in accordance with the plans or nearer the plans and standards

Management control is a process to be used by managers to achieve organisational goals. They use it in their interaction with one another and with subordinates. It is a people-oriented process. Line managers are the focal points in management control. They make plans for attaining goals, and they are the persons who must influence others and whose performance is measured. Staff people collect, summarise and present information that is useful in the process and make calculations that translate management judgements into the format of the system. Such a staff may be large in numbers. Indeed, the control department is often the largest staff department in a company, but the significant decisions are made by the line managers. The goals, strategies and policies are taken as given in the management control process. Management control aims to implement strategies and is concerned with the actions of managers and employees in their efforts to achieve organisational goals.

The planning and control requirements of business units pursuing different strategies are quite different. Shank and Govindrajan state that for effective implementation, there should be congruence between the mission chosen and the type of control used[14].

Shank and Govindrajan develop the control-mission fit using the following line of reasoning:

> The mission of the business unit influences the uncertainties that its general manager faces and the short-term versus long-term tradeoffs that he or she makes.
>
> Management control systems can be systematically varied to help motivate the manager to cope effectively with uncertainty and make appropriate short-term versus long-term tradeoffs.
>
> Thus, different missions often require systematically different management control systems.

Management control is generally based on budgets and standards. However, if the circumstances which were used to plan have changed, management control should look at the actions as compared with new conditions. Also, management control should permit the managers, if he finds better ways of doing, to deviate from the plans if that would help in achieving the firm's objectives.

Difference between Strategy Formulation and Management Control

The following are the differences between strategy formulation and management control:

1. Strategy formulation is primarily unsystematic. Business strategies are formulated after noticing some new opportunities or perceiving some threat to the business from the competitors and environment. The new opportunities or threats do not emerge in a regular and systematic manner but may be detected abruptly. Therefore, strategy decisions are unsystematic and can be made at any time.

   Management control is essentially systematic, follows defined control procedures and steps as decided by the management in advance. It is a regular, ongoing process used by all organisations.
2. Strategy decisions involve rough approximations and estimates and judgement. There is no set method to make strategy analysis. Management Control is based on clear time-table and guidelines and uses information developed within the organisation.
3. Strategy decisions involve less persons, usually at the higher management level. In management control, the entire staff at different levels of the organisation participate and becomes involved.
4. Strategy formulations do not affect all the strategies and policies simultaneously. Generally, strategy may relate to one of the firm's activities and may affect one or more strategies.

   Management control affects the whole organisation. Management Control requires effective coordination among different departments and activities to ensure that remedial actions are effective and results are as planned.

TASK OR OPERATIONAL CONTROL

> **Task control or operational control** means the evaluation of operating-level employees by mid-level managers.

Task control is also known as action control, operational control, input control, and pretransaction control Task control or operational control means the evaluation of operating-level employees by mid-level managers. Task control focuses on the control of works performed byindividuals in an organisation. It aims at detailed controls of all procedures used by individuals while performing tasks, especially at lower level of management. Task control includes the process of correcting or preventing variation of performed scheduled (laid down) activities from the objectives, procedures or standards set in advance. In other words, task control emphasises on correspondence between the actual activities and results with the standards.

Difference between Task (Operational) Control and Management Control

Task or operational control focuses on detailed short-term performance measures whereas management control focuses on higher-level managers and long-term, strategic issues. Operational Control has a management by exception approach, that is, it identifies units or individuals whose performance does not comply with expectations so that the problem can be promptly corrected. In contrast, management control is more consistent with the management-by-objectives approach in which long-term objectives such as growth and profitability are determined and performance is periodically measured against these goals.

Management control also has a broader and more strategic objective: to evaluate the unit's overall profitability as well as the performance of its managers, to decide whether the unit should be retained or closed and to motivate the manager to achieve top management's goals. Because of this broad focus, various objectives for management control generally have multiple measures of performance rather than a single financial or operating measure, as is sometimes true in operational control[18].

The following are the distinctions between task or operational control and management control.

1. Management control focuses on the control of the whole organisation whereas task control is directed towards the control of one individual, one unit of the organisation.
2. The management control, functions and steps within it, are framed in terms of strategies formulated by top/senior management. The task control functions are based on procedures and rules which are derived from management control and its requirements.
3. In task control, standards set for evaluating procedures, rules and activities are more precise and objective than that of management control where standards set for evaluation are not that much precise.
   The compactness and objectivity in task control standards helps in developing definite conclusions whether the results are or are not as planned.
4. Task control aims primarily at controlling things and performance, and such control may be purely direct, for example, to place an order for purchase of merchandise if inventory level falls below a point which can be indicated by a manual or computerised accounting system. On the other hand, management control primarily focuses on controlling individuals and involves human dynamics.
5. In task control, most often, non-financial measures such as labour hours, number of units, quantity of waste, are used for control purposes. In task control, different types of measures can be used in different units or departments depending on the requirements. But, in management control, mostly financial or monetary measures are used for control purposes.
6. Task control requires minute or transaction-based information such as inventory level of an item, requisition for an item, repair of a specific machine etc. On the other hand, management control is done on the basis of summaries of transactions, consolidated or summarised reports, total sales or total production cost for a month, total repair costs, total marketing expenses etc.
7. Information used for task control are immediate and developed as the tasks are being performed, whereas information for management control contains summaries and schedules of past performances and activities. Task control uses exact and real situation data, but management control may also use approximations and estimates.

The activities to which operational control can be exercised in an organisation generally are order processing, inventory control, production activities of different machines, production scheduling, storekeeping, oil refineries, power production. The activities which are generally subject to management control are legal services, employees welfare and benefits programmes, training, supervision, job enrichment, advertising, sales promotion, pricing, marketing activities, research and development, financing decision activities, activities of top and senior management, total production of all plants.

Anthony and Govindrajan[19] have summarised the distinctions between strategy formulation, management control and task control in the following manner:

> Management control fits between strategy formulation and task control in several ways. Strategy formulation is the least systematic of the three, task control is the most systematic, and management control is in between. Strategy formulation focuses on the long-run, task control focuses on short-run operating activities, and management control is in between. Strategy formulation uses rough approximations of the future, task control uses current accurate data and management control is in between. Each activity involves both planning and control; but the emphasis varies with the type of activity. The planning process is much more important in strategy formulation, the control process is much more important in task control, and planning and control are of approximately equal importance in management control.

MANAGEMENT CONTROL SYSTEMS

Broadly, management control system (MCS) refers to the design, installation and operation of management planning and control systems. The term 'management control systems' emphasises on two distinct, but highly interrelated and sometimes indistinguishable, subdivisions of controls systems:

> **Management Control System (MCS)** refers to the design, installation and operation of management planning and control systems.

1. Structure or organisation structure or relationships among the units in the organisation, more specifically the responsibility centres, the relationship among responsibility centres, performance measures and the information that flows among these responsibility centres.
2. Process or set of activities, or steps or decisions that are taken by an organisation or managers to establish purposes, allocate resources and achieve organisational purposes. The process consists of interrelated phases of programming (programme selection), budgeting, execution, measurement and evaluation of actual performance.

The structure of a management control system indicates what the system "is" and process of a management control system indicates what the system "does." The management control systems knits the organisation together so that each part, by exercising the autonomy given to it, fulfils a purpose that is consistent with and contributes to the fulfillment of the overall purpose of the organisation. The control system should be designed to achieve unity of purpose through the use of the diverse talents of individuals in the organisation. The constant requirement of management control is the achievement of unity in diversity through coordination, in pursuit of short-term objectives and long-term goals.

MANAGEMENT CONTROL STRUCTURE

As stated earlier, management control structure consists of different responsibility centres such as cost centre, revenue centre, profit centre, investment centre; measurement of performances of different responsibility centres and different methods of transfer pricing.

The above topics have been discussed thoroughly in the chapter 'Performance Measurement in Divisionalised Companies'. Hence, they are not being discussed here.

MANAGEMENT CONTROL PROCESS

The following are the steps in the management control process in sequence as they are found in practice.

1. Programming or Strategic Planning
2. Budgeting
3. Execution
4. Evaluation

Programming

Programming is defined as making programmes by top/senior management in terms of organisational goals and strategies and deciding the funds and resources needed to accomplish the programmes. Programmes can be made about developments of new products, research and development activities, merger, takeover, other activities that are not related much with the existing product lines. In service organisations, such

> **Programming** is making programmes by top/senior management in terms of organisational goals and strategies and deciding the funds and resources needed to accomplish the programmes.

as a hotel chain, management may draw programmes for each hotel or each region where hotels are to be set up. In decentralised organisation, for each segment or centre, programming can be done.

Programming is a long-range plan, covering period of approximately five future years. The reason is that if programming is made for a shorter period, the results and benefits of programming cannot be realised within this period. Some organisations like public utilities prepare long-range plans for even a period of twenty years. Because of the relatively long-time plan, only rough estimates are possible for revenues, expenses and capital expenditure.

The task of programming is done by senior/top management and the managers of divisions or principal responsibility centres, assisted by their staffs. The managers of lower responsibility centres generally do not participate in the programming process. Although the staff of the divisions making the programming can participate, the decisions on the different aspects of the plan are made by the line managers.

Programming is time-consuming and expensive. The most significant expense is the time devoted to it by management, but it also involves a special programming staff and considerable paperwork. A formal programming process is not worthwhile in some organisations. It is desirable in organisations that have the following characteristics.[20]

1. Its top management is convinced that programming is important. Otherwise programming is likely to be, or to become, a staff exercise that has little impact on actual decision-making.
2. It is relatively large and complex. In small, simple organisations, an informal understanding of the organisation's future directions is adequate for making decisions about resource allocations, which is a principal purpose of preparing programme.
3. Considerable uncertainty about the future exists, but the organisation has the flexibility to adjust to changed circumstances. In a relatively stable organisation, a programme may be unnecessary; the future is sufficiently like the past so that the programme would be only an exercise in extrapolation. If the future is so uncertain that reasonably reliable estimates cannot be made, preparation of a formal programme is a waste of time.

In summary, a formal programming process is not needed in small, relatively stable organisations, and it is not worthwhile in organisations that can not make reliable estimates about the future or in organisations whose top management does not prefer to manage in this fashion.

Budgeting

Chapter 9 of this book discusses the different aspects of budgeting and budget preparation in details.

Budgeting is a formal financial plan for each year. A budget, known as short-range plans, is a technique of expressing revenues, expenses, physical targets like production and sales, profit, assets and liabilities usually for a period of one future year.

> **Budgeting** is a formal financial plan for each year.

Budget has the functions of motivating managers, coordinating activities, communicating to persons within an organisation, providing standards for judging actual performances and acting as a control tool.

Programming and budgeting differs from each other in the following respects[21]:

1. Programming involves senior managers; operating managers ordinarily are not involved. Budgeting involves operating managers as well as senior managers.

2. Staff personnel have a considerable input to the programming process, but relatively less input to the budgeting process. In a large organisation, the programming staff is distinct from the budget staff. The programming staff (perhaps called planning staff or analysis staff) is skilled in analysing proposed new programmes; the budget staff is skilled in finding soft spots in proposed budgets.
3. The programme structure consists of programme and major project; it includes both capital expenditure and operating items; and it covers a period of several years. The budget is structured by responsibility centres (which may or may not cut across programme), the focus is on operating revenues and expenses; and it typically is for a single year.
4. Budget preparation is done under greater time pressure and is more hectic than programming.
5. A programme is a broad-brush sketch of the future. A budget has more detail, both because it is a fairly specific guide to operating decisions and also because it will be used subsequently to evaluate the performance of individual managers. Also, "management by objectives" are incorporated in the budget, but not usually in the programme.
6. Programming decisions can have consequences of great magnitude. Budgeting decisions are typically much less significant, because they are made within the context of the current level of operating activities, except as those activities will be affected by programme decisions.
7. Behavioural considerations are much more important in the budget preparation process than in the programming process. The approved budget is a bilateral commitment; the programme is not a commitment. Because the budget will be used to evaluate performance, operating managers tend to be much more concerned with the numbers in the budget than with the numbers in the programme.

Readers are advised to refer to chapter 9 to have an understanding of advantages of budgeting, features of budgeting, types of budget, preparation of functional and financial budgets, etc.

Executing

After the budget preparation, budgeting is used as a tool for coordinating the actions of individuals and department within the organisation. In fact, within the execution phase, task control is done to ensure that actions and performances match with the planned or desired results. While performing, the manager's goal is to achieve budgeted targets. However, compliance to budget is not necessary if the plans given in the budget are found as not the best way of achieving the objectives. Adherence to budget is not necessarily good, and departure from it is not necessarily bad.

After execution, actual performances and results are compared with the budgeted plans and targets and variances reports are prepared which highlight the variances between the two and the causes for such variances. Variance reports should separate controllable items from non-controllable items, determine the effect of changes in volume on revenues and costs and if possible, should mention changes in other circumstances affecting the variances. Variance reports lead to corrective actions subsequently. Variance reports should be prepared timely and promptly and contain all useful information for helping the managers to take corrective actions.

Evaluation

Management control process ends with the evaluation phase in which the performances of managers are evaluated. Since, it is an after-event exercise, the evaluation does not affect what has happened. However, evaluation phase acts like a powerful stimulus as employees know that their performances will be subsequently evaluated. Also, on the basis of performance evaluation, the future budgets and plans are revised.

The chapter 'Performance Measurement in Divisionalised Companies' has touched upon a few issues relating to measuring the performance of a division or responsibility centre.

It is in the interest of organisation as well as employees that managers should discuss regularly the performance reports (or control reports) with their subordinates. The management control process developed in an organisation will fail if subordinates do not attach importance to performance reports or not convinced that the reports are important. In order to build up confidence among the managers for the performance reports, it is necessary that such performance reports (*i*) should measure fairly the performances of managers, to the extent possible, and (*ii*) should allow for adjustments on account of unavoidable circumstances, noncontrollable factors and justified departures from the budget. Anthony[22] observes:

> The performance reported for a given period rarely reflects the managers' actual performance in that period. Quite apart from the difficulty of measuring the performance of the responsibility centre in a period, the performance report cannot allow for two factors that are relevant to the manager's performance: (1) performance in the period was affected by actions taken by managers in prior periods that influence both the resources available and also the control climate in the current period; and (2) in the current period, the manager takes actions that will affect performance in future periods, and the report can not show the ultimate consequences of these actions. The first point is especially important if a different manager headed the responsibility center in the earlier period. The second point is an inherent limitation on all reports of current performance and is probably the greatest weakness in the whole management control process.

CASES

Case 1

Quantum Computers Co. produces and sells laptop computers. The company is currently deciding whether or not to continue concentrating on the laptop computer market or to expand by entering the highly competitive computer desktop workstation market.

Most of the management staff has been with Quantum for a long time. Michael Mitchem, Quantum's president, wants his management staff to assist him in Quantum's strategic planning process. Mitchem has scheduled a three-day offsite meeting for the management staff to join together for the company's strategic planning process.

Required:

A. What functional areas should be discussed during the strategic planning process?

B. Identify at least six factors to be considered in a thorough strategic planning process that will move a company such as Quantum Computers Inc. to another level of product development.

C. Identify at least three benefits that Quantum Computers Inc. can derive from a participatory strategic planning process.

D. Discuss the expected behaviour of the managers at Quantum Computer Inc. who participate in the three-day offsite strategic planning meeting. (*CMA, USA, Adapted with permission*)

Solution:

A. Several different functional areas should be discussed during the strategic planning process. This would include product research and development, production, marketing, and administrative support areas.

B. At least six factors that should be considered in a thorough strategic planning process that will move a company such as Quantum Computers Co. to another level of product development include the following.

- Define the mission of the organisation. State the fundamental, unique purpose that sets the company apart from other firms of its type and identify the scope of its operation in product and market terms.
- Develop organisational objectives. State the specific aims that management seeks to achieve for the organisation within a stated period of time. Objectives improve the effectiveness of the organisation by providing direction, serving as standards for evaluating performance, and motivating members of the organisation. Objectives can be short and long range, and internal and external.
- Evaluate current and projected risks and opportunities in the firm's environment and business culture, including trends in the competitive, economic, demographic, social, technological, and regulatory areas.
- Assess the organisation's strengths and weaknesses in comparison with those of other organisations. Identify the firm's core competencies. Strengths, weaknesses, opportunities, threats (SWOT) analysis is a strategic planning tool that forces managers to identify internal strengths and weaknesses and assess them in relation to external opportunities and threats.
- Determine the total company resources constraints, including human, physical, and financial.
- Formulate strategy. Select an appropriate strategy to take advantage of existing and expected external environmental conditions and the firm's internal strengths and weaknesses.

C. At least three benefits that Quantum Computers Co. can derive from a participatory strategic planning process include the following.

- Exchange of ideas between participating managers will lead to greater creativity, resulting in a better plan.
- Participation fosters increased teamwork, cohesiveness, communication and cooperation among departments and managers.
- Communication will be improved, leading to better understanding of the mission and strategy and how each area contributes to the mission. This should contribute to improved goal congruence between operating areas and the overall goals of the firm.

D. The managers at Quantum Computer Co. who participate in the three-day offsite strategic planning meeting are more likely to

- Feel that they have been part of the process and be positive about the plan.
- Be more motivated and committed to making the plan succeed because they had the opportunity to express their opinions and insights.
- Be more enthusiastic in communicating the plan to their subordinates.

Case 2

Richards Furniture Co. is a 15-store chain, concentrated in the southwest that sells living room and bedroom furniture. Each store has a full-time manager and an assistant manager, who are paid on a salary basis. The cashiers and sales personnel typically work part-time and are paid an hourly wage plus a commission based on sales volume. The company uses unsophisticated cash registers with four-part sales invoices to record each transaction. These sales invoices are used regardless of the payment type (cash, cheque, or bank credit card).

On the sales floor, the salesperson manually records his/her employee number and the transaction (furniture description, quantity and unit price), totals the sales invoice, calculates the discount when appropriate, calculates the sales tax and prepares the grand total. The salesperson then gives the sales invoice to the cashier, retaining one copy in the sales book.

The cashier reviews the invoice and inputs the sale into the cash register. The cash register automatically assigns a consecutive number to each transaction. The cashier is also responsible for obtaining credit authorization approval on bank credit card sales and approving sales paid by customer cheque. The cashier gives one copy of the invoice to the customer, retains the second copy as a store copy, and retains the third copy for a bank credit card deposit, if needed. Returns are handled in exactly the reverse manner with the cashier issuing a return slip when necessary.

At the end of each day, the cashier sequentially orders the sales invoices and provides cash register total for cash, bank credit card, and cheque sales, and cash and bank credit card returns. These totals are reconciled by the assistant manager to the cash register tapes, the total of the consecutively numbered sales invoices and the return slips. The assistant manager prepares a daily reconciled report for the store manager's review.

Cash sales, cheque sales and bank credit card sales are reviewed by the manager who then prepares the daily bank deposit (bank credit card sales invoices are included in the deposit). The manager physically deposits these at the bank and files the validated deposit slip. At the end of the month, the manager performs the bank reconciliation.

The cash register tapes, sales invoices, return slips, and reconciled report are then forwarded daily to the central Data Entry Department at corporate headquarters for processing. The Data Entry Department returns a weekly Sales and Commission Activity Report to the manager for review.

Required:

Each store in the Richards Furniture Co. chain follows this sales and cash receipts system for the control of sales transactions.

A. 1. Identify at least five strengths in the Richards Furniture Co. system for controlling sales transactions.

2. For each strength identified, explain what problem(s) Richards Furniture Co. has avoided by incorporating the strength in the system for controlling sales transactions.

Use the following format in preparing your answer.

1. Strength 2. Problem (s) Avoided

B. Identify at least two opportunities to improve Richards Furniture Co.'s system for controlling sales transactions. *(CMA, USA, Adapted with permission)*

Solution:

A. 1. & 2.

At least five strengths and the corresponding problems avoided by the system for the control of sales transactions at Richards Furniture Co. are listed below.

Strengths	Problems Avoided
• All 15 stores use the same system for controlling sales transactions.	• Avoids difficulty in auditing the stores and in incorporating chain-wide improvements.
• The separation of cashiers and sales people for completing sales invoices and returns.	• The separation of duties minimises the possibility of theft or fraud, e.g., prevents the sales people from taking the returns for their own personal use. • Helps mitigate sales invoice errors.
• Automatic sequential numbering is done by the cash register.	• Eliminates subjective, consecutive numbering minimising employee error and theft. • Avoids the undetected loss of an invoice. • Provides an audit trail for invoices.
• The reconcilation of cash receipts, cheques, bank credit cards, returns and cash register tapes is performed by the assistant manager.	• The separation of duties reduces the possibility of theft or fraud. • This review provides another opportunity to catch errors.
• The bank deposit is prepared and deposited by the manager.	• The separation of duties reduces the possibility of theft, fraud, or loss.

B. At least two opportunities to improve Richards Furniture Co.'s system for controlling sales transactions include the following.

- The bank reconciliation should be performed by someone other than the manager, since he/she deposits the cash.
- Automate the process by implementing.
  - point of sale (POS) registers, permitting automatic generation of invoices and inventory control.
  - electronic communication of sales data to headquarters.
  - computer-based reconciliations.

Case 3

MagnaTronics manufactures a prestige line of diagnostic instruments for the medical field. High quality, leading-edge design, and reasonable pricing policies have made MagnaTronics the premier company in a competitive field for many years. Recently, however, Rising Star, a relative newcomer in the industry, has begun making serious inroads into MagnaTronics' market share.

After reviewing the results of operations for the last six months of 2016. Howard Runz, vice-president of manufacturing, proposed and received approval for an incentive plan designed to lower costs sufficiently to impact pricing and subsequently, market share. The major elements of the plan are described below.

- **Purchasing Department**
  For each five per cent decrease in actual direct material purchase costs as compared to budget, purchasing supervisors will receive a one per cent salary bonus at the end of the year.
- **Manufacturing Department**
  For each five per cent decrease in actual direct material usage as compared to standard, manufacturing supervisors will receive a one per cent salary bonus at the end of the year.

For each five per cent decrease in actual direct labour cost as compared to standard, manufacturing supervisors will receive a one per cent salary bonus at the end of the year.

- **Equipment Maintenance Department**

  For each five per cent decrease in total departmental costs as compared to budget, maintenance supervisors will receive a one per cent salary bonus at the end of the year.

The plan appeared to be working initially, but after six months of operation under the new plan, costs have begun to increase, exceeding pre-plan levels, and product quality has diminished to the point where rework costs are a significant factor. MagnaTronics is considering abandoning the plan and searching for other means to reduce costs and remain competitive.

Required:

A. Identify and describe at least two consequences of MagnaTronics' new incentive plan that could cause negative results in each of the following departments.

1. Purchasing Department.
2. Manufacturing Department.
3. Equipment Maintenance Department.

B. By identifying and describing at least three characteristics of successful incentive plans, suggest ways in which MagnaTronics could improve its incentive plan.

(*CMA, USA, Adapted with permission*)

Solution:

A. At least two consequences of MagnaTronics' new incentive plan that could cause negative results in each of the three departments are identified and described below.

1. Purchasing Department

- The Purchasing Department's incentive is to obtain raw material at the lowest possible price. In an effort to reduce costs and increase the department manager's bonus, departmental personnel may have selected vendors of materials based on price alone, without considering other factors, such as reliability, quality and delivery time. The department may have also ordered inferior substitute material at a lower price. While costs may be reduced in the short term by these actions, over the long term the company may already be adversely affected by longer delivery times, higher rework costs, greater inspection costs, and unusable material or waste.
- The poor quality material also affects other departments. The Manufacturing Department needs to use more material and labour to make the product, reducing efficiency, and ultimately, raising costs. Poor quality material can also create more maintenance problems, such as excessive wear on the machinery. These interdepartmental effects could cause friction between departments and lower the overall efficiency of the company.

2. Manufacturing Department

- The incentives for the Manufacturing Department emphasise moving product through the department as quickly as possible with minimum material usage. The increasing rework costs indicates that the Manufacturing Department is not responsible for rework and is allowing poor quality product to leave the department. This is apparently increasing overall manufacturing costs. It may also cause customer complaints if the poor quality products are allowed to be shipped (especially if they cut back on inspections in an effort to reduce this labour cost).

- The departmental manager may have lowered labour work standards in order to hire less experienced workers at a lower rate. As a result, a greater amount of rework is needed to bring products up to standard. The net result is to increase direct labour costs rather than decrease them as anticipated. Pushing the experienced workers too hard or requiring them to take shortcuts could result in a similar consequence, since morale would decline along with productivity.

3. **Equipment Maintenance Department**
   - The Equipment Maintenance Department's incentive is to minimize departmental costs, which includes maintenance labour and parts. One negative consequence could be improperly (and hastily) adjusted equipment that could have led to excessive waste of material and labour. In addition, the departmental supervisor may have deferred routine maintenance on machinery and equipment to reduce costs in the short run. This causes increased breakdowns (repairs) and loss of productivity over the long run. This may already be occurring at MagnaTronics.
   - Maintenance supervisors may be encouraging premature equipment replacement since new equipment requires less maintenance than older ones. This decreases maintenance expenses, but increases capital asset depreciation.

B. MagnaTronics could improve its incentive plan with one that is understandable by the employees and reflects the company's overall goal alignment. At least three characteristics of a successful incentive plan that MagnaTronics should implement include the following.

- The incentive plan should include other measures besides cost reduction, such as profitability, customer satisfaction, innovation, productivity, quality, reliability and timeliness. These measures should be tested against the "best in class" (bench-marking), rather than the arbitrary standard of 5 per cent.
- All functions within the plant should feel part of a team working toward a common objective. MagnaTronics' current system does not recognise the relationship between departments. An effective way to begin building such teams is to have workers and supervisors participate in developing performance measures and revising these measures on a regular basis in order to encourage the employees to "buy into" the incentive system and to feel committed to the process. Cross-functional teams could be developed to work on ways to reach the overall objectives. In addition to supervisory bonuses, team members should be awarded bonuses as well.
- A plant-wide incentive programme based upon the lowest overall production costs (including quality costs) may be effective for MagnaTronics. The cost measures should be stated in terms of a given volume level (a flexible budget approach). To avoid the motivation to build inventory, there should be a charge for inventory that includes carrying costs. To avoid the motivation to ship poor quality products, customer returns should be included at a cost that reflects the full cost of handling returns and complaints from customers.

REFERENCES

1. Charles T. Horngreen, Sri Kant M.Datar and George Foster, Cost Accounting, *A Managerial Emphasis*, Prentice Hall of India Pvt Ltd., New Delhi, 2000, p. 788.
2. Joseph G. Louderback III and Jay S. Holmen, *Managerial Accounting*, Thomson South Western, 2003, p. 363.

3. Charles T. Horngreen, Sri Kant M. Datar and George Foster, *Cost/Accounting, A Managerial Emphasis*, 2001, pp. 789–790.
4. Mohinder N. Kaura, Management Control and Reportings Systems, Response Book, 2002, pp. 26–28.
5. John K. Shank and Vijay Govindarajan, Strategic Cost Management, The Free Press, 1993, pp. 94-95.
6. Richard Normann and Rafael Ramirez. "From Value Chain to Value Constellation: Designing Interactive Strategy." *Harvard Business Review* (*July–August 1993*), p. 65.
7. Robert N. Anthony and Vijay Govindrajan, *Managment Control Systems*, Irwin, Mc-Graw Hill, 1998, p. 10.
8. Joseph A. Maciariello, *Management Control Systems*, Prentice Hall, 1984, p. 39.
9. Gary Hamel and C.K. Prahalad, Competing for the Future, *Harvard Business School Press*, 1994, pp. 25–26.
10. John K. Shank and Vijay Govindrajan, Strategy Cost Management, The Free Press, pp. 95.
11. Michael E. Porter, Competitive Strategy E. Porter, Competitive Strategy, The Free Press, New York.
12. Robert Simons, *Performance Measurement and Control Systems for Implementing Strategy*, Prentice Hall, 2000, pp. 16–17.
13. Robert Simon, *Performance Measurement and Control Systems for Implementing Strategy*, Prentice Hall, 2000, pp. 27–36. Materials herein are based on Robert Simon's analysis.
14. Robert Burgelman, "A Process View of Strategic Business Exit: Implications for an Evolutionary Perspective on Strategy", Strategic Management Journal (Summer 1996), pp. 193–214.
15. Robert Simon, "Performance Measurement and Control Systems for Implementing Strategy", *Ibid*, p. 36.
16. Robert N.Anthony and Vijay Govindrajan, *Management Control Systems*, Irwin McGraw Hill, 1998, p. 6.
17. John K. Shank and Vijay Govindrajan, *Ibid*, p. 96.
18. Edward J. Blocher, Kung H. Chen, Garg Cokins and Thomas W. Lin, *Cost Management, A Strategic Approach*, McGraw Hill, 2005, p. 223.
19. Robert N. Anthony and Vijay Govidrajan, *Ibid*, p. 6.
20. Rober N. Anthony, *Management Control Function*. Harvard University Press. p. 86.
21. Robert N. Anthony, *Management Control Function, Ibid.*, p. 97.
22. Robert N. Anthony, *Management Control Functuin, Ibid*, p. 88.

CRITICAL ANALYSIS AND DISCUSSION QUESTIONS, MULTIPLE CHOICE QUESTIONS, AND CASES

CRITICAL ANALYSIS AND DISCUSSION QUESTIONS

1. Define strategic planning, management control and operational control.
2. Bring out the differences between:
   (*i*) Strategic planning and management control
   (*ii*) Management Control and task control
3. What do you mean by management control system? What are its characteristics?
4. What does management control structure consist of? Explain them fully.
5. Explain the different steps in management control process.
6. "Responsibility accounting has emerged as a tool of management control." Elaborate this statement with suitable illustrations. (*M. Com., Delhi*)
7. Give the structure and process of management control systems. How does strategic planning help in designing MCS in a large-sized organisation? (*M.Com., Delhi*)
8. "Management control systems is basically rooted in accounting or more specifically in accounting for management. Yet the field of management control systems is much broader than accounting. It also draws upon materials from economics, management science and perhaps most important, behavioural sciences." Discuss and also briefly explain its highly interrelated and sometimes indistinguishable sub-divisions of structure and process. (*M.Com., Delhi*)
9. Is it fair to describe Management Control Systems as an extension of management accounting? Give the structure and process of MCS with appropriate examples. (*M. Com., Delhi*)
10. Examine the principal characteristics of a management control system. (*M. Com., Delhi*)
11. Discuss the factors influencing the design of management control systems.
12. What is strategy? Distinguish between corporate strategy and business strategy. Discuss 4 Ps. of strategy as formulated by Robert Simon.
13. Distinguish between management control and operational control.
14. Explain the term 'mission' and 'strategy'.
15. Differentiate between strategy formulation and management control.
16. What do you believe are the organisational goals of a nonprofit hospital, or a university.
17. Think of the class you are attending as an organisation. Assume your teacher is the "owner." What are the goals of this organisation? What are your individual goals in relation to this class? Do you see a divergence between your goals and your teacher's goals? How does your teacher motivate you to perform in a way that advances course goals?
18. Special Forces such as the Navy and the Army represent group settings in which there is almost perfect alignment between team and individual goals, and where individuals often put team goals ahead of their personal well being. What unique features give rise to the difference between these organisations and the "typical" profit-making organisation?

19. Referring to an experience that we are sometimes forced to endure, we often find ourselves saying things like. "That wasn't too bad." What is the implicit plan in this statement? What is the control aspect? What implications does the assessment have for subsequent plans?
20. Why is mission statement important to an organisation?
21. Select three large publicly held companies in the same industry. Use the internet to access their websites and find a mission statement for each. How do these mission statements differ and how are they similar? Assuming that you are the president of a new company in this industry, write a mission statement for your company.
22. What is organisation strategy? Why would each organisation have a unique strategy or set of strategies?
23. Are the financial implications of strategic planning more important in a business than in a not-for-profit organisation? Why or why not?
24. Differentiate between authority and responsibility. Can you have one without the other. Explain.
25. Use the internet to find three companies that have recently changed their organisation structure. How were the companies restructured and what reasons were given for the change?
26. How can a change in government laws or regulations create a strategic opportunity for an organisation? Give an example.
27. Define each of the strategies an organisation may pursue to avoid competition, and discuss the benefits of each type of strategy.
28. You are the manager of the local Home Depot store. What are the five factors that you believe to be most critical to the success of your organisation? How would these factors influence your store's strategy?
29. Choose a company that might utilise each of the following strategies relative to its competitors and discuss the benefits that might be realised from that strategy. Indicate the industry in which the company does business and the company's primary competitors.
    (*a*) Differentiation
    (*b*) Cost leadership
    (*c*) Confrontation
30. Successful business organisations appear to be those that have clearly defined long-range goals and a well-planned strategy to reach those goals. These successful organisations understand their markets as well as the internal strengths and weaknesses of the organisations. These organisations take advantage of this knowledge to grow (through internal development or acquisitions) in a consistent and disciplined manner.
    (*a*) Discuss the need for long-range goals for business organisations
    (*b*) Discuss how long-range goals are set
    (c) Define the concepts of strategic planning and management control. Discuss how they relate to each other and contribute to progress toward the attainment of long-range goals.
31. Mission statements are supported to indicate what an organisation does and why it exists. Some of them, however, are simply empty words, with little or no substance and with few people using them to guide activities.

(*a*) Why does an organisation need a mission statement?

(*b*) How might a mission statement help an organisation in its pursuit of ethical behavior from employees?

(*c*) How might a mission statement help an organisation in its pursuit of production of high-quality products and provision of high levels of customer service?

32. Discuss the importance of mission statement for a not-for-profit organisation.
33. Distinguish between goals and objectives. What goals do you hope to achieve by taking this course? What objectives can you establish to measure the degree to which you achieve these stated goals?
34. What is a core competency and how do core competencies impact the feasible set of alternative organisational strategies?

MULTIPLE CHOICE QUESTIONS

Select the Correct Answer for the following Multiple Choice Questions

1. Strategic planning, as practiced by most modern organisations, includes all of the following except
   (*a*) top-level management participation
   (*b*) a long-term focus
   (*c*) strategies that will help in achieving long-range goals
   (*d*) analysis of the current month's actual variances from budget
   (*e*) identification of long-term key variables including external influences
2. Which one of the following management considerations is usually addressed first in strategic planning?
   (*a*) Outsourcing
   (*b*) Overall goals of the firm
   (*c*) Organisational structure
   (*d*) Recent annual budgets
   (*e*) Being an industry leader
3. Goal congruence is
   (*a*) The desire and the commitment to achieve a specific goal
   (*b*) The sharing of goals by supervisors and subordinates
   (*c*) The extent to which individuals have the authority to make decisions
   (*d*) The extent of the attempt to accomplish a specific goal
4. Motivation is
   (*a*) The desire and the commitment to achieve a specific goal
   (*b*) The sharing of goals by supervisors and subordinates
   (*c*) The extent to which individuals have the authority to make decisions
   (*d*) The extent of the attempt to accomplish a specific goal

Answer to Multiple Choice Questions

1. (*d*) 2. (*b*) 3. (*b*) 4. (*a*)

CASES

1. Jensen Corporation is a holding company with several diversified divisions operating throughout the United States. The management of Jensen has a policy of allowing its division to operate on an autonomous basis in most areas; however, the corporate office does become involved in some of the division strategies such as capital budgeting, the development of marketing campaigns, and the implementation of divisional incentive plans. The area of incentive plans has often presented problems to Jensen, as many of the companies Jensen has acquired have incentive plans already in place. These plans are not easily changed without causing discontent among employees. While Jensen has striven for consistency among its divisions with regard to bonus and incentive plans, this has not always been achievable, as discussed below.

   The Restaurant Division operates a chain of vegetarian restaurants, Hobbit Hole, in the eastern United States. Jensen acquired the chain approximately three years ago and has made very few changes in the organisation. The reputation of the restaurants was well established and, aside from nominal changes in marketing strategy, the chain has been allowed to operate in much the same manner as it did before the Jensen acquisition. In addition to a base salary, the unit managers of Hobbit Hole participate in the profits of the restaurants. This incentive plan was in place when Jensen acquired the chain, and while the profit percentage may vary among restaurant units, the overall plans are basically the same. The unit managers are satisfied with this incentive strategy, and Jensen's management does not believe any changes are necessary.

   Jensen's Motel Division was formed fifteen years ago when Jensen purchased a small group of motels in the midwest. Since that time, the division has grown significantly as Jensen acquired motels throughout the country using the name, Cruise and Snooze Inns. Since its initial motel purchase Jensen has had a policy of implementing its own incentive programme in the individual motels. The unit managers of the motels are covered by an incentive programme that provides annual bonuses based on the achievement of specified goals. These goals are not necessarily finance oriented but may pertain to areas such as improved quality control and customer service. While this programme requires administrative time. Jensen believes the results have been satisfactory.

Required:

A. Hobbit Hole's restaurant unit managers are covered by a profit participation incentive plan. Discuss the

(*i*) Benefits of this type of incentive plan to Jensen Corporation

(*ii*) Negative behavioural problems that could arise with this type of incentive plan

B. The motel unit managers of Cruise and Snooze Inns participate in an incentive programme based on goal attainment. Discuss the

(*i*) advantages of this type of incentive plan to Jensen Corporation

(*ii*) disadvantages of this type of incentive plan to Jensen Corporation

C. Having two different types of incentive plans for two operating divisions of the same holding company can create problems.

(*i*) Discuss the behavioural problems that could arise for Jensen Corporation by having different types of incentive plans for Hobbit Hole and Cruise and Snooze Inns.

(*ii*) Present the rationale that Jensen Corporation can give to the unit managers of Hobbit Hole and Cruise and Snooze Inns to justify having different incentive plans for two operating divisions of the same company. (*CMA, USA, Adapted with permission*)

2. Whitehall Company is a manufacturer of leather goods operating from several regional divisions treated individually as profit centres. A master operating plan based on divisional projections for each fiscal year is prepared at corporate headquarters. Several years ago, Whitehall implemented an incentive plan to reward the performance of key personnel; the main features of the incentive plan, presented below, were designed to avoid "managed" earnings and recognise careful planning.

- The performance of each division's manager and other key personnel is measured against the division's annual operating plan. The plan is to be prepared by the division manager but is subject to revision during the corporate budgeting process.
- Acceptable performance is defined as 90–110 per cent of the division's budgeted operating income. For every percentage point achieved above 90 per cent, one per cent of the division's operating income is placed in the division's bonus fund. The maximum bonus fund contribution is 20 per cent of operating income for achieving 110 per cent of the budgeted operating income.
- The compensation committee of the Board of Directors has the authority to increase the bonus fund calculated above by 25 per cent. The Board uses the following criteria to make its judgment: non-quantifiable achievements, uncontrollable external influences, and major expenses made in the year to benefit the division in future periods.

Whitehall's sales declined during the recent recession, and its performance has not rebounded as well as the industry as a whole. Whitehall's Income Statement for the year ended November 30, 2016, is presented below.

Whitehall Company
Income Statement for the Year Ended November 30, 2016.

	(₹ 000)	(₹ 000)
Net sales		16,800
Expenses		
Cost of goods sold	12,600	
Selling expense	1,560	
Administrative expense	1,800	
Interest expense	280	
Total expenses		16,240
Income before income taxes		560
Income taxes		224
Net income		336

Whitehalls's turnover of average assets of four times and return on average assets before interest and taxes of 20 per cent are both well below the industry average. In addition, the company's return on sales before interest and taxes was five per cent in fiscal 2016 compared to the industry average of nine per cent.

Mitchel Boyd, president of Whitehall, is unhappy with this performance and wants to improve these ratios to be more comparable to the industry averages. While preparing the master budget, Boyd established the following goals for fiscal 2017 even though the divisional projections did not support all of these targets.

Return on sales before interest and taxes	8 per cent
Turnover of average assets	5 times
Return on average assets before interest and taxes	30 per cent

When establishing these goals, Boyd issued the following operational directives for fiscal 2017 which he believes will improve profitability

- Increase unit sales five per cent.
- Increase selling prices ten per cent.
- Increase advertising by ₹ 3,00,000 while holding all other selling and administrative expenses at fiscal 2016 levels.
- Increase production capacity by increasing the average investment in inventory and equipment by ₹ 6,00,000 while holding all other assets at fiscal 2016 levels.
- Finance the additional assets at an annual interest rate of ten per cent and hold all other interest expense at fiscal 2016 levels.
- Improve the marketability of products carried which will increase the unit cost of goods sold by seven per cent.

Whitehall's 2017 effective income tax rate is expected to be 40 per cent, the same as in fiscal 2016.

These operating goals and directives have just been presented at a meeting of the divisional managers and controllers. Roberta Green, controller of the Atlantic Division, has several reservations about Boyd's plan and had the following conversation with Jack Moore, controller of the Gulf Coast Division.

Green: These directives have little resemblance to the numbers I submitted for Atlanic. Although I didn't mention anything at the meeting. I think the ratio improvements are unrealistic, don't you?"

Moore: "It'll be a reach for us to follow Boyd's plan and achieve these targets. But, if it really does improve profits, our bonuses will be better."

Green: "I don't think Boyd cares about our bonuses. All he's looking for is better corporate performance; he made no mention of the effect these directives will have on divisional performance."

Moore: "Well, I'am going to support Boyd's targets."

Green: "Not me. I think I can convince my management team at Atlantic that it will be better for us to follow the original plan we submitted to headquarters for two or three months in order to prove my point."

Required:

A. 1. Evaluate at least three strengths and at least three weaknesses of Whitehall Company's incentive plan in terms of its effectiveness in achieving the desired behaviour of avoiding "managed" earnings and preparing careful plans.

2. Describe the likely behavioural impact that Mitchell Boyd's operational directives and goals will have on the divisional management teams.

B. Assuming that Mitchell Boyd's operational directives are carried out and his projected increase in unit sales is achieved.

1. prepare a pro forma income statement for Whitehall Company for the fiscal year ending November 30, 2017.
2. determine if the goals for ratio improvement will be achieved.

C. Discuss the ethical implications of the opinions expressed by Roberta Green in her conversation with Jack Moore. *(CMA, USA, Adapted with permission)*

Return on sales before interest and taxes	8 per cent
Turnover of average assets	[illegible] times
Return on average assets before interest and taxes	30 per cent

When establishing these goals, Boyd issued the following operational directives for fiscal 2017 which he believes will improve profitability.

- Increase unit sales five per cent.
- Increase selling prices ten per cent.
- Increase advertising by ₹ 3,00,000 while holding all other selling and administrative expenses at fiscal 2016 levels.
- Increase production capacity by increasing the average investment in inventory and equipment by ₹ 6,00,000 while holding all other assets at fiscal 2016 levels.
- Finance the additional assets at an annual interest rate of ten per cent and hold all other interest expense at fiscal 2016 level.
- Improve the marketability of products carried which will increase the unit cost of goods sold by seven per cent.

Whitehall's 2017 effective income tax rate is expected to be 40 per cent, the same as in fiscal 2016.

These operating goals and directives have just been presented at a meeting of the divisional managers and controllers. Roberta Green, controller of the Atlantic Division, has several reservations about Boyd's plan and had the following conversation with Jack Moore, controller of the Gulf Coast Division.

Green: "These directives have little resemblance to the numbers I submitted for Atlantic. Although he didn't mention anything at the meeting, I think the ratio improvements are unrealistic, don't you?"

Moore: "It will be a reach for us to follow Boyd's plan and achieve these targets. But if it really does improve profits, our bonuses will be better."

Green: "I don't think Boyd cares about our bonuses. All he's looking for is better corporate performance; he made no mention of the effect these directives will have on divisional performance."

Moore: "Well, I am going to support Boyd's targets."

Green: "Not me. I think I can convince my management team at Atlantic that it will be better for us to follow the original plan we submitted to headquarters for two or three months in order to prove my point."

Required

A. 1. Evaluate at least three strengths and at least three weaknesses of Whitehall Company's incentive plan in terms of its effectiveness in achieving the desired behaviour, of avoiding "managed" earnings and preparing careful plans.

2. Describe the likely behavioural impact that Mitchell Boyd's operational directives and goals will have on the divisional management teams.

B. Assuming that Mitchell Boyd's operational directives are carried out and his projected increase in unit sales is achieved:

1. prepare a pro forma income statement for Whitehall Company for the fiscal year ending November 30, 2017.

2. determine if the goals for ratio improvement will be achieved.

C. Discuss the ethical implications of the opinions expressed by Roberta Green in her conversation with Jack Moore. (IMA, USA. Adapted with permission)

PART

5

MANAGERIAL USES OF FINANCIAL STATEMENTS

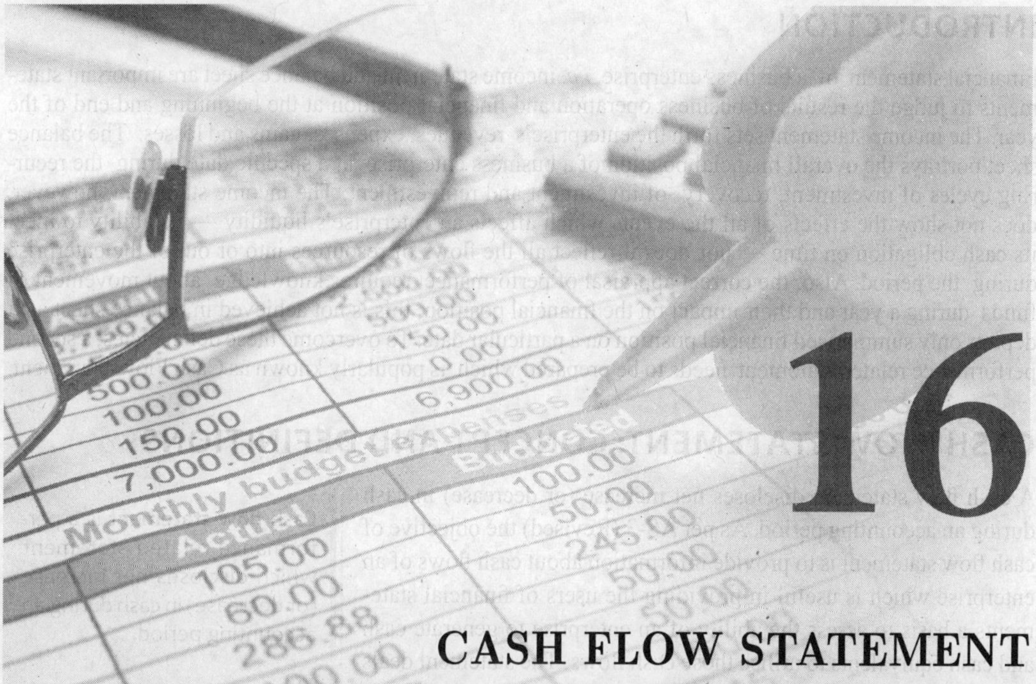

16

CASH FLOW STATEMENT

LEARNING OBJECTIVES:

After reading this chapter, you should be able to:

- Explain Cash Flow Statement and elaborate upon the Definitions given in AS 3
- Distinguish between Cash Inflows and Outflows
- Understand Direct and Indirect Methods of Presenting Cash Flow Statement
- Explain the Procedure of Preparing Cash Flow Statement
- Discuss the Importance of Cash Flow Statement

INTRODUCTION

Financial statement of a business enterprise, *i.e*, income statement and balance sheet are important statements to judge the results of business operation and financial position at the beginning and end of the year. The income statement sets forth the enterprise's revenues, expenses, gains and losses. The balance sheet portrays the overall financial position of a business enterprise at a specific date during the recurring cycles of investment, recovery of investment and reinvestment. The income statement, however, does not show the effects of all the events which affects an enterprise's liquidity — its ability to meet its cash obligation on time — nor does it reflect all the flows of resources into or out of the enterprise during the period. Also, the correct appraisal of performance requires knowledge about movement of funds during a year and their impact on the financial position; this is not achieved in balance sheet as it depicts only summarised financial position on a particular date. To overcome these deficiencies, a second performance related statement needs to be prepared which is popularly known as Cash Flow Statement.

CASH FLOW STATEMENT: CONCEPT AND DEFINITIONS

A cash flow statement discloses net increase (or decrease) in cash during an accounting period. As per AS-3 (Revised) the objective of cash flow statement is to provide information about cash flows of an enterprise which is useful in providing the users of financial statements a basis to assess the ability of an enterprise to generate cash and cash equivalents to utilise those cash flows. The statement deals with the provisions of information about the changes in cash and cash equivalents during the accounting year. It classifies Cash flows into operating, investing and financing activities.

> **Cash flow statement** is a performance related statement which discloses net increase (or decrease) in cash during an accounting period.

Definitions in AS 3

The following terms are used in this Statement with the meanings specified:

- *Cash comprises cash on hand and demand deposits with banks.*
- *Cash equivalents are short-term, highly liquid investments that are readily convertible into known amounts of cash and which are subject to an insignificant risk of changes in value.*
- *Cash flows are inflows and outflows of cash and cash equivalents.*
- *Operating activities are the principal revenue-producing activities of the enterprise and other activities that are not investing or financing activities.*
- *Investing activities are the acquisition and disposal of long-term assets and other investments not included in cash equivalents.*
- *Financing activities are activities that result in changes in the size and composition of the owners' capital (including preference share capital in the case of a company) and borrowings of the enterprise.*

Cash and Cash Equivalents

Cash equivalents are held for the purpose of meeting short-term cash commitments rather than for investment or other purposes. For an investment to qualify as a cash equivalent, it must be readily convertible to a known amount of cash and be subject to an insignificant risk of changes in value. Therefore, an investment normally qualifies as a cash equivalent only when it has a short maturity of, say, three months or less from the date of acquisition. Investments in shares are excluded from cash equivalents unless they are, in substance, cash equivalents; for example, preference shares of a company acquired shortly before their specified redemption date (provided there is only an insignificant risk of failure of the company to repay the amount at maturity).

Cash flows exclude movements between items that constitute cash or cash equivalents because these components are part of the cash management of an enterprise rather than part of its operating, investing and financing activities. Cash management includes the investment of excess cash in cash equivalents.

CLASSIFICATION OF CASH INFLOWS AND OUTFLOWS

A cash flow statement focuses on various activities and items which bring about changes in the cash balance between two balance sheet dates. This statement covers all items which increase or decrease the cash of a business enterprise. For example, this statement includes items like receipts from debtors and payments to creditors. On the contrary, this statement will not cover items which have no immediate effect on cash increase or decrease. For instance, goods purchased on credit and goods sold on credit will not be included in this statement as these transactions have no effect on inflow and outflow of cash.

A cash flow statement aims to determine the effects on cash of different types of cash inflows and outflows. In this process, all cash flows, *i.e.*, activities resulting into cash flows are classified into different categories. The ICAI's AS 3 'Cash Flow Statement' has classified cash flows into three categories:

1. Operating Activities (or Flows)
2. Investing Activities (or Flows)
3. Financing Activities (or Flows)

> **Cash Flow Statement** aims to determine the effects on cash of different types of cash inflows and outflows.

Figure 16.1 displays the classification of cash inflows and cash outflows relating to operating activities, investing activities and financing activities.

Operating Activities

Operating activities are those transactions which are considered in the determination of net income. Examples of cash inflows in this category are cash received from debtors for goods and services, interest and dividend received on loans and investment. Examples of cash outflows in this category are cash payments for goods and services; merchandise; wages; interest; taxes; supplies and others.

Classification of Cash Inflows and Cash Outflows

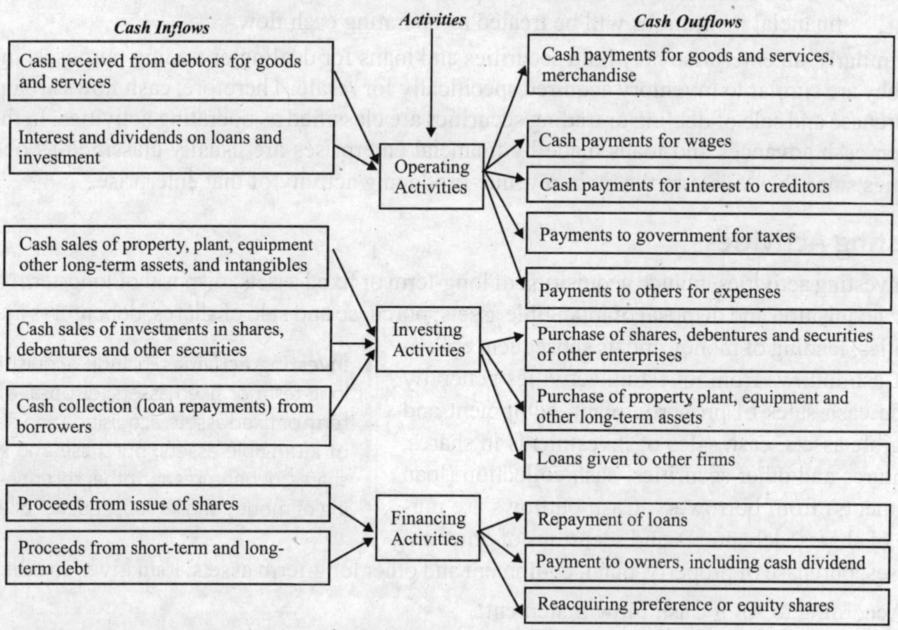

Figure 16.1: Classification of Cash Inflows and Outflows Relating to Operating Activities, Investing Activities and Financing Activities

AS 3 Cash flow statement states:

1. The amount of cash flows arising from operating activities is a key indicator of the extent to which the operations of the enterprise have generated sufficient cash flows to maintain the operating capability of the enterprise, pay dividends, repay loans and make new investments without recourse to external source of financing. Information about the specific components of historical operating cash flows is useful, in conjunction with other information, in forecasting future operating cash flows.
2. Cash flows from operating activities are primarily derived from the principal revenue-producing activities of the enterprise. Therefore, they generally result from the transactions and other events that enter into the determination of net profit or loss. Examples of cash flows from operating activities are:
   (*i*) cash receipts from the sale of goods and the rendering of services
   (*ii*) cash receipts from royalties, fees, commissions and other revenue
   (*iii*) cash payments to suppliers for goods and services
   (*iv*) cash payments to and on behalf of employees
   (*v*) cash receipts and cash payments of an insurance enterprise for premiums and claims, annuities and other policy benefits
   (*vi*) cash payments or refunds of income taxes, unless they can be specifically identified with financing and investing activities
   (*vii*) cash receipts and payments relating to future contracts, forward contracts, option contracts and swap contracts when the contracts are held for dealing or trading purposes
3. Some transactions, such as the sale of an item of plant, may give rise to a gain or loss which is included in the determination of net profit or loss. However, the cash flows relating to such transactions are cash flows from investing activities.
4. Cash flows from operating activities are determined according to the activities relating to the business in which the enterprise deals in e.g. interest and dividend received by financial institutions will be treated as operating cash flow.

Similarly, an enterprise may hold securities and loans for dealing or trading purposes, in which case they are similar to inventory acquired specifically for resale. Therefore, cash flows arising from the purchase and sale of dealing or trading securities are classified as operating activities. In the same manner, cash advances and loans made by financial enterprises are usually classified as operating activities since they relate to the main revenue-producing activity of that enterprise.

Investing Activities

Investing activities include acquisition of long-term or fixed assets; disposal of long-term or fixed assets; acquisition and disposal of intangible assets; purchase and sale of shares, debentures and other securities; lending of money and its subsequent collection. Cash inflows from investing activities generally include cash sales of property, plant, equipment and intangible assets, cash sales of investments in shares, debentures and other securities, cash collection (loan repayments) from borrowers. Cash outflows are purchase of shares, debentures and securities of other enterprises, purchase of property, plant, equipment and other long-term assets, loan given to other firms.

> **Investing activities** include acquisition of long-term or fixed assets; disposal of long-term or fixed assets; acquisition and disposal of intangible assets; purchase and sale of shares, debentures and other securities; lending of money and its subsequent collection.

According to AS 3 Cash Flow Statement:

1. The separate disclosure of cash flows arising from investing activities is important because the cash flows represent the extent to which expenditures have been made for resources

intended to generate future income and cash flows. Examples of cash flows arising from investing activities are:

(*i*) Cash payments to acquire fixed assets (including intangibles). These payments includes those relating to capitalised research and development costs and self-constructed fixed assets;

(*ii*) Cash receipts from disposal of fixed assets (including intangibles);

(*iii*) Cash payments to acquire shares, warrants or debt instruments of other enterprises and interests in joint ventures (other than payments for those instruments considered to be cash equivalents and those held for dealing or trading purposes);

(*iv*) Cash receipts from disposal of shares, warrants or debt instruments of other enterprises and interests in joint ventures (other than receipts from those instruments considered to be cash equivalents and those held for dealing or trading purposes);

(*v*) Cash advances and loans made to third parties (other than advances and loans made by a financial enterprise);

(*vi*) Cash receipts from the repayment of advances and loans made to third parties (other than advances and loans of a financial enterprise);

(*vii*) Cash payments from future contracts, forward contracts, option contracts and swap contracts except when the contracts are held for dealing or trading purposes, or the payments are classified as financing activities; and

(*viii*) Cash receipts from future contracts, forward contracts, option contracts and swap contracts except when the contracts are held for dealing or trading purposes, or the receipts are classified as financing activities.

2. When a contract is accounted for as a hedge of an identifiable position, the cash flows of the contract are classified in the same manner as the cash flow of the position being hedged.

Financing Activities

Financing activities relate to long-term liability and equity capital. A firm engages in financing activities when it obtains resources from owners, returns resources to owners, borrows resources from creditors and repays amounts borrowed. Cash inflows include proceeds from issue of shares and short-term and long-term borrowings. Cash outflows include repayment of loans and payments to owners, including cash dividends. Repayments of accounts payable or accrued liabilities are not considered repayment of loans under financing activities but are classified as cash outflows under operating activities.

> **Financing activities** relate to long-term liability and equity capital.

AS 3 Cash Flow Statement observes:

The separate disclosure of cash flows arising from financing activities is important because it is useful in predicting claims on future cash flows by providers of funds (both capital and borrowings) to the enterprise. Examples of cash flows arising from financing activities are:

1. Cash proceeds from issuing shares or other similar instruments;
2. Cash proceeds from issuing debentures, loans, notes, bonds, and other short- or long-term borrowings; and
3. Cash repayments of amounts borrowed.

CASH FLOW STATEMENT AND CASH RECEIPTS AND DISBURSEMENTS

A cash flow statement differs from the summary of cash receipts and disbursements. A cash flow statement is prepared by rearrangement of items on the income statement and balance sheet, rather than from entries made to the cash account. Cash flow statement may also highlight the amount of cash generated by the firm's operations. This is not reported in statement of cash receipts and disbursements.

CASH FLOW AND INCOME STATEMENTS

Cash flow statement apparently differs from income statement. An income statement includes adjustments in respect of expenses accrued in the calculation of periodic income, whereas cash flow statement excludes such adjustments. The largest item of difference between them is the allocation of fixed assets costs as depreciation. Also, the procedures adopted in the two statements are reflected in changes in balance sheet items. These would include changes in balances of trade debtors and trade creditors.

CASH PROFIT (CASH NET INCOME)

Accrual-based profit and loss account reveals accrual net income. By adjusting the items on the profit and loss account, one can arrive at cash profit or cash net income. It should be noted that cash profit relates to operating activities in the same way as profit and loss account focuses on net income determination from operating activities. But profit and loss account does not show cash inflow and outflow relating to operating activities because profit and loss account is prepared on accrual basis.

Cash profit and cash flow is not the same thing. Cash profit is confined to indicating cash flow relating to operating activities. But cash flow is a total concept indicating total inflows and outflows. For example, issue of equity shares is a source of cash inflow but will not be used for determining cash profit. Similarly, plant purchased will be cash outflow for its full value, but will not be used for determining cash profit.

PRESENTATION OF CASH FLOW STATEMENT

A cash flow statement can be presented in either the direct or indirect format. The investing and financing sections will be the same under either format. However, the operating section will be different.

> **Direct Method** discloses major class of gross cash receipts and gross cash payment.
>
> **Indirect Method** shows the relationship between the income statement and the balance sheet.

Direct Method

Direct method is that method whereby major class of gross cash receipts and gross cash payment are disclosed.

Enterprises that utilize the direct method should report separately the following classes of operating cash receipts and payments:

1. Cash collected from customers, including lessees, licensee, and other similar items
2. Interest and dividends received
3. Other operating cash receipts, if any
4. Cash paid to employees and other suppliers of goods or services, including insurance, advertising, and other similar expenses.

5. Interest paid
6. Income taxes paid
7. Other operating cash payments, if any

Companies that use the direct method must provide a reconciliation of net income to net cash flow from operating activities in a separate schedule in the financial statements.

According to AS 3 Cash Flow Statement:

The direct method provides information which may be useful in estimating future cash flows and which is not available under the indirect method and is, therefore, considered more appropriate than the indirect method. Under the direct method, information about major classes of gross cash receipts and gross cash payments may be obtained either:

1. from the accounting records of the enterprise; or
2. by adjusting sales, cost of sales (interest and similar income and interest expense and similar charges for a financial enterprise) and other items in the statement of profit and loss for:
   (*i*) changes during the period in inventories and operating receivables and payables;
   (*ii*) other non-cash items; and
   (*iii*) other items for which the cash effects are investing or financing cash flows.

Indirect Method

Under the indirect method, the net cash flow from operating activities is determined by adjusting net profit or loss for the effects of:

1. changes during the period in inventories and operating receivables and payables;
2. non-cash items such as depreciation, provisions, deferred taxes, and unrealised foreign exchange gains and losses; and
3. all other items for which the cash effects are investing or financing cash flows.

Alternatively, the net cash flow from operating activities may be presented under the indirect method by showing the operating revenues and expenses excluding non-cash items disclosed in the statement of profit and loss and the changes during the period in inventories and operating receivables and payables.

The indirect method starts with net income and reconciles it to net cash flow from operating activities. The cash flow from operating activities is found by adjusting net income for (*i*) changes in current assets and current liabilities and (*ii*) depreciation expense. Depreciation expense is not a cash flow. Because it decreases net income, it is added back to net income, in order to arrive at the operating cash flow. The following summarizes the process:

Change	*Adjustment to Net Income*
Decrease in a current asset	Add
Increase in a current asset	Subtract
Decrease in a current liability	Subtract
Increase in a current liability	Add

The indirect method is more widely used, since it shows the relationship between the income statement and the balance sheet and therefore aids in the analysis of these statements.

Reporting Cash Flows from Investing and Financing Activities

An enterprise should report separately major classes of gross cash receipts and gross cash payments arising from investing and financing activities.

Comparison Between Direct and Indirect Method

Both the approaches, direct and indirect result in the same amount for cash flow from operations after making necessary adjustments. However, both the approaches have the arguments, pros and cons.

The arguments in favour of direct approach are that it identifies the major categories of cash receipts and cash payments arising from operating activities; it provides a more useful basis for estimating future cash flows; and it provides information that is not otherwise available in the balance sheet and profit and loss account. The direct method is a better indicator of company solvency, has a sounder conceptual framework and reflects accepted business practice. It permits an evaluation of cash flow relating to specific line items of income statement such as sales and cost of goods sold. The empirical evidence indicates that the direct method is superior over the indirect method in predicting future operating cash flows and future net operating cash flows.

On the other hand, followers of the indirect approach argue that indirect method is less costly and more convenient to use by firms. It is argued that the direct approach would require information that is hard to collect and sensitive. One difficulty with the direct approach is that some of the cash flows may have characteristics of more than one category of cash flow.

However, the indirect method has also been criticised on two grounds. First, it contains unnecessary detail and may confuse the users. Another limitation of the indirect method is that the adding of expenses such as depreciation suggests that expenses are a source of cash. The conceptual and practical problems which underlie the indirect method are as follows:

- Ambiguity in the definition of "operations."
- Diversity in reporting practices.
- Impact of changes in the reporting entity on the non-cash current accounts.
- Use of absorption costing in accounting for manufactured inventory.
- Measurement of current portion of long-term leases.
- Reclassifications between current and non-current accounts.

Exhibit 16.1 and 16.2 show respectively direct and indirect method of preparing cash flow statement.

Exhibit 16.1: Cash Flow Statement (Direct Method)

ABC Company
for the Year Ended December 31, 2016

	₹	₹
(A) Cash Flow from Operating Activities		
Cash Receipts from:		
Sales		
Interest Received		
Cash Payments for:		
Purchases		
Operating Expenses		
Interest Payments		
Income Taxes		
Net Cash Flow from Operating Activities		
(B) Cash Flows from Investing Activities:		
Sale of Plant Assets		

Sale of Investments	
Purchase of Plant Assets	
Purchase of Investments	
Net Cash Flows Used by Investing Activities	
(C) Cash Flows from Financing Activities:	
Repayment of Bonds and Debentures	
Issue of Common Shares	
Dividends Paid	
Net Cash Flows from Financing Activities	
Net Increase (Decrease) in Cash	

Exhibit 16.2: Cash Flow Statement (Indirect Method)

ABC Company
for the Year Ended December 31, 2016

	₹	₹
(A) Cash Flows from Operating Activities		
Net Income		
Adjustments to Reconcile Net Income to Net		
Cash provided by Operating Activities:		
Depreciation		
Gain on Sale of Investments		
Loss on Sale of Plant Asset		
Decrease in Accounts Receivable		
Increase in Inventory		
Decrease in Prepaid Expenses		
Increase in Accounts Payable		
Increase in Accrued Liabilities		
Decrease in Income Taxes Payable		
Net Cash Flows from Operating Activities		
(B) Cash Flows from Investing Activities:		
Sale of Plant Assets		
Sale of Investments		
Purchase of Plant Assets		
Purchase of Investment		
Net Cash Flows Used by Investing Activities.		
(C) Cash Flows from Financing Activities		
Repayment of Bonds and Debentures		
Issue of Common Shares		
Dividends Paid		
Net Cash Flows from Financing Activities		
Net Increase (Decrease) in Cash		

PREPARING CASH FLOW STATEMENT

Before preparing cash flow statement, first of all, the following three steps have to be completed:

1. Determining cash flows from operations or operating activities
2. Determining cash flows from investing activities
3. Determining cash flows from financing activities

After obtaining information regarding the above, a cash flow statement can be prepared. The three steps have been discussed below:

Cash flow from Operations

The profit and loss account focuses on net income determination from operating activities. However, it does not show cash inflow and outflow relating to operating activities because the profit and loss account is prepared on accrual basis. In preparing profit and loss account, revenues are recorded even though cash for them has not been received. Similarly, expenses are recorded even though they may not have been paid. Therefore, to find cash flows from operations, one needs to convert accrual basis income statement figures to cash basis by making adjustments. By way of adjustments, earned revenues will be converted into cash received from sales or customers and incurred expenses will be converted into cash expended, *i.e.*, expenses actually paid in cash.

The conversion of accrual basis income statement to cash basis income statement along with required adjustment has been shown below:

The conversion process displayed in Exhibit 16.3 can be described as follows, using a short-cut calculation:

Accrual-Basis Net Income

↓

Deduct Increase in Accounts Receivable (or Add Decrease in Accounts Receivable)
Deduct Increase in Merchandise Inventory (or Add Decrease in Merchandise Inventory)
Deduct Increase in Prepaid Expenses (or Add Decrease in Prepaid Expenses)
Add Increase in Accounts Payable (Or Deduct Decrease in Accounts Payable)
Add Increase in Accrued Expenses (Or Deduct Decrease in Accrued Expenses)
Add Depreciation and Amortization Expenses for the Year

↓

Cash Basis Net Income

While making conversion, one should know the relationship between profit and loss accounts and balance sheet changes. Each individual item on the income statement should be viewed as it relates to a balance sheet account. On the accrual basis of accounting, the explanation for the difference between the amount of sales revenue and the receipts from those sales is found in the changes in accounts receivable and debtors account. Similarly, the difference between the amount of an expense and the amount of payments for that expense is found in the changes of its associated asset or liability, such as prepaid rent or rent payable. If there is no associated balance sheet account for an item on the profit and loss account, it is presumed that the amount shown on the profit and loss account resulted in a cash flow exactly equal to that revenue or expense. Table 16.1 shows relationship between some profit and loss account and balance sheet accounts.

Exhibit 16.3: Relationship of Accrual Basis and Cash Basis of Accounting

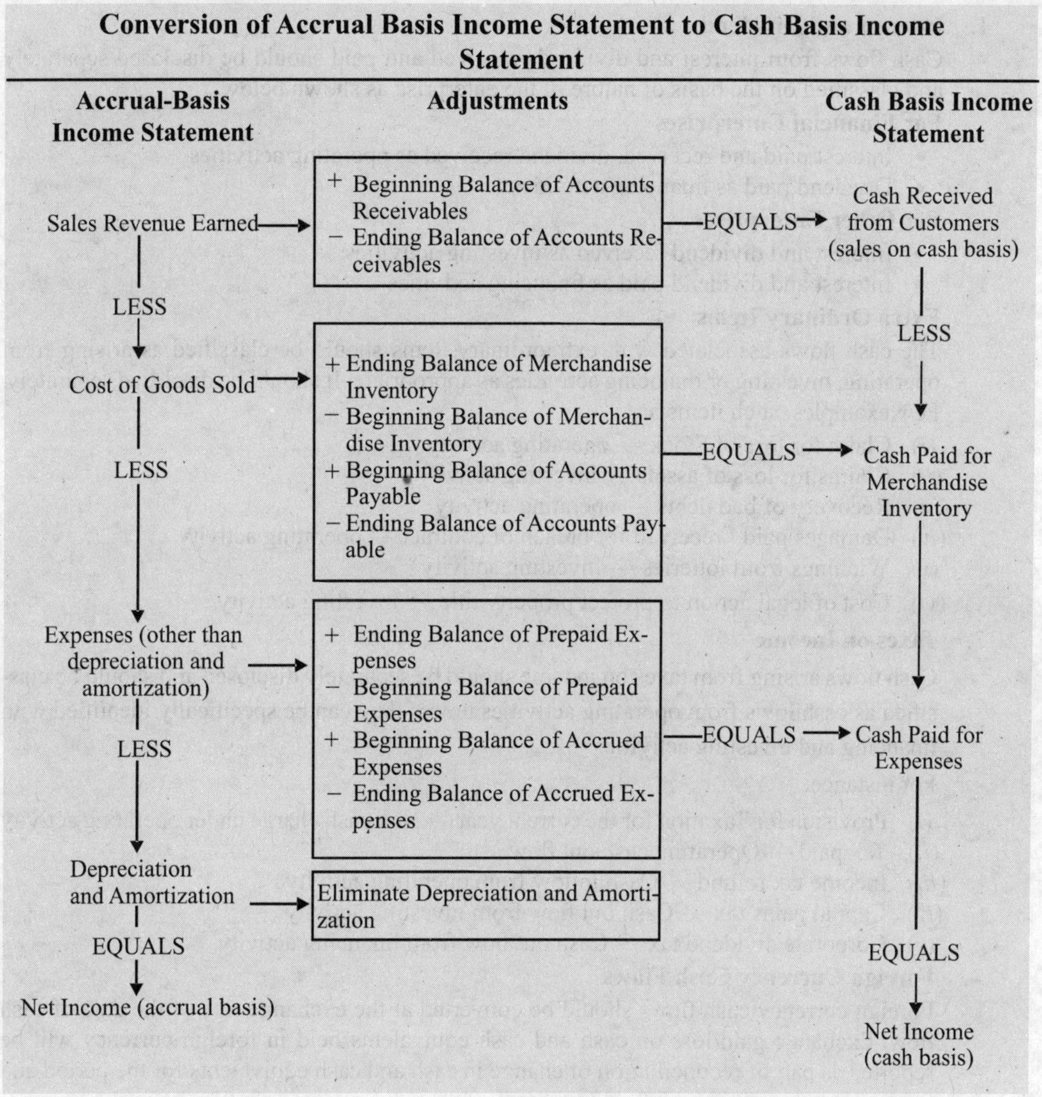

Table 16.1: Relationship Between Income Statement and Balance Sheet

Financial Statement Relationship

Profit and Loss Accounts	Related to Balance Sheet Accounts
Sales	Debtors
Cost of goods sold	(Inventory) (Creditors)
Salaries Expenses	Salaries payable
Rent Expenses	Rent payable
Depreciation Expenses	Accumulated depreciation
Insurance Expenses	Prepaid insurance
Interest Expenses	Interest payable
Income Tax Expenses	Income taxes payable

PROVISIONS OF AS-3 ON TREATMENT OF CERTAIN ITEMS

1. **Interest and Dividend**

   Cash flows from interest and dividends received and paid should be disclosed separately and classified on the basis of nature of the enterprise as shown below:

   For Financial Enterprises
   - Interest paid and received, dividend received as operating activities.
   - Dividend paid as financing activities.

   For Other Enterprises
   - Interest and dividend received as investing activities.
   - Interest and dividend paid as financing activities.

2. **Extra Ordinary Items**

   The cash flows associated with extraordinary items should be classified as arising from operating, investing or financing activities as appropriate. It should be disclosed separately. Few examples, such items are :

   (*i*) Claim for loss of Stock — operating activity
   (*ii*) Claims for loss of assets — investing activity
   (*iii*) Recovery of bad debts — operating activity
   (*iv*) Damages paid / received for breach of contract — operating activity
   (*v*) Winnings from lotteries — Investing activity
   (*vi*) Cost of legal action to protect property title — Investing activity.

3. **Taxes on Income**

   Cash flows arising from taxes on income should be separately disclosed and should be classified as cashflows from operating activities unless they can be specifically identified with financing and investing activities.

   For instance:

   (*i*) Provision for Taxation for the current year — Non cash charge under operating activity
   (*ii*) Tax paid — Operating cash out flow
   (*iii*) Income tax refund — Cash inflow from operating activity
   (*iv*) Capital gains tax — Cash out flow from investing activity
   (*v*) Corporate dividend tax — Cash out flow from financing activity.

4. **Foreign Currency Cash Flows**

   Foreign currency cash flows should be converted at the exchange rate of the date of cash flow. Exchange gain/loss on cash and cash equivalents held in foreign currency will be reported as part of reconciliation of change in cash and cash equivalents for the period and hence, not reported in cash flow statement.

5. **Non-cash Transactions**

   Investing and financing transactions that do not require the use of cash or cash equivalents are not shown in the cash flow statement. Examples of such non-cash transactions are:

   (*i*) Issue of shares or debentures for a consideration other than cash *i.e.* against building, machinery etc.
   (*ii*) Conversion of debentures into equity shares.
   (*iii*) Purchase of business by issue of shares.

   AS-3 (Revised) recommends that such transactions may be disclosed under footnote to cash flow statement.

6. **Investments in Subsidiaries, Associates and Joint Venture**

   Acquisition of interest in any subsidiary, associates or in any joint venture is treated as "Investing Activity". Similarly, sale or disposal of such interest and receipt of interest or dividends on such investments is treated as "Investing Activity".

Illustrative Problem 1

From the following Profit and Loss Account of ABC Ltd for the year ended 31st March, 2016 calculate Cash generated from "Operating Activities" by Direct Method.

Profit and Loss Account for the year ended 31st March 2016

	₹	₹		₹
To Opening Stock		1,60,000	By Sale (Cash)	42,50,000
To Purchases (Cash)		31,00,000	By Commission accrued	40,000
To Wages	4,40,000		By Dividend received	60,000
Add: Outstanding	60,000	5,00,000	By Profit on sale of Plant	2,40,000
To Salaries	2,20,000		(Sale proceeds 22,40,000	
Add: Outstanding	20,000		— book value ₹ 20,00,000)	
	2,40,000		By Closing Stock	2,20,000
Less: Prepaid	10,000	2,30,000		
To Office Expenses		80,000		
To Selling Expenses		1,20,000		
To Depreciation		1,10,000		
To Income Tax paid		20,000		
To Goodwill written		44,000		
To Preliminary Expenses written off		20,000		
To Net profit		4,26,000		
		48,10,000		48,10,000

Solution:

Cash Flow from Operations

		₹	₹
(A)	**Cash Receipts from Operating Activities:**		
	Cash Sales		42,50,000
Less:			
(B)	Cash payments due to operating activities:		
	Purchases	31,00,000	
	Wages	4,40,000	
	Salaries	2,20,000	
	Office Expenses	80,000	
	Selling Expenses	1,20,000	39,60,000
	Cash Flow from operations before Tax		2,90,000
	Less: Income Tax paid		20,000
	Net Cash inflow from Operations		2,70,000

Notes:

1. Non cash charges such as depreciations, Goodwill written off, Preliminary expenses written off have been ignored as these do not involve any outflow of cash.
2. Dividend received and profit on Sale of Plant are to be treated under cash flow from 'Investing activities'.
3. Commission Accrued does not involve any cash inflow, hence ignored.
4. Changes in current assets and current liabilities are ignored.

Illustrative Problem 2

From the following Profit and Loss A/c and additional information of M/s Anurag Enterprises, compute cash flow from operations.

Profit and Loss Account
for the Year Ended 31st March, 2016

	₹	₹		₹
To Opening Stock		1,60,000	By Sale :	
To Purchases			Cash	6,00,000
Cash	2,00,000		Credit	10,00,000
Credit	6,00,000	8,00,000	By Closing Stock	2,08,000
To Wages		48,000	By Commission	1,12,000
To Office Expenses		1,76,000	By Royalties	80,000
To Selling Expenses		96,000	By Discount Received	40,000
To Bad debts		16,000		
To Discount Allowed		32,000		
To Depreciation		1,20,000		
To Provision for Tax		2,40,000		
To Net Profit		3,52,000		
		20,40,000		20,40,000

Additional Information	March 31, 2015	March 31, 2016
	₹	₹
Debtors	1,20,000	1,44,000
Creditors	1,12,000	80,000
O/s Selling Expenses	24,000	32,000
Prepaid Office Expenses	16,000	24,000
Accrued Royalties	96,000	88,000
Advance Commission	72,000	64,000
Provision for Tax	3,20,000	4,80,000

Solution:

Cash Flow from Operations

		₹	₹
(A) Receipts from Operations :			
	Cash Sales		6,00,000
	Cash Received from Debtors*1		9,76,000
	Cash from Royalties*2		88,000
	Cash from Commission*3		1,04,000
			17,68,000
Less:			
(B) Operating Cash Payments			
	Cash Purchases	2,00,000	
	Cash paid to Creditors*4	6,32,000	
	Cash Selling Expenses	88,000	
	Cash Office Expenses	1,92,000	11,12,000
	Cash inflow from operations before tax		6,56,000
Less: Income Tax paid (on operating incomes)			80,000
	Net Cash flow from operations		5,76,000

*1 Cash Received from debtors → prepare debtors a/c

Debtors A/c

	₹		₹
To Balance b/d	1,20,000	By Cash Received (Bal. (Fig.)	9,76,000
To Sales (Credit)	10,00,000	By Balance c/d	1,44,000
	11,20,000		11,20,000

*2 **Cash from Royalties**

Opening Bal. + Royalties as per P & L A/c — Closing Bal. = Cash from Royalties

96,000 + 80,000 — 88,000 = ₹ 88,000

*3 **Cash from Commission**

Closing bal. + Commission as per P & L A/c — Opening Bal. = Cash from Commission
of Advance of Advance

64,000 + 1,12,000 – 72,000 = 1,04,000

*4 **Cash paid to Creditors**

Op. bal. + Purchases – Cl. Bal. = Cash paid to creditors

80,000 + 6,00,000 – 1,12,000 = ₹ 6,32,000

Illustrative Problem 3 (Cash Flows from Operating Activities)

The net income reported on the income statement for the year was ₹ 1,10,000 and depreciation of fixed assets for the year was ₹ 44,000. The balances of the current asset and current liability accounts at the beginning and end of the year are as follows:

	End of the Year	Beginning of the year
	₹	₹
Cash	1,30,000	1,40,000
Debtors	2,00,000	1,80,000
Inventories	2,90,000	3,00,000
Prepaid Expenses	15,000	16,000
Accounts Payable	1,02,000	1,16,000
Calculate total cash from operating activities		

Solution:

Cash from Operating Activities

	₹	₹
Net Income		1,10,000
Add: Depreciation		44,000
Operating profit before working capital changes		1,54,000
Add: Decrease in Inventories	10,000	
Decrease in prepaid expenses	1,000	11,000
		1,65,000
Deduct: Increase in Debtors	20,000	
Decrease in Accounts Payable	14,000	34,000
Net Cash Flow from Operating Activities		1,31,000

Illustrative Problem 4 (Cash flow from Operation-Indirect Method

From the following, calculate cash from operation by Indirect Method.

Profit and Loss Account
for the year ended 31st March, 2016

	₹	₹		₹
To Opening Stock		2,00,000	By Sales	45,00,000
To Purchases		36,40,000	By Closing Stock	2,40,000
To Wages	2,25,000			
+ Outstanding	25,000	2,50,000		
To Manufacturing Expenses		75,000		
To Gross Profit *c/d*		5,75,000		
		47,40,000		47,40,000
To Salaries	1,37,500			
Add: Outstanding	62,500	2,00,000	By Gross Profit *b/d*	5,75,000
To Insurance	30,000		By Rent Received	37,500
Less: Prepaid	7,500	22,500	By Commission Accrued	17,500
To Office Expenses		1,17,500	By Net Loss	55,000
To Selling Expenses		1,45,000		
To Depreciation		1,25,000		
To Share Issue Expenses w/o		75,000		
		6,85,000		6,85,000

Solution:

Calculation of Cash From Operating Activities
(Indirect Method)

		₹	₹
	Net Loss as per Profit and Loss A/c (before tax and extraordinary item)		(55,000)
	Adjustments for Non cash charges and Non-operating items.		
Add:	Depreciation	1,25,000	
Add:	Share Issue Expenses written off	75,000	2,00,000
			1,45,000
Less:	Rent Received (Non-operating)		(37,500)
	Operating profit before Working Capital Changes		1,07,500
Adjustment for current assets/liabilities:			
Add:	Increase in Current liabilities		
	Wages O/s	25,000	
	Salaries	62,500	87,500
			1,95,000
Less:	Increase in Current Assets		
	Stock	40,000	
	Prepaid Insurance	7,500	
	Accrued Commission	17,500	(65,000)
Net Cash from operating Activities			1,30,000

Illustrative Problem 5 (Cash Flows from Operating Activities)

X Ltd. has the following balance on 01.01.2016 :

	₹	₹
Fixed Assets	15,00,000	
Less: Depreciation	(5,00,000)	10,00,000
Bank		87,500
Other Current Assets		6,25,500
Current Liabilities		2,50,000

Next year's estimate are :

(*i*) The company will acquire fixed assets costing ₹ 2,50,000 after selling one machine for ₹ 70,000, costing ₹ 1,50,000 on which depreciation provided will amount to ₹ 90,000.

(*ii*) The net profits will be ₹ 1.75,000 after providing for depreciation of ₹ 1,50,000.

(*iii*) Current assets and current liabilities (other than bank balance) at 31.12.2016 are estimated to be ₹ 7,50,000 and ₹ 4,00,000 respectively.

At the end of the accounting year, the company deposits all the cash into the bank. Calculate the cash flows from operations and investing activities for the year 2016.

Solution:

Cash Flow from Operating Activities

	₹	₹
Net Profit after depreciation	1,75,000	
Add: Depreciation provided	1,50,000	
Less: Profit on sale of machinery	(10,000)	
Operating profit before working capital changes	3,15,000	
Less: Increase in assets	(1,25,000)	
Add: Increase in current liabilities	1,50,000	
Net cash from operating activities		3,40,000

Cash Flow from Investing Activities

Sale of Machine	70,000	
Purchase of Machine	(2,50,000)	
Net cash used in investing activities		(1,80,000)

Working Note

Calculation of Profit on sale of machinery: 70,000 – (1,50,000 – 90,000) = ₹ 10,000.

Illustrative Problem 6 (Cash from Operation and Extraordinary Activities)

From the following information, calculate cash from operations.

Profit and Loss Account
for the year ended 31st March, 2016

	₹		₹
To Opening Stock	1,50,000	By Sales	32,75,000
To Purchases	14,50,000	By Closing Stock	3,25,000
To Wages	70,000		
To Gross Profit c/d	19,30,000		
	36,00,000		36,00,000
To Operating Expenses	11,10,000	By Gross Profit b/d	19,30,000
To Interest on debentures	18,000	By Interest on Investments	15,000
To Depreciation	1,20,000	By Dividend Received	18,000
To Loss on Sale of Plant	40,000	By Profit on Sale of Land	20,000
To Discount on Issue of shares	10,000	By Rent Received	12,000
To Goodwill written off	15,000	By Refunds of Tax	8,000
To Provision for Tax	30,000	By Insurance claims for Loss of Stock	1,25,000
To General Reserve	25,000		
To Proposed, Dividend	1,80,000		
To Interim Dividend	70,000		
To Net Profit	5,10,000		
	21,28,000		21,28,000

Additional Information:

	31.03.2015 ₹	31.03.2016 ₹
Stock	1,40,000	1,00,000
Debtors	25,000	1,00,000
Creditors	15,000	50,000
Provision for Tax	50,000	60,000
Prepaid Expenses	18,000	20,000
Outstanding Salaries	20,000	25,000
Accrued Commission	15,000	15,000

Solution:

Cash Flow from Operating Activities

		₹	₹
	Net Profit before Tax and Extraordinary items (1)		6,82,000
	Adjustment for: Non Cash Charges and Non-operating items		
Add:	Depreciation	1,20,000	
	Goodwill	15,000	
	Discount on issue of shares	10,000	
	Loss on sale of plant	40,000	
	Interest on Debentures (2)	18,000	2,03,000
			8,85,000
Less:	Profit on Sale of Land (3)	20,000	
	Interest Received (3)	15,000	
	Dividend Received (3)	18,000	(53,000)
	Operating profit before working Capital Changes		8,32,000
Adjustment for Working Capital:			
Add:	Decrease in Current Assets and Increase in current liabilities:		
	Stock	40,000	
	Debtors	35,000	
	O/s Salaries	5,000	80,000
			9,12,000
Less:	Increase in current assets and decrease in current liabilities:		
	Debtors	75,000	
	Accrued Commission	15,000	
	Prepaid Expenses	2,000	(92,000)
			8,20,000
Less:	Tax Paid		(12,000)
	Cash flow before Extraordinary items		8,08,000
Add:	Cash from Extra ordinary items		
	(Insurance claims for loss of Stock (4)		1,25,000
	Net Cash Flow from Operations		9,33,000

Working Notes:

		₹	₹
(1)	Net Profit as per P and L A/c		5,10,000
Add:	Tax and Appropriations:		
	Provision for Tax	30,000	
	Proposed Dividend	1,80,000	
	Interim Dividend	70,000	
	General Reserve	25,000	3,05,000
			8,15,000
Less:	Tax Refund and Extra Ordinary Receipts (8,000 + 1,25,000)		1,33,000
			6,82,000

(2) Interest on Debentures to be adjusted against Financing Activities.

(3) Interest Received, Dividend Received, Profit on sale of Fixed Assets are covered by Investing Activities,

(4) Insurance claims for loss of Stock is treated under Operating Activities while loss of assets under "Investing Activities".

Illustrative Problem 7 (Indirect Method)

The following data are provided for ABC Ltd. :

Income Statement Data For 2016

	₹
Revenues	84,000
Cost of goods sold	(48,000)
Depreciation expense	(4,000)
Interest expense	(6,000)
Other expenses	(22,000)
Net income	4,000

Comparative Balance Sheets Data

	2016 ₹	2015 ₹
Current Assets		
Cash	20,000	16,000
Debtors (net)	12,000	7,000
Stock in hand	16,000	14,000
Non Current Assets		
Plant and Machinery	24,000	20,000
Less: Accumulated Depreciation	(8,000)	(4,000)
Total Assets	64,000	53,000
Liabilities		
Creditors	12,000	14,000
Non-current Note Payable	20,000	20,000
Less: Discount on Note	(1,600)	(2,000)
	30,400	32,000
Owner's Equity		
Equity Share Capital	24,000	14,000
Retained Earnings	9,600	7,000
	33,600	21,000

Required: Prepare statement of cash flows using the Indirect Method as per, [AS-3 (Revised)]

Solution:

ABC Ltd.
Cash Flow Statement for the Year Ended 31 December, 2016
[AS-3 (Revised)] (Indirect Method)

		₹	₹
(A)	**Cash Flows from Operating Activities**		
	Net Income before tax	4,000	
	Adjustments for:		
	Depreciation	4,000	
	Amortization of discount on note payable	400	
	Interest expense	6,000	
	Operating Profit before working capital changes	**14,400**	
	Increase in Debtors	(5,000)	
	Increase in Inventories	(2,000)	
	Decrease in Creditors	(2,000)	
	Net cash provided by operating activities		**5,400**
(B)	**Cash Flows from Investing Activities**		
	Purchase of Plant and Machinery	(4,000)	
	Net cash used in investing activities		**(4,000)**
(C)	**Cash Flows from Financing Activities**		
	Issues of Share Capital	10,000	
	Interest Paid	(6,000)	
	Dividends Paid	(1,400)	
	Net cash from financing activities		2,600
	Net increase in cash and cash equivalents (A + B + C)		4,000
	Cash and cash equivalents at the beginning of the period		16,000
	Cash and cash equivalents at the end of the period		20,000

Note:

Dividends paid have been calculated as under :

	₹
Retained earnings at the beginning	7,000
Add: Net Income	4,000
	11,000
Less: Retained earnings at the end	9,600
Dividend paid	1,400

Illustrative Problem 8 (Direct and Indirect Methods)

From the following particulars, prepare Cash Flow Statement for the year ended 31st March, 2016 using.

(a) Direct Method

(b) Indirect Method

(A) Income Statement for the Year Ended 31st March, 2016

		₹	₹
	Turnover		12,80,000
Less:	Cost of Goods Sold		8,00,000
			4,80,000
Add:	Other Receipts :		
	Insurance Claims for loss of Stock due to fire		20,000
			5,00,000
Less:	Operating Expenses	3,16,000	
	Interest on Debentures	6,000	
	Depreciation	84,000	
	Discount on Debentures w/o	400	4,06,400
	Profit before Tax		93,600
Less:	Provision for Tax		36,800
	Profit after Tax		56,800

(B) The Assets and Liabilities as on 31.3.2015 and 31st March, 2016 were as under :

	31.03.2015 ₹	31.03.2016 ₹
Stock	72,000	88,000
Debtors	16,000	15,200
Bills Receivable	12,000	22,000
Cash and Bank balance	44,800	99,200
Creditors	31,200	38,000
Bills Payable	8,000	6,000
O/s Expenses	12,400	17,600

(C) **Additional Information:**

(*i*) Fully paid Equity shares of the face value of ₹ 80,000 were allotted at a premium of @20%.

(*ii*) Fixed assets were acquired for ₹ 60,000 and the payment was made in 6% convertible debentures at par.

(*iii*) Income Tax paid during the year amounted to ₹ 38,000.

(*iv*) Company paid a dividend and corporate dividend tax thereon for the year ended 31st March, 2015 amounting to ₹ 44,000.

(*v*) 9% Debentures for ₹ 1,20,000 were redeemed at a premium of 2%.

Solution:

(*a*) Cash Flow Statement (Direct Method)

		₹	₹
Cash Flow from Operating Activities:			
(*a*)	Operating Cash Receipts :		
	Cash from customers (1)	12,70,800	
(*b*)	Operating cash Payments (2)	11,22,000	
	Cash Flow from Operations (a –b)	1,48,800	
	Income Tax Paid	(38,000)	
		1,10,800	
Cash Flow from Extra Ordinary items:			
Add:	Claims Received	20,000	
	Net Cash Flow from operating activities:		1,30,800
Cash Flow from Financing Activities:			
	Issue of shares at premium (3)	96,000	
•	Redemption of Debentures	(1,22,400)	
•	Interest on Debentures	(6,000)	
•	Dividend and Corporate dividend Tax	(44,000)	
	Net cash used in financing Activities		(76,400)
	Net Increase in Cash and Cash Equivalents		54,400
	Cash and Cash equivalents in the beginning		44,800
	Cash and Cash equivalents at the end		99,200

Financing and Investing Activities not affecting Cash flow—Issue of debentures against acquisition of land -	60,000

Working Notes:

(1) Receivables A/c (Debtors + Bills Receivables)

	₹		₹
To Balance b/d	28,000	By Cash Received (B.F.)	12,70,800
To Sales (credit)	12,80,000	By Balance c/d	37,200
	13,08,000		13,08,000

(2) Payables A/c (Creditors + Bills Payable)

	₹		₹
To Cash Paid	8,11,200	By Balance b/d	39,200
To Balance c/d	44,000	By Purchases*	8,16,000
	8,55,200		8,55,200

Operating Expenses A/c

	₹		₹
To Cash Paid (Bal. Figure)	3,10,800	By Balance b/d	12,400
To Balance c/d	17,600	By Profit and Loss A/c (Income statement)	3,16,000
	3,28,400		3,28,400

*Purchases = Closing Stock + Cost of Goods Sold – Opening Stock

Purchases = 88,000 + 8,00,000 – 72,000 = ₹ 8,16,000

operating cash payment	=	8,11,200	(To creditors)
and operating Expenses paid		3,10,800	
		11,22,000	

(3) Face Value of Shares issued	80,000	
Add: Premium @ 20%		16,000
		96,000

(3) CASH FLOW STATEMENT AS PER AS-3 (REVISED) (Indirect Method)

		₹	₹
I	**Cash Flow from Operating Activities:**		
	Net Profit before Tax and Extraordinary Item:	73,600	
	Adjustment for Non Cash and Non operating items :		
	Depreciation	84,000	
	Discount on Issue of Debentures	400	
	Interest on Debentures	6,000	
	Operating profit before Working Capital Changes	1,64,000	
	Adjustment for current items.		
	–Increase in Stock	(16,000)	
	–Increase in Bills Receivable	(10,000)	
	–Decrease in Bills Payable	(2,000)	
	+Decrease in Debtors	800	
	+Increase in Creditors	6,800	
	+Increase in o/s Expenses	5,200	
	Cash generated from operation	1,48,800	
	Less: Income Tax paid	38,000	
	Cash flow from operation before Extraordinary item	1,10,800	
	Add: Insurance Claim for Loss of Stock	20,000	
	Net Cash generated from operation		1,30,800
II	**Cash Flow from Investing Activities**		—

III Cash Flow from Financing Activities	—	
Issue of shares at premium	96,000	
Redemption of Debentures	(1,22,400)	
Interest on Debentures	(6,000)	
Dividend and corporate dividend Tax	(44,000)	
Net cash used in Financing Activities		(76,400)
Net Increase in Cash and Cash Equivalents		54,400
Cash and Cash Equivalents in the beginning		44,800
Cash and Cash Equivalents at the end		99,200

Illustrative Problem 9

From the following details relating to the accounts of Grow More Ltd., prepare Cash Flow Statement:

	31.03.2016 ₹	31.03.2015 ₹
Liabilities		
Share Capital	10,00,000	8,00,000
Reserve	2,00,000	1,50,000
Profit and Loss Account	1,00,000	60,000
Debentures	2,00,000	—
Provision for taxation	1,00,000	70,000
Proposed dividend	2,00,000	1,00,000
Sundry Creditors	7,00,000	8,20,000
	25,00,000	20,00,000
Assets		
Plant and Machinery	7,00,000	5,00,000
Land and Building	6,00,000	4,00,000
Investments	1,00,000	—
Sundry Debtors	5,00,000	7,00,000
Stock	4,00,000	2,00,000
Cash on hand/Bank	2,00,000	2,00,000
	25,00,000	20,00,000

(*i*) Depreciation @ 25% was charged on the opening value of Plant and Machinery.

(*ii*) During the year one old machine costing ₹ 50,000 (WDV ₹ 20,000) was sold for ₹ 35,000.

(*iii*) ₹ 50,000 was paid towards income tax during the year.

(*iv*) Building under construction was not subject to any depreciation.

Prepare Cash flow Statement.

Solution:

Grow More Ltd.
Cash Flow Statement
for The Year Ended 31 March, 2016

	₹	₹
(A) Cash Flows from Operating Activities		
Net Profit before Tax and Extra-ordinary, items*	3,20,000	
Adjustment for:		
Transfer to General Reserve	50,000	
Depreciation	1,25,000	
Profit on sale of Plant and Machinery	(15,000)	
Operating Profit before Working Capital Changes	**4,80,000**	
Increase in Stock	(2,00,000)	
Decrease in debtors	2,00,000	
Decrease in creditors	(1,20,000)	
Cash generated from operations	3,60,000	
Income tax paid	(50,000)	
Net cash provided by operating activities		**3,10,000**
(B) Cash Flows from Investing Activities		
Purchase of fixed assets	(3,45,000)	
Expenses on building	(2,00,000)	
Increase in investments	(1,00,000)	
Sale of old machine	35,000	
Net cash used in investing activities		**(6,10,000)**
(C) Cash Flows from Financing Activities		
Proceeds from issue of shares	2,00,000	
Proceeds from issue of debentures	2,00,000	
Dividend paid	(1,00,000)	
Net cash provided by financing activities		**3,00,000**
Net increase in cash and cash equivalents (A + B + C)		Nil
Cash and Cash equivalents at the beginning of the year		2,00,000
Cash and Cash equivalents at the end of the year		2,00,000

Working Notes:

Provision for Taxation Account

	₹		₹
Bank (Paid)	50,000	Balance b/d	70,000
Balance c/d	1,00,000	Profit and Loss Account (Balancing Figure)	80,000
	1,50,000		1,50,000

*₹ 40,000 + ₹ 2,00,000 (Provision for dividend) + ₹ 80,000 (Provision for Tax).

Plant and Machinery Account

	₹		₹
Balance b/d	5,00,000	Depreciation	1,25,000
Bank (Balance Fig.)	3,45,000	Bank (Sale)	20,000
		Balance C/d	7,00,000
	8,45,000	Total	8,45,000

Illustrative Problem 10

Following are the Balance Sheets of Suhani Ltd. as on 31st March, 2015 and 2016.

Liabilities	31.03.16 ₹	31.03.15 ₹
Share Capital	4,00,000	3,00,000
General Reserve	1,00,000	80,000
Profit & Loss A/c	50,000	30,000
Debentures	1,00,000	1,50,000
Provision for Taxation	40,000	50,000
Proposed Dividend	40,000	30,000
Trade Creditors	70,000	90,000
	8,00,000	7,30,000
Assets		
Goodwill	90,000	1,00,000
Plant and Machinery	4,29,250	2,98,000
Investment	60,000	1,00,000
S, Debtors	1,10,000	1,60,000
Stock	80,000	50,000
Prepaid Expenses	5,750	4,000
Cash and Bank balance	20,000	10,000
Discount on Debentures	5,000	8,000
	8,00,000	7,30,000

Additional Information

(*i*) Depreciation on Plant and Machinery has been charged @ 15%.

(*ii*) A machine costing ₹ 10,000 (W.D.V. ₹ 3,000) has been discarded. An old machine costing ₹ 50,000 (W.D.V. ₹ 20,000) has been sold for ₹ 35,000.

(*iii*) A profit of ₹ 10,000 has been earned by sale of investments.

(*iv*) Debentures have been redeemed at 5% premium.

(*v*) ₹ 45,000 income tax has been paid and adjusted against provision for taxation. Prepare Statement of Changes in Financial Position on cash basis.

Solution:

Statement of Changes in Financial Position (Cash Basis)
for the Year Ended 31st March, 2016

	₹	₹
I Cash Flow from operating Activities:		
Net Profit before tax and extraordinary items	1,75,000	
Adjustment for Non cash and Non-operating Items:		
Depreciation	75,750	
Goodwill written off	10,000	
Loss on machine discarded	3,000	
Profit on sale of Investment	(10,000)	
Profit on sale of Machine	(15,000)	
Loss (premium) on Redemption of Debentures	2,500	
Discount on Issue of Debentures	3,000	
Cash generated from operation before Tax	1,84,250	
Less: Tax paid	45,000	
Cash generated from Operating activities before Working Capital	1,39,250	
Adjustments for Working Capital		
Decrease in Debtors	50,000	
Increase in Stock	(30,000)	
Increase in Prepaid Expenses	(1,750)	
Decrease in Trade Creditors	(20,000)	
Net cash flow from Operating Activities		1,37,500
II Cash Flow from Investing Activities:		
Sale of Investments	50,000	
Sale of Machinery	35,000	
Purchase of Machinery	(2,30,000)	
Net cash used in Investing Activities		(1,45,000)
III Cash Flow from Financing Activities:		
Issue of Shares	1,00,000	
Redemption of Debentures	(52,500)	
Payment of Dividend	(30,000)	
Net Cash generated from Financing Activities		17,500
Net Increase in Cash and Cash Equivalents		10,000
Cash and Cash equivalents at the beginning		10,000
Cash and Cash equivalents at the end		20,000

Working Notes:

(1) Profit and Loss A/c (Adjusted)

	₹		₹
To Provision for Tax	35,000	By Balance b/d	30,000
To General Reserve	20,000	By Net Profit before Tax and	1,15,000
To Proposed dividend	40,000	Extraordinary items	
To Balance c/d	50,000		
	1,45,000		1,45,000

(2) Plant and Machinery A/c

	₹		₹
To Balance b/d	2,98,000	By Depreciation*	75,750
To Profit on sale	15,000	By Bank (sale)	35,000
(Tr. to P and L A/c)		By Loss on sale	3,000
To Bank (Purchases)	2,30,000	(Tr. to P and L A/c)	
(Bal. figure)		By Balance c/d	4,29,250
	5,43,000		5,43,000

		₹
	*W.D.V. as on 1.4.2015	2,98,000
Less:	W.D.V. of machine sold (20,000 + 3,000)	23,000
		2,75,000
	*Depreciation @ 15%	41,250
	W.D. V. after Depreciation	2,33,750
		₹
	Cost of Machinery acquired	2,30,000**
	*Depreciation on Machinery Purchased	34,500
	W.D.V.	1,95,500
	*Thus total Depreciation charged ₹ (41,250 + 34,500) =	75,750
	** ₹ (4,29,250 – 2,33,750) = $\left(1,95,500 \times \frac{100}{85}\right)$ =	2,30,000

(3) Provision for Tax A/c

	₹		₹
To Bank	45,000	By Balance b/d	50,000
To Balance c/d	40,000	By P and L A/c (B.F.)	35,000
	85,000		85,000

Illustrative Problem 11 (Indirect Method)

Presented below is the comparative balance sheets for Jyoti Ltd. at 31 March:

	2016 ₹	2015 ₹
Cash	40,000	57,000
Accounts Receivable	77,000	64,000
Inventory	1,32,000	1,40,000
Prepaid expenses	12,140	16,540
Land	1,25,000	1,50,000
Equipment	2,00,000	1,75,000
Accumulated Depreciation-Equipment	(60,000)	(42,000)
Building	2,50,000	2,50,000
Accumulated Depreciation-Building	(75,000)	(50,000)
	7,01,140	7,60,540
Accounts Payable	33,000	45,000
Bonds Payable	2,35,000	2,65,000
Equity Share Capital (₹ 10 per share)	2,80,000	2,50,000
Retained Earnings	1,53,140	2,00,540
	7,01,140	7,60,540

Additional Information

(*i*) Operating expenses include depreciation expense of ₹ 70,000 and amortization of prepaid expenses of ₹ 4,400.

(*ii*) Land was sold for cash at book value.

(*iii*) Cash dividends of ₹ 74,290 were paid.

(*iv*) Net income for 2016 was ₹ 26,890.

(*v*) Equipment was purchased for ₹ 65,000 cash. In addition equipment costing ₹ 40,000 with a book value of ₹ 13,000 was sold for ₹ 15,000 cash.

(*vi*) Bonds were redeemed at face value by issuing 3,000 equity shares of ₹ 10 at par.

Instructions

Prepare a statement of cash flow for 2016 using the indirect method [AS-3 (Revised)]

Solution:

Cash Flows Statement for the Year Ended 31 December, 2016
[AS-3 (Revised)] (Indirect Method)

	₹	₹
(A) Cash Flows from Operating Activities		
Net Income	26,890	
Adjustments for:		
Depreciation	70,000	
Amortization of prepaid expenses	4,400	
Gain on sale of equipment	(2,000)	

	Operating profit before working capital changes	99,290	
	Increase in Accounts Receivable	(13,000)	
	Decrease in Inventories	8,000	
	Decrease in Accounts Payable	(12,000)	
	Net cash from operating activities		**82,290**
(B)	**Cash Flow from Investing Activities:**		
	Sale of Land	25,000	
	Sale of Equipment	15,000	
	Purchase of Equipment	(65,000)	
	Net cash used in Investing activities		**(25,000)**
(C)	**Cash Flows from Financing Activities**		
	Dividends Paid	(74,290)	
	Net cash used in financing activities		**(74,290)**
	Net decrease in cash and cash equivalents (A + B + C)		(17,000)
	Cash and cash equivalents at the beginning of the period		57,000
	Cash and cash equivalents at the end of the period		40,000
	Significant Non-cash Transaction		
	Redemption of Bonds in exchange for Equity Share Capital ₹ 30,000		

Working Notes:

Equity Share Capital Account

	₹		₹
Balance c/d	2,80,000	By Balance b/d	2,50,00
		Bond Payable Account	30,000
	2,80,000		2,80,000

Bonds Payable Accounts

	₹		₹
Equity Share Capital Account	2,35,000	By Balance b/d	2,65,000
To Balance c/d	30,000		
	2,65,000		2,65,000

Illustrative Problem 12

From the following, prepare a cash flow statement for XYZ Ltd. for the year 2016.

XYZ LTD.

Balance Sheet as at March 31, 2015

Liabilities & Equity	**₹ ('000)**	***Assets***		**₹ ('000)**
Paid up capital	50	Gross Fixed Assets	1,000	
Retained earnings	350	*Less:* Accum. Deprn.	100	900
Long-term debt	500	Inventory		100
Notes payable	80	Accounts receivables		50
Accounts payable	80	Cash		10
	1,060			1,060

Balance Sheet as at March 31, 2016

Liabilities & Equity	₹ ('000)	*Assets*		₹ ('000)
Paid up capital	50	Gross Fixed Assets	1,125	
Retained earnings	415	*Less* : Accum. Deprn.	175	950
Long-term debt	550	Inventory		110
Notes payable	100	Accounts receivables		60
Accounts payable	90	Cash		85
	1,205			1,205

Income Statement, March 31, 2016

	₹ ('000)
Sales	1,200
(–) Cost of goods sold	–800
Gross Profit	400
(–) Selling, general, administration, expenses	– 150
EBIT	250
(–) Interest expenses	–50
EBT	200
(–) Taxes (50%)	–100
Net Income	100

Additional Information

(*i*) Dividend paid : 35

(*ii*) Additions to retained earnings : 65

(*iii*) Depreciation : 75

Solution:

XYZ Ltd. :

I. Change in Balance Sheet : (₹ '000)

a.	Change in receivables	:	10 (use)
b.	Change in inventory	:	10 (use)
c.	Change in Gross fixed assets	:	125 (use)
d.	Change in A/c payables	:	10 (source)
e.	Change in notes payable	:	20 (source)
f.	Change in long-term debt	:	50 (source)

II. Operating cash flow (₹ '000) : 100 + 75 – (10 + 10 – 10) = ₹ 165

XYZ Limited

III. **Cash Flow Statement for the year 2015-16**

Cash Inflows	₹ '000	*Cash Outflows*	₹ '000
Opening Balance	10		
Operating Cash flows	165	Purchase of Fixed Assets	125
Increase in notes payable	20	Dividends	35
Increase in long-term debt	50	Closing balance	85
	245		245

Illustrative Problem 13

Rockford Company's comparative balance sheet for 2016 and the company's income statement for the year follow:

Rockford Company
Comparative Balance Sheet
December 31, 2016, and 2015
(₹ in Lakhs)

	2016	2015
Assets		
Cash	₹ 260	₹ 100
Accounts receivable	1800	2700
Inventory	2050	1600
Prepaid expenses	170	200
Plant and equipment	4300	3090
Less accumulated depreciation	(2180)	(1940)
Long-term investments	600	750
Total assets	₹ 7000	₹ 6500
Liabilities and Common Equity		
Account payable	₹ 2300	₹ 3100
Accrued liabilities	700	600
Bonds payable	1350	400
Deferred income taxes	150	80
Common equity	1400	1400
Retained earnings	1100	920
Total liabilities and stockholders' equity	₹ 7000	₹ 6500

Rockford Company
Income Statement for the Year Ended December 31, 2016
(₹ in Lakhs)

Sales	₹ 10,000
Cost of goods sold	5,300
Gross margin	4,700
Selling and administrative expenses	3,520
Net operating income	1,180
Nonoperating items:	
Loss on sale of equipment	(40)
Income before taxes	1,140
Income taxes	480
Net income	₹ 660

Notes: Dividends of ₹ 480 lakhs were paid in 2016. The loss on sale of equipment of ₹ 40 lakhs reflects a transaction in which equipment with an original cost of ₹ 120 lakhs and accumulated depreciation of ₹ 50 lakhs was sold for ₹ 30 lakhs in cash.

Required:

Using the indirect method, determine the net cash provided by operating activities for 2016 and construct a statement of cash flows for the year.

Solution:

Working Notes Sheet

Rockford Company
Statement of Cash Flows for the Year Ended December 31, 2016
(₹ in Lakhs)

	(1) Change	(2) Source or Use?	(3) Cash Flow Effect	(4) Adjustments	(5) Adjusted Effect (3) + (4)	(6) Classification
Assets (except cash and cash equivalent)						
Current assets:						
Accounts receivable	– 900	Source	₹ + 900		₹ + 900	Operating
Inventory	+ 450	Use	– 450		– 450	Operating
Prepaid expenses	– 30	Source	+ 30		+ 30	Operating
Noncurrent assets:						
Property, buildings, and equipment	+ 1210	Use	– 1210	₹ – 120	–1330	Investing
Long-term investments	– 150	Source	+ 150		+ 150	Investing
Contra Assets, Liabilities, and Equity						
Contra assets:						
Accumulated depreciation	+ 240	Source	+ 240	+ 50	+ 290	Operating
Current liabilities:						
Accounts payable	– 800	Use	– 800		– 800	Operating

Accrued liabilities	+ 100	Source	+ 100	+ 100	Operating
Noncurrent liabilities:					
Bonds payable	+ 950	Source	+ 950	+ 950	Financing
Deferred income taxes	+ 70	Source	+ 70	+ 70	Operating
Equity:					
Common equity	+ 00	—	+ 00	+ 00	Financing
Retained earnings:					
Net income	+ 660	Source	+ 660	+ 660	Operating
Dividends	– 480	Use	– 480	– 480	Financing
Additional Items					
Proceeds from sale of equipment			+ 3	+ 30	Investing
Loss on sale of equipment			+ 4	+ 40	Operating
Total (net cash flow)			₹ + 160 ₹ 0	₹ +160	

Rockford Company
Statement of Cash Flows—Indirect Method
for the Year Ended December 31, 2016
(₹ in Lakhs)

Operating Activities:		
Net income		₹ 660
Adjustments to convert net income to a cash basis:		
Depreciation and amortization changes	₹ 290	
Depreciation in accounts receivable	900	
Increase in inventory	(450)	
Decrease in prepaid expenses	30	
Decrease in accounts payable	(800)	
Increase in accrued liabilities	100	
Increase in deferred income taxes	70	
Loss on sale of equipment	40	180
Net cash provided by operating activities		840
Investing Activities:		
Additions to property, buildings, and equipment	(1330)	
Decrease in long-term investments	150	
Proceeds from sale of equipment	30	
Net cash used in investing activities		(1150)
Financing Activities:		
Increase in bonds payable	950	
Cash dividends paid	(480)	
Net cash provided by financing activities		470
Net increase in cash and cash equivalents		160
Cash and cash equivalents at beginning of year		100
Cash and cash equivalents at end of year		₹ 260

Note that the ₹ 160 lakhs increase in cash and cash equivalent agrees with the ₹ 160 lakhs increase in the company's Cash account shown in the company's balance sheet and it agrees with the total in column (5) of the working note sheet.

SIGNIFICANCE OF CASH FLOW STATEMENT

Cash basis funds flow statement is important for a number of reasons.

1. First, by focusing on cash flows, it explains the nature of the financial events which have affected the cash positions. This statement explains the reasons for the difference between opening and closing cash balance.
2. The statement is important for financial planning purposes. For example, budgeted cash flow statements are crucial element in the process of budget plans. These surpluses and shortfalls are expressed sequentially over the planning period and require management to deal with the forecasted cash surplus or deficit, the former involving a short-term investment of surplus cash, the latter a short-term borrowing arrangement.
3. This statement brings into sharp focus the enterprise's earning capacity with its spending and operating activity. Accounting principles restrict the income statement to matching periodic revenues with the cost of earning those revenues. Statement of changes in cash is not restricted in this way; hence, it provides an extended view of the financial inflows and outflows by including both capital and revenue flows.
4. Cash flow statement provides an insight into the critical areas of financial management by identifying two important classes of cash flows, namely, operating cash flows and financing cash flows. This distinction draws attention to the net cash flows from operations and the net financing cash flows. The net operating cash flows classify the capability of the firm to support dividend payments to shareholders. It is these net cash flows which are of critical importance to investors and shareholders in predicting the amount of cash likely to be distributed in the future in the form of liquidation distributions or repayment of principal and in the evaluation of risk.
5. The significance of cash flow statement lies in the increased complexity of business activity. This complexity results in a greater disparity between the time when income and expense items are reported and the time when the related cash flows occur. It may also result in a greater variability of cash flows.

ICAI's AS 3 Cash Flow Statement contains the following explanations on the utility of cash flow statement:

1. Information about the cash flows of an enterprise is useful in providing users of financial statements with a basis to assess the ability of the enterprise to generate cash and cash equivalents and the needs of the enterprise to utilise those cash flows. The economic decisions that are taken by users require an evaluation of the ability of an enterprise to generate cash and cash equivalents and the timing and certainty of their generation.
2. Users of an enterprise's financial statements are interested in how the enterprise generates and uses cash and cash equivalents. This is the case regardless of the nature of the enterprise's activities and irrespective of whether cash can be viewed as the product of the enterprise, as may be the case with a financial enterprise. Enterprises need cash for essentially the same reasons, however different their principal revenue-producing activities might be. They need cash to conduct their operations, to pay their obligation, and to provide returns to their investors.

3. A cash flow statement, when used in conjunction with the other financial statements, provides information that enables users to evaluate the changes in net assets of an enterprise, its financial structure (including its liquidity and solvency) and its ability to affect the amounts and timing of cash flows in order to adapt to changing circumstances and opportunities. Cash flow information is useful in assessing the ability of the enterprise to generate cash and cash equivalents and enables users to develop models to assess and compare the present value of the future cash flows of different enterprises. It also enhances the comparability of the reporting of operating performance by different enterprises because it eliminates the effects of using different accounting treatments for the same transactions and events.
4. Historical cash flow information is often used as an indicator of the amount, timing and certainty of future cash flows. It is also useful in checking the accuracy of past assessments of future cash flows and in examining the relationship between profitability and net cash flow and the impact of changing prices.

Limitations of Cash Flow Statement

Cash flow can be more precisely measured than can other concepts of funds because the valuation problem of cash are not as great as for other financial resources. However, movement of cash may be easily influenced. For example, payment of liabilities may be temporarily delayed or marketable securities may be sold, increasing cash flow for a given period. This statement, since it does not cover non-cash items, is not useful in analysing changes in financial position of an enterprise. Cash and changes in cash are not adequate to measure change in financial position. For instance, an enterprise may possess very satisfactory financial (cash) position during a particular month. But if the firm has to pay creditors next month, or make payments for the plant purchased in the near future, the cash position of the firm will be adversely affected. In this way statement of changes in financial position measured through cash only has drawbacks and does not indicate accurately the changes in financial position. The statement has utility for making short - term financial planning but for long-term planning this statement would not be useful. Because of the limited usefulness of statement of changes in cash, the preparation of statement of changes in working capital (popularly known as funds flow statement) has been suggested.

CRITICAL ANALYSIS AND DISCUSSION QUESTIONS, MULTIPLE CHOICE QUESTIONS, AND PROBLEMS

CRITICAL ANALYSIS AND DISCUSSION QUESTIONS

1. Why is cash flow statement a useful statement?
2. Identify the three major types of activities classified on a cash flow statement and gives examples of cash inflows and cash outflows in each classification.
3. What limitations of funds flow statement are overcome by a cash flow statement?
4. What are the purposes of cash flow statement?
5. Discuss the procedures in preparing a cash flow statement.
6. What are the two methods of determining cash flows from operations? Generally which of these methods is preferable?
7. "A cash flow statement is required to explain changes in cash account balances between balance sheet dates." Explain this statement.
8. List the common sources and uses of cash in each activity area : operating, investing and financing.
9. Discuss the guidelines as contained in AS 3 on cash flow statement.
10. Discuss the main features of AS 3. What changes have been made in this standard?
11. Distinguish between cash and 'cash equivalent'.
12. Distinguish among cash flows from operating, investing and financing activities. Provide examples of each type of activity as per AS 3. Show a proforma statement of cash flows.
13. Discuss the Direct Method and Indirect Method of preparing Cash Flow Statement.
14. How do you analyse cash flow statement?
15. Discuss the different aspects of cash flow statements analysis.
16. What are the limitations of a cash flow statement.

MULTIPLE CHOICE QUESTIONS

Select the correct answer for the following multiple choice questions:

1. On a statement of changes in financial position, depreciation is treated as an adjustment to reported net earnings because depreciation—
   (*a*) is a direct source of funds
   (*b*) reduces reported net earnings but does not involve an outflow of funds
   (*c*) reduces reported net earnings and involves an inflow of funds
   (*d*) is an inflow of funds to a reserve account for replacement of assets

2. Which of the following items is included on a statement of changes in financial position only because of the total financial resources concept?
   (*a*) Depreciation
   (*b*) Issuance of equity capital
   (*c*) Purchase of government securities
   (*d*) Retirement of long-term debt by issue of preferred capital
3. A transaction which would appear as an application of funds on a conventional funds statement using the total financial resources concept , but not on a statement using the traditional working capital concept would be —
   (*a*) acquisition of property, plant and equipment for cash
   (*b*) requisition of bonds issued by the reporting entity
   (*c*) acquisition of property, plant and equipment with an issue of equity capital
   (*d*) declaration and payments of dividends
4. A statement of changes in financial position typically would not disclose the effects of:
   (*a*) share capital issued to acquire productive facilities
   (*b*) dividends on shares declared
   (*c*) cash dividends declared but not yet paid
   (*d*) a purchase and immediate retirement of government securities
5. Which of the following is not disclosed in cash flow statement?
   (*a*) Amount of cash on hand at year-end
   (*b*) Cash outflows from investing activities during the period
   (*c*) Cash inflows from financing activities during the period
   (*d*) Cash provided by operations during the period
6. Which of the following events will appear in the cash flows from financing activities section of cash flow statement?
   (*a*) Cash purchase of equipment
   (*b*) Cash purchase of bonds issued by another company
   (*c*) Cash received as repayment for funds loaned
   (*d*) Cash purchase of government securities
7. Which of the following statements is true?
   (*a*) The direct method of calculating cash flows from operations starts with net income and adjusts for non cash revenues and expenses and changes in current assets and current liabilities.
   (*b*) The indirect method of calculating cash flows from operations adjusts each item in the income statement to a cash basis
   (*c*) The description in (*a*) and (*b*) should be reversed
   (*d*) The direct method is easier to use than the indirect method
8. Investing activities include all of the following except:
   (*a*) Payment of debt
   (*b*) Collection of loans
   (*c*) Making of loans
   (*d*) Sale of available-for-sale and held-to-maturity securities

9. If sales on an accrual basis are ₹ 5,00,000 and accounts receivable increased by ₹ 30,000, the cash received from customers would be:
   (a) ₹ 5,00,000 (b) ₹ 4,70,000
   (c) ₹ 5,30,000 (d) Can not be determined
10. Assume cost of goods sold on an accrual basis is ₹ 3,00,000, accounts payable increased by ₹ 20,000, and inventory increased by ₹ 50,000. Cash paid for merchandise is:
   (a) ₹ 3,70,000 (b) ₹ 2,30,000
   (c) ₹ 2,70,000 (d) ₹ 3,30,000
11. Assume net income was ₹ 2,00,000, depreciation expense was ₹ 10,000, accounts receivable increased by ₹ 15,000, and accounts payable increased by ₹ 5,000. The amount of cash flows from operating activities is:
   (a) ₹ 2,00,000 (b) ₹ 1,80,000
   (c) ₹ 2,10,000 (d) ₹ 1,90,000
12. An example of a cash flow from a operating activity is:
   (a) receipt of cash from the sale of stock
   (b) receipt of cash from the sale of bonds
   (c) payment of cash for dividends
   (d) receipt of cash from customers on account
13. An example of a cash flow from an investing activity is:
   (a) receipt of cash from the sale of equipment
   (b) receipt of cash from the sale of stock
   (c) payment of cash for dividends
   (d) payment of cash to acquire treasury stock
14. An example of a cash flow from a financing activity is:
   (a) receipt of cash from customers on account
   (b) receipt of cash from the sale of equipment
   (c) payment of cash for dividends
   (d) payment of cash to acquire land
15. Which of the following methods of reporting cash flows from operating activities adjusts net income for revenues and expenses not involving the receipt or payment of cash?
   (a) Direct method (c) Reciprocal method
   (b) Purchase method (d) Indirect method
16. The net income reported on the income statement for the year was ₹ 55,000, and depreciation of fixed assets for the year was ₹ 22,000. The balances of the current assent and current liability accounts at the beginning and end of the year are shown below.

	End	**Beginning**
Cash	₹ 65,000	₹ 70,000
Accounts receivable	1,00,000	90,000
Inventories	1,45,000	1,50,000
Prepaid expenses	7,500	8,000
Accounts payable (merchandise creditors)	51,000	58,000

The total amount reported for cash flows from operating activities in the statement of cash flows, using the indirect method, is:

(*a*) ₹ 33,000 (*c*) ₹ 65,500.

(*b*) ₹ 55,000 (*d*) ₹ 77,000.

Answer to Multiple Choice Questions

1. (*b*)	2. (*d*)	3. (*c*)	4. (*b*)	5. (*a*)
6. (*d*)	7. (*c*)	8. (*a*)	9. (*b*)	10. (*d*)
11. (*a*)				

PROBLEMS

1. From the following particulars Calculate Cash from operating activities by applying:
   (*a*) Direct Method
   (*b*) Indirect Method

PROFIT AND LOSS A/C
for the year ended 31st March, 2016

	₹		₹
To Opening Stock	60,000	By Sales	6,00,000
To Purchases	3,00,000	By Stock	85,000
To Wages	75,000	(Closing)	
To Gross Profit c/d	2,50,000		
	6,85,000		6,85,000
To Salaries	50,000	By Gross Profit b/d	2,50,000
To General Expenses	15,000		
To Insurance	10,000		
To Depreciation	75,000		
To Provision for Tax	30,000		
To Net Profit	70,000		
	2,50,000		2,50,000

Additional Information

	31.3.2015	31.03.2016
	₹	₹
Salaries o/s	5,000	7,500
Prepaid Insurance	5,000	5,000
Debtors	50,000	70,000
Bills Receivable	25,000	15,000
Creditors	35,000	25,000
Income Tax paid during the year amounted to ₹ 25,000.		

(**Ans.** ₹ 97,500.)

2. **(Investment and Financing activities not affecting Cash)**

The Following are the Balance Sheets of Huda Ltd. as on 31st March, 2015 and 31st March, 2016.

	31.03.2015	31.03.2016
Liabilities	₹	₹
Share Capital	4,00,000	5,20,000
General Reserve	1,00,000	1,00,000
Profit & Loss Account	79,380	82,440
S. Creditors	79,000	82,270
Bills Payable	67,560	23,050
Bank Overdraft	1,19,020	—
Provision for Tax	80,000	1,00,000
	9,24,960	9,07,760
Assets		
Goodwill	—	40,000
Land & Building	2,97,000	2,88,500
Plant and Machinery	2,25,900	2,32,400
Stock	2,22,080	1,94,740
Advances	4,630	1,470
Debtors	1,70,350	1,45,250
Cash at Bank	5,000	5,400
	9,24,960	9,07,760

Additional Information

(*i*) During the year ended 31st March, 2016, an additional dividend of ₹ 52,000 was paid.

(*ii*) The assets of another company were purchased for ₹ 1,20,000 payable in fully paid shares of the company. The assets consisted of Stock ₹ 43,280, Machinery ₹ 36,720 and Goodwill ₹ 40,000. In addition plant was purchased amounting to ₹ 11,300.

(*iii*) Income tax paid during the year was ₹ 50,000.

(*iv*) The net-profit for the year before tax amounted to ₹ 1,25,060.

Prepare Cash Flow Statement as per AS-3 (Revised)

(**Ans.** Cash from Operating activities : ₹ 1,82,720;
Cash from investing activities : ₹ (11,300)
Net-increase in cash and cash equivalents ₹ 400

3. From the following Profit and Loss A/c Calculate Cash from operating activities.

	₹		₹
To Salaries	1,80,000	By Gross Profit b/d	5,40,000
To Rent	90,000	By Profit on Sale of Land	28,000
To Office Expenses	30,000	By Dividend Received	20,000
To Depreciation	24,000	By Income Tax Refund	8,000

To Loss on Sale of Plant	12,000	By Rent Received	40,000
To Goodwill w/o	30,000		
To Discount on Issue of Debentures w/o	10,000		
To Preliminary Expenses w/o	8,000		
To Proposed Dividend	60,000		
To Provision for Tax	60,000		
To Net Profit c/d	1,32,000		
	6,36,000		6,36,000

Income Tax paid during the year amounted to ₹ 50,000.

(**Ans.** Cash generated from operating activities ₹ 1,98,000)

4. From the following information compute:
   (*i*) Cash flow from Operating activities
   (*ii*) Cash flow from Investing activities
   (*iii*) Cash flow from Financing activities

		₹
(*i*)	Sales made during the year	
	Cash —	2,00,000
	Credit —	3,50,000
	Purchases, cash —	Nil
	Credit —	3,00,000
(*ii*)	Salaries incurred during the year	62,500
(*iii*)	Depreciation	1,50,000
(*iv*)	Goodwill w/o	12,500

(*v*) Issue of 1,00,000 equity shares of ₹ 10 each at premium of 20%.

(*vi*) Issue of equity shares of ₹ 25,00,000 as purchase consideration of Building of ₹ 30,00,000

(*vii*) Purchase of Machinery for cash — 4,20,000

(*viii*) Dividend of last year amounting to ₹ 1,00,000 was paid. Dividend of ₹ 2,50,000 was declared but not yet paid.

(*ix*) An equipment (Book value ₹ 50,000) sold for ₹ 60,000

(*x*) Closing Balances Debtors ₹ 85,000
Creditors ₹ 1,00,000, Salaries O/s ₹ 12,500

(**Ans.:** Cash from Operating activities — ₹ 2,15,000
Cash used in Investing activities — ₹ (3,60,000)
Cash Flow from financing activities — ₹ 11,00,000)

5. Following are the Balance Sheets of Vrinda Ltd. as on 31st March, 2015 and 2016

Liabilities	**31.3.2015** ₹	**31.3.2016** ₹
Equity Share Capital	12,00,000	12,75,000
Profit and Loss Appropriation A/c	2,17,500	3,67,500
Mortgaged Loans	—	75,000
S. Creditors	1,35,000	75,000
	15,52,500	17,92,500
Assets		
Fixed Assets	11,10,000	12,60,000
Stock	1,35,000	1,05,000
Debtors	2,47,500	2,92,500
Cash and Bank Balance	60,000	1,35,000
	15,52,500	17,92,500

Prepare Cash Flow Statement as per AS-3 (Revised).

(**Ans.** Cash From Operating Activities — ₹ 75,000
Cash used in Investing Activities — ₹ (1,50,000)
Cash flow from Financing Activities — ₹, 1,50,000

6. Usha Ltd. had the following condensed Trial Balance at the end of 31 March, 2016:

	₹		₹
Cash	7,500	Current Liabilities	15,000
Accounts Receivable	30,000	Long-term Notes Payable	25,500
Investments	20,000	Bonds Payable	25,000
Plant assets	67,500	Capital Stock	75,000
Land	40,000	Retained Earnings	24,500
	1,65,000		1,65,000

During 2016-17 the followings occurred:

(*i*) A tract of land was purchased for ₹ 7,750 cash.
(*ii*) Bonds payable in the amount of ₹ 6,000 were retired for cash at face and book value.
(*iii*) An additional ₹ 20,000 equity shares were issued at par for cash.
(*iv*) Dividends totalling ₹ 9,375 were paid.
(*v*) Net income for 2016-17 was ₹ 28,450 after allowing for depreciation of ₹ 9,500.
(*vi*) Land was purchased through the issuance of ₹ 22,500 in bonds.
(*vii*) Usha Ltd. sold part of its investments portfolio for ₹ 12,875 cash. This transaction resulted in a gain of ₹ 1,375 for the firm.
(*viii*) Current liabilities increased to ₹ 18,000 at 31.03.2017.
(*ix*) Accounts receivable at 31 March, 2017 total ₹ 38,000.
(*x*) The cash balance at 31 March, 2017 is ₹ 48,825.

Instructions

Prepare a statement of cash flows for 2016-17 with the indirect method [AS-3 (Revised)]

(**Ans.** Net-cash from operating activities — ₹ 31,575
Net-cash from investing activities — ₹ 5,125
Net-increase in cash and cash equivalent — ₹ 41,325

7. From the following Balance Sheets of Twenty First Century Ltd. and additional information prepare a Cash Flow Statement as per AS -3 (Revised)

Liabilities	**31.3.15** ₹	**31.3.16** ₹
Equity Share Capital	12,00,000	15,00,000
General Reserve	3,00,000	3,50,000
Profit and Loss A/c	1,00,000	1,50,000
9% Debentures	6,00,000	4,00,000
Creditors	4,90,000	5,60,000
Proposed Dividends	1,20,000	1,80,000
Provision for Taxation	1,00,000	1,30,000
	29,10,000	32,70,000
Assets		
Building	8,00,000	7,60,000
Machinery	5,00,000	7,20,000
Short-Term Investments	3,00,000	4,50,000
Inventories	4,00,000	4,70,000
Debtors	6,70,000	5,30,000
Cash at Bank	2,20,000	3,30,000
Prepaid Expenses	20,000	10,000
	29,10,000	32,70,000

Additional Information

(*i*) Debentures were redeemed at a premium of 10% on 1st April, 2015.

(*ii*) Income tax paid during the year amounted to ₹ 1,40,000.

(*iii*) A machine which appeared at a W.D.V. of ₹ 80,000 was sold for ₹ 1,30,000 and a new machine costing ₹ 3,60,000 was acquired during the year.

(**Ans.** Net Cash flow from operating activities : ₹ 5,66,000
Net cash used in investing activities : ₹ 3,80,000)

8. From the following Balance Sheets of Diana and Daisy Ltd. prepare a Cash Flow Statement for the year end 31st March, 2016.

Liabilities	**31.3.2015** ₹	**31.3.2016** ₹
8% Preference Share Capital	1,50,000	1,00,000
Equity Share Capital	3,00,000	4,00,000
General Reserve	40,000	70,000
Profit and Loss A/c	30,000	48,000
Proposed Dividend	42,000	50,000
Creditors	55,000	83,000
Bills Payable	20,000	16,000
Provision for Taxation	40,000	50,000
	6,77,000	8,17,000

Assets		
Goodwill	1,15,000	90,000
Land and Building	2,00,000	1,70,000
Plant and Machinery	80,000	2,00,000
Stock	77,000	1,09,000
Debtors	1,60,000	2,00,000
Bills Receivable	20,000	30,000
Cash at Bank	15,000	10,000
Cash in hand	16,000	8,000
	6,77,000	8,17,000

Additional Information

(*i*) Depreciation of ₹, 20,000 and ₹, 10,000 have been charged on Plant and Machinery and on Building respectively,

(*ii*) An interim dividend of ₹, 20,000 has been paid during the year,

(*iii*) Income Tax ₹ 35,000 was paid during the year,

(**Ans.** Cash from Operating activities — ₹ 1,25,000
Cash used in Investing activities — ₹ (1,20,000)
Cash used in Financing activities — ₹ (12,000)
Net decrease in Cash and Cash equivalent — ₹ (7,000)

9. From the summary cash account of X Ltd., prepare Cash Flow Statement for the year ended 31 March, 2015 in accordance with AS-3 (Revised) using the direct method and indirect method. The company does not have any equivalents.

Summary Cash Account
For the Year Ended 31.03.2015

(₹'000)

	₹		₹
Balance on 01.04.2014	50	Payment to Suppliers	2,000
Issue of Equity Shares	300	Purchase of Fixed Assets	200
Reccipts from Customers	2,800	Overhead Expenses	200
Sale of Fixed Assets	100	Wages and Salaries	100
		Taxation	250
		Dividend	50
		Repayment of Bank Loan	300
		Balance on 31.03.2015	150
	3,250		3,250

Ans. Net-Cash from operating activities (in ₹ '000) — ₹ 250
Net-Cash used in investing activities: — ₹ (100)
Net increase in cash: — ₹ 100

10. From the following Balance Sheets of Ahmed Ltd. prepare a Cash Flow Statement.

Liabilities	**31.3.2015** ₹	**31.3.2016** ₹
12% Preference Share Capital	—	90,000
Equity Share Capital	7,20,000	8,10,000
General Reserve	36,000	45,000
Profit and Loss Account	18,000	21,600
15% Debentures	1,08,000	1,17,000
S. Creditors	2,16,000	1,98,000
Bank overdraft	2,25,000	1,22,400
Provision for Taxation	54,000	75,600
Proposed Dividend	90,000	1,04,400
	14,67,000	15,84,000
Assets		
Fixed Assets	7,38,000	7,20,000
Less: Provision for Depreciation	(1,98,000)	(2,70,000)
	5,40,000	4,50,000
Stock	5,40,000	6,30,000
Debtors	3,60,000	4,32,000
Prepaid Expenses	5,400	9,000
Cash and Bank	21,600	63.000
	14,67,000	15,84,000

Interest paid on debentures — ₹ 16,200

Prepare Cash Flow Statement

(**Ans.** Cash from Operating activities — ₹ 43,200
Cash from Investing Activities — ₹ 18,000
Cash used in Financing Activities — ₹ 82,800
Net Increase in Cash and Cash equivalent — ₹ 1,44,000

11. From the following condensed comparative Balance Sheets of Bangalore Mills Ltd. and additional information, prepare a Cash Flow Statement for the year 2016.

Liabilities	**2015** ₹	**2016** ₹	**Assets**	**2015** ₹	**2016** ₹
Share Capital	70,000	80,000	Plant & Machinery	62,000	66,000
Security Premium	9,000	11,000	Accumulated		
Retained earnings	23,820	30,820	Depreciation on		
7% Mortgage loan	—	20,000	plant and machinery	(37,000)	(26,200)
Creditors	6,900	6,000	Building	95,000	1,16,000
Outstanding salaries	2,000	1,400	Accumulated depreciation		

Provision for taxation	1,000	1,400	on building	(43,000)	(45,000)
			Land	10,000	12,000
			Stock	10,220	9,620
			Debtors	8,600	7,600
			Prepaid expenses	720	800
			Cash	6,180	9,800
	1,12,720	1,50,620		1,12,720	1,50,620

Additional Information

(*i*) Plant costing ₹ 16,000 (accumulated depreciation ₹ 14,800) was sold during the year for ₹ 1,200.

(*ii*) Building was acquired during the year at a cost of ₹ 21,000. In addition to cash payment of ₹ 1,000, a 7% mortgage loan was raised for the balance.

(*iii*) Dividend of ₹ 8,000 was paid during the year.

(*iv*) A sum of ₹ 13,900 was transferred to provision for taxation account in 2016.

(**Ans.** Net cash generated from operations : ₹ 21,420
Net cash used in investing activities : ₹ (21,800)
Net cash from financing activities : ₹ 4000
Net increase in cash : ₹ 3,600

12. Balance sheets of M/s. Ram and Shyam as on January 1, 2016 and 31 December, 2016, were as follows :

Liabilities	**Jan. 1, 2016** ₹	**Dec. 31, 2016** ₹	***Assets***	**Jan. 1, 2016** ₹	**Dec. 31 2016** ₹
Creditors	40,000	44,000	Cash	10,000	7,000
Mrs. Ram's Loan	25,000	—	Debtors	30,000	50,000
Loan from Bank	40,000	50,000	Stock	35,000	25,000
Capital	1,25,000	1,53,000	Machinery	80,000	55,000
			Land	40,000	50,000
			Building	35,000	60,000
	2,30,000	2,47,000		2,30,000	2,47,000

During the year a machine costing ₹ 10,000 (Accumulated depreciation ₹ 3,000) was sold for ₹ 5,000. The balance of provision for depreciation against machinery as on 1 January, 2016 was ₹ 25,000 and on 31 December, 2016 ₹ 40,000. Net profit for the year amounted to ₹ 45,000.

Required : Prepare a Cash Flow Statement [AS-3 (Revised)]

(**Ans.:**	Net cash generated from operations:	₹ 59,000
	Net cash used in investing activities:	₹ (30,000)
	Net cash used in Financing activities:	₹ (32,000)
	Net decrease in cash:	₹ (3,000)

17 FINANCIAL STATEMENT ANALYSIS

LEARNING OBJECTIVES:

After reading this chapter, you should be able to:

1. Understand the Meaning and Objectives of Financial Statement Analysis
2. Explain the Techniques of Financial Statement Analysis — Horizontal Analysis, Vertical Analysis, Trend Analysis and Ratio Analysis
3. Describe Different Analyses and Ratios Considered for Making Financial Statement Analysis — Liquidity or Short Term Solvency, Movement of Assets, Profitability, Capital Structure, Market Strength and Growth and Stability
4. Explain the Limitations of Financial Ratios

FINANCIAL STATEMENT ANALYSIS: MEANING AND OBJECTIVES

> **Financial statement analysis** is an information processing system which highlights important relationships between items in the financial statements.

Financial Statement Analysis is an analysis which highlights important relationships between items in the financial statements. Financial Statement analysis embraces the methods used in assessing and interpreting the results of past performance and current financial position as they relate to particular factors of interest in investment decisions. It is an important means of assessing past performance and in forecasting and planning future performance. According to Lev:[1]

> Financial Statement Analysis is an information processing system designed to provide data for decision making models, such as the portfolio selection model, bank lending decision models, and corporate financial management models.

Objectives of Financial Statement Analysis

The major objectives of financial statement analysis is to provide decision makers information about a business enterprise for use in decision-making. Users of financial statement information are the decision makers concerned with evaluating the economic situation of the firm and predicting its future course.

Financial statement analysis can be used by different users and decision makers to achieve the following objectives:

1. ***Assessment of Past Performance and Current Position:*** Past performance is often a good indicator of future performance. Therefore, an investor or creditor is interested in the trend of past sales, expenses, net income, cash flow and return on investment. These trends offer a means for judging management's past performance and are possible indicators of future performance. Similarly, the analysis of current position indicates where the business stands today. For instance, the current position analysis will show the types of assets owned by a business enterprise and the different liabilities due against the enterprise. It will tell what the cash position is, how much debt the company has in relation to equity and how reasonable the inventories and receivables are.
2. ***Prediction of Net Income and Growth Prospects:*** The financial statement analysis helps in predicting the earning prospects and growth rates in the earnings which are used by investors while comparing investment alternatives and other users interested in judging the earning potential of business enterprises. Investors also consider the risk or uncertainty associated with the expected return. The decision makers are futuristic and are always concerned with the future. Financial statements which contain information on past performances are analysed and interpreted as a basis for forecasting future rates of return and for assessing risk.
3. ***Prediction of Bankruptcy and Failure:*** Financial statement analysis is a significant tool in predicting the bankruptcy and failure probability of business enterprises. After being aware about probable failure, both managers and investors can take preventive measures to avoid/minimise losses. Corporate managements can effect changes in operating policy, reorganise financial structure or even go for voluntary liquidation to shorten the length of time losses.

   In accounting and finance area, empirical studies conducted have suggested a set of financial ratios which can give early signal of corporate failure. Such a prediction model based on financial statement analysis is useful to managers, investors and creditors. Managers may use the ratios prediction model to assess the solvency position of their firms and thus can take appropriate corrective actions. Investors and shareholder can use the model to make the optimum portfolio selection and to bring changes in the investment strategy in accordance with their investment goals. Similarly, creditors can apply the prediction model while evaluating the creditworthiness of business enterprises.

4. ***Loan Decision by Financial Institutions and Banks:*** Financial statement analysis is used by financial institutions, loaning agencies, banks and others to make sound loan or credit decision. In this way, they can make proper allocation of credit among the different borrowers. Financial statement analysis helps in determining credit risk, deciding terms and conditions of loan if sanctioned, interest rate, maturity date etc.

TECHNIQUES OF FINANCIAL STATEMENT ANALYSIS

Various techniques are used in the analysis of financial data to emphasise the comparative and relative importance of data presented and to evaluate the position of the firm. Among the more widely used of these techniques are the following:

1. Horizontal Analysis
2. Vertical Analysis
3. Trend Analysis
4. Ratio Analysis

Horizontal Analysis

Horizontal analysis involves the computation of amount changes and percentage changes from the previous to the current year.

The percentage analysis of increases and decreases in corresponding items in comparative financial statements is called horizontal analysis. Horizontal analysis involves the computation of amount changes and percentage changes from the previous to the current year. The amount of each item on the most recent statement is compared with the corresponding item on one or more earlier statements. The increase or decrease in the amount of the item is then listed, together with the per cent of increase or decrease. When the comparison is made between two statements, the earlier statement is used as the base. If the horizontal analysis includes three or more statements, there are two alternatives in the selection of the base. First, the earliest date or period may be used as basis for comparing all later dates or periods: or second, each statement may be compared with the immediately preceding statement.

Exhibit 17.1 and 17.2 present the comparative balance sheet and profit and loss account respectively of a company with the amount of increase or decrease and percentage changes shown. The per cent change is computed as follows:

$$\text{Percentage change} = \frac{\text{Amount of change}}{\text{Previous year amount}} \times 100$$

When examining financial statements, the investment analyst focuses immediate attention on significant items only. Large percentage changes frequently occur in items whose amounts may not be significant compared with other items on the statements. *For example*, although a large percentage change occurred in Prepaid Expenses, the analyst would scarcely notice this item in an initial examination of changes. Instead, attention would be directed first to changes in totals—current assets, long-term assets, total assets, current liabilities, and so on. Next, changes in significant individual items, such as receivables and inventory, would be examined. These changes may be related to certain changes in income statement items to determine whether they are favorable.

Exhibit 17.1: Comparative Balance Sheet with Horizontal Analysis

ABC Company Ltd.
Balance Sheet, December 31, 2016 and December 31, 2015

(₹'000)

	Dec. 31, 2016	Dec. 31, 2015	Increase (Decrease)	Percent Change
Assets				
Current Assets:				
Cash	₹ 5,500	₹ 4,200	₹ 1,300	31.0
Marketable Securities	1,500	2,400	(900)	(37.5)
Accounts Receivable (less allowance for uncollectible accounts of ₹ 2,400 in 2016 and ₹ 2,000 in 2015)	61,600	52,000	9,600	18.5
Inventory [lower of cost or market]	76,000	63,000	13,000	20.6
Prepaid Expenses	900	600	300	50.0
Total Current Assets	₹ 1,45,500	₹ 1,22,200	₹ 23,300	19.1
Long-term Assets:				
Property, Plant, and Equipment (net of accumulated depreciation)	₹ 45,000	₹ 40,000	₹5,000	12.5
Investments	1,800	1,600	200	12.5
Total Long-term Assets	₹ 46,800	₹ 41,600	₹ 5,200	12.5
Total Assets	₹ 1,92,300	₹ 1,63,800	₹ 28,500	17.4
Liabilities and Shareholders' Equity				
Liabilities				
Current Liabilities:				
Notes Payable	₹ 5,700	₹ 3,000	₹ 2,700	90.0
Accounts Payable	22,000	24,100	(2,100)	(8.7)
Accrued Liabilities	30,000	27,300	2700	9.9
Total Current Liabilities	₹ 57,700	₹ 54,400	₹3,300	6.1
Long-term Liabilities:				
12% Debenture Bonds Payable	₹ 25,000	₹ 20,000	₹ 5,000	25.0
Total Liabilities	₹ 82,700	₹ 74,400	₹ 8,300	11.2
Shareholders' Equity				
10% Preferred shares, ₹ 100 Par Value	8,000	8,000	—	—
Common shares, ₹ 5 Par Value	20,000	14,000	6,000	42.9
Paid-in Capital in Excess of Par Value	7,500	5,500	2,000	36.4
Retained Earnings	74,100	61,900	12,200	19.7
Total shareholders' Equity	₹ 1,09,600	₹ 89,400	₹ 20,200	22.6
Total Liabilities and shareholders Equity	₹ 1,92,300	₹ 1,63,800	₹ 28,500	17.4

Exhibit 17.2: Comparative Profit and Loss Account with Horizontal Analysis

Comparative Profit and Loss Account with Horizontal Analysis for the Years Ended December 31, 2016 and December 31, 2015

(₹'000)

	Year Ended Dec. 31, 2016	Year Ended Dec. 31, 2015	Increase (Decrease)	Percent Change
Net Sales	₹ 4,15,000	₹ 3,20,000	₹ 95,000	29.7
Cost of Goods Sold	2,90,000	2,30,000	60,000	26.1
Gross Profit	₹ 1,25,000	₹ 90,000	₹ 35,000	38.9
Operating Expenses:				
Selling Expenses	₹ 39,500	₹ 27,300	₹ 12,200	44.7
Administrative Expenses	49,640	32,600	17,040	52.3
Total Operating Expenses	₹ 89,140	₹ 59,900	₹ 29,240	48.8
Operating Income	₹ 35,860	₹ 30,100	₹ 5,760	19.1
Interest Expense	3,000	2,400	600	25.0
Income before Income Taxes	₹ 32,860	₹ 27,700	₹ 5,160	18.6
Income Tax Expense	14,100	12,300	1,800	14.6
Net Income	₹ 18,760	₹ 15,400	₹ 3,360	21.8
Earnings per Share	₹ 5.28	₹ 5.21		
Dividends per Share	1.44	0.81		

For example, ABC Company's total assets increased 17.4% (Exhibit 17.1), and sales increased 29.7% (Exhibit 17.2). A fairly large percentage increase in sales was supported by a much smaller rate of increase in assets. Furthermore, the 20.6% increase in inventory was also considerably less than the increase in sales. These results reflect quite favourably on the firm's performaqnce. In addition, the 29.7% increase in sales was accompanied by an increase in accounts receivable of only 18.5%; on the surface, the company's sales growth was not associated with a relaxation in credit policy.

The income statement shows that the 38.9% gross profit increase out-stripped the rate of increase in sales, indicating a higher mark-up rate in the latest year. Net income, however, increased only 21.8%; therefore, expenses must have grown disproportionately. Indeed, selling and administrative expenses increased 44.7% and 52.3%, respectively.

From this limited analysis of comparative financial statements, an analyst would conclude that operating performance for the latest year appeared favourable. Further analysis using some of the techniques described later in this chapter, however, might cause the analyst to modify that opinion. The foregoing analysis has revealed one reservation—operating expenses, particularly administrative expenses, have increased at a fairly high rate. Many selling expenses—such as sales salaries, commissions, and advertising—should rise somewhat proportionately with sales, but adminsitrative expenses should not. An investigation of the reasons for the large increase in the latter expense might be indicated.

Vertical Analysis

> **Vertical analysis** sets a total figure in the statement equal to 100 per cent and computes the percentage of each component of that figure.

Vertical Analysis uses percentages to show the relationship of the different parts to the total in a single statement. Vertical analysis sets a total figure in the statement equal to 100 per cent and computes the percentage of each component of that figure. The figure to be used as 100 per cent will be total assets or total liabilities and equity capital in the case of balance sheet and revenue or sales in the case of profit and loss account.

Trend Analysis

Using the previous year's data of a business enterprise, trend analysis can be done to observe percentage changes over time in selected data. In trend analysis, percentage changes are calculated for several successive years instead of between two years. Trend analysis is important because, with its long-run view, it may point to basic changes in the nature of the business. By looking at a trend in a particular ratio, one may find whether that ratio is falling, rising or remaining relatively constant. From this observation, a problem is detected or the sign of a good management is found.

Trend analysis uses an index number over a period of time. For index numbers, one year, the base year is equal to 100 per cent. Other years are measured in relation to that amount. *For example*, an analyst may be interested in sales and earnings trends for the past five years. For this purpose, sales and earnings data of a company are given to prepare further the trend analysis or percentages.

ABC Company

Annual Performance **(₹ '000)**

	Year 1	*Year 2*	*Year 3*	*Year 4*	*Year 5*
Sales	202.0	215.0	243.0	320.0	417.0
Net Earnings	10.9	11.7	13.5	15.4	18.8

The above data show a fairly healthy growth pattern but the pattern of change from year to year can be determined more precisely by calculating trend percentages. To do this, a base year is selected and then the data are divided for each of the other years by the base year data. The resultant figures are actually indexes of the changes occurring throughout the period. If year 1 is chosen as the base year, all data for year 2 through 5 will be related to year 1, which is represented as 100%.

To create the following table, each year sales is divided-from year 2 through years 5 - by ₹ 202, the year 1 sales. Similarly, the net earnings for years 2 through 5 are divided by ₹ 10.9, the year 1 net earnings

Annual Performance (Percentage of Base Year)

	Year 1	*Year 2*	*Year 3*	*Year 4*	*Year 5*
Sales	100	106	120	158	205
Net Earnings	100	107	124	141	172

The trend percentages reveal that the growth in earnings outstripped the growth in sales for years 2 and 3, then fell below the sales growth in the last two years. It is clear in this analysis of comparative statements that a disproportionate increase in operating expenses emerged in year 5. One may analyse the year 4 data to determine if net income was affected for the same reason or if the reduced growth was caused by other factors.

Ratio Analysis

Ratio analysis is an important means of expressing the relationship between two numbers. A ratio can be computed from any pair of numbers. To be useful, a ratio must represent a meaningful relationship, but use of ratios cannot take the place of studying the underlying data.

Ratios are guides or shortcuts that are useful in evaluating the financial position and operations of a company and in comparing them to previous years or to other companies. The primary purpose of ratios is to point out areas for further investigation. They should be used in connection with a general understanding of the company and its environment.

> **Ratios** are guides or shortcuts that are useful in evaluating the financial position and operations of a company and in comparing them to previous years or to other companies.

Comparison of income statement and balance sheet numbers, in the form of ratios, can create difficulties due to the timing of the financial statements. Specifically, the profit and loss account covers the entire fiscal period, whereas the balance sheet is for a single point in time, the end of the period. Ideally then, to compare an income statement figure such as sales to a balance sheet figure such as receivable, we usually need a reasonable measure of average receivables for the year that the sales figure cover. However, these data are not available to the external analyst. In some cases, the analyst should take the next best approach, by using an average of beginning and ending balance sheet figures. This approach smooths out changes from beginning to end, but it does not eliminate problem due to seasonal and cyclical changes. It also does not reflect changes that occur unevenly throughout the year.

COMMON SIZE STATEMENTS

Common size statements involve expressing comparisons in percentages. Common size statements may be prepared in order to compare percentages of a current period with past periods, to compare individual business, or to compare one business with industry percentages published by trade associations and financial information services.

Common size financial statements contain the percentages of a key figure alone, without the corresponding amount figures. The use of percentages is usually preferable to the use of absolute figures. An illustration will make this clear. If company A earns ₹ 10,000 and Company B earns ₹ 1,000, which is more profitable? The answer is likely to be company A. However, the total shareholders equity of company A is ₹ 10,00,000 and company B is ₹ 10,000 the return on equity will be as follows:

$$\text{Return on Equity} = \frac{\text{Earnings}}{\text{Equity}}$$

$$\text{Company A} = \frac{₹\ 10{,}000}{₹\ 10{,}00{,}000} = 1\%$$

$$\text{Company B} = \frac{₹\ 1{,}000}{₹\ 10{,}000} = 10\%$$

Comparing the return on equity, it can be clearly said that company B is more profitable than company A.

The use of common size statements can make comparisons of business enterprises of different sizes much more meaningful since the numbers are brought to common base, *i.e.*, per cent. Such statement allows an analyst to compare the operating and financing characteristics of two companies of different sizes in the same industry.

Care must be exercised in the use of common size statements when the absolute figures are small, because a small absolute change can result in a very substantial percentage change. *For example*, if net profits last year amounted to ₹ 1,000 and increased this year to ₹ 5,000, this would be an increase of only ₹ 4,000 in net profits, but it represents a substantial increase in percentage terms.

Common size statements can be prepared in vertical analysis and horizontal analysis formats. In vertical analysis format, a figure from a year is compared with a base selected from the same year. *For example*, if advertising expenses were ₹ 10,000 in 2016 and sales were ₹ 10,00,000, the advertising expenses will be 1% of sales. In horizontal analysis format, the amount of an item (an account) is expressed in terms of that same account figure for a selected base year. *For example*, if sales were ₹ 8,00,000 in 2016 and ₹ 12,00,000 in 2017, then sales increased to 150% of the 2016 level in 2017, an increase of 50%.

FOCUS OF FINANCIAL STATEMENT ANALYSIS—RATIO ANALYSIS

Financial Statement Analysis involves evaluating different aspects of a business enterprise which are of great importance to different users such as management, investors, creditors, bankers, analysts, investment advisers, etc. Generally, the following analyses are made while making financial statement analysis:

1. Liquidity or Short-term Solvency Analysis
2. Analysis for Measuring the Movement of Assets — Activity Ratios
3. Profitability Analysis
4. Capital Structure or Gearing Analysis
5. Market Strength or Investor Analysis
6. Growth and Stability Analysis

Each of the above are discussed is great detail in the following sections.

LIQUIDITY OR SHORT-TERM SOLVENCY ANALYSIS (OR RATIOS)

Liquidity or short-term solvency analysis aims to determine the ability of a business to meet its financial obligations during the short-term and to maintain its short-term debt-paying ability. The aim of liquidity analysis is for a company to have adequate funds on hand to pay bills when they are due and to meet unexpected needs for cash. If a business enterprise cannot maintain its short-term debt paying ability, obviously it cannot maintain a long-term debt-paying ability or long-term solvency. Shareholders also will not be satisfied with such a state of affairs of the company. Even a business enterprise on a very profitable course will find itself bankrupt if it fails to meet its obligations to short-term creditors.

Liquidity analysis mainly focuses on balance sheet relationships that indicate the ability of a business to liquidate current and non-current liabilities. The ratios that evaluate liquidity relate to working capital or some part of it, because it is out of working capital that debts are paid as they mature. The comparisons and ratios related to evaluating liquidity or short-term solvency are as follows:

Working Capital Position

> **Working capital position** of the business is the excess of current assets over current liabilities.

The working capital of a business is the excess of current assets over current liabilities; this is computed by subtracting current liabilities from the current assets. The resulting working capital figure is taken as one of the primary indications of the short-term solvency of the business. The working capital formula is as follows:

Working Capital = Current assets – Current liabilities

The current working capital amount should be compared with past amounts to determine if working capital is reasonable. Caution must be exercised, because the relative size of the firm may be expanding or contracting. Further, the absolute amounts of working capital are difficult to use in comparing companies of different sizes or in comparing such amounts with industry figures.

Current Ratio

Current ratio is sometimes referred to as working capital ratio or banker's ratio. Current ratio expresses the relationship of current assets to current liabilities. It is widely used as a broad indicator of a company's liquidity and short-term debt-paying ability. The current ratio formula is as follows:

> **Current ratio** expresses the relationship of current assets to current liabilities.

$$\text{Current ratio} = \frac{\text{Current assets}}{\text{Current liabilities}}$$

Current ratio is a more dependable indicator of solvency than is working capital. For many years, the guideline for the minimum current ratio has been 2:1. The assumption is even if the value of current assets declines by 50%, the firm can still pay its current liabilities. But now-a-days there has been a decline in the liquidity of many firms. It can be said that in some industries, a current ratio substantially below 2 is adequate, while some other industries may require a ratio much larger than 2. In general, the shorter the operating cycle, the lower the normal current ratio. The longer the operating cycle, the higher the normal current ratio. A higher current ratio enables a firm to pay off current obligations and provides adequate margin of safety to the creditors.

A company's current ratio can be compared with the company's past current ratios and with industry averages as well. Such comparisons can help in determining if the current ratio is high or low at this period in time. However, these comparisons do not indicate why the current ratio is high or low. Possible reasons for unsatisfactory current ratio can be found from an analysis of the individual accounts and items which make up the current assets and current liability.

Example: The following are the current assets and current liabilities in respect of two companies, Company A and Company B.

	Company A ₹	*Company B* ₹
Current assets	4,50,000	1,60,000
Current liabilities	1,50,000	80,000

The current ratio will be as follows:

$$\text{Current ratio} = \frac{\text{Current assets}}{\text{Current liabilities}}$$

$$\text{Company A} = \frac{4,50,000}{1,50,000} = 3.1$$

$$\text{Company B} = \frac{1,60,000}{80,000} = 2:1$$

Acid Test Ratio or Quick Ratio

The current ratio is generally used to evaluate an enterprise's overall short-term solvency or liquidity position. The current ratio does not take into account the makeup or composition of current assets. *For example*, a rupee of cash or debtor is considered more readily available to meet obligations than a rupee of inventory. The quick ratio is designed to overcome this problem by relating the most liquid assets to current liabilities. Cash, marketable securities or short-term investments, receivables and prepaids are included within the meaning of most liquid assets; inventory is excluded. The acid test ratio is as follows:

$$\text{Acid Test} = \frac{\text{Current Assets} - \text{Inventory}}{\text{Current Liabilities}}$$

It may be preferable to have a better view of liquidity by excluding some other items in current assets that may not represent relatively current cash flow. Examples of items to be excluded are prepaids and miscellaneous items such as assets held for sale. This is considered a more conservative manner of computing the acid test ratio and the formula of acid test ratio in this situation will be as follows:

$$\text{Acid Test} = \frac{\text{Cash + Marketable Securities + Net Receivables and Debtors}}{\text{Current Liabilities}}$$

Inventory should be removed from current assets when computing the acid test ratio. Some of the reasons for this are that inventory may be slow moving or possibly obsolete and parts of the inventory may have been pledged to specific creditors. *For example*, a winery has inventory that requires considerable time for aging and therefore a considerable time before sale. To include the wine inventory in the test computation would overstate the liquidity. There is also a valuation problem with inventory, because it is stated at a cost figure that is likely to be materially different from a fair current valuation. In summary, inventory should be left out of the computation because of possible misleading liquidity indications[2].

The usual guideline for the acid test ratio is 1.00. However, some industries may find that a ratio less than 1.00 is adequate, while others need a ratio greater than 1.00. *For example*, a typical grocery store sells only for cash and therefore does not have receivables. This type of business can have an acid test substantially below the 1.00 guideline and still have adequate liquidity.

Example: A firm has the following current assets and current liabilities:

	₹
Debtors	5,000
Inventory	20,000
Cash	5,000
Total current assets	30,000

Total current liabilities ₹ 20,000

The acid test or quick ratio is as follows:

$$\text{Quick ratio} = \frac{\text{Quick assets}}{\text{Current liabilities}}$$

$$= \frac{₹\,10{,}000}{₹\,20{,}000} = 0.5 : 1$$

Cash Ratio

> **Cash ratio** is the ratio of cash and marketable securities to current liabilities.

Liquidity of a firm can be viewed from an extremely conservative point of view and the short-term liquidity of a company may be measured through cash ratio. The cash ratio relates cash and marketable securities to current liabilities. The cash ratio is computed as follows:

$$\text{Cash Ratio} = \frac{\text{Cash + Marketable Securities}}{\text{Current liabilities}}$$

Cash ratio is not given much importance unless a firm is in deep financial trouble. It is not considered pragmatic to expect a business enterprise to have enough cash and marketable securities to cover current liabilities. However, in the case of very slow-moving inventories and receivables and highly speculative companies, cash ratio is of great importance. A high cash ratio indicates that a business enterprise is not using its resource cash to best advantage. A low cash ratio reflects an immediate problem with paying bills.

ANALYSIS FOR MEASURING THE MOVEMENT OF ASSETS — ACTIVITY RATIOS

Activity ratios also known as turnover ratios indicate the efficiency with which an enterprise's resources are utilised. Liquidity or short-term analysis (current ratio and acid test ratio) will show misleading results if debtors are too high because of slow collections. Similarly, the current ratio will be misleading if inventory is not sold and thus remains at high levels. Since liquidity ratios (*i.e.* current ratio and acid test ratio) ignore the movement of current assets, it is necessary for short term creditors to make an analysis of how fast the debtors and stock are turned into cash so that their claims can be met timely. Moreover, the overall profitability of the business depends upon: (1) the rate of return of capital employed; and (2) the turnover, *i.e.*, the speed at which the capital employed in the business rotates. Hence, in order to find out which part of capital (*i.e.* assets) is efficiently employed and which part not, different activity or turnover ratios are calculated. Mainly activity ratios include:

> **Activity ratios** also known as **turnover ratios** indicate the efficiency with which an enterprise's resources are utilised.

1. Capital turnover ratio
2. Asset turnover ratio
3. Net working capital turnover ratio
4. Inventory turnover ratio
5. Debtor's turnover ratio or Receivables turnover.

Capital Turnover Ratio

This ratio measures the effectiveness with which a firm uses its financial resources. It indicates the number of times the capital has been rotated in the process of doing business. This ratio is computed as follows:

$$\frac{\text{Net Sales (or cost of goods sold)}}{\text{Capital employed or owner's equity}}$$

Net Sales = Total Sales less returns (if any)

Cost of goods sold = Opening Stock + Purchases + Direct Expenses – Closing Stock

OR

Sales – Gross profit

Example: A firm has opening and closing stock of ₹ 30,000 and ₹ 20,000 respectively. Its administrative and selling expenses are ₹ 10,000; Purchases ₹ 3,10,000; Sales ₹ 5,00,000; Debentures ₹ 50,000 (representing one-third of owner's equity). The capital turnover ratio is as follows:

$$\text{Capital turnover ratio} = \frac{\text{Cost of goods sold}}{\text{Owner's equity}}$$

$$\begin{aligned}\text{Cost of goods sold} &= \text{Opening stock + Purchases – Closing stock}\\ &= 30{,}000 + 3{,}10{,}000 - 20{,}000\\ &= ₹\,3{,}20{,}000\end{aligned}$$

$$\begin{aligned}\text{Capital or owner's equity} &= \text{3 times the amount of Debentures}\\ &= 3 \times 50{,}000 = 1{,}50{,}000\end{aligned}$$

$$\text{Capital turnover ratio} = \frac{3{,}20{,}000}{1{,}50{,}000} = 2.133 \text{ times}$$

Asset Turnover Ratio

This ratio reveals the number of times the net tangible assets (*i.e.*, total assets less current liabilities less intangibles) are turned over during the year. Strictly speaking, average net tangible assets should be used in calculating this ratio. But, invariably net tangible assets at the end of the year is used.

$$\text{Asset Turnover} = \frac{\text{Turnover}}{\text{Net Tangible Assets}}$$

An improvement in asset turnover ratio as compared to the previous year indicates that the turnover of the company has improved. In cases where assets are not revalued or replaced, its magnitude will be decreasing over the years due to depreciation. Then, obviously, the ratio will be higher as the turnover figures for the future will reflect an increasing trend.

Another form of assets turnover ratio can be computed as **fixed assets turnover ratio**. This ratio indicates the extent to which the investments in fixed assets have contributed to sales. If compared with a previous period, it indicates whether investment in fixed assets has been judicious or not.

> **Asset turnover ratio** indicates the extent to which the investments in fixed assets have contributed to sales.

The higher this ratio, better it is because it indicates higher efficiency displaying that investments in fixed assets has resulted in higher sales. A lower ratio may point to the under utilisation or non-utilisation of certain assets. The ratio is calculated as follows:

$$\frac{\text{Net sales}}{\text{Fixed assets less depreciation}}$$

Example:

The following details have been given to you for Messors ABC Ltd. for two years. You are required to find out Fixed Assets Turnover Ratio and comment on it.

	2015 ₹	2016 ₹
Fixed assets at written down value	15,00,000	30,00,000
Sales less returns	60,00,000	80,00,000

Solution:

$$\text{Fixed assets turnover ratio} = \frac{\text{Sales}}{\text{Fixed assets}}$$

For, 2015	For 2016
= 60,00,000 ÷ 15,00,000	= 80,00,000 ÷ 30,00,000
= 4 times	= 2.67 times.

Comment

There has been decline in the Fixed Assets Turnover Ratio though absolute figures of sales have gone up. It indicates that increase in the investment in Fixed Asset has not brought about proportionate gain. However, before concluding, results for next two to three years must also be seen.

Net Working Capital Turnover Ratio

This ratio indicates whether or not working capital has been effectively utilised in making sales. This ratio is computed by dividing the net sales or cost of goods sold by net working capital. Net working capital signifies the excess of current assets over current liabilities. The ratio is calculated as follows:

$$\frac{\text{Net Sales}}{\text{Net Working Capital}}$$

A high net working capital ratio (if it is expressed in percentage) indicates efficient use of working capital and quick turnover of current assets like stock and debtors. A low ratio indicates low turnover of these assets.

Inventory Turnover Ratio

Inventory turnover measures the relative size of inventory and influences the amount of cash available to pay liabilities. A smaller, faster-moving inventory means that the company has less cash tied up in inventory. On the contrary, a build up in inventory means that a recession or some other factor is preventing sales from keeping pace with purchasing and production. Ideally, inventory should be maintained at an optimum level to support production and sales. Inventory turnover ratio is calculated by using the following formula:

> **Inventory turnover** measures the relative size of inventory and influences the amount of cash available to pay liabilities.

$$\text{Inventory turnover} = \frac{\text{Cost of goods sold}}{\text{Average inventory}}$$

Average Inventory is obtained using a simple average process by dividing the opening and closing inventory by the two. Cost of goods sold is obtained by deducting gross profit from sales.

Example:

A firm has opening and closing inventory of ₹ 56,000 and ₹ 44,000 respectively. The firm has sold goods for ₹ 5,00,000 at gross profit margin of 20%. The inventory turnover ratio is as follows:

$$\text{Inventory turnover} = \frac{\text{Cost of goods sold}}{\text{Average inventory}}$$

$$= \frac{5{,}00{,}000 - 1{,}00{,}000}{1/2\,(56{,}000 + 44{,}000)}$$

$$= \frac{4{,}00{,}000}{50{,}000}$$

$$= 8 \text{ times per year}$$

Receivables Turnover Ratio

The ability of a company to collect for credit sales in a timely way affects the company's liquidity. The relationship between credit sales and accounts receivables may be stated as the receivable turnover.

Receivable turnover states the relationship between credit sales and accounts receivables.

Receivables or debtors turnover determines the liquidity of one item of current assets and finds out how faster debts are being collected. The formula for computing receivables turnover is as follows:

$$\text{Receivables Turnover} = \frac{\text{Net Credit Sales}}{\text{Average accounts receivables or debtors}}$$

Receivables turnover shows how many times, on average, the receivables were turned into cash during the period. A high debtors turnover ratio indicates shorter time span between credit sales and cash collection. This ratio requires one balance sheet account and one profit and loss account item. In case, credit sales figure is not given, total sales figure can be used to compute receivables turnover.

Example:

A firm has opening and closing debtors of ₹ 40,000 and ₹ 75,000 respectively and credit sales of ₹ 3,45,000. The debtors turnover ratio is as follows:

$$\text{Debtors turnover ratio} = \frac{\text{Credit Sales}}{\text{Average Debtors}} = \frac{₹\ 3{,}45{,}000}{₹\ 57{,}500} = 6 \text{ times per year}$$

$$\text{Debt Collection period} = \frac{12 \text{ months}}{\text{Debtors Turnover}} = \frac{12 \text{ months}}{6 \text{ times}} = 2 \text{ months}$$

PROFITABILITY ANALYSIS (OR RATIOS)

The long-term survival of a business enterprise depends on satisfactory income earned by it. An evaluation of a company's past profits may give the investors, creditors and others a better understanding for decision-making. The profitability position also affects the liquidity position which is vital to creditors as well. These ratios are:

Earnings Margin

It is the ratio of net income to turnover, expressed as a percentage.

$$\text{Earnings Margin} = \frac{\text{Net Income}}{\text{Turnover}} \times 100\%$$

Earnings margin is not the same as margin of profits. Margin of profits refers to the direct operating results only and is the amount before income tax and before non-operating income and charges. In earnings margin, only the final net profit is used.

Example:

The Profit and Loss Account of ABC Ltd. is given as follows:

ABC Ltd.
Profit and Loss Account

Particulars	₹	*Particulars*	₹
Cost of good Sold	30,00,000	Sales	50,00,000
Interest on Debentures	1,00,000	Income from investments	1,00,000
Provision for Taxation	10,00,000		
Net Profit after Tax	10,00,000		
	51,00,000		51,00,000

Calculate Earnings margin.

$$\text{Earnings Margin} = \frac{\text{Net Profit after tax}}{\text{Sales (Turnover)}} \times 100\%$$

$$= ₹\frac{10,00,000}{50,00,000} \times 100 = 20\%.$$

Return on Capital Employed (ROCE) or Return on Investment (ROI)

> **ROCE/ROI** measures profitability in relation to the total capital employed in a business enterprise.

This ratio measures profitability in relation to the total capital employed in a business enterprise. The terms invested capital, capital funds and total capital may be used interchangeably. It is a useful ratio when comparing the overall performances of companies, particularly where they have different proportions of debt in their capital structure. This ratio would also show whether the company's borrowing policy is wise economically and whether the capital had been employed fruitfully. *For example*, funds have been borrowed at 8% and return on capital is 7½%, it would be better not to borrow unless it is essential. It would also show that the firm had not been employing the funds efficiently. The business can survive only when the return on capital is more than the cost of capital employed in the business.

$$\text{Return on Capital} = \frac{\text{Profit before interest and tax}}{\text{Total capital employed}} \times 100$$

According to some analysts, short-term borrowings, such as bank loans, commercial paper, and deferred tax liability, should be included under capital. Current accrued payables which are not interest bearing should be excluded because their interest component is not observable.

Example:

Given below is the Balance Sheet of ABC Co. Ltd as on 31st March, 2016:

Liabilities	₹	*Assets*	₹
Equity Share Capital	20,00,000	Fixed Assets	30,00,000
Reserves	5,00,000	Current Assets	25,00,000
Surplus-Profit for the year	5,00,000	Discount on issue of debentures	1,00,000
10% Debentures	10,00,000		
Current liabilities	16,00,000		
	56,00,000		56,00,000

Find out Return on Capital Employed/ROI

Solution:

$$\text{Return on Investment} = \frac{\text{Profit before Interest etc.}}{\text{Capital employed}} \times 100$$

Profit before Interest = Profit (given in b/s) + interest on debentures

= 500,000 + 100,000 (10% of 10,00,000)

= ₹ 6,00,000

Capital Employed = Fixed Assets + Working Capital

= 30,00,000 + (25,00,000 – 16,00,000)

= ₹ 39,00,000

OR

Capital Employed = Equity Share Capital + Reserves + Surplus + Long term Debts – Discount on issue of debentures

= 20,00,000 + 5,00,000 + 5,00,000 + 10,00,000 – 1,00,000

= 39,00,000

$$\text{Return on Capital/ROI} = \frac{6,00,000}{39,00,000} \times 100 = 15.4\%.$$

Return on Equity

Return on equity is derived by taking net income and dividing it by the shareholders' equity. This indicates the returns which the management is realising from the shareholders' equity and shows how effectively ordinary shareholder funds are being utilised by the management. As long as it is above the current interest rates, a company is doing fairly well.

> **Return on equity** indicates the returns which the management is realising from the shareholders' equity and shows how effectively the ordinary shareholder funds are being utilised by the management.

$$\text{Return on Equity} = \frac{\text{Profit after taxation} - \text{Preference Dividends}}{\text{Ordinary shareholders' funds}} \times 100\%$$

It is obvious that both the ratios–return on capital and return on equity – will be influenced when a company has raised new capital during the course of the year. That is, in other words, the ratios will be artificially low. Also, the ratios do not take into account the effect of financial leverage which undesirably tends to increase the variability of earnings for the ordinary shares. In fact, ordinary shareholders of a company having higher dose of borrowings expect large returns to compensate for the high levels of risk. Financial analysts, sometimes in such cases, find out the trade-off between higher earnings and increased variability of earnings to determine whether the management has chosen the optimum amount of financial leverage.

Example:

Calculate Return on Equity (ROE) from the following information :

	₹
10% Preference Share Capital (fully paid up)	10,00,000
1,60,000 Equity Shares of ₹ 10 each fully paid	16,00,000
Reserves and Surplus	64,00,000
Net Profit after tax	23,75,000

Solution:

$$\text{Returns on Equity} = \frac{\text{Net Profit} - \text{Preference dividend}}{\text{Equity Shareholders' fund}}$$

Preference dividend = 10% on ₹ 10,00,000 = ₹ 1,00,000.

Equity Shareholders' funds:	₹
Paidup Equity Share Capital	16,00,000
+ Reserves & Surplus	64,00,000
	80,00,000

$$\text{Return on Equity} = \frac{23,75,000 - 1,00,000}{80,00,000} \times 100$$

$$= \frac{22,75,000}{80,00,000} \times 100 = 28.44\%.$$

CAPITAL STRUCTURE OR GEARING ANALYSIS (RATIOS)

Gearing ratio, *i.e.*, the relationship of long-term debt to total capital is considered the most important by many investors and financial analysts. Popularly known as debt-equity ratio, this ratio has utility to many including shareholders, creditors, business managers, suppliers and other user groups. Gearing ratios are used to indicate:

1. The cushion of assets/profits available to holders of fixed income capital should assets/ profits decline.
2. The gearing advantage of potentially higher assets/ profits attributable to ordinary shareholders and the correspondingly higher risk which is incurred
3. The scope for raising additional fixed-income capital at reasonable costs, from the point of view of the company.

> **Gearing ratio** is the relationship of long-term debt to total capital.

Debt-Equity Ratio

The debt-equity ratio is computed as follows:

$$\text{Debt-equity ratio} = \frac{\text{Loan capital} + \text{Preference share capital}}{\text{Net tangible assets}} \times 100$$

Net tangible assets (or total capital) is obtained by subtracting the intangible assets and the current assets from total assets. Loan capital plus preference capital constitutes the amount of long-term debt. Alternatively, long-term debt can be derived by subtracting current liabilities from total liabilities.

Other variants of Debt-Equity Ratio are as follows:

1. $\frac{\text{Long term Liabilities}}{\text{Equity (or Net Worth)}} \times 100$

2. $\frac{\text{External Equities}}{\text{Internal Equities}}$

3. $\frac{\text{Long- term debts}}{\text{Owner's equities}}$

4. $\dfrac{\text{Long term debts}}{\text{Shareholder's funds} + \text{Long term debt}}$

Sometimes capital gearing is calculated in terms of debt to equity ratio and not total capital. Capital gearing ratios, calculated in these two manners, provide essentially the same information. It is desirable that the investors select a standard method and follow it consistently throughout. It is said that as a rule of thumb, one should not opt for a company whose long-term debt exceeds two-thirds of its total capitalisation. Debt equity ratio is very helpful in assessing a company—whether the company is marching steadily into or out of debt. In younger and aggressive companies, comparatively speaking, the long-term debts may at times exceed the shareholders equity which means that a company will not be able to get out of the difficult situation easily. A company depending on large amounts of debt should manage and perform well to avoid any worse contingencies. Debt equity ratios should be analysed not for one but for many years to determine a trend. If it is found that equity component is continuously increasing than the long-term debt, there may not be any cause for concern.

Example:

From the following, calculate debt-equity ratio:

	₹
Equity Share Capital :	
10,000 Equity shares of ₹ 100 each	10,00,000
General Reserve	4,50,000
Accumulated Profits	3,00,000
Debentures	7,50,000
Sundry trade creditors	4,00,000
Outstanding expenses	1,00,000

Solution:

(1) Debt Equity Ratio $= \dfrac{\text{External equities}}{\text{Internal equities}}$

$$= \frac{\text{Debentures} + \text{Trade Creditors} + \text{Outstanding expenses}}{\text{Equity Share Capital} + \text{General Reserve} + \text{Accumulated Profit}}$$

$$= \frac{7{,}50{,}000 + 4{,}00{,}000 + 1{,}00{,}000}{10{,}00{,}000 + 4{,}50{,}000 + 3{,}00{,}000} = \frac{12{,}50{,}000}{17{,}50{,}000} = 0.71 : 1.$$

(2) Debt-Equity Ratio $= \dfrac{\text{Long-term debts}}{\text{Owners' equity}}$

$$= \frac{\text{Debentures}}{\text{Equity Share Capital} + \text{General Reserve} + \text{Accumulated Profit}}$$

$$= \frac{7{,}50{,}000}{17{,}50{,}000} = 0.43 : 1$$

(3) Debt-Equity Ratio $= \dfrac{\text{Long-term debts}}{\text{Shareholders' funds} + \text{Long-term debt}}$

$$= \frac{7{,}50{,}000}{17{,}50{,}000 + 7{,}50{,}000} = \frac{7{,}50{,}000}{25{,}00{,}000} = 0.3 : 1$$

Interest Coverage Ratio

Interest coverage ratio determines the debt servicing capacity of a business enterprise keeping in view fixed interest on long-term debt. The formula for this ratio is:

$$\text{Interest Coverage ratio} = \frac{\text{Earnings before Interest and taxes (EBIT)}}{\text{Interest}}$$

If a business enterprise is able to earn a return on the assets higher than the rate of interest on long-term debt, the enterprise makes an overall profit. However, if the enterprise runs the risk of not earning a return on assets equal to the interest cost of the long-term loan, the enterprise makes an overall loss. The interest coverage ratio measures the degree of protection creditors have from default on the payment of interest by the company.

> **Interest coverage ratio** determines the debt servicing capacity of a business enterprise keeping in view fixed interest on long-term debt.

Example:

ABC Ltd. has earned net profit of ₹ 3,50,000 during the year 2015-16. It has paid income tax of ₹ 1,50,000 and interest on debentures as ₹ 1,25,000. The interest coverage ratio may be calculated as follows:

$$\frac{\text{Profit before interest and tax}}{\text{Interest}}$$

$$= \frac{3,50,000 + 1,50,000 + 1,25,000}{1,25,000}$$

$$= \frac{6,25,000}{1,25,000} = 5 \text{ times.}$$

MARKET STRENGTH ANALYSIS OR INVESTOR ANALYSIS

The market strength analysis or investor analysis are especially important for investors while analysing information about a company. This analysis helps the investors to decide about a company as an investment opportunity at a point of time. These ratios are also known as stock market ratios, investment ratios or market test ratios. The ratios under this category are as follows:

Earnings Per Share

Earnings per share is derived by dividing the profit of a company by the total number of shares outstanding. Earnings here means the net profit, net income or the net earnings. This is the amount by which the total revenues exceed the total expenses for the year.

$$\text{Earnings per share} = \frac{\text{Earnings after tax} - \text{Preference dividends}}{\text{Number of ordinary shares}}$$

The net earnings figure is the amount which is completely free from any obligations and the company can plough it back into the company, pay to the ordinary shareholders as dividends or a combination of both. This amount is also known as the earnings available for ordinary shareholders.

Example:

Net profit before tax ₹ 1,00,000

Tax rate — 40% of Net Profit

10% Preference Share Capital (₹ 10 each) ₹ 1,00,000

Equity Shares Capital (₹ 10 per Share) ₹ 1,00,000

$$\text{Earnings Per Share} = \frac{\text{Net Profit after tax and Pref. dividend}}{\text{Number of Equity Shares}}$$

$$= \frac{₹1,00,000 - 40,000 \text{ (Tax)} - 10,000 \text{ (Pref. Div.)}}{10,000}$$

$$= \frac{50,000}{10,000} = ₹5 \text{ per share.}$$

Primary and Diluted Earnings Per Share

Earnings per share can either be primary or diluted. Primary earnings per share is the earnings per share for the number of ordinary shares outstanding as on the beginning of the report period. Diluted earnings per share, on the other hand, is calculated after taking into account convertible debentures, bonds, etc. (which have been converted into ordinary shares) during the year. It is computed in the same manner as primary earnings per share except that it assumes that all investments with the convertibility clause were converted at the beginning of the year. In case a company has bonds and debentures which are convertible into ordinary shares, it is always useful to compute fully diluted earnings per share (assuming full conversion) as well as earnings per share on a normal basis. This implies adding back the interest paid on the convertibles, recalculating the numerator and then dividing by the total number of ordinary shares on the assumption that conversion has taken place.

Dividend Per Share

The dividend per share can be net or gross. Net dividend per share is the dividend declared on a single ordinary share for the year, the net of basic rate tax.

$$\text{Net Dividend Per Share} = \frac{\text{Ordinary dividends paid to ordinary shareholders}}{\text{Number of ordinary shares}}$$

Gross dividend per share is net dividend per share together with the associated tax credit.

$$\text{Gross Dividend per share} = \frac{\text{Net dividend per share}}{1 - \text{Basic rate of tax}}$$

Alternatively,

Gross Dividend Per Share = Net Dividend Per Share + Associated Tax Credit

Gross Dividend Yield

The gross dividend yield is the gross dividend per share divided by the ordinary share price expressed as a percentage.

$$\text{Gross Dividend Yield} = \frac{\text{Gross dividend per share}}{\text{Ordinary share price}} \times 100\%$$

For example, if a company declares dividend at 20% on its shares, each having a paid-up value of ₹ 8 and market price of ₹ 25, the dividend yield ratio will be calculated as follows:

$$\text{Dividend Per Share} = \frac{20}{100} \times 8 = ₹1.60$$

$$\text{Dividend Yield Ratio} = \frac{\text{Dividend per share}}{\text{Market price per share}} \times 100$$

$$= \frac{1.6}{25} \times 100 = 6.4\%.$$

The gross dividend yield indicates the current level of income from a share. Dividend yields are normally calculated using gross dividends rather than net dividends because it helps in better analysis and comparison with other types of investments. Also, investors pay income tax at rates other than the basic rate. If the dividend yield is calculated on a net basis, the level of tax rate which has been deducted should be made clear.

Besides indicating the general level of the market, dividend yield reflects the market estimates of future dividend growth and risk. The higher the dividend growth expectations for a given share, the lower the current yield; the higher the market's estimate of risk, the higher the current yield.

Dividend Cover

Dividend cover denotes the number of times the dividend per share is covered by earnings per share

$$\text{Dividend Cover} = \frac{\text{Earnings per share}}{\text{Dividend per share}}$$

Dividend cover helps in assessing the prospects for dividend increases. Or, alternatively, the possibility of a dividend cut, should profits decline. For the purpose of dividend cover, full distribution earnings per share is normally taken into account. In other words, it is assumed that all profits are distributed as dividends. The gross dividend per share should be taken to ensure consistency in the resulting figure of dividend cover.

Payout Ratio

Payout ratio measures the proportion of earnings per share which are paid out as dividends.

$$\text{Payout Ratio} = \frac{\text{Net dividend per share}}{\text{Net earnings per share}} \times 100\%$$

The percentage of available earnings paid out as ordinary dividends has a vital influence on the market's behaviour towards those issues of shares which are not in the growth category. For those companies which have paid dividends in the form of stock dividends and cash, only the cash dividend should be included in calculating the payout ratio. In the case of dividends paid out as stock dividends, the investor receives nothing that was not already owned and the company gives up nothing of value.

Example:

Compute the Pay-out Ratio and Retained Earning Ratio from the following data:

	₹		₹
Net Profit	20,000	No. of Equity Shares	3,000
Provision for tax	10,000	Dividend per equity shares	0.80
Preference Dividend	4,000		

Solution:

$$\text{Pay out Ratio} = \frac{\text{Dividend per equity share}}{\text{Earnings per equity share}} \times 100$$

$$\text{Earnings per share} = \frac{\text{Profit available to equity shareholders}}{\text{No. of equity share}}$$

$$= \frac{20,000-10,000-4,000}{3,000} = \frac{6000}{3000} = 2$$

$$\text{Dividend Pay out Ratio} = \frac{₹\,0.80}{2} \times 100 = 40\%.$$

$$\text{Retained Earning Ratio} = \frac{\text{Retained Earnings}}{\text{Total Earnings (after tax and Pref. Div.)}} \times 100$$

$$\text{Retained Earnings} = \text{Profit available for Equity Shareholders} - \text{Dividends paid}$$

$$= 6,000 - 2,400 = ₹\,3,600$$

$$\text{Retained Earnings ratio} = \frac{3,600}{6,000} \times 100 = 60\%.$$

Dividends to Cash Flow

'Dividends to cash flow' is a more useful ratio than the payout ratio. It helps in understanding the past trend in this regard and is greatly helpful in estimating future dividends than the conventional payout ratio.

$$\text{Dividend to Cash Flow} = \frac{\text{Dividend paid on ordinary shares}}{\text{Net earnings available for ordinary share}}$$

Price/Earnings (P/E) Ratio

It is the market price of shares expressed as a multiple of earnings per share.

$$\text{Price Earnings (P/E) Ratio} = \frac{\text{Price per ordinary share}}{\text{Earnings per share}}$$

Many investors consider P/E ratio as the best indicator of the ongoing performance of a company. This ratio along with the payout ratio indicates the market estimates of future dividend growth and risk. High growth shares have high P/E ratios as investors are willing to pay a greater multiple of current earnings to achieve a higher future growth. If high risk is found in a share, it reduces its market price and hence automatically reduces its P/E ratio. Payout ratios can have a positive influence on P/E ratio. High P/Es are not always bad. If investors are willing to pay a high price for a share in relations to its earnings, then they are doing so in the belief that the company has a bright future. That it will continue to strengthen and grow in future. Buying a share with a high P/E is described as buying a security with a high multiple. It should be understood here that the common share dividends come out of the earnings per share. A drop in earnings could mean that a dividend is in trouble.

The elements which govern the P/E ratio are:

1. Those factors that are fully reflected in the financial data (tangible factors)— Growth of earnings and sales in the past; Profitability or rate of returns on invested capital; Stability of past earnings; Dividend rate and record, and; Financial strength or credit standing.
2. Those factors that are reflected to an indefinite extent in the data (intangible factors)— Quality of management; Nature and prospects of the industry, and competitive position and individual prospects of the company.

Net Asset Value Per Share

This ratio is also known as the book value per share. Net asset value per share is the value of net tangible assets attributable to one ordinary share. Net asset value is, simply put, the shareholders' equity. Net asset value or book value has nothing to do with the market value as shares usually sell in the stock market at several times its net asset or book value.

$$\text{Net Asset Value Per Share} = \frac{\text{Ordinary share capital + Reserves} - \text{Intangibles}}{\text{Number of ordinary shares outstanding at balance sheet date}}$$

Net asset value applies to ordinary shares only. However, it does not mean that investors can get that amount if the company is liquidated. The amounts attributed to the assets are only attempts at fair and systematic evaluation, not at guessing what these assets would bring if sold in the market place. Net asset or book value can be considered only as the theoretical value of ordinary shares if the assets of the company were liquidated at the amounts attributed to them on the balance sheet. It is not unusual for a share price to be very different from the net asset value per share, even where assets in the balance sheet have recently been revalued. In general, the market price of a share will be influenced by earnings and the dividend-paying potential. Share prices will not be significantly influenced by the net asset value per share except where:

1. The company is an investment vehicle for specific types of assets (e.g., investment trusts, property companies).
2. It seems probable that the company will be liquidated.
3. A takeover bid of the company seems likely.

The net asset value per share figure is useful while comparing shares of one company with shares of other companies operating in the same industry. If it is found that a company is selling shares at a much lower ratio of market price to book value than other companies in the same industry, it indicates a good investment opportunity. When a share can be bought for less than its net asset value, it is an indication that share will have good value in the future. In case of mutual funds, net asset value ratio is important as it is determined at or near the price at which the mutual fund will buy and sell its shares. In the stock market, it is often found that a share is selling five times, seven times (and more) its book value. The lower the multiple, the greater will be probable value of the share.

Cash Flow Per Share

Cash flow per share is an useful indicator of a company's general ability to leverage itself, to pay dividends, to convert accounting earnings into cash and to enjoy financial flexibility.

$$\text{Cash Flow Per Share} = \frac{\text{Cash flow from operations after taxes}}{\text{Ordinary shares outstanding at balance sheet date}}$$

The amount of cash flow does not totally belong to ordinary shareholders, as the earnings belong; it is also meant to pay the expenses and claims prior to the payment of dividend.

GROWTH AND STABILITY ANALYSIS OR RATIOS

Growth and stability ratios measure the performance and financial strength of a company apart from market valuation.

Growth and stability ratios measure the performance and financial strength of a company apart from market valuation. Stability ratios are useful in evaluating the quality of bonds, debentures, preference shares, etc. These ratios are calculated over time and relate to sales, total returns, and earnings per share. Such ratios are:

1. $\text{Growth in Sales} = \dfrac{\text{Sales in final period}}{\text{Sales in base period}}$
2. $\text{Growth in Total Returns} = \dfrac{\text{Net earned for total capital in final period}}{\text{Net earned for total capital in base period}}$

3. Growth in earnings $= \dfrac{\text{Earnings per share in final period}}{\text{Earnings per share in base period}}$

4. Maximum decline in coverage of interest charges $= \dfrac{\text{Worst year (or lowest year)}}{\text{Average of previous three years}}$

Normally interest charges may include any of the following combinations:

— Interest on short and long-term debts, including capital leases.

— Interest on expenses plus an interest component for operating leases

— Interest on expenses on short and long-term debts plus rentals on both capital and operating bases

— Total fixed charges, rentals and preferred dividends.

5. Per cent Decline in Return on Total Capital $= \dfrac{\text{Worst year (or lowest year)}}{\text{Average of previous three years}}$

6. Per cent Decline in return on Ordinary Capital $= \dfrac{\text{Worst year (or lowest year)}}{\text{Average of previous three years}}$

7. Percentage Decline in Earnings Per Share $= \dfrac{\text{Worst year (or lowest year)}}{\text{Average of previous three years}}$

LIMITATIONS OF FINANCIAL RATIOS

Financial statement analysis through ratios is useful because they highlight relationships between items in the financial statements. However, they have a number of limitations which should be kept in mind while preparing or using them.

1. Ratios are based on accounting figures given in the financial statements. However, accounting figures are themselves subject to deficiencies, approximations, diversity in practice or even manipulation to some extent. Therefore, ratios are not very helpful in drawing reliable conclusions.
2. Ratios have inherent problem of comparability. Companies otherwise similar may employ different accounting methods, which can cause problems in comparing certain key relationships. *For example*, inventory turnover can be different for a company using FIFO than for the other company using LIFO method of inventory valuation. Similarly the differences in accounting methods relating to depreciation, estimates of the life of asset, amortisation of intangibles and preliminary expenses, treatment of extraordinary items etc. can create the problem of comparability among the companies even in the same industry.
3. Inflation may limit the utility of accounting ratios. Due to inflation, historical cost-based financial statements and accounting figures do not reflect current value figures, especially in the case of assets purchased at different dates by the different enterprises. Since financial statements are not adjusted in terms of inflation effect, accounting ratios calculated (using varying cost or prices) have distortions and become deceptive. Sometimes, gains (reflected through ratios) over time in sales, net income and other key figures disappear when the accounting data are adjusted for changes in price levels.
4. Accounting ratios are not totally dependable and they must be used after giving due weightage to general economic conditions, industry situation, position of firms within the industry, mode of operations, size of firm, diversity of product which can make the business enterprises completely dissimilar and thus affect the computation of accounting ratios.

5. The different methods of computation also influence the utility of accounting ratios. The different concepts used for determining numerator and denominator in a particular accounting ratio will not help in drawing reliable conclusions even in identical situations.

Illustrative Problem 1

The working capital of ABC Ltd. has deteriorated in recent years and now stands as under:

Current Assets	₹	*Current Liabilities*	₹
Inventory	5,60,000	Creditors	4,90,000
Debtors	3,50,000	Bank loan	2,10,000
Cash	70,000		
	9,80,000		7,00,000

(*a*) Compute the current and quick ratios.

(*b*) A further bank loan of ₹ 50,000 against debtors is under negotiation. Assuming the loan is received, calculate the revised current and quick ratios.

(*c*) There is also a negotiation going on for discounting the debtors of ₹ 350,000 for ₹ 3,15,000 to a collection agency for immediate cash. Also obsolete stocks worth ₹ 1,25,000 are being sold for ₹ 80,000. Of the cash to be realised by the two transactions, the bank loan is proposed to be reduced to ₹ 1,00,000. Calculate the current ratio after the transactions are put through.

Solution:

(*a*) $$\text{Current Ratio} = \frac{\text{Current assets}}{\text{Current liabilities}} = \frac{₹\ 9{,}80{,}000}{₹\ 7{,}00{,}000} = 1.4$$

$$\text{Quick Ratio} = \frac{\text{Liquid assets}}{\text{Current liabilities}} = \frac{₹\ 4{,}20{,}000}{₹\ 7{,}00{,}000} = 0.6$$

(*b*) $$\text{Revised Current Ratio} = \frac{₹\ 10{,}30{,}000}{₹\ 7{,}50{,}000} = 1.37$$

$$\text{Revised Quick Ratio} = \frac{₹\ 4{,}70{,}000}{₹\ 7{,}50{,}000} = 0.63$$

(*c*) Financial position after the transactions:

	₹
Current Assets:	
Inventory	4,35,000
Debtors	—
Cash	3,55,000
	7,90,000
Current Liabilities:	
Creditors	4,90,000
Bank Loan	1,00,000
	5,90,000

$$\text{New Current Ratio} = \frac{₹\ 7,90,000}{₹\ 5,90,000} = 1.34$$

$$\text{New Quick Ratio} = \frac{₹\ 3,55,000}{₹\ 5,90,000} = 0.6$$

Cash balance = ₹ 70,000 + 3,15,000 + 80,000 – 1,10,000 = ₹ 3,55,000

Illustrative Problem 2

From the following annual accounts of New Horizon Limited you are required to calculate the following ratios and comment on the results, indicating what other information you require.

(*i*)	Gross profit percentage	(*vi*)	Stock turnover
(*ii*)	Net profit percentage	(*vii*)	Fixed assets: turnover
(*iii*)	Return on total assets	(*viii*)	Return on shareholders' funds
(*iv*)	Quick assets ratio	(*ix*)	Current ratio
(*v*)	Debtors collection period	(*x*)	Debt ratio

Balance Sheet as at 31 December, 2016

	(₹ *000*)
Share Capital	450
Retained Profits	240
	690
12% Debentures	700
Trade creditors	620
Proposed dividend	45
	2,055
Fixed assets net of depreciation	875
Stocks	310
Debtors	770
Bank balance	100
	2,055

Extracts from Year's Profit and Loss Account

	(₹)
Sales for the year	31,00,000
Gross profit	17,25,000
Expenses	8,05,000
Depreciation	2,50,000

Solution:

(*i*) Gross profit percentage $= \frac{1725}{3100} \times 100\% = 55.6\%$

(*ii*) Net profit percentage $= \frac{670}{3100} \times 100\% = 21.6\%$

(*iii*) Return on total assets $= \frac{670}{2055} \times 100\% = 32.6\%$

(*iv*) Quick ratio $= \frac{870}{665} = 1{\cdot}3{:}1$

(*v*) Debtors collection period $= \frac{770}{3100} \times 365 = 91$ days

(*vi*) Stock : turnover $= \frac{3100}{310} = 10$ times

(*vii*) Fixed assets : turnover $= \frac{3100}{875} = 3.5$ times

(*viii*) Return on shareholders' funds $= \frac{586}{690} \times 100\% = 84.9\%$

(*ix*) Current ratio $= \frac{1180}{665} \times 1.8{:}1$

(*x*) Debt ratio $= \frac{1365}{2055} \times 100\% = 66.4$

Very few ratios have an absolute value but they are used in a relative way in intra- and inter-firm comparisons. Both gross and net margins are calculated using the profit before tax and interest to identify the trading profit, irrespective of the capital structure in force. Both these figures seem satisfactory but knowledge of the industry is necessary. Also the returns on shareholders' funds and on total assets both appear quite satisfactory.

The quick ratio exceeds the 1:1 norm and the current ratio is near the 2:1 norm, but this requirement varies widely. On the other hand the debt ratio seems high, as two-thirds of all assets are financed by debt.

Asset turnover rates also need comparisons to make any judgement but the debtors collection period of 91 days would seem too long for most industries, especially if credit is granted on a net monthly basis.

Illustrative Problem 3

XYZ Company's financial statements contain the following information:

	2015 ₹	2016 ₹
Cash	2,00,000	1,60,000
Sundry Debtors	3,20,000	4,00,000
Temporary Investments	2,00,000	3,20,000
Stock	18,40,000	21,60,000
Prepaid Expenses	28,000	12,000
Total Current Assets	25,88,000	30,52,000
Total assets	56,00,000	64,00,000
Current Liabilities	6,40,000	8,00,000
Loans	16,00,000	16,00,000
Capital	20,00,000	20,00,000
Retained Earnings	4,68,000	8,12,000

Statement of Profit for the Current Year

	₹
Sales	40,00,000
Less cost of goods sold	(28,00,000)
Less interest	(160,000)
Net profit	10,40,000
Less taxes @ 50%	5,20,000
Profit after taxes	5,20,000
Profit distributed	2,20,000

From the above, appraise the financial position of the company from the point of view of (*i*) Liquidity, (*ii*) Profitability, and (*iii*) Activity.

Solution:

1. **Liquidity Ratios:**

(*a*) Current Ratio (2016) $= \dfrac{\text{Current Assets}}{\text{Current Liabilities}} = \dfrac{30{,}52{,}000}{8{,}00{,}000} = 3.81$

(*b*) Acid Test Ratio (2016) $= \dfrac{\text{Liquid Assets}}{\text{Current Liabilities}} = \dfrac{30{,}52{,}000 - 21{,}72{,}000}{8{,}00{,}000} = 1.1$

2. **Leverage Ratios:**

(*a*) Debt Equity Ratio (2016) $= \dfrac{\text{Long term debts}}{\text{Equity Funds}} = \dfrac{16{,}00{,}000}{28{,}12{,}000} = .57$

(*b*) Interest Coverage Ratio (2016) $= \dfrac{\text{EBIT}}{\text{Interest Charge}} = \dfrac{12{,}00{,}000}{1{,}60{,}000} = 7.5$ times.

3. **Profitability Ratios:**

(*a*) Gross Profit Ratio (2016) $= \dfrac{\text{Gross Profit}}{\text{Sales}} \times 100 = \dfrac{12{,}00{,}000}{40{,}00{,}000} \times 100 = 30\ \%$

(*b*) Net Profit Ratio (2016) $= \dfrac{\text{Net Profit}}{\text{Sales}} \times 100 = \dfrac{5{,}20{,}000}{40{,}00{,}000} \times 100 = 13\%$

(*c*) Return on Total Assets 2016 $= \dfrac{\text{Profit after Tax}}{\text{Total Assets}} \times 100 = \dfrac{5{,}20{,}000}{64{,}00{,}000} \times 100 = 8.12\%$

(*d*) Return on Cap. Emp. (2016) $= \dfrac{\text{PAT} + \text{Int}(1\text{-t})}{\text{Total Cap. Emp.}} \times 100 = \dfrac{5{,}20{,}000 + 80{,}000}{44{,}12{,}000} \times 100 = 13.6\%$

(*e*) Return on Equity Funds (2016) $= \dfrac{\text{Profit after Tax}}{\text{Equity Funds}} \times 100 = \dfrac{5{,}20{,}000}{28{,}12{,}000} \times 100 = 18.5\%$

4. Activity Ratios:

₹

(*a*) Debtors Turnover (2016) = $\dfrac{\text{Sales}}{\text{Average Debtors}} = \dfrac{40{,}00{,}000}{3{,}60{,}000}$ = 11.1 times

(*b*) Stock Turnover (2016) = $\dfrac{\text{Cost of goods sold}}{\text{Average Stock}} = \dfrac{28{,}00{,}000}{20{,}00{,}000}$ = 1.4 times

(*c*) Total Assets Turnover (2016) = $\dfrac{\text{Sales}}{\text{Average Assets}} = \dfrac{40{,}00{,}000}{60{,}00{,}000}$ = 0.67 times

On the basis of the above ratios, it can be said that the firm's positions is sound from the point of view of liquidity, solvency and profitability. However, its activity ratios do not represent a satisfactory position. Better position will be reflected only if the ratios are compared with the performance of other firms in the same industry.

Illustrative Problem 4

The balance sheet of XYZ company is given below:

(₹ in lacs)

Liabilities	*Amount*	*Assets*	*Amount*
Equity Share Capital	250	Fixed Assets	400
General Reserve	280	Investment	50
P & L A/c (Current Year)	30	Stock	460
Secured loans-Long term	300	Debtors	460
Secured loans-Short term	360	Cash in hand	10
Creditors	150	Misc. Expenditure (not written off)	20
Other liabilities	30		
	1400		1400

Additional Information:

(*a*) From the Profit and Loss Account ₹ 90 lacs was transferred to General Reserve during the year

(*b*) Interest cost amounted to ₹ 120 lacs

(*c*) Taxation @ 40%

You are required to calculate (*i*) Debt equity ratio (*ii*) Current ratio (*iii*) Interest coverage ratio.

Solution:

Current Ratio = $\dfrac{\text{Current Assets}}{\text{Current Liabilities}} = \dfrac{₹\ 930 \text{ lacs}}{₹\ 540 \text{ lacs}}$ = 1.73

Debt Equity Ratio = $\dfrac{\text{Debt}}{\text{Equity}} = \dfrac{₹\ 300 \text{ lacs}}{₹\ 560 \text{ lacs}}$ = 0.54

Interest Coverage Ratio = $\dfrac{\text{EBIT}}{\text{Interest}} = \dfrac{₹\ 320 \text{ lacs}}{₹\ 120 \text{ lacs}}$ = 2.66

Working Notes:

Current Assets	₹	***Debt***	***Equity***	₹
Stock	460 lacs	Term loan ₹ 300 lacs	Capital	250 lacs
Debtors	460 lacs		Reserve	280 lacs
Cash	10 lacs		P&L A/c	30 lacs
	930 lacs			560 lacs

Current Liabilities	₹	***EBIT***	₹
Short-term loan	360 lacs	Profit for the year (30 + 90)	120 lacs
Trade Credit	150 lacs	Interest	120 lacs
Other Liabilities	30 lacs	Tax @ 40% $\frac{120 \times 40}{60}$	80 lacs
	540 lacs		320 lacs

Illustrative Problem 5

Calculate the P/E ratio from the following:

	₹
Equity Share Capital (₹ 20 each)	50,00,000
Reserves and Surplus	5,00,000
Secured Loans at 15%	25,00,000
Unsecured Loans at 12.5%	10,00,000
Fixed Assets	30,00,000
Investments	5,00,000
Operating Profit	25,00,000
Income-tax Rate	50%
Market Price/Share	₹ 50

Solution:

	₹	
Operating Profit		25,00,000
Less: Interest on:		
Secured loans @ 15%	3,75,000	
Unsecured Loans @12.5%	1,25,000	5,00,000
Profit before Tax (PBT)		20,00,000
Less: Income Tax @ 50%		10,00,000
Profit After Tax (PAT)		10,00,000
No. of Equity Shares		250,000

$$\textbf{EPS} = \frac{\text{Profit after tax}}{\text{No. of Equity shares}} = \frac{₹\ 10,00,000}{2,50,000} = ₹\ 4$$

P/E ratio = Market price per share/EPS = ₹ 50/₹ 4 = 12.50

Illustrative Problem 6

ABC Distributors has the following Balance Sheet and Income Statement:

Balance Sheet

Liabilities	*Amount*	*Assets*	*Amount*
Shareholders Equity (50,000 shares)	3,00,000	Long Term Assets	3,50,000
		Cash	25,000
Long Term Debt	1,00,000	Accounts Receivables	60,000
Account payable	80,000	Inventory	65,000
Other Current Liabilities	20,000		
	5,00,000		5,00,000

Income Statement

Particular	*Amount*
Sales	9,00,000
Cost of Goods Sold	4,00,000
General, Administrative and Selling Expenses	1,00,000
Other Expenses	2,50,000
Net Income (PAT)	1,50,000

You are required to:

(*a*) Determine ABC distributor's liquidity position by calculating the Current ratio, Working Capital, the ratio of Current Assets to Total Assets, the ratio of Current Liabilities to Total Assets and the Cash Conversion cycle.

(*b*) Calculate the current market price per share of ABC's Stock if its P/E ratio is eight.

Solution:

Various Ratios of A B C Distributors may be found as follows :

Current assets	=	Cash + Accounts receivable + Inventory
	=	25,000 + 60,000 + 65,000 = 1,50,000
Current liabilities	=	Accounts payable + Other current liabilities
	=	80,000 + 20,000 = 1,00,000
Current Ratio	=	Current assets/Current liabilities
	=	1,50,000/1,00,000 = 1.5
Net working capital	=	1.50,000 – 1,00,000 = 50,000
Current assets/Total assets	=	1,50,000/5,00,000 = 0.30
Current liabilities/Total assets	=	1,00,000/5,00,000 = 0.20
Receivables Turnover	=	Sales / Accounts receivables = 17.00
Inventory Turnover	=	Cost of goods sold/Inventory = 6.15
Payable Turnover	=	$\frac{\text{Cost of goods sold}}{\text{Accounts Payable}} = \frac{4,00,000}{80,000} = 5.00$

Average collection period = 365/Receivables turnover = 24.33 days
Inventory conversion period = 365/Inventory turnover = 59.35 days
Payable Deferral period = 365/Payables turnover = 73 days
Cash conversion cycle = 10.68 days (24.33 + 59.35 – 73)

Calculation of market price of Share of ABC Distributors

EPS = PAT/ No. of shares = ₹ 1,50,000/50,000 = 3.00
Price = (EPS) × (P/E) = (3.00 × 8) = ₹ 24.

Illustrative Problem 7

Following is the Balance Sheet of M/s Bintex Co. Ltd. Banglore, as on 31st December, 2016:

Liabilities	₹	*Assets*	₹
Share Capital:		Land	4,00,000
Authorised, issued and fully		Building	21,00,000
paid up:		Plant and Machinery	1,19,00,000
50,000 9% preference		Furniture and Fittings	1,50,000
shares of ₹ 100 each	50,00,000	Office cars, trucks	1,50,000
5,00,000 equity shares of		Stock	1,50,00,000
₹ 10 each	50,00,000	Accounts receivable	6,00,000
	1,00,00,000	Cash and bank	2,00,000
Capital reserves	5,00,000		
General reserves	10,00,000		
Sinking fund reserves	15,00,000		
7% Debentures	50,00,000		
Bank Overdraft	85,00,000		
Notes payable	15,00,000		
Account payable	25,00,000		
	3,05,00,000		3,05,00,000

Compute the following from the above balance sheet:

1. Net worth
2. Total value of equity
3. Shareholders reserves
4. Total fixed assets
5. Total current assets
6. Working capital
7. Long-term liabilities

(Show the workings, where necessary)

Solution:

1. Net Worth

This represents the net assets of the company. It is also equivalent to proprietors' fund, viz., paid up capital plus reserves. This can be obtained by calculating both ways Assets Approach and Liabilities Approach as given below:

		₹	₹
(*a*)	Gross assets as per balance sheet		3,05,00,000
	Less: Liabilities:		
	7% Debentures	50,00,000	
	Bank overdraft	85,00,000	
	Notes payable	15,00,000	
	Accounts payable	25,00,000	
			1,75,00,000
	Net worth		1,30,00,000

Alternatively

(*a*)	Paid up capital		
	Preference share capital	50,00,000	
	Equity share capital	50,00,000	
			1,00,00,000
	Reserves:		
	Capital reserve	5,00,000	
	General reserve	10,00,000	
	Sinking fund reserve	15,00,000	
			30,00,000
	Net worth		1,30,00,000

2. Total Value of Equity

This can be obtained by adding up Equity Paid up Capital with reserves and surpluses belonging to equity shareholders. Alternatively the same can be obtained by subtracting from net worth of the company what is due to preferences shareholders:

		₹
	Net worth as calculated under 1(*a*) above	1,30,00,000
Less:	Preference share capital	50,00,000
	Total value of equity	80,00,000

3. Shareholder's reserves:

Capital reserve		5,00,000
General reserve		10,00,000
Sinking fund reserve		15,00,000
	Total	30,00,000

		₹
4. Total fixed assets:		
Land		4,00,000
Building		21,00,000
Plant and Machinery		1,19,00,000
Furniture and Fittings		1,50,000
Office cars and Trucks		1,50,000
	Total	1,47,00,000

		₹
5. Total current assets:		
Stock		1,50,00,000
Account receivable		6,00,000
Cash at bank		2,00,000
	Total	1,58,00,000

6. Working capital

This represents excess of current assets over current liabilities :

		₹	
	Current assets as calculated under (5)		1,58,00,000
Less:	Current liabilities:	₹	
	Bank Overdraft	85,00,000	
	Notes payable	15,00,000	
	Accounts payable	25,00,000	1,25,00,000
	Working Capital		33,00,000

7. Long-term liabilities

7% debentures	50,00,000
	50,00,000

Illustrative Problem 8

Calculate and comment on the rate of return on total assets from the following data of two companies:

	Go Slow Co.	*Go. Fast Co.*
	₹	₹
Sales		2,52,75,000
Total assets	42,50,000	
Net profit in sales	6%	4%
Turnover of assets	6 times	6 times
Gross margin	20,68,000	12%

Solution:

	₹	₹
Sales	42,50,000 × 6 = 2,55,00,000	2,52,75,000
Total assets	₹ 42,50,000	2,52,75,000 ÷ 6 = 42,12,500
Net profit in sales		

	6% of 2,55,00,000	4% of 2,52,75,000
	= ₹ 15,30,000	= ₹ 10,11,000
Rate of return on total assets	$\frac{₹ 15,30,000}{42,50,000}$	$\frac{₹ 10,11,000}{42,12,500}$
	= 36%	= 24%

The rate of return on total assets in respect of Go Fast Co. is less than that of Go Slow Co. as the total assets are same (approx.) in both the Companies. Net profit in sales in Go Fast Co. is 2nd/3rd of net profit of Go Slow Co. and similar is the case of rate of return on total assets.

Illustrative Problem 9

The following are the ratios relating to the activities of National Traders Ltd.:

Debtors Velocity	3 months
Stock velocity	8 months
Creditors velocity	2 months
Gross profit ratio	25%

Gross profit for the current year ended 31 December amounted to ₹ 4,00,000. Closing stock of the year is ₹ 10,000 above the opening stock. Bills Receivables amount to ₹ 25,000 and bills payable to ₹ 10,000. Find out:

(*a*) Sales
(*b*) Sundry debtors
(*c*) Closing stock
(*d*) Sundry creditors.

Solution:

(*a*) Determination of sales:

$$\text{Gross profit ratio} = \frac{\text{Gross profit}}{\text{Sales}} \times 100$$

$$25 = \frac{4,00,000}{\text{Sales}} \times 100$$

$$\text{Sales} = \frac{4,00,000}{25} \times 100 = ₹\ 16,00,000$$

(*b*) Determination of sundry debtors:

Debtors velocity is 3 months. In other words, debtors collection period is 3 months, or debtors turnover ratio is 4. Assuming all sales to be credit sales and debtors turnover ratio being calculated on the basis of the year-end figures, debtors would be determined as follows:

$$\text{Debtors turnover ratio} = \frac{\text{Credit sales}}{\text{Closing debtors} + \text{Bills receivable}}$$

or

$$\text{Closing debtors} + \text{Bills receivables} = \frac{\text{Credit sales}}{\text{Debtors turnover ratio}}$$

$$= \frac{16,00,000}{4}$$

= ₹ 4,00,000

Closing debtors = 4,00,000 – 25,000

= ₹ 3,75,000

(*c*) Determination of closing stock:

Stock velocity of 8 months signifies that the turnover is 8 months. In other words, stock turnover ratio is 1.5 = (12 months ÷ 8).

$$\text{Stock turnover} = \frac{\text{Cost of goods sold (Sales - Gross Profit)}}{\text{Average stock}}$$

$$\text{Average stock} = \frac{12,00,000}{1.5} = ₹\ 8,00,000$$

Closing Stock – Opening stock = ₹ 10,000 (1)

$$\frac{\text{Closing stock + Opening stock}}{2} = ₹\ 8,00,000 \quad (2)$$

or

Closing stock + Opening stock = 16,00,000 (3)

Subtracting equation (1) from equation (3) (*i.e.*, 16,00,000 – 10,000) = ₹ 15,90,000

	₹
Opening stock	7,95,000
Closing stock	8,05,000

(*d*) Determination of sundry creditors:

Credit velocity of 2 months signifies that the credit payment period is 2 months. In other words, creditors turnover ratio is 6 (12 months ÷ 2). Assuming all purchases to be credit purchases and creditors turnover is based on year-end figures, we have:

$$\text{Creditors turnover ratio} = \frac{\text{Credit purchases}}{\text{Creditors + Bills payable}}$$

$$6 = \frac{12,10,000}{\text{Creditors} + 10,000}$$

$$\text{Creditors} + 10,000 = \frac{12,10,000}{6} = ₹\ 2,01,667$$

Creditors = 2,01,667 – 10,000 = 1,91,667

Credit purchases are calculated as follows:

Cost of goods sold = Opening stock + Purchases – Closing stock

₹ 12,00,000 = ₹ 7,95,000 + Purchases – 8,05,000

₹ 12,00,000 + 10,000 = Purchases

₹ 12,10,000 = Purchases (credit)

Illustrative Problem 10

The capital of E. Co. Ltd., is as follows:

	(₹)
9% Preference shares of ₹ 10 each	3,00,000
Equity shares of ₹ 10 each	8,00,000
	11,00,000

The accountant has ascertained the following information:

Profit (after tax at 60%) ₹ 2,70,000 : Depreciation ₹ 60,000; Equity dividend paid 20%: market price of equity shares ₹ 40. You are required to state the following, showing the necessary workings:

(*a*) Dividend yield on the equity shares

(*b*) Cover for the preference and equity dividends

(*c*) Earnings for equity shares

(*d*) Price-earnings ratio

Solution:

(*a*) Dividend yield on the equity shares:

$$= \frac{\text{Dividend per share}}{\text{Market price per share}} \times 100$$

$$= \frac{₹\ 2\ (20\%\text{ of }₹\ 10) \times 100}{₹\ 40} \times 100 = 5\%$$

(*b*) Dividend coverage ratio:

(*i*) Preference $= \dfrac{\text{Profits after taxes}}{\text{Dividend payable to preference shareholders}}$

$$= \frac{₹\ 2,70,000}{₹\ 27,000\ (9\%\text{ of }₹\ 3,00,000)} = 10\text{ times}$$

(*ii*) Equity $= \dfrac{\text{Profits after taxes} - \text{Preference share dividends}}{\text{Dividend payable to equity shareholders at current rate of ₹ 2 per share}}$

$$= \frac{₹\ 2,70,000 - ₹\ 27,000}{₹\ 1,60,000\ (80,000\text{ shares} \times ₹\ 2)}$$

$$= \frac{₹\ 2,43,000}{₹\ 1,60,000} = 1.52\text{ times}$$

(*c*) Earnings for equity Shares:

$$= \frac{\text{Earnings available to equity shareholders}}{\text{Number of the equity share outstanding}}$$

$$= \frac{₹\ 2,43,000}{₹\ 80,000} = ₹\ 3.04\text{ per share}$$

(*d*) Price-earning (P/E) Ratio:

$$\text{P/E Ratio} = \frac{\text{Market price per share}}{\text{Earnings per share}}$$

$$= \frac{₹ 40.00}{₹ 3.04} = 13.2 \text{ times}$$

Illustrative Problem 11

With the help of the following ratios regarding ABC Company, draw the Balance Sheet of the Company for the year 2016:

Current Ratio	2.5
Liquidity Ratio	1.5
Net Working Capital	₹ 3,00,000
Stock Turnover Ratio (cost of sales/closing stock)	6 times
Gross Profit Ratio	20 per cent
Fixed Assets Turnover Ratio (on cost of sales)	2 times
Debt Collection Period	2 months
Fixed assets to shareholders net worth	0.80
Reserve and surplus to capital	0.50

Solution:

Balance Sheet as on...

Liabilities	₹	*Assets*	₹
Share capital	5,00,000	Fixed Assets	6,00,000
Reserve and surplus	2,50,000	Stocks	2,00,000
Long-term borrowings		Debtors	2,50,000
(balancing figure)	1,50,000	Bank	50,000
Current liabilities	2,00,000		
	11,00,000		11,00,000

Working Notes:

	₹
If Current Liabilities	= 1
Current Assets	= 2.5
It means the difference or working capital	= 1.5
Working Capital is 1.5	= ₹ 3,00,000
Therefore, Current Assets	= ₹ 5,00,000
Current Liabilities	= ₹ 2,00,000
Therefore, the Liquid Assets	
(Bank and debtors (2,00,000 × 1.5)	= 3,00,000
Stock (5,00,000 – 3,00,000, *i.e.*, Current Assets – Liquid Assets)	= 2,00,000
Cost of sales (as stock turnover ratio is 6)	= 12,00,000
Sales as G/P ratio is 20 per cent, 12,00,000 + 20/80 × 12,00,000)	= 15,00,000
Fixed Assets are ₹ 12,00,000/2 since Fixed Assets turnover is ratio 2	= 6,00,000
Debtors are ₹ 15,00,000/ 6 since debt collection period is 2 months	= 2,50,000

Shareholders Net Worth $\left(\dfrac{6,00,000 \times 1}{0.80}\right)$ = 7,50,000

Out of Shareholders net worth, reserves and surplus = 2,50,000

Therefore, share capital = 5,00,000

Illustrative Problem 12

With the following ratios and further information given below prepare a Trading Account, Profit and Loss Account and Balance Sheet of Shri Narain:

(i)	Gross Profit Ratio	25 per cent
(ii)	Net Profit/Sales	20 per cent
(iii)	Stock-turnover ratio	10
(iv)	Net Profit to Capital	1/5
(v)	Capital to Total Liabilities	1/2
(vi)	Fixed Assets/Capital	5/4
(vii)	Fixed Assets/Total Current Assets	5/7
(viii)	Fixed Assets	₹ 10,00,000
(ix)	Closing Stock	₹ 1,00,000

Solution:

Trading and Profit and Loss Account for the year ended...

	₹		₹
To Opening stock	20,000	By Sales	8,00,000
To Purchases (balancing figure)	6,80,000	By Closing Stock	1,00,000
To Gross Profit c/d	2,00,000		
	9,00,000		9,00,000
To Expenses	40,000	By Gross Profit b/d	2,00,000
To Net Profit	1,60,000		
	2,00,000		2,00,000

Balance Sheet as on...

Capital	₹	*Assets*	₹
		Fixed Assets	10,00,000
Opening Balance	6,40,000	Closing Stock	1,00,000
Add: Net Profit	1,60,000	Other Current Assets	13,00,000
	8,00,000	(Balancing figure)	
Liabilities	16,00,000		
	24,00,000		24,00,000

Working Notes:

1. Fixed Assets are ₹ 10,00,000

$$\frac{\text{Fixed Assets}}{\text{Capital}} = \frac{5}{4}$$

$$\text{Capital} = \frac{10,00,000}{5} \times 4 = ₹\ 8,00,000$$

2. Capital is 1/2 of total liabilities
Liabilities = 8,00,000 × 2 = ₹ 16,00,000
3. Net Profit is 1/5 of Capital
Net Profit = 8,00,000 × 1/5 = ₹ 1,60,000
4. Net Profit is 20 per cent of sales
Sales = 1,60,000 × 100/20 = ₹ 8,00,000
5. Gross Profit Ratio is 25 per cent of Sales
Gross Profit = ₹ 2,00,000.
6. Stock Turnover Ratio (*i.e.*, Cost of States/Average Inventory) is 10
Cost of Sales = Sales – Gross Profit
= ₹ 8,00,000 – 2,00,000
= ₹ 6,00,000
Average Inventory is ₹ 60,000.
7. Closing Stock is ₹ 1,00,000
Average Inventory is ₹ 60,000
Opening Stock is ₹ 20,000.
8. Fixed Assets are ₹ 10,00,000
Fixed Assets/Total Current Assets = 5/7
Total Current Assets are 10,00,000 × 7/5
= ₹ 14,00,000
Stock is ₹ 1,00,000
Other Current Assets are ₹ 13,00,000

Illustrative Problem 13

The following balances are extracted from the account of RKD Ltd. in respect of the accounting year ended on 31st March, 2016:

(Fig. in ₹)

Sales (2015-16)	1,00,00,000
Fixed Assets (31.3.2016)	25,00,000
Bank overdraft (31.3.2016)	2,50,000
Long-term debt (31.3.2016)	15,00,000
Equity shares (₹ 10 each) (31.3.2016)	5,00,000
Reserves and surplus (31.3.2016)	25,00,000

Forecasts for 2016-17:

(*i*) Sales will increase by 20%. They will spread evenly throughout the year. There will be no further increase in sales in the following year.

(*ii*) Year-end cash balance should be a minimum of 4% of annual sales.

(*iii*) Inventory Turnover – 8 times.

(*iv*) Additional capital expenditure will equal depreciation.

(*v*) Sundry creditors – 1 month's purchase.

(*vi*) Upper limit of bank borrowings – ₹ 10,00,000.

(*vii*) Accruals – 3% of sales.

(*viii*) Gross margin – 40% of sales.

(*ix*) Net profit margin (after tax) – 8% of sales.

(*x*) Average collection period – 2 months.

(*xi*) Income tax – 40%.

(*xii*) Redemption of long-term debt at the end of the year – ₹ 3,75,000.

(*xiii*) Purchases – 50% of the cost of goods sold.

From the above information, prepare a proforma profit and loss account for the year ended 31 March, 2013 and a proforma balance sheet as on that date. All relevant workings are to be shown.

Solution:

Proforma Profit & Loss Account
for the Year Ended 31 March 2017

(₹)

Sales (₹ 1,00,00,000 × 1.20)	1,20,00,000
Less: Cost of goods sold (60%)	72,00,000
Gross Profit (40%)	48,00,000
Less: Expenses [4]	32,00,000
Profit before tax (PBT)	16,00,000
Less: Tax (40%) [5]	6,40,000
Net Profit (8% of ₹ 1,20,00,000)	9,60,000

Proforma Balance Sheet as on 31 March, 2017

	₹		₹
Equity shares (₹ 10)	5,00,000	Fixed Assets (net)	25,00,000
Reserves and Surplus		Current Assets:	
₹ (25,00,000 + 9,60,000)	34,60,000	Inventory [3]	9,00,000
		Debtors [2]	20,00,000
		Cash	4,80,000
		(40%) of ₹ 1,20,00,000)	
Long-term debt			
₹ (15,00,000 – 3,75,000)	11,25,000		
Accruals (3% of sales)	3 60 000		
Sundry creditors [1]	3,00,000		
Bank overdraft (balancing)	1,35,000		
	58,80,000		58,80,000

Working Notes:

(1) (50% of CGS) × 1/12 = 36,00,000/12 = ₹ 3,00,000

(2) ₹ (120,00,000 × 2)/12 = ₹ 20,00,000

(3) ₹ 72,00,000/8 = ₹ 9,00,000

(4) Expenses = GP – tax – after tax profit = ₹ 48,00,000 – ₹ 640,000 – ₹ 960,000 = ₹ 32,00,000

(5) Tax = (After – tax profit / 0.6) × 0.4 = ₹ 6,40,000.

Illustrative Problem 14

The following information relating to a company for the year ended 31.3.2016 are given:

Credit sales for the year	:	₹ 96 lakhs	Current Ratio	:	1.8
Net Working Capital	:	₹ 12 lakhs	Quick Ratio	:	0.8
Fixed Assets turnover	:	2	Reserves to Capital	:	1:5
Average collection period for credit sales	:	One month			

Prepare the Balance Sheet of the company from the above data:

Solution:

The details required for the Balance Sheet are worked out as follows:

(*i*) $\text{Fixed Asset Turnover} = \frac{\text{Sales}}{\text{Fixed Asset}} = \frac{96}{\text{Fixed Asset}} = 2$

∴ Fixed Asset = ₹ 48 lakhs

(*ii*) Net Working Capital = ₹ 12 lakhs

∴ Current Assets – Current Liabilities = 12

$\text{But Current Ratio} = \frac{\text{Current Assets}}{\text{Current Liabilities}} = 1.8$

= 1.8 Current Liabilities – Current liabilities = 12

$\therefore \text{Current Liabilities} = \frac{12}{0.8} = ₹\ 15 \text{ lakhs}$

Current Assets = 1.8 × Current Liabilities = 1.8 × 15 = ₹ 27 lakhs

(*iii*) $\frac{\text{Current Asset} - \text{Stock}}{\text{Current Liabilities}} = \frac{27 - \text{Stock}}{15} = \text{Quick Ratio} = 0.8$

∴ Stock = 27 – 12 = ₹ 15 Lakhs

(*iv*) $\text{Average Collection Period} = \frac{\text{Average Debtors}}{\text{Average Credit Sales p.m.}} = \frac{\text{Debtors}}{\frac{96}{12}} = 1$

Debtors = ₹ 8 lakhs

(*v*) Total Assets = Fixed Assets + Current Assets = 48 + 27 = ₹ 75 lakhs

Capital + Reserves = Total Assets – Current Liabilities

= 75 – 15 = ₹ 60 lakhs

But, Reserves = $\frac{1}{5}$ Capital

$\therefore$ Capital + $\frac{1}{5}$ Capital = 60 $\therefore$ Capital = $\frac{60}{\frac{6}{5}}$ = ₹ 50 lakh

Hence, Reserves = $\frac{1}{5}$ × Capital = ₹ 10 lakhs

Balance Sheet of the Company as at 31.3.2016

Capital & Liabilities	*Amount ₹ in lakhs*	*Assets*		*Amount ₹ in lakhs*
Capital	50	Fixed Assets		48
Reserves	10	Current Assets:		
Current Liabilities	15	Stock	15	
		Debtors	8	
		Cash & Bank Balance	4	27
	75			75

Illustrative Problem 15

With the help of the following information, complete the Balance Sheet of XYZ Ltd.:

Equity ₹ 1,00,000

The relevant ratios of the firm are as follows:

Current debt to total debt	0.40
Total debt to owners equity	0.60
Fixed assets to owners equity	0.60
Total assets turnover	2 times
Inventory turnover	8 times

Solution:

Balance Sheet

Liabilities	₹	*Assets*	₹
Owners Equity	1,00,000	Fixed Assets	60,000
Current debt	24,000	Cash	60,000
Long term debt	36,000	Inventory	40,000
	1,60,000		1,60,000

Working Notes:

(*i*) Total Debt = 0.60 × Owners equity = 0.60 × ₹ 1,00,000 = ₹ 60,000

(*ii*) Fixed Assets = 0.60 × Owners equity = 0.60 × ₹ 1,00,000 = ₹ 60,000

(*iii*) Total equity = Total debt + Owners' equity = ₹ 60,000 + ₹ 1,00,000 = ₹ 1,60,000

(*iv*) Total Assets consisting of current assets and fixed assets must be equal to ₹ 1,00,000 (Assets = Liability + Owner's equity)

Fixed Assets are ₹ 60,000, therefore, current assets should be ₹ 1,60,000 – ₹ 60,000 = ₹ 1,00,000

(*v*) Sales are found as follows:

Assets Turnover = (Sales ÷ Assets) = 2

= (Sales ₹ 1,60,000) = 2

Sales = ₹ 1,60,000 × 2 = ₹ 3,20,000

(*vi*) Inventories are found as follows:

Inventory Turnover = Sales ÷ Inventory = ₹ 3,20,000 ÷ Inventory = 8

Inventory = ₹ 3,20,000 ÷ 8 = ₹ 40,000

(*vii*) Cash = Current assets – Inventory = ₹ 1,00,000 – 40,000 = 60,000

(*viii*) Current debt = 0.40 × Total debt = 0.40 × ₹ 60,000 = ₹ 24,000

(*ix*) Long term debt = Total debt – Current debt

= ₹ 60,000 – ₹ 24,000

= ₹ 36,000

Illustrative Problem 16

Some selected financial figures for the last three years are given for a company as under:

	Year 1	Year 2	Year 3
GP Ratio	40%	30%	20%
Stock Turnover	20 times	25 times	20 times
Opening Stock (₹)	90,000	1,10,000	1,30,000
Closing Stock (₹)	1,10,000	1,30,000	1,70,000

Administrative Expenses every year amounted to 10% of Sales.

The Income Tax rate is 40%.

You are required to prepare a comparative Statement of Profit for the three years and give your comments for variations in profitability.

Solution:

Computing sales:

Average stock = (Opening stock + Closing stock) ÷ 2

	Year 1	Year 2	Year 3
(*i*) Stock turnover	20 times	25 times	20 times
(*ii*) Average stock	₹ 1,00,000	₹ 1,20,000	₹ 1,50,000
(*iii*) Cost of goods sold (Stock turnover × Av. stock)	₹ 20,00,000	₹ 30,00,000	₹ 30,00,000
Sales	$= \frac{₹ 20L \times 100}{60}$	$= \frac{₹ 30L \times 100}{70}$	$= \frac{₹ 30L \times 100}{80}$
	₹ 33,33,333	₹ 42,85,714	₹ 37,50,000

L = Lakhs

Statement of Profitability

(₹ in lakhs)

	Year 1 ₹	*Year 2* ₹	*Increase over last year (%)*	*Year 3* ₹	*(Decrease) over last year %*
1. Sales	33.33	42.85	28.5	37.50	(12.5)
2. Cost of goods sold	20.00	30.00	50.0	30.00	—
3. Gross Profit (1 – 2)	13.33	12.85		7.50	
4. Admin. Expenses (10%)	3.33	4.28		3.75	
5. Profit before tax (3 – 4)	10.00	8.57		3.75	
6. Tax @ 40%	4.00	3.43		1.50	
7. Profit after tax (5 – 6)	6.00	5.14		2.25	

Comments:

The performance of the company is deteriorating from bad to worse every year. Although the sales increased in year 2, it has been offset by an increase in cost of goods sold. There has been a decline in sales in year 3 and to make the performance worse, the cost of goods as % of sales has increased further. A thorough study covering all areas of proficiency like Material Usage, Labour Productivity, possibility of revision in sales price of end product, etc. need to be done.

REFERENCES

1. Baruch Lev, Financial Statement Analysis, A New Approach, Prentice Hall, 1974, p. 5.
2. Charles H.G. Gibson, Financial Statement Analysis, South Western Publishing Co., 1992, p. 144.

CRITICAL ANALYSIS AND DISCUSSION QUESTIONS, MULTIPLE CHOICE QUESTIONS, AND PROBLEMS

CRITICAL ANALYSIS AND DISCUSSION QUESTIONS

1. What do you mean by financial statement analysis? What are its purposes?
2. Discuss the importance of financial ratios.
3. Explain the financial ratios:
   (*a*) Liquidity ratios
   (*b*) Profitability ratio
   (*c*) Capital structure ratio
4. In what way market strength ratios are useful to investors?
5. Discuss the computation and significance of the following financial ratios:
   (*a*) Current ratio
   (*b*) Quick ratio
   (*c*) Inventory turnover ratio
   (*d*) Debt-equity ratio
   (*e*) Accounts receivables ratio
   (*f*) Earnings margin
   (*g*) Earnings per share.
6. What are the limitations of accounting ratios?
7. What is meant by horizontal and vertical analysis of financial statement? Explain giving suitable examples.
8. What is asset turnover? What influence does a higher asset turnover tend to have on the rate of return on assets?
9. What is the key question in assessing liquidity? What ratios are used in this regard?
10. What are trend percentages and how are they calculated?
11. Distinguish between horizontal analysis and vertical analysis of financial statements.
12. What are commonsize percentages and how are they used?
13. Discuss the significance of equity ratio and explain how it is computed.
14. What similarities and differences exist in the objectives of investors and creditors in using financial statement analysis?
15. "Net income based on historical financial statements is a useless measurement because it is influenced by so many arbitrary decisions." Examine the rationale of this statement.
16. What are the objectives associated with horizontal and trend analysis of a company's financial statements?
17. Company A and Company B both have net income of ₹ 10,00,000. Is it possible to say that these companies are equally successful? Why or why not?

MULTIPLE CHOICE QUESTIONS

Select the correct answer for the following multiple choice questions.

I. The following data were taken from December 31, 2016 balance sheet of ABC Company:

	(₹)
Cash	1,36,000
Marketable securities	64,000
Accounts and notes receivable, net	1,84,000
Merchandise inventory	2,44,000
Prepaid expenses	12,000
Accounts and notes payable, short-term	2,56,000
Accrued liabilities	64,000
Bonds payable, long term	4,00,000

Based on the above data,

1. The current ratio is:
   (*a*) 1 : 2. (*b*) 2 : 1.
   (*c*) 1.2 : 1. (*d*) 3 : 1.
2. The acid-test ratio is:
   (*a*) 1 : 2. (*b*) 2 : 1.
   (*c*) 1.2 : 1. (*d*) 3 : 1.

II. ABC Company shows the following data on its 2016 financial statements.

	(₹)
Accounts receivable, January 1	7,20,000
Accounts receivable, December 31	9,60,000
Merchandise inventory, January 1	9,00,000
Merchandise inventory, December 31	10,20,000
Gross sales	48,00,000
Sales returns and allowances	1,80,000
Net sales	46,20,000
Cost of goods sold	33,60,000
Income before interest and taxes	7,20,000
Interest on bonds	1,92,000
Net income	3,84,000

Based on the above data

3. The accounts receivable turnover is:
   (*a*) 5.5 times per year (*b*) 5.714 times per year
   (*c*) 5 times per year (*d*) 6.667 times per year
4. The inventory turnover is:
   (*a*) 5 times per year (*b*) 4.8125 times per year
   (*c*) 3.5 times per year (*d*) 4 times per year

5. The times interest earned ratio is:
   (*a*) 4.75 times per year (*b*) 3.75 times per year
   (*c*) 2 times per year (*d*) 3 times per year

Answer to Multiple Choice Questions:

I. 1. (*b*) 2. (*c*) II. 3. (*a*) 4. (*c*) 5. (*b*)

PROBLEMS

1. From the following annual statement of Pioneer Ltd., calculate the following ratios:
   (*a*) Gross Profit Ratio; (*b*) Current Ratio; (*c*) Liquid Ratio; (*d*) Debt-Equity Ratio; and (*e*) Return on Equity Ratio.

Trading and Profit and Loss Account for the Year Ended 31 December 2016

	₹		₹
Materials Consumed:		Sales	85,000
Opening Stock	9,050	Profit on Sale of Investments	600
Purchases	54,525	Interest on Investments	300
	63,575		
Closing Stock	14,000		
	49,575		
Carriage Inwards	1,425		
Office Expenses	15,000		
Sales Expenses	3,000		
Financial Expenses	1,500		
Loss on Sale of Assets	400		
Net Profit	15,000		
	85,900		85,900

Balance Sheet as on 31 December 2016

	₹	₹		₹	₹
Share Capital:			Fixed Assets:		
2,000 Equity Shares of ` 10 each		20,000	Buildings	15,000	
Reserves		9,000	Plant	8,000	23,000
Profit and Loss Account		6,000	Current Assets:		
Bank overdraft		3,000	Stock in trade	14,000	
Sundry creditors:			Debtors	7,000	
For expenses	2,000		Bills Receivable	1,000	
For others	8,000	10,000	Bank	3,000	25,000
		48,000			48,000

Answer:

(*a*) Gross Profit Ratio. 40%; (*b*) Current Ratio - 1.92 : 1; (*c*) Liquid ratio 1.1 : 1 Bank overdraft has not been taken as a current liability; (*d*) Debt-Equity Ratio:

(*i*) $\frac{\text{All Debts}}{\text{Equity}} = 0.371:1$

(*ii*) $\frac{\text{All Debts}}{\text{All Debts} + \text{Equity}} = 0.271:1$

(*e*) Return on Investment Ratio: $= \frac{\text{Net Profit}}{\text{Capital Employed}}$

$\frac{15{,}000}{35{,}000} = 42.85\%$

2. Following is the Profit and Loss Account and balance sheet of A Limited for the year ended 31 December, 2016 and balance sheet as on that date. Calculate the different ratios and comment on the financial position of the company.

Profit and Loss Account
for the year ended 31 December, 2016

	₹	₹
Net sales		3,00,000
Less: Cost of Goods sold		2,58,000
Gross Profit		42,000
Operating Expenses:		
Selling	2,200	
General and administration	4,000	
Rent of Office	2,800	
		9,000
Gross Operating profit		33,000
Depreciation		10,000
		23,000
Other Income:		
Interest on Government Securities		1,500
Gross Income		24,500
Other Expenses:		
Interest on bank overdraft	300	
Interest on debentures	4,200	4,500
Net Income before Tax		20,000
Tax @ 50 per cent on net Income		10,000
Net Income after Tax		10,000

Balance Sheet as on 31 December, 2016

Liabilities	₹	*Assets*	₹	₹
Sundry Creditors	6,000	Cash		5,000
Bills Payable	10,000	Investments (Govt. Securities)		15,000
Outstanding Expenses	1,000	Sundry Debtors		20,000
Provision for Taxation	13,000	Stock		30,000
Total Current Liabilities	30,000	Total current Assets		70,000
6 per cent Mortgage Debentures	70,000	Fixed Assets	1,80,000	
7 per cent preference shares	10,000	*Less:* Provision for depr.	50,000	
Equity Shares	50,000			1,30,000
Reserve and surplus	40,000			
Total Claim on Assets	2,00,000			2,00,000

Answer:

Gross Profit Ratio 14 per cent, Net Profit Ratio (after considering interest on bank overdraft), 7.56 per cent, ROI 13.53 per cent, stock turnover Ratio 8.6. Debt Collection Period 24 days. Fixed Assets Turnover 2.3, Fixed Assets Ratio 7.6, Debt-equity Ratio 70/100 = .7, Current ratio 2.3)

3. Following is the balance sheet of C Ltd. as on 31st December, 2016

Liabilities		₹	*Assets*	₹
Equity Share Capital		20,000	Goodwill	12,000
Capital reserve		4,000	Fixed Assets	28,000
8% Loan on mortgage		16,000	Stocks	6,000
Trade creditors		8,000	Debtors	6,000
Bank overdraft		2,000	Investments	2,000
Taxation: Current		2,000	Bank	6,000
Future		2,000		
Profit and loss A/c:				
Profit for 2016 after taxation and interest on fixed deposits				
	12,000			
Less: Transfer to Reserve	4,000			
Dividend	2,000	6,000		
		60,000		60,000

Sales amounted to ₹ 1,20,000

Calculate ratio for:

(*i*) Testing liquidity

(*ii*) Testing solvency

(*iii*) Testing profitability

(*iv*) Testing capital gearing and

(*v*) Comment on the significance thereof.

4. From the following particulars extracted from the financial statements of Sun and Co. Ltd. Compute: (*a*) Current Ratio; (*b*) Acid Test Ratio; (*c*) Stock Turnover Ratio; (*d*) Debtors Turnover Ratio; and (*e*) Creditors Turnover Ratio for the two years 2015 and 2016 independently and comment on the liquidity position of the company:

	2015 ₹	2016 ₹
Opening Stock	47,000	53,000
Closing Stock	53,000	67,000
Sales less returns	2,52,000	3,65,000
Provision for bad debts	2,000	3,000
Sundry creditors	32,000	35,000
Purchases	1,80,000	1,90,000
Sundry debtors	42,000	63,000
Cash	10,000	15,000
Bank	8,000	10,000
Bills Receivable	15,000	20,000
Bills Payable	29,000	30,000
Marketable Securities	8,000	8,000

5. A Ltd. and B. Ltd. produce and sell the same product but under different brand names. Their profit and loss statements and Balance Sheets are given below for the year ending 2016

Profit and Loss Statement

(*Fig. in ₹ lakhs*)

			A. Ltd.	*B. Ltd.*
	Sales		25.00	30.00
Less:	Costs:	Materials	4.00	2.00
		Labour	2.00	7.00
	Overheads:	Fixed	9.00	2.00
		Variable	2.00	9.00
	Total Cost		17.00	20.00
	Gross Margin		8.00	10.00
	Interest		2.00	4.00
	Profit before taxes		6.00	6.00
	Taxes		3.00	3.00
	Profit after taxes		3.00	3.00
	Dividends declared		2.00	2.00
	Retained earnings		1.00	1.00

Balance Sheet

(Fig. in ₹ Lakhs)

	A Ltd. ₹	B. Ltd. ₹
A. Capital and Liabilities:		
1. Equity Capital	10.00	20.00
2. Debenture Capital	8.00	20.00
3. Creditors	5.00	17.00
4. Reserves	17.00	5.00
	40.00	60.00
B. Assets:		
1. Plant and Machinery	8.00	34.00
2. Buildings	6.00	16.00
3. Inventories	18.00	2.00
4. Debtors	7.00	1.00
5. Cash	1.00	7.00
	40.00	60.00

Required:

Evaluate the performance of two organizations for the current year and assess the expected problem by using the relevant ratios.

6. A condensed balance sheet and other financial data for Alpha Company appear below.

Alpha Company
Balance Sheet
December 31, 2016

	(₹)
Assets:	
Current Assets	100,000
Plant Assets	150,000
Total Assets	250,000
Liabilities and Equity:	
Current Liabilities	100,000
Long-term Liabilities	75,000
Total Liabilities	175,000
Common Equity	75,000
Total Liabilities and Equity	250,000

Income Statement Data

	₹
Net Sales	375,000
Interest Expense	4,000
Net Income	22,500

The following account balances existed at December 31, 2015: Total Assets, ₹ 200,000; Equity, ₹ 65,000. The tax rate is 35 percent.

Industry norms as of December 31, 2016 were:

Debt-equity ratio	1.75
Profit margin	0.12
Return on total Assets	0.15
Return on stockholder's equity	0.30
Total asset turnover	1.71

Calculate and evaluate the following ratios for Alpha Company as of December 31, 2016:

(*a*) Debt-equity ratio

(*b*) Profit margin

(*c*) Return on total assets

(*d*) Return on stockholders' equity

(*e*) Total asset turnover

7. Here are the income statements and balance sheet of A Company and B Company, taken from their annual reports for the year ended December 31, 2016.

Income Statement
for the Year 2016

	A Company ₹	*B Company* ₹
Sales	80,00,000	70,00,000
Cost of goods sold	60,00,000	47,00,000
Selling, general, and administrative expenses	12,00,000	19,00,000
Interest on debt	—	70,000
Income before taxes	8,00,000	3,30,000
Income taxes	3,90,000	1,60,000
Net income	4,10,000	1,70,000
Dividends declared	1,00,000	70,000

Condensed Balance Sheets
as of December 31, 2016

	A Company ₹	*B Company* ₹
Assets		
Cash	3,00,000	3,00,000
Accounts receivable	8,00,000	6,50,000
Inventory	13,00,000	8,50,000
Net plant and equipment	21,00,000	15,00,000
Total Assets	45,00,000	33,00,000

Liabilities and Equity		
	₹	₹
Accounts payable	7,10,000	4,00,000
Taxes payable	3,90,000	1,60,000
Long-term debt	—	14,00,000
Common equity	22,00,000	8,00,000
Retained earnings	12,00,000	5,40,000
Total liabilities and equity	45,00,000	33,00,000

On the basis of the available information, which do you consider to be (*i*) more liquid? (*ii*) more solvent? (*iii*) more profitable? Explain your conclusions.

8. The following summaries are prepared for you by the accountant of Adarsh Products Limited from the Balance Sheet of the Company as at 31st December, 2016

	31.12.2016	***Previous Year***
	₹	₹
Share Capital		
Equity Shares of ₹ 100 each	4,00,000	3,50,000
Reserves and Surplus:		
Premium on Shares	20,000	20,000
General Reserve	70,000	50,000
Surplus in Profit and Loss Account	12,500	7,500
Shareholders Funds	5,02,500	4,27,500
Current Assets:		
Stock-in-trade	1,70,500	81,400
Sundry Debtors	1,42,700	85,600
Cash	45,900	27,300
Current Liabilities:		
Creditors	1,97,700	45,400
Proposed Dividend	20,000	12,000
Provision for Taxation	27,000	10,000
	2,44,700	67,400
Fixed Assets (at cost)	4,70,000	3,71,100
Less: Depreciation	81,900	70,500
	3,88,100	3,00,600

The following additional information is available from company's books.

(*i*) The profit for the year was ₹ 46,000.

(*ii*) Income-tax ₹ 9,000 was paid during the year in respect of the previous year and the balance was transferred to general reserve account.

(*iii*) The proposed dividend for the year 2011 was duly paid.

You are required to prepare a statement showing (1) Current Ratio (2) Liquid Ratio and (3) Return on Proprietor's funds together with other comments.

9. From the following information you are required to prepare a Balance Sheet:

1. Current Ratio — 1.75
2. Liquid Ratio — 1.25
3. Stock Turnover Ratio (cost of sales/ closing stock) — 9
4. Gross Profit Ratio — 25 per cent
5. Debt Collection Period — 1½ months
6. Reserves and surplus to capital — 2
7. Turnover to fixed assets — 1.2
8. Capital gearing Ratio — 0.6
9. Fixed Assets to net worth — 1.25
10. Sales for the year ₹ 12,00,000.

Answer:

Liabilities	₹	*Assets*	₹
Share Capital	5,00,000	Fixed Assets	7,50,000
Long-term liabilities	3,00,000	Stock	1,00,000
Reserves and Surplus	1,00,000	Debtors	1,50,000
Current Liabilities	2,00,000	Cash and Bank balance	1,00,000
Total	11,00,000	Total	11,00,000

10. ABC Company is the leading retailer and roaster of specialty coffee in North India selling freshly brewed coffee, pastries, and coffee beans. Data from the company's financial statements are as follows:

ABC Company Comparative Balance Sheet
(₹ in lakhs)

	End of Year	*Beginning of Year*
Assets		
Current assets:		
Cash	₹ 2,810	₹ 3,130
Marketable securities	1,570	1,410
Accounts receivable	2,880	2,240
Inventories	6,920	6,360
Other current assets	2,780	2,160
Total current assets	1,69,60	1,53,00
Property and equipment, net	2,89,00	2,28,80
Other assets	7,580	6,110
Total assets	₹ 5,34,40	₹ 4,42,90
Liabilities and Shareholders Equity		
Current liabilities:		
Accounts payable	₹ 39,910	₹ 3,410
Short-term bank loans	7,100	7,000
Accrued payables	7,570	6,620

Other current liabilities	2,980	2,330
Total current liabilities	2,15,60	1,93,60
Long-term liabilities	9,040	2,650
Total liabilities	3,06,00	2,20,10
Equity		
Preferred equity	00	00
Common equity and additional paid-in capital	400	400
Retained earnings	22,440	21,880
Total shareholders equity	22,840	22,280
Total liabilities and shareholders equity	₹ 53,440	₹ 44,290

Income Statement
(₹ in lakhs)

		Current Year
Sales		₹ 94,110
Cost of goods sold		39,990
Gross margin		54,120
Selling and administrative expenses:		
Store operating expenses		32,160
Other operating expenses		2,940
Depreciation and amortization		4,670
General and administrative expenses		4,890
Total selling and administrative expenses		44,660
Net operating income		9,460
Plus interest and other income		1,100
Interest expense		00
Net income before taxes		10,560
Income taxes (about 37%)		3,840
Net income		₹ 6,720

Required:

1. Compute the return on total assets.
2. Compute the return on common stockholders's equity.
3. Is financial leverage positive or negative? Explain.
4. Compute the current ratio.
5. Compute the acid-text ratio.
6. Compute the inventory turnover.
7. Compute the average sale period.
8. Compute the debt-to-equity ratio.

Answer:

1. Return on total assets:

$$\text{Return on total assets} = \frac{\text{Net income} + [\text{Interest expense} \times (1 - \text{Tax rate})]}{\text{Average total assets}}$$

$$= \frac{₹\,6720 + [₹\,0 \times (1 - 0.36)]}{(₹\,53,440 + ₹\,44,290)/2} = 13.8\% \text{ (rounded)}$$

2. Return on common equity:

$$\text{Return on common equity} = \frac{\text{Net income} - \text{Preferred dividends}}{\text{Average common equity}}$$

$$= \frac{₹\,6720 - ₹\,0}{(₹\,22840 + ₹\,22,280)/2} = 29.8\% \text{ (rounded)}$$

3. The company has positive financial leverage because the return on common equity of 29.8% is greater than the return on total assets of 13.8%. The positive financial leverage was obtained from current and long-term liabilities.

4. Current ratio:

$$\text{Current ratio} = \frac{\text{Current assets}}{\text{Current liabilities}}$$

$$= \frac{₹\,16,960}{₹\,21,560} = 0.79 \text{ (rounded)}$$

5. Acid-test ratio:

Acid-test ratio

$$= \frac{\text{Cash} + \text{Marketable securities} + \text{Accounts receivable} + \text{Short-term notes receivable}}{\text{Current liabilities}}$$

$$= \frac{₹\,2810 + ₹\,1570 + ₹\,2880 + ₹\,0}{₹\,21,560} = 6.02 \text{ (rounded)}$$

6. Inventory turnover:

$$\text{Inventory turnover} = \frac{\text{Cost of goods sold}}{\text{Average inventory balance}}$$

$$= \frac{₹\,39,990}{(₹\,6,920 + ₹\,6,360)/2} = 6.02 \text{ (rounded)}$$

7. Average sale period:

$$\text{Average sale period} = \frac{365 \text{ days}}{\text{Inventory turnover}}$$

$$= \frac{365 \text{ days}}{6.02} = 61 \text{ days (rounded)}$$

8. Debt-to-equity ratio:

$$\text{Debt-to-equity ratio:} = \frac{\text{Total liabilities}}{\text{Shareholders equity}}$$

$$= \frac{₹\,21{,}560 + ₹\,9{,}040}{₹\,22{,}840} = 1.34 \text{ (rounded)}$$

SELECTED BIBLIOGRAPHY

Ahmed Riahi Belkaoui, *The New Foundations of Management Accounting*, New York: Quorum Books, 1992.

Ahmed Belkaoui, *Cost Accounting, A Multi Dimensional Emphasis*, New York: The Dryden Press, 1983.

Ahmed Belkaoui, *Advanced Management Accounting*, Quorum Books, 2000.

Albie Brooks, Judy Oliver and Gillian Vesty, *Contemporary Management Accounting,* John Wiley and Sons Australia Ltd, 2005.

Anthony A. Atkonson, Robert S. Kaplan, Ella Mae Matsumura, S. Mark Young, G. Arun Kumar, *Management Accounting,* 5th Edition, Pearson, Delhi, 2009.

Anthony A. At Kinson, Rajiv D-Banker, Robert S. Kaplan and S. Mark Young, *Management Accounting*, Prentice Hall International, New Jersey, 1997.

Arnold Schneider and Harold M. Sollenbarger, *Managerial Accounting*, South Western Publishing Co., 2001.

Bob Ryan and John Hobos, *Management Accounting*, London: Pitman, 1985.

Brenda M. Mallouk, Gary Spraak a man, Ceuly A. Raiborn, Jesse T. Barfield, Michael R. Kinney, *Managerial Accounting,* IInd Canadian Edition, 2007.

Brian Plowman, *Activity-based Management*, Gower, 2001.

Carl L. Moore, Robert Jaedicke and Lane K. Anderson, *Managerial Accounting*, Cincinnati: South Western Publishing Co., 1984.

Carl S. Warren and Philip E. Fess, *Principles of Financial and Management Accounting*, Cincinnati: South Western Publishing Co., 1992.

Charles T. Horngreen and Garry L. Sundem and William O. Stratton *Introduction to Management Accounting*, New Delhi, Prentice Hall of India Ltd., 2006.

Charles T. Horngreen, Srikant M. Dattar and George Faster, *Cost Accounting, A Managerial Emphasis*, Pearson Education, New Delhi, 2008.

Cheryls McWatters, Dale C. Morse and Jerold L. Zimmerman, *Management Accounting*, McGraw Hill Irwin, Boston, 2001.

Colin Drury, *Management and Cost Accounting*, Thomas Learning, 2001.

Colin Drury (Ed.), *Management Accounting Handbook, The Chartered Institute of Management Accountants*, Butter Worth, 1996.

Cyril Tomkins, *Financial Planning in Divisionalised Companies*, 1973, Basil Blackwell, 1973.

Cyril Tomkins. *Corporate Resource Allocation*, Basil Blackwell, 1991.

David Benjamin and Colin Biggs, *Management Accounting Techniques*, CIMA, UK.

David Fanning, *Handbook of Management Accounting, Gower*, 1983.

David Solomons, *Divisional Performance: Measurement and Control*, New York: FERF, 1965.

Don R. Hansen and Maryanne. M. Mowen, *Management Accounting*, Thomson South Western, 2005.

Don T. Decoster, Eldon S. Schaer and Mary T. Ziebell, *Management Accounting, A Decision Emphasis*, New York: John Wily and Sons, 1982.

D.S.J. Remenyi, *Strategic Information Systems, Development, Implementation*, Case Studies, NCC Blackwell, 1990.

Edward B. Deakin and Michael W. Maher, *Cost Accounting*, Homeward: Richard D. Irwin, 1984.

Edward J. Blocher *et al.,* Cost Management, McGraw Hill Education, 2006.

Edwin H. Caplan, *Management Accounting and Behavioural Science*, 1971.

Emerson O. Henke and Chartene W. Spoede, *Cost Accounting: Managerial Use of Accounting Data*, Bostin: PWS Kent Publishing Co. 1991.

Erich A. Hedfert, *Techniques of Financial Analysis*, Homewood: Irwin, 1991.

Gary Cokins, Activity-Based Cost Management, McGraw Hill Education, 2004.

Gorden Shilling Law, *Managerial Cost Accounting*, Homewood: Richard D. Irwin, 1982.

Graham Mott. *Management Accounting for Decision Makers*, London: Pitman, 1991.

Henry R. Anderson, Belverd Needless, Jr. and James C. Caldwell, *Managerial Accounting*, Boston: Houghton Mifflin Co., 1989.

Hugh Coombs, David Hobbs and Ellis Jenkins, Management Accounting, Sage Publications, 2005.

Jack Grey and Don Ricketts, *Cost and Managerial Accounting*, New York: McGraw Hill International Book Co., 1982.

Jack L. Smith, Robert M. Keith and William L. Stephens, *Managerial Accounting, New York*: McGraw Hill Book Co. 1992.

James H. Rossel, William W Frisure, Donald H. Taylor, *Management Accounting, An Introduction*, Columbus: Charles E. Merril Publishing Co. 1980.

James Jiambalvo, *Managerial Accounting*, John Wiley and Sons, New York, 2001.

James T. Mackey and Michael F. Thomas, *Management Accounting, A Road of Discovery*, South Western College Publishing, 2000.

Jarold L. Zimmerman, *Accounting for Decision Making and Control* Fifth Edition, McGraw Hill, Irwin, 2006.

Jerry J. Weygandt, Paul D. Kimmel and Donald E. Kiesco, *Managerial Accounting,* Sixth Edition, John Wiley and Sons, 2012.

Jesset T. Barfield, Cecily A. Baiborn and Michael R. Kinney, *Cost Accounting*, Thomson, 2003.

John Arnold and Tony Hope, *Accounting for Management Decisions*, Prentice Hall, 1990.

John Deardon, *Management Accounting,* Text and Cases, Prentice Hall, 1988.

John G. Glynn *et al.*, *Accounting for Managers*, Chapman and Hall, 1994.

John J. Burch, *Cost and Management Accounting*, West Publishing Co., Saint Paul, 1994.

John K. Shank and Vijay Govindrajan, *Strategic Cost Management*, Free Press, 1993.

Joseph A. Maciariello, *Management Control System*, Prentice Hall, New Jersey, 1984.

Joseph G. Louder back III and Jay S. Holman, *Management Accounting,* Thomson, 2003.

J. Omen Charrington, E. Dee Hubbard and David H. Luthy, *Cost and Managerial Accounting*, WMC Brown Publishers.

Kenneth A. Merchant, *Modern Management Control Systems*, Text and Cases, Prentice Hall, 1998.

Leslie G. Eldenburg and Susan K. Wolcott, *Cost Management,* John Wiley and Sons, 2005.

Lester E. Heitger and Serge Matulich, *Managerial Accounting*, Auckland, 1985.

Latricia Gayle Raburn, *Principles of Cost Accounting, Using a Cost Management Approach*, Homewood: Richard D. Irwin, 1989.

Lyman A. Keith and Richard L. Keith, Accounting, *A Management Perspective*, New Jersey: Prentice Hall, 1985.

Michael Chatfield and Dewnis Neilson, *Cost Accounting*, Harcourt Brace Javanvich, 1983.

Michael R. Tyran, *Handbook of Business and Financial Ratios*, New York: Woodhead Faulkner, 1992.

Michael W. Maher, Clyde P. Stickney and Roman L. Weil, *Managerial Accounting*, 10th Ed. Thomson South Western, 2008.

Milton E. Usry and Lawrence H. Hammer, *Cost Accounting, Planning and Control*, South Western Publishing Co., Cinncinati, 1997.

Mohinder N. Kaura, *Management Control and Reporting Systems*, *Response Books*, Sage Publications, 2002.

M. Ezzamel and H. Hart, *Advanced Management Accounting, An Organisational Emphasis*, London: Cassell, 1987.

National Association of Accountants, *Cost Accounting for the 90s, The Challange of Technological Change*, New Jersey: NAA 1986.

Peter Taylor and Brian Underdown, *Financial Accounting*, CIMA, 1986.

Pierre L. Titard, *Managerial Accounting*, Chicago: The Dryden Press, 1983.

Ramji Balakrishnan, K. Sivaram Krishnan and Geoffrey B. Sprinkle, *Managerial Accounting*, John Wiley and Sons, 2009.

Ray Fitzgerald, *A Handbook of Practical Business Finance*, Kogan Page, 1992.

Ray H. Garrison and Eric.W. Noreen, *Managerial Accounting*, Irwin: McGraw Hill, 2000.

Ray H. Garrison, Eric W. Noreen and Peter C. Brewer, *Managerial Accounting*, 12th Edition, McGraw Hill, 2008.

Ray H. Garrison, Eric W. Noreen and Peter C. Brewer, *Managerial Accounting*, 13th Edition, Indian Edition, McGraw Hill Education (India) Private Ltd, 2011.

Richard M. Lynch and Robert W. Williamson, *Accounting for Management, Planning and Control*, New York: McGraw Hill, 1983.

Richard M.S. Wilson and Wai Fong Chua, *Managerial Accounting*, Van Nostrang, Reihold Co., 1988.

R.J. Tricker, *Management Information and Control Systems*, New York: John Wiley and Sons, 1982.

R.K. Mautz and James Winjum, *Criteria for Management Control Systems*, New York: FERF, 1981.

Rober G. Eccles, *The Transfer Pricing Problems. A Theory for Practice*, Lexington: Lexington Books, 1985.

Robert H. Chenhol, *The Organisational Context of Management Accounting*, Boston: Pitman, 1981.

Robert J. Thieranf, *Decision Support Systems for Effective Planning and Control*, New Jersey: Prentice Hall, 1982.

Robert M. Grant, *Contemporary Strategy Analysis*, Basil Blackwell, 1991.

Robert N. Anthony, *Management Control Function*, Boston: Harvard Business School, 1988.

Robert N. Anthony, David F. Howkins and Kenneth A. Merchant, *Accounting, Text and Cases,* Tata McGraw Hill Publishing Co., 2008.

Robert N. Anthony, Glewn A. Welsch and James S. Reece, *Fundamentals of Management Accounting*, Homewood: Richard D. Irwin, 1985.

Robert N. Anthony and Vijay Govindrajan, *Management Control Systems*, Irwin: McGraw Hill, 1998.

Robert S. Kaplan and Thomas Johnson, Relevance Lost: *The Rise and Fall of Management Accounting*, Harvard Business School Press, 1987.

Robert S. Kaplan and David P. Norton, *Balanced Scorecard, Translating Strategy into Action*, Harvard Business School Press, 1996.

Robert S. Kaplan and Anthony A. Atkinson, *Advanced Management Accounting*, Prentice Hall, 1998.

Robert Simon, *Performance Measurement and Control Systems for Implementing Strategy*, Prentice Hall, New Jersey, 2000.

Roland Fox, Alison Kennedy and Keith Sugden, *Decision Making, A Management Accounting Perspective,* CIMA, 1990.

Roman L. Weil and Michall W. Maher, *Handbook of Cost Management,* JohnWiley & Sons, New Jersey, 2005.

Ronald W. Hilton, *Managerial Accounting,* McGraw Hill Education, 2006.

Ronald W. Hilton, Michall W. Maher and Frank H. Selto, *Cost Management*, McGraw Hill Irwin, 2006.

Ronald W Hilton and David E. Platt, *Managerial Accounting, Creating Value in a Global Business Environment,* McGraw Hill Education (India) Private Ltd., Indian Edition, 2011.

Shane Moriarity and Carl Allen, *Cost Accounting*, Harper and Row publishers, New York, 1984.

Shyam Sunder, Theory of Accounting and Control, South Western College Publishing, 1997.

Steve W. Williams, Making Better Decisions, Sage Publications, New Delhi, 2002.

T. Lucky, *Management Accounting* D. P. Publications, 1992.

Wayne J. Morse, James R. Davis and Al L. Hartgraves, *Management Accounting, A Strategic Approach*, Thomson, 2003.

William J. Bruns Jr. and Robert S. Kaplan (Eds.) *Accounting and Management, Field Study Perspective*, Harvard Business School Press, 1987.

Williamson Duncan, *Cost and Management Accounting*, Prentice Hall, 1999.

INDEX

M

N

O

P

Q

R

S